Lecture Notes in Computer Science   13275

More information about this series at https://link.springer.com/bookseries/558

Orr Dunkelman · Stefan Dziembowski (Eds.)

Advances in Cryptology – EUROCRYPT 2022

41st Annual International Conference on the Theory
and Applications of Cryptographic Techniques
Trondheim, Norway, May 30 – June 3, 2022
Proceedings, Part I

 Springer

Editors
Orr Dunkelman ⓘ
University of Haifa
Haifa, Haifa, Israel

Stefan Dziembowski ⓘ
University of Warsaw
Warsaw, Poland

ISSN 0302-9743   ISSN 1611-3349 (electronic)
Lecture Notes in Computer Science
ISBN 978-3-031-06943-7   ISBN 978-3-031-06944-4 (eBook)
https://doi.org/10.1007/978-3-031-06944-4

This Springer imprint is published by the registered company Springer Nature Switzerland AG
The registered company address is: Gewerbestrasse 11, 6330 Cham, Switzerland

Preface

The 41st Annual International Conference on the Theory and Applications of Cryptographic Techniques, Eurocrypt 2022, was held in Trondheim, Norway. Breaking tradition, the conference started on the evening of Monday, May 30, and ended at noon on Friday, June 3, 2022. Eurocrypt is one of the three flagship conferences of the International Association for Cryptologic Research (IACR), which sponsors the event. Colin Boyd (NTNU, Norway) was the general chair of Eurocrypt 2022 who took care of all the local arrangements.

The 372 anonymous submissions we received in the IACR HotCRP system were each reviewed by at least three of the 70 Program Committee members (who were allowed at most two submissions). We used a rebuttal round for all submissions. After a lengthy and thorough review process, 85 submissions were selected for publication. The revised versions of these submissions can be found in these three-volume proceedings.

In addition to these papers, the committee selected the "EpiGRAM: Practical Garbled RAM" by David Heath, Vladimir Kolesnikov, and Rafail Ostrovsky for the best paper award. Two more papers — "On Building Fine-Grained One-Way Functions from Strong Average-Case Hardness" and "Quantum Algorithms for Variants of Average-Case Lattice Problems via Filtering" received an invitation to the Journal of Cryptology. Together with presentations of the 85 accepted papers, the program included two invited talks: The IACR distinguished lecture, carried by Ingrid Verbauwhede, on "Hardware: an essential partner to cryptography", and "Symmetric Cryptography for Long Term Security" by María Naya-Plasancia.

We would like to take this opportunity to thank numerous people. First of all, the authors of all submitted papers, whether they were accepted or rejected. The Program Committee members who read, commented, and debated the papers generating more than 4,500 comments(!) in addition to a large volume of email communications. The review process also relied on 368 subreviewers (some of which submitted more than one subreivew). We cannot thank you all enough for your hard work.

A few individuals were extremely helpful in running the review process. First and foremost, Kevin McCurley, who configured, solved, answered, re-answered, supported, and did all in his (great) power to help with the IACR system. Wkdqn Brx! We are also extremely grateful to Gaëtan Leurent for offering his wonderful tool to make paper assignment an easy task. The wisdom and experience dispensed by Anne Canteaut, Itai Dinur, Bart Preneel, and François-Xavier Standaert are also noteworthy and helped usher the conference into a safe haven. Finally, we wish to thank the area chairs—Sonia Belaïd, Carmit Hazay, Thomas Peyrin, Nigel Smart, and Martijn Stam. You made our work manageable.

Finally, we thank all the people who were involved in the program of Eurocrypt 2022: the rump session chairs, the session chairs, the speakers, and all the technical support staff in Trondheim. We would also like to mention the various sponsors and thank them for the generous support. We wish to thank the continuous support of the Cryptography Research Fund for supporting student speakers.

May 2022   Orr Dunkelman
                                                                              Stefan Dziembowski

Organization

The 41st Annual International Conference on the Theory
and Applications of Cryptographic Techniques (Eurocrypt 2022)

Sponsored by the *International Association for Cryptologic Research*
Trondheim, Norway
May 30 – June 3, 2022

General Chair

Colin Boyd   NTNU, Norway

Program Chairs

Orr Dunkelman   University of Haifa, Israel
Stefan Dziembowski   University of Warsaw, Poland

Program Committee

Masayuki Abe   NTT Laboratories, Japan
Shashank Agrawal   Western Digital Research, USA
Joël Alwen   AWS Wickr, Austria
Marshall Ball   New York University, USA
Gustavo Banegas   Inria and Institut Polytechnique de Paris, France
Paulo Barreto   University of Washington Tacoma, USA
Sonia Belaïd   CryptoExperts, France
Jean-François Biasse   University of South Florida, USA
Begül Bilgin   Rambus Cryptography Research, The Netherlands
Alex Biryukov   University of Luxembourg, Luxembourg
Olivier Blazy   Ecole Polytechnique, France
Billy Bob Brumley   Tampere University, Finland
Chitchanok Chuengsatiansup   University of Adelaide, Australia
Michele Ciampi   University of Edinburgh, UK
Ran Cohen   IDC Herzliya, Israel
Henry Corrigan-Gibbs   Massachusetts Institute of Technology, USA
Cas Cremers   CISPA Helmholtz Center for Information
                                    Security, Germany
Dana Dachman-Soled   University of Maryland, USA
Jean Paul Degabriele   TU Darmstadt, Germany
Itai Dinur   Ben-Gurion University, Israel

Rafael Dowsley	Monash University, Australia
Antonio Faonio	EURECOM, France
Pooya Farshim	Durham University, UK
Sebastian Faust	TU Darmstadt, Germany
Ben Fuller	University of Connecticut, USA
Pierrick Gaudry	Loria, France
Esha Ghosh	Microsoft Research, Redmond, USA
Paul Grubbs	University of Michigan, USA
Divya Gupta	Microsoft Research India, India
Felix Günther	ETH Zurich, Switzerland
Iftach Haitner	Tel Aviv University, Israel
Shai Halevi	Algorand Foundation, USA
Carmit Hazay	Bar-Ilan University, Israel
Pavel Hubáček	Charles University, Czech Republic
Tibor Jager	University of Wuppertal, Germany
Dmitry Khovratovich	Ethereum Foundation, Luxembourg
Gregor Leander	Ruhr University Bochum, Germany
Gaëtan Leurent	Inria, France
Helger Lipmaa	Simula UiB, Norway
Shengli Liu	Shanghai Jiao Tong University, China
Alex Lombardi	Massachusetts Institute of Technology, USA
Hemanta K. Maji	Purdue University, USA
Giulio Malavolta	Max Planck Institute for Security and Privacy, Germany
Peihan Miao	University of Illinois at Chicago, USA
Pratyay Mukherjee	Visa Research, USA
David Naccache	ENS Paris, France
Svetla Nikova	KU Leuven, Belgium
Miyako Ohkubo	National Institute of Information and Communications, Japan
Arpita Patra	Indian Institute of Science, India
Alice Pellet-Mary	CNRS and University of Bordeaux, France
Thomas Peyrin	Nanyang Technological University, Singapore
Josef Pieprzyk	CSIRO Data61, Australia, and Institute of Computer Science, PAS, Poland
Bertram Poettering	IBM Research Europe - Zurich, Switzerland
Peter Rindal	Visa Research, USA
Carla Ràfols	Universitat Pompeu Fabra, Spain
Amin Sakzad	Monash University, Australia
Alessandra Scafuro	North Carolina State University, USA
Nigel Smart	KU Leuven, Belgium
Martijn Stam	Simula UiB, Norway

Meltem Sönmez Turan	National Institute of Standards and Technology, USA
Daniele Venturi	Sapienza University of Rome, Italy
Ivan Visconti	University of Salerno, Italy
Gaoli Wang	East China Normal University, China
Stefan Wolf	University of Italian Switzerland, Switzerland
Sophia Yakoubov	Aarhus University, Denmark
Avishay Yanai	VMware Research, Israel
Bo-Yin Yang	Academia Sinica, Taiwan
Arkady Yerukhimovich	George Washington University, USA
Yu Yu	Shanghai Jiao Tong University, China
Mark Zhandry	NTT Research and Princeton University, USA

Subreviewers

Behzad Abdolmaleki
Ittai Abraham
Damiano Abram
Anasuya Acharya
Alexandre Adomnicai
Amit Agarwal
Shweta Agrawal
Thomas Agrikola
Akshima
Navid Alamati
Alejandro Cabrera Aldaya
Bar Alon
Miguel Ambrona
Hiroaki Anada
Diego F. Aranha
Victor Arribas
Tomer Ashur
Gennaro Avitabile
Matilda Backendal
Saikrishna Badrinarayanan
Shi Bai
Ero Balsa
Augustin Bariant
James Bartusek
Balthazar Bauer
Carsten Baum
Ämin Baumeler
Arthur Beckers
Charles Bédard

Christof Beierle
Pascal Bemmann
Fabrice Benhamouda
Francesco Berti
Tim Beyne
Rishabh Bhadauria
Adithya Bhat
Sai Lakshmi Bhavana Obbattu
Alexander Bienstock
Erica Blum
Jan Bobolz
Xavier Bonnetain
Cecilia Boschini
Raphael Bost
Vincenzo Botta
Katharina Boudgoust
Christina Boura
Zvika Brakerski
Luís Brandão
Lennart Braun
Jacqueline Brendel
Gianluca Brian
Anne Broadbent
Marek Broll
Christopher Brzuska
Chloe Cachet
Matteo Campanelli
Federico Canale
Anne Canteaut

Ignacio Cascudo
Andre Chailloux
Nishanth Chandran
Donghoon Chang
Binyi Chen
Shan Chen
Weikeng Chen
Yilei Chen
Jung Hee Cheon
Jesus-Javier Chi-Dominguez
Seung Geol Choi
Wutichai Chongchitmate
Arka Rai Choudhuri
Sherman S. M. Chow
Jeremy Clark
Xavier Coiteux-Roy
Andrea Coladangelo
Nan Cui
Benjamin R. Curtis
Jan Czajkowski
Jan-Pieter D'Anvers
Hila Dahari
Thinh Dang
Quang Dao
Poulami Das
Pratish Datta
Bernardo David
Gareth T. Davies
Hannah Davis
Lauren De Meyer
Gabrielle De Micheli
Elke De Mulder
Luke Demarest
Julien Devevey
Siemen Dhooghe
Denis Diemert
Jintai Ding
Jack Doerner
Xiaoyang Dong
Nico Döttling
Benjamin Dowling
Yang Du
Leo Ducas
Julien Duman
Betul Durak

Oğuzhan Ersoy
Andreas Erwig
Daniel Escudero
Muhammed F. Esgin
Saba Eskandarian
Prastudy Fauzi
Patrick Felke
Thibauld Feneuil
Peter Fenteany
Diodato Ferraioli
Marc Fischlin
Nils Fleischhacker
Cody Freitag
Daniele Friolo
Tommaso Gagliardoni
Steven D. Galbraith
Pierre Galissant
Chaya Ganesh
Cesar Pereida García
Romain Gay
Kai Gellert
Craig Gentry
Marilyn George
Hossein Ghodosi
Satrajit Ghosh
Jan Gilcher
Aarushi Goel
Eli Goldin
Junqing Gong
Dov Gordon
Jérôme Govinden
Lorenzo Grassi
Johann Großschädl
Jiaxin Guan
Daniel Guenther
Milos Gujic
Qian Guo
Cyril Guyot
Mohammad Hajiabadi
Ariel Hamlin
Shuai Han
Abida Haque
Patrick Harasser
Dominik Hartmann
Phil Hebborn

Alexandra Henzinger
Javier Herranz
Julia Hesse
Justin Holmgren
Akinori Hosoyamada
Kai Hu
Andreas Hülsing
Shih-Han Hung
Vincenzo Iovino
Joseph Jaeger
Aayush Jain
Christian Janson
Samuel Jaques
Stanislaw Jarecki
Corentin Jeudy
Zhengzhong Jin
Daniel Jost
Saqib Kakvi
Vukašin Karadžić
Angshuman Karmakar
Shuichi Katsumata
Jonathan Katz
Mahimna Kelkar
Nathan Keller
John Kelsey
Mustafa Khairallah
Hamidreza Amini Khorasgani
Dongwoo Kim
Miran Kim
Elena Kirshanova
Fuyuki Kitagawa
Michael Klooß
Sebastian Kolby
Lukas Kölsch
Yashvanth Kondi
David Kretzler
Veronika Kuchta
Marie-Sarah Lacharité
Yi-Fu Lai
Baptiste Lambin
Mario Larangeira
Rio LaVigne
Quoc-Huy Le
Jooyoung Lee
Julia Len

Antonin Leroux
Hanjun Li
Jianwei Li
Yiming Li
Xiao Liang
Damien Ligier
Chengyu Lin
Dongxi Liu
Jiahui Liu
Linsheng Liu
Qipeng Liu
Xiangyu Liu
Chen-Da Liu Zhang
Julian Loss
Vadim Lyubashevsky
Lin Lyu
You Lyu
Fermi Ma
Varun Madathil
Akash Madhusudan
Bernardo Magri
Monosij Maitra
Nikolaos Makriyannis
Mary Maller
Giorgia Marson
Christian Matt
Noam Mazor
Nikolas Melissaris
Bart Mennink
Antonis Michalas
Brice Minaud
Kazuhiko Minematsu
Alberto Montina
Amir Moradi
Marta Mularczyk
Varun Narayanan
Jade Nardi
Patrick Neumann
Ruth Ng
Hai H. Nguyen
Kirill Nikitin
Ryo Nishimaki
Anca Nitulescu
Ariel Nof
Julian Nowakowski

Jorge L. Villar
Giuseppe Vitto
Sameer Wagh
Hendrik Waldner
Alexandre Wallet
Ming Wan
Xiao Wang
Yuyu Wang
Zhedong Wang
Hoeteck Wee
Mor Weiss
Weiqiang Wen
Daniel Wichs
Mathias Wolf
Lennert Wouters
Michał Wroński
David Wu
Yusai Wu
Keita Xagawa
Yu Xia

Zejun Xiang
Tiancheng Xie
Shota Yamada
Takashi Yamakawa
Lisa Yang
Kevin Yeo
Eylon Yogev
Kazuki Yoneyama
Yusuke Yoshida
William Youmans
Alexandros Zacharakis
Michał Zając
Arantxa Zapico
Greg Zaverucha
Shang Zehua
Tina Zhang
Wentao Zhang
Yinuo Zhang
Yu Zhou
Cong Zuo

Abstracts of Invited Talks

Hardware: An Essential Partner to Cryptography

Ingrid Verbauwhede

KU Leuven, Leuven, Belgium

Abstract. Cryptography is a beautiful branch of mathematics, its aim being to provide information security. To be useful in practical applications, cryptography is mapped to hardware or software, with software ultimately running also on hardware processors. This presentation covers multiple aspects of this relation between hardware and cryptography. The goal is to provide insights to the cryptographer, so that more efficient and secure algorithms and protocols are designed.

- Hardware provides the means to accelerate the computationally demanding operations, as is currently the case for the new generation of post-quantum algorithms. [We will illustrate this with some numbers.]
- A very nice aspect of cryptography is that it reduces what needs to be kept secret to the keys, while the algorithms can be publicly known. As a consequence, the hardware is responsible to keep the key(s) secret. Side-channel, fault-attacks and other physical attacks make this a challenging task. [We could show some recent results in fault and laser attacks.] [We can also illustrate this with PUFs to generate secret keys.]
- "Provable Secure" mathematical countermeasures against physical attacks rely on models on how the hardware behaves. Unfortunately, the models are often the weak link between theory and practice and it results in broken implementations. [We will illustrate this with successful attacks on several provably secure masking schemes.]
- Hardware also provides essential building blocks to security. Protocols rely on nonces and freshness from random numbers. Generating full entropy random numbers is a challenge. [We can illustrate this with the challenges of designing TRNGs].
- We will end with some trends in hardware that can benefit cryptography. [We will show tricks on how cheap noise can be generated e.g. for learning with error problems.] [Or how light weight crypto should be adapted to the not-so-perfect random but very light weight random number generators.] [What to do with process variations in deep submicron technologies, or with ultra low-power approximate computing.]

We can conclude that hardware is an essential partner to cryptography to provide the promised information security.

Symmetric Cryptography for Long Term Security

María Naya-Plasencia

Inria, Paris, France

Abstract. Symmetric cryptography has made important advances in recent years, mainly due to new challenges that have appeared, requiring some new developments. During this talk we will discuss these challenges and developments, with a particular emphasis on quantum-safe symmetric cryptography and latest results, providing the details of some particularly interesting cases. We will also discuss some related open problems.

Contents – Part I

Homomorphic Encryption

Obfuscation

Contents – Part II

Cryptographic Primitives

Real-World Systems

Contents – Part III

Post-Quantum Cryptography

Information-Theoretic Security

Best Paper Award

EPiGRAM: Practical Garbled RAM

David Heath[1($\boxtimes$)], Vladimir Kolesnikov[1], and Rafail Ostrovsky[2]

[1] Georgia Tech, Atlanta, USA
{heath.davidanthony,kolesnikov}@gatech.edu
[2] UCLA, Los Angeles, USA
rafail@cs.ucla.edu

Abstract. Garbled RAM (GRAM) is a powerful technique introduced
by Lu and Ostrovsky that equips Garbled Circuit (GC) with a sublinear
cost RAM without adding rounds of interaction. While multiple GRAM
constructions are known, none are suitable for practice, due to costs that
have high constants and poor scaling.

We present the first GRAM suitable for practice. For computational
security parameter κ and for a size-n RAM that stores blocks of size
$w = \Omega(\log^2 n)$ bits, our GRAM incurs amortized $O(w \cdot \log^2 n \cdot \kappa)$ communication and computation per access. We evaluate the concrete cost
of our GRAM; our approach outperforms trivial linear-scan-based RAM
for as few as 512 128-bit elements.

Keywords: MPC · Garbled circuits · Oblivious RAM · Garbled RAM

1 Introduction

Secure multiparty computation (MPC) allows mutually untrusting parties to
compute functions of their combined inputs while revealing nothing but the
outputs. MPC protocols traditionally consider functions encoded as circuits.
While this does not limit expressivity, it does limit efficiency: many interesting
computations are best expressed as RAM programs, not as circuits, and the
reduction from RAM programs to circuits is expensive.

Fortunately, we can combine MPC with oblivious RAM (ORAM). ORAM is
a technology that allows a client to outsource an encrypted database to a server;
the client can then access the database while both (1) incurring only sublinear overhead and (2) hiding the access pattern from the server. By running an
ORAM client inside MPC, we can augment circuits with random access memory.
This powerful combination allows us to run RAM programs inside MPC.

Garbled Circuit (GC) is a foundational and powerful MPC technique that
allows two parties to achieve secure computation while consuming only constant
rounds of interaction. One party, the GC generator G, "encrypts" the circuit
and sends it to the other party, the GC evaluator E. E is given an encryption of
each party's input and steps through the circuit gate-by-gate under encryption.
At each gate, E propagates encryptions of input wire values to encryptions of

© International Association for Cryptologic Research 2022
O. Dunkelman and S. Dziembowski (Eds.): EUROCRYPT 2022, LNCS 13275, pp. 3–33, 2022.
https://doi.org/10.1007/978-3-031-06944-4_1

output wire values. Once E finishes, E and G can jointly decrypt the output wire values, revealing the circuit output.

It is natural to consider adding RAM to GC while preserving GC's constant rounds. However, the constant round requirement means that adding RAM to GC is seemingly more difficult than adding RAM to interactive protocols. Nevertheless, it is possible to run an ORAM client inside the GC and to let E play an ORAM server. This technique is called Garbled RAM (GRAM) [LO13].

While GRAM constructions are known [LO13, GHL+14, GLOS15, GLO15], none are suitable for practice: existing constructions simply cost too much. All existing GRAMs suffer from at least two of the following problems:

- **Use of non-black-box cryptography.** [LO13] showed that GRAM can be achieved by evaluating a PRF *inside GC* in a non-black-box way. Unfortunately, this non-black-box cryptography is extremely expensive, and on each access the construction must evaluate the PRF *repeatedly*. [LO13] requires a circular-security assumption on GC and PRFs. Follow-up works removed this circularity by replacing the PRF with even more expensive non-black-box techniques [GHL+14, GLOS15].
- **Factor-κ blowup.** Let κ denote the computational security parameter. In practical GC, we generally assume that we will incur factor κ overhead due to the need to represent each bit as a length-κ *encoding* (i.e. a GC label). However, existing GRAMs suffer from yet another factor κ. This overhead follows from the need to represent GC labels (which have length κ) *inside the GC* such that we can manipulate them with Boolean operations. The GC labels that encode a GC label together have length κ^2. In practice, where we generally use $\kappa = 128$, this overhead is intolerable.
- **High factor scaling.** Existing GRAMs operate as follows. First, they give an array construction that leaks access patterns to E. This leaky array already has high cost. Then, they compile this array access into GRAM using off-the-shelf ORAM. This compilation is problematic: off-the-shelf ORAMs require that, on each access, E access the leaky array a polylogarithmic (or more) number of times. Thus, existing GRAMs incur *multiplicative* overhead from the composition of the leaky array with the ORAM construction.

Prior GRAM works do not attempt to calculate their concrete or even asymptotic cost, other than to claim cost sublinear or polylogarithmic in n. In the full version of this paper, we (favorably to prior work) estimate their cost: for a GRAM that stores 128-bit blocks, the best prior GRAM breaks even with trivial linear-scan based GRAM when the RAM size reaches $\approx 2^{20}$ elements. As noted, our analysis discounts many potentially expensive steps of prior constructions, giving an estimate favorable to them. In particular, this conservative estimate indicates that by the time it is worthwhile to use existing GRAM, each and every access requires a 4GB GC.

1.1 Contribution

We present the first practical garbled RAM. Our GRAM, which we call EPI-GRAM, uses only $O(w \cdot \log^2 n \cdot \kappa)$ computation and communication per access. EPIGRAM circumvents all three of the above problems:

- **No use of non-black-box cryptography.** Our approach routes array elements using novel, yet simple, techniques. These techniques are light-weight, and non-black-box cryptography is not required.
- **No factor-κ blowup.** While we, like previous GRAMs, represent GC labels inside the GC itself, we give a novel generalization of existing GC gates that eliminates the additional factor κ overhead.
- **Low polylogarithmic scaling.** Like previous GRAMs, we present a leaky construction that reveals access patterns to E. However, we do not compile this into GRAM using off-the-shelf ORAM. Instead, we construct a custom ORAM designed with GC in mind. Our GRAM minimizes use of our leaky construction. The result is a highly efficient technique.

In the remainder of this paper we:

- Informally and formally describe the first practical GRAM. For an array with n elements each of size w such that $w = \Omega(\log^2 n)$, the construction incurs amortized $O(w \cdot \log^2 n \cdot \kappa)$ communication and computation per access.
- Prove our GRAM secure by incorporating it in a *garbling scheme* [BHR12]. Our scheme handles arbitrary computations consisting of AND gates, XOR gates, and array accesses. Our scheme is secure under a typical GC assumption: a circular correlation robust hash function [CKKZ12].
- Analyze EPIGRAM's concrete cost. Our analysis shows that EPIGRAM outperforms trivial linear-scan based RAM for as few as 512 128-bit elements.

2 Technical Overview

In this section, we explain our construction informally but with sufficient detail to understand our approach. This overview covers four topics:

- First, we explain a problem central to GRAM: *language translation*.
- Second, we informally explain our *lazy permutation network*, which is a construction that efficiently solves the language translation problem.
- Third, as a stepping stone to our full construction, we explain how to construct *leaky* arrays from the lazy permutation network. This informal construction securely implements an array with the caveat that we let E learn the array access pattern.
- Fourth, we upgrade the leaky array to full-fledged GRAM: the presented construction hides the access pattern from E.

2.1 The Language Translation Problem

For each GC wire x_i the evaluator E holds one of two κ-bit strings: either X_i, which encodes a logical zero, or $X_i \oplus \Delta$, which encodes one. Meanwhile, G holds each such X_i and the global secret Δ. We refer to the wire-specific value X_i as the *language* of that wire, and to the pair $\langle X_i, X_i \oplus x_i \Delta \rangle$ jointly held by G and E as the *GC encoding*, or the *garbling*, of x_i. We present this notation formally in

Sect. 4.4. To produce a garbled gate that takes as input a particular wire value x_i, G must know the corresponding language X_i. Normally this is not a problem: the structure of the circuit is decided statically, and G can easily track which languages go to which gates.

However, consider representing an array as a collection of such garbled labels. That is, there are n values x_i where E holds $X_i \oplus x_i \Delta$. Suppose that at runtime the GC requests access to a particular index α. We could use a static circuit to select x_α, but this would require an expensive linear-cost circuit. A different method is required to achieve the desired sublinear access costs.

Instead, suppose we disclose α to E in cleartext – we later add mechanisms that hide RAM indices from E. Since she knows α, E can jump directly to the αth wire and retrieve the value $X_\alpha \oplus x_\alpha \Delta$. Recall, to use a wire as input to a gate, G and E must agree on that wire's language. Unfortunately, it is *not possible* for G to predict the language X_α: α is computed during GC evaluation and, due to the constant round requirement, E cannot send messages to G.

Therefore, we instead allow G to select a fresh uniform language Y. If we can convey to E the value $Y \oplus x_\alpha \Delta$, then G will be able to garble gates that take the accessed RAM value as input, and we can successfully continue the computation.

Thus, our new goal is to *translate* the language X_α to the language Y. Mechanically, this translation involves giving to E the value $X_\alpha \oplus Y$. Given this, E simply XORs the translation value with her label and obtains $Y \oplus x_\alpha \Delta$. Keeping the circuit metaphor, providing such translation values to E allows her to take two wires – the wire out of the RAM and the wire into the next gate – and to solder these wires together *at runtime*. However, the problem of efficiently conveying these translation values remains.

In the full version of this paper, we discuss natural attempts at solving the language translation problem. Translation can be achieved by a linear-sized gadget (suggesting dynamic conversion is possible), or by a non-black box PRF [LO13] (suggesting the ability to manipulate languages inside the GC). Our *lazy permutation network* (discussed next) achieves dynamic language translation more cheaply, but its underpinnings are the same: the network carefully manipulates languages inside the GC.

2.2   Lazy Permutations

Recall that our current goal is to translate GC languages. Suppose that the GC issues n accesses over its runtime. Further suppose that the GC accesses a *distinct location* on each access – in the end we reduce general RAM to a memory with this restriction. To handle the n accesses, we wish to convey to E n translation values $X_i \oplus Y_j$ where Y_j is G's selected language for the jth access.

What we need then is essentially a permutation on n elements that routes between RAM locations (with language X_i) and accesses (with language Y_j). However, a simple permutation network will not suffice, since at the time of RAM access j, the location of each subsequent access will, in general, not yet be known. Therefore, we need a *lazy* permutation whereby we can decide and apply the routing of the permutation one input at a time. We remind the reader

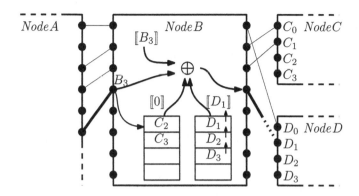

Fig. 1. An internal node of our lazy permutation network, realizing a "garbled switch". We depict the fourth access to this switch. The encoded input uses language B_3. The first encoded input bit is a flag that indicates to proceed left or right. Our objective is to forward the remaining input to either the left or right node. Each node stores two oblivious stacks that hold encodings of the unused languages of the two children. We conditionally pop both stacks. In this case, the left stack is unchanged whereas the right stack yields D_1, the next language for the target child. Due to the pop, the remaining elements in the right stack move up one slot. By XORing these values with an encoding of the input language, then opening the resulting value to E, we convert the message to the language of the target child, allowing E to solder a wire to the child.

that we assume that E knows each value α. I.e., we need only achieve a lazy permutation where E learns the permutation.

Given this problem, it may now be believable that algorithms and data structures exist such that the total cost is $O(\kappa \cdot n \cdot \text{polylog}(n))$, and hence only amortized $O(\kappa \cdot \text{polylog}(n))$ per access. Indeed we present such a construction. However, our solution requires that we apply this lazy permutation *to the GC languages themselves*, not to bits stored in the RAM. Thus, we need a logic in which we can encode GC languages: E must obliviously and authentically manipulate GC languages. GC gives us these properties, so we can encode languages bit-by-bit inside the GC. I.e., for a language of length w, we would add w GC wires, each of which would hold a single bit of the language.

Unfortunately, this bit-by-bit encoding of the languages leads to a highly objectionable factor κ blowup in the size of the GC: the encoding of a length-w language has length $w \cdot \kappa$. We later show that the factor κ blowup is unnecessary. Under particular conditions, existing GC gates can be generalized such that we can represent a length-w language using an encoding of only length w. These special and highly efficient GC gates suffice to build the gadgetry we need. We formalize the needed gate in Sect. 5.1.

The ability to encode languages inside the GC is powerful. Notice that since we can dynamically solder GC wires, and since wires can hold languages needed to solder other wires, we can arrange for E to repeatedly and dynamically lay down new wiring in nearly arbitrary ways.

With this high level intuition, we now informally describe our lazy permutation network. Let n be a power of two. Our objective is to route between the languages of n array accesses and the languages of n array elements.

G first lays out a full binary tree with n leaves. Each node in this tree is a GC with static structure. However, the inputs and outputs to these circuits are loose wires, ready to be soldered at runtime by E. At runtime, seeking to read array element x_α with language X_α into a wire with language Y, E begins at the root of the tree, which holds a GC encoding of the target language Y. (Note, G knows the target language Y of the j-th access, and can accordingly program the tree root.) Based on the GC encoding of the first bit of α, E is able to dynamically decrypt a translation value to either the left or the right child node. Now, E can solder wires to this child, allowing her to send to the child circuit both the encoding of Y and the remaining bits of α. E repeatedly applies this strategy until she reaches the αth leaf node. This leaf node is a special circuit that computes $\mathcal{C}(x) = x \oplus X_\alpha$ and then reveals the output to E.[1] Since we have pushed the encoding of Y all the way to this leaf, E obtains $Y \oplus X_\alpha$, the translation value that she needs to read x_α.

In yet more detail, each internal node on level k of the tree, which we informally call a *garbled switch*, is a static circuit with $2^{\log n - k}$ loose sets of input wires. Each node maintains two *oblivious stacks* [ZE13]. The first stack stores encodings of the languages for the $2^{\log n - k - 1}$ loose input wires of the left child, and the second stack similarly stores languages for the right child (see Fig. 1). On the j-th access and seeking to compute $Y_j \oplus X_\alpha$, E dynamically traverses the tree to leaf α (recall, we assume E knows α in cleartext), forwarding an encoding of Y_j all the way to the αth leaf. At each internal node, she uses a bit of the encoding of α to conditionally pop the two stacks, yielding an encoding of the language of the correct child. The static circuit uses this encoding to compute a translation value to the appropriate child.

By repeatedly routing inputs over the course of n accesses, we achieve a lazy permutation. Crucially, the routing between nodes is not decided until runtime.

This construction is affordable. Essentially the only cost comes from the oblivious stacks. For a stack that stores languages of length w, each pop costs only $O(w \cdot \log n)$ communication and computation (Sect. 5.2). Thus, the full lazy permutation costs only $O(w \cdot n \cdot \log^2 n)$ communication, which amortizes to sublinear cost per access. We describe our lazy permutation network in full formal detail in Sect. 5.3.

Our lazy permutation networks route the language of each RAM slot to the access where it is needed, albeit in a setting where E views the routing in cleartext. Crucially, the lazy permutation network avoids factor κ additional overhead that is common in GRAM approaches. To construct a secure GRAM, we build on this primitive and hide the RAM access pattern.

---

[1] Our actual leaf circuit is more detailed. See Sects. 2.4 and 5.3.

2.3 Pattern-Leaking (Leaky) Arrays

As a stepping stone to full GRAM, we informally present an intermediate array which leaks access patterns. For brevity, we refer to it as *leaky* array. This construction handles arbitrary array accesses in a setting where E is allowed to learn the access pattern. We demonstrate a reduction from this problem to our lazy permutation network.

We never *formally* present the resulting construction. Rather, we explain the construction now for expository reasons: we decouple our explanation of *correctness* from our explanation of *obliviousness*. I.e., this section builds a correct GRAM that leaks the access pattern to E. The ideas for this leaky construction carry to our secure GRAM (Sect. 2.4).

Suppose the GC wishes to read index α. Recall that our lazy permutation network is a mechanism that can help translate GC languages: E can dynamically look up an encoding of the language X_α. However, because the network implements a *permutation*, it alone does not solve our problem: an array should allow multiple accesses to the same index, but the permutation can route each index to *only one* access. To complete the reduction, more machinery is needed.

To start, we simplify the problem: consider an array that handles at most n accesses. We describe an array that works in this restricted setting and later upgrade it to handle arbitrary numbers of accesses.

Logical Indices → One-Time Indices. The key idea is to introduce a level of indirection. While the GC issues queries via logical indices α, our array stores its content according to a different indexing system: the content for each logical index α is stored at a particular *one-time index* p. As the name suggests, each one-time index may be written to and read at most once. This limitation ensures compatibility with a lazy permutation: since each one-time index is read only once, a permutation suffices to describe the read pattern. We remark that this reduction from general purpose RAM to a permuted read order was inspired by prior work on efficient RAM for Zero Knowledge [HK21].

Each one-time index can be read only once, yet each logical index can be read multiple times. Thus, over the course of n accesses, a given logical index might correspond to *multiple* one-time indices.

Neither party can *a priori* know the mapping between logical indices and one-time indices. However, to complete an access the GC must compute the relevant one-time index. Thus, we implement the mapping as a recursively instantiated *index map*.[2] The index map is itself a leaky array where each index α holds the corresponding one-time index p. We are careful that the index map is strictly smaller than the array itself, so the recursion terminates; when the next needed index map is small enough, we instantiate it via simple linear scans.

A leaky array with n elements each of size w and that handles at most n accesses is built from three pieces:

1. A block of $2n$ GC encodings each of size w called the one-time array. We index into the one-time array using one-time indices.

---

[2] Recursive index/position maps are typical in ORAM constructions, see e.g. [SvS+13].

2. A size-$2n$ lazy permutation $\tilde{\pi}$ where each leaf i stores the language for one-time array slot i.
3. The recursively instantiated index map.

Let $\{\!|x_i|\!\}$ denote the GC encoding of bitstring x_i where G holds X_i and E holds $X_i \oplus x_i \Delta$ (see also Sect. 4.4). Suppose the parties start with a collection of n encodings $\{\!|x_0|\!\}, ..., \{\!|x_{n-1}|\!\}$ which they would like to use as the array content. The parties begin by sequentially storing each value $\{\!|x_i|\!\}$ in the corresponding one-time index i. The initial mapping from logical indices to one-time indices is thus statically decided: each logical index i maps to one-time index i. The parties recursively instantiate the index map with content $\{\!|0|\!\}, ..., \{\!|n-1|\!\}$.

When the GC performs its j-th access to logical index $\{\!|\alpha|\!\}$, we perform the following steps:

1. The parties recursively query the index map using input $\{\!|\alpha|\!\}$. The result is a one-time index $\{\!|p|\!\}$. The parties simultaneously write back into the index map $\{\!|n+j|\!\}$, indicating that α will next correspond to one-time index $n+j$.
2. The GC reveals p to E in cleartext. This allows E to use the lazy permutation network $\tilde{\pi}$ to find a translation value for the pth slot of the one-time array.
3. E jumps to the pth slot of the array and translates its language, soldering the value to the GC and completing the read. Note that the GC may need to access index α again, so the parties perform the next step:
4. The parties write back to the $(n+j)$-th slot of the one-time array. If the access is a read, they write back the just-read value. Otherwise, they write the written value.

In this way, the parties can efficiently handle n accesses to a leaky array.

Handling More than n Accesses. If the parties need more than n accesses, a reset step is needed. Notice that after n accesses, we have written to each of the $2n$ one-time indices (n during initialization and one per access), but we have only read from n one-time indices. Further notice that on an access to index α, we write back a new one-time index for α; hence, it must be the case that the n remaining unread one-time array slots hold the current array content.

Going beyond n accesses is simple. First, we one-by-one read the n array values in the sequential *logical* order (i.e. with $\alpha = 0, 1, .., n-1$), flushing the array content into a block $\{\!|x_0|\!\}, ..., \{\!|x_{n-1}|\!\}$. Second, we initialize a new leaky array data structure, using the flushed block as its initial content. This new data structure can handle n more accesses. By repeating this process every n accesses, we can handle arbitrary numbers of accesses.

Summarizing the Leaky Array. Thus, we can construct an efficient garbled array, which leaks access patterns. Each access to the leaky array costs amortized $O(w \cdot \log^2 n \cdot \kappa)$ bits of communication, due to the lazy permutation network. We emphasize the key ideas that carry over to our secure GRAM:

– We store the array data according to *one-time indices*, not according to logical indices. This ensures compatibility with our lazy permutation network.

- We recursively instantiate an *index map* that stores the mapping from logical indices to one-time indices.
- We store the GC languages of the underlying data structure in a lazy permutation network such that E can dynamically access slots.
- Every n accesses, we *flush* the current array and instantiate a fresh one.

2.4 Garbled RAM

In Sect. 2.3 we demonstrated that we can reduce random access arrays to our lazy permutation network, so long as E is allowed to learn the access pattern. In this section we strengthen that construction by hiding the access patterns, therefore achieving secure GRAM.

Note that this strengthening is clearly possible, because we can simply employ off-the-shelf ORAM. In ORAM, the server learns a physical access pattern, but the ORAM protocol ensures that these physical accesses together convey no information about the logical access pattern. Thus, we can use our leaky array to implement physical ORAM storage, implement the ORAM client inside the GC, and the problem is solved.

We are not content with this solution. The problem is that our leaky array already consumes $O(\log^2 n)$ overhead, due to lazy permutations. In ORAM, each logical access is instantiated by at least a logarithmic number of physical reads/writes. Thus, compiling our leaky array with off-the-shelf ORAM incurs *at least* an additional $O(\log n)$ *multiplicative factor*. In short, this off-the-shelf composition is expensive.

We instead directly improve the leaky array construction (Sect. 2.3) and remove its leakage. This modification incurs only additive overhead, so our GRAM has the same asymptotic cost as the leaky array: $O(w \cdot \log^2 n \cdot \kappa)$ bits per access.

The key idea of our full GRAM is as follows: In regular ORAM, we assume that the client is significantly weaker than the server. In our case, too, the GC – which plays the client – *is* much weaker than E – who plays the server. However, we have a distinct advantage: the GC generator G can act as a powerful advisor to the GC, directly informing most of its decisions.

More concretely, our GRAM carefully arranges that the locations of almost all of the physical[3] reads and writes are decided *statically* and are independent of the logical access pattern. Thus, G can *a priori* track the static schedule and prepare for each of the static accesses. Our GRAM incurs $O(\log^2 n)$ physical reads/writes per logical access. However, only a *constant number*[4] of these reads cannot be predicted by G, as we will soon show.

Each physical read/write requires that G and E agree on the GC language of the accessed element. For each statically decided read/write, this agreement

---

[3] I.e. reads and writes to the lowest level underlying data structure, where access patterns are visible to E.

[4] To be pedantic, if we account for recursively instantiated index maps, each map incurs this constant number of unpredictable reads, so there are total a logarithmic number of unpredictable reads.

is reached trivially. Therefore, we only need our lazy permutation network for reads that G cannot predict. There are only a constant number of these, so we only need a constant number of calls to the lazy permutation network.

Upgrading the Leaky Array. We now informally describe our GRAM. Our description is made by comparison to the leaky array described in Sect. 2.3.

In the leaky array, we stored all $2n$ one-time indices in a single block. In our GRAM, we instead store the $2n$ one-time indices across $O(\log n)$ *levels* of exponentially increasing size: each level i holds 2^{i+1} elements, though some levels are vacant. As we will describe later, data items are written to the smallest level and then slowly move from small levels to large levels. Each populated level of the GRAM holds 2^i one-time-indexed data items and 2^i *dummies*. Dummies are merely encodings of zero. Each level of the GRAM is stored shuffled. The order of items on each level is unknown to E but, crucially, *is known to G*. This means that at all times G knows which one-time index is stored where and knows which elements are dummies.

In the leaky array, E was pointed directly to the appropriate one-time index. In our GRAM, we need to hide the identity of the level that holds the appropriate index. Otherwise, since elements slowly move to larger levels, E will learn an approximation of the time at which the accessed element was written. Hence we arrange that E will read from *each* level on each access. However, all except one of these accesses will be to a dummy, and the indices of the accessed dummies are *statically scheduled by G*. More precisely, G a priori chooses one dummy on *each* populated level and enters their addresses as input to the GC. The GC then conditionally replaces one dummy address by the real address, then reveals each address to E. (Note that G *does not know* which dummy goes unaccessed – we discuss this later.)

In the leaky array and when accessing logical index α, we used the index map to find corresponding one-time index p. p was then revealed to E. In our GRAM, it is not secure for E to learn one-time indices corresponding to accesses. Thus, we introduce a new uniform permutation π of size $2n$ that is held by G and secret from E. Our index map now maps each index $\{\!|\alpha|\!\}$ to the corresponding *permuted* one-time index $\{\!|\pi(p)|\!\}$. We can safely reveal $\pi(p)$ to E – the sequence of such revelations is indistinguishable from a uniform permutation.

In the leaky array, we used the lazy permutation network $\tilde{\pi}$ to map each one-time index p to a corresponding GC language. Here, we need two changes:

1. Instead of routing p to the metadata corresponding to p, we instead route $\pi(p)$ to the metadata corresponding to p. G can arrange for this by simply initializing the content of the lazy permutation in permuted order.
2. We slowly move one-time indexed array elements from small levels to large levels (we have not yet presented how this works). Thus, each one-time index no longer corresponds to a single GC language. Instead, each one-time index now corresponds to a *collection* of physical addresses. Moreover, each time we move a one-time index to a new physical address, it is crucial to security that we encode the data with a different GC language. Fortunately, we ensure

that G knows the entire history of each one-time index. Thus, he can garble a circuit that takes as input the number of accesses so far and outputs the *current* physical address and GC language. We place these per-one-time-index circuits at the leaves of a lazy permutation network.

Remark 1 (Indices). Our GRAM features three kinds of indices:

- *Logical indices* α refer to simple array indices. The purpose of the GRAM is to map logical indices to values.
- Each time we access a logical index, we write back a corresponding value to a fresh *one-time index* p. Thus, each logical index may correspond to multiple one-time indices. The mapping from logical indices to one-time indices is implemented by the recursively instantiated *index map*.
- One-time indices are not stored sequentially, but rather are stored permuted such that we hide access patterns from E. A *physical address* @ refers to the place where a one-time index p is currently held. Because we repeatedly move and permute one-time indices, each one-time index corresponds to multiple physical addresses. The mapping from one-time indices to physical addresses is known to G and is stored in a lazy permutation network.

In the leaky array and on access j, we write back an element to one-time index $n + j$. In our GRAM, we similarly perform this write. We initially store this one-time index in the smallest level. Additionally, the parties store a fresh dummy in the smallest level. After each write, the parties permute a subset of the levels of RAM using a traditional permutation network. The schedule of permutations – see next – is carefully chosen such that the access pattern is hidden but cost is low. Over the course of n accesses, the n permutations together consume only $O(n \cdot \log^2 n)$ overhead.

The Permutation Schedule. Recall that we arrange the RAM content into $O(\log n)$ levels of exponentially increasing size. After each access, G applies a permutation to a subset of these levels. These permutations prevent E from learning the access pattern.

Recall that on each access, E is instructed to read from each populated level. All except one of these reads is to a dummy. Further recall that after being accessed once, a one-time index is never used again. Thus, it is important that each dummy is similarly accessed at most once. Otherwise, E will notice that doubly-accessed addresses must hold dummies.

Since we store only 2^i dummies on level i, level i can only support 2^i accesses: after 2^i accesses it is plausible that all dummies have been exhausted. To continue processing, G therefore re-permutes the level, mixing the dummies and real elements such that the dummies can be safely reused. More precisely, on access j we collect those levels i such that 2^i divides j. Let k denote the largest such i. We concatenate each level $i \leq k$ together into a block of size 2^{k+1} and permute its contents into level $k + 1$ (this level is guaranteed to be vacant). This leaves each level $i \leq k$ vacant and ready for new data to flow up. Now that the data has been permuted, it is safe to once again use the shuffled dummies, since they are shuffled and each is given a new GC language.

As a security argument, consider E's view of a particular level i over all 2^i accesses between permutations. Each such access could be to a dummy or to a real element, but these elements are uniformly shuffled. Hence, E's view can be simulated by uniformly sampling, without replacement, a sequence of 2^i indices.

Remark 2 (Permutations). Our RAM features three kinds of permutations:

- $\tilde{\pi}$ is a *lazy* permutation whose routing is revealed to E over the course of n accesses. The lazy permutation allows E to efficiently look up the physical address and language for the target one-time index.
- π is a uniform permutation chosen by G whose sole purpose is to ensure that $\tilde{\pi}$ does not leak one-time indices to E. Let π' denote the *actual* routing from RAM accesses to one-time indices. E does not learn π', but rather learns $\tilde{\pi} = \pi' \circ \pi$. Since π is uniform, $\tilde{\pi}$ is also uniform.
- $\pi_0, ..., \pi_{n-1}$ is a sequence of permutations chosen by G and applied to levels of GRAM. These ensure that the physical access pattern leaks nothing to E.

Accounting for the Last Dummy per Access. One small detail remains. Recall that on each access, G statically chooses a dummy on each of the $O(\log n)$ levels. E will be pointed to each of these dummies, save one: E will not read the dummy on the same level as the real element. The identity of the real element is dynamically chosen, so G cannot know which dummy is not read. The parties must somehow account for the GC language of the unread dummy to allow E to proceed with evaluation. (We expand on this need in a moment.)

This accounting is easily handled by a simple circuit C_{hide}. C_{hide} takes as input an encoding of the real physical address and outputs an encoding of the language of the unaccessed dummy.

We now provide more detail (which can be skipped at the first reading) explaining why E must recover an encoding of the language of the unaccessed dummy. Suppose the real element is on level j. G selects $O(\log n)$ dummy languages D_i for this access, and E reads one label in each language $D_{i \neq j}$, and reads the real value. To proceed, G and E must obtain the real value in some agreed language, and this language must depend on all languages D_i (since G cannot know which dummy was not read). Therefore, D_j must be obtained and used by E as well. In even more detail, in the mind of G, the "output" language includes the languages D_i XORed together; to match this, in addition to XORing all labels she already obtained, E XORs in the encoding of the missing dummy language. The validity of this step relies heavily on Free XOR [KS08].

The High Level Procedure. To conclude our overview, we enumerate the steps of the RAM. Consider an arbitrary access to logical index α.

1. E first looks up α's current one-time index p by consulting the index map. The index map returns an encoding of $\pi(p)$ where π is a uniform permutation that hides one-time indices from E.

2. The GC reveals $\pi(p)$ to E in cleartext such that she can route the lazy permutation $\tilde{\pi}$. E uses $\tilde{\pi}$ to route the current RAM time to a leaf circuit that computes encodings of the appropriate physical address @ and GC language. Let ℓ denote the RAM level that holds address @.

3. A per-access circuit $\mathcal{C}_{hide}$ is used to compute (1) encodings of physical addresses of dummies on each populated level $i \neq \ell$ and (2) the GC language of the dummy that *would* have been accessed on level ℓ, had the real element been on some other level.

4. The GC reveals addresses to E and E reads each address. E XORs the results together. (Recall, dummies are garblings of zero.) Each read value is a GC label with a distinct language. To continue, G and E must agree on the language of the resulting GC label. G can trivially account for the GC language of each dummy except for the unaccessed dummy. E XORs on the encoded language for the accessed element and the encoded language for the unaccessed dummy. This allows E to solder the RAM output to the GC such that computation can continue.

5. Parties write back an encoding either of the just-accessed-element (for a read) or of the written element (for a write). This element is written to the smallest level. Parties also write a fresh dummy to the smallest level.

6. G applies a permutation to appropriate RAM levels.

7. After the nth access, E flushes the RAM by reading each index without writing anything back, then initializes a new RAM with the flushed values.

We formalize our GRAM in Sect. 5.4.

3 Related Work

Garbled RAM. [LO13] were the first to achieve sublinear random access in GC. As already mentioned, their GRAM evaluates a PRF inside the GC and also requires a circular-security assumption.

This circularity opened the door to further improvements. [GHL+14] gave two constructions, one that assumes identity-based-encryption and a second that assumes only one-way functions, but that incurs super-polylogarithmic overhead. [GLOS15] improved on this by constructing a GRAM that simultaneously assumes only one-way functions and that achieves polylog overhead. Both of these works avoid the [LO13] circularity assumption, but are expensive because they repeatedly evaluate cryptographic primitives inside the GC.

[GLO15] were the first to achieve a GRAM that makes only black-box use of crypto-primitives. Our lazy permutation network is inspired by [GLO15]: the authors describe a network of GCs, each of which can pass the program control flow to one of several other circuits. In this way they translate between GC languages. Our approach improves over the [GLO15] approach in several ways:

- The [GLO15] GRAM incurs factor κ blowup when passing messages through their network of GCs. Our lazy permutation network avoids this blowup.
- [GLO15] uses a costly probabilistic argument. Each node of their network is connected to a number of other nodes; this number scales with the statistical security parameter. The authors show that the necessary routing can be achieved at runtime with overwhelming probability.[5] This approach uses a network that is *significantly* larger than is needed for any particular routing, and most nodes are ultimately wasted. In contrast, our lazy permutation network is direct. Each node connects to exactly two other nodes, and all connections are fully utilized over n accesses.
- [GLO15] compile their GRAM using off-the-shelf ORAM, incurring multiplicative overhead between their network of GCs and the ORAM. We build a custom RAM that makes minimal use of our lazy permutation network.

In this work, we focus on RAM access in the standard GC setting. A number of other works have explored other dimensions of GRAM, such as parallel RAM access, adaptivity, and succinctness [CCHR16, CH16, LO17, GOS18].

Practical GC and ORAM. Due to space, we defer discussion of works in the areas of practical GC and ORAM to the full version of this paper.

4   Preliminaries, Notation, and Assumptions

4.1   Common Notation

- G is the circuit generator. We refer to G as he/him.
- E is the circuit evaluator. We refer to E as she/her.
- We denote by $\langle x, y \rangle$ a pair of values where G holds x and E holds y.
- κ is the computational security parameter (e.g. 128).
- We write $x \overset{\Delta}{=} y$ to denote that x is defined to be y.
- $\overset{c}{=}$ is the computational indistinguishability relation.
- $x \leftarrow y$ denotes that variable x is assigned to value y; x can later be reassigned.
- We generally use n to denote the number of elements and w to denote the bit-width of those elements.
- $[x]$ denotes the natural numbers $0, ..., x - 1$.

Our construction is a garbling scheme [BHR12], not a protocol. I.e., our construction is merely a tuple of procedures that can be plugged into GC protocols. However, it is often easier to think of G and E as participating in a semi-honest protocol. Thus, we often write that the parties "send messages". We make two notes about this phrasing:

- We will never write that E sends a message to G: all information flows from G to E. In this way, we preserve the constant round nature of GC.
- 'G sends x to E' formally means that (1) our garbling procedure appends x to the GC and (2) our evaluation procedure extracts x from the GC.

---

[5] The [GLO15] probabilistic argument *requires* that indices be accessed randomly. I.e., the [GLO15] leaky array cannot be used except by plugging it into ORAM.

4.2 Cryptographic Assumptions

We use the Free XOR technique [KS08], so we assume a circular correlation robust hash function H [CKKZ12, ZRE15]. In practice, we instantiate H using fixed-key AES [GKWY20].

4.3 Garbling Schemes

A *garbling scheme* [BHR12] is a method for securely computing a class of circuits in constant rounds. A garbling scheme is *not* a protocol; rather, it is a tuple of procedures that can be plugged into a variety of protocols.

Definition 1 (Garbling Scheme). *A garbling scheme for a class of circuits* $\mathbb{C}$ *is a tuple of procedures:*

$$(Gb, En, Ev, De)$$

where (1) Gb maps a circuit $\mathcal{C} \in \mathbb{C}$ *to a garbled circuit* $\tilde{\mathcal{C}}$, *an input encoding string* e, *and an output decoding string* d; *(2) En maps an input encoding string* e *and a cleartext bitstring* x *to an encoded input; (3) Ev maps a circuit* $\mathcal{C}$, *a garbled circuit* $\tilde{\mathcal{C}}$, *and an encoded input to an encoded output; and (4) De maps an output decoding string* d *and encoded output to a cleartext output string.*

A garbling scheme must be *correct* and may satisfy any combination of *obliviousness*, *privacy*, and *authenticity* [BHR12]. We include formal definitions of these properties in the full version of this paper. Our scheme satisfies each definition and hence can be plugged into GC protocols.

4.4 Garblings and Sharings

We work with two kinds of encodings of logical values: 'garblings' and simple XOR shares. Garblings correspond to the traditional notion of garbled labels; i.e., a garbling is a length-κ value held by each party.

Recall from Sect. 2 that we manipulate languages inside the GC. This is why we work also with simple XOR sharings: we use XOR sharings to encode and move languages inside the GC. We define notation for both types of shares, and we emphasize the compatibility of garblings and sharings.

Garblings are Free XOR-style garbled circuit labels [KS08]. G samples a uniform value $\Delta \in \{0,1\}^{\kappa-1}1$. I.e., Δ is uniform except that the least significant bit is one. Δ is *global* to the entire computation. A garbling of $x \in \{0,1\}$ is a tuple $\langle X, X \oplus x\Delta \rangle$, where the first element (here, X) is held by G, and the second by E.

Definition 2 (Garbling). *Let* $x \in \{0,1\}$ *be a bit. Let* $X \in \{0,1\}^{\kappa}$ *be a bitstring held by* G. *We say that the pair* $\langle X, X \oplus x\Delta \rangle$ *is a* garbling *of* x *over (usually implicit)* $\Delta \in \{0,1\}^{\kappa-1}1$. *We denote a garbling of* x *by writing* $\{\!\lvert x \rvert\!\}$:

$$\{\!\lvert x \rvert\!\} \triangleq \langle X, X \oplus x\Delta \rangle$$

Definition 3 (Sharing). *Let* $x, X \in \{0,1\}$ *be two bits. We say that the pair* $\langle X, X \oplus x \rangle$ *is a* sharing *of* x. *We denote a sharing of* x *by writing* $[\![x]\!]$:

$$[\![x]\!] \triangleq \langle X, X \oplus x \rangle$$

We refer to G's share X as the *language* of the garbling (resp. sharing). Except in specific circumstances, we use uniformly random languages both for garblings and for sharings.

Note, XOR is homomorphic over garblings [KS08] and sharings:

$$\{\!|a|\!\} \oplus \{\!|b|\!\} = \{\!|a \oplus b|\!\} \qquad [\![a]\!] \oplus [\![b]\!] = [\![a \oplus b]\!]$$

We extend our garbling and sharing notation to vectors of values. That is, a garbling (resp. sharing) of a vector is a vector of garblings (resp. sharings):

$$\{\!|a_0, ..., a_{n-1}|\!\} \triangleq (\{\!|a_0|\!\}, ..., \{\!|a_{n-1}|\!\}) \qquad [\![a_0, ..., a_{n-1}]\!] \triangleq ([\![a_0]\!], ..., [\![a_{n-1}]\!])$$

Remark 3 (Length of garblings/sharings). Garblings are longer than sharings. I.e., let $x \in \{0,1\}$ be a bit. Then $\{\!|x|\!\}$ is a pair of length-κ strings held by G and E. Meanwhile, $[\![x]\!]$ is a pair of bits held by G and E.

Remark 4 (Sharings contain garblings). Notice that the space of sharings contains the space of garblings. Indeed, this will be important later: we will in certain instances reinterpret a garbling $\{\!|x|\!\}$ as a sharing $[\![x\Delta]\!]$. This will allow us to operate on the garbling as if it is a sharing.

We frequently deal with values that are known to a particular party. We write x^G (resp. x^E) to denote that x is a value known to G (resp. to E) in cleartext. E.g., $\{\!|x^E|\!\}$ indicates a garbling of x where E knows x.

Operations on Sharings/Garblings.

- $\{\!|x|\!\} \mapsto [\![x]\!]$. Recall that G ensures that the least significant bit of Δ is one. Suppose each party takes the least significant bit of his/her part of $\{\!|x|\!\}$:

$$lsb(\{\!|x|\!\}) = lsb(\langle X, X \oplus x\Delta \rangle) \triangleq \langle lsb(X), lsb(X \oplus x\Delta) \rangle$$
$$= \langle lsb(X), lsb(X) \oplus x \cdot lsb(\Delta) \rangle = \langle lsb(X), lsb(X) \oplus x \rangle = [\![x]\!]$$

That is, if both parties compute lsb on their parts of a garbling, the result is a valid sharing of the garbled value. This idea was first used to implement the classic point and permute technique.
- $[\![x]\!] \mapsto x^E$ and $\{\!|x|\!\} \mapsto x^E$. G can open the cleartext value of a sharing by sending his share to E. Similarly, we can open a garbling by first computing lsb (see above) and then opening the resulting share.
- $x^G \mapsto [\![x]\!]$ and $x^G \mapsto \{\!|x|\!\}$. G can easily introduce fresh inputs. Specifically, let x be a bit chosen by G and unknown to E. The parties can construct $\langle x, 0 \rangle = [\![x]\!]$. Similarly, the parties can construct $\langle x\Delta, 0 \rangle = \{\!|x|\!\}$.
- $\{\!|x|\!\} \cdot \{\!|y|\!\} \mapsto \{\!|x \cdot y|\!\}$. Garblings support AND gates. This operation can be implemented using two ciphertexts [ZRE15] (or 1.5 ciphertexts [RR21]).

- INPUT:
  - G inputs a permutation on n elements π.
  - A garbled array $\{x_0, ..., x_{n-1}\}$ where $x_i \in \{0,1\}^w$.
- OUTPUT:
  - The permuted array $\{\pi(x_0, ..., x_{n-1})\}$.

Fig. 2. Interface to the procedure G-*permute* which permutes n values using a permutation π chosen by G. For power of two n, permuting n garbled values each of length w costs $w \cdot (n \log n - n + 1) \cdot \kappa$ bits of communication via a permutation network [Wak68].

- $x^G \cdot \{y\} \mapsto \{x \cdot y\}$. It is possible to instantiate a cheaper AND gate if G knows in cleartext one of the arguments. This operation can be implemented using one ciphertext [ZRE15].
- $\{x^E\} \cdot [\![y]\!] \mapsto [\![x \cdot y]\!]$. This novel operation scales a vector of sharings by a garbling whose cleartext value is known to E. Section 5.1 gives the procedure.
- $\{x\} \cdot y^G \mapsto [\![x \cdot y]\!]$. This operation follows simply from the above scaling procedure. See Sect. 5.1.

4.5 Oblivious Permutation

We permute garbled arrays using permutations chosen by G. A permutation on $n = 2^k$ width-w elements can be implemented using $w(n \log n - n + 1)$ AND gates via a classic construction [Wak68]. Since G chooses the permutation, we can use single ciphertext AND gates and implement the permutation for only $w \cdot (n \log n - n + 1) \cdot \kappa$ bits. Figure 2 lists the interface to this procedure.

5   Approach

In this section we formalize the approach described in Sect. 2. Our formalism covers four topics:

- Section 5.1 formalizes our generalized GC gates. These gates allow us to avoid the factor-κ blowup that is common to prior GRAMs.
- Section 5.2 uses these new gates to modify an existing pop-only stack construction [ZE13]. Our modified pop-only stacks leak their access pattern to E but can efficiently store GC languages.
- Section 5.3 uses pop-only stacks to formalize our lazy permutation network.
- Section 5.4 builds on the lazy permutation network to formalize our GRAM.

We package the algorithms and definitions in this section into a garbling scheme [BHR12] that we call EPIGRAM. EPIGRAM handles arbitrary circuits with AND gates, XOR gates, and array accesses, and is defined as follows:

Construction 1. (EPIGRAM). EPIGRAM *is a garbling scheme (Definition 1) that handles circuits with four kinds of gates:*

- *XOR gates take as input two bits and output the XOR of the two inputs.*
- *AND gates take as input two bits and output the AND of the two inputs.*
- *ARRAY gates are parameterized over power of two n and positive integer w. The gate outputs a zero-initialized array of n elements each of width w.*
- *ACCESS gates take as input (1) an array A, (2) a $(\log n)$-bit index α, (3) a w-bit value y to store in the case of a write, and (4) a bit r that indicates if this is a read or write. The gate outputs $A[\alpha]$. As a side effect, A is mutated:*

$$A[\alpha] \leftarrow \begin{cases} y & \text{if } r = 0 \\ A[\alpha] & \text{otherwise} \end{cases}$$

The garbling scheme procedures are defined as follows:

- *En and De are standard; formally, our scheme is* projective *[BHR12], which allows us to implement En and De as simple maps between cleartext and encoded values. We formalize En and De in the full version of this paper.*
- *Ev and Gb each proceed gate-by-gate through the circuit. For each XOR gate, each procedure XORs the inputs [KS08]. For each AND gate, the procedures compute the half-gates approach [ZRE15]. For each ARRAY gate, Gb (resp. Ev) invokes G's (resp. E's) part of the array initialization procedure (Fig. 9). For each ACCESS gate, Gb (resp. Ev) invokes G's (resp. E's) part of the array access procedure (Fig. 10).*

In the full version of this paper, we prove lemmas and theorems that together imply the following result:

Theorem 1 (Main Theorem). *If H is a circular correlation robust hash function, then* EPIGRAM *is a correct, oblivious, private, and authentic garbling scheme. For each ACCESS gate applied to an array of n elements each of size $w = \Omega(\log^2 n)$, Gb outputs a GC of amortized size $O(w \cdot \log^2 n \cdot \kappa)$ and both Gb and Ev consume amortized $O(w \cdot \log^2 n \cdot \kappa)$ computation.*

5.1   Avoiding Factor κ Blowup

Recall from Sect. 2 that we avoid the factor-κ overhead that is typical in GRAMs. We now give the crucial operation that enables this improvement.

Our operation scales a vector of κ sharings by a garbled bit whose value is known to E. The scaled vector remains hidden from E. The operation computes $\{x^E\} \cdot [\![y]\!] \mapsto [\![x \cdot y]\!]$ for $y \in \{0,1\}^\kappa$ (see Fig. 3). Crucially, the operation only requires that G send to E κ total bits. While this presentation is novel, the procedure in Fig. 3 is a simple generalization of techniques given in [ZRE15]. This generalization allows us to scale an encoded GC language of length w (when $w = c \cdot \kappa$ for some c) for only w bits. This is how we avoid factor-κ blowup.

Formally, we have a *vector space* where the vectors are sharings and the scalars are garblings whose value is known to E. Vector space operations cannot compute arbitrary functions of sharings, but they can arbitrarily move sharings around. These data movements suffice to build our lazy permutation network.

Given Fig. 3, we can also compute $\{x\} \cdot y^G \mapsto [\![x \cdot y]\!]$ for $y \in \{0,1\}^\kappa$:

- INPUT:
  - A garbled bit known to E: $\{x^E\}$.
  - A shared vector $[\![y]\!]$ for $y \in \{0,1\}^\kappa$.
- OUTPUT:
  - A sharing of the scaled vector $[\![x \cdot y]\!]$.
- PROCEDURE $\{x^E\} \cdot [\![y]\!]$:
  - Parties agree on a gate-specific nonce i.
  - Let $\langle X, X \oplus x\Delta \rangle = \{x^E\}$.
  - Let $\langle Y, Y \oplus y \rangle = [\![y]\!]$.
  - G computes and sends to E $row \triangleq H(X \oplus \Delta, i) \oplus H(X, i) \oplus Y$.
  - E computes the following:

$$H(X \oplus x\Delta, i) \oplus x \cdot (row \oplus (Y \oplus y))$$

$$= H(X \oplus x\Delta, i) \oplus \begin{cases} row \oplus (Y \oplus y) & \text{if } x = 1 \\ 0 & \text{otherwise} \end{cases}$$

$$= \begin{cases} H(X \oplus \Delta, i) \oplus (H(X \oplus \Delta, i) \oplus H(X, i) \oplus Y) \oplus Y \oplus y & \text{if } x = 1 \\ H(X, i) & \text{otherwise} \end{cases}$$

$$= H(X, i) \oplus x \cdot y$$

  - Parties output (respective shares of) $\langle H(X, i), H(X, i) \oplus x \cdot y \rangle = [\![x \cdot y]\!]$.

Fig. 3. Scaling a shared κ-bit vector by a garbling where E knows in cleartext the scalar. Scaling a κ-bit sharing requires that G send to E κ bits. We prove the construction secure when G's share of the vector $[\![y]\!]$ is either (1) a uniform bitstring Y or (2) a bitstring $z\Delta$ for $z \in \{0,1\}$. The latter case arises when G introduces a garbled input.

- PROCEDURE $\{x\} \cdot y^G$:
  - Parties compute $[\![x]\!] = lsb(\{x\})$. Let $\langle X, X \oplus x \rangle = [\![x]\!]$.
  - G introduces inputs $\{X\}$, $[\![y]\!]$ and $[\![X \cdot y]\!]$.
  - Parties compute $\{X\} \oplus \{x\} = \{X \oplus x\}$. Note that E knows $X \oplus x$.
  - Parties compute (using Fig. 3) and output:

$$\{X \oplus x\} \cdot [\![y]\!] \oplus [\![X \cdot y]\!] = [\![(X \oplus x) \cdot y]\!] \oplus [\![X \cdot y]\!] = [\![x \cdot y]\!]$$

This procedure is useful in our lazy permutation network and in the $\mathcal{C}_{hide}$ circuit.

5.2 Pop-only Oblivious Stacks

Our lazy permutation network uses pop-only oblivious stacks [ZE13], a data structure with a single pop operation controlled by a garbled bit. If the bit is one, then the stack indeed pops. Otherwise, the stack returns an encoded zero and is left unchanged. Typically, both the data stored in the stack *and* the access pattern are hidden. For our purposes, we only need a stack where the stored data is hidden from E, but where E learns the access pattern.

[ZE13] gave an efficient circuit-based stack construction that incurs only $O(\log n)$ overhead per pop. This construction stores the data across $O(\log n)$

- INPUT:
  • A block of n elements $[\![x_0, ..., x_{n-1}]\!]$ where $x_i \in \{0,1\}^w$.
- OUTPUT:
  • A capacity n stack $Stack(x_0, ..., x_{n-1})$.

- INPUT:
  • A size n stack $Stack(x_0, ..., x_{n-1})$.
  • A garbled bit known to E $\{\!\{p^E\}\!\}$ that indicates whether or not to pop.
- OUTPUT:
  • The popped value $[\![p \cdot x_0]\!]$.
  • The updated stack:

$$\begin{cases} Stack(x_1, ..., x_{n-1}, 0^w) & \text{if } p = 1 \\ Stack(x_0, ..., x_{n-1}) & \text{otherwise} \end{cases}$$

Fig. 4. Interface to stack procedures *stack-init* (top) and *pop* (bottom). For a stack of size n with width-w entries, parties locally initialize using $O(w \cdot n)$ computation; each pop costs amortized $O(w \cdot \log n)$ communication and computation.

levels of exponentially increasing size; larger levels are touched exponentially less often than smaller levels, yielding low logarithmic overhead.

If E is allowed to learn the access pattern, we can implement the [ZE13] construction where the stack holds arbitrary sharings, not just garblings. This is done by replacing AND gates – which move data towards the top of the stack – with our scaling gate (Fig. 3). Since we simply replace AND gates by scaling gates, we do not further specify. A modified stack with n elements each of width w costs amortized $O(w \cdot \log n)$ bits of communication per pop.

Construction 2 (Pop-only Stack). *Let* $x_0, ..., x_{n-1}$ *be a n elements such that* $x_i \in \{0,1\}^w$. *$Stack(x_0, ..., x_{n-1})$ is a pop-only stack of elements* $x_0, ..., x_{n-1}$. *Pop-only stacks support the procedures stack-init and pop (Fig. 4).*

5.3   Lazy Permutations

Recall from Sect. 2 that our lazy permutation network allows E to look up an encoded physical address and an encoded language for the needed RAM slot. The network is a binary tree where each inner node holds two pop-only oblivious stacks. Each inner node forwards messages to its children. Once a message is forwarded all the way to a leaf, the leaf node interprets the message as (1) an encoding of the current RAM time and (2) an encoding of an output language. This leaf node accordingly computes encodings of the appropriate physical address and language, then translates these to the output language. The encoded address and language are later used to allow E to read from RAM.

Inner Nodes and Implementation of Garbled Switches. For simplicity of notation, let level 0 denote the tree level that holds the leaves; level $\log n$ holds

- INPUT:
  - Let i denote the node id and k denote the tree level. Level 0 holds leaves; level $\log n$ holds the root.
  - Parties input two stacks $s_0 = Stack(L_{2i}^\ell, ...)$ and $s_1 = Stack(L_{2i+1}^r, ...)$ such that each language L_a^b is an independent uniform string unknown to E.
  - Parties input message $[\![m]\!]$ such that $m \in \{0,1\}^{k \cdot \kappa + w}$
  - E inputs a bit d indicating if m should be sent to the left or right child.
- OUTPUT:
  - E outputs $L_{2i+d}^{(\bar{d}\ell + dr)} \oplus m'$ for $m' \in \{0,1\}^{(k-1)\kappa + w}$. I.e., she outputs a share that encodes the last $(k-1)\kappa + w$ bits of the incoming message m and that is encoded by a language for child d.
  - Parties output updated stacks $Stack(L_{2i}^{\ell + \bar{d}}, ...)$ and $Stack(L_{2i+1}^{r+d}, ...)$.
- PROCEDURE $inner(s_0, s_1, [\![m]\!], d)$:
  - Parties parse $[\![m]\!]$ as $\{\![d^E]\!\}, [\![m']\!]$.
  - Parties pop both stacks (Figure 4):

  $$([\![\bar{d} \cdot L_{2i}^\ell]\!], s_0') = pop(s_0, \{\![\bar{d}]\!\}) \qquad ([\![d \cdot L_{2i+1}^r]\!], s_1') = pop(s_1, \{\![d]\!\})$$

  - Parties compute:

  $$[\![\bar{d} \cdot L_{2i}^\ell \oplus d \cdot L_{2i+1}^r \oplus m']\!] = [\![L_{2i+d}^{(\bar{d}\ell + dr)} \oplus m']\!]$$

  - G opens his share to E and E outputs $L_{2i+d}^{(\bar{d}\ell + dr)} \oplus m'$.
  - Parties output s_0' and s_1'.

Fig. 5. Procedure for inner nodes of a lazy permutation network, implementing garbled switches.

the root. Consider an arbitrary inner node i on level k. This node can 2^k times receive a message $[\![m]\!]$ of a fixed, arbitrary length. On each message, the node strips the first κ bits from the message and interprets them as the garbling of a bit $\{\![d]\!\}$. d is a direction indicator: if $d = 0$, then the node forwards the remaining message to its left child; otherwise it forwards to its right child. Over its lifetime, the inner node forwards 2^{k-1} messages to its left child and 2^{k-1} messages to its right child. Crucially, the *order* in which a node distributes its 2^k messages to its children is not decided until runtime.

Each of the 2^k messages are sharings with a particular language. I.e., the jth message $[\![m_j]\!]$ has form $\langle L_j, L_j \oplus m_j \rangle$ where each language L_j is distinct. The node must convert each message to a language next expected by the target child.

Assume that a particular node has so far forwarded ℓ messages to its left child and r messages to its right child. Let L_a^b denote the bth input language for node a. Note that the current language is thus $L_i^{\ell+r}$ and the language expected by the left (resp. right) child is L_{2i}^ℓ (resp. L_{2i+1}^r).

To forward m_j based on d, the node computes the following translation value:

$$[\![\bar{d} \cdot L_{2i}^\ell \oplus d \cdot L_{2i+1}^r]\!] = [\![L_{2i+d}^{(\bar{d}\ell + dr)}]\!] \tag{1}$$

- INPUT:
  - Let this node be leaf $\pi(p)$ where π is a permutation chosen by G.
  - G inputs the storage metadata (Definition 4) $\mathcal{M}_p$ for one-time index p.
  - Parties input $\{\!|T|\!\}$, a garbling of the current RAM time.
  - Parties input $[\![Y]\!]$, a sharing of an output language such that Y is uniform.
- OUTPUT:
  - Let $(t_i^p, @_i^p, X_i^p)_{i \in [\log n]} = \mathcal{M}_p$. Let t_j^p be the largest metadata timer such that $t_j^p \leq T$. E outputs $Y \oplus (@_j^p \cdot \Delta, X_j^p)$. I.e., she outputs a sharing of the appropriate physical address and language for one-time index p.
- PROCEDURE $leaf(\mathcal{M}_p, \{\!|T|\!\}, [\![Y]\!])$:
  - Parties set $\{\!|@|\!\} \leftarrow \{\!|@_0^p|\!\}$ and $[\![X]\!] \leftarrow [\![X_0^p]\!]$.
  - For each $i \in \{1 .. \log n - 1\}$ parties compute $\{\!|t_i^p \leq T|\!\}$ via a Boolean circuit.
  - For each $i \in \{1 .. \log n - 1\}$ the parties update $[\![X]\!]$:

$$
\begin{aligned}
[\![X]\!] &\leftarrow [\![X]\!] \oplus \{\!|t_i^p \leq T|\!\} \cdot (X_{i-1}^p \oplus X_i^p) \\
&= [\![X \oplus (t_i^p \leq T) \cdot (X_{i-1}^p \oplus X_i^p)]\!] \qquad G \text{ knows } (X_{i-1}^p \oplus X_i^p) \\
&= \begin{cases} [\![X \oplus X \oplus X_i^p]\!] & \text{if } t_i^p \leq T \\ [\![X]\!] & \text{otherwise} \end{cases} \quad (t_i^p \leq T) \Rightarrow (t_{i-1}^p \leq T) \text{ (Defn. 4)} \\
&= \begin{cases} [\![X_i^p]\!] & \text{if } t_i^p \leq T \\ [\![X]\!] & \text{otherwise} \end{cases}
\end{aligned}
$$

We elaborate the above step carefully to show this conditional update can be achieved using efficient sharing procedures given in Section 5.1.
  - For each $i \in \{1 .. \log n - 1\}$ the parties update $\{\!|@|\!\}$ via a Boolean circuit:

$$
\{\!|@|\!\} \leftarrow \begin{cases} \{\!|@_i^p|\!\} & \text{if } t_i^p \leq T \\ \{\!|@|\!\} & \text{otherwise} \end{cases}
$$

  - Let $[\![m]\!] \triangleq \{\!|@|\!\}, [\![X]\!]$ be the concatenated output. Then parties compute $[\![m \oplus Y]\!]$ and G opens his share to E.
  - E outputs $m \oplus Y = Y \oplus (@_j^p \cdot \Delta, X_j^p)$.

Fig. 6. Procedure for leaf nodes of a lazy permutation network.

To compute the above, node i maintains two oblivious pop-only stacks (see Sect. 5.2) of size 2^{k-1}. The first stack stores, in order, sharings of the 2^{k-1} languages for the left child. The second stack similarly stores languages for the right child. By popping both stacks based on $\{\!|d|\!\}$, the node computes Eq. (1). Figure 5 specifies the formal procedure for inner nodes.

Leaf Nodes. Once a message has propagated from the root node to a leaf, we are ready to complete a lookup. Each leaf node of the lazy permutation network is a static circuit that outputs the encoding of a physical address and a language.

As the parties access RAM, G repeatedly permutes the physical storage to hide the access pattern from E. Each one-time index p has $O(\log n)$ different

- INPUT:
  - Let i denote the node id and k denote the tree level. Level 0 holds leaves; level $\log n$ holds the root.
  - Parties input two stacks $s_0 = Stack(L_{2i}^{\ell}, ...)$ and $s_1 = Stack(L_{2i+1}^{r}, ...)$ such that each language L_a^b is an independent uniform string unknown to E.
  - Parties input message $[\![m]\!]$ such that $m \in \{0, 1\}^{k \cdot \kappa + w}$
  - E inputs a bit d indicating if m should be sent to the left or right child.
- OUTPUT:
  - E outputs $L_{2i+d}^{(\bar{d}\ell + dr)} \oplus m'$ for $m' \in \{0, 1\}^{(k-1)\kappa + w}$. I.e., she outputs a share that encodes the last $(k-1)\kappa + w$ bits of the incoming message m and that is encoded by a language for child d.
  - Parties output updated stacks $Stack(L_{2i}^{\ell + \bar{d}}, ...)$ and $Stack(L_{2i+1}^{r+d}, ...)$.
- PROCEDURE $inner(s_0, s_1, [\![m]\!], d)$:
  - Parties parse $[\![m]\!]$ as $\{\!\!\{d^E\}\!\!\}, [\![m']\!]$.
  - Parties pop both stacks (Figure 4):

$$([\![\bar{d} \cdot L_{2i}^{\ell}]\!], s_0') = pop(s_0, \{\!\!\{\bar{d}\}\!\!\}) \qquad ([\![d \cdot L_{2i+1}^{r}]\!], s_1') = pop(s_1, \{\!\!\{d\}\!\!\})$$

  - Parties compute:

$$[\![\bar{d} \cdot L_{2i}^{\ell} \oplus d \cdot L_{2i+1}^{r} \oplus m']\!] = [\![L_{2i+d}^{(\bar{d}\ell + dr)} \oplus m']\!]$$

  - G opens his share to E and E outputs $L_{2i+d}^{(\bar{d}\ell + dr)} \oplus m'$.
  - Parties output s_0' and s_1'.

Fig. 7. Lazy permutation network initialization. When initializing with leaves that store languages of length w, G sends to E a GC of size $O(w \cdot n \cdot \log^2 n)$ bits.

physical addresses and languages; the needed address and language depends on how many accesses have occurred. Thus, each leaf node must conditionally output one of $O(\log n)$ values depending on how many accesses have occurred.

G chooses all permutations and storage languages before the first RAM access. Hence, G can precompute metadata indicating which one-time index will be stored where and with what language at which point in time:

Definition 4 (Storage Metadata). *Consider a one-time index p. The storage metadata $\mathcal{M}_p$ for one-time index p is a sequence of $\log n$ three-tuples:*

$$\mathcal{M}_p \triangleq (t_i^p, @_i^p, L_i^p)_{[i \in \log n]}$$

where each t_i^p is a natural number that indicates a point in time, $@_i^p$ is a physical address, and L_i^p is a uniform language. Each time $t_i \leq t_{i+1}$.

In our construction, each one-time index p may have fewer than $\log n$ corresponding physical addresses. G pads storage metadata by repeating the last entry until all $\log n$ slots are filled. G uses the storage metadata for each one-time index to configure each leaf. Figure 6 specifies the procedure for leaf nodes.

- INPUT:
  - A size n lazy permutation network $\tilde{\pi}$.
  - A garbled index $\{\!\{\pi(p)\}\!\}$ such that $\pi(p)$ has not yet been routed.
  - The current RAM time T.
- OUTPUT:
  - A physical address $\{\!\{@^p\}\!\}$.
  - A shared language $[\![X^p]\!]$.
  - The updated lazy permutation network (i.e., where $\pi(p)$ has been routed).
- PROCEDURE $route(\tilde{\pi}, \{\!\{\pi(p)\}\!\}, T)$:
  - Let v denote the number of times $\tilde{\pi}$ has already been used.
  - G and E parse the input lazy permutation network:

  $$\left([\![L_0^{j\in[n]}]\!], (s_{i\in[n-1]}^{\ell}, s_{i\in[n-1]}^{r}) \right) = \tilde{\pi}$$

  - G samples a uniform value Y with length appropriate for the output; the parties trivially hold $[\![Y]\!]$. The parties also hold $[\![L_0^v]\!]$.
  - Parties collect $[\![m]\!] \triangleq \{\!\{\pi(p)\}\!\}, \{\!\{T\}\!\}, [\![Y]\!]$ and then compute $[\![L_0^v \oplus m]\!]$; G opens his share to E such that E holds $L_0^v \oplus m$.
  - Recall from Figure 7 that at initialization, E stored 2^k GCs for each level k node. Let E initialize $M \leftarrow L_0^v \oplus m$. E now traverses the tree from root to leaf $\pi(p)$. At each node i on the path to $\pi(p)$, G invokes:

  $$(M, s_j^{\ell}, s_j^{r}) \leftarrow inner(s_j^{\ell}, s_j^{r}, M, d)$$

  where j is the id of the ith node on the path to $\pi(p)$ and d is the ith bit of $\pi(p)$. To perform each invocation, E loads in the jth GC stored at initialization. This propagates E's share of $\{\!\{T\}\!\}$ and $[\![Y]\!]$ to leaf $\pi(p)$.
  - E invokes (using the appropriate GC) the leaf node procedure:

  $$Y \oplus (@^p \cdot \Delta, X^p) \leftarrow leaf(\cdot, \{\!\{T\}\!\}, [\![Y]\!])$$

  - The parties output the updated $\tilde{\pi}$.
  - The parties compute and output:

  $$\langle Y, Y \oplus (@^p \cdot \Delta, X^p) \rangle = [\![@^p \cdot \Delta, X^p]\!] = \{\!\{@^p\}\!\}, [\![X^p]\!]$$

Fig. 8. Procedure to route one value through a lazy permutation network.

Putting the Network Together. We now formalize the top level lazy permutation network. To instantiate a new network, G and E agree on a size n and a width w and G provides storage metadata, conveying the information that should be stored at the leaves of the network. From here, G proceeds node-by-node through the binary tree, fully garbling each node. E receives all such GCs from G, but crucially she does not yet begin to evaluate. Instead, she stores the GCs for later use, remembering which GCs belong to each individual node.

Recall that G selects a uniform permutation π that prevents E from viewing the one-time index access pattern: when the GC requests access to one-time index p, E is shown $\pi(p)$. Now, let us consider the ith access to the network. At the time of this access, a garbled index $\{\!\{\pi(p)\}\!\}$ is given as input by the parties.

G selects a uniform language Y to use as the output language, and the parties trivially construct the sharing $[\![Y]\!]$. The parties then concatenate the message $[\![m_i]\!] \triangleq \{\!|\pi(p)|\!\}, \{\!|T|\!\}, [\![Y]\!]$ where T is the number of RAM writes performed so far. Let L_0^i denote the ith input language for the root node 0. The parties compute $[\![L_0^i]\!] \oplus [\![m_i]\!]$ and G sends his resulting share, giving to E a valid share of m_i with language configured for the root node. E now feeds this value into the tree, starting from the root node and traversing the path to leaf $\pi(p)$. Note that G does not perform this traversal, since he already garbled all circuits.

Each inner node strips off one garbled bit of $\pi(p)$. This propagates the message to leaf $\pi(p)$. Finally, the leaf node computes the appropriate physical address and language for one-time index p and translates them to language Y. Let $Y \oplus (@^p \cdot \Delta, L^p)$ denote E's output from the leaf node. The parties output:

$$\langle Y, Y \oplus (@^p \cdot \Delta, L^p) \rangle = [\![@^p \cdot \Delta, L^p]\!] = \{\!|@^p|\!\}, [\![L^p]\!]$$

Thus, the parties successfully read an address and a language from the network.

Construction 3. (Lazy Permutation Network). *Let n be a power of two. A size-n lazy permutation network $\tilde{\pi}$ is a two-tuple consisting of:*

1. *Sharings of the input languages to the root node $[\![L_0^{j \in [n]}]\!]$.*
2. *$2n - 2$ stacks belonging to the $n - 1$ inner nodes, $s_{i \in [n-1]}^{\ell}$ and $s_{i \in [n-1]}^r$.*

Here, each input language $L_0^{j \in [n]}$ and each language stored in each stack is an independently sampled uniform string. Lazy permutation networks support initialization (Fig. 7) and routing of a single input (Fig. 8).

5.4   Our GRAM

We formalize our GRAM on top of our lazy permutation network:

Construction 4. (GRAM). *Let n – the RAM size – be a power of two and let w – the word size – be a positive integer. Let $x_0, ..., x_{n-1}$ be n values such that $x_i \in \{0, 1\}^w$. Then $Array(x_{i \in [n]})$ denotes a size-n GRAM holding the content $x_{i \in [n]}$. Concretely, a GRAM is a tuple consisting of:*

1. *A timer T denoting the number of writes performed so far.*
2. *A sequence of languages $\mathcal{X}$ held by G and used as the languages for the permuted RAM content. Each language has length $w \cdot \kappa$, sufficient to encode a single garbled word.*
3. *A size-$2n$ uniform permutation π held by G.*
4. *A sequence of $n + 1$ uniform permutations $\pi_0, ..., \pi_n$ held by G and used to permute the physical storage. These hide the RAM access pattern from E.*
5. *A size-$2n$ lazy permutation $\tilde{\pi}$.*
6. *A recursively instantiated RAM called the index map that maps each logical index α to $\pi(p)$: the (permuted) one-time index where α is currently saved. For each recursive RAM of size n, we instantiate the index map with word size $w = 2(\log n + 1)$. To bound the recursion, we use a linear-scan based RAM when instantiating a index map that stores only $O(w \cdot \log^2 n)$ bits.*

- INPUT:
  - Let n denote a number of elements and let w denote the width of each element. The parties input a vector $\{x_0, ..., x_{n-1}\}$ where $x_i \in \{0,1\}^w$
- OUTPUT:
  - A length n random access array $Array(x_{i \in [n]})$.
- PROCEDURE $array\text{-}init(\{x_{i \in [n]}\})$:
  - Parties initialize the timer T to n, indicating the n initial writes.
  - G schedules all accesses and computes his needed metadata:

  $$(\mathcal{X}, \mathcal{M}_{p \in [2n]}, \pi_{i \in [n+1]}) \leftarrow G\text{-}schedule(n, w)$$

  - G uniformly samples a size-$2n$ permutation π.
  - Parties instantiate the lazy permutation network: $\tilde{\pi} \leftarrow \tilde{\pi}\text{-}init(\pi, \mathcal{M}_{p \in [2n]})$
  - G and E recursively initialize the index map with content $\{0, 1, ..., n-1\}$, indicating that each index i starts in one-time index i:

  $$index\text{-}map \leftarrow array\text{-}init(\{0, 1, ..., n-1\})$$

  - Parties zero initialize the stash and each of the $\log n + 2$ levels of storage.
  - Parties store the initial data $\{x_{i \in [n]}\}$ on level $\log n - 1$.[a]

  ---
  [a] This is a simple trick. On each access, we shuffle RAM levels (see Figure 10) By initializing the content on level $\log n - 1$, we ensure that the first access will shuffle the n items with n dummies and place them on level $\log n$.

Fig. 9. RAM initialize.

7. $\log n + 2$ levels *of physical storage where level i is a garbling of size $w \cdot 2^{i+1}$. Each level i is either vacant or stores 2^i real elements and 2^i dummies. The physical storage is permuted according to permutations $\pi_0, ..., \pi_n$.*

8. *A garbling of size $2w$ called the* stash. *Parties write back to the stash; on each access, items are immediately moved from the stash into a level of storage.*

GRAMs support initialization (Fig. 9) and access (Fig. 10).

Our top level garbling scheme is defined with respect to this data structure; EPIGRAM makes explicit calls to *array-init* (Fig. 9) and *access* (Fig. 10). We call attention to *G-schedule*, *shuffle*, *flush*, and *hide*:

- *G-schedule* is a local procedure run by G where he plans ahead for the next n accesses. Specifically, G selects uniform permutations on storage, chooses uniform languages with which to store the RAM content, and computes the storage metadata $\mathcal{M}_p$ for each one-time index $p \in [2n]$. The full version of this paper gives the explicit interface to *G-schedule*.
- *shuffle* describes how G permutes levels of storage. By doing so, we ensure that the revealed physical addresses give no information to E. *shuffle* is a straightforward formalization of the permutation schedule given in Sect. 2.4 and is formalized in the full version of this paper.

- INPUT:
  - A length n array $A = Array(x_0, ..., x_{n-1})$.
  - A garbled index $\{\!|\alpha|\!\}$ such that $\alpha \in \{0,1\}^{\log n}$.
  - A garbled value $\{\!|y|\!\}$ to store in the case of a write.
  - A garbled bit $\{\!|r|\!\}$ that indicates if this is a read; else this is a write.
- OUTPUT:
  - The indexed value $\{\!|x_\alpha|\!\}$.
  - The updated array $Array(x_0, ..., x_{\alpha-1}, (r \cdot x_\alpha \oplus \bar{r} \cdot y), x_{\alpha+1}, ..., x_{n-1})$.
- PROCEDURE $access(A, \{\!|\alpha|\!\}, \{\!|y|\!\}, \{\!|r|\!\})$:
  - Parties appropriately permute levels of storage: $A \leftarrow shuffle(A)$
  - If $T = 2n$ then the parties reinitialize and try again, returning that result:

  $$access(array\text{-}init(flush(A)), \{\!|\alpha|\!\}, \{\!|y|\!\}, \{\!|r|\!\})$$

  Otherwise, the parties continue as follows:

  - Parties recursively access the index map and update the one-time index for index α by writing back a garbling $\{\!|\pi(T)|\!\}$ (G knows $\pi(T)$):

  $$\{\!|\pi(p)|\!\} \leftarrow access(index\text{-}map, \{\!|\alpha|\!\}, \{\!|\pi(T)|\!\}, \{\!|0|\!\})$$

  - G opens his share of $\{\!|\pi(p)|\!\}$ to reveal $\pi(p)$ to E.
  - E uses $\tilde{\pi}$ to route time T to leaf $\pi(p)$. This returns the current physical address and language corresponding to p.

  $$(\{\!|@|\!\}, [\![X]\!]) \leftarrow route(\tilde{\pi}, \{\!|\pi(p)|\!\}, T)$$

  - For each populated storage level i, G chooses a previously unaccessed dummy element with address $@'_i$ and language D_i.
  - Let j denote the level that holds $@$. Parties compute (See the full version for details of $hide$):

  $$(\{\!|@_i|\!\}, [\![D_j]\!]) \leftarrow hide(@'_i, D_i, \{\!|@|\!\})$$

  I.e., $hide$ computes one physical address per populated storage level.
  - G reveals to E each physical address $@_i$ by sending his share.
  - E reads each physical address and XORs the values together. I.e., E reads each dummy language $D_{i \neq j}$ and the desired element $X \oplus x_\alpha \Delta$. This yields:

  $$\left(\bigoplus_{i \neq j} D_i \right) \oplus X \oplus x_\alpha \Delta$$

  - Let $\langle L, L \oplus X \rangle = [\![X]\!]$ and $\langle L', L' \oplus D_j \rangle = [\![D_j]\!]$. Parties compute and output:

  $$\left\langle L \oplus L' \oplus \left(\bigoplus_i D_i \right), L \oplus X \oplus L' \oplus D_j \oplus \left(\bigoplus_{i \neq j} D_i \right) \oplus X \oplus x_\alpha \Delta \right\rangle$$
  $$= \left\langle L \oplus L' \oplus \left(\bigoplus_i D_i \right), L \oplus L' \oplus \left(\bigoplus_i D_i \right) \oplus x_\alpha \Delta \right\rangle = \{\!|x_\alpha|\!\}$$

  - Parties compute $\{\!|r \cdot x_\alpha \oplus \bar{r} \cdot y|\!\}$ and place their shares in the first slot of the stash. Parties place $\{\!|0|\!\}$, a fresh dummy, in the second slot of the stash.
  - Parties increment the timer: $T \leftarrow T + 1$.

Fig. 10. RAM access.

- INPUT:
  - A length n array $A = Array(x_0, ..., x_{n-1})$.
- OUTPUT:
  - The flushed content $\{x_0, ..., x_{n-1}\}$.
- PROCEDURE $flush(A)$:
  - Parties recursively flush the index map:

  $$\{\pi(p_0), ..., \pi(p_{n-1})\} \leftarrow flush(index\text{-}map)$$

  - For each $i \in [n]$ the parties route time T to leaf $\pi(p_i)$, returning the current physical address and language corresponding to p_i:

  $$(\{@_i\}, [\![X_i]\!]) \leftarrow route(\tilde{\pi}, \{\pi(p_i)\}, T)$$

  When flushing, each level $i \neq \log n + 1$ is vacant, so we need not use extra machinery to hide the accessed level: E knows each item is on level $\log n + 1$.
  - G reveals to E each physical address $@_i$ by sending his share.
  - E reads each address $@_i$, yielding $X_i \oplus x_i \Delta$.
  - For each i, let $\langle L_i, L_i \oplus X_i \rangle = [\![X_i]\!]$. Parties compute and output:

  $$\langle L_i, L_i \oplus X_i \oplus X_i \oplus x_i \Delta \rangle = \{x_i\}$$

Fig. 11. *flush* is a helper procedure used to reset the array after n accesses. *flush* recovers the n array elements and places them into a contiguous block.

- After each n-th access, we invoke *flush* (Fig. 11) to reinitialize GRAM. We also mention that our proof of correctness defines correctness of the GRAM data structure with respect to *flush*: a GRAM is *valid* if we can flush and recover its content.
- On each access, *hide* picks a dummy on each storage level, the conveys to E (1) a physical address on each level of storage and (2) a sharing of the language of the unaccessed dummy. The precise procedure is formalized in the full version of this paper.

With these four helper procedures defined, we formalize GRAM initialization (Fig. 9) and GRAM access (Fig. 10). Initialization is straightforward, and GRAM access is a formalization of the high level procedure given in Sect. 2.4.

6   Evaluation

In this section, we analyze EPIGRAM's performance. We leave implementation and low-level optimization as important future work.

To estimate cost, we implemented a program that modularly computes the communication cost of each of EPIGRAM's subcomponents. E.g., a permutation network on n width-w elements uses $w \cdot (n \log n - n + 1)$ ciphertexts [Wak68].

Figure 12 fixes the word size w to 128. That is, each RAM slot stores 128 *garbled* bits. We plot the estimated communication cost as a function of n. For comparison, we also plot the cost of a linear scan; a linear scan on n elements of

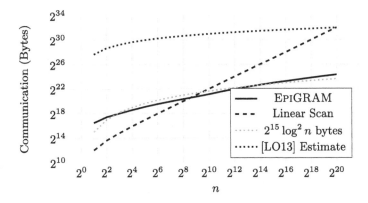

Fig. 12. Estimated concrete communication cost of our GRAM. We fix the word size $w = 128$ and plot per-access amortized communication as a function of n. For comparison we include an estimate of [LO13]'s performance (our estimate is favorable to [LO13], see the full version for our analysis).

width w and while using [ZRE15] AND gates can be achieved for (slightly more than) $2 \cdot w \cdot (n-1)$ ciphertexts. We also plot the function $2^{15} \log^2 n$ bytes, a close approximation of EpiGRAM's cost for $w = 128$.

Figure 12 clearly demonstrates EpiGRAM's low polylogarithmic scaling. Note that our communication grows slightly faster than the function $2^{15} \log^2 n$. This can be explained by the fact that we *fixed* a relatively low and constant word size $w = 128$; recall that to achieve $O(\log^2 n)$ scaling, we must choose $w = \Omega(\log^2 n)$. Still, our cost is closely modeled by $O(\log^2 n)$.

EpiGRAM is practical even for small n. The breakeven point with trivial GRAM (i.e., GRAM implemented by linear scans) is only $n = 512$ elements. Even non-garbled ORAMs have similar breakeven points. For example, Circuit ORAM [WCS15] gives the breakeven point $w = 128, n = 128$. At $n = 2^{20}$, EpiGRAM consumes $\approx 200\times$ less communication than trivial GRAM.

Acknowledgements. This work was supported in part by NSF award #1909769, by a Facebook research award, a Cisco research award, and by Georgia Tech's IISP cybersecurity seed funding (CSF) award. This material is also based upon work supported in part by DARPA under Contract No. HR001120C0087. Work of the third author is supported in part by DARPA under Cooperative Agreement HR0011-20-2-0025, NSF grant CNS-2001096, US-Israel BSF grant 2015782, Google Faculty Award, JP Morgan Faculty Award, IBM Faculty Research Award, Xerox Faculty Research Award, OKAWA Foundation Research Award, B. John Garrick Foundation Research Award, Teradata Research Award, Lockheed-Martin Research Award and Sunday Group. The views and conclusions contained herein are those of the authors and should not be interpreted as necessarily representing the official policies, either expressed or implied, of DARPA, the Department of Defense, or the U.S. Government. Distribution Statement "A" (Approved for Public Release, Distribution Unlimited). The U.S. Government is authorized to reproduce and distribute reprints for governmental purposes not withstanding any copyright annotation therein.

References

[BHR12] Bellare, M., Hoang, V.T., Rogaway, P.: Foundations of garbled circuits. In: Yu, T., Danezis, G., Gligor, V.D. (eds.) ACM CCS 2012, pp. 784–796. ACM Press, October 2012

[CCHR16] Canetti, R., Chen, Y., Holmgren, J., Raykova, M.: Adaptive succinct garbled RAM or: how to delegate your database. In: Hirt, M., Smith, A. (eds.) TCC 2016. LNCS, vol. 9986, pp. 61–90. Springer, Heidelberg (2016). https://doi.org/10.1007/978-3-662-53644-5_3

[CH16]   Canetti, R., Holmgren, J.: Fully succinct garbled RAM. In: Sudan, M., (ed.) ITCS 2016, pp. 169–178. ACM, January 2016

[CKKZ12] Choi, S.G., Katz, J., Kumaresan, R., Zhou, H.-S.: On the security of the "Free-XOR" technique. In: Cramer, R. (ed.) TCC 2012. LNCS, vol. 7194, pp. 39–53. Springer, Heidelberg (2012). https://doi.org/10.1007/978-3-642-28914-9_3

[GHL+14] Gentry, C., Halevi, S., Steve, L., Ostrovsky, R., Raykova, M., Wichs, D.: Garbled RAM revisited. In: Nguyen, P.Q., Oswald, E. (eds.) EUROCRYPT 2014. LNCS, vol. 8441, pp. 405–422. Springer, Heidelberg (2014)

[GKWY20] Guo, C., Katz, J., Wang, X., Yu, Y.: Efficient and secure multiparty computation from fixed-key block ciphers. In: 2020 IEEE Symposium on Security and Privacy, pp. 825–841. IEEE Computer Society Press, May 2020

[GLO15] Garg, S., Lu, S., Ostrovsky, R.: Black-box garbled RAM. In: Guruswami, V. (ed.) 56th FOCS, pp. 210–229. IEEE Computer Society Press, October 2015

[GLOS15] Garg, S., Lu, S., Ostrovsky, R., Scafuro, A.: Garbled RAM from one-way functions. In: Servedio, R.A., Rubinfeld, R. (eds.) 47th ACM STOC, pp. 449–458. ACM Press, June 2015

[GOS18] Garg, S., Ostrovsky, R., Srinivasan, A.: Adaptive garbled RAM from laconic oblivious transfer. Cryptology ePrint Archive, Report 2018/549 (2018). https://eprint.iacr.org/2018/549

[HK21]   Heath, D., Kolesnikov, V.: PrORAM: Fast $O(\log n)$ private coin ZK ORAM (2021)

[KS08]   Kolesnikov, V., Schneider, T.: Improved garbled circuit: free XOR gates and applications. In: Aceto, L., Damgård, I., Goldberg, L.A., Halldórsson, M.M., Ingólfsdóttir, A., Walukiewicz, I. (eds.) ICALP 2008. LNCS, vol. 5126, pp. 486–498. Springer, Heidelberg (2008). https://doi.org/10.1007/978-3-540-70583-3_40

[LO13]   Steve, L., Ostrovsky, R.: How to garble RAM programs. In: Johansson, T., Nguyen, P.Q. (eds.) EUROCRYPT 2013. LNCS, vol. 7881, pp. 719–734. Springer, Heidelberg (2013)

[LO17]   Steve, L., Ostrovsky, R.: Black-box parallel garbled RAM. In: Katz, J., Shacham, H. (eds.) CRYPTO 2017. Part II, volume 10402 of LNCS, pp. 66–92. Springer, Heidelberg (2017)

[RR21]   Rosulek, M., Roy, L.: Three halves make a whole? beating the half-gates lower bound for garbled circuits. In: Malkin, T., Peikert, C. (eds.) CRYPTO 2021. LNCS, vol. 12825, pp. 94–124. Springer, Cham (2021). https://doi.org/10.1007/978-3-030-84242-0_5

[SvS+13] Stefanov, E., et al.: Path ORAM: an extremely simple oblivious RAM protocol. In: Sadeghi, A.-R., Gligor, V.D., Yung, M. (eds.) ACM CCS 2013, pp. 299–310. ACM Press, November 2013

[Wak68] Waksman, A.: A permutation network. J. ACM **15**(1), 159–163 (1968)

[WCS15] Xiao Wang, T.-H. Chan, H., Shi, E.: Circuit ORAM: On tightness of the Goldreich-Ostrovsky lower bound. In: Ray, I., Li, N., Kruegel, C. (eds.) ACM CCS 2015, pp. 850–861. ACM Press, October 2015

[ZE13] Zahur, S., Evans, D.: Circuit structures for improving efficiency of security and privacy tools. In: 2013 IEEE Symposium on Security and Privacy, pp. 493–507. IEEE Computer Society Press, May 2013

[ZRE15] Zahur, S., Rosulek, M., Evans, D.: Two halves make a whole - reducing data transfer in garbled circuits using half gates. In: Oswald, E., Fischlin, M. (eds.) EUROCRYPT 2015. LNCS, vol. 9057, pp. 220–250. Springer, Heidelberg (2015). https://doi.org/10.1007/978-3-662-46803-6_8

Secure Multiparty Computation

Garbled Circuits with Sublinear Evaluator

Abida Haque[1], David Heath[2]([✉]), Vladimir Kolesnikov[2], Steve Lu[3],
Rafail Ostrovsky[4], and Akash Shah[4]

[1] NC State, Raleigh, USA
ahaque3@ncsu.edu
[2] Georgia Tech, Atlanta, USA
{heath.davidanthony,kolesnikov}@gatech.edu
[3] Stealth Software Technologies, Inc., Los Angeles, USA
steve@stealthsoftwareinc.com
[4] UCLA, Los Angeles, USA
rafail@cs.ucla.edu, akashshah08@ucla.edu

Abstract. A recent line of work, Stacked Garbled Circuit (SGC), showed that Garbled Circuit (GC) can be improved for functions that include conditional behavior. SGC relieves the communication bottleneck of 2PC by only sending enough garbled material for a single branch out of the b total branches. Hence, communication is sublinear in the circuit size. However, both the evaluator and the generator pay in computation and perform at least factor $\log b$ *extra* work as compared to standard GC.

We extend the sublinearity of SGC to *also* include the work performed by the GC evaluator E; thus we achieve a fully sublinear E, which is essential when optimizing for the online phase. We formalize our approach as a garbling scheme called GCWise: *GC WIth Sublinear Evaluator*.

We show one attractive and immediate application, Garbled PIR, a primitive that marries GC with Private Information Retrieval. Garbled PIR allows the GC to non-interactively and sublinearly access a privately indexed element from a publicly known database, and then use this element in continued GC evaluation.

1 Introduction

Garbled Circuit (GC) is a foundational cryptographic technique that allows two parties to jointly compute arbitrary functions of their private inputs while revealing nothing but the outputs. GC allows the parties to securely compute while using only constant rounds of communication. The technique requires that one party, the GC generator G, send to the other party, the GC evaluator E, a large "encryption" of a circuit that expresses the desired function. We refer to these circuit encryptions as GC material. The bandwidth consumed when sending GC material is typically understood to be the GC bottleneck.

A. Shah—Work partially done while at Microsoft Research, India.

O. Dunkelman and S. Dziembowski (Eds.): EUROCRYPT 2022, LNCS 13275, pp. 37–64, 2022.
https://doi.org/10.1007/978-3-031-06944-4_2

Stacked Garbling [HK20a, HK21] – or Stacked GC, SGC – is a recent GC improvement that reduces bandwidth consumption for functions with conditional behavior. We review SGC in Sect. 3.1. In SGC, G sends material proportional to only the single longest branch, not to the entire circuit. Thus, SGC achieves sublinear communication for certain circuits.

Unfortunately, SGC's improved communication comes at the cost of increased computation. Let b denote the number of branches. The parties each incur at least $O(b \log b)$ computation, as compared to $O(b)$ when using standard GC [HK21].

In this work, we focus on improving the SGC computation cost of E. We mention two reasons why it is sensible to focus on E.

- **Weak E.** First, G and E may have different computational resources. We argue that E will often have weaker hardware. GC offers built-in protection against malicious E, but more sophisticated and expensive techniques are needed to protect against malicious G, see e.g., [WRK17]. Thus, the more trusted party should play G to avoid the cost of these techniques.

  We argue that in many natural scenarios, the more trusted party (e.g., a server, or a bank), is also computationally more powerful than the less trusted one (e.g., bank's client, a cell phone, an IoT device).

  In such scenarios, E will have weaker hardware, and E's computational power will be the bottleneck.

- **Online/offline 2PC.** Second, GC naturally allows to offload most work to an offline phase (i.e., before function inputs are available): G can construct and transmit the GC in advance. However, E can only evaluate once inputs become available in an online phase. Thus, E's computation is essentially the *only* cost in the online phase.

1.1   Our Contribution

We show that GC conditional branching can be achieved while incurring only sublinear communication *and* sublinear computation cost for E. More precisely, for a conditional with b branches, our construction requires that G send to E material of size $\tilde{O}(\sqrt{b})$ and E uses $\tilde{O}(\sqrt{b})$ computation. Our G uses $\tilde{O}(b)$ computation. Importantly, the *entire online phase* has only $\tilde{O}(\sqrt{b})$ cost.

Our construction is formalized and proved secure as a *garbling scheme* [BHR12] assuming one-way functions. (To compose our technique with Free-XOR-based schemes, we need a stronger circular correlation-robust hash function [CKKZ12].) Since it is a garbling scheme, our construction can be plugged into GC protocols. We name our garbling scheme GCWise, for GC WIth Sublinear Evaluator.

Our construction can be immediately used to build an efficient *Garbled PIR*, described next in Sect. 1.2. Garbled PIR allows the GC to non-interactively and sublinearly access a privately indexed element from a publicly known database, and then use this element in continued GC evaluation.

1.2   Garbled PIR

Our construction is best applied when the target conditional has high branching factor. We mention an interesting application where high branching factor naturally arises.

Suppose G and E agree on a public database with elements $(x_0, ..., x_{n-1})$. They wish to include the database as part of their GC computation by reading one of its elements. Namely, suppose the GC computes a garbled index i that is known to neither party. The parties wish to efficiently recover the value x_i *inside the GC* such that the value can be used in further computation. Such a capability is essentially Private Information Retrieval (PIR), but where the selected index and the value are compatible with GC. One can view this as the GC playing the PIR receiver and G and E jointly playing the PIR sender. We emphasize that G and E must publicly agree on the contents of the database, but they do not learn which element is accessed. For completeness, we include the following formal definition of Garbled PIR:

Definition 1 (Garbling Scheme with PIR (Garbled PIR)). *A garbling scheme [BHR12] $\mathcal{G}$ is considered a* garbling scheme with PIR *if its circuits may include the following G_{pir} gates:*

$$G_{pir}[x_0, ..., x_{n-1}](i) \mapsto x_i$$

Here G_{pir} is parameterized by the public constant array $[x_0, ..., x_{n-1}]$, and the gate input i is computed inside the evaluated circuit.

Constructing Garbled PIR from conditional branching. Efficient Garbled PIR can be immediately constructed from conditional branching. In particular, we define n conditionally composed circuits $\mathcal{C}_0, ..., \mathcal{C}_{n-1}$ such that each circuit $\mathcal{C}_i$ takes no inputs and outputs the constant x_i.

We thus obtain Garbled PIR incurring only $\tilde{O}(\sqrt{n})$ communication and $\tilde{O}(\sqrt{n})$ E computation.

Our Garbled PIR can be upgraded to store private data by using one non-black-box PRF call per access. Indeed, each x_i can be stored masked with $F_k(i)$; the GC simply accesses the i-th position, unmasks the computed PRF, and proceeds with subsequent GC evaluation.

Comparison with Garbled RAM (GRAM). It is important (and easy) to see that GRAM, introduced by [LO13], does not solve the problem of efficient Garbled PIR. Indeed, GRAM performance is *amortized* over a sequence of RAM queries. A single GRAM access will require players to jointly build and then access a superlinear data structure, a far more expensive task than a simple linear scan. Thus GRAM *does not* imply Garbled PIR with sublinear communication and E computation.

1.3   Compact 2PC and Garbled PIR

For functions with conditional behavior, we achieve communication and computation for one of the parties that is sublinear in the size of the function description (i.e., function's circuit size). We find it convenient to assign a name to this property. We call this double sublinearity *compactness*.

For example, Sect. 1.2 describes a compact Garbled PIR, and our garbling scheme GCWise allows to achieve compact 2PC.

1.4   High-Level Intuition for Our Approach

Let b denote the number of branches in a conditional. Rather than sending garbled material for each conditional branch, our G randomly organizes the branches into $\tilde{O}(\sqrt{b})$ *buckets* and *stacks* the branches inside each bucket. Each bucket contains $\tilde{O}(\sqrt{b})$ branches, with the constraint that each branch appears at least once (with overwhelming probability). For each bucket, G stacks the material for that bucket's branches and sends the SGC to E. This achieves sublinear $\tilde{O}(\sqrt{b})$ communication.

To achieve E's sublinear computation, we ensure that E needs to only consider a single bucket, one (possibly of several) that contains the active branch. E processes only the $\tilde{O}(\sqrt{b})$ circuits in this single bucket.

The GC simply reveals to E the ID of the active bucket and the IDs of the inactive branches in it. E then unstacks the active branch material and evaluates using the remaining material.

The above description elides many details. For instance, we must route GC wire labels to 1-out-of-b circuits while maintaining sublinear communication and E computation. Additionally, we must ensure that E does not learn the identity of the active branch. We present a detailed overview of our approach in Sect. 4.

2   Related Work

Stacked Garbling. The most closely related works are those that developed Stacked Garbled Circuit (SGC) [Kol18, HK20b, HK20a, HK21], a GC primitive that reduces the communication cost of branching. We review the SGC technique in Sect. 3.1.

Our construction builds on SGC. Like prior work, we also achieve communication sublinear in the number of branches. However, we *also* achieve sublinear evaluation: our construction is compact. Prior SGC techniques are not compact.

Online-offline MPC. MPC of large functions can be expensive, and is unacceptable for certain time-sensitive (e.g., real-time) applications. One often-acceptable solution to this is to take advantage of the idle time before MPC inputs are available (the *offline* phase) by performing input-independent computation and data transfers. This often dramatically reduces the cost of the *online* phase.

MPC with preprocessing, aka online/offline MPC, is widely seen as a central setting for MPC, and is considered in many lines of work and protocol families, such as SPDZ [DPSZ12, BNO19]. Our protocol is the first one to achieve sublinear online phase for GC.

Other Garbled Circuit Optimizations. Originally, GCs required G send to E four ciphertexts per fan-in two gate.

This number of needed ciphertexts has been improved by a long line of works. While our emphasis is sublinear cost branching, not the efficiency of individual GC gates, we review such works for completeness.

- [NPS99] introduced *garbled row-reduction* (GRR3), which reduced the cost to three ciphertexts per gate.
- Much later, [KS08a] introduced the Free XOR technique which allows XOR gates to be computed without extra ciphertexts.
- [PSSW09] introduced a polynomial interpolation-based technique that uses only two ciphertexts per gate (GRR2).
- While GRR3 is compatible with Free XOR, GRR2 is not. This opened the door to further improvements: [KMR14] generalized Free XOR into "fleXOR", a technique that uses heuristics to mix GRR2 with Free XOR and GRR3.
- [ZRE15] superceded prior improvements with their half-gates technique. Half-gates consumes only two ciphertexts per AND gate and compatible with Free XOR. [ZRE15] also gave a matching lower bound in a model that seemed difficult to circumvent.
- Very recently – and quite suprisingly – [RR21] found a new approach outside the [ZRE15] lower bound model. Their technique requires only 1.5 ciphertexts per AND gate and is compatible with Free XOR.

This line of work improves the cost of individual gates; in contrast to our work, the total cost remains proportional to the circuit size.

Garbled RAM (GRAM). Most GC constructions operate in the circuit model of computation, rather than using Turing machines or RAM machines. Exceptions include the line of work on garbling schemes for RAM programs: Garbled RAM (GRAM) [LO13], outsourced RAM [GKK+12], and the TM model of [GKP+13]. RAM-based 2PC is motivated by the prohibitively expensive cost of generic program-to-circuit unrolling.

GRAM and our Garbled PIR are incomparable: while GRAM achieves sublinear RAM, its costs are amortized. Meanwhile, Garbled PIR is less expressive, but achieves sublinear cost without amortization.

Private Information Retrieval (PIR). Private information retrieval (PIR), introduced by Chor et al. [CGKS95, CKGS98], allows a client to retrieve an item from a public database stored at a server without revealing which item is requested. The communication complexity of PIR is sublinear in the size n of the database, and the computation of the server is linear in n. [KO97] designed a PIR scheme with communication $O(n^\epsilon)$ for an arbitrary constant ϵ; subsequent works achieved polylogarithmic communication.

We achieve Garbled PIR; i.e., private information retrieval that is compatible with GC (Sect. 1.2).

Table 1. Table of notation.

Symbol	Denotation
κ	Computational security parameter (e.g., 128)
$\mathcal{C}$	Function/circuit
$\hat{\mathcal{C}}$	Garbled circuit on $\mathcal{C}$ (uses ˆsymbol)
x, y	Small Latin letters for plain inputs/outputs
X, Y	Capital Latin letters for garbled inputs/outputs
G	GC Generator (he/him)
E	GC Evaluator (she/hers)
b	Number of conditional branches
ℓ, i	Number of buckets ℓ indexed by i
m, j	Number of elements in a bucket indexed by j (bucket size)
α	Active branch ID
β	Active bucket ID
γ	The index of active instance for $\mathcal{C}_\alpha$ in active bucket B_β (see Sect. 5.1)
n	Number of gates in a branch
S	Pseudorandom seed
K	Encryption key

Compact 2PC from Fully Homomorphic Encryption (FHE). The breakthrough work on FHE by Gentry [Gen09] and Brakerski and Vaikuntanathan [BV11] can be used to achieve compact 2PC. Using FHE, one party encrypts its input and sends it to the other party. The other party then computes the function *homomorphically* over these encrypted inputs and its own inputs. Hence, the communication and computation complexity of one of the parties is proportional to the size of its inputs and is independent of the size of the circuit. Despite concrete improvements, e.g., [BV11, GSW13], FHE remain expensive in practice, compared to GC.

3 Preliminaries

This section reviews stacked garbling [HK20a, HK20b] and introduces basic notation and concepts needed to understand our approach.

Notational Preliminaries. For an integer n, we use $[n]$ to denote the set $\{0, 1, \ldots, n-1\}$. PPT stands for probabilistic polynomial time. The base two logarithm of x is denoted $\log x$. We use $\overset{c}{=}$ to show two distributions are computationally indistinguishable. Table 1 lists various naming conventions used throughout this work.

3.1   Reducing GC Communication

A recent line of works showed that GC communication can be asymptotically improved for circuits with conditional behavior. This line began with 'Free If' [Kol18]. To reduce communication, Kolesnikov decoupled the circuit *topology* from the garbled circuit *material*. The topology is the circuit description, describing how the gates are laid out as a graph. The material is the collection of encrypted truth tables that support secure evaluation

Free If only works when G knows the identity of the active conditional branch but ensures that E does not learn the active branch.

Building on the topology-decoupling idea, Heath and Kolesnikov showed improvements both when only E knows the active branch [HK20b] and when *neither* player knows the active branch [HK20a]. Both [HK20b] and [HK20a] consume communication proportional to only the program's longest execution path rather than to the entire circuit.

By using these stacked garbling techniques (sometimes called stacked garbled circuit, SGC), we need not send separate material for each conditional branch. Instead, a single *stacked* (via bitwise XOR) string of material can be sent for all branches. After receiving the stacked material, E is given enough information to efficiently and locally reconstruct the material for each inactive branch. This allows her to *unstack* (again, by bitwise XORing) the material for the single active branch. E can then correctly execute the active branch. By stacking the branch material, SGC greatly reduces bandwidth consumption.

[HK20b] **Review.** Like [HK20a], we target secure computation in the setting where neither party knows the active branch. Thus, our setting is closest to [HK20a]. While our approach is for general 2PC, our construction is more closely related to that of [HK20b], which was used to improve GC-based zero knowledge proofs [JKO13,FNO15]. The core idea given by [HK20b] does not *require* the ZK setting; it simply requires that the GC evaluator E knows the identity of each active conditional branch. Hence, we elide the ZK details and present the [HK20b] technique as one for secure 2PC.

For reference, Table 1 lists variables used to describe circuits and GCs.

Consider b branches $C_0, \ldots, C_{b-1}$ and let α denote the index of the active branch. Let E know α. The [HK20b] approach is as follows: G selects b PRG seeds $S_0, \ldots, S_{b-1}$ and uses each respective seed to derive all randomness used while constructing a garbling of the respective branch. Let $\hat{C}_0, \ldots, \hat{C}_{b-1}$ denote the b resultant GC materials (i.e., the collections of encrypted truth tables). Before [HK20b], each of these b materials would be sent to E, requiring communication proportional to the number of branches.

[HK20b] improves over this as follows: G pads the shorter materials with extra 0s until each material has the same length. G computes $\hat{C} \leftarrow \bigoplus_i \hat{C}_i$ and sends $\hat{C}$ to E. G additionally conveys to E each seed $S_{i \neq \alpha}$ corresponding to the $b - 1$ inactive branches.[1] If E were to obtain *all* GC seeds, she could use them

---

[1] [HK20b] use oblivious transfer to convey these seeds, but they can also be encrypted according to the active branch GC labels in a GC gadget.

to learn all circuit labels. This would not be secure since this would allow E to decrypt intermediate circuit values. However, it *is* secure to send seeds to E, so long as each seed is not used in an active branch [HK20b]. We ensure this is secure by using garbled gadgets to enforce that no inactive branch holds semantic values on its wires. Hence, there are no wire labels for E to illegally decrypt.

E uses the $b - 1$ seeds to reconstruct the materials $\hat{C}_{i \neq \alpha}$ and then computes $\hat{C}_\alpha \leftarrow \hat{C} \oplus (\bigoplus_{i \neq \alpha} \hat{C}_i)$, unstacking the active branch material. E uses this active branch material and the appropriate input labels (which are conveyed separately) to evaluate the active branch.

Although we consider the setting where neither E nor G know the active branch, we leverage the above technique: we also stack GC material and reveal to E to the stacked index of the active branch. Crucially, our approach decouples the stacked index of the active branch from its index in the program. Thus, learning the former does not break security by revealing the identity of the active branch. We discuss our approach further in Sect. 4.

3.2   Universal and Set-Universal Circuits

To evaluate a circuit C inside the GC, E must both hold the material $\hat{C}$ *and* know the *topology* for that circuit. However, we need to ensure that the differing topology *across* branches does not leak the identity of the active branch. This leakage can be prevented by using *universal circuits* (UC). A UC can hide the structure of the evaluated circuit.

A UC can emulate any circuit with size up to a parameterized maximum number of gates n. A UC takes as input the description of the desired circuit C encoded as a *programming string* c. On input x and programming string c that encodes C, a UC $\mathcal{U}$ computes $\mathcal{U}(c, x) = C(x)$.

Valiant [Val76] achieved the first UC construction, which was of size $O(n \log n)$. More recent works have improved the constant overhead of UC constructions. The current best construction [LYZ+20] achieves UCs of size $3n \log n$. A simpler construction with size $O(n \log^2 n)$ also exists and is better for small n [KS08b].

We note that UCs do not directly solve our compactness problem, since in addition to the garbled UC itself we must convey a garbling of the UC *programming string*. This programming string is proportional to the size of the UC. In general, b programming strings are needed to encode the possibility of evaluating any branch. Nevertheless, UCs are core to our approach.

Set-Universal Circuits. When we handle conditional branching, we know statically that the active branch is an element from the small set of circuits in the conditional. Thus, using a general purpose UC that emulates *any* size n circuit is overkill. *Set-universal* circuits [KKW17] construct a single circuit that can emulate any circuit from a specific *set* of circuits S. A set-universal circuit can be less costly than a full universal circuit.

Note that for Garbled PIR (Sect. 1.2), the relevant set-universal circuit is incredibly simple: each "circuit" in Garbled PIR simply outputs a constant value. Hence, all such circuits already share a fixed topology and the set-universal topology is trivially constructed without overhead.

3.3 Garbled Circuit Formalization

Our approach achieves compact 2PC by using garbled circuits (GCs). Yao [Yao86] first introduced garbled circuits, with subsequent works like Lindell and Pinkas [LP09] and Bellare, Hoang, and Rogaway [BHR12] formalizing the syntax, methods, and proofs. Garbled circuit techniques are often formalized as *garbling schemes*, not as protocols. We take the same approach, formalizing our technique as a garbling scheme in the framework given by [BHR12]. In practice, the parties G and E run these algorithms as part of a protocol that uses the scheme as a black box. We present the [BHR12] garbling scheme definitions.

Definition 2 (Garbling Scheme). *A garbling scheme $\mathcal{G}$ is a tuple of algorithms:*

$$\mathcal{G} = (\mathsf{Gb}, \mathsf{En}, \mathsf{De}, \mathsf{Ev}, \mathsf{ev})$$

such that:

1. *$(\hat{\mathcal{C}}, e, d) \leftarrow \mathsf{Gb}(1^\kappa, \mathcal{C})$: Gb maps a function $\mathcal{C} : \{0,1\}^\ell \to \{0,1\}^m$ to a triple $(\hat{\mathcal{C}}, e, d)$ such that $\mathsf{De}(d, \cdot) \circ \mathsf{Ev}(\mathcal{C}, \hat{\mathcal{C}}, \cdot) \circ \mathsf{En}(e, \cdot) = \mathcal{C}$. We often make garbling randomness explicit via pseudorandom seed S: $(\hat{\mathcal{C}}, e, d) \leftarrow \mathsf{Gb}(1^\kappa, \mathcal{C}; S)$*
2. *$X \leftarrow \mathsf{En}(e, x)$: En maps a cleartext input $x \in \{0,1\}^\ell$ to garbled labels X by looking up labels from the encoding string e according to x.*
3. *$y \leftarrow \mathsf{De}(d, Y)$: De maps garbled output labels Y to the cleartext output y by comparing values in Y to values in the decoding string d.*
4. *$Y \leftarrow \mathsf{Ev}(\mathcal{C}, \hat{\mathcal{C}}, X)$: Ev securely evaluates a circuit $\mathcal{C}$ using its garbled material $\hat{\mathcal{C}}$ and garbled input X.*
5. *$y \leftarrow \mathsf{ev}(\mathcal{C}, x)$: ev evaluates the function $\mathcal{C}$ on input x in cleartext and is used to evaluate correctness. We sometimes instead write $\mathcal{C}(x)$ for simplicity.*

We formally define the security notions of a garbling scheme and show that our construction satisfies them in Sect. 6.

Projectivity. Our scheme only considers Boolean values and is *projective* [BHR12]. In a projective garbling scheme, each circuit wire is associated with two labels that respectively encode zero and one. Projective schemes enjoy simple definitions for En and De that map between GC labels and cleartext bits.

The encoding string e is a list of $2n$ tokens $e = (X_0^0, X_0^1, \ldots, X_{n-1}^0, X_{n-1}^1)$, two for each bit of an input $x \in \{0,1\}^n$. For a given $x = (x_0, \ldots, x_{n-1})$, $\mathsf{En}(e, x)$ selects a subvector $(X_0^{x_0}, \ldots, X_{n-1}^{x_{n-1}})$ for the encoding. Similarly, the decryption De compares output labels to the content of the decoding string d and outputs appropriate cleartext values.

3.4 Circuit Syntax

Traditionally, Boolean circuits refer to a collection of gates with specified connections. Unfortunately, this notion does not make explicit the function's conditional behavior. Therefore, we follow [HK20a] and instead refer to the above notion as a *netlist*. Our garbling scheme (Sect. 5.3) handles conditionals built from a vector of netlists.

A circuit $\mathcal{C}$ is a vector of constituent netlists $\mathcal{C}_0, \ldots, \mathcal{C}_{b-1}$. As in [HK20a], we leave the syntax of netlists unspecified. This allows us to plug different low-level garbling techniques into our construction, even if the technique uses novel gates. The only restriction we place on netlists is that given a vector of netlists $\mathcal{C}_0, \ldots, \mathcal{C}_{b-1}$, it is possible to construct a universal netlist (see Sect. 3.2) that can be programmed (e.g., by part of its input) as any branch $\mathcal{C}_i$. By convention, the first $\lceil \log b \rceil$ bits of input to a conditional are *condition* bits that encode the active branch ID α. Semantically, on input (α, x), the conditional outputs $\mathcal{C}_\alpha(x)$.

Sequentially composed conditionals. It is often useful to sequentially compose multiple circuits, e.g., the output of one conditional is fed as input to another. While our syntax does not directly handle sequential composition, such handling can be easily laid on top of our approach, see e.g., [HK20a]. Thus, the fact that we do not further discuss sequential composition simplifies presentation but does not limit expressivity.

Nesting conditionals. We do not handle nested conditionals: it is not clear how to express a universal circuit that captures arbitrary explicit conditional branching. We note that in many cases it is possible to efficiently rewrite nested conditionals as a single top-level conditional via safe program transformations.

4   Technical Overview

In this section, we present our construction at a high level. Formal algorithms and proofs are in Sects. 5 and 6. Consider b conditionally composed circuits $\mathcal{C}_{i \in [b]}$. We call these circuits *branches*. Let α denote the index of the *active branch*, i.e., the branch whose output appears at the end of the conditional. Suppose that neither G nor E knows α. Our goal is to securely compute and propagate the output of $\mathcal{C}_\alpha$ while using communication and E computation *sublinear* in the number of branches.

Standard stacked garbling. To recap Sect. 3.1, in standard SGC [HK20a], G constructs for each branch $\mathcal{C}_i$ a garbling $\hat{\mathcal{C}}_i$ from a seed S_i and then sends to E the stacked garbling $\bigoplus_i \hat{\mathcal{C}}_i$. At runtime, the GC conveys to E each seed $S_{i \neq \alpha}$ (via a garbled gadget programmed by G). E uses these seeds to garble each inactive branch and constructs the value $\bigoplus_{i \neq \alpha} \hat{\mathcal{C}}_i$. This value allows her to *unstack* the material for the active branch:

$$\left(\bigoplus_i \hat{\mathcal{C}}_i \right) \oplus \left(\bigoplus_{i \neq \alpha} \hat{\mathcal{C}}_i \right) = \hat{\mathcal{C}}_\alpha$$

She uses the resultant material to correctly evaluate the active branch $\mathcal{C}_\alpha$. Unfortunately, the above procedure is not compact: E must garble *each branch*, so her work is linear in b. We adopt a different strategy.

G's handling. Instead of stacking all b garblings into a *single* stack of garbled material, G constructs *multiple* stacks. Specifically, he considers a sublinear number $\ell = \tilde{O}(\sqrt{b})$ of *buckets*, each of which is simply a collection of some of the branches. G fills each bucket with $m = \tilde{O}(\sqrt{b})$ branches via a garbled gadget called the *bucket table* (see Sect. 5.1). The bucket table ensures that each branch appears at least once with overwhelming probability. For each bucket B_i, G garbles the m constituent branches using m distinct seeds and stacks the resultant material. G separately sends to E the stacked material for each bucket B_i. At runtime, E will consider only *one* of these buckets. Since the considered bucket holds only $\tilde{O}(\sqrt{b})$ branches, E's work is sublinear in b.

Terminology. In our construction, a particular branch may be stacked more than once. Indeed, each branch may appear in multiple buckets and even multiple times within the *same bucket*. Each copy of a branch is called an *instance*. There are more instances than there are branches and (with overwhelming probability) there exists at least one instance of each branch. All instances in the same bucket are called *siblings*.

E need not evaluate all instances: many are *dummies* that prevent E from learning the active branch ID. At runtime, E will evaluate a garbling of exactly one instance of branch $\mathcal{C}_\alpha$. We call this evaluated instance the *active* instance. The active instance resides in a bucket that we call the *active bucket*; we denote the active bucket ID by β.

E's handling of buckets. Recall that the GC computes the value α and that E holds stacked material for each bucket. The garbled material for the active instance is in the active bucket B_β. We proceed as follows: The GC reveals to E the following information via the *bucket table*:

1. The identity of the active bucket β.
2. The identity of the active instance's $m - 1$ siblings: i.e., which inactive branches are in B_β.
3. The $m - 1$ seeds used to garble the active instance's siblings.

E, crucially, is *not* given information about any inactive buckets $B_{i \neq \beta}$ and is *not* told the identity of the active instance. We show that the above information can be compactly and securely computed by our carefully arranged bucket table gadget (see Sect. 5.1).

With this information, E garbles each sibling instance and unstacks the active instance's material. Crucially, our bucket table ensures that the branches within a single bucket are sampled *with replacement*, so even learning that branch $\mathcal{C}_j$ is a sibling of the active instance does not allow E to rule out the fact that $\mathcal{C}_j$ might be the active branch. From here, we would like E to evaluate the active instance. However, one important problem remains: to evaluate, E needs both the active instance's material (which she has) *and* the active branch *topology*.

As discussed so far, E cannot learn this topology, since this would immediately imply the identity of the active branch.

Universal topology. To avoid the above problem, we ensure each branch C_i uses *the same topology*. We achieve this by expressing each branch as the programming of a *universal circuit* (UC) (see Sect. 3.2). Since each branch has the same topology, E can evaluate the active branch without learning its identity.

This raises a question: Why not instead simply use one UC to directly express the conditional instead of stacking garbled material? The crucial problem with using UCs for conditional branching is that E must somehow obtain a garbled *programming string* corresponding to the active branch. Standard techniques for conveying 1-out-of-b programming strings require communication proportional to b, and so are not compact.

In our approach, programming strings are sent efficiently: G incorporates the programming string directly into each garbling. Thus, when E unstacks, she obtains a garbling with the proper programming for the active branch, but without learning the active branch ID and without needing to consider all b possible functions.

Summary of our approach.

- G and E agree on a circuit $\mathcal{U}$ that is universal to each branch C_i.
- G considers $\tilde{O}(\sqrt{b})$ buckets and fills each bucket with $\tilde{O}(\sqrt{b})$ branch IDs.
- For each instance, G accordingly programs $\mathcal{U}$ and garbles programmed $\mathcal{U}$. For each bucket, G stacks the $\tilde{O}(\sqrt{b})$ materials.
- G sends $\tilde{O}(\sqrt{b})$ materials to E. The materials include the stacked garbling for each bucket and the garbled gadgets, including the *bucket table*. The bucket table tells E how to unstack the active instance.
- E evaluates the bucket table and learns the active bucket, the identities of the siblings of the active instance, and seeds for these siblings.
- E considers *only* the active bucket, garbles the siblings, unstacks the active instance material, and evaluates the active instance.

By running the above high-level procedure, E evaluates a conditional with b branches, but while using only $\tilde{O}(\sqrt{b})$ communication and computation. The technique does require a garbled bucket table gadget (and a demultiplexer and multiplexer gadget), but we show that the gadgets can be constructed with size sublinear in the number of branches. Hence, G and E obliviously execute a conditional while using only sublinear communication and E computation: we achieve compact 2PC.

5 Our Construction

In this section, we present our technique in detail. We start by describing the bucket table gadget. Then we introduce our multiplexer (mux) and demultiplexer (demux) gadgets. One key idea (similar to SGC) is different parts of the circuit are garbled with different seeds. This creates the problem that different circuit wires are associated with two different GC *labels*. Garbling even the same circuit starting from a different seed will result in different GC wire labels: we say that different GCs have different *vocabularies*. The mux/demux gadgets handle a problem of *vocabulary translation* needed to evaluate one out of many different garbled circuits.

Finally, we combine our gadgets and the high level ideas from Sect. 4 into a *garbling scheme* [BHR12]. Section 6 then proves this garbling scheme is secure.

5.1 Bucket Table Gadget

In this section, we formalize the *bucket table* gadget, which is the garbled gadget that tells E the information needed to evaluate the active branch $\mathcal{C}_\alpha$. Given a garbled encoding of the branch id α, the bucket table gives the following information to E:

- The active bucket's identity, β.
- The identity of the siblings of $\mathcal{C}_\alpha$ in B_β.
- $m - 1$ seeds corresponding to the garbling of each sibling.
- A *bucket key* K_β corresponding to the active bucket. Each bucket's garbling is encrypted by a distinct key that ensures E can only view the active bucket's garbling.

To implement the bucket table using only sublinear work, we use a key insight: we only need to sample enough randomness for *one bucket* as we can reuse this sampled randomness across buckets.

In our bucket table gadget, we sample m uniform offsets $\delta_i \in [b]$. These m offsets comprise the choices of branches for each bucket. Specifically, we place each branch id $(\delta_i + j) \bmod b$ at the ith index of bucket B_j. That is, we use the same m random offsets for each bucket but apply a deterministic per-bucket linear shift. Figure 2 depicts the assignment of branches to buckets. As the random choices are made *with replacement*, a branch may appear more than once in a bucket. This approach is similar to a technique used to achieve PIR with sublinear online time [CK20].

Besides assigning branches to buckets, the bucket table also samples m garbling seeds S_i and ℓ encryption keys K_j uniformly at random. Each seed S_i will be used to garble the ith branch in every bucket B_j. Key K_j will be used to encrypt the stacked material corresponding to bucket B_j (see Sect. 5.3).

At runtime, the bucket table takes as argument a garbling of the active branch id α and computes, based on the list δ_i, the identity of the active bucket β *and* an index γ within the active bucket that holds the active instance. In this procedure, we must ensure that E learns no information about α. Since our bucket table will often include multiple instances corresponding to active branch $\mathcal{C}_\alpha$, we must choose among these instances uniformly. Moreover, we must make this choice using work sublinear in the number of branches. We define the bucket table procedure below:

1. Identify each instance of the active branch $\mathcal{C}_\alpha$. To perform this in sublinear time, iterate over the list of offsets $\delta_{i \in [m]}$ and build a list instances of those indices i for which some bucket holds a garbling of $\mathcal{C}_\alpha$ at position i. The instances list can be built by computing

$$\gamma_i = (\alpha - \delta_i) \bmod b, \text{ for } i \in [m].$$

If $\gamma_i \in [\ell]$, then set instances$[i] = 1$, indicating that there is a bucket that holds an instance of $\mathcal{C}_\alpha$ at a position corresponding to γ_i; else set instances$[i] = 0$ to indicate that there does not exist a bucket id j such that $(\delta_i + j) \bmod b = \alpha$.

2. Select a single active instance by uniformly sampling among the non-zero indices of instances. This can be achieved as follows (1) Compute the hamming weight HW(instances), (2) Select a large uniform value r (this can be done outside the GC by G), (3) Compute $t = r \bmod$ HW(instances) which, for $r \gg$ HW(instances) is statistically indistinguishable from uniform, and (4) Linearly scan the list δ_i to select the tth non-zero index of instances which is denoted by γ. Select the value δ_γ via a linear scan over each δ_i.

3. Identify the active bucket $\beta \leftarrow (\alpha - \delta_\gamma) \bmod B$. The index of the active instance within the active bucket is γ.

4. Compute each sibling $y_{i \neq \gamma} = \delta_{i \neq \gamma} + \beta$, each sibling seed $S_{i \neq \gamma}$, and the bucket key K_β: each of these values is computed by linearly scanning lists of offsets $\delta_{i \in [m]}$, garbling seeds $S_{i \in [m]}$, and encryption keys $K_{j \in [\ell]}$ respectively, with respect to β and γ.

Let $\mathcal{C}_{\mathsf{bt}}$ denote the circuit that computes the above procedure. To summarize, $\mathcal{C}_{\mathsf{bt}}$ takes as input the active branch id α and outputs the active bucket id $\beta \in [\ell]$, the index of active instance in that bucket $\gamma \in [m]$, the siblings of the active instance $y_{i \neq \gamma}$, the seeds $S_{i \neq \gamma}$, and the encryption key K_β. Observe that $\mathcal{C}_{\mathsf{bt}}$ has size $\tilde{O}(\ell + m)$ as it only consists of linear scans of lists of length ℓ and m.

Let BT.Gb denote the procedure that takes as input lists of offsets $\delta_{i \in [m]}$, garbling seeds $S_{i \in [m]}$, encryption keys $K_{j \in [\ell]}$, the GC vocabulary for the possible active branch labels $\hat{\gamma}$ and constructs a garbled circuit $\hat{\mathcal{C}}_{\mathsf{bt}}$ for circuit $\mathcal{C}_{\mathsf{bt}}$. Let BT.Ev denote the evaluation procedure that takes as input the garbled circuit $\hat{\mathcal{C}}_{\mathsf{bt}}$ and an encoding of the active branch id $\hat{\alpha}$ and outputs $\mathcal{C}_{\mathsf{bt}}(\alpha)$.

We define an additional subprocedure Proc$_{\mathsf{Bkt}}$ which G uses to sample necessary random values used in the bucket table. Specifically, Proc$_{\mathsf{Bkt}}$ samples (1) samples the m offsets $\delta_{i \in [m]}$, (2) assigns branches to each of the buckets, (3) samples the m garbling seeds $S_{i \in [m]}$, and (4) samples ℓ encryption keys $K_{j \in [\ell]}$. Proc$_{\mathsf{Bkt}}$ is described in Fig. 1. In Lemma 1, we prove that by setting ℓ and m to $\tilde{O}(\sqrt{b})$, all branches appear with overwhelming probability. Hence, the size of circuit $\mathcal{C}_{\mathsf{bt}}$ is $\tilde{O}(\sqrt{b})$.

Lemma 1. *If $\ell = \tilde{O}(\sqrt{b})$ and $m = \tilde{O}(\sqrt{b})$, then the bucket table (Fig. 1) places each branch $\mathcal{C}_\eta$ (for $\eta \in [b]$) into a bucket with overwhelming probability.*

$\mathsf{Proc_{Bkt}}(m, \ell, b)$:

1: Uniformly sample m offsets $\delta_{i \in [m]} \in [b]$.
2: Uniformly sample m garbling seeds $S_{i \in [m]}$ and ℓ encryption keys $K_{j \in [\ell]}$.
3: For each $j \in [\ell]$, build bucket $B_j = [\delta_i + j]_{i \in [m]}$.
4: **Return** $\delta_{i \in [m]}, S_{i \in [m]}, B_{j \in [\ell]}, K_{j \in [\ell]}$.

Fig. 1. Procedure to construct bucket table, $\mathsf{Proc_{Bkt}}$.

Table 2. The Bucket Table assigns branches to buckets. Each branch id $(\delta_i + j) \bmod b$ is placed at index i of bucket B_j.

Bucket B_0	δ_0	$\dots$	δ_i	$\dots$	δ_{m-1}
$\vdots$					
Bucket B_j	$\delta_0 + j$	$\dots$	$\delta_i + j$	$\dots$	$\delta_{m-1} + j$
$\vdots$					
Bucket $B_{\ell-1}$	$\delta_0 + \ell - 1$	$\dots$	$\delta_i + \ell - 1$	$\dots$	$\delta_{m-1} + \ell - 1$

All arithmetic operations are in $\mathbb{Z}_b$.

Proof. Let $m = \sqrt{b}\kappa$ and $\ell = \sqrt{b}$. We analyze the probability that branch $\eta \in [b]$ does not belong to any of the ℓ buckets $B_{j \in [\ell]}$. Let $\gamma_j = \eta - \delta_j \bmod b$, where $j \in [m]$. Since each δ_j is uniform at random,

$$\Pr[\gamma_j \notin [\ell]] = 1 - \frac{\ell}{b}.$$

Moreover, since each δ_j is independent:

$$\Pr[\eta \notin B_1 \wedge \cdots \wedge \eta \notin B_\ell] = \Pr[\gamma_1 \notin [\ell] \wedge \cdots \wedge \gamma_m \notin [\ell]]$$

$$= \left(1 - \frac{\ell}{b}\right)^m = \left(1 - \frac{\sqrt{b}}{b}\right)^{\sqrt{b}\kappa} = \frac{1}{e^\kappa} = \mathsf{negl}(\kappa).$$

$\square$

5.2   Demultiplexer and Multiplexer

The bucket table allows E to unstack material for the active instance γ in the active bucket β, but it does not suffice to route inputs to (resp. outputs from) the active instance. E needs more information to evaluate the active branch $\mathcal{C}_\alpha$.

In general, the conditional composition of b branches can occur in the middle of a circuit, with sequentially composed circuits occurring before and after the conditional. To route input and output GC labels to enter and exit the conditional, we design an additional demultiplexer (demux) and multiplexer (mux) gadget.

The demux and mux map the vocabulary of the surrounding circuit (i.e., the circuit that holds the conditional branch) to the vocabulary of each instance. Both the demux and mux operate at the level of a particular bucket: they translate the vocabulary of the surrounding circuit to the vocabulary of one instance in that bucket. Thus, the demux and mux are compact, since their size is proportional to the number of elements in a bucket. We can reuse the same demux and mux across all buckets, and hence our vocabulary translation for the full conditional is compact.

The demultiplexer computes the following function for each input wire to the conditional x and each bucket index i:

$$\mathsf{demux}(x, i, \gamma) = \begin{cases} x & \text{if } i = \gamma \\ \bot & \text{otherwise} \end{cases}$$

where $\bot$ indicates that the demultiplexer makes no promise if the instance is inactive. In other words, the demultiplexer delivers valid labels to the active instance, but not to any inactive instance. In the GC, the demux is an encrypted truth table that maps each input label X to a corresponding label X_i for each ith instance. The truth table is encrypted by the GC labels that encode γ such that E can *only* decrypt valid input labels for the active instance X_γ, and not for any inactive instance.

Similarly, the multiplexer computes the following simple function that selects outputs from the active instance

$$\mathsf{mux}(y_1, ..., y_b, \gamma) = y_\gamma$$

In the GC, the mux is, again, built by encrypted truth tables that map each output label from each ith instance Y_i to an output label for the surrounding circuit Y. Again, this truth table is encrypted according to GC labels that encode γ such that E can *only* translate outputs labels Y_γ of the active instance, not any inactive instance.

Both the demultiplexer and multiplexer can be built as simple garbled gadgets that use encrypted truth tables, like techniques used in [HK20a]. However, one crucial observation ensures both gadgets are compact: it is sufficient to sample only m total garbling seeds S_i. These same m seeds can be reused across the ℓ buckets. Because the buckets reuse the seeds and every circuit uses the same universal topology, there are only m total vocabularies: each ith garbling in a given bucket is garbled starting from the ith seed S_i, so the ith circuits across all buckets share the same vocabulary. This fact means that the demultiplexer (resp. multiplexer) need only translate to (resp. from) m different vocabularies, and so is compact.

Our construction uses four procedures:

- demux.Gb garbles the demux. It takes as arguments (1) the input vocabulary for each ith instance e_i and (2) the GC label vocabulary for the active instance id γ. It outputs (1) the input vocabulary from the overall conditional e and (2) a garbled circuit $\hat{\mathcal{C}}_{\text{dem}}$ that encodes the demux procedure. demux.Gb samples the input encoding string e uniformly, with the exception that each pair of labels for a given label have differing least significant bits.

- demux.Ev evaluates the demux. It takes as arguments (1) a GC $\hat{C}_{\text{dem}}$, (2) GC labels that encode the active branch id γ, and (3) surrounding circuit inputs X. It outputs inputs for the active instance X_γ.

- mux.Gb garbles the mux. It takes as arguments (1) the output vocabulary for each ith instance d_i and (2) the GC label vocabulary for the active instance id γ. It outputs (1) the output vocabulary from the overall conditional d and (2) a garbled circuit $\hat{C}_{\text{mux}}$ that encodes the mux procedure. mux.Gb samples the output decoding string d uniformly, with the exception that each pair of labels for a given label have differing least significant bits.

- mux.Ev evaluates the mux. It takes as arguments (1) a GC $\hat{C}_{\text{mux}}$, (2) GC labels that encode the active branch id γ, and (3) GC output labels from the active instance Y_γ. It outputs output labels for the overall conditional Y.

5.3 Our Garbling Scheme

Following our syntax from Definition 2, we construct our garbling scheme GCWise:

Construction 1 (GCWise Garbling Scheme). *Let* Base *be an underlying garbling scheme that satisfies the GC properties of correctness, obliviousness, privacy, authenticity, and sequential composability (see Sect. 3.3). Then* GCWise *is the five tuple of algorithms:*

(GCWise.Gb, GCWise.En, GCWise.De, GCWise.Ev, GCWise.ev)

as defined in Fig. 2.

Construction 1 supports compact 2PC for conditional circuits. Specifically, for a conditional with b branches each with n gates, GCWise.Gb outputs a material of size $\tilde{O}(\sqrt{b} \cdot n)$ and GCWise.Ev runs in $\tilde{O}(\sqrt{b} \cdot n)$ time.

Construction 1 is the relatively straightforward formalization of our technique as explained in Sect. 4. The key algorithmic details arise from our garbled gadgets, particularly the bucket table, and were formalized in Sects. 5.1 and 5.2. We note some of the interesting details of Construction 1:

- Our garbling scheme is *projective* [BHR12]. As discussed in Sect. 3.3, a projective garbling scheme has a simplified input and output vocabulary, so we can use standard algorithms to implement GCWise.En and GCWise.De. We simply reuse the encoding and decoding algorithms of Base.

- Our algorithms GCWise.Gb and GCWise.Ev formalize the core of our approach as explained in Sect. 4.

- Notice that we call Base.Gb with an additional seed argument. Recall from Definition 2 that this denotes that we configure the randomness of the procedure with an explicit seed.

- Our scheme passes the universal circuit $\mathcal{U}$ to both Base.Gb and Base.Ev. In the former case we write $\mathcal{U}[\mathcal{C}_i]$ to denote that Gb hardcodes the programming string inputs based on $\mathcal{C}_i$. This ensures that the garbled material $\hat{\mathcal{C}}_i$ includes the garbled programming string for the UC. In the latter case, therefore, E can evaluate $\mathcal{U}$ without knowing $\mathcal{C}_\alpha$.

6   Security

In this section, we first introduce the security notions of a garbling scheme [BHR12], then formally prove that Construction 1 satisfies these notions. Informally, the GC security notions are as follows:

- Privacy: $(\hat{\mathcal{C}}, X, d)$ reveals no more about x than $\mathcal{C}(x)$. Formally, there must exist a simulator Sim_{pr} that takes the input $(1^\kappa, \mathcal{C}, \mathcal{C}(x))$ and produces an output that is indistinguishable from $(\hat{\mathcal{C}}, X, d)$.
- Obliviousness: $(\hat{\mathcal{C}}, X)$ reveals no information about x. Formally, there must exist a simulator Sim_{ob} that takes input $(1^\kappa, \mathcal{C})$ and produces an output that is indistinguishable from $(\hat{\mathcal{C}}, X)$.
- Authenticity: Given only $(\hat{\mathcal{C}}, X)$ no adversary should be able to produce $Y' \neq \mathsf{Ev}(\hat{\mathcal{C}}, X)$ such that $\mathsf{De}(d, Y') \neq \bot$ except with negligible probability.

The games for privacy and obliviousness are illustrated in Fig. 3.

Definition 3 (Correctness). *For* $\mathcal{C} \in \{0,1\}^*$, $\kappa \in \mathbb{N}$, *and* $x \in \{0,1\}^n$, *and* $(\hat{\mathcal{C}}, e, d) \leftarrow \mathsf{Gb}(1^\kappa, \mathcal{C})$:

$$\mathsf{De}(d, \mathsf{Ev}(\mathcal{C}, \hat{\mathcal{C}}, \mathsf{En}(e, x))) = \mathcal{C}(x).$$

Definition 4 (Obliviousness). *A garbling scheme* $\mathcal{G}$ *is oblivious if for all* λ *large enough, there exists a polynomial-time simulator* Sim *such that for any PPT adversary* $\mathcal{A}$:

$$Pr[\mathsf{ObvSim}^{\mathcal{A}}_{\mathcal{G},\mathsf{Sim}}(1^\kappa) = 1] \leq \mathsf{negl}(\kappa).$$

Definition 5 (Privacy). *A garbling scheme* $\mathcal{G}$ *is private if for all* λ *large enough, there exists a polynomial-time simulator* Sim *such that for any PPT adversary* $\mathcal{A}$:

$$Pr[\mathsf{PrivSim}^{\mathcal{A}}_{\mathcal{G},\mathsf{Sim}}(1^\kappa) = 1] \leq \mathsf{negl}(\kappa).$$

Definition 6 (Authenticity). *A garbling scheme* $\mathcal{G}$ *is authentic if for all sufficiently large* λ *and for any polynomial time adversary* $\mathcal{A}$:

$$Pr[\mathcal{A} \ wins \ \mathsf{AuthGame}(1^\lambda)] \leq \mathsf{negl}(\kappa)$$

$\mathsf{GCWise.Gb}(1^\kappa, \mathcal{C}_0, ..., \mathcal{C}_{b-1})$

1: $\delta_{i\in[m]}, S_{i\in[m]}, B_{j\in[\ell]}, K_{j\in[\ell]} \leftarrow \mathsf{Proc}_{\mathsf{Bkt}}(m, \ell, b)$
2: $(\hat{\alpha}, \hat{\gamma}, \hat{\mathcal{C}}_{\mathsf{bt}}) \leftarrow \mathsf{BT.Gb}(\delta_{i\in[m]}, S_{i\in[m]}, K_{j\in[\ell]})$
3: **for** $j \in [\ell]$ **do**
4:    $\mathcal{M}_j \leftarrow 0$
5:    **for** $i \in [m]$ **do**
6:       $\mathsf{ix} \leftarrow B_j[i]$
7:       $(\hat{\mathcal{C}}_{\mathsf{ix}}, e_i, d_i) \leftarrow \mathsf{Base.Gb}(1^\kappa, \mathcal{U}[\mathcal{C}_{\mathsf{ix}}]; S_i)$
8:       $\mathcal{M}_j \leftarrow \mathcal{M}_j \oplus \hat{\mathcal{C}}_{\mathsf{ix}}$
9:    $\tilde{\mathcal{M}}_j \leftarrow \mathsf{Encrypt}(\mathcal{M}_j, K_i)$
10: $(e', \hat{\mathcal{C}}_{\mathsf{dem}}) \leftarrow \mathsf{demux.Gb}(\hat{\gamma}, e_{i\in[m]})$
11: $(d, \hat{\mathcal{C}}_{\mathsf{mux}}) \leftarrow \mathsf{mux.Gb}(\hat{\gamma}, d_{i\in[m]})$
12: $e \leftarrow (\hat{\alpha}, e')$
13: $\hat{\mathcal{C}} \leftarrow (\tilde{\mathcal{M}}_{j\in[\ell]}, \hat{\mathcal{C}}_{\mathsf{bt}}, \hat{\mathcal{C}}_{\mathsf{dem}}, \hat{\mathcal{C}}_{\mathsf{mux}})$
14: **return** $(\hat{\mathcal{C}}, e, d)$

$\mathsf{GCWise.Ev}(\mathcal{C}_0, ..., \mathcal{C}_{b-1}, \hat{\mathcal{C}}, X)$

1: Parse $\hat{\mathcal{C}}$ as $(\tilde{\mathcal{M}}_{j\in[\ell]}, \hat{\mathcal{C}}_{\mathsf{bt}}, \hat{\mathcal{C}}_{\mathsf{dem}}, \hat{\mathcal{C}}_{\mathsf{mux}})$
2: Parse X as $(\hat{\alpha}, X')$
3: $(\beta, \gamma, \hat{\gamma}, (B_\beta \setminus \gamma), S_{i\in[m]\setminus\gamma}, K_\beta) \leftarrow \mathsf{BT.Ev}(\hat{\mathcal{C}}_{\mathsf{bt}}, \hat{\alpha})$
4: $X_\gamma \leftarrow \mathsf{demux.Ev}(\hat{\mathcal{C}}_{\mathsf{dem}}, \hat{\gamma}, X')$
5: $\mathcal{M}_\beta \leftarrow \mathsf{Decrypt}(\tilde{\mathcal{M}}_\beta, K_\beta)$
6: **for** $i \in [m] \setminus \gamma$ **do**
7:    $\mathsf{ix} \leftarrow B_\beta[i]$
8:    $(\hat{\mathcal{C}}_{\mathsf{ix}}, \cdot, \cdot) \leftarrow \mathsf{Base.Gb}(1^\kappa, \mathcal{U}[\mathcal{C}_{\mathsf{ix}}]; S_i)$
9:    $\mathcal{M}_\beta \leftarrow \mathcal{M}_\beta \oplus \hat{\mathcal{C}}_{\mathsf{ix}}$
10: $\hat{\mathcal{C}}_\alpha \leftarrow \mathcal{M}_\beta$
11: $Y_\gamma \leftarrow \mathsf{Base.Ev}(\mathcal{U}, \hat{\mathcal{C}}_\alpha, X_\gamma)$
12: $Y \leftarrow \mathsf{mux.Ev}(\hat{\mathcal{C}}_{\mathsf{mux}}, \hat{\gamma}, Y_\gamma)$
13: **return** Y

Fig. 2. Our garbling scheme GCWise. Recall from Sect. 3.4 that our scheme considers the conditional composition of b netlists. Let $\mathcal{U}$ be a circuit universal to $\mathcal{C}_0, ..., \mathcal{C}_{b-1}$; $\mathcal{U}[\mathcal{C}_i]$ denotes hardcoding the programming string of $\mathcal{U}$ according to the circuit description $\mathcal{C}_i$. Since GCWise is a projective garbling scheme [BHR12], procedures GCWise.En and GCWise.De are standard constructions that implement straightforward mappings between cleartext Boolean values and GC labels (see Sect. 3.3). The semantic function GCWise.ev gives the straightforward semantics of a conditional and is defined as follows: $\mathsf{GCWise.ev}(\mathcal{C}_0, ..., \mathcal{C}_{b-1}, \alpha, x) \mapsto \mathcal{C}_\alpha(x)$. Our construction uses our three garbled gadgets: the bucket table BT (see Sect. 5.1) as well as the demux and mux (see Sect. 5.2). Our scheme is parameterized over an underlying garbling scheme Base which we use to handle the individual conditional branches.

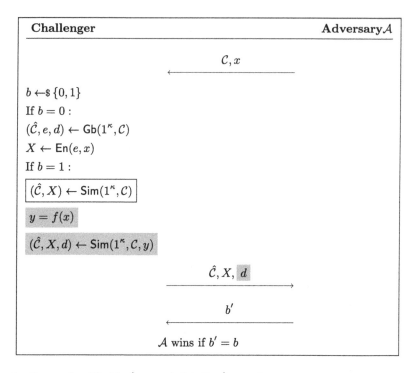

Fig. 3. Games for ObvSim$_{\mathcal{G},\mathsf{Sim}}^{\mathcal{A}}$ and PrivSim$_{\mathcal{G},\mathsf{Sim}}^{\mathcal{A}}$. The steps in boxes only apply to ObvSim, and the highlighted steps only apply to PrivSim. Unmarked text means the steps appear in both games.

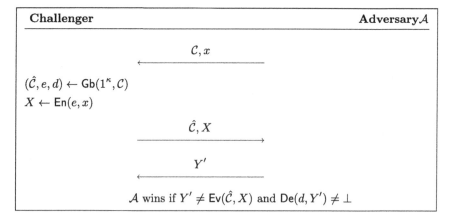

Fig. 4. Game for AuthGame$_{\mathcal{G}}^{\mathcal{A}}$.

Sequential Composability. As explained in Sect. 3.4, we do not directly manage the low level handling of individual gates. We instead adopt an approach given by [HK20a], where we leave the handling of netlists to a parameterized *underlying* garbling scheme. Arbitrary garbling schemes are not candidates for the underlying scheme because they do not export the format of their GC labels. To interface with the underlying scheme, we need to build *garbled gadgets* such that we can route wire labels into and out of conditional branches. Therefore, we define a concept of *sequentially composable* garbling schemes, a weakening of the *strong stackability* property given by [HK21]. Informally, sequential composability requires the garbling scheme to export the format of its labels such that they can be directly manipulated (i.e., used as PRF keys) by higher level garbling schemes. A sequentially composable scheme is projective and has a color and key function colorPart and keyPart. Many traditional garbling schemes, such as the classic 4-row Yao scheme, or the more recent half-gates [ZRE15], are sequentially composable or can be trivially adjusted (in a formal sense, meaning that only syntactic changes are needed) to meet the requirements.

As with [HK20a], we use the output labels of the underlying scheme as keys in subsequent garbled gadgets. We explain these gadgets in Sect. 5.2, but basically, they are implemented as garbled rows. The keyPart procedure gives us a key for each label. The colorPart procedure tells us the bits to instruct E as to which garbled row to decrypt. We 'split' each output label into a key and a color.

Definition 7 (Sequential Composability). *A garbling scheme is sequentially composable if:*

1. *The scheme is projective, including with respect to decoding. I.e., the output decoding string d is a vector of pairs of labels, and the procedure $\mathsf{De}(d, Y)$ is a simple comparison that, for each output label $Y_i \in Y$, computes the following output bit:*

$$\begin{cases} 0 & \textit{if } Y_i = d_i^0 \\ 1 & \textit{if } Y_i = d_i^1 \\ \bot & \textit{otherwise} \end{cases}$$

2. *There exists an efficient deterministic procedure colorPart that maps bitstrings to $\{0,1\}$ such that for all projective label pairs $X^0, X^1 \in d$:*

$$\mathsf{colorPart}(X^0) \neq \mathsf{colorPart}(X^1)$$

for the projective label pairs of the garbling scheme.

3. *There exists an efficient deterministic function keyPart that maps bitstrings to $\{0,1\}^\kappa$. Let k be the concatenation of the result of applying keyPart to each label in the output decoding string d. Let $R \in_\$ \{0,1\}^{|k|}$ be a uniform string:*

$$k \stackrel{c}{=} R$$

Note that the definition discusses the output decoding string d. Normally, d is used at the final layer of the GC to reveal outputs to E. *This is not our intent here.* We will not reveal the underlying scheme's d to E. Rather, we use d as a hook by which our garbling scheme can syntactically manipulate the labels of the underlying scheme to glue the output of the underlying scheme with the next layer of gates.

Free XOR [KS08a] based schemes (e.g., [ZRE15]) might appear to violate sequential composability: in Free XOR, each pair of internal wire labels is related by single global constant. Note, Free XOR-based schemes must *not* use the global constant as an offset for the output decoding string d, since otherwise the scheme would clearly fail to satisfy privacy (Definition 5). To resolve this issue, Free XOR-based schemes usually apply a hash function H to break correlation between labels inside the De function. To meet the letter of Definition 7, we simply push these hash function calls into the Ev function. Thus, these schemes effectively do generate output labels that are indistinguishable from uniformly random strings (i.e., that meet requirement 3 of Definition 7). This syntactic reinterpretation does not imply semantic change in [KS08a, ZRE15].

6.1 Proofs

In this section, we prove that GCWise satisfies the above garbled circuit security notions. Recall that Base is the underlying garbling scheme used to handle the content of individual branches. Our theorems have the form "If Base satisfies property X and sequential composability (Definition 7), then GCWise satisfies property X." The additional assumption of sequential composability is needed to so our garbling scheme can manipulate the GC labels of Base. Specifically, the sequential composability property allows us to use the colorPart and keyPart procedures to construct encrypted truth tables.

We first prove a lemma that our scheme is itself sequentially composable. This lemma can be used to embed GCWise inside a higher level scheme such that, for example, many conditionals can be sequentially composed (see discussion in Sect. 3.4).

Lemma 2. GCWise *is sequentially composable (Definition 7).*

Proof. The sequential composability of our scheme follows trivially from the definition of mux.Gb (Sect. 5.2). This procedure samples a uniform projective decoding string d with the constraint that the least significant bit of each label pair differs. Thus, we can use the least significant bit of each label as its color and the remaining bits as the key.   □

We next prove our scheme satisfies the properties of *correctness, authenticity, obliviousness,* and *privacy.* By satisfying these properties we ensure that our scheme can be securely plugged into GC protocols that use garbling schemes as a black box.

Theorem 1. *If the underlying garbling scheme* Base *is correct and sequentially composable then* GCWise *is correct.*

Proof. Correctness follows from (1) the discussion in Sect. 4, (2) the correctness of Base, and (3) the correctness of our garbled gadgets, as implied by the sequential composability of Base.

Let $\mathcal{C}_0, ..., \mathcal{C}_{b-1}$ be a vector of arbitrary circuits. Each branch $\mathcal{C}_i$ is garbled using Base. By construction, the $\mathcal{C}_i$ is stacked in buckets, and E obtains the material only for the active branch $\mathcal{C}_\alpha$.

Going in steps, the bucket table (Sect. 5.1) first reveals to E the information needed to extract material for the active instance:

- The identity of the active bucket, β.
- The identity of the siblings of $\mathcal{C}_\alpha$ in B_β.
- $m - 1$ seeds corresponding to the garbling of each sibling.
- A *bucket key* K_β corresponding to the active bucket.

E uses this information to decrypt and unstack the material $\hat{\mathcal{C}}_\alpha$ and properly translate the encoding into the encoding for $\hat{\mathcal{C}}_\alpha$.

The demux gadget routes GC label inputs to the active branch. The demux is implemented as a garbled gadget that properly translates the encoding of the input. Now, since E holds a GC for the UC $\mathcal{U}$ (programmed as $\mathcal{C}_\alpha$) and holds inputs X_γ, she can evaluate. As Base is correct, this yields the appropriate output labels Y_γ. Finally, the mux properly translates the output; this translation table can be correctly constructed thanks to the sequential composability of Base. Therefore, GCWise is correct.   □

Theorem 2. *If* Base *is oblivious and sequentially composable then* GCWise *is oblivious.*

Proof. By construction of a simulator $\mathcal{S}_{\text{obv}}$.

The goal of the simulator is to produce a tuple $(\mathcal{C}, \hat{\mathcal{C}}', X')$ such that:

$$(\mathcal{C}, \hat{\mathcal{C}}', X') \overset{c}{=} (\mathcal{C}, \hat{\mathcal{C}}, X)$$

where $\hat{\mathcal{C}}$ and X arise in the real world execution.

Our simulator uses Base's obliviousness simulator as a black box. There is one crucial detail in this use: we have carefully ensured that there is only one universal topology $\mathcal{U}$. Hence, the call to Base.$\mathcal{S}_{\text{obv}}(1^\kappa, \mathcal{U})$ indistinguishably simulates *any* of the conditional branches.

Our definition of $\mathcal{S}_{\text{obv}}$ closely matches the definition of Ev (Fig. 2). Specifically, $\mathcal{S}_{\text{obv}}$ proceeds as follows:

- Simulate the input string X by drawing uniform bits. This is trivially indistinguishable from real, since our input encoding string e is also chosen uniformly.
- Parse X as $(\hat{\alpha}, X')$.
- Simulate the bucket table and its garbled material $\hat{\mathcal{C}}_{\text{bt}}$ by calling a modular simulator $\text{Sim}_{\text{bt}}(\hat{\alpha})$ (described later). Let $(\beta, \gamma, \hat{\gamma}, (B_\beta \setminus \gamma), S_{i \in [m] \setminus \gamma}, K_\beta)$ be the simulated output.

- Simulate each stack of material $\mathcal{M}_{j \neq \beta}$ by a uniform string. This is indistinguishable from real: E obtains the decryption key K_β, but does not obtain any decryption key $K_{j \neq \beta}$, so in the real world she cannot decrypt. Simulating the active bucket is more nuanced.
- Simulate the demultiplexer and its garbled material $\hat{\mathcal{C}}_{\mathsf{demux}}$ via a modular simulator $\mathsf{Sim}_{\mathsf{demux}}(\hat{\gamma}, X')$ (described later). Let X_γ be the simulated output.
- Proceed by garbling each of the (simulated) $m-1$ siblings as described in Ev. Stack each material into $\mathcal{M}_\beta$.
- Simulate the material for the active instance by calling Base's obliviousness simulator: $\hat{\mathcal{C}}_\alpha \leftarrow \mathsf{Base}.\mathcal{S}_{\mathsf{obv}}(1^\kappa, \mathcal{U})$. Stack $\hat{\mathcal{C}}$ into $\mathcal{M}_\beta$ to complete the simulation of $\mathcal{M}_\beta$. We argue indistinguishability shortly.
- Evaluate the active instance normally: $Y_\gamma \leftarrow \mathsf{Base}.\mathsf{Ev}(\mathcal{U}, \hat{\mathcal{C}}_\alpha, X_\gamma)$.
- Simulate the multiplexer and its garbled material $\hat{\mathcal{C}}_{\mathsf{mux}}$ via a modular simulator $\mathsf{Sim}_{\mathsf{demux}}(\hat{\gamma}, Y_\gamma)$ (described later).
- Output all simulated GC material.

First, note that the simulated stacked material for the active bucket $\mathcal{M}_\beta$ is indistinguishable from real. This is because (1) the materials for the $m-1$ siblings are generated by garbling, which matches the real world and hence are clearly indistinguishable, and (2) the material for the active instance $\hat{\mathcal{C}}_\alpha$ is generated by Base's obliviousness simulator. By assumption, Base is oblivious, so this additional simulated material is indistinguishable from real.

Now, the above simulation refers to three modular simulators for our GC gadgets: $\mathsf{Sim}_{\mathsf{bt}}$, $\mathsf{Sim}_{\mathsf{demux}}$, and $\mathsf{Sim}_{\mathsf{mux}}$. Each of these gadgets are implemented from typical GC techniques: namely, encrypting output values by masking the output value with a PRF applied to the correct input value. These techniques are simple and well known, so we do not fully flesh out these component simulators. However, there are two important points which we must address.

Simulation of information revealed by the bucket table. The bucket table gadget reveals information in cleartext to E: E sees the active bucket ID β and the active instance id γ. These values must be simulated.

We argue that $\mathsf{Sim}_{\mathsf{bt}}$ (1) can simulate β by uniformly sampling a value from $[\ell]$ and (2) can simulate γ by uniformly sampling a value from $[m]$. This simulation is valid because in the real world (1) we sample each offset value δ_i uniformly at random, and (2) we uniformly choose the active instance from the set of all candidate instances (see discussion in Sect. 5.1). This means that a given branch ID is equally likely to reside in each bucket. Moreover, we sample among each of these instances uniformly, so each bucket is equally likely to be the active bucket. Hence uniformly sampling β and γ is a good simulation.

Security of using a PRF on labels from Base. Our multiplexer gadget (Sect. 5.2) takes as input output labels from the underlying scheme Base. Our multiplexer is a typical gadget that encrypts garbled rows using a PRF. Hence, we must be careful: we use output labels from Base as PRF keys. To simulate, the PRF definition requires PRF keys to be chosen uniformly. Here is where we make use of sequential composability (Definition 7). Sequential composability insists that all output labels, even jointly, are uniformly random. Thus, we can use the output labels as PRF keys without breaking the security of the PRF. GCWise is oblivious.   □

Theorem 3. *If* Base *is oblivious and sequentially composable then* GCWise *is private.*

Proof. By construction of a simulator $\mathcal{S}_{\mathrm{prv}}$.

By Theorem 2, GCWise is oblivious, so there exists an obliviousness simulator $\mathcal{S}_{\mathrm{obv}}$. $\mathcal{S}_{\mathrm{prv}}$ first runs $\mathcal{S}_{\mathrm{obv}}(1^{\kappa}, \mathcal{C})$ and obtains $(\mathcal{C}, \hat{\mathcal{C}}', X')$. From here, $\mathcal{S}_{\mathrm{prv}}$ must simulate an output decoding string d' such that

$$(\hat{\mathcal{C}}, X, d) \stackrel{c}{=} (\hat{\mathcal{C}}', X', d')$$

$\mathcal{S}_{\mathrm{prv}}$ computes $Y' \leftarrow \mathsf{Ev}(\mathcal{C}, M', X', t)$. Now, $\mathcal{S}_{\mathrm{prv}}$ constructs d' in a straight-forward manner: for each wire y, $\mathcal{S}_{\mathrm{prv}}$ fills one of the two labels in d' with Y' at position y such that decoding the label results in cleartext output y. The other label is set to be uniform with the restriction that its least significant bit differs from Y'. This simulation is indistinguishable from the real execution. The simulated d' decodes the true output y and is indistinguishable from d.   □

Theorem 4. *If the underlying garbling scheme* Base *is oblivious and sequentially composable then* GCWise *is authentic.*

Proof. Authenticity (Fig. 4) demands that an adversary $\mathcal{A}$ with only $\hat{\mathcal{C}}$ and X cannot construct a garbled output Y' that is different from the one allowed by X and $\hat{\mathcal{C}}$, i.e., where $Y' \neq \mathsf{Ev}(\hat{\mathcal{C}}, X)$ and $\mathsf{De}(d, Y) \neq \perp$, except with negligible probability.

Our authenticity proof is like existing GC proofs, e.g., [ZRE15].

Authenticity follows from the definition of the privacy simulator $\mathcal{S}_{\mathrm{prv}}$, from our choice of output decoding string d, and from De. Assume, to reach a contradiction, that a polytime $\mathcal{A}$ can indeed forge a proof. We demonstrate that such an adversary allows a privacy distinguisher. Specifically, on input $(\hat{\mathcal{C}}, X, d)$ the distinguisher (1) evaluates the GC normally to obtain Y, (2) forges an output Y' by invoking $\mathcal{A}$, and (3) outputs 1 if and only if $Y \neq Y'$ and both Y and Y' successfully decode.

If we give to this distinguisher a circuit garbling produced by $\mathcal{S}_{\mathrm{prv}}$, the distinguisher will output one with negliglible probability. Indeed, $\mathcal{A}$ must guess $Y' \neq Y$ that successfully decodes. However, for each bit in d, $\mathcal{S}_{\mathrm{prv}}$ uniformly samples the inactive decoding string. Thus $\mathcal{A}$ must simply *guess* such a value, since these uniformly drawn values are independent of the adversary's view. This only succeeds with probability $\frac{1}{2^{\kappa}}$.

Hence, if the $\mathcal{A}$ can succeed on a *real* garbling with non-negligible probability, then we indeed have distinguisher. But GCWise is private, so the distinguisher should not exist, and we have a contradiction.

GCWise is authentic.   □

Acknowledgements. This work was supported in part by NSF award #1909769, by a Facebook research award, a Cisco research award, and by Georgia Tech's IISP cybersecurity seed funding (CSF) award. This material is also based upon work supported in part by DARPA under Contract No. HR001120C0087. This work is also supported by DARPA under Cooperative Agreement HR0011-20-2-0025, NSF grant CNS-2001096, CNS-1764025, CNS-1718074, US-Israel BSF grant 2015782, Google Faculty Award, JP Morgan Faculty Award, IBM Faculty Research Award, Xerox Faculty Research Award, OKAWA Foundation Research Award, B. John Garrick Foundation Award, Teradata Research Award, Lockheed-Martin Research Award and Sunday Group. The views and conclusions contained herein are those of the authors and should not be interpreted as necessarily representing the official policies, either expressed or implied, of DARPA, the Department of Defense, or the U.S. Government. The U.S. Government is authorized to reproduce and distribute reprints for governmental purposes not withstanding any copyright annotation therein.

References

[BHR12] Bellare, M., Hoang, V.T., Rogaway, P.: Foundations of garbled circuits. In: Yu, T., Danezis, G., Gligor, V.D. (eds.) ACM CCS 2012, pp. 784–796. ACM Press, October 2012

[BNO19] Ben-Efraim, A., Nielsen, M., Omri, E.: Turbospeedz: double your online SPDZ! improving SPDZ using function dependent preprocessing. In: Deng, R.H., Gauthier-Umaña, V., Ochoa, M., Yung, M. (eds.) ACNS 2019. LNCS, vol. 11464, pp. 530–549. Springer, Cham (2019). https://doi.org/10.1007/978-3-030-21568-2_26

[BV11] Brakerski, Z., Vaikuntanathan, V.: Efficient fully homomorphic encryption from (standard) LWE. In: Ostrovsky, R. (ed.) 52nd FOCS, pp. 97–106. IEEE Computer Society Press, October 2011

[CGKS95] Chor, B., Goldreich, O., Kushilevitz, E., Sudan, M.: Private information retrieval. In: 36th Annual Symposium on Foundations of Computer Science, Milwaukee, Wisconsin, USA, 23–25 October 1995, pp. 41–50. IEEE Computer Society (1995)

[CK20] Corrigan-Gibbs, H., Kogan, D.: Private information retrieval with sublinear online time. In: Canteaut, A., Ishai, Y. (eds.) EUROCRYPT 2020. LNCS, vol. 12105, pp. 44–75. Springer, Cham (2020). https://doi.org/10.1007/978-3-030-45721-1_3

[CKGS98] Chor, B., Kushilevitz, E., Goldreich, O., Sudan, M.: Private information retrieval. J. ACM **45**(6), 965–981 (1998)

[CKKZ12] Choi, S.G., Katz, J., Kumaresan, R., Zhou, H.-S.: On the security of the "Free-XOR" technique. In: Cramer, R. (ed.) TCC 2012. LNCS, vol. 7194, pp. 39–53. Springer, Heidelberg (2012). https://doi.org/10.1007/978-3-642-28914-9_3

[DPSZ12] Damgård, I., Pastro, V., Smart, N., Zakarias, S.: Multiparty computation from somewhat homomorphic encryption. In: Safavi-Naini, R., Canetti, R. (eds.) CRYPTO 2012. LNCS, vol. 7417, pp. 643–662. Springer, Heidelberg (2012). https://doi.org/10.1007/978-3-642-32009-5_38

[FNO15] Frederiksen, T.K., Nielsen, J.B., Orlandi, C.: Privacy-free garbled circuits with applications to efficient zero-knowledge. In: Oswald, E., Fischlin, M. (eds.) EUROCRYPT 2015. LNCS, vol. 9057, pp. 191–219. Springer, Heidelberg (2015). https://doi.org/10.1007/978-3-662-46803-6_7

[Gen09] Gentry, C.: Fully homomorphic encryption using ideal lattices. In: Mitzenmacher, M. (ed.) 41st ACM STOC, pp. 169–178. ACM Press, May/June 2009

[GKK+12] Dov Gordon, S., et al.: Secure two-party computation in sublinear (amortized) time. In: Yu, T., Danezis, G., Gligor, V.D. (eds.) ACM CCS 2012, pp. 513–524. ACM Press, October 2012

[GKP+13] Goldwasser, S., Kalai, Y.T., Popa, R.A., Vaikuntanathan, V., Zeldovich, N.: How to run turing machines on encrypted data. In: Canetti, R., Garay, J.A. (eds.) CRYPTO 2013. LNCS, vol. 8043, pp. 536–553. Springer, Heidelberg (2013). https://doi.org/10.1007/978-3-642-40084-1_30

[GSW13] Gentry, C., Sahai, A., Waters, B.: Homomorphic encryption from learning with errors: conceptually-simpler, asymptotically-faster, attribute-based. In: Canetti, R., Garay, J.A. (eds.) CRYPTO 2013. LNCS, vol. 8042, pp. 75–92. Springer, Heidelberg (2013). https://doi.org/10.1007/978-3-642-40041-4_5

[HK20a] Heath, D., Kolesnikov, V.: Stacked garbling. In: Micciancio, D., Ristenpart, T. (eds.) CRYPTO 2020. LNCS, vol. 12171, pp. 763–792. Springer, Cham (2020). https://doi.org/10.1007/978-3-030-56880-1_27

[HK20b] Heath, D., Kolesnikov, V.: Stacked garbling for disjunctive zero-knowledge proofs. In: Canteaut, A., Ishai, Y. (eds.) EUROCRYPT 2020. LNCS, vol. 12107, pp. 569–598. Springer, Cham (2020). https://doi.org/10.1007/978-3-030-45727-3_19

[HK21] Heath, D., Kolesnikov, V.: LogStack: stacked garbling with $O(b \log b)$ computation. In: Canteaut, A., Standaert, F.-X. (eds.) EUROCRYPT 2021. LNCS, vol. 12698, pp. 3–32. Springer, Cham (2021). https://doi.org/10.1007/978-3-030-77883-5_1

[JKO13] Jawurek, M., Kerschbaum, F., Orlandi, C.: Zero-knowledge using garbled circuits: how to prove non-algebraic statements efficiently. In: Sadeghi, A.-R., Gligor, V.D., Yung, M. (eds.) ACM CCS 2013, pp. 955–966. ACM Press, November 2013

[KKW17] Kennedy, W.S., Kolesnikov, V., Wilfong, G.: Overlaying conditional circuit clauses for secure computation. In: Takagi, T., Peyrin, T. (eds.) ASIACRYPT 2017. LNCS, vol. 10625, pp. 499–528. Springer, Cham (2017). https://doi.org/10.1007/978-3-319-70697-9_18

[KMR14] Kolesnikov, V., Mohassel, P., Rosulek, M.: FleXOR: flexible garbling for XOR gates that beats free-XOR. In: Garay, J.A., Gennaro, R. (eds.) CRYPTO 2014. LNCS, vol. 8617, pp. 440–457. Springer, Heidelberg (2014). https://doi.org/10.1007/978-3-662-44381-1_25

[KO97] Kushilevitz, E., Ostrovsky, R.: Replication is NOT needed: SINGLE database, computationally-private information retrieval. In: 38th FOCS, pp. 364–373. IEEE Computer Society Press, October 1997

[Kol18] Kolesnikov, V.: Free IF: how to omit inactive branches and implement $\mathcal{S}$-universal garbled circuit (almost) for free. In: Peyrin, T., Galbraith, S. (eds.) ASIACRYPT 2018. LNCS, vol. 11274, pp. 34–58. Springer, Cham (2018). https://doi.org/10.1007/978-3-030-03332-3_2

[KS08a] Kolesnikov, V., Schneider, T.: Improved garbled circuit: free XOR gates and applications. In: Aceto, L., Damgård, I., Goldberg, L.A., Halldórsson, M.M., Ingólfsdóttir, A., Walukiewicz, I. (eds.) ICALP 2008. LNCS, vol. 5126, pp. 486–498. Springer, Heidelberg (2008). https://doi.org/10.1007/978-3-540-70583-3_40

[KS08b] Kolesnikov, V., Schneider, T.: A practical universal circuit construction and secure evaluation of private functions. In: Tsudik, G. (ed.) FC 2008. LNCS, vol. 5143, pp. 83–97. Springer, Heidelberg (2008). https://doi.org/10.1007/978-3-540-85230-8_7

[LO13] Lu, S., Ostrovsky, R.: How to garble RAM programs? In: Johansson, T., Nguyen, P.Q. (eds.) EUROCRYPT 2013. LNCS, vol. 7881, pp. 719–734. Springer, Heidelberg (2013). https://doi.org/10.1007/978-3-642-38348-9_42

[LP09] Lindell, Y., Pinkas, B.: A proof of security of Yao's protocol for two-party computation. J. Cryptol. **22**(2), 161–188 (2009)

[LYZ+20] Liu, H., Yu, Y., Zhao, S., Zhang, J., Liu, W.: Pushing the limits of valiant's universal circuits: simpler, tighter and more compact. Cryptology ePrint Archive, Report 2020/161 (2020). https://eprint.iacr.org/2020/161

[NPS99] Naor, M., Pinkas, B., Sumner, R.: Privacy preserving auctions and mechanism design. In: Proceedings of the 1st ACM Conference on Electronic Commerce, EC 1999, pp. 129–139, 1999. Association for Computing Machinery, New York (1999)

[PSSW09] Pinkas, B., Schneider, T., Smart, N.P., Williams, S.C.: Secure two-party computation is practical. In: Matsui, M. (ed.) ASIACRYPT 2009. LNCS, vol. 5912, pp. 250–267. Springer, Heidelberg (2009). https://doi.org/10.1007/978-3-642-10366-7_15

[RR21] Rosulek, M., Roy, L.: Three halves make a whole? beating the half-gates lower bound for garbled circuits. In: Malkin, T., Peikert, C. (eds.) CRYPTO 2021. LNCS, vol. 12825, pp. 94–124. Springer, Cham (2021). https://doi.org/10.1007/978-3-030-84242-0_5

[Val76] Valiant, L.G.: Universal circuits (preliminary report). In: STOC, pp. 196–203. ACM Press, New York (1976)

[WRK17] Wang, X., Ranellucci, S., Katz, J.: Authenticated garbling and efficient maliciously secure two-party computation. In: Thuraisingham, B.M., Evans, D., Malkin, T., Xu, D. (eds.) ACM CCS 2017, pp. 21–37. ACM Press, October/November 2017

[Yao86] Yao, A.C.-C.: How to generate and exchange secrets (extended abstract). In: 27th FOCS, pp. 162–167. IEEE Computer Society Press, October 1986

[ZRE15] Zahur, S., Rosulek, M., Evans, D.: Two halves make a whole. In: Oswald, E., Fischlin, M. (eds.) EUROCRYPT 2015. LNCS, vol. 9057, pp. 220–250. Springer, Heidelberg (2015). https://doi.org/10.1007/978-3-662-46803-6_8

Round-Optimal and Communication-Efficient Multiparty Computation

Michele Ciampi[1] , Rafail Ostrovsky[2] , Hendrik Waldner[1(✉)] ,
and Vassilis Zikas[3]

[1] The University of Edinburgh, Edinburgh, UK
{michele.ciampi,hendrik.waldner}@ed.ac.uk
[2] University of California, Los Angeles, CA, USA
rafail@cs.ucla.edu
[3] Purdue University, West Lafayette, IN, USA
vzikas@cs.purdue.edu

Abstract. Typical approaches for minimizing the round complexity of multiparty computation (MPC) come at the cost of increased communication complexity (CC) or the reliance on setup assumptions. A notable exception is the recent work of Ananth *et al.* [TCC 2019], which used Functional Encryption (FE) combiners to obtain a round optimal (two-round) semi-honest MPC in the plain model with a CC proportional to the depth and input-output length of the circuit being computed—we refer to such protocols as *circuit scalable*. This leaves open the question of obtaining communication efficient protocols that are secure against *malicious* adversaries in the plain model, which we present in this work. Concretely, our two main contributions are:

1) We provide a round-preserving black-box compiler that compiles a wide class of MPC protocols into *circuit-scalable* maliciously secure MPC protocols in the plain model, assuming (succinct) FE combiners.

2) We provide a round-preserving black-box compiler that compiles a wide class of MPC protocols into *circuit-independent*—i.e., with a CC that depends only on the input-output length of the circuit—maliciously secure MPC protocols in the plain model, assuming Multi-Key Fully-Homomorphic Encryption (MFHE). Our constructions are based on a new compiler that turns a wide class of MPC protocols into k-delayed-input function MPC protocols (a notion we introduce), where the function that is being computed is specified only in the k-th round of the protocol.

As immediate corollaries of our two compilers, we derive (1) the first round-optimal and circuit-scalable maliciously secure MPC, and (2) the first round-optimal and circuit-independent maliciously secure MPC in the plain model. The latter MPC achieves the best to-date CC for a round-optimal malicious MPC protocol. In fact, it is even communication-optimal when the output size of the function being evaluated is smaller than its input size (e.g., for boolean functions). All of our results are based on standard polynomial time assumptions.

© International Association for Cryptologic Research 2022
O. Dunkelman and S. Dziembowski (Eds.): EUROCRYPT 2022, LNCS 13275, pp. 65–95, 2022.
https://doi.org/10.1007/978-3-031-06944-4_3

1   Introduction

Secure multiparty computation (MPC) [23,42] allows different parties to jointly evaluate any circuit over private inputs in such a way that each party learns the output of the computation and nothing else. Many improvements in this area have led to better protocols in terms of complexity assumptions and round complexity in the case of malicious adversaries[1] [5,12,13,23,24,27–30,37,38,41].

Recently, the design of round-optimal MPC has attracted a lot of attention. Concretely, for semi-honest adversaries, two rounds are necessary for secure MPC in the plain model (as any one-round protocol is trivially broken). A lower bound was matched by [6,21], where the authors present a two-round MPC protocol in the semi-honest model from standard assumptions. Note that the above lower bound holds even when a correlated-randomness setup is assumed. The works [6,9,16,21,34] show that the same bound holds even for maliciously secure MPC, assuming a trusted correlated-randomness setup. However, Garg et al. [18] proved that in the plain model four rounds are necessary for maliciously secure MPC with a black-box simulator. This four-round lower-bound was matched by several constructions for a range of common (polynomial) complexity assumptions [4,11,25]. Notwithstanding, a common drawback in all the above constructions is that their communication complexity is proportional to the size (of the description) of the circuit being evaluated. For malicious adversaries, under the assumption that parties have access to correlated randomness, Quach et al. [39] proved that it is possible to design a two-round circuit-scalable MPC protocol that is secure against malicious adversaries under the learning with errors assumption (LWE). Also in the correlated randomness model, Morgan et al. [33] showed that it is possible to construct a two-round circuit-independent[2] two-party computation protocol in which only one party gets the output, by relying only on LWE.[3]

In the case of semi-honest adversaries (without a setup) the works of Ananth et al. [1] and Quach et al. [39] proposed a round-optimal (two-round) circuit-scalable MPC protocol under standard assumptions. Interesting, and most related to our results, Ananth et al. [1] obtained their result by leveraging a connection between round-optimal semi-honest MPC and *functional encryption combiners*. However, their construction does not achieve security against

---

[1] A malicious adversary attacks the protocol following an arbitrary probabilistic polynomial-time strategy. Unless stated differently, when we talk about the security of an MPC protocol against semi-honest or malicious adversaries we assume that up to $n - 1$ parties can be corrupted, where n is the number of parties.

[2] We stress that in our work the size of the circuit is always related to the security parameter via a polynomial p. We use the term circuit-independent for MPC protocols whose communication complexity depend on the security parameter, the size of the input and output, and does not depend on p. The same argument holds for circuit-scalable MPC protocols.

[3] In the communication model used in [33] in each round only one party can speak. Hence they obtain the best possible security guarantees in such a communication model.

malicious adversaries. The mentioned results raise the following important open question:

> Is there a round-optimal maliciously MPC protocol secure against dishonest majority[4] in the plain model based on standard complexity assumptions that achieves circuit-scalability, i.e. has a communication complexity that depends only on the depth of the circuit being evaluated and its input and output length?

As the first of our two main contributions, we answer the above question in the affirmative by extending the investigation of the relation between FE combiners and MPC to the malicious setting. This completes the landscape of circuit-scalable and round-optimal maliciously secure MPC in the plain model. More concretely, we provide a round-preserving black-box compiler that compiles a wide class of MPC protocols into circuit-scalable protocols assuming any *succinct* FE combiner (see below). Such FE combiners are known to exist based on the learning with errors assumption. We next investigate whether our result can be strengthened to achieve *circuit-independent* MPC:

> Is there a round-optimal and circuit-independent maliciously secure MPC protocol in the plain model from standard (polynomial) complexity assumptions?

Although the connection between MPC and FE does not seem to help here, we still answer the above question in the affirmative. Concretely, we propose a round-preserving *black-box compiler* that compiles a wide class of MPC protocols[5] into a circuit-independent protocol assuming the existence of any *compact* Multi-Key Fully-Homomorphic Encryption (MFHE) scheme that enjoys perfect correctness. Informally, the compactness property, here, requires that the size of the ciphertexts and the size of the description of the encryption and decryption algorithms depend only on the input-output size of the function being computed.

For the special case of constant parties, the MFHE scheme required for our compiler exists based on perfect correct FHE [32], which, in turn, can be instantiated from the LWE assumption [10]. Hence our result yields the first circuit-independent round-optimal malicious MPC in the plain model for a constant number of parties—and therefore specifically to the first two-party-computation protocol—based on standard polynomial-time assumptions. For the case of arbitrary many parties, to our knowledge, compact MFHE is only known to exist based on the Ring-LWE and the Decisional Small Polynomial Ratio (DSPR) assumption [32]. Hence, under these assumptions, we obtain a circuit-independent round-optimal MPC protocol for arbitrary many parties. Deriving compact MFHE for arbitrary many parties—and hence also a circuit-independent round-optimal MPC—from standard polynomial-time assumptions (e.g., LWE) is an interesting open problem.

---

[4] Unless otherwise specified, all our results are proved secure in the dishonest majority setting.

[5] We require the first 2 rounds of the MPC protocol to be independent from the inputs.

We highlight that all our constructions require the input protocol to achieve a special notion called k-delayed-input function, which we introduce in this work. Informally, in a k-delayed-input function protocol each party has two inputs: 1) a private input (known at the beginning of the protocol) and 2) the function to be computed whose description is needed only to compute the rounds $k, k+1, \ldots$. A k-delayed-input function protocol guarantees that the adversary does not learn more than what it can infer from the evaluation of the function f on the honest parties' input, where f can be adversarially (and adaptively) chosen.

We further show how to turn any MPC protocol that does not require the input to compute the first $k - 1$ rounds into a k-delayed-input function protocol.

1.1 Related Work

Functional encryption (FE) [8,35,40] is a primitive that enables fine-grained access control over encrypted data. In more detail, a FE scheme is equipped with a key generation algorithm that allows the owner of a master secret key to generate a *secret key* sk_f associated with a circuit f. Using such a secret key sk_f for the decryption of a ciphertext $\mathsf{ct} \leftarrow \mathsf{Enc}(\mathsf{msk}, x)$ yields *only* $f(x)$. In other terms, the security of a functional encryption scheme guarantees that no other information except for $f(x)$ is leaked.

A functional encryption combiner allows for the combination of many FE candidates in such a way that the resulting FE protocol is secure as long as any of the initial FE candidates is secure. Ananth et al. [1] show how to construct an FE combiner, based on the learning with errors (LWE) assumption, that enjoys the property of *succinctness* and *decomposability* (we elaborate more on the latter property in the next section). The property of succinctness states that 1) the length of each secret key is related to the depth and the length of the output of the circuit being evaluated and 2) the encryption complexity is proportional to the depth of the circuit being evaluated and to the length of the message being encrypted.

Given such a succinct FE combiner and an ℓ-round semi-honest MPC (not necessarily communication efficient), Ananth et al. show how to obtain an ℓ-round *circuit-scalable* MPC protocol that is secure against semi-honest adversaries. Given that such a combiner —as well as a round optimal semi-honest MPC—can be constructed from LWE, this result can be instantiated from the LWE assumption. In [2] the authors also explore the relation between MFHE and MPC and, among other results, the authors also show how to obtain a circuit-independent MPC protocol that is secure against semi-malicious adversary assuming Ring LWE, DSPR and 2-round OT.[6] Cohen et al. [15] proposed a round-optimal *circuit-scalable* MPC protocol which tolerates adaptive corruption (i.e., the identities of the corrupted parties can be decided during the protocol execution). The security of this protocol is proven in the correlated-randomness

---

[6] We recall that a semi-malicious adversary behaves like a semi-honest adversary with the exception that it decides the randomness and the input used to run the protocol.

model under the adaptive LWE assumption and secure erasures (alternatively, sub-exponential indistinguishability obfuscation). We recall that it is not possible to achieve security with adaptive corruption (with black-box simulation) in the plain model with a constant number of rounds [19]. For this reason, our work focuses on static corruption only.

1.2 Overview of Our Results

In this work we provide two main results which close the gap between communication-efficient and round-optimal maliciously secure MPC. We present two compilers that amplify existing protocols in terms of their communication complexity while preserving their round complexity, which results in the first class of maliciously secure MPC protocols that are communication-efficient and round-optimal.

From FE Combiners to Circuit-Scalable MPC. The first is a round optimal MPC protocol that 1) is secure against malicious adversaries, 2) tolerates arbitrary many parties, 3) is secure under standard polynomial time assumptions and 4) is circuit-scalable, i.e., has a communication complexity proportional to the depth of the circuit and the length of the input and output of the circuit being evaluated.[7] In summary, we prove the following theorem.

Theorem 1 (informal). *If there exists a 3-delayed-input function ℓ-round MPC protocol Π that is secure against malicious adversaries and a succinct FE combiner, then there exists an ℓ-round MPC protocol Π' that is secure against malicious adversaries whose communication complexity depends only on the security parameter, the depth, the input length and the output length of the circuit being evaluated, and that makes black-box use of Π.*

We argue that the four-round protocols proposed in [4,11] can be turned into 3-delayed-input function protocols, which in turn implies that we can obtain a circuit-scalable round optimal MPC protocol from the LWE assumption, since the maliciously-secure four-round OT that the protocol of [11] relies on can also be instantiated using LWE [17]. This allows us to prove the following corollary.

Corollary 1 (informal). *If the LWE assumption holds, then there exists a round optimal MPC protocol that is secure against malicious adversaries whose communication complexity depends only on the security parameter, the depth, the input length and the output length of the circuit being evaluated.*

---

[7] All our result are with respect to black-box simulation.

From Circuit-Independent MPC. For the second contribution we show how to combine an MPC protocol with a perfectly correct, compact MFHE scheme to obtain a *circuit-independent* MPC protocol. The notion of MFHE extends the notion of Fully-Homomorphic Encryption (FHE) to the multi-party setting by allowing each party to generate a public-secret key pair. All the ciphertexts generated using the public keys of the MFHE scheme can be homomorphically combined to obtain a single ciphertext, which can be decrypted only using all the secret keys. The output of our compiler is a circuit-independent round-optimal MPC protocol that supports $\min\{n_0, n_1\}$ parties where n_0 and n_1 is the number of parties supported by the input MPC protocol and the MFHE scheme respectively. Our second contribution can be summarized as follows.

Theorem 2 (informal). *If there exists a 2-delayed-input function ℓ-round MPC protocol Π that is secure against malicious adversaries which supports n_0 number of parties and a perfectly correct, compact MFHE scheme that supports n_1 number of parties, then there exists an ℓ-round MPC protocol Π' that is secure against malicious adversaries whose communication complexity depends (polynomially) only on the security parameter, the input length and the output length of the circuit being evaluated, and that makes black-box use of Π and supports $\min\{n_0, n_1\}$ number of parties.*

Additionally, it is possible to improve the above result and to obtain a protocol whose communication complexity is only linear in the length of the inputs (and polynomially in the length of the output and the security parameter), by relying on pseudorandom generators (PRGs). Hence, we obtain an MPC protocol that is optimal in terms of round and communication complexity for all the functions whose input-size is bigger than the output-size (e.g., boolean functions).

Given that a MFHE scheme for a constant number of parties can be instantiated from LWE and that a scheme for arbitrary many parties can be instantiated from Ring-LWE and DSPR [32] we obtain the following additional corollary.

Corollary 2 (informal). *If the LWE assumption holds (resp. Ring LWE and DSPR hold and any of the assumptions DDH, QR, N^{th} Residuosity, LWE hold, or malicious-secure OT exists), then there exists a round optimal circuit-independent MPC protocol for a constant (resp. arbitrarily) number of parties that is secure against malicious adversaries.*

For completeness we have included a comprehensive comparison of our results with existing round-optimal MPC protocols proven secure in the plain model, under standard polynomial-time complexity assumptions in Table 1.

2   Technical Overview

Our treatment advances the state of the art in communication-efficient and round-optimal MPC. Toward this goal, we combine and substantially extend

Table 1. Communication complexity of two-round semi-honest secure and four-round maliciously secure n-party protocols in the plain- and all-but-one corruption model, with black-box simulation, based on polynomial-time assumptions. We denote by $|f|$ and d the size and depth of the circuit representing the MPC functionality f, respectively. L_{in} and L_{out} denote, respectively, the input and output lengths of the circuit and piO stands for probabilistic indistinguishability obfuscation. We recall that we can replace 4-round maliciously secure OT with either DDH, QR, N^{th} Residuosity, or LWE.

	Communication complexity	Assumptions	Adversarial model	Rounds
[1,39]	$\text{poly}(\lambda, n, d, L_{in}, L_{out})$	LWE	Semi-honest	2
[6,21]	$\text{poly}(\lambda, n, |f|)$	Semi-honest OT	Semi-honest	2
[16]	$\text{poly}(\lambda, n, d, L_{in}, L_{out})$	piO and lossy encryption	Semi-honest	2
[20]	$\text{poly}(\lambda, n, |f|)$	Bilinear Maps	Semi-honest	2
[25]	$\text{poly}(\lambda, n, |f|)$	QR	Malicious	4
[4]	$\text{poly}(\lambda, n, |f|)$	DDH/QR/ N^{th} Residuosity	Malicious	4
[11]	$\text{poly}(\lambda, n, |f|)$	Malicious 4-round OT	Malicious	4
[2]	$\text{poly}(\lambda, n, L_{in}, L_{out})$	Ring LWE and DSPR and 2-round OT	Semi-malicious	2
This work	$\text{poly}(\lambda, n, d, L_{in}, L_{out})$	LWE	Malicious	4
This work[*]	$\text{poly}(\lambda, n, L_{in}, L_{out})$	LWE	Malicious	4
This work	$\text{poly}(\lambda, n, L_{in}, L_{out})$	Ring LWE and DSPR and malicious 4-round OT	Malicious	4

[*]Constant number of parties only.

several recent techniques in the literature of FE and MFHE as well as delayed-input MPC. In this section, to assist the reader better navigate through the many technical challenges and details of our result and evaluate its novelty, we review the main technical challenges and our approach to tackling them.

From FE Combiners to Circuit-Scalable MPC. Towards our construction of circuit-scalable MPC, we rely on the recent work of Ananth et al. [1]. In order to build a better intuition for our final solution, we briefly recap their compiler here.

The main building blocks of that compiler are an ℓ-round semi-honest secure MPC protocol and a succinct decomposable FE combiner. The property of decomposability requires the functional key for f to be of the form $(\mathsf{sk}_1^f, \ldots, \mathsf{sk}_n^f)$, and the master secret key needs to be $(\mathsf{msk}_1, \ldots, \mathsf{msk}_n)$, where sk_i and msk_i are the secret key and master secret key produced by the i-th FE candidate.

Compiler of Ananth et al. [1]. The construction of Ananth et al. [1] is very intuitive, and roughly works as follows. The MPC protocol computes the function g which takes n inputs, one for each party P_i with $i \in [n]$. The input of each party consists of a master secret key msk_i, a value x_i and a randomness r_i. The function g uses the n master secret keys to compute an encryption of $x_1, \ldots, x_n$ using the randomness $r_1, \ldots, r_n$.

Let x_i be the input of the party P_i with $i \in [n]$. Each party P_i samples a master secret key msk_i for the FE combiner, a random string r_i and runs the MPC protocol Π using $(\mathsf{msk}_i, x_i, r_i)$ as an input. In parallel, P_i computes the secret key sk_i^f and sends it to all the parties (we recall that sk_i^f can be computed by party P_i due to the decomposability property of the FE combiner). Let ct be the output of Π received by P_i, and let $(\mathsf{sk}_1^f, \ldots, \mathsf{sk}_{i-1}^f, \mathsf{sk}_{i+1}^f, \ldots, \mathsf{sk}_n^f)$ be the keys received from all the other parties, then P_i runs the decryption algorithm of the FE combiner on input $(\mathsf{sk}_1^f, \ldots, \mathsf{sk}_n^f)$ and ct thus obtaining $f(x_1, \ldots, x_n)$.

Given that the MPC protocol computes a function g whose complexity is $\mathrm{poly}(\lambda, d, L_{\mathsf{in}})$ and the size of each one of the secret keys sent on the channel is $\mathrm{poly}(\lambda, d, L_{\mathsf{out}})$ the final protocol has a communication complexity of $\mathrm{poly}(\lambda, n, d, L_{\mathsf{in}}, L_{\mathsf{out}})$, where λ is the security parameter, d is the depth of f, L_{in} is the length of the input of f and L_{out} is the output length of f (we recall that this is due to the succinctness of the FE combiner).

Achieving Malicious Security. Starting from the above approach, we now show how to obtain a circuit-scalable MPC protocol in the case of malicious adversaries (instead of semi-honest) in the plain model.

As a first approach one can try to simply replace the semi-honest MPC protocol with a maliciously secure one. Unfortunately, this does not work as a corrupted party $P_j^\star$ might create an ill formed master secret key msk_j (i.e., msk_j is not generated accordingly to the setup procedure of the j-th FE candidate) and sample r_j according to an arbitrary strategy. However, we note that the second problem is straightforward to solve as we can modify the function g, evaluated by the MPC protocol Π, in such a way that it uses the randomness $r_1 \oplus \cdots \oplus r_n$ to compute the encryption ct (we note that in this case each party needs to sample a longer r_i compared to the semi-honest protocol described earlier).

To solve the first problem, we follow a similar approach. Each party P_i inputs an additional random value r_i^{Setup} to the MPC protocol and the function g is modified such that it generates the master secret keys using the randomness $R = r_1^{\mathsf{Setup}} \oplus \cdots \oplus r_n^{\mathsf{Setup}}$ and outputs to the party P_i the ciphertext ct.[8] Unfortunately, this approach is not round preserving, as the knowledge of the master secret key msk_i, which becomes available only in the end of the execution of Π, is required to generate the secret key sk_i^f. Hence, if Π requires ℓ-rounds, our final protocol would consist of $\ell + 1$ rounds as each party P_i needs to send its functional secret key sk_i^f in the $(\ell + 1)$-th round.

Besides this, the described protocol is also still not secure, since a corrupted party $P_j^\star$ might generate an ill formed secret key sk_j^f, that could decrypt ct incorrectly, yielding an incorrect output for the honest parties. However, we can prove that this protocol protects the inputs of the honest parties. That

---

[8] R is parsed as n strings and each of the strings is used to generate a different master secret key.

is, it achieves *privacy with knowledge of outputs (PKO)* [26,36]. This notion guarantees that the input of the honest parties are protected as in the standard definition of secure MPC, but the output of the honest parties might not be the correct one (e.g., the adversary can force the honest party to output a string of its choice).

Round Preserving Construction: Privacy with Knowledge of Outputs. The first step towards our final construction is to adapt the above idea in such a way that the round complexity of the resulting protocol is kept down to ℓ, while achieving a somewhat reduced security, namely *privacy with knowledge of outputs* [26]. Looking ahead, in the following paragraph, we discuss how to elevate this to full security. For simplicity, we describe our protocol considering only two parties P_0 and P_1 and consider as a building block an MPC protocol Π which consists of ($\ell = 4$)-rounds (which is optimal). The protocol then can be trivially extended to the case of n-parties and an arbitrary $\ell \geq 4$ as we show in the technical part of the paper.

For our construction we need the first two rounds of Π to be independent of the inputs (i.e., the input is required only to compute the last two rounds in our simplified example). Assuming that the parties have access to a simultaneous broadcast channel where every party can simultaneously broadcast a message to all other parties, our compiler works, at a high level, as follows (we refer to Fig. 1 for a pictorial representation).

In the first step, the parties run two instances of Blum's coin tossing protocol [7]. In the first instance the party P_0 acts as the sender and in the other instance the party P_1 acts as the sender. In more detail, each party P_i commits to two random strings in the first round $c_i^0 := \mathsf{com}(r_i^0; \rho_i^0)$ and $c_i^1 := \mathsf{com}(r_i^1; \rho_i^1)$ and sends, in the second round, r_{1-i}^i to P_{1-i}.[9] Then P_i uses the randomness $R_i := r_0^i \oplus r_1^i$ to generate a master secret key msk_i, and uses it to compute the secret key sk_i^f which it sends in the fourth round.

In parallel, P_0 and P_1 execute the MPC protocol Π that evaluates the function g'. The function g' takes the inputs of each party, where the input corresponding to party P_i (for each $i \in \{0,1\}$) is of the form $\left(x_i, (r_i^0; \rho_i^0, r_i^1; \rho_i^1, r_{1-i}^i, r_i,), (c_1^0, c_1^1, c_2^0, c_2^1)\right)$. In more detail, the input of each party P_i corresponds to its actual input x_i, all the commitments generated (by P_0 and P_1) in the first round, the message r_{1-i}^i received in the second round from P_{1-i} and the randomness used to generate the commitments c_i^0, c_i^1. The function g' checks that 1) the commitments $(c_1^0, c_1^1, c_2^0, c_2^1)$ (that are part of the inputs of the two parties) are the same, 2) the value r_i^{1-i} sent in the second round by the party P_i is committed in c_i^{1-i} for each $i \in \{0,1\}$ and 3) the randomness used to generate the commitments is correct. If all these checks are successful then g' outputs a ciphertext $\mathsf{ct} = \mathsf{Enc}((\mathsf{msk}_i)_{i \in \{0,1\}}, (x_0, x_1); r_0 \oplus r_1)$ for the FE combiner computed using the randomness $r_0 \oplus r_1$. We highlight that the check that the commitments generated outside of the MPC protocol are generated correctly is not possible in the standard security definition of MPC. To

---

[9] Note that only the committed message is sent, not the randomness ρ_i^{1-i}.

perform these checks we require the underlying MPC to achieve our new notion of k-delayed-input function, which we explain in the end of this section.

Upon receiving the output of g' (evaluated by Π), P_i computes the output running the decryption algorithm of the FE combiner. Using this approach we guarantee that: 1) the ciphertext ct is honestly computed using honestly generated master secret keys and randomnesses, 2) each party can compute its own master secret key already in the third round so that a functional key can be generated and output in the last round and 3) the value r_{1-i}^i that P_i receives in the second round corresponds to the value used in the commitment c_{1-i}^i (hence, the master secret key that P_i obtains as part of the output of Π is consistent with the master secret key it has created *outside* of Π).

Unfortunately, we can only prove that the above protocol preserves the privacy of the inputs of the honest parties, but the output computed by the honest parties might still be incorrect. This is due to the fact that a corrupted party can generate an ill formed secret key sk_i^f and send it to the honest parties. We finally note that it might look like our approach yields to malleability attacks (i.e., the adversary might bias its commitments using honest-parties commitments). Intuitively, such attacks are prevented since we require the adversary to provide the correct opening as part of the input to the MPC protocol. Hence, we delegate to the MPC the prevention of any such malleability attacks.

From PKO to Full Security. The next step is to elevate PKO security to full security. To achieve this, we utilize the PKO-secure to fully-secure compiler of Ishai et al. [26] to turn the above described protocol into a protocol that achieves standard security in a black-box way.

Besides achieving privacy with knowledge of outputs, our protocol also only realizes single-output functionalities instead of multi-output functionalities. In this case, we can also rely on existing compilers to make our protocol supporting multi-output functionalities [3,31].

We note that we can apply those compilers only if they are 1) round-preserving and 2) do not increase the communication complexity by more than a factor of $\mathrm{poly}(\lambda)$. For the sake of completeness we formally argue that this is indeed the case and refer the interested reader to the full version [14].

From to Circuit-Independent MPC. To obtain a circuit-independent MPC protocol, we combine a multi-key fully-homomorphic encryption scheme (MFHE) with a (non-necessarily communication-efficient) MPC protocol Π.

Let us first briefly recall MFHE: A MFHE scheme consists of four algorithms: (1) a setup algorithm Setup that allows for the generation of public-secret key pairs; (2) an encryption algorithm Enc that takes as input a public key and a message and outputs a ciphertext; (3) an evaluation algorithm Eval that takes as input a list of public keys PK, a set of ciphertexts CT (generated using the list of public keys PK) and a function f, and outputs a ciphertexts ct that contains the evaluation of f on input the messages encrypted in the list CT; (4) a decryption algorithm Dec that on input all the secret keys, associated

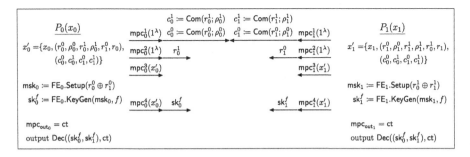

Fig. 1. FE_i, with $i \in \{0,1\}$, denotes a functional encryption candidate. The master secret key for the combiner corresponds to the master secret keys of FE_0 and FE_1. A secret key for the combiner required to evaluate the function f is generated by combining a secret key for FE_0 (sk_0^f) and a secret key for FE_1 (sk_1^f). Dec denotes the decryption algorithm of the combiner which takes as input a combined secret key for the function f and a ciphertext ct generated accordingly to a combined master secret key represented by $(\mathsf{msk}_0, \mathsf{msk}_1)$. mpc_i^k, with $i \in \{0,1\}$ and $k \in [4]$, represents the k-th message of the MPC protocol Π computed by P_i. The protocol Π evaluates a function $g'(x_0', x_1')$ where $x_i' = \{x_i, (r_i^0, \rho_i^0, r_i^1, \rho_i^1, r_{1-i}^i, r_i), (c_0^0, c_0^1, c_1^0, c_1^1)\}$ with $i \in \{0,1\}$. The function g checks if the commitments that are part of the two inputs x_0', x_1' are the same and if c_i^b has been computed accordingly to the message r_i^b and the randomness ρ_i^b for each $i, b \in \{0,1\}$. If the check is successful, then g computes two master secret keys msk_0 and msk_1 using respectively the randomnesses $r_0^1 \oplus r_1^1$ and $r_0^0 \oplus r_1^0$, and computes an encryption ct of $x_0 || x_1$ for the FE combiner using those master secret keys and the randomness $r_0 \oplus r_1$. The output of Π for P_i consists of $\mathsf{mpc}_{\mathsf{out}_i} = \mathsf{ct}$.

with the public keys of PK, and the ciphertext ct outputs the decryption of ct. Additionally, we require the MFHE scheme to be *compact*, i.e. we require the size of the keys, the ciphertexts and the description of the algorithms Enc and Dec to dependent only on the input-output size of f.

Once again, to keep the description simple and to focus on the core ideas, we stick to the two-party case and refer to Sect. 6 for the description of the protocol that supports arbitrary many parties. We provide a pictorial description of our protocol in Fig. 2.

At a high level, our compiler works as follows. Let x_i be the secret input of the party P_i with $i \in \{0,1\}$. Each party P_i runs the setup algorithm using the randomness r_i thus obtaining a private-secret key pair $(\mathsf{pk}_i, \mathsf{sk}_i)$ and encrypts its input using Enc with some randomness r_i', obtaining ct_i. Then P_i sends the public key together with its encrypted input and the first message of the MPC protocol Π to party P_{1-i}. Upon receiving pk_{1-i} and ct_{1-i} from P_{i-1}, P_i runs the evaluation algorithm on input $\mathsf{pk}_0, \mathsf{pk}_1, f, \mathsf{ct}_0, \mathsf{ct}_1$, obtaining ct_i'. At this point P_i keeps executing the protocol Π on input x_i which consists of the randomness used to generate the MFHE keys, the randomness used to generate ct_i, the list of all the ciphertexts (received and generated) $\mathsf{CT} = (\mathsf{ct}_0, \mathsf{ct}_1)$ and the evaluated ciphertext ct_i'. The function g computed by the MPC protocol Π does the following: 1) checks that both P_0 and P_1 have input the same list of ciphertexts CT,

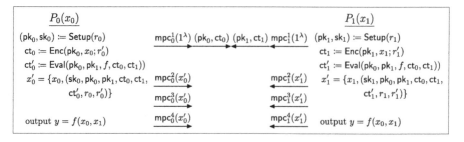

Fig. 2. (Setup, Enc, Dec, Eval) represents a MFHE scheme. The MPC protocol checks that the cipthertexes ct_0 and ct_1 are in the domain of Enc and that both parties have input the same list of cipthertexes ct_0, ct_1. Then the MPC protocol decrypts ct_0' and ct_1' and if the decrypted values corresponds to the same value y then the protocol outputs y.

2) for each $i \in \{0, 1\}$ it uses the randomness r_i and r_i' to check that pk_i and ct_i are in the domain of the setup and of the encryption algorithm. If these checks are successful, then the function g decrypts ct_0' and ct_1' using the secret keys (sk_0, sk_1) (which can be generated using the randomnesses r_0, r_1) thus obtaining y_0 and y_1. If $y_0 = y_1$ then g outputs y, otherwise it outputs $\perp$.

In a nutshell, we use Π to check that all ciphertexts and public keys have been generated correctly and that all the parties have obtained an encryption of the same value when running the MFHE evaluation algorithm. As in the circuit-scalable compiler described before, the check that the public keys and ciphertexts outside of the MPC protocol are generated correctly is not possible in the standard security definition of MPC. To perform these checks we require the underlying MPC protocol to achieve our new notion of k-delayed-input function. The protocol that we have just described is circuit-independent since the size of the public keys and the ciphertexts depends only on the input-output size of f and the protocol Π evaluates a function g whose description size depends only on the input-output size of f and the description of the circuits for Enc and Dec.

The communication complexity of this protocol is $poly(\lambda, n, L_{in}, L_{out})$, where L_{in} is the input-size and L_{out} is the output size of the function being evaluated. We can slightly modify the protocol above to achieve a communication complexity of $O(L_{in}) + poly(\lambda, n, L_{out})$. To do that, we rely on a folklore technique to reduce the size of the ciphertexts of the MFHE scheme using pseudorandom generators (PRGs). In more detail, instead of providing an encryption of the input x_i under the MFHE scheme, each party P_i encrypts a short seed s_i of a PRG PRG using the FHE scheme, i.e. $Enc(pk_i, s_i; r_i^s)$, and sends this encryption along with the value $w_i = PRG(s_i) \oplus x_i$ to the other party. The size of the resulting message is then $O(L_{in}) + poly(\lambda)$. The party P_i, upon receiving $(Enc(pk_{1-i}, s_{1-i}; r_{1-i}^s), w_{1-i})$ computes $Enc(pk_{1-i}, PRG(s_{1-i}))$, using homomorphic operations, $Enc(pk_{1-i}, w_{1-i})$ by encrypting w_{1-i} using pk_{1-i}, and then homomorphically XORs the resulting ciphertexts to receive $Enc(pk_{1-i}, x_{1-i})$. This ciphertext can now be used to run the evaluation algorithm and compute

$\mathsf{Enc}(\mathsf{pk}_0, \mathsf{pk}_1, f(x_0, x_1))$. The parties now check that the ciphertexts (w_0, w_1) are well formed by running the MPC protocol, exactly as in the previous protocol.

k-Delayed-Input Function MPC. As already mentioned in the description of the compilers, we need to rely on an MPC protocol Π that needs the input of the parties only to compute the last two rounds (three in the case of the construction of Fig. 2). Indeed, for the protocol of Fig. 1 for example, the input of each party consists of its actual input, the randomness used to generate its commitments, and *all* the commitments that it has seen (even those generated by the adversary). We note that many existing MPC protocols (e.g., [4,6,11]) indeed do not require the input to compute the first two rounds. However, the fact that the input of the honest parties might be adversarially influenced (e.g., in our protocol some commitments are generated from the adversary) makes it impossible to rely on the standard security notion achieved by such MPC protocols. This is because the standard security notion of MPC requires the inputs of the honest parties to be specified before the real (ideal) world experiment starts. Therefore, the honest parties cannot choose an input that depends on (for example) the first two messages of the protocol, and is, therefore, adversarially influenced.

However, we observe that even if P_i needs to provide all the commitments it has received as part of its input to Π, we do not care about protecting the privacy of this part of P_i's input, we just want to achieve a correct evaluation of Π. That is, these commitments could be thought of as being hardwired in the function evaluated by the MPC protocol Π.

To capture this aspect, we consider a more general notion called k-delayed-input function, where the input of each party consists of two parts, a private input x and a function f. The private part x is known at the beginning of the protocol, whereas the function f does not need to be known before the protocol starts and it is needed only to compute the rounds $k, k+1, \ldots$ of the protocol. We want to guarantee that in the real-world experiment the adversary does not learn more than what it could infer from the output of f, even in the case where it chooses the function f. Equipped with an MPC protocol that satisfies such a definition, we can modify our constructions by letting the parties specify the function that needs to be computed. For example, in the case of the protocol of Fig. 1, the function will contain, in its description, the set of commitments sent in the first round and the messages r_1^1, r_1^2 and uses these values to check that the opening of the commitments are valid with respect to (r_0^1, r_1^2) and only in this case returns a ciphertext for the FE protocol.

To construct a k-delayed-input function protocol, we use a standard $2n$-party ℓ-round MPC protocol Π, where the first $k-1$ rounds can be computed without requiring any input, and a one-time MAC. We refer to the technical part of the paper for more details on how this construction works.

3 Preliminaries

We denote the security parameter with $\lambda \in \mathbb{N}$. A randomized algorithm $\mathcal{A}$ is running in *probabilistic polynomial time* (PPT) if there exists a polynomial $p(\cdot)$ such that for every input x the running time of $\mathcal{A}(x)$ is bounded by $p(|x|)$. We use "$=$" to check equality of two different elements (i.e. $a = b$ then...) and "$:=$" as the assigning operator (e.g. to assign to a the value of b we write $a := b$). A randomized assignment is denoted with $a \leftarrow A$, where A is a randomized algorithm and the randomness used by A is not explicit. If the randomness is explicit we write $a := A(x; r)$ where x is the input and r is the randomness. When it is clear from the context, to not overburden the notation, we do not specify the randomness used in the algorithms unless needed for other purposes.

3.1 Functional Encryption

Definition 3.1 (Functional Encryption [8,35,40]). *Let* $\mathcal{C} = \{\mathcal{C}_\lambda\}_{\lambda \in \mathbb{N}}$ *be a collection of circuit families (indexed by* λ*), where every* $C \in \mathcal{C}_\lambda$ *is a polynomial time circuit* $C \colon \mathcal{X}_\lambda \to \mathcal{Y}_\lambda$*. A (secret-key) functional encryption scheme (FE) for the circuit family* $\mathcal{C}_\lambda$ *is a tuple of four algorithms* $\mathsf{FE} = (\mathsf{Setup}, \mathsf{KeyGen}, \mathsf{Enc}, \mathsf{Dec})$*:*

$\mathsf{Setup}(1^\lambda)$*: Takes as input a unary representation of the security parameter* λ *and generates a master secret key* msk*. It also outputs the randomness* r *that has been used to generate the master secret key.*

$\mathsf{KeyGen}(\mathsf{msk}, C)$*: Takes as input the master secret key* msk *and a circuit* $C \in \mathcal{C}_\lambda$*, and outputs a functional key* sk_C*.*

$\mathsf{Enc}(\mathsf{msk}, x)$*: Takes as input the master secret key* msk*, a message* $x \in \mathcal{X}_\lambda$ *to encrypt, and outputs a ciphertext* ct*.*

$\mathsf{Dec}(\mathsf{sk}_C, \mathsf{ct})$*: Is a deterministic algorithm that takes as input a functional key* sk_C *and a ciphertext* ct *and outputs a value* $y \in \mathcal{Y}_\lambda$*.*

A scheme FE *is (approximate) correct, if for all* $\lambda \in \mathbb{N}$*,* $\mathsf{msk} \leftarrow \mathsf{Setup}(1^\lambda)$*,* $C \in \mathcal{C}_\lambda$*,* $x \in \mathcal{X}_\lambda$*, when* $\mathsf{sk}_C \leftarrow \mathsf{KeyGen}(\mathsf{msk}, C)$*, we have* $\Pr[\mathsf{Dec}(\mathsf{sk}_C, \mathsf{Enc}(\mathsf{msk}, x)) = C(x)] \geq 1 - \mathrm{negl}(\lambda)$*.*

In this work, we define the setup algorithm in such a way that it also outputs the randomness r that has been used to generate the master secret key. This has no effects on the security definition of the scheme since the master secret key msk and the randomness r both remain in the control of the challenger.

Definition 3.2 (Single Key Simulation Security of FE [1]). *Let* FE *be a functional encryption scheme,* $\mathcal{C} = \{\mathcal{C}_\lambda\}_{\lambda \in \mathbb{N}}$ *a collection of circuit families indexed by* λ*. We define the experiments* $\mathrm{Real}^{\mathsf{DFEC}}$ *and* $\mathrm{Ideal}^{\mathsf{DFEC}}$ *in Fig. 3. A functional encryption scheme* FE *is single key simulation secure, if for any polynomial-time adversary* $\mathcal{A} = (\mathcal{A}_1, \mathcal{A}_2, \mathcal{A}_3)$*, there exists a PPT simulator* $\mathcal{S}$ *and a negligible function* negl *such that:* $|\Pr[\mathrm{Real}^{\mathsf{FE}}(1^\lambda, \mathcal{A}) = 1] - \Pr[\mathrm{Ideal}^{\mathsf{FE}}(1^\lambda, \mathcal{A}, \mathcal{S}) = 1]| \leq \mathrm{negl}(\lambda)$*.*

$\mathbf{Real}^{\mathsf{FE}}(1^\lambda, \mathcal{A})$	$\mathbf{Ideal}^{\mathsf{FE}}(1^\lambda, \mathcal{A}, \mathcal{S})$
$\mathsf{msk} \leftarrow \mathsf{Setup}(1^\lambda)$	$\mathsf{msk} \leftarrow \mathsf{Setup}(1^\lambda)$
$(C, \mathsf{st}_1) \leftarrow \mathcal{A}_1(1^\lambda)$	$(C, \mathsf{st}_1) \leftarrow \mathcal{A}_1(1^\lambda)$
$\mathsf{sk}_C \leftarrow \mathsf{KeyGen}(\mathsf{msk}, C)$	$\mathsf{sk}_C \leftarrow \mathsf{KeyGen}(\mathsf{msk}, C)$
$(x, \mathsf{st}_2) \leftarrow \mathcal{A}_2(\mathsf{sk}_C, \mathsf{st}_1)$	$(x, \mathsf{st}_2) \leftarrow \mathcal{A}_2(\mathsf{sk}_C, \mathsf{st}_1)$
$\mathsf{ct} \leftarrow \mathsf{Enc}(\mathsf{msk}, x)$	$\mathsf{ct} \leftarrow \mathcal{S}(\mathsf{msk}, C, C(x))$
$\alpha \leftarrow \mathcal{A}_3(\mathsf{ct}, \mathsf{sk}_C, \mathsf{st}_2)$	$\alpha \leftarrow \mathcal{A}_3(\mathsf{ct}, \mathsf{sk}_C, \mathsf{st}_2)$
Output: α	Output: α

Fig. 3. Single Key Simulation Security of FE

The succinctness definition provided in [1] requires some restrictions on the circuit size of the encryption algorithm, as well as on the size of the functional key. In our work, we also require a bounded circuit size for the setup algorithm and we refer to this notion as strong succinctness.

Definition 3.3 (Strong Succinctness). *A functional encryption scheme* FE = (Setup, KeyGen, Enc, Dec) *for a circuit class $\mathcal{C}$ containing circuits C that take inputs of length ℓ_{in} bits, outputs strings of length ℓ_{out} bits and are of depth at most d is succinct if the following holds:*

- *The size of the circuit for* Setup(1^λ) *is upper bounded by* $\mathrm{poly}(\lambda, d, \ell_{\mathsf{in}})$ *for some polynomial* poly.
- *Let* msk $\leftarrow$ Setup(1^λ), *then the size of the circuit for* Enc(msk, $\cdot$) *is upper bounded by* $\mathrm{poly}(\lambda, d, \ell_{\mathsf{in}}, \ell_{\mathsf{out}})$ *for some polynomial* poly.
- *The functional key* $\mathsf{sk}_C \leftarrow$ KeyGen(msk, C) *is of the form* (C, aux) *where* $|\mathsf{aux}| \leq \mathrm{poly}(\lambda, d, \ell_{\mathsf{out}}, n)$ *for some polynomial* poly.

3.2 Decomposable Functional Encryption Combiner

In this section, we recap the notion of a decomposable functional encryption combiner (DFEC) as introduced by Ananth et al. [1]. In this definition, we rely on the definition of a functional encryption scheme, introduced before (Sect. 3.1).

Definition 3.4 (Decomposable Functional Encryption Combiner). *Let* $\mathcal{C} = \{\mathcal{C}_\lambda\}_{\lambda \in \mathbb{N}}$ *be a collection of circuit families (indexed by λ), where every $C \in \mathcal{C}_\lambda$ is a polynomial time circuit $C \colon \mathcal{X}_\lambda \to \mathcal{Y}_\lambda$ and let $\{\mathsf{FE}_i\}_{i \in [n]}$ be the description of n FE candidates. A decomposable functional encryption combiner (DFEC) for the circuit family $\mathcal{C}_\lambda$ is a tuple of five algorithms* DFEC = (Setup, Partition, KeyGen, Enc, Dec):

Setup($1^\lambda, \{\mathsf{FE}_i\}_{i \in [n]}$): *Takes as input a unary representation of the security parameter λ and the description of n FE candidates $\{\mathsf{FE}_i\}_{i \in [n]}$ and generates a master key msk_i for each FE candidate $\mathsf{msk}_i \leftarrow \mathsf{FE.Setup}_i(1^\lambda)$ and outputs* $\mathsf{msk} := \{\mathsf{msk}_i\}_{i \in [n]}$.

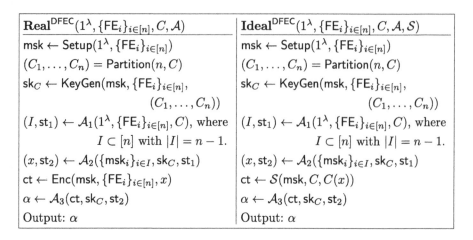

Fig. 4. Single Key Simulation Security of DFEC

Partition(n, C): *Takes as input the number of parties n and a circuit C and outputs $(C_1, \ldots, C_n)$, where each C_i is a circuit of depth polynomial in the depth of C.*

KeyGen(msk, $\{FE_i\}_{i\in[n]}, (C_1, \ldots, C_n)$): *Takes as input the master secret key* msk, *the description of n FE candidates $\{FE_i\}_{i\in[n]}$ and a partitioned circuit $(C_1, \ldots, C_n)$, and generates a functional key* sk_{C_i} *for each FE candidate* $sk_{C_i} \leftarrow$ FE.KeyGen$_i$(msk$_i, C_i$) *and outputs* $sk_C := \{sk_{C_i}\}_{i\in[n]}$.

Enc(msk, $\{FE_i\}_{i\in[n]}, x$): *Takes as input the master secret key* msk, *the description of n FE candidates $\{FE_i\}_{i\in[n]}$, a message $x \in \mathcal{X}_\lambda$ to encrypt, and outputs a ciphertext* ct.

Dec($sk_C, \{FE_i\}_{i\in[n]}, ct$): *Is a deterministic algorithm that takes as input a functional key* sk_C, *the description of n FE candidates $\{FE_i\}_{i\in[n]}$ and a ciphertext* ct *and outputs a value $y \in \mathcal{Y}_\lambda$.*

A scheme DFEC is *(approximate) correct, if for all $\lambda \in \mathbb{N}$,* msk $\leftarrow$ Setup($1^\lambda, \{FE_i\}_{i\in[n]}$), $C \in \mathcal{C}_\lambda$, $x \in \mathcal{X}_\lambda$, *when* $sk_C \leftarrow$ KeyGen(msk, C), *we have*

$$\Pr\left[\mathsf{Dec}(sk_C, \mathsf{Enc}(\mathsf{msk}, x)) = C(x)\right] \geq 1 - \mathsf{negl}(\lambda).$$

To ensure that all the algorithms of the functional encryption combiner are still polynomial in the security parameter λ and the number of parties n, we introduce the notion of polynomial slowdown.

Definition 3.5 (Polynomial Slowdown [1]). *A decomposable functional encryption combiner* DFEC = (Setup, Partition, KeyGen, Enc, Dec) *satisfies polynomial slowdown, if the running time of all its algorithms are at most* poly(λ, n), *where n is the number of FE candidates that are being combined.*

The definition of single key simulation security of a functional encryption combiner should capture the case that if at least one of the FE candidates is secure, then the combiner is also secure. In the case of decomposability we give the adversary even more power by letting it choose a set I of all the corrupted candidates, which contains all but one party.

Definition 3.6 (Single Key Simulation Security of DFEC [1]). *Let* DFEC *be a decomposable functional encryption combiner,* $C = \{C_\lambda\}_{\lambda \in \mathbb{N}}$ *a collection of circuit families indexed by* λ *and* $\{FE_i\}_{i \in [n]}$ n *FE candidates of which at least one is guaranteed to be secure. We define the experiments* $\mathrm{Real}^{\mathrm{DFEC}}$ *and* $\mathrm{Ideal}^{\mathrm{DFEC}}$ *in Fig. 4. A decomposable functional encryption combiner* DFEC *is single key simulation secure, if for any polynomial-time adversary* $\mathcal{A} = (\mathcal{A}_1, \mathcal{A}_2, \mathcal{A}_3)$ *there exists a PPT simulator* $\mathcal{S}$ *and a negligible function* negl *such that:*

$$| \Pr[\mathrm{Real}^{\mathrm{DFEC}}(1^\lambda, \{FE_i\}_{i \in [n]}, C, \mathcal{A}) = 1] - \Pr[\mathrm{Ideal}^{\mathrm{DFEC}}(1^\lambda, \{FE_i\}_{i \in [n]}, C, \mathcal{A}, \mathcal{S}) = 1]| \leq \mathrm{negl}(\lambda) .$$

Definition 3.7 (Strong Succinctness). *A decomposable FE combiner* DFEC = (Setup, Partition, KeyGen, Enc, Dec) *for a circuit class* C *containing circuits* C *that take inputs of length* ℓ_{in} *bits, outputs strings of length* ℓ_{out} *bits and are of depth at most* d *is succinct if for every set of succinct FE candidates* $\{FE_i\}_{i \in [n]}$, *the following holds:*

- *For the circuit of* Setup$(1^\lambda, \{FE_i\}_{i \in [n]})$ *it holds that* Setup$(1^\lambda, \{FE_i\}_{i \in [n]}) \leq$ poly$(\lambda, n, d, \ell_{\mathrm{in}})$.
- *Let* msk $\leftarrow$ Setup$(1^\lambda, \{FE_i\}_{i \in [n]})$. *For the circuit of* Enc$(\mathrm{msk}, \{FE_i\}_{i \in [n]}, \cdot)$ *it holds that* Enc$(\mathrm{msk}, \{FE_i\}_{i \in [n]}, \cdot) \leq$ poly$(\lambda, d, \ell_{\mathrm{in}}, \ell_{\mathrm{out}}, n)$ *for some polynomial* poly.
- *The functional key* $\mathrm{sk}_C \leftarrow$ KeyGen$(\mathrm{msk}, \{FE_i\}_{i \in [n]}, (C_1, \ldots, C_n))$, *with* $(C_1, \ldots, C_n) =$ Partition(n, C), *is of the form* (C, aux) *where* $|\mathrm{aux}| \leq$ poly$(\lambda, d, \ell_{\mathrm{out}}, n)$ *for some polynomial* poly.

3.3 Multi Key Fully Homomorphic Encryption

Definition 3.8 (Multi-Key Fully Homomorphic Encryption [32]). *Let* $C = \{C_\lambda\}_{\lambda \in \mathbb{N}}$ *be a collection of circuit families (indexed by* λ*), where every* $C \in C_\lambda$ *is a polynomial time circuit* $C \colon \mathcal{X}_\lambda \to \mathcal{Y}_\lambda$ *and* n *the number of participating parties. A multi-key fully homomorphic encryption (MFHE) for the circuit family* C_λ *is a tuple of four algorithms* MFHE = (Setup, Enc, Eval, Dec)*:*

Setup(1^λ)*: Takes as input a unary representation of the security parameter* λ *and generates a public key* pk *and a secret key* sk.

Enc(pk, x)*: Takes as input a public key* pk *and a message* $x \in \mathcal{X}_\lambda$ *to encrypt, and outputs a ciphertext* ct.

Eval$(C, (\mathrm{pk}_i, \mathrm{ct}_i)_{i \in [\ell]})$*: Takes as input a circuit* C, ℓ *different public keys* pk_i *and ciphertexts* ct_i *and outputs a ciphertext* ct.

Dec$(\{\mathrm{sk}_i\}_{i \in [n]}, \mathrm{ct})$*: Is a deterministic algorithm that takes as input* n *secret keys* $\{\mathrm{sk}_i\}_{i \in [n]}$ *and a ciphertext* ct *and outputs a value* y.

A *scheme* MFHE *is perfectly correct, if for all* $\lambda \in \mathbb{N}$, $i \in [n]$, $\ell \leq n$, $r_i^{\mathsf{Setup}} \leftarrow \{0,1\}^\lambda$, $r_i^{\mathsf{Enc}} \leftarrow \{0,1\}^\lambda$, $(\mathsf{pk}_i, \mathsf{sk}_i) \leftarrow \mathsf{Setup}(1^\lambda; r_i^{\mathsf{Setup}})$, $C \in \mathcal{C}_\lambda$, $x_i \in \mathcal{X}_\lambda$, *we have*

$$\Pr\left[\mathsf{Dec}(\{\mathsf{sk}_i\}_{i \in [n]}, \mathsf{Eval}(C, (\mathsf{pk}_i, \mathsf{Enc}(\mathsf{pk}_i, x_i; r_i^{\mathsf{Enc}}))_{i \in [\ell]})) = C(x_1, \ldots, x_\ell)\right] = 1.$$

For $n = 1$ multi-key FHE is equivalent to FHE. In the introductory paper of López-Alt, Tromer, and Vaikuntanathan [32], the setup algorithm also outputs an evaluation key together with the public and secret key. In our work we assume that the information of the evaluation key is contained in the public key.

Definition 3.9 (IND-CPA security of MFHE). *A multi-key fully homomorphic encryption scheme* MFHE = (Setup, Enc, Eval, Dec) *is secure, if for any PPT adversary* $\mathcal{A}$, *it holds that*

$$\left| \Pr\left[\mathcal{A}(\mathsf{pk}, \mathsf{Enc}(\mathsf{pk}, x_0)) = 1 \,\middle|\, \begin{matrix} (\mathsf{pk}, \mathsf{sk}) \leftarrow \mathsf{Setup}(1^\lambda) \\ (x_0, x_1) \leftarrow \mathcal{A}(\mathsf{pk}) \end{matrix}\right] \right.$$
$$\left. - \Pr\left[\mathcal{A}(\mathsf{pk}, \mathsf{Enc}(\mathsf{pk}, x_1)) = 1 \,\middle|\, \begin{matrix} (\mathsf{pk}, \mathsf{sk}) \leftarrow \mathsf{Setup}(1^\lambda) \\ (x_0, x_1) \leftarrow \mathcal{A}(\mathsf{pk}) \end{matrix}\right] \right| \leq \mathrm{negl}(\lambda).$$

Besides the security of a multi-key FHE scheme, we also need to define what it means for a multi-key FHE scheme to be compact.

Definition 3.10 (Compactness). *A multi-key FHE scheme* MFHE = (Setup, Enc, Eval, Enc, Dec) *for a circuit class* $\mathcal{C}$ *and* n *participating parties is called compact, if* $|\mathsf{ct}| \leq \mathrm{poly}(\lambda, n)$, *where* $\mathsf{ct} := \mathsf{Eval}(C, (\mathsf{pk}_i, \mathsf{ct}_i)_{i \in [\ell]})$ *with* $\ell \leq n$ *and with the description of the circuits* Setup, Enc *and* Dec *being polynomial in the security parameter* λ.

We note that this definition implies that public- and secret-key pairs are also independent from the size of the circuit. We assume familiarity with the notion of negligible functions, symmetric encryption, digital signatures and commitments and refer to the full version [14] for the formal definitions.

3.4 Secure Multiparty Computation

The security of a protocol (with respect to a functionality f) is defined by comparing the real-world execution of the protocol with an ideal-world evaluation of f by a trusted party. More concretely, it is required that for every adversary $\mathcal{A}$, which attacks the real execution of the protocol, there exist an adversary $\mathcal{S}$, also referred to as a simulator, which can *achieve the same effect* in the ideal-world. In this work, we denote an ℓ-round MPC protocol as $\pi = (\pi.\mathsf{Next}_1, \ldots, \pi.\mathsf{Next}_\ell, \pi.\mathsf{Out})$, where $\pi.\mathsf{Next}_j$, with $j \in [\ell]$ denotes the *next-message function* that takes as input all the messages generated by π in the rounds $1, \ldots, j-1$ (that we denote with τ_{j-1}) the randomness and the input of the party P_i and outputs the message $\mathsf{msg}_{j,i}$. Additionally, we assume that all the parties run the same next message function algorithms (the only difference is the randomness and the input provided by each party). π.Out denotes the algorithm used to compute the final output of the protocol. We assume that readers arc familiar with standard simulation-based definitions of secure multiparty computation in the standalone setting. For self-containment we provide the definition in the full version [14] and refer to [22] for a more detailed treatment.

In this work we also consider a relaxed notion of security known as *privacy with knowledge of outputs* [26,36]. In this the input of the honest parties is protected in the standard simulation based sense, but the output of these parties might be incorrect. To formalize this notion we need to slightly modify the ideal execution as follows.

1. **Send inputs to the trusted party:** The parties send their inputs to the trusted party, and we let x_i' denote the value sent by P_i.
2. **Ideal functionality sends output to the adversary:** The ideal functionality computes $(y_1, \ldots, y_n) := f(x_1, \ldots, x_n)$ and sends $\{y_i\}_{i \in I}$ to the adversary $\mathcal{A}$.
3. **Output of the honest parties:** The adversary $\mathcal{S}$ sends either a continue or abort message or arbitrary values $\{y_i'\}_{i \in [n] \setminus I}$ to the ideal functionality. In the case of a continue message the ideal functionality sends y_i to the party P_i, in the case of an abort message every uncorrupted party receives $\perp$ and in the case that the ideal functionality receives arbitrary values $\{y_i'\}_{i \in [n] \setminus I}$ it forwards them to the honest parties.
4. **Outputs:** $\mathcal{S}$ outputs an arbitrary function of its view, and the honest parties output the values obtained from the trusted party.

The interaction of $\mathcal{S}$ with the trusted party defines a random variable $\mathrm{Ideal}_{f,\mathcal{S}(z)}^{\mathsf{PKO}}(k, \boldsymbol{x})$ as above.

Having defined the real and the ideal world, we now proceed to define our notion of security.

Definition 3.11 *Let λ be the security parameter. Let f be an n-party randomized functionality, and π be an n-party protocol for $n \in \mathbb{N}$.*

We say that π securely realizes f with knowledge of outputs in the presence of malicious adversaries if for every PPT adversary $\mathcal{A}$ there exists a PPT adversary $\mathcal{S}$ such that for any $I \subset [n]$ the following ensembles are computational indistinguishable:

$$\{\mathrm{Real}_{\pi,\mathcal{A}(z),I}(k, \boldsymbol{x})\}_{k \in \mathbb{N}, \langle \boldsymbol{x}, z \rangle \in \{0,1\}^*}, \{\mathrm{Ideal}_{f,\mathcal{S}(z),I}^{\mathsf{PKO}}(k, \boldsymbol{x})\}_{k \in \mathbb{N}, \langle \boldsymbol{x}, z \rangle \in \{0,1\}^*}.$$

4 k-Delayed-Input Function MPC

In this section, we introduce the new notion of *k-Delayed-Input Function*. The classical simulation-based definition of secure MPC requires that the function to be computed is known at the beginning of the real (and ideal) world experiment, before the protocol starts. In our construction we are not in this setting, as we need an MPC protocol in which the parties can influence the function to be computed by giving an extra input mid-protocol. Concretely, in our protocols, the function computed by the MPC protocol becomes fully defined in the third round (i.e., for the circuit-scalable construction the function incorporates the commitments and the random values sent in the second round).

To capture this, we devise a variant of secure MPC where each party P_i has two inputs x_i and f, where 1) the input x_i is known at the beginning of the real (ideal) world experiment (as in the standard definition of MPC) but 2) the input f can be any function and it becomes known only in the k-th round. In this setting we want to guarantee that if all the honest parties input the same function f, then the adversary either learns the output of f or nothing at all. More formally, we require the input of the honest parties to be protected in the standard simulation based manner for the case where the ideal world evaluates the function f.

A strawman's approach for such a protocol would be to rely on an ℓ-round MPC protocol that does not require the input of the parties to compute the first $k-1$ rounds with $k \leq \ell - 1$. We call such protocols *delayed-input* protocols. More precisely, one could consider a delayed-input MPC protocol Π for the universal function g where g takes a pair of inputs from each party P_i denoted with (x, f) and returns $f(x_1, \ldots, x_n)$.

Unfortunately, it is not guaranteed that this approach works since the standard security definition of MPC does not capture the scenario in which an input f for an honest party is chosen adaptively based on the first $k-1$ rounds of the protocol. Therefore, even if all the honest parties follow the naive approach we have just described and use the function f as their input, the adversary might be able compute the output of a function $\tilde{f} \neq f$. It should be noted that the description of the computed function can be part of the output as well, hence, the honest parties will notice that the wrong function has been computed and will reject the output. However, the adversary might have gained much more information from the evaluation of $\tilde{f}$ than it would have gotten by evaluating f.

Syntax & Correctness. Before defining the real and ideal execution, we need to define the syntax of an ℓ-Round k-Delayed-Input Function MPC protocol and its correctness. An ℓ-Round k-Delayed-Input Function MPC protocol is defined as $\Pi = (\mathsf{Next}_1, \ldots, \mathsf{Next}_\ell, \mathsf{Out})$. The next message function Next_1 takes as an input the security parameter in unary form, the input of the party, its randomness and a parameter m that represents the size of the function that will be computed, and returns the first message of the protocol. The next-message function Next_j, with $j \in [k-1]$ takes as input all the messages generated by Π in the rounds $1, \ldots, j-1$ (that we denote with τ_{j-1}) the input and the randomness of P_i and outputs the message $\mathsf{msg}_{j,i}$. The next message function Next_j with $j \in \{k, \ldots, \ell\}$ takes the input of the party P_i, a function f (together with τ_{k-1}) and the randomness of P_i, and returns the message $\mathsf{msg}_{j,i}$. To compute the final output, each party P_i runs Out on input τ_ℓ, its input and randomness. We now define the correctness and the security property that a k-delayed-input function protocol must satisfy.

Definition 4.1 (Perfect Correctness for ℓ-Round k-Delayed-Input Function MPC Protocols). *For any $\lambda, m \in \mathbb{N}$, for any inputs $(x_1, \ldots, x_n) \in (\{0,1\}^\lambda)^n$ and for any set of functions $\{f_\gamma\}_{\gamma \in [n]}$ with $|f_\gamma| = m$ for all $\gamma \in [n]$, it must hold for all $i \in [n]$ that*

- *if $f_1 = \cdots = f_n$ then $\Pr\left[(\mathsf{Out}(\tau_\ell, x_i, r_i) \neq f(x_1, \ldots, x_n)\right] = 0$,*
- *if there exists $\alpha, \beta \in [n]$ s.t. $f_\alpha \neq f_\beta$ then $\Pr\left[(\mathsf{Out}(\tau_\ell, x_i, r_i) \neq \bot\right] = 0$,*

where $\mathsf{msg}_{1,i} \leftarrow \mathsf{Next}_1(1^\lambda, x_i, m; r_i)$, $\mathsf{msg}_{c,i} \leftarrow \mathsf{Next}_c(\tau_{c-1}, x_i; r_i)$ and $\mathsf{msg}_{j,i} \leftarrow \mathsf{Next}_j(\tau_{j-1}, x_i, f_i; r_i)$ where $r_i \leftarrow \{0,1\}^\lambda$, $c \in \{1, \ldots, k-1\}$ and $j \in [k, \ldots, \ell]$.

We now proceed to defining the security of k-delayed-input function protocols, by describing how the real and the ideal world look like.

The Real Execution. Let us denote $\boldsymbol{x} = (x_1, \ldots, x_n)$ where x_i denotes the input of the party P_i. In the real execution the n-party protocol Π is executed in the presence of an adversary $\mathcal{A}$. The honest parties follow the instructions of Π. The adversary $\mathcal{A}$ takes as input the security parameter λ, the size of the function m, the set $I \subset [n]$ of corrupted parties, the inputs of the corrupted parties, and an auxiliary input z. $\mathcal{A}$ sends all messages in place of corrupted parties and may follow an arbitrary polynomial-time strategy. At round $k - 1$, $\mathcal{A}$ picks a function f and sends it to the honest parties. Then each honest party P_i uses f to compute the rounds $k, k+1, \ldots, \ell$ of Π. The adversary $\mathcal{A}$ continues its interaction with the honest parties following an arbitrary polynomial-time strategy. The interaction of $\mathcal{A}$ with a protocol Π defines a random variable $\mathsf{Real}^{\mathsf{DIF\text{-}MPC}}_{\Pi, \mathcal{A}(z), I}(k, \boldsymbol{x})$ whose value is determined by the coin tosses of the adversary and the honest players. This random variable contains the output of the adversary (which may be an arbitrary function of its view), the outputs of the uncorrupted parties as well as the function f chosen by the adversary. We let $\mathsf{Real}^{\mathsf{DIF\text{-}MPC}}_{\Pi, \mathcal{A}(z), I}$ denote the distribution ensemble $\{\mathsf{Real}^{\mathsf{DIF\text{-}MPC}}_{\Pi, \mathcal{A}(z), I}(k, \boldsymbol{x})\}_{k \in \mathbb{N}, \langle \boldsymbol{x}, z \rangle \in \{0,1\}^*}$.

The Ideal Execution

- **Send inputs to the trusted party:** Each honest party P_i sends x_i to the ideal functionality. The simulator sends $\{x_j\}_{j \in I}$ and f to the ideal functionality.
- **Ideal functionality sends output to the adversary:** The ideal functionality computes $(y_1, \ldots, y_n) := f(x_1, \ldots, x_n)$ and sends $\{y_i\}_{i \in I}$ to the simulator $\mathcal{S}$ and f to P_i for each $i \in [n] \setminus I$.
- **Output of the honest parties:** The simulator $\mathcal{S}$ sends either a continue or abort message to the ideal functionality. In the case of a continue message the ideal functionality sends y_i to the party P_i, in the case of an abort message every uncorrupted party receives $\bot$.
- **Outputs:** $\mathcal{S}$ outputs an arbitrary function of its view, and the honest parties output the values obtained from the trusted party.

The interaction of $\mathcal{S}$ with the trusted party defines a random variable $\text{Ideal}_{\mathcal{S}(z),I}^{\text{DIF-MPC}}(k, \boldsymbol{x})$ as above. Having defined the real and the ideal world, we now proceed to define our notion of security.

Definition 4.2 (k-Delayed-Input Function MPC). *Let λ be the security parameter. We say that a protocol Π satisfying Definition 4.1 is k-delayed-input function in the presence of malicious adversaries if for every PPT adversary $\mathcal{A}$ attacking in the real world (as defined above) there exists an expected PPT ideal-world adversary $\mathcal{S}$ restricted to query the ideal functionality with the same function f that will appear in the real world experiment output such that for any $I \subset [n]$ the following ensembles are computational indistinguishable*

$$\{\text{Real}_{\Pi,\mathcal{A}(z),I}^{\text{DIF-MPC}}(k, \boldsymbol{x})\}_{k\in\mathbb{N},\langle\boldsymbol{x},z\rangle\in\{0,1\}^*}, \{\text{Ideal}_{\mathcal{S}(z),I}^{\text{DIF-MPC}}(k, \boldsymbol{x})\}_{k\in\mathbb{N},\langle\boldsymbol{x},z\rangle\in\{0,1\}^*}.$$

Remark 4.3. We note that Definition 4.2 is very similar to the standard notion of MPC. Indeed, our ideal world can be thought of as the ideal world of the standard definition of MPC for the case where the parties want to evaluate the universal function. We also note that in the ideal world there is no notion of rounds, hence it is not immediately clear how to translate what happens in the real world (where the function f is adaptively chosen in the k-th round by the adversary) into the ideal world (where the ideal world adversary has all the information it needs from the beginning of the experiment). The way we break this asymmetry between the ideal and the real world is exactly by restricting the power of the simulator (i.e., the power of the ideal-world adversary) depending on an event that happens in the real world. In our specific case, we require the admissible simulators (i.e., the admissible ideal world adversaries) to be those that query the ideal world functionality using the same function that will appear in the output of the real world experiment. We note that without this requirement this definition becomes useless since the simulator might query the ideal functionality using a function $\tilde{f}$ that is different from the function f used in the real world, which would allow the simulator to learn more about the honest parties' inputs then it would have by querying the ideal functionality with the function f.

Input: $((x_i, k_i), (f_i, \tau_i))_{i\in[n]}$.
    If $\mathsf{Verify}(k_i, f_i, \tau_i) = 0$ or $f_i \neq f_j$ for any $i, j \in [n]$, then output $\bot$.
    Compute $y_1, \ldots, y_n := f'(x_1, \ldots, x_n)$ with $f' = f_i$ for any $i \in [n]$ and set $y_i := y_i^0 := y_i^1$ for all $i \in [n]$.
Output: (y_i^0, y_i^1) to the party P_i for each $i \in [n]$.

Fig. 5. Description of the function g.

From MPC Protocols to k-Delayed-Input Function MPC Protocols. To construct an n party ℓ-round k-Delayed-Input Function MPC protocol

Π^{DIF}, we rely on a $2n$ party ℓ-round MPC protocol Π that does not require the input to compute the first $k - 1$ rounds and a one-time MAC scheme $\mathsf{MAC} = (\mathsf{Setup}, \mathsf{Auth}, \mathsf{Verify})$. In our protocol Π^{DIF}, each party P_i controls two parties of Π. One party uses the private input and a MAC key (which is known from the beginning) as its input and the other party uses the function f (received at the end of round $k - 1$) authenticated with the MAC key as its input. The MPC protocol Π then checks that the functions are authenticated accordingly to the MAC key and that they are all equal. If this check is successful, Π evaluates the function f over the secret inputs of the parties. Finally, the individual outputs of the function evaluation are returned to one of the two parties of Π controlled by the party P_i. To show that the described protocol Π^{DIF} is indeed k-delayed-input function, we rely on the security of the MPC protocol Π and the unforgeability of the MAC. The security of the MPC protocol Π ensures that the private inputs of the parties are protected and the unforgeability of the MAC is used to enforce that the correct function is used in the protocol execution. Intuitively, if, by contradiction, there exists an adversary that manages to evaluate the function $\tilde{f}$ instead of f then we would be able to construct a reduction to the security of the MAC since the only condition in which Π does not output $\bot$ is the one in which all the parties input the same authenticated function f. If there exists an adversarial strategy that makes Π parse f as $\tilde{f}$, then it must be that $\tilde{f}$ has been authenticated using the MAC key of an honest party. We can extract such a forgery using the simulator of Π (that extracts the input from the parties declared as corrupted).

Now, we describe the construction more formally. Let Π be a $2n$-party MPC protocol that realizes the $2n$-input function g described in Fig. 5 with the property that it needs the input of the parties only to compute the rounds $k, k+1, \ldots, \ell$ with $0 \le k \le \ell - 1$ where $\ell \in \mathbb{N}$ represents the round complexity of Π. In our k-Delayed-Input Function MPC protocol Π^{DIF}, each party P_i emulates two parties P_i^0 and P_i^1 of Π. Let x_i be the private input of P_i, then P_i performs the following steps.

1. Run Setup to sample a MAC key k_i.
2. Run the party P_i^0 using the input (x_i, k_i) and P_i^1 until the round $k - 1$.[10]
3. Upon receiving the function f_i compute $\tau_i \leftarrow \mathsf{Auth}(\mathsf{k}_i, f_i)$ and run P_i^1 using the input (f_i, τ_i).
4. When the protocol Π is finished, P_i outputs the output obtained by P_i^0.

Theorem 4.4. *Let Π be a $2n$-party ℓ-round MPC protocol that securely realizes the function f of Fig. 5 and that requires the input only to compute the rounds $k, k+1, \ldots, \ell$ with $0 \le k \le \ell - 1$ and let $\mathsf{MAC} = (\mathsf{Setup}, \mathsf{Auth}, \mathsf{Verify})$ be a one-time secure MAC scheme, then the protocol Π^{DIF} described above is an n-party ℓ-round k-Delayed-Input Function MPC protocol.*

The proof for this theorem can be found in the full version [14].

---

[10] We recall that P_0^i and P_1^i do not need to use the input to compute the first $k - 1$ rounds, nonetheless we can specify the input of P_i^1 at the very beginning of the protocol.

5   Our Compiler: Circuit-Scalable MPC

In this section we prove our main theorems on how to construct a circuit-scalable MPC protocol that realizes any functionality f with privacy with knowledge of outputs. We refer to Sect. 2 for a simplified description of the protocol for the two-party case and to Fig. 6 for the formal description of our compiler. Our construction makes use of the following cryptographic tools:

- An ℓ-round k-delayed-input function MPC protocol $\Pi^M = (\Pi^M.\mathsf{Next}_1, \ldots, \Pi^M.\mathsf{Next}_\ell, \Pi^M.\mathsf{Out})$ (not necessarily communication efficient) with $k \geq 3$. In the description of our compiler we assume, without loss of generality, that Π^M is 3-delayed-input function.[11]
- A strong succinct single-key simulation secure decomposable FE combiner DFEC = (DFEC.Setup, DFEC.Enc, DFEC.KeyGen, DFEC.Dec, DFEC.Partition) for n FE candidates.
- A non-interactive computationally hiding commitment scheme Com.

Theorem 5.1. *Let* DFEC *be a single-key simulation secure decomposable FE combiner with circuit size cs_Setup for the setup algorithm* DFEC.Setup, *circuit size cs_ct for the encryption algorithm* DFEC.Enc *and functional key size s_sk, let* Com *be a commitment scheme and let Π^M be the ℓ-round MPC protocol k-delayed-input function protocol described in Sect. 4 that realizes $C^\mathsf{ct}_{,\mathsf{Setup},i,R^i_\mathsf{Setup}}$ (Fig. 7), then Π^FE is an ℓ-round MPC protocol that realizes the single-output functionality C with knowledge of outputs which has communication complexity* $\mathrm{poly}(\lambda, n, cs_\mathsf{Setup}, cs_\mathsf{Enc}, s_\mathsf{sk})$.

We refer to the full version [14] for the formal proof of the theorem.

The following theorem follows immediately from Theorem 5.1 and the definition of strong succinct FE combiners.

Theorem 5.2. *Let* DFEC *be a succinct single-key simulation secure decomposable FE combiner, then Π^FE is a circuit-scalable secure MPC protocol that realizes any single-output functionality with knowledge of outputs.*

In the full version [14], we give more details on how our compiler can be instantiated, which leads to the following theorem.

Theorem 5.3. *If the LWE assumption holds, then there exists a round optimal (4-round) circuit-scalable MPC protocol that realizes any single-output functionality with knowledge of outputs.*

By relying on the compilers proposed in [3,26,31] we can turn our protocol into one that computes any function under the standard simulation based definition of MPC.

---

[11] Any k'-delayed-input function MPC with $k' > 3$ can be turned into a 3-delayed-input function MPC protocol since the function received in round 2 can be ignored up to round $k' - 1$.

$$\Pi^{\mathsf{FE}}$$

Each $i \in [n]$ party P_i has input $x_i \in \{0,1\}^*$ as its secret input.

Round 1.
1. Sample $r_{\mathsf{Setup}}^{i \leftarrow i}, r_{\mathsf{com}}^{i \to k}, r_i^{\mathsf{Enc}} \leftarrow \{0,1\}^\lambda$ for all $k \in [n]$ and set $R_{\mathsf{com}}^i := (r_{\mathsf{com}}^{i \to k})_{k \in [n]}$.
2. Set $x_i' := (x_i, r_{\mathsf{Setup}}^{i \leftarrow i}, R_{\mathsf{com}}^i, r_i^{\mathsf{Enc}})$ and compute $\mathsf{msg}_{1,i} \leftarrow \Pi^{\mathsf{M}}.\mathsf{Next}_1(1^\lambda, x_i')$.
3. Sample $r_{\mathsf{Setup}}^{i \to k} \leftarrow \{0,1\}^\lambda$ for all $k \in [n] \setminus \{i\}$, compute $\mathsf{com}_{\mathsf{Setup}}^{i \to k} := \mathsf{Com}(r_{\mathsf{Setup}}^{i \to k}; r_{\mathsf{com}}^{i \to k})$ and set $\mathsf{com}_{\mathsf{Setup}}^i := \{\mathsf{com}_{\mathsf{Setup}}^{i \to k}\}_{k \in [n]}$.
4. Send $(\mathsf{msg}_{1,i}, \mathsf{com}_{\mathsf{Setup}}^i)$.

Round 2.
1. Let τ_1 denote the transcript of the protocol Π^{M} up to round 1.
2. Compute $\mathsf{msg}_{2,i} \leftarrow \Pi^{\mathsf{M}}.\mathsf{Next}_2(\tau_1)$.
3. Send $(\mathsf{msg}_{2,i}, (r_{\mathsf{Setup}}^{i \to j})_{j \in [n] \setminus \{i\}})$.

Round 3.
1. Let τ_2 denote the transcript of the protocol Π^{M} up to round 2.
2. Compute $\mathsf{msg}_{3,i} \leftarrow \Pi^{\mathsf{M}}.\mathsf{Next}_3(C_{\mathsf{com}_{\mathsf{Setup},i}, R_{\mathsf{Setup}}^i}^{\mathsf{ct}}, \tau_2)$, with $\mathsf{com}_{\mathsf{Setup},i} := \{\mathsf{com}_{\mathsf{Setup}}^k\}_{k \in [n]}$ and $R_{\mathsf{Setup}}^i := (r_{\mathsf{Setup}}^{j \to k})_{j \in [n], k \in [n] \setminus \{j\}}$.
3. Send $\mathsf{msg}_{3,i}$.

For each round $k \in \{4, \ldots, \ell - 1\}$.
1. Let τ_{k-1} denote the transcript of the protocol Π^{M} up to round $k - 1$.
2. Compute the second round message $\mathsf{msg}_{k,i} \leftarrow \Pi^{\mathsf{M}}.\mathsf{Next}_k(\tau_{k-1})$.
3. Send $\mathsf{msg}_{k,i}$.

Round ℓ.
1. Let $\tau_{\ell-1}$ denote the transcript of the protocol Π^{M} up to round $\ell - 1$.
2. Compute $r_i^{\mathsf{Setup}} = \bigoplus_{k \in [n]} r_{\mathsf{Setup}}^{k \to i}$.
3. Generate $\mathsf{msk}_i \leftarrow \mathsf{FE}_i.\mathsf{Setup}(1^\lambda; r_i^{\mathsf{Setup}})$, compute the partition of C, i.e. $(C_1 \ldots, C_n) \leftarrow \mathsf{DFEC.Partition}(1^\lambda, C)$ and generate $\mathsf{sk}_i \leftarrow \mathsf{FE}_i.\mathsf{KeyGen}(\mathsf{msk}_i, C_i; r_i^{\mathsf{KeyGen}})$ with $r_i^{\mathsf{KeyGen}} \leftarrow \{0,1\}^\lambda$.
4. Compute the fourth round message $\mathsf{msg}_{\ell,i} \leftarrow \Pi^{\mathsf{M}}.\mathsf{Next}_\ell(\tau_{\ell-1})$.
5. Send $(\mathsf{msg}_{\ell,i}, \mathsf{sk}_i)$.

Output Computation.
1. Let τ_ℓ denote the transcript of the protocol Π^{M} up to round ℓ.
2. Compute the output of Π^{M} as $(\mathsf{ct}, (\tilde{r}_{\mathsf{Setup}}^{k \to i})_{i \in [n], k \in [n] \setminus \{i\}}) \leftarrow \Pi^{\mathsf{M}}.\mathsf{Out}(\tau_\ell)$.
3. Output $\mathsf{DFEC.Dec}(\mathsf{sk}_C, \mathsf{ct})$ with $\mathsf{sk}_C = (\mathsf{sk}_1, \ldots, \mathsf{sk}_n)$.

Fig. 6. Description of the protocol Π^{FE} that securely realizes any functionality with knowledge of outputs.

6 Our Compiler: Circuit-Independent MPC

We now show how to construct a communication efficient MPC protocol that realizes any single-output functionality f. We refer to Sect. 2 for a simplified description of the protocol for the two-party case and to Fig. 8 for the formal description of our compiler We make use of the following tools:

Input: $(x_i, r_{\mathsf{Setup}}^{i \to i}, R_{\mathsf{com}}^i, r_i^{\mathsf{Enc}})_{i \in [n]}$

- Parse $\mathsf{com}_{\mathsf{Setup},i}$ as $\{\mathsf{com}_{\mathsf{Setup}}^k\}_{k \in [n]}$ and
  $\mathsf{com}_{\mathsf{Setup}}^i$ as $\{\mathsf{com}_{\mathsf{Setup}}^{i \to k}\}_{k \in [n]}$.
- Parse R_{Setup}^i as $(r_{\mathsf{Setup}}^{j \to k})_{j \in [n], k \in [n] \setminus \{j\}}$.
- Parse R_{com}^i as $(r_{\mathsf{com}}^{i \to k})_{k \in [n]}$ for all $i \in [n]$.
- For all $i, j \in [n]$ check that $\mathsf{com}_{\mathsf{Setup}}^{i \to j} = \mathsf{Com}(r_{\mathsf{Setup}}^{i \to j}; r_{\mathsf{com}}^{i \to j})$.
  If one of the above checks fails then output $\bot$, continue
  as follows otherwise.
  For each $i \in [n]$, compute $r_{\mathsf{Setup}}^i = \bigoplus_{k \in [n]} r_{\mathsf{Setup}}^{k \to i}$ and generate
  $\mathsf{msk}_i \leftarrow \mathsf{FE}_i.\mathsf{Setup}(1^\lambda; r_i^{\mathsf{Setup}})$
  Let $\mathsf{msk} := (\mathsf{msk}_1, \dots, \mathsf{msk}_n)$, $x = (x_1, \dots, x_n)$, $r^{\mathsf{Enc}} := \bigoplus_{i \in [n]} r_i^{\mathsf{Enc}}$.

Output: $\mathsf{ct} := \mathsf{DFEC}.\mathsf{Enc}(\mathsf{msk}, x; r^{\mathsf{Enc}})$ and $\{r_{\mathsf{Setup}}^{k \to j}\}_{j \in [n], k \in [n] \setminus \{j\}}$ to P_i.

Fig. 7. Circuit $C_{\mathsf{com}_{\mathsf{Setup}}, i, R_{\mathsf{Setup}}^i}^{\mathsf{ct}}$.

- An ℓ-round k-delayed-input function MPC protocol $\Pi^{\mathsf{M}} = (\Pi^{\mathsf{M}}.\mathsf{Next}_1, \dots, \Pi^{\mathsf{M}}.\mathsf{Next}_\ell, \Pi^{\mathsf{M}}.\mathsf{Out})$ (not necessarily communication efficient) with $k \geq 2$.
- A multi-key fully homomorphic encryption scheme $\mathsf{MFHE} = (\mathsf{Setup}, \mathsf{Enc}, \mathsf{Eval}, \mathsf{Dec})$ for n keys.

Theorem 6.1. *Let* MFHE *be a multi-key fully homomorphic encryption scheme with circuit size* cs_{Setup} *for the setup algorithm* $\mathsf{MFHE}.\mathsf{Setup}$, *circuit size* cs_{Enc} *for the encryption algorithm* $\mathsf{MFHE}.\mathsf{Enc}$, *circuit size* cs_{Dec} *for the decryption algorithm* $\mathsf{MFHE}.\mathsf{Dec}$ *and ciphertext size* s_{ct}, *let* Π^{M} *be the* ℓ-*round MPC protocol* k-*delayed-input function protocol that realizes the circuit* $C_{\mathsf{ct}^i, K^i}^{\mathsf{Dec}}$ *(Fig. 9), then* Π^{FHE} *is an* ℓ-*round MPC protocol that securely realizes the single-output functionality* C *with communication complexity* $\mathrm{poly}(\lambda, n, cs_{\mathsf{Setup}}, cs_{\mathsf{Enc}}, cs_{\mathsf{Dec}}, s_{\mathsf{ct}})$.

We refer to the full version [14] for the formal proof.

Due to Theorem 6.1 and the definition of a compact multi-key FHE scheme we have the following.

Theorem 6.2. *Let* MFHE *be a compact multi-key FHE scheme, then* Π^{FHE} *is a circuit-independent secure MPC protocol that realizes any single-output functionality.*

We can easily modify Π^{FHE} to obtain a protocol $\Pi^{\mathsf{FHE}'}$ which has a communication complexity of $O(L_{\mathsf{in}}) + \mathrm{poly}(\lambda, n, L_{\mathsf{out}})$. The protocol $\Pi^{\mathsf{FHE}'}$ works exactly as Π^{FHE} with the following differences. Every party P_i encrypts a short seed s_i of a PRG PRG using the FHE scheme, i.e. $\mathsf{Enc}(\mathsf{pk}_i, s_i; r_i^s)$, and sends it together with the value $w_i = \mathsf{PRG}(s_i) \oplus x_i$ to all the other parties P_j with $j \in [n] \setminus \{i\}$. The party P_i, upon receiving $(\mathsf{Enc}(\mathsf{pk}_j, s; r_j^s), w_j)$ from all the other parties P_j with $j \in [n] \setminus \{i\}$, computes $\mathsf{Enc}(\mathsf{pk}_j, \mathsf{PRG}(s_j))$, using homomorphic operations, $\mathsf{Enc}(\mathsf{pk}_j, w_j)$ by encrypting w_j using pk_j, and then homomorphically XORs the resulting ciphertexts to receive $\mathsf{Enc}(\mathsf{pk}_j, x_j)$. This ciphertext can now

$$\Pi^{\mathsf{FHE}}$$

Initialization: Each $i \in [n]$ party P_i has input $x_i \in \{0,1\}^*$ as its secret input.

Round 1.
1. Sample r_i^{Setup} and $r_i^{\mathsf{Enc}} \leftarrow \{0,1\}^\lambda$.
2. Set $x_i' := (x_i, r_i^{\mathsf{Setup}}, r_i^{\mathsf{Enc}})$ and compute $\mathsf{msg}_{1,i} \leftarrow \Pi^{\mathsf{M}}.\mathsf{Next}_1(1^\lambda, x_i')$.
3. Compute $(\mathsf{pk}_i, \mathsf{sk}_i) := \mathsf{Setup}(1^\lambda; r_i^{\mathsf{Setup}})$.
4. Compute $\mathsf{ct}_i := \mathsf{Enc}(\mathsf{pk}_i, x_i; r_i^{\mathsf{Enc}})$.
5. Send $(\mathsf{msg}_{1,i}, \mathsf{pk}_i, \mathsf{ct}_i)$.

Round 2.
1. Let τ_1 denote the transcript of the protocol Π^{M} up to round 1.
2. Compute $\mathsf{ct}^i := \mathsf{Eval}(C, (\mathsf{pk}_1, \mathsf{ct}_1), \ldots, (\mathsf{pk}_n, \mathsf{ct}_n))$.
3. Compute $\mathsf{msg}_{2,i} \leftarrow \Pi^{\mathsf{M}}.\mathsf{Next}_2(C_{\mathsf{ct}^i, K^i}^{\mathsf{Dec}}, \tau_1)$, where $K^i := (\mathsf{pk}_j, \mathsf{ct}_j)_{j \in [n]}$.
4. Send $\mathsf{msg}_{2,i}$.

For each round $k \in \{3, \ldots, \ell\}$.
1. Let τ_{k-1} denote the transcript of the protocol Π^{M} up to round $k-1$.
2. Compute the k-th round message $\mathsf{msg}_{k,i} \leftarrow \Pi^{\mathsf{M}}.\mathsf{Next}_k(\tau_{k-1})$.
3. Send $\mathsf{msg}_{k,i}$.

Output Computation.
1. Let τ_ℓ denote the transcript of the protocol Π^{M} up to round ℓ.
2. Compute the output of Π^{M} as $y \leftarrow \Pi^{\mathsf{M}}.\mathsf{Out}(\tau_\ell)$.
3. Output y.

Fig. 8. The protocol Π^{FHE} that securely realizes f.

Input: $(x_i, r_i^{\mathsf{Setup}}, r_i^{\mathsf{Enc}})_{i \in [n]}$.
- Parse K^i as $(\mathsf{pk}_i, \mathsf{ct}_i)_{i \in [n]}$.
- For all $i \in [n]$, check that $(\mathsf{pk}_i, \cdot) = \mathsf{Setup}(1^\lambda; r_i^{\mathsf{Setup}})$ and $\mathsf{ct}_i = \mathsf{Enc}(\mathsf{pk}_i, x_i; r_i^{\mathsf{Enc}})$ and compute $(\cdot, \mathsf{sk}_i) = \mathsf{Setup}(1^\lambda; r_i^{\mathsf{Setup}})$.
- Compute $y := \mathsf{Dec}(\mathsf{sk}_1, \ldots, \mathsf{sk}_n, \mathsf{ct}^i)$.
  If one of the above checks fails then output $\bot$ else return y to P_i.

Fig. 9. Circuit $C_{\mathsf{ct}^i, K^i}^{\mathsf{Dec}}$

be used to run the evaluation algorithm and compute $\mathsf{Enc}(\{\mathsf{pk}_j\}, f(x_1, \ldots, x_n))$. The parties now check that the ciphertexts $\{w_j\}_{j \in [n]}$ are well formed by running the MPC protocol as described in Fig. 9.

Theorem 6.3. *Let* MFHE *be a compact multi-key FHE scheme, then* $\Pi^{\mathsf{FHE}'}$ *is a secure MPC protocol with communication complexity* $O(L_{\mathsf{in}}) + \mathrm{poly}(\lambda, n, L_{\mathsf{out}})$ *that realizes any single-output functionality.*

Due to [3,31,32] we can claim the following.

Corollary 6.4. *If the LWE and DSPR assumptions hold and any of the DDH, QR, N^{th} Residuosity or LWE assumption hold, or there exists a malicious-secure*

OT, then there exists a round optimal (4-round) circuit-independent *MPC protocol that realizes any functionality.*

Acknowledgments. Work done in part while the fourth author was at the University of Edinburgh.

The first author is supported in part by the European Union's Horizon 2020 Research and Innovation Programme under grant agreement 780477 (PRIVILEDGE). The second author is supported in part by DARPA under Cooperative Agreement HR0011-20-2-0025, NSF grant CNS-2001096, US-Israel BSF grant 2015782, Cisco Research Award, Google Faculty Award, JP Morgan Faculty Award, IBM Faculty Research Award, Xerox Faculty Research Award, OKAWA Foundation Research Award, B. John Garrick Foundation Award, Teradata Research Award, Lockheed-Martin Research Award and Sunday Group. The third author is supported in part by the European Union's Horizon 2020 Research and Innovation Programme under grant agreement 780108 (FENTEC). The fourth author is supported in part by NSF grant no. 2055599 and by Sunday Group.

The views and conclusions contained herein are those of the authors and should not be interpreted as necessarily representing the official policies, either expressed or implied, of DARPA, the Department of Defense, or the U.S. Government. The U.S. Government is authorized to reproduce and distribute reprints for governmental purposes not withstanding any copyright annotation therein.

References

1. Ananth, P., Badrinarayanan, S., Jain, A., Manohar, N., Sahai, A.: From FE combiners to secure MPC and back. In: Hofheinz, D., Rosen, A. (eds.) TCC 2019, Part I. LNCS, vol. 11891, pp. 199–228. Springer, Cham (2019). https://doi.org/10.1007/978-3-030-36030-6_9
2. Ananth, P., Jain, A., Jin, Z., Malavolta, G.: Multikey fhe in the plain model. Cryptology ePrint Archive, Report 2020/180 (2020). https://eprint.iacr.org/2020/180
3. Asharov, G., Jain, A., Wichs, D.: Multiparty computation with low communication, computation and interaction via threshold FHE. Cryptology ePrint Archive, Report 2011/613 (2011). https://eprint.iacr.org/2011/613
4. Badrinarayanan, S., Goyal, V., Jain, A., Kalai, Y.T., Khurana, D., Sahai, A.: Promise zero knowledge and its applications to round optimal MPC. In: Shacham, H., Boldyreva, A. (eds.) CRYPTO 2018, Part II. LNCS, vol. 10992, pp. 459–487. Springer, Cham (2018). https://doi.org/10.1007/978-3-319-96881-0_16
5. Beaver, D., Micali, S., Rogaway, P.: The round complexity of secure protocols (extended abstract). In: 22nd ACM STOC, pp. 503–513. ACM Press, May 1990. https://doi.org/10.1145/100216.100287
6. Benhamouda, F., Lin, H.: k-round multiparty computation from k-round oblivious transfer via garbled interactive circuits. In: Nielsen, J.B., Rijmen, V. (eds.) EUROCRYPT 2018, Part II. LNCS, vol. 10821, pp. 500–532. Springer, Cham (2018). https://doi.org/10.1007/978-3-319-78375-8_17
7. Blum, M.: Coin flipping by telephone. In: Gersho, A. (ed.) CRYPTO'81, vol. ECE Report 82-04, pp. 11–15. U.C. Santa Barbara, Dept. of Elec. and Computer Eng. (1981)

8. Boneh, D., Sahai, A., Waters, B.: Functional encryption: definitions and challenges. In: Ishai, Y. (ed.) TCC 2011. LNCS, vol. 6597, pp. 253–273. Springer, Heidelberg (2011). https://doi.org/10.1007/978-3-642-19571-6_16

9. Boyle, E., Gilboa, N., Ishai, Y.: Group-based secure computation: optimizing rounds, communication, and computation. In: Coron, J.-S., Nielsen, J.B. (eds.) EUROCRYPT 2017, Part II. LNCS, vol. 10211, pp. 163–193. Springer, Cham (2017). https://doi.org/10.1007/978-3-319-56614-6_6

10. Brakerski, Z., Gentry, C., Vaikuntanathan, V.: (Leveled) fully homomorphic encryption without bootstrapping. In: Goldwasser, S. (ed.) ITCS 2012, pp. 309–325. ACM, January 2012. https://doi.org/10.1145/2090236.2090262

11. Rai Choudhuri, A., Ciampi, M., Goyal, V., Jain, A., Ostrovsky, R.: Round optimal secure multiparty computation from minimal assumptions. In: Pass, R., Pietrzak, K. (eds.) TCC 2020, Part II. LNCS, vol. 12551, pp. 291–319. Springer, Cham (2020). https://doi.org/10.1007/978-3-030-64378-2_11

12. Choudhuri, A.R., Ciampi, M., Goyal, V., Jain, A., Ostrovsky, R.: Oblivious transfer from trapdoor permutations in minimal rounds. In: Nissim, K., Waters, B. (eds.) TCC 2021, Part II. LNCS, vol. 13043, pp. 518–549. Springer, Cham (2021). https://doi.org/10.1007/978-3-030-90453-1_18

13. Ciampi, M., Ostrovsky, R., Siniscalchi, L., Visconti, I.: Round-optimal secure two-party computation from trapdoor permutations. In: Kalai, Y., Reyzin, L. (eds.) TCC 2017, Part I. LNCS, vol. 10677, pp. 678–710. Springer, Cham (2017). https://doi.org/10.1007/978-3-319-70500-2_23

14. Ciampi, M., Ostrovsky, R., Waldner, H., Zikas, V.: Round-optimal and communication-efficient multiparty computation. Cryptology ePrint Archive, Report 2020/1437 (2020). https://eprint.iacr.org/2020/1437

15. Cohen, R., Shelat, A., Wichs, D.: Adaptively secure MPC with sublinear communication complexity. In: Boldyreva, A., Micciancio, D. (eds.) CRYPTO 2019, Part II. LNCS, vol. 11693, pp. 30–60. Springer, Cham (2019). https://doi.org/10.1007/978-3-030-26951-7_2

16. Dodis, Y., Halevi, S., Rothblum, R.D., Wichs, D.: Spooky encryption and its applications. In: Robshaw, M., Katz, J. (eds.) CRYPTO 2016, Part III. LNCS, vol. 9816, pp. 93–122. Springer, Heidelberg (2016). https://doi.org/10.1007/978-3-662-53015-3_4

17. Friolo, D., Masny, D., Venturi, D.: A black-box construction of fully-simulatable, round-optimal oblivious transfer from strongly uniform key agreement. In: Hofheinz, D., Rosen, A. (eds.) TCC 2019, Part I. LNCS, vol. 11891, pp. 111–130. Springer, Cham (2019). https://doi.org/10.1007/978-3-030-36030-6_5

18. Garg, S., Mukherjee, P., Pandey, O., Polychroniadou, A.: The exact round complexity of secure computation. In: Fischlin, M., Coron, J.-S. (eds.) EUROCRYPT 2016, Part II. LNCS, vol. 9666, pp. 448–476. Springer, Heidelberg (2016). https://doi.org/10.1007/978-3-662-49896-5_16

19. Garg, S., Sahai, A.: Adaptively secure multi-party computation with dishonest majority. In: Safavi-Naini, R., Canetti, R. (eds.) CRYPTO 2012. LNCS, vol. 7417, pp. 105–123. Springer, Heidelberg (2012). https://doi.org/10.1007/978-3-642-32009-5_8

20. Garg, S., Srinivasan, A.: Garbled protocols and two-round MPC from bilinear maps. In: Umans, C. (ed.) 58th FOCS, pp. 588–599. IEEE Computer Society Press, October 2017. https://doi.org/10.1109/FOCS.2017.60

21. Garg, S., Srinivasan, A.: Two-round multiparty secure computation from minimal assumptions. In: Nielsen, J.B., Rijmen, V. (eds.) EUROCRYPT 2018, Part II. LNCS, vol. 10821, pp. 468–499. Springer, Cham (2018). https://doi.org/10.1007/978-3-319-78375-8_16

22. Goldreich, O.: The Foundations of Cryptography - Volume 2 Basic Applications. Cambridge University Press, Cambridge (2004)

23. Goldreich, O., Micali, S., Wigderson, A.: How to play any mental game or A completeness theorem for protocols with honest majority. In: Aho, A. (ed.) 19th ACM STOC, pp. 218–229. ACM Press, May 1987. https://doi.org/10.1145/28395.28420

24. Goyal, V.: Constant round non-malleable protocols using one way functions. In: Fortnow, L., Vadhan, S.P. (eds.) 43rd ACM STOC, pp. 695–704. ACM Press, June 2011. https://doi.org/10.1145/1993636.1993729

25. Halevi, S., Hazay, C., Polychroniadou, A., Venkitasubramaniam, M.: Round-optimal secure multi-party computation. In: Shacham, H., Boldyreva, A. (eds.) CRYPTO 2018, Part II. LNCS, vol. 10992, pp. 488–520. Springer, Cham (2018). https://doi.org/10.1007/978-3-319-96881-0_17

26. Ishai, Y., Kushilevitz, E., Paskin, A.: Secure multiparty computation with minimal interaction. In: Rabin, T. (ed.) CRYPTO 2010. LNCS, vol. 6223, pp. 577–594. Springer, Heidelberg (2010). https://doi.org/10.1007/978-3-642-14623-7_31

27. Ishai, Y., Prabhakaran, M., Sahai, A.: Founding cryptography on oblivious transfer – efficiently. In: Wagner, D. (ed.) CRYPTO 2008. LNCS, vol. 5157, pp. 572–591. Springer, Heidelberg (2008). https://doi.org/10.1007/978-3-540-85174-5_32

28. Katz, J., Ostrovsky, R.: Round-optimal secure two-party computation. In: Franklin, M. (ed.) CRYPTO 2004. LNCS, vol. 3152, pp. 335–354. Springer, Heidelberg (2004). https://doi.org/10.1007/978-3-540-28628-8_21

29. Katz, J., Ostrovsky, R., Smith, A.: Round efficiency of multi-party computation with a dishonest majority. In: Biham, E. (ed.) EUROCRYPT 2003. LNCS, vol. 2656, pp. 578–595. Springer, Heidelberg (2003). https://doi.org/10.1007/3-540-39200-9_36

30. Kilian, J.: Founding cryptography on oblivious transfer. In: 20th ACM STOC, pp. 20–31. ACM Press, May 1988. https://doi.org/10.1145/62212.62215

31. Lindell, Y., Pinkas, B.: A proof of security of yao's protocol for two-party computation. J. Cryptol. **22**(2), 161–188 (2008). https://doi.org/10.1007/s00145-008-9036-8

32. López-Alt, A., Tromer, E., Vaikuntanathan, V.: On-the-fly multiparty computation on the cloud via multikey fully homomorphic encryption. In: Karloff, H.J., Pitassi, T. (eds.) 44th ACM STOC, pp. 1219–1234. ACM Press, May 2012. https://doi.org/10.1145/2213977.2214086

33. Morgan, A., Pass, R., Polychroniadou, A.: Succinct non-interactive secure computation. In: Canteaut, A., Ishai, Y. (eds.) EUROCRYPT 2020, Part II. LNCS, vol. 12106, pp. 216–245. Springer, Cham (2020). https://doi.org/10.1007/978-3-030-45724-2_8

34. Mukherjee, P., Wichs, D.: Two round multiparty computation via multi-key FHE. In: Fischlin, M., Coron, J.-S. (eds.) EUROCRYPT 2016, Part II. LNCS, vol. 9666, pp. 735–763. Springer, Heidelberg (2016). https://doi.org/10.1007/978-3-662-49896-5_26

35. O'Neill, A.: Definitional issues in functional encryption. Cryptology ePrint Archive, Report 2010/556 (2010). https://eprint.iacr.org/2010/556

36. Paskin-Cherniavsky, A.: Secure computation with minimal interaction. Ph.D. thesis, Computer Science Department, Technion (2012)

37. Pass, R.: Bounded-concurrent secure multi-party computation with a dishonest majority. In: Babai, L. (ed.) 36th ACM STOC, pp. 232–241. ACM Press, June 2004. https://doi.org/10.1145/1007352.1007393

38. Pass, R., Wee, H.: Constant-round non-malleable commitments from subexponential one-way functions. In: Gilbert, H. (ed.) EUROCRYPT 2010. LNCS, vol. 6110, pp. 638–655. Springer, Heidelberg (2010). https://doi.org/10.1007/978-3-642-13190-5_32

39. Quach, W., Wee, H., Wichs, D.: Laconic function evaluation and applications. In: Thorup, M. (ed.) 59th FOCS, pp. 859–870. IEEE Computer Society Press, October 2018. https://doi.org/10.1109/FOCS.2018.00086

40. Sahai, A., Waters, B.: Fuzzy identity-based encryption. In: Cramer, R. (ed.) EUROCRYPT 2005. LNCS, vol. 3494, pp. 457–473. Springer, Heidelberg (2005). https://doi.org/10.1007/11426639_27

41. Wee, H.: Black-box, round-efficient secure computation via non-malleability amplification. In: 51st FOCS, pp. 531–540. IEEE Computer Society Press, October 2010. https://doi.org/10.1109/FOCS.2010.87

42. Yao, A.C.C.: How to generate and exchange secrets (extended abstract). In: 27th FOCS, pp. 162–167. IEEE Computer Society Press, October 1986. https://doi.org/10.1109/SFCS.1986.25

Round-Optimal Byzantine Agreement

Diana Ghinea[1], Vipul Goyal[2], and Chen-Da Liu-Zhang[3(✉)]🆔

[1] ETH Zurich, Zürich, Switzerland
ghinead@ethz.ch
[2] Carnegie Mellon University and NTT Research, Pittsburgh, USA
vipul@cmu.edu
[3] Carnegie Mellon University, Pittsburgh, USA
cliuzhan@andrew.cmu.edu

Abstract. Byzantine agreement is a fundamental primitive in cryptography and distributed computing, and minimizing its round complexity is of paramount importance. It is long known that any randomized r-round protocol must fail with probability at least $(c \cdot r)^{-r}$, for some constant c, when the number of corruptions is linear in the number of parties, $t = \theta(n)$. On the other hand, current protocols fail with probability at least 2^{-r}. Whether we can match the lower bound agreement probability remains unknown.

In this work, we resolve this long-standing open question. We present a protocol that matches the lower bound up to constant factors. Our results hold under a (strongly rushing) adaptive adversary that can corrupt up to $t = (1 - \epsilon)n/2$ parties, and our protocols use a public-key infrastructure and a trusted setup for unique threshold signatures. This is the first protocol that decreases the failure probability (overall) by a *super-constant* factor per round.

1 Introduction

Byzantine agreement (BA) is an essential building block and an extensively studied problem in distributed protocols: it allows a set of n parties to achieve agreement on a common value even when up to t of the parties may arbitrarily deviate from the protocol. BA was first formalized in the seminal work of Lamport et al. [LSP82], and since then, it has been the subject of a huge line of work (e.g. [DS83, PW96, FM97, CL99, KK06]).

A crucial efficiency metric for distributed protocols is their round complexity. That is, the number of synchronous communication rounds that are needed for a protocol to terminate. As shown by Dolev and Strong [DS83], any deterministic protocol for BA requires at least $t + 1$ rounds. Fortunately, the seminal results of Ben-Or [Ben83] and Rabin [Rab83] show that such limitation can be

V. Goyal and C.-D. Liu-Zhang—Supported in part by the NSF award 1916939, DARPA SIEVE program, a gift from Ripple, a DoE NETL award, a JP Morgan Faculty Fellowship, a PNC center for financial services innovation award, and a Cylab seed funding award.

O. Dunkelman and S. Dziembowski (Eds.): EUROCRYPT 2022, LNCS 13275, pp. 96–119, 2022.
https://doi.org/10.1007/978-3-031-06944-4_4

circumvented by the use of randomization. In this regime, there are protocols that achieve *expected constant* number of rounds [FM97,KK06].

It is also known that any r-round randomized protocol must fail with probability at least $(c \cdot r)^{-r}$, for some constant c, when the number of corruptions, $t = \theta(n)$, is linear in the number of parties [KY84,CMS89,CPS19].

The seminal work of Feldman and Micali (FM) [FM97] introduced an unconditional protocol, secure up to $t < n/3$ corruptions, that achieves agreement in $O(r)$ rounds except with probability 2^{-r}. Assuming an initial trusted setup and for the case of binary input domain, the protocol requires $2r$ rounds to achieve the same agreement probability. Despite the extensive line of works [FG03,KK06,CM19,MV17,ADD+19] improving different parameters of the original FM protocol, the agreement probability was not improved until the very recent work of Fitzi, Liu-Zhang and Loss [FLL21], which showed a binary BA protocol that uses a trusted setup and requires $r+1$ rounds to achieve agreement except with probability 2^{-r}.

To the best of our knowledge, up to date, there is no r-round protocol that fails with probability less than 2^{-r} after r rounds.

It is therefore natural to ask whether one can achieve a protocol that increases the agreement probability by more than a constant per round, hopefully matching the known lower bounds. Concretely, we ask whether one can achieve a round-optimal Byzantine agreement given a target probability of error; alternatively achieving the optimal probability within a fixed number of rounds r:

Is there an r-round BA protocol that achieves agreement except with probability $(c \cdot r)^{-r}$, for some constant c, and secure up to some $t = \theta(n)$ corruptions?

We answer this question in the affirmative. We show an optimal protocol up to constants. Concretely, our protocol achieves the optimal agreement probability and simultaneous termination[1] within $3r + 1$ rounds and is secure against a strongly rushing adaptive adversary that can corrupt any $t = (1 - \epsilon)n/2$ parties, for any constant $\epsilon > 0$, assuming a public-key infrastructure (PKI) setup and a trusted setup for unique threshold signatures.

Note that, to the best of our knowledge, this is the first protocol that decreases the failure probability (overall) by a **super-constant** factor per round. No previous r-round protocol achieved less than 2^{-r} failure probability, even for any setup assumptions, and even against a static adversary corrupting up to any fraction $t = \theta(n)$ of parties.

1.1 Technical Overview

We give an overview of the main techniques used in our protocol.

Expand-and-Extract. Our starting point is the recent work by Fitzi, Liu-Zhang and Loss [FLL21], where the authors provide a new elegant way to design round-efficient BA protocols, called Expand-and-Extract.

---

[1] All parties simultaneously terminate in the same round.

The Expand-and-Extract iteration paradigm consists of three steps. The first step is an expansion step, where an input bit is expanded into a value with range ℓ, via a so-called Proxcensus protocol. This protocol guarantees that the outputs of honest parties lie within two consecutive values (see Definition 2).

The second step is a multi-valued coin-flip, and the last step is an extraction technique, where the output bit is computed from the coin and the output of Proxcensus. The steps are designed such that parties are guaranteed to reach agreement except with probability $1/\ell$, assuming that the coin returns a common uniform ℓ-range value. See Sect. 3 for a recap.

Our main technical contribution is a new Proxcensus protocol that expands the input bit into $\ell = (c \cdot r)^r$ values in $3r$ rounds, for any $t = (1 - \epsilon)n/2$ corruptions, for some constant c that depends on ϵ. Combining this with a 1-round coin-flip protocol [CKS05,LJY14], which can be instantiated using a trusted setup for unique threshold signatures, the desired result follows.

Round-Optimal Proxcensus. The protocol starts by positioning the honest parties into one of the extremes of a large interval $[0, M]$ of natural values (for some large value M specified below). If the input of party P_i is $x_i = 0$, then P_i positions himself in value 0, and if the input is $x_i = 1$, then P_i positions himself in the value $v = M$.

The protocol then proceeds in iterations of 3 rounds each. At each iteration, each party P_i distributes its current value within the interval, and updates its value according to some deterministic function f. Importantly, each iteration guarantees that the values between any two honest parties get closer (overall) by a *super-constant* factor. Concretely, we achieve a protocol in which, after any sufficiently large number L of iterations, the distance between any two honest values is roughly at most L. By setting the initial range to $M \approx L^{L+1}$ values, we can group every L consecutive values into batches, to obtain a total of roughly L^L batches, which will constitute the output values for the Proxcensus protocol.

To handle this high number of values, we will need to devise two ingredients: a mechanism that limits the adversary's cheating capabilities, and a function f that allows the iteration-outputs of the honest parties to get closer, even when the function is evaluated on sets of values that are different (in a limited way).

Cheating-Limitation Mechanism. We specify a mechanism that, for each party $\widetilde{P}$, allows honest parties to decide at a specific iteration whether to take into account the value received from $\widetilde{P}$ or not. This mechanism provides two guarantees. First, if there is an honest party P_i that takes into account the value received from $\widetilde{P}$, and another honest party P_j that does not, then $\widetilde{P}$ is necessarily corrupted and all honest parties will ignore $\widetilde{P}$'s values in all future iterations. Second, if all honest parties consider the value received by $\widetilde{P}$, then $\widetilde{P}$ actually distributed the same consistent value to all honest parties.

These two guarantees have the effect that any corrupted party can cause differences between the values taken into consideration by honest parties **at most once**. That is, the amount of discrepancy between any two honest parties depends on the actual number of corrupted parties that actively cheated in that iteration.

In order to implement such a mechanism, we introduce a modification of the well-known graded broadcast [FM97] primitive, which we denote *conditional graded broadcast*. In this primitive, the sender has an input to be distributed, and every recipient holds an input bit b_i. The primitive then achieves the same properties as graded broadcast, but with a few differences. When all honest parties have as input $b_i = 0$, then the output of all honest parties has grade 0 (we call this property "no honest participation"). Moreover, even when a subset of honest parties have $b_i = 0$, graded consistency is achieved. See Definition 3 for more details and Sect. 4 for a construction.

The mechanism can then be implemented as follows. Each party P_i keeps track of a set of corrupted parties $\mathcal{C}$ that it identified as corrupted. At each iteration, P_i distributes its current value x_i via a conditional graded broadcast; P_i only considers those values that have grade 1 or 2 to update its value via the function f, and ignores the values with grade 0. On top of that, P_i updates its local set $\mathcal{C}$ with those parties that sent grade 0 or 1 (these parties are guaranteed to be corrupted by the graded broadcast primitive). Moreover, P_i sets $b_i = 0$ in any future conditional graded broadcast from any sender in $\mathcal{C}$.

Observe that if a dishonest sender $\widetilde{P}$ distributes values such that an honest party P_i takes into account the value from $\widetilde{P}$ (P_i receives grade at least 1), and another honest party P_j does not consider $\widetilde{P}$'s value (P_j gets grade 0), then necessarily $\widetilde{P}$ is corrupted, and all honest parties add $\widetilde{P}$ to their corrupted sets (this is because P_j got grade 0, so graded broadcast guarantees that no honest party gets grade 2). It follows by "no honest participation" that all values from $\widetilde{P}$ will be ignored in future iterations. Moreover, if all honest parties take into account the value from $\widetilde{P}$, it means no honest party received grade 0, and therefore all parties obtain the same value (with grade 1 or 2). Note that in this case, $\widetilde{P}$ can still distribute values that are considered in further iterations; however it did not cause discrepancies in the current iteration.

Deterministic Function f. With the above mechanism, we reach a situation where at each iteration $\mathtt{it}$, the set of values considered by different honest parties P_i and P_j differ in at most $l_{\mathtt{it}}$ values, where $l_{\mathtt{it}}$ is the number of corrupted parties that distributed grade 1 to a party and grade 0 to the other party.

In order to compute the updated value, P_i discards the lowest and the highest $t - c$ values from the set of considered values (those with grade at least 1), where c represents the number of values received with grade 0. Then, the new value is computed as the average of the remaining values.

Observe that because those c parties (that sent grade 0) are corrupted, then among the $n - c$ parties at most $t - c$ are corrupted. This implies that the updated value is always within the range of values from honest parties. Moreover, if the adversary doesn't distribute different values at an iteration, the honest parties' updated values will be the same, and will never diverge again.

With technical combinatorial lemmas (see Lemmas 6 and 7), we will show that with this deterministic update function, the distance between any two honest parties' updated values decreases by a factor proportional to the number of corrupted parties l_{it}. After L iterations, and bounding the sum of l_{it} terms by the corruption threshold t, we will show that the distance between honest values is bounded by $M \cdot (\frac{n-2t}{t} \cdot L)^{-L} + L$. Hence, by grouping every $2L$ consecutive values, we will be able to handle approximately $(\frac{n-2t}{t} \cdot L)^L = (\frac{2\epsilon}{1-\epsilon} \cdot L)^L$ values in Proxcensus within $3L$ rounds when $t = (1-\epsilon)n/2$. See more details in Sect. 5.

1.2 Related Work

The literature on round complexity of Byzantine agreement is huge, and different protocols achieve different levels of efficiency depending on many aspects, including the setup assumptions, the corruption threshold, input domain, etc.

In the following, we focus on the round-complexity of binary BA protocols, noting that these can be extended to multivalued BA using standard techniques [TC84], at the cost of an additional 2 rounds in the $t < n/3$ case, and 3 rounds in the $t < n/2$ case. Some of the constructions also use an ideal 1-round coin-flip protocol with no error nor bias, which can be instantiated using a trusted setup for unique threshold signatures [CKS05, LJY14].

Feldman and Micali [FM97] gave an unconditional protocol for $t < n/3$ with expected constant number of rounds. This protocol achieves agreement in $O(r)$ rounds except with probability 2^{-r}. Assuming an ideal coin, the protocol achieves the same agreement probability within (the smaller number of) $2r$ rounds for binary inputs.

Fitzi and Garay [FG03] gave the first expected constant-round protocol for $t < n/2$ assuming a PKI, under specific number-theoretic assumptions. This result was later improved by Katz and Koo [KK06], where they gave a protocol relying solely on a PKI. Assuming threshold signatures, Abraham et al. [ADD+19] extended the above results to achieve the first expected constant-round BA with expected $O(n^2)$ communication complexity, improving the communication complexity by a linear factor. These protocols can be adapted to achieve in $O(r)$ rounds agreement except with probability 2^{-r}. The concrete efficiency was improved by Micali and Vaikuntanathan [MV17], where the authors achieve agreement in $2r$ rounds except with probability 2^{-r}, assuming an ideal coin for binary inputs.

Recently, Fitzi, Liu-Zhang and Loss [FLL21] generalized the Feldman and Micali iteration paradigm, and gave improvements in the concrete efficiency of fixed-round protocols, assuming an ideal coin. For binary inputs, the protocols incur a total of $r+1$ rounds for $t < n/3$, and $\frac{3}{2}r$ for $t < n/2$, to achieve agreement except with probability 2^{-r}.

A line of work focused on achieving round-efficient solutions for *broadcast*, the single-sender version of BA, in the dishonest majority setting [GKKO07, FN09, CPS20, WXSD20, WXDS20].

Karlin and Yao [KY84], and also Chor, Merritt and Shmoys [CMS89] showed that any r-round randomized protocol must fail with probability at least $(c \cdot r)^{-r}$, for some constant c, when the number of corruptions, $t = \theta(n)$, is linear in the number of parties. This bound was extended to the asynchronous model by Attiya and Censor-Hillel [AC10].

Protocols with *expected* constant round complexity have probabilistic termination, where parties (possibly) terminate at different rounds. It is known that composing such protocols in a round-preserving fashion is non-trivial. Several works analyzed protocols with respect to parallel composition [Ben83, FG03], sequential composition [LLR06], and universal composition [CCGZ16, CCGZ17].

Cohen et al. [CHM+19] showed lower bounds for Byzantine agreement with probabilistic termination. The authors give bounds on the probability to terminate after one and two rounds. In particular, for a large class of protocols and a combinatorial conjecture, the halting probability after the second round is $o(1)$ (resp. $1/2 + o(1)$) for the case where there are up to $t < n/3$ (resp. $t < n/4$) corruptions.

2   Model and Definitions

We consider a setting with n parties $\mathcal{P} = \{P_1, P_2, \ldots, P_n\}$.

2.1   Communication and Adversary Model

Parties have access to a complete network of point-to-point authenticated channels. The network is *synchronous*, meaning that any message sent by an honest party is delivered within a known amount of time. In this setting, protocols are typically described in rounds.

We consider an adaptive adversary that can corrupt up to t parties at any point in the protocol's execution, causing them to deviate arbitrarily from the protocol. Moreover, the adversary is strongly rushing: it can observe the messages sent by honest parties in a round before choosing its own messages for that round, and, when an honest party sends a message during some round, it can immediately corrupt that party and replace the message with another of its choice.

2.2   Cryptographic Primitives

Public-Key Infrastructure. We assume that all the parties have access to a public key infrastructure (PKI). That is, parties hold the same vector of public keys $(pk_1, pk_2, \ldots, pk_n)$, and each honest party P_i holds the secret key sk_i associated with pk_i.[2]

A signature on a value v using secret key sk is computed as $\sigma \leftarrow \mathsf{Sign}_{sk}(v)$; a signature is verified relative to public key pk by calling $\mathsf{Ver}_{pk}(v, \sigma)$. For simplicity, we assume in our proofs that the signatures are perfectly unforgeable. When

---

[2] This is a *bulletin-board* PKI, where the keys from corrupted parties can be chosen adversarially. See [BCG21] for a nice discussion.

replacing the signatures with real-world instantiations, the results hold except with a negligible failure probability.

Coin-Flip. Parties have access to an ideal coin-flip protocol CoinFlip that gives the parties a common uniform random value (in some range depending on the protocol of choice). This value remains uniform from the adversary's view until the first honest party has queried CoinFlip. Such a primitive can be achieved from a trusted setup of unique threshold signatures [CKS05, LJY14].

2.3   Agreement Primitives

Byzantine Agreement. We first recall the definition of Byzantine agreement.

Definition 1 (Byzantine Agreement). *A protocol Π where initially each party P_i holds an input value $x_i \in \{0, 1\}$ and terminates upon generating an output y_i is a Byzantine agreement protocol, resilient against t corruptions, if the following properties are satisfied whenever up to t parties are corrupted:*

- *Validity: If all honest parties have as input x, then every honest party outputs $y_i = x$.*
- *Consistency: Any two honest parties P_i and P_j output the same value $y_i = y_j$.*

Proxcensus. Relaxations of Byzantine agreement have been proposed in the past, where the output value is typically augmented with a *grade*, indicating the level of agreement achieved in the protocol (see e.g. [FM97]). Proxcensus [CFF+05, FLL21] can be seen as a generalization of these primitives, where the grade is an arbitrary but finite domain. We consider a simplified version of the definition of Proxcensus [FLL21], to the case where the input is binary.

Definition 2 (Binary Proxcensus). *Let $\ell \geq 2$ be a natural number. A protocol Π where initially each party P_i holds an input bit $x_i \in \{0, 1\}$ and terminates upon generating an output $y_i \in \{0, 1, \ldots, \ell - 1\}$ is a binary Proxcensus protocol with ℓ slots, resilient against t corruptions, if the following properties are satisfied whenever up to t parties are corrupted:*

- *Validity: If all honest parties input $x_i = 0$ (resp. $x_i = 1$), then every honest party outputs $y_i = 0$ (resp. $y_i = \ell - 1$).*
- *Consistency: The outputs of any two honest parties P_i and P_j lie within two consecutive slots. That is, there exists a value $v \in \{0, 1, \ldots, \ell - 2\}$ such that each honest party P_i outputs $y_i \in \{v, v + 1\}$.*

Conditional Graded Broadcast. Graded broadcast [FM97, KK06, Fit03] is a relaxed version of broadcast. The primitive allows a sender to distribute a value to n recipients, each with a grade of confidence.

In our protocols, it will be convenient to have a slightly modified version of graded broadcast, where each party P_i has an additional bit b_i, which intuitively indicates whether P_i will send any message during the protocol. There are two main differences with respect to the usual graded broadcast definition. First, if all honest parties have $b_i = 0$ as input, then all honest parties output some value with grade 0. Second, we require the usual graded consistency property in the dishonest sender case even when any subset of honest parties have $b_i = 0$.

Definition 3. *A protocol Π where initially a designated party P_s (called the sender) holds a value x, each party P_i holds a bit b_i, and each party P_i terminates upon generating an output pair (y_i, g_i) with $g_i \in \{0, 1, 2\}$, is a conditional graded broadcast protocol resilient against t corruptions if the following properties hold whenever up to t parties are corrupted:*

1. *Conditional Validity: If P_s is honest and each honest party has $b_i = 1$, then every honest party outputs $(x, 2)$.*
2. *Conditional Graded Consistency: For any two honest parties P_i and P_j:*
   - *$|g_i - g_j| \leq 1$.*
   - *If $g_i > 0$ and $g_j > 0$, then $y_i = y_j$.*
3. *No Honest Participation: If all honest parties input $b_i = 0$, then every honest party outputs $(\perp, 0)$.*

Assuming a public-key infrastructure, conditional gradecast can be achieved up to $t < n/2$ corruptions in 3 rounds (see Sect. 4).

3 Expand-and-Extract Paradigm

In this section we briefly recap the Expand-and-Extract paradigm, introduced by Fitzi, Liu-Zhang and Loss [FLL21].

The Expand-and-Extract paradigm consists of three steps. The first step is an expansion step, where parties jointly execute an ℓ-slot binary Proxcensus protocol Prox_ℓ. That is, each party P_i has as input bit x_i, and obtains an output $z_i = \mathsf{Prox}_\ell(x_i) \in \{0, 1, \ldots, \ell - 1\}$. At this point, the outputs of honest parties satisfy validity and consistency of Proxcensus.

The second step is a multi-valued coin-flip. Let $c_i \in \{0, 1, \ldots, \ell - 2\}$ denote the coin value that the parties obtain.

The last step is a cut, where the output bit is computed from the coin c_i and the output z_i of Proxcensus, simply as $y_i = 0$ if $z_i \leq c_i$, and $y_i = 1$ otherwise (Fig. 1).

$$\underbrace{0 \vdots 1 \vdots 2 \vdots 3 \vdots 4}_{y_i = 0} \underbrace{\Big|}_{c_i} \underbrace{5 \vdots 6 \vdots \cdots \vdots l-2 \vdots l-1}_{y_i = 1}$$

Fig. 1. Party P_i outputs a slot-value in $\{0, \ldots, \ell - 1\}$, and the coin can "cut" the array of slots in any of the $\ell - 2$ intermediate positions (indicated with dotted lines). If the obtained value lies on the left of the cut made by c_i (indicated with a red line), the output is $y_i = 0$. Otherwise, the output is $y_i = 1$.

Assuming that the coin is ideal (no error and no bias), i.e. returns a common uniform value in the range $\{0, 1, \ldots, \ell - 2\}$, it is easy to see that parties reach agreement except with probability $1/(\ell - 1)$:

– If all honest parties have input $x_i = 0$, then after the first step the output of Proxcensus is $z_i = 0$, and the final output is $y_i = 0$ no matter what the coin value is. Similarly, if the input is $x_i = 1$, then $z_i = \ell - 1$ and the output is $y_i = 1$ because the largest coin value is $\ell - 2$.
– Moreover, since honest parties lie in two adjacent slots after the invocation of Prox_ℓ, there is only one possible coin value (out of $\ell - 1$) that lead to parties having different inputs.

We formally describe the protocol below.

Protocol $\Pi_{\mathsf{EE}}^\ell(P_i)$

Let $\ell \geq 2$ be a natural number. The protocol is described from the point of view of party P_i, with input bit $x_i \in \{0, 1\}$.

1: $z_i = \mathsf{Prox}_\ell(x_i)$
2: $c_i = \mathsf{CoinFlip}$
3: **if** $z_i \leq c_i$ **then**
4:     Output 0
5: **else**
6:     Output 1
7: **end if**

Theorem 1 ([FLL21]). *Let $t < n$. Let Prox_ℓ be an ℓ-slot Proxcensus protocol, and $\mathsf{CoinFlip}$ be an $(\ell - 1)$-valued ideal Coin-Flip protocol, secure up to t corruptions. Then, protocol Π_{EE}^ℓ achieves binary Byzantine Agreement against an adaptive, strongly rushing adversary with probability $1 - \frac{1}{\ell - 1}$.*

4 Conditional Graded Broadcast

We describe our conditional graded broadcast protocol below, which is based on previous graded broadcast protocols [MV17, FLL21].

The protocol takes three rounds. The rounds are executed only if the input bit is $b_i = 1$. In the first round, the sender distributes its input signed. Then, when each party receives a value from the sender, it adds its own signature and echoes the pair of signatures along with the value to all parties. The third round consists of simply echoing all received pairs to every other party.

At the end of the third round, every party executes the output determination phase (this is executed irrespective of the value of b_i). A party outputs with grade 2 if it received from each of a total of $n - t$ parties a set of $n - t$ signatures on a value v, and no signature on any other value $v' \neq v$. Note that if an honest party outputs v with grade 2, then it is guaranteed that every honest party received at least one set of $n - t$ signatures on v, and no echo signature on any $v' \neq v$ in the second round. This constitutes exactly the condition to output grade 1. In any other case, the output is $(\perp, 0)$.

Protocol cGBC(P_s)

Code for sender P_s with input x

1: **if** $b_s = 1$ **then**
2:     Round 1: Compute $\sigma = \mathsf{Sign}_{sk_s}(x)$, and send (x, σ) to all the parties.
3: **end if**

Code for party P_i

1: **if** $b_i = 1$ **then**
2:     Round 2: Upon receiving (x', σ_s) with valid signature from P_s, compute
       $\sigma_i = \mathsf{Sign}_{sk_i}(x)$ and send (x, σ_s, σ_i) to all the parties.
3:     Round 3: Forward all valid tuples received in the previous round to all
       parties. Let Σ_j be the set of valid signature tuples received from party P_j.
4: **end if**

Code for party P_i: Output Determination We say that a set of valid signatures Σ on v is consistent if it contains valid signatures on v from at least $n - t$ distinct parties.

1: **if** at least $n - t$ consistent signature sets Σ_j on v have been received from
   distinct parties, and no valid tuple (v', σ_s, σ_j) on any $v' \neq v$ was received at
   any previous round **then**
2:     Output $(v, 2)$.
3: **else if** at least one consistent set Σ for v has been received, and no valid
   tuple (v', σ_s, σ) on $v' \neq v$ was received at round 2 **then**
4:     Output $(v, 1)$.
5: **else**
6:     Output $(\bot, 0)$.
7: **end if**

We show that cGBC(P_s) is a conditional gradecast protocol in a sequence of lemmas.

Theorem 2. *Assuming a PKI infrastructure, cGBC(P_s) is a 3-round conditional graded broadcast protocol resilient against $t < n/2$ corruptions.*

Lemma 1. cGBC(P_s) *satisfies conditional validity.*

Proof. Let x be the input of the sender. If the sender is honest and all honest parties have as input $b_i = 1$, then the sender sends its input to all parties, who then forward a signature on this value to everyone. Therefore, all parties collect a signature set on x of size at least $n - t$ and forward all these. At the end of round 3, they all collect at least $n - t$ consistent signature sets. Further note that since the sender is honest, no honest party can collect a tuple (x', σ_s, σ) containing a valid signature from the sender for any other value $x' \neq x$.

Lemma 2. cGBC(P_s) *satisfies conditional graded consistency.*

Proof. We first show that if an honest party P_i outputs $(y_i, g_i) = (v, 2)$, then every honest party P_j outputs (y_j, g_j) with $y_j = y_i$ and $g_j \geq 1$.

Since $g_i = 2$, P_i received $n - t > t$ consistent signature sets Σ_k for the same value y_i. As at least one of these sets is sent by an honest party, P_j received at least one consistent Σ_k on y_i. Moreover, P_j does not receive any tuple (y', σ_s, σ) with valid signatures for any value $y' \neq y_i$ at round 2. This is because P_i did not receive any such tuple (y', σ_s, σ) on $y' \neq y_i$ at round 3.

It remains to show that there cannot be two honest parties P_i and P_j that output y_i and $y_j \neq y_i$, both with grade 1. In this case, P_i received a set of $n - t$ signatures on y_i. This implies that there was at least one honest party that sent a tuple (y_i, σ_s, σ) with valid signatures at round 2. Therefore, at the end of round 2, P_j received this tuple and could not have output y_j with grade 1.

Lemma 3. $\mathsf{cGBC}(P_s)$ *satisfies no honest participation.*

Proof. Assume that $b_i = 0$ for every honest party P_i. Since the honest parties do not send any messages at Round 1, and a consistent signature set Σ requires at least $n - t > t$ signatures, no party receives any consistent signature set. Therefore, every honest party outputs $(\bot, 0)$.

5 Round-Optimal Proxcensus

In this section, we introduce a round-optimal Proxcensus protocol, for any $t < (1-\epsilon)n/2$, for constant $\epsilon > 0$. The protocol achieves a super-exponential number of slots with respect to the number of rounds.

5.1 Protocol Description

The protocol is deterministic and runs for L iterations of 3 rounds each.

At the start of the protocol, parties position themselves into a large set $[0, M]$ of integer values, which we denote as *mini-slots*. ($M = \left(\frac{n-2t}{t}\right)^L \cdot L^{L+1}$ to be exact.)

If the input of party P_i is $x_i = 0$, then P_i positions himself in the mini-slot $v = 0$, and if the input is $x_i = 1$, then P_i positions himself in the mini-slot $v = M$.

At each iteration, each party P_i invokes an instance of conditional graded broadcast (see Definition 3 and Sect. 4 for a construction) to distribute the current mini-slot value. Given the outputs of these graded broadcasts, each party deterministically updates its mini-slot value (within $[0, M]$). Each iteration guarantees that the mini-slot values between any two honest parties get closer. Our process guarantees that after any number $L \geq \frac{1-\epsilon}{\epsilon}$ of iterations, the honest mini-slot values differ in at most $2L$ positions. To achieve that the honest parties lie within two consecutive final slots, each final slot will group every $2L$ consecutive mini-slots. The final number of slots will then be $\ell = \frac{M}{2L} = \frac{1}{2}\left(\frac{n-2t}{t}\right)^L \cdot L^L$.

Cheating Limitation Mechanism. At the core of our efficient Proxcensus protocol lies a mechanism to limit the adversary's cheating capabilities.

Each party P_i (locally) keeps track of a set of parties $\mathcal{C}$ that it identified as corrupted. The mechanism allows P_i to select parties from whom P_i should take into account their value, with two guarantees: For any corrupted party $\widetilde{P}$, it holds that 1) if there are honest parties P_i and P_j such that P_i takes into account the value received from $\widetilde{P}$ but P_j does not, then all honest parties identify $\widetilde{P}$ as corrupted and no honest party will further consider the values from $\widetilde{P}$ in the rest of the protocol. And 2) if all honest parties consider their respective received values from $\widetilde{P}$, then it is guaranteed that the received values are the same. These two properties heavily limit the adversary's capabilities in influencing the output value.

We show how to implement this mechanism. At each iteration it, parties distribute a value via conditional graded broadcast, and P_i takes into account values with grade 1 or 2, but does not take into account values with grade 0. On top of that, P_i updates its set $\mathcal{C}$ adding all parties from whom it received a value with grade 0 or 1 (these are clearly corrupted, since Conditional Graded Validity ensures that honest parties distribute grade 2). Moreover, P_i does not participate in any conditional graded broadcast invocation where the sender is a party in $\mathcal{C}$.

The effect of this is as follows. Consider the case where a corrupted sender $\widetilde{P}$ distributes (possibly different values) to some honest parties P_i and P_j, such that P_i takes into account the value received from $\widetilde{P}$, but P_j does not. In this case, P_i received grade 1 and P_j received grade 0, and both parties add $\widetilde{P}$ to their respective corrupted sets. This implies that no honest party will participate in any following conditional graded broadcast from $\widetilde{P}$ (this is because by Conditional Graded Consistency no honest party received grade 2), and therefore all parties obtain grade 0 by the No Honest Participation property of conditional graded broadcast in the following iterations. Moreover, if $\widetilde{P}$'s value is taken into account by all honest parties, this implies that all honest parties receive grade at least 1, and therefore Graded Consistency ensures that all honest parties receive the same value.

It follows that any corrupted party can cause differences between the values taken into consideration by honest parties at most once.

Mini-Slot Update Function. In order to compute the updated mini-slot value, P_i discards the lowest and the highest $t - c$ values from the values received with grade at least 1, where c represents the number of values received with grade 0. Then, the new value is computed as the average of the remaining values. Note that all those c parties with grade 0 are actually corrupted, and among the $n - c$ parties there are at most $t - c$ corrupted. This implies that the updated value is always within the range of values from honest parties. In particular, if the adversary doesn't send different values at an iteration, the honest parties' updated values are exactly the same, and will never diverge again.

Let l_{it} be the number of corrupted parties that are identified for the first time by every honest party at iteration it. We will show that the distance between any two honest parties' updated values decreases essentially by a factor of $\frac{l_{\text{it}}}{n-2t+\sum_{i=1}^{\text{it}} l_i}$. After L iterations, the values from honest parties will have distance at most $M \cdot \frac{t^L}{L^L} \cdot \frac{1}{(n-2t)^L} + L = 2L$. See Lemmas 6 and 7.

We formally describe the protocol below.

Protocol OptimalProx$_L$

Initialization

1: $\ell = \lfloor \frac{1}{2} \cdot \left(\frac{n-2t}{t}\right)^L \cdot L^L \rfloor$ // Protocol achieves $\ell + 1$ slots in Proxcensus
2: $M = \lceil \left(\frac{n-2t}{t}\right)^L \cdot L^{L+1} \rceil$ // Auxiliar number of minislots

Code for party P_i with input $x_i \in \{0,1\}$

$v_0 = x_i \cdot M$
$C_0 = \varnothing$ (the set of parties P has identified as corrupted)
1: **for** it $= 1 \ldots L$ **do**
2:    Participate in cGBC(P_i) as the sender with input $v_{\text{it}-1}$ and $b_i = 1$. Moreover, participate in all instances of cGBC(P_j) as a receiver as well, with input $b_i = 0$ if $P_j \in C_{\text{it}-1}$, and otherwise with input $b_i = 1$.
3:    Let (v^j, g^j) be the output obtained in the instance of graded broadcast cGBC(P_j) where P_j is the sender.
4:    $C_{\text{it}}^0 = \{P_j \mid g^j = 0\}$; $C_{\text{it}}^1 = \{P_j \mid g^j = 1\}$
5:    Let V_{it} be the multiset containing the values v^j with grade $g^j \geq 1$.
6:    Let T_{it} be the multiset obtained by discarding the lowest and highest $t - |C_{\text{it}}^0|$ values of V_{it}.
7:    $v_{\text{it}} = \lfloor \frac{\sum_{v \in T_{\text{it}}} v}{|T_{\text{it}}|} \rfloor$
8:    $C_{\text{it}} = C_{\text{it}-1} \cup C_{\text{it}}^0 \cup C_{\text{it}}^1$
9: **end for**
10: Output $\lfloor \frac{v_L \cdot \ell}{M} \rfloor$

We now prove that OptimalProx is an optimal Proxcensus for any $t = (1-\epsilon)\frac{n}{2}$ in a sequence of lemmas. The claim on the round complexity follows from the fact that the protocol runs for L iterations, and each iteration involves an instance of parallel graded conditional broadcast, which takes 3 rounds.

Theorem 3. *Let $\epsilon > 0$ be a constant, and let $L \geq \frac{1-\epsilon}{\epsilon}$ and $\ell = \lfloor \frac{1}{2} \left(\frac{2\epsilon}{1-\epsilon}\right)^L L^L \rfloor$ be natural numbers. Assuming a PKI infrastructure, OptimalProx$_L$ is a $3L$-round Proxcensus protocol with $\ell + 1$ slots, resilient against $t = (1-\epsilon)\frac{n}{2}$ corruptions.*

Let us denote by $C_{\text{it},P}$ the (local) set of parties that P identified as corrupted at iteration it. We denote $C_{\text{it}}^\cap = \bigcap_{P \text{ honest}} C_{\text{it},P}$ to be the set of corrupted parties discovered by all honest parties up to iteration it. Then, $l_{\text{it}} = |C_{\text{it}}^\cap \setminus C_{\text{it}-1}^\cap|$ represents the number of corrupted parties that are newly discovered by every honest party exactly at iteration it. These contain the parties that can cause differences in the updated mini-slot values obtained by honest parties.

Let us denote by U_{it} the set of updated mini-slot values v_{it} computed by honest parties at iteration it ≥ 1. Additionally, let $U_0 = \{0, M\}$.

Lemma 4. *At every iteration* it, $T_{it} \subseteq [\min U_{it-1}, \max U_{it-1}]$ *for every honest party.*

Proof. Let P_i be an honest party. Note that its local set $\mathcal{C}_{it}^0$ only contains parties from whom P_i obtained grade 0. Conditional Graded Validity implies that these parties are corrupted (all instances with honest senders output grade 2 at all iterations, and no honest party stops participating in any of these instances).

Therefore, $c = |\mathcal{C}_{it}^0| \leq t$. The values in V_{it} are sent by the parties in $\mathcal{P} \setminus \mathcal{C}_{it}^0$, and hence $|V_{it}| = n - c$. These values contain all values in U_{it-1} sent by the (at least) $n - t$ honest parties, and the values from at most $t - c$ corrupted parties.

Therefore, the multiset T_{it}, obtained by discarding the highest and the lowest $t - c$ values within V_{it}, contains only values within $[\min U_{it-1}, \max U_{it-1}]$. $\qquad\blacksquare$

Lemma 5. OptimalProx$_L$ *achieves Validity.*

Proof. We assume that every honest party starts with input b. Then, $U_0 = \{b \cdot M\}$, and from Lemma 4 we obtain that $U_L \subseteq U_0$ and hence the set containing the value v_L computed by every honest party is $U_L = \{b \cdot M\}$. Therefore, each honest party outputs $\frac{v_L \cdot \ell}{M} = \frac{b \cdot M \cdot \ell}{M} = b \cdot \ell$. $\qquad\blacksquare$

Lemma 6. *Let P and P' denote two honest parties, and let v_{it} and v'_{it} be their respective updated mini-slot values (computed in line 7 of the protocol) at iteration* it. *Then,*

$$|v_{it} - v'_{it}| \leq \frac{l_{it}}{n - 2t + \sum_{i=1}^{it} l_i} \cdot (\max U_{it-1} - \min U_{it-1}) + 1.$$

Proof. Since $v_{it} = \lfloor \text{avg } T_{it} \rfloor$, where $\text{avg } T_{it} = \frac{\sum_{v \in T_{it}} v}{|T_{it}|}$, it is enough to show:

$$|\text{avg } T_{it} - \text{avg } T'_{it}| \leq \frac{l_{it}}{n - 2t + \sum_{i=1}^{it} l_i} \cdot (\max U_{it-1} - \min U_{it-1}).$$

(The last additive term "+1" in the theorem statement accounts for the floor operation.)

Fix iteration it. Consider the values that are received with grade at least 1 by P or P'. It will be convenient to arrange these values in an increasing order in an array A. The array contains exactly $k = n - c$ values, where $c = |\mathcal{C}_{it}^0 \cap \mathcal{C}_{it}'^0|$ is the number of values that both P and P' discard (they both receive grade 0).

Within this array of values, we denote by I_1 (resp. I_2) the set of indices containing the values that were received with grade 0 by P (resp. P') and grade 1 by P' (resp. P).

We then denote the resulting array T^1 (resp. T^2) created by 1) substituting the values at indices in I_1 (resp. I_2) in A by the special symbol $\perp$ and afterwards 2) further substituting the lowest and highest $(t - c) + |I_1|$ (resp. $(t - c) + |I_2|$) values also by $\perp$.

It is easy to see that T^1 (resp. T^2) was created using the exact same process as in the protocol and contains exactly the same values as the multiset T_{it} (resp. T'_{it}), but conveniently arranged in an array.

Let $s = t - c$. Assuming that $|I_1| \geq |I_2|$ (the argument holds symmetrically when $|I_2| \geq |I_1|$), the technical combinatorial Lemma 8 and Lemma 4 imply that:

$$
\begin{aligned}
|\mathrm{avg}\, T^1 - \mathrm{avg}\, T^2| &= |\mathrm{avg}\, T_{\mathrm{it}} - \mathrm{avg}\, T'_{\mathrm{it}}| \\
&\leq \frac{|I_1|}{k - 2s + |I_1|} \cdot (\max U_{\mathrm{it}-1} - \min U_{\mathrm{it}-1}) \\
&\leq \frac{l_{\mathrm{it}}}{k - 2s + l_{\mathrm{it}}} \cdot (\max U_{\mathrm{it}-1} - \min U_{\mathrm{it}-1}) \\
&\leq \frac{l_{\mathrm{it}}}{n - 2t + \sum_{i=1}^{\mathrm{it}} l_i} \cdot (\max U_{\mathrm{it}-1} - \min U_{\mathrm{it}-1}),
\end{aligned}
$$

where in the second inequality we used that $|I_1| \leq l_{\mathrm{it}}$[3], and in the last inequality we used that $k - 2s + l_{\mathrm{it}} = n - 2t + c + l_{\mathrm{it}}$, and the fact that $c \geq |C^{\cap}_{\mathrm{it}-1}| = \sum_{i=1}^{\mathrm{it}-1} l_i$ (any corrupted party in $C^{\cap}_{\mathrm{it}-1}$ that is identified as corrupted by all honest parties distributes a grade 0 to all honest parties by the No Honest Participation property of conditional graded broadcast).

Lemma 7. OptimalProx$_L$ *achieves Consistency.*

Proof. Lemma 4 implies that the honest parties' outputs are within $\lfloor \frac{\ell}{M} \min U_L \rfloor$ and $\lfloor \frac{\ell}{M} \max U_L \rfloor$. Then, to prove that the honest parties' outputs lie within two consecutive slots, it is enough to show that $\frac{\ell}{M}(\max U_L - \min U_L) \leq 1$.

By iteratively applying Lemma 6, and using the fact that $U_0 = \{0, M\}$ and $\frac{l_{\mathrm{it}}}{n - 2t + \sum_{i=1}^{\mathrm{it}} l_i} < 1$ for any $\mathrm{it} \leq L$, we obtain:

$$
\begin{aligned}
\max U_L - \min U_L &\leq M \cdot \prod_{\mathrm{it}=1}^{L} \frac{l_{\mathrm{it}}}{n - 2t + \sum_{i=1}^{\mathrm{it}} l_i} + L \\
&\leq M \cdot \prod_{\mathrm{it}=1}^{L} l_{\mathrm{it}} \cdot \frac{1}{(n - 2t)^L} + L \\
&\leq M \cdot \frac{t^L}{L^L} \cdot \frac{1}{(n - 2t)^L} + L,
\end{aligned}
$$

where the last step follows from inequality of arithmetic and geometric means, and the fact that the sum of identified corrupted parties is at most t:

$$
\left(\prod_{\mathrm{it}=1}^{L} l_{\mathrm{it}} \right)^{\frac{1}{L}} \leq \frac{l_1 + l_2 + \cdots + l_L}{L} \leq \frac{t}{L} \implies \prod_{\mathrm{it}=1}^{L} l_{\mathrm{it}} \leq \frac{t^L}{L^L}
$$

---

[3] Note that $\frac{x}{x+a} \leq \frac{x+b}{x+a+b}$ for any positive real numbers x, a and b.

Then, we bound $\frac{\ell}{M}\left(\max U_L - \min U_L\right)$ as follows:

$$\frac{\ell}{M}\left(\max U_L - \min U_L\right) \leq \ell \cdot \frac{1}{L^L}\left(\frac{t}{n-2t}\right)^L + \frac{\ell}{M} \cdot L$$

$$\leq \ell \cdot \frac{1}{L^L}\left(\frac{t}{n-2t}\right)^L + \frac{\ell}{\left(\frac{n-2t}{t}\right)^L \cdot L^{L+1}} \cdot L$$

$$\leq \ell \cdot \frac{1}{L^L}\left(\frac{t}{n-2t}\right)^L + \ell \cdot \frac{1}{L^L} \cdot \left(\frac{t}{n-2t}\right)^L$$

$$= 2\ell \cdot \frac{1}{L^L}\left(\frac{t}{n-2t}\right)^L \leq \ell \cdot \ell^{-1} = 1,$$

where in the last inequality we used that $\ell \geq 1$, which follows from the fact that $t = (1-\epsilon) \cdot \frac{n}{2}$ and $L \geq \frac{1-\epsilon}{\epsilon}$.

6   Technical Combinatorial Lemma

In this section we prove the technical combinatorial lemma that allows to prove that the updated mini-slot values from honest parties get closer by the required amount, as stated in Lemma 6.

Consider an array A of k values sorted by increasing order and a number $s < k/2$. Further consider the array T^1 created as follows: T^1 has some of the values missing in indices from a fixed set I_1 and then the lowest and highest $s - |I_1|$ values are removed. Similarly, consider the array T^2 created in the same way, but with indices in I_2. See Fig. 2 for an example.

Let b be the maximum value among those remaining in array T^1 or T^2, and let a be the minimum value. Then, the following combinatorial lemma states that the averages of the remaining values in T^1 and T^2 differ in at most a fraction $\frac{\max(|I_1|,|I_2|)}{k-2s+\max(|I_1|,|I_2|)}$ of $b - a$.

$$
\begin{array}{llllllllll}
A: & A_0 & A_1 & A_2 & A_3 & A_4 & A_5 & A_6 & A_7 & A_8 & A_9 \\
T^1: & \bot & A_1 & \bot & A_3 & A_4 & \bot & A_6 & \bot & A_8 & \bot \\
T^2: & \bot & \bot & \bot & A_3 & A_4 & A_5 & \bot & \bot & \bot & \bot
\end{array}
$$

Fig. 2. An example of A, T^1, and T^2, for $k = 10$, $s = 4$, $I^1 = \{2, 5, 7\}$, and $I^2 = \{6\}$.

Lemma 8. *Let $A = [A_0, A_1, \ldots, A_{k-1}]$ denote an array where $A_0 \leq A_1 \leq \cdots \leq A_{k-1}$. Let $s < k/2$ and let $I_1, I_2 \subseteq \{0, 1, \ldots, k-1\}$ denote two sets of indices such that $|I_1 \cup I_2| \leq s$. Consider the arrays $T^1 = [T_0^1, T_1^1, \ldots, T_{k-1}^1]$ and $T^2 = [T_0^2, T_1^2, \ldots, T_{k-1}^2]$ constructed as follows: for $j \in \{1, 2\}$, we first set T_i^j to*

A_i if $i \notin I_j$ and otherwise to $\perp$, and afterwards we replace the lowest and the highest non-$\perp$ $(s - |I_j|)$ values in T^j by $\perp$. Then,

$$\left| avg\ \{T_i^1 \neq \perp\}_{i \in [0,k-1]} - avg\ \{T_i^2 \neq \perp\}_{i \in [0,k-1]} \right|$$
$$\leq \frac{\max\left(|I_1|, |I_2|\right)}{k - 2s + \max\left(|I_1|, |I_2|\right)}(b - a),$$

where $b = \max\{T_i^j \neq \perp\}_{j \in \{1,2\}, i \in [0,k-1]}$ and $a = \min\{T_i^j \neq \perp\}_{j \in \{1,2\}, i \in [0,k-1]}$.

Proof. Let $m_1 := |I_1|$ and $m_2 := |I_2|$. Without loss of generality, we assume that $m_1 \geq m_2$, meaning that T^1 contains at least as many non-$\perp$ values as T^2. Let

$$v_1 := avg\ \{T_i^1 \neq \perp\}_{i \in [0,k-1]} = \frac{1}{|\{T_i^1 \neq \perp\}|} \sum_{\{i:T_i^1 \neq \perp\}} T_i^1,$$

$$v_2 := avg\ \{T_i^2 \neq \perp\}_{i \in [0,k-1]} = \frac{1}{|\{T_i^2 \neq \perp\}|} \sum_{\{i:T_i^2 \neq \perp\}} T_i^2.$$

We first note that the number of non-$\perp$ values in T^1 is:

$$|\{T_i^1 \neq \perp\}| = k - 2(s - m_1) - m_1 = k - 2s + m_1.$$

Similarly, $|\{T_i^2 \neq \perp\}| = k - 2s + m_2$.

We then obtain the following:

$$
\begin{aligned}
v_1 - v_2 &= \frac{\sum_{\{i:T_i^1 \neq \perp\}} T_i^1}{k - 2s + m_1} - v_2 = \frac{\sum_{\{i:T_i^1 \neq \perp\}} T_i^1 - (k - 2s + m_1) \cdot v_2}{k - 2s + m_1} \\
&= \frac{\sum_{\{i:T_i^1 \neq \perp\}} T_i^1 - (k - 2s + m_2) \cdot v_2 - (m_1 - m_2) \cdot v_2}{k - 2s + m_1} \\
&= \frac{\sum_{\{i:T_i^1 \neq \perp\}} T_i^1 - \sum_{\{i:T_i^2 \neq \perp\}} T_i^2 - (m_1 - m_2) \cdot v_2}{k - 2s + m_1}.
\end{aligned}
\tag{1}
$$

Analyzing the Term $\sum_{\{i:T_i^1 \neq \perp\}} T_i^1$. In order to analyze this sum, it will be convenient to look at the values in T_i^1 within three regions, separated by the indices start $= s - m_2$ and end $= k - (s - m_2) - 1$. Note that by construction, at least the lowest and the highest $s - m_2$ indices in T^2 contain $\perp$ as its value.

- Indices $i <$ start. In this region, $T_i^2 = \perp$. Moreover, since the values are ordered increasingly and $\{T_i^2 \neq \perp\} \neq \varnothing$, we can bound any non-$\perp$ value $T_i^1 = A_i \leq A_{\text{start}} \leq \min\{T_j^2 \neq \perp\}$.
- Indices $i >$ end. Similarly as above, $T_i^2 = \perp$. Moreover, any non-$\perp$ value $T_i^1 = A_i \geq A_{\text{end}} \geq \max\{T_j^2 \neq \perp\}$.

– Indices $\texttt{start} \leq i \leq \texttt{end}$. Here non-$\bot$ values in T^1 and T^2 are within the values $A_{\texttt{start}}$ and $A_{\texttt{end}}$. In this region, we define the sets of subindices where exactly either T^1 or T^2 contain non-$\bot$ values. That is, $M^1 := \{\texttt{start} \leq i \leq \texttt{end} : T_i^1 = \bot$ and $T_i^2 \neq \bot\}$ and $M^2 := \{\texttt{start} \leq i \leq \texttt{end} : T_i^1 \neq \bot$ and $T_i^2 = \bot\}$.

We can then express the sum of values in T^1 as:

$$\sum_{\{i : T_i^1 \neq \bot\}} T_i^1 = \sum_{\{i < \texttt{start} : T_i^1 \neq \bot\}} T_i^1 + \sum_{\{\texttt{start} \leq i \leq \texttt{end} : T_i^1 \neq \bot\}} T_i^1 + \sum_{\{\texttt{end} < i : T_i^1 \neq \bot\}} T_i^1$$

$$= \sum_{\{i < \texttt{start} : T_i^1 \neq \bot\}} T_i^1 + \sum_{\{\texttt{end} < i : T_i^1 \neq \bot\}} T_i^1 + \sum_{\{i : T_i^2 \neq \bot\}} T_i^2 - \sum_{i \in M^1} T_i^2 + \sum_{i \in M^2} T_i^1,$$

since $\sum_{\{\texttt{start} \leq i \leq \texttt{end} : T_i^1 \neq \bot\}} T_i^1 = \sum_{\{i : T_i^2 \neq \bot\}} T_i^2 - \sum_{i \in M^1} T_i^2 + \sum_{i \in M^2} T_i^1$ (Fig. 3).

$$
\begin{array}{llllllllll}
A : & A_0 & A_1 & A_2 & A_3 & A_4 & A_5 & A_6 & A_7 & A_8 & A_9 \\
T^1 : & [\bot & A_1 & \bot] & [A_3 & A_4 & \bot & A_6] & [\bot & A_8 & \bot] \\
T^2 : & \bot & \bot & \bot & [A_3 & A_4 & A_5 & \bot] & \bot & \bot & \bot \\
& & & & \texttt{start} & & & \texttt{end}
\end{array}
$$

Fig. 3. In the example from Fig. 2, $\texttt{start} = 3$ and $\texttt{end} = 6$. The brackets show how we split the indices of T^1 and T^2.

Using Eq. (1), we have:

$$|v_1 - v_2| = \frac{1}{k - 2s + m_1} \cdot |d|,$$

where

$$d = \sum_{\{i < \texttt{start} : T_i^1 \neq \bot\}} T_i^1 - \sum_{i \in M^1} T_i^2 + \sum_{\{\texttt{end} < i : T_i^1 \neq \bot\}} T_i^1 + \sum_{i \in M^2} T_i^1 - (m_1 - m_2) \cdot v_2. \quad (2)$$

In order to upper bound $|d|$, we find bounds for each of the summands.

Bounds for $\sum_{\{i < \texttt{start} : T_i^1 \neq \bot\}} T_i^1$. In this region, any summand T_i^1 satisfies: $a = \min\{T_i^j \neq \bot\}_{j \in \{1,2\}} \leq T_i^1 \leq A_{\texttt{start}}$.

Within this region of indices, the first $s - m_1$ indices have $\bot$ as their value (by construction of T^1). Therefore, the number of summands is

$$|\{i < \texttt{start} : T_i^1 \neq \bot\}| = \texttt{start} - (s - m_1) - l = (m_1 - m_2 - l),$$

where $l = |\{s - m_1 \leq i < \texttt{start} : T_i^1 = \bot\}|$.

Therefore, we have:

$$(m_1 - m_2 - l) \cdot a \leq \sum_{\{i < \text{start}: T_i^1 \neq \perp\}} T_i^1 \leq (m_1 - m_2 - l) \cdot A_{\text{start}}. \qquad (3)$$

Bounds for $\sum_{\{\text{end} < i: T_i^1 \neq \perp\}} T_i^1$. Similarly, in this region, any summand T_i^1 satisfies $A_{\text{end}} \leq T_i^1 \leq \max\{T_i^j \neq \perp\}_{j \in \{1,2\}} = b$.
Since the last $s - m_1$ indices have $\perp$ as their value:

$$|\{\text{end} < i : T_i^1 \neq \perp\}| = k - (s - m_1) - 1 - \text{end} - h = m_1 - m_2 - h,$$

where $h = |\{\text{end} < i \leq k - (s - m_1) - 1 : T_i^1 = \perp\}|$.
Therefore, we have:

$$(m_1 - m_2 - h) \cdot A_{\text{end}} \leq \sum_{\{\text{end} < i: T_i^1 \neq \perp\}} T_i^1 \leq (m_1 - m_2 - h) \cdot b. \qquad (4)$$

Bounds for $\sum_{i \in M^1} T_i^2$. From the definition of M^1, any index $i \in M^1$ satisfies $\text{start} \leq i \leq \text{end}$. Moreover, any summand T_i^2, $i \in M^1$, satisfies that $A_{\text{start}} \leq T_i^2 \leq A_{\text{end}}$.
By construction of T_i^1, we have that $|\{T_i^1 = \perp : s - m_1 \leq i \leq k - (s - m_1) - 1\}| = m_1$. This is because T^1 has $2(s - m_1) + m_1$ indices with $\perp$ in total, including the lowest and highest $s - m_1$ indices.
It follows that $|\{\text{start} \leq i \leq \text{end} : T_i^1 = \perp\}| = m_1 - l - h$.
Then, $|M^1| = |\{\text{start} \leq i \leq \text{end} : T_i^1 = \perp\}| - c = m_1 - l - h - c$, where c is the number of indices $\text{start} \leq i \leq \text{end}$ such that $T_i^1 = T_i^2 = \perp$. We obtain that

$$(m_1 - l - h - c) \cdot A_{\text{start}} \leq \sum_{i \in M^1} T_i^2 \leq (m_1 - l - h - c) \cdot A_{\text{end}}. \qquad (5)$$

Bounds for $\sum_{i \in M^2} T_i^1$. The bounds are derived similarly as in the previous case. Any index $i \in M^2$ satisfies $\text{start} \leq i \leq \text{end}$, and any summand T_i^1, $i \in M^2$, satisfies that $A_{\text{start}} \leq T_i^1 \leq A_{\text{end}}$.
By construction of T_i^2, we have that $|\{T_i^2 = \perp : \text{start} \leq i \leq \text{end}\}| = m_2$. Then, $|M^2| = |\{\text{start} \leq i \leq \text{end} : T_i^2 = \perp\}| - c = m_2 - c$, where c is the number of indices $\text{start} \leq i \leq \text{end}$ such that $T_i^1 = T_i^2 = \perp$. We obtain that

$$(m_2 - c) \cdot A_{\text{start}} \leq \sum_{i \in M^2} T_i^1 \leq (m_2 - c) \cdot A_{\text{end}}. \qquad (6)$$

Bounds for $(m_1 - m_2) \cdot v_2$. Since v_2 is the average of the non-$\perp$ values in T^2, $A_{\text{start}} \leq \min\{T_i^2 \neq \perp\} \leq v_2 \leq \max\{T_i^2 \neq \perp\} \leq A_{\text{end}}$. Then, we have

$$(m_1 - m_2) \cdot A_{\text{start}} \leq (m_1 - m_2) \cdot v_2 \leq (m_1 - m_2) \cdot A_{\text{end}}. \qquad (7)$$

Upper Bounding $|d|$. In order to upper bound $|d|$, we distinguish two cases.

- $v_1 \geq v_2$. Here, $|d| = d$. By using the inequalities (3) to (7) in Eq. (2) and simplifying the terms, we obtain that:

$$|d| \leq c \cdot (A_{\mathtt{start}} - A_{\mathtt{end}}) + m_2 \cdot (A_{\mathtt{end}} - b)$$
$$+ h \cdot (A_{\mathtt{start}} - b) + m_1 \cdot (b - A_{\mathtt{start}}) \leq m_1 \cdot (b - a),$$

where in the last inequality we used that $c, h, m_1, m_2 \geq 0$ and $a \leq A_{\mathtt{start}} \leq A_{\mathtt{end}} \leq b$.

- $v_1 \leq v_2$. In this case, $|d| = -d$. By using the inequalities (3) to (7) in Eq. (2) and simplifying the terms, we obtain that:

$$|d| \leq c \cdot (A_{\mathtt{start}} - A_{\mathtt{end}}) + l \cdot (a - A_{\mathtt{end}}) +$$
$$m_2 \cdot (a - A_{\mathtt{start}}) + m_1 \cdot (A_{\mathtt{end}} - a) \leq m_1 \cdot (b - a),$$

where in the last inequality we used that $c, l, m_1, m_2 \geq 0$ and $a \leq A_{\mathtt{start}} \leq A_{\mathtt{end}} \leq b$.

It follows that $|d| \leq m_1 \cdot (b - a)$, and therefore $|v_1 - v_2| \leq \frac{m_1}{k - 2s + m_1} \cdot (b - a)$, which concludes the proof.

7   Putting It All Together

By instantiating the Proxcensus protocol from Theorem 3 in the Expand-and-Extract iteration paradigm from Theorem 1, we achieve the desired result.

Theorem 4. *Let $\epsilon > 0$ be a constant. Assuming a PKI infrastructure and an ideal 1-round Coin-Flip protocol, there is a $(3r + 1)$-round Byzantine agreement protocol that achieves agreement except with probability at most $\left[\lfloor \frac{1}{2} \left(\frac{2\epsilon}{1-\epsilon} r \right)^r \rfloor \right]^{-1}$ and is resilient against $t = (1 - \epsilon)n/2$ corruptions, for any $r \geq \frac{1-\epsilon}{\epsilon}$.*

Note that one can instantiate the 1-round ideal coin-flip from a trusted setup of unique threshold signatures (see [CKS05, LJY14]).

7.1   Comparison to Previous Protocols

We add a comparison to previous protocols in Fig. 4 for our setting with an ideal 1-round Coin-Flip. Our protocol achieves a lower failure probability when the number of honest parties is high. We therefore depict how the failure probability decreases with the number of rounds in three regimes: $t < n/10$, $t < n/3$ and $t = 0.49n$. In each of the regimes, we compare our protocol with the two more efficient known protocols.

Our figures show that in the regimes $t < n/10$ and $t < n/3$, our protocol achieves a lower failure probability than the previous protocols [FM97] and [FLL21] after a few tens of rounds. Concretely, after 6 (resp. 27) rounds compared to [FLL21], and 4 (resp. 13) rounds compared to [FM97]. On the other hand, when $t = 0.49n$, our protocol achieves a lower failure probability only after more than 200 rounds, compared to previous solutions [MV17, FLL21].

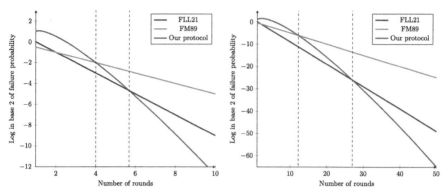

(a) $t < n/10$: The failure probability of our protocol becomes lower than that of [FM97] after 4 rounds, and lower than that of [FLL21] after 6 rounds.

(b) $t < n/3$: The failure probability of our protocol becomes lower than that of [FM97] after 13 rounds, and lower than that of [FLL21] after 27 rounds.

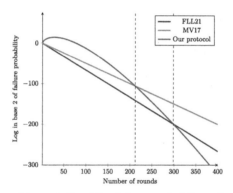

(c) $t = 0.49n$: The failure probability of our protocol becomes lower than that of [MV17] after 212 rounds, and lower than that of [FLL21] after 299 rounds.

Fig. 4. Comparison to previous protocols.

7.2 Open Problems

Our results leave a number of very exciting open problems.

Improving Constants. We leave open whether one can get similar results for the optimal threshold $t < n/2$. In a similar direction, our protocol is optimal *up to constants*, i.e. it achieves the optimal agreement probability for an r-round protocol within $c \cdot r$ rounds for some constant c. It would be interesting to see whether one can match the exact constants obtained from the known lower bounds.

Setup Assumptions. Another exciting direction would be to see whether similar results can be achieved from weaker setup assumptions. In particular, it would be interesting to see whether one can instantiate an ideal common-coin from plain PKI, or even with specific number-theoretic assumptions, within a constant (or even linear in r) number of rounds.

Early Termination. Finally, another interesting open question is to investigate whether one can leverage our protocols to achieve *early termination*. That is, a protocol that in expectation terminates in a constant number of rounds, but in the worst case it still achieves the optimal agreement probability.

Communication Complexity. Our protocol incurs a communication complexity of $O(n^4(\kappa + r \log(r)))$ bits, where κ is the size of a signature and r is the number of rounds. Using threshold signatures for the (conditional) graded broadcast primitive, we can save a linear factor n. It remains open to explore solutions with improved communication.

References

[AC10]   Attiya, H., Censor-Hillel, K.: Lower bounds for randomized consensus under a weak adversary. SIAM J. Comput. **39**(8), 3885–3904 (2010)

[ADD+19]   Abraham, I., Devadas, S., Dolev, D., Nayak, K., Ren, L.: Synchronous byzantine agreement with expected $O(1)$ rounds, expected $O(n^2)$ communication, and optimal resilience. In: Goldberg, I., Moore, T. (eds.) FC 2019. LNCS, vol. 11598, pp. 320–334. Springer, Cham (2019). https://doi.org/10.1007/978-3-030-32101-7_20

[BCG21]   Boyle, E., Cohen, R., Goel, A.: Breaking the $O(\sqrt{n})$-bit barrier: Byzantine agreement with polylog bits per party. In: Proceedings of the 2021 ACM Symposium on Principles of Distributed Computing, PODC 2021, pp. 319–330. Association for Computing Machinery, New York (2021)

[Ben83]   Ben-Or, M.: Another advantage of free choice: completely asynchronous agreement protocols (extended abstract). In: Probert, R.L., Lynch, N.A., Santoro, N. (eds.) 2nd ACM PODC, pp. 27–30. ACM, August 1983

[CCGZ16]   Cohen, R., Coretti, S., Garay, J., Zikas, V.: Probabilistic termination and composability of cryptographic protocols. In: Robshaw, M., Katz, J. (eds.) CRYPTO 2016, Part III. LNCS, vol. 9816, pp. 240–269. Springer, Heidelberg (2016). https://doi.org/10.1007/978-3-662-53015-3_9

[CCGZ17]   Cohen, R., Coretti, S., Garay, J.A., Zikas, V.: Round-preserving parallel composition of probabilistic-termination cryptographic protocols. In: Chatzigiannakis, I., Indyk, P., Kuhn, F., Muscholl, A. (eds.) ICALP 2017. LIPIcs, vol. 80, pp. 37:1–37:15. Schloss Dagstuhl, July 2017

[CFF+05]   Considine, J., Fitzi, M., Franklin, M.K., Levin, L.A., Maurer, U.M., Metcalf, D.: Byzantine agreement given partial broadcast. J. Cryptol. **18**(3), 191–217 (2005)

[CHM+19] Cohen, R., Haitner, I., Makriyannis, N., Orland, M., Samorodnitsky, A.: On the round complexity of randomized Byzantine agreement. In: Suomela, J. (ed.) 33rd International Symposium on Distributed Computing (DISC 2019). Leibniz International Proceedings in Informatics (LIPIcs), vol. 146, pp. 12:1–12:17. Schloss Dagstuhl-Leibniz-Zentrum fuer Informatik, Dagstuhl, Germany (2019)

[CKS05] Cachin, C., Kursawe, K., Shoup, V.: Random oracles in constantinople: practical asynchronous Byzantine agreement using cryptography. J. Cryptol. 18(3), 219–246 (2005)

[CL99] Castro, M., Liskov, B.: Practical Byzantine fault tolerance. In: OSDI, vol. 99, pp. 173–186 (1999)

[CM19] Chen, J., Micali, S.: Algorand: a secure and efficient distributed ledger. Theoret. Comput. Sci. 777, 155–183 (2019)

[CMS89] Chor, B., Merritt, M., Shmoys, D.B.: Simple constant-time consensus protocols in realistic failure models. J. ACM (JACM) 36(3), 591–614 (1989)

[CPS19] Hubert Chan, T.-H., Pass, R., Shi, E.: Round complexity of Byzantine agreement, revisited. Cryptology ePrint Archive, Report 2019/886 (2019). https://ia.cr/2019/886

[CPS20] Chan, T.-H.H., Pass, R., Shi, E.: Sublinear-round Byzantine agreement under corrupt majority. In: Kiayias, A., Kohlweiss, M., Wallden, P., Zikas, V. (eds.) PKC 2020, Part II. LNCS, vol. 12111, pp. 246–265. Springer, Cham (2020). https://doi.org/10.1007/978-3-030-45388-6_9

[DS83] Dolev, D., Raymond Strong, H.: Authenticated algorithms for Byzantine agreement. SIAM J. Comput. 12(4), 656–666 (1983)

[FG03] Fitzi, M., Garay, J.A.: Efficient player-optimal protocols for strong and differential consensus. In: Borowsky, E., Rajsbaum, S. (eds.) 22nd ACM PODC, pp. 211–220. ACM, July 2003

[Fit03] Fitzi, M.: Generalized Communication and Security Models in Byzantine Agreement. Ph.D. thesis, ETH Zurich, 3 2003. Reprint as, vol. 4 of ETH Series in Information Security and Cryptography, ISBN 3-89649-853-3, Hartung-Gorre Verlag, Konstanz (2003)

[FLL21] Fitzi, M., Liu-Zhang, C.-D., Loss, J.: A new way to achieve round-efficient Byzantine agreement. In: Proceedings of the 2021 ACM Symposium on Principles of Distributed Computing, PODC 2021, pp. 355–362. Association for Computing Machinery, New York (2021)

[FM97] Feldman, P., Micali, S.: An optimal probabilistic protocol for synchronous Byzantine agreement. SIAM J. Comput. 26(4), 873–933 (1997)

[FN09] Fitzi, M., Nielsen, J.B.: On the number of synchronous rounds sufficient for authenticated byzantine agreement. In: Keidar, I. (ed.) DISC 2009. LNCS, vol. 5805, pp. 449–463. Springer, Heidelberg (2009). https://doi.org/10.1007/978-3-642-04355-0_46

[GKKO07] Garay, J.A., Katz, J., Koo, C.-Y., Ostrovsky, R.: Round complexity of authenticated broadcast with a dishonest majority. In: 48th FOCS, pp. 658–668. IEEE Computer Society Press, October 2007

[KK06] Katz, J., Koo, C.-Y.: On expected constant-round protocols for Byzantine agreement. In: Dwork, C. (ed.) CRYPTO 2006. LNCS, vol. 4117, pp. 445–462. Springer, Heidelberg (2006). https://doi.org/10.1007/11818175_27

[KY84]   Karlin, A.R., Yao, A.C.: Probabilistic lower bounds for Byzantine agreement and clock synchronization (1984)

[LJY14] Libert, B., Joye, M., Yung, M.: Born and raised distributively: fully distributed non-interactive adaptively-secure threshold signatures with short shares. In: Halldórsson, M.M., Dolev, S. (eds.) 33rd ACM PODC, pp. 303–312. ACM, July 2014

[LLR06] Lindell, Y., Lysyanskaya, A., Rabin, T.: On the composition of authenticated Byzantine agreement. J. ACM (JACM) **53**(6), 881–917 (2006)

[LSP82] Lamport, L., Shostak, R., Pease, M.: The Byzantine generals problem. ACM Trans. Program. Lang. Syst. **4**(3), 382–401 (1982)

[MV17]   Micali, S., Vaikuntanathan, V.: Optimal and player-replaceable consensus with an honest majority (2017)

[PW96]   Pfitzmann, B., Waidner, M.: Information-theoretic pseudo signatures and Byzantine agreement for $t \geq n/3$. IBM (1996)

[Rab83] Rabin, M.O.: Randomized Byzantine generals. In: 24th FOCS, pp. 403–409. IEEE Computer Society Press, November 1983

[TC84]   Turpin, R., Coan, B.A.: Extending binary Byzantine agreement to multivalued Byzantine agreement. Inf. Process. Lett. **18**(2), 73–76 (1984)

[WXDS20] Wan, J., Xiao, H., Devadas, S., Shi, E.: Round-efficient byzantine broadcast under strongly adaptive and majority corruptions. In: Pass, R., Pietrzak, K. (eds.) TCC 2020, Part I. LNCS, vol. 12550, pp. 412–456. Springer, Cham (2020). https://doi.org/10.1007/978-3-030-64375-1_15

[WXSD20] Wan, J., Xiao, H., Shi, E., Devadas, S.: Expected constant round byzantine broadcast under dishonest majority. In: Pass, R., Pietrzak, K. (eds.) TCC 2020, Part I. LNCS, vol. 12550, pp. 381–411. Springer, Cham (2020). https://doi.org/10.1007/978-3-030-64375-1_14

A Complete Characterization
of Game-Theoretically Fair, Multi-Party
Coin Toss

Ke Wu[1](✉)(iD), Gilad Asharov[2](✉)(iD), and Elaine Shi[1]

[1] Computer Science Department, Carnegie Mellon University, Pittsburgh, USA
kew2@andrew.cmu.edu
[2] Department of Computer Science, Bar-Ilan University, Ramat Gan, Israel
Gilad.Asharov@biu.ac.il

Abstract. Cleve's celebrated lower bound (STOC'86) showed that a *de facto* strong fairness notion is impossible in 2-party coin toss, i.e., the corrupt party always has a strategy of biasing the honest party's outcome by a noticeable amount. Nonetheless, Blum's famous coin-tossing protocol (CRYPTO'81) achieves a strictly weaker "game-theoretic" notion of fairness—specifically, it is a 2-party coin toss protocol in which neither party can bias the outcome *towards its own preference*; and thus the honest protocol forms a Nash equilibrium in which neither party would want to deviate. Surprisingly, an n-party analog of Blum's famous coin toss protocol was not studied till recently. The work by Chung et al. (TCC'18) was the first to explore the feasibility of game-theoretically fair n-party coin toss in the presence of corrupt majority. We may assume that each party has a publicly stated preference for either the bit 0 or 1, and if the outcome agrees with the party's preference, it obtains utility 1; else it obtains nothing.

A natural game-theoretic formulation is to require that the honest protocol form a coalition-resistant Nash equilibrium, i.e., no coalition should have incentive to deviate from the honest behavior. Chung et al. phrased this game-theoretic notion as "cooperative-strategy-proofness" or "CSP-fairness" for short. Unfortunately, Chung et al. showed that under $(n - 1)$-sized coalitions, it is impossible to design such a CSP-fair coin toss protocol, unless all parties except one prefer the same bit.

In this paper, we show that the impossibility of Chung et al. is in fact not as broad as it may seem. When coalitions are majority but not $n - 1$ in size, we can indeed get feasibility results in some meaningful parameter regimes. We give a complete characterization of the regime in which CSP-fair coin toss is possible, by providing a matching upper- and lower-bound. Our complete characterization theorem also shows that the mathematical structure of game-theoretic fairness is starkly different from the *de facto* strong fairness notion in the multi-party computation literature.

The author ordering is randomized. The full version of this paper is available at [38].

ⓒ International Association for Cryptologic Research 2022
O. Dunkelman and S. Dziembowski (Eds.): EUROCRYPT 2022, LNCS 13275, pp. 120–149, 2022.
https://doi.org/10.1007/978-3-031-06944-4_5

1   Introduction

Coin toss protocols, first proposed by Blum [9], are at the heart of cryptography and distributed computing. Imagine that Murphy and Mopey simultaneously solve the same long-standing open problem in cryptography, and they both submit a paper with identical results to EUROCRYPT'22. The program committee of EUROCRYPT'22 decide to recommend Murphy and Mopey to merge their papers. Now, Murphy and Mopey want to toss a coin to elect one of them to present the result at EUROCRYPT'22. How can Murphy and Mopey accomplish this task remotely? Clearly, we can use Blum's coin toss protocol. Murphy and Mopey each commit to a random bit, and post the commitment to a public bulletin board (e.g., a blockchain). They then each open their commitments. If the XOR of the two opened bits is 1, Murphy wins; else, Mopey wins. If either player aborts any time during the protocol or does not provide a valid opening for its commitment, it automatically forfeits and the other player wins. Although not explicitly stated in his ground-breaking paper [9], Blum's protocol actually achieves a natural, *game-theoretic* notion of fairness. Since both players want to get elected, we may assume that the winner obtains utility 1, and the loser obtains utility 0. Observe that a rational player who aims to maximize its utility has no incentive to deviate from the honest protocol. Any deviation (including aborting or opening the commitment wrongly) would cause it to lose.

Although this game-theoretic notion of fairness is very natural, it seems to have been overlooked in the subsequent long line of work on multi-party computation (MPC) [21,39,40]. Specifically, the MPC line of work instead switched to considering a *strictly* stronger notion of fairness henceforth called *unbiasability*. Unbiasability requires that an adversary controlling a corrupt coalition cannot bias the outcome of the coin toss whatsoever. Blum's protocol actually does not satisfy this strong, unbiasability notion: a player can indeed bias the outcome in Blum's protocol, although the bias would never be in its own favor. This unbiasability notion has been thoroughly explored in the cryptography literature. It is well-known that in general, if the majority of the players are honest, then unbiasability is indeed attainable [7,12,21,37]. On the other hand, the celebrated lower bound of Cleve [15] shows that if half or more of the players are corrupt, unbiasability is impossible—in particular, this lower bound applies to the two-party case where one party can be corrupt.

Despite Cleve's lower bound, the fact that Blum's protocol can achieve meaningful fairness in the two-party case is thought provoking. A natural question arises:

can we achieve game-theoretically fair coin toss in the multi-party setting in the presence of a majority coalition?

Somewhat surprisingly, this question was not explored till the very recent work of Chung et al. [14].

Imagine that each player has a publicly stated preference for either the bit 0 or 1. If the coin toss outcome agrees with the player's preference, it obtains utility 1; else it obtains nothing. This formulation can have interesting applications. For example, imagine that n parties in a blockchain protocol want to jointly elect a random block proposer among two possible candidates, and users have different preferences among the two depending on which one they are geographically closer to. Another example is where n investors who have invested money into a crowd-funding smart contract want to randomly choose a kick-starter to fund among two candidates, and each player may have a different preference in mind.

In many applications, the preference profiles are public. For example, suppose some blockchain community wants to randomly choose among two governance proposals. Here, the voters are public figures/community leaders whose affiliations, opinions, and past forum posts are publicly known. In general, when the voters' identities/reputations are known to the public and identities do not come for free, voters' preferences are usually public. Another example is games where players must put in stake to play. For example, suppose n players play binary roulette on a blockchain. Here, their preferences are made explicit by their public bets which they cannot lie about.

Chung et al. suggested the following natural formulations of game theoretic fairness for multi-party coin toss, both of which would equate to Blum's notion in the 2-party special case:

- **CSP-fairness:** *Cooperative-strategy-proofness* (or "CSP-fairness" for short) requires that no coalition can *increase* its own expected utility, *no matter how it deviates from the prescribed protocol*. In this way, the honest protocol forms a *coalition-resistant Nash equilibrium*, and no profit-seeking coalition of players would be incentivized to deviate from this equilibrium.
- **Maximin fairness:** Another natural notion is called *maximin fairness*, which requires that no coalition can *harm* any honest party (no matter how the coalition deviates from the prescribed protocol). More precisely, for any (computational) strategy adopted by a coalition of players, the expected utility of any honest party is at most negligibly apart from its utility in an all-honest execution. As motivated by Chung et al. [14], maximin fairness guarantees that no coalition aiming to monopolize the eco-system by harming and driving away small individual players has incentives to deviate; moreover, no defensive individual aiming to protect itself in the worst-case scenario has incentives to deviate.

Unfortunately, Chung et al. [14] showed very broad lower bounds which seem to crush our original hope of using game-theoretic fairness to circumvent Cleve's impossibility [15] in the corrupt majority setting. Specifically, Chung et al. proved that unless all parties except one have the same preference, it would be impossible to realize either CSP-fair coin toss or maximin-fair coin toss.

1.1   Our Results and Contributions

It may seem that Chung et al.'s results have put a pessimistic closure to this direction. However, upon more careful examination, their lower bound proofs implicitly assume that all but one parties can be corrupt and form a coalition.

It is not immediately clear whether the impossibility would still hold if majority but not $n - 1$ parties are corrupt. We therefore revisit the question originally posed by Chung et al., i.e., whether one can rely on game-theoretic fairness to overcome Cleve's impossibility for coin toss protocols in the corrupt majority setting. Specifically, we focus on the following refinement of the question:

Can we achieve game-theoretically fair coin toss under for majority but not necessarily $(n - 1)$-sized coalitions?

In this paper, we give a complete characterization of the landscape of game-theoretically fair coin toss, including for the CSP-fair and the maximin-fair notions. At a very high level, we show the following results:

- For CSP-fairness, the pessimistic view of Chung et al. [14] poorly reflects the actual state of affairs. In contrast, we show that under a broad range of parameter regimes, CSP-fairness is possible in the presence of a majority coalition; moreover, we give a complete characterization of the parameter regimes under which CSP-fairness is possible.
- For maximin-fairness, we show that the pessimistic view of Chung et al. indeed applies quite broadly. Roughly speaking, we show that except for the cases when all parties but one prefer the same outcome, or when exactly half of the players are corrupt, maximin-fairness is impossible to attain. We fully characterize maximin fairness as well.

Note that in cases when there is an honest individual with an opposite preference as the coalition, maximin-fairness would directly imply CSP-fairness. This partly explains why maximin-fairness is harder to attain than CSP-fairness.

Our work sheds new light on the intriguing mathematical structure of game-theoretic fairness, which differs fundamentally from the mathematical structure of the *de facto* unbiasability notion that is widely adopted in the cryptography literature. Since coin toss protocols [9] have been the cornerstone of the long line of work on multi-party computation protocols, we hope that our work can inspire future work in the exciting space of "game theory meets multi-party protocols" in general. We now give more formal statements of our results.

CSP Fairness. For CSP fairness, we design a new protocol and explore for which range of parameters the upper bound holds. In addition, we generalize the lower bound proof of Chung et al. [14], and give the range of parameters in which impossibility holds. Our upper- and lower-bounds tightly match in their stated parameter regimes. Therefore, our two main results jointly provide a complete characterization of CSP fairness. It is worth noting that our upper bound holds in the presence of a *malicious* coalition that may deviate from the prescribed protocol arbitrarily to increase its own gain; whereas our lower bound holds for a *fail-stop* coalition whose only possible deviation is to have some of its players abort from the protocol. This makes both the upper- and lower-bound stronger.

Our results can be summarized with the following theorem statements— below, let n_0 be the number of players that prefer 0 (also called 0-supporters), and let n_1 be the number of players that prefer 1 (also called 1-supporters). Throughout the paper, *without loss of generality, we may assume that $n_1 \geq n_0 \geq$ 1* since the other direction is symmetric. Additionally, we assume $n_0 + n_1 > 2$, since for 2-parties, we can just run Blum's coin toss.

Theorem 1.1 (Upper bound). *Assume the existence of Oblivious Transfer (OT), and without loss of generality, assume that $n_1 \geq n_0 \geq 1$, and $n_0 + n_1 > 2$. There exists a CSP-fair coin toss protocol which tolerates up to t-sized non-uniform p.p.t. coalitions where*

$$t := \begin{cases} n_1 - \lfloor \frac{1}{2} n_0 \rfloor, & \text{if } n_1 \geq \frac{5}{2} n_0; \\ \lfloor \frac{2}{3} n_1 - \frac{1}{6} n_0 \rfloor + \lceil \frac{1}{2} n_0 \rceil + 1 = n_1 + 1, & \text{if } n_1 = n_0 = \text{odd}; \\ \lfloor \frac{2}{3} n_1 - \frac{1}{6} n_0 \rfloor + \lceil \frac{1}{2} n_0 \rceil, & \text{otherwise.} \end{cases} \tag{1}$$

Our upper bound holds even when the coalition may deviate arbitrarily from the prescribed protocol to increase its gain.

Theorem 1.2 (Lower bound). *Without loss of generality, assume that $n_1 \geq n_0 \geq 1$ and $n_0 + n_1 > 2$. There does not exist a CSP-fair n-party coin toss which tolerates coalitions of size $t + 1$ or greater where t is same as Eq. (1).*

Further, this lower bound holds even for fail-stop coalitions whose only possible deviations are aborting from the honest protocol, and it holds even allowing computational hardness assumptions and restricting the coalition to be computationally bounded.

Previously, the work of [14] shows possibility only for the case where where $n_0 = 1$ or $n_1 = 1$ and $t = n_0 + n_1 - 1$. Moreover, it showed that it is impossible to tolerate $n_0 + n_1 - 1$ corruptions only for the case where both $n_0, n_1 \geq 2$ (i.e., there are at least two parties among the set of 0-supporters and at least two parties among the set of 1-supporters).

Observe that the optimal resilience parameter t (specified in Eq. (1)) is a function of n_0 and n_1. Intriguingly, its dependence as a function of n_0 and n_1 changes when $n_1 = \frac{5}{2} n_0$. This intriguing *phase transition* partly suggests that *the mathematical structure of game theoretic fairness is starkly different the classical notion of unbiasability.* The reason for this phase transition is related to the concrete techniques we adopt to prove our theorems. We will explain why this phase transition occurs as we describe our protocol to help the reader gain intuition (see Remark 2.4 of Sect. 2.1 for more explanations). Note also that the transition has a continuous boundary, i.e., at exactly $n_1 = \frac{5}{2} n_0$, the two expressions $n_1 - \lfloor \frac{1}{2} n_0 \rfloor$ and $\lfloor \frac{2}{3} n_1 - \frac{1}{6} n_0 \rfloor + \lceil \frac{1}{2} n_0 \rceil$ are equal (to $2n_0$).

Maximin Fairness. The work of [14] shows that maximin fairness is possible against $t \leq n - 1$ corruptions only when all but one of the parties are interested in the same outcome. We next show that this is essentially the only interesting setting which does not behave as in the crypto settings. We show that even when allowing a more liberate security threshold, we cannot push the barriers much further than relying on an honest majority. We show the following possibility and its complementary impossibility result:

Theorem 1.3. *Without loss of generality, assume that the number of 1-supporters n_1 is at least the number of 0-supporters, n_0, and assume that $n_0 + n_1 > 2$. Then:*

- *For $n_0 \geq 2$, there does not exist a maximin-fair n-party coin toss protocol which tolerates more than $\lceil \frac{1}{2}(n_0 + n_1) \rceil$ number of fail-stop adversaries. Moreover, there exists a (statistically-secure) maximin-fair n-party coin toss protocol which tolerates up to $\lceil \frac{1}{2}(n_0 + n_1) \rceil - 1$ malicious corruptions.*
- *For the special case where $n_0 = 1$, we show that there does not exist a maximin-fair n party coin toss protocol which tolerates more than $\lceil \frac{1}{2}n_1 \rceil + 1$ number of (semi-malicious) players. Assuming Oblivious Transfer, there exists a maximin fair-coin tossing protocol tolerating up to $\lceil \frac{1}{2}n_1 \rceil$ malicious corruptions.*

Public Verifiability. Our positive results are achieved in a model that allowed *public verifiability*. In particular, the output of the protocol can be computed from messages that were sent over the broadcast medium (e.g., a public blockchain), and therefore also external *observers*, i.e., parties that do not take part of the computation, can also learn the output. Such public verifiability is often needed in blockchain and decentralized smart contract applications.

1.2 Related Work

Game Theory Meets Cryptography. Although game theory [27,33] and multi-party computation [21,39] originated from different academic communities, some recent efforts have investigated the connections of the two areas (e.g., see the excellent surveys by Katz [28] and by Dodis and Rabin [17]). At a high level, this line of work focuses on two broad classes of questions.

First, a line of works [1,3,5,24,29,34] explored how to define game-theoretic notions of security (as opposed to cryptography-style security notions) for distributed computing tasks such as secret sharing and secure function evaluation. Earlier works in this space considered *a different notion of utility* than our work. Utility functions are often defined with the following assumptions regarding players' perference: players prefer to compute the function correctly; they prefer to learn others' secret data, and prefer that other players do not learn their own secrets. In light of such utility functions, earlier works in this space explored whether we can design protocols such that rational players will be incentivized to follow the honest protocol. Inspired by this line of work, Garay et al. propose a new paradigm called Rational Protocol Design (RPD) [19], and this paradigm was developed further in several subsequent works [18,20] (we will comment on the relationship of our notion and RPD shortly).

Second, another central question is how cryptography can help traditional game theory. Classical works in game theory [27,33] assumed the existence of a trusted mediator. Therefore, recent works considered how to realize this trusted mediator using cryptography [6,16,23,26].

It is well-understood that the notion of Nash equilibrium may predict unstable outcomes since it may rely on empty threats. Our CSP notion adopts the (coalition-resistant) Nash equilibrium paradigm and therefore it does not eliminate the issue of empty threats. In other words, for a CSP-fair protocol, it could be that a player threatens to deviate from the honest protocol (possibly at a harm to itself), making other players reconsider their strategies too. A couple works proposed new notions in the context of computationally bounded agents, aiming to eliminate empty threats. Gradwohl, Livne and Rosen [22] suggested a notion called computational threat-free Nash equilibrium, which can be viewed as a relaxation of the classical notion of subgame perfect equilibrium for computationally bounded agents. This work does not consider coalition resistance. Pass and shelat [35] suggest a new notion called renegotiation-safe equilibrium, which they show to be incomparable to Nash equilibrium. Their work captures some notion of coalition resistance in the sense that coalitions do not want to renegotiate to strategies that are themselves resilient to future renegotiations. Our protocol is not a threat-free Nash/renegotiation safe under the same resilience parameter—it is interesting to study what resilience parameters our protocol can tolerate under these notions. In fact, Threat-Free Nash and Renegotiation Safety have not been explored in a coalition setting before. It would also be an interesting future direction to explore the (in)feasiblity of threat-free or renegotiation-safe notions in the context of multi-party coin toss.

Recent Efforts. More recently, there has been renewed interest in the connection of game theory and cryptography, partly due to the success of decentralized blockchains. Besides the work of Chung et al. [14] which provided direct inspiration of our work, the recent work of Chung, Chan, Wen, and Shi [13] suggested an alternative formulation of game-theoretically fair multi-party coin toss. Specifically, they consider the task of electing a leader among n players, where everyone is competing to get elected. Therefore, if a user gets elected, its utility is 1, else its utility is 0. Their formulation can be viewed as tossing an n-way dice whereas our formulation and that of Chung et al. consider a binary coin. Intriguingly, for the leader election formulation, it is indeed possible to achieve CSP-fairness under any number of corruptions, and thus Chung et al. [13] focus on understanding the round complexity of such protocols. Chung et al. also explore how to define *approximate* notions of game-theoretic fairness in a distributed protocol context, and they point out that further subtleties exist in defining an *approximate* notion, and thus they suggest new notions called sequential CSP fairness and sequential maximin fairness. These technicalities only pertain to approximate notions with non-negligible slack, and are *not* relevant for us since we consider (1-negligible)-fairness.

Other recent works, also inspired by blockchain applications, consider a financial fairness notion through the use of collateral and penalities [2,8,30–32]. In comparison, the protocols in this paper can ensure game theoretic fairness even *without* the use of collateral or penalties if applied in blockchain contexts.

Relationship to RPD. Chung, Chan, Wen, and Shi [13] also show a connection between their approximate game-theoretic notion and the elegant RPD notion by Garay et al. [18–20]. The same connection also applies to our notion. More specifically, the RPD framework models a meta-game, i.e., a Stackelberg game between the protocol designer and an attacker: the designer first picks a protocol Π, then the attacker can decide which coalition to corrupt and its strategy after examining this protocol Π. They want a solution concept that achieves a subgame perfect equilibrium in this Stackelberg meta-game, but consider classical-style utility functions related to breaking privacy or correctness. Essentially, Chung et al. [13] showed that the CSP-fairness notion can be an equivalent interpretation in the RPD framework if we alter their utility notion accordingly to match our notion. We refer the readers to Chung et al. [13] for a detailed statement and proof of this equivalence.

Other Related Works. Finally, we can also circumvent Cleve's impossibility of strongly fair (i.e., unbiasable) coin toss under corrupt majority by introducing a trusted setup, or introducing non-standard cryptographic assumptions such as Verifiable Delay Functions [10,11]. In this paper, we focus on *the plain model without trusted setup, without any common reference string (CRS), and standard cryptographic hardness assumptions.*

2 Technical Overview

2.1 Upper Bound

Glimpse of Hope. In light of the pessimistic view of Chung et al. [14], we start with a relatively simple protocol that gives us a glimpse of hope. As a special case, consider the scenario when $n_0 = n_1 = 2$—recall that for $b \in \{0,1\}$, n_b denotes the number of players that prefer b (also called b-supporters). In this case, there is a very simple protocol that achieves CSP-fairness against any coalition of at most 2 players. Imagine that we elect one 0-supporter and one 1-supporter arbitrarily as two representatives each preferring 0 and 1, respectively. We now have the two representatives duel with each other using Blum's coin toss, where if the b-supports aborts then the protocol outputs $1 - b$ for $b \in \{0,1\}$. A simple argument proves that this protocol satisfies CSP-fairness:

- If a coalition controls only 1 player, it makes no sense to deviate whether or not the corrupt player is elected representative.
- If the coalition controls 2 players with opposing preferences, then the coalition is indifferent to the outcome and has no incentive to deviate.
- Finally, if the coalition controls 2 players with the same preference, then one of the two will be elected as representative, and the representative should not have incentive to deviate (whereas the non-representative's behavior has no influence to the outcome).

This very simple teaser already shows that Chung et al. [14]'s impossibility proof does not hold when there is no $(n - 1)$-sized coalition. Moreover, it also shows that this notion is weaker than cryptographic fairness, as there is no honest majority and still there is a possibility result.

Warmup Protocol for a Semi-malicious Coalition. Unfortunately, the approach taken by the above teaser protocol for $n_0 = n_1 = 2$ does not easily generalize to larger choices of n_0 and n_1. We next give a warmup protocol that is somewhat more sophisticated, but it suggests a more general paradigm which inspires our final upper bound result. Chung et al. [14] gave a protocol against a coalition of size up to n_1 players for $n_0 = 1$, thus we only consider $n_0 \geq 2$ in our construction. For simplicity, we start with the *semi-malicious* model [4], i.e., the coalition is restricted to the following two types of deviations:

1. It can abort from the protocol in some round, after looking at the honest messages of that round. Moreover, once a player has aborted, it stops participating from that point on.
2. The coalition can choose its random coins to be used in each round after inspecting the honest messages of that round.

Besides these two possible deviations, the coalition would otherwise follow the protocol faithfully.

The HalfToss *Sub-protocol.* Consider the following sub-protocol called HalfToss$^b[k]$ where $b \in \{0, 1\}$, and k is a threshold parameter whose purpose will become clear shortly. At a very high level, the sub-protocol chooses a random coin for the group of players that invoke this sub-protocol. Later on, this HalfToss^b protocols will be executed twice: first among the 0-supporters and all the 1-supporters act as silent observers; and then among the 1-supporters where the 0-supporters act as silent observers. We use HalfToss^0 and HalfToss^1 to distinguish the two instances. Henceforth, let $\mathcal{P}_b \subset [n]$ denote the set of b supporters for $b \in \{0, 1\}$. The final coin would be the XOR of the coins of the two groups.

Protocol 2.1: HalfToss$^b[k]$ **sub-protocol (semi-malicious version)**

Sharing Phase.

1. Each b-supporter $i \in \mathcal{P}_b$ chooses a random bit coin$_i \xleftarrow{\$} \{0, 1\}$. It then uses $(k + 1)$-out-of-n Shamir secret sharing[3] to split the coin coin$_i$ into n_b shares, denoted $\{[\text{coin}_i]_j\}_{j \in \mathcal{P}_b}$, respectively. Player i then sends $[\text{coin}_i]_j$ to each player $j \in \mathcal{P}_b$ over a private channel.
2. If a b-supporter has not aborted, post a heartbeat message to the broadcast channel. At this moment, the *active set* $\mathcal{O}_b$ is defined to be the set of all b-supporters that indeed posted a heartbeat to the broadcast channel. Each player $i \in [\mathcal{P}_b]$ computes $s_i := \oplus_{j \in \mathcal{O}_b}[\text{coin}_j]_i$ where $[\text{coin}_j]_i$ is the share player i has received from player j.

Reconstruction Phase.

---

1. Every b-supporter $i \in \mathcal{P}_b$ posts the reconstruction message (i, s_i) to the broadcast channel.
2. If at least $k+1$ number of b-supporters posted a reconstruction message, then reconstruct the final secret s using Shamir secret sharing. Specifically, interpret each reconstruction message of the form (j, s_j) as jointly defining some polynomial f such that $f(j) = s_j$ and the reconstructed secret $s := f(0)$. Output s.
3. Else if fewer than $k + 1$ number of b-supporters posted a reconstruction message, output $\bot$.

Properties of the HalfToss *Sub-protocol.* The $\mathsf{HalfToss}^b[k]$ sub-protocol satisfies the following properties:

- *Binding.* The sharing phase uniquely defines a secret s, such that the reconstruction phase either succeeds and outputs s, or it fails and outputs $\bot$.
- *Knowledge threshold.* If at least $k+1$ number of b-supporters are corrupt, then the coalition can control the outcome of the coin toss. Specifically, during the sharing phase, the coalition will know the coin_i value for every honest i, and thus it can choose the coalition's coin values accordingly to program the outcome to its own liking.
  On the other hand, if at most k number of b-supporters are corrupt, then the coin value s that the sharing phase binds to is uniform and independent of the coalition's view in the sharing phase (i.e., the coalition is completely unaware of this random coin value).
- *Liveness threshold.* If the coalition controls at least $n_b - k_b$ number of b-supporters, it can cause the reconstruction to fail and output $\bot$.
  On the other hand, if the coalition controls fewer than $n_b - k$ number of b-supporters, then the reconstruction phase must succeed.

Our Warmup Protocol. Our warmup protocol makes use of two instances of the $\mathsf{HalfToss}^b$ sub-protocol among the 0-supporters and 1-supporters, respectively. The two instances are parametrized with the thresholds k_0 and k_1—we shall first describe the protocol leaving k_0 and k_1 unspecified, we then explain how to choose k_0 and k_1 to get CSP fairness.

Protocol 2.2: Warmup protocol with semi-malicious security

Sharing phase.

1. (0-supporters participate, 1-supporters observe). Run the sharing phase of $\mathsf{HalfToss}^0[k_0]$.
2. (1-supporters participate, 0-supporters observe). Run the sharing phase of $\mathsf{HalfToss}^1[k_1]$.

Reconstruction Phase.

---

[0] For concreteness, in $(k+1)$-out-of-n secret sharing, a subset of k parties learn nothing about the secret while each subset of $k + 1$ can reconstruct the secret.

1. (0-supporters participate, 1-supporters observe). Run the reconstruction phase of $\mathsf{HalfToss}^0[k_0]$, and let its outcome be s_0 if reconstruction is successful. In case the reconstruction outputs $\bot$, then let $s_0 := 0$.
2. (1-supporters participate, 0-supporters observe). Run the reconstruction phase of $\mathsf{HalfToss}^1[k_1]$. If the reconstruction phase outputs $\bot$, then output 0 as the final coin value. Else let s_1 be the reconstructed value, and output $s_0 + s_1$ as the final coin value.

Choosing the Thresholds k_0 and k_1. Suppose we want to have a CSP-fair protocol for coalitions of size at most t. Let t_0 and t_1 denote the number of corrupted 0-supporters and 1-supporters, respectively. Our idea is to choose the thresholds k_0 and k_1 in light of n_0, n_1, and t, such that the following conditions are satisfied (and recall that we assume without loss of generality that $n_1 \geq n_0$):

(C1) The coalition cannot control both coin values s_0 and s_1. That is, for either $b \in \{0, 1\}$, if the coalition controls at least $k_b + 1$ number of b-supporters, then because it is subject to the corruption budget t, the coalition must control at most k_{1-b} number of $(1 - b)$-supporters, such that the coin value s_{1-b} is uniform and independent of the coalition's view at the end of the sharing phase.

(C2) If the coalition can control the s_1 coin, i.e., it controls at least $k_1 + 1$ number of 1-supporters, then it cannot hamper the reconstruction of the coin s_0 due to the corruption budget. That is, the coalition must control at most $n_0 - k_0 - 1$ number of 0-supporters.

(C3) If the coalition controls at least $n_1 - k_1$ number of 1-supporters such that it can cause the reconstruction of s_1 to fail, then the coalition must prefer 1 or is indifferent to the outcome. In other words, denoting by t_b the number of corrupted b-supporters and letting $t_1 \geq n_1 - k_1$ then we have two cases: (a) if $n_1 - k_1 \geq n_0$, then this implies that the coalition prefers 1 (since $t_0 \leq n_0 \leq n_1 - k_1 \leq t_1$) and there is no new constraint; otherwise (b) if $n_1 - k_1 < n_0$, then we simply require that $t \leq 2t_1$. This implies that $t_0 \leq t_1$ (and the coalition prefers 1 or is indifferent) since $t = t_0 + t_1$.

If parameters k_0, k_1, t satisfy the following constraints, then they satisfy the above conditions.

Paramete Constraints 5.1 (semi-malicious version).
Assume: $0 \leq k_0 \leq n_0$, $0 \leq k_1 \leq n_1$

(C1) $t \leq k_0 + k_1 + 1$,
(C2) $t \leq k_1 + 1 + n_0 - k_0 - 1 = n_0 + k_1 - k_0$,
(C3) if $n_1 - k_1 < n_0$, then $t \leq 2(n_1 - k_1)$.

Given the above constraints and the parameters n_0, n_1, and t, if a feasible solution for k_0 and k_1 exists, the above warmup protocol (parametrized with the feasible solution k_0 and k_1) would be CSP-fair against t-sized coalitions. The reasoning is as follows.

- First, due to condition (C3), it never makes sense for the coalition to prevent the reconstruction of the s_1 coin (in which case 0 would be the declared output). If the coalition controls enough 1-supporters such that it is capable of failing the reconstruction of s_1, then it either prefers 1 or is indifferent.
- Henceforth we may assume that s_1 is successfully reconstructed. Now, due to condition (C1), there are two cases: 1) either the value of s_1 is uniform and independent of the coalition's view at the end of the sharing phase, or; 2) the coalition can control the value of s_1.

  In the former case, since the coin s_1 is assumed to be successfully reconstructed, the final outcome must be random. It is important that s_1 is reconstructed at the very end, after s_0 is reconstructed. Otherwise, this argument will not hold, since the coalition may examine the reconstructed s_1 value, and then decide whether to abort the reconstruction of s_0. In the latter case, due to conditions (C1) and (C2), it must be that s_0 is uniform and independent of the coalition's view at the end of the sharing phase, and moreover, the coalition cannot hamper the reconstruction of s_0. In this case, the final outcome $s_0 \oplus s_1$ must be random, too.

Optimal Resilience for the Warmup Protocol. Given n_0 and n_1, we may ask what is the optimal resilience for this warmup protocol? Solving for the optimal resilience is equivalent to solving for the maximum t such that there exists a feasible solution for k_0 and k_1 given the above constraints. It turns out that t is maximized under the following choices of k_0 and k_1, depending on n_0 and n_1 where $n_1 \geq n_0 \geq 1$:

Case	k_0	k_1	t
If $n_1 \geq \frac{5}{2}n_0$	$\lfloor \frac{n_0}{2} \rfloor$	$n_1 - n_0$	$n_1 - \lfloor \frac{1}{2}n_0 \rfloor$
Otherwise	$\lfloor \frac{n_0}{2} \rfloor$	$\lfloor \frac{2}{3}n_1 - \frac{1}{6}n_0 \rfloor$	$\lfloor \frac{2}{3}n_1 - \frac{1}{6}n_0 \rfloor + \lceil \frac{n_0}{2} \rceil$

Remark 2.4. *The intuition for the phase transition at $n_1 = \frac{5}{2}n_0$ follows from the implications of the different constraints. In particular, when $n_1 \geq \frac{5}{2}n_0$, then to corrupt a coalition that prefers 0, the adversary does not have to corrupt too many parties, and the conditions are easily satisfied. If the coalition prefers 1, then Condition (C3) does not add any constraint. In that case t is maximized subject to only the constraints corresponding to Condition (C1) and (C2). When $n_1 < \frac{5}{2}n_0$, then it is possible that a coalition corrupting majority parties prefers 0. Therefore, we need to maximize t under the three constraints corresponding to Condition (C1), (C2) and (C3).*

In Appendix A, we visualize the choice of t as a function of n_0 and n_1, to help understand the intriguing mathematical structure of game-theoretic fairness in multi-party coin toss.

A Corner Case of $n_0 = n_1 = odd$. It turns out that the above solution for t is optimal (even for semi-malicious coalitions) in light of our lower bound in Sect. 5, except for the corner case $n_0 = n_1 = odd$. This is because the above conditions (C1), (C2) and (C3) are slightly too stringent—in cases when the adversary corrupts exactly the same number of 0-supporters and 1-supporters, the coalition is actually indifferent (i.e., have no preference). In such cases, the coalition is allowed to bias the coin towards either direction, and therefore we do not need the above conditions to hold. Taking this corner case into account, we obtain that the number of corruptions that can be tolerated is:

Case	k_0	k_1	t
If $n_1 \geq \frac{5}{2}n_0$	$\lfloor \frac{n_0}{2} \rfloor$	$n_1 - n_0$	$n_1 - \lfloor \frac{1}{2}n_0 \rfloor$
If $n_1 = n_0 = $ odd	$\lfloor \frac{n_0}{2} \rfloor$	$\lfloor \frac{1}{2}n_1 \rfloor$	$n_1 + 1$
Otherwise	$\lfloor \frac{n_0}{2} \rfloor$	$\lfloor \frac{2}{3}n_1 - \frac{1}{6}n_0 \rfloor$	$\lfloor \frac{2}{3}n_1 - \frac{1}{6}n_0 \rfloor + \lceil \frac{n_0}{2} \rceil$

The final protocol against malicious coalition who may deviate arbitrarily from the prescribed protocol is described in Sect. 4.

2.2 Lower Bound

Our lower bound techniques are inspired by that of Chung et al. [14], who proved that there is no CSP-fair n-party coin toss protocol for $n \geq 3$ even against *fail-stop* coalitions, unless all parties except one prefer the same bit.

We may assume $n_1 \geq n_0 \geq 2$, since the corner cases where $n_0 = 1$ has already been treated by Chung et al. [14]. Our idea is to partition the players into three partitions denoted S_1, S_2, and S_3, respectively. We may assume that there is an ordering for the identities of all parties and that the preferences are public. Then:

- S_1 runs the code of the first α_0 number of 0-supporters, and the first α_1 number of 1-supporters.
- S_2 runs the code of the next $(n_0 - 2\alpha_0)$ number of 0-supports and the next $(n_1 - 2\alpha_1)$ number of 1 supporters.
- S_3 runs the code of the next (last) α_0 number of 0-supporters and the last α_1 number of 1-supporters.

This means that each party S_i internally emulates the execution of all parties it runs; all messages that are sent between theses parties are dealt internally by S_i and all messages that are sent between parties that are controlled by different S_i, S_j are sent as a message from S_i to S_j (with a clear labeling that states which message is intended to which internal party). The idea of the lower bound is to show that as long as α_0, α_1 and t satisfy a set of conditions defined with respect to n_0, n_1, then for any n-party protocol Π achieving CSP-fairness against any non-uniform fail-stop coalition of size t, its corresponding three-party coin-toss protocol must satisfy the following properties:

(LBC1) *Lone-wolf condition*: a fail-stop coalition controlling S_1 (or S_3) alone adopting any non-uniform p.p.t. strategy cannot bias the output towards *either* direction by a non-negligible amount.

(LBC2) *Wolf-minion condition*: a fail-stop coalition controlling S_1 and S_2 (or S_2 and S_3), adopting any non-uniform p.p.t. strategy, cannot bias the output towards 1 by a non-negligible amount.

(LBC3) T_2-*equity condition*: Consider an honest execution of the protocol conditioned on the fact that S_2 has its randomness fixed to T_2, and let $f(T_2)$ denote the expected outcome (where the probability is taken over S_1 and S_3's randomness). T_2-equity condition states that there exists a negligible function $\mathsf{negl}(\cdot)$ such that for all but $\mathsf{negl}(\lambda)$ fraction of T_2, $|f(T_2) - 1/2|$ is negligible.

We use Π to denote both the n-party CSP-fair protocol and the three-party coin toss protocol when the context is clear. The following generalized theorem is implicit in Chung et al. [14]'s lower bound proof—the full proof is available in the full version.

Theorem 2.5 (Generalized Theorem 21 of Chung et al. [14]). *There is no protocol Π among three super nodes S_1, S_2 and S_3 such that Π satisfies the above lone-wolf condition (LBC1), the wolf-minion condition (LBC2), and the T_2-equity condition (LBC3) simultaneously.*

If we can figure out the constraints that the parameters α_0, α_1 and t should satisfy, such that for any coin toss protocol among n_0 number of 0-supporters and n_1 number of 1-supporters that achieves CSP fairness against a coalition of size up to t, it's corresponding three-party coin toss protocol (after partition with respect to α_0 and α_1 as specified), must satisfy the lone-wolf condition (LBC1), the wolf-minion condition (LBC2), as well as the T_2 equity condition (LBC3) simultaneously. Then by Theorem 2.5, we can show that there is no coin toss protocol that can achieve CSP fairness against a coalition of size up to t. The constraint system is shown in Sect. 5 with proofs that the constraint system implies the three conditions.

3 Definitions

The Model. In an n-party coin toss protocol, n players interact through pairwise private channels as well as a public broadcast channel. We assume that all communication channels are authenticated, i.e., messages always carry the true sender's identity. Without loss of generality, we assume the players are numbered $1, 2, \ldots, n$, respectively. We assume that the network is synchronous and the protocol proceeds in rounds. Each player has a publicly stated preference for either the bit 0 or the bit 1. We call the vector of players' preferences as *the preference profile*, denoted as $\mathcal{P}$. At the end of the protocol, the coin toss outcome is defined as a deterministic, polynomial-time function over *the set of public messages posted to the broadcast channel*. The utility function that we consider is defined as follows:

The utility function: If the outcome agrees with a player's preference, the player obtains utility 1; else it obtains 0.

The utility of a coalition $A \subset [n]$ is the sum of the utilities of all coalition members.

The protocol execution is parametrized with a security parameter λ, and we may assume that n is polynomially bounded in λ. We assume that the coalition A (also called the *adversary*) may perform a *rushing* attack: in any round r, it can wait for honest players (i.e., those not in A) to send messages, and then decide what round-r messages the corrupt players in A want to send.

Correctness. We let $\sigma^* = (\sigma_1^*, \ldots, \sigma_n^*)$ denote the strategy (the code) of the all honest execution. That is, σ_i^* can be viewed as the code that party P_i is supposed to run according to the protocol specifications. We say that the protocol is *correct* if, unless all players have the same preference (in which case we can simply output the preferred bit with probability 1), the coin toss outcome is some fixed $b \in \{0,1\}$ with probability at most $1/2 \pm \mathsf{negl}(\lambda)$ for some negligible function $\mathsf{negl}(\cdot)$.

Notations. For a coalition $A \subset [n]$, we let U_A denote the utility of the coalition. We let $\sigma^* = (\sigma_1^*, \ldots, \sigma_n^*)$ denote the strategy (the code) of the all honest execution. For a coalition $A \subset [n]$, we denote by $U_A(\sigma_A, \sigma_{-A}^*)$ the expected utility of all members in A where the members of A follow some σ_A and the members that are not in A follow the honest strategy σ_{-A}^*. We denote by $U_A(\sigma_A^*, \sigma_{-A}^*)$ the expected utility of all members in A where all parties follow the honest strategy. All executions are considered with respect to some utility function and some public preference profile $\mathcal{P}$.

CSP Fairness. Recall that in CSP fairness we require that no coalition can increase its own expected utility no matter how it deviates from the prescribed strategy. This is formalized as follows:

Definition 3.1 (CSP-fairness [14]). *We say that a coin toss protocol σ^* satisfies* cooperative-strategy-proofness *(or CSP-fairness) against any for t-sized coalitions with respect to a preference profile $\mathcal{P}$, iff for all $A \subseteq [n]$ of cardinality at most t, any non-uniform probabilistic polynomial-time (p.p.t.) strategy σ_A' adopted by the coalition A, there is a negligible function $\mathsf{negl}(\cdot)$, such that[1]*

$$U_A(\sigma_A', \sigma_{-A}^*) \leq U_A(\sigma_A^*, \sigma_{-A}^*) + \mathsf{negl}(\lambda) .$$

---

[1] Like earlier works [1,3,5,14,18–20,24,29,34,36], our CSP-fair notion considers the deviation of *a single* coalition. Such a definitional approach is standard and dominant in the game theory literature, and the philosophical motivation is that the honest protocol would then become an *equilibrium* such that no coalition (of a certain size) would be incentivized deviate. In fact, many earlier works (including the standard Nash equilibrium notion) would even consider deviation of a single individual rather than a coalition.

Note that in this definition, if the coalition controls the same number of 0-supporters and 1-supporters, then we allow it to bias the output arbitrarily since it has no preference.

Maximin Fairness. Maximin fairness requires that no coalition can harm any honest party. This is formalized as follows:

Definition 3.2. *We say that a coin-toss protocol σ^* satisfies* maximin fairness *for t-sized coalitions with respect to a preference profile $\mathcal{P}$, iff for any p.p.t. adversary $\mathcal{A}$ controlling at most t parties, there exists a negligible function $\mathsf{negl}(\cdot)$ such that, in an execution of the protocol involving the adversary $\mathcal{A}$, the expected utility of any honest party i is at least $U_i(\sigma^*) - \mathsf{negl}(\lambda)$, where $U_i(\sigma^*)$ is the expected utility of party i in an honest execution of the protocol with respect to $\mathcal{P}$.*

4 Upper Bound

Our starting point is the warmup protocol for semi-malicious adversary, as presented in Sect. 2.1, which leads to the following optimal resilience:

Case	k_0	k_1	t
If $n_1 \geq \frac{5}{2} n_0$	$\lfloor \frac{n_0}{2} \rfloor$	$n_1 - n_0$	$n_1 - \lfloor \frac{1}{2} n_0 \rfloor$
Otherwise	$\lfloor \frac{n_0}{2} \rfloor$	$\lfloor \frac{2}{3} n_1 - \frac{1}{6} n_0 \rfloor$	$\lfloor \frac{2}{3} n_1 - \frac{1}{6} n_0 \rfloor + \lceil \frac{n_0}{2} \rceil$

A Corner Case of $n_0 = n_1 = odd$. It turns out that the above solution for t is optimal (even for semi-malicious coalitions) in light of our lower bound in Sect. 5, except for the corner case $n_0 = n_1 = odd$. This is because the above conditions (C1), (C2) and (C3) are slightly too stringent—in cases when the adversary corrupts exactly the same number of 0-supporters and 1-supporters, the coalition is actually indifferent (i.e., have no preference). In such cases, the coalition is allowed to bias the coin towards either direction, and therefore we do not need the above conditions to hold. Taking this corner case into account, we obtain that the number of corruptions that can be tolerated is:

Case	k_0	k_1	t
If $n_1 \geq \frac{5}{2} n_0$	$\lfloor \frac{n_0}{2} \rfloor$	$n_1 - n_0$	$n_1 - \lfloor \frac{1}{2} n_0 \rfloor$
If $n_1 = n_0 = odd$	$\lfloor \frac{n_0}{2} \rfloor$	$\lfloor \frac{1}{2} n_1 \rfloor$	$n_1 + 1$
Otherwise	$\lfloor \frac{n_0}{2} \rfloor$	$\lfloor \frac{2}{3} n_1 - \frac{1}{6} n_0 \rfloor$	$\lfloor \frac{2}{3} n_1 - \frac{1}{6} n_0 \rfloor + \lceil \frac{n_0}{2} \rceil$

Due to our lower bound in Sect. 5, the above resilience parameter is optimal for CSP fairness, even for semi-malicious corruptions.

4.1 Our Final Protocol for Malicious Coalitions

We now present our final construction ensures CSP-fairness against malicious coalitions that may deviate arbitrarily from the prescribed protocol.

Maliciously Secure HalfToss^b Sub-Protocol. To lift the warmup protocol to malicious security, the main challenge is how to realize a counterpart of the HalfToss^b protocol for the malicious corruption model. Recall that in the semi-malicious model, we relied on the players themselves to send heartbeats to identify which players have aborted. In this malicious model, we can no longer rely on such self-identification because players can lie. In a corrupt majority model, we also cannot easily take majority vote to determine who remains online and honest.

Our final solution relies on MPC with identifiable abort [21,25] which can be accomplished assuming the existence of Oblivious Transfer (OT). Recall that in MPC with identifiable abort, either the players successfully evaluate some ideal functionality, or if the protocol aborted, then all honest players receive the identity of an offending player. The idea is that the honest players can now kick out the offending player and retry, until the protocol succeeds in producing output.

Specifically, we will replace our earlier HalfToss^b[k] sub-protocol with the following maliciously secure counterpart, in which the b-supporters participate and the $(1-b)$-supporters observe.

Protocol 4.1: HalfToss^b[k] sub-protocol with malicious security

Sharing phase.

1. Initially, define the active set $\mathcal{O} := \mathcal{P}_b$. Repeat the following until success:
   (a) The active set $\mathcal{O}$ use MPC with identifiable abort to securely compute the ideal functionality $\mathcal{F}_{\text{sharegen}}^{b,\mathcal{O}}[k]$ to be described below (Functionality 4.2:).
   (b) If the protocol aborts, then every honest player obtains the identity of a corrupt player $j^* \in \mathcal{O}$. Remove j^* from $\mathcal{O}$.
2. At this moment, each player $i \in \mathcal{O}$ has obtained the tuple $(\mathsf{vk}, [s]_i, [r]_i, [\mathsf{com}]_i, \sigma_i, \sigma_i')$ from $\mathcal{F}_{\text{sharegen}}^{b,\mathcal{O}}[k]$.

Vote phase.

1. Each player posts vk to the broadcast channel — henceforth this is also called a vote for vk. Let vk' be the verification key that has gained the most number of votes, breaking ties arbitrarily.
2. If vk' has not gained at least $k + 1$ votes, declare that the vote phase failed and return. Else, if $\mathsf{vk}' = \mathsf{vk}$, then player i posts $[\mathsf{com}]_i$ and σ_i to the broadcast channel.
3. Everyone gathers all $([\mathsf{com}]_j, \sigma_j)$ pairs posted to the broadcast channel such that σ_j is a valid signature of $[\mathsf{com}]_j$ under vk'. If there are at least

$k + 1$ such tuples and all shares $[\text{com}]_j$ reconstruct uniquely to the value com, then record the reconstructed commitment com. Else we say that the vote phase failed.

Reconstruction phase.

1. If the vote phase failed, output the reconstructed value $\bot$. Else, continue with the following.
2. For each player $i \in \mathcal{O}$, if $\text{vk}' = \text{vk}$, then post to the broadcast channel the tuple $([s]_i, [r]_i, \sigma_i')$.
3. Every player does the following: gather all tuples $([s]_j, [r]_j, \sigma_j')$ posted to the broadcast channel such that σ_j' is a valid signature for $([s]_j, [r]_j)$ under vk'. If all such $([s]_j, [r]_j)$ tuples reconstruct to a unique value (s, r) and moreover, (s, r) is a valid opening of com, then output the reconstructed value s. Else output $\bot$ as the reconstructed value.

Functionality 4.2: The $\mathcal{F}_{\text{sharegen}}^{b,\mathcal{O}}[k]$ ideal functionality

1. Sample $(\text{sk}, \text{vk}) \leftarrow \text{Sig.KeyGen}(1^\lambda)$ where $\text{Sig} := (\text{KeyGen}, \text{Sign}, \text{Vf})$ denotes a signature scheme.
2. Sample $s \xleftarrow{\$} \{0, 1\}$, and randomness $r \in \{0, 1\}^\lambda$, let $\text{com} := \text{Commit}(s, r)$.
3. Use a $(k+1)$-out-of-$|\mathcal{O}|$ Shamir secret sharing scheme to split the terms (s, r) and com into $|\mathcal{O}|$ shares, denoted $\{[s]_i, [r]_i, [\text{com}]_i\}_{i \in \mathcal{O}}$, respectively. Let $\sigma_i := \text{Sig.Sign}(\text{sk}, [\text{com}]_i)$ and $\sigma_i' := \text{Sig.Sign}(\text{sk}, ([s]_i, [r]_i))$ for $i \in \mathcal{O}$.
4. Each player in $\mathcal{O}$ receives the output $(\text{vk}, [s]_i, [r]_i, [\text{com}]_i, \sigma_i, \sigma_i')$.

The maliciously secure $\text{HalfToss}^b[k]$ protocol satisfies the following properties:

- *Binding.* If the vote phase does not fail, then the messages on the broadcast channel in the sharing and vote phases uniquely define a coin $s \neq \bot$ such that reconstruction must either output s or $\bot$.
- *Knowledge threshold.* We now have a computationally secure version of the knowledge threshold property.
  - If at least $k + 1$ number of b-supporters are corrupt, then the coalition can bias coin values s that the sharing and vote phases uniquely bind to (assuming that the voting phase did not fail). Specifically, if the coalition controls $k + 1$ number of b-supporters, it can decide whether to abort $\mathcal{F}_{\text{sharegen}}^{b,\mathcal{O}}[k]$ after seeing the corrupt players' shares $\{[s]_j\}_{j \in A}$ where $A \subset [n]$ denotes the coalition. If it controls $\max(k + 1, n_b/2)$ number of b-supporters, it can control the verification key vk' and thus alter the coin s the sharing and vote phases bind to as well.
  - If fewer than $k + 1$ number of b-supporters are corrupt, then the coalition's view at the end of the voting phase is computationally independent of the coin value s that the sharing and vote phases bind to. More formally, either the vote phase fails, or there exists a p.p.t. simulator Sim such that:

$$(s, \text{view}_A) \approx_c (\text{Uniform}, \text{Sim}(1^\lambda))$$

where s denotes the unique coin value that the sharing phase and vote phases bind to, view_A denotes the coalition's view at the end of the vote phase, Uniform denotes a random bit sampled from $\{0,1\}$, and $\approx_c$ denotes computational indistinguishability.

- *Liveness threshold.* If the coalition controls at least $\min(n_b - k, n_b/2)$ number of b-supporters, it can cause the reconstruction to output $\bot$. On the other hand, if the coalition controls fewer than $\min(n_b - k, n_b/2)$ number of b-supporters, then the reconstruction phase must succeed.

In comparison with the earlier semi-malicious version, the knowledge threshold and liveness threshold property now become weaker. One relaxation is the computational security relaxation in the knowledge threshold property whereas previously in the semi-malicious version, the property was information theoretic. Another relaxation is that the thresholds for the two properties have changed. Now, the coalition may be able to control the coin value and hamper reconstruction with a smaller threshold.

Final Protocol. Our final protocol is described as follows:

Protocol 4.3: Final protocol with malicious security

Sharing phase.

1. 0-supporters run the sharing phase of $\mathsf{HalfToss}^0[k_0]$.
2. 1-supporters run the sharing phase of $\mathsf{HalfToss}^1[k_1]$.

Vote phase.   (*The order of the two instances is important.*)

1. 1-supporters run the vote phase of $\mathsf{HalfToss}^1[k_1]$.
2. 0-supporters run the vote phase of $\mathsf{HalfToss}^0[k_0]$.

Reconstruction Phase.   (*The order of the two instances is important.*)

1. 0-supporters run the reconstruction phase of $\mathsf{HalfToss}^0[k_0]$, and let its outcome be s_0 if reconstruction is successful. In case the reconstruction outputs $\bot$, then let $s_0 := 0$.
2. 1-supporters run the reconstruction phase of $\mathsf{HalfToss}^1[k_1]$. If the reconstruction phase outputs $\bot$, then output 0 as the final coin value. Else let s_1 be the reconstructed value, and output $s_0 + s_1$ as the final coin value.

In the above, the order of the two instances in the vote and reconstruction phases is important due to a similar reason as in the semi-malicious version.

Setting aside the computational security issue for the time being (which can be formally dealt with using a standard computational reduction argument), in light of the properties for our maliciously secure $\mathsf{HalfToss}^b$ sub-protocol, we can now rewrite the earlier (C1), (C2), (C3) conditions as follows (recall that t_0 and t_1 are number of corrupted 0-supporters and 1-supporters, respectively):

(C1*) The coalition cannot control both s_0 and s_1, i.e., the coin values the sharing and vote phases of $\mathsf{HalfToss}^0[k_0]$ and $\mathsf{HalfToss}^1[k_1]$ bind to (assuming that it did not fail), respectively. This means that if the coalition controls at least k_b+1 number of b-supporters, then it does not have enough corruption budget to control $k_{1-b} + 1$ number of $(1-b)$-supporters.

(C2*) If the coalition controls the s_1 coin, i.e., it controls at least k_1+1 number of 1-supporters, then it cannot hamper the reconstruction of the coin s_0 due to the corruption budget. That is, the coalition must control fewer than $\min(n_0 - k_0, n_0/2)$ number of 0-supporters.

(C3*) If the coalition controls at least $\min(n_1 - k_1, n_1/2)$ number of 1-supporters such that it can cause the reconstruction of s_1 to fail, then the coalition must prefer 1 or is indifferent to the outcome—in other words, either $n_0 \le t_1$ or $t \le 2t_1$ ($t_0 \le t_1$ and so $t = t_0 + t_1 \le 2t_1$).

These conditions can be rewritten as the following expressions:

Paramete Constraints 4.4 (malicious version).
Assume: $0 \le k_0 \le n_0$, $0 \le k_1 \le n_1$

(C1*) $t \le k_0 + k_1 + 1$,
(C2*) $t < k_1 + 1 + \min(n_0 - k_0, n_0/2)$,
(C3*) if $\min(n_1 - k_1, \lceil \frac{n_1}{2} \rceil) < n_0$, then $t \le 2 \cdot \min(n_1 - k_1, \lceil \frac{n_1}{2} \rceil)$.

One can verify that any k_0, k_1, t that satisfy (C1*), (C2*), (C3*) must also satisfy the earlier conditions (C1), (C2) and (C3). This means that the new malicious version of the protocol cannot tolerate more corruptions than the semi-malicious version. Intriguingly, it turns out that there exists a choice of k_0 and k_1 that maximizes t for conditions (C1), (C2) and (C3), such that the same (k_0, k_1, t) also satisfy (C1*), (C2*), and (C3*). This means that our maliciously secure protocol can achieve the same resilience parameter as the semi-malicious version.[2] More specifically, there exists a choice satisfying $k_0 = \lceil (n_0 - 1)/2 \rceil$ and $k_1 \ge \lfloor n_1/2 \rfloor$ such that t is maximized for conditions (C1), (C2) and (C3). One can then verify that as long as $k_0 = \lceil (n_0 - 1)/2 \rceil$ and $k_1 \ge \lfloor n_1/2 \rfloor$, a feasible solution (k_0, k_1, t) for conditions (C3), (C2) and (C3) would also be a feasible solution for conditions (C1*), (C2*), and (C3*).

Just like the earlier semi-malicious setting, the above constraints (C1*), (C2*), and (C3*) are in fact slightly too stringent; thus, for the special case $n_0 = n_1 = odd$, the resulting solution of t would have a gap of 1 away from optimal. This gap can be bridged by observing that if the same number of 0-supporters and 1-supporters are corrupt, the coalition would then be indifferent, and it would be fine if the coalition could bias the coin towards either direction.

The formal proof of the following theorem (Theorem 1.1 in the introduction) is available in the full version.

---

[2] Note that since our lower bound holds even for fail-stop adversaries, only when the malicious version matches the resilience of the semi-malicious version can it be tight.

Theorem 4.5 (Upper bound). *Assume the existence of Oblivious Transfer (OT), and without loss of generality, assume that $n_1 \geq n_0 \geq 1$, and $n_0 + n_1 > 2$. Protocol 4.3: is CSP-fair coin toss protocol which tolerates up to t-sized non-uniform p.p.t. malicious coalitions where*

$$t := \begin{cases} n_1 - \lfloor \frac{1}{2}n_0 \rfloor, & \text{if } n_1 \geq \frac{5}{2}n_0; \\ \lfloor \frac{2}{3}n_1 - \frac{1}{6}n_0 \rfloor + \lceil \frac{1}{2}n_0 \rceil + 1 = n_1 + 1, & \text{if } n_1 = n_0 = \text{odd}; \\ \lfloor \frac{2}{3}n_1 - \frac{1}{6}n_0 \rfloor + \lceil \frac{1}{2}n_0 \rceil, & \text{otherwise}. \end{cases}$$

5   Lower Bound

5.1   Parameter Constraints

We now show that, if the parameters α_0, α_1 and t satisfy the following constraints, then for any coin toss protocol among n_0 number of 0-supporters and n_1 number of 1-supporters that achieves CSP fairness against a coalition of size up to t,[3] it's corresponding three-party coin toss protocol (after partition with respect to α_0 and α_1 as specified), must satisfy the lone-wolf condition (LBC1), the wolf-minion condition (LBC2), as well as the T_2 equity condition (LBC3) simultaneously.

Paramete Constraints 5.1 (Constraint system for lower bound proof).

Non-negative	Lone-wolf	Wolf-minion	T_2-equity
$0 \leq \alpha_0 \leq \frac{1}{2}n_0$	$\alpha_1 + 1 \leq n_0$	$n_0 - \alpha_0 < n_1 - \alpha_1$	$1 \leq \alpha_0$
$0 \leq \alpha_1 \leq \frac{1}{2}n_1$	$\alpha_0 + 1 \leq n_1$	$n_0 + n_1 - \alpha_0 - \alpha_1 \leq t$	$1 \leq \alpha_1$
	$\alpha_0 + \alpha_1 \leq t$		$3 \leq t$
	$2\alpha_0 + 1 \leq t$		$1 \leq n_0 + n_1 - 2\alpha_0 - 2\alpha_1 \leq t$
	$2\alpha_1 + 1 \leq t$		

In the above set of conditions, the first set (i.e., non-negative) makes sure that the number of 0-supporters and 1-supporters in each partition is non-negative. The next three sets of conditions are required to prove the corresponding three conditions, respectively. We show how the conditions lead to this set of parameter constraints in Sect. 5.2. Then, given any fixed n_0 and n_1, it suffices to solve for the best partition strategy (i.e., choice of α_0 and α_1) that minimizes t, and this minimal choice of t gives rise to our lower bound in light of Theorem 2.5. We explore that in Sect. 5.3. It turns out that the minimal t value satisfying the above constraint system coincides with our upper bound stated in Eq. (1).

5.2   Constraint System Implies the Lone-Wolf, Wolf-Minion, and T_2-Equality Conditions

Below we focus on proving that the three lower bound conditions hold provided the constraint system.

---

[3] Our main lower bound theorem, i.e., Theorem 1.2, states the impossibility for coalitions of size $t+1$ or greater. For convenience, in this section, we switch the notation to t rather than $t+1$.

Lemma 5.2 (Generalized lone-wolf lemma). *Let Π be a protocol that is CSP-fair against any non-uniform p.p.t., fail-stop coalition of size t. If α_0, α_1 and t satisfy the non-negative and lone-wolf constraints in Parameter Constraints 5.1, then Π satisfies the lone-wolf condition (LBC1).*

Proof. Suppose for the sake of contradiction that the long-wolf condition is violated, i.e., there exists a non-uniform p.p.t. fail-stop adversary $\mathcal{A}$ corrupting only $\mathcal{S}_1$ (the same argument holds for $\mathcal{S}_3$) that can bias the output towards $b \in \{0,1\}$ by a non-negligible amount. We show that then Π is not CSP fair against t fail-stop adversaries. There are two cases:

- If $\alpha_b > \alpha_{1-b}$ then $\mathcal{S}_1$ (resp. $\mathcal{S}_3$) prefers b. The number of parties in $\mathcal{S}_1$ is $\alpha_0 + \alpha_1$. According to the lone-wolf constraints in Parameter Constraints 5.1 we have that $\alpha_0 + \alpha + 1 \leq t$ and thus this coalition is supposed to be tolerated.
- If $\alpha_b \leq \alpha_{1-b}$, consider the following coalition in the CSP-fair protocol. The coalition corrupts $\mathcal{S}_1$ and in addition $\alpha_{1-b} + 1 - \alpha_b$ number of b-supporters outside $\mathcal{S}_1$. From the lone-wolf constraint in Parameter Constraints 5.1, we have that $n_b \geq \alpha_{1-b} + 1$. This implies that the number of b-supporters outside $\mathcal{S}_1$ is $n_b - \alpha_b \geq \alpha_{1-b} + 1 - \alpha_b$. Then, this coalition consists of α_{1-b} number of $(1-b)$-supporters and $\alpha_{1-b} + 1$ number of b-supporters. From the lone-wolf constraint in Parameter Constraints 5.1 we have that $2\alpha_{1-b} + 1 \leq t$. Then, this coalition contains less than t parties and it prefers b. If there exists a fail-stop adversary in the three-party protocol that controls $\mathcal{S}_1$ and can bias towards b, then this coalition in the CSP-protocol can also bias towards b. Note that the additional parties in the coalition that are outside of $\mathcal{S}_1$ act honestly and are used just to change the preference of the coalition, i.e., it is enough to consider the existence of a fail-stop adversary that corrupts only one party in the corresponding three-party protocol.

$\square$

Lemma 5.3 (Generalized wolf-minion lemma). *Let Π be a protocol that is CSP-fair against any non-uniform p.p.t., fail-stop coalition of size t. If α_0, α_1 and t satisfy the non-negative and wolf-minion constraints in Parameter Constraints 5.1, then Π satisfies the wolf-minion condition (LBC2).*

Proof. The non-negative constraints make sure that the number of parties in $\mathcal{S}_1$, $\mathcal{S}_2$ and $\mathcal{S}_3$ are non-negative, as $\mathcal{S}_2$ contains $(n_0 - 2\alpha_0)$ number of 0-supporters and $(n_1 - 2\alpha_1)$ number of 1-supporters. If the wolf-minion constrains hold, then the coalition of $\mathcal{S}_1$ and $\mathcal{S}_2$ (or $\mathcal{S}_3$ and $\mathcal{S}_2$) prefers 1 since in total it contains $n_0 - \alpha_0$ number of 0-supporters and $n_1 - \alpha_1$ number of 1-supporters and according to the constraints, $n_1 - \alpha_1 > n_0 - \alpha_0$. Moreover, the number of parties in this coalition is $n_1 + n_0 - \alpha_0 - \alpha_1$, which is at most t according to the condition. Therefore, any fail-stop adversary corrupting $\mathcal{S}_1$ and $\mathcal{S}_2$ (or $\mathcal{S}_3$ and $\mathcal{S}_2$) cannot bias the output towards 1 by a non-negligible amount, according to the CSP fairness of Π against t fail-stop adversaries. This means that the protocol Π satisfies the wolf-minion condition. $\square$

Lemma 5.4 (Generalized T_2-equity lemma). *Let Π be a protocol that is CSP-fair against any non-uniform p.p.t., fail-stop coalition of size t. If α_0, α_1 and t satisfy the non-negative and the T_2-equity constraints in Parameter Constraints 5.1, then protocol Π satisfies the T_2-equity condition (LBC3). That is, for all but a negligible fraction of S_2's randomness T_2, $|f(T_2) - \frac{1}{2}|$ is negligible.*

Proof. By correctness of the protocol, $\mathbb{E}_{T_2}[f(T_2)] = \frac{1}{2}$. Note that T_2 consists of the randomness of all players in S_2, we can view T_2 as a vector $\{t_Q\}_{Q \in S_2}$ where t_Q is player Q's randomness. For any fixed party Q in S_2, consider a protocol Π^Q that is same with Π except that Q aborts at the very beginning of the protocol and all other parties behave honestly. Let $g^Q(T_2)$ be the expected output of Π^Q conditioned on S_2's randomness T_2.

Claim 5.5. *For any $Q \in S_2$, $|\mathbb{E}_{T_2}[g^Q(T_2)] - \frac{1}{2}|$ is negligible.*

Proof. Suppose for the sake of contradiction that the claim is not true. Then this single aborting party Q can bias the outcome of Π towards $b \in \{0,1\}$ by a non-negligible amount. This violates the CSP-fairness of the n-party protocol: Consider a coalition that consists of the Q party and two b-supporters. This coalition prefers the coin b, and can bias towards it by having Q abort at the very beginning of the protocol Π. Note that according to T_2-equity constraints in Parameter Constraints 5.1, $\alpha_b \geq 1$, which implies that there are at least two b-supporters outside S_2. Moreover, the size of the coalition is 3, and thus we require that $t \geq 3$. □

Claim 5.6. *For any Q in S_2, for all but a negligible fraction of T_2, $|g^Q(T_2) - f(T_2)|$ is also negligible.*

Proof. Note that for all but a negligible fraction of T_2, $|\mathbb{E}_{T_2}[g^Q(T_2) - f(T_2)]| = |\mathbb{E}_{T_2}[g^Q(T_2)] - \mathbb{E}_{T_2}[f(T_2)]| = |\mathbb{E}_{T_2}[g^Q(T_2)] - \frac{1}{2}|$ is negligible. Suppose that there exists a non-negligible fraction of T_2 such that $f(T_2) - g^Q(T_2)$ is positive and non-negligible, then there must also exists a non-negligible fraction of T_2 such that $g^Q(T_2) - f(T_2)$ is positive and non-negligible. This indicates that for a non-negligible fraction of T_2, Q can bias the output of Π towards 1 (or 0) by a non-negligible amount by aborting at the beginning of the protocol.

Suppose that S_2 prefers 1 (the same argument holds if S_2 prefers 0). Consider an adversary $\mathcal{A}^*$ that receives a polynomial $p(\cdot)$ as an advice where $p(\cdot)$ is chosen such that for a non-negligible fraction of T_2, $g^Q(T_2) - f(T_2) \geq 1/p(\lambda)$. $\mathcal{A}^*$ corrupts S_2 and acts as follows:

- $\mathcal{A}^*$ randomly samples a T_2.
- $\mathcal{A}^*$ repeats the following for $p^2(\lambda)$ times: $\mathcal{A}^*$ samples T_1 and T_3 for S_1 and S_3 and simulates an honest execution with the randomness T_1, T_2, T_3. $\mathcal{A}^*$ also simulates an execution in which Q always aborts at the beginning of the protocol. Then $\mathcal{A}^*$ gets estimates of $\tilde{g}^Q(T_2)$ and $\tilde{f}(T_2)$.
- If $\tilde{g}^Q(T_2) > \tilde{f}(T_2)$, $\mathcal{A}^*$ instructs Q to abort at the very beginning of the protocol. Otherwise it follows the honest execution.

Note that for any T_2 such that $g^Q(T_2) - f(T_2) \geq \frac{1}{p(\lambda)}$, by the Chernoff bound, except with a negligible probability, it must be that $\widetilde{g}^Q(T_2) > \widetilde{f}(T_2)$. Therefore, $\mathcal{A}^*$ can bias the output of Π towards 1 by a non-negligible amount. This breaks the CSP fairness of Π since, according to the T_2-equity constraint in Parameter Constraints 5.1, $\mathcal{S}_2$, which contains $n_0 + n_1 - 2\alpha_0 - 2\alpha_1$ contains parties which is at most t, and it prefers 1. Therefore, for all but a negligible fraction of T_2, $|g^Q(T_2) - f(T_2)|$ is negligible. $\qquad \square$

For any fixed $Q \in \mathcal{S}_2$, for any pair of T_2 and T_2' that only differ in Q's randomness, it must be that $g^Q(T_2) = g^Q(T_2')$. Let ℓ denote the length of T_2, we have:

Claim 5.7. *For any fixed $i \in [\ell]$, for all but a negligible fraction of T_2, $|f(T_2) - f(\widetilde{T}_2^i)|$ is negligible, where $\widetilde{T}_2^i$ is same as T_2 except with the i-th bit flipped.*

Proof of Claim 5.7. Suppose that the i-th bit is contributed by party $Q \in \mathcal{S}_2$. For any polynomial $p(\cdot)$, define bad_1^p to be the event $|f(T_2) - g^Q(T_2)| \geq \frac{1}{p(\lambda)}$, and bad_2^p to be the event $|f(\widetilde{T}_2^i) - g^Q(\widetilde{T}_2^i)| \geq \frac{1}{p(\lambda)}$. Since for all but a negligible fraction of T_2, $|f(T_2) - g^Q(T_2)|$ is negligible, the probability that bad_1^p happens is negligible. The probability that bad_2^p happens is also negligible. Thus by a union bound, the probability that both bad_1^p and bad_2^p do not happen is $1 - \mathsf{negl}(\lambda)$ for some negligible function $\mathsf{negl}(\cdot)$. This indicates that for any polynomial $p(\cdot)$, $|f(T_2) - f(\widetilde{T}_i)| \leq |f(T_2) - g^Q(T_2)| + |f(\widetilde{T}_2^i) - g^Q(\widetilde{T}_2^i)| \leq \frac{2}{p(\lambda)}$ with probability $1 - \mathsf{negl}(\lambda)$. The claim thus follows. $\qquad \square$

Claim 5.8. *Pick a random T_2 and a random T_2'. Then except with a negligible probability over the random choice of T_2 and T_2', $|f(T_2) - f(T_2')|$ is negligible.*

Proof. Pick a random T_2 and a random T_2', we define hybrids T^i, $i = 0, \ldots, \ell+1$ as follows:

$$T^i = \{t_1, \ldots, t_i, t_{i+1}', \ldots, t_\ell'\},$$

where t_i is the i-th bit of T_2 and t_i' is the i-th bit of T_2'. Then, $T^0 = T_2'$ and $T^\ell = T_2$. For any fixed polynomial $p(\cdot)$, define bad_i^p to be the event that $|f(T^i) - f(T^{i+1})| \geq \frac{1}{p(\lambda)}$. Note that the marginal distribution of T^i is uniform, for any polynomial $p(\cdot)$, the probability that bad_i^p happens is negligible over the choice of T_2 and T_2', according to Claim 5.7. Therefore, for any $p(\cdot)$, by the union bound, the probability that none of bad_i^p happens is $1 - \mathsf{negl}(\lambda)$ for some negligible function $\mathsf{negl}(\cdot)$. Observe that for any fixed polynomial $p(\cdot)$, if none of the events bad_i^p happen, then $|f(T_2) - f(T_2')| \leq \frac{\ell+1}{p(\lambda)}$ by triangle inequality. Hence, for any random T_2 and any random T_2', $|f(T_2) - f(T_2')|$ is negligible except with a negligible probability over the random choices over T_2 and T_2'. $\qquad \square$

Together with the fact that $\mathbb{E}_{T_2}[f(T_2)] = \frac{1}{2}$, we have that for all but a negligible fraction of T_2, $|f(T_2) - \frac{1}{2}|$ is negligible. Otherwise if for some polynomial $p(\cdot), q(\cdot)$, there exists $1/p(\lambda)$ fraction of T_2 such that $f(T_2) - \frac{1}{2} \geq 1/q(\lambda)$, then there must exist $1/p'(\lambda)$ fraction of T_2 such that $\frac{1}{2} - f(T_2) \geq 1/q'(\lambda)$ for some polynomial $p'(\cdot), q'(\cdot)$. Then for any random T_2 and T_2', with a non-negligible probability, $|f(T_2) - f(T_2')| \geq 1/q(\lambda) + 1/q'(\lambda)$, which violates the above conclusion. To conclude, for all but a negligible fraction of T_2, $|f(T_2) - \frac{1}{2}|$ is negligible.

$\square$

5.3   Minimizing t Subject to Constraints

The full proof of the following lemma is available in the full version.

Lemma 5.9 (Solving the constraint system and minimizing t). *For Parameter Constraint 5.1, the parameter t is minimized when α_0 and α_1 are chosen as follows, and the corresponding t is:*

Case	α_0	α_1	t
$n_1 \geq \frac{5}{2}n_0, n_0 \geq 2$	$\lfloor \frac{1}{2}n_0 \rfloor$	$n_0 - 1$	$n_1 - \lfloor \frac{1}{2}n_0 \rfloor + 1$
$2 \leq n_0 < n_1 < \frac{5}{2}n_0$	$\lfloor \frac{1}{2}n_0 \rfloor$	$\lceil \frac{1}{3}n_1 + \frac{1}{6}n_0 \rceil - 1$	$\lceil \frac{1}{2}n_0 \rceil + \lfloor \frac{2}{3}n_1 - \frac{1}{6}n_0 \rfloor + 1$
$2 \leq n_0 = n_1$	$\lfloor \frac{1}{2}n_0 \rfloor$	$\lfloor \frac{1}{2}n_0 \rfloor - 1$	$2\lceil \frac{1}{2}n_0 \rceil + 1$

Note that for the case $t = 2\lceil \frac{1}{2}n_0 \rceil + 1$, this expression is equal to $\lfloor \frac{2}{3}n_1 - \frac{1}{6}n_0 \rfloor + \lceil \frac{1}{2}n_0 \rceil + 1$ when $n_0 = n_1$ is even, and is equal to $n_0 + 2$ when $n_0 = n_1$ is odd.

6   Complete Characterization of Maximin Fairness

In this section we give a complete characterization of the maximin fairness defined by Chung et al. [14]. Intuitively, maximin fairness requires that a corrupted coalition cannot harm the expected reward of any honest party, compared to an all-honest execution. This definition is formalized in Definition 3.2.

6.1   Lower Bound

Unlike CSP-fairness, maximin-fairness is impossible under a broad range of parameters. More specifically, we prove the following theorem, which says that unless $n_0 = 1$ and $n_1 = odd$, for maximin fairness, we cannot tolerate *fail-stop* coalitions of half of the parties or more. The special case $n_0 = 1$ and $n_1 = odd$ is slightly more subtle. Chung et al. [14] showed that for the special case $n_0 = 1$, it is indeed possible to achieve maximin fairness against all but one *fail-stop* corruptions. We prove that for $n_0 = 1$, we cannot tolerate *semi-malicious* coalitions that are majority in size.

Theorem 6.1 (Lower bound for maximin fairness). *Without loss of generality, assume that $n_1 \geq n_0 \geq 1$ and $n_0 + n_1 > 2$. Then there does not exist a maximmin-fair n-party coin toss protocol that can:*

$$\textit{tolerate } \textbf{fail-stop} \textit{ coalition of size } t \geq \lceil \tfrac{1}{2}(n_0 + n_1) \rceil \qquad \textit{for } n_0 \geq 2$$
$$\textit{tolerate } \textbf{semi-malicious} \textit{ coalition of size } t \geq \lceil \tfrac{1}{2}n_1 \rceil + 1 \textit{ for } n_0 = 1$$

Proof Sketch. For the case where $n_0 \geq 2$, we show that if there exists a coin toss protocol that achieves maximin-fairness against $\lceil \tfrac{1}{2}(n_0 + n_1) \rceil$ fail-stop adversaries, then we can construct a two-party protocol that violates Cleve's lower bound [15]. Consider any preference profile that contains at least two 0-supporters and in which $n_1 \geq n_0$. Then, we partition the 0-supporters and 1-supporters as evenly as possible into two partitions, and the two party protocol is simply an emulation of the n-party protocol with respect to this preference profile. Each party internally emulates the execution of all parties it runs in the outer protocol, in a similar manner as in Sect. 5. Since $n_1 \geq n_0 \geq 2$, each partition must contain at least one 0-supporter and at least one 1-supporter. By maximin fairness, if either partition is controlled by a non uniform p.p.t. adversary $\mathcal{A}$, it should not be able to bias the outcome towards either 0 or 1 by a non-negligible amount—otherwise if $\mathcal{A}$ was able to bias the coin towards $b \in \{0, 1\}$, it would be able to harm an individual b-support in the other partition. Now, if we view the coin toss protocol as a two-party coin toss protocol between the two partitions, the above requirement would contradicts Cleve's impossibility result [15].

For the case where $n_0 = 1$, the proof is similar to that of the CSP-fairness. We partition the players into three partitions: $\mathcal{S}_1$ and $\mathcal{S}_3$ each contains half of 1-supporters and $\mathcal{S}_2$ contains the single 0-supporter. We can show that if a coin toss protocol is maximin-fair against $\lceil \tfrac{1}{2}n_1 \rceil + 1$ fail-stop adversaries, then it should satisfy the wolf-minion condition, the lone-wolf condition and the T_2-equity condition simultaneously. The full proof is available in the full version.

□

6.2   Upper Bound

As mentioned, except for the special case $n_0 = 1$ and $n_1 = \textit{odd}$, for maximin fairness, we cannot hope to tolerate half or more fail-stop corruptions. However, if majority are honest, we can simply run honest-majority MPC with guaranteed output delivery [21,37].

Therefore, the only non-trivial case is when $n_0 = 1$ and $n_1 = \textit{odd}$. Chung et al. [14] showed that for $n_0 = 1$, there is a maximin-fair coin toss protocol against up to $(n - 1)$ *fail-stop* adversaries. Here, we construct a maximin-fair coin toss protocol tolerates exactly half or fewer *malicious* corruptions.

In our protocol, first, the single 0-supporter commits to a random coin, and moreover, the 1-supporters jointly toss a coin s_1 such that the outcome is secret shared among the 1-supporters. Only if $\lceil n_1/2 \rceil$ number of 1-supporters get together, can they learn s_1, influence the value of s_1, or hamper its reconstruction later. Next, the 1-supporters reconstruct the secret-shared coin s_1. If the reconstruction fails, the reconstructed value is set to a canonical value $s_1 := 0$. Finally, the single 0-supporter opens its commitment and let the opening be s_0.

If the single 0-supporter aborts any time during the protocol, the outcome is declared to be 1. Else, the outcome is declared to be $s_0 + s_1$. More formally, the protocol is as below.

Protocol 6.2: Protocol for maximin-fairness: special case when $n_0 = 1$ and $n_1 = odd$

1. The single 0-supporter randomly choose $s_0 \xleftarrow{\$} \{0,1\}$ and compute the commitment $\mathsf{com} = \mathsf{Commit}(s_0, r)$ with some randomness $r \in \{0,1\}^\lambda$. It then sends the commitment com to the broadcast channel. If the 0-supporter fails to send the commitment, set $s_0 = \bot$.
2. The 1-supporters run an honest-majority MPC with guaranteed output delivery to toss a coin s_1. Each player $i \in \mathcal{P}_1$ (the set of 1-supporters) receives $\widetilde{s}_i$ as the output of the MPC.
3. Every 1-supporter $i \in \mathcal{P}_1$ posts the output $\widetilde{s}_i$ it receives to the broadcast channel. Let s_1 be the majority vote. If no coin gains majority vote, set $s_1 = 0$.
4. The 0-supporter opens its coin s_0. If it fails to open the coin correctly, set $s_0 = \bot$.
5. If $s_0 = \bot$, output 1. Otherwise, output $s_0 \oplus s_1$.

Observe that if the single 0-supporter is honest, then we need to make sure that the coalition cannot bias the coin towards either direction; however, in this case, since the 0-supporter is guaranteed to choose a random coin and open it at the end, this can be ensured. If, on the other hand, the single 0-supporter is corrupt, then we only need to ensure that the coalition cannot bias the coin towards 0. We may therefore assume that the single 0-supporter does not abort because otherwise the outcome is just declared to be 1. Further, in this case, the coalition only has budget to corrupt $\lceil n_1/2 \rceil$ number of 1-supporters, which means that we have honest majority in 1-supporters. Therefore, if the 0-supporter does not abort, then the outcome will be a uniformly random coin.

This gives rise to the following theorem. The full proof to the theorem is available in the full version.

Theorem 6.2 (Upper bound for maximin fairness). *Assume the existence of Oblivious Transfer. Without loss of generality, assume that $n_1 \geq n_0 \geq 1$ and $n_0 + n_1 > 2$. There exists a maximin-fair n-party coin toss protocol among n_0 players who prefer 0 and n_1 players who prefer 1, which tolerates up to t malicious adversaries where*

$$
t := \begin{cases} \lceil \frac{1}{2}(n_0 + n_1) \rceil - 1, & \text{if } n_0 \geq 2, \\ \lceil \frac{1}{2} n_1 \rceil, & \text{if } n_0 = 1. \end{cases} \tag{2}
$$

Acknowledgments. This work is in part supported by NSF under the award numbers CNS-1601879 and CNS-1561209, a Packard Fellowship, an ONR YIP award, a DARPA SIEVE grant, by the ISRAEL SCIENCE FOUNDATION (grant No. 2439/20), by JPM Faculty Research Award, and by the BIU Center for Research in Applied Cryptography and Cyber Security in conjunction with the Israel National Cyber Bureau in the Prime Minister's Office. This project has received funding from the European Union's Horizon 2020 research and innovation programme under the Marie Skłodowska-Curie grant agreement No. 891234.

A   Visualization of the Resilience Parameter

We visualize the choice of t as a function of n_0 and n_1, to help understand the mathematical structure of game-theoretic fairness in multi-party coin toss (Fig. 1).

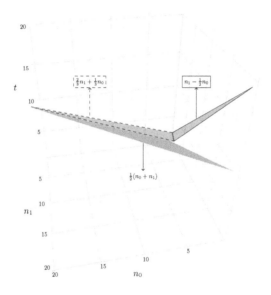

Fig. 1. Visualization of the maximum t as a function of n_0 and n_1 in comparison to $\frac{1}{2}(n_0 + n_1)$. For simplicity we ignore the rounding in the plot. The blue plane is $\frac{1}{2}(n_0 + n_1)$, while the red plane with the dashes boundary is $\frac{2}{3}n_1 + \frac{1}{3}n_0$ when $n_1 < \frac{5}{2}n_0$, and the red plane with the solid boundary is $n_1 - \frac{1}{2}n_0$ when $n_1 \geq \frac{5}{2}n_0$. (Color figure online)

References

1. Abraham, I., Dolev, D., Gonen, R., Halpern, J.: Distributed computing meets game theory: Robust mechanisms for rational secret sharing and multiparty computation. In: PODC (2006)
2. Andrychowicz, M., Dziembowski, S., Malinowski, D., Mazurek, U.: Secure multiparty computations on bitcoin. Commun. ACM **59**(4), 76–84 (2016). https://doi.org/10.1145/2896386

3. Asharov, G., Canetti, R., Hazay, C.: Towards a game theoretic view of secure computation. In: Paterson, K.G. (ed.) EUROCRYPT 2011. LNCS, vol. 6632, pp. 426–445. Springer, Heidelberg (2011). https://doi.org/10.1007/978-3-642-20465-4_24

4. Asharov, G., Jain, A., López-Alt, A., Tromer, E., Vaikuntanathan, V., Wichs, D.: Multiparty computation with low communication, computation and interaction via threshold FHE. In: Pointcheval, D., Johansson, T. (eds.) EUROCRYPT 2012. LNCS, vol. 7237, pp. 483–501. Springer, Heidelberg (2012). https://doi.org/10.1007/978-3-642-29011-4_29

5. Asharov, G., Lindell, Y.: Utility dependence in correct and fair rational secret sharing. J. Cryptology 24(1), 157–202 (2011)

6. Beimel, A., Groce, A., Katz, J., Orlov, I.: Fair computation with rational players. https://eprint.iacr.org/2011/396.pdf, full version of Eurocrypt'12 version (2011)

7. Ben-Or, M., Goldwasser, S., Wigderson, A.: Completeness theorems for non-cryptographic fault-tolerant distributed computation (extended abstract). In: Proceedings of the 20th Annual ACM Symposium on Theory of Computing, 2–4 May, 1988, Chicago, Illinois, USA, pp. 1–10 (1988)

8. Bentov, I., Kumaresan, R.: How to use bitcoin to design fair protocols. In: Garay, J.A., Gennaro, R. (eds.) CRYPTO 2014. LNCS, vol. 8617, pp. 421–439. Springer, Heidelberg (2014). https://doi.org/10.1007/978-3-662-44381-1_24

9. Blum, M.: Coin flipping by telephone. In: CRYPTO (1981)

10. Boneh, D., Bonneau, J., Bünz, B., Fisch, B.: Verifiable delay functions. In: Shacham, H., Boldyreva, A. (eds.) CRYPTO 2018. LNCS, vol. 10991, pp. 757–788. Springer, Cham (2018). https://doi.org/10.1007/978-3-319-96884-1_25

11. Boneh, D., Bünz, B., Fisch, B.: A survey of two verifiable delay functions. Cryptology ePrint Archive, Report 2018/712 (2018)

12. Chaum, D., Crépeau, C., Damgård, I.: Multiparty unconditionally secure protocols (extended abstract). In: Proceedings of the 20th Annual ACM Symposium on Theory of Computing, 2–4 May, 1988, Chicago, Illinois, USA, pp. 11–19. ACM (1988)

13. Chung, K.M., Chan, T.H.H., Wen, T., Shi, E.: Game-theoretic fairness meets multi-party protocols: the case of leader election. In: CRYPTO (2021). https://eprint.iacr.org/2020/1591

14. Chung, K., Guo, Y., Lin, W., Pass, R., Shi, E.: Game theoretic notions of fairness in multi-party coin toss. In: TCC (2018)

15. Cleve, R.: Limits on the security of coin flips when half the processors are faulty. In: STOC (1986)

16. Dodis, Y., Halevi, S., Rabin, T.: A cryptographic solution to a game theoretic problem. In: Bellare, M. (ed.) CRYPTO 2000. LNCS, vol. 1880, pp. 112–130. Springer, Heidelberg (2000). https://doi.org/10.1007/3-540-44598-6_7

17. Dodis, Y., Rabin, T.: Cryptography and game theory. In: AGT (2007)

18. Garay, J., Katz, J., Tackmann, B., Zikas, V.: How fair is your protocol? a utility-based approach to protocol optimality. In: PODC (2015)

19. Garay, J.A., Katz, J., Maurer, U., Tackmann, B., Zikas, V.: Rational protocol design: cryptography against incentive-driven adversaries. In: FOCS (2013)

20. Garay, J., Tackmann, B., Zikas, V.: Fair distributed computation of reactive functions. In: Moses, Y. (ed.) DISC 2015. LNCS, vol. 9363, pp. 497–512. Springer, Heidelberg (2015). https://doi.org/10.1007/978-3-662-48653-5_33

21. Goldreich, O., Micali, S., Wigderson, A.: How to play any mental game. In: ACM Symposium on Theory of Computing (STOC) (1987)

22. Gradwohl, R., Livne, N., Rosen, A.: Sequential rationality in cryptographic protocols. ACM Trans. Econ. Comput. (TEAC) **1**(1), 1–38 (2013)
23. Groce, A., Katz, J.: Fair computation with rational players. In: Pointcheval, D., Johansson, T. (eds.) EUROCRYPT 2012. LNCS, vol. 7237, pp. 81–98. Springer, Heidelberg (2012). https://doi.org/10.1007/978-3-642-29011-4_7
24. Halpern, J., Teague, V.: Rational secret sharing and multiparty computation. In: STOC (2004)
25. Ishai, Y., Ostrovsky, R., Zikas, V.: Secure multi-party computation with identifiable abort. In: Garay, J.A., Gennaro, R. (eds.) CRYPTO 2014. LNCS, vol. 8617, pp. 369–386. Springer, Heidelberg (2014). https://doi.org/10.1007/978-3-662-44381-1_21
26. Izmalkov, S., Micali, S., Lepinski, M.: Rational secure computation and ideal mechanism design. In: FOCS (2005)
27. J. Aumann, R.: Subjectivity and correlation in randomized strategies. J. Math. Econ. **1**(1), 67–96 (1974)
28. Katz, J.: Bridging game theory and cryptography: recent results and future directions. In: TCC (2008)
29. Kol, G., Naor, M.: Cryptography and game theory: designing protocols for exchanging information. In: TCC (2008)
30. Kosba, A.E., Miller, A., Shi, E., Wen, Z., Papamanthou, C.: Hawk: The blockchain model of cryptography and privacy-preserving smart contracts. In: IEEE Symposium on Security and Privacy, SP 2016, San Jose, CA, USA, 22–26 May, 2016, pp. 839–858. IEEE Computer Society (2016)
31. Kumaresan, R., Bentov, I.: How to use bitcoin to incentivize correct computations. In: Proceedings of the 2014 ACM SIGSAC Conference on Computer and Communications Security, Scottsdale, AZ, USA, 3–7 November, 2014, pp. 30–41. ACM (2014)
32. Kumaresan, R., Vaikuntanathan, V., Vasudevan, P.N.: Improvements to secure computation with penalties. In: ACM CCS (2016)
33. Nash, J.: Non-cooperative games. Ann. Math. **54**(2), 286–295 (1951)
34. Ong, S.J., Parkes, D.C., Rosen, A., Vadhan, S.P.: Fairness with an honest minority and a rational majority. In: TCC (2009)
35. Pass, R., Shelat, A.: Renegotiation-safe protocols. In: ICS, pp. 61–78. Citeseer (2011)
36. Pass, R., Shi, E.: Fruitchains: a fair blockchain. In: PODC (2017)
37. Rabin, T., Ben-Or, M.: Verifiable secret sharing and multiparty protocols with honest majority (extended abstract). In: Proceedings of the 21st Annual ACM Symposium on Theory of Computing, 14–17 May, 1989, Seattle, Washington, USA, pp. 73–85. ACM (1989)
38. Wu, K., Asharov, G., Shi, E.: A complete characterization of game-theoretically fair, multi-party coin toss. IACR Cryptol. ePrint Arch, p. 748 (2021). https://eprint.iacr.org/2021/748
39. Yao, A.C.C.: Protocols for secure computations. In: FOCS (1982)
40. Yao, A.C.C.: How to generate and exchange secrets. In: FOCS (1986)

Lightweight, Maliciously Secure Verifiable Function Secret Sharing

Leo de Castro[1($\boxtimes$)] and Anitgoni Polychroniadou[2]

[1] MIT, Cambridge, USA
ldec@mit.edu
[2] J.P. Morgan AI Research, New York, USA
antigoni.polychroniadou@jpmorgan.com

Abstract. In this work, we present a lightweight construction of verifiable two-party function secret sharing (FSS) for point functions and multi-point functions. Our verifiability method is lightweight in two ways. Firstly, it is concretely efficient, making use of only symmetric key operations and no public key or MPC techniques are involved. Our performance is comparable with the state-of-the-art *non-verifiable* DPF constructions, and we outperform all prior DPF verification techniques in both computation and communication complexity, which we demonstrate with an implementation of our scheme. Secondly, our verification procedure is essentially unconstrained. It will verify that distributed point function (DPF) shares correspond to some point function irrespective of the output group size, the structure of the DPF output, or the set of points on which the DPF must be evaluated. This is in stark contrast with prior works, which depend on at least one and often all three of these constraints. In addition, our construction is the first DPF verification protocol that can verify general DPFs while remaining secure even if one server is malicious. Prior work on maliciously secure DPF verification could only verify DPFs where the non-zero output is binary and the output space is a large field.

As an additional feature, our verification procedure can be batched so that verifying a polynomial number of DPF shares requires the *exact* same amount of communication as verifying one pair of DPF shares. We combine this packed DPF verification with a novel method for packing DPFs into shares of a multi-point function where the evaluation time, verification time, and verification communication are *independent* of the number of non-zero points in the function.

An immediate corollary of our results are two-server protocols for PIR and PSI that remain secure when any one of the three parties is malicious (either the client or one of the servers).

1 Introduction

Function secret sharing (FSS), first introduced by Boyle, Gilboa, and Ishai [2], is a cryptographic primitive that extends the classical notion of secret-sharing a scalar value to secret sharing a function. FSS allows a party to secret-share

© International Association for Cryptologic Research 2022
O. Dunkelman and S. Dziembowski (Eds.): EUROCRYPT 2022, LNCS 13275, pp. 150–179, 2022.
https://doi.org/10.1007/978-3-031-06944-4_6

a function $f : \mathcal{D} \to \mathbb{G}$ and produce function shares k_0 and k_1. These shares have several useful properties. Firstly, viewing either share alone computationally hides the function f. Secondly, the function shares can be evaluated at points in the domain $\mathcal{D}$ to produce additive shares of the output of f. In other words, for $x \in \mathcal{D}$, we have $k_0(x) + k_1(x) = f(x)$.

A point function $f : \mathcal{D} \to \mathbb{G}$ is defined by a single point $(\alpha, \beta) \in \mathcal{D} \times \mathbb{G}$ such that $f(\alpha) = \beta$ and for all $\gamma \neq \alpha$ we have $f(\gamma) = 0$. We will often denote the point function f defined by (α, β) as $f_{\alpha,\beta}$. Distributed point functions (DPFs), first introduced by Gilboa and Ishai [9], are a special case of FSS that supports point functions. Boyle, Gilboa, and Ishai [3] gave an efficient construction of a distributed point function.

An FSS construction is immediately applicable to the problem of constructing two-server protocols, where a client interacts with two servers that are assumed to not collude. Despite the simplicity of point functions, DPFs give rise to a rich class of two-server protocols, including private information retrieval (PIR) [3], private set intersection (PSI) [6], Oblivious-RAM [8], contact-tracing [7], and many more [1,13]. These two-server protocols often have a similar structure. For example, a simple, semi-honest PIR construction from a DPF begins with a client generating DPF shares for the function $f_{i,1}$, where i is the query index, and the servers begin with identical copies of a database of size N. The client sends one function share to each server, and the servers evaluate the share on each index $i \in [N]$ to obtain a secret sharing of a one-hot vector. The servers then take the inner product with their copy of the database to obtain an additive share of the ith element, which is returned to the client.

Verifiable DPF. A crucial barrier that must be overcome in order for many applications to be deployed in the real world is achieving some form of malicious security. For the two-server model, this often means verifying that the client's inputs are well-formed in order to ensure that the client does not learn unauthorized information about the servers' database or modify the database in an unauthorized way. A DPF scheme that supports this well-formedness check is called a verifiable DPF (VDPF).

In addition to constructing DPFs, the work of Boyle et al. [3] also constructs VDPFs that are secure when the servers are semi-honest; a malicious server is able to learn non-trivial information about the client's chosen point (α, β) through the verification procedure. Even to achieve semi-honest security, the VDPF protocol of [3] requires a constant-sized MPC protocol (consisting of several OLEs) to be run between the servers to verify the DPF. The recent work of Boneh, Boyle, Corrigan-Gibbs, Gilboa, and Ishai [1] achieves maliciously secure VDPFs when $\beta \in \{0, 1\}$ and the output group has size at least 2^λ, but they do not extend their protocol to support general β values or smaller output groups. They also require a constant sized MPC (also a few OLEs) to be run between the servers to verify a single DPF share. More detail on these protocols is given in Sect. 1.2. These works leave open the problem of constructing a maliciously-secure VDPF for general β values, which we solve in this work.

Distributed Multi-Point Functions. While DPFs result in a surprisingly rich class of two-server protocols, in many applications [6,7] it is desirable to have FSS for functions with more than one nonzero point. We call these multi-point functions (MPFs) (see Sect. 4.2 for more details). Naively, this requires constructing a DPF for each nonzero point. To evaluate the naive MPF share the servers must perform a DPF evaluation for each nonzero point in the function. In other words, if a function contains t non-zero points and the servers wish to evaluate the MPF share at η points, then they must perform $t \cdot \eta$ DPF evaluations. This clearly wastes a tremendous amount of work, since we know that for each of the t DPF shares, at most one of the η evaluation points will map to a non-zero value, and yet each share is evaluated the full η times. To maintain efficient FSS for these multi-point functions, it is clear that a more efficient manner of batching DPF shares is required. Furthermore, the naive verifiable DMPF construction is simply a concatenation of many verifiable DPF shares, which means the complexity of the verification procedure grows linearly in t. Prior works have left open the problem of constructing DMPF shares with evaluation time and verification complexity sublinear in the number of nonzero points, which we solve in this work.

1.1   Our Contributions

Lightweight Verifiable DPF. We give a lightweight construction of a verifiable DPF, which admits a very efficient way to verify that DPF shares are well-formed. This construction is light-weight in two ways. First, it's performance is comparable with the state-of-the-art non-verifiable DPF constructions (within a factor of 2 in both communication and computation), as we show in Sect. 5. In addition, we strictly outperform all prior DPF verification methods in both communication and computation. These verification methods often have strictly stronger or incomparable constraints, such as remaining secure when the servers are semi-honest or only verifying if $\beta \in \{0, 1\}$. Unlike all other DPF verification methods [1,3], we do not make use of any public key operations or arithmetic MPC; for a security parameter λ, our verification procedure is a simple exchange of 2λ bits.

Second, the constraints on the verification procedure are essentially non-existent. We can verify that a DPF share is well-formed regardless of output field size, regardless of the value of the non-zero output element, and regardless of the set of evaluation points the servers choose. This is in stark contrast to prior works [1,3], which depend on at least one and often all of these constraints, as we describe in Sect. 1.2. Our method is able to verify that there is at most one non-zero value in any set of outputs of the DPF share, even if the set is adversarially chosen.

Efficient Batched Verification. Another novel feature of our verification procedure is efficient batching. When verifying any polynomial number of shares in our VDPF scheme, the communication for the verification procedure remains only an exchange of 2λ bits. This is because our verification procedure for a single pair of VDPF shares is to check if two 2λ-bit strings are equal (we explain how these strings are generated in Sect. 3), so the two servers are able to check if many pairs of 2λ-bit strings are equal by simply hashing all strings down into a single pair of 2λ-bit strings. This batching requires no additional computational overhead beyond hashing the strings together. Furthermore, this means that the communication to verify VDPF shares from *many different clients* is bounded at 2λ bits, and, to our knowledge, this is the first efficient cross-client batched VDPF verification procedure of its kind.

Verifiable FSS for Multi-Point Functions. Another immediate consequence of our batched verification procedure is verifiable FSS for multi-point functions. Our VDMPF scheme goes beyond the naive construction, which is to simply generate a pair of VDPF shares for each non-zero point in the multi-point function. As mentioned above, when using this naive method for an MPF with t non-zero points, a sever evaluating the MPF at η points needs to perform $t \cdot \eta$ VDPF evaluations. We show how a simple application of Cuckoo-hashing can reduce the number of VDPF evaluations to 3η *regardless* of the value of t. This is at the cost of the client needing to produce and send roughly $2\times$ the number of VDPF shares as in the naive case, where these VDPF shares are at most the same size as in the naive case. For even moderately sized t (e.g. $t > 30$) this provides a tremendous savings in the overall computation time. Due to our batched verification, the communication between the two servers never grows beyond 2λ bits.

Ultimately, we will show the following two theorems.

Theorem 1 (Verifiable DPF (informal)). *There exists a verifiable DPF for any point function $f\colon \{0,1\}^n \to \mathbb{G}$ that remains secure even when one server is malicious. For security parameter λ, the runtime of share generation is $O(n\lambda)$, and the size of a function share is $O(n\lambda)$. For any $x \in \{0,1\}^n$, the runtime of share evaluation $O(n\lambda)$. For the verification procedure with η outputs, additional runtime is $O(\eta\lambda)$ and the communication between the two servers is $O(\lambda)$.*

Theorem 2 (Verifiable DMPF (informal)). *There exists is a verifiable DMPF for multi-point functions $f\colon [N] \to \mathbb{G}$ with at most t non-zero evaluation points that remains secure even when one server is malicious. For security parameter λ and a number of hash table buckets $m = O(t\lambda + t\log(t))$, the runtime of share generation is $O\left(m\lambda \log(N/m)\right)$. The runtime of share evaluation is $O(\lambda \log(N/m))$. For the verification procedure with η outputs, the additional runtime is $O(\eta\lambda)$ and the communication between the two servers is $O(\lambda)$.*

We implement our VDPF and VDMPF schemes and present benchmarks in Sect. 5.

Applications. As a direct result of our verifiable FSS construction, we obtain several protocols in the two-server model that are secure against any one malicious corruption. More specifically, our verifiable DPF directly results in a maliciously-secure two-server PIR scheme and our verifiable DMPF directly results in a maliciously-secure two-server PSI scheme. We exclude the presentation of the constructions due to space constraints and because these protocol follow immediately from our constructions. We give these constructions in the full version.

1.2 Related Work

The most relevant related work is the verifiable DPF constructions of Boyle, Gilboa, and Ishai [3] and the subsequent work of Boneh, Boyle, Corrigan-Gibbs, Gilboa, and Ishai [1]. We begin with an overview of the DPF construction of [3], then discuss the semi-honest verification protocols presented in [3]. We also briefly discuss the malicious verification procedure in [1], which handles the case where $\beta \in \{0, 1\}$ and the DPF output space is a large field.

Overview of the Boyle et al. [3] Construction. The DPF construction of Boyle et al. [3] is a function secret sharing scheme for point functions in the two-server model. As described in Sect. 2.2, a distributed point function scheme allows a client to run an algorithm $(k_0, k_1) \leftarrow \mathsf{Gen}(1^\lambda, f_{\alpha,\beta})$, where $f_{\alpha,\beta} \colon \{0,1\}^n \to \mathbb{G}$ is a point function. This client can then send k_0 to a server $\mathcal{S}_0$ and send k_1 to a server $\mathcal{S}_1$. A single share k_b completely hides the function $f_{\alpha,\beta}$; it completely hides the location and value of the non-zero point, but not necessarily the fact that $f_{\alpha,\beta}$ is a point function. For any $x \in \{0,1\}^n$, the servers are able to compute $y_b = \mathsf{Eval}(b, k_b, x)$, such that $y_0 + y_1 = f_{\alpha,\beta}(x)$.

The construction of [3] begins with the observation that a point function differs from the zero function (the function that outputs zero on every input) on at most a single point. Therefore, they begin with the following protocol to share the zero function. The zero function can be shared by giving each server an identical copy of a PRF along with an additional bit that indicates if the output should be negated. The servers $\mathcal{S}_0$ and $\mathcal{S}_1$ can then evaluate their PRF on the same input x, then server $\mathcal{S}_1$ negates the output. The scheme will produce outputs from the same input x that sum to zero, making this a secret sharing of the zero function.

We can then instantiate this PRF using the GGM [10] construction, where the PRF is evaluated by expanding a tree of PRGs, and the output of the PRF is a leaf of this tree. Each input to the PRF will arrive at a unique leaf and will have a distinct path through the tree. To turn this zero function into a point function, we need to puncture a single path in this tree. In other words, we need to ensure that there is exactly one path in the tree where the values at the GGM nodes differ. For a point function $f_{\alpha,\beta}$, the path through the tree and the location of the leaf corresponds to α, and the value at the leaf corresponds to β. Since all other paths will have matching nodes, they will result in matching leaves, which become additive shares of zero. The GGM nodes along the punctured path will differ, which will result in this path terminating in leaves that do not match. We will discuss in Sect. 3 how to arrange operations at the final level to turn this one specific mismatched pair into additive shares of the desired non-zero output β.

As we traverse the tree, we maintain the following invariant. If we are along the punctured path (the path leading to the leaf at position α), the PRG seeds should differ. If we are not along the punctured path, then the PRG seeds should be the same. At each level in the tree, we need to ensure that as soon as we diverge from the punctured path, the seeds will match again, bringing us back to the zero-function state. To achieve this, a *correction operation* is applied at each GGM node as we traverse the tree. One of the core contributions of [3] is a method to achieve this correction operation. We make use of the same correction operation and exploit its useful properties to obtain our VDPF construction. More details are provided in Sect. 1.3.

Verification Procedure of [3]. We will now provide a high-level overview of the verification procedures for the DPF construction of [3]. One of the main features of these verification procedures is that they view the DPF as a black-box. With this view, the task becomes taking a secret-shared vector $y = y_0 + y_1$ of length N and verifying that the shared values are non-zero in at-most one location. There are several different protocols presented in [3] to achieve this, although all follow a basic template. These verification procedures all begin by sampling a linear sketching matrix L from a distribution $\mathcal{L}$ with N columns and a small constant number of rows. Each server $\mathcal{S}_b$ multiplies their share y_b by L to obtain a short vector z_b. The servers then run a simple MPC procedure is run to verify that z_0 and z_1 are well-formed. These verification procedures are only secure when the servers are semi-honest.

To give an example, the verification for $\beta \in \{0,1\}$ with an output field $\mathbb{F}$ begins by defining a matrix $L \in F^{3 \times N}$. Each column j of L is defined to be $L_{1,j} = r_j$, $L_{2,j} = s_j$, and $L_{3,j} = r_j s_j$, where r_j and s_j are sampled uniformly at random over $\mathbb{F}$. The two servers begin with PRG seeds to locally generate this L matrix. The servers then locally compute $L \cdot y_b = z_b$, which is a secret sharing of three elements z_1, z_2, and z_3. Finally, the servers run an MPC protocol to check if $z_3 = z_1 z_2$. In [3], it is shown that the probability this check passes if y is not the zero-vector or a unit vector is at most $2/|\mathbb{F}|$. For security parameter λ, this means that $|\mathbb{F}|$ must be at least $2^{\lambda+1}$; all verification procedures given in [3] require that $|\mathbb{F}|$ must be $O(2^\lambda)$.

To obtain a verification for a general β, we can simply take the protocol for $\beta \in \{0,1\}$ and slightly modify the verification procedure to account for a $\beta \neq \beta^2$. In particular, the servers run the same protocol as above, but the final MPC check now verifies that $\beta \cdot z_3 = z_1 z_2$. The client provides a secret-sharing of β to the servers to allow them to compute shares of the product $\beta \cdot z_3$. We conclude this description by noting that this construction is vulnerable to additive attacks, where a malicious server can learn non-trivial information about the client's point (α, β).

Verification Procedure of [1]. We now briefly describe the maliciously secure verification procedure of [1]. Recall that this approach verifies if DPF shares are well formed and if $\beta \in \{0,1\}$. At a high level, this approach is an extension of the check for binary β described above with checksum values added to defend against additive attacks from a malicious server. Instead of sending a single

DPF share corresponding to the point (α, β), this VDPF scheme consists of two DPF shares: one defined by the original point (α, β) and the other defined by the point $(\alpha, \kappa \cdot \beta)$, where κ is a uniformly random element of the output field $\mathbb{F}$. Intuitively, the purpose of this κ value is to defend against a malicious server learning information about the non-zero point by applying additive shifts to candidate α locations. However, the value κ must also be included in the sketching checks in order to verify the consistency of the two DPF shares. This task is prone to error. For example, if the servers were simply given shares of κ directly, then a malicious server could learn if β was 0 if it applied an additive shift to κ and the verification still passed. This would occur because both β and $\kappa \cdot \beta$ are 0 when β is 0. The overcome this, the method of [1] embeds the κ value in an OLE correlation that the client sends to the servers. We omit the details, but we note that, at the time of this writing, there is no published method to extend this binary check to a general check in the same way as in [3]. We conclude this description by summarizing the complexity of this approach. The computational overhead of the verification includes evaluating the second DPF share that encodes the checksum, as well as sampling the sketching matrix. Then the sketching matrix must be multiplied by the output DPF vectors, which is a constant number of length N inner-products. The communication of the verification procedure consists of 4 elements of $\mathbb{F}$ sent by each server over two rounds of communication.

1.3   Technical Overview

We now give a brief technical overview of our verification methods.

Our DPF Verification Procedure. In our work, we observe that the correction operation of [3] is limited in a way that is useful for us. In particular, the correction operation is designed to correct *at most* one difference per level. With this observation, we can construct a simple verification procedure by extending the GGM tree by one level. This level takes each leaf in the original tree and produces two children: a left leaf and a right leaf. The left leaves can all be equivalent to the parent, while the right leaves should all correspond to a zero output. This means that all pairs of right leaves in the two DPF shares should be *equal.* Since the correction word can only correct one difference, if all the right leaves are the same, then there can be at most one difference in the previous level, meaning that all but one of the left leaves must be the same. The location of the differing left leaf is the α value, and the value produced by the differing leaves is the β value. All other left leaves will be equal, thus corresponding to the zero output. Since the DPF evaluation is completely deterministic, the α and β values that define the point function can be deterministically extracted from any pair of DPF shares that pass this verification check, meaning that regardless of the method a malicious client uses to generate the DPF shares, if the verification check passes then the servers have the guarantee that the shares encode a DPF defined by this (α, β) pair.

Furthermore, the servers need only check that all of their right leaves (which they can hash down into a single string of length 2λ) are equal, meaning that if the DPF shares are well formed the servers' messages to each other are perfectly simulatable. Therefore, this verification method introduces zero additional privacy risk to an honest client even when one of the servers is malicious. This security extends to verifying a polynomial number of DPF shares from the same client or different clients, since an equality check that will always pass for honest clients will not leak information about the honest clients' choices of α and β.

For more details and intuition about this approach, see Sect. 3.

Multi-point Function Packing. A natural application of our packed verification technique is to verify multi-point functions, since the communication for the verification will not increase as the number of non-zero points grows. As discussed above, the naive construction of a multi-point function with t non-zero points requires time linear in t for each evaluation. This is prohibitively expensive for applications where the servers must evaluate the DMPF at many points. To avoid this linear scaling of the evaluation time, we observe that in the list of tuples $(\alpha_1, \beta_1), \ldots, (\alpha_t, \beta_t)$ all of the α values are unique. Therefore, for each evaluation point x, the output of at most one of the DPFs will be nonzero, which occurs if $x = \alpha_i$. This means that our DMPF evaluation algorithm only needs to guarantee that the evaluation point x will be evaluated on the DPF with $\alpha_i = x$ if this point is nonzero in the MPF.

Towards this goal, we have the client insert the values $\alpha_1, \ldots, \alpha_t$ into a Cuckoo-hash table. At a high level, a Cuckoo-hash table is defined by a list of m buckets and $\kappa = O(1)$ of hash functions $h_1, \ldots, h_\kappa$ (in our case we use $\kappa = 3$). Each hash function has an output space that is $\{1, \ldots, m\}$, and each element α inserted in the table is at an index $i = h_j(\alpha)$ for some $1 \leq j \leq \kappa$.

The client constructs a DMPF share from this Cuckoo-hash table by creating a DPF share for each bucket in the table. The empty buckets will hold a DPF that shares the zero function, and the buckets that hold an index α_i hold a DPF that shares f_{α_i, β_i}. The domain of this DPF can be the same as the domain of the MPF, so the index of this non-zero point is simply α_i. The client then sends these m DPF shares to the server along with the hash functions defining the Cuckoo-hash table. To evaluate a point x on these shares, the servers simply hash x with each of the κ hash functions to get κ candidate buckets. If $x = \alpha_i$ for one of the non-zero points in the MPF, the guarantee is that α_i is in one of these buckets, so the servers evaluate only these κ DPFs at x then sum the result. This is an MPF evaluation procedure with a runtime that does not grow with the number of non-zero points in the MPF. In Sect. 4, we discuss a variant of this method that allows the domain of the DPFs for Cuckoo-hash buckets to *shrink* as the number of nonzero points grows, further speeding up evaluation time.

To maintain client privacy, we must ensure that the Cuckoo-hash table does not leak information about the client's choice of $\alpha_1, \ldots, \alpha_t$ values. The only information that is leaked from the Cuckoo-hash table is that the client's choice of non-zero indices did not fail to be inserted in this Cuckoo-hash table. Therefore, we must choose parameters for the Cuckoo-hash table such that the probability of failure is at most $2^{-\lambda}$ for security parameter λ. For a fixed κ, the failure probability of a Cuckoo-hash table shrinks as the number of buckets m increases. For $\kappa = 3$ and $\lambda = 80$, we get an upper bound on the number of buckets as $m \leq 2t$ for nearly all practical values of t. Therefore, for less than a $2\times$ growth in the client computation and the client-server communication, we can achieve this significant improvement in the servers' evaluation time.

To verify that these DMPF shares are well-formed, we can simply put verifiable DPF shares in the buckets. Since the DPF verification method can be packed, the communication between the two servers never grows beyond the 2λ equality check, and the security against a malicious server is maintained. Our only sacrifice is in the verification of the number of nonzero points in the DMPF. The naive approach would allow the servers to verify that there are at most t nonzero points in the MPF, while the Cuckoo-hashing approach only allows the servers to verify that there are at most m nonzero points in the MPF. However, as we mentioned, for nearly all settings of t we get $m \leq 2t$, and we believe this gap is acceptable for many applications.

2   Background

2.1   Notation

Let $\mathcal{T}$ be a complete binary tree with 2^n leaves. If we index each leaf from 0 to $2^n - 1$, let $v_\alpha^{(n)}$ be the leaf at index $\alpha \in \{0, 1\}^n$. Let $v_\alpha^{(i)}$ be the node at the ith level of $\mathcal{T}$ such that $v_\alpha^{(n)}$ is in the subtree rooted at $v_\alpha^{(i)}$. We will sometimes refer to $v_\alpha^{(i)}$ as the ith node along the path to α.

For a finite set S, we will denote sampling a uniformly random element x as $x \xleftarrow{\$} S$.

For $n \in \mathbb{N}$, we denote the set $[n] := \{1, \ldots, n\}$.

We will denote a set of n-bit strings as either $\{x_i\}_{i=1}^L$ or simply as $\mathbf{x}$ if the length is not relevant or clear from context.

For a parameter λ, we say that a function $\mathsf{negl}(\lambda)$ is *negligible* in λ if it shrinks faster than all polynomials in λ. In other words, for all polynomials $\mathsf{poly}(\lambda)$, there exists a λ' such that for all $\lambda > \lambda'$ we have $\mathsf{negl}(\lambda) < \mathsf{poly}(\lambda)$.

2.2   Function Secret Sharing

In this section, we give a high level definition of function secret sharing and distributed point functions. A function secret sharing scheme takes a function $f \colon \mathcal{D} \to \mathcal{R}$ and generates two *function shares* f_0 and f_1. These function shares can be evaluated a points $x \in \mathcal{D}$ such that $f_b(x) = y_b$ and $y_0 + y_1 = y = f(x)$. In other words, when evaluated at an input x the function shares produce additive secret shares of the function output. It is currently an open problem to construct an efficient FSS scheme where the function is split into more than two shares [4].

Definition 1 (Function Secret Sharing, Syntax & Correctness [2,3]**).** *A function secret sharing scheme is defined by two PPT algorithms. These algorithms are parametrized by a function class $\mathcal{F}$ of functions between a domain $\mathcal{D}$ and a range $\mathcal{R}$.*

– FSS.Gen($1^\lambda, f \in \mathcal{F}$) → ($k_0, k_1$)
  The FSS.Gen *algorithm takes in a function $f \in \mathcal{F}$ and generates two FSS keys k_0 and k_1.*
– FSS.Eval($b, k_b, x \in \mathcal{D}$) → y_b
  The FSS.Eval *algorithm takes in an $x \in \mathcal{D}$ and outputs an additive share $y_b \in \mathcal{R}$ of the value $y = f(x)$. In other words, $y_0 + y_1 = y = f(x)$.*

We now give the basic security property that an FSS scheme must satisfy.

Definition 2 (FSS Security: Function Privacy [2,3]**).** *Let* FSS *be a function secret sharing scheme for the function class $\mathcal{F}$, as defined in Definition 1. For any $f, f' \in \mathcal{F}$, the following should hold:*

$$\{k_b \mid (k_0, k_1) \leftarrow \text{FSS.Gen}(\{0,1\}, f)\} \approx_c$$
$$\{k'_b \mid (k'_0, k'_1) \leftarrow \text{FSS.Gen}(\{0,1\}, f')\}, \quad for\ b \in \{0,1\}$$

In words, the marginal distribution of one of the FSS keys computationally hides the function used to compute the share.

We now give the definition of a distributed point function (DPF) in terms of the FSS definitions above. We begin by defining a point function.

Definition 3 (Point Function). *A function $f: \mathcal{D} \to \mathcal{R}$ is a point function if there is $\alpha \in \mathcal{D}$ and $\beta \in \mathcal{R}$ such that the following holds:*

$$f_{\alpha,\beta}(x) = \begin{cases} \beta & x = \alpha \\ 0 & x \neq \alpha \end{cases}$$

Throughout this work, we will be interested in point functions with domain $\mathcal{D} = \{0,1\}^n$ and range $\mathcal{R} = \mathbb{G}$ for a group $\mathbb{G}$.

Definition 4 (Distributed Point Function). *Let $\mathcal{F}_{n,\mathcal{G}}$ be the class of point functions with domain $\mathcal{D} = \{0,1\}^n$ and range $\mathcal{R} = \mathbb{G}$. We call an FSS scheme a Distributed Point Function scheme if it supports the function class $\mathcal{F}$.*

3 Lightweight, Verifiable DPF

3.1 Definitions

We begin by defining a verifiable DPF. We define correctness and security for a batched evaluation, since the verification procedure operates is defined over a set of outputs. The procedure ensures that at-most one of these outputs is non-zero.

Definition 5 (Verifiable DPF, denoted $\text{VerDPF}_{n,\mathbb{G}}$). *A verifiable distributed point function scheme $\text{VerDPF}_{n,\mathbb{G}}$ supports the function class $\mathcal{F}$ of point functions $f\colon \{0,1\}^n \to \mathbb{G}$. It is defined by three PPT algorithms. Define $\text{VerDPF} := \text{VerDPF}_{n,\mathbb{G}}$.*

- $\text{VerDPF.Gen}(1^\lambda, f_{\alpha,\beta}) \to (\mathsf{k}_0, \mathsf{k}_1)$
  This is the FSS share generation algorithm. It takes in a function $f_{\alpha,\beta}$ and generates two shares k_0 and k_1.
- $\text{VerDPF.BVEval}(b, \mathsf{k}_b, \{x_i\}_{i=1}^L) \to \left(\{y_b^{(x_i)}\}_{i=1}^L, \pi_b \right)$
  This is the verifiable evaluation algorithm, denoted BVEval for batch verifiable evaluation. It takes in a set of L inputs $\{x_i\}_{i=1}^L$, where each $x_i \in \{0,1\}^n$, and outputs a tuple of values. The first set of values are the FSS outputs, which take the form $y_b^{(x_i)}$ for $i \in [L]$ satisfying $y_0^{(x_i)} + y_1^{(x_i)} = f(x_i)$. The second output is a proof π_b that is used to verify the well-formedness of the output.
- $\text{VerDPF.Verify}(\pi_0, \pi_1) \to \text{Accept/Reject}$
  For some pair of VerDPF keys $(\mathsf{k}_0, \mathsf{k}_1)$, the VerDPF.Verify algorithm takes in the proofs π_0 and π_1 from $(y_b, \pi_b) \leftarrow \text{BVEval}(b, \mathsf{k}_b, \{x_i\}_{i=1}^L)$ and outputs either Accept or Reject. The output should only be Accept if $y_0 + y_1$ defines the truth table of some point function, which occurs if it is non-zero in at most one location.

Correctness for a verifiable DPF is defined in the same way as correctness for any FSS scheme, as in Definition 1. To verify that the entire share is well-formed, the BVEval algorithm can be run on the whole domain. We give a more efficient algorithm for evaluating our verifiable DPF on the whole domain in Algorithm 3, which uses techniques from Boyle et al. [3] to save a factor of n on the overall runtime.

We now define security for a verifiable DPF. Note that we are only interested in detecting a malformed share when the evaluators are semi-honest. However, we do require that even a malicious evaluator does not learn any information about the shared function; in other words, we require that the verification process does not compromise the function privacy of an honestly generated DPF share if one of the evaluators is malicious.

Definition 6 (Verifiable DPF Share Integrity, or Security Against Malicious Share Generation). *Let $\text{VerDPF} := \text{VerDPF}_{n,\mathbb{G}}$, and let k_b be the (possibly maliciously generated) share received by server S_b. For an adversarially chosen set of inputs $\{x_i\}_{i=1}^\eta$, let $(\{y_b^{(x_i)}\}_{i=1}^\eta, \pi_b) \leftarrow \text{VerDPF.BVEval}(b, \mathsf{k}_b, \{x_i\}_{i=1}^\eta)$. We say that VerDPF is secure against malicious share generation if the the following holds with all but negligible probability over the adversary's choice of randomness. If $\text{VerDPF.Verify}(\pi_0, \pi_1)$ outputs Accept, then the values $y_0^{(x_i)} + y_1^{(x_i)}$ must be non-zero in at most one location.*

Definition 7 (Verifiable DPF Function Privacy, or Security Against a Malicious Evaluator). *Let $\text{VerDPF} := \text{VerDPF}_{n,\mathbb{G}}$ support the class of point functions $\mathcal{F}$ with domain $\{0,1\}^n$ and range $\mathbb{G}$. For a set of function inputs $\mathbf{x}$,* define the distribution representing the view of server $\mathcal{S}_b$ for a fixed function $f \in \mathcal{F}$.

$$\mathsf{View}_{\mathsf{VerDPF}}(b, f, \mathbf{x}) :=$$
$$\left\{ (\mathsf{k}_b, \pi_{1-b}) \;\middle|\; \begin{array}{l} (\mathsf{k}_0, \mathsf{k}_1) \leftarrow \mathsf{VerDPF.Gen}(1^\lambda, f), \\ (\_, \pi_{1-b}) \leftarrow \mathsf{VerDPF.BVEval}(1 - b, \mathsf{k}_{1-b}, \mathbf{x}) \end{array} \right\}$$

We say that VerDPF maintains function privacy if there exists a PPT simulator Sim such that for any adversarially chosen $\mathbf{x}$ the following two distributions are computationally indistinguishable for any $f \in \mathcal{F}$.

$$\left\{ (\mathsf{k}_b, \pi_{1-b}) \mid (\mathsf{k}_b, \pi_{1-b}) \leftarrow \mathsf{View}_{\mathsf{VerDPF}}(b, f, \mathbf{x}) \right\} \approx_c$$
$$\left\{ (\mathsf{k}^*, \pi^*) \mid (\mathsf{k}^*, \pi^*) \leftarrow \mathsf{Sim}(1^\lambda, b, n, \mathbb{G}, \mathbf{x}) \right\}$$

3.2 Our Construction

In this DPF scheme, the shares of the point function are k_0 and k_1. Each key k_b contains a starting seed $s_b^{(0)}$ that defines the root of a GGM-style binary tree, where at each node there is a PRG seed that is expanded into two seeds that comprise the left and the right child of that node. However, the seeds that define the left and right children are not the direct output of the PRG; instead, we apply a correction operation to the PRG output in order to maintain the required property of these trees, which we call the "DPF invariant."

In addition to the PRG seed, each node is associated with a *control bit*, which is one additional bit of information that is updated along with the seed during the correction operation. This control bit is used in the correction operation, and its purpose is to maintain the DPF invariant.

Definition 8 (DPF Invariant). *Let* $\mathsf{DPF} = \mathsf{DPF}_{n,\mathbb{G}}$, *and let*

$$(\mathsf{k}_0, \mathsf{k}_1) \leftarrow \mathsf{DPF.Gen}(1^\lambda, f_{\alpha,\beta})$$

for $\alpha \in \{0,1\}^n$. *Each key* k_b *defines a binary tree* $\mathcal{T}_b$ *with* 2^n *leaves, and each node in the tree is associated with a PRG seed and a control bit.*

For a fixed node location, let s_0, t_0 *be the seed and control bit associate with the node in* $\mathcal{T}_0$, *and let* s_1, t_1 *be the seed and control bit associated with the node in* $\mathcal{T}_1$. *The DPF invariant is defined as the following:*

$$s_0 = s_1 \text{ and } t_0 = t_1 \qquad \text{if the node is not along the path to } \alpha.$$
$$t_0 \neq t_1 \qquad\qquad\qquad \text{if the node is along the path to } \alpha.$$

In our construction, it is also very likely that $s_0 \neq s_1$ *if the node is along the path to* α, *but this requirement is not necessary for the invariant.*

From this invariant, we maintain that at each level there is exactly one place in which the two trees differ, which is the node in that level corresponding to the path to α. At the final level, all of the 2^n leaves in both trees will be the

---

Algorithm 1. VerDPF$_{n,\mathbb{G}}$ node expansion, denoted NodeExpand. This algorithm describes generating the child nodes from the parent node in the DPF tree.

Input: PRG $\mathcal{G}\colon \{0,1\}^\lambda \to \{0,1\}^{2\lambda+2}$
    Seed $s \in \{0,1\}^\lambda$, control bit $t \in \{0,1\}$.
    Correction word $\mathsf{cw} = (s_c, t_c^L, t_c^R)$.
1: Expand $(s^L, t^L, s^R, t^R) \leftarrow \mathcal{G}(s)$
2: $s_0' \leftarrow \mathsf{correct}(s^L, s_c, t)$ and $t_0' \leftarrow \mathsf{correct}(t^L, t_c^L, t)$
3: $s_1' \leftarrow \mathsf{correct}(s^R, s_c, t)$ and $t_1' \leftarrow \mathsf{correct}(t^R, t_c^R, t)$
Output: $(s_0', t_0'), (s_1', t_1')$

---

same, except at position α. We can define deterministic transformations on the values at the leaves such that leaves with the same value produce additive shares of zero. These transformations are each determined by the control bit, and symmetry in the control bits results in symmetric application of these deterministic operations. At the leaf where the values differ, the invariant tells us that the control bits will differ, and we can take advantage of this asymmetry to produce additive shares of β at this pair of leaves.

In order to maintain the invariant in Definition 8, we perform a correction operation at each node as we traverse the tree. Each level of the tree is associated with a correction word. At each node, we perform the PRG expansion defined in Definition 9, then apply the correction operation define in Definition 10 to compute the seeds and control bits for the left and right children.

Definition 9 (VerDPF PRG Expansion [3]). *Let $s \in \{0,1\}$ be a seed for the PRG $\mathcal{G}\colon \{0,1\}^\lambda \to \{0,1\}^{2\lambda+2}$. Define the PRG expansion of the seed s as follows:*

$$s^L\|t^L\|s^R\|t^R \leftarrow \mathcal{G}(s)$$

where $s^L, s^R \in \{0,1\}^\lambda$ and $t^L, t^R \in \{0,1\}$.

Definition 10 (VerDPF Correction Operation [3]). *The VerDPF correction operation*

$$\mathsf{correct}_{\mathbb{G}}\colon \mathbb{G} \times \mathbb{G} \times \{0,1\} \to \mathbb{G}$$

is defined as follows:

$$\mathsf{correct}_{\mathbb{G}}(\xi_0, \xi_1, t) = \begin{cases} \xi_0 & if \quad t = 0 \\ \xi_0 + \xi_1 & if \quad t = 1 \end{cases}$$

When $\mathbb{G}$ is not defined, the group $\mathbb{G}$ is taken to be $\mathbb{Z}_2^\ell$ for some positive integer ℓ. In particular, this makes the group addition operation the component-wise XOR of ξ_0 and ξ_1.

From the node expansion described in Algorithm 1, it becomes clear what the correction word must be in order to maintain that only one pair of nodes differ at each level of the tree. In particular, if the bit x_i disagrees with α_i, the corresponding bit of α, then the correction word must ensure that seeds and controls bits in the next level match. We define the correction word generation algorithm in Algorithm 2.

Algorithm 2. VerDPF$_{n,\mathbb{G}}$ correction word generation, denoted CWGen.

Input: PRG $\mathcal{G} \colon \{0,1\}^\lambda \rightarrow \{0,1\}^{2\lambda+2}$
        Left seed s_0, left control bit t_0.
        Right seed s_1, right control bit t_1.
        Bit x of the input.
1: Expand $(s_b^L, t_b^L, s_b^R, t_b^R) \leftarrow \mathcal{G}(s_b)$ for $b \in \{0,1\}$.
2: **if** $x = 0$ **then** Diff $\leftarrow L$, Same $\leftarrow R$ ▷ Set the right children to be equal.
3: **else** Diff $\leftarrow R$, Same $\leftarrow L$ ▷ Set the left children to be equal.
4: $s_c \leftarrow s_0^{\mathsf{Same}} \oplus s_1^{\mathsf{Same}}$
5: $t_c^L \leftarrow t_0^L \oplus t_1^L \oplus 1 \oplus x$ ▷ Ensure that the left control bits are not equal iff $x = 0$.
6: $t_c^R \leftarrow t_0^R \oplus t_1^R \oplus x$ ▷ Ensure that the right control bits are not equal iff $x = 1$.
7: cw $\leftarrow s_c || t_c^L || t_c^R$
8: $s_b' \leftarrow \mathsf{correct}(s_b^{\mathsf{Diff}}, s_c, t_b^{(i-1)})$ for $b \in \{0,1\}$.
9: $t_b' \leftarrow \mathsf{correct}(t_b^{\mathsf{Diff}}, t_c^{\mathsf{Diff}}, t_b)$ for $b \in \{0,1\}$.
Output: cw, (s_0', t_0'), (s_1', t_1')

Intuitively, our construction takes advantage of the fact that the correction words in the DPF construction of Boyle et al. can only correct at most one difference in each level. In our construction, we extend the GGM tree by one level, extending the DPF evaluation to all of the left children. In addition, at the final level we replace the PRG with a hash function H sampled from a family $\mathcal{H}$ that is collision-resistant and correlation-intractable for an XOR correlation defined below. We then have the servers check that all of their right children are the same by hashing all right children and exchanging the hash value.

In an honest pair of function shares, the trees should only differ at one node at each level, and in the final level the only difference should be in one of the left children. The collision resistance of the hash function ensures that any difference in the second-to-last level will result in a difference in the right children. This forces the correction word to correct these right children in order for the consistency check to pass. Since the correction word can correct at most one difference in the right children, this will guarantee that all other right children are the same because their parents are the same, which, in turn, implies that all corresponding left children are the same.

As discussed above, it is straightforward to turn matching leaf nodes into additive shares of zero, although we will have to generate the final control bit slightly differently in this final level to ensure that this conversion is performed correctly. In particular, we generate these control bits deterministically from the seeds, which ensures that matching seeds will result in matching control bits. For the non-zero output, we will have the honest client generate the function shares until the control bits at the non-zero point are different. If a malicious client samples shares such that these bits are the same, this will simply correspond to a different choice of β.

To securely instantiate the final level of the tree, our hash function family must be collision resistant, which will ensure that a difference in the previous level will translate to a difference in the children. We will also require the hash function to be secure against a similar, but incomparable, correlation, which we call *XOR-collision resistance*. Intuitively, satisfying this definition will ensure that each correction seed will only be able to correct one difference in the right children.

Definition 11 (XOR-Collision Resistance). *We say a function family $\mathcal{F}$ is XOR-collision resistant if no PPT adversary given a randomly sampled $f \in \mathcal{F}$ can find four values $x_0, x_1, x_2, x_3 \in \{0,1\}^\lambda$ such that $(x_0, x_1) \neq (x_2, x_3)$, $(x_0, x_1) \neq (x_3, x_2)$, and $f(x_0) \oplus f(x_1) = f(x_2) \oplus f(x_3) \neq 0$ with probability better than some function $\mathsf{negl}(\lambda)$ that is negligible in λ.*

To satisfy this definition, our hash function output has length 4λ, since we must defend against a birthday-attack where the adversary is searching for a colliding 4-tuple. We expand on this more in the full version. With a hash function satisfying this definition, we will be able to argue that if an adversary can construct invalid VerDPF keys that pass the consistency check, then this adversary has found either a collision or an XOR-collision in the hash function.

We define the VerDPF key in Definition 12. The full verifiable DPF construction is given in Fig. 1.

Definition 12 (VerDPF Function Share). *Let $\mathsf{VerDPF}_{n,\mathbb{G}}$ be our verifiable DPF scheme. Let λ be the security parameter. A function share contains the following elements.*

- *Starting seed $s^{(0)} \in \{0,1\}^\lambda$.*
- *Correction words $\mathsf{cw}_1, \ldots, \mathsf{cw}_n$, where each $\mathsf{cw}_i \in \{0,1\}^\lambda \times \{0,1\} \times \{0,1\}$.*
- *One additional correction seed $\mathsf{cs} \in \{0,1\}^{4\lambda}$, which corrects differences in the final level. Corrections to the control bits are not necessary at the final level.*
- *A final output correction group element $\mathsf{ocw} \in \mathbb{G}$.*

Lemma 1 (VerDPF Correctness). *The VerDPF scheme defined in Fig. 1 defines a correct verifiable DPF scheme.*

Proof. If we ignore the last level of the DPF expansion, our DPF is essentially the same as the DPF construction of Boyle et al. [3]. The only difference is the way the final control bits are generated. The control bits for the nodes that correspond to zero outputs will be the same, since the seeds for these leaves will also be the same. In the key generation, the seeds are sampled such that the control bits for the leaf at position α will differ, allowing the selective XOR of the final correction word. Since the correct operation is deterministic, the nodes

Verifiable Distributed Point Function $\mathsf{VerDPF}_{n,\mathbb{G}}$.

Let $\mathsf{VerDPF} := \mathsf{VerDPF}_{n,\mathbb{G}}$. Let $\mathcal{G}\colon \{0,1\}^\lambda \to \{0,1\}^{2\lambda+2}$ be a PRG. Let $\mathsf{H}\colon \{0,1\}^{n+\lambda} \to \{0,1\}^{4\lambda}$ be a hash function sampled from a family $\mathcal{H}$ that is both collision-resistant and XOR-collision-resistant. Let $\mathsf{H}'\colon \{0,1\}^{4\lambda} \to \{0,1\}^{2\lambda}$ be a hash function sampled from a family $\mathcal{H}'$ that is collision-resistant. Let $\mathsf{convert}\colon \{0,1\}^\lambda \to \mathbb{G}$ be a map converting a random λ-bit string to a pseudorandom element of $\mathbb{G}$. Let $\mathsf{LSB}\{0,1\}^\ell \to \{0,1\}$ be the function that takes any bit-string and extracts the least significant bit.

The $\mathsf{VerDPF.Verify}$ algorithm simply checks if the two input proofs are equal.

VerDPF.Gen

Input: Security parameter 1^λ and point function $f_{\alpha,\beta}\colon \{0,1\}^n \to \mathbb{G}$

1: Sample $s_0^{(0)} \leftarrow \{0,1\}^\lambda$ and $s_1^{(0)} \leftarrow \{0,1\}^\lambda$. Set $t_0^{(0)} = 0$ and $t_1^{(0)} = 1$.
2: Let $\alpha_1, \ldots \alpha_n$ be the bits of α.
3: **for** i from 1 to n **do**
4:     vals $\leftarrow \mathsf{CWGen}(\mathcal{G}, s_0^{(i-1)}, t_0^{(i-1)}, s_1^{(i-1)}, t_1^{(i-1)}, \alpha_i)$
5:     Parse $\mathsf{cw}_i, (s_0^{(i)}, t_0^{(i)}), (s_1^{(i)}, t_1^{(i)}) \leftarrow$ vals
6: $\tilde{\pi}_b \leftarrow \mathsf{H}(\alpha \| s_b^{(n)})$ for $b \in \{0,1\}$.
7: $\mathsf{cs} \leftarrow \tilde{\pi}_0 \oplus \tilde{\pi}_1$.
8: $s_b^{(n+1)} \leftarrow s_b^{(n)}$ ▷ True output always extends to left child.
9: $t_b^{(n+1)} \leftarrow \mathsf{LSB}(s_b^{(n+1)})$
10: **if** $t_0^{(n+1)} = t_1^{(n+1)}$ **then goto** 1
11: Compute output correction word: $\mathsf{ocw} \leftarrow (-1)^{t_1^{(n+1)}} [\beta - \mathsf{convert}(s_0^{(n+1)}) + \mathsf{convert}(s_1^{(n+1)})]$
12: Set $\mathsf{k}_b \leftarrow (s_b^{(0)}, \{\mathsf{cw}_i\}_{i=1}^n, \mathsf{cs}, \mathsf{ocw})$ for $b \in \{0,1\}$
Output: $(\mathsf{k}_0, \mathsf{k}_1)$

VerDPF.BVEval

Input: $b \in \{0,1\}$ and VerDPF key k_b.
        Set of L distinct evaluation points $x_1, \ldots, x_L$.

1: Parse the VerDPF key $(s^{(0)}, \{\mathsf{cw}_i\}_{i=1}^n, \mathsf{cs}, \mathsf{ocw}) \leftarrow \mathsf{k}_b$.
2: Define $\mathsf{y} \leftarrow \{\}$ and $\pi \leftarrow \mathsf{cs}$
3: **for** ℓ from 1 to L **do**
4:     Let $s \leftarrow s^{(0)}$ and $t \leftarrow b$.
5:     Let $\beta_1 = \mathsf{MSB}(x_\ell), \ldots, \beta_n = \mathsf{LSB}(x_\ell)$ be the bits of x_ℓ.
6:     **for** i from 1 to n **do**
7:         $(s_0', t_0'), (s_1', t_1') \leftarrow \mathsf{NodeExpand}(\mathcal{G}, s, t)$
8:         **if** $\beta_i = 0$ **then** $(s,t) \leftarrow (s_0', t_0')$
9:         **else** $(s,t) \leftarrow (s_1', t_1')$
10:     $\tilde{\pi} \leftarrow \mathsf{H}(x_\ell \| s)$ and $t \leftarrow \mathsf{LSB}(s)$
11:     $\mathsf{y}.\mathsf{append}\left((-1)^b \cdot \mathsf{correct}_{\mathbb{G}}(\mathsf{convert}(s), \mathsf{ocw}, t)\right)$
12:     $\pi \leftarrow \pi \oplus \mathsf{H}'(\pi \oplus \mathsf{correct}(\tilde{\pi}, \mathsf{cs}, t))$
Output: (y, π)

Fig. 1. Verifiable distributed point function $\mathsf{VerDPF}_{n,\mathbb{G}}$.

Algorithm 3 . VerDPF.FDEval. The verifiable full-domain evaluation function for our verifiable DPF construction. The hash functions H and H′ are as in Figure 1.

Input: $b \in \{0, 1\}$ and VerDPF key k_b.
 1: Parse the VerDPF key $(s^{(0)}, \{cw_i\}_{i=1}^n, cs, ocw) \leftarrow k_b$.
 2: Let $s \leftarrow s^{(0)}$ and $t \leftarrow b$
 3: Define nodes $\leftarrow \{(s, t)\}$
 4: **for** i from 1 to n **do**
 5:     Define nodes′ $\leftarrow \{\}$
 6:     **for** (s, t) in nodes **do**
 7:         $(s'_0, t'_0), (s'_1, t'_1) \leftarrow$ NodeExpand$(\mathcal{G}, s, t)$
 8:         nodes′.append$((s'_0, t'_0))$
 9:         nodes′.append$((s'_1, t'_1))$
10:     nodes $\leftarrow$ nodes′
11: Define y $\leftarrow \{\}$ and $\pi \leftarrow cs$
12: **for** i from 1 to N **do**
13:     $(s, \_) \leftarrow$ nodes$[i]$.
14:     $\tilde{\pi} \leftarrow H(i \| s)$
15:     $t \leftarrow LSB(s)$
16:     y.append $\left((-1)^b \cdot \text{correct}_\mathbb{G}(\text{convert}(s), ocw, t)\right)$
17:     $\pi \leftarrow \pi \oplus H'(\pi \oplus \text{correct}(\tilde{\pi}, cs, t))$

Output: (y, π)

---

with matching seeds and control bits will produce shares of zero. This can be seen below, where we set $s_0 = s_1$ and $t_0 = t_1$.

$$y_b = (-1)^b \cdot \text{correct}_\mathbb{G}(\text{convert}(s_b), ocw, t_b) = -1 \cdot y_{1-b}$$

For the leaf at position α, we have that $t_0 \neq t_1$. Here, the output values will be a secret sharing of β. For simplicity, we write $g_b = \text{convert}(s_b)$.

$$ocw = (-1)^{t_1} [\beta - g_0 + g_1]$$
$$y_0 + y_1 = \text{correct}_\mathbb{G}(g_0, ocw, t_0) + \text{correct}_\mathbb{G}(g_1, ocw, t_1)$$
$$= g_0 - g_1 + (-1)^{t_0} \cdot ocw = g_0 - g_1 + \beta - g_0 + g_1 = \beta$$

where we get that $(-1)^{t_0} \cdot ocw = \beta - g_0 + g_1$ from $t_0 \neq t_1$.

3.3   VDPF Security Proof

We will now prove that the verifiable DPF construction given in Fig. 1 is secure. We will focus on proving the following theorem.

Lemma 2 (Detection of Malicious Function Shares). *Except with probability negligible in the security parameter* λ, *no PPT adversary* $\mathcal{A}$ *can generate VerDPF keys* $(k_0^*, k_1^*) \leftarrow \mathcal{A}(1^\lambda)$ *where the final level uses a hash function* $H \leftarrow \mathcal{H}$ *sampled from a family* $\mathcal{H}$ *of collision-resistant and XOR-collision-resistant hash* *functions such that the following holds. For an adversarially chosen set of evaluation points* $\{x_i\}_{i=1}^L$, *let* $(y_b, \pi_b) \leftarrow$ VerDPF.BVEval$(b, k_b^*, \{x_i\}_{i=1}^L)$ *such that* Accept $\leftarrow$ VerDPF.Verify(π_0, π_1) *passes but* $y_0 + y_1$ *is nonzero in more than one location.*

Proof. The approach to proving this theorem will be to focus on the final level of the GGM tree. At the second-to-last level, each server has a set of seeds $\{s_0^{(x_i)}\}_{i=1}^L$ and $\{s_1^{(x_i)}\}_{i=1}^L$. The servers also have the *same* correction seed cs. Let $\tilde{\pi}_b^{(x)} \leftarrow$ H$(x||s_b^{(x)})$, let $t_b^{(x)} \leftarrow$ LSB$(s_b^{(x)})$, and let $\pi_b^{(x)} \leftarrow$ correct$(\tilde{\pi}_b^{(x)}, cs, t_b^{(x)})$. The bulk of this proof is covered by the following lemma.

Lemma 3. *For* $L \geq 2$, *let* $\mathbf{x} := \{x_i\}_{i=1}^L$. *Suppose there exists two distinct inputs* $u, v \in \mathbf{x}$ *such that* $s_0^{(u)} \neq s_1^{(u)}$ *and* $s_0^{(v)} \neq s_1^{(v)}$. *If* H *is sampled from a collision-resistant and XOR-collision-resistant family, then no PPT adversary can find a correction seed* cs *such that for all* $x \in \mathbf{x}$ *we will have* $\pi_0^{(x)} = \pi_1^{(x)}$.

Proof. Suppose for contradiction that there exists two inputs $u, v \in \mathbf{x}$ such that $s_0^{(u)} \neq s_1^{(u)}$ and $s_0^{(v)} \neq s_1^{(v)}$ and for all $x \in \mathbf{x}$ we have $\pi_0^{(x)} = \pi_1^{(x)}$. By collision-resistance, we have that $\tilde{\pi}_0^{(u)} \neq \tilde{\pi}_1^{(u)}$ and $\tilde{\pi}_0^{(v)} \neq \tilde{\pi}_1^{(v)}$. In order to get $\pi_0^{(u)} = \pi_1^{(u)}$ and $\pi_0^{(v)} = \pi_1^{(v)}$, we need the following:

$$\textsf{cs} = \tilde{\pi}_0^{(u)} \oplus \tilde{\pi}_1^{(u)} = \tilde{\pi}_0^{(v)} \oplus \tilde{\pi}_1^{(v)} \neq 0$$

From the XOR-collision-resistance of $\mathcal{H}$, in order to get this equality we must have one of the following two cases.

- Case (i): $\tilde{\pi}_0^{(u)} = \tilde{\pi}_0^{(v)}$ and $\tilde{\pi}_1^{(u)} = \tilde{\pi}_1^{(v)}$
- Case (ii): $\tilde{\pi}_0^{(u)} = \tilde{\pi}_1^{(v)}$ and $\tilde{\pi}_1^{(u)} = \tilde{\pi}_0^{(v)}$

We can show that any one of these four equalities violates the collision-resistance of H. Suppose we have H$(u||s_b^{(u)}) = \tilde{\pi}_b^{(u)} = \tilde{\pi}_{b'}^{(v)} = $ H$(v||s_{b'}^{(v)})$ for any $b, b' \in \{0, 1\}$. Since $u \neq v$, any equality between these hash outputs violates the collision resistance of $\mathcal{H}$.

Therefore, no value of cs will result in $\pi_0^{(x)} = \pi_1^{(x)}$ for all $x \in \mathbf{x}$.

From the collision resistance of H$'$, if the proofs produced by the BVEval algorithm match, then $\pi_0^{(x)} = \pi_1^{(x)}$ for all $x \in \mathbf{x}$. From Lemma 3, this implies that there is at most one $u \in \mathbf{x}$ such that $s_0^{(u)} \neq s_1^{(u)}$, and for all $x \in \mathbf{x}$ such that $x \neq u$, we have $s_0^{(x)} = s_1^{(x)}$.

Define $\alpha = u$ for the unique u such that $s_0^{(u)} \neq s_1^{(u)}$. If no such u exists (which occurs if all outputs are zero), set $u = x_1$. Define

$$\beta = \textsf{correct}_{\mathbb{G}}\left(\textsf{convert}(s_0^{(u)}), \textsf{ocw}, t_0^{(u)}\right) - \textsf{correct}_{\mathbb{G}}\left(\textsf{convert}(s_1^{(u)}), \textsf{ocw}, t_1^{(u)}\right)$$

Note that this β is well-defined for any $s_b^{(u)}$ and $t_b^{(u)}$. For all other $x \neq u$, observing that $t_b^{(x)} = \mathsf{LSB}(s_b^{(x)})$ implies the following:

$$s_0^{(x)} = s_1^{(x)} \implies t_0^{(x)} = t_1^{(x)} \implies \mathsf{correct}_\mathbb{G}\left(\mathsf{convert}(s_0^{(x)}), \mathsf{ocw}, t_0^{(x)}\right)$$
$$= \mathsf{correct}_\mathbb{G}\left(\mathsf{convert}(s_1^{(x)}), \mathsf{ocw}, t_1^{(x)}\right)$$
$$\implies \mathsf{y}_0^{(x)} + \mathsf{y}_1^{(x)} = 0$$

Since $s_0^{(x)} = s_1^{(x)}$ for all $x \neq u$, $\mathsf{y}_0 + \mathsf{y}_1$ defines the truth table of $f_{\alpha,\beta}$. Therefore, the construction in Fig. 1 satisfies Definition 6.

Lemma 4 (VerDPF Function Privacy). *The VDPF construction* VerDPF *satisfies Definition 7.*

Proof. All elements of a VerDPF key are computationally indistinguishable from random elements. The starting seed is randomly sampled from $\{0,1\}^\lambda$. Each correction word is XOR'd with the output of a PRG where the seed is not known to the evaluator, and hence is also indistinguishable from random. Finally, the inclusion of the correct proof from the other party does not add any information, since the evaluator holding the share k_b can locally compute the correct proof $\pi_{1-b} = \pi_b$. Therefore, the simulator Sim can set all elements of the key k^* to be randomly sampled elements, then compute $(\_, \pi^*) \leftarrow \mathsf{VerDPF.BVEval}(b, \mathsf{k}^*, \mathbf{x})$ to output $(\mathsf{k}^*, \pi^*) \approx_c (\mathsf{k}_b, \pi_{1-b})$.

Combining Lemma 2 and Lemma 4 gives the proof of the following theorem.

Theorem 3 (Verifiable Distributed Point Function). *The construction in Fig. 1 is a secure verifiable DPF for the class of point functions $\mathcal{F}_{n,\mathbb{G}}$. For any $f \in \mathcal{F}_{n,\mathbb{G}}$, the runtime of $(\mathsf{k}_0, \mathsf{k}_1) \leftarrow \mathsf{VerDPF.Gen}(1^\lambda, f)$ is $O(n\lambda)$, and the size of a function share is $O(n\lambda)$. For any $x \in \{0,1\}^n$, the runtime of $\mathsf{VerDPF.Eval}(b, \mathsf{k}_b, x)$ is $O(n\lambda)$, and the runtime of $\mathsf{VerDPF.BVEval}(b, \mathsf{k}_b, \mathbf{x})$ is $O(n \cdot \lambda \cdot |\mathbf{x}|)$.*

4   Verifiable Distributed Multi-Point Function

In this section, we present a novel method for efficiently batching many verifiable DPF queries to obtain a verifiable FSS scheme for multi-point functions (MPFs). Multi-point functions are defined as the sum of several point functions. While any function can be viewed as an MPF, we will focus here on MPFs that have a small number of non-zero points relatively to the domain size. This scheme will also be verifiable in a similar, although more relaxed, manner as in the verifiable DPF from Sect. 3. Our construction is based on a novel Cuckoo-hashing scheme described below.

4.1   Cuckoo-hashing from PRPs

Our technique is inspired by the use of Cuckoo-hashing schemes that are common throughout the PSI [5,6] and DPF [12] literature. In particular, it is common for the Cuckoo-hashing scheme to have two modes: a *compact* mode and an *expanded* mode. Both modes are parameterized by m buckets and κ hash functions $h_1, \ldots, h_\kappa \colon \{0,1\}^* \to [m]$.

Compact Cuckoo-hashing Mode. In the compact mode, the input is t elements $x_1, \ldots, x_t$ to be inserted into a table of m buckets. To insert an element x_i, an index $k \in [\kappa]$ is randomly sampled and x_i is inserted at index $h_k(x_i)$. If this index is already occupied by some other element x_j, then x_j is replaced by x_i and x_j is reinserted using this same method. After some limit on the number of trials, the insertion process is deemed to have failed. The purpose of the compact mode is to efficiently pack t elements into the table of size m. This algorithm, denoted CHCompact, is given in Algorithm 4.

Algorithm 4. CHCompact Compact Cuckoo-hashing scheme. The algorithm is given a fixed time to run before it is deemed to have failed.

Input: Domain elements $\alpha_1, \ldots, \alpha_t$
          Hash functions $h_1, \ldots, h_\kappa \colon \{0,1\}^* \to m$
          Number of buckets $m \geq t$

1: Define an empty array of m elements Table where each entry is initialized to $\bot$.
2: **for** ω from 1 to t **do**
3:      Set $\beta \leftarrow \alpha_\omega$ and set success $\leftarrow$ False
4:      **while** success is False **do**
5:          Sample $k \xleftarrow{\$} [\kappa]$
6:          $i \leftarrow h_k(\beta)$.
7:          **if** Table$[i] = \bot$ **then**
8:              Table$[i] = \beta$ and success $\leftarrow$ True
9:          **else** Swap β and Table$[i]$

Output: Table

We consider $m = e \cdot t$ for $e > 1$, where the size of e determines the probability over the choice of hash functions of failing to insert any set of t elements. More specifically, from the empirical analysis of Demmler et al. [6], we have the following lemma.

Lemma 5 (Cuckoo-hashing Failure Probability [6]). *Let $\kappa = 3$ and $t \geq 4$. Let $m = e \cdot t$ for $e > 1$. Let $\mathcal{H}$ be a family of collision-resistant hash functions, and let $h_1, \ldots, h_\kappa \leftarrow \mathcal{H}$ be randomly sampled from $\mathcal{H}$. We have that t elements will fail to be inserted into a table of size m with probability $2^{-\lambda}$, where*

$$\lambda = a_t \cdot e - b_t - \log_2(t)$$
$$a_t = 123.5 \cdot \mathsf{CDF}_{\mathsf{Normal}}(x = t, \mu = 6.3, \sigma = 2.3)$$
$$b_t = 130 \cdot \mathsf{CDF}_{\mathsf{Normal}}(x = t, \mu = 6.45, \sigma = 2.18)$$

Here, $\mathsf{CDF}_{\mathsf{Normal}}(x, \mu, \sigma)$ *refers to the cumulative density function of the normal distribution with mean μ and standard deviation σ up to the point x.*

Remark 1 (Cuckoo-hash parameters). Asymptotically, we have the number of Cuckoo-hash buckets as $m = O(t\lambda + t\log(t))$; however, concretely, the picture is much nicer than the asymptotics suggest. For sufficiently large t (i.e. $t \geq 30$), we can simplify Lemma 5 to be $\lambda = 123.5 \cdot e - 130 - \log_2(t)$, since the $\mathsf{CDF}_{\mathsf{Normal}}$ factors become effectively one. Then, for $\lambda = 80$, we have that $m \leq 2t$ for all $30 \leq t \leq 2^{37}$, which we believe captures nearly all practical use cases.

Expanded Cuckoo-hashing mode. In the expanded Cuckoo-hashing mode, the hashing scheme takes as input t elements and produces a matrix of dimension $m \times B$ that contains $\kappa \cdot t$ elements. This mode is produced by hashing all t elements with each of the κ hash functions, then inserting each of the t elements in all κ buckets as indicated by the hash functions. The parameter B is the maximum size of these buckets.

Our PRP Cuckoo-hashing. In the Cuckoo-hashing schemes from the prior literature, the design of the scheme is focused on the compact mode, and the extended mode is added without much change to the overall design. In our Cuckoo-hashing scheme, we begin with an efficient construction of the expanded mode, then show how we maintain efficiency of the compact mode. For a domain of elements $\mathcal{D}$ of size $n = |\mathcal{D}|$, we define the expanded mode of our Cuckoo-hashing scheme with a PRP of domain size $n\kappa$. Let m be the number of bins in the Cuckoo-hash table. Define $B := \lceil n\kappa/m \rceil$. The PRP then defines an expanded Cuckoo-hash table of dimension $m \times B$ by simply arranging the $n\kappa$ outputs of the PRP into the entries of an $m \times B$ matrix. More specifically, let $\mathsf{PRP}\colon \{0,1\}^\lambda \times [n\kappa] \to [n\kappa]$ be the PRP. Let $\sigma \leftarrow \{0,1\}^\lambda$ be the seed of the PRP. Define entry (i, j) of the $m \times B$ matrix A to be $A_{i,j} := \mathsf{PRP}(\sigma, (i-1) \cdot m + j)$. Note that the last row of the matrix may have some empty entries, but this turns out to have little consequence on the overall scheme.

To define the compact mode of this Cuckoo-hashing scheme, we explicitly define the hash functions in terms of the PRP. As above, let $\mathsf{PRP}\colon \{0,1\}^\lambda \times [n\kappa] \to [n\kappa]$ be the PRP, and let $\sigma \leftarrow \{0,1\}^\lambda$ be the seed of the PRP. For $i \in [\kappa]$, define the hash function $h_i\colon [n] \to [m]$ as follows:

$$h_i(x) := \lfloor \mathsf{PRP}(\sigma, x + n \cdot (i-1))/B \rfloor \tag{1}$$

The hash functions $h_1, \ldots, h_\kappa$ can then be used in the original compact Cuckoo-hashing scheme with m buckets. The main benefit of our construction comes with the next feature, which allows a party to learn the location of an element within a specific bucket of the expanded Cuckoo-hash table without directly constructing the expanded table. More specifically, for $i \in [\kappa]$, we define the function $\mathsf{index}_i\colon [n] \to [B]$ as follows:

$$\mathsf{index}_i(x) := \mathsf{PRP}(\sigma, x + n \cdot (i-1)) \mod B \tag{2}$$

With these functions $\mathsf{index}_1, \ldots, \mathsf{index}_\kappa$ in addition to the hash functions h_1, $\ldots$, h_κ, we can compute the locations $\{(i, j)_k \in [m] \times [B]\}_{k=1}^\kappa$ for each of the κ locations of an element $x \in [n]$ in the expanded Cuckoo-hash table. In particular, we have $(i, j)_k = (h_k(x), \mathsf{index}_k(x))$.

4.2 Verifiable Distributed MPFs via PRP Hashing

We now present our verifiable MPF scheme that makes use of the Cuckoo-hashing scheme described in the previous section. Let N be the MPF domain size. Our input will be an MPF f defined by t point functions $f_{\alpha_i, \beta_i} : [N] \to \mathbb{G}$ for $i \in [t]$. Without loss of generality, we consider $\alpha_1, \ldots, \alpha_t$ as distinct points. We would like to efficiently support an FSS scheme for the function $f : [N] \to \mathbb{G}$ that is defined as follows:

$$f(x) = \sum_{i=1}^{t} f_{\alpha_i, \beta_i}(x)$$

Naively, we would generate t different DPF shares, one for each point function. Evaluation of this naive distributed MPF (DMPF) share at a single point would require t DPF share evaluations.

To improve over this naive construction, the idea is to pack our point functions into a Cuckoo-hash table with m buckets. We begin by instantiating our PRP-based Cuckoo-hashing scheme with a PRP of domain size $N\kappa$ and define $B = \lceil N\kappa/m \rceil$. The client can then use the compact mode to pack the values $\alpha_1, \ldots, \alpha_t$ into a Cuckoo-hash table of size m. For each bucket at index $i \in [m]$, let α_i' be the value in the bucket. We can either have $\alpha_i' = \alpha_j$ for one of the input α_j, or $\alpha_i' = \bot$ if the bucket is empty. If $\alpha_i' = \alpha_j$, let $k \in [\kappa]$ be the index of the hash function used to insert α_j to bucket i. In other words, $h_k(\alpha_j) = i$. Define the index $\gamma_i = \mathsf{index}_k(\alpha_j)$, which is the index of α_j in the ith bucket in the expanded Cuckoo-hash mode. Next, define the point function $g_{\gamma_i, \beta_j} : [B] \to \mathbb{G}$, which evaluates to β_j at the index of α_j within the ith bucket. This point function is then shared to create $(\mathsf{k}_0^{(i)}, \mathsf{k}_1^{(i)}) \leftarrow \mathsf{VerDPF.Gen}(1^\lambda, g_{\gamma_i, \beta_j})$. In the case where $\alpha_i' = \bot$, the shared function is set to be the zero function. The verifiable distributed MPF (VDMPF) share has the form $\mathsf{mpk}_b = (\sigma, \mathsf{k}_b^{(1)}, \ldots, \mathsf{k}_b^{(m)})$ where σ is the PRP seed.

To evaluate this multi-point function share at a point $x \in [N]$, the evaluator first computes the κ possible buckets in which x could lie, denoted $i_k = h_k(x)$ for $k \in [\kappa]$. Next, the evaluator computes the index of x in each bucket, denoted $j_k = \mathsf{index}_k(x)$ for $k \in [\kappa]$. Finally, the evaluator computes the sum of the VDPF in each of the buckets at $i_1, \ldots, i_k$ evaluated at $j_1, \ldots, j_k$. This gives the output

$$\mathsf{y}_b = \mathsf{VerDMPF.Eval}(b, \mathsf{mpk}_b, x) = \sum_{k \in [\kappa]} \mathsf{VerDPF.Eval}(b, \mathsf{k}_b^{(i_k)}, j_k)$$

In addition, this VDMPF inherits all of the features of the VDPF construction from Sect. 3, including the $O(\log(B))$ savings when evaluating the full domain (via tree traversal), as well as verifiability of share well-formedness. We note that the verifiability is a bit weaker than the definition achieved for point functions. More specifically, for point functions we showed how the servers can ensure that at most one evaluation point is nonzero when evaluating any subset of the domain. For this VDMPF construction, we can show that there are no more than m non-zero points in any subset of evaluations by showing there is no more than one non-zero point in the VDPF in each bucket. This is slightly weaker than the best-possible guarantee, which would be that there are no more than t non-zero points in any set of evaluations. However, as discussed in Sect. 4.1, we will essentially always have $m \leq 2t$ (see Remark 1), so we consider this gap acceptable for most applications. In addition, we can achieve an exact guarantee by reverting to the naive construction using the VDPFs from Sect. 3. We leave for future work the challenge of closing this gap while maintaining similar performance.

Our VDMPF construction is given in Fig. 2.

Lemma 6 (VerDMPF Correctness). *Let $\mathcal{F}$ be the function class of multi-point functions with at most t non-zero points. Figure 2 gives a correct function secret sharing scheme for $\mathcal{F}$.*

Proof. This follows directly from the correctness of the VerDPF shares in each bucket and the low statistical failure probability of the Cuckoo-hashing scheme.

Lemma 7 (VerDMPF Function Privacy). *Let $\mathcal{F}$ be the function class of multi-point functions with at most t non-zero points. Figure 2 gives a function-private FSS scheme for $\mathcal{F}$, as defined in Definition 2*

Proof. The VerDPF shares in this construction computationally hide all information regarding the non-zero evaluation points. The only additional leakage is that these t evaluation points fit into a Cuckoo-hash table with the hash functions specified by the PRP seed σ. Lemma 5 gives us a way to set the number of buckets so that any t inputs will fail to hash with $2^{-\lambda}$ probability. Setting λ to be the computational security parameter maintains the adversary's negligible distinguishing advantage.

Lemma 8 (VerDMPF Share Integrity). *Let VerDPF be a secure verifiable point function scheme. Let $\mathsf{VerDMPF} := \mathsf{VerDMPF}_{N,\mathbb{G}}$ be a verifiable multi-point function scheme as defined in Fig. 2 that uses VerDPF for the Cuckoo-hash buckets. No PPT adversary $\mathcal{A}$ can generate VerDMPF keys $(\mathsf{k}_0^*, \mathsf{k}_1^*) \leftarrow \mathcal{A}(1^\lambda)$ along with $L \geq 1$ distinct evaluation points $x_1, \ldots, x_L \in [N]$ such that the following holds. Let $(\mathsf{y}_b, \pi_b) \leftarrow \mathsf{VerDMPF.BVEval}(b, \mathsf{k}_b^*, \{x_i\}_{i=1}^L)$ such that $\mathsf{Accept} \leftarrow \mathsf{VerDMPF.Verify}(\pi_0, \pi_1)$ but there are $\omega > m$ indices $i_1, \ldots, i_\omega$ such that $\mathsf{y}_0^{(i_j)} + \mathsf{y}_1^{(i_j)} \neq 0$ for $j \in [\omega]$. In other words, the output of the batched evaluation contains more than m non-zero outputs.*

Proof. This follows directly from the verifiability of the VerDPF shares, which guarantees that there is at most one non-zero evaluation for each of the m buckets.

Lemma 6, Lemma 7, and Lemma 8 combine to give the following theorem.

Theorem 4. *The construction in Fig. 2 is a secure verifiable DMPF for the class $\mathcal{F}$ of multi-point functions $f\colon [N] \to \mathbb{G}$ with at most t non-zero evaluation points. For any $f \in \mathcal{F}$ and $m = O(t\lambda + t\log(t))$, the runtime of* VerDMPF.Gen *is $O\left(m\lambda \log(N/m)\right)$. For η inputs, the runtime of* VerDMPF.BVEval *is $O(\eta\lambda \log(N/m))$.*

Proof. The asymptotics follow from the fact that generating a single VerDPF share in this scheme takes time $O(\lambda \log(N/m))$, and evaluation of a VerDPF share at one point is also $O(\lambda \log(N/m))$, where we take the PRP and PRG evaluations to be $O(\lambda)$.

Remark 2. We note briefly that if a PRP for the domain κN is not available, our method will work just as well utilizing a generic Cuckoo-hashing scheme and setting all $\mathsf{index}_j(i) = i$. The difference will be that the domain size of the DPF in each Cuckoo-hash bucket will not shrink as the number of nonzero points grows, resulting in a VerDMPF.Gen time of $O\left(m\lambda \log(N)\right)$ and a VerDMPF.BVEval time of $O(\eta\lambda \log(N))$.

In Appendix A, we give an alternate evaluation mode of our VDMPF, which we call "match-mode" evaluation. This mode has identical performance to the regular batch verifiable evaluation mode with the same verification guarantee. The difference is that for each of the m buckets, match-mode evaluation computes additive shares of whether or not any of the inputs matched with the nonzero point in that bucket. This mode is useful in two-server PSI protocols, among others.

5   Implementation & Performance

In this section, we present an implementation of our verifiable DPF and verifiable MPF constructions and compare them to their non-verifiable and non-batched counterparts.

Implementation Details. We implemented our VDPF and VDMPF constructions in C++. We follow the approach of Wang et al. [13] by using a fixed-key AES cipher to construct a Matyas-Meyer-Oseas [11] one-way compression function. We use AES-based PRFs to construct our PRGs, our hash functions, and our PRP. Using an AES-based PRP implicitly fixes our DMPF domain size to be 128 bits, and we leave for future work the task of implementing an efficient small-domain PRP. Our implementation is accelerated with the Intel AES-NI instruction, and all benchmarks were run on a single thread on an Intel i7-8650U CPU. For comparison, we also implemented a non-verifiable DPF following the constructions of Boyle et al. [3] and Wang et al. [13], which we refer to as the "textbook" DPF. We implement the "textbook" distributed MPF by naively applying the textbook DPF; namely, our textbook DMPF share contains one DPF share per non-zero point, and evaluating the share requires evaluation all DPF shares and summing their results.

Verifiable Distributed Multi-Point Function $\mathsf{VerDMPF}_{N,\mathbb{G}}$.

For a domain $\mathcal{D}$ of size N and output group $\mathbb{G}$, let $\mathsf{VerDMPF} := \mathsf{VerDMPF}_{N,\mathbb{G}}$. Let domain: $\mathcal{D} \to [N]$ be an injective function mapping domain elements to indices in $[N]$. Unless otherwise specified, we will consider a domain element as its index. For $\kappa = 3$, let $\mathsf{PRP}: \{0,1\}^{\lambda} \times [N\kappa] \to [N\kappa]$ be a pseudorandom permutation. Let $\mathsf{CHBucket}(t, \kappa, \lambda) \to \mathbb{N}$ be the function that outputs the number of cuckoo hash buckets required so that inserting t elements with κ hash functions fails with probability at most $2^{-\lambda}$. The hash function H' is as in Figure 1.

The $\mathsf{VerDMPF.Verify}$ algorithm simply checks that the two input proofs are equal.

$\mathsf{VerDMPF.Gen}$

Input: Security parameter 1^{λ} and t point functions $\{f_{\alpha_i,\beta_i}\}_{i=1}^{t}$

1: $m \leftarrow \mathsf{CHBucket}(t, 3, \lambda)$, where $\kappa = 3$.
2: Sample a random PRP seed $\sigma \leftarrow \{0,1\}^{\lambda}$ and let $B \leftarrow \lceil N\kappa/m \rceil$.
3: From σ, m, B, define $h_1, \ldots, h_{\kappa}: [N\kappa] \to [m]$ as in Equation (1) and $\mathsf{index}_1, \ldots, \mathsf{index}_{\kappa}: [N\kappa] \to B$ in Equation (2).
4: $\mathsf{Table} \leftarrow \mathsf{CHCompact}\left(\{\alpha_i\}_{i=1}^{t}, \{h_k\}_{k=1}^{\kappa}, m\right)$. If this algorithm fails, return to step 2 to sample a fresh PRP seed.
5: Let $n' = \lceil \log(B) \rceil$ and let $\mathsf{VerDPF} := \mathsf{VerDPF}_{n',\mathbb{G}}$. Let $\mathsf{k}_0 \leftarrow \{\sigma\}$ and $\mathsf{k}_1 \leftarrow \{\sigma\}$.
6: **for** i from 1 to m **do**
7:     **if** $\mathsf{Table}[i] = \bot$ **then** Define $\alpha' \leftarrow 0$ and $\beta' \leftarrow 0$
8:     **else**
9:         Let $\alpha_j = \mathsf{Table}[i]$, for $j \in [t]$, and let $k \in [\kappa]$ be such that $h_k(\alpha_j) = i$.
10:         Let $\alpha' \leftarrow \mathsf{index}_k(\alpha_j)$ and $\beta' \leftarrow \beta_j$
11:     Sample $(\mathsf{k}_0^{(i)}, \mathsf{k}_1^{(i)}) \leftarrow \mathsf{VerDPF.Gen}(1^{\lambda}, f_{\alpha',\beta'})$
12:     Append $\mathsf{k}_0^{(i)}$ to k_0 and $\mathsf{k}_1^{(i)}$ to k_1.

Output: $(\mathsf{k}_0, \mathsf{k}_1)$

$\mathsf{VerDMPF.BVEval}$

Input: Bit b and VerDMPF key k_b and η inputs $x_1, \ldots, x_{\eta} \in \mathcal{D}$.

1: Parse $\sigma, \mathsf{k}_b^{(1)}, \ldots, \mathsf{k}_b^{(m)} \leftarrow \mathsf{k}_b$ and define $B \leftarrow \lceil N\kappa/m \rceil$, $n' \leftarrow \lceil \log(B) \rceil$.
2: Let $\mathsf{VerDPF} := \mathsf{VerDPF}_{n',\mathbb{G}}$ and initialize an array inputs of length m.
3: **for** ω from 1 to η **do**
4:     Let $i_1, \ldots, i_{\kappa} \leftarrow h_1(x_{\omega}), \ldots, h_{\kappa}(x_{\omega})$
5:     Let $j_1, \ldots, j_{\kappa} \leftarrow \mathsf{index}_1(x_{\omega}), \ldots, \mathsf{index}_{\kappa}(x_{\omega})$
6:     Append (j_k, ω) to $\mathsf{inputs}[i_k]$ for each $k \in [\kappa]$, ignoring duplicates.
7: Initialize an array $\mathsf{outputs}$ of length η to all zeros and Initialize a proof $\pi \leftarrow 0$.
8: **for** i from 1 to m **do**
9:     Parse $(j_1, \omega_1), \ldots, (j_L, \omega_L) \leftarrow \mathsf{inputs}[i]$
10:     $\{y_{\ell}\}_{\ell=1}^{L}, \pi^{(i)} \leftarrow \mathsf{VerDPF.BVEval}(b, \mathsf{k}_b^{(i)}, \{j_{\ell}\}_{\ell=1}^{L})$
11:     $\mathsf{outputs}[\omega_{\ell}] \leftarrow \mathsf{outputs}[\omega_{\ell}] + \mathsf{y}_{\ell}$ for $\ell \in [L]$
12:     $\pi \leftarrow \pi \oplus \mathsf{H}'(\pi \oplus \pi^{(i)})$

Output: $\mathsf{outputs}, \pi$

Fig. 2. Verifiable distributed multi-point function.

DPF Comparisons. We now present the results of our DPF comparisons. For various domain sizes 2^n, we benchmarked the share generation time, the evaluation time, and the full-domain evaluation time for the textbook DPF and the verifiable DPF. All benchmarks of the verifiable DPF include the generation of the verification proof. The share evaluation comparison runs the verifiable DPF at 100 random points in $\{0,1\}^n$ and generates the proof verifying this set of evaluations. The runtime reported is the time per evaluation point. Benchmarks are given in Fig. 4.

The slowdown for the verifiable evaluation time is quite small, as it essentially only requires evaluating one additional level of the GGM tree. The slowdown for the share generation time is a bit greater, since the verifiable share generation has a 50% chance of failure, at which point it must be restarted. This can be seen by the roughly factor of 2 slowdown in the runtime of the verifiable share generation.

Overall, our comparisons show that our techniques introduce relatively little overhead to the textbook DPF procedures. We view these results as an affirmation of our claim that our verifiable DPF can replace the textbook DPF in any application to provide a meaningful & robust malicious security claim without seriously impacting performance. Our results are displayed in Fig. 3.

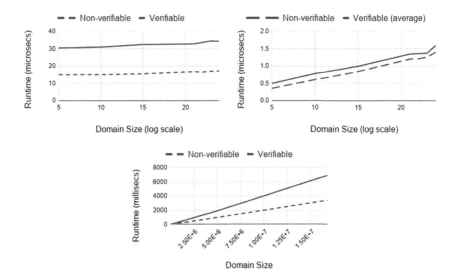

Fig. 3. In this figure, we present the benchmarks of the textbook DPF and the verifiable DPF presented in this work. The top-left graph plots runtimes for the share generation time. As can be seen, the slowdown for verifiability is roughly 2×. The top-right graph plots the runtimes for the share evaluation. As discussed in Sect. 5, the verifiable runtime was computed by taking the runtime of the verifiable batch evaluation procedure (Fig. 1) for 100 random points and dividing it by 100. The bottom graph plots the runtimes for the full domain evaluation operation.

DMPF Comparisons. We now present the results of our DMPF comparisons. We benchmarked the share generation and evaluation time for MPFs with various numbers of nonzero points t. As with the DPF comparisons, all benchmarks of the VDMPFs include the time required to generate the verification proof. Recall that our "textbook" benchmark uses neither the batching nor the verification techniques presented in this work. The batched, verifiable share generation time is about 2× slower than the textbook share generation time. This is a balancing between the increased runtime due to the overhead of the verifiable share generation, the overhead due to the number of buckets being greater than the nonzero values, and the savings due to the domain size shrinking thanks to the PRP savings. To display benchmarks that demonstrate this optimization, we chose a domain size of $N = 2^{126}$. This is so that the $\kappa \cdot N$ elements of the permutation fit in the 128-bit domain of AES PRP. These benchmarks are given in Fig. 4.

The real savings, and what we view as one of the main results of this section, comes in the share evaluation. As discussed in Sect. 4, the performance of the batched VDMPF evaluation effectively does not grow with the number of nonzero points t in the shared multi-point function. This is in stark contrast to the textbook version, where evaluation time grows linearly with the number of nonzero points t in the shared multi-point function. This leads to a dramatic difference in the evaluation times, even when considering the time to generate the verification proof, even for a small number of nonzero points (e.g. 10 points). These results are displayed in Fig. 5.

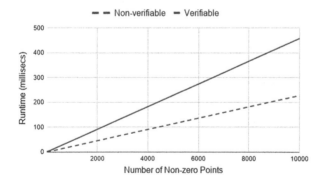

Fig. 4. This graph plots the share generation time for the textbook DMPF and the batched, verifiable DMPF presented in this work.

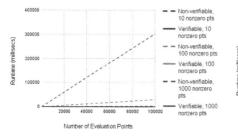
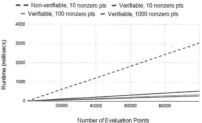

Fig. 5. This figure plots the evaluation times for the textbook DMPF and the batched, verifiable DMPF presented in this work. The domain sizes of these functions were 126 bits. Both graphs in this figure plot the same data; the first graph shows all plots while the second graph is only a plot of the smallest four lines so that the batched VDMPF runtimes can be viewed. The x-axis for these graphs is the number of points η on which the shares are evaluated, and the colors of each line represent the number of nonzero points t in the shared multi-point functions. The number of points is indicated in the legends of the graphs. Note in the second graph that the evaluation time decreases as the number of nonzero points on in the MPF grows.

Acknowledgments. We would like to thank Vinod Vaikuntanathan and Henry Corrigan-Gibbs for helpful conversations and insights.

Leo de Castro was supported by a JP Morgan AI Research PhD Fellowship.

This paper was prepared for informational purposes by the Artificial Intelligence Research group of JPMorgan Chase & Co. and its affiliates ("JP Morgan"), and is not a product of the Research Department of JP Morgan. JP Morgan makes no representation and warranty whatsoever and disclaims all liability, for the completeness, accuracy or reliability of the information contained herein. This document is not intended as investment research or investment advice, or a recommendation, offer or solicitation for the purchase or sale of any security, financial instrument, financial product or service, or to be used in any way for evaluating the merits of participating in any transaction, and shall not constitute a solicitation under any jurisdiction or to any person, if such solicitation under such jurisdiction or to such person would be unlawful. 2021 JPMorgan Chase & Co. All rights reserved.

A   Match-Mode VDMPF: Point Matching

In this section, we present an alternative evaluation mode for our VDMPF scheme that is be useful in various applications. In the "main" evaluation mode, which was presented in Fig. 2, the servers produce one output for each input element to the batched evaluation algorithm. In the "match" evaluation mode discussed in this section, the servers produce one output for each of the cuckoo-hash buckets in the VDMPF key. The purpose of this evaluation mode is to determine if one of the server's input elements matches one of the non-zero points of the multi-point function.

In more detail, during the evaluation algorithm the servers still produce a set of inputs for each of the m buckets and evaluate the corresponding VDPF keys on these inputs. Instead of summing the VDPF outputs according to a matching input, the servers sum the outputs of each VDPF to create a single output for each of the m buckets. From the verifiability of the point function share in each bucket, the servers can easily ensure that the evaluation of at most one of their inputs is being revealed for each bucket. The algorithm is given in Algorithm 5.

Algorithm 5. VDMPF Match-Mode Evaluation, denoted VerDMPF.MatchEval. The setting for this algorithm is the same as the VDMPF construction in Figure 2.

Input: bit b and VerDMPF key k_b

η inputs $x_1, \ldots, x_\eta$

1: Parse $\sigma, k_b^{(1)}, \ldots, k_b^{(m)} \leftarrow k_b$
2: Define $B \leftarrow \lceil N\kappa/m \rceil$, $n' \leftarrow \lceil \log(B) \rceil$.
3: Let VerDPF $:=$ VerDPF$_{n',\mathbb{G}}$.
4: Initialize an array inputs of length m.
5: **for** ω from 1 to η **do**
6:    Let $i_1, \ldots, i_\kappa \leftarrow h_1(x_\omega), \ldots, h_\kappa(x_\omega)$
7:    Let $j_1, \ldots, j_\kappa \leftarrow \mathsf{index}_1(x_\omega), \ldots, \mathsf{index}_\kappa(x_\omega)$
8:    Append j_k to inputs$[i_k]$ for each $k \in [\kappa]$, ignoring duplicates.
9: Initialize an array outputs of length m to all zeros.
10: Initialize a proof $\pi \leftarrow 0$
11: **for** i from 1 to m **do**
12:    $\{y_\ell\}_{\ell=1}^L, \pi^{(i)} \leftarrow$ VerDPF.BVEval$(b, k_b^{(i)}, \mathsf{inputs}[i])$
13:    outputs$[i] \leftarrow$ outputs$[i] + y_\ell$ for $\ell \in [L]$
14:    $\pi \leftarrow \pi \oplus \mathsf{H}'(\pi \oplus \pi^{(i)})$

Output: outputs, π

References

1. Boneh, D., Boyle, E., Corrigan-Gibbs, H., Gilboa, N., Ishai, Y.: Lightweight techniques for private heavy hitters. Cryptology ePrint Archive, Report 2021/017 (2021). https://eprint.iacr.org/2021/017
2. Boyle, E., Gilboa, N., Ishai, Y.: Function secret sharing. In: Oswald, E., Fischlin, M. (eds.) EUROCRYPT 2015. LNCS, vol. 9057, pp. 337–367. Springer, Heidelberg (2015). https://doi.org/10.1007/978-3-662-46803-6_12
3. Boyle, E., Gilboa, N., Ishai, Y.: Function secret sharing: improvements and extensions. In: Proceedings of the 2016 ACM SIGSAC Conference on Computer and Communications Security, CCS 2016, pp. 1292–1303. Association for Computing Machinery, New York, NY (2016)
4. Bunn, P., Kushilevitz, E., Ostrovsky, R.: CNF-FSS and its applications. IACR Cryptol. ePrint Arch. 163, (2021)
5. Chen, H., Laine, K., Rindal, P.: Fast private set intersection from homomorphic encryption. In: CCS 2017 Proceedings of the 2017 ACM SIGSAC Conference on Computer and Communications Security, pp. 1243–1255. ACM New York, NY 2017, October 2017

6. Demmler, D., Rindal, P., Rosulek, M., Trieu, N.: Pir-psi: scaling private contact discovery. Proc. Priv. Enhanc. Technol. **159–178**(10) (2018)
7. Dittmer, S., et al.:. Function secret sharing for psi-ca: with applications to private contact tracing. Cryptology ePrint Archive, Report 2020/1599 (2020). https:// eprint.iacr.org/2020/1599
8. Doerner, J., Shelat, A.: Scaling ORAM for secure computation. In: Proceedings of the 2017 ACM SIGSAC Conference on Computer and Communications Security, CCS 2017, pp. 523–535. Association for Computing Machinery, New York, NY (2017)
9. Gilboa, N., Ishai, Y.: Distributed point functions and their applications. In: Nguyen, P.Q., Oswald, E. (eds.) EUROCRYPT 2014. LNCS, vol. 8441, pp. 640–658. Springer, Heidelberg (2014). https://doi.org/10.1007/978-3-642-55220-5_35
10. Goldreich, O., Goldwasser, S., Micali, S.: How to construct random functions. J. ACM **33**(4), 792–807 (1986)
11. Matyas, S.M., Meyer, C.H., Oseas, J.: Generating strong one-way functions with cryptographic algorithm. IBM Tech. Discl. Bull. **27**, 5658–5659 (1985)
12. Schoppmann, P., Gascón, A., Reichert, L., Raykova, M.: Distributed vector-ole: improved constructions and implementation. In: Proceedings of the 2019 ACM SIGSAC Conference on Computer and Communications Security, CCS 2019, pp. 1055–1072. Association for Computing Machinery, New York, NY (2019)
13. Wang, F., Yun, C., Goldwasser, S., Vaikuntanathan, V., Zaharia, M.: Splinter: practical private queries on public data. In: 14th USENIX Symposium on Networked Systems Design and Implementation (NSDI 17), pp. 299–313. USENIX Association, Boston, MA, March 2017

Highly Efficient OT-Based Multiplication Protocols

Iftach Haitner[1,2], Nikolaos Makriyannis[3], Samuel Ranellucci[4], and Eliad Tsfadia[1,5(✉)]

[1] School of Computer Science, Tel Aviv University, Tel Aviv, Israel
iftachh@taux.tau.ac.il, eliadtsf@tau.ac.il
[2] Check Point Institute for Information Security, Tel Aviv, Israel
[3] Fireblocks, New York, USA
nikos@fireblocks.com
[4] Coinbase, San Francisco, USA
samuel.ranellucci@coinbase.com
[5] Google Research, Tel Aviv, Israel

Abstract. We present a new OT-based two-party multiplication protocol that is almost as efficient as Gilboa's semi-honest protocol (Crypto '99), but has a high-level of security against malicious adversaries without further compilation. The achieved security suffices for many applications, and, assuming DDH, can be cheaply compiled into full security.

1 Introduction

In a two-party multiplication protocol, each party's output is a random additive share of the multiplication of the parties' private inputs. Two-party multiplication is a fundamental building-block of arithmetic secure computation, holding a role analogous to that oblivious transfer (OT) has in Boolean secure computation. We present a new, highly efficient (maliciously secure) OT-based two-party multiplication protocol below, but first start with some background.

1.1 Background on OT-Based Two-Party Multiplication

There are a several known techniques to obtain two-party multiplication, historically falling in one of two categories: protocols based on homomorphic encryption (HE), or protocols based on (Boolean) OT. The two classes of protocols offer different tradeoffs between efficiency and underlying security assumption; HE-based protocols are typically more efficient communication-wise, while OT-based are more efficient computation-wise. Also, HE-based protocols typically require stronger assumptions. In recent years, new paradigms [1,4–6,14] have emerged for realizing two-party multiplication,[1] where the underlying "machinery" is

---

[1] Actually, most papers in the space focus on the related functionalities of OLE and VOLE, discussed later on.

© International Association for Cryptologic Research 2022
O. Dunkelman and S. Dziembowski (Eds.): EUROCRYPT 2022, LNCS 13275, pp. 180–209, 2022.
https://doi.org/10.1007/978-3-031-06944-4_7

based on *homomorphic* [7,8] or *function* [6] secret sharing. The two notions may be viewed as analogues of respectively HE and *functional encryption* [3] in the secret sharing realm. In this paper, we focus on OT-based protocols, and we refer the reader to Sect. 1.4 for further discussion on protocols that do not rely on OT.

Recall that OT is the functionality that takes two inputs $x_0, x_1 \in \mathbb{Z}_q$ from the sender, a bit β from the receiver, and returns x_β to the receiver (and nothing to the sender). To the best of our knowledge, there are essentially two basic templates for honest-but-curious OT-based multiplication: the Gilboa [15] protocol, and the Ishai, Prabhakaran, and Sahai [19] protocol. We refer the reader to Fig. 1 for a side by side comparison of the two protocols. For clarity of exposition, we focus our attention on multiplications over the field $\mathbb{Z}_q = \mathbb{Z}/q\mathbb{Z}$ for an odd prime q (i.e., the arithmetic field of integers modulo an odd prime).

Malicious Security. As far as we know, all OT-based multiplication protocols only achieve honest-but-curious (passive) security.[2] To achieve malicious security, these protocols can be compiled in a number of generic ways, e.g., using SNARKSs, cut-and-choose, and/or MPC-in-the-head techniques. For concrete efficiency, however, it is often preferable to design tailor-made solutions [14,20]. For instance, motivated by applications to MPC in the preprocessing model, Keller et al. [20] (MASCOT) design various cut-and-choose techniques, on top of Gilboa's protocol, for maliciously realizing various useful functionalities in the preprocessing model. We discuss MASCOT in detail in Sect. 1.3.

1.2   Our Contributions

We present a new OT-based two-party multiplication protocol that achieves a high level of security against malicious adversaries. The protocol may be viewed as a noisy generalization of Gilboa [15]'s protocol (or, alternatively, as a hybrid between Gilboa [15] and Ishai et al. [19] protocols).

Let $a, b \in \mathbb{Z}_q$ be the inputs of P_1 and P_2, respectively, and let $n = \lceil \log q \rceil + \kappa$ for a (statistical) security parameter κ. Our protocol requires no initialization stage, and the parties make n parallel OT-calls. In the ith call, P_2's input index is a random value $t_i \leftarrow \{-1, 1\}$ (i.e., we switch conventions regarding the OT-receiver's input),[3] and P_1's input pair is $(-a + \delta_i, a + \delta_i)$ for a random mask $\delta_i \leftarrow \mathbb{Z}_q$. Notice that this differs from Ishai et al. [19] protocol in which P_1's input in for OT-calls depends on the vectors sent by P_2. After these calls are done, P_2 uniformly samples $\boldsymbol{v} = (v_1, \ldots, v_n) \leftarrow \mathbb{Z}_q^n$ subject to $b = \sum_i v_i t_i$, and sends $\boldsymbol{v}$, but not the t_i's, to P_1. See Protocol 1 for a more detailed description.

---

[2] The OT-based protocol of Ghosh, Nielsen, and Nilges [14] does achieve malicious security (without further compilation), but its security proof relies on an additional hardness assumption (a rather non-standard coding assumption). Interestingly, the security analysis in [14] is somewhat reminiscent of the security analysis of our protocol.

[3] The choice of $\{-1, 1\}$ instead of $\{0, 1\}$ significantly simplifies our security analysis, but it is also what limits it to fields of characteristic greater than two (see Theorem 2).

Gilboa's Protocol

- **Init.** Let $\ell = \lceil \log q \rceil$.

  P_2 sets $t_1, \ldots t_\ell \in \{0, 1\}$ to the bit-decomposition of $b = \sum_i t_i \cdot 2^{i-1}$.

- **OT.** The parties make ℓ parallel OT-calls, P_1 as sender, P_2 as receiver. In the ith call:
  1. P_1 uses input $(\delta_i, a + \delta_i)$, for $\delta \leftarrow \mathbb{Z}_q$. (It receives no output).
  2. P_2 uses input index t_i.

     It receives output $z_i \in \mathbb{Z}_q$.
- **Outputs.**
  1. P_1 outputs $-\sum_i \delta_i \cdot 2^{i-1}$.
  2. P_2 outputs $\sum_i z_i \cdot 2^{i-1}$.

Ishai et al.'s Protocol

- **Init.** Let $\ell = \lceil \log q \rceil$ and $n = \ell + \kappa$.
  1. P_2 samples $\boldsymbol{u}_0, \boldsymbol{u}_1 \leftarrow \mathbb{Z}_q^n$ and $\boldsymbol{t} \leftarrow \{0,1\}^n$, subject to $b = \sum_i u_{t_i, i}$.
  2. P_2 sends $(\boldsymbol{u}_0, \boldsymbol{u}_1)$ to P_1.
- **OT.** The parties make n parallel OT-calls, P_1 as sender, P_2 as receiver. In the ith call:
  1. P_1 uses input $(au_{0,i} + \delta_i, au_{1,i} + \delta_i)$, for $\delta_i \leftarrow \mathbb{Z}_q$. (It receives no output).
  2. P_2 uses input index t_i.

     It receives output $z_i \in \mathbb{Z}_q$.
- **Outputs.**
  1. P_1 outputs $-\sum_i \delta_i$.
  2. P_2 outputs $\sum_i z_i$.

Fig. 1. Honest-But-Curious multiplication protocols between party P_1, holding input $a \in \mathbb{Z}_q$, and party P_2, holding input $b \in \mathbb{Z}_q$. Gilboa's protocol consists of $\ell = \lceil \log(q) \rceil$ parallel OT-calls, where Ishai et al. [19]' protocol consists on $n = \ell + \kappa$ calls, where κ is a (statistical) security parameter. We remark that Gilboa's protocol can be cast as a variant of Ishai et al. [19]' protocol, where the pair of vectors $(\boldsymbol{u}_0, \boldsymbol{u}_1)$, which P_2 uses for encoding its input in Ishai et al. [19] are implicitly hardcoded as $\boldsymbol{u}_0 = (0, \ldots, 0)$ and $\boldsymbol{u}_1 = (1, 2^1, 2^2, \ldots, 2^{\ell-1})$. Gilboa [15], however, dispenses of the communication round prior to the OT, since the two vectors are known in advance to both parties, and achieves perfect security (in the OT-hybrid model).

Protocol 1 (Our OT-based multiplication protocol (P_1, P_2))

- **Inputs.** *The parties hold common input 1^κ. Party P_1 holds private input $a \in \mathbb{Z}_q$, and party P_2 holds private input $b \in \mathbb{Z}_q$. Let $n = \lceil \log q \rceil + \kappa$.*
- **OT.** *The parties makes n parallel OT-calls. In the i-th call:*
  1. *P_1, as the sender, inputs pair $(-a + \delta_i, a + \delta_i)$ for a uniform $\delta_i \leftarrow \mathbb{Z}_q$.*
     (It receives no output.)
  2. *P_2, as the receiver, inputs index $t_i \leftarrow \{-1, 1\}$, and receives output $z_i \in \mathbb{Z}_q$.*

- **Outputs.**
    1. P_2 samples $\boldsymbol{v} = (v_1, \ldots, v_n) \leftarrow \mathbb{Z}_q^n$ subject to $b = \sum_i v_i \cdot t_i$. It sends $\boldsymbol{v}$ to P_1.
    2. P_1 outputs $-\sum_i \delta_i \cdot v_i$.
    3. P_2 outputs $\sum_i z_i \cdot v_i$.

Before we discuss the merits of our protocol, we briefly touch on the correctness and security analysis. It is easy to see that the protocol is correct (when invoked by honest parties). Indeed,

$$s_2 = \langle \boldsymbol{v}, (z_1, \ldots, z_n) \rangle = \langle \boldsymbol{v}, \underbrace{(\delta_1, \ldots, \delta_n)}_{\delta} + a \cdot \underbrace{(t_1, \ldots, t_n)}_{t} \rangle$$
$$= a \cdot \langle \boldsymbol{v}, \boldsymbol{t} \rangle + \langle \boldsymbol{v}, \boldsymbol{\delta} \rangle = a \cdot b - s_1,$$

making $s_1 + s_2 = a \cdot b$. Second, (similarly to Gilboa's protocol mentioned earlier) the protocol is fully secure for a malicious P_2: the only way P_2 may deviate from the protocol is by choosing a different value for $\boldsymbol{v}$ (unrelated to b) at the last stage of the protocol. This behavior, however, is equivalent to choosing a different input, and thus does not violate the security of the protocol. The analysis for a malicious P_1 is more involved. Effectively, P_1 is limited to choosing inconsistent inputs for the OT-calls: instead of using (a_i, a_i') of the form $(\delta_i - a, \delta_i + a)$, a corrupted P_1 may choose pairs of inputs which are not consistent across different OT-calls i.e., for some $i \neq j$, it holds that $a_i - a_i' \neq a_j - a_j'$, and it seems this attack cannot be simulated using access to the (standard) multiplication functionality.[4] Instead, we show that it exhibits the following useful dichotomy: depending on the number of inconsistent inputs in the OT-calls provided by P_1, either the execution can be simulated using the standard multiplication functionality (with $2^{-\kappa/4}$ statistical-closeness), or, P_2's output has *min-entropy* at least $\kappa/4$, when conditioning jointly on P_2's input and P_1's view. That is, P_2's output is highly unpredictable, even when knowing its input. This property is technically captured by the following informally stated theorem.

Theorem 2 (Security of our multiplication protocol, informal). *For adversary* A *corrupting* P_1, *consider a random execution of Protocol 1 in the presence of* A, *where* P_2 *is holding input* b, *and let* $\mathrm{out}_2^A(b)$ *denote* P_2's *output and* $\mathrm{view}^A(b)$ *denote* A's *view in this execution. Assume* $q \geq 2^{\kappa/2}$,[5] *then at least one of the following holds (depending on its inputs to the OT-calls):*

1. A *can be simulated given access to the perfect (standard) multiplication functionality. (By extracting the input to the perfect multiplication from* A's *inputs to the OT-calls.)*

---

[4] It is not too hard to get convinced that our protocol does not realize the multiplication functionality with *statistical* security (in the OT-hybrid model), but we defer the rather tedious proof of this fact to the next version of this paper. It seems plausible, however, that under the right *Subset-Sum* hardness assumption, the protocol does realize the multiplication functionality with *computational* security. Proving it is an intriguing open question.

[5] We discuss how our results extend to arbitrary fields of characteristic greater than two in Sect. 2.

2. $H_\infty\left(\text{out}_2^A(b) \mid \text{view}^A(b), b\right) \geq \kappa/4$. (i.e., $P_2(b)$'s output is unpredictable from A's point of view, even if A knows b.)

We prove Theorem 2 by showing that our protocol realizes a "weak" ideal multiplication functionality that formally captures the two conditions above (see Sect. 4 for details). The above security guarantee makes our protocol very desirable for a number of reasons, enumerated below.

1. First, via a simple reduction from (standard) designated-input multiplication to random-input multiplication, we can compile our protocol into a maliciously secure protocol by performing an *a posteriori* check on the shares. Such a check does not seem to exist for Gilboa [15], Ishai et al. [19] protocols.
2. Second, and more importantly, we claim that the security notion achieved out-of-the-box by our protocol is sufficient for a number of applications, e.g., within protocols where some kind of correctness check is performed obliviously on the parties' outputs. For instance, in the threshold ECDSA of Lindell and Nof [23], the output is released only after it is checked for correctness. Consequently our protocol can readily be used as a multiplication protocol therein.

Batching. We show that our protocol enjoys the following performance improvement when performing m multiplications with P_1 using the same input in each instance; this task essentially corresponds to the important VOLE functionality discussed in Sect. 1.3. Instead of running the protocol m times (and thus paying $m \cdot n = m \cdot (\ell + \kappa)$ OT's), our protocol can be batched so that it requires only $\kappa + m \cdot \ell$ calls to the underlying OT functionality. The batched version of our protocol exhibits a similar dichotomy to the non-batched version: either the protocol is secure (with $2^{-\kappa/4}$ closeness to the ideal world), or, if not, each one of the honest outputs has *min-entropy* at least $\kappa/4$, *even when conditioning on all of the honest party's inputs* (albeit there may be dependencies between the outputs). For large m, our approach almost matches the number of OT-calls from Gilboa's honest-but-curious protocol, while achieving a stronger security notion. Moreover, in the Random Oracle Model (ROM), it is possible to also bring down the communication complexity of our protocol to match [15] by instructing P_2 to communicate $\boldsymbol{v} = (v_1, \ldots, v_n)$ succinctly via the oracle, e.g., by sending a short seed instead of the entire vector. Furthermore, for malicious security, it is enough to perform a single *a posteriori* check on the shares of only one of the underlying multiplications (say the first multiplication). Indeed, our dichotomy result guarantees that the check is successful only if the attack can be simulated in the ideal world (and thus all outputs are well-formed).

As a concrete efficiency example, for a prime q for which there exists a q-size group where DDH is assumed to hold (say secp256k1 – the Bitcoin curve – with prime $q \approx 2^{256}$), we instantiate the correctness-check using El-Gamal commitments (these commitments were thoroughly used in [23] in the context of threshold ECDSA). We estimate that the correctness-check requires computational-complexity of around 30 exponentiations in the group and communication-complexity of 20 group elements (assuming the encodings of field elements and group elements have essentially the same size). Since this penalty is independent of the number of multiplications in the batch, performing a batch of m multiplications with (full) malicious security $2^{-\kappa/4}$ in the ROM incurs the following cost:

OT's	Communication (bits)	Computation (group exp.)
$m \cdot \ell + \kappa$	$(m + 20) \cdot \ell$ bits	30

Hence, even with the correctness-check, the complexity-penalty of our protocol compared to Gilboa's honest-but-curious protocol is insignificant for large m.[6]

1.3 Applications

In this section, we discuss several applications where our protocol may be of interest.

OLE and VOLE. The oblivious linear evaluation (OLE) functionality may be viewed as a variant of two-party multiplication where one party (say P_2) has full control over its share. Namely, on input a for P_1 and (b, σ) for P_2, the functionality returns $ab + \sigma$ to party P_1 and nothing to party P_2. An important generalization of OLE is *vector* oblivious linear evaluation (VOLE), where it is now assumed that P_2 holds a pair of vectors $(\boldsymbol{b}, \boldsymbol{\sigma})$ and P_1 learns the combination $a\boldsymbol{b} + \boldsymbol{\sigma}$. There is a straightforward reduction from OLE and VOLE to multiplication and batch-multiplication respectively and thus our protocol (compiled for malicious security) can readily be used for this purpose.

MACs and Multiplication Triplets. Motivated by applications of arithmetic MPC in the preprocessing model, i.e., generating function-independent correlated random data that can be later used by the parties to achieve statistically secure MPC for any functionality, there is a rich line of work ([2,10,11,13,20,22] to name but a few) for generating message authentication codes (MACs) and authenticated multiplication triplets. For convenience, we recall the definition of each notion. On secret input x from P_1 (only one party provides input), the two-party MAC functionality returns $\tau \in \mathbb{Z}_q$ to P_1 and a pair $(k, \sigma) \in \mathbb{Z}_q^2$ to P_2 such that $\tau = x \cdot k + \sigma$. Thus, a corrupted P_1 is effectively committed to x which can be authenticated by revealing the pair (x, τ). Notice that P_2 accepts the decommitment if and only if $\tau = x \cdot k + \sigma$ which uniquely determines x (unless P_1 can guess k, which happens with negligible probability). For reference, σ and τ are referred to as the MAC shares and k is referred to as the MAC key. Next, we define authenticated multiplication triplets. On empty inputs, the authenticated multiplication triplets functionality (Beaver) returns (a_1, b_1, c_1) and (a_2, b_2, c_2) to P_1 and P_2 respectively such that $(a_1 + a_2) \cdot (b_1 + b_2) = c_1 + c_2$, together with

---

[6] Without the oracle the penalty is rather noticeable, since there is a $(\ell \cdot m + \kappa)$-multiplicative blowup in the communication complexity.

MAC keys and shares for all the relevant data, i.e., P_2 holds a key k and shares $\sigma, \sigma', \sigma''$, and P_1 holds τ, τ', τ'' as MAC data for the triplet (a_1, b_1, c_1), and the MAC data for P_2's triplet (a_2, b_2, c_2) is analogously defined (where the parties' roles are reversed). It goes without saying, our base protocol can be used to generate MACs and triplets in a straightforward way (explained further below). For comparison, we briefly outline MASCOT [20], the only purely OT-based work for generating triplets with malicious security.

MASCOT [20]. To realize the two functionalities described above in the presence of malicious adversaries, [20] employs a number of cut-and-choose techniques on top of Gilboa's protocol. Specifically, for the MAC functionality, the authors propose the following process: P_2 samples a random MAC key k and the parties run Gilboa's protocol twice; once with inputs (x, k) and once with inputs (x_0, k) where x_0 denotes a random dummy input sampled by P_1. At the end of the protocol the parties (are supposed to) obtain MAC shares for both x and x_0 under key k. To verify that P_1 behaved honestly (as we discussed earlier, only P_1 is capable of cheating), P_1 is instructed to reveal a random combination of x_0 and x as well as the same random combination of its MAC shares. If P_2 accepts, then, with all but negligible probability, P_2 is holding the right MAC data for x. The protocol for the Beaver functionality follows a similar template, however the added redundancy and check procedure (to verify correctness) is more involved. For brevity, we do not describe it here but we mention that it requires 6 or 8 executions (depending on the target security) of Gilboa's protocol on top of the required runs to obtain the MAC data (In total, Gilboa's protocol is ran 18 or 20 times depending on the target security for a single authenticated multiplication triple).

Using our protocol to generate MACs and Triplets maliciously. MAC-generation essentially coincides with batch-multiplication (where a single k is used as a MAC-key to authenticate many values $x_1, x_2, \ldots$). Thus, our batch-multiplication protocol (with the correctness-check) can readily be used for this purpose. Next, we turn to the triplets.

Analogously to standard multiplication, if we allow for an a posteriori check on the shares (more involved than the one presented earlier), we show how our protocol can be used to generate triplets. In particular, a single triplet can be generated by running our base protocol 2 times in its non-batched version (to generate the triplet) and 2 times in the batched version with batches of size 3 (to generate all the MAC-data), and then performing a correctness-check on the shares. For concreteness, we instantiate this check for prime q when there is an accompanying group where DDH is hard. We estimate that the correctness-check requires computational-complexity of around 90 exponentiations in the group and communication-complexity of 60 group elements. In total, this process incurs the following costs for generating a single triplet in the random oracle model.[7]

---

[7] Since it is not the focus of our paper, we have not examined how to optimize the protocol or correctness-check when many triplets are being generated, and we speculate that several optimizations are possible.

OT's	Communication (bits)	Computation (group exp.)
$4\kappa + 8\ell$	70ℓ	90

As an example, for $\ell \approx 512$, our protocol is 53% cheaper in usage of the underlying OT compared to MASCOT when aiming for security 2^{-64}.

Comparison to 2PC Multiplication from [12]. We note that our multiplication protocol may also improve the efficiency of the threshold ECDSA protocol of Doerner et al. [12]. In more detail, the core two-party multiplication protocol in [12] is a variant of MASCOT where the parties multiply (random) dummy values which are then opened in a cut-and-choose way to check for correctness. Specifically, for each (designated-input) multiplication, [12] instructs the parties to perform *two* random multiplications using the OT. Our protocol only prescribes one random multiplication and avoids this redundancy. Thus, our protocol enjoys an x2 improvement in the underlying use of OT.[8]

1.4 Related Work

Multiplication from Noisy Encoding. Drawing from [24], Ishai et al. [19] generalize their protocol so that it supports many types of encodings for P_2 input. Thus, instead of the two u-vectors from Fig. 1, P_2 may use different *noisy encoding* to encode its input prior to the OT. Under various coding assumption (e.g., [21]), Ishai et al. [19] show that several coding schemes give rise to honest-but-curious multiplication protocols with much improved complexity. As mentioned earlier, this approach was later shown to be sufficient by [14] for achieving malicious security under a specific coding assumption.

Non OT-based multiplication. Here we distinguish between HE-based and the more recent approaches based on homomorphic and function secret sharing. HE-Multiplication can be based on either somewhat homomorphic encryption or fully homomorphic encryption. We refer the reader to [25] for a discussion on HE-based multiplication in the context of a specific general-purpose MPC (the SPDZ protocol [11]). The work on the two newer notions (homomorphic and function secret sharing) is motivated by applications to correlated data generation in the prepossessing model (in the spirit of multiplication triplets). For instance, Boyle et al. [5] show how to generate OLE-correlations using homomorphic secret sharing (under various coding assumptions), and Boyle et al. [4] show how to generate long VOLE instances (again under various coding assumptions). These new approaches offer improvements over previous ones, especially in communication costs.

---

[8] When using OT-extensions, this improvement automatically translates into an x2 improvement in communication complexity, which is the most expensive resource in [12].

Paper Organization

In Sect. 2, we describe the high-level approach for analyzing the security of P_2 in Protocol 1, as stated in Theorem 2. Notations, definitions and general statements used throughout the paper are given in Sect. 3. Theorem 2 is formally stated and proved in Sect. 4, and its batching extension is formally stated in Sect. 5. Finally, in Sect. 6, we show how to compile our protocol generically for a number of applications (including, e.g., perfect multiplication). We note that we also provide (non-generic) group-theoretic instantiations in the supplementary material.

2   Our Techniques

In this section, we describe the high-level approach for analyzing the security of P_2 in Protocol 1, as stated in Theorem 2. For the formal proof of this theorem see Sect. 4.

Recall that a malicious A corrupting P_1 can deviate from the protocol by providing inputs to the OT-calls that are not consistent with any $a \in \mathbb{Z}_q$. Our security proof consist of a case-by-case analysis depending on how "far from consistent" A's inputs to the OT are. Let (w_i^-, w_i^+) denote the inputs that A uses in the ith OT-call, let $a_i = (w_i^+ - w_i^-)/2$ and let $\delta_i = w_i^+ - a_i$. Let $\hat{a}$ be the value that appears the most often in $\boldsymbol{a} = (a_1, \ldots, a_n)$, and let $\boldsymbol{d} = \boldsymbol{a} - \hat{a} \cdot \boldsymbol{1}$. Intuitively, the hamming distance of $\boldsymbol{d}$ from $\boldsymbol{0}$ measures how much A deviates from honest behaviour. In particular, $\boldsymbol{d} = \boldsymbol{0}$ if P_1 uses the same a in all OT-calls, and the hamming weight of $\boldsymbol{d}$ is $n-1$ if P_1 never uses the same input twice. Let $\boldsymbol{t} = (t_1, \ldots, t_n)$, $\boldsymbol{z} = (z_1, \ldots, z_n)$ and $\boldsymbol{v}$ be the values that are sampled/obtained by P_2 in the execution, and let s_2 denote its final output. By definition, it holds that

$$s_2 = \langle \boldsymbol{v}, \boldsymbol{z} \rangle = \langle \boldsymbol{v}, \boldsymbol{\delta} + \boldsymbol{a} * \boldsymbol{t} \rangle = \langle \boldsymbol{v}, \boldsymbol{\delta} + \hat{a} \cdot \boldsymbol{t} \rangle + \langle \boldsymbol{v}, \boldsymbol{d} * \boldsymbol{t} \rangle$$
$$= (\langle \boldsymbol{v}, \hat{a} \cdot \boldsymbol{t} \rangle + \langle \boldsymbol{v}, \boldsymbol{\delta} \rangle) + \langle \boldsymbol{v}, \boldsymbol{d} * \boldsymbol{t} \rangle$$
$$= (\hat{a} \cdot b + \langle \boldsymbol{v}, \boldsymbol{\delta} \rangle) + \langle \boldsymbol{v}, \boldsymbol{d} * \boldsymbol{t} \rangle,$$

letting $*$ stand for point-wise multiplication and $\boldsymbol{\delta} = (\delta_1, \ldots, \delta_n)$. The last equation holds by the definition of $\boldsymbol{v}$. Thus, given P_1's view along with the value of b, notice that the value of s_2 is the addition of the following two summands: the constant[9] $(\hat{a} \cdot b + \langle \boldsymbol{v}, \boldsymbol{\delta} \rangle)$ (viewed as a single summand) and $\langle \boldsymbol{v}, \boldsymbol{d} * \boldsymbol{t} \rangle$.

We say that $\boldsymbol{a} \in \mathbb{Z}_q^n$ is m-*polychromatic*, if for every $y \in \mathbb{Z}_q$ it holds that $\text{Ham}(\boldsymbol{d}, y^n) \geq m$ (e.g., $(0, 1, 2, 3, 0)$ is 3-polychromatic but not 4-polychromatic). We show that if $\boldsymbol{a}$ is *not* $\kappa/2$-polychromatic, hereafter *almost monochromatic*, then the execution of the protocol can be simulated using oracle-access to the perfect (i.e., standard) multiplication functionality (which provides the right share to each party, without any offset). Otherwise, if $\boldsymbol{a}$ is $\kappa/2$-polychromatic, hereafter *polychromatic*, then $\langle \boldsymbol{v}, \boldsymbol{d} * \boldsymbol{t} \rangle$ has high min-entropy, given A's view and the value of b.

---

[9] Given P_1's view and P_2's input.

Before we further elaborate on each of the above two cases, we introduce the following notation. To distinguish between the values fixed adversarially by A and those sampled (honestly) by P_2, in the remainder we treat the adversary's inputs as fixed values and the honest party's input as random variables. Namely, it is assumed that $a \in \mathbb{Z}_q^n$ is fixed (and thus also the vector d), and we let V and T denote the random variables where v and t are drawn from (i.e., uniform distribution over $\mathbb{Z}_q^n$ and $\{-1,1\}^n$, respectively).

Almost-Monochromatic a yields statistical security. We prove this part by showing that, given V, the value of $\langle V, d * T \rangle$ is close to being *independent* of b. Namely, for any $b, b' \in \mathbb{Z}_q$,

$$\text{SD}\left((V, \langle V, d * T \rangle)|_{\langle V, d*T \rangle = b}, \; (V, \langle V, d * T \rangle)|_{\langle V, d*T \rangle = b'}\right) \le 2^{-\kappa/4} \quad (1)$$

Equation (1) yields that the simulation of P_2 in the ideal world, given access to the perfect multiplication functionality, can be simply done by emulating P_2 on an arbitrary input.

To see why Eq. (1) holds, let $\mathcal{I} := \{i \in [n]: d_i \ne 0\}$, and assume $T_{\mathcal{I}}$ (the value of T in the coordinate of $\mathcal{I}$) is fixed to some $s \in \{-1,1\}^{|\mathcal{I}|}$. Since, given this fixing, $\langle V, d * T \rangle = \langle V_{\mathcal{I}}, d_{\mathcal{I}} * s \rangle$ is a deterministic function of V, proving the monochromatic case is reduced to proving that

$$\text{SD}(V|_{\langle V,T \rangle = b}, V) \le 2^{-\kappa/4} \quad (2)$$

Since d is almost-monochromatic, then, given the above fixing of $T_{\mathcal{I}}$, it still holds that $\text{H}_\infty(T) \ge n - |\mathcal{I}| \ge \lceil \log q \rceil + \kappa/2$. Thus, by the leftover hash lemma

$$\text{SD}\left((V, \langle V, T \rangle), (V, U)\right) \le 2^{-\kappa/4} \quad (3)$$

for a uniformly sampled $U \leftarrow \mathbb{Z}_q$. In other words, the value of V is $2^{-\kappa/4}$-close to uniform given $\langle V, T \rangle$, and Eq. (2) follows by a not-too-complicated chain of derivations (see proof of Lemma 3).

Polychromatic a yields unpredictable offset. Fix $b \in \mathbb{Z}_q$, and for $t \in \{-1,1\}^n$ let W^t be the indicator random variable of the event $\{\langle V, t \rangle = b\}$, and let $W := \sum_{t \in \{-1,1\}^n} W^t$. In addition, for $t \in \{-1,1\}^n$ and $x \in \mathbb{Z}_q$, let Z_x^t be the indicator random variable of the event $\{\langle V^b, t \rangle = b \wedge \langle V, d * t \rangle = x\}$, and let $Z_x := \sum_{t \in \{-1,1\}^n} Z_b^t$. We show that for a polychromatic a, with probability $1 - 2^{-\kappa/4}$ over V it holds that

$$Z_x / W \le 2^{-\kappa/4} \quad (4)$$

for *every* $x \in \mathbb{Z}_q$ (simultaneously). It follows that for such vector a, with high probability over V, the probability that $\langle V, d * T \rangle = x$, for *any* value of x, is small. In other words, $\langle V, d * T \rangle$ has high min-entropy given (V, b).[10]

---

[10] Actually, since the value of v sent to P_1 is not uniform, but rather distributed according to $V^b := V|_{\langle V,T \rangle = b}$, to argue about the security of the protocol one needs to argue about the min-entropy of $\langle V^b, d * T \rangle$ given (b, V^b). We ignore this subtlety in this informal exposition.

We prove Eq. (4) by upper-bounding $E[W^3]$ and $E[Z_x^3]$, for any x, and then we use a third moment concentration inequality to derive Eq. (4). The harder part is bounding $E[Z_x^3]$. To get the gist of this bound, we give the intuition for bounding $E[Z_x^2]$. This bound is derived by proving that the number of pairs (t, t') with $E[Z_x^t \cdot Z_x^{t'}] > 1/q^4$ is small. These pairs are identified by relating the correlation of the indicator random variables of the events $\{\langle V, t \rangle = b\}$, $\{\langle V, t' \rangle = b\}$, $\{\langle V, d * t \rangle\}$ and $\{\langle V, d * t' \rangle\}$ to the dimension of space spanned by the vectors in $\mathcal{S}_{t,t'} := \{t, t', d * t, d * t'\}$. In particular, it is not hard to see that

$$\mathrm{rank}(\mathcal{S}_{t,t'}) = j \implies E[Z_x^t \cdot Z_x^{t'}] \le 1/q^j$$

Hence, upper-bounding $E[Z_x^2]$ reduces to upper-bounding to number of pairs (t, t') with $\mathrm{rank}(\mathcal{S}_{t,t'}) < 4$. Upper-bounding the number of such pairs is done using linear algebra arguments, exploiting the fact that d has at least $\kappa/2$ non-zero elements (since it is polychromatic). Specifically, we show that the number of pairs (t, t') with $E[Z_x^t \cdot Z_x^{t'}] < 1/q^4$ decreases *exponentially* with the weight of d. This bound is sufficient for calculating the second moment of Z_x (deducing a weaker bound than Eq. (4), cf., Sect. 4.2). Calculating the third moment of Z_x, however, for deriving Eq. (4) is more involved, and requires a more detailed case-by-case analysis in the counting argument, cf., the full version of this paper [17].

Extension to Arbitrary Fields. Our results extend trivially to *large* finite fields (i.e., of size greater than $2^{\kappa/2}$). Next, we briefly explain how to use our protocol for multiplying in a small field, denoted $\mathbb{F}$. Unfortunately, as is, the protocol does not enjoy the same unpredictability under attack since the entropy of the offset is constrained by the size of the field, i.e., the offset has min-entropy at most $\log(|\mathbb{F}|)$. To circumvent this issue, we instruct the parties to embed $\mathbb{F}$ into a larger field $\mathbb{H}$ of size $2^{\kappa/2}$ and perform the multiplication in $\mathbb{H}$ (of course, the parties' shares then reside in the larger field).

To obtain additive shares over the smaller field $\mathbb{F}$, it is enough to perform a local transformation to the output. This way, we enjoy the unpredictability under attack (and thus the correctness-check can be performed over the larger field) and we obtain correct shares of the output in $\mathbb{F}$.

3   Preliminaries

3.1   Notations

We use calligraphic letters to denote sets, uppercase for random variables, lowercase for values and functions, and boldface for vectors. All logarithms considered here are in base 2. For a vector $v = (v_1, \ldots, v_n)$ and a set $\mathcal{I} \subseteq [n]$, let $v_{\mathcal{I}}$ be the *ordered sequence* $(v_i)_{i \in \mathcal{I}}$, let $v_{-\mathcal{I}} := v_{[n] \setminus \mathcal{I}}$, and let $v_{-i} := v_{-\{i\}}$ (i.e., $(v_1, \ldots, v_{i-1}, v_{i+1}, \ldots, v_n)$). For two vectors $u = (u_1, \ldots, u_n)$ and $v = (v_1, \ldots, v_n)$, let $u * v := (u_1 \cdot v_1, \ldots, u_n \cdot v_n)$, and let $\langle u, v \rangle := \sum_{i=1}^n u_i v_i$. Let b^n denote the n-size all b vector, or just b when the size is clear from the context. For a field $\mathbb{F}$ and a sequence of vectors $v_1, \ldots, v_m \in \mathbb{F}^n$, let

$\text{span}\{v_1, \ldots, v_m\} := \{\sum_{j=1}^{m} \lambda_j v_j : \lambda_1, \ldots, \lambda_m \in \mathbb{F}\}$ (i.e., the vector space that is spawn by vectors $v_1, \ldots, v_m$), and let $\text{rank}\{v_1, \ldots, v_m\}$ denote the dimension of $\text{span}\{v_1, \ldots, v_m\}$. For a function f taking $1^\kappa \in \mathbb{N}$ as its first input, we let $f_\kappa(\cdot)$ stand for $f(1^\kappa, \cdot)$. Let PPT stand for probabilistic polynomial time, and PPTM stand for PPT (uniform) algorithm Turing Machine).

3.2 Distributions and Random Variables

The support of a distribution P over a finite set $\mathcal{S}$ is defined by $\text{Supp}(P) := \{x \in \mathcal{S} : P(x) > 0\}$. For a (discrete) distribution D, let $d \leftarrow D$ denote that d is sampled according to D. Similarly, for a set $\mathcal{S}$, let $x \leftarrow \mathcal{S}$ denote that x is drawn uniformly from $\mathcal{S}$. The statistical distance (also known as, variation distance) of two distributions P and Q over a discrete domain $\mathcal{X}$ is defined by $\text{SD}(P, Q) := \max_{\mathcal{S} \subseteq \mathcal{X}} |P(\mathcal{S}) - Q(\mathcal{S})| = \frac{1}{2} \sum_{x \in \mathcal{S}} |P(x) - Q(x)|$. The min-entropy of a distribution P over a discrete domain $\mathcal{X}$ is defined by $H_\infty(P) := \min_{x \in \text{Supp}(P)} \{\log(1/P(x))\}$.

3.3 Two-Party Protocols and Functionalities

A two-party protocol consists of two *interactive* Turing Machines (TMs). In each round, only one party sends a message. At the end of protocol, each party outputs some value. This work focuses on static adversaries: before the beginning of the protocol, the adversary corrupts one of the parties that from now on may arbitrarily deviate from the protocol. Thereafter, the adversary sees the messages sent to the corrupted party and controls its messages. A party is honest, with respect to a given protocol, if it follows the prescribed protocol. A party is semi-honest, if it follows the prescribed protocol, but might output additional values.

We mark inputs to protocols and functionalities as **optional**, if they do not have to be defined by the caller, and in this case they are set to $\perp$.

3.3.1 Security

We define the security of our two-party protocols in the *real* vs. *ideal* paradigm [9,16]. In this paradigm, the *real-world model*, in which protocols is executed, is compared to an *ideal model* for executing the task at hand. The latter model involves a trusted party whose functionality captures the security requirements of the task. The security of the real-world protocol is argued by showing that it "emulates" the ideal-world protocol, in the following sense: for any real-life adversary A, there exists an ideal-model oracle-aided adversary (also known as, simulator) S, such that the global output of an execution of the protocol with A in the real-world model is distributed similarly to the global output of running S^A in the ideal model. In the following we only consider *non*-reactive functionalities, i.e., random functions.

The Ideal Model. In the ideal execution model, the parties do not interact, but rather make a single joint call to a two-party functionality. An ideal execution of a two-party functionality f with respect to an adversary A taking the role of P_1 and inputs $(1^\kappa, x_1, x_2)$, denoted by $\text{IDEAL}_{P_1}^f (A, \kappa, x_1, x_2)$, is the output of A and that of the trusted party, in the following experiment (the case of malicious P_2 is analogously defined):

Experiment 3 (Ideal execution)

1. On input $(1^\kappa, x_1)$, A sends an arbitrary message $\widehat{x}_1$ to the trusted party.
2. The trusted party computes $(y_1, y_2) = f(1^\kappa, \widehat{x}_1, x_2)$ and sends y_1 to $A(1^\kappa, x_1)$.
3. A sends the message Continue/ Abort to the trusted party, and locally outputs some value.
4. If A instructs Abort, the trusted party outputs $\perp$. Otherwise, it outputs y_2.

The real model. We focus on security of protocols in the *g-hybrid model*, in which the parties are given access to two-party functionality g. In executions of such protocols, a malicious party can instruct the functionality g to abort after seeing its output (which it gets first). Let $\Pi = (P_1, P_2)$ be an two-party protocol in the g-hybrid model, and let A be an adversary controlling party P_1 (the case of malicious P_2 is analogously defined). We define $\text{REAL}_{P_1}^\Pi (A, \kappa, x_1, x_2)$ as the output of A (i.e., without loss of generality its view: its random input, the messages it received, and the output of the g calls) and the prescribed output of P_2, in a random execution of $(A^g(x_1), P_2^g(x_2))(1^\kappa)$.

Hybrid-model security.

Definition 1 (α-security). *A two-party protocol $\Pi = (P_1, P_2)$ (black-boxly) α-computes a two-party functionality f in the g-hybrid model with respect to input domain $\mathcal{D}_1 \times \mathcal{D}_2$, if there exists a* PPT *oracle-aided algorithm S (simulator), such that for every adversary A, $\kappa \in \mathbb{N}$ and inputs $(x_1, x_2) \in \mathcal{D}_1 \times \mathcal{D}_2$, it holds that*

$$\text{SD}\left(\text{REAL}_{P_1}^\Pi (A, \kappa, x_1, x_2)), \text{IDEAL}_{P_1}^f (S^A, \kappa, x_1, x_2)\right) \leq \alpha(\kappa).$$

Furthermore, if A is semi-honest then so is S^A: it sends its (real) input to the trusted party, and does not ask to abort. Security is defined analogously for P_2.

Extension to UC security. The above security notions are defined in the so-called "standalone" model. However, we mention that the security analysis for our main results (realizing WeakMult and WeakBatch) as well as for our applications (e.g. Realizing PerfectMult from WeakMult and auxiliary "helper" functionalities) uses *straightline simulators* exclusively, i.e., the simulator does not rewind the adversary at any point of the simulation. Therefore, our results can be extended to the UC setting.

3.3.2 Oblivious Transfer (OT)

We use the (perfect) one-out-two oblivious transfer functionality (OT) defined as follows: on input (σ_{-1}, σ_1) sent by the first party (the sender), and input $i \in \{-1, 1\}$ sent by the second party (the receiver), it sends σ_i to the receiver. The functionality gets no security parameter.

3.3.3 Two-Party Multiplication

In multiplication over the field $\mathbb{Z}_q = \mathbb{Z}/q\mathbb{Z}$, where q is an odd prime, party P_1 holds private input $a \in \mathbb{Z}_q$, party P_2 holds private input $b \in \mathbb{Z}_q$, and the goal is to securely computes random shares $s_1, s_2 \in \mathbb{Z}_q$ for P_1 and P_2 (respectively), such that $s_1 + s_2 = a \cdot b$ (for the ease of notation, we assume that operations are made over the field $\mathbb{Z}_q$, i.e., modulo q). The following is what we address as the *perfect multiplication functionality*.

Functionality 4 (PerfectMult)

P_1's input: $a \in \mathbb{Z}_q$.
P_2's input: $b \in \mathbb{Z}_q$ and **optional** $s_2 \in \mathbb{Z}_q$.
Operation:

1. If $s_2 = \perp$, sample $s_2 \leftarrow \mathbb{Z}_q$.
2. Output (s_1, s_2) for $s_1 \leftarrow a \cdot b - s_2$.

Note that it is always holds that $s_1 + s_2 = a \cdot b$. Also note that an adversary controlling P_1 can do no harm, and adversary controlling party P_2 may choose the value of its share s_2, but no information about the other party's input is leaked. It seems that allowing one party to control its output is unavoidable, and is also harmless for all the applications we are aware of.

3.3.4 Batching

In a *batch-multiplication*, a single input provided by one party is multiplied with several inputs provided by the other party. Such multiplication is interesting if the batching is more efficient than parallel executions of the (single input per party) multiplication protocol. For this case, we define the *perfect batch-multiplication functionality* below.

Functionality 5 (PerfectMultBatching)

P_1's input: $a \in \mathbb{Z}_q$.
P_2's input: $\boldsymbol{b} = (b_1, \dots, b_m) \in \mathbb{Z}_q^m$ and **optional** $(s_2^1, \dots, s_2^m) \in \mathbb{Z}_q^m$.
Operation:

1. If $(s_2^1, \dots, s_2^m) = \perp$, sample $(s_2^1, \dots, s_2^m) \leftarrow \mathbb{Z}_q^m$.
2. Output $(s_1^1, \dots, s_1^m)$ to P_1 and $(s_2^1, \dots, s_2^m)$ to P_2 for $(s_1^1, \dots, s_1^m) \leftarrow a \cdot \boldsymbol{b} - (s_2^1, \dots, s_2^m)$.

3.4 Some Inequalities

We use the following inequalities.

Lemma 1 (Chebyshev's inequality). *Let X be a random variable with $E[X] \in (-\infty, \infty)$ and $\mathrm{Var}(X) \in (0, \infty)$. Then*

$$\forall k > 0 : \quad \Pr\left[|X - E[X]| \geq k\right] \leq \mathrm{Var}(X)/k^2.$$

Definition 2 (Universal hash functions). *A family $\mathcal{H} = \{h \colon \mathcal{D} \to \mathcal{R}\}$ of (hash) functions is called* universal *if for every $x, y \in \mathcal{D}$ with $x \neq y$,*

$$\Pr_{h \leftarrow \mathcal{H}}[h(x) = h(y)] \leq 1/|\mathcal{R}|.$$

Lemma 2 (The leftover hash lemma [18]). *Let X be a random variable over a universe $\mathcal{D}$, let $\mathcal{H} = \{h \colon \mathcal{D} \to \mathcal{R}\}$ be a universal hash family. Then for $H \leftarrow \mathcal{H}$ it holds that*

$$\mathrm{SD}((H, H(X)), (H, U)) \leq 2^{-(H_\infty(X) - \log|\mathcal{R}|)/2},$$

where $U \leftarrow \mathcal{R}$ (independent of H).

The following lemma is similar both in statement and proof to [19, Lemma 1]. It states that for a uniform universal hash function H conditioned on its output for a uniform input X, does not affect its distribution by much. This is in a sense the converse of the leftover hash lemma that states that $(H, H(X))$ is close to uniform. For simplicity, we only state the lemma for the inner-product hash family.

Lemma 3. *Let $(\mathcal{R}, +, \cdot)$ be a finite ring of size r, let $n = \lceil \log r \rceil + \kappa$, let $\boldsymbol{d} \in \mathcal{R}^n$, let $\ell = \mathrm{dist}(\boldsymbol{d}, 0^n)$ and let $\boldsymbol{V} \leftarrow \mathcal{R}^n$ and $\boldsymbol{T} \leftarrow \{-1, 1\}^n$ be two independent random variables. Then for every $x \in \mathcal{R}$ it holds that:*

$$\mathrm{SD}(\boldsymbol{V}, \boldsymbol{V}|_{\langle \boldsymbol{V}, \boldsymbol{T} \rangle = x}) \leq 2^{-(\kappa-1)/2}.$$

The proof of the above can be found in the full-version of this paper [17].

4   Multiplication with Unpredictable Output Under Attack

In this section, we formally describe our "weak" OT-based multiplication protocol introduced in Sect. 1; we state and analyze its security guarantee. We show that our protocol securely realizes a multiplication functionality that guarantees *unpredictable honest-party output under attack*, which, for lack of a better short name, we will address as WeakMult. Intuitively, WeakMult allows the adversary to either act honestly, or to induce an unpredictable offset on the honest party's output. As discussed in the introduction, such a security guarantee suffices in many settings where "secure multiplication" is needed, and, with some additional effort (see Sect. 6), can be compiled into perfect i.e., standard multiplication.

In Sect. 4.1, we define the WeakMult functionality and analyze the security guarantee it provides. In Sect. 4.2, we formally define our OT-based multiplication protocol, and we prove that it securely realizes WeakMult. Hereafter, we fix $q \in \mathrm{PRIMES}_{>2}$ (i.e., the size of the field), and all arithmetic operations are done over the field $\mathbb{Z}_q = \mathbb{Z}/q\mathbb{Z}$ (i.e., modulo q). Let $\mathrm{Ham}(\boldsymbol{x}, \boldsymbol{y})$ stand for the hamming distance between the vectors $\boldsymbol{x}$ and $\boldsymbol{y}$.

4.1   The Ideal Functionality

We start by describing the ideal functionality WeakMult. Recall that PerfectMult is the perfect (standard) multiplication functionality defined in Sect. 3.3.3.

Definition 3 (polychromatic vector). *A vector $d \in \mathbb{Z}_q^n$ is m-polychromatic if for every $y \in \mathbb{Z}_q$ it holds that $\mathrm{Ham}(d, y^n) \geq m$.*

Functionality 6 (WeakMult)
Common input: a security parameter 1^κ. Let $n = \lceil \log q \rceil + \kappa$.
P_1*'s input: $a \in \mathbb{Z}_q$, and optional $d \in \mathbb{Z}_q^n$.*
P_2*'s input: $b \in \mathbb{Z}_q$, and optional $s_2 \in \mathbb{Z}_q$.*
Operation:
  If d is **not** $\kappa/2$*-polychromatic (or $d = \perp$), act according to* PerfectMult$(a, (b, s_2))$.

  Else:

1. *Sample $(v, t) \leftarrow \mathbb{Z}_q^n \times \{-1, 1\}^n$ such that $\langle v, t \rangle = b$.[11]*
2. *Sample $s_2 \leftarrow \mathbb{Z}_q$.*
3. *Output $((s_1, v), s_2)$ for $s_1 = a \cdot b - s_2 + \langle v, d * t \rangle$.*

It is clear that WeakMult outputs the shares of $a \cdot b$ correctly on a non $\kappa/2$-polychromatic d. The following lemma states the security guarantee of WeakMult against a "cheating" P_1 that uses a $\kappa/2$-polychromatic vector d.

Lemma 4. *Let $q \in \mathrm{PRIMES}_{>2}$, $\kappa \in \mathbb{N}$ and $n := \lceil \log q \rceil + \kappa$. Let $d \in \mathbb{Z}_q^n$, let $\ell = \min_{y \in \mathbb{Z}_q}\{\mathrm{Ham}(d, y^n)\}$, let $\lambda := \min\{\ell, \kappa - 5, \log q, n/3\}$, and let $(V, T) \leftarrow \mathbb{Z}_q^n \times \{-1, 1\}^n$. Then for every $b \in \mathbb{Z}_q$, with probability $1 - 2^{-\lambda/2+3}$ over $v \leftarrow V|_{\langle V, T \rangle = b}$, it holds that*

$$\mathrm{H}_\infty(\langle v, d * T \rangle \mid \langle v, T \rangle = b) \geq \lambda/2 - 4.$$

When $\lambda \geq \kappa/2$ (by the definition of λ this happens when the field is not too small), for a $\kappa/2$-polychromatic d, Lemma 4 yields that for such d, conditioned on $\langle v, T \rangle = b$, the min-entropy of $\langle v, d*T \rangle$ is at least $\kappa/4 - 4$. The rather tedious proof of Lemma 4 is given in the full version of this paper [17]. Below, we state and prove a weaker, but easier to read, variant.

Lemma 5 (A weak variant of Lemma 4). *Let κ, n, d, ℓ, V, T be as in Lemma 4, and let $\lambda := \min\{\ell, \kappa, \log q, n/3\}$. Then for any $b \in \mathbb{Z}_q$, with probability $1 - 2^{-\lambda/3+2}$ over $v \leftarrow V|_{\langle V, T \rangle = b}$, it holds that*

$$\mathrm{H}_\infty(\langle v, d * T \rangle \mid \langle v, T \rangle = b) \geq \lambda/3 - 4.$$

In words, compared to Lemma 4, Lemma 5 yields a slightly smaller min-entropy guarantee which occurs with a slightly smaller probability.

---

[11] This sampling can be done efficiently by sampling the two item uniformly, and then adjusting one coordinate of v.

Proof. We assume without loss of generality that

$$\underset{x \in \mathbb{Z}_q}{\operatorname{argmax}} |\{i \in [n] \colon d_i = x\}| = 0,$$

i.e., 0 is the most common element in $\boldsymbol{d}$. (Otherwise, we prove the lemma for the vector $\boldsymbol{d}' = \boldsymbol{d} - y^n$, where $y \in \mathbb{Z}_q$ be the most common element). We also assume that $\boldsymbol{d}$ is not the all-zero vector, as otherwise the proof trivially holds.

Let $\kappa, n, \boldsymbol{d}, \ell, \lambda, \boldsymbol{V}, \boldsymbol{T}$ be as in Lemma 4, and fix $b \in \mathbb{Z}_q$. In addition, for $t \in \{-1,1\}^n$, let W^t be the indicator random variable for the event $\{\langle \boldsymbol{V}, \boldsymbol{t} \rangle = b\}$, and let $W := \sum_{t \in \{-1,1\}^n} W^t$. For $\boldsymbol{t} \in \{-1,1\}^n$ and $x \in \mathbb{Z}_q$, let Z_x^t be the indicator random variable for the event $\{\langle \boldsymbol{V}, \boldsymbol{t} \rangle = b \wedge \langle \boldsymbol{V}, \boldsymbol{d} * \boldsymbol{t} \rangle = x\}$, and let $Z_x := \sum_{t \in \{-1,1\}^n} Z_x^t$. We start by proving that with high probability over $\boldsymbol{V}$, for every $x \in \mathbb{Z}_q$, it holds that

$$Z_x / W \leq 2^{-\lambda/3+4} \tag{5}$$

and we will complete the proof of the lemma by showing that the above inequality still holds when defining Z_x and W with respect to the random variable $\boldsymbol{V}^b := \boldsymbol{V}|_{\langle \boldsymbol{V}, \boldsymbol{T} \rangle = b}$ (rather than with respect to $\boldsymbol{V}$). We prove Eq. (5) by bounding the variance of W and Z_x, and then use Chebyshev's inequality (Lemma 1). Specifically, we use the following claims (proven below).

Claim 7. *For every* $x \in \mathbb{Z}_q$: $\mathrm{E}[Z_x] = 2^n/q^2$ *and* $\mathrm{Var}(Z_x) \leq 2^{2n-\lambda+4}/q^3$.

Claim 8. $\mathrm{E}[W] = 2^n/q$ *and* $\mathrm{Var}(W) \leq 2^{n+1}/q$.

By Chebyshev's inequality and Claim 7, for every $x \in \mathbb{Z}_q$:

$$\Pr\left[|Z_x - 2^n/q^2| \geq 2^{n-\lambda/3+2}/q\right] \leq \frac{q^2 \cdot \mathrm{Var}(Z_x)}{2^{2n-2\lambda/3+4}} \leq \frac{2^{-\lambda/3}}{q},$$

and thus by a union bound

$$\Pr\left[\exists x \text{ s.t. } |Z_x - 2^n/q^2| \geq 2^{n-\lambda/3+2}/q\right] \leq 2^{-\lambda/3}. \tag{6}$$

Applying Chebyshev's inequality with respect to Claim 8, we get that

$$\Pr\left[W \leq 2^{n-1}/q\right] \leq \Pr\left[|W - 2^n/q| \geq 2^{n-1}/q\right] \leq \frac{q^2 \cdot \mathrm{Var}(W)}{2^{2n-2}} \leq 2^{-\kappa+3}, \tag{7}$$

where the last inequality holds since, be definition, $n \geq \log q + \kappa$. Combining Eqs. (6) and (7) yields that with probability at least $1 - (2^{-\lambda/3} + 2^{-\kappa+3}) \geq 1 - 2^{-\lambda/3+1}$ over $\boldsymbol{v} \leftarrow \boldsymbol{V}$, it holds that:

1. $\forall x \in \mathbb{Z}_q : Z_x \leq 2^{n-\lambda/3+3}/q$, and
2. $W \geq 2^{n-1}/q$.

Note that for every v satisfying Items 1 and 2, and every $x \in \mathbb{Z}_q$, it holds that

$$\Pr\left[\langle v, d * T \rangle = x \mid \langle v, T \rangle = b\right] = \frac{\Pr\left[\langle v, d * T \rangle = x \wedge \langle v, T \rangle = b\right]}{\Pr\left[\langle v, T \rangle = b\right]} \tag{8}$$

$$= \frac{Z_x}{W}|_{V=v}$$

$$\leq 2^{-\lambda/3+4}.$$

We now turn to the distribution $V^b = V|_{\langle V,T \rangle=b}$. Applying Lemma 3 with respect to the ring $\mathcal{R} = \mathbb{Z}_q$ with addition and multiplication modulo q, yields that

$$\mathrm{SD}(V, V^b) \leq 2^{-(\kappa-1)/2} \tag{9}$$

It follows that Eq. (8) holds with probability at least $1 - 2^{-\lambda/3+1} - 2^{-(\kappa-1)/2} \geq 1 - 2^{-\lambda/3+2}$ over $v \leftarrow V^b$, as required.

4.1.1 Proving Claim 8

Proof. Recall that $W := \sum_{t\in\{-1,1\}^n} W^t$ for W^t being the indicator random variable for the event $\{\langle V, t \rangle = b\}$. Therefore, it is clear that $\mathrm{E}[W] = 2^n/q$, and a simple calculation yields that

$$\mathrm{Var}(W) = \mathrm{Var}\left(\sum_{t\in\{-1,1\}^n} W^t\right) \tag{10}$$

$$= \sum_{t\in\{-1,1\}^n} (\mathrm{E}[(W^t - 1/q)^2] + \mathrm{E}[(W^t - 1/q) \cdot (W^{-t} - 1/q)])$$

$$\leq 2 \cdot \sum_{t\in\{-1,1\}^n} \mathrm{Var}(W^t)$$

$$\leq 2^{n+1}/q,$$

as required. The second equality holds since for every t, t' with $t' \notin \{-t, t\}$, the random variables W^t and $W^{t'}$ are independent (because t and t' are linearly independent).

4.1.2 Proving Claim 7

Recall that $Z_x := \sum_{t\in\{-1,1\}^n} Z_x^t$ for Z_x^t being the indicator random variable for the event $\{\langle V, t \rangle = b \wedge \langle V, d * t \rangle = x\}$. For any $t \in \{-1,1\}^n$, since the vectors t and $d * t$ are linearly independent (recall that d contains zero and non-zero elements) it holds that $\mathrm{E}[Z_x^t] = 1/q^2$, and therefore, $\mathrm{E}[Z_x] = 2^n/q^2$. It is left to bound $\mathrm{Var}(Z_x)$. For $j \in [4]$, let

$$\mathcal{B}_j := \{(t, t') \in \{-1,1\}^{2n} : \mathrm{rank}\{t, t', d * t, d * t'\} = j\}$$

Note that the only possible values for $E[Z_x^t \cdot Z_x^{t'}]$ are $\{0\} \cup \{1/q^j\}_{j=1}^4$, where $E[Z_x^t \cdot Z_x^{t'}] = 1/q^j \implies (t, t') \in \mathcal{B}_j$. We relate $\mathrm{Var}\left(\sum_{t \in \{-1,1\}^n} Z_x^t\right)$ to size $\{\mathcal{B}_j\}$ as follows:

$$\mathrm{Var}\left(Z_x\right) = \sum_{t,t' \in \{-1,1\}^n} E[(Z_x^t - 1/q^2)(Z_x^{t'} - 1/q^2)] \tag{11}$$

$$\leq \sum_{t,t' \in \{-1,1\}^n} E[Z_x^t \cdot Z_x^{t'}]$$

$$\leq \sum_{j=1}^4 |\mathcal{B}_j| / q^j.$$

We complete the proof by bounding the size of $\mathcal{B}_j$ for each $j \in [3]$ (for $\mathcal{B}_4$ we use the trivial bound $|\mathcal{B}_4| \leq 2^{2n}$).

Claim 9. $|\mathcal{B}_1| = 0$.

Proof. Since d contains zeros and non-zeros elements, the vectors t and $d * t$, for any $t \in \{-1, 1\}^n$, are linearly independent over $\mathbb{Z}_q^n$, yielding that $|\mathcal{B}_1| = 0$.

Claim 10. $|\mathcal{B}_2| \leq 2^{n+2}$.

Proof. Since there are exactly 2^{n+1} linearly dependent pairs (t, t'), i.e., the pairs $\cup_{t \in \{-1,1\}^n} \{(t, t), (t, -t)\}$, we deduce the bound by proving that there are at most 2^{n+1} independent pairs (t, t') in $\mathcal{B}_2$.

Fix an independent pair $(t, t') \in \mathcal{B}_2$, let $\mathcal{E} = \{i \in [n]: t_i = t_i'\}$ and let $\mathcal{N} = [n] \setminus \mathcal{E}$. Up to reordering of the coordinates, we can write $t = (t_\mathcal{E}, t_\mathcal{N})$, $t' = (t_\mathcal{E}, -t_\mathcal{N})$ and $d = (d_\mathcal{E}, d_\mathcal{N})$. It is easy to verify that

$$\mathrm{span}\{t, t', d * t, d * t'\} = \mathrm{span}\{(t_\mathcal{E}, 0), (0, t_\mathcal{N}), (d_\mathcal{E} * t_\mathcal{E}, 0), (0, d_\mathcal{N} * t_\mathcal{N})\}.$$

Since (t, t') are independent and $\mathrm{rank}\{t, t', d * t, d * t'\} = 2$, the above yields that

$$d_\mathcal{E} \in \mathrm{span}\{1\} \wedge d_\mathcal{N} \in \mathrm{span}\{1\} \tag{12}$$

Since, by assumption, d is d is not the all-zero vector, Eq. (12) yields that $(d_\mathcal{E}, d_\mathcal{N}) = (u \cdot 1, 0)$ or $d = (0, u \cdot 1)$, for some $u \in \mathbb{Z}_q \setminus \{0\}$.

Assuming that $\mathcal{B}_2$ contains an independent pair, otherwise we are done, the above yields that the non-zero coordinates of d are all equal to some $u \in \mathbb{Z}_q \setminus \{0\}$. It follows that for each vector $t \in \{-1, 1\}^n$ there are at most *two* vectors t^1 and t^2, such that (t, t^j) is an independent pair in $\mathcal{B}_2$ (actually, each t has exactly two such vectors, with $t^1 = -t^2$). We conclude that the number of independent pairs $(t, t') \in \mathcal{B}_2$ is at most 2^{n+1}.

Claim 11. $|\mathcal{B}_3| \leq 2^{2n - \min\{n/3, \ell\} + 2}$ *(recall that $\ell = \mathrm{Ham}(d, 0)$).*

Proof. Let $\mu := \min\{n/3, \ell\}$, fix $(\boldsymbol{t}, \boldsymbol{t}') \in \mathcal{B}_3$, let $\mathcal{E} = \{i \in [n]: t_i = t_i'\}$ and let $\mathcal{N} = [n] \setminus \mathcal{E}$. Up to reordering of the coordinates, we can write $\boldsymbol{t} = (\boldsymbol{t}_\mathcal{E}, \boldsymbol{t}_\mathcal{N})$, $\boldsymbol{t}' = (\boldsymbol{t}_\mathcal{E}, -\boldsymbol{t}_\mathcal{N})$ and $\boldsymbol{d} = (\boldsymbol{d}_\mathcal{E}, \boldsymbol{d}_\mathcal{N})$. It holds that

$$\mathrm{span}\{\boldsymbol{t}, \boldsymbol{t}', \boldsymbol{d} * \boldsymbol{t}, \boldsymbol{d} * \boldsymbol{t}'\} = \mathrm{span}\{(\boldsymbol{t}_\mathcal{E}, \boldsymbol{0}), (\boldsymbol{0}, \boldsymbol{t}_\mathcal{N}), (\boldsymbol{d}_\mathcal{E} * \boldsymbol{t}_\mathcal{E}, \boldsymbol{0}), (\boldsymbol{0}, \boldsymbol{d}_\mathcal{N} * \boldsymbol{t}_\mathcal{N})\}.$$

Since the assumed dimension is 3, then

$$\boldsymbol{d}_\mathcal{E} \in \mathrm{span}\{\boldsymbol{1}\} \ \vee \ \boldsymbol{d}_\mathcal{N} \in \mathrm{span}\{\boldsymbol{1}\} \tag{13}$$

We next show how to partition the coordinates of $\boldsymbol{d}$ into sets $\mathcal{I}_0$ and $\mathcal{I}_1$, each of size at least μ, such that for all $i \in \mathcal{I}_0$ it holds that $d_i \notin \{d_j : j \in \mathcal{I}_1\}$ and vice versa. If $\ell \leq n - \mu$, then we are done by taking $\mathcal{I}_0 = \{i: d_i = 0\}$ and $\mathcal{I}_1 = [n] \setminus \mathcal{I}_0$. Assume that $\ell > n - \mu$, which implies that $\mu \leq n - 2\mu < 2\ell - n$. For $\alpha \in \mathbb{Z}_q$ define $\mathcal{J}_\alpha = \{i: d_i = \alpha\}$ and notice that $|\mathcal{J}_\alpha| < (n - \mu)/2$ because otherwise

$$|\mathcal{J}_\alpha| \geq (n - \mu)/2 > (n - (2\ell - n))/2 = n - \ell$$

which contradicts the definition of ℓ (recall that 0 is the element with maximal number of appearances in $\boldsymbol{d}$, and there are exactly $n - \ell$ zero coordinates). Finally, define $s \in \mathbb{Z}_q$ to be the minimal value such that $\cup_{\alpha=0}^s \mathcal{J}_\alpha \geq \mu$ and let $\mathcal{I}_0 = \cup_{\alpha=0}^s \mathcal{J}_\alpha$ and $\mathcal{I}_1 = [n] \setminus \mathcal{I}_0$. By definition, $\mathcal{I}_0$ is bigger than μ and it remains to show that $\mathcal{I}_1 \geq \mu$. It holds that

$$|\mathcal{I}_1| = n - |\mathcal{I}_0| = n - \left| \cup_{\alpha=0}^{s-1} \mathcal{J}_\alpha \right| - |\mathcal{J}_s| \geq n - \mu - (n - \mu)/2 \geq \mu.$$

Back to the proof, Eq. (13) yields that either $\mathcal{E} \subseteq \mathcal{I}_0$, or $\mathcal{E} \subseteq \mathcal{I}_1$, or $\mathcal{N} \subseteq \mathcal{I}_0$, or $\mathcal{N} \subseteq \mathcal{I}_1$. Since $|\mathcal{I}_0|, |\mathcal{I}_1| \geq \mu$, the number of pairs $(\boldsymbol{t}, \boldsymbol{t}') \in \{-1, 1\}^n$ that satisfy this condition is at most $4 \cdot 2^{2n-\mu}$, which ends the proof of the claim.

Putting it Together. Given the above claims, we are ready to prove Claim 7.

Proof (Proof of Claim 7). Recall that $\lambda := \min\{\ell, \kappa, \log q, n/3\}$. By Eq. (11) and Claims 9 to 11, we conclude that

$$\begin{aligned}
\mathrm{Var}(Z_x) &\leq \sum_{j=1}^{4} |\mathcal{B}_j| / q^j \\
&\leq 2^{n+2}/q^2 + 2^{2n-\lambda+2}/q^3 + 2^{2n}/q^4 \\
&\leq 2^{2n-\lambda+4}/q^3,
\end{aligned}$$

as required. The last inequality holds since $\lambda \leq \kappa$ implies that $2^{n+2}/q^2 \leq 2^{2n-\lambda+2}/q^3$, and $\lambda \leq \log q$ implies that $2^{2n}/q^4 \leq 2^{2n-\lambda+2}/q^3$.

4.2 The OT-Based Protocol

In the following we describe our OT-based implementation of the functionality WeakMult. Recall that throughout this section we fix a field size $q > 2$ and assume that all operation are made over the field $\mathbb{Z}_q = \mathbb{Z}/q\mathbb{Z}$ (i.e., modulo q).

Protocol 12 ($\Pi = (\mathsf{P}_1, \mathsf{P}_2)$).
Oracle: (one-out-of-two) OT.
Common input: security parameter 1^κ. Let $n = \lceil \log q \rceil + \kappa$.
P_1*'s private input: $a \in \mathbb{Z}_q$.*
P_2*'s private input: $b \in \mathbb{Z}_q$.*
Operations:

1. *For each $i \in [n]$, in parallel:*
   (a) P_1 *samples $\delta_i \leftarrow \mathbb{Z}_q$, and P_2 samples $t_i \leftarrow \{-1, 1\}$.*
   (b) *The parties jointly call $\mathrm{OT}((\delta_i - a, \delta_i + a), t_i)$.*
       Let z_i be the output obtained by P_2 in this call.
2. P_2 *samples $\boldsymbol{v} \leftarrow \mathbb{Z}_q^n$ such that $\langle \boldsymbol{v}, (t_1, \ldots, t_n) \rangle) = b$, samples $\sigma \leftarrow \mathbb{Z}_q$, and sends $(\boldsymbol{v}, \sigma)$ to P_1.*
3. P_1 *outputs $s_1 := -\langle \boldsymbol{v}, \boldsymbol{\delta} \rangle - \sigma$.*
4. P_2 *outputs $s_2 := \langle \boldsymbol{v}, (z_1, \ldots, z_n) \rangle + \sigma$.*

Note that, unlike in the simplified version of the protocol presented in the introduction, party P_2 in the above adds an additional mask σ to the shares. The role of this additional mask is rather technical, but it appears necessary for simulating of the above protocol using WeakMult (Functionality 6).

Lemma 6 (Security). *Protocol 12 ($\alpha(\kappa) := 2^{-\kappa/4+1.5}$)-computes WeakMult in the OT-hybrid model with respect to input domain $\mathbb{Z}_q \times \mathbb{Z}_q$. Furthermore, if both parties act honestly, then their joint output equals the output of WeakMult on their joint inputs.*

Proof. We start with proving correctness (correct output when acting honestly). Indeed, for any possible values of $a, b, \kappa, s_2, \boldsymbol{\delta} = (\delta_1, \ldots, \delta_n), \boldsymbol{t} = (t_1, \ldots, t_n), \boldsymbol{z} = (z_1, \ldots, z_n), \boldsymbol{v}$ an σ in a honest execution of $\Pi(a, b)(1^\kappa)$, it holds that

$$s_2 = \langle \boldsymbol{v}, \boldsymbol{z} \rangle + \sigma = \langle \boldsymbol{v}, \boldsymbol{\delta} + a \cdot \boldsymbol{t} \rangle + \sigma = a \cdot \langle \boldsymbol{v}, \boldsymbol{t} \rangle + \langle \boldsymbol{v}, \boldsymbol{\delta} \rangle + \sigma = a \cdot b - s_1,$$

and thus $s_1 + s_2 = a \cdot b$.

For security, fix a security parameter $\kappa \in \mathbb{N}$ and inputs $a, b \in \mathbb{Z}_q$.

We only prove security for corrupted P_1 (the proof for corrupted P_2 is straightforward and can be found in the full version of this paper [17]).

Corrupted P_1: Given an oracle access to (the next-message function of) an interactive adversary A controlling P_1, its ideal-model simulator S, which uses the functionality WeakMult, is described as follows:

Algorithm 13 (Ideal-model S)
Inputs: 1^κ and $a \in \mathbb{Z}_q$.
Oracles: (real-model) attacker A.
Operations:

1. *Simulate a random execution of $(\mathsf{A}(a), \mathsf{P}_2(0))(1^\kappa)$ till the end of Step 1.*
2. *If the simulation ends prematurely (e.g., on invalid behavior), send Abort to $\mathsf{WeakMult}_\kappa$, output A's output and halt the execution.*

3. Let (w_i^-, w_i^+) and t_i denote the inputs that A and P_2 use (respectively) in the ith OT execution of the simulation (Step 1b). Let $a_i = (w_i^+ - w_i^-) \cdot 2^{-1}$ (where 2^{-1} stands for the inverse of 2 in $\mathbb{Z}_q$), let $\boldsymbol{a} = (a_1, \ldots, a_n)$, let $\boldsymbol{\delta} = (w_1^+ - a_1, \ldots, w_n^+ - a_n)$, let $\hat{a} \in \mathbb{Z}_q$ denote the value that appears the most often in $\boldsymbol{a}$, and let $\boldsymbol{d} = \boldsymbol{a} - \hat{a} \cdot \mathbf{1}$.

4. If $\mathrm{Ham}(\boldsymbol{d}, 0^n) < \kappa/2$:
   (a) Send $(\hat{a}, \boldsymbol{d})$ to $\mathsf{WeakMult}_\kappa$.
   (b) Receive s_1 from $\mathsf{WeakMult}_\kappa$.
   (c) Sample $\boldsymbol{v} \leftarrow \mathbb{Z}_q^n$ such that $\langle \boldsymbol{v}, (t_1, \ldots, t_n) \rangle = 0$, and send $(\boldsymbol{v}, \sigma := -\langle \boldsymbol{v}, \boldsymbol{\delta} \rangle - \langle \boldsymbol{v}, \boldsymbol{d} * \boldsymbol{t} \rangle - s_1)$ to A.

5. Else:
   (a) Send $(\hat{a}, \boldsymbol{d})$ to $\mathsf{WeakMult}_\kappa$.
   (b) Receive $(s_1, \hat{\boldsymbol{v}})$ from $\mathsf{WeakMult}_\kappa$.
   (c) Send $(\hat{\boldsymbol{v}}, \sigma := -s_1 - \langle \hat{\boldsymbol{v}}, \boldsymbol{\delta} \rangle)$ to A.

6. Output A's output in the simulation.

It is clear that S is efficient. We next bound the statistical distance between $\mathrm{REAL}_{\mathsf{P}_1}^\Pi(\mathsf{A}, \kappa, a, b)$ and $\mathrm{IDEAL}_{\mathsf{P}_1}^{\mathsf{WeakMult}}(\mathsf{S}^\mathsf{A}, \kappa, a, b)$. Assuming without loss of generality that A is deterministic (a randomized adversary is just a convex combination of deterministic adversaries), the values of $\boldsymbol{d}$, $\hat{a}$ and $\boldsymbol{\delta}$ that it uses are fixed, and it either uses an $\kappa/2$-polychromatic $\boldsymbol{d}$, or not (i.e., an almost all-zeros $\boldsymbol{d}$). We handle each of these cases separately. In the following let $\boldsymbol{V} \leftarrow \mathbb{Z}_q^n$, $\boldsymbol{T} \leftarrow \{-1, 1\}^n$ and $S_1 \leftarrow \mathbb{Z}_q$ be independent random variables.

Polychromatic $\boldsymbol{d}$. If A uses an $\kappa/2$-polychromatic $\boldsymbol{d}$, then $\mathrm{REAL}_{\mathsf{P}_1}^\Pi(\mathsf{A}, \kappa, a, b)$, the view of A and the output of P_2 in the real execution $(\mathsf{A}(a), \mathsf{P}_2(b))(1^\kappa)$, are jointly distributed according to

$$((\boldsymbol{V}, -S_1 - \langle \boldsymbol{V}, \boldsymbol{\delta} \rangle), \ \hat{a} \cdot b - S_1 + \langle \boldsymbol{V}, \boldsymbol{d} * \boldsymbol{T} \rangle) |_{\langle \boldsymbol{V}, \boldsymbol{T} \rangle = b} \tag{14}$$

Let $(\hat{\boldsymbol{v}}, \hat{\boldsymbol{t}})$ be the pair that is sampled in Step 1 of $\mathsf{WeakMult}_\kappa$. Since this pair is sampled according to $(\boldsymbol{V}, \boldsymbol{T})|_{\langle \boldsymbol{V}, \boldsymbol{T} \rangle = b}$, in the ideal execution it holds that $\mathrm{IDEAL}_{\mathsf{P}_1}^{\mathsf{WeakMult}}(\mathsf{S}^\mathsf{A}, \kappa, a, b)$ (A's view and the output of the trusted party in the ideal execution) are jointly distributed according to Eq. (14). This concludes the proof of this case.

Almost-monochromatic $\boldsymbol{d}$. Assume A uses a non $\kappa/2$-polychromatic vector $\boldsymbol{d}$, i.e., ℓ, the hamming distance of $\boldsymbol{d}$ from 0^n, is less than $\kappa/2$. In this case, A's view in the real execution, i.e., the pair $(\boldsymbol{v}, \sigma)$, and the output s_2 of P_2, are jointly distributed according to $((\boldsymbol{V}, \Sigma), \hat{a} \cdot b - S_1)|_{\langle \boldsymbol{V}, \boldsymbol{T} \rangle = b}$, for $\Sigma = -S_1 - \langle \boldsymbol{V}, \boldsymbol{\delta} \rangle - \langle \boldsymbol{V}, \boldsymbol{d} * \boldsymbol{T} \rangle$. On the other hand, the output of S^A and that of the trusted party in the ideal execution, are jointly distributed according to $((\boldsymbol{V}, \Sigma), \ \hat{a} \cdot b - S_1)|_{\langle \boldsymbol{V}, \boldsymbol{T} \rangle = 0}$ (i.e., now the conditioning is over $\langle \boldsymbol{V}, \boldsymbol{T} \rangle$ equals 0 and not b). Therefore

$$\mathrm{SD}\left(\mathrm{REAL}_{\mathsf{P}_1}^\Pi(\mathsf{A}, \kappa, a, b), \ \mathrm{IDEAL}_{\mathsf{P}_1}^{\mathsf{WeakMult}}(\mathsf{S}^\mathsf{A}, \kappa, a, b)\right) \tag{15}$$

$$= \mathrm{SD}\left(((\boldsymbol{V}, \Sigma), \ \hat{a} \cdot b - S_1)|_{\langle \boldsymbol{V}, \boldsymbol{T} \rangle = b}, \ (((\boldsymbol{V}, \Sigma), \ \hat{a} \cdot b - S_1)|_{\langle \boldsymbol{V}, \boldsymbol{T} \rangle = 0}\right)$$

$$\leq \mathrm{SD}\left((\boldsymbol{V}, \langle \boldsymbol{V}, \boldsymbol{d} * \boldsymbol{T} \rangle)|_{\langle \boldsymbol{V}, \boldsymbol{T} \rangle = b}, \ (\boldsymbol{V}, \langle \boldsymbol{V}, \boldsymbol{d} * \boldsymbol{T} \rangle)|_{\langle \boldsymbol{V}, \boldsymbol{T} \rangle = 0}\right).$$

The inequality holds since each pair is a randomized function of V and $\langle V, d * T \rangle$ (recall that $\hat{a}, b, \delta$ are fixed, S_1 is independent, and Σ is a function of S_1, $\langle V, d * T \rangle$ and $\langle V, \delta \rangle$). Recall that $\ell = \text{Ham}(d, 0^n) < \kappa/2$, and let $\mathcal{I} := \{i \in [n]: d_i \neq 0\}$. Since $\langle V, d * T \rangle$ is a deterministic function of V and $T_{\mathcal{I}}$, it suffices to prove that

$$\text{SD}((V, T_{\mathcal{I}})|_{\langle V, T \rangle = b}, \ (V, T_{\mathcal{I}})|_{\langle V, T \rangle = 0}) \leq 2^{-(\kappa - \ell - 3)/2} \tag{16}$$

Since $\mathcal{I} \subsetneq [n]$, for every $x \in \mathbb{Z}_q$ it holds that

$$(V_{\mathcal{I}}, T_{\mathcal{I}})|_{\langle V, T \rangle = x} \equiv (V_{\mathcal{I}}, T_{\mathcal{I}}) \tag{17}$$

Hence, it suffices to prove that Eq. (16) holds for every fixing of $(V_{\mathcal{I}}, T_{\mathcal{I}}) = (v_{\mathcal{I}}, t_{\mathcal{I}})$. Indeed,

$$\begin{aligned}
&\text{SD}(V_{-\mathcal{I}}|_{\langle V_{-\mathcal{I}}, T_{-\mathcal{I}} \rangle = x}, \ V_{-\mathcal{I}}|_{\langle V_{-\mathcal{I}}, T_{-\mathcal{I}} \rangle = x'}) \\
&\leq \text{SD}(V_{-\mathcal{I}}, \ V_{-\mathcal{I}}|_{\langle V_{-\mathcal{I}}, T_{-\mathcal{I}} \rangle = x}) + \text{SD}(V_{-\mathcal{I}}, \ V_{-\mathcal{I}}|_{\langle V_{-\mathcal{I}}, T_{-\mathcal{I}} \rangle = x'}) \\
&\leq 2 \cdot 2^{-(\kappa - \ell - 1)/2} \\
&= 2^{-(\kappa - \ell - 3)/2}.
\end{aligned}$$

The second inequality holds by applying Lemma 3 with a vector size $\tilde{n} = n - \ell = \lceil \log q \rceil + (\kappa - \ell)$, over the ring $\mathcal{R} = \mathbb{Z}_q$ with addition and multiplication modulo q.

5   Batching

In this section we consider the case that the parties $\hat{P}_1$ and $\hat{P}_2$ would like to perform $m > 1$ multiplications, where $\hat{P}_1$ uses the same input $a \in \mathbb{Z}_q$ and $\hat{P}_2$ uses different inputs $b_1, \ldots, b_m \in \mathbb{Z}_q$. A naive solution is to perform m independent executions of our single multiplication protocol Π (Protocol 12), where the overall cost is $m \cdot (\log q + \kappa)$ OT calls. In this section we present our batching protocol which performs m such multiplications using only $m \cdot \log q + \kappa$ OT calls, at the cost of relaxing the security requirement. In Sect. 5.1 we describe the relaxed ideal functionality WeakBatch that we consider for our batching task, and in Sect. 5.2 we describe our OT-Based implementation (Protocol 15).

5.1   The Ideal Functionality

In the following we describe the ideal functionality WeakBatch.

Functionality 14 (WeakBatch)
Parameters: Multiplications number $m \in \mathbb{N}$ and a security parameter $\kappa \in \mathbb{N}$.
    Let $n := \lceil m \cdot \log q \rceil + \kappa$.
$\hat{P}_1$'s input: $a \in \mathbb{Z}_q$, and **optional** $d \in \mathbb{Z}_q^n$.
$\hat{P}_2$'s input: $b = (b_1, \ldots, b_m) \in \mathbb{Z}_q^m$, and **optional** $s_2 = (s_2^1, \ldots, s_2^m) \in \mathbb{Z}_q^m$.

Operation:

If $\boldsymbol{d}$ is **not** $\kappa/2$-polychromatic (or $\boldsymbol{d} = \perp$), act according to PerfectMultBatching$(a, (\boldsymbol{b}, \boldsymbol{s}_2))$.

Else:

1. Sample $(\boldsymbol{v}^1, \ldots, \boldsymbol{v}^m, \boldsymbol{t}) \leftarrow (\mathbb{Z}_q^n)^m \times \{-1, 1\}^n$ such that $\forall i \in [m] : \langle \boldsymbol{v}^i, \boldsymbol{t} \rangle = b_i$.
2. Sample $\boldsymbol{s}_2 = (s_2^1, \ldots, s_2^m) \leftarrow \mathbb{Z}_q^m$.
3. Output $(\{(s_1^i, \boldsymbol{v}^i)\}_{i=1}^m, \{(s_2^i)\}_{i=1}^m)$ for $s_1^i = a \cdot b_i - s_2^i + \langle \boldsymbol{v}^i, \boldsymbol{d} * \boldsymbol{t} \rangle$.

Note that for $m = 1$, WeakBatch is identical to WeakMult (Sect. 4.1). For $m > 1$, WeakBatch achieves perfect correctness and security whenever $\boldsymbol{d}$ is not $\kappa/2$-polychromatic. In particular, when $\hat{\mathsf{P}}_1$ is honest (i.e., $\boldsymbol{d} = \perp$), the functionality is perfectly secure against a cheating $\hat{\mathsf{P}}_2$. As in WeakMult, the more complicated security guarantee is against a cheating $\hat{\mathsf{P}}_1$, which may use a $\kappa/2$-polychromatic vector $\boldsymbol{d}$.

The security guarantee against a cheating $\hat{\mathsf{P}}_1$ that chooses an $\kappa/2$-polychromatic $\boldsymbol{d}$ is characterized by the following result.

Lemma 7 *Let* $q \in \mathsf{PRIMES}_{>2}$, $\kappa \in \mathbb{N}$, $m \in \mathbb{N}$ *and* $n := \lceil m \cdot \log q \rceil + \kappa$. *Let* $\boldsymbol{d} \in \mathbb{Z}_q^n$, *let* $\ell := \min_{y \in \mathbb{Z}_q} \{\mathrm{Ham}(\boldsymbol{d}, y^n)\}$ *and let* $\lambda := \min\{\ell, \kappa - 5, \log q, n/3\}$. *Let* $(\boldsymbol{V} = (\boldsymbol{V}^1, \ldots, \boldsymbol{V}^m), \boldsymbol{T}) \leftarrow (\mathbb{Z}_q^n)^m \times \{-1, 1\}^n$. *Then for any* $b_1, \ldots, b_m \in \mathbb{Z}_q$, *w.p.* $1 - m \cdot 2^{-\lambda/2+3}$ *over* $\boldsymbol{v} = (\boldsymbol{v}^1, \ldots, \boldsymbol{v}^m) \leftarrow \boldsymbol{V}|_{\forall j \in [m] : \langle \boldsymbol{V}^j, \boldsymbol{T} \rangle = b_j}$, *it holds that*

$$\forall i \in [m] \colon \mathrm{H}_\infty(\langle \boldsymbol{v}^i, \boldsymbol{d} * \boldsymbol{T} \rangle \mid \forall j \in [m] : \langle \boldsymbol{v}^j, \boldsymbol{T} \rangle = b_j) \geq \lambda/2 - 4.$$

We remark that the security guarantee that is obtained by Lemma 7 is weaker than m independent calls to WeakMult, i.e., the functionality WeakMults$_{m,\kappa}((a, \boldsymbol{d}), (\boldsymbol{b}, \boldsymbol{s}_2)) := (\mathsf{WeakMult}_\kappa((a, \boldsymbol{d}), (b_i, s_2^i)))_{i=1}^m$. The reason is that Lemma 7 does not guarantee independence between the m shares of $\hat{\mathsf{P}}_2$. While each share, without knowing the other shares, has high min-entropy, it might be that this is not the case when revealing some of the other shares.

The proof of Lemma 4 is given in the full version of this paper [17].

5.2   The OT-Based Protocol

In the following we describe our OT-based implementation of the functionality WeakBatch. We remind that throughout this section we fix a field size $q \in \mathsf{PRIMES}_{>2}$ and assume that all operation are made over the field $\mathbb{Z}_q = \mathbb{Z}/q\mathbb{Z}$ (i.e., modulo q).

Protocol 15 $(\varGamma = (\hat{\mathsf{P}}_1, \hat{\mathsf{P}}_2))$

Oracles: One-out-of-two OT protocol OT.
Common inputs: $m \in \mathbb{N}$ *and* 1^κ *for* $\kappa \in \mathbb{N}$. *Let* $n = \lceil m \cdot \log q \rceil + \kappa$.
$\hat{\mathsf{P}}_1$*'s private input:* $a \in \mathbb{Z}_q$.
$\hat{\mathsf{P}}_2$*'s private inputs:* $b_1, \ldots, b_m \in \mathbb{Z}_q$.

Operations:

1. *For each* $i \in [n]$, *in parallel:*
   (a) $\hat{P}_1$ *samples* $\delta_i \leftarrow \mathbb{Z}_q$, *and* $\hat{P}_2$ *samples* $t_i \leftarrow \{-1, 1\}$.
   (b) *The parties jointly call* $\text{OT}((\delta_i - a, \delta_i + a), t_i)$. .
       Let z_i *be the output obtained by* $\hat{P}_2$ *in this call.*
2. $\hat{P}_2$ *samples* $v^1, \ldots, v^m \leftarrow \mathbb{Z}_q^n$ *such that* $\forall i \in [m] : \langle v^i, t \rangle = b_i$, *samples*
   $\sigma_1, \ldots, \sigma_m \leftarrow \mathbb{Z}_q$, *and sends* $(v^1, \sigma_1), \ldots, (v^m, \sigma_m)$ *to* $\hat{P}_1$.
3. $\hat{P}_1$ *outputs* $(s_1^1, \ldots, s_1^m)$ *for* $s_1^i = -\langle v^i, \delta \rangle - \sigma_i$.
4. $\hat{P}_2$ *outputs* $(s_2^1, \ldots, s_2^m)$ *for* $s_2^i = \langle v^i, z \rangle + \sigma_i$.

Namely, as in Protocol 12 (single multiplication), $\hat{P}_1$ samples random values $(\delta_1, \ldots, \delta_n)$ and $\hat{P}_2$ samples random values $(t_1, \ldots, t_n)$, and the OT calls (i.e., Step 1) are performed the same (except from the fact that in Protocol 15, the value of n is larger than the one used in Protocol 12). But now, in Step 2, instead of sampling a single vector v a single σ, $\hat{P}_2$ now samples m independent random vectors $v^1, \ldots, v^m$, where each v^i satisfy $\langle v^i, t \rangle = b_i$, and samples m independent random offsets $\sigma_1, \ldots, \sigma_m$ (instead of a single one).

Lemma 8 (Security). *For every* $m \in \mathbb{N}$, $\Gamma_m = (\hat{P}_1, \hat{P}_2)(m, \cdot)$ *(Protocol 12)* $(\alpha(\kappa) := 2^{-\kappa/4 + 1.5})$*-computes* $\mathsf{WeakBatch}_m = \mathsf{WeakBatch}(m, \cdot, \cdot, \cdot)$ *in the OT-hybrid model, with respect to input domain* $\mathbb{Z}_q \times \mathbb{Z}_q^m$. *Furthermore, if both parties act honestly, then their joint output equals* $\mathsf{WeakBatch}_m$*'s output on their joint input.*

The proof of Lemma 8 is given in the full version of this paper [17].

6   Applications

In this section, we show how our protocol can be used in several applications. To be more precise, we show how to realize several functionalities of interest (Perfect Multiplication, OLE, VOLE, MACs, Authenticated Triplets) in a hybrid model with oracle access to the functionality WeakMult, which can be compiled into a real-world protocol by substituting the oracle with our protocol (as per the composition theorem of Canetti [9]).

6.1   Realizing Perfect Multiplication

We begin by showing how to realize perfect batch-multiplication maliciously where the definition of perfect batch-multiplication is according Functionality 5 (It is stressed that perfect multiplication is simply a special case). We will distinguish between large and small fields (where a field $\mathbb{F}$ is small if $|\mathbb{F}| < 2^{\kappa/2}$). Thus, we will assume here that $q \geq 2^{\kappa/2}$. In the full version of this paper [17] we discuss the technicalities for small fields (it is stressed that our results extend trivially to large fields that are not prime order).

To realize malicious security for Functionality 5, we will be needing the following "helper" functionalities: One commitment functionality denote $\mathcal{F}_{\mathsf{com}}$

(Functionality 16) that allows the parties to commit to certain values that can be revealed at a later time, and another functionality ShareCheck (Functionality 17) that enables the parties to verify whether their shares where computed correctly. In Sect. 6.1.2 we define our protocol in the hybrid model with ideal access to WeakBatch, ShareCheck and $\mathcal{F}_{com}$ and we prove that it realizes PerfectMultBatching.[12] In the full version of this paper [17], we show how to realize ShareCheck cheaply using group-theoretic cryptography. A real world protocol with minimal overhead can thus be derived by substituting the oracles with the relevant protocols herein.[13]

6.1.1 Ideal Commitment and Share-Correctness Functionalities

The functionality below receives one input from each party. These values are revealed at a later time once the functionality receives approval by both parties.

Functionality 16 (Commitment Functionality $\mathcal{F}_{com}$)

- P_1's input: $\alpha \in \mathbb{Z}_q$.
- P_2's input: $\beta \in \mathbb{Z}_q$
- Operation: Upon receiving continue from both parties, $\mathcal{F}_{com}$ outputs β to P_1 and α to P_2.

The functionality below receives one input and one share from each party. It simply checks whether the additive shares sum up to the product of the inputs.

Functionality 17 (ShareCheck)
P_1's input: $(x_1, s_1) \in \mathbb{Z}_q^2$.
P_2's input: $(x_2, s_2) \in \mathbb{Z}_q^2$
Operation: Output 1 if $x_1 \cdot x_2 = s_1 + s_2$ and 0 otherwise.

6.1.2 Secure Multiplication Protocol

Protocol 18 ($\Psi = (P_1, P_2)$)
Oracles: WeakBatch and ShareCheck
Parameters: Multiplications number $m \in \mathbb{N}$ and a security parameter $\kappa \in \mathbb{N}$.
    Let $n := \lceil m \cdot \log q \rceil + \kappa$.
P_1's input: $a \in \mathbb{Z}_q$.
P_2's input: $\boldsymbol{b} = (b_1, \ldots, b_m) \in \mathbb{Z}_q^m$.
Operations:

1. P_1 samples $x \leftarrow \mathbb{Z}_q$, sets $\alpha = a - x$ and sends α to $\mathcal{F}_{com}$.
2. P_2 samples $y \leftarrow \mathbb{Z}_q$, sets $\beta = b_1 - y$ and sends β to $\mathcal{F}_{com}$.
3. P_1 and P_2 invoke WeakBatch on inputs $(1^\kappa, x)$ and $(1^\kappa, y, b_2, \ldots, b_m)$ respectively. Let $(\hat{s}_1^1, \ldots, \hat{s}_1^m)$, $(\hat{s}_1^2, \ldots, \hat{s}_2^m)$ denote the respective outputs.

---

[12] We note that the definition of $\mathcal{F}_{com}$ is reactive. This feature does not interfere with composition [9].

[13] Typically, $\mathcal{F}_{com}$ is realized via a hash function modelled as a random oracle.

4. P_1 *and* P_2 *invoke* ShareCheck *on inputs* $(1^\kappa, x, \hat{s}_1^1)$ *and* $(1^\kappa, y, \hat{s}_2^1)$ *respectively.*
5. P_1 *and* P_2 *send* continue *to* $\mathcal{F}_{\mathsf{com}}$.
6. P_1 *locally outputs* $(x \cdot \beta + \hat{s}_1^1, \hat{s}_1^2, \ldots, \hat{s}_1^m)$ *and* P_2 *locally outputs* $(b_1 \cdot \alpha + \hat{s}_2^1, \ldots, b_m \cdot \alpha + \hat{s}_2^m)$.

Theorem 19. *Protocol 18* α-*computes* PerfectMultBatching *(Functionality 5) for*

$$\alpha(\kappa) = 2^{-\kappa/4+4}.$$

The proof of Theorem 19 can be found in the suplementary material.

6.1.3   Realizing OLE and VOLE

Recall that in VOLE (OLE is just single-instance VOLE), P_1 holds an input a and P_2 holds $\boldsymbol{b}, \boldsymbol{\sigma} \in \mathbb{Z}_q^m$, and the functionality returns $ab + \boldsymbol{\sigma}$ to P_1 and nothing to P_2. Using a straightforward reduction from VOLE to batch-multiplication, it is enough to run Protocol 18 with parties using inputs a and $\boldsymbol{b}$ respectively. Then, once the protocol concludes, we instruct P_2 to add $\boldsymbol{\sigma}$ to its output and reveal the result to P_1. The resulting protocol is a secure realization of VOLE (or OLE for $m = 1$). We omit the formal details since they are rather straightforward.

6.2   Generating Correlated Data in the Preprocessing Model

In this section, we show how to use our protocol for generating correlated preprocessed data for general purpose MPC (namely MACs and Beaver Triplets). For an informal discussion of the two concepts, we refer the reader to the introduction (Sect. 1.3). Since MACs are just a special instance of batch-multiplication (and thus Protocol 18 can readily be used for this purpose) we only focus here on Beaver triplets. Similarly to PerfectMult, we will be using another "helper" functionality denote BeaverCheck which is analogous the ShareCheck, except that it is more complicated because it involves many more checks. Still, in the full version of this paper [17], we show that it can be cheaply realized using group-theoretic cryptography.

Functionality 20 (Beaver)
Inputs: Empty for both parties with the following optional inputs.

1. P_1's *optional input* opt_1: $(x_1^1, x_1^2, x_1^3, k_1) \in \mathbb{Z}_q^2$ *and* $(\sigma_1^i, \tau_1^i) \in \mathbb{Z}_q^2$ *for* $i \in [3]$.
2. P_2's *optional input* opt_2: $(x_2^1, x_2^2, x_2^3, k_2) \in \mathbb{Z}_q^2$ *and* $(\sigma_2^i, \tau_2^i) \in \mathbb{Z}_q^2$ *for* $i \in [3]$.

Operation:

– *Verify* $\mathsf{opt}_1 = \perp$ *or* $\mathsf{opt}_2 = \perp$, *otherwise abort (wlog say* $\mathsf{opt}_1 \neq \perp$).
– *Sample* $(x_2^1, x_2^2, k_2) \leftarrow \mathbb{Z}_q^3$.

– *Output* $(x_i^1, x_i^2, x_i^3, k_i, \sigma_i^1, \sigma_i^2, \sigma_i^3, \tau_i^1, \tau_i^2, \tau_i^3)$ *to* P_i *where unassigned values are set subject to*

$$\begin{cases} (x_1^1 + x_2^1)(x_1^2 + x_2^2) = x_1^3 + x_2^3 \\ \tau_i^j = k_{3-i} x_i^j + \sigma_{3-i}^j \quad \text{for } i \in \{1, 2\}, \ j \in \{1, 2, 3\} \end{cases}.$$

Functionality 21 (BeaverCheck)
Common input: 1^κ *for a security parameter* $\kappa \in \mathbb{N}$.
P_1 *'s input:* $(x_1^1, x_1^2, x_1^i, k_1) \in \mathbb{Z}_q^2$ *and* $(\sigma_1^i, \tau_1^i) \in \mathbb{Z}_q^2$ *for* $i \in \{1, 2, 3\}$.
P_2 *'s input:* $(x_2^1, x_2^2, x_2^i, k_2) \in \mathbb{Z}_q^2$ *and* $(\sigma_2^i, \tau_2^i) \in \mathbb{Z}_q^2$ *for* $i \in \{1, 2, 3\}$.
Operation: Output 1 if the inputs satisfy the following (output 0 otherwise)

$$\begin{cases} (x_1^1 + x_2^1)(x_1^2 + x_2^2) = x_1^3 + x_2^3 \\ \tau_i^j = k_{3-i} x_i^j + \sigma_{3-i}^j \quad \text{for } i \in \{1, 2\}, \ j \in \{1, 2, 3\} \end{cases}.$$

6.2.1 Authenticated (Beaver) Triplets Protocol

As mentioned in the introduction, the protocol below simply preforms two weak multiplications to calculate the triplet and two (weak) batch-multiplications each to obtain all the MAC data. In the end, the parties perform the correctness-check on their shares.

Protocol 22 $(\Phi = (\mathsf{P}_1, \mathsf{P}_2))$
Oracles: WeakMult, WeakBatch *and* BeaverCheck.
Inputs: Statistical parameter κ.
Operations:

1. *Each* P_i *samples* $k_i, a_i, b_i \leftarrow \mathbb{Z}_q$.
2. P_1 *and* P_2 *invoke* WeakMult (a_1, b_2) *and* WeakMult (b_1, a_2).
   Write γ_1, δ_1 *and* γ_2, δ_2 *for their respective outputs.*
3. *Each* P_i *sets* $c_i = a_i b_i + \gamma_i + \delta_i$.
4. P_1 *and* P_2 *invoke* WeakBatch$(k_1, (a_2, b_2, c_2))$ *and* WeakBatch$(k_2, (a_1, b_1, c_1))$.
   Write $(\tau_i, \tau_i', \tau_i'')$, *and* $(\sigma_i, \sigma_i', \sigma_i'')$ *for* P_i *'s outputs in each execution.*
5. P_1 *and* P_2 *invoke* BeaverCheck *on the relevant inputs.*
6. P_i *outputs* $(a_i, b_i, c_i, k_i, \tau_i, \tau_i', \tau_i'', \sigma_i, \sigma_i', \sigma_i'')$.

Theorem 23. *Protocol 22* α-*computes* Beaver *(Functionality 20) for*

$$\alpha(\kappa) = 2^{-\kappa/4 + 4}.$$

The proof of the above is very similar to the proof of Theorem 19 and it is omitted.

References

1. Baum, C., Escudero, D., Pedrouzo-Ulloa, A., Scholl, P., Troncoso-Pastoriza, J.R.: Efficient protocols for oblivious linear function evaluation from ring-LWE. In: Galdi, C., Kolesnikov, V. (eds.) SCN 2020. LNCS, vol. 12238, pp. 130–149. Springer, Cham (2020). https://doi.org/10.1007/978-3-030-57990-6_7

2. Beaver, D.: Efficient multiparty protocols using circuit randomization. In: Feigenbaum, J. (ed.) CRYPTO 1991. LNCS, vol. 576, pp. 420–432. Springer, Heidelberg (1992). https://doi.org/10.1007/3-540-46766-1_34

3. Boneh, D., Sahai, A., Waters, B.: Functional encryption: definitions and challenges. In: Ishai, Y. (ed.) TCC 2011. LNCS, vol. 6597, pp. 253–273. Springer, Heidelberg (2011). https://doi.org/10.1007/978-3-642-19571-6_16

4. Boyle, E., Couteau, G., Gilboa, N., Ishai, Y.: Compressing vector OLE. In: Proceedings of the 2018 ACM SIGSAC Conference on Computer and Communications Security. CCS 2018, pp. 896–912. ACM (2018)

5. Boyle, E., et al.: Efficient two-round OT extension and silent non-interactive secure computation. In: Proceedings of the 2019 ACM SIGSAC Conference on Computer and Communications Security. CCS 2019, pp. 291–308. ACM (2019)

6. Boyle, E., Gilboa, N., Ishai, Y.: Function secret sharing. In: Oswald, E., Fischlin, M. (eds.) EUROCRYPT 2015. LNCS, vol. 9057, pp. 337–367. Springer, Heidelberg (2015). https://doi.org/10.1007/978-3-662-46803-6_12

7. Boyle, E., Gilboa, N., Ishai, Y.: Breaking the circuit size barrier for secure computation under DDH. In: Robshaw, M., Katz, J. (eds.) CRYPTO 2016. LNCS, vol. 9814, pp. 509–539. Springer, Heidelberg (2016). https://doi.org/10.1007/978-3-662-53018-4_19

8. Boyle, E., Kohl, L., Scholl, P.: Homomorphic secret sharing from lattices without FHE. In: Ishai, Y., Rijmen, V. (eds.) EUROCRYPT 2019. LNCS, vol. 11477, pp. 3–33. Springer, Cham (2019). https://doi.org/10.1007/978-3-030-17656-3_1

9. Canetti, R.: Security and composition of multiparty cryptographic protocols. J. Cryptol. **13**(1), 143–202 (2000)

10. Damgard, I., Orlandi, C.: Multiparty computation for dishonest majority: from passive to active security at low cost. In: Rabin, T. (ed.) CRYPTO 2010. LNCS, vol. 6223, pp. 558–576. Springer, Heidelberg (2010). https://doi.org/10.1007/978-3-642-14623-7_30

11. Damgard, I., Pastro, V., Smart, N., Zakarias, S.: Multiparty computation from somewhat homomorphic encryption. In: Safavi-Naini, R., Canetti, R. (eds.) CRYPTO 2012. LNCS, vol. 7417, pp. 643–662. Springer, Heidelberg (2012). https://doi.org/10.1007/978-3-642-32009-5_38

12. Doerner, J., Kondi, Y., Lee, E., Shelat, A.: Threshold ECDSA from ECDSA assumptions: the multiparty case. In: 2019 IEEE Symposium on Security and Privacy, SP 2019, San Francisco, CA, USA, 19–23 May 2019, pp. 1051–1066. IEEE (2019)

13. Frederiksen, T.K., Pinkas, B., Yanai, A.: Committed MPC - maliciously secure multiparty computation from homomorphic commitments. In: Abdalla, M., Dahab, R. (eds.) PKC 2018. LNCS, vol. 10769, pp. 587–619. Springer, Cham (2018). https://doi.org/10.1007/978-3-319-76578-5_20

14. Ghosh, S., Nielsen, J.B., Nilges, T.: Maliciously secure oblivious linear function evaluation with constant overhead. In: Takagi, T., Peyrin, T. (eds.) ASIACRYPT 2017. LNCS, vol. 10624, pp. 629–659. Springer, Cham (2017). https://doi.org/10.1007/978-3-319-70694-8_22

15. Gilboa, N.: Two party RSA key generation. In: Wiener, M. (ed.) CRYPTO 1999. LNCS, vol. 1666, pp. 116–129. Springer, Heidelberg (1999). https://doi.org/10.1007/3-540-48405-1_8
16. Goldreich, O.: Foundations of Cryptography - Volume 2: Basic Applications. Cambridge University Press, Cambridge (2004)
17. Haitner, I., Makriyannis, N., Ranellucci, S., Tsfadia, E.: Highly efficient ot-based multiplication protocols. Cryptology ePrint Archive, Report 2021/1373 (2021). https://ia.cr/2021/1373
18. Impagliazzo, R., Levin, L.A., Luby, M.: Pseudo-random generation from one-way functions. In: Proceedings of the Twenty-First Annual ACM Symposium on Theory of Computing, pp. 12–24 (1989)
19. Ishai, Y., Prabhakaran, M., Sahai, A.: Secure arithmetic computation with no honest majority. In: Reingold, O. (ed.) TCC 2009. LNCS, vol. 5444, pp. 294–314. Springer, Heidelberg (2009). https://doi.org/10.1007/978-3-642-00457-5_18
20. Keller, M., Orsini, E., Scholl, P.: MASCOT: faster malicious arithmetic secure computation with oblivious transfer. In: Proceedings of the 2016 ACM SIGSAC Conference on Computer and Communications Security, pp. 830–842. ACM (2016)
21. Kiayias, A., Yung, M.: Cryptographic hardness based on the decoding of Reed-Solomon codes. IEEE Trans. Inf. Theory **54**(6), 2752–2769 (2008)
22. Lindell, Y., Nof, A.: A framework for constructing fast MPC over arithmetic circuits with malicious adversaries and an honest-majority. In: Proceedings of the 2017 ACM SIGSAC Conference on Computer and Communications Security. CCS 2017, pp. 259–276. ACM (2017)
23. Lindell, Y., Nof, A.: Fast secure multiparty ECDSA with practical distributed key generation and applications to cryptocurrency custody. In: Proceedings of the 2018 ACM SIGSAC Conference on Computer and Communications Security. CCS 2018, pp. 1837–1854. ACM (2018)
24. Naor, M., Pinkas, B.: Oblivious polynomial evaluation. SIAM J. Comput. **35**(5), 1254–1281 (2006)
25. Rotaru, D., Smart, N.P., Tanguy, T., Vercauteren, F., Wood, T.: Actively secure setup for SPDZ. IACR Cryptology ePrint Archive, p. 1300 (2019)

Round-Optimal Black-Box Protocol Compilers

Yuval Ishai[1], Dakshita Khurana[2], Amit Sahai[3],
and Akshayaram Srinivasan[4(✉)]

[1] Technion, Haifa, Israel
[2] UIUC, Champaign, USA
dakshita@illinois.edu
[3] UCLA, Los Angeles, USA
[4] Tata Institute of Fundamental Research, Mumbai, India
akshayaram.srinivasan@tifr.res.in

Abstract. We give black-box, round-optimal protocol compilers from semi-honest security to malicious security in the Random Oracle Model (ROM) and in the 1-out-of-2 OT correlations model. We use our compilers to obtain the following results:

- A two-round, two-party protocol secure against malicious adversaries in the random oracle model making black-box use of a two-round semi-honest secure protocol. Prior to our work, such a result was not known even considering special functionalities such as a two-round oblivious transfer. This result also implies the first constructions of two-round malicious (batch) OT/OLE in the random oracle model based on the black-box use of two-round semi-honest (batch) OT/OLE.
- A three-round multiparty secure computation protocol in the random oracle model secure against malicious adversaries that is based on the black-box use of two-round semi-honest OT. This protocol matches a known round complexity lower bound due to Applebaum et al. (ITCS'20) and is based on a minimal cryptographic hardness assumption.
- A two-round, multiparty secure computation protocol in the 1-out-of-2 OT correlations model that is secure against malicious adversaries and makes black-box use of cryptography. This gives new round-optimal protocols for computing arithmetic branching programs that are statistically secure and makes black-box use of the underlying field.

As a contribution of independent interest, we provide a new variant of the IPS compiler (Ishai, Prabhakaran and Sahai, Crypto 2008) in the two-round setting, where we relax requirements on the IPS "inner protocol" by strengthening the "outer protocol".

1 Introduction

Minimizing the round complexity of cryptographic protocols in the presence of malicious parties has been a major theme of research in recent years. While

© International Association for Cryptologic Research 2022
O. Dunkelman and S. Dziembowski (Eds.): EUROCRYPT 2022, LNCS 13275, pp. 210–240, 2022.
https://doi.org/10.1007/978-3-031-06944-4_8

most feasibility questions have been answered, there are still big efficiency gaps between known round-optimal protocols and their best counterparts with security against semi-honest parties.

This line of research produced many innovative ideas for bridging the efficiency gap in special cases of interest. For instance, Peikert et al. [33] proposed concretely efficient 2-round oblivious transfer (OT) protocols under several standard assumptions. Other concretely efficient 2-round OT protocols were proposed in [26,27]. Chase et al. [10] and Branco et al. [7] designed such protocols for oblivious linear evaluation (OLE), a natural arithmetic extension of OT. Recent techniques improve the efficiency of 2-round protocols in the batch setting, where multiple instances of OT or OLE are generated together [5,6]. In all these cases, efficiently obtaining security against malicious parties (without resorting to general-purpose NIZK) requires ingenious ideas that are carefully tailored to the structure of the underlying primitives. In some cases, this requires using more aggressive (and sometimes nonstandard) flavors of the assumptions that underlie the semi-honest protocols. For instance, Boyle et al. [5] present a communication-efficient 2-round "batch-OT" protocol, realizing polynomially many instances of OT, with semi-honest security based on the Learning Parity with Noise (LPN) assumption. In the case of malicious security, they present a similar protocol in the random oracle model, but require a stronger leakage-resilient variant of LPN.

The goal of this work is to propose new general techniques for bridging the "semi-honest vs. malicious" gap without increasing round complexity, without strengthening the underlying assumptions, and *without significantly hurting concrete efficiency*. A clean theoretical model for capturing the latter is a *black-box construction*. Such a construction builds a malicious-secure protocol by using an underlying semi-honest protocol *as an oracle*. The latter restriction ensures that the efficiency gap does not depend on the complexity or structure of the semi-honest protocol. This paradigm has been successfully applied not only in the context of theoretical feasibility results, but also in the context of concretely efficient protocols. Indeed, black-box constructions can typically be optimized to have a very low overhead, at least in an amortized sense.

There is a large body of research on such black-box constructions, including a black-box construction of constant-round *honest-majority* secure computation from one-way functions [11] (replacing an earlier non-black-box construction from [4]), a black-box construction of malicious-secure OT from semi-honest OT [18] or trapdoor permutations [29] (replacing a non-black-box construction of [17]), and a black-box construction for OT extension [20] (replacing the earlier non-black-box protocol [3]).

One major shortcoming of most previous black-box constructions is that they inherently increase the round complexity. In particular, they cannot be used to obtain 2-round protocols. Thus, the main question we ask is:

Can we construct round-optimal black-box transformations from semi-honest secure protocols to malicious secure variants?

The recent work of [19], building upon the IPS compiler of [24], made partial progress towards settling the question. In particular, it gave a round-preserving black-box compiler that relies on a random OT correlation setup in the 2-party case, or a more complex correlated OT setup in the multiparty case. Two significant caveats are that the underlying semi-honest protocol should satisfy: *(i)* semi-malicious security;[1] and *(ii)* adaptive security with erasures, a limitation inherited from [24]. This latter property is typically easy to achieve by increasing the round complexity. However, it poses a major challenge in the 2-round setting. While natural two-round protocols *in the OT-hybrid model* already satisfy the adaptive security requirement, standard 2-round protocols in the plain model, including semi-honest OLE or batch-OT protocols, do not.

The above state of affairs raises the following natural questions: Can we eliminate the adaptive security requirement? Can we eliminate the setup completely, or replace it by a standard OT setup in the multiparty case?

Since we are targeting 2-round protocols with security against malicious adversaries, we cannot hope to obtain results in the plain model. But since the aim of achieving black-box protocols is efficiency, this raises the natural question: can we build such round-preserving black-box protocol compilers in the *random oracle model*?

1.1   Our Results

In this work, we tackle both kinds questions: eliminating the adaptive security requirement and eliminating the need for correlated randomness completely in the random oracle model. In the multiparty case, we also address the goal of replacing the complex correlation setup from [19] by standard OT correlations. We now give a more detailed account of our results.

Round-Preserving Compilers in the OT Correlations Model. In the case of two-party protocols in the OT correlations model, we remove the need for adaptive security with erasures and obtain the following result.

Informal Theorem 1. *There exists a black-box compiler from any two-round semi-malicious two-party protocol to a two-round malicious two-party computation protocol given a setup that consists of random 1-out-of-2 OT correlations (alternatively, Rabin-OT correlations).*

See Theorem 3 for a formal statement. As in the case of the IPS compiler [24], the functionality f' realized by the semi-malicious protocol may depend on the target functionality f we want the malicious protocol to realize. From a feasibility point of view, it suffices to consider a semi-malicious protocol for OT (which can

---

[1] Semi-malicious security is a strengthening of semi-honest security where the adversary is allowed to choose the random tape of the corrupted parties in an arbitrary manner before the protocol begins. In the context of 2-round protocols, most (but not all) natural semi-honest protocols also satisfy this stronger security property.

be used in parallel to realize f' via Yao's protocol [34]). But when f is a "simple" functionality such as batch-OT[2] or batch-OLE, we can in fact use f' that consists of only a *constant* number of instances of f.

We note that the required setup is minimal in the sense that both the number of random OT correlations and their size only depend on the security parameter and not on the circuit being computed. Moreover, recent techniques for efficient "silent" OT extension [6] can make the setup reusable without additional interaction.

To obtain this result, we build a *new* version of the black-box protocol compiler of [24], where we replace the outer protocol with one that can be simpler and more efficient than the state-of-the-art [23] protocol previously used in this setting. Besides eliminating the need for adaptive security from the semi-honest MPC protocol, the improved outer protocol may be of independent interest.

However, our primary contribution (that also uses the techniques developed above) is the construction of round-optimal compilers in the Random Oracle model, as we discuss next.

Round-Preserving Compilers in the Random Oracle Model. The semi-malicious to malicious protocol compilers, described above, rely on OT correlations to perform cut-and-choose (using the watchlists mechanism introduced in [24]). Our key contribution in this work is to remove the need for watchlists/OT correlations, and to instead give a novel adaptation of the *Fiat-Shamir* paradigm in the Random Oracle model to perform the watchlist function. This gives rise to new round-optimal malicious secure protocols in the random oracle model from black-box use of semi-honest secure protocol.[3]

The Two-Party Setting. We obtain the following results in the two-party setting. Here, non-interactive secure computation (NISC) denotes a two-round 2-party secure computation protocol for general functionalities where only one party obtains an output. A two-sided non-interactive secure computation (NISC) denotes a two-round 2-party secure computation protocol for general functionalities where both parties obtain an output.

Informal Theorem 2 (BB Malicious NISC). *There exists a construction of NISC with malicious security in the random oracle model that makes black-box use of NISC with semi-honest security.*

Informal Theorem 3 (BB Malicious 2-sided NISC). *In the random oracle model, there exists a construction of two-sided NISC with malicious security that makes black-box use of two-sided NISC with semi-honest security.*

---

[2] Batch-OT is not trivialized in the OT correlations model because the number of OTs in this setup is a fixed polynomial in the security parameter.

[3] In the random oracle model, we additionally remove the need for semi-malicious security.

As before, the functionality computed by the semi-honest protocol depends on the target functionality computed by the malicious protocol. For the case of simple functionalities such as (batch)-OT and (batch)-OLE, these two functions are identical. The formal statement of the transformation in the random oracle model can be found in Theorem 2 and its extension to the two-sided setting appears in Sect. 5.3.

We note that [28] also used the Fiat-Shamir transform to collapse the number of rounds of a NISC protocol but their final protocol was not two-round and their assumptions were stronger than semi-honest two-round, two-party computation (specifically, they needed homomorphic commitments and two-round malicious secure OT protocol). Finally, NISC with semi-honest security can be obtained based on the black-box use of any two-round semi-honest oblivious transfer (OT) protocol, by relying on Yao's garbled circuits [34]. This implies the following corollaries of Informal Theorem 2:

Informal Corollary 1. *There exists a construction of two-round OT with malicious security in the random oracle model that makes black-box use of two-round OT with semi-honest security.*

Informal Corollary 2. *There exists a construction of two-round OLE/batch OT/batch OLE respectively with malicious security in the random oracle model that makes black-box use of two-round OLE/batch OT/batch OLE respectively with semi-honest security.*

Prior to our work, the only known construction of two-round malicious OLE relied on specialized assumptions such as N^{th} residuosity [10] or LWE [7]. The black-box constructions of OT required assumptions stronger than semi-honest security in the random oracle model [26,27] or in the plain model [13] (such as strongly uniform key agreement).

Protocol Compilers in the Multi-party Setting. In the multiparty setting, we give a construction of a three round protocol in the random oracle model that makes black-box use of the minimal cryptographic hardness assumption which is a two-round semi-honest OT protocol.

Informal Theorem 4. *There exists a construction of three-round MPC with malicious security in the random oracle model that makes black-box use of two-round OT with semi-honest security.*

The formal statement can be found in Theorem 4. Applebaum et al.[1] showed that even considering only semi-honest security such a protocol is round-optimal (in the random oracle model). A recent work of Patra and Srinivasan [32] gave a construction of a three-round malicious secure protocol from any two-round oblivious transfer that satisfied a certain form of adaptive security on the receiver side. In this work, we construct a malicious secure protocol by relying only a two-round semi-honest OT (in the random oracle model).

As an additional contribution, we show how to remove the complex multi-party watchlist correlations setup from the work of [19] and replace it with a simple 1-out-of-2 random OT correlations setup. As a corollary, this gives the first constructions of statistical secure protocols against malicious adversaries for computing arithmetic branching programs making black-box use of the underlying field in the OLE correlations model. The formal statement appears in Theorem 5.

2   Technical Overview

In this section, we describe the key ideas and techniques used in the construction of our protocol compilers.

2.1   IPS Compiler

The starting point of our work is the black-box compiler given by Ishai, Prabhakaran, and Sahai [24] (henceforth, referred to as the IPS compiler). This compiler transforms a semi-honest secure protocol (with certain special properties) into a malicious secure protocol. The (simplified version of the) IPS compiler for computing a function f in the two-party setting consists of the following components:

- A client-server MPC protocol for computing f that is secure against any malicious adversary corrupting an arbitrary subset of the clients and a constant fraction of the servers. Such a protocol, requiring only two rounds, was constructed by Ishai, Kushilevitz, and Paskin [23] (see also [30]) making black-box use of a PRG. This protocol is referred to as the *outer protocol*.
- A semi-honest secure[4] protocol where the functionality computed by this protocol is the computation done by the servers in the outer protocol. This is referred to as the *inner protocol*.

In the IPS compiler, each party takes the role of a client in the outer MPC protocol and generates the first round messages to be sent to the servers. The computation performed by the servers in the outer protocol is emulated by the inner protocol. Specifically, we run m instances of the inner protocol (where m is the number of servers) in parallel. In the i-th instance, the parties use as input the messages to be sent to the i-th server and use the inner protocol to compute the functionality of the i-th server. At the end of this emulation, the parties can obtain the second round message generated by each server from the inner protocol and finally, compute the output of f using the output decoder of the outer protocol.

If the adversary cheats in an instance of the inner protocol, then this cheating translates to a corruption of the corresponding server in the outer protocol. However, a malicious adversary can cheat in all the inner protocol instances, thereby breaking the security of each one of them. Note that the outer protocol

---

[4] The IPS compiler required this semi-honest protocol to satisfy a variant of adaptive security with erasures property and we will come back to this point soon.

is only guaranteed to be secure as long as a constant fraction of the servers are corrupted. To ensure this property, the IPS compiler uses a special "cut-and-choose" mechanism referred to as *watchlists*.

The simplest version of watchlist mechanism involves a Rabin-OT channel with a carefully chosen erasure probability. For each of the m executions of the inner protocol, each party sends its input, randomness pair used in that particular execution to the other party via the Rabin OT channel. The other party then checks if the input, randomness pair for the executions it received via the channel is consistent with the transcript seen so far and aborts the execution if it detects any inconsistency. The erasure probability of the Rabin-OT channel is chosen in such a way that:

- The adversary cannot learn the private inputs of the honest parties from the information it receives via the Rabin-OT channel.
- If the adversary cheats in more than a constant fraction of the inner protocol instances, then with overwhelming probability this cheating is detected via an inconsistency by the honest party.

Thus, the watchlist mechanism ensures that a malicious adversary that cheats in more than a constant fraction of the inner protocol executions is caught and this allows us to argue the security of the compiled protocol against malicious adversaries.

Need for Adaptive Security of the Inner Protocol. As mentioned earlier, in the IPS compiler, it is not sufficient for the inner protocol to satisfy standard semi-honest security. We actually need the inner protocol to satisfy so-called "semi-malicious" security with a certain variant of adaptive security with erasures. As already noted in [24], it is possible to replace semi-malicious security with standard semi-honest security using additional rounds. However, the need for adaptive security with erasure seems somewhat inherent in the proof of security. In the two-round setting, which is the primary focus of this work, this security requirement translates to a natural property of the receiver called as *equivocal receiver security* [15]. Specifically, we require the existence of an equivocal simulator that can equivocate the first round message of the receiver to any input. Before proceeding further, let us give some more details on why is equivocality property is needed in the security proof.

Consider an adversary that corrupts the sender and cheats in a small number of inner protocol instances. The number of such cheating executions is small enough so that it goes undetected by the watchlist mechanism. At the point of generating the first round message from the receiver, we do not know in which executions the adversary is planning to cheat, as the receiver sends its message before the sender. Only after receiving the message from the adversary, we realize that in some executions the adversary has cheated, thereby breaking the security of the inner protocol. Hence, we need to equivocate the first round receiver message in these cheating executions to the actual receiver input so that we can derive the same output that an honest receiver obtains.

We note that this property could be added generically to certain types of protocols such two-round semi-honest oblivious transfer. However, it is not known how to add this property to general protocols by making black-box use of cryptography. Even for special cases such as Oblivious Linear Evaluation (OLE), we do not know of any method to add this property to natural semi-honest OLE instantiations.

2.2 A New Compiler: Removing Equivocality

In this work, we give a new IPS-style compiler in the two-round setting where the inner protocol need not satisfy the equivocal receiver message property.

Strengthening the Outer Protocol. Our main idea to achieve this is to strengthen the requirements from the outer MPC protocol. Namely, we show that if the outer protocol satisfies a certain output error-correction property, then we do not need equivocal receiver security from the inner protocol. Our output error-correction property requires that for all choices of second round messages from the (few) corrupted servers, the output of the honest receiver remains the same. Indeed, we can substitute the outputs of those cheating executions with any default value and still we are guaranteed to obtain the same output as that of an honest receiver. This removes the need to equivocate the first round message of the receiver for the executions where the adversary is cheating and instead, we can rely on any semi-malicious inner protocol. The main question we are now tasked with solving is to construct an outer protocol in the client-server setting that runs in two rounds and satisfies the output error-correction property.

Barriers. We first observe that if the outer protocol satisfies guaranteed output delivery, then it satisfies the error correction property as well. Unfortunately, Gennaro et al. [16] showed that in the two round setting, if more than one party is corrupted, then it is impossible to construct protocols that have guaranteed output delivery. Indeed, we do not know of any ways to bypass this impossibility result even to achieve the weaker goal of error correction.

Pairwise Verifiable Adversaries. To overcome this barrier, we show that it is sufficient to achieve error correction against a restricted class of adversaries, that we call *pairwise verifiable*. In this model, the adversary that is corrupting either one of the two clients and a constant fraction of the servers is forced to send a first round message from the corrupted client to the honest servers such that these messages pass a specified pairwise predicate check. Namely, there is a predicate that takes the first round messages sent to any two servers and outputs either accept or reject. We require the first round messages sent by the adversary to each pair of honest servers to pass this predicate check. However, the first round messages sent between corrupted servers or between a honest server and a corrupted server need not satisfy the pairwise verification check. Additionally, second round messages from corrupted servers can be generated arbitrarily. We show that once we restrict the adversary to be pairwise verifiable, we can construct extremely efficient outer protocols that also satisfy output error correction. In particular, we show that the semi-honest secure protocol from [21] is secure against pairwise verifiable adversaries if we replace the plain Shamir secret sharing with a bi-variate Shamir secret sharing. The error correction property of this construction can be shown by viewing Shamir secret sharing as an instance of the Reed-Solomon error correcting codes.

Why is Security Against Pairwise Verifiable Adversaries Sufficient? We now explain why this weaker security notion is sufficient to instantiate the IPS compiler for two rounds. To see why this is the case, we modify the watchlist mechanism checks so that it not only checks if the pair of input and randomness it received via the Rabin-OT channel is consistent with the transcript, but also checks if the inputs (a.k.a. the first round messages sent to the servers) pass the pairwise verification check. Using standard statistical arguments, we show that if all the inputs received via the Rabin-OT channel pass the pairwise verification check, then a large fraction of the other messages also pass the pairwise verification checks. This translates to the adversary only corrupting a small fraction of the servers and we can rely on the security of the outer protocol against pairwise verifiable adversaries.

Instantiating the Rabin-OT Channel. We now explain how to instantiate a Rabin-OT channel if we have access to 1-out-of-2 OT correlations:

1. We first transform the 1-out-2 OT correlations non-interactively to 1-out-of-p correlations. Such a transformation is implicit in the work of [8].
2. We then use the transformation described in [24, Section 2] to convert 1-out-of-p random OT correlations into a single round Rabin OT protocol with erasure probability $1 - 1/p$.

We show that such a rational erasure probability is sufficient to instantiate the IPS compiler.

2.3   Protocol Compiler in the Random Oracle Model

To give a compiler in the random oracle model, we first observe that the Rabin OT channel can be replaced with a k-out-of-m OT channel (for an appropriate choice of k) and the same arguments go through. Our key idea here is to replace the k-out-of-m OT channel with the Fiat-Shamir transformation [12] applied using a random oracle. Specifically, we require both parties to additionally send a non-interactive and extractable commitment to their input and randomness used in each of the inner protocol instances[5]. In each round, we require the party sending the message to hash the transcript seen so far along with the messages generated in this round to obtain a set of executions (called the opened executions) of size k. The party, in addition to sending the messages of the

---

[5] Such a commitment can be constructed unconditionally in the random oracle model [31].

inner protocol instances in that particular round, must also reveal the input–randomness pair (via an opening of the commitments) for the opened executions. The other party checks if the openings are correct, if the random oracle output is correctly computed, if the input–randomness pair in the opened executions are consistent with the transcript seen so far, and if the pairwise consistency checks pass.

In the security proof, we rely on the correlation-intractability of the random oracle [9] to show that if the adversary cheats in more than a constant fraction of the inner protocol instances, then with overwhelming probability the opened executions will intersect with the cheating executions. This will therefore be detected by the honest party forcing it to abort. In our proof of security, we also rely on the programmability of the random oracle to pre-determine the set of opened executions of the honest parties.

Relying on a Semi-honest Secure Protocol. We observe that in the random oracle model, it is sufficient for the inner protocol to satisfy semi-honest security rather than semi-malicious security. Specifically, the random tape used by each party in an instance of the inner protocol is set to be the output of the random oracle on the party index, the instance number, and a randomly chosen salt. This ensures that even if the salt is not uniformly random, the adversarial parties will query the random oracle on different inputs which implies that the outputs obtained from the oracle will be uniform and uncorrelated.

2.4 Two-Sided NISC

In the protocol compiler described earlier, at the end of the second round, the receiver obtains the output of the two-party functionality whereas the sender does not obtain any output. To extend this protocol to the setting where both parties get the output (called the two-sided NISC setting [19]), we cannot use the naïve idea of running the one-sided protocol in parallel but in opposite directions. Specifically, nothing prevents a cheating adversary from using inconsistent inputs in both these executions, thereby, breaking the security of the overall protocol. To prevent this attack, we further refine the IPS compiler methodology. We modify the first round commitments/message sent via the Rabin-OT channel to include the inputs and the randomness used on both sides of the inner protocols. In the opened/non-erased executions, in addition to the checks that are already performed, each party checks if the inputs used on both sides are the same and if it is not the case, then the honest parties abort. This prevents the adversary from using inconsistent inputs in "many" instances of the inner protocol, and if that is the case, we can rely on the security of the outer protocol to show that this adversary does not learn any additional information about the honest party inputs.

2.5 The Multiparty Setting

In extending the above ideas to the multiparty setting, we face two main challenges:

1. First, we do not know of any two-round black-box inner protocol in the semi-honest setting (and indeed [1] gave some barriers). Moreover, in existing three-round protocols [32], if the adversary cheats in generating the first round message, then the adversary can recover the private inputs of the honest parties. Thus, we need the first message in the (3-round) inner protocol to satisfy a certain form of adaptive security with erasures even if the outer protocol has the output error correction property.

2. Recall that to use the security of the semi-honest inner protocol, we need to additionally give the simulator the power to program the random tape of the corrupted parties in some intermediate hybrids. Note that in our compiler we rely on the random oracle to perform this programming. However, a cheating adversary on behalf of a corrupted party i could query the random oracle on many different salts where the first two parts of the query are fixed to the same i and instance number j. It could then use the output of any one of these queries as the random tape in the j-th inner protocol instance. A natural idea to deal with this is to choose one of these queries uniformly at random and "embed" the programmed random tape as the output of the chosen query. The hope is that the adversary chooses this particular query with non-negligible probability and we can use this to come up with a reduction that breaks the security of the inner protocol. But this idea quickly runs into trouble in the multiparty setting as the adversary could potentially corrupt an arbitrary subset of the parties, and we require the adversary on behalf of each malicious party to correctly choose this embedded query. This only happens with probability that is exponential in n (where n is the number of parties) and is not sufficient to break the security of the inner protocol.

To solve the first issue, we show how to add the required equivocal properties to the protocol of [32] in a black-box manner relying only on two-round semi-honest OT. This allows us to use it as the inner protocol and instantiate the IPS compiler.

To solve the second issue, we rely on the fact that the semi-honest secure protocol in [32] has a special structure. Namely, it is a parallel composition of a sub-protocol that computes a special functionality called 3MULTPlus. Importantly, for this discussion it is sufficient to note that 3MULTPlus is a three-party functionality. The security of the composed protocol is argued via a hybrid argument where we switch each one of these sub-protocols for computing the 3MULTPlus functionality to the ideal world. Now, relying on this special structure, we show that in the intermediate hybrids, it is sufficient to program the random tapes of the corrupted parties that participate in a single instance of the sub-protocol. Since the number of such parties is only a constant, we can show that adversary chooses the "correct" random oracle outputs with non-negligible probability and this allows us to provide a reduction that breaks the security of the sub-protocol.

3   Preliminaries

Let λ denote the cryptographic security parameter. We assume that all cryptographic algorithms implicitly take 1^λ as input. A function $\mu(\cdot) : \mathbb{N} \to \mathbb{R}^+$ is said to be negligible if for any polynomial $\mathsf{poly}(\cdot)$, there exists λ_0 such that for all $\lambda > \lambda_0$, we have $\mu(\lambda) < \frac{1}{\mathsf{poly}(\lambda)}$. We will use $\mathsf{negl}(\cdot)$ to denote an unspecified negligible function and $\mathsf{poly}(\cdot)$ to denote an unspecified polynomial function.

We say that two distribution ensembles $\{X_\lambda\}_{\lambda \in \mathbb{N}}$ and $\{Y_\lambda\}_{\lambda \in \mathbb{N}}$ are computationally indistinguishable if for every non-uniform PPT distinguisher D there exists a negligible function $\mathsf{negl}(\cdot)$ such that $|\Pr[D(1^\lambda, X_\lambda) = 1]| - \Pr[D(1^\lambda, Y_\lambda) = 1]| \leq \mathsf{negl}(\lambda)$.

3.1   Semi-honest Two-Round Two-Party Computation

We now give the syntax and definition for a two-round semi-honest two-party computation protocol.

Syntax. Consider two parties, a sender with input y and a receiver with input x. Let f be an arbitrary two-party functionality. A two-party protocol Π for computing f is given by a tuple of algorithms $(\Pi_1, \Pi_2, \mathsf{out}_\Pi)$. Π_1 is run by the receiver and takes as input 1^λ and the receiver input x and outputs (π_1, sk). The receiver sends π_1 to the sender in the first round. Π_2 is run by the sender and it takes as input 1^λ, π_1, and the sender input y and outputs π_2. The sender sends π_2 to the receiver in the second round. The receiver then runs out_Π on inputs π_2 and sk and obtains the output z. Let $\mathsf{View}_R(\langle R(1^\lambda, x), S(1^\lambda, y)\rangle)$ and $\mathsf{View}_S(\langle R(1^\lambda, x), S(1^\lambda, y)\rangle)$ be the views of the receiver and the sender during the protocol interaction with inputs x and y respectively. Here, View of a party (either the sender or the receiver) includes its private input, its random tape, and the transcript of the protocol. The protocol Π satisfies the definition given below.

Definition 1 (Semi-Honest Security). *A two-round, two-party protocol $\Pi = (\Pi_1, \Pi_2, \mathsf{out}_\Pi)$ is said to securely compute f against semi-honest adversaries if it satisfies the following properties:*

- **Correctness:** *For every receiver's input x and for every sender input y, we have:*
$$\Pr[\mathsf{out}_\Pi(\pi_2, sk) = f(x, y)] = 1$$
  where $(\pi_1, sk) \leftarrow \Pi_1(1^\lambda, x)$ and $\pi_2 \leftarrow \Pi_2(1^\lambda, \pi_1, y)$.
- **Security:** *There exists a simulator Sim_Π such that for any receiver's input x and sender's input y, we have:*

$$\mathsf{View}_S(\langle R(1^\lambda, x), S(1^\lambda, y)\rangle) \approx_c (y, r, \mathsf{Sim}_\Pi(1^\lambda, R, y))$$

$$\mathsf{View}_R(\langle R(1^\lambda, x), S(1^\lambda, y)\rangle) \approx_c (x, r, \mathsf{Sim}_\Pi(1^\lambda, S, (x, r), f(x, y)))$$

  where the random tape r of the sender/receiver in the second distribution is uniformly chosen.

Remark 1. In the standard definition of semi-honest security, Sim_Π is allowed to additionally set the random tape of the corrupted receiver. Here, we consider a slightly stronger definition where the random tape of the corrupted receiver is chosen uniformly and this is provided as input to Sim_Π and Sim_Π is required to produce the transcript of the protocol. We note that this definition is implied by the standard definition whenever f is reverse sampleable. Specifically, given $(x, f(x, y))$, if there is an efficient algorithm I that outputs some y' s.t. $f(x, y) = f(x', y')$ then the weaker definition implies the stronger definition described above. Indeed, for most natural functionalities, such as Oblivious Transfer (OT), Oblivious Linear Evaluation (OLE), their batched versions, batch-OT and batch-OLE, there exists such a reverse sampler, and the above definition is satisfied by all semi-honest secure protocols.

3.2   Semi-malicious Two-Round Two-Party Computation

Semi-Malicious security [2] is a strengthening of the semi-honest security definition where we additionally allow the adversary to choose the random tape of the corrupted party arbitrarily. However, the adversary is restricted to follow the protocol specification. Such an adversary is called as a semi-malicious adversary. A two-round semi-malicious secure two-party protocol has the same syntax of a semi-honest protocol and satisfies the definition given below.

Definition 2 (Semi-Malicious Security). *A two-round, two-party protocol $\Pi = (\Pi_1, \Pi_2, \mathsf{out}_\Pi)$ is said to securely compute f against semi-malicious adversaries if it satisfies the following properties:*

– **Correctness:** *For every receiver's input x and for every sender input y, we have:*
$$\Pr[\mathsf{out}_\Pi(\pi_2, sk) = f(x, y)] = 1$$
where $(\pi_1, sk) \leftarrow \Pi_1(1^\lambda, x)$ and $\pi_2 \leftarrow \Pi_2(1^\lambda, \pi_1, y)$.
– **Security:** *There exists a simulator Sim_Π such that for any semi-malicious adversary $\mathcal{A}$ corrupting either the sender or the receiver and for any receiver's input x, sender's input y and for any random tape r, we have:*

$$\mathsf{View}_\mathcal{A}(\langle R(1^\lambda, x), \mathcal{A}(1^\lambda, y)\rangle) \approx_c \mathsf{View}_\mathcal{A}(\langle R(1^\lambda, \mathbf{0}), \mathcal{A}(1^\lambda, y)\rangle)$$

$$\mathsf{View}_\mathcal{A}(\langle \mathcal{A}(1^\lambda, x), S(1^\lambda, y)\rangle) \approx_c (x, r, \mathsf{Sim}_\Pi(1^\lambda, S, (x, r), f(x, y)))$$

where $\mathbf{0}$ is a default input.

3.3   Extractable Commitments in ROM

In our protocol compilers, we make use of non-interactive, straight-line extractable commitments in the random oracle model. Namely, the commitments are computationally hiding and straight-line extractable by observing the queries that the adversary makes to the random oracle. Such commitments were constructed in [31].

3.4 Pairwise Verifiable Secret Sharing

Consider a linear t-out-of-m threshold secret sharing scheme where the secrets are over a finite field $\mathbb{F}$ and the shares are over another finite field $\mathbb{F}'$. We use $+$ and $\cdot$ to denote the addition and multiplication operations over both the fields.

Definition 3 (Pairwise Verifiable Predicate). *A predicate P is a pairwise verifiable predicate if it takes a threshold t, two indices $j, k \in [m]$ and the purported j-th and k-th shares x_j and x_k and outputs 1/0. Further, if $P(t, j, k, (x_j, x_k)) = 1$ and $P(t, j, k, (x'_j, x'_k)) = 1$, then $P(t, j, k, (x_j + x'_j, x_k + x'_k)) = 1$ and $P(2t, j, k, (x_j \cdot x'_j, x_k \cdot x'_k)) = 1$.*

In the main body, we also extend the definition of the pairwise verifiable predicate P to take in a vector of pair of shares and apply the above pairwise check for each pair.

Definition 4 (Pairwise Verifiable and Error Correctable Secret Sharing). *A t-out-of-m threshold linear secret sharing scheme $(\mathsf{Share}_{(t,m)}, \mathsf{Rec}_{(t,m)})$ is said to be k-multiplicative and ℓ-error-correctable w.r.t. pairwise predicate P if:*

1. *k-**Multiplicative**: Given m shares of elements $x_1, \ldots, x_k$ arranged as a matrix M of k rows and m columns, the row vector obtained by computing the product of each column of M is a kt-out-of-m secret sharing of $x_1 \cdot x_2 \ldots \cdot x_k$.*
2. ***Pairwise Verifiable Error Correction**: Let T be a subset of $[m]$ of size at most ℓ. Let $(x_1, \ldots, x_m)$ be arbitrary elements such that for any threshold $t' \leq kt$ and for any $j, k \in [m] \backslash T$, $P(t', j, k, x_j, x_k) = 1$. Then, for any $\{\overline{x}_i\}_{i \in T}$, $\mathsf{Rec}_{(t',m)}(\{x_i\}_{i \in T}, \{x_i\}_{i \notin T}) = \mathsf{Rec}_{(t',m)}(\{\overline{x}_i\}_{i \in T}, \{x_i\}_{i \notin T}) = x$. Furthermore, there exists an efficient procedure $\mathsf{Extrapolate}$ that on input $t', \{x_i\}_{i \notin T}$ outputs $\{x'_i\}_{i \in T}$ such that $(\{x_i\}_{i \notin T}, \{x'_i\}_{i \in T})$ belongs to $\mathsf{supp}(\mathsf{Share}_{(t',m)}(x))$.*

We note that the above definition of pairwise verifiable secret sharing is the same as the one given in [23] except that We note that bivariate Shamir secret sharing is a t-out-of-m secret sharing scheme that is k-multiplicative and ℓ-error correctable as long as $m \geq kt + 2\ell + 1$.

4 Two-Round Client-Server Protocol with Pairwise Verifiability

In this section, we give a construction of a two-round, pairwise verifiable MPC protocol in the client-server model. We start with the Definition of this protocol in Sect. 4.1.

4.1   Definition

Syntax. Let f be an arbitrary n-party functionality. Consider the standard client-server MPC setting [11] with n clients and m servers. A two-round protocol $\Phi = (\mathsf{Share}, \mathsf{Eval}, \mathsf{Dec})$ for computing a function f in this model has the following syntax:

- $\mathsf{Share}(1^\lambda, i, x_i)$: It outputs a set of shares $(x_1^i, \ldots, x_m^i)$ along with a verification key vk_i.
- $\mathsf{Eval}(j, (x_j^1, \ldots, x_j^n))$: It outputs a string ϕ_j.
- $\mathsf{Dec}(i, vk_i, (\phi_1, \ldots, \phi_m))$: It outputs a string z or the special symbol $\perp$.

In the first round of the protocol, each client $i \in [n]$ runs the algorithm Share on its private input x_i and obtains a set of shares $(x_1^i, \ldots, x_m^i)$ and a verification key vk_i. It then sends x_j^i as the first round message to the j-th server for each $j \in [m]$. In the second round, each server $j \in [m]$ runs the Eval algorithm on the first round messages received from each client and obtains the string ϕ_j. A subset of the clients are designated as output clients in the protocol. The j-th server sends ϕ_j to each of the output clients in the second round. To obtain the output, each output client i runs Dec on its verification key vk_i and the second round messages received from all the servers to obtain the output z.

Security Definition. Below we provide the security definition of a client-server MPC protocol that is pairwise verifiable w.r.t. predicate P.

Definition 5 (Admissible Adversary). *Let P be a pairwise predicate that takes a client index $i \in [n]$, two server indices $j, k \in [m]$, the first round message (x_j^i, x_k^i) sent by the i-th client to the servers j and k and outputs $1/0$. An adversary $\mathcal{A}$ corrupting a subset of the clients and up to t servers is said to be admissible w.r.t. pairwise predicate P if for every honest pair of servers j, k and every corrupted client i, the output of the predicate P on input $(i, j, k, (x_j^i, x_k^i))$ is 1.*

Definition 6 (Pairwise Verifiable MPC). *Let f be a n-party functionality. A protocol $\Phi = (\mathsf{Share}, \mathsf{Eval}, \mathsf{Dec})$ is a two-round, n-client, m-server pairwise verifiable MPC protocol for computing f against t server corruptions if there exists a pairwise predicate P such that:*

1. ***Error Correction:*** *If $\mathcal{A}$ is any admissible adversary (see Definition 5) w.r.t. P corrupting a subset T (where $|T| \leq t$) of the servers and for any two sets of second round messages $\{\phi_j\}_{j \in T}$ and $\{\overline{\phi}_j\}_{j \in T}$ and for any honest client $i \in [n]$, $\mathsf{Dec}(i, vk_i, \{\phi_j\}_{j \notin T}, \{\phi_j\}_{j \in T}) = \mathsf{Dec}(i, vk_i, \{\phi_j\}_{j \notin T}, \{\overline{\phi}_j\}_{j \in T})$ where $\{\phi_j\}_{j \notin T}$ are the second round messages generated by the honest servers in the interaction with $\mathcal{A}$ and vk_i is the verification key output by Share algorithm.*

2. ***Security:*** *For any admissible adversary $\mathcal{A}$ (see Definition 5) w.r.t. P corrupting a subset of the clients and (adaptively) corrupting upto t servers, there exists an ideal world simulator Sim_Φ such that for any choice of inputs of the honest clients, the following two distributions are computationally indistinguishable:*

- **Real Execution.** *The admissible adversary $\mathcal{A}$ interacts with the honest parties who follow the protocol specification. The output of the real execution consists of the output of the admissible adversary $\mathcal{A}$ and the output of the honest output clients.*
- **Ideal Execution.** *This corresponds to the ideal world interaction where Sim_Φ and the honest client have access to the trusted party implementing f. Each honest client sends its input to f and each honest output client outputs whatever the trusted functionality sends back. For every honest output client, Sim_Φ sends a special instruction to the trusted functionality to either give the output of f to the output client or the special symbol $\perp$. The output of the ideal execution corresponds to the output of Sim_Φ and the output of all the honest outputs clients.*

We state the main theorem about constructing pairwise verifiable MPC protocol and defer the proof to the full version.

Theorem 1. *Let $(\mathsf{Share}_{(t,m)}, \mathsf{Rec}_{(t,m)})$ be a t-out-of-m, 4-multiplicative, t-error-correctable secret sharing scheme w.r.t. pairwise predicate P (see Definition 4). Let f be an arbitrary n-party functionality. Then, there exists a construction of an n-client, m-server pairwise verifiable MPC protocol for computing f against t server corruptions (see Definition 6) that makes black-box use of a PRF. Furthermore, Eval algorithm does not perform any cryptographic operations. The computational cost of the protocol is polynomial in the circuit size of f, the security parameter 1^λ, and the number of parties.*

5 Black-Box Protocol Compilers in the Two-Party Setting

In this section, we give our black-box protocol compilers to construct round-optimal malicious-secure protocols in the two-party setting. In Sect. 5.1, we give our compiler in the random oracle model. In Sect. 5.2, we give our compiler in the OT correlations model. Finally, in Sect. 5.3, we show how to extend these compilers to give a round-optimal, malicious-secure, two-party protocol in the two-sided setting.

5.1 Protocol Compiler in the Random Oracle Model

In this subsection, we give a black-box compiler that transforms from any two-round semi-honest two-party protocol to a two-round malicious secure protocol in the random oracle model. We state the formal theorem statement below.

Theorem 2. *Let f be an arbitrary two-party functionality. Assume the existence of:*

- *A two-round, 2-client, m-server pairwise verifiable MPC protocol $\Phi =$ ($\mathsf{Share}, \mathsf{Eval}, \mathsf{Dec}$) for computing f against t server corruptions (see Definition 6).*

– A two-round semi-honest protocol $\Pi_i = (\Pi_{i,1}, \Pi_{i,2}, \text{out}_{\Pi_i})$ for each $i \in [m]$ (see Definition 1) where Π_i computes the function $\text{Eval}(i, \cdot)$.

Then, there exists a two-round protocol Γ for computing f that makes black-box use of $\{\Pi_i\}_{i \in [n]}$ and is secure against static, malicious adversaries in the random oracle model. The communication and computation costs of the protocol are $\text{poly}(\lambda, |f|)$, where $|f|$ denotes the size of the circuit computing f.

Instantiating the pairwise verifiable MPC protocol from Theorem 1, we get the following corollary.

Corollary 1. *Let f be an arbitrary two-party functionality. There exists a two-round protocol Γ for computing f that makes black-box use of $\{\Pi_i\}_{i \in [n]}$ and is secure against static, malicious adversaries in the random oracle model. The communication and computation costs of the protocol are $\text{poly}(\lambda, |f|)$, where $|f|$ denotes the size of the circuit computing f.*

In Sect. 5.1, we describe the construction of the above malicious-secure protocol and in Sect. 5.1, we give the proof of security.

Construction. We start with the description of the building blocks used in the construction.

Building Blocks. The construction makes use of the following building blocks.

1. A protocol $\Phi = (\text{Share}, \text{Eval}, \text{Dec})$ that is a two-round, 2-client, m-server pairwise verifiable MPC protocol w.r.t. predicate P for computing the function f against t server corruptions (see Definition 6). We set $t = 4\lambda$ and $m = 6t + 1$.
2. An two-round semi-honest inner protocol $\Pi_i = (\Pi_{i,1}, \Pi_{i,2}, \text{out}_{\Pi_i})$ for each $i \in [m]$ (see Definition 1) where Π_i computes the function $\text{Eval}(i, \cdot)$ (i.e., the function computed by the i-th server).
3. A non-interactive, straight-line extractable commitment $(\text{Com}, \text{Open})$. Such a commitment scheme can be constructed unconditionally in the random oracle model (see Sect. 3.3).
4. Two hash functions $H_1 : \{0,1\}^* \to \{0,1\}^\lambda$ and $H_2 : \{0,1\}^* \to \mathcal{S}_{m,\lambda}$ that are modelled as random oracles where $\mathcal{S}_{m,\lambda}$ is the set of all subsets of $[m]$ of size λ.

Description of the Protocol. Let P_0 be the receiver that has private input x_0 and P_1 be the sender that has private input x_1. The common input to both parties is a description of a two-party function f. We give the formal description of a two-round, malicious-secure protocol for computing f in Figs. 1 and 2.

Proof of Security. Let $\mathcal{A}$ be the malicious adversary that is corrupting either P_0 or P_1. We start with the description of the simulator Sim. Let P_i be the honest client.

- **Round 1:** The receiver P_0 does the following:
  1. It computes $(x_1^0, \ldots, x_m^0, vk_0) \leftarrow \mathsf{Share}(1^\lambda, 0, x_0)$.
  2. For each $j \in [m]$,
     (a) It computes $r_j^0 := H_1(0, j, x_j^0, s_j^0)$ for uniformly chosen $s_j^0 \leftarrow \{0, 1\}^\lambda$.
     (b) It computes $\mathsf{com}_j^0 \leftarrow \mathsf{Com}((x_j^0, s_j^0))$.
     (c) It computes $(\pi_{j,1}, sk_j) \leftarrow \Pi_{j,1}(1^\lambda, x_j^0; r_j^0)$.
  3. It computes $K_0 = H_2(0, \{\mathsf{com}_j^0, \pi_{j,1}\}_{j\in[m]}, \mathsf{tag}_0)$ where $\mathsf{tag}_0 \leftarrow \{0, 1\}^\lambda$.
  4. It sends $\{\mathsf{com}_j^0, \pi_{j,1}\}_{j\in[m]}$, tag_0, and $\{(x_j^0, s_j^0), \mathsf{Open}(\mathsf{com}_j^0)\}_{j\in K_0}$.
- **Round-2:** The sender does the following:
  1. It runs $\mathsf{chkConsistency}(0, \mathbb{T})$ where $\mathsf{chkConsistency}$ is described in Figure 2 and $\mathbb{T}$ is the transcript in the first round. If $\mathsf{chkConsistency}$ outputs 0, then it aborts.
  2. Else, it computes $(x_1^1, \ldots, x_m^1, vk_1) \leftarrow \mathsf{Share}(1^\lambda, 1, x_1)$.
  1. For each $j \in [m]$,
     (a) It computes $r_j^1 := H_1(1, j, x_j^1, s_j^1)$ for uniformly chosen $s_j^1 \leftarrow \{0, 1\}^\lambda$.
     (b) It computes $\mathsf{com}_j^1 \leftarrow \mathsf{Com}((x_j^1, s_j^1))$.
     (c) It computes $\pi_{j,2} \leftarrow \Pi_{j,2}(1^\lambda, x_j^1, \pi_{j,1}; r_j^1)$.
  2. It computes $K_1 = H_2(1, \{\mathsf{com}_j^1, \pi_{j,2}\}_{j\in[m]}, \mathsf{tag}_1)$ where $\mathsf{tag}_1 \leftarrow \{0, 1\}^\lambda$.
  3. It sends $\{\mathsf{com}_j^1, \pi_{j,2}\}_{j\in[m]}$, tag_1, and $\{(x_j^1, s_j^1), \mathsf{Open}(\mathsf{com}_j^1)\}_{j\in K_1}$.
- **Output:** To compute the output, the receiver does the following:
  1. It runs $\mathsf{chkConsistency}(1, \mathbb{T})$ where $\mathbb{T}$ is the transcript in the first two rounds. If $\mathsf{chkConsistency}$ outputs 0, then it aborts and outputs $\bot$.
  2. For each $j \in [m]$,
     (a) It runs $\mathsf{out}_{\Pi_j}(\pi_{j,2}, sk_j)$ to obtain ϕ_j.
  3. It runs $\mathsf{Dec}(0, vk_0, \phi_1, \ldots, \phi_m)$ and outputs whatever Dec outputs.

Fig. 1. Description of r-round malicious 2PC

Input: A party index $i \in \{0, 1\}$ and the transcript $\mathbb{T}$.

1. Compute K_i from the transcript $\mathbb{T}$ and the hash function H_2.
2. For each $j \in K_i$,
   (a) It obtains $\{(x_j^i, s_j^i), \mathsf{Open}(\mathsf{com}_j^i)\}$ from $\mathbb{T}$.
   (b) It checks if $\mathsf{Open}(\mathsf{com}_j^i)$ is valid.
   (c) It then checks if $(x_j^i, H_1(i, j, x_j^i, s_j^i))$ is a valid (input,randomness) pair for the protocol Π_j consistent with the transcript $\mathbb{T}$.
   (d) For each $j' \in K_i$, it checks if $P(i, j, j', x_j^i, x_{j'}^i) = 1$.
3. If any of the checks fail, it outputs 0. Else, if all the checks pass, it outputs 1.

Fig. 2. Description of $\mathsf{chkConsistency}$

Description of Sim.

1. **Interaction with the Environment.** For every input value corresponding to the corrupted P_{1-i} that Sim receives from the environment, it writes these values to the input tape of the adversary $\mathcal{A}$. Similarly, the contents of the output tape of $\mathcal{A}$ is written to Sim's output tape.

2. Sim chooses uniform subset K_i of size λ and programs the random oracle H_2 to output this set when queried on the message generated by P_i.

3. Sim starts interacting with the simulator Sim$_\Phi$ for the outer protocol by corrupting the client P_{1-i} and the set of servers indexed by K_i. It obtains the first round messages $\{x_j^i\}_{j \in K_i}$ sent by the honest client P_i to the corrupted servers.

4. For each $j \in K_i$, it uses the input x_j^i and uniformly chosen s_j^i to generate the messages in the protocol Π_j as described in Fig. 1. For each $j \notin K_i$, it runs the simulator for the inner protocol Π_j to generate the messages on behalf of P_i. To generate the commitments, for each $j \in K_i$, it uses (x_j^i, s_j^i) to compute com$_j^i$. However, for each $j \notin K_i$, it commits to some dummy values.

5. For each of the unique random oracle queries made by $\mathcal{A}$, Sim samples a uniform element in the range of the oracle and outputs it as the response. Each time Sim generates query to the random oracle on behalf of honest P_i, Sim checks if adversary has already made that query. If that is the case, then it aborts the execution and outputs a special symbol ABORT.

6. On obtaining the protocol message from $\mathcal{A}$, Sim uses the straightline extractor for the extractable commitment Com and obtains $(x_1^{1-i}, s_1^{1-i}), \ldots, (x_m^{1-i}, s_m^{1-i})$ from com$_1^{1-i}, \ldots,$ com$_m^{1-i}$ respectively.

7. It initializes two empty sets I_1 and I_2.

8. For each $j \in [m]$, if $(x_j^{1-i}, H_1(1-i, j, x_j^{1-i}, s_j^{1-i}))$ is not a valid (input,randomness) pair for the protocol Π_j w.r.t. the messages sent by $\mathcal{A}$, then it adds j to the set I_1. It adaptively corrupts the server j in the outer protocol and obtains x_j^i. It uses this as the input to compute the second round message of the protocol Π_j when $i = 1$.

9. It constructs an inconsistency graph G where the vertices correspond to $[m]$ and it adds an edge between j and k if $P(1-i, j, k, x_j^{1-i}, x_k^{1-i}) = 0$. It then computes a 2-approximation for the minimum vertex cover in this graph and calls this vertex cover as I_2. For each $j \in I_2$, it adaptively corrupts the server j in the outer protocol and obtains x_j^i. It uses this as the input to generate the second round message of the protocol Π_j when $i = 1$.

10. If $|I_1| \geq \lambda$ or if $|I_2| \geq \lambda$, then it sends $\bot$ to its ideal functionality.

11. It completes the interaction with $\mathcal{A}$ and if at any point of time, $\mathcal{A}$'s messages do not pass chkConsistency then Sim sends $\bot$ to the trusted functionality.

12. It provides $\{x_j^{1-i}\}_{j \notin I_1 \cup I_2 \cup K_i}$ to Sim$_\Phi$ as the messages sent by the adversary to the honest servers. Sim$_\Phi$ queries the ideal functionality on an input x_{1-i} and Sim forwards this to its trusted functionality.

13. If $i = 0$, then if Sim$_\Phi$ instructs the ideal functionality to deliver the output to honest P_0, then Sim forwards this message. Otherwise, if Sim$_\Phi$ instructs the ideal functionality to deliver $\bot$, Sim sends $\bot$ to the ideal functionality.

14. If $i = 1$, then Sim obtains $z = f(x_0, x_1)$ from the ideal functionality and forwards this to Sim_Φ. Sim_Φ sends the second round protocol messages $\{\phi_j\}_{j \notin I_1 \cup I_2 \cup K_1}$ from the honest servers. For each $j \notin I_1 \cup I_2 \cup K_1$, Sim uses ϕ_j as the output of Π_j and gives this as input to the simulator for Π_j along with $(x_j^0, H_1(0, j, x_j^0, s_j^0))$ as the (input, randomness) pair. We get the final round message for Π_j for each $j \notin I_1 \cup I_2 \cup K_1$ from the inner protocol simulators and we use this to generate the final round message in the protocol.

Proof of Indistinguishability. We now argue that the real execution and the ideal execution are computationally indistinguishable via a hybrid argument.

- Real : This corresponds to the output of the real execution of the protocol.
- Hyb_0 : This hybrid corresponds to the distribution where the random oracle queries of the adversary are answered with a uniformly chosen random element from the image of the oracle. Further, if the adversary makes any queries to the hash functions H_1, H_2 before the exact same query was made by the honest party, we abort. We note that since each query made to the hash functions H_1, H_2 has a component which is a uniformly chosen random string of length λ, the probability that an adversary is able to make a query that exactly matches this string queried by an honest party is $q \cdot 2^{-\lambda}$ (where q is the total number of queries made by the adversary to the random oracles). Hence, this hybrid is statistically close to the previous one.
- Hyb_1 : In this hybrid, we make the following changes:
  1. We use the extractor for the extractable commitment Com to obtain $(x_1^{1-i}, s_1^{1-i}), \ldots, (x_m^{1-i}, s_m^{1-i})$ from $\mathsf{com}_1^{1-i}, \ldots, \mathsf{com}_m^{1-i}$ respectively.
  2. We construct the sets I_1 and I_2 as described in the simulation.
  3. If $|I_1| \geq \lambda$ or $|I_2| \geq \lambda$, we abort the execution and instruct the honest party to output $\bot$.
  4. If $i = 0$ and if $|I_1| < \lambda$ and $|I_2| < \lambda$, then for each $j \in I_1 \cup I_2 \cup K_i$, we set ϕ_j to be some default value and compute the output of honest P_0.
  In Lemma 1, we show that Hyb_0 and Hyb_1 are statistically indistinguishable from the error correction properties of Φ (see Definition 4.1).
- Hyb_2 : In this hybrid, we make the following changes:
  1. We sample a uniform subset K_i (of size λ) and program the random oracle H_2 to output this set when queried on the messages generated by P_i.
  2. For each $j \notin K_i$, we change the commitments com_j^i to be commitments to some dummy values instead of (x_j^i, s_j^i).
  This hybrid is computationally indistinguishable to the previous hybrid from the hiding property of the non-interactive commitment scheme.
- Hyb_3 : In this hybrid, we do the following:
  1. We choose uniform subset K_i of $[m]$ of size λ and program the random oracle H_2 to output this set when queried on the messages generated by P_i.
  2. For each $j \notin K_i$, we run the simulator for the inner protocol and generate the messages from P_i for the protocol Π_j using this simulator.

3. We compute the sets I_1 and I_2 as before.
4. If some $j \notin K_i$ is added to I_1 or I_2 and if $i = 1$, we use x_j^i to compute the second round sender message.
5. If $|I_1| \geq \lambda$ or if $|I_2| \geq \lambda$, we abort as in the previous hybrid.
6. For $j \notin K_i \cup I_1 \cup I_2$, we use the input x_j^{1-i} extracted from the extractable commitment to compute $\phi_j = \mathsf{Eval}(1^\lambda, j, x_j^0, x_j^1)$.
7. If $i = 0$, for each $j \in K_i \cup I_1 \cup I_2$, we set ϕ_j to be a default value and use these values instead to compute the output of the receiver P_0.
8. If $i = 1$, then for each $j \notin K_1 \cup I_1 \cup I_2$, we send the input x_j^0, randomness $H_1(0, j, x_j^0, s_j^0)$ and the output ϕ_j to the simulator for Π_j and obtain the final round message in Π_j. We use this to generate the final round message in the overall protocol.

In Lemma 2, we show that $\mathsf{Hyb}_2 \approx_c \mathsf{Hyb}_3$ from the semi-honest sender security of the inner protocol.

- Hyb_4 : In this hybrid, we make the following changes:
  1. We (adaptively) corrupt the set of servers corresponding to the indices $K_i \cup I_1 \cup I_2$ and the client P_{1-i}. We run the simulator Sim_Φ for the outer protocol and obtain the first round messages sent by the honest client to these corrupted servers. We use this to complete the execution with $\mathcal{A}$.
  2. We provide $\{x_j^{1-i}\}_{j \notin K_i \cup I_1 \cup I_2}$ (extracted from the extractable commitment) to Sim_Φ as the messages sent by the adversary to the honest servers. Sim_Φ queries the ideal functionality on an input x_{1-i}.
  3. If $i = 0$ then if Sim_Φ instructs the ideal functionality to deliver the output to honest P_0, then we instruct P_0 to output $f(x_0, x_1)$. Otherwise, if Sim_Φ instructs the ideal functionality to deliver $\bot$, we instruct P_0 to output $\bot$.
  4. If $i = 1$, we compute $z = f(x_0, x_1)$ and send this to Sim_Φ as the output from the ideal functionality. Sim_Φ sends the second round protocol messages $\{\phi_j\}_{j \notin K_i \cup I_1 \cup I_2}$ from the honest servers. We use this to generate the final round message of the protocol as in the previous hybrid.

In Lemma 3, we show that $\mathsf{Hyb}_3 \approx_c \mathsf{Hyb}_4$ from the security of the outer protocol. We note that output of Hyb_4 is identically distributed to the output of the ideal execution with Sim.

Lemma 1. *Assuming the error correction properties of Φ, we have* $\mathsf{Hyb}_0 \approx_s \mathsf{Hyb}_1$.

Proof. We show that if $|I_1| \geq \lambda$ or if $|I_2| \geq \lambda$ then the honest client in Hyb_0 also aborts with overwhelming probability.

- **Case-1:** $|I_1| \geq \lambda$: Note that K_{1-i} is chosen by the random oracle after the adversary generates the message on behalf of the corrupted party in the protocol. We show that since K_{1-i} is uniformly chosen random subset of $[m]$ of size λ, the probability that $|I_1 \cap K_{1-i}| = 0$ is $2^{-O(\lambda)}$. Note that if this event doesn't happen, then the honest client P_i aborts in Hyb_0.

$$\Pr[|K_{1-i} \cap I_1| = 0] \leq \frac{\binom{m-\lambda}{\lambda}}{\binom{m}{\lambda}}$$

$$= \left(1 - \frac{\lambda}{m}\right)\left(1 - \frac{\lambda}{(m-1)}\right) \cdots \left(1 - \frac{\lambda}{(m-(\lambda-1))}\right)$$

$$< \left(1 - \frac{\lambda}{m}\right)^\lambda < e^{-O(\lambda)}.$$

where the last inequality follows since $m = O(\lambda)$. By an union bound over the set of all the q queries that adversary makes to the random oracle H_2, the probability that there exists some K_{1-i} which is the response of the RO such that $|K_{1-i} \cap I_1| = 0$ is upper bounded by $q \cdot e^{-O(\lambda)}$.

- **Case-2:** $|I_2| \geq \lambda$: Since $|I_2| \geq \lambda$, the size of the minimum vertex cover is at least $\lambda/2$. This means that in the inconsistency graph, there exists a maximum matching of size at least $\lambda/4$. Let M be the set of vertices for this matching. Note that K_{1-i} is uniformly chosen random subset of $[m]$ of size λ. If any edge of this matching is present in K_{1-i}, then the honest client P_i aborts in Hyb_0. [22, Theorem 4.1] shows that probability that no edge of this matching is present in K_{1-i} is $2^{-O(\lambda)}$. Again, by an union bound over the set of all the q queries that adversary makes to the random oracle H_2, the probability that there exists some K_{1-i} which is the response of the RO such that no edge in M is in K_{1-i} is upper bounded by $q \cdot 2^{-O(\lambda)}$.

In the case, where $|I_1| \leq \lambda$ and $|I_2| \leq \lambda$, consider an admissible adversary $\mathcal{A}'$ against the protocol Φ that corrupts the set of servers indexed by $I_1 \cup I_2 \cup K_i$. By definition for every server $j, k \notin I_1 \cup I_2 \cup K_i$, it follows that $P(1 - i, j, k, x_j^{1-i}, x_k^{1-i}) = 1$. Thus, it follows from the error correction property of Φ that $\mathsf{Hyb}_2 \approx_s \mathsf{Hyb}_3$.

Lemma 2. *Assuming the semi-honest security of the inner protocol, we have that* $\mathsf{Hyb}_2 \approx_c \mathsf{Hyb}_3$.

Proof. We sample a uniform subset K_i of $[m]$ of size λ and program the random oracle H_2 to output the this set when queried on the messages generated by P_i.

Let $I = [m]\backslash K_i$. We consider a sequence of $|I|$ hybrids between Hyb_2 and Hyb_3 where we change from real to simulated executions of the inner protocol for each $j \in I$ one by one. If Hyb_2 and Hyb_3 are computationally distinguishable, then by a standard hybrid argument, there exists two sub-hybrids $\mathsf{Hyb}_{2,j-1}$ and $\mathsf{Hyb}_{2,j}$ which differ only in the j-th execution and are computationally distinguishable. Specifically, in $\mathsf{Hyb}_{2,j}$, the messages in the protocol Π_j is generated as in the ideal execution and in the $\mathsf{Hyb}_{2,j-1}$ it is generated as in the real execution. We now show that this contradicts the semi-honest security of the inner protocol.

We begin interacting with external challenger and provide x_j^i as the input used by P_i in Π_j. Amongst all the queries made by $\mathcal{A}$ to the random oracle H_1 where the first two inputs are $(1 - i, j)$, we choose one of these queries

$(1 - i, j, x_j^{1-i}, s_j^{1-i})$ at random and give x_j^{1-i} as the input of the corrupted party. The challenger provides with a random tape r_j^{1-i} to be used by P_{1-i}. We provide r_j^{1-i} as the response from the random oracle. On receiving the protocol message from $\mathcal{A}$, we run the extractor for the extractable commitment Com on com_j^{1-i} and obtain $(\overline{x}_j^{1-i}, \overline{s}_j^{1-i})$. We consider the following cases.

1. If j is added to I_1 or I_2 then:
   - If $i = 1$, we use x_j^i to generate the second round sender message. We generate the view of the adversary and run the distinguisher between $\text{Hyb}_{2,j}$ and $\text{Hyb}_{2,j-1}$ on this view and output whatever it outputs.
   - If $i = 0$, we set ϕ_j to be an arbitrary value and generate the view of the adversary and the output of the honest party as before. We run the distinguisher between $\text{Hyb}_{2,j}$ and $\text{Hyb}_{2,j-1}$ on these values and output whatever it outputs.
2. If j is not added to I_1 or I_2 but $(\overline{x}_j^{1-i}, \overline{s}_j^{1-i}) \neq (x_j^{1-i}, s_j^{1-i})$, then we output a random bit to the external challenger.
3. If j is not added to I_1 or I_2 and $(\overline{x}_j^{1-i}, \overline{s}_j^{1-i}) = (x_j^{1-i}, s_j^{1-i})$, then we continue with the rest of the execution using the messages from the challenger ($i = 1$) or the output from the challenger ($i = 0$) to compute the view of the adversary and output of the honest party. We run the distinguisher between $\text{Hyb}_{2,j}$ and $\text{Hyb}_{2,j-1}$ and output whatever it outputs.

We note that if j is not added to I_1 or I_2 and $(\overline{x}_j^{1-i}, \overline{s}_j^{1-i}) = (x_j^{1-i}, s_j^{1-i})$, then the input to the distinguisher is identical to $\text{Hyb}_{2,j-1}$ if the challenger generated the messages of Π_j as in the real execution and otherwise, it is identical to $\text{Hyb}_{2,j}$. Similarly, if j is added to I_1 or I_2, then the input to the distinguisher is identical to $\text{Hyb}_{2,j-1}$ if the challenger generated the messages of Π_j as in the real execution and otherwise, it is identical to $\text{Hyb}_{2,j}$.

Finally, conditioning on j not added to I_1 or I_2, the probability that $(\overline{x}_j^{1-i}, \overline{s}_j^{1-i}) \neq (x_j^{1-i}, s_j^{1-i})$ is at least $1 - 1/q - \text{negl}(\lambda)$ (and at most $1 - 1/q + \text{negl}(\lambda)$) where q is the total number of queries made by the adversary to the random oracle H_1. Let us assume that the probability that the distinguisher correctly predicts whether it is given a sample from $\text{Hyb}_{2,j}$ and $\text{Hyb}_{2,j-1}$ to be $1/2 + \mu(\lambda)$ (for some non-negligible $\mu(\lambda)$). Let ϵ be the probability that j is added to I_1 or I_2. Let p be the probability that the above reduction correctly predicts whether it is interacting with the real execution or the ideal execution. Then,

$$p \geq (1/2 + \mu(\lambda))\epsilon + (1 - \epsilon)((1 - 1/q - \text{negl}(\lambda))(1/2) + (1/q - \text{negl}(\lambda))(1/2 + \mu(\lambda)))$$
$$\geq (1/2 + \mu(\lambda))\epsilon + (1 - \epsilon)(1/2 + \mu(\lambda)/q) - \text{negl}(\lambda)$$
$$\geq 1/2 + \mu(\lambda)/q + \epsilon(\mu(\lambda) - \mu(\lambda)/q) - \text{negl}(\lambda)$$
$$\geq 1/2 + \mu(\lambda)/q - \text{negl}(\lambda)$$

and this contradicts the semi-honest security of the inner protocol.

Lemma 3. *Assuming the security of the outer protocol Φ, we have $\mathsf{Hyb}_3 \approx_c \mathsf{Hyb}_4$.*

Proof. Assume for the sake of contradiction that Hyb_3 and Hyb_4 are computationally distinguishable. We give a reduction to breaking the security of the outer protocol.

We begin interacting with the external challenger by providing the input x_i of the honest client P_i. We then corrupt the other client P_{1-i} and the set of servers indexed by K_i. We obtain the first round messages sent from the honest client P_i to the corrupted servers and we begin interacting with $\mathcal{A}$ using these messages. For each server that is added to I_1 or I_2, we adaptively corrupt that server and obtain the first round message sent from the honest client to this server. We use this message to continue with the rest of the execution as in Hyb_3. At the end of the protocol execution, we send $\{x_j^{1-i}\}_{j\notin K_i \cup I_1 \cup I_2}$ as the first round messages sent by the corrupted client P_{1-i} to the honest servers. If P_0 is uncorrupted, we send $\{\phi_j\}_{j\in K_i \cup I_1 \cup I_2}$ (set to be arbitrary values as in Hyb_3) to the challenger and it provides the output of P_0 and we instruct P_0 to output the same. If P_0 is corrupted, we obtain $\{\phi_j\}_{j\notin K_i \cup I_1 \cup I_2}$ from the external challenger and we use this to generate the final round message in the protocol. We finally run the distinguisher between Hyb_2 and Hyb_3 on the view of $\mathcal{A}$ and the output of P_0 (if it is uncorrupted) and output whatever the distinguisher outputs.

The above reduction emulates an admissible adversary as by definition the first round message sent to the honest servers pass the pairwise verification w.r.t. predicate P. Since $|K_i \cup I_1 \cup I_2| \leq |K_i| + |I_1| + |I_2| = 3\lambda = t$, the reduction emulates an admissible adversary that corrupts at most t servers. Thus, if the messages generated by the external challenger are done as in the real execution then input to the distinguisher is identical to Hyb_3. Else, it is identically distributed to Hyb_4. This implies that the reduction breaks the security of the protocol Φ and this is a contradiction.

5.2   Protocol Compiler in the OT Correlations Model

In this section, we describe a protocol compiler that transforms two-round semi-malicious two-party protocol to a two-round malicious-secure protocol. This transformation is in the standard 1-out-of-2 OT correlations model. We state the formal theorem below.

Theorem 3. *Let f be an arbitrary two-party functionality. Assume the existence of:*

- *A two-round, 2-client, m-server pairwise verifiable MPC protocol $\Phi = (\mathsf{Share}, \mathsf{Eval}, \mathsf{Dec})$ for computing f against t server corruptions (see Definition 6).*
- *A two-round semi-malicious protocol $\Pi_i = (\Pi_{i,1}, \Pi_{i,2}, \mathsf{out}_{\Pi_i})$ for each $i \in [m]$ (see Definition 2) where Π_i computes the function $\mathsf{Eval}(i, \cdot)$.*

Then, there exists a two-round protocol Γ for computing f that makes black-box use of $\{\Pi_i\}_{i \in [n]}$ and is secure against static, malicious adversaries in the 1-out-of-2 OT correlations model. The communication and computation costs of the protocol are $\mathsf{poly}(\lambda, |f|)$, where $|f|$ denotes the size of the circuit computing f and the size of the OT correlations shared between the parties is a fixed polynomial in the security parameter and is independent of the size of the function f.

Instantiating the pairwise verifiable MPC protocol from Theorem 1, we get the following corollary.

Corollary 2. *Let f be an arbitrary two-party functionality. There exists a two-round protocol Γ for computing f that makes black-box use of $\{\Pi_i\}_{i \in [n]}$ and is secure against static, malicious adversaries in the 1-out-of-2 OT correlations model. The communication and computation costs of the protocol are $\mathsf{poly}(\lambda, |f|)$, where $|f|$ denotes the size of the circuit computing f and the size of the OT correlations shared between the parties is a fixed polynomial in the security parameter and is independent of the size of the function f.*

We defer the proof of Theorem 3 to the full version.

5.3 Extension to the Two-Sided Setting

In this subsection, we explain how to extend the protocol described in Sect. 5.1 to the bidirectional communication model. Specifically, we want to construct an two-round protocol where in each round, both parties can send a message and we require both parties get the output at the end of the second round. The extension for the protocol in the OT correlations model is similar.

Construction. The construction is very similar to the one described in Fig. 1 except that we run two instances of the inner protocol for each $j \in [m]$, namely, Π_j^0 and Π_j^1 where the parties use the same input in both the executions (but use independently chosen randomness). Here, Π_j^0 is the protocol that delivers output to P_0 and Π_j^1 is the protocol that delivers output to P_1. Additionally, for each $j \in [m]$, the parties send an extractable commitment to the input and the random strings used in Π_j^0 and Π_j^1 respectively. In each round $u \in [2]$, the parties use the random oracle H_2 to derive a set K_0^u, K_1^u respectively as in the previous protocol description. The party P_i (for each $i \in \{1, 2\}$) then opens the above generated extractable commitment for those executions indexed by K_i^u. The chkConsistency run by P_i is modified so that it checks if the input, randomness pair is consistent in Π_j^0 and Π_j^1 for each $j \in K_{1-i}^u$. The output computation by both parties is done exactly as described in Fig. 1.

We defer the proof of security of this construction to the full version.

6 Black-Box Protocol Compilers in the Multiparty Setting

We state our main theorems about our protocol compiler in the multiparty case. The proof of these theorems are given in the Appendix.

6.1 Protocol Compiler in the Random Oracle Model

In this subsection, we give a construction of a three-round malicious-secure MPC protocol in the random oracle model that makes black-box use of a two-round semi-honest OT. It was shown in [1] that even considering only semi-honest security in the random oracle model, such a black-box protocol for the case of three parties is round-optimal. Recently, [32] gave a malicious-secure construction in the CRS model assuming a two-round malicious secure oblivious transfer protocol that additionally satisfies equivocal receiver security [15].

We give the formal statement of our theorem below.

Theorem 4. *Let f be an arbitrary n-party functionality. Assuming the existence of:*

- *A two-round, 2-client, m-server pairwise verifiable MPC protocol $\Phi = (\mathsf{Share}, \mathsf{Eval}, \mathsf{Dec})$ for computing f against t server corruptions (see Definition 6).*
- *A two-round semi-honest oblivious transfer protocol $\mathsf{OT} = (\mathsf{OT}_1, \mathsf{OT}_2, \mathsf{out}_{\mathsf{OT}})$.*

Then, there exits a three-round protocol Γ for computing f over point-to-point channels that makes black-box use OT and satisfies security with selective abort against static, malicious adversaries in the random oracle model. The communication and computation costs of the protocol are $\mathsf{poly}(\lambda, n, |f|)$, where $|f|$ denotes the size of the circuit computing f.

Instantiating the pairwise verifiable MPC protocol from Theorem 1, we get the following corollary.

Corollary 3. *Let f be an arbitrary n-party functionality. There exits a three-round protocol Γ for computing f over point-to-point channels that makes black-box use OT and satisfies security with selective abort against static, malicious adversaries in the random oracle model. The communication and computation costs of the protocol are $\mathsf{poly}(\lambda, n, |f|)$, where $|f|$ denotes the size of the circuit computing f.*

We give the proof of Theorem 4 in the full version.

6.2 Protocol Compiler in the OT Correlations Model

In this subsection, we improve the result from [19] and give a construction of a two-round black-box protocol for computing multiparty functionalities that are secure against malicious adversaries in the OT correlations model. This compiler makes black-box use of a two-round semi-malicious secure inner protocol that has first message equivocality (defined in [19] and recalled in Definition 7).

Building Blocks. The construction makes use of the following building blocks.

1. A two-round n-client, m-sever protocol $\Phi = (\Phi_1, \Phi_2, \mathsf{out}_\Phi)$ satisfying privacy with knowledge of outputs[6] for computing the function $g((x_1, k_1), \ldots, (x_n, k_n)) = (y = f(x_1, \ldots, x_n), \{\mathsf{MAC}(k_i, y)\}_{i \in [n]})$ where MAC is a strongly unforgeable one-time MAC scheme. This protocol is secure against t server corruptions and has publicly decodable transcript. We set $t = (m - 1)/3$ and $m = 16\lambda n^3$. Such a protocol was constructed in [23, 30] by making black-box use of a PRG. As noted in [19], we can delegate the PRG computations made by the servers to the client and ensure that the computation done by the servers do not involve any cryptographic operations.

2. A two-round inner protocol $\Pi_j = (\Pi_{j,1}, \Pi_{j,2}, \mathsf{out}_\Pi)$ with publicly decodable transcript for each $j \in [m]$ where Π_j computes the function $\Phi_2(j, \cdot)$ (i.e., the function computed by the j-th server). For each $j \in [m]$, we require protocol Π_j to satisfy the following definition.

Definition 7 [19]. *We say that $(\Pi_1, \Pi_2, \mathsf{out}_\Pi)$ is a two-round, inner protocol for computing a function f with publicly decodable transcript if it satisfies the following properties:*

- **Correctness:** *We say that the protocol Π correctly computes a function f if for every choice of inputs x_i for party P_i and for any choice of random tape r_i, we require that for every $i \in [n]$,*

$$\Pr[\mathsf{out}_\Pi(i, \pi(2)) = f(x_1, \ldots, x_n)] = 1$$

where $\pi(2)$ denotes the transcript of the protocol Π when the input of P_i is x_i with random tape r_i and sk_i is the output key generated by Π_1.

- **Security.** *Let $\mathcal{A}$ be an adversary corrupting a subset of the parties indexed by the set M and let H be the set of indices denoting the honest parties. We require the existence of a simulator Sim_Π such that for any choice of honest parties inputs $\{x_i\}_{i \in H}$, we have:*

$$\mathsf{Real}(\mathcal{A}, \{x_i, r_i\}_{i \in H}) \approx_c \mathsf{Ideal}(\mathcal{A}, \mathsf{Sim}_\Pi, \{x_i\}_{i \in H})$$

where the real and ideal experiments are described in Fig. 3 and for each $i \in H$, r_i is uniformly chosen.

[19] showed that the protocol from [14] in the OT correlations model and [25] in the OLE correlations model satisfy the above definition.

3. A single round Rabin OT protocol RabinOT with erasure probability $1 - \lambda \cdot n/m$. We extend the syntax of the Rabin OT protocol to take in m strings and each of these strings are independently erased with probability $1 - \lambda \cdot n/m$.

---

[6] Privacy with knowledge of outputs is a weaker notion than security with selective abort and allows the adversary to select the output given by the trusted functionality to the honest parties. We refer the reader to [23] for the formal definition.

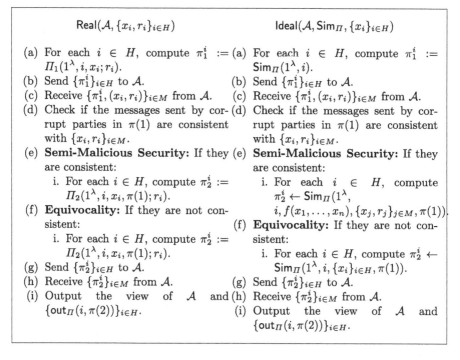

Fig. 3. Security game for the two-round inner protocol

Theorem 5. *Let f be an arbitrary n-party functionality. Assume the existence of:*

- *A two-round n-client, m-sever protocol $\Phi = (\Phi_1, \Phi_2, \text{out}_\Phi)$ satisfying privacy with knowledge of outputs against t server corruptions for computing the function g defined above.*
- *A two-round inner protocol $\Pi_j = (\Pi_{j,1}, \Pi_{j,2}, \text{out}_\Pi)$ with publicly decodable transcript for each $j \in [m]$ where Π_j computes the function $\Phi_2(j, \cdot)$ (i.e., the function computed by the j-th server) satisfying Definition 7.*

Then, there exists a two-round protocol Γ that makes black box use of $\{\Pi_j\}_{j \in [m]}$ and computes f against static, malicious adversaries satisfying security with selective abort in the 1-out-of-2 OT correlations model and access to point-to-point channels. Further, if only $(\Phi_1, \text{out}_\Phi)$ makes black-box use of a PRF and Φ_2 does not perform any cryptographic operations, then Γ is fully black-box. The communication and computation costs of the protocol are $\text{poly}(\lambda, n, |f|)$, where $|f|$ denotes the size of the circuit computing f and the size of the OT correlations shared between the parties is a fixed polynomial in the security parameter and number of parties and is independent of the size of the function f.

We give the proof of this theorem in the full version.

Acknowledgments. Y. Ishai was supported in part by ERC Project NTSC (742754), BSF grant 2018393, and ISF grant 2774/20. D. Khurana was supported in part by DARPA SIEVE award, a gift from Visa Research, and a C3AI DTI award. A. Sahai was supported in part from a Simons Investigator Award, DARPA SIEVE award, NTT Research, NSF Frontier Award 1413955, BSF grant 2012378, a Xerox Faculty Research Award, a Google Faculty Research Award, and an Okawa Foundation Research Grant. This material is based upon work supported by the Defense Advanced Research Projects Agency through Award HR00112020024. A. Srinivasan was supported in part by the SERB startup grant.

References

1. Applebaum, B., Brakerski, Z., Garg, S., Ishai, Y., Srinivasan, A.: Separating two-round secure computation from oblivious transfer. In: ITCS 2020. LIPIcs, vol. 151, pp. 71:1–71:18. Schloss Dagstuhl - Leibniz-Zentrum für Informatik (2020). https://doi.org/10.4230/LIPIcs.ITCS.2020.71

2. Asharov, G., Jain, A., López-Alt, A., Tromer, E., Vaikuntanathan, V., Wichs, D.: Multiparty computation with low communication, computation and interaction via threshold FHE. In: Pointcheval, D., Johansson, T. (eds.) EUROCRYPT 2012. LNCS, vol. 7237, pp. 483–501. Springer, Heidelberg (2012). https://doi.org/10.1007/978-3-642-29011-4_29

3. Beaver, D.: Correlated pseudorandomness and the complexity of private computations. In: Miller, G.L. (ed.) STOC 1996, pp. 479–488. ACM (1996). https://doi.org/10.1145/237814.237996

4. Beaver, D., Micali, S., Rogaway, P.: The round complexity of secure protocols (extended abstract). In: 22nd ACM STOC, pp. 503–513. ACM Press, Baltimore, 14–16 May 1990

5. Boyle, E., et al.: Efficient two-round OT extension and silent non-interactive secure computation. In: CCS 2019, pp. 291–308. ACM (2019). https://doi.org/10.1145/3319535.3354255

6. Boyle, E., Couteau, G., Gilboa, N., Ishai, Y., Kohl, L., Scholl, P.: Efficient pseudorandom correlation generators: silent OT extension and more. In: Boldyreva, A., Micciancio, D. (eds.) CRYPTO 2019. LNCS, vol. 11694, pp. 489–518. Springer, Cham (2019). https://doi.org/10.1007/978-3-030-26954-8_16

7. Branco, P., Döttling, N., Mateus, P.: Two-round oblivious linear evaluation from learning with errors. IACR Cryptology ePrint Archive, p. 635 (2020). https://eprint.iacr.org/2020/635

8. Brassard, G., Crépeau, C., Robert, J.M.: Information theoretic reductions among disclosure problems. In: 27th FOCS, pp. 168–173. IEEE Computer Society Press, Toronto, 27–29 October 1986

9. Canetti, R., Goldreich, O., Halevi, S.: The random oracle methodology, revisited. J. ACM **51**(4), 557–594 (2004). https://doi.org/10.1145/1008731.1008734

10. Chase, M., et al.: Reusable non-interactive secure computation. In: Boldyreva, A., Micciancio, D. (eds.) CRYPTO 2019. LNCS, vol. 11694, pp. 462–488. Springer, Cham (2019). https://doi.org/10.1007/978-3-030-26954-8_15

11. Damgård, I., Ishai, Y.: Constant-round multiparty computation using a black-box pseudorandom generator. In: Shoup, V. (ed.) CRYPTO 2005. LNCS, vol. 3621, pp. 378–394. Springer, Heidelberg (2005). https://doi.org/10.1007/11535218_23

12. Fiat, A., Shamir, A.: How to prove yourself: practical solutions to identification and signature problems. In: Odlyzko, A.M. (ed.) CRYPTO 1986. LNCS, vol. 263, pp. 186–194. Springer, Heidelberg (1987). https://doi.org/10.1007/3-540-47721-7_12

13. Friolo, D., Masny, D., Venturi, D.: A black-box construction of fully-simulatable, round-optimal oblivious transfer from strongly uniform key agreement. In: Hofheinz, D., Rosen, A. (eds.) TCC 2019. LNCS, vol. 11891, pp. 111–130. Springer, Cham (2019). https://doi.org/10.1007/978-3-030-36030-6_5

14. Garg, S., Ishai, Y., Srinivasan, A.: Two-round MPC: information-theoretic and black-box. In: Beimel, A., Dziembowski, S. (eds.) TCC 2018, Part I. LNCS, vol. 11239, pp. 123–151. Springer, Cham (2018). https://doi.org/10.1007/978-3-030-03807-6_5

15. Garg, S., Srinivasan, A.: Two-round multiparty secure computation from minimal assumptions. In: Nielsen, J.B., Rijmen, V. (eds.) EUROCRYPT 2018. LNCS, vol. 10821, pp. 468–499. Springer, Cham (2018). https://doi.org/10.1007/978-3-319-78375-8_16

16. Gennaro, R., Ishai, Y., Kushilevitz, E., Rabin, T.: On 2-round secure multiparty computation. In: Yung, M. (ed.) CRYPTO 2002. LNCS, vol. 2442, pp. 178–193. Springer, Heidelberg (2002). https://doi.org/10.1007/3-540-45708-9_12

17. Goldreich, O., Micali, S., Wigderson, A.: How to play any mental game or A completeness theorem for protocols with honest majority. In: Aho, A. (ed.) 19th ACM STOC, pp. 218–229. ACM Press, New York City, 25–27 May 1987

18. Haitner, I., Ishai, Y., Kushilevitz, E., Lindell, Y., Petrank, E.: Black-box constructions of protocols for secure computation. SIAM J. Comput. **40**(2), 225–266 (2011). https://doi.org/10.1137/100790537

19. Ishai, Y., Khurana, D., Sahai, A., Srinivasan, A.: On the round complexity of black-box secure MPC. In: Malkin, T., Peikert, C. (eds.) CRYPTO 2021. LNCS, vol. 12826, pp. 214–243. Springer, Cham (2021). https://doi.org/10.1007/978-3-030-84245-1_8

20. Ishai, Y., Kilian, J., Nissim, K., Petrank, E.: Extending oblivious transfers efficiently. In: Boneh, D. (ed.) CRYPTO 2003. LNCS, vol. 2729, pp. 145–161. Springer, Heidelberg (2003). https://doi.org/10.1007/978-3-540-45146-4_9

21. Ishai, Y., Kushilevitz, E.: Randomizing polynomials: a new representation with applications to round-efficient secure computation. In: 41st FOCS, pp. 294–304. IEEE Computer Society Press, Redondo Beach, 12–14 November 2000

22. Ishai, Y., Kushilevitz, E., Ostrovsky, R., Sahai, A.: Zero-knowledge from secure multiparty computation. In: Johnson, D.S., Feige, U. (eds.) 39th ACM STOC, pp. 21–30. ACM Press, San Diego, 11–13 June 2007

23. Ishai, Y., Kushilevitz, E., Paskin, A.: Secure multiparty computation with minimal interaction. In: Rabin, T. (ed.) CRYPTO 2010. LNCS, vol. 6223, pp. 577–594. Springer, Heidelberg (2010). https://doi.org/10.1007/978-3-642-14623-7_31

24. Ishai, Y., Prabhakaran, M., Sahai, A.: Founding cryptography on oblivious transfer – efficiently. In: Wagner, D. (ed.) CRYPTO 2008. LNCS, vol. 5157, pp. 572–591. Springer, Heidelberg (2008). https://doi.org/10.1007/978-3-540-85174-5_32

25. Lin, H., Liu, T., Wee, H.: Information-theoretic 2-round MPC without round collapsing: adaptive security, and more. In: Pass, R., Pietrzak, K. (eds.) TCC 2020. LNCS, vol. 12551, pp. 502–531. Springer, Cham (2020). https://doi.org/10.1007/978-3-030-64378-2_18

26. Masny, D., Rindal, P.: Endemic oblivious transfer. In: CCS 2019, pp. 309–326. ACM (2019). https://doi.org/10.1145/3319535.3354210

27. McQuoid, I., Rosulek, M., Roy, L.: Minimal symmetric PAKE and 1-out-of-n OT from programmable-once public functions. In: CCS 2020, pp. 425–442. ACM (2020). https://doi.org/10.1145/3372297.3417870

28. Mohassel, P., Rosulek, M.: Non-interactive Secure 2PC in the Offline/Online and Batch Settings. In: Coron, J.-S., Nielsen, J.B. (eds.) EUROCRYPT 2017. LNCS, vol. 10212, pp. 425–455. Springer, Cham (2017). https://doi.org/10.1007/978-3-319-56617-7_15

29. Ostrovsky, R., Richelson, S., Scafuro, A.: Round-optimal black-box two-party computation. In: Gennaro, R., Robshaw, M. (eds.) CRYPTO 2015, Part II. LNCS, vol. 9216, pp. 339–358. Springer, Heidelberg (2015). https://doi.org/10.1007/978-3-662-48000-7_17

30. Paskin-Cherniavsky, A.: Secure computation with minimal interaction. Ph.D. thesis, Technion (2012). http://www.cs.technion.ac.il/users/wwwb/cgi-bin/tr-get.cgi/2012/PHD/PHD-2012-16.pdf

31. Pass, R.: On deniability in the common reference string and random oracle model. In: Boneh, D. (ed.) CRYPTO 2003. LNCS, vol. 2729, pp. 316–337. Springer, Heidelberg (2003). https://doi.org/10.1007/978-3-540-45146-4_19

32. Patra, A., Srinivasan, A.: Three-round secure multiparty computation from black-box two-round oblivious transfer. In: Malkin, T., Peikert, C. (eds.) CRYPTO 2021. LNCS, vol. 12826, pp. 185–213. Springer, Cham (2021). https://doi.org/10.1007/978-3-030-84245-1_7

33. Peikert, C., Vaikuntanathan, V., Waters, B.: A framework for efficient and composable oblivious transfer. In: Wagner, D. (ed.) CRYPTO 2008. LNCS, vol. 5157, pp. 554–571. Springer, Heidelberg (2008). https://doi.org/10.1007/978-3-540-85174-5_31

34. Yao, A.C.: How to generate and exchange secrets (extended abstract). In: 27th Annual Symposium on Foundations of Computer Science, Toronto, Canada, 27–29 October 1986, pp. 162–167. IEEE Computer Society (1986). https://doi.org/10.1109/SFCS.1986.25

Guaranteed Output in $O(\sqrt{n})$ Rounds for Round-Robin Sampling Protocols

Ran Cohen[1], Jack Doerner[2]([✉]), Yashvanth Kondi[2], and Abhi Shelat[2]

[1] Reichman University, Herzliya, Israel
[2] Northeastern University, Boston, UK
j@ckdoerner.net

Abstract. We introduce a notion of *round-robin* secure sampling that captures several protocols in the literature, such as the "powers-of-tau" setup protocol for pairing-based polynomial commitments and zk-SNARKs, and certain verifiable mixnets.

Due to their round-robin structure, protocols of this class inherently require n sequential broadcast rounds, where n is the number of participants.

We describe how to compile them generically into protocols that require only $O(\sqrt{n})$ broadcast rounds. Our compiled protocols guarantee output delivery against *any* dishonest majority. This stands in contrast to prior techniques, which require $\Omega(n)$ sequential broadcasts in most cases (and sometimes many more). Our compiled protocols permit a certain amount of adversarial bias in the output, as all sampling protocols with guaranteed output must, due to Cleve's impossibility result (STOC'86). We show that in the context of the aforementioned applications, this bias is harmless.

1 Introduction

In many settings it is desirable for a secure multiparty computation (MPC) protocol to *guarantee output delivery*, meaning that regardless of the actions taken by an adversary who may corrupt up to $n-1$ parties, all honest parties always learn their outputs from the computation. This property, for example, is needed in any use of secure computation that creates a critical *public output*, such as securely sampling the setup parameters needed for a blockchain system, etc. However, the seminal result of Cleve [23] showed that unless a majority of parties are assumed to be honest, certain functions cannot be computed even with *fairness* (meaning that if the adversary learns the output then so do all honest parties).

In the two-party setting, a series of works culminated with a full characterization of all finite-domain Boolean functions that can be computed with guaranteed output delivery [2–4,35,49]. Our understanding is limited in the multiparty setting: only a handful of functions are known to be securely computable with guaranteed output delivery (e.g., the Boolean-OR and majority

---

The full version of this paper is available at https://eprint.iacr.org/2022/257.

© International Association for Cryptologic Research 2022
O. Dunkelman and S. Dziembowski (Eds.): EUROCRYPT 2022, LNCS 13275, pp. 241–271, 2022.
https://doi.org/10.1007/978-3-031-06944-4_9

functions) [25,26,36]. In fact, for $n > 3$, only Boolean OR is known to achieve guaranteed output delivery against $n - 1$ corruptions without bias.

The Boolean-OR protocol of Gordon and Katz [36] inherently requires a *linear* number of broadcast rounds relative to the party count. It extends the folklore "player-elimination technique" (originally used in the honest-majority setting [33,34]) to the dishonest-majority case by utilizing specific properties of the Boolean-OR function. In a nutshell, the n parties iteratively run a related secure computation protocol with *identifiable abort* [25,42], meaning that if the protocol aborts without output, it is possible to identify at least one dishonest party. Since the abort may be conditioned on learning the putative output, this paradigm only works if the putative output is simulatable, which is the case for Boolean OR. If the protocol aborts, the dishonest party is identified and expelled, and the remaining parties restart the computation with a default input for the cheater (0 in case of Boolean OR). Because $n - 1$ dishonest parties can force this process to repeat $n - 1$ times, the overall round complexity must be $\Omega(n)$.[1]

The $1/p$ relaxation. A closer look at Cleve's attack [23] reveals that *any r-round* coin-tossing protocol that completes with a common output bit is exposed to an inverse-polynomial bias of $\Omega(1/r)$; it is a natural line of inquiry to attempt to achieve as tight a bias in the output as possible. Unfortunately, as far as we know, this approach creates a dependence of the round complexity on the number of parties that is typically *much worse* than linear. The state of the art for coin-tossing is the work of Buchbinder et al. [16] where the bias is $\tilde{O}\big(n^3 \cdot 2^n / r^{0.5 + 1/(2^{n-1}-2)}\big)$, which improves upon prior works [5,23] for $n = O(\log \log r)$, i.e., when the number of rounds is *doubly exponential* in n (e.g., for a constant number of parties the bias translates to $O(1/r^{1/2+\Theta(1)})$).

Towards generalizing the coin-tossing results, Gordon and Katz [37] relaxed the standard MPC security definition to capture bias via $1/p$-*secure computation*, where the protocol is secure with all but inverse-polynomial probability, as opposed to all but negligible.[2] They showed feasibility for any randomized two-party functionality with a polynomial-sized range and impossibility for certain functionalities with super-polynomial-sized domains and ranges. Beimel et al. [8] extended $1/p$-secure computation to the multiparty setting and presented protocols realizing certain functionalities with polynomial-sized ranges. However, their protocols again have round counts *doubly exponential* in n and only support a constant number of parties. Specifically, if the size of the range of a function is $g(\lambda)$, then the round complexity for computing that function with $1/p$-security is $(p(\lambda) \cdot g(\lambda))^{2^{O(n)}}$.

In sum, the $1/p$-relaxation requires many more rounds and is limited to functionalities with a polynomial-sized range. Many useful tasks, such as the

---

[1] Surprisingly, if a *constant fraction* of the parties are assumed to be honest, this linear round complexity can be reduced to any super-constant function; e.g., $O(\log^* n)$ [24].

[2] Formally, there exists a polynomial p such that every attack on the "real-world" execution of the protocol can be simulated in the "ideal-world" computation such that the output of both computations cannot be distinguished in polynomial-time with more than $1/p(\lambda)$ probability.

sampling of cryptographic keys (which must be drawn from a range of super-polynomial size) cannot be achieved via this technique.

Biased-Sampling of Cryptographic Keys. Fortunately, some applications of MPC that require guaranteed output delivery can indeed tolerate quite large bias. A long line of works in the literature consider the problem of random sampling of *cryptographic objects* in which each party contributes its *own* public share in such a way that combining the public shares yields the public output, but even the joint view of $n - 1$ secret shares remains useless. Protocols that follow this pattern give a rushing adversary the ability to see the public contribution of the honest parties first, and only later choose the secrets of the corrupted parties. This approach permits the adversary to inflict a statistically large bias on the distribution of the public output (for example, forcing the output to always end in 0). However, the effect of this bias on the corresponding secret is hidden from the adversary due to the hardness of the underlying cryptographic primitive.

For some simple cryptographic objects (e.g., collectively sampling $x \cdot G^3$), there are *single-round* sampling protocols, known as *Non-Interactive Distributed Key Generation (NIDKG)* schemes [28,54]. Interestingly, a classic construction for (interactive) distributed key generation by Pedersen [51] in the honest major-ity setting was found by Gennaro et al. [31] to unintentionally permit adversarial bias, which the same authors later proved can be tolerated in a number of appli-cations [32].

For more complex cryptographic objects, the contributions of the parties can-not come in parallel. A few protocols are known in which the parties must each contribute only once, but they must contribute sequentially. We refer to these as *round-robin* protocols. Among them are the "powers-of-tau" protocol [13,39,47] and variants of Abe's verifiable mixnets [1,14], about which we will have more to say below. The round-robin approach inherently requires $\Omega(n)$ broadcast rounds.

For some cryptographic objects, the state-of-the-art sampling protocols do not guarantee output, but achieve security with identifiable abort. Multi-party RSA modulus generation [20,21] is a key example. Applying the player-elimination technique in this setting gives the adversary *rejection-sampling* capa-bilities, since the adversary can repeatedly learn the outcome of an iteration of the original protocol and then decide whether to reject it by actively cheating with a party (who is identified and eliminated), or accept it by playing honestly. An adversary that controls $n-1$ parties can reject $n-1$ candidate outputs before it must accept one. This *may* be different than inducing a plain bias, since the adversary can affect the distribution of the honest parties' contributions, but in this work we show that for certain tasks the two are the same. Regardless, the broadcast-round complexity of this approach is, again, inherently $\Omega(n)$.

To summarize, with the exception of NIDKG protocols a few specific tasks, all known techniques in the study of guaranteed output delivery with bias inherently require $\Omega(n)$ broadcast rounds. It was our initial intuition that $\Omega(n)$ rounds were

---

[3] Where G is a generator of a group of order q written in additive notation, and x is a shared secret from $\mathbb{Z}_q$.

a barrier. Our main result is overcoming this intuitive barrier for an interesting class of functionalities.

1.1   Our Contributions

Our main contribution is to develop a new technique for constructing secure computation protocols that guarantee output delivery with bias using $O(\sqrt{n})$ broadcast rounds while tolerating an arbitrary number of corruptions. Prior state-of-the-art protocols for the same tasks require n broadcast rounds. Moreover, our work stands in contrast to the folklore belief that realizing such functionalities with guaranteed output delivery *inherently* requires $\Omega(n)$ rounds.

Our technique applies to the sampling of certain cryptographic objects for which there exist *round-robin* sampling protocols, with a few additional properties. This class is nontrivial: it includes both the powers-of-tau and verifiable mixnet constructions mentioned previously. The combination of scalability in n with security against $n - 1$ corruptions is particularly important as it allows for better distribution of trust (given that there need only be a single honest party) than is possible with $\Omega(n)$-round protocols. Indeed, well-known real-world ceremonies for constructing the powers-of-tau-based setup parameters for zk-SNARK protocols involved just a few participants [10] and later one hundred participants [13]. Our aim is to develop methods that allow thousands to millions of participants to engage in such protocols, which naturally requires a sublinear round complexity.

Though our techniques are model-agnostic, we formulate all of our results in the UC model. Specifically, we construct a *compiler* for round-robin protocols, and formally incorporate the adversary's bias into our ideal functionalities, as opposed to achieving only $1/p$-security [37].

The Basic Idea. The transformation underlying our compiler uses the "player-simulation technique" that goes back to Bracha [15] and is widely used in the Byzantine agreement and MPC literature (e.g., [41,43]) as well as the "player-elimination framework" [33,34]. We partition the set of n players into $\sqrt{n}$ subsets of size $\sqrt{n}$ each, and then construct a protocol that proceeds in at most $O(\sqrt{n})$ phases, with $O(1)$ rounds per phase. The key invariant of our technique is that in each phase, either one subset is able to *make progress* towards an output (and are thus able to halt), or if no subset succeeds, then at least one player from each active subset can be identified as cheating and removed from the next phase.

Applying our technique requires two key properties of the original protocol which we group under the moniker "strongly player-replaceable round-robin." We do not know precisely what kinds of functions can be computed by such protocols, but the literature already contains several examples. This issue is not new, as prior works in the literature must also resort to describing function classes by the "presence of an embedded XOR" [35] or the "size of domain or range" [8]. In our case, the restriction is defined by the existence of an *algorithm* with certain properties that can be used to compute the function.

Motivating Protocol: Powers of Tau. Before we give a more detailed explanation of our technique, it will be useful to recall a simplified version of the *powers-of-tau* protocol of Bowe, Gabizon, and Miers [13]. Throughout, we assume synchronous communication, and a malicious adversary that can statically corrupt an arbitrary subset of the parties. The powers-of-tau protocol was designed for generating setup parameters for Groth's zk-SNARK [38]. Given an elliptic curve group $\mathbb{G}$ generated by the point G, our simplified version will output $\{\tau \cdot G, \tau^2 \cdot G, \ldots, \tau^d \cdot G\}$, where d is public and τ is secret.

The protocol's invariant is to maintain as an intermediate result a vector of the same form as the output. In each round, the previous round's vector is rerandomized by a different party. For example, if the intermediate result of the first round is a vector $\{\tau_1 \cdot G, \tau_1^2 \cdot G, \ldots, \tau_1^d \cdot G\}$, then in round two the second party samples τ_2 uniformly and broadcasts $\{\tau_1 \cdot \tau_2 \cdot G, \tau_1^2 \cdot \tau_2^2 \cdot G, \ldots, \tau_1^d \cdot \tau_2^d \cdot G\}$, which it can compute by exponentiating each element of the previous vector. It also broadcasts a zero-knowledge proof that it knows the discrete logarithm of each element with respect to the corresponding element of the previous vector, and that the elements are related in the correct way.

It is not hard to see that a malicious party can bias the output, as Cleve's impossibility requires, and variants of this protocol have attempted to reduce the bias by forcing parties to speak twice [10,12], using "random beacons" as an external source of entropy [13], or considering restricted forms of *algebraic adversaries* [29,47] in the random oracle model.

Round-Robin Sampling Protocols. The powers-of-tau protocol has a simple structure shared by other (seemingly unrelated) protocols [1,14], which we now attempt to abstract. First, observe that it proceeds in a round-robin fashion, where in every round a single party speaks over a broadcast channel, and the order in which the parties speak can be arbitrary. Furthermore, the message that each party sends depends only on public information (such as the transcript of the protocol so far, or public setup such as a common random string) and freshly-tossed private random coins known only to the sending party. The next-message function does not depend on private-coin setup such as a PKI, or on previously-tossed coins. *Strongly player-replaceable round-robin protocols—* the kind supported by our compiler—share these properties.

Next, we generalize this protocol-structure to arbitrary domains. We denote the "public-values" domain by $\mathbb{V}$ (corresponding to $\mathbb{G}^d$ in our simplified example) and the "secret-values" domain by $\mathbb{W}$ (corresponding to $\mathbb{Z}_q$). Consider an *update function* $f : \mathbb{V} \times \mathbb{W} \to \mathbb{V}$ (corresponding to the second party's "rerandomization" function, *sans proofs*) and denote by $\pi_{RRSample}(f, n, u)$ the corresponding n-party round-robin protocol for some common public input value $u \in \mathbb{V}$ (corresponding to, e.g., $\{G, \ldots, G\}$). In addition to the basic powers-of-tau protocol and its variants [13,39,47], this abstraction captures an additional interesting protocol from the literature: verifiable mixnets [14], where the parties hold a vector of ciphertexts and need to sample a random permutation.

Generalizing to Pre-transformation Functionality. Having defined the class of protocols, we specify a corresponding ideal functionality that these protocols realize in order to apply our compiler. This "pre-transformation functionality" is rather simple and captures the inherent bias that can be induced by the adversary. Specifically, the functionality starts with the common public input u, and then samples a uniform secret value $w \in \mathbb{W}$ and updates u with w to yield a new public (intermediate) value $v := f(u, w)$. The functionality shows v to the adversary, and allows the adversary free choice of a bias value $x \in \mathbb{W}$ with which it updates v to yield the final output $y := f(v, x)$. For the specific case of powers-of-tau, this corresponds to an honest party picking a secret τ_1 and broadcasting $\{\tau_1 \cdot G, \tau_1^2 \cdot G, \ldots, \tau_1^d \cdot G\}$, and then the *adversary* choosing τ_2 (conditioned on the honest party's output) and broadcasting $\{\tau_1 \cdot \tau_2 \cdot G, \tau_1^2 \cdot \tau_2^2 \cdot G, \ldots, \tau_1^d \cdot \tau_2^d \cdot G\}$.

For update function $f : \mathbb{V} \times \mathbb{W} \to \mathbb{V}$ and common public input $u \in \mathbb{V}$, we denote by $\mathcal{F}_{PreTrans}(f, n, u)$ the n-party variant of the pre-transformation functionality. Proving that the round-robin protocol realizes this functionality boils down to realizing the a zero-knowledge proof that f has been correctly applied. We prove the following theorem:

Theorem 1.1 (Pre-Transformation Security, Informal). Let $n \in \mathbb{N}$, let $f : \mathbb{V} \times \mathbb{W} \to \mathbb{V}$ be an update function, and let $u \in \mathbb{V}$. Under these conditions, $\pi_{RRSample}(f, n, u)$ realizes $\mathcal{F}_{PreTrans}(f, n, u)$ in the $\mathcal{F}_{\mathsf{NIZK}}$-hybrid model within n broadcast rounds.

Theorem 1.1 gives the first *modular* analysis in the simulation paradigm of (a version of) the powers-of-tau protocol; this is opposed to other security analyses (e.g., [13,47]) that give a monolithic security proof and explicitly avoid simulation-based techniques. On one hand, the modular approach allows the use of the powers-of-tau protocol to generate setup for other compatible constructions that otherwise rely on a trusted party, such as polynomial commitments [44]. On the other hand, different instantiations of $\mathcal{F}_{\mathsf{NIZK}}$ give different security guarantees for the protocol: a universally composable (UC) NIZK in the CRS model yields a corresponding UC-secure protocol, a random-oracle-based NIZK yields security in the random-oracle model, and a knowledge-of-exponent-based NIZK yields stand-alone, non-black-box security in the plain model.

Round-Reducing Compiler. Let us now return to our main conceptual contribution: a compiler that reduces the round complexity of the round-robin protocols described above from n broadcast rounds to $O(\sqrt{n})$.

Let $f : \mathbb{V} \times \mathbb{W} \to \mathbb{V}$ be an update function and $u \in \mathbb{V}$ a common public input as before, and let $m < n$ be integers (without loss of generality, consider n to be an exact multiple of m). Given an m-party protocol $\pi_{RRSample}(f, m, u)$ executed in m rounds by parties $\mathcal{Q}_1, \ldots, \mathcal{Q}_m$ (who speak sequentially), let $\mathbf{g}_j$ be the next-message function of $\mathcal{Q}_j$. The compiled protocol $\pi_{Compiler}(\pi_{RRSample}(f, m, u), n, u, m)$ will be executed by n parties $\mathcal{P}_1, \ldots, \mathcal{P}_n$.

The compiled protocol will organize its parties into m committees, and each committee will execute a (n/m)-party MPC protocol in order to *jointly* evaluate the next-message functions of parties in the original protocol. For ease of exposition, we will say that each committee in this new protocol acts as a *virtual party* in the original, which proceeds in virtual rounds. The MPC protocol must be secure with *identifiable abort* [25,42] against any number of corruptions; that is, either all honest parties obtain their outputs or they all identify at least one cheating party.

Furthermore the MPC must provide *public verifiability* [6,53] in the sense that every party that is *not* in a particular committee must also learn that committee's output (or the identities of cheating parties), and be assured that the output is well-formed (i.e., compatible with the transcript, for some set of coins) even if the entire committee is corrupted. This is similar to the notions of *publicly identifiable abort* [46] and *restricted identifiable abort* [24].

In the ith round, *all* of the committees will attempt to emulate the party $\mathcal{Q}_i$ of the original protocol, in parallel. If a party is identified as a cheater at any point, it is excluded from the rest of the computation. At the conclusion of all MPC protocols for the first round, one of two things must occur: either all committees aborted, in which case at least m cheating parties are excluded, and each committee re-executes the MPC protocol with the remaining parties, or else at least one committee completed with an output. In the latter case, let j be the minimal committee-index from those that generated output, and denote the output of committee j by $\mathbf{a}_i$. Next, all committees (except for committee j, which disbands) proceed as if the virtual party $\mathcal{Q}_i$ had broadcasted $\mathbf{a}_i$ in the ith round, and continue in a similar way to emulate party $\mathcal{Q}_{i+1}$ in round $i+1$. Note that at a certain point all remaining committees may be fully corrupted, and cease sending messages. This corresponds to the remaining virtual parties being corrupted and mute in the virtual protocol; in this case all of the remaining committee members are identified as cheaters. The compiled protocol proceeds in this way until the virtualized copy of $\pi_{RRSample}(f, m, u)$ is complete.

If the generic MPC protocol that underlies each virtual party requires constant rounds, then the entire protocol completes in $O(m + n/m)$ rounds, and if we set $m = \sqrt{n}$, we achieve a round complexity of $O(\sqrt{n})$, as desired. So long as there is at least one honest party, one virtual party is guaranteed to produce an output at some point during this time, which means that the compiled protocol has the same output delivery guarantee as the original.

Post-Transformation Functionality. Although the compiled protocol $\pi_{Compiler}(\pi_{RRSample}(f, m, u), n, u, m)$ emulates the original $\pi_{RRSample}(f, m, u)$ in some sense, it does not necessarily realize $\mathcal{F}_{PreTrans}(f, m, u)$ as the original protocol does, because the adversary has additional rejection-sampling capabilities that allow for additional bias. We therefore specify a second ideal functionality $\mathcal{F}_{PostTrans}(f, n, u, r)$, where r is a bound on the number of rejections the adversary is permitted; setting this bound to 0 coincides with $\mathcal{F}_{PreTrans}(f, n, u)$.

As in $\mathcal{F}_{PreTrans}(f, n, u)$, the functionality begins by sampling $w \leftarrow \mathbb{W}$, computing $v = f(u, w)$ and sending v to the adversary, who can either accept or reject. If the adversary accepts then it returns $x \in \mathbb{W}$ and the functionality outputs $y = f(v, x)$ to everyone; if the adversary rejects, then the functionality samples another $w \leftarrow \mathbb{W}$, computes $v = f(u, w)$, and sends v to the adversary, who can again either accept or reject. The functionality and the adversary proceed like this for up to r iterations, or until the adversary accepts some value.

Theorem 1.2 (Post-Transformation Security, Informal). Let $m < n$ be integers and let $f : \mathbb{V} \times \mathbb{W} \to \mathbb{V}$ and $u \in \mathbb{V}$ be as above. Assume that $\pi_{RRSample}(f, m, u)$ realizes $\mathcal{F}_{PreTrans}(f, m, u)$ using a suitable NIZK protocol within m broadcast rounds, and that the next-message functions of $\pi_{RRSample}(f, m, u)$ can be securely computed with identifiable abort and public verifiability in a constant-number of rounds. Let $r = m + \lceil n/m \rceil$. Under these conditions, $\pi_{Compiler}(\pi_{RRSample}(f, m, u), n, u, m)$ realizes $\mathcal{F}_{PostTrans}(f, n, u, r)$ within $O(r)$ broadcast rounds.

Although $\pi_{Compiler}(\pi_{RRSample}(f, m, u), n, u, m)$ does not necessarily realize $\mathcal{F}_{PreTrans}(f, m, u)$ for every f, we show that it somewhat-unexpectedly does if the update function f satisfies certain properties. Furthermore, we show that these properties are met in the cases of powers-of-tau and mixnets.

Theorem 1.3 (Equivalence of Pre- and Post-Transformation Security, Informal). Let $n, r \in \mathbb{N}$, let $f : \mathbb{V} \times \mathbb{W} \to \mathbb{V}$ be a *homomorphic* update function, and let $u \in \mathbb{V}$ be a common public input. If a protocol π realizes $\mathcal{F}_{PostTrans}(f, n, u, r)$ then π also realizes $\mathcal{F}_{PreTrans}(f, n, u)$.

Powers of Tau and Polynomial Commitments. A polynomial-commitment scheme enables one to commit to a polynomial of some bounded degree d, and later open evaluations of the polynomial. The pairing-based scheme of Kate et al. [44] requires trusted setup of the form $\{G, \tau \cdot G, \tau^2 \cdot G, \ldots, \tau^d \cdot G\} \in \mathbb{G}^{d+1}$, for some elliptic curve group $\mathbb{G}$. The security of the scheme reduces to the d-strong Diffie-Hellman assumption (d-SDH) [11]. We show that if the setup is not sampled by a trusted party, but instead computed (with bias) by our protocol (either the round-robin or compiled variation), there is essentially no security loss.

Theorem 1.4 (Generating Setup for SDH, Informal). If there exists a PPT adversary that can break a d-SDH challenge generated by an instance of our protocol in which it has corrupted $n-1$ parties, then there exists a PPT adversary that can win the standard (unbiased) d-SDH game with the same probability.

SNARKs with Updateable Setup. Several recent Succinct Non-interactive Arguments (zk-SNARKs) have featured *updatable* trusted setup, and have security proofs that hold so long as at least one honest party has participated in the update process [22,30,39,50]. Since their proofs already account for adversarial bias and the form of their trusted setup derives from the setup of Kate et al. [44], our protocols can be employed for an asymptotic improvement upon the best previously known update procedure.

Verifiable Mixnets. A verifiable mixnet is a multiparty protocol by which a group of parties can shuffle a set of encrypted inputs, with the guarantee that no corrupt subset of the parties can learn the permutation that was applied or prevent the output from being delivered, and the property that non-participating observers can be convinced that the shuffle was computed correctly. Prior constructions, such as the work of Boyle et al. [14], involve random shuffling and re-encryption in a round-robin fashion, and their security proofs already consider bias of exactly the sort our protocol permits. Thus, it is natural to apply our compiler, yielding the first verifiable mixnet that requires sublinear broadcast rounds.

Concrete Efficiency. While our primary goal in this work is optimizing round complexity, a round-efficient protocol is not useful in practice if it has unfeasibly high (but polynomially bounded) communication or computation complexity. As evidence of the practicality of our technique, the full version of this paper will include an additional, non-generic construction that specifically computes the powers-of-tau, and an analysis of its concrete costs. We give a summary of this additional result in Sect. 5.

2   Preliminaries

Notation. We use $=$ for equality, $:=$ for assignment, $\leftarrow$ for sampling from a distribution, $\equiv$ for distributional equivalence, $\approx_c$ for computational indistinguishability, and $\approx_s$ for statistical indistinguishability. In general, single-letter variables are set in *italic* font, function names are set in sans-serif font, and string literals are set in slab-serif font. We use $\mathbb{V}$, $\mathbb{W}$, $\mathbb{X}$, and $\mathbb{Y}$ for unspecified domains, but we use $\mathbb{G}$ for a group, $\mathbb{F}$ for a field, $\mathbb{Z}$ for the integers, $\mathbb{N}$ for the natural numbers, and Σ_d for the permutations over d elements. We use λ to denote the computational security parameter.

Vectors and arrays are given in bold and indexed by subscripts; thus $\mathbf{a}_i$ is the ith element of the vector $\mathbf{a}$, which is distinct from the scalar variable a. When we wish to select a row or column from a multi-dimensional array, we place a $*$ in the dimension along which we are not selecting. Thus $\mathbf{b}_{*,j}$ is the jth column of matrix $\mathbf{b}$, $\mathbf{b}_{j,*}$ is the jth row, and $\mathbf{b}_{*,*} = \mathbf{b}$ refers to the entire matrix. We use bracket notation to generate inclusive ranges, so $[n]$ denotes the integers from 1 to n and $[5,7] = \{5,6,7\}$. On rare occasions, we may use one vector to index another: if $\mathbf{a} := [2,7]$ and $\mathbf{b} := \{1,3,4\}$, then $\mathbf{a}_{\mathbf{b}} = \{2,4,5\}$. We use $|x|$ to denote the bit-length of x, and $|\mathbf{y}|$ to denote the number of elements in the vector $\mathbf{y}$. We use $\mathcal{P}_i$ to indicate an actively participating party with index i; in a typical context, there will be a fixed set of active participants denoted $\mathcal{P}_1, \ldots, \mathcal{P}_n$. A party that observes passively but remains silent is denoted $\mathcal{V}$.

For convenience, we define a function GenSID, which takes *any* number of arguments and deterministically derives a unique Session ID from them. For example GenSID(sid, x, x) derives a Session ID from the variables sid and x, and the string literal "x."

Universal Composability, Synchrony, Broadcast, and Guaranteed Output Delivery. We consider a malicious PPT adversary who can statically corrupt any subset of parties in a protocol, and require all of our constructions to guarantee output delivery. Guaranteed output delivery is traditionally defined in the *stand-alone model* (e.g., [25]) and *cannot* be captured in the inherently asynchronous UC framework [17]. For concreteness, we will consider the synchronous UC modeling of Katz et al. [45], which captures guaranteed termination in UC, but for clarity we will use standard UC notation. We note that our techniques do not rely on any specific properties of the model, and can be captured in any composable framework that supports synchrony, e.g., those of Liu-Zhang and Maurer [48] or Baum et al. [7].

In terms of communication, we consider all messages to be sent over an authenticated broadcast channel, sometimes denoted by $\mathcal{F}_{BC}$, and do not consider any point-to-point communication. This is standard for robust MPC protocols in the dishonest-majority setting. Our protocols proceed in rounds, where all parties receive the messages sent in round $i - 1$ before anyone sends a message for round i.

3   A Round-Reducing Compiler

The main result of our paper is a round-reducing compiler for round-robin sampling protocols. To be specific, our compiler requires three conditions on any protocol ρ that it takes as input: ρ must have a *broadcast-only round-robin structure*, it must be *strongly player-replaceable*, and it must UC-realize a specific functionality $\mathcal{F}_{PreTrans}(f, \cdot, \cdot)$ for some function f. We define each of these conditions in turn, before describing the compiler itself in Sect. 3.1.

Definition 3.1 (Broadcast-Only Round-Robin Protocol). A protocol has a *broadcast-only round-robin structure* if the parties in the protocol send exactly one message each in a predetermined order, via an authenticated broadcast channel. We often refer to such protocols simply as *round-robin* protocols.

Definition 3.2 (Strong Player-Replaceability). A protocol is *strongly player-replaceable* if no party has any secret inputs or keeps any secret state. That is, the next-message functions in a *strongly player-replaceable* protocol may take as input only public values and a random tape.

Remark 3.3 (Strongly Player-Replaceable Round-Robin Protocols). If a protocol $\rho(n, u)$ for n parties with some common input $u \in \mathbb{V}$ conforms to Definitions 3.1 and 3.2, then it can be represented as a vector of functions $\mathbf{g}_1, \ldots, \mathbf{g}_{n+1}$ such that $\mathbf{g}_i$ for $i \in [n]$ is the next-message function of the ith party. $\mathbf{g}_1$ takes $u \in \mathbb{V}$ and a vector of η uniform coins for some $\eta \in \mathbb{N}$ as input, and each succeeding function $\mathbf{g}_i$ for $i \in [2, n]$ takes u concatenated with the outputs of all previous functions in the sequence, plus η additional uniform coins. The last function, $\mathbf{g}_{m+1}$, does not take any coins, and can be run locally by anyone to extract the protocol's output from its transcript. We refer to protocols that meet these criteria as SPRRR *protocols* hereafter.

Note that Definition 3.2 is somewhat more restrictive than the (non-strong) player-replaceability property defined by Chen and Micali [19]. Their definition forbids secret state but allows players to use some kinds of secret inputs (in particular, secret signature keys) in the next-message function, so long as every player is capable of computing the next message for any given round. We forbid such secret inputs, giving parties only an ideal authenticated broadcast channel by which to distinguish themselves from one another.

Finally, we define the biased sampling functionality that any input protocol ρ is required to realize. This functionality is parameterized by a function f which takes an input value from some space (denoted $\mathbb{V}$) and a randomization witness (from some space $\mathbb{W}$) and produces an output value (again in $\mathbb{V}$) deterministically. The functionality models sampling with adversarial bias by selecting a randomization witness w from $\mathbb{W}$ uniformly, rerandomizing the input value using w, and then providing the resulting intermediate v to the adversary, who can select a second (arbitrarily biased) randomization witness x from $\mathbb{W}$ to apply to v using f, in order to produce the functionality's output y. Note that the *only* requirement on f is that it has the same input and output domains, so that it can be applied repeatedly. It is not required to have any other properties (such as, for example, one-wayness).

Functionality 3.4. $\mathcal{F}_{PreTrans}(f, n, u)$. **Biased Sampling**

This functionality interacts with n actively participating parties denoted by $\mathcal{P}_1 \ldots \mathcal{P}_n$ and with the ideal adversary $\mathcal{S}$. It is also parameterized by an update function $f : \mathbb{V} \times \mathbb{W} \to \mathbb{V}$ and an arbitrary value $u \in \mathbb{V}$.

Sampling: On receiving (sample, sid) from at least one $\mathcal{P}_i$ for $i \in [n]$,

1. If a record of the form (unbiased, sid, $*$) exists in memory, then ignore this message. Otherwise, continue with steps 2 and 3.
2. Sample $w \leftarrow \mathbb{W}$ and compute $v := f(u, w)$.
3. Store (unbiased, sid, v) in memory and send (unbiased, sid, v) to $\mathcal{S}$.

Bias: On receiving (proceed, sid, x) from $\mathcal{S}$, where $x \in \mathbb{W}$,

4. If the record (done, sid) exists in memory, or if the record (unbiased, sid, v) does not exist in memory, then ignore this message. Otherwise, continue with steps 5 and 6.
5. Compute $y := f(v, x)$.
6. Store (done, sid) in memory and broadcast (output, sid, y) to all parties.

Note that this functionality never allows an abort or adversarially delayed output to occur, and thus it has guaranteed output delivery.[4] Now that all of the constraints on input protocols for our compiler are specified, and we can introduce a second functionality, which will be UC-realized by the compiled protocol, given a constraint-compliant input protocol. This second functionality is similar to $\mathcal{F}_{PreTrans}$ and likewise has guaranteed output delivery, but it takes an additional parameter r, and allows the adversary to reject up to r potential honest randomizations before it supplies its bias and the output is delivered.

Functionality 3.5. $\mathcal{F}_{PostTrans}(f, n, u, r)$. Rejection Sampling

This functionality interacts with n actively participating parties denoted by $\mathcal{P}_1 \ldots \mathcal{P}_n$ and with the ideal adversary $\mathcal{S}$. It is also parameterized by an update function $f : \mathbb{V} \times \mathbb{W} \to \mathbb{V}$, an arbitrary value $u \in \mathbb{V}$, and a rejection bound $r \in \mathbb{N}$.

Sampling: On receiving (sample, sid) from at least one $\mathcal{P}_i$ for $i \in [n]$,

1. If a record of the form (candidate, sid, $*$, $*$) exists in memory, then ignore this message. Otherwise, continue with steps 2 and 3.
2. Sample $\mathbf{w}_1 \leftarrow \mathbb{W}$ and compute $\mathbf{v}_1 := f(u, \mathbf{w}_1)$.
3. Store (candidate, sid, 1, $\mathbf{v}_1$) in memory and send the same tuple to $\mathcal{S}$.

Rejection: On receiving (reject, sid, i) from $\mathcal{S}$, where $i \in \mathbb{N}$,

4. If $i > r$, or if either of the records (done, sid) or (candidate, sid, $i + 1, \mathbf{v}_{i+1}$) exists in memory, or if the record (candidate, sid, $i, \mathbf{v}_i$) does not exist in memory, then ignore this message. Otherwise, continue with steps 5 and 6.
5. Sample $\mathbf{w}_{i+1} \leftarrow \mathbb{W}$ and compute $\mathbf{v}_{i+1} := f(u, \mathbf{w}_{i+1})$.
6. Store (candidate, sid, $i + 1, \mathbf{v}_{i+1}$) in memory and send the same tuple to $\mathcal{S}$.

Bias: On receiving (accept, sid, i, x) from $\mathcal{S}$, where $i \in \mathbb{N}$ and $x \in \mathbb{W}$,

7. If either of the records (done, sid) or (candidate, sid, $i + 1, \mathbf{v}_{i+1}$) exists in memory, or if the record (candidate, sid, $i, \mathbf{v}_i$) does not exist in memory, then ignore the message. Otherwise, continue with steps 8 and 9.
8. Compute $y := f(\mathbf{v}_i, x)$.
9. Store (done, sid) in memory and broadcast (output, sid, y) to all parties.

Finally, we must discuss the property of public verifiability. We model public verifiability as an abstract modifier for other functionalities. The parties interacting with any particular session of an unmodified functionality become the *active*

---

[4] Formally, every party requests the output from the functionality, and the adversary can instruct the functionality to ignore a polynomially-bounded number of such requests [45].

participants in the modified functionality, but there may be additional parties, known as *observing verifiers*, who may register to receive outputs (potentially unbeknownst to the active participants) but do not influence the functionality in any other way. This corresponds to the protocol property whereby a protocol instance can be verified as having been run correctly by third parties who have access to only a transcript (obtained, for example, by monitoring broadcasts).

Functionality 3.6. $[\![\mathcal{F}]\!]_{\mathsf{PV}}$. **Public Verifiability for** $\mathcal{F}$

The functionality $[\![\mathcal{F}]\!]_{\mathsf{PV}}$ is identical to the functionality $\mathcal{F}$, except that it interacts with an arbitrary number of additional *observing verification parties* (all of them denoted by $\mathcal{V}$, as distinct from the *actively participating parties* $\mathcal{P}_1$, $\mathcal{P}_2$, etc.). Furthermore, if *all* actively participating parties are corrupt, then $[\![\mathcal{F}]\!]_{\mathsf{PV}}$ receives its random coins from the adversary $\mathcal{S}$.

Coin Retrieval: Whenever the code of $\mathcal{F}$ requires a random value to be sampled from the domain $\mathbb{X}$, then sample as $\mathcal{F}$ would if at least one of the active participants is honest. If all active participants are corrupt, then send $(\texttt{need-coin}, \mathsf{sid}, \mathbb{X})$ to $\mathcal{S}$, and upon receiving $(\texttt{coin}, \mathsf{sid}, x)$ such that $x \in \mathbb{X}$ in response, continue behaving as $\mathcal{F}$, using x as the required random value.

Observer Registration: Upon receiving $(\texttt{observe}, \mathsf{sid})$ from $\mathcal{V}$, remember the identity of $\mathcal{V}$, and if any message with the same sid is broadcasted to all active participants in the future, then send it to $\mathcal{V}$ as well.

In the introduction, we have omitted discussion of public verifiability for the sake of simplicity and clarity, but in fact, all known input protocols for our compiler have this property (that is, they UC-realize $[\![\mathcal{F}_{PreTrans}]\!]_{\mathsf{PV}}$, which is strictly stronger than $\mathcal{F}_{PreTrans}$). Furthermore, we will show that given an input protocol that realizes $[\![\mathcal{F}_{PreTrans}]\!]_{\mathsf{PV}}$, the compiled protocol realizes $[\![\mathcal{F}_{PostTrans}]\!]_{\mathsf{PV}}$.

Note that when proving that a protocol realizes a functionality with public verifiability, we do not typically need to reason about security against malicious observing verifiers, since honest parties ignore any messages they send, and therefore there can be nothing in their view that the adversary cannot already obtain by monitoring the relevant broadcast channel directly.

3.1   The Compiler

We now turn our attention to the compiler itself. We direct the reader to Sect. 1.1 for an intuitive view of the compiler, via virtual parties and virtual rounds. With this intuitive transformation in mind, we now present a compiler which formalizes it and addresses the unmentioned corner cases. The compiler takes the form of a multiparty protocol $\pi_{Compiler}(\rho, n, u, m)$ that is parameterized by a description of the original protocol ρ for m parties, and by the number of real, active participants n, the public input u for the original protocol, and the number of committees (i.e., virtual parties) m. Before describing $\pi_{Compiler}$, we must formalize the tool that each committee uses to emulate a virtual party. We do this via a UC functionality for generic MPC with identifiable abort.

Functionality 3.7. $\mathcal{F}_{SFE\text{-}IA}(f, n)$. SFE with Identifiable Abort [42]

This functionality interacts with n actively participating parties denoted by $\mathcal{P}_1 \ldots \mathcal{P}_n$ and with the ideal adversary $\mathcal{S}$. It is also parameterized by a function, $f : \mathbb{X}_1 \times \ldots \times \mathbb{X}_n \to \mathbb{Y}$.

SFE: On receiving $(\texttt{compute}, \mathsf{sid}, \mathbf{x}_i)$ where $x_i \in \mathbb{X}_i$ from every party $\mathcal{P}_i$ for $i \in [n]$,

1. Compute $y := f\left(\{\mathbf{x}_i\}_{i \in [n]}\right)$.
2. Send $(\texttt{candidate-output}, \mathsf{sid}, y)$ to $\mathcal{S}$, and receive $(\texttt{stooge}, \mathsf{sid}, c)$ in response.
3. If c is the index of a corrupt party, then broadcast $(\texttt{abort}, \mathsf{sid}, c)$ to all parties. Otherwise, broadcast $(\texttt{output}, \mathsf{sid}, y)$ to all parties.

In order to ensure that every party can identify the cheaters in committees that it is not a member of, we must apply $[\![\cdot]\!]_{\mathsf{PV}}$ to $\mathcal{F}_{SFE\text{-}IA}$, which gives us *publicly verifiable identifiable abort*. We discuss a method for realizing this functionality in Sect. 3.2; see Lemma 3.12 for more details. We can now give a formal description of our compiler.

Protocol 3.8. $\pi_{Compiler}(\rho, n, u, m)$. Round-reducing Compiler

This compiler is parameterized by ρ, which is a player-replaceable round-robin protocol with two parameters: the number of participants, which may be hardcoded as m, and a common public input value from the domain $\mathbb{V}$. Let $\mathbf{g}_1, \ldots, \mathbf{g}_{m+1}$ be the vector of functions corresponding to ρ as described in Remark 3.3, and let η be the number of coins that the first m functions require. The compiler is also parameterized by the party count $n \in \mathbb{N}^+$, the common public input $u \in \mathbb{V}$, and the committee count $m \in \mathbb{N}^+$ such that $m \le n$. In addition to the actively participating parties $\mathcal{P}_\ell$ for $\ell \in [n]$, the protocol involves the ideal functionality $[\![\mathcal{F}_{SFE\text{-}IA}]\!]_{\mathsf{PV}}$, and it may involve one or more observing verifiers, denoted by $\mathcal{V}$.

Sampling: Let $\mathbf{a}_0 := u$ and let $\mathbf{C}_{1,*,*}$ be a deterministic partitioning of $[n]$ into m balanced subsets. That is, for $i \in [m]$, let $\mathbf{C}_{1,i,*}$ be a vector indexing the parties in the ith committee. Upon receiving $(\texttt{sample}, \mathsf{sid})$ from the environment $\mathcal{Z}$, each party repeats the following sequence of steps, starting with $k := 1$ and $\mathbf{j}_1 := 1$, incrementing k with each loop, and terminating the loop when $\mathbf{j}_k > m$

1. For all $i \in [m]$ (in parallel) each party $\mathcal{P}_\ell$ for $\ell \in \mathbf{C}_{k,i,*}$ samples $\omega_\ell \leftarrow \{0,1\}^\eta$ and sends $(\texttt{compute}, \mathsf{GenSID}(\mathsf{sid}, k, i), \omega_\ell)$ to

$\llbracket \mathcal{F}_{SFE\text{-}IA}(\gamma_{\mathbf{j}_k}, |\mathbf{C}_{k,i,*}|) \rrbracket_{\mathsf{PV}}$, where $\gamma_{\mathbf{j}_k}$ is a function such that

$$\gamma_{\mathbf{j}_k}\left(\{\omega_\ell\}_{\ell \in \mathbf{C}_{k,i,*}}\right) \mapsto \mathbf{g}_{\mathbf{j}_k}\left(\mathbf{a}_{[0,\mathbf{j}_k]}, \bigoplus_{\ell \in \mathbf{C}_{k,i,*}} \omega_\ell\right)$$

2. For all $i \in [m]$ (in parallel) each party $\mathcal{P}_\ell$ for $\ell \in [n] \setminus \mathbf{C}_{k,i,*}$ sends (observe, GenSID(sid, k, i)) to $\llbracket \mathcal{F}_{SFE\text{-}IA}(\gamma_{\mathbf{j}_k}, |\mathbf{C}_{k,i,*}|) \rrbracket_{\mathsf{PV}}$ (thereby taking the role of verifier).

3. For all $i \in [m]$, all parties receive either (abort, GenSID(sid, k, i), $\mathbf{c}_{k,i}$) or (output, GenSID(sid, k, i), $\hat{\mathbf{a}}_{k,i}$) from $\llbracket \mathcal{F}_{SFE\text{-}IA}(\gamma_{\mathbf{j}_k}, |\mathbf{C}_{k,i,*}|) \rrbracket_{\mathsf{PV}}$. In the latter case, let $\mathbf{c}_{k,i} := \bot$.

4. If any outputs were produced in the previous step, then let ℓ be the smallest integer such that (output, GenSID(sid, k, ℓ), $\hat{\mathbf{a}}_{k,\ell}$) was received. Let $\mathbf{j}_{k+1} := \mathbf{j}_k + 1$ and let $\mathbf{a}_{\mathbf{j}_{k+1}} := \hat{\mathbf{a}}_{k,\ell}$ and for every $i \in [m]$ let

$$\mathbf{C}_{k+1,i,*} := \begin{cases} \mathbf{C}_{k,i,*} \setminus \{\mathbf{c}_{k,i}\} & \text{if } i \neq \ell \\ \varnothing & \text{if } i = \ell \end{cases}$$

5. If no outputs were produced in Step 3, then let $\mathbf{j}_{k+1} := \mathbf{j}_k$ and for every $i \in [m]$ let

$$\mathbf{C}_{k+1,i,*} := \mathbf{C}_{k,i,*} \setminus \{\mathbf{c}_{k,i}\}$$

Finally, each party outputs (output, sid, $\mathbf{g}_{m+1}(\mathbf{a}_m)$) to the environment when the loop terminates.

Verification: If there is an observing verifier $\mathcal{V}$, then upon receiving (observe, sid) from the environment $\mathcal{Z}$, it repeats the following sequence of steps, starting with $k := 1$ and $\mathbf{j}_1 := 1$, incrementing k with each loop, and terminating the loop when $\mathbf{j}_k > m$.

6. $\mathcal{V}$ sends (observe, GenSID(sid, k, i)) to $\llbracket \mathcal{F}_{SFE\text{-}IA}(\gamma_{\mathbf{j}_k}, |\mathbf{C}_{k,i,*}|) \rrbracket_{\mathsf{PV}}$ for all $i \in [m]$, and receives either (abort, GenSID(sid, k, i), $\mathbf{c}_{k,i}$) or (output, GenSID(sid, k, i), $\hat{\mathbf{a}}_{k,i}$) in response.

7. $\mathcal{V}$ determines the value of $\mathbf{j}_{k+1}$ and $\mathbf{C}_{k+1,*,*}$ per the method in Steps 4 and 5.

Finally, $\mathcal{V}$ outputs (output, sid, $\mathbf{g}_{m+1}(\mathbf{a}_m)$) to the environment when the loop terminates.

3.2   Proof of Security

In this section we provide security and efficiency proofs for our compiler. Our main security theorem (Theorem 3.9) is split into two sub-cases: the case that there is at least one honest active participant is addressed by Lemma 3.10, and the case that there are no honest active participants (but there is one or more honest observing verifiers) is addressed by Lemma 3.11. After this, we give a folklore method for realizing $[\![\mathcal{F}_{SFE\text{-}IA}]\!]_{\mathsf{PV}}$ in Lemma 3.12, and use it to prove our main efficiency result in Corollary 3.13.

Theorem 3.9. *Let* $f : \mathbb{V} \times \mathbb{W} \to \mathbb{V}$ *be an update function, let* $u \in \mathbb{V}$, *let* $m \in \mathbb{N}^+$, *and let* ρ *be an SPRRR protocol such that* $\rho(m, u)$ *UC-realizes* $[\![\mathcal{F}_{PreTrans}(f, m, u)]\!]_{\mathsf{PV}}$ *in the presence of a malicious adversary statically corrupting any number of actively participating parties. For every integer* $n \geq m$, *it holds that* $\pi_{Compiler}(\rho, n, u, m)$ *UC-realizes* $[\![\mathcal{F}_{PostTrans}(f, n, u, m + n/m)]\!]_{\mathsf{PV}}$ *in the presence of a malicious adversary statically corrupting any number of actively participating parties in the* $[\![\mathcal{F}_{SFE\text{-}IA}]\!]_{\mathsf{PV}}$-*hybrid model.*

Proof. By conjunction of Lemmas 3.10 and 3.11. Since corruptions are static, a single simulator can be constructed that follows the code of either $\mathcal{S}_{\mathsf{Compiler}}$ or $\mathcal{S}_{\mathsf{CompilerPV}}$ depending on the number of active participants corrupted by the real-world adversary $\mathcal{A}$. □

Lemma 3.10. *Let* $f : \mathbb{V} \times \mathbb{W} \to \mathbb{V}$ *be an update function, let* $u \in \mathbb{V}$, *let* $m \in \mathbb{N}^+$, *and let* ρ *be an SPRRR protocol such that* $\rho(m, u)$ *UC-realizes* $[\![\mathcal{F}_{PreTrans}(f, m, u)]\!]_{\mathsf{PV}}$ *in the presence of a malicious adversary statically corrupting up to* $m - 1$ *actively participating parties. For every integer* $n \geq m$, *it holds that* $\pi_{Compiler}(\rho, n, u, m)$ *UC-realizes* $[\![\mathcal{F}_{PostTrans}(f, n, u, m + n/m)]\!]_{\mathsf{PV}}$ *in the presence of a malicious adversary statically corrupting up to* $n - 1$ *actively participating parties in the* $[\![\mathcal{F}_{SFE\text{-}IA}]\!]_{\mathsf{PV}}$-*hybrid model.*

Note that the above lemma also holds if the $[\![\cdot]\!]_{\mathsf{PV}}$ modifier is removed from *both* functionalities. This is straightforward to see, given the proof of the lemma as written, so we elide further detail. Regardless, because the proof of this lemma is our most interesting and subtle proof, upon which our other results rest, we will sketch it first, to give the reader an intuition, and *then* present the formal version in the full version of this paper.

Proof Sketch. In this sketch give an overview of the simulation strategy followed by the simulator $\mathcal{S}_{\mathsf{Compiler}}$ against a malicious adversary who corrupts up to $n-1$ parties, using the same terminology and simplified, informal protocol description that we used to build an intuition about the compiler in Sect. 1.1. Recall that with the ith protocol committee we associate an emulated "virtual" party $\mathcal{Q}_i$, for the purposes of exposition. We are guaranteed by the premise of Theorem 3.10, that there exists an ideal adversary $\mathcal{S}_{\rho, \mathcal{D}}$ that simulates a transcript of ρ for the dummy adversary $\mathcal{D}$ that corrupts up to $m - 1$ parties, while engaging in an ideal interaction with functionality $[\![\mathcal{F}_{PreTrans}(f, m, u)]\!]_{\mathsf{PV}}$ on $\mathcal{D}$'s behalf. The compiled protocol $\pi_{Compiler}(\rho, n, u, m)$ represents a single instance of the original protocol ρ, but in each virtual round there is an m-way fork from which a single definitive outcome is selected (by the adversary) to form the basis of the next virtual round. The main idea behind $\mathcal{S}_{\mathsf{Compiler}}$ is that the forking tree can be pruned in each virtual round to include only the single path along which the a real honest party's contribution lies (or might lie, if no honest contribution has yet become a definitive outcome), and then $\mathcal{S}_{\rho, \mathcal{D}}$ can be used to translate between the protocol instances represented by these path and the functionality $[\![\mathcal{F}_{PostTrans}(f, m, u, m)]\!]_{\mathsf{PV}}$.

For each fresh candidate $\mathbf{v}_i$ produced by $[\![\mathcal{F}_{PostTrans}(f, m, u, m)]\!]_{\mathsf{PV}}$, the simulator $\mathcal{S}_{\mathsf{Compiler}}$ will invoke an instance of $\mathcal{S}_{\rho, \mathcal{D}}$, feed it all the (definitive-output) messages produced by the protocol thus far, and then feed it $\mathbf{v}_i$ in order to generate a corresponding honest-party message that can be sent to the corrupted parties. It repeats this process until the adversary accepts the honest party's contribution in some virtual round κ, whereafter the last instance of $\mathcal{S}_{\rho, \mathcal{D}}$ (which was created in round κ) is fed the remaining protocol messages in order to extract the adversary's bias y. Let $h \in [n]$ index an honest party, and let θ index the committee in to which it belongs, (corresponding to $\mathcal{Q}_\theta$). The outline for $\mathcal{S}_{\mathsf{Compiler}}$ is as follows (dropping Session IDs for the sake of simplification):

1. Initialize $j := 1$, $k := 1$, $\mathbf{a}_0 := u$, $\kappa := \perp$.
2. Obtain a candidate $\mathbf{v}_k$ by sending either $\mathtt{sample}$ (only when $k = 1$) or $(\mathtt{reject}, k - 1)$ to $[\![\mathcal{F}_{PostTrans}]\!]_{\mathsf{PV}}$, and receiving $(\mathtt{candidate}, k, \mathbf{v}_k)$ in response.
3. Invoke $\mathcal{S}_{\rho, \mathcal{D}}$ on protocol transcript $\mathbf{a}_*$ (each message being sent on behalf of a different corrupt party, and then send it $(\mathtt{unbiased}, \mathbf{v}_k)$ on behalf of $[\![\mathcal{F}_{PreTrans}]\!]_{\mathsf{PV}}$ in order to obtain the tentative protocol message $\hat{\mathbf{a}}_{k, \theta}$ of $\mathcal{Q}_\theta$.
4. Send $(\mathtt{candidate\text{-}output}, \hat{\mathbf{a}}_{k, \theta})$ on behalf of $[\![\mathcal{F}_{SFE\text{-}IA}]\!]_{\mathsf{PV}}$ to the corrupt parties in the committee indexed by θ, and wait for the adversary to either accept this output, or abort by blaming a corrupt committee-member.
5. Simultaneously, interact with the fully corrupt committees indexed by $[m] \setminus \{\theta\}$ on behalf of $[\![\mathcal{F}_{SFE\text{-}IA}]\!]_{\mathsf{PV}}$ to learn the values of $\hat{\mathbf{a}}_{k, i}$ for $i \in [m] \setminus \{\theta\}$.
6. If any virtual parties produced non-aborting output during this virtual round, then let $i' \in [m]$ be the smallest number that indexes such a virtual party. Let $\mathbf{a}_j := \hat{\mathbf{a}}_{k, i'}$ (making the output of $\mathcal{Q}_{i'}$ definitive) and if $i' = \theta$ then set $\kappa := j$ and skip to Step 8; otherwise, increment j and k and return to Step 2, updating the committee partitioning to remove the committee corresponding to $\mathcal{Q}_{i'}$ (and to remove any cheating real parties from the other committees) as per the protocol.
7. If no virtual parties produced non-aborting output during this virtual round, then increment k (but *not* j), update the committee partitioning to remove the cheaters as per the protocol, and return to Step 2.
8. Once $\mathcal{Q}_\theta$ has produced a definitive output (in virtual round κ) and its underlying committee has disbanded, continue interacting with the other (fully corrupt) committees on behalf of $[\![\mathcal{F}_{SFE\text{-}IA}]\!]_{\mathsf{PV}}$ until they have all either produced a definitive output (which is appended to $\mathbf{a}$) or become depleted of parties due to cheating. At this point, $\mathbf{a}_*$ should comprise a full transcript of protocol ρ. Some prefix of this transcript has already been transmitted to the final instance of $\mathcal{S}_{\rho, \mathcal{D}}$ (which was spawned in Step 2 during virtual round κ); send the remaining messages (those not in the prefix) to the last instance of $\mathcal{S}_{\rho, \mathcal{D}}$ as well, and it should output $(\mathtt{proceed}, x)$ along with its interface to $[\![\mathcal{F}_{PreTrans}]\!]_{\mathsf{PV}}$. Send $(\mathtt{accept}, \kappa, x)$ to $[\![\mathcal{F}_{PostTrans}]\!]_{\mathsf{PV}}$ and halt.

The only non-syntactic aspect in which the above simulation differs from the real protocol is as follows: whereas in the real protocol Q_θ computes its message $\hat{a}_{k,\theta}$ by running its honest code as per ρ (recall that this virtual party is realized by an invocation of $[\![\mathcal{F}_{PreTrans}]\!]_{PV}$ by committee θ), in the simulation this value is produced by $\mathcal{S}_{\rho,\mathcal{D}}$ in consultation with $[\![\mathcal{F}_{PostTrans}]\!]_{PV}$. Observe, first, that the $\mathtt{reject}$ interface of $[\![\mathcal{F}_{PostTrans}]\!]_{PV}$ functions identically to an individual invocation of $[\![\mathcal{F}_{PreTrans}]\!]_{PV}$ and second that the transcript produced by $\mathcal{S}_{\rho,\mathcal{D}}$ in its interaction with $[\![\mathcal{F}_{PreTrans}]\!]_{PV}$ is indistinguishable from a real execution of ρ. From these two observations, we can conclude that the above simulation is indistinguishable from a real execution of $\pi_{Compiler}$ to any efficient adversary.

The formal proof of Lemma 3.10 is given in the full version of this paper, where we also prove a similar lemma holds when there are no honest participants, but at least one honest verifier, and sketch a proof for the folklore construction of secure function evaluation with publicly verifiable identifiable abort.

Lemma 3.11. Let $f : \mathbb{V} \times \mathbb{W} \to \mathbb{V}$ be an update function, let $u \in \mathbb{V}$, let $m \in \mathbb{N}^+$, and let ρ be an SPRRR protocol such that $\rho(m, u)$ UC-realizes $[\![\mathcal{F}_{PreTrans}(f, m, u)]\!]_{PV}$ in the presence of an honest *observing verifier* and a malicious adversary statically corrupting all m actively participating parties. For every integer $n \geq m$, it holds that $\pi_{Compiler}(\rho, n, u, m)$ UC-realizes $[\![\mathcal{F}_{PostTrans}(f, n, u, m + n/m)]\!]_{PV}$ in the presence of an honest observing verifier and a malicious adversary statically corrupting all n actively participating parties in the $[\![\mathcal{F}_{SFE\text{-}IA}]\!]_{PV}$-hybrid model.

Lemma 3.12 (Folklore: NIZK + OT + BC $\implies$ $[\![\mathcal{F}_{SFE\text{-}IA}]\!]_{PV}$). The functionality $[\![\mathcal{F}_{SFE\text{-}IA}]\!]_{PV}$ can be UC-realized in the $(\mathcal{F}_{NIZK}, \mathcal{F}_{BC})$-hybrid model using a constant number of sequential authenticated broadcasts and no other communication, assuming the existence of a protocol that UC-realizes $\mathcal{F}_{OT}$.

Corollary 3.13. If there exists a protocol that UC-realizes $\mathcal{F}_{OT}$ and a strongly-player-replaceable round-robin protocol that UC-realizes $[\![\mathcal{F}_{PreTrans}(f, n, u)]\!]_{PV}$ using n sequential authenticated broadcasts and no other communication, then there is a player-replaceable protocol in the $(\mathcal{F}_{NIZK}, \mathcal{F}_{BC})$-hybrid model that UC-realizes $[\![\mathcal{F}_{PostTrans}(f, n, u, m+n/m)]\!]_{PV}$ and uses $O(m+n/m)$ sequential authenticated broadcasts and no other communication. Setting $m = \sqrt{n}$ yields the efficiency result promised by the title of this paper.

Proof. Observe that $\pi_{Compiler}(\rho, n, u, m)$ requires at most $m + n/m$ sequential invocations of the $[\![\mathcal{F}_{SFE\text{-}IA}]\!]_{PV}$ functionality, and involves no other communication. Thus the corollary follows from Theorem 3.9 and Lemma 3.12.   □

4   A Round-Robin Protocol

In this section we present a simple protocol that meets our requirements (and therefore can be used with our compiler), which is parametric over a class of update functions that is more restrictive than the compiler demands, but nevertheless broad enough to encompass several well-known sampling problems. After presenting the protocol in Sect. 4.1 and proving that it meets our requirements in Sect. 4.2, we discuss how it can be parameterized to address three different applications: sampling structured reference strings for polynomial commitments in Sect. 4.3, sampling structured reference strings for zk-SNARKs in Sect. 4.4, and constructing verifiable mixnets in Sect. 4.5. We begin by defining the restricted class of update functions that our protocol supports.

Definition 4.1. (Homomorphic Update Function). A deterministic polynomial-time algorithm $f : \mathbb{V} \times \mathbb{W} \to \mathbb{V}$ is a *Homomorphic Update Function* if it satisfies:

1. Perfect Rerandomization: for every pair of values $v_1 \in \mathbb{V}$ and $w_1 \in \mathbb{W}$, $\{f(f(v_1, w_1), w_2) : w_2 \leftarrow \mathbb{W}\} \equiv \{f(v_1, w_3) : w_3 \leftarrow \mathbb{W}\}$. If distributional equivalence is replaced by statistical or computational indistinguishability, then the property achieved is Statistical or Computational Rerandomization, respectively.
2. Homomorphic Rerandomization: there exists an efficient operation $\star$ over $\mathbb{W}$ such that for every $v \in \mathbb{V}$, and every pair of values $w_1, w_2 \in \mathbb{W}$, $f(v, w_1 \star w_2) = f(f(v, w_1), w_2)$. Furthermore, there exists an identity value $0_{\mathbb{W}} \in \mathbb{W}$ such that $f(v, 0_{\mathbb{W}}) = v$.

4.1   The Protocol

Our example is straightforward: each party (in sequence) calls the update function f on the previous intermediate output to generate the next intermediate output. To achieve UC-security, the protocol must be simulatable even if f is one-way. We specify that each party uses a UC-secure NIZK to prove that it evaluated f correctly; this allows the simulator to extract the randomization witness w for f even in the presence of a malicious adversary. Specifically, we define a relation for correct evaluation for any update function f:

$$\mathcal{R}_f = \{((v_1, v_2), w) \ : \ v_2 = f(v_1, w)\}$$

We make use of the standard UC NIZK functionality $\mathcal{F}_{\mathsf{NIZK}}$, originally formulated by Groth et al. [40]. For any particular f, there may exist an efficient bespoke proof system that realizes $\mathcal{F}_{\mathsf{NIZK}}^{\mathcal{R}_f}$. For example, if there is a sigma protocol for $\mathcal{R}_f$, then $\mathcal{F}_{\mathsf{NIZK}}^{\mathcal{R}_f}$ can (usually) be UC-realized by applying the Fischlin transform [27] to that sigma protocol. There are also a number of generic ways to UC-realize $\mathcal{F}_{\mathsf{NIZK}}^{\mathcal{R}_f}$ for any polynomial-time function f [18,40,52]. Regardless, we give our protocol description next.

Protocol 4.2. $\pi_{RRSample}(f, n, u)$. **Round-robin Sampling**

This protocol is parameterized by the number of actively participating parties $n \in \mathbb{N}^+$, by a homomorphic update function $f : \mathbb{V} \times \mathbb{W} \to \mathbb{V}$ (as per Definition 4.1), and by a common public input $u \in \mathbb{V}$. In addition to the actively participating parties $\mathcal{P}_p$ for $p \in [n]$, the protocol involves the ideal functionality $\mathcal{F}_{\mathsf{NIZK}}^{\mathcal{R}f}$, and it may involve one or more observing verifiers, denoted by $\mathcal{V}$.

Sampling: Let $\mathbf{v}_0 := u$. Upon receiving $(\mathsf{sample}, \mathsf{sid})$ from the environment $\mathcal{Z}$, each party $\mathcal{P}_i$ for $i \in [n]$ repeats the following loop for $j \in [n]$:

1. If $j = i$, $\mathcal{P}_i$ samples $\mathbf{w}_j \leftarrow \mathbb{W}$, computes $\mathbf{v}_j := f(\mathbf{v}_{j-1}, \mathbf{w}_j)$ and submits $(\mathsf{prove}, \mathsf{sid}, \mathsf{GenSID}(\mathsf{sid}, j), (\mathbf{v}_{j-1}, \mathbf{v}_j), \mathbf{w}_j)$ to $\mathcal{F}_{\mathsf{NIZK}}^{\mathcal{R}f}$. Upon receiving $(\mathsf{proof}, \mathsf{sid}, \mathsf{GenSID}(\mathsf{sid}, j), \pi_j)$ in response, $\mathcal{P}_i$ broadcasts $(\mathbf{v}_j, \pi_j).^a$

2. If $j \neq i$, $\mathcal{P}_i$ waits to receive $(\hat{\mathbf{v}}_j, \pi_j)$ from $\mathcal{P}_j$, whereupon it submits $(\mathsf{verify}, \mathsf{GenSID}(\mathsf{sid}, j), (\mathbf{v}_{j-1}, \hat{\mathbf{v}}_j), \pi_j)$ to $\mathcal{F}_{\mathsf{NIZK}}^{\mathcal{R}f}$. If $\mathcal{F}_{\mathsf{NIZK}}^{\mathcal{R}f}$ replies with $(\mathsf{accept}, \mathsf{sid}, \mathsf{GenSID}(\mathsf{sid}, j))$, then $\mathcal{P}_i$ assigns $\mathbf{v}_j := \hat{\mathbf{v}}_j$. If $\mathcal{F}_{\mathsf{NIZK}}^{\mathcal{R}f}$ replies with $(\mathsf{reject}, \mathsf{sid}, \mathsf{GenSID}(\mathsf{sid}, j))$ (or if no message is received from $\mathcal{P}_j$), then $\mathcal{P}_i$ assigns $\mathbf{v}_j := \mathbf{v}_{j-1}$.

Finally, when the loop terminates, all actively participating parties output $(\mathsf{output}, \mathsf{sid}, \mathbf{v}_n)$ to the environment.^{b}

Verification: If there is an observing verifier $\mathcal{V}$, then on receiving $(\mathsf{observe}, \mathsf{sid})$ from the environment $\mathcal{Z}$, it listens on the broadcast channel and follows the instructions in Step 2 for *all* $j \in [n]$. At the end, it outputs $(\mathsf{output}, \mathsf{sid}, \mathbf{v}_n)$ to the environment.

---

^{a} Note that when our compiler is applied to this protocol, $\mathbf{a}_j = (\mathbf{v}_j, \pi_j)$.
^{b} This implies that the "output extraction" function $\mathbf{g}_{n+1}$ described in Remark 3.3 simply returns $\mathbf{v}_n$, given the protocol transcript.

4.2   Proof of Security

In this section, we present the security theorem for the above protocol, a corollary concerning the application of our compiler under various generic realizations of $\mathcal{F}_{\mathsf{NIZK}}$, and a theorem stating that for the specific class of functions covered by Definition 4.1, the compiled protocol realizes the *original* functionality. Proofs of the theorems in this section are given in the full version of this paper.

Theorem 4.3. Let $f : \mathbb{V} \times \mathbb{W} \to \mathbb{V}$ be a homomorphic update function per Definition 4.1. For any $n \in \mathbb{N}^+$ and $u \in \mathbb{V}$, it holds that $\pi_{RRSample}(f, n, u)$ UC-realizes $[\![\mathcal{F}_{PreTrans}(f, n, u)]\!]_{\mathsf{PV}}$ in the presence of a malicious adversary corrupting any number of actively participating parties in the $\mathcal{F}_{\mathsf{NIZK}}^{\mathcal{R}f}$-hybrid model.

Corollary 4.4. Let $f : \mathbb{V} \times \mathbb{W} \to \mathbb{V}$ be a homomorphic update function per Definition 4.1. For any $u \in \mathbb{V}$ and $m, n \in \mathbb{N}^+$ such that $m \leq n$, there exists a protocol in the $\mathcal{F}_{\mathsf{CRS}}$-hybrid model that UC-realizes $[\![\mathcal{F}_{PostTrans}(f, n, u, m + n/m)]\!]_{\mathsf{PV}}$ and that requires $O(m + n/m)$ sequential broadcasts and no other communication, under any of the conditions enumerated in Remark 4.5.

Remark 4.5. $\mathcal{F}_{\mathsf{NIZK}}^{\mathcal{R}_f}$ is realizable for any polynomial-time f in the $\mathcal{F}_{\mathsf{CRS}}$-hybrid model under the existence of enhanced trapdoor permutations, or the existence of homomorphic trapdoor functions and the decisional linear assumption in a bilinear group, or the LWE assumption, or the LPN and DDH assumptions.

Theorem 4.6. Let $f : \mathbb{V} \times \mathbb{W} \to \mathbb{V}$ be a homomorphic update function per Definition 4.1. For any value of $r \in \mathbb{N}$, the ideal-world protocol involving $[\![\mathcal{F}_{PostTrans}(f, n, u, r)]\!]_{\mathsf{PV}}$ perfectly UC-realizes $[\![\mathcal{F}_{PreTrans}(f, n, u)]\!]_{\mathsf{PV}}$ in the presence of a malicious adversary corrupting any number of active participants.

4.3   Application: Powers of Tau and Polynomial Commitments

In this section we specialize $\pi_{RRSample}$ to the case of sampling the powers of tau, which was previously introduced in Sect. 1.1. Specifically, we define an update function for the powers of tau in any prime-order group $\mathbb{G}$ with maximum degree $d \in \mathbb{N}^+$ as follows:

$$\mathbb{V} = \mathbb{G}^d \qquad \mathbb{W} = \mathbb{Z}_{|\mathbb{G}|}$$
$$f : \mathbb{V} \times \mathbb{W} \to \mathbb{V} = \mathsf{PowTau}_{\mathbb{G},d}(\mathbf{V}, \tau) \mapsto \left\{ \tau^i \cdot \mathbf{V}_i \right\}_{i \in [d]}$$

It is easy to see that if G is a generator of $\mathbb{G}$, then $\mathsf{PowTau}_{\mathbb{G},d}(\{G\}_{i \in [d]}, \tau)$ computes the powers of τ in $\mathbb{G}$ up to degree d. Proving that this function satisfies Definition 4.1 will allow us to apply our results from Sect. 4.2.

Lemma 4.7. For any prime-order group $\mathbb{G}$ and any $d \in \mathbb{N}^+$, $\mathsf{PowTau}_{\mathbb{G},d}$ is a homomorphic update function with perfect rerandomization, per Definition 4.1.

Proof. It can be verified by inspection that the homomorphic rerandomization property of $\mathsf{PowTau}_{\mathbb{G},d}$ holds if the operator $\star$ is taken to be multiplication modulo the group order. That is, if $q = |\mathbb{G}|$, then for any $\alpha, \beta \in \mathbb{Z}_q$ and any $\mathbf{V} \in \{\mathbb{G}\}_{i \in [d]}$, we have $\mathsf{PowTau}_{\mathbb{G},d}(\mathsf{PowTau}_{\mathbb{G},d}(\mathbf{V}, \alpha), \beta) = \mathsf{PowTau}_{\mathbb{G},d}(\mathbf{V}, \alpha \cdot \beta \mod q)$. If we combine this fact with the fact that $\{\mathsf{PowTau}_{\mathbb{G},d}(\mathbf{V}, \tau) : \tau \leftarrow \mathbb{Z}_q\}$ is uniformly distributed over the image of $\mathsf{PowTau}_{\mathbb{G},d}(\mathbf{V}, \cdot)$, then perfect rerandomization follows as well. $\qquad\square$

As we have previously discussed, the powers of tau are useful primarily as a structured reference string for other protocols. In light of this fact, it does not make sense to construct a sampling protocol that itself requires a structured reference string. This prevents us from realizing $\mathcal{F}_{\mathsf{NIZK}}^{\mathcal{R}\mathsf{PowTau}_{\mathbb{G},d}}(n)$ via the constructions of Groth et al. [40], or Canetti et al. [18]. Fortunately, the NIZK construction of De Santis et al. [52] requires only a uniform common random string. Thus we achieve our main theoretical result with respect to the powers of tau:

Corollary 4.8. For any prime-order group $\mathbb{G}$ and any $d \in \mathbb{N}^+$, $n \in \mathbb{N}^+$, $m \in [n]$, and $\mathbf{V} \in \mathbb{G}^d$, there exists a protocol in the $\mathcal{F}_{\mathsf{CRS}}$-hybrid model (with a uniform CRS distribution) that UC-realizes $[\![\mathcal{F}_{PreTrans}(\mathsf{PowTau}_{\mathbb{G},d}, n, \mathbf{V})]\!]_{\mathsf{PV}}$ and that requires $O(m + n/m)$ sequential broadcasts and no other communication, under the assumption that enhanced trapdoor permutations exist.

Proof. By conjunction of Lemma 4.7 and Theorems 4.4 and 4.6 under the restriction that the CRS distribution be uniform. □

The above corollary shows that if we set $m := \sqrt{n}$, then we can sample well-formed powers-of-tau structured reference strings with guaranteed output delivery against $n - 1$ malicious corruptions in $O(\sqrt{n})$ broadcast rounds. However, most schemes that use structured reference strings with this or similar structures assume that the strings have been sampled (in a trusted way) with *uniform* trapdoors. Our protocol does *not* achieve this, and indeed cannot without violating the Cleve bound [23]. Instead, our protocol allows the adversary to introduce some bias. In order to use a reference string sampled by our protocol in any particular context, it must be proven (in a context-specific way) that the bias does not give the adversary any advantage.

Although previous work has proven that the bias in the reference string induced by protocols for distributed sampling can be tolerated by SNARKs [12, 47], such proofs have thus far been monolithic and specific to the particular combination of SNARK and sampling scheme that they address. Moreover, because SNARKs are proven secure in powerful idealized models, prior distributed sampling protocols were analyzed in those models as well. Unlike SNARKs, which require knowledge assumptions, the security of the Kate et al. [44] polynomial-commitment scheme can be reduced to a concrete falsifiable assumption. This presents a clean, standalone context in which to examine the impact adversarial bias in the trapdoor of a powers-of-tau reference string. We do not recall the details of the polynomial-commitment construction,[5] but note that its security follows from the d-Strong Diffie-Hellman (or d-SDH) Assumption [44, Theorem 1]. We show that replacing an ideal bias-free powers-of-tau reference string with a reference string that is adversarially biased as permitted by our functionality $\mathcal{F}_{PostTrans}(\mathsf{PowTau}_{\mathbb{G},d}, n, \{G\}_{i \in [d]}, r)$ yields *no advantage* in breaking the d-SDH assumption, regardless of the value of r, so long as no more than $n - 1$ parties are corrupt. We begin by recalling the d-SDH assumption:

Definition 4.9 (d-Strong Diffie-Hellman Assumption [11]). Let the security parameter λ determine a group $\mathbb{G}$ of prime order q that is generated by G. For every PPT adversary $\mathcal{A}$,

$$\Pr\left[(c, G/(\tau + c)) = \mathcal{A}\left(\{\tau^i \cdot G\}_{i \in [d]}\right) : \tau \leftarrow \mathbb{Z}_q\right] \in \mathsf{negl}(\lambda)$$

---

[5] Kate et al. actually present two related schemes. The first uses the powers of tau, exactly as we have presented it, and the second requires the powers, plus the powers again with a secret multiplicative offset (or, alternatively, relative to a second group generator). It is easy to modify our construction to satisfy the second scheme, and so for clarity we focus on the first, simpler one.

We wish to formulate a variant of the above assumption that permits the same bias as $\mathcal{F}_{PostTrans}(\mathsf{PowTau}_{\mathbb{G},d}, n, \{G\}_{i\in[d]}, r)$. In order to do this, we define a sampling algorithm that uses the code of the functionality. We then give a formal definition of the biased assumption, which we refer to as the (n, r)-Biased d-Strong Diffie-Hellman (or (n, r, d)-SDH) assumption.

Algorithm 4.10. $\mathsf{AdvSample}^{\mathcal{Z}}_{\mathcal{F}_{PostTrans}}(\mathsf{PowTau}_{\mathbb{G},d,n,\{G\}_{i\in[d]},r})(1^\lambda)$

Let $\mathcal{Z}$ be a PPT adversarial algorithm that is compatible with the environment's interface to an ideal-world UC experiment involving $\mathcal{F}_{PostTrans}$ and the dummy adversary $\mathcal{D}$. Let $\mathcal{Z}$ be guaranteed to corrupt no more than $n - 1$ parties, and let it output some state s on termination.

1. Using the code of $\mathcal{F}_{PostTrans}$, begin emulating an instance of the ideal-world experiment for $\mathcal{F}_{PostTrans}(\mathsf{PowTau}_{\mathbb{G},d}, n, \{G\}_{i\in[d]}, r)$, with $\mathcal{Z}$ as the environment. Let $\mathcal{P}_h$ be the honest party guaranteed in this experiment by the constraints on $\mathcal{Z}$.

2. In the emulated experiment, on receiving (sample, sid) from $\mathcal{Z}$ on behalf of $\mathcal{P}_h$, forward this message to $\mathcal{F}_{PostTrans}$ on behalf of $\mathcal{P}_h$ as a dummy party would, and then wait to receive (output, sid, $z = \{\tau \cdot G, \tau^2 \cdot G, \ldots, \tau^d \cdot G\}$) for some $\tau \in \mathbb{Z}_q$ from $\mathcal{F}_{PostTrans}$ in reply.

3. Extract τ from the internal state of $\mathcal{F}_{PostTrans}$, and wait for $\mathcal{Z}$ to terminate with output s.

4. Output (s, τ)

Definition 4.11 (((n, r)-**Biased** d-**Strong Diffie-Hellman Assumption**). Let the security parameter λ determine a group $\mathbb{G}$ of prime order q that is generated by G. For every pair of PPT adversaries $(\mathcal{Z}, \mathcal{A})$,

$$\Pr\left[\begin{array}{l} \mathcal{A}\left(s, \{\tau^i \cdot G\}_{i\in[d]}\right) = (c, G/(\tau+c)) \; : \\[6pt] (s, \tau) \leftarrow \mathsf{AdvSample}^{\mathcal{Z}}_{\mathcal{F}_{PostTrans}}(\mathsf{PowTau}_{\mathbb{G},d,n,\{G\}_{i\in[d]},r})(1^\lambda) \end{array}\right] \in \mathsf{negl}(\lambda)$$

Note that per Canetti [17], the dummy adversary $\mathcal{D}$ can be used to emulate any other adversary. Thus if one were to use an n-party instance of $\mathcal{F}_{PostTrans}$ to generate the structured reference string for a protocol that uses the polynomial commitments of Kate et al. [44], the hardness assumption that would underlie the security of the resulting scheme is (n, r, d)-SDH. We show that for all parameters n, r, the (n, r, d)-SDH assumption is *exactly* as hard as d-SDH.

Theorem 4.12. For every $n, r, d \in \mathbb{N}^+$ and t-time adversary $(\mathcal{Z}, \mathcal{A})$ that succeeds with probability ε in the (n, r, d)-SDH experiment, there exists a t'-time adversary $\mathcal{B}$ for the d-SDH experiment that succeeds with probability ε, where $t' \approx t$.

The proof of the above theorem appears in the full version of this document.

4.4   Application: Sampling Updateable SRSes

In this section we discuss the specialization of our protocol to the application of sampling updateable structured reference strings for SNARKs. The game-based notion of updateable security with respect to structured reference strings was defined recently by Groth et al. [39]. Informally, if a SNARK has an updateable SRS, then any party can publish and update to the SRS at any time, along with a proof of well-formedness, and the security properties of the SNARK hold so long as at least one honest party has contributed at some point. We direct the reader to Groth et al. for a full formal definition. Because the update operation is defined to be a local algorithm producing a new SRS and a proof of well-formedness, which takes as input only a random tape and the previous SRS state, it is tempting to consider the protocol comprising sequentially broadcasted SRS updates by every party as a pre-existing specialization of $\pi_{RRSample}$. However, we require that the proof of well-formedness be a realization of $\mathcal{F}_{NIZK}^{\mathcal{R}f}$ for whatever f maps the previous SRS to the next one, and the update algorithm of Groth et al. (also used by later works [22,30,50]) does not have straight-line extraction. Modifying any updateable SNARK to fit into our model is beyond the scope of this work. Nevertheless, we discuss two alternatives that do not involve modifying the SNARK.

First, we observe that if the proofs of well-formedness of the Groth et al. update procedure [39] are taken to be part of the SRS itself, then the entire update function (let it be called GrothUpdate) is in fact a homomorphic update procedure per Definition 4.1, by an argument similar to our proof of Lemma 4.7. This implies a result similar to Corollary 4.8: for any $n, m \in \mathbb{N}^+$ such that $m \leq n$, there exists a protocol in the uniformly distributed CRS model that UC-realizes $\mathcal{F}_{PostTrans}(\mathsf{GrothUpdate}, n, 1_{SRS}, m + n/m)$ while using only $O(m + n/m)$ broadcasts under the assumption that enhanced trapdoor permutations exist, where 1_{SRS} is the "default" SRS. Furthermore, the well-formedness of SRSes generated via this protocol can be verified without checking the entire protocol transcript.

Second, we can define the functions f mapping the previous SRS to the next one (without the proofs), specialize our protocol $\pi_{RRSample}$ for that function (realizing $\mathcal{F}_{NIZK}^{f}$ generically), and rely on the public verifiability of $[\![\mathcal{F}_{PostTrans}]\!]_{PV}$ to ensure that the resulting SRS has the well-formedness property required. In service of this approach, we present the update functions for three recent zk-SNARKs. The update function $\mathsf{BilinearSRS}_{\mathbb{G}_1,\mathbb{G}_2,d}$ is a simple modification of $\mathsf{PowTau}_{\mathbb{G},d}$ that is compatible with both Marlin [22] and Plonk [30]:

$$\mathbb{V} = \mathbb{G}_1^d \times \mathbb{G}_2 \qquad \mathbb{W} = \mathbb{Z}_q$$

$$f : \mathbb{V} \times \mathbb{W} \to \mathbb{V} = \mathsf{BilinearSRS}_{\mathbb{G}_1,\mathbb{G}_2,d}((\mathbf{X}, Y), \tau) \mapsto \left(\left\{ \tau^i \cdot \mathbf{X}_i \right\}_{i \in [d]}, \tau \cdot Y \right)$$

whereas Sonic [50] has a more complex SRS with a more complex update function

$$\mathbb{V} = \mathbb{G}_1^{4d} \times \mathbb{G}_2^{4d+1} \times \mathbb{G}_\mathsf{T} \qquad \mathbb{W} = \mathbb{Z}_q^2 \qquad f : \mathbb{V} \times \mathbb{W} \to \mathbb{V} = \mathsf{SonicSRS}_{\mathbb{G}_1,\mathbb{G}_2,d}$$

$$\mathsf{SonicSRS}_{\mathbb{G}_1,\mathbb{G}_2,d}((\mathbf{X},\mathbf{Y},Z),(\tau,\beta))$$

$$\mapsto \left(\begin{array}{l} \left\{\tau^{i-d-1}\cdot\mathbf{X}_i\right\}_{i\in[d]} \| \left\{\tau^i\cdot\mathbf{X}_{i+d}\right\}_{i\in[d]} \| \left\{\beta\cdot\tau^i\cdot\mathbf{X}_{i+3d+1}\right\}_{i\in[-d,d]\setminus\{0\}}, \\ \left\{\tau^{i-d-1}\cdot\mathbf{Y}_i\right\}_{i\in[d]} \| \left\{\tau^i\cdot\mathbf{Y}_{i+d}\right\}_{i\in[d]} \| \left\{\beta\cdot\tau^i\cdot\mathbf{Y}_{i+3d+1}\right\}_{i\in[-d,d]}, \beta\cdot Z \end{array} \right)$$

and all three have homomorphic rerandomization per Definition 4.1, by an argument similar to our proof of Lemma 4.7.

Because SNARKs with updateable SRSes must tolerate adversarial updates, it seems natural to assume that they can tolerate the adversarial bias induced by either of the above sampling methods. However, as we have mentioned, their proofs tend to be in powerful idealized models that are incompatible with UC, and so formalizing this claim is beyond the scope of this work.

4.5   Application: Verifiable Mixnets

Finally, we discuss the specialization of $\pi_{RRSample}$ to the mixing procedure of verifiable mixnets. Most mixnet security definitions, whether game-based or simulation based, encompass a suite of algorithms (or interfaces, in the simulation-based case) for key generation, encryption, mixing, and decryption. We reason only about the mixing function, via an exemplar: the game-based protocol of Boyle et al. [14]. Though we do not give formal proofs, and argue that the security of the overall mixnet construction is preserved under our transformation.

Boyle et al. base their mixnet upon Bellare et al.'s [9] *lossy* variant of El Gamal encryption for constant-sized message spaces. Let the message space size be given by ϕ. Given a group $\mathbb{G}$ (chosen according to the security parameter λ) of prime order q and generated by G, it is as follows:

$$\mathsf{KeyGen}_\mathbb{G}(\mathsf{sk} \in \mathbb{Z}_q) \mapsto (\mathsf{sk},\mathsf{pk}) : \mathsf{pk} := \mathsf{sk}\cdot G$$

$$\mathsf{Enc}_\mathsf{pk}(m \in [\phi], r \in \mathbb{Z}_q) \mapsto (R,C) : R := r\cdot G,\ C := r\cdot\mathsf{pk} + m\cdot G$$

$$\mathsf{ReRand}_\mathsf{pk}((R,C) \in \mathbb{G}^2, r \in \mathbb{Z}_q) \mapsto (S,D) : S := R + r\cdot G,\ D := r\cdot\mathsf{pk} + C$$

$$\mathsf{Dec}_\mathsf{sk}((R,C) \in \mathbb{G}^2) \mapsto m \in [\phi]\ \text{s.t.}\ m\cdot G = C + R/\mathsf{sk}$$

Note that we have given the random values (sk and r) for each function as inputs, but they must be sampled uniformly and secretly in order to prove that the above algorithms constitute an encryption scheme. Boyle et al. define the notion of a (perfectly) rerandomizable encryption scheme and assert that the above scheme satisfies it. We claim that given any $\mathsf{pk} \in \mathbb{G}$, if the homomorphic operator $\star$ is taken to be addition over $\mathbb{Z}_q$, then $\mathsf{ReRand}_\mathsf{pk}$ is a homomorphic update function per Definition 4.1. Given $\mathsf{ReRand}_\mathsf{pk}$, the ciphertext mixing function for a vector of d ciphertexts in the Boyle et al. mixnet is as follows:

$$\mathbb{V} = (\mathbb{G} \times \mathbb{G})^d \qquad \mathbb{W} = \Sigma_d \times \mathbb{Z}_q^d$$

$$f = \mathsf{Mix}_{\mathsf{pk},d}(\mathbf{c},(\sigma,\mathbf{r})) \mapsto \left\{\mathsf{ReRand}_\mathsf{pk}(\mathbf{c}_{\sigma^{-1}(i)},\mathbf{r}_i)\right\}_{i\in[d]}$$

where Σ_d is the set of all permutations over d elements. We claim that this function is a homomorphic update function.

Lemma 4.13. For any $\mathsf{pk} \in \mathbb{G}$ and any $d \in \mathbb{N}^+$, $\mathsf{Mix}_{\mathsf{pk},d}$ is a homomorphic update function with perfect rerandomization, per Definition 4.1.

Proof Sketch. Perfect rerandomization holds because all elements in the vector of ciphertexts are individually perfectly rerandomized. The homomorphic operator is defined to be

$$\star : ((\sigma_1, \mathbf{r}), (\sigma_2, \mathbf{s})) \mapsto \left(\sigma_1 \circ \sigma_2, \left\{\mathbf{s}_i + \mathbf{r}_{\sigma_2^{-1}(i)}\right\}_{i \in [d]}\right)$$

where $\circ$ is the composition operator for permutations. □

In the mixnet design of Boyle et al., every mixing server runs $\mathsf{Mix}_{\mathsf{pk},d}$ in sequence and broadcasts the output along with a proof that the function was evaluated correctly. In other words, their protocol is round-robin and player replaceable. Because their proofs of correct execution achieve only witness-indistinguishability (which is sufficient for their purposes), whereas we require our proofs to UC-realize $\mathcal{F}_{\mathsf{NIZK}}^{\mathcal{R}\mathsf{Mix}_{\mathsf{pk},d}}$, their protocol is not a pre-existing specialization of $\pi_{RRSample}$. Nevertheless, we can realize $\mathcal{F}_{\mathsf{NIZK}}^{\mathcal{R}\mathsf{Mix}_{\mathsf{pk},d}}$ generically as we have in our previous applications.

Corollary 4.14. For any prime-order group $\mathbb{G}$ and any $d \in \mathbb{N}^+$, $n, m \in \mathbb{N}^+$ such that $m \leq n$, $\mathsf{pk} \in \mathbb{G}$, and $\mathbf{c} \in \mathrm{image}(\mathsf{Enc}_{\mathsf{pk}})^d$, there exists a protocol in the $\mathcal{F}_{\mathsf{CRS}}$-hybrid model that UC-realizes $[\![\mathcal{F}_{PreTrans}(\mathsf{Mix}_{\mathsf{pk},d}, n, \mathbf{c})]\!]_{\mathsf{PV}}$ and that requires $O(m + n/m)$ sequential broadcasts and no other communication, under any of the conditions enumerated in Remark 4.5.

Proof. By conjunction of Lemma 4.13 and Theorems 4.4 and 4.6. □

We remark that the public-verifiability aspect of the functionality ensures that the mixnet that results from integrating it into the scheme of Boyle et al. is verifiable in the sense that they require [14, Definition 7]. Furthermore, the game-based security definition of Boyle et al. [14, Definition 12] permits the adversary to induce *precisely* the same sort of bias as $[\![\mathcal{F}_{PreTrans}(\mathsf{Mix}_{\mathsf{pk},d}, \cdot, \cdot)]\!]_{\mathsf{PV}}$. It follows naturally that their construction retains its security properties when mixing is done via our functionality. Setting $m := \sqrt{n}$, we have achieved a verifiable mixnet with guaranteed output delivery against $n - 1$ maliciously-corrupt mix servers in $O(\sqrt{n})$ broadcast rounds.

5   With Concrete Efficiency

The previous sections of this paper were concerned with optimizing round efficiency to the exclusion of all else. In practice, this may lead to protocols that are concretely round-efficient, but prohibitively expensive due to large concrete communication or computation costs. Consider, for example, the powers of tau in an elliptic curve: in practice, $d \in [2^{10}, 2^{20}]$ [13]. This implies that the $\mathsf{PowTau}_{\mathbb{G},d}$ function involves many thousands of elliptic curve scalar multiplications; if rendered into a boolean circuit, it could easily require trillions of gates. Evaluating circuits of such size is at or beyond the edge of feasibility with current techniques even in the security-with-abort setting, and our compiler requires the circuit to be evaluated many times with identifiable abort.

We believe that this concrete inefficiency is a shortcoming of our *compiler* and not the technique that underlies it. In evidence of this, we use this section to sketch a new protocol, $\pi_{\mathsf{BilinearSRS}}$, which realizes $\mathcal{F}_{PostTrans}(\mathsf{BilinearSRS}_{\mathbb{G}_1,\mathbb{G}_2,d}, n, (\mathbf{X}, Y), 2\sqrt{n}-1)$ *directly*, where $(\mathbf{X}, Y)$ is any well-formed SRS. Our new protocol requires $O(\sqrt{n} \cdot \log d)$ sequential broadcast rounds and avoids the major concrete costs implied by compiling the round-robin protocol. Here we will give a simple sketch and make a few high-level efficiency claims. The full version of this paper contains a full protocol description, an in-depth concrete cost analysis, and a proof of security.

$\pi_{\mathsf{BilinearSRS}}$ will leverage the fact that the well-formedness of SRSes sampled by the $\mathsf{BilinearSRS}$ update function can be checked using the pairing operation of the underlying bilinear group, without any additional protocol artifacts or external information. $\pi_{\mathsf{BilinearSRS}}$ is structured similarly to $\pi_{Compiler}$, with two major differences. First, when a committee's intermediate output is chosen to become definitive, it is first double-checked for well-formedness by *all* parties in the protocol (the check is performed via the pairing operation and therefore incurs only computational costs), and the entire committee is ejected for cheating if this check fails. Second, we replace instances of $[\![\mathcal{F}_{SFE-IA}]\!]_{\mathsf{PV}}$ that evaluate the $\mathsf{BilinearSRS}_{\mathbb{G}_1,\mathbb{G}_2,d}$ update function as a circuit with instances of a new functionality $[\![\mathcal{F}_{\mathsf{ExtSRS}}]\!]_{\mathsf{PV}}$ that directly computes the same update function. $[\![\mathcal{F}_{\mathsf{ExtSRS}}]\!]_{\mathsf{PV}}$ maintains most of the public-verifiability properties of $[\![\mathcal{F}_{SFE-IA}]\!]_{\mathsf{PV}}$, but unlike the latter it allows the adversary to choose the output arbitrarily if all active participants are corrupted.

In order to realize $[\![\mathcal{F}_{\mathsf{ExtSRS}}]\!]_{\mathsf{PV}}$ with reasonable concrete efficiency, each committee samples shares of a uniform secret τ and uses a generic *reactive, arithmetic* MPC functionality $[\![\mathcal{F}_{\mathsf{MPC-IA}}]\!]_{\mathsf{PV}}$ to compute secret sharings of the powers of τ. The functionality $[\![\mathcal{F}_{\mathsf{MPC-IA}}]\!]_{\mathsf{PV}}$ is similar to $[\![\mathcal{F}_{SFE-IA}]\!]_{\mathsf{PV}}$, except that it is *reactive* (that is, it allows the circuit to be determined dynamically after inputs are supplied), it allows the adversary to choose outputs arbitrarily if all active participants are corrupted, and it natively supports arithmetic computations over an arbitrary field, which implies that this computation requires only $O(d)$ multiplication gates arranged in a circuit of depth $O(\log d)$. Using these shares of the powers of τ, the committee engages in a round of distributed EC scalar operations to generate its intermediate SRS, which is checked for well-formedness by the members of the committee (but *not* by any passive verifiers). If any active participants are honest, and the intermediate SRS is not well-formed, then they broadcast a message indicating as much, along with information that allows passive verifiers to efficiently confirm which active participant has cheated. Known techniques for realizing $[\![\mathcal{F}_{\mathsf{MPC-IA}}]\!]_{\mathsf{PV}}$ require a round count proportionate to the circuit's multiplicative depth, and so the protocol realizing $[\![\mathcal{F}_{\mathsf{ExtSRS}}]\!]_{\mathsf{PV}}$ runs in $O(\log d)$ rounds overall.

In practice, bilinear groups are realized by certain elliptic curves, and both the pairing operation and the scalar-multiplication operation have large concrete computational costs; thus we must use them judiciously. In $\pi_{\mathsf{BilinearSRS}}$, these two operations incur the vast majority of concrete computational costs that are not due to the protocol realizing $[\![\mathcal{F}_{\mathsf{MPC-IA}}]\!]_{\mathsf{PV}}$. We define a metric of the overall wall-clock latency incurred by EC pairings and, similarly, a metric of the latency incurred by EC scalar operations. For $\pi_{\mathsf{BilinearSRS}}$, the former cost is in $O(\sqrt{n})$ and the latter is in $O(d \cdot \sqrt{n} + n \cdot \lambda / \log \lambda)$ for active participants or $O(n + d \cdot \sqrt{n})$ for passive verifiers; this is an improvement upon the round-robin SRS sampling technique, which (after optimization) has a pairing latency in $O(n)$ and a scalar latency in $O(d \cdot n)$.

It should be noted that our protocol is not a strict improvement upon prior techniques in all respects: it requires $O(n^{1.5} \cdot d \cdot \lambda + n^{1.5} \cdot \lambda^2 / \log \lambda)$ bits to be broadcasted in total, *not including* the communication costs of the protocol that realizes $[\![\mathcal{F}_{\mathsf{MPC-IA}}]\!]_{\mathsf{PV}}$; in this respect our approach is strictly worse than prior work. The protocol that realizes $[\![\mathcal{F}_{\mathsf{MPC-IA}}]\!]_{\mathsf{PV}}$ must evaluate $O(d \cdot n^{1.5})$ input and output gates and $O(d \cdot n)$ multiplication gates in total, among groups of $\sqrt{n}$ active participants. We identify this as our most significant concrete bottleneck. Substantial progress has recently been made toward optimizing generic MPC in the security-with-abort setting, but the publicly-verifiable identifiable-abort setting has received less attention thus far. We hope and expect that this will change, and $\pi_{\mathsf{BilinearSRS}}$ will move toward practicality as a result.

Acknowledgements. We thank Alon Rosen for a helpful discussion. We furthermore thank an anonymous reviewer for making us aware of certain practical optimizations used in the full version of this paper. Ran Cohen's research is supported in part by NSF grant no. 2055568. The other authors are supported in part by NSF grants 1816028 and 1646671.

References

1. Abe, M.: Mix-networks on permutation networks. In: Lam, K.-Y., Okamoto, E., Xing, C. (eds.) ASIACRYPT 1999. LNCS, vol. 1716, pp. 258–273. Springer, Heidelberg (1999). https://doi.org/10.1007/978-3-540-48000-6_21

2. Asharov, G.: Towards characterizing complete fairness in secure two-party computation. In: Lindell, Y. (ed.) TCC 2014. LNCS, vol. 8349, pp. 291–316. Springer, Heidelberg (2014). https://doi.org/10.1007/978-3-642-54242-8_13

3. Asharov, G., Beimel, A., Makriyannis, N., Omri, E.: Complete characterization of fairness in secure two-party computation of Boolean functions. In: Dodis, Y., Nielsen, J.B. (eds.) TCC 2015. LNCS, vol. 9014, pp. 199–228. Springer, Heidelberg (2015). https://doi.org/10.1007/978-3-662-46494-6_10

4. Asharov, G., Lindell, Y., Rabin, T.: A full characterization of functions that imply fair coin tossing and ramifications to fairness. In: Sahai, A. (ed.) TCC 2013. LNCS, vol. 7785, pp. 243–262. Springer, Heidelberg (2013). https://doi.org/10.1007/978-3-642-36594-2_14

5. Awerbuch, B., Blum, M., Chor, B., Goldwasser, S., Micali, S.: How to implement Bracha's $O(\log n)$ Byzantine agreement algorithm (1985). Unpublished manuscript
6. Baum, C., Damgård, I., Orlandi, C.: Publicly auditable secure multi-party computation. In: Abdalla, M., De Prisco, R. (eds.) SCN 2014. LNCS, vol. 8642, pp. 175–196. Springer, Cham (2014). https://doi.org/10.1007/978-3-319-10879-7_11
7. Baum, C., David, B., Dowsley, R., Nielsen, J.B., Oechsner, S.: TARDIS: a foundation of time-lock puzzles in UC. In: Canteaut, A., Standaert, F.-X. (eds.) EURO-CRYPT 2021. LNCS, vol. 12698, pp. 429–459. Springer, Cham (2021). https://doi.org/10.1007/978-3-030-77883-5_15
8. Beimel, A., Lindell, Y., Omri, E., Orlov, I.: $1/p$-secure multiparty computation without honest majority and the best of both worlds. In: Rogaway, P. (ed.) CRYPTO 2011. LNCS, vol. 6841, pp. 277–296. Springer, Heidelberg (2011). https://doi.org/10.1007/978-3-642-22792-9_16
9. Bellare, M., Hofheinz, D., Yilek, S.: Possibility and impossibility results for encryption and commitment secure under selective opening. In: Joux, A. (ed.) EURO-CRYPT 2009. LNCS, vol. 5479, pp. 1–35. Springer, Heidelberg (2009). https://doi.org/10.1007/978-3-642-01001-9_1
10. Ben-Sasson, E., Chiesa, A., Green, M., Tromer, E., Virza, M.: Secure sampling of public parameters for succinct zero knowledge proofs. In: IEEE S&P (2015)
11. Boneh, D., Boyen, X.: Short signatures without random oracles. In: Cachin, C., Camenisch, J.L. (eds.) EUROCRYPT 2004. LNCS, vol. 3027, pp. 56–73. Springer, Heidelberg (2004). https://doi.org/10.1007/978-3-540-24676-3_4
12. Bowe, S., Gabizon, A., Green, M.D.: A multi-party protocol for constructing the public parameters of the Pinocchio zk-SNARK. In: Zohar, A., et al. (eds.) FC 2018. LNCS, vol. 10958, pp. 64–77. Springer, Heidelberg (2019). https://doi.org/10.1007/978-3-662-58820-8_5
13. Bowe, S., Gabizon, A., Miers, I.: Scalable multi-party computation for zk-SNARK parameters in the random beacon model. IACR Cryptol. ePrint Arch., 2017 (2017)
14. Boyle, E., Klein, S., Rosen, A., Segev, G.: Securing Abe's mix-net against malicious verifiers via witness indistinguishability. In: Catalano, D., De Prisco, R. (eds.) SCN 2018. LNCS, vol. 11035, pp. 274–291. Springer, Cham (2018). https://doi.org/10.1007/978-3-319-98113-0_15
15. Bracha, G.: An O(log n) expected rounds randomized Byzantine generals protocol. JACM **34**(4), 910–920 (1987)
16. Buchbinder, N., Haitner, I., Levi, N., Tsfadia, E.: Tighter analysis and the many-party case. In: SODA, Fair coin flipping (2017)
17. Canetti, R.: Universally composable security: a new paradigm for cryptographic protocols. In: FOCS (2001)
18. Canetti, R., Sarkar, P., Wang, X.: Triply adaptive UC NIZK. IACR Cryptol. ePrint Arch. (2020)
19. Chen, J., Micali, S.: Algorand: a secure and efficient distributed ledger. Theoret. Comput. Sci. **777**, 155–183 (2019)
20. Chen, M., et al.: Multiparty generation of an RSA modulus. In: Micciancio, D., Ristenpart, T. (eds.) CRYPTO 2020. LNCS, vol. 12172, pp. 64–93. Springer, Cham (2020). https://doi.org/10.1007/978-3-030-56877-1_3
21. Chen, M., et al.: Diogenes: lightweight scalable RSA modulus generation with a dishonest majority. In: IEEE S&P, pp. 590–607 (2021)
22. Chiesa, A., Hu, Y., Maller, M., Mishra, P., Vesely, N., Ward, N.: Marlin: preprocessing zkSNARKs with universal and updatable SRS. In: Canteaut, A., Ishai, Y. (eds.) EUROCRYPT 2020. LNCS, vol. 12105, pp. 738–768. Springer, Cham (2020). https://doi.org/10.1007/978-3-030-45721-1_26

23. Cleve, R.: Limits on the security of coin flips when half the processors are faulty (extended abstract). In: STOC (1986)

24. Cohen, R., Haitner, I., Omri, E., Rotem, L.: From fairness to full security in multiparty computation. J. Cryptol. **35**(1), 1–70 (2022)

25. Cohen, R., Lindell, Y.: Fairness versus guaranteed output delivery in secure multiparty computation. J. Cryptol. **30**(4), 1157–1186 (2017)

26. Dachman-Soled, D.: Revisiting fairness in MPC: polynomial number of parties and general adversarial structures. In: Pass, R., Pietrzak, K. (eds.) TCC 2020. LNCS, vol. 12551, pp. 595–620. Springer, Cham (2020). https://doi.org/10.1007/978-3-030-64378-2_21

27. Fischlin, M.: Communication-efficient non-interactive proofs of knowledge with online extractors. In: Shoup, V. (ed.) CRYPTO 2005. LNCS, vol. 3621, pp. 152–168. Springer, Heidelberg (2005). https://doi.org/10.1007/11535218_10

28. Fouque, P.-A., Stern, J.: One round threshold discrete-log key generation without private channels. In: Kim, K. (ed.) PKC 2001. LNCS, vol. 1992, pp. 300–316. Springer, Heidelberg (2001). https://doi.org/10.1007/3-540-44586-2_22

29. Fuchsbauer, G., Kiltz, E., Loss, J.: The algebraic group model and its applications. In: Shacham, H., Boldyreva, A. (eds.) CRYPTO 2018. LNCS, vol. 10992, pp. 33–62. Springer, Cham (2018). https://doi.org/10.1007/978-3-319-96881-0_2

30. Gabizon, A, Williamson, Z.J., Ciobotaru, O.: PLONK: permutations over lagrangebases for oecumenical noninteractive arguments of knowledge. IACR Cryptol. ePrint Arch. (2019)

31. Gennaro, R., Jarecki, S., Krawczyk, H., Rabin, T.: Secure distributed key generation for discrete-log based cryptosystems. J. Cryptol. **20**(1), 51–83 (2006). https://doi.org/10.1007/s00145-006-0347-3

32. Gennaro, R., Jarecki, S., Krawczyk, H., Rabin, T.: Secure applications of Pedersen's distributed key generation protocol. In: Joye, M. (ed.) CT-RSA 2003. LNCS, vol. 2612, pp. 373–390. Springer, Heidelberg (2003). https://doi.org/10.1007/3-540-36563-X_26

33. Goldreich, O.: Foundations of Cryptography - VOLUME 2: Basic Applications. Cambridge University Press, Cambridge (2004)

34. Goldreich, O., Micali, S., Wigderson, A.: How to play any mental game or a completeness theorem for protocols with honest majority. In: STOC (1987)

35. Dov Gordon, S., Hazay, C., Katz, J., Lindell, Y.: Complete fairness in secure two-party computation. In: STOC (2008)

36. Gordon, S.D., Katz, J.: Complete fairness in multi-party computation without an honest majority. In: Reingold, O. (ed.) TCC 2009. LNCS, vol. 5444, pp. 19–35. Springer, Heidelberg (2009). https://doi.org/10.1007/978-3-642-00457-5_2

37. Gordon, S.D., Katz, J.: Partial fairness in secure two-party computation. In: Gilbert, H. (ed.) EUROCRYPT 2010. LNCS, vol. 6110, pp. 157–176. Springer, Heidelberg (2010). https://doi.org/10.1007/978-3-642-13190-5_8

38. Groth, J.: On the size of pairing-based non-interactive arguments. In: Fischlin, M., Coron, J.-S. (eds.) EUROCRYPT 2016. LNCS, vol. 9666, pp. 305–326. Springer, Heidelberg (2016). https://doi.org/10.1007/978-3-662-49896-5_11

39. Groth, J., Kohlweiss, M., Maller, M., Meiklejohn, S., Miers, I.: Updatable and universal common reference strings with applications to zk-SNARKs. In: Shacham, H., Boldyreva, A. (eds.) CRYPTO 2018. LNCS, vol. 10993, pp. 698–728. Springer, Cham (2018). https://doi.org/10.1007/978-3-319-96878-0_24

40. Groth, J., Ostrovsky, R., Sahai, A.: New techniques for noninteractive zero-knowledge. JACM **59**(3), 1–35 (2012)

41. Hirt, M., Maurer, U.: Player simulation and general adversary structures in perfect multiparty computation. J. Cryptol. **13**(1), 31–60 (2000). https://doi.org/10.1007/s001459910003

42. Ishai, Y., Ostrovsky, R., Zikas, V.: Secure multi-party computation with identifiable abort. In: Garay, J.A., Gennaro, R. (eds.) CRYPTO 2014. LNCS, vol. 8617, pp. 369–386. Springer, Heidelberg (2014). https://doi.org/10.1007/978-3-662-44381-1_21

43. Ishai, Y., Prabhakaran, M., Sahai, A.: Founding cryptography on oblivious transfer – efficiently. In: Wagner, D. (ed.) CRYPTO 2008. LNCS, vol. 5157, pp. 572–591. Springer, Heidelberg (2008). https://doi.org/10.1007/978-3-540-85174-5_32

44. Kate, A., Zaverucha, G.M., Goldberg, I.: Constant-size commitments to polynomials and their applications. In: Abe, M. (ed.) ASIACRYPT 2010. LNCS, vol. 6477, pp. 177–194. Springer, Heidelberg (2010). https://doi.org/10.1007/978-3-642-17373-8_11

45. Katz, J., Maurer, U., Tackmann, B., Zikas, V.: Universally composable synchronous computation. In: Sahai, A. (ed.) TCC 2013. LNCS, vol. 7785, pp. 477–498. Springer, Heidelberg (2013). https://doi.org/10.1007/978-3-642-36594-2_27

46. Kiayias, A., Zhou, H.-S., Zikas, V.: Fair and robust multi-party computation using a global transaction ledger. In: Fischlin, M., Coron, J.-S. (eds.) EUROCRYPT 2016. LNCS, vol. 9666, pp. 705–734. Springer, Heidelberg (2016). https://doi.org/10.1007/978-3-662-49896-5_25

47. Kohlweiss, M., Maller, M., Siim, J., Volkhov, M.: Snarky ceremonies. IACR Cryptol. ePrint Arch., 2021 (2021)

48. Liu-Zhang, C.-D., Maurer, U.: Synchronous constructive cryptography. In: Pass, R., Pietrzak, K. (eds.) TCC 2020. LNCS, vol. 12551, pp. 439–472. Springer, Cham (2020). https://doi.org/10.1007/978-3-030-64378-2_16

49. Makriyannis, N.: On the classification of finite Boolean functions up to fairness. In: Abdalla, M., De Prisco, R. (eds.) SCN 2014. LNCS, vol. 8642, pp. 135–154. Springer, Cham (2014). https://doi.org/10.1007/978-3-319-10879-7_9

50. Maller, M., Bowe, S., Kohlweiss, M., Meiklejohn, S.: Sonic: zero-knowledge snarks from linear-size universal and updatable structured reference strings. In: CCS (2019)

51. Pedersen, T.P.: A threshold cryptosystem without a trusted party. In: Davies, D.W. (ed.) EUROCRYPT 1991. LNCS, vol. 547, pp. 522–526. Springer, Heidelberg (1991). https://doi.org/10.1007/3-540-46416-6_47

52. De Santis, A., Di Crescenzo, G., Ostrovsky, R., Persiano, G., Sahai, A.: Robust non-interactive zero knowledge. In: Kilian, J. (ed.) CRYPTO 2001. LNCS, vol. 2139, pp. 566–598. Springer, Heidelberg (2001). https://doi.org/10.1007/3-540-44647-8_33

53. Schoenmakers, B., Veeningen, M.: Universally verifiable multiparty computation from threshold homomorphic cryptosystems. In: Malkin, T., Kolesnikov, V., Lewko, A.B., Polychronakis, M. (eds.) ACNS 2015. LNCS, vol. 9092, pp. 3–22. Springer, Cham (2015). https://doi.org/10.1007/978-3-319-28166-7_1

54. Stadler, M.: Publicly verifiable secret sharing. In: Maurer, U. (ed.) EUROCRYPT 1996. LNCS, vol. 1070, pp. 190–199. Springer, Heidelberg (1996). https://doi.org/10.1007/3-540-68339-9_17

Universally Composable Subversion-Resilient Cryptography

Suvradip Chakraborty[1], Bernardo Magri[2(✉)], Jesper Buus Nielsen[3], and Daniele Venturi[4]

[1] ETH Zurich, Zürich, Switzerland
[2] The University of Manchester, Manchester, UK
bernardo.magri@manchester.ac.uk
[3] Aarhus University, Aarhus, Denmark
[4] Sapienza University of Rome, Rome, Italy

Abstract. Subversion attacks undermine security of cryptographic protocols by replacing a legitimate honest party's implementation with one that leaks information in an undetectable manner. An important limitation of all currently known techniques for designing cryptographic protocols with security against subversion attacks is that they do not automatically guarantee security in the realistic setting where a protocol session may run concurrently with other protocols.

We remedy this situation by providing a foundation of *reverse firewalls* (Mironov and Stephens-Davidowitz, EUROCRYPT'15) in the *universal composability* (UC) framework (Canetti, FOCS'01 and J. ACM'20). More in details, our contributions are threefold:

- We generalize the UC framework to the setting where each party consists of a core (which has secret inputs and is in charge of generating protocol messages) and a firewall (which has no secrets and sanitizes the outgoing/incoming communication from/to the core). Both the core and the firewall can be subject to different flavors of corruption, modeling different kinds of subversion attacks. For instance, we capture the setting where a subverted core looks like the honest core to any efficient test, yet it may leak secret information via covert channels (which we call *specious subversion*).
- We show how to sanitize UC commitments and UC coin tossing against specious subversion, under the DDH assumption.
- We show how to sanitize the classical GMW compiler (Goldreich, Micali and Wigderson, STOC 1987) for turning MPC with security in the presence of semi-honest adversaries into MPC with security in the presence of malicious adversaries. This yields a completeness theorem for maliciously secure MPC in the presence of specious subversion.

S. Chakraborty—Work done while at IST Austria; supported in part by ERC grant 724307.
B. Magri—Work done while at Aarhus University.
D. Venturi—Supported by the grant SPECTRA from Sapienza University of Rome.

O. Dunkelman and S. Dziembowski (Eds.): EUROCRYPT 2022, LNCS 13275, pp. 272–302, 2022.
https://doi.org/10.1007/978-3-031-06944-4_10

Additionally, all our sanitized protocols are *transparent*, in the sense that communicating with a sanitized core looks indistinguishable from communicating with an honest core. Thanks to the composition theorem, our methodology allows, for the first time, to design subversion-resilient protocols by sanitizing different sub-components in a modular way.

1   Introduction

Cryptographic schemes are typically analyzed under the assumption that the machines run by honest parties are fully trusted. Unfortunately, in real life, there are a number of situations in which this assumption turns out to be false. In this work, we are concerned with one of these situations, where the adversary is allowed to subvert the implementation of honest parties in a stealthy way. By stealthy, we mean that the outputs produced by a subverted machine still look like honestly computed outputs, yet, the adversary can use such outputs to completely break security. Prominent examples include back-doored implementations [15,16,18] and algorithm-substitution (or *kleptographic*) attacks [2–4,22,23]. The standardization of the pseudorandom number generator Dual_EC_DRBG, as exposed by Snowden, is a real-world instantiation of the former, while Trojan horses, as in the case of the Chinese hack chip attack, are real-world instantiations of the latter.

1.1   Subversion-Resilient Cryptography

Motivated by these situations, starting from the late 90s, cryptographers put considerable effort into building cryptographic primitives and protocols that retain some form of security in the presence of *subversion attacks*.

Yet, after nearly 30 years of research, all currently known techniques to obtain subversion resilience share the limitation of only implying *standalone* security, *i.e.* they only guarantee security of a protocol in isolation, but all bets are off when such a protocol is used in a larger context in the presence of subversion attacks. This shortcoming makes the design of subversion-resilient cryptographic protocols somewhat cumbersome and highly non-modular. For instance, Ateniese, Magri, and Venturi [1] show how to build subversion-resilient signatures, which in turn were used by Dodis, Mironov and Stephens-Davidowitz [17] to obtain subversion-resilient key agreement protocols, and by Chakraborty, Dziembowski and Nielsen [11] to obtain subversion-resilient broadcast; however, the security analysis in both [17] and [11] reproves security of the construction in [1] from scratch. These examples bring the fundamental question:

Can we obtain subversion resistance in a composable *security framework?*

A positive answer to the above question would dramatically simplify the design of subversion-resilient protocols, in that one could try to first obtain security under subversion attacks for simpler primitives, and then compose such primitives in an arbitrary way to obtain protocols for more complex tasks, in a modular way.

1.2 Our Contributions

In this work, we give a positive answer to the above question using so-called *cryptographic reverse firewalls*, as introduced by Mironov and Stephens-Davidowitz [21]. Intuitively, a reverse firewall is an external party that sits between an honest party and the network, and whose task is to sanitize the incoming/outgoing communication of the party it is attached to, in order to annhilate subliminal channels generated via subversion attacks. The main challenge is to obtain sanitation while maintaining the correctness of the underlying protocol, and in a setting where other parties may be completely under control of the subverter itself.

While previous work showed how to build reverse firewalls for different cryptographic protocols in *standalone* security frameworks we provide a foundation of reverse firewalls in the framework of universal composability (UC) of Canetti [6,7]. More in details, our contributions are threefold:

- We generalize the UC framework to the setting where each party consists of a core (which has secret inputs and is in charge of generating protocol messages) and a firewall (which has no secrets and sanitizes the outgoing/incoming communication from/to the core). Both the core and the firewall can be subject to different flavors of corruption, modeling different kinds of subversion attacks. For instance, we capture the setting where a subverted core looks like the honest core to any efficient test, yet it may leak secret information via covert channels (which we call *specious subversion*).
- We show how to sanitize UC commitments and UC coin tossing against specious subversion, under the decisional Diffie-Hellman (DDH) assumption in the common reference string (CRS) model. Our sanitized commitment protocol is non-interactive, and requires 2λ group elements in order to commit to a λ-bit string; the CRS is made of 3 group elements.
- We show how to sanitize the classical compiler by Goldreich, Micali and Wigderson (GMW) [20] for turning multiparty computation (MPC) with security against semi-honest adversaries into MPC with security against malicious adversaries. This yields a completeness theorem for maliciously secure MPC in the presence of specious subversion.

Additionally, all our sanitized protocols are *transparent*, in the sense that communicating with a sanitized core looks indistinguishable from communicating with an honest core. Thanks to the composition theorem, our methodology allows, for the first time, to design subversion-resilient protocols by sanitizing different sub-components in a modular way.

1.3 Technical Overview

Below, we provide an overview of the techniques we use in order to achieve our results, starting with the notion of subversion-resilient UC security, and then explaining the main ideas behind our reverse firewalls constructions.

Subversion-resilient UC Security. At a high level we model each logical party P_i of a protocol Π as consisting of two distinct parties of the UC framework, one called the core C_i and one called the firewall F_i. These parties can be independently corrupted. For instance, the core can be subverted and the firewall honest, or the core could be honest and the firewall corrupted. The ideal functionalities $\mathcal{F}$ implemented by such a protocol will also recognize two UC parties per virtual party and can let their behavior depend on the corruption pattern. For instance, $\mathcal{F}$ could specify that if C_i is subverted and F_i honest, then it behaves as if P_i is honest on $\mathcal{F}$. Or it could say that if C_i is honest and F_i corrupt, then it behaves as if P_i is honest but might abort on $\mathcal{F}$. This is a reasonable choice as a corrupt firewall can always cut C_i off from the network and force an abort. We then simply ask that Π UC-realizes $\mathcal{F}$. By asking that Π UC-realizes $\mathcal{F}$ we exactly capture that if the core is subverted and the firewall is honest, this has the same effect as P_i being honest. See Table 1 for all possible corruption combinations for C_i and F_i at a glance, and how they translate into corruptions for P_i in an ideal execution with functionality $\mathcal{F}$.

Unfortunately, it turns out that for certain functionalities it is just impossible to achieve security in the presence of *arbitrary* subversion attacks. For instance, a subverted prover in a zero-knowledge proof could simply output an honestly computed proof or the all-zero string depending on the first bit of the witness. Since the firewall would not know a valid witness, these kind of subversion attacks cannot be sanitized. For this reason, following previous work [11,17,19,21], we focus on classes of subversion attacks for which a subverted core looks like an honest core to any efficient test, yet it may signal private information to the subverter via subliminal channels. We call such corruptions *specious*. We note that testing reasonably models a scenario in which the core has been built by an untrusted manufacturer who wants to stay covert, and where the user tests it against a given specification before using it in the wild.

By defining subversion resilience in a black-box way, via the standard notion of UC implementation, we also get composition almost for free via the UC composition theorem. One complication arises to facilitate modular composition of protocols. When doing a modular construction of a subversion-resilient protocol, both the core and the firewall will be built by modules. For instance, the core could be built from a core for a commitment scheme and the core for an outer protocol using the commitment scheme. Each of these cores will come with their own firewall: one sanitizes the core of the commitment scheme; the other sanitizes the core of the outer protocol. The overall firewall is composed of these two firewalls. It turns out that it is convenient that these two firewalls can coordinate, as it might be that some of the commitments sent need to have the message randomized, while others might only have their randomness refreshed. The latter can be facilitated by giving the firewall of the commitment scheme a sanitation interface where it can be instructed by the outer firewall to do the right sanitation. Note that the protocol implementing the commitment ideal functionality now additionally needs to implement this sanitation interface.

We refer the reader to Sect. 2 for a formal description of our model. Note that another natural model would have been to have P_i split into three parts (or tiers), C_i, U_i, and F_i, where: (i) U_i is a user program which gets inputs and sends messages on the network; (ii) C_i is a core holding cryptographic keys and implementations of, *e.g.*, signing and encryption algorithms; and (iii) F_i is a firewall used by U_i to sanitize messages to and from C_i in order to avoid covert channels. The above better models a setting where we are only worried that some part of the computer might be subverted. The generalisation to this case is straightforward given the methodology we present for the case with no user program U_i. Since we only look at subversions which are indistinguishable from honest implementations, having the "unsubvertable" U_i appears to give no extra power. We therefore opted for the simpler model for clarity. Further discussion on the three-tier model can be found the full version [12].

Strong sanitation. The main challenge when analyzing subversion security of a protocol in our framework is that, besides maliciously corrupting a subset of the parties, the adversary can, *e.g.*, further speciously corrupt the honest parties. To overcome this challenge, we introduce a simple property of reverse firewalls which we refer to as *strong sanitation*. Intuitively, this property says that no environment, capable of doing specious corruptions of an honest core in the real world, can distinguish an execution of the protocol with one where an honest core is replaced with a so-called *incorruptible* core (that simply behaves honestly in case of specious corruption). The latter, of course, requires that the firewall of the honest core is honest.

We then prove a general lemma saying that, whenever a firewall has strong sanitation, it is enough to prove security in our model without dealing with specious corruptions of honest parties. This lemma significantly simplifies the security analysis of protocols in our model.

Commitments In Sect. 3, we show how to obtain subversion-resilient UC commitments. First, we specify a sanitizable string commitment functionality $\widehat{\mathcal{F}}_{\mathsf{sCOM}}$. This functionality is basically identical to the standard functionality for UC commitments [8], except that the firewall is allowed to sanitize the value s that the core commits to, using a blinding factor r; the effect of this sanitation is that, when the core opens the commitment, the ideal functionality reveals $\hat{s} = s \oplus r$. Note that this is the sanitation allowed by the sanitation interface. An implementation will further have to sanitise the randomness of outgoing commitments to avoid covert channels.

Second, we construct a protocol $\widehat{\Pi}_{\mathsf{sCOM}}$ that UC realizes $\widehat{\mathcal{F}}_{\mathsf{sCOM}}$ in the presence of subversion attacks. Our construction borrows ideas from a recent work by Canetti, Sarkar and Wang [10], who showed how to construct efficient non-interactive UC commitments with adaptive security. The protocol, which is in the CRS model and relies on the standard DDH assumption, roughly works as follows. The CRS is a tuple of the form (g, h, T_1, T_2), such that $T_1 = g^x$ and $T_2 = h^{x'}$ for $x \neq x'$ (*i.e.*, a non-DH tuple). In order to commit to a single bit b, the core of the committer encodes b as a value $u \in \{-1, 1\}$ and outputs $B = g^\alpha \cdot T_1^u$ and $H = h^\alpha \cdot T_2^u$, where α is the randomness. The firewall sanitizes a pair (B, H) by outputting $\widehat{B} = B^{-1} \cdot g^\beta$ and $\widehat{H} = H^{-1} \cdot h^\beta$, where β is chosen randomly; note that, upon receiving an opening (b, α) from the core, the firewall can adjust it by returning $(1-b, -\alpha+\beta)$. Alternatively, the firewall can choose to leave the bit b unchanged and only refresh the randomness of the commitment; this is achieved by letting $\widehat{B} = B \cdot g^\beta$ and $\widehat{H} = H \cdot h^\beta$; in this case, the opening is adjusted to $(b, \alpha + \beta)$. In the security proof, we distinguish two cases:

- In case the committer is maliciously corrupt, the simulator sets the CRS as in the real world but additionally knows the discrete log t of h to the base g. Such a trapdoor allows the simulator to extract the bit b corresponding to the malicious committer by checking whether $H/T_2 = (B/T_1)^t$ (in which case $b = 1$) or $H \cdot T_2 = (B \cdot T_1)^t$ (in which case $b = 0$). If none of the conditions hold, no opening exists.
- In case the committer is honest, the simulator sets the CRS as a DH-tuple. Namely, now $T_1 = g^x$ and $T_2 = h^x$ for some x known to the simulator. The latter allows the simulator to fake the commitment as $B = g^\alpha$ and $H = h^\alpha$, and later adjust the opening to any given $u \in \{-1, 1\}$ (and thus $b \in \{0, 1\}$) by letting $\alpha' = \alpha - u \cdot x$.

The above ideas essentially allow to build a simulator for the case of two parties, where one is maliciously corrupt and the other one has an honest core and a semi-honest firewall. These ideas can be generalized to n parties (where up to $n - 1$ parties are maliciously corrupt, while the remaining party has an honest core and a semi-honest firewall) using an independent CRS for each pair of parties. Finally, we show that the firewall in our protocol is strongly sanitizing and thus all possible corruption cases reduce to the previous case. In particular, strong sanitation holds true because a specious core must produce a pair (B, H) of the form $B = g^\alpha \cdot T_1^{\tilde{u}}$ and $H = h^\alpha \cdot T_2^{\tilde{u}}$ for some $\tilde{u} \in \{-1, 1\}$ (and thus $\tilde{b} \in \{0, 1\}$), as otherwise a tester could distinguish it from an honest core by asking it to open the commitment; given such a well-formed commitment, the firewall perfectly refreshes its randomness (and eventually blinds the message).

As we show in Sect. 3, the above construction can be extended to the case where the input to the commitment is a λ-bit string by committing to each bit individually; the same CRS can be reused across all of the commitments.

Coin Tossing. Next, in Sect. 4, we show a simple protocol that UC realizes the standard coin tossing functionality $\mathcal{F}_{\mathsf{Toss}}$ in the presence of subversion attacks. Recall that the ideal functionality $\mathcal{F}_{\mathsf{Toss}}$ samples a uniformly random string $s \in \{0, 1\}^\lambda$ and sends it to the adversary, which can then decide which honest party gets s (i.e., the coin toss output).

Our construction is a slight variant of the classical coin tossing protocol by Blum [5]; the protocol is in the $\widehat{\mathcal{F}}_{\mathsf{sCOM}}$-hybrid model, and roughly works as follows. The core of each party commits to a random string $s_i \in \{0, 1\}^\lambda$ through the ideal functionality $\widehat{\mathcal{F}}_{\mathsf{sCOM}}$. Then, the firewall of the coin toss instructs the firewall of the commitment to blind s_i using a random blinding factor $r_i \in \{0,1\}^\lambda$ which is revealed to the core. At this point, each (willing) party opens the commitment, which translates into $\widehat{\mathcal{F}}_{\mathsf{sCOM}}$ revealing $\hat{s}_j = s_j \oplus r_j$, and each party finally outputs $s = s_i \oplus r_i \oplus \bigoplus_{j \neq i} \hat{s}_j$.

In the security proof, the simulator can fake the string s_i of an honest party so that it matches the output of the coin tossing s (received from $\mathcal{F}_{\mathsf{TOSS}}$), the strings s_j received from the adversary (on behalf of a malicious core), and the blinding factor r_i received from the adversary (on behalf of a semi-honest firewall). This essentially allows to build a simulator for the case where up to $n-1$ parties are maliciously corrupt, while the remaining party has an honest core and a semi-honest firewall. Finally, we show that the firewall in our protocol is strongly sanitizing and thus all possible corruption cases reduce to the previous case. Strong sanitation here holds because any string s_i chosen by a specious core is mapped to a uniformly random string $\hat{s}_i$ via the sanitation interface of the functionality $\widehat{\mathcal{F}}_{\mathsf{sCOM}}$.

Completeness Theorem. Finally, in Sect. 5, we show how to sanitize the GMW compiler, which yields a completeness theorem for UC subversion-resilient MPC. Recall that in the classical GMW compiler one starts with an MPC protocol Π tolerating $t < n$ semi-honest corruptions and transforms it into an MPC protocol tolerating t malicious corruptions as follows. First, the players run an augmented coin-tossing protocol, where each party receives a uniformly distributed string (to be used as its random tape) and the other parties receive a commitment to that string. Second, each party commits to its own input and proves in zero knowledge that every step of the protocol Π is executed correctly and consistently with the random tape and input each party is committed to.

As observed by Canetti, Lindell, Ostrovsky and Sahai [9], the above compilation strategy cannot immediately be translated in the UC setting, as the receiver of a UC commitment obtains no information about the value that was committed to. Hence, the parties cannot prove in zero knowledge statements relative to their input/randomness commitment. This issue is resolved by introducing a commit-and-prove ideal functionality, which essentially allows each party to commit to a witness and later prove arbitrary NP statements relative to the committed witness.

In order to sanitize the GMW compiler in the presence of subversion attacks, we follow a similar approach. Namely, we first introduce a sanitazable commit-and-prove functionality $\widehat{\mathcal{F}}_{\mathsf{C\&P}}$. This functionality is very similar in spirit to the standard commit-and-prove functionality, except that the firewall can decide to blind the witness that the core commits to. In the full version [12], we show how to realize the sanitizable commit-and-prove functionality in the CRS model from the DDH assumption, using re-randomizable non-interactive zero-knowledge arguments for all of NP [13]. In fact, there we exhibit a much more general construction that can be instantiated from any so-called *malleable mixed commitment*, a new notion that we introduce and that serves as a suitable abstraction of our DDH-based construction from Sect. 3.

In the actual protocol, we use both the coin tossing functionality $\mathcal{F}_{\mathsf{TOSS}}$ and the sanitizable commit-and-prove functionality $\widehat{\mathcal{F}}_{\mathsf{C\&P}}$ to determine the random tape of each party as follows. Each core commits to a random string s_i via $\widehat{\mathcal{F}}_{\mathsf{C\&P}}$; the corresponding firewall blinds s_i with a random r_i that is revealed to the core. Thus, the players use $\mathcal{F}_{\mathsf{TOSS}}$ to generate public randomness s_i^* that can be used to derive the random tape of party P_i as $s_i^* \oplus (s_i \oplus r_i)$. Moreover each core commits to its own input x_i, which however is not blinded by the firewall. The above allows each party, during the protocol execution, to prove via $\widehat{\mathcal{F}}_{\mathsf{C\&P}}$ that each message has been computed correctly and consistently with the committed input and randomness derived from the public random string s_i^* received from $\mathcal{F}_{\mathsf{TOSS}}$.

The security analysis follows closely the one in [9], except that in our case we show that any adversary corrupting up to t parties maliciously, and the firewall of the remaining honest parties semi-honestly, can be reduced to a semi-honest adversary attacking Π. Since we additionally show that our firewall is strongly sanitizing, which essentially comes from the ideal sanitation interface offered by $\widehat{\mathcal{F}}_{\mathsf{C\&P}}$, all possible corruption cases reduce to the previous case.

2   A UC Model of Reverse Firewalls

In this section we propose a foundation of reverse firewalls in the UC model [7]. We use the UC framework for concreteness as it is the *de facto* standard. However, we keep the description high level and do not depend on very particular details of the framework. Similar formalizations could be given in other frameworks defining security via comparison to ideal functionalities, as long as these ideal functionalities are corruption aware: they know which parties are corrupted and their behavior can depend on it.

2.1   Quick and Dirty Recap of UC

A protocol Π consists of code for each of the parties $\mathsf{P}_1, \ldots, \mathsf{P}_n$. The parties can in turn make calls to ideal functionalities $\mathcal{G}$. More precisely, the code of the program is a single machine. As part of its input, it gets a party identifier pid which tells the code which party it should be running the code for. This allows more flexibility for dynamic sets of parties. Below, we will only consider programs with a fixed number of parties. We are therefore tacitly identifying n parties identifiers $\mathsf{pid}_1, \ldots, \mathsf{pid}_n$ with the n parties $\mathsf{P}_1, \ldots, \mathsf{P}_n$, *i.e.*, $\mathsf{P}_i = \mathsf{pid}_i$. We prefer the notation P_i for purely idiomatic reasons.

A party P_i can call an ideal functionality. To do so it will specify which $\mathcal{G}$ to call (technically it writes down the code of $\mathcal{G}$ and a session identifier sid distinguishing different calls), along with an input x. Then, $(\mathsf{sid}, \mathsf{pid}, x)$ is given to $\mathcal{G}$. If $\mathcal{G}$ does not exists, then it is created from its code.

There is an adversary $\mathcal{A}$ which attacks the protocol. It can corrupt parties via special corruption commands. How parties react to these corruptions is flexible; the parties can in principle be programmed to react in any efficient way. As an example, in response to input `active-corrupt`, we might say that the party in the future will output all its inputs to the adversary, and that it will let the adversary specify what messages the party should send. The adversary can also control ideal functionalities, if the ideal functionalities expose an interface for that. It might for instance be allowed to influence at what time messages are delivered on an ideal functionality of point-to-point message transmission.

There is also an environment $\mathcal{E}$ which gives inputs to the parties and sees their outputs. The environment can talk freely to the adversary. A real world execution $\text{EXEC}_{\Pi,\mathcal{A},\mathcal{E}}$ is driven by the environment which can activate parties or ideal functionalities. The parties and ideal functionalities can also activate each other. The details of activation are not essential here, and can be found in [7].

The protocol Π is meant to implement an ideal functionality $\mathcal{F}$. This is formulated by considering a run of $\mathcal{F}$ with dummy parties which just forward messages between $\mathcal{E}$ and $\mathcal{F}$. In addition, there is an adversary $\mathcal{S}$, called the simulator, which can interact with $\mathcal{F}$ on the adversarial interface, and which can interact freely with $\mathcal{E}$ as an adversary can. The simulation is the process $\text{EXEC}_{\mathcal{F},\mathcal{S},\mathcal{E}}$, where we do not specify the dummy protocol but use $\mathcal{F}$ for the dummy protocol composed with $\mathcal{F}$. We say that Π UC-realizes $\mathcal{F}$ if there exists an efficient simulator which makes the simulation look like the real world execution to any efficient environment:

$$\exists \mathcal{S} \forall \mathcal{E} : \text{EXEC}_{\Pi,\mathcal{A},\mathcal{E}} \approx \text{EXEC}_{\mathcal{F},\mathcal{S},\mathcal{E}},$$

where $\mathcal{A}$ is the dummy adversary (that simply acts as a proxy for the environment), and where the quantifications are over poly-time interactive Turing machines.

Consider a protocol Π that realizes an ideal functionality $\mathcal{F}$ in a setting where parties can communicate as usual, and additionally make calls to an unbounded number of copies of some other ideal functionality $\mathcal{G}$. (This model is called the $\mathcal{G}$-hybrid model.) Furthermore, let Γ be a protocol that UC-realizes $\mathcal{G}$ as sketched above, and let $\Pi^{\mathcal{G}\to\Gamma}$ be the composed protocol that is identical to Π, with the exception that each interaction with the ideal functionality $\mathcal{G}$ is replaced with a call to (or an activation of) an appropriate instance of the protocol Γ. Similarly, any output produced by the protocol Γ is treated as a value provided by the functionality $\mathcal{G}$. The composition theorem states that in such a case, Π and $\Pi^{\mathcal{G}\to\Gamma}$ have essentially the same input/output behavior. Namely, Γ behaves just like the ideal functionality $\mathcal{G}$ even when composed with an arbitrary protocol Π. A special case of this theorem states that if Π UC-realizes $\mathcal{F}$ in the $\mathcal{G}$-hybrid model, then $\Pi^{\mathcal{G}\to\Gamma}$ UC-realizes $\mathcal{F}$.

2.2 Modeling Reverse Firewalls

To model reverse firewalls, we will model each party P_i as two separate parties in the UC model: the core C_i and the firewall F_i. To be able to get composability for our framework via UC composition, we model them as separate parties each with their own party identifier $(\mathsf{pid}, \mathsf{F})$ and $(\mathsf{pid}, \mathsf{C})$. We use pid to denote the two

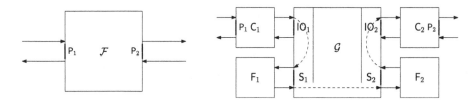

Fig. 1. Implementing a normal functionality $\mathcal{F}$ using a sanitizable hybrid functionality $\mathcal{G}$ and a sanitizing protocol $\Pi = (\mathsf{C}, \mathsf{F})$. Cores and firewalls talk to sanitizable functionalities directly. Cores can additionally talk to the environment to exchange inputs and outputs. Firewalls only talk to ideal functionalities. We think of ideal functionalities as sanitizing the communication with the core via the firewall. This is illustrated in the figure by information from the core going to the firewall, and information to the core coming via the firewall. There is no formal requirement to what extent this happens; it is up to the ideal functionality to decide what type of sanitation is possible, if any.

of them together. Below we write, for simplicity, P_i to denote the full party, C_i to denote the core, and F_i to denote the firewall. Being two separate parties, the core and the firewall cannot talk directly. It will be up to the ideal functionality $\mathcal{G}$ used for communication to pass communication with the core through the corresponding firewall before acting on the communication. It might be that when $\mathcal{G}$ gets a message from C_i it will output this message to F_i and allow F_i to change the message, possibly under some restrictions. We say that F_i sanitizes the communication, and we call the interface connecting F_i for $\mathcal{G}$ the sanitation interface of $\mathcal{G}$. We call such an ideal functionality a "sanitizable" ideal functionality.

Consider a party $(\mathsf{C}_i, \mathsf{F}_i)$ with core C_i and firewall F_i connected to a sanitizing ideal functionality $\mathcal{G}$. The idea is that the firewall gets to sanitize all communication of the core C_i. The UC model seemingly allows a loophole, as the core could make a call to some other ideal functionality $\mathcal{H}$ instead of talking to $\mathcal{G}$. As we discuss later, this behavior is ruled out if C_i is specious, so we will not explicitly disallow it. If our model is later extended to allow stronger (non-specious) types of subversion, then one would probably have to explicitly forbid C_i to use this loophole.

When using a sanitizable ideal functionality, it is convenient to be able to distinguish the interface of the ideal functionality from the parties using the interface. We call the interface of $\mathcal{G}$ to which the core of P_i is connected the input-output interface, IO. We call the party connected to it C_i. We call the interface of $\mathcal{G}$ to which the firewall of P_i is connected the sanitation interface, S. We call the party connected to it F_i. This is illustrated in Fig. 1.

2.3 Specious Corruptions

A major motivation for studying subversion resilience is to construct firewalls which ensure that security is preserved even if the core is subverted. In this section, we describe and discuss how we model subversion in the UC framework.

In a nutshell, we let the adversary replace the code of the core. Clearly, if the core is arbitrarily corrupted, it is impossible to guarantee any security. We therefore have to put restrictions on the code used to subvert the core. One can consider different types of subversions. In this work, we will consider a particularly "benign" subversion, where the subverted core looks indistinguishable from the honest core to any efficient test. This is a particularly strong version of what has been called "functionality preservation" in other works [11,17,19,21]. As there are slightly diverting uses of this term we will coin a new one to avoid confusion.

The central idea behind our notion is that we consider corruptions where a core C_i has been replaced by another implementation $\widetilde{C}_i$ which cannot be distinguished from C_i by black-box access to $\widetilde{C}_i$ or C_i. We use the term *specious* for such corruptions, as they superficially appear to be honest, but might not be.

More in details, we define specious corruptions via testing. Imagine a test T which is given non-rewinding black-box access to either C_i or $\widetilde{C}_i$, and that tries to guess which one it interacted with. We say that a subversion is specious if it survives all efficient tests. This is a very strong notion. One way to motivate this notion could be that $\widetilde{C}_i$ might be built by an untrusted entity, but the buyer of $\widetilde{C}_i$ can test it up against a specification. If the untrusted entity wants to be sure to remain covert, it would have to do a subversion that survives all tests. We assume that the test does not have access to the random choices made by $\widetilde{C}_i$. This makes the model applicable also to the case where $\widetilde{C}_i$ is a blackbox or uses an internal physical process to make random choices. We will allow the entity doing the subversion to have some auxiliary information about the subversion and its use of randomness. This will, for instance, allow the subversion to communicate with the subverter in a way that cannot be detected by any test (*e.g.*, using a secret message acting as a trigger).

For a machine T and an interactive machine $\widetilde{C}$, we use $T^{\widetilde{C}}$ to denote that T has non-rewinding black-box access to $\widetilde{C}$. If during the run of $T^{\widetilde{C}}$ the machine $\widetilde{C}$ requests a random bit, then a uniformly random bit is sampled and given to $\widetilde{C}$. Such randomness is not shown to T. We define the following game for an efficiently sampleable distribution D and a test T.

- Sample $(\widetilde{C}, a) \leftarrow D$, where a is an auxiliary string.
- Sample a uniformly random bit $b \in \{0, 1\}$:
    - If $b = 0$, then run $T^{\widetilde{C}}$ to get a guess $g \in \{0, 1\}$.
    - If $b = 1$, then run T^{C} to get a guess $g \in \{0, 1\}$.
- Output $c = b \oplus g$.

Let $\text{TEST}_{D,T}$ denote the probability that $c = 0$, *i.e.*, the probability that the guess at b is correct.

Definition 1 (Specious subversion). *We say that D is computationally specious if for all PPT tests T it holds that $\text{TEST}_{D,T} - 1/2$ is negligible.*

We return to the discussion of the loophole for specious cores of creating other ideal functionalities $\mathcal{H}$ that are not sanitizing. Note that if a core creates an ideal functionality that it is not supposed to contact, then this can be seen by testing. Therefore, such a core is not considered specious. Hence, the notion of specious closes the loophole.

The notion of specious is strong, as it requires that no test T can detect the subversion. At first glance it might even look too strong, as it essentially implies that the subversion is correct. However, as we show next, a specious subversion can still signal to the outside in an undetectable manner. To formalize this notion, we define the following game for an efficiently sampleable distribution D, an adversary A and a decoder Z.

- Sample $(\widetilde{\mathsf{C}}, a) \leftarrow \mathsf{D}$, where a is an auxiliary string.
- Sample a uniformly random bit $b \in \{0,1\}$:
    - If $b = 0$, then run $\mathsf{A}^{\widetilde{\mathsf{C}}}$ to get a signal $s \in \{0,1\}^*$.
    - If $b = 1$, then run A^{C} to get a signal $s \in \{0,1\}^*$.
- Run $\mathsf{Z}(a, s)$ to get a guess $g \in \{0,1\}$.
- Output $c = b \oplus g$.

Let $\text{SIGNAL}_{\mathsf{D},\mathsf{A},\mathsf{Z}}$ denote the probability that $c = 0$, *i.e.*, the probability that the guess at b is correct.

Definition 2 (Signaling). *We say that D is computationally signalling if there exists a PPT adversary A and a PPT decoder Z such that $\text{SIGNAL}_{\mathsf{D},\mathsf{A},\mathsf{Z}} - 1/2$ is non-negligible.*

Lemma 1. *There exist a machine C, and an efficiently sampleable distribution D, such that D is both computationally specious and signaling.*

Proof (Proof sketch). Consider a machine C that when queried outputs a fresh uniformly random $y \in \{0,1\}^\lambda$. Let $\Phi = \{\phi_\kappa : \{0,1\}^\lambda \to \{0,1\}^\lambda\}_{\kappa \in \{0,1\}^\lambda}$ be a family of pseudorandom permutations. Consider the subversion $\widetilde{\mathsf{C}}$ of C that hardcodes a key $\kappa \in \{0,1\}^\lambda$ and: (i) when initialised samples a uniformly random counter $x \in \{0,1\}^\lambda$; (ii) when queried, it returns $\phi_\kappa(x)$ and increments x. Moreover, let D be the distribution that picks $\kappa \in \{0,1\}^\lambda$ at random and outputs $(\widetilde{\mathsf{C}}, a = \kappa)$.

Note that the distribution D is specious, as the key κ is sampled at random *after* T has been quantified. In particular, the outputs of ϕ_κ are indistinguishable from random to T. The distribution D is also clearly signaling, as it can be seen by taking the adversary A that queries its target oracle twice and sends the outputs y_1 and y_2 as a signal to the decoder. The decoder Z, given $a = \kappa$, computes $x_i = \phi_\kappa^{-1}(y_i)$ (for $i = 1, 2$) and outputs 0 if and only if $x_2 = x_1 + 1$.

We can also define what it means for a set of subversions to be specious.

Definition 3 (Specious subversions). *Given an efficiently sampleable distribution D with outputs of the form $(\widetilde{\mathsf{C}}_1, \ldots, \widetilde{\mathsf{C}}_m, a) \leftarrow \mathsf{D}$, we let D_i be the distribution sampling $(\widetilde{\mathsf{C}}_1, \ldots, \widetilde{\mathsf{C}}_m, a) \leftarrow \mathsf{D}$ and then outputting $(\widetilde{\mathsf{C}}_i, (i, a))$. We say that D is specious if each D_i is specious.*

We now define the notion of a specious corruption. In this paper, we assume that all specious corruptions are static.

Definition 4 (Specious corruption). *We say that a party accepts specious corruptions if, whenever it gets input* (SPECIOUS, $\widetilde{C}$) *from the adversary, it replaces its code by* $\widetilde{C}$. *If the input* (SPECIOUS, $\widetilde{C}$) *is not the first one received by the party, then it ignores it. We say that an environment $\mathcal{E}$ prepares specious corruptions if it operates as follows. First, it writes* (SPECIOUS, D) *on a special tape, where D is specious. Then, it samples* $(\widetilde{C}_1, \ldots, \widetilde{C}_m, a) \leftarrow D$ *and writes this on the special tape too. Finally, it inputs* (SPECIOUS, $\widetilde{C}_1, \ldots, \widetilde{C}_m$) *to the adversary. The above has to be done on the first activation, before any other communication with protocols or the adversary. We call this a specious environment.*

In case of emulation with respect to the dummy adversary, we further require that if the environment instructs the dummy adversary to input (SPECIOUS, $\widetilde{C}$) *to a party, then $\widetilde{C}$ is from the list in* (SPECIOUS, $\widetilde{C}_1, \ldots, \widetilde{C}_m$). *We say that an adversary interacting with a specious environment does specious corruptions if whenever the adversary inputs* (SPECIOUS, $\widetilde{C}$) *to a party, then $\widetilde{C}$ is from the list* (SPECIOUS, $\widetilde{C}_1, \ldots, \widetilde{C}_m$) *received from the specious environment. We call such an adversary specious. In particular, an adversary which never inputs* (SPECIOUS, $\widetilde{C}$) *to any party is specious. We also call an environment specious if it does not write* (SPECIOUS, D) *on a special tape as the first thing, but in this case we require that it does not input anything of the form* (SPECIOUS, $\widetilde{C}_1, \ldots, \widetilde{C}_m$) *to the adversary, and that it never instructs the dummy adversary to input* (SPECIOUS, $\widetilde{C}$) *to any party.*

In addition we require that specious environments and adversaries only do static corruptions and that all corruptions are of the form.

- *Core* MALICIOUS *and firewall* MALICIOUS.
- *Core* HONEST *and firewall* SEMIHONEST.
- *Core* SPECIOUS *and firewall* HONEST.
- *Core* HONEST *and firewall* MALICIOUS.

We assume that all cores accept specious corruptions, and no other parties accept specious corruptions.

We add a few comments to the definition. First, let us explain why we only require security for the above four corruption patterns. Of all the corruption patterns shown in Table 1 giving rise to a MALICIOUS party, the one with core MALICIOUS and firewall MALICIOUS gives the adversary strictly more power than any of the other ones, so we only ask for simulation of that case. Similarly, of the 3 corruption patterns giving rise to an HONEST party, the ones with the core HONEST and SPECIOUS and the firewall SEMIHONEST and HONEST respectively are different, as neither gives powers to the adversary which are a subset of the other, so we ask for simulation of both. The remaining case of HONEST core and HONEST firewall we can drop, as it is a special case of the HONEST core and SEMIHONEST firewall. The only corruption pattern giving rise to an ISOLATE

Table 1. Corruption patterns for cores and firewalls in our model, and their translation in the ideal world. The highlighted rows are the cases that one needs to consider when proving security using our framework.

Core C	Firewall F	Party P in $\mathcal{F}$
HONEST	HONEST	HONEST
HONEST	SEMIHONEST	HONEST
SPECIOUS	HONEST	HONEST
HONEST	MALICIOUS	ISOLATE
SPECIOUS	SEMIHONEST	MALICIOUS
SPECIOUS	MALICIOUS	MALICIOUS
MALICIOUS	HONEST	MALICIOUS
MALICIOUS	SEMIHONEST	MALICIOUS
MALICIOUS	MALICIOUS	MALICIOUS

party is when the core is HONEST and the firewall is MALICIOUS; we therefore ask to simulate this case too.

Second, note that it might look odd that we ask the environment to sample the subversion $\tilde{C}_i$. Could we not just ask that, when it inputs (SPECIOUS, $\tilde{C}_i$) to a core, then $\tilde{C}_i$ is specious? It turns out that this would give a trivial notion of specious corruption. Recall that in the notion of specious, we quantify over all tests. If we first fix $\tilde{C}$, and then quantify over all tests when defining that it is specious, then the universal quantifier could be used to guess random values shared between $\tilde{C}$ and the adversary, like the key κ used in Lemma 1 (demonstrating that a specious subversion can still be signaling). Therefore, a single $\tilde{C}$ specious subversion cannot be signalling. Hence, asking for a specific subversion to be specious would make the notion of specious corruption trivial. By instead asking that a distribution D is specious, we can allow $\tilde{C}$ and the adversary to sample joint randomness (like a secret key κ) after the test T has already been quantified. Namely, recall that in the test game we first fix a T, and only then do we sample D. This allows specious corruptions which can still signal to the adversary, as demonstrated above. The reason why we ask the environment to sample D and not the adversary has to do with UC composition, which we return to later.

2.4 Sanitizing Protocols Implementing Regular Ideal Functionalities

For illustration, we first describe how to implement a regular ideal functionality given a sanitizing ideal functionality. Later, we cover the case of implementing a sanitizing ideal functionality given a sanitizing ideal functionality, see Fig. 1.

Consider a sanitizing protocol Π, using a sanitizable ideal functionality $\mathcal{G}$, that implements a regular ideal functionality $\mathcal{F}$ with n parties $\mathsf{P}_1, \ldots, \mathsf{P}_n$. By regular, we mean that $\mathcal{F}$ itself does not have a sanitation interface. Note that it makes perfect sense for a sanitizing protocol Π, using a sanitizable ideal functionality $\mathcal{G}$, to implement a regular ideal functionality. The firewall is an aspect of the implementation Π and the sanitizable hybrid ideal functionality $\mathcal{G}$. In particular, this aspect could be completely hidden by the implementation of Π. However, typically the behavior when the firewall is honest and corrupted is not the same. A corrupted firewall can isolate the core by not doing its job. We therefore call a party P_i where C_i is honest and F_i is corrupt an "isolated" party. We insist that if C_i is specious and F_i is honest, then it is as if P_i is honest. Hence, $\mathcal{F}$ should behave as if P_i is honest. We would therefore like the behavior of $\mathcal{F}$ to depend only on whether P_i is honest, isolated, or corrupt. To add some structure to this, we introduce the notion of a wrapped ideal functionality and a wrapper.

A wrapped ideal functionality $\mathcal{F}$ should only talk to parties P_i. The wrapper Wrap will talk to a core C_i and a firewall F_i. The wrapper runs $\mathcal{F}$ internally, and we write $\mathsf{Wrap}(\mathcal{F})$. The inputs to and from C_i on $\mathsf{Wrap}(\mathcal{F})$ are forwarded to the interface for P_i on $\mathcal{F}$. The only job of Wrap is to introduce the same parties as in the protocol and translate corruptions of C_i and F_i into corruptions on P_i. We say that parties P_i in an ideal execution with $\mathcal{F}$ can be HONEST, MALICIOUS or ISOLATE. The wrapped ideal functionality $\mathsf{Wrap}(\mathcal{F})$ translates corruptions using the following *standard corruption translation table*.

Honest: If C_i is HONEST and F_i HONEST, let P_i be HONEST on $\mathcal{F}$.
Malicious: If C_i is MALICIOUS, corrupt P_i as MALICIOUS on $\mathcal{F}$.
Isolated: If C_i is HONEST and F_i is MALICIOUS, corrupt P_i as ISOLATE on $\mathcal{F}$.
Sanitation: If C_i is SPECIOUS and F_i is HONEST, let P_i be HONEST on $\mathcal{F}$.
No Secrets: If C_i is HONEST and F_i is SEMIHONEST, let P_i be HONEST on $\mathcal{F}$.

We discuss the five cases next. The **Honest** and **Malicious** cases are straightforward; if both the core and the firewall are honest, then treat P_i as an honest party on $\mathcal{F}$. Similarly, if the core is malicious, then treat P_i as a malicious party on $\mathcal{F}$. The **Isolated** case corresponds to the situation where the core is honest and the firewall is corrupted, and thus the firewall is isolating the core from the network. This will typically correspond to a corrupted party. However, in some cases, some partial security might be obtainable, like the inputs of the core being kept secret. We therefore allow an ISOLATE corruption as an explicit type of corruption. The standard behavior of $\mathcal{F}$ on an ISOLATE corruption is to do a MALICIOUS corruption of P_i in $\mathcal{F}$.

The **Sanitation** case essentially says that the job of the firewall is to turn a specious core into an honest core. This, in particular, means that the firewall should remove any signaling. We add the **No Secrets** case to avoid trivial solutions where the firewall is keeping, *e.g.*, secret keys used in the protocol. We want secret keys to reside in the core, and that firewalls only sanitize communication of the core. We also do not want that the core just hands the inputs to the firewall and lets it run the protocol. A simple way to model this is to require that the protocol should tolerate a semi-honest corruption of the firewall when the core is honest. We do not require that we can tolerate a specious core and a semi-honest firewall. Removing signaling from a core will typically require randomizing some of the communication. For this, the firewall needs to be able to make secret random choices. Note that, with this modeling, a core and a firewall can be seen as a two-party implementation of the honest party, where one can tolerate either a specious corruption of the core or a semi-honest corruption of the firewall.

Definition 5 (Wrapped subversion-resilient UC security). *Let $\mathcal{F}$ be an ideal functionality for n parties $\mathsf{P}_1, \ldots, \mathsf{P}_n$. Let Π be a sanitizing protocol with n cores $\mathsf{C}_1, \ldots, \mathsf{C}_n$ and n firewalls $\mathsf{F}_1, \ldots, \mathsf{F}_n$. Let $\mathcal{G}$ be a sanitizable ideal functionality which can be used by Π as in Fig. 1. We say that Π wsrUC-realizes $\mathcal{F}$ in the $\mathcal{G}$-hybrid model if Π UC-realizes $\mathsf{Wrap}(\mathcal{F})$ in the $\mathcal{G}$-hybrid model with the restriction that we only quantify over specious environments and specious adversaries.*

The typical behavior of a sanitizing ideal functionality is that, when it receives a message from the core, it will output the received message to the firewall, or output some partial information about the message to the firewall. Later, it will receive some new message or sanitation instruction from the firewall. Given this, it constructs the actual information to pass to the core functionality of $\mathcal{G}$. This might later end up at a firewall of another party, and after sanitation end up at the core of that party. The latter is illustrated in Fig. 1, and an example is given below. Note that this is not a formal requirement, but just a description of idiomatic use of sanitation to give an intuition on the use of the model.

To illustrate the use of sanitizable ideal functionalities, we specify an ideal functionality $\mathcal{F}_{\mathsf{SAT}}$ for sanitizable authenticated communication. The communication between cores goes via the firewall which might change the messages. Note that firewalls can be sure which other firewall they talk to, but corrupted firewalls can lie to their local core about who sent a message. In fact, they can pretend a message arrived out of the blue. We also equip $\mathcal{F}_{\mathsf{SAT}}$ with the possibility for distributing setup, as this is needed in some of our protocols. We assume a setup generator Setup which samples the setup and gives each party their corresponding value. The firewalls also get a value. This, *e.g.*, allows to assume that the firewalls know a CRS. Since we do not want firewalls to keep secrets, we leak their setup values to the adversary. This would not be a problem if the setup values is a CRS.

Functionality $\mathcal{F}_{\mathsf{SAT}}$

- Initially sample $((v_1, w_1), \ldots, (v_n, w_n)) \leftarrow \mathsf{Setup}()$ and output v_i on IO_i and w_i on S_i. Leak w_i to the adversary.
- On input $(\mathrm{SEND}, a, \mathsf{P}_j)$ on IO_i, output $(\mathrm{SEND}, a, \mathsf{P}_j)$ on S_i. To keep the description simple we assume honest parties sends the same a at most once. Adding fresh message identifiers can be used for this in an implementation.

- On input (SEND, b, P_k) on S_i, leak (SEND, P_i, b, P_k) to the adversary and store (SEND, P_i, b, P_k).
- On input (DELIVER, (SEND, P_i, b, P_k)) from the adversary, where (SEND, P_i, b, P_k) is stored, delete this tuple and output (RECEIVE, P_i, b) on S_k.
- On input (RECEIVE, P_m, c) on S_k, output (RECEIVE, P_m, c) on IO_i.

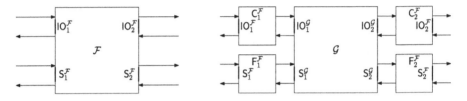

Fig. 2. Implementing $\mathcal{F}$ via protocol $\Pi = (\mathsf{C}^{\mathcal{F}}, \mathsf{F}^{\mathcal{F}})$ using $\mathcal{G}$.

Remark 1 (on $\mathcal{F}_{\mathsf{SAT}}$). We note that all protocols in this work, even if not explicitly stated, are described in the $\mathcal{F}_{\mathsf{SAT}}$-hybrid model. Moreover, whenever we say that the core sends a message to the firewall (or vice-versa) we actually mean that they communicate using $\mathcal{F}_{\mathsf{SAT}}$.

2.5   General Case

We now turn our attention to implementing sanitizable ideal functionalities. When a protocol Π implements a sanitizable ideal functionality, we call Π a sanitizable protocol. Notice the crucial difference between being a *sanitizable* protocol and a *sanitizing* protocol. A sanitizable protocol Π *implements* the sanitization interface S_i of $\mathcal{F}$. Whereas a sanitizing protocol Π would have a firewall *using* the sanitization interface S_i of $\mathcal{G}$.

When implementing a sanitizable ideal functionality $\mathcal{F}$, the protocol should implement the sanitation interface $\mathsf{S}^{\mathcal{F}}$ for F. This means that the protocol will be of the form $\Pi = (\mathsf{IO}, \mathsf{S})$ where $\mathsf{IO} = (\mathsf{IO}_1, \ldots, \mathsf{IO}_n)$ and $\mathsf{S} = (\mathsf{S}_1, \ldots, \mathsf{S}_n)$. Notice that C_i and F_i formally are separate parties, so they cannot talk directly.

It is natural that it is the firewall of the implementation $\Pi = (\mathsf{IO}, \mathsf{S})$ which handles this. The firewall has access to the sanitation interface of $\mathcal{G}$, which it can use to sanitize Π. This means that F gets what could look like a double role now. First, it sanitizes Π using $\mathsf{S}^{\mathcal{G}}$. Second, it has to implement the sanitation interface $\mathsf{S}^{\mathcal{F}}$ of Π (matching that of $\mathcal{F}$). Note, however, that this is in fact the same job. The sanitation interface $\mathsf{S}^{\mathcal{F}}$ of Π is used to specify how Π should be sanitized. It is natural that $\mathsf{F}^{\mathcal{F}}$ needs to knows this specification. It then uses $\mathsf{S}^{\mathcal{G}}$ to implement the desired sanitation. This is illustrated in Fig. 2.

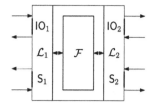

Fig. 3. The wrapper $\mathsf{Wrap}(\mathcal{F}, \mathcal{L}_1, \ldots, \mathcal{L}_n)$.

When defining security of a protocol implementing a sanitizable ideal functionality, we do not need to use a wrapper as when implementing a normal ideal functionality, as $\mathcal{F}$ already has the same parties as in the protocol. It is however still convenient to use a wrapper to add some structure to how we specify a sanitizable ideal functionality. We assume a central part which does the actual computation, and outer parts which sanitize the inputs from P_i before they are passed to the central part.

Definition 6 (Well-formed sanitizing ideal functionality). *A well-formed sanitizing ideal functionality consists of an ideal functionality $\mathcal{F}$, called the central part, with an interface P_i for each party. The interface P_i can be* HONEST, MALICIOUS, *or* ISOLATE. *There are also n outer parts $\mathcal{L}_1, \ldots, \mathcal{L}_n$ where $\mathcal{L}_i$ has an interface IO_i for the core and S_i for the firewall. The outer part $\mathcal{L}_i$ can only talk to the central part on P_i and the outer parts cannot communicate with each other. The interface IO_i can be* HONEST, MALICIOUS, *or* SPECIOUS. *The interface S_i can be* HONEST, MALICIOUS, *or* SEMIHONEST. *The corruption of $\mathcal{F}.\mathsf{IO}_i$ is computed from that of $\mathcal{L}_i.\mathsf{IO}_i$ and $\mathcal{L}_i.\mathsf{S}_i$ using the standard corruption translation table (Table 1).*

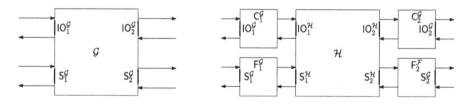

Fig. 4. Implementing $\mathcal{G}$ via protocol $\Gamma = (\mathsf{C}^{\mathcal{G}}, \mathsf{F}^{\mathcal{G}})$ using $\mathcal{H}$.

Definition 7 (Subversion-resilient UC security). *Let $\mathcal{F}$ be an ideal functionality for n cores $\mathsf{C}_1^{\mathcal{F}}, \ldots, \mathsf{C}_n^{\mathcal{F}}$ and n firewalls $\mathsf{F}_1^{\mathcal{F}}, \ldots, \mathsf{F}_n^{\mathcal{F}}$, and let Π be a sanitizing protocol with n cores $\mathsf{C}_1^{\mathcal{F}}, \ldots, \mathsf{C}_n^{\mathcal{F}}$ and n firewalls $\mathsf{F}_1^{\mathcal{F}}, \ldots, \mathsf{F}_n^{\mathcal{F}}$. Let $\mathcal{G}$ be a sanitizable ideal functionality which can be used by Π as in Fig. 2. We say that Π srUC-realizes $\mathcal{F}$ in the $\mathcal{G}$-hybrid model if $\mathcal{F}$ can be written as a well-formed sanitizing ideal functionality, and Π UC-realizes $\mathcal{F}$ in the $\mathcal{G}$-hybrid model with the restriction that we only quantify over specious environments and specious adversaries.*

2.6   Composition

We now address composition. In Fig. 2, we illustrate implementing $\mathcal{F}$ in the $\mathcal{G}$-hybrid model. Similarly, in Fig. 4, we implement $\mathcal{G}$ given $\mathcal{H}$. In Fig. 5, we illustrate the effect of composition. We can let $C_i = C_i^{\mathcal{F}} \circ C_i^{\mathcal{G}}$ and $F_i = F_i^{\mathcal{F}} \circ F_i^{\mathcal{G}}$. Then, we again have a sanitizing protocol $\Pi^{\mathcal{G} \to \Gamma} = (C, F)$. For composition to work, we need that specious corruptions respect the composition of a core.

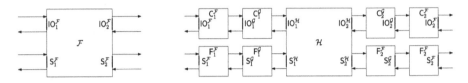

Fig. 5. Implementing $\mathcal{F}$ via protocol $\Pi^{\mathcal{G} \to \Gamma}$ using $\mathcal{H}$.

Definition 8 (Specious corruption of a composed core). *We say that an adversary does a specious corruption of a composed core* $C_i = C_i^{\mathcal{F}} \circ C_i^{\mathcal{G}}$ *if it inputs* (Specious, $\widetilde{C}_i^{\mathcal{F}}, \widetilde{C}_i^{\mathcal{G}}$), *where both* $C_i^{\mathcal{F}}$ *and* $C_i^{\mathcal{G}}$ *are specious. In response* $C_i^{\mathcal{F}}$ *replaces its code with* $\widetilde{C}_i^{\mathcal{F}}$, *and* $C_i^{\mathcal{G}}$ *replaces its code with* $\widetilde{C}_i^{\mathcal{G}}$.

Note that one could imagine a specious corruption of a composed core C_i which could not be written as the composition of specious subversions $\widetilde{C}_i^{\mathcal{F}}$ and $\widetilde{C}_i^{\mathcal{G}}$.

Theorem 1 (srUC Composition). *Let* $\mathcal{F}$ *and* $\mathcal{G}$ *be ideal functionalities, and let* Π *and* Γ *be protocols. Assume that all are subroutine respecting and subroutine exposing as defined in [6]. If* Π *srUC-realizes* $\mathcal{F}$, *and* Γ *srUC-realizes* $\mathcal{G}$, *then* $\Pi^{\mathcal{G} \to \Gamma}$ *srUC-realizes* $\mathcal{F}$.

The proof of Theorem 1 appears in the full version [12].

Note that if, *e.g.*, $\mathcal{G}$ in the composition is well-formed and therefore wrapped, then it is the wrapped functionality which is considered at all places. Therefore, in Fig. 4 the ideal functionality $\mathcal{G}$ being implemented will be the wrapped ideal functionality, and in Fig. 2 the hybrid ideal functionality $\mathcal{G}$ being used would again be the wrapped one. There is no notion of "opening up the wrapping" during composition. If $\mathcal{F}$ is a regular ideal functionality then $\mathsf{Wrap}(\mathcal{F})$ can be written as a well-formed sanitizing ideal functionality. Therefore wsrUC security relative to $\mathcal{F}$ implies srUC security relative to $\mathsf{Wrap}(\mathcal{F})$. During composition it would be $\mathsf{Wrap}(\mathcal{F})$ which is used as a hybrid functionality. This is basically the same as having $\mathcal{F}$ under the standard corruption translation.

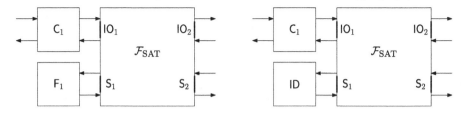

Fig. 6. A core with its matching firewall or with the identity firewall.

2.7 Computational Transparency

A central notion in the study of reverse firewalls is the notion of transparency. The firewall is only supposed to modify the behavior of a subverted core. If the firewall is attached to an honest core, it must not change the behavior of the core. We define transparency in line with [21], namely, an honest core without a firewall attached should be indistinguishable from an honest core with a firewall attached.

Notice that this does not make sense if the party is implementing a sanitizable ideal functionality, like in Fig. 2. Without a firewall $\mathsf{F}_1^{\mathcal{F}}$, no entity would implement the interface $\mathsf{S}_1^{\mathcal{F}}$, which would make a core without a firewall trivially distinguishishable from a core with a firewall. Presumably, the interface $\mathsf{S}_1^{\mathcal{F}}$ is present because different inputs on this interface will give different behaviors. We therefore only define transparency of firewalls implementing a regular ideal functionality, as in Fig. 1. Note also that if $\mathcal{G}$ in Fig. 1 has a complex interaction with F_i, then an execution without F_i might not make sense. Therefore, we additionally only consider transparency in the $\mathcal{F}_{\mathsf{SAT}}$-hybrid model. In this model we can let F_i be an *identity firewall* which does not modify the communication. This has the desired notion of no firewall being present.

Definition 9 (Transparency). *Let* $(\mathsf{C}_i, \mathsf{F}_i)$ *be a party for the* $\mathcal{F}_{\mathsf{SAT}}$*-hybrid model. Let* Π_i *be the protocol for the* $\mathcal{F}_{\mathsf{SAT}}$*-hybrid model where party number* i *is* $(\mathsf{C}_i, \mathsf{F}_i)$, *and all other parties are dummy parties. Let* ID *be the firewall which always outputs any message it receives as input. Let* Π_i' *be the protocol for the* $\mathcal{F}_{\mathsf{SAT}}$*-hybrid model where party number* i *is* $(\mathsf{C}_i, \mathsf{ID})$, *and all other parties are dummy parties. These two protocols are illustrated in Fig. 6. We say that* F_i *is computationally transparent if, for all poly-time environments* $\mathcal{E}$ *which do not corrupt* C_i *or* F_i/ID, *it holds that* $\mathrm{EXEC}_{\mathcal{E}, \Pi_i, \mathcal{A}} \approx \mathrm{EXEC}_{\mathcal{E}, \Pi_i', \mathcal{A}}$, *where* $\mathcal{A}$ *is the dummy adversary.*

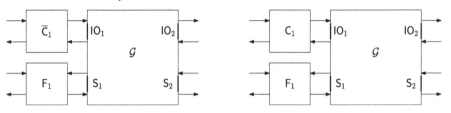

Fig. 7. An honest core with its matching firewall or a specious core with the same firewall.

2.8 Strong Sanitation

Another central notion in the study of reverse firewalls is the notion that we call sanitation. Namely, if you hide a specious core behind a firewall, then it looks like an honest core behind a firewall. So far, we have defined this implicitly by saying that a specious corruption of a core plus an honest firewall should be simulatable by having access to an honest party on the ideal functionality being implemented. This actually does not imply that the network cannot distinguish between a specious core or an honest core behind the firewall. It only says that the effect of a specious core behind a firewall are not dire enough that you cannot simulate given an honest party in the ideal world.

In this section, we give a game-based definition of sanitation capturing the stronger notion that, behind a firewall, a specious core looks like an honest core. Recall that a core C_i is capable of receiving a specious corruption (SPECIOUS, $\widetilde{C}$) from the environment, in which case it replaces its code by $\widetilde{C}$. For such a core, let $\widehat{C}$ be the *incorruptible core* which when it receives a specious corruption (SPECIOUS, $\widetilde{C}$) will ignore it and keep running the code of C.

Definition 10 (Strong sanitation). *Let (C_i, F_i) by a party for the $\mathcal{G}$-hybrid model. Let $\widehat{C}_i$ be the corresponding incorruptible core. Let Π_i be the protocol for the $\mathcal{F}_{\mathsf{SAT}}$-hybrid model where party number i is (C_i, F_i), and all other parties are dummy parties. Let Π_i' be the protocol for the $\mathcal{F}_{\mathsf{SAT}}$-hybrid model where party number i is $(\widehat{C}_i, F_i)$, and all other parties are dummy parties. Note that if the environment does a (SPECIOUS, $\widetilde{C}$) corruption of core number i, then in Π_i core i will run $\widetilde{C}$, whereas in Π_i' it will run C_i. These two outcomes are illustrated in Fig. 7. We say that F_i is strongly sanitising if, for all poly-time environments $\mathcal{E}$ which do not corrupt F_i, but which are allowed a specious corruption of the core, it holds that $\mathrm{EXEC}_{\mathcal{E},\Pi_i,\mathcal{A}} \approx \mathrm{EXEC}_{\mathcal{E},\Pi_i',\mathcal{A}}$, where $\mathcal{A}$ is the dummy adversary.*

It is easy to see that the definition is equivalent to requiring that, for all poly-time environments $\mathcal{E}$ which do not corrupt C_i or F_i/ID, it holds that $\mathrm{EXEC}_{\mathcal{E},\Pi_i,\mathcal{A}} \approx \mathrm{EXEC}_{\mathcal{E},\Pi_i',\mathcal{A}}$, where $\mathcal{A}$ is the dummy adversary.

Lemma 2. *Consider a protocol Π where for all parties (C_i, F_i) it holds that F_i has strong sanitation. Then it is enough to prove security for these cases:*

- *Core MALICIOUS and firewall MALICIOUS.*
- *Core HONEST and firewall SEMIHONEST.*

- *Core* HONEST *and firewall* MALICIOUS.

If in addition we assume the standard corruption behavior for ISOLATE, *it is enough to prove the cases:*

- *Core* MALICIOUS *and firewall* MALICIOUS.
- *Core* HONEST *and firewall* SEMIHONEST.

If in addition the protocol Π is for the $\mathcal{F}_{\mathsf{SAT}}$-hybrid model and has computational transparency, then it is enough to prove the case:

- *Core* MALICIOUS *and firewall* MALICIOUS.
- *Core* HONEST *and firewall* HONEST.

Proof. We prove the first claim. Note that relative to Definition 7 we removed the case with the core SPECIOUS and the firewall HONEST. We show that this reduces to the case with core HONEST and the firewall HONEST. First replace each C_i by $\widehat{C}_i$. This cannot be noticed due to strong sanitation. Then notice that we can replace an environment $\mathcal{E}$ doing specious corruption by $\mathcal{E}'$ which just internally do not pass on (SPECIOUS, $\widetilde{C}$) to the core. Namely, it does not matter if $\widehat{C}_i$ ignores the commands or we let $\mathcal{E}'$ do it. Then, we can replace $\widehat{C}_i$ by C_i as there are no commands to ignore. So it is enough to prove security for the core HONEST and the firewall HONEST. This case follows from the case with the core SPECIOUS and the firewall HONEST as being honest is a special case of being specious.

The second claim follows from the fact that under standard corruption behavior for ISOLATE the party P_i on the ideal functionality is MALICIOUS when the firewall is MALICIOUS. So the simulator has the same power when simulating an honest core and malicious firewall as when simulating a malicious core and a malicious firewall. Then note that being an honest core is a special case of being a malicious core.

In the last claim, we have to prove that assuming computational transparency one does not have to prove the case with the core HONEST and the firewall SEMIHONEST. One can instead prove the case with the core HONEST and the firewall HONEST. To see this note that, by definition of transparency, we can replace the firewall with the identity firewall ID. For this firewall, an HONEST corruption is as powerful as a SEMIHONEST corruption. This is because the only effect of a semi-honest corruption of ID is to leak the internal value w_i from the setup and the communication sent via ID. The ideal functionality $\mathcal{F}_{\mathsf{SAT}}$ already leaks that information when ID is honest.

3   String Commitment

In this section, we show how to build UC string commitments with security in the presence of subversion attacks. In particular, after introducing the sanitizable commitment functionality, we exhibit a non-interactive commitment (with an associated reverse firewall) that UC realizes this functionality in the CRS model, under the DDH assumption.

3.1   Sanitizable Commitment Functionality

The sanitazable commitment functionality $\widehat{\mathcal{F}}_{\mathsf{sCOM}}$, which is depicted below, is an extension of the standard functionality for UC commitments [8]. Roughly, $\widehat{\mathcal{F}}_{\mathsf{sCOM}}$ allows the core of a party to commit to a λ-bit string s_i; the ideal functionality stores s_i and informs the corresponding firewall that the core has sent a commitment. Hence, via the sanitation interface, the firewall of that party is allowed to forward to the functionality a blinding factor $r_i \in \{0,1\}^\lambda$ that is used to blind s_i, yielding a sanitized input $\hat{s}_i = s_i \oplus r_i$. At this point, all other parties are informed by the functionality that a commitment took place. Finally, each party is allowed to open the commitment via the functionality, in which case all other parties learn the sanitized input $\hat{s}_i$.

Functionality $\widehat{\mathcal{F}}_{\mathsf{sCOM}}$

The sanitizable string commitment functionality $\widehat{\mathcal{F}}_{\mathsf{sCOM}}$ runs with parties $\mathsf{P}_1, \ldots, \mathsf{P}_n$ (each consisting of a core C_i and a firewall F_i), and an adversary $\mathcal{S}$. The functionality consists of the following communication interfaces for the cores and the firewalls respectively.

Interface IO
- Upon receiving a message $(\textsc{Commit}, \mathsf{sid}, \mathsf{cid}, \mathsf{C}_i, s_i)$ from C_i, where $s_i \in \{0,1\}^\lambda$, record the tuple $(\mathsf{sid}, \mathsf{cid}, \mathsf{C}_i, s_i)$ and send the message $(\textsc{Receipt}, \mathsf{sid}, \mathsf{cid}, \mathsf{C}_i)$ to F_i. Ignore subsequent commands of the form $(\textsc{Commit}, \mathsf{sid}, \mathsf{cid}, \mathsf{C}_i, \cdot)$.
- Upon receiving a message $(\textsc{Open}, \mathsf{sid}, \mathsf{cid}, \mathsf{C}_i)$ from C_i, proceed as follows: If the tuple $(\mathsf{sid}, \mathsf{cid}, \mathsf{C}_i, \hat{s}_i)$ is recorded and the message $(\textsc{Blind}, \mathsf{sid}, \mathsf{cid}, \mathsf{C}_i, \cdot)$ was sent to $\widehat{\mathcal{F}}_{\mathsf{sCOM}}$, then send the message $(\textsc{Open}, \mathsf{sid}, \mathsf{cid}, \mathsf{C}_i, \hat{s}_i)$ to all $\mathsf{C}_{j \neq i}$ and $\mathcal{S}$. Otherwise, do nothing.

Interface S
- Upon receiving a message $(\textsc{Blind}, \mathsf{sid}, \mathsf{cid}, \mathsf{C}_i, r_i)$ from F_i, where $r_i \in \{0,1\}^\lambda$, proceed as follows: If the tuple $(\mathsf{sid}, \mathsf{cid}, \mathsf{C}_i, s_i, \cdot)$ is recorded, then modify the tuple to be $(\mathsf{sid}, \mathsf{cid}, \mathsf{C}_i, \hat{s}_i = s_i \oplus r_i)$ and send the message $(\textsc{Blinded}, \mathsf{sid}, \mathsf{cid}, \mathsf{C}_i, r_i)$ to C_i, and $(\textsc{Receipt}, \mathsf{sid}, \mathsf{cid}, \mathsf{C}_i)$ to all $\mathsf{C}_{j \neq i}$ and $\mathcal{S}$; otherwise do nothing. Ignore future commands of the form $(\textsc{Blind}, \mathsf{sid}, \mathsf{cid}, \mathsf{C}_i, \cdot)$.

3.2   Protocol from DDH

Next, we present a protocol that UC-realizes $\widehat{\mathcal{F}}_{\mathsf{sCOM}}$ in the $\mathcal{F}_{\mathsf{SAT}}$-hybrid model. For simplicity, let us first consider the case where there are only two parties. The CRS in our protocol is a tuple $\mathsf{crs} = (g, h, T_1, T_2)$ satisfying the following properties:

- The element g is a generator of a cyclic group $\mathbb{G}$ with prime order q, and $h, T_1, T_2 \in \mathbb{G}$. Moreover, the DDH assumption holds in $\mathbb{G}$.[1]
- In the real-world protocol, the tuple (g, h, T_1, T_2) corresponds to a non-DH tuple. Namely, it should be the case that $T_1 = g^x$ and $T_2 = h^{x'}$, for $x \neq x'$.
- In the security proof, the simulator will set the CRS as (g, h, T_1, T_2), where $T_1 = g^x$ and $T_2 = h^x$. By the DDH assumption, this distribution is computationally indistinguishable from the real-world distribution. In addition, the simulator will be given the trapdoor (x, t) for the CRS $\mathsf{crs} = (g, h, T_1, T_2)$, such that $h = g^t$ and $T_1 = g^x$.

As explained in Sect. 1.3, the above ideas can be generalized to the multiparty setting by using a different CRS for each pair of parties.

Protocol $\widehat{\Pi}_{\mathsf{sCOM}}$ (Sanitizable UC Commitment Protocol)

The protocol is executed between parties $\mathsf{P}_1, \ldots, \mathsf{P}_n$ each consisting of a core C_i and a firewall F_i. In what follows, let party $\mathsf{P}_j = (\mathsf{C}_j, \mathsf{F}_j)$ be the committer, and all other parties $\mathsf{P}_{k \neq j}$ act as verifiers.

Public inputs: Group $\mathbb{G}$ with a generator g, field $\mathbb{Z}_q$, and $\mathsf{crs} = (\mathsf{crs}_{j,k})_{j,k \in [n], k \neq j} = (g_{j,k}, h_{j,k}, T_{1,j,k}, T_{2,j,k})_{j,k \in [n], k \neq j}$.

Private inputs: The committer (or core) C_j has an input $s \in \{0,1\}^\lambda$ which we parse as $s = (s[1], \cdots, s[\lambda])$. We will encode each bit $s[i] \in \{0,1\}$ with a value $u[i] \in \{-1,1\}$, so that $u[i] = 1$ if $s[i] = 1$ and $u[i] = -1$ if $s[i] = 0$. The firewall F_j has an input $r = (r[1], \cdots, r[\lambda]) \in \{0,1\}^\lambda$ (*i.e.*, the blinding factor).

Commit phase: For all $i \in [\lambda]$, the core C_j samples a random $\alpha_{j,k}[i] \leftarrow \mathbb{Z}_q$ and computes the values $B_{j,k}[i] = g_{j,k}^{\alpha_{j,k}[i]} \cdot T_{1,j,k}^{u[i]}$ and $H_{j,k}[i] = h_{j,k}^{\alpha_{j,k}[i]} \cdot T_{2,j,k}^{u[i]}$. Hence, it sends $c_{j,k} = (c_{j,k}[1], \cdots, c_{j,k}[\lambda])$ to the firewall F_j where $c_{j,k}[i] = (B_{j,k}[i], H_{j,k}[i])$. For all $i \in [\lambda]$, the firewall F_j picks random $\beta_{j,k} = (\beta_{j,k}[1], \cdots, \beta_{j,k}[\lambda]) \in \mathbb{Z}_q^\lambda$ and does the following:

- If $r[i] = 0$, it lets $\widehat{B}_{j,k}[i] = B_{j,k}[i] \cdot g_{j,k}^{\beta_{j,k}[i]}$ and $\widehat{H}_{j,k}[i] = H_{j,k}[i] \cdot h_{j,k}^{\beta_{j,k}[i]}$;
- Else if $r[i] = 1$, it lets $\widehat{B}_{j,k}[i] = B_{j,k}[i]^{-1} \cdot g_{j,k}^{\beta_{j,k}[i]}$ and $\widehat{H}_{j,k}[i] = H_{j,k}[i]^{-1} \cdot h_{j,k}^{\beta_{j,k}[i]}$.

Hence, F_j sends $\hat{c}_{j,k} = (\hat{c}_{j,k}[1], \cdots, \hat{c}_{j,k}[\lambda])$ to all other parties $\mathsf{P}_{k \neq j}$, where $\hat{c}_{j,k}[i] = (\widehat{B}_{j,k}[i], \widehat{H}_{j,k}[i])$.

Opening phase: The core C_j sends $(s, \alpha_{j,k})$ to the firewall F_j, where $s \in \{0,1\}^\lambda$ and $\alpha_{j,k} \in \mathbb{Z}_q^\lambda$. Upon receiving $(s, \alpha_{j,k})$ from C_j, the firewall F_j parses $s = (s[1], \cdots, s[\lambda])$ and $\alpha_{j,k} = (\alpha_{j,k}[1], \cdots, \alpha_{j,k}[\lambda])$. Thus, for all $i \in [\lambda]$, it does the following:

- If $r[i] = 0$, it lets $\hat{s}[i] = s[i]$ and $\hat{\alpha}_{j,k}[i] = \alpha_{j,k}[i] + \beta_{j,k}[i]$;
- Else if $r[i] = 1$, it lets $\hat{s}[i] = -s[i]$ and $\hat{\alpha}_{j,k}[i] = -\alpha_{j,k}[i] + \beta_{j,k}[i]$.

Hence, F_j sends $(\hat{s}, \hat{\alpha}_{j,k})$ to all other parties $\mathsf{P}_{k \neq j}$, where $\hat{s} = (\hat{s}[1], \cdots, \hat{s}[\lambda])$ and $\hat{\alpha}_{j,k} = (\hat{\alpha}_{j,k}[1], \cdots, \hat{\alpha}_{j,k}[\lambda])$.

---

[1] Recall that the DDH assumption states that the distribution ensembles $\{g, h, g^x, h^x : x \leftarrow \mathbb{Z}_q\}$ and $\{g, h, g^x, h^{x'} : x, x' \leftarrow \mathbb{Z}_q\}$ are computationally indistinguishable.

Verification phase: Upon receiving $(\hat{c}_{j,k}, (\hat{s}, \hat{\alpha}_{j,k}))$ from P_j, each party $\mathsf{P}_{k \neq j}$ parses $\hat{c}_{j,k} = ((\widehat{B}_{j,k}[1], \widehat{H}_{j,k}[1]), \cdots, (\widehat{B}_{j,k}[\lambda], \widehat{H}_{j,k}[\lambda]))$, $\hat{\alpha}_{j,k} = (\hat{\alpha}_{j,k}[1], \cdots, \hat{\alpha}_{j,k}[\lambda])$, and encodes $\hat{s} = (\hat{s}[1], \cdots, \hat{s}[\lambda]) \in \{0,1\}^\lambda$ as $\hat{u} = (\hat{u}[1], \cdots, \hat{u}[\lambda]) \in \{-1,1\}^\lambda$. Hence, for all $i \in [\lambda]$, it verifies whether $\widehat{B}_{j,k}[i] = g_{j,k}^{\hat{\alpha}_{j,k}[i]} \cdot T_{1,j,k}^{\hat{u}[i]}$ and $\widehat{H}_{j,k}[i] = h_{j,k}^{\hat{\alpha}_{j,k}[i]} \cdot T_{2,j,k}^{\hat{u}[i]}$. If for any $i \in [\lambda]$, the above verification fails, party P_k aborts; otherwise P_k accepts the commitment.

Theorem 2. *The protocol $\widehat{\Pi}_{\mathsf{sCOM}}$ srUC-realizes the $\widehat{\mathcal{F}}_{\mathsf{sCOM}}$ functionality in the $\mathcal{F}_{\mathsf{SAT}}$-hybrid model in the presence of up to $n-1$ static malicious corruptions.*

We defer the proof of Theorem 2 to the full version [12].

4   Coin Tossing

In this section, we build a sanitizing protocol that implements the regular coin tossing functionality. Our protocol is described in the $\widehat{\mathcal{F}}_{\mathsf{sCOM}}$-hybrid model, and therefore must implement the firewall that interacts with the $\widehat{\mathcal{F}}_{\mathsf{sCOM}}$ functionality.

4.1   The Coin Tossing Functionality

We start by recalling the regular $\mathcal{F}_{\mathsf{TOSS}}$ functionality below. Intuitively, the functionality waits to receive an initialization message from all the parties. Hence, it samples a uniformly random λ-bit string s and sends s to the adversary. The adversary now can decide to deliver s to a subset of the parties. The latter restriction comes from the fact that it is impossible to toss a coin fairly so that no adversary can cause a premature abort, or bias the outcome, without assuming honest majority [14].

Functionality $\mathcal{F}_{\mathsf{TOSS}}$

The coin tossing functionality $\mathcal{F}_{\mathsf{TOSS}}$ runs with parties $\mathsf{P}_1, \ldots, \mathsf{P}_n$, and an adversary $\mathcal{S}$. It consists of the following communication interface.

– Upon receiving a message $(\text{INIT}, \mathsf{sid}, \mathsf{P}_i)$ from P_i: If this is the first such message from P_i then record $(\mathsf{sid}, \mathsf{P}_i)$ and send $(\text{INIT}, \mathsf{P}_i)$ to $\mathcal{S}$. If there exist records $(\mathsf{sid}, \mathsf{P}_j)$ for all $(\mathsf{P}_j)_{j \in [n]}$, then sample a uniformly random bit string $s \in \{0,1\}^\lambda$ and send s to the adversary $\mathcal{S}$.
– Upon receiving a message $(\text{DELIVER}, \mathsf{sid}, \mathsf{P}_i)$ from $\mathcal{S}$ (and if this is the first such message from $\mathcal{S}$), and if there exist records $(\mathsf{sid}, \mathsf{P}_j)$ for all $(\mathsf{P}_j)_{j \in [n]}$, send s to P_i; otherwise do nothing.

4.2 Sanitizing Blum's Protocol

Next, we show how to sanitize a variation of the classical Blum coin tossing protocol [5]. In this protocol, each party commits to a random string s_i and later opens the commitment, thus yielding $s = s_1 \oplus \cdots \oplus s_n$. The firewall here samples an independent random string r_i which is used to blind the string s_i chosen by the (possibly specious) core. We defer the security proof to the full version [12].

Protocol $\widehat{\Pi}_{\mathsf{TOSS}}$ (Sanitizing Blum's Coin Tossing)

The protocol is described in the $\widehat{\mathcal{F}}_{\mathsf{sCOM}}$-hybrid model, and is executed between parties $\mathsf{P}_1, \ldots, \mathsf{P}_n$ each consisting of a core C_i and a firewall F_i. Party $\mathsf{P}_i = (\mathsf{C}_i, \mathsf{F}_i)$ proceeds as follows (the code for all other parties is analogous).

1. The core C_i samples a random string $s_i \in \{0,1\}^\lambda$ and sends $(\mathrm{COMMIT}, \mathsf{sid}_i, \mathsf{cid}_i, \mathsf{C}_i, s_i)$ to $\widehat{\mathcal{F}}_{\mathsf{sCOM}}$.
2. Upon receiving $(\mathrm{RECEIPT}, \mathsf{sid}_i, \mathsf{cid}_i, \mathsf{C}_i)$ from $\widehat{\mathcal{F}}_{\mathsf{sCOM}}$, the firewall F_i samples a random string $r_i \in \{0,1\}^\lambda$ and sends $(\mathrm{BLIND}, \mathsf{sid}_i, \mathsf{cid}_i, \mathsf{C}_i, r_i)$ to $\widehat{\mathcal{F}}_{\mathsf{sCOM}}$.
3. Upon receiving $(\mathrm{BLINDED}, \mathsf{sid}_i, \mathsf{cid}_i, \mathsf{C}_i, r_i)$ from $\widehat{\mathcal{F}}_{\mathsf{sCOM}}$, as well as $(\mathrm{RECEIPT}, \mathsf{sid}_j, \mathsf{cid}_j, \mathsf{C}_j)$ for all other cores $\mathsf{C}_{j \neq i}$, the core C_i sends the message $(\mathrm{OPEN}, \mathsf{sid}_i, \mathsf{cid}_i, \mathsf{C}_i)$ to $\widehat{\mathcal{F}}_{\mathsf{sCOM}}$.
4. Upon receiving $(\mathrm{OPEN}, \mathsf{sid}_j, \mathsf{cid}_j, \mathsf{C}_j, \hat{s}_j)$ from $\widehat{\mathcal{F}}_{\mathsf{sCOM}}$, for each core $\mathsf{C}_{j \neq i}$, the core C_i outputs $s := s_i \oplus r_i \oplus \bigoplus_{j \neq i} \hat{s}_j$. (If any of the cores C_j do not open its commitment, then C_i sets $\hat{s}_j = 0^\lambda$.)

Theorem 3. *The protocol $\widehat{\Pi}_{\mathsf{TOSS}}$ wsrUC-realizes the $\mathcal{F}_{\mathsf{TOSS}}$ functionality in the $(\mathcal{F}_{\mathsf{SAT}}, \widehat{\mathcal{F}}_{\mathsf{sCOM}})$-hybrid model in the presence of up to $n-1$ malicious corruptions.*

5 Completeness Theorem

In this section, we show how to sanitize the classical compiler by Goldreich, Micali and Wigderson (GMW) [20], for turning MPC protocols with security against *semi-honest* adversaries into ones with security against *malicious adversaries*. On a high level, the GMW compiler works by having each party commit to its input. Furthermore, the parties run a coin tossing protocol to determine the randomness to be used in the protocol; since the random tape of each party must be secret, the latter is done in such a way that the other parties only learn a commitment to the other parties' random tape. Finally, the commitments to each party's input and randomness are used to enforce semi-honest behavior: Each party computes the next message using the underlying semi-honest protocol, but also proves in zero knowledge that this message was computed correctly using the committed input and randomness.

5.1   Sanitizable Commit and Prove

The GMW compiler was analyzed in the UC setting by Canetti, Lindell, Ostro-vsky and Sahai [9]. A difficulty that arises is that the receiver of a UC commit-ment obtains no information about the value that was committed to. Hence, the parties cannot prove in zero knowledge statements relative to their input/ran-domness commitment. This issue is solved by introducing a more general commit-and-prove functionality that essentially combines both the commitment and zero-knowledge capabilities in a single functionality. In turn, the commit-and-prove functionality can be realized using commitments and zero-knowledge proofs.

In order to sanitize the GMW compiler, we follow a similar approach. Namely, we introduce a sanitazable commit-and-prove functionality (denoted $\widehat{\mathcal{F}}_{\mathsf{C\&P}}$ and depicted below) and show that this functionality suffices for our purpose. Intu-itively, $\widehat{\mathcal{F}}_{\mathsf{C\&P}}$ allows the core C_i of each party P_i to (i) commit to multiple secret inputs x, and (ii) prove arbitrary NP statements y (w.r.t. an underlying rela-tion R that is a parameter of the functionality) whose corresponding witnesses consist of all the values x. Whenever the core C_i commits to a value x, the fire-wall F_i may decide to blind x with a random string r (which is then revealed to the core). Similarly, whenever the core proves a statement y, the firewall F_i may check if the given statement makes sense, in which case, and assuming the statement is valid, the functionality informs all other parties that y is indeed a correct statement proven by P_i.

Functionality $\widehat{\mathcal{F}}_{\mathsf{C\&P}}$

The sanitizable commit-and-prove functionality $\widehat{\mathcal{F}}_{\mathsf{C\&P}}$ is parameterized by an NP relation R, and runs with parties $\mathsf{P}_1, \ldots, \mathsf{P}_n$ (each consisting of a core C_i and a firewall F_i) and an adversary $\mathcal{S}$. The functionality consists of the following communication interfaces for the cores and the firewalls respectively.

Interface IO
- Upon receiving a message $(\textsc{Commit}, \mathsf{sid}, \mathsf{cid}, \mathsf{C}_i, x)$ from C_i, where $x \in \{0,1\}^*$, record the tuple $(\mathsf{sid}, \mathsf{cid}, \mathsf{C}_i, x)$ and send the message $(\textsc{Receipt}, \mathsf{sid}, \mathsf{cid}, \mathsf{C}_i)$ to F_i. Ignore future commands of the form $(\textsc{Commit}, \mathsf{sid}, \mathsf{cid}, \mathsf{C}_i, \cdot)$.
- Upon receiving a message $(\textsc{Prove}, \mathsf{sid}, \mathsf{C}_i, y)$ from C_i, if there is at least one record $(\mathsf{sid}, \mathsf{cid}, \mathsf{C}_i, \cdot)$ and a corresponding $(\textsc{Blind}, \mathsf{sid}, \mathsf{cid}, \mathsf{C}_i, \cdot)$ message was sent to $\widehat{\mathcal{F}}_{\mathsf{C\&P}}$, then send the message $(\textsc{Sanitize}, \mathsf{sid}, \mathsf{C}_i, y)$ to F_i.

Interface S
- Upon receiving a message $(\textsc{Blind}, \mathsf{sid}, \mathsf{cid}, \mathsf{C}_i, r)$ from F_i, where $r \in \{0,1\}^*$, proceed as follows: if the tuple $(\mathsf{sid}, \mathsf{cid}, \mathsf{C}_i, x)$ is recorded, modify the tuple to be $(\mathsf{sid}, \mathsf{cid}, \mathsf{C}_i, \hat{x} = x \oplus r)$ and send the message $(\textsc{Blinded}, \mathsf{sid}, \mathsf{cid}, \mathsf{C}_i, r)$ to C_i, and $(\textsc{Receipt}, \mathsf{sid}, \mathsf{cid}, \mathsf{C}_i)$ to all $\mathsf{C}_{j \neq i}$ and $\mathcal{S}$; otherwise do nothing. Ignore future commands of the form $(\textsc{Blind}, \mathsf{sid}, \mathsf{cid}, \mathsf{C}_i, \cdot)$.
- Upon receiving a message $(\textsc{Continue}, \mathsf{sid}, \mathsf{C}_i, y)$ from F_i, retrieve all tuples of the form $(\mathsf{sid}, \cdot, \mathsf{C}_i, \hat{x})$ and let $\overline{x}$ be the list containing all (possibly sani-

tized) witnesses $\hat{x}$. Then compute $R(y, \overline{x})$: if $R(y, \overline{x}) = 1$ send the message (PROVED, $\mathsf{sid}, \mathsf{C}_i, y$) to all $\mathsf{C}_{j \neq i}$ and $\mathcal{S}$, otherwise ignore the command.

In the full version [12], we show how to realize the sanitazable commit-and-prove functionality from *malleable dual-mode commitments*, a primitive which we introduce, and re-randomizable NIZKs for all of NP. Our commitment protocol from Sect. 3 can be seen as a concrete instantiation of malleable dual-mode commitments based on the DDH assumption.

5.2 Sanitizing the GMW Compiler

We are now ready to sanitize the GMW compiler. Let Π be an MPC protocol. The (sanitized) protocol $\widehat{\Pi}_{\mathsf{GMW}}$ is depicted below and follows exactly the ideas outlined above adapted to the UC framework with reverse firewalls.

Protocol $\widehat{\Pi}_{\mathsf{GMW}}$ (Sanitizing the GMW compiler)

The protocol is described in the $(\widehat{\mathcal{F}}_{\mathsf{C\&P}}, \mathcal{F}_{\mathsf{TOSS}})$-hybrid model, and is executed between parties $\mathsf{P}_1, \ldots, \mathsf{P}_n$ each consisting of a core C_i and a firewall F_i. Party $\mathsf{P}_i = (\mathsf{C}_i, \mathsf{F}_i)$ proceeds as follows (the code for all other parties is analogous).

Random tape generation: When activated for the first time, party P_i generates its own randomness with the help of all other parties:
1. The core C_i picks a random $s_i \in \{0,1\}^\lambda$ and sends (COMMIT, $\mathsf{sid}_i, \mathsf{cid}_i, s_i$) to $\widehat{\mathcal{F}}_{\mathsf{C\&P}}$.
2. Upon receiving (RECEIPT, $\mathsf{sid}_i, \mathsf{cid}_i, \mathsf{C}_i$) from $\widehat{\mathcal{F}}_{\mathsf{C\&P}}$, the firewall F_i picks a random $r_i \in \{0,1\}^\lambda$ and sends (BLIND, $\mathsf{sid}_i, \mathsf{cid}_i, \mathsf{C}_i, r_i$) to $\widehat{\mathcal{F}}_{\mathsf{C\&P}}$.
3. All the cores interact with $\mathcal{F}_{\mathsf{TOSS}}$ in order to obtain a public random string s_i^* that is used to determine the random tape of C_i. Namely, each core C_j, for $j \in [n]$, sends (INIT, $\mathsf{sid}_{i,j}, \mathsf{P}_j$) to $\mathcal{F}_{\mathsf{TOSS}}$ and waits to receive the message (DELIVERED, $\mathsf{sid}_{i,j}, \mathsf{P}_j, s_i^*$) from the functionality.
4. Upon receiving (BLINDED, $\mathsf{sid}_i, \mathsf{cid}_i, \mathsf{C}_i, r_i$) from $\widehat{\mathcal{F}}_{\mathsf{C\&P}}$, the core C_i defines $\hat{r}_i = s_i^* \oplus (s_i \oplus r_i)$.

Input commitment: When activated with input x_i, the core C_i sends (COMMIT, $\mathsf{sid}_i, \mathsf{cid}_i', x_i$) to $\widehat{\mathcal{F}}_{\mathsf{C\&P}}$ and adds x_i to the (initially empty) list of inputs $\overline{x}_i$ (containing the inputs from all the previous activations of the protocol). Upon receiving (RECEIPT, $\mathsf{sid}_i, \mathsf{cid}_i', \mathsf{C}_i$) from $\widehat{\mathcal{F}}_{\mathsf{C\&P}}$, the firewall F_i sends (BLIND, $\mathsf{sid}_i, \mathsf{cid}_i', \mathsf{C}_i, 0^{|x_i|}$) to $\widehat{\mathcal{F}}_{\mathsf{C\&P}}$.

Protocol execution: Let $\tau \in \{0,1\}^*$ be the sequence of messages that were broadcast in all activations of Π until now (where τ is initially empty).
1. The core C_i runs the code of Π on its input list $\overline{x}_i$, transcript τ, and random tape $\hat{r}_i$ (as determined above). If Π instructs P_i to broadcast a message, proceed to the next step.
2. For each outgoing message μ_i that P_i sends in Π, the core C_i sends (PROVE, $\mathsf{sid}_i, \mathsf{C}_i, (\mu_i, s_i^*, \tau)$) to $\widehat{\mathcal{F}}_{\mathsf{C\&P}}$, where the relation parameterizing the

functionality is defined as follows:

$$R := \{((\mu_i, s_i^*, \tau), (\overline{x}_i, s_i, r_i)) : \mu_i = \Pi(\overline{x}_i, \tau, s_i^* \oplus (s_i \oplus r_i))\}.$$

In words, the core C_i proves that the message μ_i is the correct next message generated by Π when the input sequence is $\overline{x}_i$, the random tape is $\hat{r}_i = s_i^* \oplus (s_i \oplus r_i)$, and the current transcript is τ. Thus, C_i appends μ_i to the current transcript τ.

3. Upon receiving (SANITIZE, sid_i, C_i, (μ_i, s_i^*, τ)) from $\widehat{\mathcal{F}}_{\mathsf{C\&P}}$, the firewall F_i verifies that s_i^* is the same string obtained via $\mathcal{F}_{\mathsf{TOSS}}$ and that τ consists of all the messages that were broadcast in all the activations up to this point. If these conditions are not met, F_i ignores the message and otherwise it sends (CONTINUE, sid_i, C_i, (μ_i, s_i^*, τ)) to $\widehat{\mathcal{F}}_{\mathsf{C\&P}}$ and appends μ_i to the current transcript τ.

4. Upon receiving (PROVED, sid_j, C_j, (μ_j, s_i^*, τ)) from $\widehat{\mathcal{F}}_{\mathsf{C\&P}}$, both the core C_i and the firewall F_i append μ_j to the transcript τ and repeat the above steps.

Output: Whenever Π outputs a value, $\widehat{\Pi}_{\mathsf{GMW}}$ generates the same output.

A few remarks are in order. First, and without loss of generality, we assume that the underlying protocol Π is reactive and works by a series of activations, where in each activation, only one of the parties has an input; the random tape of each party is taken to be a λ-bit string for simplicity. Second, each party needs to invoke an independent copy of $\widehat{\mathcal{F}}_{\mathsf{C\&P}}$; we identify these copies as sid_i, where we can for instance let $\mathsf{sid}_i = \mathsf{sid}\|i$. Third, we slightly simplify the randomness generation phase using the coin tossing functionality $\mathcal{F}_{\mathsf{TOSS}}$. In particular, each core C_i commits to a random string s_i via $\widehat{\mathcal{F}}_{\mathsf{C\&P}}$; the corresponding firewall F_i blinds s_i with a random string r_i. Thus, the parties obtain public randomness s_i^* via $\mathcal{F}_{\mathsf{TOSS}}$, yielding a sanitized random tape $\hat{r}_i = s_i^* \oplus (s_i \oplus r_i)$ for party P_i. Note that it is crucial that the parties obtain independent public random strings s_i^* in order to determine the random tape of party P_i. In fact, if instead we would use a single invocation of $\mathcal{F}_{\mathsf{TOSS}}$ yielding common public randomness s, two malicious parties P_i and P_j could pick the same random tape by choosing the same values s_i, r_i, s_j, r_j. Clearly, the latter malicious adversary cannot be reduced to a semi-honest adversary.

The theorem below states the security of the GMW compiler with reverse firewalls. The proof is deferred to the full version [12].

Theorem 4. *Let $\mathcal{F}$ be any functionality for n parties. Assuming that Π UC realizes $\mathcal{F}$ in the presence of up to $t \leq n - 1$ semi-honest corruptions, then the compiled protocol $\widehat{\Pi}_{\mathsf{GMW}}$ wsrUC realizes $\mathcal{F}$ in the $(\mathcal{F}_{\mathsf{SAT}}, \widehat{\mathcal{F}}_{\mathsf{C\&P}}, \mathcal{F}_{\mathsf{TOSS}})$-hybrid model in the presence of up to t malicious corruptions.*

6 Conclusions and Future Work

We have put forward a generalization of the UC framework by Canetti [6,7], where each party consists of a core (which has secret inputs and is in charge of generating protocol messages) and a reverse firewall (which has no secrets and sanitizes the outgoing/incoming communication from/to the core). Both the core and the firewall can be subject to different flavors of corruption, modeling the strongly adversarial setting where a subset of the players is maliciously corrupt, whereas the remaining honest parties are subject to subversion attacks. The main advantage of our approach is that it comes with very strong composition guarantees, as it allows, for the first time, to design subversion-resilient protocols that can be used as part of larger, more complex protocols, while retaining security even when protocol sessions are running concurrently (under adversarial scheduling) and in the presence of subversion attacks.

Moreover, we have demonstrated the feasibility of our approach by designing UC reverse firewalls for cryptographic protocols realizing pretty natural ideal functionalities such as commitments and coin tossing, and, in fact, even for arbitrary functionalities. Several avenues for further research are possible, including designing UC reverse firewalls for other ideal functionalities (such as oblivious transfer and zero knowledge), removing (at least partially) trusted setup assumptions, and defining UC subversion-resilient MPC in the presence of adaptive corruptions.

References

1. Ateniese, G., Magri, B., Venturi, D.: Subversion-resilient signature schemes. In: ACM CCS 2015. ACM Press, October 2015
2. Bellare, M., Jaeger, J., Kane, D.: Mass-surveillance without the state: strongly undetectable algorithm-substitution attacks. In: ACM CCS 2015. ACM Press, October 2015
3. Bellare, M., Paterson, K.G., Rogaway, P.: Security of symmetric encryption against mass surveillance. In: Garay, J.A., Gennaro, R. (eds.) CRYPTO 2014, Part I. LNCS, vol. 8616, pp. 1–19. Springer, Heidelberg (2014). https://doi.org/10.1007/978-3-662-44371-2_1
4. Berndt, S., Liskiewicz, M.: Algorithm substitution attacks from a steganographic perspective. In: ACM CCS 2017. ACM Press, October/November 2017
5. Blum, M.: Coin flipping by telephone. In: CRYPTO 1981. U.C. Santa Barbara, Dept. of Elec. and Computer Eng. (1981)
6. Canetti, R.: Universally composable security: a new paradigm for cryptographic protocols. Cryptology ePrint Archive, Report 2000/067 (2000). https://eprint.iacr.org/2000/067
7. Canetti, R.: Universally composable security: a new paradigm for cryptographic protocols. In: 42nd FOCS. IEEE Computer Society Press, October 2001
8. Canetti, R., Fischlin, M.: Universally composable commitments. In: Kilian, J. (ed.) CRYPTO 2001. LNCS, vol. 2139, pp. 19–40. Springer, Heidelberg (2001). https://doi.org/10.1007/3-540-44647-8_2
9. Canetti, R., Lindell, Y., Ostrovsky, R., Sahai, A.: Universally composable two-party and multi-party secure computation. In: 34th ACM STOC. ACM Press, May 2002
10. Canetti, R., Sarkar, P., Wang, X.: Efficient and round-optimal oblivious transfer and commitment with adaptive security. In: Moriai, S., Wang, H. (eds.) ASIACRYPT 2020, Part III. LNCS, vol. 12493, pp. 277–308. Springer, Cham (2020). https://doi.org/10.1007/978-3-030-64840-4_10

11. Chakraborty, S., Dziembowski, S., Nielsen, J.B.: Reverse fire-walls for actively secure MPCs. In: Micciancio, D., Ristenpart, T. (eds.) CRYPTO 2020, Part II. LNCS, vol. 12171, pp. 732–762. Springer, Cham (2020). https://doi.org/10.1007/978-3-030-56880-1_26

12. Chakraborty, S., Magri, B., Nielsen, J.B., Venturi, D.: Universally composable subversion-resilient cryptography. Cryptology ePrint Archive (2022). https://www.iacr.org

13. Chase, M., Kohlweiss, M., Lysyanskaya, A., Meiklejohn, S.: Malleable proof systems and applications. In: Pointcheval, D., Johansson, T. (eds.) EUROCRYPT 2012. LNCS, vol. 7237, pp. 281–300. Springer, Heidelberg (2012). https://doi.org/10.1007/978-3-642-29011-4_18

14. Cleve, R.: Limits on the security of coin flips when half the processors are faulty (extended abstract). In: 18th ACM STOC. ACM Press, May 1986

15. Degabriele, J.P., Paterson, K.G., Schuldt, J.C.N., Woodage, J.: Backdoors in pseudorandom number generators: possibility and impossibility results. In: Robshaw, M., Katz, J. (eds.) CRYPTO 2016, Part I. LNCS, vol. 9814, pp. 403–432. Springer, Heidelberg (2016). https://doi.org/10.1007/978-3-662-53018-4_15

16. Dodis, Y., Ganesh, C., Golovnev, A., Juels, A., Ristenpart, T.: A formal treatment of backdoored pseudorandom generators. In: Oswald, E., Fischlin, M. (eds.) EUROCRYPT 2015, Part I. LNCS, vol. 9056, pp. 101–126. Springer, Heidelberg (2015). https://doi.org/10.1007/978-3-662-46800-5_5

17. Dodis, Y., Mironov, I., Stephens-Davidowitz, N.: Message transmission with reverse firewalls—secure communication on corrupted machines. In: Robshaw, M., Katz, J. (eds.) CRYPTO 2016, Part I. LNCS, vol. 9814, pp. 341–372. Springer, Heidelberg (2016). https://doi.org/10.1007/978-3-662-53018-4_13

18. Fischlin, M., Janson, C., Mazaheri, S.: Backdoored hash functions: immunizing HMAC and HKDF. In: CSF 2018 Computer Security Foundations Symposium. IEEE Computer Society Press (2018)

19. Ganesh, C., Magri, B., Venturi, D.: Cryptographic reverse firewalls for interactive proof systems. In: ICALP 2020. LIPIcs, Schloss Dagstuhl, July 2020

20. Goldreich, O., Micali, S., Wigderson, A.: How to play any mental game or A completeness theorem for protocols with honest majority. In: 19th ACM STOC. ACM Press, May 1987

21. Mironov, I., Stephens-Davidowitz, N.: Cryptographic reverse firewalls. In: Oswald, E., Fischlin, M. (eds.) EUROCRYPT 2015, Part II. LNCS, vol. 9057, pp. 657–686. Springer, Heidelberg (2015). https://doi.org/10.1007/978-3-662-46803-6_22

22. Young, A., Yung, M.: The dark side of "black-box" cryptography or: should we trust capstone? In: Koblitz, N. (ed.) CRYPTO 1996. LNCS, vol. 1109, pp. 89–103. Springer, Heidelberg (1996). https://doi.org/10.1007/3-540-68697-5_8

23. Young, A., Yung, M.: Kleptography: using cryptography against cryptography. In: Fumy, W. (ed.) EUROCRYPT 1997. LNCS, vol. 1233, pp. 62–74. Springer, Heidelberg (1997). https://doi.org/10.1007/3-540-69053-0_6

Asymptotically Quasi-Optimal Cryptography

Leo de Castro[1]([✉]), Carmit Hazay[2], Yuval Ishai[3], Vinod Vaikuntanathan[1], and Muthu Venkitasubramaniam[4]

[1] MIT, Cambridge, UK
ldec@mit.edu
[2] Bar-Ilan University, Ramat Gan, Israel
[3] Technion, Haifa, Israel
[4] Georgetown University, Washington, USA

Abstract. The question of minimizing the *computational overhead* of cryptography was put forward by the work of Ishai, Kushilevitz, Ostrovsky and Sahai (STOC 2008). The main conclusion was that, under plausible assumptions, most cryptographic primitives can be realized with *constant* computational overhead. However, this ignores an additive term that may depend polynomially on the (concrete) computational security parameter λ. In this work, we study the question of obtaining optimal efficiency, up to polylogarithmic factors, for *all* choices of n and λ, where n is the size of the given task. In particular, when $n = \lambda$, we would like the computational cost to be only $\tilde{O}(\lambda)$. We refer to this goal as *asymptotically quasi-optimal* (AQO) cryptography.

We start by realizing the first AQO semi-honest batch oblivious linear evaluation (BOLE) protocol. Our protocol applies to OLE over small fields and relies on the near-exponential security of the ring learning with errors (RLWE) assumption. Building on the above and on known constructions of AQO PCPs, we design the first AQO zero-knowledge (ZK) argument system for Boolean circuit satisfiability. Our construction combines a new AQO ZK-PCP construction that respects the AQO property of the underlying PCP along with a technique for converting statistical secrecy into soundness via OLE reversal. Finally, combining the above results, we get AQO secure computation protocols for Boolean circuits with security against malicious parties under RLWE.

1 Introduction

The work of Ishai, Kushilevitz, Ostrovsky and Sahai [IKOS08] put forward the goal of minimizing the *computational overhead* of cryptography. This was defined as the asymptotic ratio between the amount of work (say, Boolean circuit size) required to securely realize a given cryptographic task of size n and the amount of work required to realize the same task without any security at all. Here, n denotes the size of a Boolean circuit specifying a functionality, for primitives such as secure computation or zero-knowledge proofs, and just message size for

© International Association for Cryptologic Research 2022
O. Dunkelman and S. Dziembowski (Eds.): EUROCRYPT 2022, LNCS 13275, pp. 303–334, 2022.
https://doi.org/10.1007/978-3-031-06944-4_11

simpler primitives such as encryption or commitment. The main conclusion of [IKOS08] is that, under plausible assumptions, most cryptographic primitives can be realized with *constant* computational overhead.

However, this ignores the significant additive term that may depend polynomially on the (concrete) computational security parameter λ.[1] That is, the computational cost of the constant overhead protocol could be $O(n + \lambda^c)$ for some constant $c > 1$. As a consequence, amortized efficiency may only kick in when $n \gg \lambda$, namely when the problem size is very big. For smaller instances, efficiency (measured in terms of communication, computation, or other resources) can be far from optimal. This is not only a theoretical concern, but also a practical concern for many primitives that have good amortized efficiency.

Asymptotically Quasi-Optimal Cryptography. The question that motivates our work is whether this is inherent. Can we get close to the best possible efficiency for *all* choices of n and λ, in particular when $n = \lambda$? We refer to the goal of achieving this up to polylogarithmic factors as *asymptotically quasi-optimal* (AQO) cryptography. AQO requires that solving a problem of size n with λ bits of security has computational cost (measured by Boolean circuit size) of $\tilde{O}(n+\lambda)$. Modulo polylogarithmic factors, this represents the *best possible* solution, as the costs of n and λ are both inherent for natural primitives.

We will sometimes also refer to the relaxed goal of *AQO communication*, where the communication (or ciphertext size) is $\tilde{O}(n+\lambda)$, but the computational cost may be larger. Here n refers to the *communication complexity* of realizing the same task without security requirements.

We view AQO as a clean theoretical abstraction of a practically relevant question, with an appealingly simple one-line description:

Solve a size-n cryptographic problem with efficiency $\tilde{O}(n + \lambda)$.

AQO Cryptography: What's Known and What Isn't. In the domain of *symmetric cryptography*, the AQO goal is relatively easy to achieve. For instance, natural generalizations of popular block ciphers such as AES are conjectured to be AQO [MV15]. In fact, even with a *constant* (rather than polylogarithmic) overhead, most symmetric primitives can be realized under plausible hardness assumptions. This includes one-way functions [Gol00], pseudorandom generators [AIK08, BIO14], collision-resistant hashing [AHI+17], and pseudorandom functions [BIP+18]. For public-key encryption and statistically binding commitments, we have AQO schemes from Ring-LWE [LPR10, LPR13, LS19, GHKW17],

---

[1] Throughout this paper, the security parameter λ refers to bits of *concrete security*, requiring that no adversary of circuit size 2^λ can gain better than $2^{-\lambda}$ advantage. This is a natural and robust notion of concrete security. An alternative notion that settles for *negligible* advantage is not as robust, analogously to relaxing standard security definitions by requiring that every polynomial-time adversary has $o(1)$ advantage (rather than negligible in the sense of sub-polynomial).

Table 1. Some representative examples in the AQO Landscape.

Primitive	Assumption	Reference
Secret-key Encryption	Generalized AES	[DR02, MV15]
	Ring-LWE	[LPR10]
	Ring-LPN	[HKL+12]
	Mod-2/Mod-3 PRFs*	[BIP+18]
Public-key Encryption	Elliptic Curve CDH/DDH†	[Gam85]
	Ring-LWE	[LPR10]
String-OT	Elliptic Curve DDH†	[NP01, AIR01]
	Ring-LWE	Folklore‡
Batch-OT	Ring-LWE	This work
Single-OLE	Ring-LWE	This work
Batch-OLE	Ring-LWE	This work
Additively Homomorphic Encryption**	Ring-LWE	[LPR10]
(Malicious-Verifier) Zero-Knowledge	Ring-LWE	This work
(Malicious) Two-party Computation	Ring-LWE	This work

Entry labeled with * was conjectured to achieve asymptotically optimal security (i.e., same as AQO but without the polylog factors).
† denotes solutions with AQO communication but not AQO computation, e.g. elliptic curves that employ exponentiation, making their computational complexity at least quadratic.
‡ The folklore protocol for string-OT uses the fact that the [LPR10] Ring-LWE-based PKE is additively homomorphic which gives us a leaky-OT. This can in turn be corrected via randomness extraction.
** indicates measuring the complexity of (non-function-private) homomorphic pointwise addition or scalar multiplication of two vectors of plaintexts.

and for collision-resistant hashing and statistically hiding commitments, we have AQO schemes from Ring-SIS [Mic02, PR06, LM06].

Besides these, the case for other central cryptographic primitives such as zero-knowledge proofs and secure computation, seems to be wide open and for good reasons, as we discuss below. We refer to Table 1 for more examples in the AQO landscape. By "batch-OT" and "batch-OLE" we refer to a semi-honest secure two-party protocol for n copies of oblivious transfer (OT) or its generalization to oblivious linear-function evaluation (OLE) modulo $p \leq \mathsf{poly}(\lambda)$, which will be discussed in detail later.

Where Do Previous Techniques Fail? The main technical challenge in achieving AQO is the question of how to *amplify soundness or privacy without naïve repetition (or similar techniques)*. Traditional techniques such as statistical noise-flooding (for lattice-based OLE), arithmetization over big fields, or cut-and-choose (for zero knowledge and secure computation) all fall short of this goal. Even techniques that do achieve this goal in an amortized sense (such as "constant-overhead" semi-honest 2PC from a local PRG [IKOS08] or ZK based on robust honest-majority MPC [IKOS07, DIK10]) incur quadratic (in λ) additive terms, seemingly for inherent reasons.

An additional challenge for public-key AQO cryptography is that standard "number-theoretic" constructions fail for two reasons. First, common number-theoretic operations, such as modular exponentiation over a λ-bit modulus, are only known to have circuits of size $\widetilde{O}(\lambda^2)$. Second, factoring λ-bit integers or discrete logarithm modulo a λ-bit prime can be done in time 2^{λ^c} for $c < 1$, which requires working with numbers of size $\lambda^{c'}$ for $c' > 1$.

This leaves us with essentially elliptic curve discrete logarithms and (ring) learning with errors. In the case of elliptic curves, computations typically require exponentiation, and in the case of learning with errors, computations typically require matrix multiplication, both of which require superlinear time which rules out *computational* quasi-optimality. This leaves us the ring learning with errors assumption [LPR10, LPR13] with the unique status of helping us go beyond communication AQO. On the one hand, the problem is believed to be quasi-exponentially hard in the bit-length of the instance; and on the other hand, operations typically involve multiplication of two $O(\lambda)$-degree polynomials over a number field, which can be performed in quasi-linear $\widetilde{O}(\lambda)$ time using the (number-field version of) fast Fourier transform. Finally, Ring LWE has proven itself to be versatile not only in theory, having helped us construct fully homomorphic encryption [BV11b, BGV12, GHS12], but also in practice with the NIST standardization effort for post-quantum-secure public-key cryptography [Moo16].

Challenges for Secure Computation. In the semi-honest model, AQO secure computation reduces to an AQO batch-OT via classical techniques [GMW87, Gol04]. This in turn reduces to AQO batch-OLE, which is a more natural target in the context of lattice-based constructions. Several Ring-LWE based batch-OLE protocols have been proposed in the literature. The vanilla batch-OLE from Ring-LWE uses noise-flooding to ensure sender privacy, and this causes the communication and computation to be of size $O(n \cdot \lambda)$ where λ is a statistical security parameter, and hence is not AQO. Alternative techniques for circuit-private FHE without noise-flooding also fall short of the AQO goal: [DS16] involves λ iterations of bootstrapping to "rinse out" the noise, and [BPMW16] requires homomorphic evaluation of a branching program of size $\Omega(\lambda)$. Even ignoring AQO, these approaches do not seem attractive from a *concrete efficiency* viewpoint.

Challenges for Security Against Malicious Parties. Going beyond semi-honest security and achieving security against *malicious* parties in the AQO setting poses additional challenges. Common cut-and-choose techniques in zero-knowledge proofs and secure computation protocols [LPS08, HKE13, Lin16, WRK17] incur a *multiplicative overhead* of at least λ to achieve simulation error $2^{-\lambda}$. This is also the case when embedding a Boolean computation into an arithmetic computation over a big field $\mathbb{F}$ to achieve soundness $O(1/|\mathbb{F}|)$ [BCG+17, XZZ+19, CDI+].

MPC-in-the-head techniques [IKOS07, IPS08, AHIV17, HIMV19] can improve over standard cut-and-choose techniques by achieving a better *amortized* overhead, as low as polylog(λ) [DIK10]. However, the underlying MPC protocols incur an additive communication overhead of at least $\Omega(\lambda^2)$. This also applies to all known *succinct* zero-knowledge argument systems, including those based on classical PCPs and IOPs (e.g., [Kil92, BCS16, BBHR19, BCR+19, ZXZS20, CY21, RR21]) and linear PCPs [IKO07, Gro10, GGPR13, BCI+13, BISW18].

Finally, there is a rich and productive literature constructing zero-knowledge protocols for $\mathcal{NP}$ statements assuming RLWE [BKLP15, LS18, BBC+18, BLS19, BLNS20]. To the best of our knowledge, these protocols cannot even achieve AQO communication, let alone computation. The reason is subtle. Focusing on ZK protocols for RLWE statements, the protocols seem to fall into one of two categories. The first type incurs large soundness error which is then repeated $\widetilde{O}(\lambda)$ times to get $2^{-\lambda}$ soundness, and thus has at least a quadratic in λ overhead. The second type is a direct proof with exponentially small soundness error and AQO efficiency, but for a weaker $\mathcal{NP}$ statement related to RLWE which does not seem directly applicable to constructing ZK proofs for general $\mathcal{NP}$ statements.[2] We refer the reader to an extensive discussion in [BLS19] who, with a great deal of ingenuity, reduce the number of parallel repetitions required in the first type of protocols in order to achieve $2^{-\lambda}$ soundness from λ to $\lambda/\log\lambda$.

1.1 Our Results and Techniques

Our Results, in a Nutshell. Our results are three-fold. First, we show AQO protocols for batch-oblivious linear evaluation (batch-OLE) and batch-oblivious transfer (batch-OT)[3] which are secure against semi-honest corruptions under the Ring Learning with Errors (RLWE) assumption.

Secondly, in the case of batch-OLE, we improve this to obtain asymptotic download rate that approaches 1. This gives an AQO variant of recent rate-1 constructions from [DGI+19, BDGM19, GH19], which require uncompressing batched ciphertexts. In contrast, our construction is a simple tweak on an old encryption scheme due to Peikert, Vaikuntanathan and Waters [PVW08], a batched version of Regev's encryption [Reg05]. The high rate of our construction gives rise (via a simple extractor-based transformation [BGI+17]) to an AQO construction of statistically sender-private (SSP) 2-message OT from RLWE. Beyond the AQO feature, this gives an alternative route to recent lattice-based constructions of SSP OT [BD18, DGI+19, MS20].

Finally, we use the batch-OT to construct AQO zero-knowledge and secure computation protocols for Boolean circuits with security against malicious parties. These protocols too are secure under RLWE.

Our goal was to answer a clean theoretical question. However, as it turned out, our solution for AQO batch-OLE is competitive in practice, especially for small instance sizes (and small fields). While the *AQO definition* may not say

---

[2] We remark that the statements we want are proofs (of knowledge) of a short secret s such that $As = t$ over a ring. On the other hand, the second type of protocols prove that there is a short secret s such that As *equals a short multiple of* t.

[3] Recall that Batch-OT/OLE refers to multiple OT/OLE instances carried out in parallel.

anything about concrete efficiency for real-world parameters, we view this empirical data point of correlation between "AQO security" and "concrete efficiency" as a promising sign.

We now proceed to describe our results and techniques in more detail.

Semi-Honest Batch-OLE: AQO and Concretely Efficient. Oblivious linear evaluation (OLE) is a protocol between two parties S, the sender who has a linear function $L_{\alpha,\beta}(x) = \alpha x + \beta$ over a finite ring $\mathcal{R}$, and R, the receiver who has an input $m \in \mathcal{R}$. At the end of the protocol, R gets $L_{\alpha,\beta}(m) = \alpha m + \beta$, and the sender gets nothing. OLE is a generalization of oblivious transfer (OT) over fields (and rings) larger than $\mathbb{F}_2$, and has numerous applications, notably in secure computation. We consider the n-fold repetition of the OLE functionality, called *batch-OLE*, where the sender has $\alpha, \beta \in \mathcal{R}^n$, the receiver has $m \in \mathcal{R}$ and gets $\alpha \circ m + \beta \in \mathcal{R}^n$ where $\circ$ denotes a coordinate-wise product. Here we consider the case of batch-OLE over a polynomial-size modulus, namely where $\mathcal{R} = \mathbb{Z}_p$ for $p \leq \mathsf{poly}(\lambda)$.

We show the first construction of a semi-honest batch-OLE protocol which is asymptotically quasi-optimal. Our protocol has minimal interaction of just two rounds, and its security is based on the ring learning with errors (RLWE) assumption. In the parameter regimes in which our protocol has competitive concrete efficiency, it can be useful for realizing the distributed seed generation of pseudorandom correlation generators (PCGs) for OLE and multiplication triples based on Ring-LPN [BCG+20].

Our starting point is a folklore batch-OLE scheme using a batched version of the classical Lyubashevsky-Peikert-Regev [LPR10] encryption scheme (henceforth called LPR encryption). The encryption scheme works over a message space $\mathcal{R}_p := \mathbb{Z}_p[x]/(x^k + 1)$ where k is a power of 2 and $x^k + 1$ factors completely into linear factors mod p.[4] To encrypt a vector $m \in \mathbb{Z}_p^k$, we first find, using the number theoretic transform (NTT), a polynomial $\widehat{m}$ such that $\widehat{m}(\zeta_i) = m_i \pmod{p}$ for all $i \in [k]$. Here, $\zeta_i \in \mathbb{Z}_p$ are the k roots of the polynomial $x^k + 1 \pmod{p}$ which exist by our choice of $p = 1 \pmod{2k}$. The ciphertext

$$ct = (a, as + e + \Delta\widehat{m}) := (a, b)$$

where $\Delta = \lceil q/p \rceil$,[5] s is a random ring element and e is a short ring element.

The receiver in our OLE generates a ciphertext ct that encrypts his input m and sends ct to the sender. By the semantic security of LPR encryption, which relies on RLWE, the sender learns nothing about m.

The sender has $\alpha, \beta \in \mathbb{Z}_p^k$ and wishes to homomorphically compute the (linear) OLE function. They do this by computing and returning to the receiver

$$ct_{eval} = (\widehat{\alpha}a, \widehat{\alpha}b + \Delta\widehat{\beta})$$

which one can easily check is an encryption of $\alpha \circ m + \beta$.

---

[4] We denote the Ring-LWE dimension by k, and the OLE batch-size by n.

[5] We typically pick q to be a multiple of p so the rounding is not necessary.

The main problem with this idea is the lack of *function privacy*. That is, the homomorphically evaluated ciphertext could contain information not just about $\alpha \circ m + \beta$, but about α and β themselves. Indeed, this is not hard to see as the first component of ct' reveals α already. This can be solved using rerandomization: the receiver can send a rerandomization key that allows the sender to generate a pair $(a', b' := a's + e')$ with a (statistically close to) random a', which they add to ct_{eval}. This results in a rerandomized ciphertext

$$ct'_{eval} = (\widehat{\alpha}a + a', \widehat{\alpha}b + b' + \Delta\widehat{\beta})$$

where the first component is statistically close to random. Still, we are not done: the receiver who knows s can retrieve terms such as $\widehat{\alpha}e + e'$ which could reveal significant information about α.

The typical way to get around this problem is to add to ct' a very-high-noise encryption of 0 (namely, one with a very large e') that will mask such terms. In particular, one appeals to the so-called noise-flooding lemmas [Gen09, AJL+12, GKPV10] that requires adding noise that is a factor 2^λ larger than $\widehat{\alpha}e$ to achieve $2^{-\lambda}$ (statistical) security. Unfortunately, this blows up ciphertext sizes by a multiplicative factor of λ, resulting in a communication of $O(k\lambda)$, violating the demands of AQO efficiency. (Recall that we need $\widetilde{O}(k + \lambda)$.)

At a high level, our main observation is that noise flooding is too strong a hammer to achieve function privacy and therefore sender privacy. Instead, our main contribution is a *gentle noise-flooding* procedure that gives us AQO efficiency. We start by imagining what happens if we only add a small amount of noise to each coordinate, in fact, just a constant factor larger than $\|\widehat{\alpha}e\|_\infty$.

To illustrate this concretely, imagine that each coordinate t of $\widehat{\alpha}e$ lives in the interval $[0, 10]$ and we add a noise term η chosen randomly from the interval $[0, 20]$. If $r = t + \eta$ lands up in the interval $[10, 20]$, it reveals no information about what t was to begin with! Indeed, all values of t in the interval $[0, 10]$ are equally likely conditioned on such a "good" r. In other words, by adding noise that is a constant factor larger than $\|\widehat{\alpha}e\|_\infty$, one could hope to hide a constant fraction of the coordinates of $\widehat{\alpha}e$. This is formalized as our gentle noise-flooding lemma (Lemma 3).

This is still not enough as leaking a constant fraction of $\widehat{\alpha}e'$ is not acceptable. However, this predicament we are in should point to secret-sharing as a possible way out. Indeed, our solution is to use a suitable modification of the OLE extractors of [IKOS09a, BMN18a] to extract fresh OLE instances from these "leaky" OLE instances. In a nutshell, to achieve AQO efficiency, we instantiate the compiler of Block, Gupta, Maji and Nguyen [BGMN18] with a Reed-Solomon code which admits quasi-linear time encoding and erasure-decoding. We can also achieve AQO batch-OT by embedding OT into OLE using a standard technique.

Finally, we show a simple modification of (a ring version of) the PVW encryption scheme [PVW08] which, when used in place of LPR encryption, gives us a download-rate-$(1 - \epsilon)$ batch-OLE. Namely, the sender message has length $(1 + \epsilon)k\log p$ for any constant $\epsilon > 0$. Note that this is smaller than the total length of the sender input (namely, $2k\log p$), thus the sender input is somewhat *statistically hidden* even if the receiver is malicious.

On Asymptotic Quasi-Optimality vs. Concrete Efficiency. Asymptotic quasi-optimality is a theoretical framework to capture efficiency of cryptographic protocols, *with an eye towards practicality.* To demonstrate the latter, we provide an implementation of our batch-OLE protocol and benchmark it against several competing approaches [BDOZ11,dCJV21,BEP+20], demonstrating that it achieves as good or better communication and/or computational overhead than the competing approaches. Due to lack of space, we defer detailed performance results and comparisons to the full version of this paper. The computational and communication complexity is as good as the rounding protocol in [dCJV21] and considerably better than other competing approaches [BDOZ11,BEP+20]. For example, doing 10,000 OLEs over a 16-bit field requires a communication of 1.17 MB in our protocol versus 1.31 MB in the protocol of [dCJV21] and 2.09 MB in the protocol of [BEP+20].

AQO Zero Knowledge. We show the first construction of a zero-knowledge proof for all of $\mathcal{NP}$ that is asymptotically quasi-optimal in both computation and communication. Furthermore, our protocol is constant-round. Our starting point is an asymptotically quasi-optimal PCP that is implicit in prior works on near-optimal PCPs [BS08,BCGT13]. We abstract such an AQO PCP via a gap version of Cook's theorem (cf. Theorem 4). Our construction proceeds in three steps:

1. We first compile the AQO PCP into an honest-verifier AQO zero-knowledge PCP (ZKPCP). Recall that in such a ZKPCP, the view of an honest verifier can be simulated without knowing the witness. Our construction relies on the "MPC-in-the-head" technique from [IKOS07,IW14]. For the compilation, we design a specialized MPC protocol that preserves the AQO property of the underlying PCP.
2. In the next step, we construct an AQO honest-verifier ZK from our ZKPCP, using batch-OT to emulate the PCP queries. As we are constructing a proof (with unconditional soundness), we need the batch-OT to be unconditionally secure against a malicious sender. However, we are unable to obtain such a protocol directly from our semi-honest batch-OT protocol (in fact, our malicious batch-OT protocol will rely on the zero-knowledge proof system designed here). Instead, we design a new AQO batch-OT protocol based on Ring-LWE with two caveats: it is unconditionally secure against a malicious receiver as opposed to the sender, and it is only *entropically secure* in the sense that a malicious receiver obtains some bounded leakage on the sender's input. By reversing the OT direction [WW06], we solve the problem of getting security against a malicious sender. Finally, we show that the entropy loss in the sender's input only reduces the ZKPCP soundness in our honest-verifier ZK proof system by essentially the loss in entropy. By appropriately instantiating the parameters, we preserve AQO in this reduction.
3. Finally, to handle a malicious verifier, we have the verifier commit to its randomness for the honest-verifier ZK system and reveal it to demonstrate

honest behavior. As the verifier can abort at reveal, we need to ensure that the actual proof is not learned by the verifier before it demonstrates honest behavior. We achieve this by having the prover commit to the proof and reveal it after the verifier reveals its randomness. By using an AQO commitment, we ensure this step preserves the AQO property.

Thus, a key insight in this construction is that a leaky (entropically secure) batch-OLE scheme is good enough because we only use it for *soundness*.

AQO Secure Function Evaluation. Finally, we discuss how to achieve AQO secure function evaluation (SFE) for Boolean circuits in the presence of semi-honest and malicious adversaries. Loosely speaking, semi-honest SFE is implied directly by instantiating a variant of the classic GMW protocol [GMW87, Gol04] with our AQO semi-honest batch-OT. Next, to compile it to achieve malicious security, we first compile our semi-honest batch-OT protocol to be secure against malicious parties using our AQO ZK. Our protocol then relies on the semi-honest GMW protocol where the OTs are instantiated using our maliciously secure OT protocol. Next, we rely on the observation from [GIP+14] that if we remove the final output reconstruction round from the *semi-honest* GMW protocol in the OT-hybrid model, then it does not reveal any information even to malicious parties. This allows us to use a *single* zero-knowledge proof (rather than one in each step of the protocol) to be provided just before the output shares are revealed. As a corollary, we get an AQO *single* OLE over an arbitrary modulus.

1.2   Perspectives and Open Problems

Theoretical Motivation. Our original motivation for this work was to design efficient solutions when the instance size n was small, i.e. $n = O(\lambda)$ where λ is the security parameter. We expect that studying this question will lead to *creative* ways to solve problems such as OT, OLE, ZK, and MPC.

Our optimism is based on past examples. Several lines of research have started from clean questions of this kind and turned out to have unexpected theoretical and practical applications. Some examples include lattice-based cryptography, black-box reductions and, closer to our work, low-complexity cryptography. A common feature is that a new theoretical challenge has led to a rich landscape of new techniques, which have then found other applications.

Practical Motivation. As already mentioned, our (semi-honest) batch-OLE protocol gives a promising evidence for relevance of the asymptotic AQO question to concrete efficiency. Batch-OLE can serve as a useful building block for secure arithmetic computation, and can be used to bootstrap pseudorandom correlation generators for OLE [BCG+20]. In contrast, our current AQO zero-knowledge protocol is impractical because of its reliance on a classical PCP.

Open Problems. The central creative challenge in achieving AQO is to find new ways of amplification. While we succeeded in some cases, many questions about

AQO cryptography remain open and motivate future research. We include here some open questions.

First, while there are AQO constructions of minicrypt objects from a variety of assumptions, the only AQO public-key encryption scheme we are aware of is based on Ring-LWE. There are likely to be other ways to achieve AQO cryptomania, and we believe this is an interesting challenge for future research. A second question is obtaining concretely efficient AQO zero-knowledge proofs. A possible route is by employing a suitable AQO variant of a *linear* PCP (such as the one of Gennaro et al. [GGPR13]), where the field size is kept small and soundness is amplified by using λ queries, but with only a polylogarithmic increase in computation. Third, the notion of *AQO reductions* (which we used to construct AQO semi-honest SFE from AQO batch-OT) leaves several open questions. For instance, is there an information-theoretic AQO reduction of zero-knowledge proofs to batch-OT? Finally, the idea of using leaky functionalities (such as batch-OT or batch-OLE) in downstream applications, which we used to construct our AQO ZK protocol, could be useful in other contexts.

2   Preliminaries

Basic Notations and Conventions. We denote the security parameter by λ and by the abbreviation PPT to denote probabilistic polynomial-time. We write $\tilde{O}(\cdot)$ to suppress polylogarithmic factors. In this work we consider nonuniform adversaries that are modeled by Boolean circuits.

2.1   Asymptotic Quasi-Optimality

In this section, we define the notion of asymptotic quasi-optimality (AQO) for the cryptographic primitives we explore in this work. Recall that a major distinction between this notion and some earlier notions of asymptotic (quasi)-optimality from the literature [IKOS08, DIK10, BCG+17, BISW18] is that here, we demand (and obtain) a near-optimal tradeoff between security and efficiency for *every instance size and security level*, as opposed to sufficiently big polynomial-size (in the security parameter) instances. In contrast, previous works neglect additive terms that depend polynomially on the security parameter. For all primitives, we define a notion of *instance size* that we denote by n and a security parameter λ. Informally, asymptotic quasi-optimality demands that the algorithms for the primitives run in time $\tilde{O}(n + \lambda)$ and provides $2^{-\lambda}$-security against adversaries of size 2^{λ}.

We now describe how such a definition manifests in the case of two-party secure function evaluation. Here, the instance size n refers to the size of a Boolean circuit implementing the underlying functionality. Such protocols are formally captured by a polynomial-time *protocol compiler* that, given inputs the security parameter 1^{λ} and a circuit C, outputs a pair of circuits (P_0, P_1) that implements the next message function of the two parties in the protocol. The AQO efficiency requirement is that the size of the circuits P_0 and P_1 output by the compiler is quasilinear in $n + \lambda$.

While the correctness requirement (when no party is corrupted) should hold irrespective of the choice of λ, C, the security requirement only considers adversaries of size at most 2^λ. The definition follows the standard definition of security for two-party secure function evaluation [Gol04] with the exception that we use the following "exact" notion of 2^λ-indistinguishability:

Definition 1. *Let $X = \{X(\lambda, a)\}_{\lambda \in \mathbb{N}, a \in \{0,1\}^*}$ and $Y = \{Y(\lambda, a)\}_{\lambda \in \mathbb{N}, a \in \{0,1\}^*}$ be two distribution ensembles. We say that the ensembles X and Y are 2^λ-indistinguishable, denoted $X \approx_{2^\lambda} Y$, if for every non-uniform circuit $\mathcal{D}$ of size at most 2^λ, every $a \in \{0,1\}^*$, and all sufficiently large λ,*

$$\left| \Pr\left[\mathcal{D}(X(\lambda, a), 1^\lambda, a) = 1 \right] - \Pr\left[\mathcal{D}(Y(\lambda, a), 1^\lambda, a) = 1 \right] \right| \leq 2^{-\lambda}.$$

The definitions for other AQO primitives considered in this paper follow as special cases of AQO secure function evaluation. We defer the formal definitions to the full version of this paper.

2.2   Ring Learning with Errors

Define the ring $\mathcal{R} := \mathbb{Z}[x]/(x^k + 1)$, where we take k to be a positive power of 2. For a modulus q, let $\mathcal{R}_q = \mathbb{Z}_q[x]/(x^k + 1)$. Let $\mathcal{U}(\mathcal{R}_q)$ be the uniform distribution over $\mathcal{R}_q$. For $\sigma \in \mathbb{R}^+$, let χ denote the *error distribution*, which is a discrete, zero-centered Gaussian distribution with variance σ^2 over $\mathcal{R}$. A sample $e \leftarrow \chi$ is produced by sampling each coefficient from a discrete, zero-centered Gaussian with variance σ^2. We now define the decisional Ring-LWE problem [LPR10], borrowing formalisms from [BEP+20].

Definition 2 (Decisional Ring Learning with Errors Problem). *For a modulus $q \in \mathbb{N}^+$, k a power of 2, and a standard deviation $\sigma \in \mathbb{R}^+$, let $\mathcal{R}_q$ and χ be as defined above. We say that an algorithm $\mathcal{A}$ has advantage ϵ in solving the problem $\mathsf{RLWE}_{n,q,\chi}$ if the following holds:*

$$\left| \Pr[b = 1 \mid \mathbf{a} \leftarrow \mathcal{U}(\mathcal{R}_q), \; \mathbf{s}, \mathbf{e} \leftarrow \chi, \; b \leftarrow \mathcal{A}(\mathbf{a}, \mathbf{as} + \mathbf{e})] \right.$$

$$\left. - \Pr[b = 1 \mid \mathbf{a} \leftarrow \mathcal{U}(\mathcal{R}_q), \; \mathbf{u} \leftarrow \mathcal{U}(\mathcal{R}_q)), \; b \leftarrow \mathcal{A}(\mathbf{a}, \mathbf{u})] \right| \geq \epsilon$$

The decisional ring-LWE assumption postulates that every 2^λ-time adversary has advantage at most $2^{-\lambda}$ in the distinguishing game above.

In order to achieve the definition, one would set $k = k(\lambda)$ to be a large enough polynomial function of λ. The cryptanalytic state of the art suggests that $k(\lambda)$ can be *quasi-linear* in λ.

2.3   Ring-LWE Encryption

We describe a batched version of an encryption scheme from Lyubashevsky, Peikert and Regev [LPR10] (henceforth called batch-LPR). There are four parameters that define the scheme: $k = k(\lambda)$, the ring dimension; $q = q(\lambda)$, the ciphertext modulus; $p = p(\lambda)$, the plaintext modulus; and χ, an error distribution. There are several constraints on these parameters that we will describe in the sequel.

The scheme operates over the polynomial ring $\mathcal{R}_q = \mathbb{Z}_q[x]/(f(x))$ where $f(x)$ is a degree-k polynomial that is irreducible over $\mathbb{Q}[x]$. Typically, and throughout this paper, we consider $f(x) = x^k + 1$ where k is a power of two.

We will let χ be a (truncated) discrete Gaussian distribution over $\mathbb{Z}^k$ which is interpreted as a distribution over the coefficient embedding of $\mathcal{R} = \mathbb{Z}[x]/(x^k+1)$. Thus, a polynomial $v \in \mathcal{R}$ is sampled according to the distribution by sampling each coefficient independently from a truncated discrete Gaussian, namely a discrete Gaussian with standard deviation σ whose support is contained in an Euclidean ball of radius $\sigma\sqrt{k}$. Note that we truncate the Gaussian distribution to have statistical distance of at most $2^{-k} \leq 2^{-\lambda}$ from the untruncated Gaussian distribution [MR04], hence truncation adds a $2^{-\lambda}$ factor in security games, which we typically ignore. Let $U(\mathcal{R}_q)$ be the uniform distribution over $\mathcal{R}_q$.

Encryption Scheme. The encryption scheme proceeds as follows. The parameters k, p, q and σ are assumed to be known to all the algorithms.

- LPR.KeyGen(1^λ): Choose $a_1, \ldots, a_\ell, s \leftarrow U(\mathcal{R}_q)$ and $e_1, \ldots, e_\ell \leftarrow \chi$, where ℓ is a tunable parameter that will be set later during the rerandomization procedure. Output the secret key $sk = s$ and the rerandomization key $rk = (a_1, \ldots, a_\ell, a_1 s + e_1, \ldots, a_\ell s + e_\ell)$.
- LPR.Encode(p, m) and LPR.Decode($p, \widehat{m}$): The public, deterministic, encoding algorithm transforms the message into a form that will be used by the encryption algorithm, and the public decoding algorithm is its inverse operation. Both operations are linear.
  The plaintext space for batch-LPR is $\mathbb{Z}_p^k$. To encode $m \in \mathbb{Z}_p^k$, apply the number-theoretic transform (NTT) over $\mathcal{R}_p := \mathbb{Z}_p[x]/(x^k + 1)$ to convert it into $\widehat{m} \in \mathcal{R}_q$. The key property is that for every $m_1, m_2 \in \mathbb{Z}_p^k$, $m_1 \circ m_2 = $ LPR.Decode($\widehat{m}_1 \cdot \widehat{m}_2$) where $\cdot$ denotes multiplication of polynomials in $\mathcal{R}_p$ and $\circ$ denotes coordinate-wise multiplication of vectors in $\mathbb{Z}_p^k$.
- LPR.Enc(sk, m): Sample $a \leftarrow \mathcal{R}_q$ and $e \leftarrow \chi$. Let $\Delta = \lceil q/p \rceil$ and let $\widehat{m} = $ LPR.Encode(p, m). Output the ciphertext

$$ct = (a, as + e + \Delta\widehat{m}) \in \mathcal{R}_q^2$$

  (In this paper, q will be chosen as a multiple of p, so $\Delta = q/p$.)
- LPR.Dec(sk, ct): Parse $sk = s$. Decryption of a ciphertext $ct = (a, b)$ proceeds by computing

$$\widehat{m} = \left\lfloor \frac{b - as}{\Delta} \right\rceil$$

Output LPR.Decode$(p, \widehat{m})$.

Correctness, Security and Parameter Settings. There are several interrelated constraints on the parameters that must be balanced when instantiating the scheme. For correctness, we need that

$$||b - as||_\infty \leq \Delta/2 \approx q/2p$$

This places a lower bound on $q = \Omega(p\sigma^2\sqrt{k})$. Since we insist on full utilization of all k plaintext slots, we require $\mathbb{Z}[x]/(x^k+1)$ to split completely mod p, requiring us to have $p = 1 \pmod{2k}$. Thus, we have $q > p \geq 2k + 1$. (Additionally to support quasi-linear time operations, we will also need to support NTT mod q, so we requires the factors of q to be 1 $\pmod{2k}$ as well.)

The relationship between parameters is further complicated because of homomorphic operations, which can grow the error term in the ciphertext. To maintain correctness, this may require the ciphertext modulus q to grow. Increasing q can raise the lower bound on k since the known attacks on Ring-LWE improve in quality as the ratio between q and σ increases; to compensate for it, one needs to increase k. In turn, this increases the smallest p that can be supported.

Homomorphic Operations. We now define two basic homomorphic operations on the encryption scheme that allow us to construct a batch-OLE protocol. The first operation Lin supports linear functions of the form $f_{\alpha,\beta}(m) = \alpha \circ m + \beta$. It is often desirable that homomorphic operations produce a ciphertext that does not leak the circuit computed to generate the ciphertext, even to the party that generated the input ciphertext and who knows the secret key. This property is often called *function privacy* [Gen09, GHV10] and is not satisfied by the Lin algorithm. To achieve this function-hiding property, we need a rerandomization algorithm ReRand.

– LPR.Lin(ct, α, β): The homomorphic addition algorithm outputs a ciphertext ct' that decrypts to $\alpha \circ m + \beta$ if ct encrypts m. Letting $ct = (a, b)$, the algorithm outputs

$$ct' = (\widehat{\alpha}a, \widehat{\alpha}b + \Delta\widehat{\beta})$$

where $\widehat{\alpha} = $ LPR.Encode(p, α) and $\widehat{\beta} = $ LPR.Encode(p, β). Note that while we think of the output of LPR.Encode as living in $\mathcal{R}_p$, we think of it as a polynomial over $\mathcal{R}$ when multiplying it with a and b.

Denoting $\widehat{\alpha}a$ by a', the ciphertext ct' is of the form $(a', a's + \widehat{\alpha}e + \Delta(\widehat{\alpha}\widehat{m} + \widehat{\beta}))$. Assuming that $\widehat{\alpha}e$ is small enough, decrytion recovers $\widehat{\alpha}\widehat{m} + \widehat{\beta}$ and decoding it recovers $\alpha \circ m + \beta$.

– LPR.ReRand(rk, ct, B): Let χ_{flood} be the uniform distribution over $[-B, \ldots, B]$. The rerandomization operation parses $rk = (a_1, a_2, \ldots, a_\ell, b_1, b_2, \ldots, b_\ell)$ and $ct = (a, b)$ and outputs

$$\left(a + \sum_{i=1}^{\ell} r_i a_i + r_0, b + \sum_{i=1}^{\ell} r_i b_i + f\right)$$

where r_i are polynomials with coefficients from a discrete Gaussian distribution, and f is a random polynomial with coefficients chosen from χ_{flood}.
Denoting the first component of the above ciphertext by a', and assuming that $b = as + e + \Delta\widehat{m}$, the second component can be written as $a's + e + \sum_{i=1}^{\ell} r_i e_i + \Delta\widehat{m}$. This is an encryption of $\widehat{m}$ as long as the error $e + \sum_{i=1}^{\ell} r_i e_i$ is small enough.

The rerandomization procedure is often used with $B > 2^\lambda \cdot p\sigma^2 k$. Indeed, $p\sigma^2 k$ is an upper bound on the ℓ_∞ norm of the noise term in the output of Lin. By the noise-flooding lemma [Gen09, GKPV10, AJL+12], this gives us $2^{-\lambda}$ statistical security of LPR.ReRand. In this work, we will use a narrower flooding distribution.

2.4 Entropy and Extraction

The min-entropy of a random variable X is $H_\infty(X) = -\log \max_x \Pr[X = x]$. The conditional min-entropy of X given Y, defined in [DORS08], is $\tilde{H}_\infty(X|Y) = -\log \mathbb{E}_y[\max_x \Pr[X = x|Y = y]]$. We need the following fact.

Lemma 1 (Lemma 2.2 in [DORS08]). *Let X, Y, Z be random variables where Y takes at most 2^ℓ possible values. Then,*

$$\tilde{H}_\infty(A|B, C) \geq \tilde{H}_\infty(A, B|C) - \ell \geq \tilde{H}_\infty(A|C) - \ell .$$

We also need the following regularity lemma [Mic02, LPR13].

Lemma 2 (Corollary 7.5 in [LPR13]). *Let $a_1, \ldots, a_\ell$ be chosen at random from $\mathcal{R}_q = \mathbb{Z}[x]/(x^k + 1)$ where k is a power of two, and let $r_0, r_1, \ldots, r_\ell$ be ring elements each of whose coefficients is chosen from a discrete Gaussian with parameter $\sigma \geq 2k \cdot q^{(n+2)/n\ell}$. Then the distribution of $r_0 + \sum_{i=1}^{\ell} r_i a_i$ (given $a_1, \ldots, a_\ell$) has statistical distance at most $2^{-\Omega(k)}$ from the uniform distribution over $\mathcal{R}_q$.*

3 AQO Semi-Honest Batch-OLE and Batch-OT

We begin this section with our first technical contribution, namely a gentle noise-flooding procedure. We then use this to construct our asymptotically quasi-optimal batch-OLE and batch-OT schemes in Sect. 3.3.

3.1 Gentle Noise-Flooding

The noise-flooding lemma (e.g. [Gen09, GKPV10]) states that for every integer $x \in [-P, P]$, the distribution of $x + y$ where the integer y is chosen uniformly at random from the interval $[-Q, Q]$ is statistically close to the uniform distribution over the interval $[-Q, Q]$. Specifically, the statistical distance is $O(P/Q)$. Typically, this lemma is used with $Q \geq P \cdot 2^\lambda$ so as to result in exponentially small statistical distance. Our gentle noise-flooding lemma below shows a qualitatively stronger statement: the distribution of $x + y$ can be *perfectly* simulated by an algorithm that gets x with probability $2P/(2Q + 1)$ (and $\perp$ otherwise). This is a specific, simple, instance of a statistical-to-perfect lemma as in [IKO+11].

Let $\mathcal{D} = \{D_a\}_{a \in A}$ be an ensemble of distributions indexed by a variable $a \in A$. An ϵ-leaky perfect simulator for $\mathcal{D}$ is an algorithm S such that the distribution obtained by outputting $S(a)$ with probability ϵ and $S(\perp)$ with probability $1 - \epsilon$ is *identically distributed* to D_a.

Lemma 3 (Gentle Noise Flooding Lemma). *Let P, Q be integers with $P < Q$. Let the encoding of $a \in [-P, P]$, denoted $\mathsf{Encode}(a)$ be $s = a + r$ where r is chosen uniformly from $[-Q, Q]$. Then, there exists a $2P/(2Q + 1)$-leaky perfect simulation for the encoding scheme.*

Proof. We first analyze the distribution $\mathsf{Encode}(a)$. Consider two cases.

- **Case 1:** $P - Q \leq s \leq Q - P$. In this case, we argue that no information about a is leaked. For any s such that $P - Q \leq s \leq Q - P$, and any $a \in [-P, P]$, there is a unique $r \leftarrow [-Q, Q]$ such that $s = a + r$. This implies that for any a,

$$\Pr[\mathsf{Encode}(a) = s \mid s \in [Q - P, P - Q]] = 1/(2Q - 2P).$$

  Furthermore, the probability that we are in Case 1, i.e., $s \in [P - Q, Q - P]$ is exactly $(2Q - 2P + 1)/(2Q + 1)$.
- **Case 2:** $s < P - Q$ or $s > Q - P$. In this case, s leaks something about a. As the number of r's that result in Case 1 is exactly $2Q - 2P + 1$, the number of *bad* r's is exactly $2P$. Therefore, the probability that this case occurs is $2P/(2Q + 1)$.

We now define S to be the algorithm that works as follows. On input $\perp$, it simply outputs a uniformly random value in $[P - Q, Q - P]$; and on input a, it outputs $a + r$ conditioned on $a + r \notin [P - Q, Q - P]$ where r is chosen uniformly at random from $[-Q, Q]$. The distributions induced by $S(\perp)$ and $S(a)$ are identical to the distributions from Cases 1 and 2 respectively. Since Case 2 occurs with $2P/(2Q + 1)$ probability, we achieve $2P/(2Q + 1)$-leaky perfect simulation. $\square$

Corollary 1. *Let $Q \geq kP$. Let $\vec{a} \in [-P, P]^k$ be arbitrary and let $\vec{s} = \vec{a} + \vec{r}$ where $\vec{r} \leftarrow [-Q, Q]^k$ is chosen at random. Then, there exists a simulator S that takes $O(\lambda \cdot (\log P + \log k))$ bits of information on $\vec{a}$ and simulates the distribution of $\vec{s}$ to within statistical distance $2^{-\Omega(\lambda)}$.*

The statistical-to-perfect simulator S in the proof of Lemma 3 uses $2P/(2Q + 1) \cdot k < 2$ coordinates of $\vec{a}$ (their values together with their locations) in expectation. The corollary follows by a Chernoff bound.

3.2 Entropically Secure Batch-OLE Protocol

We first present a "leaky" batch-OLE protocol which guarantees that the sender's input has residual entropy given the (semi-honest) receiver's view. The receiver is guaranteed simulation security against a semi-honest sender.

The receiver starts with input $m \in \mathbb{Z}_p^k$ and the sender has input $\alpha, \beta \in \mathbb{Z}_p^k$. For convenience, one can imagine that α and β are random. At the end of the protocol, the receiver gets $\gamma = \alpha \circ m + \beta$, where all operations are component-wise. Let k, p, q and σ be the parameters of the LPR scheme.

1. The receiver generates a key pair $(sk, rk) \leftarrow \mathsf{LPR.KeyGen}(1^\lambda)$. It encrypts m into a ciphertext $ct \leftarrow \mathsf{LPR.Enc}(sk, m)$, and sends (rk, ct) to the sender.
2. The sender computes a ciphertext $ct' \leftarrow \mathsf{ReRand}(rk, \mathsf{Lin}(ct, \alpha, \beta), Q)$ where $Q = \Omega(pk^2\sigma)$ and returns ct' to the client.
3. The receiver outputs $\gamma \leftarrow \mathsf{Dec}(sk, ct')$.

Correctness follows from the properties of the LPR encryption scheme in Sect. 2.3. The entropic security statement is captured by the lemma below.

Lemma 4 (Entropically Secure Semi-Honest Batch OLE). *Let the parameters $k = k(\lambda), p = p(\lambda), \sigma = \sigma(\lambda)$, $Q = \widetilde{\Omega}(pk^2\sigma)$ and $q = \Omega(pQ)$. Conditioned on the receiver's view, the sender input α has residual entropy at least $H_\infty(\alpha) - O(\lambda \log Q)$.*

Proof. The receiver's view consists of the LPR secret key s, the public polynomials $a, a_1, \dots, a_\ell$, the error polynomials $e_1, \dots, e_\ell$, the input m (which we collectively denote by view_0) and the sender message ct'. The latter is

$$ct' = (a', b') = \left(\widehat{\alpha}a + \sum_{i=1}^\ell r_i a_i + r_0, \widehat{\alpha}b + \Delta\widehat{\beta} + \sum_{i=1}^\ell r_i b_i + f\right)$$

$$= \left(\widehat{\alpha}a + \sum_{i=1}^\ell r_i a_i + r_0, (\widehat{\alpha}a + \sum_{i=1}^\ell r_i a_i + r_0)s + (\widehat{\alpha}e + \sum_{i=1}^\ell r_i e_i + f) + \Delta(\widehat{\alpha}\widehat{m} + \widehat{\beta})\right)$$

Note that ct' can be generated given $A := \widehat{\alpha}a + \sum_{i=1}^\ell r_i a_i + r_0$, $E := \widehat{\alpha}e + \sum_{i=1}^\ell r_i e_i + f$ and $\widehat{\alpha}\widehat{m} + \widehat{\beta}$. Since $\widehat{\beta}$ is random and independent of $\widehat{\alpha}$, so is $\widehat{\alpha}\widehat{m} + \widehat{\beta}$. Since the coordinates of $\widehat{\alpha}e + \sum_{i=1}^\ell r_i e_i$ are bounded by $\widetilde{O}(pk\sigma)$, an application of the gentle noise-flooding lemma (Corollary 1) tells us that E can be simulated given $O(\lambda)$ of its coordinates, and therefore $O(\lambda \log Q)$ bits. An application of Lemma 1 tells us that $\widetilde{H}_\infty(\alpha | A, E) \geq H_\infty(\alpha | A) - O(\lambda \log Q)$. (We implicitly condition all entropy expressions on view_0.) Finally, the regularity lemma (Lemma 2) tells us that A is $2^{-\Omega(\lambda)}$-close to uniform. Putting this together, we get that $\widetilde{H}_\infty(\alpha | A, E) \geq H_\infty(\alpha) - O(\lambda \log Q)$. $\square$

Finally, we note that for a sufficiently large value of k (as a function of λ), the residual entropy is a constant fraction of the entropy of α.

3.3 Our Batch-OLE and Batch-OT Schemes

AQO Batch-OLE. Block et al. [BGMN18], building on [IKOS09a, BMN18a], showed a compiler that converts leaky OLE to fresh OLE. Our main observation is that their compiler preserves asymptotic quasi-optimality as long as one uses an error-correcting code that permits quasi-linear time encoding and erasure-decoding, both of which are satisfied by the Reed-Solomon code. This gives us the following theorem. We defer details and concrete optimizations to the full version of this paper.

Theorem 1. *There exists an asymptotically quasi-optimal BOLE protocol under the 2^λ-hardness of the RLWE assumption.*

AQO Batch-OT. Since our Batch-OLE protocol works over polynomial-sized fields, we can get a batch-OT protocol by naïvely embedding a single-bit OT into a single instance of OLE over $\mathbb{Z}_p$. The naïve embedding loses a factor of $\log p$ in the rate. We remark that it may be possible to reclaim this and achieve a constant rate by working with an extension field of $\mathbb{F}_2$, i.e., $\mathbb{F}_{2^\ell}$ for some ℓ, and using ideas from [CCXY18, BMN18a] to embed $\mathbb{F}_2^{\ell'}$ into $\mathbb{F}_{2^\ell}$. We leave the exploration of this avenue to a future work. An alternative approach that achieves a near-constant rate is described in Sect. 4.1.

4   AQO Batch-OLE: The Malicious Setting

In this section, we show how to achieve a two-round AQO leaky batch-OLE that is entropically secure against a *malicious* receiver. In particular, we will show that for every (possibly maliciously chosen) receiver message, the sender input **a** has residual entropy conditioned on his message to the receiver. The sender will be assumed to be semi-honest. We defer the exact notion of entropic security to Theorem 2 and instead start with the protocol itself.

4.1   Entropically Secure OLE Against a Malicious Receiver

Our starting point is to develop an additively homomorphic encryption scheme with good "post-evaluation rate", namely one where the size of *homomorphically evaluated ciphertexts* are approximately the same as the size of the messages they encrypt. Such schemes were developed very recently in a collection of independent works [BDGM19, GH19, DGI+19]. We observe that a simple tweak on an encryption scheme due to Peikert, Vaikuntanathan and Waters [PVW08] *already* gives us good post-evaluation rate together with good concrete efficiency. In contrast, all the cited works construct somewhat more complex and concretely less efficient schemes. We do pay a price, namely, freshly encrypted ciphertexts are not rate-1; in fact, they are somewhat larger than they would be otherwise. Yet, this does not matter much for us: indeed for our application to entropically secure OLE, only the size of the homomorphically evaluated ciphertext matters.

Our scheme, denoted EntOLE, is parametrized by a dimension k, plaintext modulus p, ciphertext (Ring-LWE) modulus q and a noise parameter σ. We define two additional parameters: η that will govern the message sizes, and a compressed ciphertext modulus q'. One challenge that must be overcome to achieve a low post-evaluation rate is a reduction of the ciphertext modulus. Since our homomorphic computation must support one plaintext-ciphertext multiplication, our starting ciphertext modulus q must be greater than p^2, since we must have $\log p$ bits for the message and an additional $\log p$ bits to account for the growth of the error term. The resulting ciphertext modulus q' will only be a few bits larger than p. To switch to this modulus we employ the modulus reduction operation from Brakerski & Vaikuntanathan [BV11a].

Modulus Reduction [BV11a, BGV12]. For ciphertext moduli q, q' such that q' divides q, the modulus reduction operation $\mathsf{ModRed}_{q,q'}$ takes in an element $a \in \mathcal{R}_q$ and outputs $a' \in \mathcal{R}_{q'}$ where $a' = \left\lfloor \frac{q'}{q} a \right\rceil$.

$$\mu = \left\lfloor \frac{b' - a's \mod q'}{\Delta'} \right\rceil$$

We now describe a secret-key linearly homomorphic encryption scheme with post-evaluation rate close to 1.

- $\mathsf{EntOLE.KeyGen}(1^\lambda, \eta)$: For each $i \in [\eta]$, sample $s_i \leftarrow \chi$ and output

$$sk = (s_1, \ldots, s_\eta) \in \mathcal{R}_q^\eta$$

- $\mathsf{EntOLE.Enc}\,(sk, (\mu_1, \ldots, \mu_\eta))$: Takes as input a secret key and a message vector $(\mu_1, \ldots, \mu_\eta)$ where each μ_i is in $\mathbb{Z}_p^k$. For $i \in [\eta]$, sample $a_i \leftarrow \mathcal{U}(\mathcal{R}_q)$, where $\mathcal{U}$ denotes the uniform distribution. Let $\vec{a}$ denote the column vector of length η consisting of the a_i polynomials. Similarly, let $\vec{s}$ be a row vector of length η consisting of the secret polynomials. Define the matrix $\mathcal{M} \in \mathcal{R}_q^{\eta \times \eta}$ where $\mathcal{M}[i, j] = 0$ for $i \neq j$ and $\mathcal{M}[i, i] = \mathsf{LPR.Encode}(\mu_i)$ for each $i \in [\eta]$. Finally, sample a matrix $E \in \mathcal{R}_q^{\eta \times \eta}$ such that each $E[i, j] \leftarrow \chi$ is an independently sampled error polynomial. Output the following ciphertext:

$$ct = (\vec{a} \mid \vec{a} \cdot \vec{s} + \mathcal{M}\Delta + E) \in \mathcal{R}_q^{\eta \times (\eta+1)}$$

(Note that $\vec{a} \cdot \vec{s}$ is an $\eta \times \eta$ matrix which is the outer product of the vectors $\vec{a}$ and $\vec{s}$.)

- $\mathsf{EntOLE.Eval}(ct, \{\alpha_i\}_{i=1}^\eta, \{\beta_i\}_{i=1}^\eta)$: Takes as input a ciphertext ct and the sender's BOLE inputs where each input is in $\mathbb{Z}_p^k$. Let $\vec{\alpha}$ be the column vector of length η such that $\vec{\alpha}[i] = \mathsf{LPR.Encode}(\alpha_i)$ for $i \in [\eta]$. Let $\vec{\beta}$ be the column vector of length $\eta + 1$ such that $\vec{\beta}[i+1] = \mathsf{LPR.Encode}(\beta_i)$ for $i \in [\eta]$, and set $\vec{\beta}[1] = 0$. Compute an encryption of the BOLE result as follows:

$$ct_{bole} = (\vec{\alpha})^T \cdot ct + \Delta \vec{\beta} \in \mathcal{R}_q^{\eta+1}$$

This ciphertext consists of $\eta + 1$ elements in $\mathcal{R}_q$.

To achieve a high rate for the output ciphertext, we perform the modulus switching operation [BV11a, BGV12] to reduce our modulus from q to q'. We define the output ciphertext $ct_{res} \in \mathcal{R}_{q'}^{\eta+1}$ as follows:

$$ct_{res}[i] := \mathsf{ModRed}_{q,q'}(ct_{bole}[i]) \quad \text{for } i \in [\eta+1]$$

– EntOLE.Dec(sk, ct_{res}) : Takes as input a vector of η secret keys and a cipher-text in $\mathcal{R}_{q'}^{\eta+1}$. Decryption proceeds by first computing $\overline{\mu}_i$ for $i \in [\eta]$ as follows:

$$\overline{\mu}_i := \left\lfloor \frac{ct_{res}[i+1] - ct_{res}[1] \cdot sk[i]}{\Delta'} \right\rceil$$

where $\Delta' = \lfloor q'/p \rfloor$. Set $\mu_i := \mathsf{LPR.Decode}(\overline{\mu}_i)$, and output $\{\mu_i\}_{i=1}^{\eta} \in \mathcal{R}_p^{\eta}$.

Entropically Sender-Secure Batch OLE protocol

Receiver Input: $\mathbf{m} = (m_1, \ldots, m_{k\eta}) \in \mathbb{Z}_p^{k\eta}$.
Sender Input: $\mathbf{a} = (a_1, \ldots, a_{k\eta}) \in \mathbb{Z}_p^{k\eta}$ and $\mathbf{b} = (b_1, \ldots, b_{k\eta}) \in \mathbb{Z}_p^{k\eta}$.

Receiver does the following:

- Splits $\mathbf{m}$ into η vectors in $\mathbb{Z}_p^k$ to get $\{\mu_i\}_{i=1}^{\eta}$, where each μ_i is in $\mathbb{Z}_p^k$.
- Samples $sk \leftarrow \mathsf{EntOLE.KeyGen}(1^\lambda, \eta)$.
- Computes $ct \leftarrow \mathsf{EntOLE.Enc}(sk, \{\mu_i\}_{i=1}^{\eta})$ and sends ct to the receiver.

Sender does the following:

- Splits $\mathbf{a}$ and $\mathbf{b}$ each into η vectors in $\mathbb{Z}_p^k$ to get $\{\alpha_i\}_{i=1}^{\eta}$ and $\{\beta_i\}_{i=1}^{\eta}$, where each α_i and β_i is in $\mathbb{Z}_p^k$.
- Compute $ct_{res} = \mathsf{EntOLE.EvalOLE}(ct, \{\alpha_i\}_{i=1}^{\eta}, \{\beta\}_{i=1}^{\eta})$ and return ct_{res} to the receiver.

Receiver computes $\{y_i\}_{i=1}^{\eta} \leftarrow \mathsf{EntOLE.Dec}(sk, ct_{res})$ and concatenates the result vectors into a single vector $\mathbf{y} \in \mathbb{Z}_p^{k\eta}$. Outputs $\mathbf{y}$.

Fig. 1. Entropically secure batch-OLE scheme

The entropically secure OLE protocol is described in Fig. 1. The following theorem states the correctness and security properties of the protocol; the proof is deferred to the full version of this paper.

Theorem 2. *Fix $\eta \in \mathbb{N}$. For a security parameter λ, let k, σ, q be parameters that give 2^λ security of ring LWE. Let p be the plaintext modulus, and let q' be a ciphertext modulus such that p divides q' and q' divides q. In addition, let $q' > pk\sigma$ and let $q > p^2 k^2 \sigma$. Then, there exists a BOLE protocol with batch size $n = k\eta$ with the following properties.*

1. *The communication from the receiver to the sender is $(\eta+1)\eta \cdot k \cdot \log q$ bits.*
2. *The communication from the sender to the receiver is $k(\eta+1)\log q'$ bits.*
3. *The receiver's runtime is $\Theta(\eta^2 k \log(k) \log(q))$.*
4. *The sender's runtime is $\Theta(\eta^2 \log(k) \log(q) + \eta k \log(k) \log(q'))$.*

5. *For every malicious receiver* R^* *that outputs a ciphertext* $ct \in \mathcal{R}_q^{\eta \times (\eta + 1)}$, *the entropy of the sender's first input for any distribution of* **a** *is at least*

$$\tilde{H}_\infty(\mathbf{a}|ct_{res}) \geq \tilde{H}_\infty(\mathbf{a}) - (\log(q')k(\eta + 1)) - \log(p)k\eta)$$
$$\geq \tilde{H}_\infty(\mathbf{a}) - O(n\log(k) + k\log(p)) \tag{1}$$

The last bullet shows that with a large enough η, there is considerable residual entropy in **a** given the receiver's view. Indeed, **a** has entropy $n\log p$, and the residual entropy is (up to multiplicative constants) at least $n\log p - n\log k - k\log p$ which is a constant fraction of the entropy of **a** if $p = \mathsf{poly}(k)$ and $\eta = n/k$ is a constant, or even a $1 - 1/\log^c k$ fraction if p is superpolynomial in k and η is polylogarithmic in k. The first four bullets show that the protocol has AQO efficiency.

By relying on a simple extension of [WW06], we also obtain an entropically secure OLE w.r.t malicious sender. In slight more detail, in the "reversed" protocol, the receiver will play the role of the sender and the sender the role of the receiver in the underlying batch OLE. For each instance of the batch OLE, the receiver with input x sets its input as x, r where r is chosen uniformly at random and the sender with input a, b sets its input as a. The sender learns $z = a \cdot x + r$ and sends $w = z + b$ to the receiver which can compute its output as $w - r$. If the underlying batch OLE is entropically secure against a malicious receiver with entropy loss ϵ, then the reversed protocol will be entropically secure against a malicious sender with entropy loss ϵ.

Leaky Batch-OTs from Leaky Batch-OLE. We now show how to obtain a entropically secure batch OT protocol from a batch OLE protocol.

We begin by observing that a naïve embedding of n OT instances into n OLE's does not work. From Theorem 2, we have that the entropy loss with a batch size n is $\omega(n)$. The maximum entropy of the sender's message in n OT instances is $2 \cdot n$, therefore, the sender's entire input could potentially be leaked. Next, we provide a tighter reduction from batch-OT to batch-OLE.

Let c be any integer. We will design an m-batch OT protocol that is entropically secure against a malicious receiver where the entropy loss in the sender's "a" message is at most $(1/\log^c(n)) \cdot m$. Our compilation proceeds as follows:

1. We compile a batch OLE with batch size n over a prime p of length $\log^{c+2}\lambda$ bits to n OLEs over the ring modulo $p' = p_1 \cdot p_2 \cdots p_\tau$ where $p_1, \ldots, p_\tau$ are the first $\tau = \log^c \lambda$ prime numbers with the guarantee that except with probability $2^{-\lambda}$ at least $n - \lambda$ OLEs over p' are secure against a malicious receiver. If the original batch OLE is only entropically secure against a malicious receiver w.r.t "a"-message, then the entropy loss in the "a" message will decrease further by at most $\lambda \cdot \log(p')$.

2. Next, we reduce OLE over ring modulo $p' = p_1 \cdot p_2 \cdots p_\tau$ to τ OLEs over each of the primes $p_1, \ldots, p_\tau$ using a standard application of the Chinese Remainder Theorem.

3. Finally, we employ the näive reduction of OLE modulo any prime p to a bit OT, namely, the receiver feeds its input bit b as is in the OLE protocol, while the sender maps its input s_0, s_1 to $a = (s_1 - s_0), b = s_0$.

We provide details only for the first step as the remaining steps follow standard techniques.

The sender and receiver will essentially use their inputs a, b, x modulo p' as their inputs for the OLE modulo p. Recall that p' is the product of the first $\log^c \lambda$ primes,[6] which implies $\log(p') < \log^{c+1} \lambda$. This in turn means the maximum value of $a \cdot x + p$ computed over integers is $O(2^{\log^{c+1} \lambda}) < p$. So the receiver learns $a \cdot x + p$ computed over integers. This however induces a leakage as the receiver is only supposed to learn the value $\mod(p')$. In order to reduce the leakage, we will have the sender modify its inputs to $a' = a, b' = b + r \cdot p'$ where r is chosen uniformly at random from $[-\lambda \cdot p', \lambda \cdot p']$. By the gentle noise-flooding Lemma 3, we can conclude that the probability that the OLE leaks is at most $O(1/\lambda)$. By a Chernoff bound, we can conclude that except with probability $2^{-\lambda}$ at most λ of the OLE instances are leaky.

We now analyze the entire compilation. We instantiate the batch OLE with batch size $n = k \log^c \lambda$ over a prime p of length $\log^{c+2} \lambda$ bits (where k is the Ring LWE dimension set as λ). Recall from Theorem 2 that the entropy loss of the senders "α"-message is at most $n \log k + k \log p = n \log \lambda + \lambda \log p$. The length of p' is at most $\log^{c+1} \lambda$ bits. Since at most λ OLEs are leaky, the maximum entropy loss in the "α"-message can be bounded by $n \log \lambda + \lambda \log p + \lambda \log(p') = O(\lambda \log^{c+2} \lambda)$.

Finally, we obtain a batch-OT protocol with a batch size of $n \cdot \tau = \lambda \log^{2c} \lambda$ and entropy loss of $O(\lambda \log^{c+2} \lambda)$. Therefore, we have the following theorem.

Theorem 3. *For any constant c, there exists a batch-OT protocol over $n = \lambda \log^{2c} \lambda$ instances such that for every malicious receiver R^*, and arbitrary distribution over sender's inputs, the entropy of sender's "a" input at the end of the protocol is at least: $H_\infty(a) - O(\lambda \log^{c+2} \lambda)$.*

5   AQO Zero-Knowledge Arguments

In this section we construct an AQO zero-knowledge argument system. Our starting point is a stronger version of Cook's theorem that follows implicitly from the PCP literature which we compile into an (honest verifier) ZKPCP. In the next step we convert our ZKPCP into a ZK argument system. The former is achieved based on the MPC-in-the-head paradigm whereas the later transformation uses AQO batch OT protocol to emulate the query phase from the ZKPCP oracle.

We begin by recalling Cook's theorem which states that there exists a pair of algorithms (A, B) where given any Boolean circuit C of size s, A maps C to a 3CNF formula F and B maps an input w for C to an input z for F such that the following properties hold:

1. Algorithms A and B run in time $\mathsf{poly}(s)$.

---

[6] The product of the first n primes is $e^{O(n \log n)}$.

2. If w satisfies C then z satisfies F.
3. If C is unsatisfiable, then F is unsatisfiable.

Next, we state a stronger version of the Cook's theorem which is implicit in constructions of near-optimal PCPs from the literature [BS08, BCGT13].

Theorem 4. *There exists a pair of algorithms (A, B) and constants $a, b, c \in \mathbb{N}$ where given any Boolean circuit C of size s, A maps C to a 3CNF formula F and B maps an input w for C to an input z for F such that:*

1. *Algorithms A and B run in time $\tilde{O}(s)$. Let the number of clauses in F be $s \cdot \log^a(s)$.*
2. *If w satisfies C then z satisfies F.*
3. *If C is unsatisfiable, so is F. Furthermore, for any assignment of the variables of F, at most $(1 - 1/\log^b(s))$ fraction of the clauses of F are satisfied.*
4. *Finally, each variable in F appears at most $\log^c(s)$ times.*

The last property can be enforced generically by replacing each variable in F by a distinct variable and then using expander-based consistency checks [PY91].

Next, we design an honest verifier (HV) ZKPCP for the language $\mathcal{L}_C$ by relying on Theorem 4 and the MPC-in-the-head paradigm [IKOS07, IKOS09b]. Note that prior approaches for converting PCP to (HV) ZKPCP either used an ad-hoc and inefficient approach [DFK+92] or used MPC-in-the-head for achieving PCP of proximity with a focus on feasibility and did not attempt to optimize the asymptotic efficiency [IW14]. Achieving AQO based on MPC-in-the-head requires taking a different approach.

We begin by describing our MPC model and then provide our compilation.

Our MPC Model. In the original work of [IKOS07] which introduced the MPC-in-the-head paradigm, the main results implies a zero-knowledge PCP over a large alphabet for a relation $\mathcal{R}$ starting from any honest majority MPC protocol that computes a functionality related to $\mathcal{R}$. In this work, we consider a specific MPC topology and apply the MPC-in-the-head paradigm. Next, we describe our MPC model and the security.

Consider an arbitrary 3CNF formula F with m clauses and t variables $x_1, \ldots, x_t$. We specify an MPC model for the formula F. In our model, we consider a set of *input clients* $C_1, \ldots, C_d$ and d distinct parties per clause of F, servers $(S_1^i, \ldots, S_d^i)$ $(i \in [m])$, an aggregator party A and an output client o. Only the input clients will receive inputs and the final output will be output by the output client. Each input client receives a share corresponding to each variable in F. Namely, C_i receives as input $(x_i^1, \ldots, x_i^t)$ for $i \in [d]$. At the onset of the protocol, each client C_i transmits x_i^j to server S_i^k if the kth clause of F contains the literal x_j. In other words, for every $k \in [m]$, the servers $S_1^k, \ldots, S_d^k$ have the shares corresponding to the (three) literals occurring in the kth clause. Upon receiving inputs from the input clients, the servers $S_1^k, \ldots, S_d^k$ securely compute the functionality f specified by k^{th} clause, where the assignments to the literals are obtained by first XORing the corresponding shares from the servers. We denote the MPC protocol that realizes f by Π. Namely, if the jth literal occurs in the kth clause, the assignment is given by $\bigoplus_{i=1}^{d} x_i^j$. All servers learn the result, and the result of the computation is then forwarded to the aggregator party by server S_1^k for each k. Then, the aggregator party computes the AND of the k values its received and relays that to the output client. The output client finally outputs whatever it receives from the aggregator.

From the description of the MPC model, it follows that if the input clients are given as inputs (XOR) additive shares of the assignment of the variables in F, and all parties behave honestly, then the result output by the output client is the evaluation of F under the corresponding assignment.

Security Model: We will require the protocol to be secure against a passive corruption of at most $\lfloor \frac{d-1}{2} \rfloor$ servers among $S_1^k, \ldots, S_d^k$ for any k. In particular, this means the input clients and aggregator cannot be corrupted. It now follows that if we instantiate Π with any honest majority MPC protocol secure against passive adversaries we have that no adversary can learn anything beyond the result output by the output client.

Compiling to ZKPCP. We defer the proof of Theorem 5 to the full version.

Theorem 5. *Given a Boolean circuit of size s, there exists a non-adaptive $s \cdot \log^a(s)$-query AQO honest verifier ZKPCP over the binary alphabet. More precisely, the PCP achieves perfect simulation w.r.t an honest verifier, soundness $2^{-\frac{s}{\log^b(c)}}$ and a proof of size $s \cdot \log^c(s)$, where a, b, c are constants.*

5.1 AQO-Honest Verifier ZK from AQO-Honest Verifier ZKPCP

In this section, we transform the AQO-honest verifier ZKPCP into an (interactive) AQO honest-verifier ZK proof using the entropic-secure batch OT protocol discussed in Sect. 4.

We consider an interactive ZK proof where the verifier queries each bit of the PCP via the OT protocol, where the verifier sets its input as 1 if it wants to query the proof bit and 0 otherwise. The prover on the other hand sets the sender's input as the proof bit corresponding to the receiver's 1 input and a random bit corresponding to the receiver's 0 input. It now follows that the honest-verifier zero-knowledge property follows directly from the security of the OT protocol against semi-honest receivers. Furthermore, if the underlying batch OT and the honest verifier ZKPCP are AQO then the resulting ZK will also be AQO.

Ideally, we would like to conclude the soundness of the ZK protocol from the soundness of the underlying ZKPCP. However, we instantiate the underlying batch OT protocol with one that is only entropically secure. Nevertheless, since the entropic loss in sender's privacy (played by the ZK verifier) against a malicious receiver (played by the ZK prover) in the underlying OT is information-theoretic, we can argue that the soundness loss can be bounded by the loss in entropy of the OT sender's input.

In more detail, the verifier first runs the underlying PCP verifier to obtain the set of queries. It next sets its input to the OT as $x \oplus r, r$ where x is a bit vector such that $x_i = 0$ if the PCP Verifier queries that location and 1 otherwise. The vector r is set uniformly at random. The sender, on the other hand, sets each element of its input vector a uniformly at random. The prover receives $a \cdot x \oplus r$ at the end of the OT executions. It then transmits $y = a \cdot x \oplus r \oplus b$ where b is the vector incorporating the symbols of the PCP proof. Finally, the verifier will be able to retrieve the ith proof bit by computing $y_i \oplus r_i$.

Zero-knowledge against an honest verifier follows directly from the computational privacy of the underlying OT protocol.

We argue soundness next. Specifically, given a (possibly unbounded) prover $\mathcal{P}^*$ for the HVZK, we construct a PCP prover $\mathcal{B}$ that internally incorporates $\mathcal{P}^*$, runs an honest interaction with $\mathcal{P}^*$, emulating the honest verifier with input x, extracts the PCP as $y \oplus a \cdot x \oplus r$ by extracting a and r (in exponential time) from the OT transcript and feeds that as the PCP oracle.

Let h be the min-entropy of the distribution of the honest PCP verifier queries. We make a simplification assumption that holds for most ZKPCPs in the literature including the one built in the previous section. Namely, we assume that there is a family of subsets Q of indices (of PCP locations) such that the verifier's query distribution is uniform over Q. In particular, this implies $h \geq \log(|Q|)$.[7]

Let the soundness in the real world where the prover and verifier interact using the protocol be ϵ. We now identify the success probability of $\mathcal{B}$ as a function of ϵ and bound it by the soundness of the ZKPCP to conclude the soundness of the HVZK. We consider an intermediate experiment which proceeds like the real world, where the honest verifier after the OT protocol resamples its random tape consistent with the transcript and the leakage (in possibly exponential time) and uses the new random tape to verify the proof. The soundness of this verifier must be identical to the soundness of the real verifier. By construction, in an execution of the intermediate experiment, the distribution of the verifier's queries is the conditional distribution of the honest PCP verifier query distribution conditioned on the partial transcript of the OT interaction. Let X' denote this distribution. By Theorem 3 and observing h is $\tilde{\Omega}(n)$, we can conclude that

$$H_\infty(X') \geq \left(1 - \frac{1}{\log^c(n)}\right) \cdot h$$

---

[7] For example, in the classic MPC-in-the-head based ZKPCP [IKOS07], the verifier queries a random t subset out of n. Here Q contains all t subsets of $[n]$.

We know that the soundness of the ZKPCP system is 2^{-s}. This implies that for any proof oracle generated by a prover, the number of queries in Q on which the verifier accepts a false proof, i.e. bad queries is at most $|Q|/2^s$. Furthemore, given an OT transcript, each of the $|Q|/2^s$ bad queries can have a probability mass of at most $1/2^{H_\infty(X')}$ in X' by the definition of min-entropy. Therefore, we have

$$\epsilon \leq \frac{|Q|}{2^s} \cdot \frac{1}{2^{H_\infty(X')}} = \frac{2^h}{2^s} \cdot \frac{1}{2^{(1-1/\log^c(n)) \cdot h}} = \frac{1}{2^{s-h/\log^c(n)}}$$

We have that $|Q|$ is $2^{\widetilde{O}(s)}$ as the length of the ZKPCP is $\widetilde{O}(s)$. Therefore by setting c appropriately we have that soundness is $2^{-\widetilde{\Omega}(s)}$.

Security Against Malicious Verifiers. The ZK protocol described above is insecure if the verifier acts dishonestly. In particular, it may query beyond the privacy threshold of the underlying ZKPCP and violate the zero-knowledge property. In order to enforce correct behaviour and restrict a dishonest verifier to a certain query pattern, we add another phase in which the verifier commits to its randomness used both for sampling the PCP queries and for generating the OT messages. As the verifier does not have any secret input, it can reveal (decommit) this randomness upon concluding the OT phase and the prover can check if the verifier sampled the queries and participated in the OT correctly. (In fact, to enforce correct sampling of the verifier's randomness, the parties run a coin-tossing in the well, where only the verifier learns the outcome of the coin-tossing. This protocol can be implemented using commitments schemes). Recall that the prover sends the masked proof at the end of the OT phase. The prover needs to check the verifier's randomness prior to sending this message as the verifier could cheat in the OT phase, learn the proof and abort before revealing its randomness. At the same time, if the prover sees the verifier's PCP queries before sending the masked proof it can cheat. We prevent this by requiring the prover to first commit to its masked proof at the end of the OT phase before the verifier reveals its randomness and the decommit to the proof after it checks the verifier's actions in the OT phase. Our complete protocol can be found in Fig. 2. We conclude with the following theorem whose proof is deferred to the full version.

Theorem 6. *Let $(\mathcal{P}_{\mathrm{PCP}}, \mathcal{V}_{\mathrm{PCP}})$ be an AQO honest verifier ZKPCP system (cf. Theorem 5), Com be an AQO commitment scheme, Com_h be an AQO statistically hiding commitment scheme and Π_{OT} be a entropic-secure AQO batch-OT scheme (cf. Sect. 4). Then the interactive proof from Fig. 2 is a ZK argument system with soundness error $2^{-\Omega(s)}$.*

Input: Public Boolean circuit C and statement $x \in \mathcal{L}_C$ for both, and a witness $w \in \mathcal{R}_C$ for the prover $\mathcal{P}$.

Building blocks: (1) AQO honest verifier ZKPCP system $(\mathcal{P}_{\text{PCP}}, \mathcal{V}_{\text{PCP}})$ (cf. Theorem 5). (2) AQO commitment scheme Com (3) AQO statistically hiding commitment scheme Com_h (4) AQO semi-honest batch OT Π_{OT}.

The protocol:
Coin-Tossing in the Well. The parties engage in a coin-tossing protocol where only the verifier learns the outcome of the coin-tossing R which it sets as its random tape for the OT Phase.

The OT Phase: Let $|\pi| = \tau$. Then the parties engage in τ instances of OT protocol Π_{OLE} where the prover plays the role of the receiver and the sender plays the role of the sender. The verifier runs $\mathcal{V}_{\text{PCP}}$ to obtain a set of query positions. The verifier chooses its input to the ith OT as $(x_i \oplus r_i, r_i)$ where x_i is set to 0 if the PCP verifier queries the ith location and 1 otherwise and r_i is chosen uniformly at random from $\{0, 1\}$. The prover on the other hand chooses its input to the ith OT instance a_i uniformly at random. Let the vector $\mathbf{w}$ denote the output of the prover in the τ OT instances.

Committing to the PCP: Prover $\mathcal{P}$ invokes the ZKPCP prover $\mathcal{P}_{\text{PCP}}$ on (x, w) and generates a PCP proof vector $\mathbf{b}$. The prover commits to $\mathbf{y} = \mathbf{w} \oplus \mathbf{b}$ using Com.

The Reveal Phase: The verifier decommits to R. If the verifier successfully decommits and R is consistent with an honest behavior of the verifier in the OT phase, then the prover decommits to $\mathbf{y}$.

Concluding the Output: For every index i the PCP verifier queries, the verifier identifies the proof bit as $y_i \oplus r_i$. The verifier then runs the PCP verifier on the responses and accepts iff the PCP verifier accepts.

Fig. 2. ZK argument system

Acknowledgements. We thank Henry Corrigan-Gibbs for helpful comments and Hemanta Maji for answering our questions on [BGMN18]. C. Hazay was supported by the BIU Center for Research in Applied Cryptography and Cyber Security in conjunction with the Israel National Cyber Bureau in the Prime Minister's Office, and by ISF grant No. 1316/18. Y. Ishai was supported in part by ERC Project NTSC (742754), BSF grant 2018393, and ISF grant 2774/20. L. de Castro and V. Vaikuntanathan were supported by grants from MIT-IBM Watson AI Labs and Analog Devices, by a Microsoft Trustworthy AI grant, and by DARPA under Agreement No. HR00112020023.

References

[AHI+17] Applebaum, B., Haramaty, N., Ishai, Y., Kushilevitz, E., Vaikuntanathan, V.: Low-complexity cryptographic hash functions. In: ITCS 2017, vol. 67, pp. 7:1–7:31 (2017)

[AHIV17] Ames, S., Hazay, C., Ishai, Y., Venkitasubramaniam, M.: Ligero: lightweight sublinear arguments without a trusted setup. In: CCS 2017, pp. 2087–2104. ACM (2017)

[AIK08] Applebaum, B., Ishai, Y., Kushilevitz, E.: On pseudorandom generators with linear stretch in NC0. Comput. Complex. **17**, 38–69 (2008)

[AIR01] Aiello, B., Ishai, Y., Reingold, O.: Priced oblivious transfer: how to sell digital goods. In: Pfitzmann, B. (ed.) EUROCRYPT 2001. LNCS, vol. 2045, pp. 119–135. Springer, Heidelberg (2001). https://doi.org/10.1007/3-540-44987-6_8

[AJL+12] Asharov, G., Jain, A., López-Alt, A., Tromer, E., Vaikuntanathan, V., Wichs, D.: Multiparty computation with low communication, computation and interaction via threshold FHE. In: Pointcheval, D., Johansson, T. (eds.) EUROCRYPT 2012. LNCS, vol. 7237, pp. 483–501. Springer, Heidelberg (2012). https://doi.org/10.1007/978-3-642-29011-4_29

[BBC+18] Baum, C., Bootle, J., Cerulli, A., del Pino, R., Groth, J., Lyubashevsky, V.: Sub-linear lattice-based zero-knowledge arguments for arithmetic circuits. In: Shacham, H., Boldyreva, A. (eds.) CRYPTO 2018. LNCS, vol. 10992, pp. 669–699. Springer, Cham (2018). https://doi.org/10.1007/978-3-319-96881-0_23

[BBHR19] Ben-Sasson, E., Bentov, I., Horesh, Y., Riabzev, M.: Scalable zero knowledge with no trusted setup. In: Boldyreva, A., Micciancio, D. (eds.) CRYPTO 2019. LNCS, vol. 11694, pp. 701–732. Springer, Cham (2019). https://doi.org/10.1007/978-3-030-26954-8_23

[BCG+17] Bootle, J., Cerulli, A., Ghadafi, E., Groth, J., Hajiabadi, M., Jakobsen, S.K.: Linear-time zero-knowledge proofs for arithmetic circuit satisfiability. In: Takagi, T., Peyrin, T. (eds.) ASIACRYPT 2017. LNCS, vol. 10626, pp. 336–365. Springer, Cham (2017). https://doi.org/10.1007/978-3-319-70700-6_12

[BCG+20] Boyle, E., Couteau, G., Gilboa, N., Ishai, Y., Kohl, L., Scholl, P.: Efficient pseudorandom correlation generators from ring-LPN. In: Micciancio, D., Ristenpart, T. (eds.) CRYPTO 2020. LNCS, vol. 12171, pp. 387–416. Springer, Cham (2020). https://doi.org/10.1007/978-3-030-56880-1_14

[BCGT13] Ben-Sasson, E., Chiesa, A., Genkin, D., Tromer, E.: On the concrete efficiency of probabilistically-checkable proofs. In: STOC 2013 (2013)

[BCI+13] Bitansky, N., Chiesa, A., Ishai, Y., Ostrovsky, R., Paneth, O.: Succinct non-interactive arguments via linear interactive proofs. In: Sahai, A. (ed.) TCC 2013. LNCS, vol. 7785, pp. 315–333. Springer, Heidelberg (2013). https://doi.org/10.1007/978-3-642-36594-2_18

[BCR+19] Ben-Sasson, E., Chiesa, A., Riabzev, M., Spooner, N., Virza, M., Ward, N.P.: Aurora: transparent succinct arguments for R1CS. In: Ishai, Y., Rijmen, V. (eds.) EUROCRYPT 2019. LNCS, vol. 11476, pp. 103–128. Springer, Cham (2019). https://doi.org/10.1007/978-3-030-17653-2_4

[BCS16] Ben-Sasson, E., Chiesa, A., Spooner, N.: Interactive oracle proofs. In: Hirt, M., Smith, A. (eds.) TCC 2016. LNCS, vol. 9986, pp. 31–60. Springer, Heidelberg (2016). https://doi.org/10.1007/978-3-662-53644-5_2

[BD18] Brakerski, Z., Döttling, N.: Two-message statistically sender-private OT from LWE. In: Beimel, A., Dziembowski, S. (eds.) TCC 2018. LNCS, vol. 11240, pp. 370–390. Springer, Cham (2018). https://doi.org/10.1007/978-3-030-03810-6_14

[BDGM19] Brakerski, Z., Döttling, N., Garg, S., Malavolta, G.: Leveraging linear decryption: rate-1 fully-homomorphic encryption and time-lock puzzles. In: Hofheinz, D., Rosen, A. (eds.) TCC 2019, Part II. LNCS, vol. 11892, pp. 407–437. Springer, Cham (2019). https://doi.org/10.1007/978-3-030-36033-7_16

[BDOZ11] Bendlin, R., Damgård, I., Orlandi, C., Zakarias, S.: Semi-homomorphic encryption and multiparty computation. In: Paterson, K.G. (ed.) EURO-CRYPT 2011. LNCS, vol. 6632, pp. 169–188. Springer, Heidelberg (2011). https://doi.org/10.1007/978-3-642-20465-4_11

[BEP+20] Baum, C., Escudero, D., Pedrouzo-Ulloa, A., Scholl, P., Troncoso-Pastoriza, J.R.: Efficient protocols for oblivious linear function evaluation from ring-LWE. In: Galdi, C., Kolesnikov, V. (eds.) SCN 2020. LNCS, vol. 12238, pp. 130–149. Springer, Cham (2020). https://doi.org/10.1007/978-3-030-57990-6_7

[BGI+17] Badrinarayanan, S., Garg, S., Ishai, Y., Sahai, A., Wadia, A.: Two-message witness indistinguishability and secure computation in the plain model from new assumptions. In: Takagi, T., Peyrin, T. (eds.) ASI-ACRYPT 2017, Part III. LNCS, vol. 10626, pp. 275–303. Springer, Cham (2017). https://doi.org/10.1007/978-3-319-70700-6_10

[BGMN18] Block, A.R., Gupta, D., Maji, H.K., Nguyen, H.H.: Secure computation using leaky correlations (asymptotically optimal constructions). In: Beimel, A., Dziembowski, S. (eds.) TCC 2018. LNCS, vol. 11240, pp. 36–65. Springer, Cham (2018). https://doi.org/10.1007/978-3-030-03810-6_2

[BGV12] Brakerski, Z., Gentry, C., Vaikuntanathan, V.: (leveled) fully homomorphic encryption without bootstrapping. In: ITCS (2012)

[BIO14] Baron, J., Ishai, Y., Ostrovsky, R.: On linear-size pseudorandom generators and hardcore functions. Theor. Comput. Sci. **554**, 50–63 (2014)

[BIP+18] Boneh, D., Ishai, Y., Passelègue, A., Sahai, A., Wu, D.J.: Exploring crypto dark matter: new simple PRF candidates and their applications. In: Beimel, A., Dziembowski, S. (eds.) TCC 2018. LNCS, vol. 11240, pp. 699–729. Springer, Cham (2018). https://doi.org/10.1007/978-3-030-03810-6_25

[BISW18] Boneh, D., Ishai, Y., Sahai, A., Wu, D.J.: Quasi-optimal SNARGs via linear multi-prover interactive proofs. In: Nielsen, J.B., Rijmen, V. (eds.) EUROCRYPT 2018. LNCS, vol. 10822, pp. 222–255. Springer, Cham (2018). https://doi.org/10.1007/978-3-319-78372-7_8

[BKLP15] Benhamouda, F., Krenn, S., Lyubashevsky, V., Pietrzak, K.: Efficient zero-knowledge proofs for commitments from learning with errors over rings. In: Pernul, G., Ryan, P.Y.A., Weippl, E. (eds.) ESORICS 2015. LNCS, vol. 9326, pp. 305–325. Springer, Cham (2015). https://doi.org/10.1007/978-3-319-24174-6_16

[BLNS20] Bootle, J., Lyubashevsky, V., Nguyen, N.K., Seiler, G.: A Non-PCP approach to succinct quantum-safe zero-knowledge. In: Micciancio, D., Ristenpart, T. (eds.) CRYPTO 2020. LNCS, vol. 12171, pp. 441–469. Springer, Cham (2020). https://doi.org/10.1007/978-3-030-56880-1_16

[BLS19] Bootle, J., Lyubashevsky, V., Seiler, G.: Algebraic techniques for short(er) exact lattice-based zero-knowledge proofs. In: Boldyreva, A., Micciancio, D. (eds.) CRYPTO 2019. LNCS, vol. 11692, pp. 176–202. Springer, Cham (2019). https://doi.org/10.1007/978-3-030-26948-7_7

[BMN18a] Block, A.R., Maji, H.K., Nguyen, H.H.: Secure computation with constant communication overhead using multiplication embeddings. In: Chakraborty, D., Iwata, T. (eds.) INDOCRYPT 2018. LNCS, vol. 11356, pp. 375–398. Springer, Cham (2018). https://doi.org/10.1007/978-3-030-05378-9_20

[BPMW16] Bourse, F., Del Pino, R., Minelli, M., Wee, H.: FHE circuit privacy almost for free. In: Robshaw, M., Katz, J. (eds.) CRYPTO 2016. LNCS, vol. 9815, pp. 62–89. Springer, Heidelberg (2016). https://doi.org/10.1007/978-3-662-53008-5_3

[BS08] Ben-Sasson, E., Sudan, M.: Short PCPS with polylog query complexity. SIAM J. Comput. **38**(2), 551–607 (2008)

[BV11a] Brakerski, Z., Vaikuntanathan, V.: Efficient fully homomorphic encryption from (standard) LWE. In: FOCS (2011)

[BV11b] Brakerski, Z., Vaikuntanathan, V.: Fully homomorphic encryption from ring-LWE and security for key dependent messages. In: Rogaway, P. (ed.) CRYPTO 2011. LNCS, vol. 6841, pp. 505–524. Springer, Heidelberg (2011). https://doi.org/10.1007/978-3-642-22792-9_29

[CCXY18] Cascudo, I., Cramer, R., Xing, C., Yuan, C.: Amortized complexity of information-theoretically secure MPC revisited. In: Shacham, H., Boldyreva, A. (eds.) CRYPTO 2018. LNCS, vol. 10993, pp. 395–426. Springer, Cham (2018). https://doi.org/10.1007/978-3-319-96878-0_14

[CDI+] Chase, M., et al.: Reusable non-interactive secure computation. In: Boldyreva, A., Micciancio, D. (eds.) CRYPTO 2019. LNCS, vol. 11694, pp. 462–488. Springer, Cham (2019). https://doi.org/10.1007/978-3-030-26954-8_15

[CY21] Chiesa, A., Yogev, E.: Subquadratic SNARGs in the random oracle model. In: Malkin, T., Peikert, C. (eds.) CRYPTO 2021, Part I. LNCS, vol. 12825, pp. 711–741. Springer, Cham (2021). https://doi.org/10.1007/978-3-030-84242-0_25

[dCJV21] de Castro, L., Juvekar, C., Vaikuntanathan, V.: Fast vector oblivious linear evaluation from ring learning with errors. In: WAHC (2021)

[DFK+92] Dwork, C., Feige, U., Kilian, J., Naor, M., Safra, M.: Low communication 2-prover zero-knowledge proofs for NP. In: Brickell, E.F. (ed.) CRYPTO 1992. LNCS, vol. 740, pp. 215–227. Springer, Heidelberg (1993). https://doi.org/10.1007/3-540-48071-4_15

[DGI+19] Döttling, N., Garg, S., Ishai, Y., Malavolta, G., Mour, T., Ostrovsky, R.: Trapdoor hash functions and their applications. In: Boldyreva, A., Micciancio, D. (eds.) CRYPTO 2019. LNCS, vol. 11694, pp. 3–32. Springer, Cham (2019). https://doi.org/10.1007/978-3-030-26954-8_1

[DIK10] Damgård, I., Ishai, Y., Krøigaard, M.: Perfectly secure multiparty computation and the computational overhead of cryptography. In: Gilbert, H. (ed.) EUROCRYPT 2010. LNCS, vol. 6110, pp. 445–465. Springer, Heidelberg (2010). https://doi.org/10.1007/978-3-642-13190-5_23

[DORS08] Dodis, Y., Ostrovsky, R., Reyzin, L., Smith, A.D.: Fuzzy extractors: how to generate strong keys from biometrics and other noisy data. SIAM J. Comput. **38**(1), 97–139 (2008)

[DR02] Daemen, J., Rijmen, V.: The Design of Rijndael: AES - The Advanced Encryption Standard. Springer, Heidelberg (2002). https://doi.org/10.1007/978-3-662-04722-4

[DS16]   Ducas, L., Stehlé, D.: Sanitization of FHE ciphertexts. In: Fischlin, M., Coron, J.-S. (eds.) EUROCRYPT 2016. LNCS, vol. 9665, pp. 294–310. Springer, Heidelberg (2016). https://doi.org/10.1007/978-3-662-49890-3_12

[Gam85]   El Gamal, T.: A public key cryptosystem and a signature scheme based on discrete logarithms. IEEE Trans. Inf. Theory **31**(4), 469–472 (1985)

[Gen09]   Gentry, C.: Fully homomorphic encryption using ideal lattices. In: Mitzenmacher, M. (ed.) STOC 2009, pp. 169–178. ACM (2009)

[GGPR13]   Gennaro, R., Gentry, C., Parno, B., Raykova, M.: Quadratic span programs and succinct NIZKs without PCPs. In: Johansson, T., Nguyen, P.Q. (eds.) EUROCRYPT 2013. LNCS, vol. 7881, pp. 626–645. Springer, Heidelberg (2013). https://doi.org/10.1007/978-3-642-38348-9_37

[GH19]   Gentry, C., Halevi, S.: Compressible FHE with applications to PIR. In: Hofheinz, D., Rosen, A. (eds.) TCC 2019. LNCS, vol. 11892, pp. 438–464. Springer, Cham (2019). https://doi.org/10.1007/978-3-030-36033-7_17

[GHKW17]   Goyal, R., Hohenberger, S., Koppula, V., Waters, B.: A generic approach to constructing and proving verifiable random functions. In: Kalai, Y., Reyzin, L. (eds.) TCC 2017. LNCS, vol. 10678, pp. 537–566. Springer, Cham (2017). https://doi.org/10.1007/978-3-319-70503-3_18

[GHS12]   Gentry, C., Halevi, S., Smart, N.P.: Fully homomorphic encryption with polylog overhead. In: Pointcheval, D., Johansson, T. (eds.) EUROCRYPT 2012. LNCS, vol. 7237, pp. 465–482. Springer, Heidelberg (2012). https://doi.org/10.1007/978-3-642-29011-4_28

[GHV10]   Gentry, C., Halevi, S., Vaikuntanathan, V.: i-hop homomorphic encryption and rerandomizable Yao circuits. In: Rabin, T. (ed.) CRYPTO 2010. LNCS, vol. 6223, pp. 155–172. Springer, Heidelberg (2010). https://doi.org/10.1007/978-3-642-14623-7_9

[GIP+14]   Genkin, D., Ishai, Y., Prabhakaran, M., Sahai, A., Tromer, E.: Circuits resilient to additive attacks with applications to secure computation. In: STOC (2014)

[GKPV10]   Goldwasser, S., Kalai, Y.T., Peikert, C., Vaikuntanathan, V.: Robustness of the learning with errors assumption. In: ICS (2010)

[GMW87]   Goldreich, O., Micali, S., Wigderson, A.: How to play any mental game or a completeness theorem for protocols with honest majority. In: STOC (1987)

[Gol00]   Goldreich, O.: Candidate one-way functions based on expander graphs. Electron. Colloquium Comput. Complex. (90) (2000)

[Gol04]   Goldreich, O.: Foundations of Cryptography, vol. 2. Cambridge University Press, Cambridge (2004)

[Gro10]   Groth, J.: Short pairing-based non-interactive zero-knowledge arguments. In: Abe, M. (ed.) ASIACRYPT 2010. LNCS, vol. 6477, pp. 321–340. Springer, Heidelberg (2010). https://doi.org/10.1007/978-3-642-17373-8_19

[HIMV19]   Hazay, C., Ishai, Y., Marcedone, A., Venkitasubramaniam, M.: Leviosa: lightweight secure arithmetic computation. In: CCS 2019, pp. 327–344. ACM (2019)

[HKE13]   Huang, Y., Katz, J., Evans, D.: Efficient secure two-party computation using symmetric cut-and-choose. In: Canetti, R., Garay, J.A. (eds.) CRYPTO 2013. LNCS, vol. 8043, pp. 18–35. Springer, Heidelberg (2013). https://doi.org/10.1007/978-3-642-40084-1_2

[HKL+12] Heyse, S., Kiltz, E., Lyubashevsky, V., Paar, C., Pietrzak, K.: Lapin: an efficient authentication protocol based on ring-LPN. In: Canteaut, A. (ed.) FSE 2012. LNCS, vol. 7549, pp. 346–365. Springer, Heidelberg (2012). https://doi.org/10.1007/978-3-642-34047-5_20

[IKO07] Ishai, Y., Kushilevitz, E., Ostrovsky, R.: Efficient arguments without short PCPs. In: CCC 2007, pp. 278–291 (2007)

[IKO+11] Ishai, Y., Kushilevitz, E., Ostrovsky, R., Prabhakaran, M., Sahai, A., Wullschleger, J.: Constant-rate oblivious transfer from noisy channels. In: Rogaway, P. (ed.) CRYPTO 2011. LNCS, vol. 6841, pp. 667–684. Springer, Heidelberg (2011). https://doi.org/10.1007/978-3-642-22792-9_38

[IKOS07] Ishai, Y., Kushilevitz, E., Ostrovsky, R., Sahai, A.: Zero-knowledge from secure multiparty computation. In: STOC (2007)

[IKOS08] Ishai, Y., Kushilevitz, E., Ostrovsky, R., Sahai, A.: Cryptography with constant computational overhead. In: STOC (2008)

[IKOS09a] Ishai, Y., Kushilevitz, E., Ostrovsky, R., Sahai, A.: Extracting correlations. In: FOCS (2009)

[IKOS09b] Ishai, Y., Kushilevitz, E., Ostrovsky, R., Sahai, A.: Zero-knowledge proofs from secure multiparty computation. SIAM J. Comput. **39**(3), 1121–1152 (2009)

[IPS08] Ishai, Y., Prabhakaran, M., Sahai, A.: Founding cryptography on oblivious transfer – efficiently. In: Wagner, D. (ed.) CRYPTO 2008. LNCS, vol. 5157, pp. 572–591. Springer, Heidelberg (2008). https://doi.org/10.1007/978-3-540-85174-5_32

[IW14] Ishai, Y., Weiss, M.: Probabilistically checkable proofs of proximity with zero-knowledge. In: Lindell, Y. (ed.) TCC 2014. LNCS, vol. 8349, pp. 121–145. Springer, Heidelberg (2014). https://doi.org/10.1007/978-3-642-54242-8_6

[Kil92] Kilian, J.: A note on efficient zero-knowledge proofs and arguments (extended abstract). In: STOC 1992, pp. 723–732 (1992)

[Lin16] Lindell, Y.: Fast cut-and-choose-based protocols for malicious and covert adversaries. J. Cryptol. **29**(2), 456–490 (2016)

[LM06] Lyubashevsky, V., Micciancio, D.: Generalized compact knapsacks are collision resistant. In: Bugliesi, M., Preneel, B., Sassone, V., Wegener, I. (eds.) ICALP 2006. LNCS, vol. 4052, pp. 144–155. Springer, Heidelberg (2006). https://doi.org/10.1007/11787006_13

[LPR10] Lyubashevsky, V., Peikert, C., Regev, O.: On ideal lattices and learning with errors over rings. In: Gilbert, H. (ed.) EUROCRYPT 2010. LNCS, vol. 6110, pp. 1–23. Springer, Heidelberg (2010). https://doi.org/10.1007/978-3-642-13190-5_1

[LPR13] Lyubashevsky, V., Peikert, C., Regev, O.: A toolkit for ring-LWE cryptography. In: Johansson, T., Nguyen, P.Q. (eds.) EUROCRYPT 2013. LNCS, vol. 7881, pp. 35–54. Springer, Heidelberg (2013). https://doi.org/10.1007/978-3-642-38348-9_3

[LPS08] Lindell, Y., Pinkas, B., Smart, N.P.: Implementing two-party computation efficiently with security against malicious adversaries. In: Ostrovsky, R., De Prisco, R., Visconti, I. (eds.) SCN 2008. LNCS, vol. 5229, pp. 2–20. Springer, Heidelberg (2008). https://doi.org/10.1007/978-3-540-85855-3_2

[LS19] Lombardi, A., Schaeffer, L.: A note on key agreement and non-interactive commitments. Cryptology ePrint Archive, Report 2019/279 (2019)

[LS18] Lyubashevsky, V., Seiler, G.: Short, invertible elements in partially splitting cyclotomic rings and applications to lattice-based zero-knowledge proofs. In: Nielsen, J.B., Rijmen, V. (eds.) EUROCRYPT 2018. LNCS, vol. 10820, pp. 204–224. Springer, Cham (2018). https://doi.org/10.1007/978-3-319-78381-9_8

[Mic02] Micciancio, D.: Generalized compact knapsacks, cyclic lattices, and efficient one-way functions from worst-case complexity assumptions. In: FOCS (2002)

[Moo16] Moody, D.: Post-quantum crypto: NIST plans for the future (2016)

[MR04] Micciancio, D., Regev, O.: Worst-case to average-case reductions based on gaussian measures. In: FOCS 2004, pp. 372–381. IEEE Computer Society (2004)

[MS20] Micciancio, D., Sorrell, J.: Simpler statistically sender private oblivious transfer from ideals of cyclotomic integers. In: Moriai, S., Wang, H. (eds.) ASIACRYPT 2020, Part II. LNCS, vol. 12492, pp. 381–407. Springer, Cham (2020). https://doi.org/10.1007/978-3-030-64834-3_13

[MV15] Miles, E., Viola, E.: Substitution-permutation networks, pseudorandom functions, and natural proofs. J. ACM **62**(6), 46:1-46:29 (2015)

[NP01] Naor, M., Pinkas, B.: Efficient oblivious transfer protocols. In: Rao Kosaraju, S. (ed.) SODA, pp. 448–457 (2001)

[PR06] Peikert, C., Rosen, A.: Efficient collision-resistant hashing from worst-case assumptions on cyclic lattices. In: Halevi, S., Rabin, T. (eds.) TCC 2006. LNCS, vol. 3876, pp. 145–166. Springer, Heidelberg (2006). https://doi.org/10.1007/11681878_8

[PVW08] Peikert, C., Vaikuntanathan, V., Waters, B.: A framework for efficient and composable oblivious transfer. In: Wagner, D. (ed.) CRYPTO 2008. LNCS, vol. 5157, pp. 554–571. Springer, Heidelberg (2008). https://doi.org/10.1007/978-3-540-85174-5_31

[PY91] Papadimitriou, C.H., Yannakakis, M.: Optimization, approximation, and complexity classes. JCSS **43**(3), 425–440 (1991)

[Reg05] Regev, O.: On lattices, learning with errors, random linear codes, and cryptography. In: STOC (2005)

[RR21] Ron-Zewi, N., Rothblum, R.: Proving as fast as computing: Succinct arguments with constant prover overhead. In: ECCC, p. 180 (2021)

[WRK17] Wang, X., Ranellucci, S., Katz, J.: Global-scale secure multiparty computation. In: ACM CCS (2017)

[WW06] Wolf, S., Wullschleger, J.: Oblivious transfer is symmetric. In: Vaudenay, S. (ed.) EUROCRYPT 2006. LNCS, vol. 4004, pp. 222–232. Springer, Heidelberg (2006). https://doi.org/10.1007/11761679_14

[XZZ+19] Xie, T., Zhang, J., Zhang, Y., Papamanthou, C., Song, D.: Libra: succinct zero-knowledge proofs with optimal prover computation. In: Boldyreva, A., Micciancio, D. (eds.) CRYPTO 2019, Part III. LNCS, vol. 11694, pp. 733–764. Springer, Cham (2019). https://doi.org/10.1007/978-3-030-26954-8_24

[ZXZS20] Zhang, J., Xie, T., Zhang, Y., Song, D.: Transparent polynomial delegation and its applications to zero knowledge proof. In: 2020 IEEE Symposium on Security and Privacy (2020)

Round-Optimal Multi-party Computation with Identifiable Abort

Michele Ciampi[1] , Divya Ravi[2] , Luisa Siniscalchi[2,3(✉)] ,
and Hendrik Waldner[1]

[1] The University of Edinburgh, Edinburgh, UK
{michele.ciampi,hendrik.waldner}@ed.ac.uk
[2] Aarhus University, Aarhus, Denmark
{divya,lsiniscalchi}@cs.au.dk
[3] Concordium Blockchain Research Center, Aarhus, Denmark

Abstract. Secure multi-party computation (MPC) protocols that are resilient to a dishonest majority allow the adversary to get the output of the computation while, at the same time, forcing the honest parties to abort. Aumann and Lindell introduced the enhanced notion of *security with identifiable abort*, which still allows the adversary to trigger an abort but, at the same time, it enables the honest parties to agree on the identity of the party that led to the abort. More recently, in Eurocrypt 2016, Garg et al. showed that, assuming access to a simultaneous message exchange channel for all the parties, at least four rounds of communication are required to securely realize non-trivial functionalities in the plain model.

Following Garg et al., a sequence of works has matched this lower bound, but none of them achieved security with identifiable abort. In this work, we close this gap and show that four rounds of communication are also sufficient to securely realize any functionality with identifiable abort using standard and generic polynomial-time assumptions. To achieve this result we introduce the new notion of *bounded-rewind secure MPC* that guarantees security even against an adversary that performs a mild form of reset attacks. We show how to instantiate this primitive starting from *any* MPC protocol and by assuming trapdoor-permutations.

The notion of bounded-rewind secure MPC allows for easier parallel composition of MPC protocols with other (interactive) cryptographic primitives. Therefore, we believe that this primitive can be useful in other contexts in which it is crucial to combine multiple primitives with MPC protocols while keeping the round complexity of the final protocol low.

1 Introduction

Secure multi-party computation (MPC) [25,46] allows a group of mutually distrustful parties to jointly evaluate any function over their private inputs in such

---

D. Ravi—Funded by the European Research Council (ERC) under the European Unions's Horizon 2020 research and innovation programme under grant agreement No. 803096 (SPEC).

O. Dunkelman and S. Dziembowski (Eds.): EUROCRYPT 2022, LNCS 13275, pp. 335–364, 2022.
https://doi.org/10.1007/978-3-031-06944-4_12

a way that no one learns anything beyond the output of the function. Since its introduction, MPC has been extensively studied in terms of assumptions, complexity, security definitions, and execution models [2,6,7,11,12,22,25,26,33–35,37,39,41,45].

One interesting line of research concerns proving the security of MPC protocols in the case of a dishonest majority. In this model, unfortunately, it is in general impossible to obtain *guaranteed output delivery* or even *fairness* [13], which are particularly useful properties. The former guarantees that the honest parties always receive the output of the computation and the latter guarantees that either all the parties receive the output or none does (not even the corrupted parties). Due to the impossibility of Cleve et al. [13], most of the MPC protocols proven secure in the dishonest majority setting only satisfy the notion of *unanimous abort*. This notion guarantees that either all the honest parties receive the output, or none of them does. Another recent line of works has established that *four rounds* are both necessary [22] and sufficient [2,4,7,10,29] for MPC with unanimous abort (with respect to black-box simulation) while relying on broadcast.[1] However, none of these works study the notion of *MPC with identifiable abort*.

The notion of MPC with identifiable abort, which was first considered by Aumann and Lindell [3], ensures that either the honest parties receive the output of the computation or they unanimously identify the (corrupted) party that led to the abort. Subsequently, Ishai, Ostrovsky, and Zikas [32] showed how to achieve this notion in the information theoretic and computational setting, and propose a construction (in the computational setting) that does not rely on any setup assumptions. The work of Ishai et al. led to a sequence of works that proposed improved protocols realizing security with identifiable abort [5,8,9,16,43]. All of these works either require a trusted setup (e.g., correlated randomness) or require more than a constant number of rounds.

Moreover, the new recent lower bounds on MPC with unanimous abort and the new results on MPC with identifiable abort leave open the following question:

> *What is the best-possible round complexity for securely evaluating any function with identifiable abort (with black-box simulation) in the plain model when the majority of the parties are corrupted and broadcast channels are assumed?*

In this work, we answer the above question[2] and match the lower bound proven in [22] by presenting a four-round protocol with identifiable abort relying only on standard polynomial-time cryptographic assumptions (i.e., one-way

---

[1] In each round all the parties can send a message. That is, the channel allows for a simultaneous exchange of messages in each round. Unless otherwise specified we implicitly refer to this model of communication when referring to broadcast.

[2] All our results are with respect to black-box simulation. Hereafter we assume that this is implicitly stated in our claims.

trapdoor permutations).[3] To the best of our knowledge, prior to our work, no protocol achieved security with identifiable abort in the plain model in four rounds of communication.

To achieve this result, we define and construct a four-round *bounded-rewind secure MPC* protocol as an intermediate step. A bounded-rewind secure MPC protocol enjoys the same security as a standard MPC protocol (with unanimous abort), and is additionally resilient to *rewind attacks*. More precisely, the protocol remains secure even if the adversary is allowed to receive a (bounded) number of third rounds in response to multiple (adversarially chosen) second-round messages. The reason why we define (and construct a protocol that satisfies) this new security notion is to obtain an MPC protocol that can be easily composed in parallel with other interactive cryptographic primitives. We see this as a result of independent interest and we believe that this notion is also useful in other contexts where MPC protocols need to be combined with other interactive primitives (e.g., key distribution protocols, proof-of-knowledge or even other MPC protocols). This notion becomes instrumental in our construction, since we will execute an MPC protocol and a zero-knowledge-like protocol in parallel. We give more details on the notion and the constructions later in this section.

1.1 Our Results

As previously mentioned, the stepping stone of our construction is a four-round bounded-rewind secure MPC protocol. We realize this notion using a compiler that turns, in a round-preserving manner, *any* four-round MPC protocol into a bounded-rewind secure MPC protocol. Our compiler relies on a bounded-rewind secure oblivious transfer (OT) protocol (similar to the one proposed by Choudhuri et al. [10]), on Yao's Garbled Circuits (GC) and public-key encryption. Unfortunately, we cannot directly use the OT protocol of Choudhuri et al. [10], since we need the OT to be simulation-based secure against malicious receivers.[4] Hence, we also need to prove that such a bounded-rewind secure OT protocol is indeed simulatable. The bounded-rewind secure OT protocol and the public-key encryption scheme can be instantiated from trapdoor permutations (TDPs), and GCs can be based on one-way functions. Given the above, we can claim the following:

Theorem 1 (informal). *Assuming TDPs and the existence of a 4-round MPC protocol that realizes the function f with unanimous abort over broadcast channels against a dishonest majority, then there exists a bounded-rewind secure 4-round MPC protocol that realizes the same function (relying on the same communication channel) with unanimous abort against a dishonest majority.*

---

[3] Some of the tools used in our constructions require the trapdoor permutations to be certifiable. Any time that we refer to trapdoor permutations we implicitly assume that such trapdoor permutations can be instantiated using RSA with suitable parameters [21].

[4] We require an additional property on the OT, which we elaborate further in the next section.

To finally obtain our round-optimal MPC protocol that is secure with identifiable abort, we compose the bounded-rewind secure MPC protocol, in parallel, with a combination of two-round witness-indistinguishable proofs, signature schemes and three-round non-malleable commitment schemes. We provide more detail regarding this in the next section. To obtain our final construction we require the bounded-rewind secure MPC protocol to be perfectly correct. Finally, observing that all the additional tools we need can be based on TDPs, we can claim the following.

Theorem 2 (informal). *Assuming TDPs and the existence of a perfectly correct 4-round bounded-rewind secure MPC protocol that realizes the function f with* unanimous abort *over broadcast channels against a dishonest majority, then there exists a 4-round MPC protocol that realizes the same function (relying on the same communication channel) with* identifiable abort *against a dishonest majority.*

To state our main theorem, we argue that the four-round MPC protocol proposed in [10] is perfectly correct and that the final bounded-rewind MPC protocol we obtain from Theorem 1 preserves the perfect correctness of the input protocol. Given that the protocol of Choudhuri et al. [10] is based on OT, which in turn can be based on TDPs, we can state the following.

Corollary (informal). *Assuming TDPs then there exists a 4-round MPC protocol that realizes any function f with* identifiable abort *over broadcast channels against a dishonest majority.*

1.2   Technical Overview

The Challenge of Obtaining MPC with Identifiable Abort. Among many other interesting results, in [32] the authors propose a protocol that realizes any function with identifiable abort in the plain model. In more detail, Ishai et al. propose a generic approach to turn any MPC protocol with identifiable abort, that relies on correlated randomness as a setup assumption, into a secure MPC protocol with identifiable abort in the plain model. Their compiler is quite straightforward: the parties use an MPC protocol Π^{CR} to generate correlated randomness, which is then used to run the previously mentioned protocol of [32], which we denote as Π^{IOZ}. In the case that some parties abort during the execution of Π^{IOZ} the property of identifiable abort is trivially maintained since Π^{IOZ} is proven secure under the assumption that correlated randomness exists which, in turn, has been generated using by the protocol Π^{CR}. On the other hand, if an abort occurs during the execution of Π^{CR} then all the parties could simply disclose the randomness used to run Π^{CR} and check which party did not follow the protocol description. Note that the randomness of the parties can be disclosed at this stage of the protocol since Π^{CR} does not require the parties' input to be executed and therefore privacy is still guaranteed. However, such an approach crucially needs the protocol Π^{CR} to be secure against *adaptive* corruptions.[5] Indeed, without this property it is not clear how to prove the security of the protocol. This is due to the fact that, during the simulation of Π^{CR}, it might be necessary to output the random coins used by the honest parties, which are controlled by the simulator. Revealing the random coins of the simulator might make the simulated execution trivially distinguishable from the real one. Unfortunately, it is not clear how to use such an approach to obtain a constant round protocol since it has been shown in [23] that it is impossible to achieve security with adaptive corruptions in a constant number of rounds in the plain model.

Another approach that one could follow is to start from a protocol Π that is proven secure in the plain model and attach a public coin zero-knowledge (ZK) proof to each round of Π. That is, each party computes one message of Π and then runs a ZK proof to show that the computed message has been generated accordingly to Π. We first note that such an approach does not immediately work if Π is not perfectly correct. Indeed, if Π is not perfectly correct then there might exist randomness that, if used to compute a message of Π, would make the receiver of this message abort. However, the adversary would be able to complete the proof since it has followed the protocol. Instead of using a perfectly correct protocol Π one could add a coin-tossing protocol, but this would create additional issues since the coin-tossing protocol needs to be secure with identifiable abort.

Another issue with the above approach is that, even in the case where Π is perfectly correct, we cannot just use a standard public-coin ZK proof, given that the adversary might maul the ZK proof received from an honest party. To account for this, using a public-coin non-malleable ZK in combination with a perfectly correct Π seems to be a reasonable direction. But, also in this case, if we want a constant round protocol we need to require the public-coin ZK to be executable in a constant number of rounds and, as shown in [24], only trivial languages admit constant round public-coin black-box ZK protocols (with negligible soundness error). Therefore, if we want to use such an approach, we need to relax the public-coin requirement, and, indeed, *public verifiability* suffices. We say that a ZK protocol is publicly verifiable if, by looking at the messages of the protocol exchanged between a prover and a verifier, it is possible to infer whether the honest verifier would accept the proof without knowing its random coins. Moreover, it must be possible to detect whether the verifier is sending valid messages (i.e., messages that would not make the honest prover abort) without knowing the randomness of the prover and by just looking at the transcript. This property is particularly important for our purposes since it allows a party P, that is not involved in the execution of the non-malleable ZK protocol between two parties (in which one is acting as a prover and the other as the verifier), to detect which party caused the abort (if any). If the prover is malicious and the verifier rejects, then P notices this and it can tag the party acting as the prover as being corrupted. If instead the verifier sends a message that the prover would reject then, also due to the public verifiability, P can tag the party acting as the verifier as corrupted.

---

[5] In this model, the identities of the corrupted parties are not fixed at the beginning of the experiment and the adversary can decide which party to corrupt during the execution of the protocol.

Assuming that there are constant round ZK protocols with all these properties (hereafter we refer to them as *special ZK* protocols) and that Π is a perfectly correct constant round protocol, we can finally construct an MPC protocol with identifiable abort (in a constant number of rounds) in the plain model.

However, in this work, we want to study the optimal round complexity for MPC with identifiable abort. In particular, we want to prove that four rounds are sufficient to securely realize any function with identifiable abort. We start by observing that it is not needed to run a ZK proof after each round of the protocol. Indeed, we could just let the parties run the protocol Π and only at the end, in the case a party aborts, each party generates its zero-knowledge proof (proving that all the messages of Π that it has sent over the broadcast channel have been computed correctly). If the ZK protocol is four-round (which is the best we can hope for) and Π needs four rounds as well (which, again, is the best we can hope for) then we have obtained an 8-round MPC protocol with identifiable abort.

The next natural step, to reduce the round complexity of the above protocol, is to parallelize the messages of Π and the messages of the special ZK protocol. This natural approach fails for two reasons. First, the special ZK protocol now needs to be delayed-input. That is, the statement the parties prove in the case someone aborts is not defined until the fourth round and, second, there is no reason to expect that Π and a zero-knowledge protocol would compose in parallel. Even if there are four-round special ZK protocols that enjoy the property of delayed-input, like the one in [11], at the same time it is unclear how to prove that this protocol composes with Π due to well-known *rewinding issues*. Indeed, one approach to prove the security of this candidate MPC protocol would be to consider a first hybrid experiment in which we run the simulator of the special ZK proof. This step is a straightforward reduction and does not seem to cause issues. Note that, in this intermediate hybrid experiment, the simulator of the ZK protocol is rewinding the adversary and, in particular, we can assume that the simulator rewinds (at least) from the third to the second round. We now proceed to the next hybrid where we run the simulator of Π. Proving the indistinguishability between the two hybrid experiments is problematic. The reason is that the rewinds made by the ZK simulator could make the adversary ask for multiple second rounds with respect to Π. However, the reduction can only receive one set of second round messages from the challenger and it is unclear whether the reduction can fake these messages of Π during the rewinds.

In this work, we solve this issue by constructing an MPC protocol (with unanimous abort) that is *bounded-rewind secure*. That is, such an MPC protocol remains secure even if an adversary asks to receive multiple third-round messages as a reply to multiple (adversarially generated) second round messages. Equipped with this tool we can make the reduction work and complete the proof. We note that this approach works only under the assumption that the ZK simulator rewinds from the third to the second round, which we will argue to be sufficient for our construction. In more detail, in this work we simply combine the bounded-rewind secure MPC protocol with witness-indistinguishable proofs and non-malleable commitments. These tools guarantee a mild form of non-malleability (which is sufficient for our purposes) that is achieved by requiring rewinds only from the third to the second round in the security proof. The way we achieve non-malleability has become quite standard recently and has been used in [4,10,11,22]. For this reason, we do not give more details on these aspects and refer the interested reader to the technical section. Instead, we dedicate the last part of this section to explain how we construct our bounded-rewind secure MPC protocol.

Bounded-Rewind Secure MPC. Our compiler turns a four-round MPC protocol Π, that only relies on a broadcast channel, into a four-round bounded-rewind-secure MPC protocol Π_{rmpc} (that, again, works over a broadcast channel). We start by discussing how the protocol works for the two-party case (with parties P_1 and P_2), and then discuss how to extend our approach to the multi-party case. For reference, in Fig. 1 we provide a pictorial description of the protocol Π_{rmpc}.

As already mentioned, a protocol is bounded-rewind secure if it retains its security even in the case that the adversary queries the honest party on multiple second rounds, and receives an honestly generated third round for each of these queries. It is easy to imagine that most of the existing four-round MPC protocols have no resiliency against such types of attacks. Indeed, usually the simulation strategy adopted to prove the security of these protocols is to rewind from the third to the second round and extract the input of the corrupted parties. Regardless of that, we aim to provide a compiler that works on any four-round MPC protocol without making any additional assumptions on the input protocol.

To prevent the adversary from gaining an advantage, using its rewinds, we adopt a strategy to hide the third round message of Π and only reveal it in the fourth round. To do that we follow an approach similar to [1,14,18], by embedding the next-message function of Π inside a garbled circuit (GC). More precisely, each party (e.g., P_1) upon receiving the second round message of Π creates a GC that contains all the messages of Π generated so far, its input and randomness. Note that the GC embeds almost all the information needed to compute the fourth round of Π. The only thing that is missing is the third round of the other party (P_2 in our example). The GC, on input the third round message of P_2 for Π, runs the next-message function and returns the fourth round of Π for P_1.

As one might expect, to securely evaluate the GC, P_1 and P_2 need to run an OT protocol in which, in this example, P_2 acts as the receiver and P_1 acts as the sender. The input of P_1 (which acts as a sender) to the OT protocol are the labels of the GC we have just described, while the input of P_2 (which acts as the receiver) is its third round of the protocol Π. In other words, in the third round of the protocol we have just described each party does not send the third round message of Π over the channel, but it sends the OT receiver message which encodes the third round of Π.

The above approach, however, has an issue. To prove its security we need to use an OT protocol that is simulation-based secure against malicious receivers. This is required because in the simulation we need to use the OT simulator to

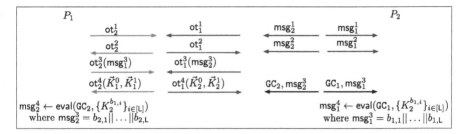

Fig. 1. Our rewindable-secure protocol for the two-party case. msg_i^j represents the j-th message of the MPC protocol Π computed by the party P_i. ot_i^j represents the j-th message of the bounded-rewind secure OT protocol in which P_i acts as the sender and P_{3-i} acts as the receiver with $i \in [2]$. The pairs of inputs $(\boldsymbol{K}_i^0, \boldsymbol{K}_i^1)$ that the party P_i uses as input when acting as the sender of the OT represent the labels of the wire for the garbled circuit that computes the next-message function of Π. This garbled circuit GC_i has hardwired-in the input of P_i, its randomness and all the messages of P_i generated up to the second round. The algorithm eval is the GC evaluation algorithm, that on input the encoding of the GC and a set of labels (one per each wire) returns the output of the GC (the last message of Π in this case). Note that the parties in the last round also send the third message of Π. This is because to compute the output of Π the parties might need all the messages generated from Π.

extract the third round of Π (and forward it to the simulator of Π). Existing OTs that achieve this property require at least four rounds, and this means that our construction is not secure unless the OT protocol is resilient against rewinding attacks. Interestingly, in [10] the authors propose a four-round OT protocol that is secure even in the presence of an adversary that does a bounded number of rewinds. One drawback of the protocol proposed in [10] is that it is not proved to be simulation-based secure against malicious receivers. This should not come as a surprise since it seems to be contradictory to have a primitive that allows extraction through rewinds (since we are in the plain model), but at the same time is secure against adversaries that make rewinds. Fortunately, we can prove that the protocol of [10] is also simulation-based secure against malicious receivers. This proof requires a non-trivial simulator and analysis to argue that the simulated transcript remains indistinguishable from a real one. Our OT simulator and proof crucially rely on the elegant analysis of the simulator for the zero-knowledge protocol proposed by Hazay et al. [30]. We refer the reader to Sect. 6 for more details.

The Multi-party Case. A natural extension of the above 2-party approach to the n-party case would be for each pair of parties to engage in an OT instance as a receiver and sender respectively, to retrieve the labels which are needed to query each other GC and to obtain the fourth round of Π. More precisely, each party now prepares a garbled circuit as before with the difference that its GC now accepts $n-1$ inputs ($n-1$ third round messages of the remaining $n-1$ parties).

This approach does not immediately work since, for example, the party P_i would be able to get only the labels for the wires of the garbled circuit of P_j that encodes its own third round. However, to query the garbled circuit of P_j, the party P_i needs at least one label per wire. To allow P_i to get those labels, we use an approach similar to the one proposed in [10], in which, in the fourth round, all the parties broadcast the randomness and the input used when acting as the OT receiver. In this way P_i can finally query P_j's garbled circuit since it has the labels that correspond to the third round messages of all the parties.

However, since we need to rely on the rewindable-security of the OT protocol, we cannot simply let the parties disclose their randomness contrary to what happens in [10]. For this reason we propose a simple modification of the rewind-secure OT that retains an adequate level of security even in the case that part of the randomness used in the computation is disclosed.

Even if the above approach looks promising, it is vulnerable to the following attack by a potentially corrupted $P^\star$: $P^\star$ could use different third-round messages in each of the n OT instances when acting as the OT receiver. This behaviour is problematic since it allows the adversary to recover the fourth-round messages of the honest parties (via the evaluation of their respective garbled circuits) computed with respect to different third-round messages, which could compromise the security of the underlying MPC protocol Π. Indeed, in the case that Π is normally executed over a broadcast channel, honest parties compute their fourth-round message with respect to the same third-round messages.

To solve this problem, we break this one-to-one dependency such that the labels of the garbled circuit (GC) are secret shared among the OT executions in such a way that it is guaranteed that the labels of a party's GC can only be reconstructed if and only if each party has used the same input across the OT executions where it was acting as the receiver. For more details on how this secret sharing works we refer the reader to Sect. 4.

1.3   Related Work

As already mentioned, the notion of security with identifiable abort was first considered by Aumann and Lindell [3]. This notion was subsequently studied in [15,31,32].

Ishai et al. [32] show that in the correlated randomness model MPC with identifiable abort can be realized information-theoretically. In the information-theoretic setting Ishai et al. require all the n parties to be in possession of some shared randomness and leave open the question of whether information-theoretic ID-MPC can be realized assuming oracles that return correlated randomness shares to less than n parties. This question has been answered in the affirmative in recent works [8,9,43].

The idea of using the SPDZ protocol [17,19] to realize ID-MPC has been used in a few follow-up works. In the work of Spini and Fehr [44] the authors aim to adapt the SDPZ protocol to allow for identifiable abort without increasing the complexity of the protocol too much. Their protocol achieves a communication and computation complexity that polynomially depends on the number of the participating parties. In another work by Cunningham et al. [16], the authors extend the results of Spini and Fehr and obtain a protocol that requires n messages instead of $O(n)$ messages [16, Table 1], where n is the number of parties. Furthermore, their protocol also realizes the notion of *completely* identifiable abort, which is introduced in the same work. The notion of completely identifiable abort extends the existing notion of identifiable abort by not only guaranteeing that a single cheating party is identified but that all the cheating parties are identified.

In the work of Scholl et al. [42] the authors present a compiler that takes any passively secure preprocessing protocol and turns it into one with covert security and identifiable abort. A protocol that fulfills these conditions is, again, the SPDZ protocol [17,19]. In Baum et al. [5] the authors present a constant round ID-MPC protocol with concrete efficiency. Their protocol only makes black-box use of OT and a circular 2-correlation robust hash function. The security of their protocol is proven in the UC framework and they also present an efficiency analysis of their construction.

The notion of bounded-rewind security has been considered in previous works with respect to simpler primitives, like witness-indistinguishable proofs, commitment schemes [4,28,36] and the mentioned oblivious transfer [10]. In [10] the authors also propose a notion (and instantiation) of a rewindable secure MPC protocol. However, their rewind-secure protocol is only secure against a weaker class of adversaries called *semi-malicious adversaries*. Without getting too technical, such an adversary provides its randomness and inputs to the simulator which can then simulate in a straight-line manner. In our work, we do not have this luxury since we require our construction to be secure against any probabilistic polynomial-time adversarial strategy which creates many additional technical challenges.

2   Preliminaries and Standard Definitions

Notation. We denote the security parameter with $\lambda \in \mathbb{N}$. A randomized algorithm $\mathcal{A}$ is running in *probabilistic polynomial time* (PPT) if there exists a polynomial $p(\cdot)$ such that for every input x the running time of $\mathcal{A}(x)$ is bounded by $p(|x|)$. Let A and B be two interactive probabilistic algorithms. We denote by $\langle A(\alpha), B(\beta) \rangle(\gamma)$ the distribution of B's output after running on private input β with A using private input α, both running on common input γ. Typically, one of the two algorithms receives 1^λ as an input. A *transcript* of $\langle A(\alpha), B(\beta) \rangle(\gamma)$ consists of the messages exchanged during an execution where A receives a private input α, B receives a private input β and both A and B receive a common input γ. Moreover, we will define the *view* of A (resp. B), denoted by $\text{view}^A_{(A,B)}$ (resp. $\text{view}^B_{(A,B)}$), as the messages it received during the execution of the protocol (A, B), along with its randomness and its input. We say that the transcript τ of an execution $b = \langle A(z), B \rangle(x)$ is *accepting* if $b = 1$. We say that a protocol (A, B) is public coin if B only sends random bits to A. If the randomness is explicit we write $a := A(x; r)$ where x is the input and r is the randomness.

A protocol is defined to be *delayed-input* if it requires the input of the protocol only in the last round of communication.

We assume familiarity with the notion of negligible functions, garbled circuits, CPA encryptions, extractable commitments, public-coin WI proofs and oblivious transfers and refer the reader to the full version for more details.

2.1 Non-malleable Commitments Scheme

We follow the definition of non-malleable commitments used in [26,38,40] (these definitions are build upon the original definition of Dwork et al. [20]). In the real experiment, the adversary, called man-in-the-middle MIM, interacts with a committer C in the left session, and with a receiver R in the right session. We assume w.l.o.g. that each session has a tag and non-malleability holds only if the tag from the left session is different from the one in the right session.

At the beginning of the experiment, C receives an input v and MIM receives an auxiliary input z, which could contain a priori information about v. For the real experiment, we denote with $\mathsf{MIM}_{\langle C,R \rangle}(\tilde{v}, z)$ the random variable that describes the message that MIM commits to in the right session, jointly with the view of MIM. In the ideal experiment, MIM interacts with a PPT simulator $\mathcal{S}$. There, we denote with $\mathsf{SIM}_{\langle C,R \rangle}(1^\lambda, z)$ the random variable describing the value $\tilde{v}$ that $\mathcal{S}$ committed to and the output view of $\mathcal{S}$. In either of the two experiments, the value $\tilde{v}$ is defined to be $\bot$ if the tags in the left and right session are equal.

Definition 2.1 (Synchronous Non-malleable Commitments). *A* 3-*round commitment scheme* $\langle C, R \rangle$ *is said to be synchronous non-malleable if for every PPT synchronizing adversary*[6] *MIM, there exists a PPT simulator $\mathcal{S}$ such that the following ensembles are computationally indistinguishable:*

$$\{\mathsf{MIM}_{\langle C,R \rangle}(\tilde{v}, z)\}_{\lambda \in \mathbb{N}, v \in \{0,1\}^\lambda, z \in \{0,1\}^*} \text{ and } \{\mathsf{SIM}_{\langle C,R \rangle}(1^\lambda, z)\}_{\lambda \in \mathbb{N}, v \in \{0,1\}^\lambda, z \in \{0,1\}^*}$$

Additionally, we require the following properties to hold for the synchronous non-malleable commitments: 1) *Non-malleability with respect to extraction*: this notion requires the existence of an extractor $\mathsf{Ext}_{\mathsf{NMCom}}$ that is able to extract a message from a well-formed commitment generated by MIM. Moreover, the output distribution of $\mathsf{Ext}_{\mathsf{NMCom}}$ remains the same independently of whether the adversary is receiving honest or simulated commitments. 2) *Last-message pseudo-randomness*: the last message generated by C is computationally indistinguishable from a random string.

Formal definitions of this properties can be found in the full version. In the work of Choudhuri et al. [10], it is observed that the (synchronous version of the) 3-round non-malleable commitments of [27] satisfies all the mentioned properties.

2.2 Trapdoor Generation Protocol with Bounded Rewind Security

This section is taken almost verbatim from [4,10] and introduces the notion of trapdoor generation protocols with bounded rewind security.

---

[6] A synchronizing adversary is an adversary that sends its message for every round before obtaining the honest party's message for the next round.

Syntax. A trapdoor generation protocol $\mathsf{TDGen} = (\mathsf{TDGen}_1, \mathsf{TDGen}_2, \mathsf{TDGen}_3,$ $\mathsf{TDOut}, \mathsf{TDValid}, \mathsf{TDExt})$ is a three round protocol between two parties - a sender (trapdoor generator) S and a receiver R that proceeds as follows:

1. **Round 1 - $\mathsf{TDGen}_1(\cdot)$:**
   S computes and sends $\mathsf{td}_1^{S \to R} \leftarrow \mathsf{TDGen}_1(R_S)$ using a random string R_S.
2. **Round 2 - $\mathsf{TDGen}_2(\cdot)$:**
   R computes and sends $\mathsf{td}_2^{R \to S} \leftarrow \mathsf{TDGen}_2(\mathsf{td}_1^{S \to R}; R_R)$ using randomness R_R.
3. **Round 3 - $\mathsf{TDGen}_3(\cdot)$:**
   S computes and sends $\mathsf{td}_3^{S \to R} \leftarrow \mathsf{TDGen}_3(\mathsf{td}_2^{R \to S}; R_S)$.
4. **Output - $\mathsf{TDOut}(\cdot)$:**
   The receiver R outputs $0/1 \leftarrow \mathsf{TDOut}(\mathsf{td}_1^{S \to R}, \mathsf{td}_2^{R \to S}, \mathsf{td}_3^{S \to R})$.
5. **Trapdoor Validation Algorithm - $\mathsf{TDValid}(\cdot)$:**
   Taking as an input $(\mathsf{trap}, \mathsf{td}_1^{S \to R})$, output a single bit 0 or 1 that determines whether the value trap is a valid trapdoor corresponding to the message td_1 sent in the first round of the trapdoor generation protocol.

In the remainder of this work, to not overburden the notation, we indicate td_1 to be $\mathsf{td}_1^{S \to R}$, td_2 to be $\mathsf{td}_2^{R \to S}$, and td_3 to be $\mathsf{td}_3^{S \to R}$.

The algorithm $\mathsf{TDValid}$ is public and everyone can verify that trap is a valid trapdoor for a first round message td_1.

Extraction. Furthermore, we require the existence of a PPT extractor algorithm TDExt that, given a set of values[7] $(\mathsf{td}_1, \{\mathsf{td}_2^i, \mathsf{td}_3^i\}_{i=1}^3)$ such that $\mathsf{td}_2^1, \mathsf{td}_2^2, \mathsf{td}_2^3$ are distinct and $\mathsf{TDOut}(\mathsf{td}_1, \mathsf{td}_2^i, \mathsf{td}_3^i) = 1$ for all $i \in [3]$, outputs a trapdoor trap such that $\mathsf{TDValid}(\mathsf{trap}, \mathsf{td}_1) = 1$.

1-Rewinding Security. Roughly speaking, if a trapdoor generation protocol is 1-rewind secure then no cheating PPT receiver $R^\star$ can learn a valid trapdoor even when $R^\star$ queries S on two (possibly adaptive) different second-round messages, thereby receiving two different third round responses from the sender. The formal definition of this notion can be found in the full version.

3 Rewind-Secure OT and MPC

We assume familiarity with the standard notions of multi-party computation secure with unanimous and identifiable abort under black-box simulation in the plain model. We refer to the full version for more details. In this section, we introduce the definitions of two rewind-secure primitives, namely oblivious transfer (OT) and MPC. We start with the definition of our new notion of special rewindable OT. Afterwards, we define what it means for an MPC protocol to be rewindable secure.

---

[7] These values can be obtained from the malicious sender via an expected PPT rewinding procedure. The expected PPT simulator in our applications performs the necessary rewindings and then inputs these values to the extractor TDExt.

Definition 3.1 (Special B-Rewindable OT Security). *Let* $\mathsf{OT} = (\mathsf{OT}_1, \mathsf{OT}_2, \mathsf{OT}_3, \mathsf{OT}_4)$ *be an OT protocol, then we say that* OT *is special B-rewindable secure against malicious senders with B rewinds if the output distributions of the adversary in the experiments* E_k^0 *and* E_k^1 *(where* E_k^σ *is defined below) are computationally indistinguishable for any* $k \in [B]$ *and all* $\{b^0[j], b^1[j]\}_{j \in [B]}$ *with* $b^\sigma[j] \in \{0,1\}^\lambda$ *for all* $j \in [B]$ *and* $\sigma \in \{0,1\}$ *and with* $b^0[k] = b^1[k]$.

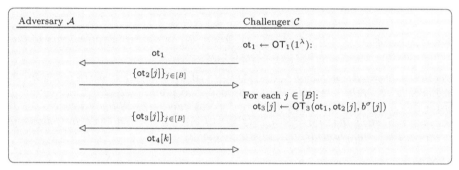

We note that this definition is equal to the one proposed in [10] except for the fact that we require the adversary to pick the same input in the k-th slot.

Definition 3.2 (Bounded Rewind-Secure MPC with unanimous abort). *A 4-round MPC protocol* MPC *for f is a tuple of deterministic polynomial-time algorithms* $\mathsf{MPC} = \{(\mathsf{Next}_i^1, \mathsf{Next}_i^2, \mathsf{Next}_i^3, \mathsf{Next}_i^4, \mathsf{output}_i)\}_{i \in [n]}$ *(where the algorithms are defined as in the standard definition of MPC:*

Similar to the standard security definition of MPC, we define the real-world and ideal-world execution.

Ideal Computation. *Let* $f : (\{0,1\}^*)^n \to (\{0,1\}^*)^n$ *be an n-party function and let* $\mathcal{I} \subset [n]$, *of size at most $n-1$, be the set of indices of the corrupt parties. Then, the joint ideal execution of f under $(\mathcal{S}, \mathcal{I})$ on input vector* $x = (x_1, \ldots, x_n)$, *auxiliary input* aux *and security parameter λ, denoted by* $\mathrm{IDEAL}_{f,\mathcal{I},\mathcal{S}(\mathsf{aux})}^{\text{un-abort}}(x, \lambda)$, *is defined as in the standard definition of MPC.*

Real Execution. *Let* $\Pi = (P_1, \ldots, P_n)$ *be an n-party 4-round MPC protocol and let* $\mathcal{I} \subseteq [n]$, *of size at most $n-1$, denote the set of indices of the parties corrupted by $\mathcal{A}$. The joint execution of Π under $(\mathcal{A}, \mathcal{I})$ in the real world, on input vector* $x = (x_1, \ldots, x_n)$, *auxiliary input* aux *and security parameter λ, denoted by* $\mathrm{REAL}_{\Pi,\mathcal{I},\mathcal{A}(\mathsf{aux})}(x, \lambda)$, *is defined as the output vector of $P_1, \ldots, P_n$ and $\mathcal{A}(\mathsf{aux})$ resulting from the following 4-round protocol interaction. Let $\mathcal{H}$ denote the set of indices of honest parties* $\mathcal{H} = [n] \setminus \mathcal{I}$.

- *Interaction in Round 1: $\mathcal{A}$ receives* $\{\mathsf{msg}_j^1 = \mathsf{Next}_j(1^\lambda, x_j, \rho_j)\}_{j \in \mathcal{H}}$ *and sends messages* $\{\mathsf{msg'}_i^1\}_{i \in \mathcal{I}}$ *of its choice. Let* $\overline{\mathsf{msg}}^{<2} = \{\{\mathsf{msg}_j^1\}_{j \in \mathcal{H}}, \{\mathsf{msg'}_i^1\}_{i \in \mathcal{I}}\}$.
- *Interaction in Round 2 and 3 with B rewinds:*
  - *$\mathcal{A}$ is given* $\{\mathsf{msg}_j^2 = \mathsf{Next}_j^2(1^\lambda, x_j, \rho_j, \overline{\mathsf{msg}}^{<2})\}_{j \in \mathcal{H}}$.
  - *$\mathcal{A}$ chooses B second-round messages, namely* $\{\mathsf{msg'}_i^2[k]\}_{i \in \mathcal{I}, k \in [B]}$.

- $\mathcal{A}$ is given $\{msg_j^3[k] = \mathsf{Next}_j^3(1^\lambda, x_j, \rho_j, \overline{msg}^{<3}[k])\}_{j \in \mathcal{H}, k \in [B]}$, where $\overline{msg}^{<3}[k] = \{\overline{msg}^{<2}, \{msg_j^2\}_{j \in \mathcal{H}}, \{msg'^2_i[k]\}_{i \in \mathcal{I}}\}$.
- $\mathcal{A}$ sends third-round message $\{msg'^3_i\}_{i \in \mathcal{I}}$ of its choice.
- Let $\overline{msg}^{<4} = \{\overline{msg}^{<3}[1], \{msg_j^3[1]\}_{j \in \mathcal{H}}, \{msg'^3_i\}_{i \in \mathcal{I}}\}$.
- Interaction in Round 4: $\mathcal{A}$ is given fourth-round messages $\{msg_j^4 = \mathsf{Next}_j^4(1^\lambda, x_j, \rho_j, \overline{msg}^{<4})\}_{j \in \mathcal{H}}$. $\mathcal{A}$ sends fourth-round messages $\{msg'^4_i\}_{i \in \mathcal{I}}$ of its choice.

$\mathsf{REAL}_{\mathcal{I}, \mathcal{A}(aux)}(\overline{x}, \lambda)$ is defined as $(\overline{y}_\mathcal{H}, z)$, where $\overline{y}_\mathcal{H}$ is the vector of outputs of the honest parties while z is the output of the adversary.

Security Definition. Let $f : (\{0,1\}^*)^n \to (\{0,1\}^*)^n$ be an n-party function. A protocol Π securely computes the function f with unanimous abort and bounded B-rewind security if for every PPT real-world adversary $\mathcal{A}$ there exists a PPT simulator $\mathcal{S}$ such that for every $\mathcal{I} \subset [n]$ of size at most $n-1$, the following ensembles are computationally indistinguishable:

$$\left\{\mathsf{REAL}_{\Pi, \mathcal{I}, \mathcal{A}(aux)}(x, \lambda)\right\}_{x \in (\{0,1\}^*)^n, \lambda \in \mathbb{N}} \quad and \quad \left\{\mathsf{IDEAL}^{un\text{-}abort}_{f, \mathcal{I}, \mathcal{S}(aux)}(x, \lambda)\right\}_{x \in (\{0,1\}^*)^n, \lambda \in \mathbb{N}}.$$

4 From MPC with Unanimous Abort to B-rewindable MPC with Unanimous Abort

In this section, we present a compiler that makes a four-round MPC protocol Π_{MPC} secure with unanimous abort in the plain model bounded-rewind-secure, resulting in the protocol Π_{rmpc}, while preserving all its other security properties. We begin with a high-level overview of the compiler and establish some notation for simplicity. Let msg_i^r denote the message broadcast by P_i in Round r ($r \in [4]$) of Π_{MPC}.

The Two-Party Case. For simplicity, we start by considering the 2-party case, where one of the parties, here P_2, is corrupted. To make Π_{MPC} bounded-rewind-secure, we need to ensure that security is maintained even if P_2 receives a set of multiple third-round messages from P_1 (namely, msg_1^3) as a response to its chosen set of second-round messages (namely, msg_2^2).

In our protocol the party P_i ($i \in [2]$) computes a garbled circuit GC_i that has hard-coded inside its input x_i, randomness r_i and the protocol transcript of Π_{MPC} until Round 2 i.e. $\{msg_i^1, msg_j^2\}_{j \in [2]}$ and takes as input the set of third-round messages $\{msg_j^3\}_{j \in [2]}$ and outputs P_i's fourth-round message i.e. msg_i^4. In the last round of Π_{rmpc}, these garbled circuits are then evaluated to obtain the fourth-round messages of Π_{MPC}. For the evaluation of these garbled circuits, we need the parties to be able to obtain the labels corresponding to $\{msg_j^3\}_{j \in [2]}$. For this purpose we rely on an oblivious transfer OT protocol.[8] In the above context, P_1 does not send msg_1^3 directly in Round 3 of Π_{rmpc} but instead participates in

---

[8] For the wires corresponding to their own third-round message (i.e. msg_i^3 in GC_i), the labels can be broadcasted directly in the last round.

an OT instance as an OT receiver with input msg_1^3; while P_2 participates as the sender using as its input the labels of GC_2 that were used to encode the input msg_1^3. Similarly, there would be another OT instance with P_2 as the receiver and P_1 as the sender for the labels of msg_2^3 corresponding to GC_1. It is now evident that the parties can proceed to evaluate the garbled circuits, obtain the fourth-round messages of Π_{MPC} and compute the output. Intuitively, the above approach helps to achieve rewind-security because, in the security game, the honest party P_1 has to send multiple third-round messages (in round 3 of Π_{rmpc}) which, in our protocol, contain msg_1^3 messages under the hood of OT and are thereby 'hidden' from the adversary. In the fourth-round only one among these third-round messages is 'opened' to the adversary which effectively reduces the security to a single execution of Π_{MPC}.

The Multi-party Case. A natural extension of the above 2-party approach to the multi-party case would be to let each pair of parties, P_i and P_j, engage in an OT instance (say $\mathsf{OT}^{j,i}$) as an OT receiver and sender respectively to retrieve labels of msg_i^3 corresponding to GC_j (which would output the fourth-round message of P_j). However, unlike the 2-party case, a party, for example, P_i is not able to obtain the labels for all the inputs of GC_j, and therefore cannot evaluate GC_j. In more detail, P_i would not have access to the labels corresponding to the input msg_k^3 in GC_j (where $k, j \neq i$). To enable P_i (and everyone else) to recover these labels, we make P_k reveal the OT randomness that is used as an OT receiver during the instance $\mathsf{OT}^{j,k}$ so that everyone can learn the output of this OT (i.e. the labels of GC_j corresponding to msg_k^3). Note that this randomness can be safely revealed because the adversary learns the OT receiver's input msg_k^3 also in the protocol Π_{MPC} which is secure with unanimous abort. In light of the above, we define the security notion of OT with rewindable security against a malicious sender. This notion is a slightly modified variant of the one used in [10] and their construction can be easily adapted with minor tweaks to satisfy our notion. This rewind-secure OT construction also satisfies *public verifiability*, enabling all the parties to check the correctness of the OT receiver messages, for all pairwise instances of the OT, by just checking the transcripts.

Next, we observe that the above approach of using pairwise OTs is vulnerable to the following attack by a potentially corrupted party P_i : P_i could use different third-round messages (i.e. msg_i^3) as its input across the n OT instances where it acts as an OT receiver (one instance for every other party as the sender). This behaviour violates the security of the underlying MPC since it allows the adversary to recover the fourth-round messages of honest parties (via evaluation of their respective garbled circuits) computed with respect to different third-round messages msg_i^3. Note that in the underlying protocol Π_{MPC} the adversary cannot launch this attack since honest parties compute their fourth-round message with respect to the same msg_i^3 (which is broadcast in round 3 of Π_{MPC}).

The crux of the above issue is that the labels of GC_j corresponding to msg_i^3 are tied to a single instance of OT, i.e. the one between P_i and P_j. To resolve this, we break this one-to-one dependency such that the labels of GC_j corresponding to msg_i^3 are obtained in a distributed manner across all n OTs where P_i acts as a receiver. For simplicity, assume that msg_i^3 contains only a single bit $b \in \{0,1\}$ and corresponds to wire w in each of the n garbled circuits. Each garbler P_j additively shares the labels of wire w of GC_j among the parties for $b \in \{0,1\}$. Now, each P_k has an additive share for each of the n garbled circuits corresponding to wire w and each bit $b \in \{0,1\}$. Accordingly, the OT instances between P_i, acting as the receiver, (who participates with the actual value of bit b as input) and P_k, acting as the sender, would now involve P_k participating with the two tuples of n additive shares as its input, where the first tuple comprises of the n additive shares for $b = 0$, while the other tuple contains the n additive shares for $b = 1$. The above technique ensures that if P_i participates with inconsistent inputs b across its instances as an OT receiver then neither the label for $b = 0$ nor for $b = 1$ will be recovered for any honest party's garbled circuit. This is due to the fact that the OT instances with a subset of honest parties as OT senders would output additive shares corresponding to 0, while the others would output additive shares corresponding to 1; which is insufficient to reconstruct either of the labels. The transfer of the additive shares is done using public-key encryption i.e. by encrypting the relevant share using the public key of the intended recipient. This allows us to maintain the property that all messages in Π_{rmpc} are sent over a broadcast channel.

Looking ahead, this is useful to achieve identifiable abort security as it allows the parties to give a corresponding proof of correctness for these messages in such a way that it can be verified by everyone. In our final construction, however, the relevant additive shares of the garbled circuits are not used directly in the OT instances. Instead, the OT senders encrypt each of their tuple of n additive shares using one-time pads, broadcast these encryptions and use the corresponding one-time pad keys as inputs to the OT. Note that if the additive shares were used directly, some of the components of an honest sender's input (corresponding to the additive shares given by a corrupt garbler) are adversarially chosen. However, the above described modification using one-time pads allows us to rely on standard OT security where an honest sender's input is not adversarially chosen. This completes the high-level description of our compiler.

Lastly, we highlight an important aspect related to the security of the above described bounded-rewind-secure MPC construction. Since we allow the adversary to proceed to the evaluation of the garbled circuits and obtain the output only if it used consistent third-round messages in all the OT instances where it participated as a receiver, we require the property of 'simultaneous extractability' from the rewind-secure OT. In more detail, consider multiple OT instances running in parallel where the receiver is corrupted and the sender is honest. We require that the simulator of the OT should be able to extract the input of the malicious receivers in the same rewinding thread for multiple OT instances. This is needed to check if the adversary used consistent inputs on behalf of the same malicious receiver or not, as the latter would result in abort. We show in Sect. 6 that the modified variant of the rewind-secure OT of [10] satisfies this property of simultaneous extractability.

We now formally describe our compiler in Fig. 2.

Notation. - Let Circuit $C_{i,x,\rho,\overline{msg}^{<3}}(msg_1^3, msg_2^3, \ldots, msg_n^3)$ denote the boolean circuit with hard-wired values i, x, ρ and the transcript $\overline{msg}^{<3}$ of the first two rounds of an execution of Π_{MPC} that upon receiving n inputs $msg_1^3, msg_2^3, \ldots, msg_n^3$ (i.e. the third-round broadcast messages of the execution of Π_{MPC}) computes $Next_i^4(x, \rho, \overline{msg}^{<4} = \{\overline{msg}^{<3}, msg_1^3, msg_2^3, \ldots, msg_n^3\})$. For simplicity, we assume that each third-round broadcast message is ℓ bits long – so the circuit has $L = n\ell$ input bits.

- Let $OT^{j,k}$ denote an instance of a B-rewind secure OT (denoted as $(rOT_1, rOT_2, rOT_3, rOT_4, rOT_5, rOT_6)$) where P_j acts as the sender and P_k acts as the receiver.

Private Input. P_i has private input $x_i \in \{0,1\}^\lambda$ and randomness ρ_i.

Output. $y = f(x_1, \ldots, x_n)$ or $\bot$.

Round 1. Each P_i does the following:

1. Run the setup of the PKE scheme as $(pk_i, sk_i) \leftarrow keygen(1^\lambda; R_{PKE})$.
2. Compute the first-round message of Π_{MPC} as $msg_i^1 \leftarrow Next_i^1(x_i; \rho_i)$.
3. Compute the first-round OT message as the receiver – i.e. for each $j \in [n]$ corresponding to the instance $OT^{j,i}$ (where P_i acts as the receiver), sample randomness $R_{j,i}^1$ and compute $rot_1^{j,i} \leftarrow rOT_1(1^\lambda; R_{j,i}^1)$.
4. Broadcast $(pk_i, msg_i^1, \{rot_1^{j,i}\}_{j \in [n]})$.

Round 2. Each P_i does the following:

1. If any party aborts in the previous round, honest parties output $\bot$. [a]
2. Compute the second-round message of Π_{MPC} as $msg_i^2 \leftarrow Next_i^2(x_i, \rho_i, \overline{msg}^{<2})$, where $\overline{msg}^{<2} = \{msg_j^1\}_{j \in [n]}$.
3. Compute the second-round OT message as the sender – for each $j \in [n]$ corresponding to the instance $OT^{i,j}$ (where P_i acts as the sender), sample randomness $S_{i,j}$ and compute $rot_2^{i,j} \leftarrow rOT_2(rot_1^{i,j}; S_{i,j})$.
4. Broadcast $(msg_i^2, \{rot_2^{i,j}\}_{j \in [n]})$.

Round 3. Each P_i does the following:

1. Compute the garbled circuit as $(GC_i, \boldsymbol{K}_i) \leftarrow garble(C_{i,x,\rho,\overline{msg}^{<3}}, 1^\lambda; R_{GC})$, where $\boldsymbol{K}_i$ denotes the set of labels $\{K_{i,\alpha}^{(0)}, K_{i,\alpha}^{(1)}\}_{\alpha \in [L]}$.
2. For each $\alpha \in [L]$ and $b \in \{0,1\}$, compute an additive sharing $(K_{i,\alpha,1}^{(b)}, K_{i,\alpha,2}^{(b)}, \ldots, K_{i,\alpha,n}^{(b)})$ of the label $K_{i,\alpha}^{(b)}$.
3. For each $\alpha \in [L]$, $b \in \{0,1\}$ and $j \in [n] \setminus \{i\}$, compute the ciphertexts $ct_{i,\alpha,j}^{(b)} \leftarrow enc(pk_j, K_{i,\alpha,j}^{(b)})$.
4. Compute the third-round message of Π_{MPC} as $msg_i^3 \leftarrow Next_i^3(x_i, \rho_i, \overline{msg}^{<3})$, where $\overline{msg}^{<3} = \{msg_j^1, msg_j^2\}_{j \in [n]}$.
5. Compute the third-round OT message as the receiver using as an input the string msg_i^3 – for each $j \in [n]$ corresponding to the OT instance $OT^{j,i}$, sample randomness $R_{j,i}^3$ and run $rot_3^{j,i} \leftarrow rOT_3(msg_i^3, rot_1^{j,i}, rot_2^{j,i}; R_{j,i}^3)$.
6. Broadcast $(\{ct_{i,\alpha,j}^{(b)}\}_{\alpha \in [L], j \in [n] \setminus i, b \in \{0,1\}}, \{rot_3^{j,i}\}_{j \in [n]})$.

Fig. 2. Π_{rmpc}

Round 4. Each P_i does the following:

1. For each $\alpha \in [L], b \in \{0,1\}$ and $j \in [n] \setminus \{i\}$, compute $\mathsf{K}^{(b)}_{j,\alpha,i} \leftarrow \mathsf{dec}(\mathsf{sk}_i, \mathsf{ct}^{(b)}_{j,\alpha,i})$.

2. For each $j, k \in [n]$, check the correctness of $\mathsf{rot}^{j,k}_3$ sent by P_k (this is possible due to public verifiability of the OT). If the check does not pass, broadcast 'abort' and output $\bot$, else, continue.

3. // Recall that the input wires of each GC_k ($k \in [n]$) at indices $[(j-1)\ell+1, j\ell]$ correspond to msg^3_j and $\mathsf{K}^{(b)}_{k,\alpha,i}$ denotes P_i's additive share of the label of GC_k corresponding to index α and bit b.

   For each $j \in [n]$ and $\beta \in [\ell]$ – let $m^{(0)}_{j,\beta,i} = (\mathsf{K}^{(0)}_{1,(j-1)\ell+\beta,i}, \ldots, \mathsf{K}^{(0)}_{n,(j-1)\ell+\beta,i})$ and $m^{(1)}_{j,\beta,i} = (\mathsf{K}^{(1)}_{1,(j-1)\ell+\beta,i}, \ldots, \mathsf{K}^{(1)}_{n,(j-1)\ell+\beta,i})$. Sample random strings $q^{(0)}_{j,\beta,i}$ and $q^{(1)}_{j,\beta,i}$ (to be used as one-time pad keys) and compute $M^{(0)}_{j,\beta,i} = m^{(0)}_{j,\beta,i} + q^{(0)}_{j,\beta,i}$ and $M^{(1)}_{j,\beta,i} = m^{(1)}_{j,\beta,i} + q^{(1)}_{j,\beta,i}$.

4. For each $j \in [n]$ corresponding to the OT instance $\mathsf{OT}^{i,j}$ (where P_j participated as a receiver with input msg^3_j) – Compute the fourth-round OT message as the sender as follows: run $\mathsf{rot}^{i,j}_4 \leftarrow \mathsf{rOT}_4\Big((q^{(0)}_{j,1,i}, q^{(1)}_{j,1,i}), (q^{(0)}_{j,2,i}, q^{(1)}_{j,2,i}), \ldots, (q^{(0)}_{j,\ell,i}, q^{(1)}_{j,\ell,i}), \mathsf{rot}^{i,j}_1, \mathsf{rot}^{i,j}_2, \mathsf{rot}^{i,j}_3;$
$S_{i,j}\Big)$.

5. For all OT instances $\mathsf{OT}^{j,i}$ where P_i participated as the receiver, compute $\mathsf{rot}^{j,i}_5 \leftarrow \mathsf{rOT}_5\Big(R^1_{j,i}, R^3_{j,i}\Big)$ for all $j \in [n]$.

6. Broadcast $(GC_i, \mathsf{msg}^3_i, \{\mathsf{rot}^{i,j}_4\}_{j\in[n]}, \{\mathsf{rot}^{j,i}_5\}_{j\in[n]}, \{M^{(0)}_{j,\beta,i}, M^{(1)}_{j,\beta,i}\}_{j\in[n],\beta\in[\ell]})$.

Output Computation. Each P_i does the following:

1. If any party broadcasted 'abort' in Round 4, output $\bot$.

2. Compute the output of each OT instance where P_j acts as the receiver and P_k acts as the sender as follows (where $j, k \in [n]$):
   - Compute $(q_{j,1,k}, q_{j,2,k}, \ldots, q_{j,\ell,k}) \leftarrow \mathsf{rOT}_6(\mathsf{rot}^{k,j}_1, \mathsf{rot}^{k,j}_2, \mathsf{rot}^{k,j}_3, \mathsf{rot}^{k,j}_4, \mathsf{rot}^{k,j}_5, \mathsf{msg}^3_j)$.
   - Let msg^3_j be the third-round message of Π_{MPC} broadcast by P_j in Round 4. Parse msg^3_j as $\mathsf{msg}^3_j = b_{j,1}||b_{j,2}||\ldots b_{j,\ell}$.
   - For each $\beta \in [\ell]$, set $\{\mathsf{K}_{1,(j-1)\ell+\beta,k}, \ldots, \mathsf{K}_{n,(j-1)\ell+\beta,k}\} = q_{j,\beta,k} \oplus M^{(b_{j,\beta})}_{j,\beta,k}$, where $M^{(b_{j,\beta})}_{j,\beta,k}$ was broadcast by P_k in Round 4.

3. For each garbled circuit GC_j ($j \in [n]$) – compute $\mathsf{K}_{j,\alpha} = \sum^n_{k=1} \mathsf{K}_{j,\alpha,k}$ for each $\alpha \in [L]$.

4. For each GC_j ($j \in [n]$), compute $\mathsf{msg}^4_j \leftarrow \mathsf{eval}(GC_j, \mathsf{K}_{j,1}, \ldots, \mathsf{K}_{j,L})$.

5. Output $y_i \leftarrow \mathsf{output}_i(x_i, \rho_i, \{\mathsf{msg}^1_j, \mathsf{msg}^2_j, \mathsf{msg}^3_j, \mathsf{msg}^4_j\}_{j\in[n]})$.

---

[a] we assume that honest parties execute this step in the beginning of each round.

Fig. 2. (*continued*)

The compiler makes use of the following tools:

- A 4-round MPC protocol Π_{MPC} with unanimous abort security represented by the set of functions $\{(\mathsf{Next}_i^1, \mathsf{Next}_i^2, \mathsf{Next}_i^3, \mathsf{Next}_i^4, \mathsf{output}_i)\}_{i \in [n]}$, where all the messages are assumed to be sent over a broadcast channel.
- A garbling scheme $(\mathsf{garble}, \mathsf{eval}, \mathsf{simGC})$ that is assumed to satisfy properties of privacy (a set of labels, together with the garbled circuit, reveals nothing about the input the labels correspond to), correctness (the correct evaluation of the garbled circuit matches the evaluation of the plain circuit), authenticity of input labels (it is not possible to 'forge' a different set of valid input labels from a set of valid input labels) and partial evaluation resiliency (unless at least one label corresponding to every bit is obtained, nothing about the output is revealed). We defer details of these notions to the full version.
- A delayed-input OT protocol, instantiated by the construction in Sect. 6, denoted as a sequence of algorithms $(\mathsf{rOT}_1, \mathsf{rOT}_2, \mathsf{rOT}_3, \mathsf{rOT}_4, \mathsf{rOT}_5, \mathsf{rOT}_6)$, where rOT_r $(r \in [5])$ denotes the algorithm to compute the r-th round messages and rOT_6 denotes the algorithm for the output computation. The OT protocol satisfies special 2-B rewindable security and sender simulatability.
- A CPA-secure public-key encryption scheme $\mathsf{PKE} = (\mathsf{keygen}, \mathsf{enc}, \mathsf{dec})$.

Theorem 4.1 *Assume the existence of a 4-round MPC protocol with unanimous abort security against dishonest majority, a CPA-secure public key encryption scheme, a garbling scheme that is assumed to satisfy properties of privacy, correctness, authenticity of input labels and partial evaluation resiliency and a 5-round delayed-input oblivious transfer protocol (described in Sect. 6) satisfying special 2-B rewindable security and sender simulatability. Then, Π_{rmpc} is a 4-round B-rewindable secure MPC with unanimous abort against dishonest majority in the plain model.*

The above construction can be built based on trapdoor permutations (we refer to the full version for details on the instantiations of each of the building blocks). The formal proof of Theorem 4.1 can be found in the full version.

5   Our Construction: MPC with Identifiable Abort

In this section we present the four-round MPC protocol secure with identifiable abort. The idea of our construction is to let every participating party prove, during the execution of the MPC protocol, that it is generating all of its messages according to the protocol description. To prove the correctness of the generated messages, each party, in the last round, executes a zap (i.e., a two-round public-coin WI proof) with every other participating party. These zaps prove that either all the messages of the MPC protocol are generated correctly or the party has, earlier in the protocol execution, generated a non-malleable commitment with respect to a trapdoor, that has been generated using a trapdoor generation protocol later in the protocol execution. Both, the trapdoor generation protocol and the non-malleable commitment scheme are also executed in parallel to the MPC protocol.

To allow the simulator in the security proof of this construction to generate a valid zap it needs to prove the second part of the relation, i.e. that the non-malleable commitment is a commitment to the trapdoor generated using the trapdoor generation protocol. To create such a commitment, the simulator needs to rewind the overall protocol to extract the trapdoor from the trapdoor generation protocol. To guarantee that during these rewinds the underlying MPC protocol is preserved, we can rely on its rewindable security. After the trapdoor is extracted, the simulator can commit to it in the non-malleable commitment and, finally, finishes the execution of the zap. We need to require the commitment scheme to be non-malleable to prevent an adversary from malleability attacks. An adversary could, for example, if these commitments were malleable, maul one of them during the simulation and use it to create its own commitment to the trapdoor of the trapdoor generation protocol and use it to provide an accepting zap even though it did not behave accordingly to the protocol description. In Fig. 3 we provide the formal description of our protocol Π^{ID}, for which we make use of the following tools.

- A public-coin perfectly correct trapdoor generation protocol $\mathsf{TDGen} = (\mathsf{TDGen}_1, \mathsf{TDGen}_2, \mathsf{TDGen}_3, \mathsf{TDOut}, \mathsf{TDValid}, \mathsf{TDExt})$.
- A perfectly correct 3-round special non-malleable commitment scheme $\mathsf{NMCom} = (C, R)$.
- A perfectly correct 4-round MPC protocol that is 3-rewindable secure with unanimous abort Π. W.l.o.g. we assume that whenever a party aborts in Π (i.e., its next message function outputs $\bot$) then the party keeps interacting with the other parties by sending $\bot$ anytime that it is suppose to send a message for Π and replace its output with $\bot$. Moreover, if a party receives $\bot$ from any other party, it will replace any message of Π (as well as its output) with $\bot$. The construction of Π is described in Sect. 4 and we argue that it satisfies perfect correctness in the full version.
- A perfectly correct 2-round public coin WI proof $\mathsf{RWI} = (\mathcal{P}, \mathcal{V})$ for the NP-language L characterized by the relation R specified below (we denote statements and witnesses as $\mathtt{st}$ and $\mathtt{w}$, respectively).

$\mathtt{st} := \left(\overline{\mathsf{msg}}^{<5}, \{\mathsf{msg}_\ell\}_{\ell \in [4]}, \{\mathsf{nmc}_\ell\}_{\ell \in [3]}, \mathsf{td}_1, r \right)$ and $\mathtt{w} := (x, R, \tilde{r}, R_{\mathsf{NMCom}})$
$R(\mathtt{st}, \mathtt{w}) = 1$ if *either* of the following conditions is satisfied:

1. **Honest:** for every $\ell \leq 4$, msg_ℓ is an honestly computed ℓ^{th} round message in the protocol Π w.r.t. input x, randomness R and the first $(\ell-1)$ round protocol transcript $\overline{\mathsf{msg}}^{<5}$.
2. **Trapdoor:** $\{\mathsf{nmc}_\ell\}_{\ell \in [3]}$ is an honest transcript of NMCom w.r.t. input $\tilde{r}$ and randomness R_{NMCom} (AND) $\mathsf{trap} = r \oplus \tilde{r}$ is a valid trapdoor w.r.t. td_1

We also require the domain of the messages of the receivers/verifier of TDGen, NMCom and RWI to be $\{0,1\}^\lambda$.

In each round if a set of parties stops replying then all the honest parties stop and output $(\bot, i)$, where P_i is the party with the smallest index that did not reply.

Round 1. P_i computes and broadcasts the *first* round messages of the following protocols:
1. Rewindable secure MPC Π: $\mathsf{msg}_{1,i} \leftarrow \mathsf{Next}_{1,i}(1^\lambda, x_i, R_i, \bot)$.
2. Sender message of TDGen: $\mathsf{td}_{1,i} \leftarrow \mathsf{TDGen}_1(R_{\mathsf{td},i})$.

For every $j \neq i$:
3. Sender message of the non-malleable commitment scheme $\mathsf{NMCom}_1^{i \to j} \leftarrow \mathsf{NMCom}_1(\tilde{r}^{i \to j}, R_{\mathsf{NMCom}}^{i \to j})$ where $\tilde{r}^{i \to j} \leftarrow \{0,1\}^\lambda$.

Round 2. P_i computes and broadcasts the *second* round messages of the following protocols:
1. MPC Π: $\mathsf{msg}_{2,i} \leftarrow \mathsf{Next}_{2,i}(1^\lambda, x_i, R_i, \overline{\mathsf{msg}}^{<2})$.

For every $j \neq i$:
2. Receiver message of TDGen: $\mathsf{td}_2^{i \to j} \leftarrow \mathsf{TDGen}_2(\mathsf{td}_{1,j})$.
3. Receiver message of the non-malleable commitment scheme $\mathsf{NMCom}_2^{j \to i} \leftarrow \mathsf{NMCom}_2(\mathsf{nmc}_1^{j \to i})$.

Round 3. P_i computes and broadcasts the following messages of the following protocols:
1. Third round of Π: $\mathsf{msg}_{3,i} \leftarrow \mathsf{Next}_{3,i}(1^\lambda, x_i, R_i, \overline{\mathsf{msg}}^{<3})$
2. The third round of TDGen: set $\mathsf{td}_{2,i} = \mathsf{td}_2^{1 \to i} || \ldots || \mathsf{td}_2^{n \to i}$ where $\mathsf{td}_2^{i \to i} = \bot$. Compute $\mathsf{td}_{3,i} \leftarrow \mathsf{TDGen}_3(\mathsf{td}_{2,i})$.

   For every $j \neq i$:
   (a) The third round of NMCom: $\mathsf{NMCom}_3^{i \to j} \leftarrow \mathsf{NMCom}_3(\mathsf{nmc}_2^{i \to j}, \tilde{r}^{i \to j}; R_{\mathsf{NMCom}}^{i \to j})$.
   (b) The first round of RWI: $\mathsf{zap}_1^{j \to i} \leftarrow \{0,1\}^\lambda$.

Round 4. P_i does the following: If $\exists j \neq i$ such that $\mathsf{TDValid}(\mathsf{td}_{1,j}, \mathsf{td}_{2,j}, \mathsf{td}_{3,j}) \neq 1$ then output (abort, j) and **stop** else compute and broadcast the following messages
// where $\mathsf{td}_{2,j} := (\mathsf{td}_2^{1 \to j} || \cdots || \mathsf{td}_2^{n \to j})$.
1. Fourth round message of the MPC protocol Π: $\mathsf{msg}_{4,i} \leftarrow \mathsf{Next}_{4,i}(1^\lambda, x_i, R_i, \overline{\mathsf{msg}}^{<4})$

For every $j \neq i$
2. A random value $r^{i \to j} \leftarrow \{0,1\}^\lambda$.
3. The second round of RWI: Define $\mathtt{st} := \left(\overline{\mathsf{msg}}^{<5}, \{\mathsf{msg}_{\ell,i}\}_{\ell \in [4]}, \{\mathsf{nmc}_\ell^{i \to j}\}_{\ell \in [3]}, \mathsf{td}_{1,j}, r^{i \to j} \right)$ and $\mathtt{w} := (x_i, R_i, \bot, \bot)$ and compute $\mathsf{zap}_2^{i \to j} \leftarrow \mathcal{P}(\mathtt{st}, \mathtt{w}, \mathsf{zap}_1^{i \to j})$.

Output Computation P_i computes the following:
1. If $\exists j \neq i$ and k, s.t. $\mathcal{V}(\mathtt{st}, \mathsf{zap}_2^{j \to k}, \mathsf{zap}_1^{j \to k}, \mathtt{st}) = 0$ where $\mathtt{st} := \left(\overline{\mathsf{msg}}^{<5}, \{\mathsf{msg}_{\ell,j}\}_{\ell \in [4]}, \{\mathsf{nmc}_\ell^{j \to k}\}_{\ell \in [3]}, \mathsf{td}_{1,k}, r_j \right)$, output j and **stop**.
2. Output $\mathsf{output}(1^\lambda, x_i, R_i, \overline{\mathsf{msg}}^{<5})$

Fig. 3. Π^{ID}

Unless otherwise specified, in each round if a set of parties stops replying then all the honest parties stop and output **abort** together with the index of the party with the smallest index to indicate which is the aborting party.

Initialization Run $\mathcal{A}$ using the randomness $\rho_{\mathcal{A}}$ and use the randomness ρ to compute all the messages described below.

Round 1.

- Upon receiving the message $\mathsf{msg}_{1,i}$ from the right session where $i \in \overline{\mathcal{I}}$ do the following.
  1. Compute $\mathsf{td}_{1,i} \leftarrow \mathsf{TDGen}_1 (R_{\mathsf{td},i})$.
     For every $j \neq i$:
  2. Compute $\mathsf{NMCom}_1^{i \rightarrow j} \leftarrow \mathsf{NMCom}_1(\tilde{r}^{i \rightarrow j}, R_{\mathsf{NMCom}}^{i \rightarrow j})$ where $\tilde{r}^{i \rightarrow j} \leftarrow \{0,1\}^{\lambda}$.
  3. Broadcast $\{\mathsf{NMCom}_1^{i \rightarrow j}\}_{j \in [n] \setminus \{i\}}, \mathsf{td}_{1,i}, \mathsf{msg}_{1,i}$.
- Upon receiving the first round from $\mathcal{A}$, for each $i \in \mathcal{I}$ forward $\mathsf{msg}_{1,i}$ to the right interface and continue as follows.

Round 2.

- Upon receiving the message $\mathsf{msg}_{2,i}$ from the right interface where $i \in \overline{\mathcal{I}}$ do the following:
  1. Compute the receiver message of TDGen: $\mathsf{td}_2^{i \rightarrow j} \leftarrow \mathsf{TDGen}_2(\mathsf{td}_{1,j})$.
  2. Compute the receiver message of the non-malleable commitment scheme $\mathsf{NMCom}_2^{j \rightarrow i} \leftarrow \mathsf{NMCom}_2(\mathsf{nmc}_1^{j \rightarrow i})$.
- Broadcast $\{\mathsf{NMCom}_1^{j \rightarrow i}, \mathsf{td}_2^{i \rightarrow j}\}_{j \in [n] \setminus \{i\}}, \mathsf{msg}_{2,i}$.
- Upon receiving the second round from $\mathcal{A}$, for each $i \in \mathcal{I}$ forward $\mathsf{msg}_{2,i}$ to the right interface and continue as follows.

Round 3.

- Upon receiving the message $\mathsf{msg}_{3,i}$ from the right session where $i \in \overline{\mathcal{I}}$ do the following:
  1. Compute the third round of TDGen: set $\mathsf{td}_{2,i} = \mathsf{td}_2^{1 \rightarrow i} || \ldots || \mathsf{td}_2^{n \rightarrow i}$ where $\mathsf{td}_2^{i \rightarrow i} = \bot$ and compute $\mathsf{td}_{3,i} \leftarrow \mathsf{TDGen}_3(\mathsf{td}_{2,i})$
     For every $j \neq i$:
     (a) Compute the third round of NMCom: $\mathsf{NMCom}_3^{i \rightarrow j} \leftarrow \mathsf{NMCom}_3(\mathsf{nmc}_2^{i \rightarrow j}, \tilde{r}^{i \rightarrow j}; R_{\mathsf{NMCom}}^{i \rightarrow j})$.
     (b) Compute the first round of RWI: $\mathsf{zap}_1^{j \rightarrow i} \leftarrow \{0,1\}^{\lambda}$.
  2. Broadcast $\{\mathsf{NMCom}_3^{i \rightarrow j}, \mathsf{zap}_1^{j \rightarrow i}\}_{j \in [n] \setminus \{i\}}, \mathsf{td}_{3,i}, \mathsf{msg}_{3,i}$

Upon receiving the third round from $\mathcal{A}$, for each $i \in \mathcal{I}$ do the following.

Check abort. On the behalf of the honest party P_i do the following: If $\exists j \neq i$ such that $\mathsf{TDValid}(\mathsf{td}_{1,j}, \mathsf{td}_{2,j}, \mathsf{td}_{3,j}) \neq 1$ then let j be the smallest of such indexes, send (abort, j) to the ideal functionality and output the view generated so far and stop. Else for each $i \in \overline{\mathcal{I}}$ do the following:

Check if the trapdoor has been already extracted. Send $\mathsf{get\_trap}$ to the right interface. If the reply received from the right interface is $0^{2\lambda}$ then go to **Rewinds**. Else, if the reply is $\{\mathsf{trap}_j\}_{j \in \mathcal{I}}$ such that for each $j \in \mathcal{I}$ $\mathsf{TDValid}(\mathsf{trap}_j, \mathsf{td}_j) = 1$ then send $\{\mathsf{msg}_{3,i}\}_{i \in \mathcal{I}}$ to the right interface, and upon receiving the message $\mathsf{msg}_{4,i}$ for all $i \in \overline{\mathcal{I}}$ from the right interface go to **Round 4**.

Fig. 4. $\mathcal{M}(\rho_{\mathcal{A}}, \rho)$

Rewinds.

1. Rewind $\mathcal{A}$ to the end of round 1 and freeze the main thread at this point. Then, create a set of T (to be determined later) rewinding threads, where on each thread, only rounds 2 and 3 of the protocol are executed using fresh randomness for each primitive.

2. For each look-ahead thread, define a thread to be GOOD with respect to P_i if for all malicious parties P_j
   - P_j does send its third round messages.
   - $\mathsf{TDValid}(\mathsf{td}_{1,j}, \mathsf{td}_{2,j}, \mathsf{td}_{3,j}) = 1$ where $\mathsf{td}_{2,j}$ is as computed in round 3.

3. The number of threads T created is such that at least 3 GOOD threads exist.

Trapdoor extraction.

1. For every corrupted party P_j , extract a trapdoor trap_j by running the trapdoor extractor TDExt using the transcript of the trapdoor generation protocol with P_j playing the role of the trapdoor generator from any 3 GOOD threads. Specifically, compute $\mathsf{trap}_j \leftarrow \mathsf{TDExt}(\mathsf{td}_1, \{\mathsf{td}_2^k, \mathsf{td}_3^k\}_{k=1}^3)$ where $(\mathsf{td}_1, \mathsf{td}_2^k, \mathsf{td}_3^k)$ denotes the transcript of the trapdoor generation protocol with P_j as the sender of the k-th GOOD thread.

2. Send $(\mathsf{set\_trap}, \{\mathsf{trap}_j\}_{j\in\mathcal{I}})$ to the right interface.

3. Go back to the pre-rewinds thread, send $\{\mathsf{msg}_{3,i}\}_{i\in\mathcal{I}}$ to the right interface. Upon receiving the message $\mathsf{msg}_{4,i}$ from the right interface for all $i \in \overline{\mathcal{I}}$ continue as follows

Round 4. For all $i \in \overline{\mathcal{I}}$

4. Set $r^{i\to j} \leftarrow \mathsf{trap}_j \oplus \tilde{r}^{i\to j}$

5. Compute RWI:
   Define $\mathsf{st} := \left(\overline{\mathsf{msg}}^{<5}, \{\mathsf{msg}_{\ell,i}\}_{\ell\in[4]}, \{\mathsf{nmc}_\ell^{i\to j}\}_{\ell\in[3]}, \mathsf{td}_{1,i}, r^{i\to j}\right)$ and
   $\mathsf{w} := \left(\bot, \bot, \tilde{r}^{i\to j}, R_{\mathsf{NMCom}}^{i\to j}\right)$ and compute $\mathsf{zap}_2^{i\to j} \leftarrow \mathcal{P}(\mathsf{st}, \mathsf{w}, \mathsf{zap}_1^{i\to j})$.

End of the simulation For all $i \in \overline{\mathcal{I}}$

1. If $\exists j \neq i$ and k, s.t. $\mathcal{V}(\mathsf{st}, \mathsf{zap}_2^{j\to k}, \mathsf{zap}_1^{j\to k}, \mathsf{st}) = 0$ where $\mathsf{st} := \left(\overline{\mathsf{msg}}^{<5}, \{\mathsf{msg}_{\ell,j}\}_{\ell\in[4]}, \{\mathsf{nmc}_\ell^{j\to k}\}_{\ell\in[3]}, \mathsf{td}_{1,k}, r^{j\to k}\right)$, let j be the smallest of such indexes such that this holds, then send (abort, j) to the ideal functionality and output the view generated so far.

Fig. 4. (*continued*)

Theorem 5.1. *Assuming the existence of a public-coin perfectly correct trapdoor generation protocol, a perfectly correct 3-round special non-malleable commitment, a perfectly correct 4-round MPC protocol that is three-rewindable secure with abort against dishonest majority in the plain model, a perfectly correct 2-*

- Start $\mathcal{S}$ using randomness of appropriate length and initialize trap $= 0^{2\lambda}$.
- Forward any query made by $\mathcal{S}$ directed to the adversarial interface to the right interface of $\mathcal{M}$.
- Upon receiving a query from $\mathcal{S}$ directed to the ideal functionality forward the query to it.
- Upon receiving (set_trap, y) from $\mathcal{M}$ set trap $\leftarrow y$.
- Upon receiving the command get_trap from $\mathcal{M}$ send trap to the right interface of $\mathcal{M}$.
- Upon receiving the command (abort, j) from $\mathcal{M}$ forward it to the ideal functionality.
- Upon receiving the messages $\{\mathsf{msg}_{k,i}\}_{i \in \mathcal{I}}$ from the right interface of $\mathcal{M}$, rewind $\mathcal{S}$ up to the k-th round and forward $\{\mathsf{msg}_{k,i}\}_{i \in \mathcal{I}}$ to $\mathcal{S}$.[a]
- Whenever $\mathcal{S}$ stops, stop and output whatever $\mathcal{S}$ outputs.

---

[a] Note that $\mathcal{S}$ has full control of $\Pi.\mathcal{S}$, hence it can rewind $\Pi.\mathcal{S}$ at its will. In the security proof such rewinds need to be handled with some care as we will show in the formal proof.

Fig. 5. $\mathcal{S}$

round public-coin WI proof, then Π^{ID} is a four-round MPC secure protocol with identifiable abort against dishonest majority in the plain model.

The above construction Π^{ID} can be built based on trapdoor permutations (we refer to the full version for details on the instantiations of each of the building blocks).

To describe the simulation, we denote the set that contains the indices of all the corrupted parties as $\mathcal{I}$. Before describing how our simulator $\mathcal{S}$ works, we define an algorithm $\mathcal{M}$ that we refer to as the *augmented machine*. The augmented machine internally runs the adversary $\mathcal{A}$ (we refer to this as the *left interface*), and acts as a proxy between $\mathcal{A}$ and its external interface (which we denote as the *right interface*) with respect to the messages of Π. At a high level, $\mathcal{M}$ filters the messages of Π that will be forwarded to the simulator of Π denoted by $\Pi.\mathcal{S}$, and forwards the replies received from $\Pi.\mathcal{S}$ to $\mathcal{A}$. The way in which $\mathcal{M}$ and $\Pi.\mathcal{S}$ interact with each other is regulated by our simulator $\mathcal{S}$, that internally runs (and has full control of) $\mathcal{M}$ and $\Pi.\mathcal{S}$.

The reason why we describe our simulator via the augmented machine $\mathcal{M}$ is to deal with the rewinds that the simulator of Π might do. We refer to Fig. 4 and Fig. 5 for the formal description of $\mathcal{M}$ and $\mathcal{S}$ respectively.

The indistinguishability proof of Theorem 5.1 can be found in the full version.

6   Special B_{OT}-Rewindable Secure Oblivious Transfer

Now, we present a modified version of the compiler of Choudhuri et al. [10] that achieves our new notion of special B_{OT}-rewindable security and sender simulatability. The compiler makes use of the following tools:

Private Inputs. The sender uses as its private input two lists (L_0, L_1), where each list consists of l bit strings of length λ, i.e. $L_b = \{y_{i,b}\}_{i \in [l]}$ and $y_{i,b} \in \{0,1\}^\lambda$. The receiver uses as its private input a vector $\boldsymbol{x}$ that consists of l bits, i.e. $\boldsymbol{x} = (x_1, \ldots, x_l)$.

Output. The receiver obtains the values $\{y_{i,x_i}\}_{i \in [l]}$.

Round 1. (Receiver)

1. Compute the first round message of all the OTs, i.e. for all $i \in [n], k \in [B_{OT}]$, $\mathsf{ot}_1^{i,k} \leftarrow \mathsf{OT}_1(1^\lambda, r_{i,k}^1)$. We refer to index i as the outer index and k as the inner index.
2. Output $\{\mathsf{ot}_1^{i,k}\}_{i \in [n], k \in [B_{OT}]}$ to the sender.

Round 2. (Sender)

1. Compute the second round message of all the OTs, i.e. for all $i \in [n], k \in [B_{OT}], \mathsf{ot}_2^{i,k} \leftarrow \mathsf{OT}_1'(\mathsf{ot}_1^{i,k}; r_{i,k}^2)$.
2. Output $\{\mathsf{ot}_2^{i,k}\}_{i \in [n], k \in [B_{OT}]}$ to the receiver.

Round 3. (Receiver)

1. Encode the input $\boldsymbol{x}$ using n additive shares, i.e. sample $\boldsymbol{b}_j \leftarrow \{0,1\}^l$ for all $j \in [n-1]$ and compute $\boldsymbol{b}_n := \bigoplus_{j=1}^{n-1} \boldsymbol{b}_j$.
2. Select one of the OT' instances for all of the outer indexes i, i.e. sample $\sigma_i \leftarrow [B_{OT}]$ for all $i \in [n]$.
3. Use the input $\boldsymbol{b}_i$ to compute $\mathsf{ot}_3^{i,\sigma_i} \leftarrow \mathsf{OT}_3'(\boldsymbol{b}_i, \{\mathsf{ot}_j^{i,\sigma_i}\}_{j \in [2]}; r_i^3)$. The other OTs are discontinued.
4. Output $\{\mathsf{ot}_3^{i,\sigma_i}\}_{i \in [n]}$ to the sender.

Round 4. (Sender)

1. Compute the garbled circuit $(\mathsf{GC}, \{K_{i,b}\}_{i \in [n], b \in \{0,1\}}) := \mathsf{garble}(\mathsf{C}_{OT}[\{y_{i,0}\}_{i \in [l]}, \{y_{i,1}\}_{i \in [l]}])$, where the circuit $\mathsf{C}_{OT}[\{y_{i,0}\}_{i \in [l]}, \{y_{i,1}\}_{i \in [l]}]$ on input $\boldsymbol{x}_1, \ldots, \boldsymbol{x}_l$ outputs $\{y_{i,x_i}\}_{i \in [l]}$ with $\boldsymbol{x} = (\boldsymbol{x}_1, \ldots, \boldsymbol{x}_l) := \bigoplus_{i=1}^n \boldsymbol{b}_i$.
2. For all $i \in [n]$, compute $\mathsf{ot}_4^{i,\sigma_i} \leftarrow \mathsf{OT}_4'(\{K_{i,b}\}_{b \in \{0,1\}}, \{\mathsf{ot}_j^{i,\sigma_i}\}_{j \in [3]}; r_i^4)$
3. Output $\{\mathsf{ot}_4^{i,\sigma_i}\}_{i \in [n]}$ and GC to the receiver.

Round 5. (Receiver)

1. Output $(r_{\sigma_i,i}^1, r_i^3)_{i \in [n]}$ to the sender.

Output Computation. (Receiver)

1. For all $i \in [n]$, compute $\widetilde{K}_i := \mathsf{OT}_5'(\boldsymbol{b}_i, \{\mathsf{ot}_j^{i,\sigma_i}\}_{j \in [4]})$.
2. Output $\{y_i'\}_{i \in [l]} := \mathsf{eval}(\mathsf{GC}, \{\widetilde{K}_i\}_{i \in [n]})$.

Fig. 6. B_{OT}-rewindable Compiler OT

- A delayed-input oblivious transfer protocol $\mathsf{OT}' = (\mathsf{OT}'_1, \mathsf{OT}'_2, \mathsf{OT}'_3, \mathsf{OT}'_4, \mathsf{OT}'_5)$ with the following properties: one-sided simulation security, and 2-extractability. In the full version we recall the oblivious transfer protocol of [34] and observe that it has the desired properties.
- A garbled circuit (garble, eval, simGC) that is assumed to satisfy privacy, perfect correctness, authenticity of input labels and partial evaluation resiliency.

Theorem 6.1. *Assuming the existence of a delayed-input oblivious transfer protocol that satisfies one-sided simulation security, and 2-extractability, and a garbled circuit that satisfies privacy, perfect correctness, authenticity of input labels and partial evaluation resiliency, then the OT (described above) is an oblivious transfer protocol with special B_{OT}-rewindableand sender simulatability.*

The above construction can be built based on trapdoor permutations (we refer to the full version for details on the instantiations of each of the building blocks). In the remainder of this section we argue informally about sender simulatability, the proof can be found in the full version.

Sender Simulatability for Parallel Executions of OT. Our construction of B-rewindable secure MPC Π_{rmpc} in Sect. 4 uses the OT defined in this section as a building block. It is crucial for proving the security of Π_{rmpc} that it is possible to extract from all the malicious receivers at the same time. In more detail, the simulator $\mathcal{S}_{\mathsf{OT}}$ of OT proceeds to the extraction via rewinds (i.e. sending to the adversary a 2nd round of OT computed with new randomness), therefore the simulator of the OT should be able to extract the inputs of malicious receivers in the same rewinding thread for multiple OT instances that are executed in parallel. We refer to this property informally as *simultaneous extractability*. We therefore define $\mathcal{S}_{\mathsf{OT}}$ when multiple, say m^2, executions of the protocol OT of Fig. 6 are executed in parallel, with a single execution corresponding to each pair of parties, where m denotes the number of parties. Let us indicate with OT' the underlying OT protocol that is used in Fig. 6. We discuss now the high-level overview of $\mathcal{S}_{\mathsf{OT}}$. Recall that in the rewind-secure OT construction of Fig. 6, the OT receiver chooses a set of indices among the underlying OT' instances that it wishes to continue. However, the adversary acting on behalf of the OT receiver can choose to reveal a different set of indices across different rewinds of the simulator. Note that, to extract the receiver's input used in an instance of OT', the simulator requires two transcripts where the receiver chooses the same index. Therefore, in order to extract the input of malicious receivers across multiple OT instances in the same rewind thread, it is crucial that the indices for all the OT instances have appeared at least once previously in the rewind thread in which we are able to extract. Based on the above, the natural simulation strategy would be to continue rewinds until the above condition occurs i.e. until there occurs a rewinding thread such that the indices for all the OT instances have appeared at least once previously (we refer to this as a collision). It is important to notice that if in a rewinding thread a collision does not appear, then $\mathcal{S}_{\mathsf{OT}}$ obtains a transcript with a new index. Therefore, it is sufficient for $\mathcal{S}_{\mathsf{OT}}$ to rewind until it finds a collision. Unfortunately, simulation based on the above natural halting condition suffers from the following issue: if the simulator stops the first time it sees a transcript having the set of indices seen earlier, then the distribution of the transcripts output by the simulator is biased towards more frequently appearing indices that appeared in earlier rewinds. Therefore, the simulated view is not indistinguishable from the real view of the adversary. A similar issue was observed in the zero-knowledge protocol of [30], where the authors proposed a new halting condition of the simulator to maintain the indistinguishability of the views. We adopt their solution in the design of our simulation strategy. In more detail, for a better understanding, we elaborate on the issue of [30] and describe how their scenario is analogous to us. The authors of [30] consider N parallel instances of the following four-round ZK protocol: the verifier commits to a challenge in the 1st round and opens it in the 3rd round. In the 4th round the prover answers to the challenge. In particular, the verifier chooses t among the N instances for which it opens the challenge. The prover, in round 4, finishes the ZK protocol for the revealed challenges. The simulator S on behalf of the honest prover should be able to cheat w.r.t. all the indices (of the instances) opened by the verifier. In order to do that S rewinds the malicious verifier V^*, and succeeds if each of the t indices opened by V^* has appeared in at least one of the earlier rewinds (a collision occurs). Note that V^* can choose different indices during different rewinds. However, when S fails to cheat it learns at least one new index that did not occur in any of the previous rewinds. In [30] it is pointed out that if S stops as soon as it can simulate successfully, then the simulated view could be distinguishable from the real world view of V^* due to the same reasons explained above (in the context of OT). It is easy to see that $\mathcal{S}_{\mathsf{OT}}$ could collect the indices in the same way as S. It remains to argue that the strategies with which the malicious receiver can open the OT' indices are a subset of the one that V^* can perform. Consider an execution of OT where the malicious receiver opens n indices $k_1, \ldots, k_n$ as opposed to t indices $i_1, \ldots, i_t$ given by V^*. It easy to see that N of [30] corresponds to nB in our case. For simplicity, let us assume that the underlying OT' instances are labeled $\{1, \ldots, nB\}$, then each k_j has a value only in $\{(j-1) \cdot B + 1, \ldots, j \cdot B\}$, with $j \in [n]$. Therefore, this corresponds to a strategy of V^* where for each i_j, V^* chooses value only in $\{j - 1 \cdot (\frac{N}{t}) + 1, \ldots, j \cdot \frac{N}{t}\}$, with $j \in [t]$.

Acknowledgements. We are grateful to Maciej Obremski, our tall lighthouse who illuminated our path toward proving the complexity of our simulators.

References

1. Ananth, P., Choudhuri, A.R., Goel, A., Jain, A.: Two round information-theoretic MPC with malicious security. In: Ishai, Y., Rijmen, V. (eds.) EUROCRYPT 2019. LNCS, vol. 11477, pp. 532–561. Springer, Cham (2019). https://doi.org/10.1007/978-3-030-17656-3_19
2. Ananth, P., Choudhuri, A.R., Jain, A.: A new approach to round-optimal secure multiparty computation. In: Katz, J., Shacham, H. (eds.) CRYPTO 2017. LNCS, vol. 10401, pp. 468–499. Springer, Cham (2017). https://doi.org/10.1007/978-3-319-63688-7_16

3. Aumann, Y., Lindell, Y.: Security against covert adversaries: efficient protocols for realistic adversaries. J. Cryptol. **23**(2), 281–343 (2009). https://doi.org/10.1007/s00145-009-9040-7

4. Badrinarayanan, S., Goyal, V., Jain, A., Kalai, Y.T., Khurana, D., Sahai, A.: Promise zero knowledge and its applications to round optimal MPC. In: Shacham, H., Boldyreva, A. (eds.) CRYPTO 2018. LNCS, vol. 10992, pp. 459–487. Springer, Cham (2018). https://doi.org/10.1007/978-3-319-96881-0_16

5. Baum, C., Orsini, E., Scholl, P., Soria-Vazquez, E.: Efficient constant-round MPC with identifiable abort and public verifiability. In: Micciancio, D., Ristenpart, T. (eds.) CRYPTO 2020. LNCS, vol. 12171, pp. 562–592. Springer, Cham (2020). https://doi.org/10.1007/978-3-030-56880-1_20

6. Beaver, D., Micali, S., Rogaway, P.: The round complexity of secure protocols (extended abstract). In: 22nd ACM STOC, pp. 503–513. ACM Press, May 1990. https://doi.org/10.1145/100216.100287

7. Brakerski, Z., Halevi, S., Polychroniadou, A.: Four round secure computation without setup. In: Kalai, Y., Reyzin, L. (eds.) TCC 2017. LNCS, vol. 10677, pp. 645–677. Springer, Cham (2017). https://doi.org/10.1007/978-3-319-70500-2_22

8. Brandt, N.: Tight setup bounds for identifiable abort. Cryptology ePrint Archive, Report 2021/684 (2021). https://eprint.iacr.org/2021/684

9. Brandt, N.P., Maier, S., Müller, T., Müller-Quade, J.: Constructing secure multiparty computation with identifiable abort. Cryptology ePrint Archive, Report 2020/153 (2020). https://eprint.iacr.org/2020/153

10. Rai Choudhuri, A., Ciampi, M., Goyal, V., Jain, A., Ostrovsky, R.: Round optimal secure multiparty computation from minimal assumptions. In: Pass, R., Pietrzak, K. (eds.) TCC 2020. LNCS, vol. 12551, pp. 291–319. Springer, Cham (2020). https://doi.org/10.1007/978-3-030-64378-2_11

11. Ciampi, M., Ostrovsky, R., Siniscalchi, L., Visconti, I.: Delayed-input non-malleable zero knowledge and multi-party coin tossing in four rounds. In: Kalai, Y., Reyzin, L. (eds.) TCC 2017. LNCS, vol. 10677, pp. 711–742. Springer, Cham (2017). https://doi.org/10.1007/978-3-319-70500-2_24

12. Ciampi, M., Ostrovsky, R., Siniscalchi, L., Visconti, I.: Round-optimal secure two-party computation from trapdoor permutations. In: Kalai, Y., Reyzin, L. (eds.) TCC 2017. LNCS, vol. 10677, pp. 678–710. Springer, Cham (2017). https://doi.org/10.1007/978-3-319-70500-2_23

13. Cleve, R.: Limits on the security of coin flips when half the processors are faulty (extended abstract). In: 18th ACM STOC, pp. 364–369. ACM Press, May 1986. https://doi.org/10.1145/12130.12168

14. Cohen, R., Garay, J., Zikas, V.: Broadcast-optimal two-round MPC. In: Canteaut, A., Ishai, Y. (eds.) EUROCRYPT 2020. LNCS, vol. 12106, pp. 828–858. Springer, Cham (2020). https://doi.org/10.1007/978-3-030-45724-2_28

15. Cohen, R., Lindell, Y.: Fairness versus guaranteed output delivery in secure multiparty computation. In: Sarkar, P., Iwata, T. (eds.) ASIACRYPT 2014. LNCS, vol. 8874, pp. 466–485. Springer, Heidelberg (2014). https://doi.org/10.1007/978-3-662-45608-8_25

16. Cunningham, R.K., Fuller, B., Yakoubov, S.: Catching MPC cheaters: identification and openability. In: Shikata, J. (ed.) ICITS 17. LNCS, vol. 10681, pp. 110–134. Springer, Heidelberg (2017)

17. Damgård, I., Keller, M., Larraia, E., Pastro, V., Scholl, P., Smart, N.P.: Practical covertly secure MPC for dishonest majority – or: breaking the SPDZ limits. In: Crampton, J., Jajodia, S., Mayes, K. (eds.) ESORICS 2013. LNCS, vol. 8134, pp. 1–18. Springer, Heidelberg (2013). https://doi.org/10.1007/978-3-642-40203-6_1

18. Damgård, I., Magri, B., Ravi, D., Siniscalchi, L., Yakoubov, S.: Broadcast-optimal two round MPC with an honest majority. In: Malkin, T., Peikert, C. (eds.) CRYPTO 2021. LNCS, vol. 12826, pp. 155–184. Springer, Cham (2021). https://doi.org/10.1007/978-3-030-84245-1_6
19. Damgård, I., Pastro, V., Smart, N., Zakarias, S.: Multiparty computation from somewhat homomorphic encryption. In: Safavi-Naini, R., Canetti, R. (eds.) CRYPTO 2012. LNCS, vol. 7417, pp. 643–662. Springer, Heidelberg (2012). https://doi.org/10.1007/978-3-642-32009-5_38
20. Dolev, D., Dwork, C., Naor, M.: Non-malleable cryptography (extended abstract). In: 23rd ACM STOC, pp. 542–552. ACM Press. May 1991. https://doi.org/10.1145/103418.103474
21. Dwork, C., Naor, M.: Zaps and their applications. In: 41st FOCS, pp. 283–293. IEEE Computer Society Press, November 2000. https://doi.org/10.1109/SFCS.2000.892117
22. Garg, S., Mukherjee, P., Pandey, O., Polychroniadou, A.: The exact round complexity of secure computation. In: Fischlin, M., Coron, J.-S. (eds.) EUROCRYPT 2016. LNCS, vol. 9666, pp. 448–476. Springer, Heidelberg (2016). https://doi.org/10.1007/978-3-662-49896-5_16
23. Garg, S., Sahai, A.: Adaptively secure multi-party computation with dishonest majority. In: Safavi-Naini, R., Canetti, R. (eds.) CRYPTO 2012. LNCS, vol. 7417, pp. 105–123. Springer, Heidelberg (2012). https://doi.org/10.1007/978-3-642-32009-5_8
24. Goldreich, O., Krawczyk, H.: On the composition of zero-knowledge proof systems. SIAM J. Comput. 25(1), 169–192 (1996)
25. Goldreich, O., Micali, S., Wigderson, A.: How to play any mental game or A completeness theorem for protocols with honest majority. In: Aho, A. (ed.) 19th ACM STOC. pp. 218–229. ACM Press, May 1987. https://doi.org/10.1145/28395.28420
26. Goyal, V.: Constant round non-malleable protocols using one way functions. In: Fortnow, L., Vadhan, S.P. (eds.) 43rd ACM STOC, pp. 695–704. ACM Press, June 2011. https://doi.org/10.1145/1993636.1993729
27. Goyal, V., Pandey, O., Richelson, S.: Textbook non-malleable commitments. In: Wichs, D., Mansour, Y. (eds.) 48th ACM STOC. pp. 1128–1141. ACM Press (Jun 2016), https://doi.org/10.1145/2897518.2897657
28. Goyal, V., Richelson, S., Rosen, A., Vald, M.: An algebraic approach to non-malleability. In: 55th FOCS, pp. 41–50. IEEE Computer Society Press, October 2014. https://doi.org/10.1109/FOCS.2014.13
29. Halevi, S., Hazay, C., Polychroniadou, A., Venkitasubramaniam, M.: Round-optimal secure multi-party computation. In: Shacham, H., Boldyreva, A. (eds.) CRYPTO 2018. LNCS, vol. 10992, pp. 488–520. Springer, Cham (2018). https://doi.org/10.1007/978-3-319-96881-0_17
30. Hazay, C., Venkitasubramaniam, M.: Round-optimal fully black-box zero-knowledge arguments from one-way permutations. In: Beimel, A., Dziembowski, S. (eds.) TCC 2018. LNCS, vol. 11239, pp. 263–285. Springer, Cham (2018). https://doi.org/10.1007/978-3-030-03807-6_10
31. Ishai, Y., Ostrovsky, R., Seyalioglu, H.: Identifying cheaters without an honest majority. In: Cramer, R. (ed.) TCC 2012. LNCS, vol. 7194, pp. 21–38. Springer, Heidelberg (2012). https://doi.org/10.1007/978-3-642-28914-9_2

32. Ishai, Y., Ostrovsky, R., Zikas, V.: Secure multi-party computation with identifiable abort. In: Garay, J.A., Gennaro, R. (eds.) CRYPTO 2014. LNCS, vol. 8617, pp. 369–386. Springer, Heidelberg (2014). https://doi.org/10.1007/978-3-662-44381-1_21

33. Ishai, Y., Prabhakaran, M., Sahai, A.: Founding cryptography on oblivious transfer – efficiently. In: Wagner, D. (ed.) CRYPTO 2008. LNCS, vol. 5157, pp. 572–591. Springer, Heidelberg (2008). https://doi.org/10.1007/978-3-540-85174-5_32

34. Katz, J., Ostrovsky, R.: Round-optimal secure two-party computation. In: Franklin, M. (ed.) CRYPTO 2004. LNCS, vol. 3152, pp. 335–354. Springer, Heidelberg (2004). https://doi.org/10.1007/978-3-540-28628-8_21

35. Katz, J., Ostrovsky, R., Smith, A.: Round efficiency of multi-party computation with a dishonest majority. In: Biham, E. (ed.) EUROCRYPT 2003. LNCS, vol. 2656, pp. 578–595. Springer, Heidelberg (2003). https://doi.org/10.1007/3-540-39200-9_36

36. Khurana, D.: Round optimal concurrent non-malleability from polynomial hardness. In: Kalai, Y., Reyzin, L. (eds.) TCC 2017. LNCS, vol. 10678, pp. 139–171. Springer, Cham (2017). https://doi.org/10.1007/978-3-319-70503-3_5

37. Kilian, J.: Founding cryptography on oblivious transfer. In: 20th ACM STOC, pp. 20–31. ACM Press, May 1988. https://doi.org/10.1145/62212.62215

38. Lin, H., Pass, R., Venkitasubramaniam, M.: Concurrent non-malleable commitments from any one-way function. In: Canetti, R. (ed.) TCC 2008. LNCS, vol. 4948, pp. 571–588. Springer, Heidelberg (2008). https://doi.org/10.1007/978-3-540-78524-8_31

39. Pass, R.: Bounded-concurrent secure multi-party computation with a dishonest majority. In: Babai, L. (ed.) 36th ACM STOC, pp. 232–241. ACM Press, Jun 2004. https://doi.org/10.1145/1007352.1007393

40. Pass, R., Rosen, A.: Concurrent non-malleable commitments. In: 46th FOCS, pp. 563–572. IEEE Computer Society Press, October 2005. https://doi.org/10.1109/SFCS.2005.27

41. Pass, R., Wee, H.: Constant-round non-malleable commitments from subexponential one-way functions. In: Gilbert, H. (ed.) EUROCRYPT 2010. LNCS, vol. 6110, pp. 638–655. Springer, Heidelberg (2010). https://doi.org/10.1007/978-3-642-13190-5_32

42. Scholl, P., Simkin, M., Siniscalchi, L.: Multiparty computation with covert security and public verifiability. Cryptology ePrint Archive, Report 2021/366 (2021). https://eprint.iacr.org/2021/366

43. Simkin, M., Siniscalchi, L., Yakoubov, S.: On sufficient oracles for secure computation with identifiable abort. Cryptology ePrint Archive, Report 2021/151 (2021). https://eprint.iacr.org/2021/151

44. Spini, G., Fehr, S.: Cheater detection in SPDZ multiparty computation. In: Nascimento, A.C.A., Barreto, P. (eds.) ICITS 2016. LNCS, vol. 10015, pp. 151–176. Springer, Cham (2016). https://doi.org/10.1007/978-3-319-49175-2_8

45. Wee, H.: Black-box, round-efficient secure computation via non-malleability amplification. In: 51st FOCS, pp. 531–540. IEEE Computer Society Press, October 2010. https://doi.org/10.1109/FOCS.2010.87

46. Yao, A.C.C.: How to generate and exchange secrets (extended abstract). In: 27th FOCS, pp. 162–167. IEEE Computer Society Press, October 1986. https://doi.org/10.1109/SFCS.1986.25

On the Security of ECDSA with Additive Key Derivation and Presignatures

Jens Groth and Victor Shoup$^{(\boxtimes)}$

DFINITY, Zurich, Switzerland
{jens,victor.shoup}@dfinity.org

Abstract. Two common variations of ECDSA signatures are *additive key derivation* and *presignatures*. Additive key derivation is a simple mechanism for deriving many subkeys from a single master key, and is already widely used in cryptocurrency applications with the Hierarchical Deterministic Wallet mechanism standardized in Bitcoin Improvement Proposal 32 (BIP32). Because of its linear nature, additive key derivation is also amenable to efficient implementation in the threshold setting. With presignatures, the secret and public nonces used in the ECDSA signing algorithm are precomputed. In the threshold setting, using presignatures along with other precomputed data allows for an extremely efficient "online phase" of the protocol. Recent works have advocated for both of these variations, sometimes combined together. However, somewhat surprisingly, we are aware of no prior security proof for additive key derivation, let alone for additive key derivation in combination with presignatures.

In this paper, we provide a thorough analysis of these variations, both in isolation and in combination. Our analysis is in the generic group model (GGM). Importantly, we do not modify ECDSA or weaken the standard notion of security in any way. Of independent interest, we also present a version of the GGM that is specific to elliptic curves. This EC-GGM better models some of the idiosyncrasies (such as the conversion function and malleability) of ECDSA. In addition to this analysis, we report security weaknesses in these variations that apparently have not been previously reported. For example, we show that when both variations are combined, there is a cube-root attack on ECDSA, which is much faster than the best known, square-root attack on plain ECDSA. We also present two mitigations against these weaknesses: re-randomized presignatures and homogeneous key derivation. Each of these mitigations is very lightweight, and when used in combination, the security is essentially the same as that of plain ECDSA (in the EC-GGM).

1 Introduction

Let us recall the basic ECDSA signature scheme [17]. Let E be an elliptic curve defined over $\mathbb{Z}_p$ and generated by a point $\mathcal{G}$ of prime order q, and let E^* be the set of points (x, y) on the curve excluding the point at infinity $\mathcal{O}$. The **unreduced conversion function** $C : E^* \rightarrow \mathbb{Z}_p$ maps a point $\mathcal{P}$ to its x-coordinate. The

© International Association for Cryptologic Research 2022
O. Dunkelman and S. Dziembowski (Eds.): EUROCRYPT 2022, LNCS 13275, pp. 365–396, 2022.
https://doi.org/10.1007/978-3-031-06944-4_13

reduced conversion function $\bar{C} : E^* \to \mathbb{Z}_q$ maps a point $\mathcal{P}$ to the canonical representative of $C(\mathcal{P})$ (i.e., an integer in the range $[0, p)$) reduced mod q.

The secret key for ECDSA is a random $d \in \mathbb{Z}_q^*$, the public key is $\mathcal{D} = d\mathcal{G} \in E$. The scheme makes use of a hash function $Hash : \{0, 1\}^* \to \mathbb{Z}_q$. The signing and verification algorithms are shown in Fig. 1. The signing algorithm will *fail* with only negligible probability.

Sign message m:	Verify signature $(s, t) \in \mathbb{Z}_q^* \times \mathbb{Z}_q^*$ on m:
$h \leftarrow Hash(m) \in \mathbb{Z}_q$	$h \leftarrow Hash(m) \in \mathbb{Z}_q$
$r \xleftarrow{\$} \mathbb{Z}_q^*, \ \mathcal{R} \leftarrow r\mathcal{G} \in E, \ t \leftarrow \bar{C}(\mathcal{R}) \in \mathbb{Z}_q$	$\mathcal{R} \leftarrow s^{-1}h\mathcal{G} + s^{-1}t\mathcal{D}$
if $t = 0$ or $h + td = 0$ then return *fail*	check that $\mathcal{R} \neq \mathcal{O}$ and $\bar{C}(\mathcal{R}) = t$
$s \leftarrow r^{-1}(h + td)$	
return the signature (s, t)	

Fig. 1. ECDSA signing and verification algorithms

The security of ECDSA has only been analyzed in idealized models of computation. Specifically, Brown [4] showed that under standard intractability assumptions on *Hash* (collision resistance and random/zero preimage resistance), ECDSA is secure in the generic group model [14,16]. In addition, Fersch, Kiltz, and Pottering [10] have also showed that ECDSA is secure under somewhat different intractability assumptions on *Hash* if the conversion function is modeled as an idealized function (but one that captures some idiosyncrasies of the actual conversion function). In this paper, we will also analyze ECDSA and several variants in the generic group model. However, we shall work in a specific version of the generic group model that more accurately models some of the idiosyncrasies of elliptic curves and the corresponding conversion function. We call this the **elliptic curve generic group model (EC-GGM)**, which may be of independent interest. By working in this model, we overcome objections raised in [10] and elsewhere [18] that Brown's analysis was incomplete. For example, it was pointed out that Brown's analysis ruled out any malleability in the signature scheme, whereas ECDSA signatures are in fact malleable.

Several variations of ECDSA have been proposed, notably **additive key derivation** and **presignatures**. We are mainly interested in these variations because of the optimizations they enable in the threshold setting, where the signing functionality is implemented as a secure distributed protocol by parties that each hold a share of the secret key. However, these variations also enable optimizations in the single-signer setting as well.

Additive Key Derivation. With additive key derivation, the secret-key/public-key pair $(d, \mathcal{D})$ is viewed as a **master key pair** from which **subkey pairs** can be derived using a simple additive shift. Specifically, we can derive a secret subkey of the form $d + e$ by using a "tweak" $e \in \mathbb{Z}_q$. For such a derived secret subkey, we can compute the corresponding derived public subkey from the public key $\mathcal{D}$ as $\mathcal{D} + e\mathcal{G}$. In the context of cryptocurrency, this type of additive key derivation is used in so-called **Hierarchical Deterministic Wallets** using the Bitcoin Improvement Proposal 32 (BIP32) standard [20], which is a specific way of deriving a tweak e via a chain of hashes applied to the public key and other public data. Note that BIP32 also specifies so-called "hardened" subkeys, which derives subkeys using the secret key—we do not consider such "hardened" subkeys in this paper.

There is a cost to storing secret keys, and additive key derivation is useful in reducing that cost, since it allows several distinct public keys to be used while only having to store a single secret key. This secret-key storage cost manifests itself in both the threshold and non-threshold settings. In the non-threshold setting, there is the obvious cost of maintaining the secret key in some kind of secure storage. In the threshold setting, there is the cost of running the key generation algorithm and storing secret shares in some kind of secure storage. There may be additional costs in the threshold setting: for example, the cost of resharing the secret key periodically, both to provide proactive security and to allow for dynamic changes in the share-holder membership. Because of the linearity of the key derivation, implementing additive key derivation in the threshold setting comes at essentially no cost.

Unfortunately, and somewhat surprisingly, we are aware of no prior proofs of security for ECDSA with additive key derivation. While [21] purports to present such a proof (via a direct reduction to the security of ECDSA), their proof seems to be fundamentally flawed: their simulator apparently needs to "reprogram" a random oracle that has already been "programmed". The more recent work [8] analyzes additive key derivation with respect to a variant of ECDSA in which the derived public key is prepended to the message to be signed, and with a restricted attack model in which an attacker is only allowed to ask for one signature per message and derived public key.

Presignatures. In the signing algorithm, the values r and $\mathcal{R} := r\mathcal{G}$ are independent of the message to be signed (or the tweak), and so they can be precomputed in advance of an actual signing request. In the threshold setting, it is tempting to not only precompute a sharing of r, but to also to precompute $\mathcal{R}$ itself. This can greatly simplify the online signing phase of the protocol. Indeed, several papers, including [7] and [11] present protocols that use presignatures. Moreover, [7] advocates for the combination of presignatures and additive key derivation, even though the security of additive key derivation, let alone additive key derivation in combination with presignatures, has never been analyzed.

The paper [5] considers the security of presignatures (in isolation). They give an explicit definition and they briefly sketch a proof of security in the GGM with *Hash* also modeled as a random oracle (an earlier version of [5] had an incorrect security bound).

1.1   Our Contributions

Security Proofs. We carry out a careful and detailed security analysis of ECDSA and several variants, including ECDSA with additive key derivation, ECDSA with presignatures, and ECDSA with both additive key derivation and presignatures. This analysis is done in the generic group model (more precisely, the EC-GGM) under concrete assumptions for the hash function *Hash*. Importantly, we do not modify ECDSA or weaken the standard notion of security in any way. Unlike [5], we do not model *Hash* as a random oracle (and we give somewhat tighter security bounds). Our analysis carries over immediately to any threshold implementation of ECDSA whose security reduces to that of the non-threshold scheme (which is typically the case).

For additive key derivation, we mainly assume that the set $\mathfrak{E}$ of all valid tweaks is not too large and is determined in advance. In practice (such as with BIP32), tweaks are derived, via a hash, from identifiers (possibly combined with a "root" public key). This assumption on $\mathfrak{E}$ can be justified if the set of valid identifiers, and in particular, the set of identifiers with respect to which we are concerned about forgeries, is indeed small. It can also be further justified by modeling the hash function used to derive tweaks as a random oracle. That said, our analysis also works without this assumption, and we describe how our security results can be stated in terms of concrete security properties of the hash used to derive the tweaks—this is discussed in the full version [12]. We also provide an analysis of the BIP32 key derivation function in the full version [12], which justifies modeling it as a (public use) random oracle.

Attacks. While we are able to prove security results under reasonable assumptions for all of the variations listed above, in the course of our analysis, we discovered that the concrete security of some of these variants is substantially worse than plain ECDSA.

An Attack on ECDSA with Additive Key Derivation and Presignatures. For example, consider ECDSA with both additive key derivation and presignatures. Consider the following attack:

1. Make one presignature query to get the group element $\mathcal{R}$ and let $t := \bar{C}(\mathcal{R})$.
2. Find m, e, m^*, e^* such that $h + te = h^* + te^*$, where $e \neq e^*$ and $h := Hash(m)$ and $h^* := Hash(m^*)$
3. Ask for a signature (s, t) using this presignature on message m with tweak e.

Observe that (s, t) being a valid signature on m with respect to the tweak e means that

$$\mathcal{R} = s^{-1}h\mathcal{G} + s^{-1}t(\mathcal{D} + e\mathcal{G}) = s^{-1}(h + te)\mathcal{G} + s^{-1}t\mathcal{D} = s^{-1}(h^* + te^*)\mathcal{G} + s^{-1}t\mathcal{D},$$

which means that (s, t) is also a valid signature on m^* with respect to e^*.

Also observe that Step 2 above is essentially a 4-sum problem of the type studied by Wagner [19] and others [2,15]. Indeed, Wagner's algorithm allows us to implement Step 2 in time significantly less than $O(q^{1/2})$ if the set $\mathfrak{E}$ is sufficiently large. In particular, if $|\mathfrak{E}| = \Theta(q^{1/3})$, then we can solve this 4-sum problem and forge a signature in time roughly $O(q^{1/3})$. While not a polynomial-time attack, this is clearly a much more efficient attack than the best-known attack on plain ECDSA, which runs in time roughly $O(q^{1/2})$.

An Attack on ECDSA with Presignatures. Even with presignatures alone, ECDSA has potential security weaknesses that plain ECDSA does not. Consider the following attack:

1. Make one presignature query to get the group element $\mathcal{R}$ and let $t := \bar{C}(\mathcal{R})$.
2. Compute $\mathcal{R}^* \leftarrow c\mathcal{R}$ for some $c \in \mathbb{Z}_q^*$ and let $t^* := \bar{C}(\mathcal{R}^*)$.
3. Find m, m^* such that $h/t = h^*/t^*$, where $h := Hash(m)$ and $h^* := Hash(m^*)$ and $m \neq m^*$.
4. Ask for a signature (s, t) using the presignature $\mathcal{R}$ on message m.
5. Compute s^* satisfying $(s^*)^{-1}t^* = cs^{-1}t$, and output (s^*, t^*).

Observe that (s, t) being a valid signature on m means that $\mathcal{R} = s^{-1}h\mathcal{G} + s^{-1}t\mathcal{D}$. Moreover,

$$
\begin{aligned}
\mathcal{R}^* = cR = cs^{-1}h\mathcal{G} + cs^{-1}t\mathcal{D} &= cs^{-1}t(h/t)\mathcal{G} + cs^{-1}t\mathcal{D} \\
&= (s^*)^{-1}t^*(h/t)\mathcal{G} + (s^*)^{-1}t^*\mathcal{D} = (s^*)^{-1}t^*(h^*/t^*)\mathcal{G} + (s^*)^{-1}t^*\mathcal{D} \\
&= (s^*)^{-1}h^*\mathcal{G} + (s^*)^{-1}t^*\mathcal{D},
\end{aligned}
$$

which means that (s^*, t^*) is a valid signature on m^*.

To implement Step 3, for fixed t and t^*, there is no obvious way to find h, h^* satisfying $h/t = h^*/t^*$ in time faster than $O(q^{1/2})$. However, the inability to do so requires an assumption on *Hash* that is not needed for plain ECDSA. Moreover, it is clear that ECDSA with presignatures is *completely insecure* if we allow a "raw" signing oracle, i.e., a signing oracle that takes as input the purported hash h rather than the message m. There are settings where allowing such "raw" signing queries may be useful (e,g., in a remote signing service to avoid the cost of message transmission), and plain ECDSA is secure in the EC-GGM even with raw signing queries.

Note that one could extend the above attack so that the attack iterates Steps 3 and 4 for many values of c. This would give us an attack that is essentially a multiplicative variant of a 3-sum problem, for which there is no known algorithm that runs in time $O(q^{1-\epsilon})$ for any $\epsilon > 0$ [15]. However, this is again an attack vector that is not available for plain ECDSA.

Mitigations. In addition to the analysis and attacks above, we present several mitigations.

Re-randomized Presignatures. A presignature of the form $r' \in \mathbb{Z}_q$ and $\mathcal{R}' := r'\mathcal{G} \in E$ is computed as before. However, when a signing request is made, the actual presignature used is $r := r'+\delta$ and $\mathcal{R} := \mathcal{R}'+\delta\mathcal{G}$, where $\delta \in \mathbb{Z}_q$ is a public value that is pseudo-randomly generated at the time of the signing request (the key property is that δ is not predictable). This mitigation may be deployed both with and without additive key derivation.

We prove much stronger security results with this mitigation. Specifically, we prove a security result for re-randomized presignatures without additive key derivation that is essentially equivalent to the security result for plain ECDSA. With additive key derivation, the concrete security degrades by a factor of $|\mathfrak{E}|$, where $\mathfrak{E}$ is the set of valid tweaks, but the resulting scheme is no longer vulnerable to the 4-sum attack described above. Both with and without additive key derivation, we can also prove security even with respect to a raw signing oracle.

We are mainly interested in the use of re-randomized presignatures in the threshold setting. Since the re-randomization is linear, in terms of working with linear secret sharing, the impact is negligible (computing $(r'+\delta)^{-1}$ in the threshold setting is no harder than computing r^{-1}, assuming one is using standard techniques, such as [1]). However, the parties will still need access to a source of public randomness to generate δ. Accessing this public randomness may or may not introduce some extra latency, depending on details of the system. For example, in the Internet Computer (IC) [9], which motivated our work, there is already a mechanism for accessing public, unpredictable randomness via a "random tape" (which is implemented using a threshold BLS signature [3]). Moreover, in the IC architecture, when a subprotocol (such as a threshold ECDSA signing protocol) is launched, we can access this public randomness with no additional latency.

Instead of generating δ at the time of the signing request, as an alternative approach, one might also derive δ from a hash applied to (among other things) the public key, the (hash of) the message to be signed, and (if using additive key derivation) the tweak. This approach for re-randomizing presignatures comes at essentially no cost, either in terms of computation or latency. However, while it heuristically appears to offer more security than plain presignatures, and in particular foils the 4-sum attack described above, we have not formally analyzed the security of this approach.

Homogeneous Key Derivation. We also propose an alternative additive key derivation mechanism with better security properties. The master secret key now consists of a randomly chosen pair $(d, d') \in \mathbb{Z}_q \times \mathbb{Z}_q$. The corresponding master public key is $(\mathcal{D}, \mathcal{D}') := (d\mathcal{G}, d'\mathcal{G})$. Given a tweak $e \in \mathbb{Z}_q$, the derived secret key is $d + ed'$, and the derived public key is $\mathcal{D} + e\mathcal{D}'$.

Clearly, just as for additive key derivation, we can easily derive a public key from the master public key. Moreover, since key derivation is linear, implementing homogeneous key derivation in the threshold setting comes at very little cost. Compared to additive key derivation, the only downsides are (1) some small additional computational and communication complexities, and (2) the lack of compatibility with existing standards, such as BIP32.

One can combine homogeneous key derivation with either plain ECDSA, ECDSA with presignatures, and ECDSA with re-randomized presignatures. We give security proofs for all three of these variations. The upshot is that with homogeneous key derivation, for each variation, we get a security result for that variation *with* homogeneous key derivation that is essentially equivalent to that variation *without* key derivation. In particular, unlike with additive key derivation, our security results do not degrade linearly with $|\mathfrak{E}|$, where $\mathfrak{E}$ is the set of valid tweaks, and we do not need to insist that the set $\mathfrak{E}$ is determined in advance. In particular, we may just assume that the tweaks are derived by a collision resistant hash.

Table 1. Summary of concrete security theorems

	No presigs	Presigs	Re-randomized presigs
No derivation	$\mathcal{E}_{cr} + N\mathcal{E}_{rpr} + \mathcal{E}_{zpr} + N^2/q$	$\mathcal{E}_{cr} + UN\mathcal{E}_{rpr} + N\mathcal{E}_{rr} + \mathcal{E}_{zpr} + N^2/q$ ⊠	$\mathcal{E}_{cr} + N\mathcal{E}_{rpr} + \mathcal{E}_{zpr} + N^2/q$
Additive	$\mathcal{E}_{cr} + N|\mathfrak{E}|\mathcal{E}_{rpr} + \mathcal{E}_{zpr} + N^2/q$	$\mathcal{E}_{cr} + UN|\mathfrak{E}|\mathcal{E}_{rpr} + N_{psig}\mathcal{E}_{4sum1} + N\mathcal{E}_{4sum2} + \mathcal{E}_{zpr} + N^2/q$ ⊠	$\mathcal{E}_{cr} + N|\mathfrak{E}|\mathcal{E}_{rpr} + \mathcal{E}_{zpr} + N^2/q$
Homogeneous	$\mathcal{E}_{cr} + N\mathcal{E}_{rpr} + \mathcal{E}_{zpr} + N^2/q$	$\mathcal{E}_{cr} + UN\mathcal{E}_{rpr} + N\mathcal{E}_{rr} + \mathcal{E}_{zpr} + N^2/q$ ⊠	$\mathcal{E}_{cr} + N\mathcal{E}_{rpr} + \mathcal{E}_{zpr} + N^2/q$

Summary of Concrete Security Bounds. Table 1 summarizes our concrete security theorems. Each table entry gives an upper bound on an adversary's success in producing a forgery (ignoring small constants) in the EC-GCM (and in the PDF file, each table entry also contains a hyperlink to the actual theorem). These upper bounds are stated in terms of:

- q: the order of the group E;
- N: the number of oracle queries (group, signing, or presignature);
- N_{psig}: the number of presignature requests;
- U: the maximum number of *unused* presignature requests outstanding at any point in time;
- $|\mathfrak{E}|$: the size of the set of valid tweaks;
- $\mathcal{E}_{cr}$: the probability of successfully finding a collision in *Hash*;
- $\mathcal{E}_{rpr}$: the probability of successfully finding a preimage under *Hash* of a random element in $\mathbb{Z}_q$;
- $\mathcal{E}_{zpr}$: the probability of successfully finding a preimage under *Hash* of 0;
- $\mathcal{E}_{rr}$: the probability, given random $\rho \in \mathbb{Z}_q^*$, of finding m, m^* such that $h/h^* = \rho$, where $h := Hash(m)$ and $h^* := Hash(m^*)$ and $h^* \neq 0$;
- $\mathcal{E}_{4sum1}$: the probability, given random $t \in \mathbb{Z}_q$, of successfully finding m, e, m^*, e^* such that $h + te = h^* + te^*$, where $e, e^* \in \mathfrak{E}$, $e \neq e^*$ and $h := Hash(m)$ and $h^* := Hash(m^*)$;
- $\mathcal{E}_{4sum2}$: the probability of successfully finding m, e, m^*, e^* such that $h/t + e = h^*/t^* + e^*$, where $e, e^* \in \mathfrak{E}$, $(m, e) \neq (m^*, e^*)$ and $h := Hash(m)$ and $h^* := Hash(m^*)$, where $t \in \mathbb{Z}_q^*$ is selected by the adversary from one of several random samples, and $t^* \in \mathbb{Z}_q^*$ is a random value given after t is selected.

The success probabilities $\mathcal{E}_{cr}, \mathcal{E}_{rpr}, \mathcal{E}_{zpr}, \mathcal{E}_{rr}, \mathcal{E}_{4sum1}, \mathcal{E}_{4sum2}$ are stated in terms of an adversary whose running time is essentially that of the forging adversary (or that time plus UN, in either of the presignature settings). Also, the symbol ⊠ in the table indicates that this mode of operation is insecure with "raw" signing.

We make some quick observations about this table. First, observe that the first and third rows are identical, as are the first and third columns. Second, we see that the best security bounds are in the upper left cell and the lower right cell, and these bounds are the same—this suggests that ECDSA with homogeneous key derivation and re-randomized presignatures is just as secure as plain ECDSA. Third, we see that the worst security result is in the middle cell, corresponding to the setting of additive key derivation combined with (non-re-randomized) presignatures; moreover, this is not just a case of sloppy analysis, as we have already seen that in this setting, there is an actual attack that produces a forgery in time significantly faster than $O(q^{1/2})$. Finally, we see that "raw" signing is insecure for all modes of operation in the middle column. Each other mode is secure even with "raw" signing, meaning that the mode is just as secure if the signing algorithm is given an arbitrary hash value $h \in \mathbb{Z}_q$ (not necessarily the output of $Hash$) and, in the case of key derivation, and arbitrary tweak $e \in \mathbb{Z}_q$ (not necessarily in $\mathfrak{E}$ or satisfying any other constraint).

2   The EC-GGM

We propose the following **elliptic curve generic group model (EC-GGM)**.

We assume an elliptic curve E is defined by an equation $y^2 = F(x)$ over $\mathbb{Z}_p$ and that the curve contains q points including the point at infinity $\mathcal{O}$. Here, p and q are odd primes. Let E^* be the set of non-zero points (excluding the point at infinity) on the curve, i.e., $(x, y) \in \mathbb{Z}_p \times \mathbb{Z}_p$ that satisfy $y^2 = F(x)$. From now on, we shall not be making any use of the usual group law for E, but simply treat E as a set; however, for a point $\mathcal{P} = (x, y) \in E^*$, we write $-P$ to denote the point $(x, -y) \in E^*$. Note that because we are assuming q is prime, there are no points of the form $(x, 0) \in E$ (these would be points of order 2 under the usual group law).

An **encoding function** for E is a function $\pi : \mathbb{Z}_q \mapsto E$ that is injective, **identity preserving**, meaning that $\pi(0) = \mathcal{O}$, and **inverse preserving**, meaning that for all $i \in \mathbb{Z}_q$, $\pi(-i) = -\pi(i)$.

In the EC-GGM, parties know E and interact with a **group oracle** $\mathcal{O}_{\mathrm{grp}}$ that works as follows:

- $\mathcal{O}_{\mathrm{grp}}$ on initialization chooses an encoding function π at random from the set of all encoding functions
- $\mathcal{O}_{\mathrm{grp}}$ responds to two types of queries:
  - $(\mathtt{map}, i)$, where $i \in \mathbb{Z}_q$: return $\pi(i)$
  - $(\mathtt{add}, \mathcal{P}_1, \mathcal{P}_2)$, where $\mathcal{P}_1, \mathcal{P}_2 \in E$: return $\pi\big(\pi^{-1}(\mathcal{P}_1) + \pi^{-1}(\mathcal{P}_2) \big)$

Notes. 1. The intuition is that the random choice of encoding function hides relations between group elements.

2. However, to make things more realistic in terms of the ECDSA conversion function, the encodings themselves have the same format as in a concrete elliptic curve, even though we do not at all use the group law of an elliptic curve.

3. Also to make things more realistic, the trivial relationship between a point and its inverse (that they share the same x-coordinate) is preserved.
4. Our model only captures the situation of elliptic curves over $\mathbb{Z}_p$ of prime order and cofactor 1. This is sufficient for many settings, and it covers all of the "secp" curves in [6].
5. It would be possible to extend the model to elliptic curves of non-prime order as well, in which case the domain of the encoding function π would have to be adjusted to match the structure of the group.

3 Properties of the ECDSA Conversion Function

For a random variable T taking values in some finite set $\mathfrak{X}$, we define its **guessing probability** to be $\max\{\Pr[T = x] : x \in \mathfrak{X}\}$.

Recall again the ECDSA signature scheme as described in Sect. 1 and Fig. 1. The unreduced conversion function $C : E^* \to \mathbb{Z}_p$ is a 2-to-1 map (recall that there are no points of the form $(x, 0) \in E$). Therefore, the distribution of $C(\mathcal{R})$, for random $\mathcal{R} \in E^*$, is uniform over a subset of $\mathbb{Z}_p$ of size $(q-1)/2$. In particular, the guessing probability of $C(\mathcal{R})$ is $2/(q-1)$.

Hasse's theorem says that $q - 1 = p + 2\theta p^{1/2}$ for some $\theta \in [-1, 1]$. This implies that for $p \geq 13$ we have $p/2 \leq q \leq 2p$. We shall implicitly assume this from now on. The bound $p \leq 2q$ and the fact that C is 2-to-1 imply that every element of $\mathbb{Z}_q$ has at most four preimages under the reduced conversion function $\bar{C} : E^* \to \mathbb{Z}_q$; therefore, the guessing probability of $t := \bar{C}(\mathcal{R})$ is at most $4/(q-1)$. The ECDSA signing algorithm fails if $t = 0$ or $h + td = 0$. Thus, the probability that the signing algorithm fails is at most $8/(q-1)$.

Hasse's theorem also implies that the probability that $x \in C(E^*)$, for random $x \in \mathbb{Z}_p$, is equal to $1/2 + \theta p^{-1/2}$. We can use this to design an efficient probabilistic **sampling algorithm $Samp$**, which takes as input $t \in \mathbb{Z}_q$ and returns either fail or a point $\mathcal{R} \in \bar{C}^{-1}(t)$, with the following properties:

- For randomly chosen $t \in \mathbb{Z}_q$, we have

$$\Pr[Samp(t) = \texttt{fail}] \leq \tfrac{3}{4} + \tfrac{1}{2}p^{-1/2}.$$

- For randomly chosen $t \in \mathbb{Z}_q$, the conditional distribution of $Samp(t)$, given that $Samp(t) \neq \texttt{fail}$, is uniform over E^*.

The algorithm works as follows:

1. Let $t' \in \mathbb{Z}$ be the canonical representative of t in the interval $[0, q)$. (*Assume t is uniform over $\mathbb{Z}_q$. t' is uniform over $\{0, \ldots, q-1\}$.*)
2. If $q < p$, then with probability $1/2$ add q to t'. (*t' is uniform over an interval $\{0, \ldots, u-1\}$, where $p \leq u \leq 2p$.*)
3. If $t' \geq p$ then return fail. (*Failure occurs with probability at most $1/2$; otherwise, t' is uniform over $\{0, \ldots, p-1\}$.*)
4. Set $x \leftarrow [t' \bmod p] \in \mathbb{Z}_p$. (*$x$ is uniform over $\mathbb{Z}_p$.*)

5. If $F(x)$ is not a square, return **fail**. (*Failure occurs with probability* $1/2 - \theta p^{-1/2}$.)
6. Choose a random square root y of $F(x)$ and return $\mathcal{R} := (x, y)$. ($\mathcal{R}$ *is uniform over* E^*.)

4   Notions of Security

Definition 1 (CMA security). *For a signature scheme $\mathcal{S}$ and an adversary $\mathcal{A}$, we denote by* CMAadv$[\mathcal{A}, \mathcal{S}]$ *the advantage that $\mathcal{A}$ has in forging a signature in a chosen message attack against $\mathcal{S}$. This is the probability that $\mathcal{A}$ wins the following game.*

- *The challenger runs the key generation algorithm for $\mathcal{S}$ to obtain a public key pk and a secret key sk and gives pk to $\mathcal{A}$.*
- *$\mathcal{A}$ makes a sequence of **signing requests** to the challenger. Each such request is a message m, which the challenger signs using sk, giving the resulting signature σ to $\mathcal{A}$.*
- *At the end of the game, $\mathcal{A}$ outputs (m^*, σ^*).*
- *We say $\mathcal{A}$ **wins the game** if σ^* is a valid signature on m^* under pk, and m^* was not submitted as a signing request.*

Definition 2 (CMA security in GGM). *If $\mathcal{S}$ is based on computations in a certain group, we can also model such a CMA attack in the **generic group model**, in which all computations in the group done by $\mathcal{A}$ and the challenger are performed using the group oracle as described in Sect. 2. In this case, $\mathcal{A}$'s advantage in the corresponding CMA attack game is denoted* CMA^{ggm}adv$[\mathcal{A}, \mathcal{S}]$.

Definition 3 (Random-preimage resistance). *Let Hash be a hash function whose output space is $\mathbb{Z}_q$. Let $\mathcal{A}$ be an adversary. We define* RPRadv$[\mathcal{A}, \mathit{Hash}]$ *to be the advantage of $\mathcal{A}$ in breaking the **random-preimage resistance** of Hash. This is defined as the probability that $\mathcal{A}$ wins the following game.*

- *The challenger chooses $h \in \mathbb{Z}_q$ uniformly at random and gives h to $\mathcal{A}$.*
- *$\mathcal{A}$ outputs m.*
- *We say $\mathcal{A}$ **wins the game** if $\mathit{Hash}(m) = h$.*

Definition 4 (Zero-preimage resistance). *Let Hash be a hash function whose output space is $\mathbb{Z}_q$. Let $\mathcal{A}$ be an adversary. We define* ZPRadv$[\mathcal{A}, \mathit{Hash}]$ *to be the advantage of $\mathcal{A}$ in breaking the **zero-preimage resistance** of Hash. This is defined as the probability that $\mathcal{A}$ wins the following game.*

- *$\mathcal{A}$ outputs m.*
- *We say $\mathcal{A}$ **wins the game** if $\mathit{Hash}(m) = 0$.*

Definition 5 (Collision resistance). *Let Hash be a hash function. Let $\mathcal{A}$ be an adversary. We define* CRadv$[\mathcal{A}, \mathit{Hash}]$ *to be the advantage of $\mathcal{A}$ in breaking the **collision resistance** of Hash. This is defined as the probability that $\mathcal{A}$ wins the following game.*

- *$\mathcal{A}$ outputs m, m'.*
- *We say $\mathcal{A}$ **wins the game** if $\mathit{Hash}(m) = \mathit{Hash}(m')$ but $m \neq m'$.*

5   Proof of Security of ECDSA in the EC-GGM

In the EC-GGM model, the generator $\mathcal{G}$ is encoded as $\pi(1)$ and the public key $\mathcal{D}$ is encoded as $\pi(d)$ for randomly chosen $d \in \mathbb{Z}_q^*$. We assume that $d \neq 0$. These encodings of $\mathcal{G}$ and $\mathcal{D}$ are given to the adversary at the start of the signing attack game.

The adversary then interacts makes a sequence of queries to both the group and signing oracles. The signing oracle on a message m itself works as usual, computing $h = Hash(m)$, but it uses the group oracle to compute the encoding of $\mathcal{R} = r\mathcal{G}$. Note that we have $\mathcal{R} = s^{-1}h\mathcal{G} + s^{-1}t\mathcal{D}$, where (s,t) is the signature. For simplicity, let us assume that $\mathcal{R}$ is output by the signing oracle as well.

At the end of the signing attack game, the adversary outputs a forgery (s^*, t^*) on a message m^*. The signature is then verified using the verification algorithm, computing $h^* = Hash(m^*)$, and then again making use of the group oracle to compute the encoding of $\mathcal{R}^* = (s^*)^{-1}h^*\mathcal{G} + (s^*)^{-1}t^*\mathcal{D}$.

We define three types of forgers.

Type I. $\mathcal{R}^* = \pm\mathcal{R}$ for some $\mathcal{R}$ computed by the signing oracle.
Type II. $\mathcal{R}^* \neq \pm\mathcal{R}$ for any $\mathcal{R}$ computed by the signing oracle, and $h^* \neq 0$.
Type III. Neither Type I or Type II.

A Lazy Simulator. Instead of choosing the encoding function π at random at the beginning of the attack game, we can lazily construct π a bit at a time. That is, we represent π as a set of pairs $(i, \mathcal{P})$ which grows over time—such a pair $(i, \mathcal{P})$ represents the relation $\pi(i) = \mathcal{P}$. Here, we give the entire logic for both the group and signing oracles in the forgery attack game. Figure 2 gives the details of **Lazy-Sim**.

1. Initialization:
   (a) $\pi \leftarrow \{(0, \mathcal{O})\}$.
   (b) $d \overset{\$}{\leftarrow} \mathbb{Z}_q^*$
   (c) invoke (map, 1) to obtain $\mathcal{G}$
   (d) invoke (map, d) to obtain $\mathcal{D}$
   (e) return $(\mathcal{G}, \mathcal{D})$
2. To process a group oracle query (map, i):
   (a) if $i \notin Domain(\pi)$:
      i. $\mathcal{P} \overset{\$}{\leftarrow} E^*$;
         while $\mathcal{P} \in Range(\pi)$ do: $\mathcal{P} \overset{\$}{\leftarrow} E^*$
      ii. add $(-i, -\mathcal{P})$ and $(i, \mathcal{P})$ to π
   (b) return $\pi(i)$

3. To process a group oracle query (add, $\mathcal{P}_1, \mathcal{P}_2$):
   (a) for $j = 1, 2$: if $\mathcal{P}_j \notin Range(\pi)$:
      i. $i \overset{\$}{\leftarrow} \mathbb{Z}_q^*$;
         while $i \in Domain(\pi)$ do: $i \overset{\$}{\leftarrow} \mathbb{Z}_q^*$
      ii. add $(-i, -\mathcal{P}_j)$ and $(i, \mathcal{P}_j)$ to π
   (b) invoke (map, $\pi^{-1}(\mathcal{P}_1) + \pi^{-1}(\mathcal{P}_2)$) and return the result
4. To process a request to sign m:
   (a) $h \leftarrow Hash(m) \in \mathbb{Z}_q$
   (b) $r \overset{\$}{\leftarrow} \mathbb{Z}_q^*$
   (c) invoke (map, r) to get $\mathcal{R}$
   (d) $t \leftarrow \bar{C}(\mathcal{R}) \in \mathbb{Z}_q$
   (e) if $t = 0$ then return *fail*
   (f) if $h + td = 0$ then return *fail*
   (g) $s \leftarrow r^{-1}(h + td)$
   (h) return $(\mathcal{R}, s, t)$

Fig. 2. Lazy-Sim

At the end of the attack game, the adversary will output a forgery (s^*, t^*) on a message m^*. The verification routine will be used to verify this signature, and this will use the add queries to perform the computation, which will take $O(\log q)$ group oracle queries. We denote by N_{grp} the total number of group oracle queries explicitly made by the adversary, with the understanding that this includes the group oracle queries used to verify the forgery, as well as the group oracle queries used to generate $\mathcal{G}$ and $\mathcal{D}$, but not including group oracle queries used in the signing queries. We let N_{sig} denote the number of signing queries made by the adversary, and set $N := N_{sig} + N_{grp}$.

This lazy simulation is perfectly faithful. Specifically, the advantage of any adversary in the signature attack game using this lazy simulation of the group oracle is identical to that using the group oracle as originally defined.

A Symbolic Simulator. We now define a **symbolic** simulation of the attack game. The essential difference in this game is that $Domain(\pi)$ will now consist of polynomials of the form $a + b\mathsf{D}$, where $a, b \in \mathbb{Z}_q$ and D is an indeterminant. Here, D symbolically represents the value of d. Note that π will otherwise still satisfy all of the requirements of an encoding function. Figure 3 gives the details of **Symbolic-Sym**.

---

1. Initialization:
   (a) $\pi \leftarrow \{(0, \mathcal{O})\}$.
   (b) invoke $(\mathtt{map}, 1)$ to obtain $\mathcal{G}$
   (c) invoke $(\mathtt{map}, \mathsf{D})$ to obtain $\mathcal{D}$
   (d) return $(\mathcal{G}, \mathcal{D})$
2. To process a group oracle query $(\mathtt{map}, i)$:
   (a) if $i \notin Domain(\pi)$:
      i. $\mathcal{P} \xleftarrow{\$} E^*$;
         if $\mathcal{P} \in Range(\pi)$ then **abort**
      ii. add $(-i, -\mathcal{P})$ and $(i, \mathcal{P})$ to π
   (b) return $\pi(i)$
3. To process a group oracle query $(\mathtt{add}, \mathcal{P}_1, \mathcal{P}_2)$:
   (a) for $j = 1, 2$: if $\mathcal{P}_j \notin Range(\pi)$:
      i. $i \xleftarrow{\$} \mathbb{Z}_q^*$;
         if $i \in Domain(\pi)$ then **abort**
      ii. add $(-i, -\mathcal{P}_j)$ and $(i, \mathcal{P}_j)$ to π
   (b) invoke $(\mathtt{map}, \pi^{-1}(\mathcal{P}_1) + \pi^{-1}(\mathcal{P}_2))$ and return the result

4. To process a request to sign m:
   (a) $h \leftarrow Hash(m) \in \mathbb{Z}_q$
   (b) $\mathcal{R} \xleftarrow{\$} E^*$
   (c) if $\mathcal{R} \in Range(\pi)$ then **abort**
   (d) $t \leftarrow \bar{C}(\mathcal{R}) \in \mathbb{Z}_q$
   (e) if $t = 0$ then **abort**
   (f) $s \xleftarrow{\$} \mathbb{Z}_q^*$
   (g) $r \leftarrow s^{-1}(h + t\mathsf{D})$
   (h) if $r \in Domain(\pi)$ then **abort**
   (i) add $(-r, -\mathcal{R})$ and $(r, \mathcal{R})$ to π
   (j) return $(\mathcal{R}, s, t)$

Fig. 3. Symbolic-Sim

Lemma 1. *The difference between the adversary's forging advantage in the Lazy-Sim and Symbolic-Sim games (as described in Figs. 2 and 3) is $O(N^2/q)$.*

Proof. See the full version [12]. □

Theorem 1. *Let $\mathcal{A}$ be an adversary attacking $\mathcal{S}_{\mathrm{ecdsa}}$ as in Definition 2 that makes at most N signing or group queries. Then there exist adversaries $\mathcal{B}_{\mathrm{I}}$, $\mathcal{B}_{\mathrm{II}}$, and $\mathcal{B}_{\mathrm{III}}$, whose running times are essentially the same as $\mathcal{A}$, such that*

$$\mathrm{CMA}^{\mathrm{ggm}}\mathrm{adv}[\mathcal{A}, \mathcal{S}_{\mathrm{ecdsa}}] \le \mathrm{CRadv}[\mathcal{B}_{\mathrm{I}}, \mathit{Hash}] + (4 + o(1))N \cdot \mathrm{RPRadv}[\mathcal{B}_{\mathrm{II}}, \mathit{Hash}]$$
$$+ \mathrm{ZPRadv}[\mathcal{B}_{\mathrm{III}}, \mathit{Hash}] + O(N^2/q).$$

Proof. Consider a Type I forger playing against our symbolic simulator (see Fig. 3), where $\mathcal{R}^* = \pm\mathcal{R}$ for some $\mathcal{R}$ produced by the signing oracle (which must be unique). This means $(s^*)^{-1}(h^* + t^*\mathsf{D}) = \pm s^{-1}(h + t\mathsf{D})$ and $t^* = t$. In other words, for $\eta \in \{\pm 1\}$, we have $(s^*)^{-1}(h^* + t\mathsf{D}) = \eta s^{-1}(h + t\mathsf{D})$, which gives us the two equations $(s^*)^{-1}h^* = \eta s^{-1}h$ and $(s^*)^{-1}t = \eta s^{-1}t$. These two equations imply $h^* = h$, which implies a collision on the hash function *Hash*. This gives us the adversary $\mathcal{B}_{\mathrm{I}}$ in the theorem.

Now consider a Type II forger playing against our symbolic simulator, where $\mathcal{R}^* \ne \pm\mathcal{R}$ for any $\mathcal{R}$ produced by the signing oracle. Suppose $\pi^{-1}(\mathcal{R}^*) = a + b\mathsf{D}$. By the verification equation, we also have $\pi^{-1}(\mathcal{R}^*) = (s^*)^{-1}(h^* + t^*\mathsf{D})$. Thus, we have $a = (s^*)^{-1}h^*$ and $b = (s^*)^{-1}t^*$. These identities, along with the assumption that $h^* \ne 0$, imply that $b \ne 0$, $a \ne 0$, and $t^* = h^* a^{-1}b$. The group element $\mathcal{R}^*$ must have been generated at random by some group oracle query made directly by the adversary (this follows from the fact that $b \ne 0$). Since the coefficients a, b were already determined before this query, it follows that the value of $\mathcal{R}^*$ is independent of these coefficients. We want to use this Type II forger to break the random-preimage resistance of *Hash*. That is, we are given random $h^\dagger \in \mathbb{Z}_q$ and want to find a preimage of $h^\dagger$ under *Hash*. To do this, we will **guess the group oracle query** that will produce the value $\mathcal{R}^*$ in the forgery, and then we will **run our sampling algorithm** to compute $t^\dagger \leftarrow h^\dagger a^{-1}b$, $\mathcal{R}^\dagger \overset{\$}{\leftarrow} \mathit{Samp}(t^\dagger)$. If the sampler fails, then we abort. Otherwise, we set $\mathcal{R}^* := \mathcal{R}^\dagger$ and $t^* := t^\dagger$ and proceed as usual: if the adversary forges a signature, we succeed in finding a preimage of $h^\dagger$. This is adversary $\mathcal{B}_{\mathrm{II}}$ in the theorem.

A Type III forger produces a forgery with $h^* = 0$. This gives us adversary $\mathcal{B}_{\mathrm{III}}$ in the theorem.

The above analysis was with respect to the symbolic simulator. To get the result with respect to the lazy simulator, we use Lemma 1, which gives us the term $O(N^2/q)$ in the theorem. □

Notes. 1. All three assumptions we make—collision resistance, random-preimage resistance, and zero-preimage resistance—are necessary conditions, in the sense that it is trivial to break the scheme if any of them are false.
2. The above analysis shows that ECDSA is secure under the same assumptions, even if we give the adversary access to a "raw" signing oracle, where the input is h, not m. Of course, in this model, the notion of a forgery must be modified appropriately, to disallow forgery on any message m^* for which $H(m^*)$ was submitted as a "raw" signing query.

6   ECDSA with Additive Key Derivation

We assume that the secret key $d \in \mathbb{Z}_p$ is used as a master key to derive secret subkeys of the form $d + e$ for a "tweak" $e \in \mathbb{Z}_q$. For such a derived secret subkey, we can compute the corresponding derived public subkey from the public key $\mathcal{D}$ as $\mathcal{D} + e\mathcal{G}$.

As we will see, it is impossible to achieve security without some restriction on the choice of tweaks. We assume that any tweak must come from a set $\mathfrak{E} \subseteq \mathbb{Z}_q$ of allowed tweaks that is chosen before the attack game starts. This can be enforced in several ways, one of which is to obtain tweaks as the output of a hash function which is modeled as a random oracle. In the full version [12] we provide an analysis of the BIP32 key derivation function, which justifies modeling it as a (public use) random oracle. As we will see, security will degrade linearly in $|\mathfrak{E}|$. In the full version [12], we provide an alternative analysis in terms of concrete security properties of the hash function used to derive tweaks.

The CMA security game in Definition 1 (as well as Definition 2) is modified so that the signing oracle takes a message m and a tweak e. Similarly, the adversary must output a forgery on a specific message m^* under specific tweak e^*, and the forgery only counts if the pair (m^*, e^*) was not given to the signing oracle.

We define $\mathrm{CMA}_{\mathrm{akd}}^{\mathrm{ggm}}\mathrm{adv}[\mathcal{A}, \mathcal{S}, \mathfrak{E}]$ to be adversary $\mathcal{A}$'s advantage in winning this modified CMA game in the EC-GGM.

Lemma 1 is seen to hold as well in this setting, where to process a signing query (h, e), the symbolic simulator runs the same algorithm as before, but with $e + \mathsf{D}$ in place of D.

Theorem 2. *Let $\mathcal{A}$ be an adversary attacking $\mathcal{S}_{\mathrm{ecdsa}}$ as in Definition 2 with* **additive key derivation** *that makes at most N signing or group queries, of which N_{sig} are signing queries. Then there exist adversaries $\mathcal{B}_{\mathrm{Ia}}$, $\mathcal{B}_{\mathrm{Ib}}$, $\mathcal{B}_{\mathrm{II}}$, and $\mathcal{B}_{\mathrm{III}}$, whose running times are essentially the same as $\mathcal{A}$, such that*

$$\mathrm{CMA}_{\mathrm{akd}}^{\mathrm{ggm}}\mathrm{adv}[\mathcal{A}, \mathcal{S}_{\mathrm{ecdsa}}, \mathfrak{E}] \leq \mathrm{CRadv}[\mathcal{B}_{\mathrm{Ia}}, Hash] + (4 + o(1))N_{\mathrm{sig}}|\mathfrak{E}| \cdot \mathrm{RPRadv}[\mathcal{B}_{\mathrm{Ib}}, Hash]$$
$$+ (4 + o(1))N|\mathfrak{E}| \cdot \mathrm{RPRadv}[\mathcal{B}_{\mathrm{II}}, Hash] + \mathrm{ZPRadv}[\mathcal{B}_{\mathrm{III}}, Hash] + O(N^2/q).$$

Proof. Consider a Type I forger playing against our symbolic simulator, where $\mathcal{R}^* = \pm\mathcal{R}$ for some $\mathcal{R}$ produced by the signing oracle (which must be unique). This means $(s^*)^{-1}(h^* + t^*(e^* + \mathsf{D})) = \pm s^{-1}(h + t(e + \mathsf{D}))$ and $t^* = t$. In other words, for $\eta \in \{\pm 1\}$, we have $(s^*)^{-1}(h^* + te^* + t\mathsf{D}) = \eta s^{-1}(h + te + t\mathsf{D})$, which gives us the two equations $(s^*)^{-1}(h^* + te^*) = \eta s^{-1}(h + te)$ and $(s^*)^{-1}t = \eta s^{-1}t$. These two equations imply

$$h^* + te^* = h + te. \tag{1}$$

If $e^* = e$, then we have $h^* = h$. Let us call this a **Type Ia forgery**. In this case, we can use the forging adversary to break the collision resistance of $Hash$ as in Theorem 1. This is adversary $\mathcal{B}_{\mathrm{Ia}}$ in Theorem 2.

Otherwise, we have $t = (h^* - h)/(e - e^*)$. Let us call this a **Type Ib forgery**. We want to use this Type Ib forger to break the random-preimage resistance of

Hash. That is, we are given random $h^\dagger \in \mathbb{Z}_q$ and want to find a preimage of $h^\dagger$ under *Hash.* To do this, we will **guess the relevant signing query and the tweak** e^*. We then we will run our sampling algorithm to compute $t^\dagger \leftarrow (h^\dagger - h)/(e - e^*)$, $\mathcal{R}^\dagger \xleftarrow{\$} Samp(t^\dagger)$. If the sampler fails, then our forger fails. Otherwise, we set $\mathcal{R} := \mathcal{R}^\dagger$ and $t := t^\dagger$ and proceed as usual: if the adversary forges a signature, we succeed in finding a preimage of $h^\dagger$. This is adversary $\mathcal{B}_{\mathrm{Ib}}$ in Theorem 2.

Now consider a Type II forger playing against our symbolic simulator, where $\mathcal{R}^* \neq \pm\mathcal{R}$ for any $\mathcal{R}$ produced by the signing oracle. Suppose $\pi^{-1}(\mathcal{R}^*) = a + b\mathsf{D}$. By the verification equation, we also have $\pi^{-1}(\mathcal{R}^*) = (s^*)^{-1}(h^* + t^*(e^* + \mathsf{D}))$. Thus, we have $a = (s^*)^{-1}(h^* + t^*e^*)$ and $b = (s^*)^{-1}t^*$. These identities, along with the assumption that $h^* \neq 0$, imply $b \neq 0$, $a - be^* \neq 0$, and

$$t^* = \frac{bh^*}{a - be^*}. \tag{2}$$

The group element $\mathcal{R}^*$ must have been generated at random by some group oracle query made directly by the adversary (this follows from the fact that $b \neq 0$). Since the coefficients a, b were already determined before this query, it follows that the value of $\mathcal{R}^*$ is independent of these coefficients. We want to use this Type II forger to break the random-preimage resistance of *Hash.* That is, we are given random $h^\dagger \in \mathbb{Z}_q$ and want to find a preimage of $h^\dagger$ under *Hash.* To do this, we will **guess the relevant group oracle query that will produce the value** $\mathcal{R}^*$ **in the forgery, as well as the tweak** e^*. Then we will run our sampling algorithm to compute $t^\dagger \leftarrow (bh^\dagger)/(a - be^*)$, $\mathcal{R}^\dagger \xleftarrow{\$} Samp(t^\dagger)$. If the sampler fails, then our forger fails. Otherwise, we set $\mathcal{R}^* := \mathcal{R}^\dagger$ and $t^* := t^\dagger$ and proceed as usual: if the adversary forges a signature, we succeed in finding a preimage of $h^\dagger$. This is adversary $\mathcal{B}_{\mathrm{Ib}}$ in Theorem 2.

Type III forgers are handled just as in Theorem 1.   □

Notes. 1. This analysis also shows that ECDSA with additive key derivation is secure under the same assumptions, even if we give the adversary access to a "raw" signing oracle, where the input is h, not m. It even remains secure if the signing tweak e is not constrained to lie in the set $\mathfrak{E}$. It is really only the forging tweak e^* that must be constrained.
2. Security really does degrade as $|\mathfrak{E}|$ gets large. In particular, if $|\mathfrak{E}| = \Theta(q^{1/2})$, then for fixed h, t, and e, a Type Ib forger can expect to find $(h^*, e^*) \neq (h, e)$ satisfying (1) in time $O(q^{1/2})$, which is enough to forge a signature. Similarly, for fixed a, b, and t^*, a Type II forger can expect to find (h^*, e^*) satisfying (2) in time $O(q^{1/2})$, which is enough to forge a signature.

7   ECDSA with Presignatures

In some settings, it is convenient to precompute various pairs $(r, \mathcal{R})$, where $r \xleftarrow{\$} \mathbb{Z}_q^*$ and $\mathcal{R} \leftarrow r\mathcal{G}$. When processing a request to sign a message, we can allocate one such precomputed pair and use it to finish the computation of the signature. So long as neither $\mathcal{R}$ is not revealed to the adversary before he makes a signing query, our proof of security goes through unchanged. However, there are optimizations in some settings (especially in threshold signing protocols) that can be exploited if we do in fact reveal $\mathcal{R}$ to the adversary before he chooses which message to sign using the value of $\mathcal{R}$.

In the forgery game, we allow the adversary to make presig queries, which generate a pair $(r, \mathcal{R})$ as above. In a signing request, the adversary also specifies an index k to specify that the kth presignature should be used to sign the given message. The adversary is not allowed to specify the same presignature index for two distinct signing requests.

A Lazy Simulator. We start with the analog of Lazy-Sim in Fig. 2, but now with presignatures. Figure 4 gives the details of **Lazy-Sim**.

---

1. Initialization:
   (a) $\pi \leftarrow \{(0, \mathcal{O})\}$.
   (b) $d \stackrel{\$}{\leftarrow} \mathbb{Z}_q^*$
   (c) invoke $(\mathtt{map}, 1)$ to obtain $\mathcal{G}$
   (d) invoke $(\mathtt{map}, d)$ to obtain $\mathcal{D}$
   (e) $k \leftarrow 0$; $K \leftarrow \emptyset$
   (f) return $(\mathcal{G}, \mathcal{D})$
2. To process a group oracle query $(\mathtt{map}, i)$:
   (a) if $i \notin Domain(\pi)$:
      i. $\mathcal{P} \stackrel{\$}{\leftarrow} E^*$;
         while $\mathcal{P} \in Range(\pi)$ do: $\mathcal{P} \stackrel{\$}{\leftarrow} E^*$
      ii. add $(-i, -\mathcal{P})$ and $(i, \mathcal{P})$ to π
   (b) return $\pi(i)$
3. To process a group oracle query $(\mathtt{add}, \mathcal{P}_1, \mathcal{P}_2)$:
   (a) for $j = 1, 2$: if $\mathcal{P}_j \notin Range(\pi)$:
      i. $i \stackrel{\$}{\leftarrow} \mathbb{Z}_q^*$;
         while $i \in Domain(\pi)$ do: $i \stackrel{\$}{\leftarrow} \mathbb{Z}_q^*$
      ii. add $(-i, -\mathcal{P}_j)$ and $(i, \mathcal{P}_j)$ to π
   (b) invoke $(\mathtt{map}, \pi^{-1}(\mathcal{P}_1) + \pi^{-1}(\mathcal{P}_2))$ and return the result

4. To process a presignature request:
   (a) $k \leftarrow k + 1$
   (b) $r_k \stackrel{\$}{\leftarrow} \mathbb{Z}_q^*$
   (c) invoke $(\mathtt{map}, r_k)$ to get $\mathcal{R}_k$
   (d) $t_k \leftarrow \bar{C}(\mathcal{R}_k) \in \mathbb{Z}_q$
   (e) if $t_k = 0$ then return *fail*
   (f) $K \leftarrow K \cup \{k\}$; return $\mathcal{R}_k$
5. To process a request to sign m_k using presignature number $k \in K$:
   (a) $K \leftarrow K \setminus \{k\}$
   (b) $h_k \leftarrow Hash(m_k) \in \mathbb{Z}_q$
   (c) if $h_k + t_k d = 0$ then return *fail*
   (d) $s_k \leftarrow r_k^{-1}(h_k + t_k d)$
   (e) return (s_k, t_k)

Fig. 4. Lazy-Sim (with presignatures)

A Symbolic Simulator. We now define a **symbolic** simulation of the attack game, which is the analog of Symbolic-Sim in Fig. 3. In this setting, however, $Domain(\pi)$ will now consist of polynomials of the form $a + b\mathrm{D} + c_1\mathrm{R}_1 + c_2\mathrm{R}_2 + \cdots$, where $a, b, c_1, c_2, \ldots \in \mathbb{Z}_q$, and $\mathrm{D}, \mathrm{R}_1, \mathrm{R}_2, \ldots$ are indeterminants. Here, D symbolically represents the value of d, and R_k symbolically represents the value of r_k. Figure 5 gives the details of **Symbolic-Sim**.

Lemma 2. *The difference between the adversary's forging advantage in the Lazy-Sim and Symbolic-Sim games (as described in Figs. 4 and 5) is $O(N^2/q)$.*

---

1. Initialization:
   - (a) $\pi \leftarrow \{(0, \mathcal{O})\}$.
   - (b) invoke $(\mathtt{map}, 1)$ to obtain $\mathcal{G}$
   - (c) invoke $(\mathtt{map}, \mathtt{D})$ to obtain $\mathcal{D}$
   - (d) $k \leftarrow 0; K \leftarrow \emptyset$
   - (e) return $(\mathcal{G}, \mathcal{D})$
2. To process a group oracle query $(\mathtt{map}, i)$:
   - (a) if $i \notin Domain(\pi)$:
      - i. $\mathcal{P} \xleftarrow{\$} E^*$;
         if $\mathcal{P} \in Range(\pi)$ then abort
      - ii. add $(-i, -\mathcal{P})$ and $(i, \mathcal{P})$ to π
   - (b) return $\pi(i)$
3. To process a group oracle query $(\mathtt{add}, \mathcal{P}_1, \mathcal{P}_2)$:
   - (a) for $j = 1, 2$: if $\mathcal{P}_j \notin Range(\pi)$:
      - i. $i \xleftarrow{\$} \mathbb{Z}_q^*$;
         if $i \in Domain(\pi)$ then abort
      - ii. add $(-i, -\mathcal{P}_j)$ and $(i, \mathcal{P}_j)$ to π
   - (b) invoke $(\mathtt{map}, \pi^{-1}(\mathcal{P}_1) + \pi^{-1}(\mathcal{P}_2))$ and return the result

4. To process a presignature request:
   - (a) $k \leftarrow k + 1$
   - (b) invoke $(\mathtt{map}, \mathtt{R}_k)$ to get $\mathcal{R}_k$
   - (c) $t_k \leftarrow \bar{C}(\mathcal{R}_k) \in \mathbb{Z}_q$
   - (d) if $t_k = 0$ then abort
   - (e) $K \leftarrow K \cup \{k\}$; return $\mathcal{R}_k$
5. To process a request to sign m_k using presignature number $k \in K$:
   - (a) $K \leftarrow K \setminus \{k\}$
   - (b) $h_k \leftarrow Hash(m_k) \in \mathbb{Z}_q$
   - (c) $s_k \xleftarrow{\$} \mathbb{Z}_q^*$
   - (d) substitute $s_k^{-1}(h_k + t_k \mathtt{D})$ for $\mathtt{R}_k$ throughout $Domain(\pi)$, and abort if any two polynomials collapse
   - (e) return (s_k, t_k)

Fig. 5. Symbolic-Sim (with presignatures)

Proof. See the full version [12]. □

Since our symbolic simulation is used in our reductions to various hardness assumptions about *Hash*, we have to take into account the extra cost associated with computing with polynomials in the variables $\mathtt{D}, \mathtt{R}_1, \mathtt{R}_2, \ldots$. Let U denote the maximum number of *unused* presignatures at any point in time, i.e., the maximum size of the set K attained throughout the game. Assuming we use hash tables as appropriate, the symbolic simulation can be implemented so as to have an expected running time that is $O(UN)$ (with good tail bounds on the running time as well). This degradation in the running time by a factor of U for the extra bookkeeping seems unavoidable. If one views *Hash* as a random oracle, then this degradation plays no role, as then we have a perfectly information-theoretic result.

The results proved on basic ECDSA (without key derivation) do not carry through without modification. To analyze security in the setting, we need a new assumption on *Hash*:

Definition 6 (Ratio resistance). *Let Hash be a hash function whose output space is $\mathbb{Z}_q$. Let $\mathcal{A}$ be an adversary. We define $\mathrm{RRadv}[\mathcal{A}, Hash]$ to be the advantage of $\mathcal{A}$ in breaking the **ratio resistance** of Hash. This is defined as the probability that $\mathcal{A}$ wins the following game.*

- *The challenger chooses $\rho \in \mathbb{Z}_q^*$ uniformly at random and gives ρ to $\mathcal{A}$.*
- *$\mathcal{A}$ outputs messages m and m^*.*
- *We say $\mathcal{A}$ **wins the game** if $Hash(m^*) \neq 0$ and $Hash(m)/Hash(m^*) = \rho$.*

If we view *Hash* as a random oracle, then the best type of ratio resistance attack is a birthday attack.

We define $\mathrm{CMA}_{\mathrm{ps}}^{\mathrm{ggm}}\mathrm{adv}[\mathcal{A}, \mathcal{S}]$ to be adversary $\mathcal{A}$'s advantage in winning the CMA game with presignatures in the EC-GGM. Theorem 1 then becomes:

Theorem 3. *Let $\mathcal{A}$ be an adversary attacking $\mathcal{S}_{\mathrm{ecdsa}}$ as in Definition 2 with* **presignatures** *that makes at most N presignature, signing, or group queries. Let U denote the maximum number of unused presignatures at any point in time. Then there exist adversaries $\mathcal{B}_{\mathrm{I}}$, $\mathcal{B}_{\mathrm{IIa}}$, $\mathcal{B}_{\mathrm{IIb}}$, $\mathcal{B}_{\mathrm{IIc}}$, and $\mathcal{B}_{\mathrm{III}}$, whose running times are essentially the same as $\mathcal{A}$ plus $O(UN)$, such that $\mathrm{CMA}_{\mathrm{ps}}^{\mathrm{ggm}}\mathrm{adv}[\mathcal{A}, \mathcal{S}_{\mathrm{ecdsa}}]$ is bounded by*

$$
\begin{aligned}
&\mathrm{CRadv}[\mathcal{B}_{\mathrm{I}}, \mathit{Hash}] + (4 + o(1))N \cdot \mathrm{RPRadv}[\mathcal{B}_{\mathrm{IIa}}, \mathit{Hash}] \\
&+ (4 + o(1))N \cdot \mathrm{RRadv}[\mathcal{B}_{\mathrm{IIb}}, \mathit{Hash}] + UN \cdot \mathrm{RPRadv}[\mathcal{B}_{\mathrm{IIc}}, \mathit{Hash}] \\
&+ \mathrm{ZPRadv}[\mathcal{B}_{\mathrm{III}}, \mathit{Hash}] + O(N^2/q).
\end{aligned}
$$

Proof. Everything goes through as in the proof of Theorem 1, except for the analysis of Type II forgeries.

Consider the point in time when the adversary queries the group oracle to obtain $\mathcal{R}^*$ for the first time. Let us call this a **Type IIa** forgery if at this time, $\pi^{-1}(\mathcal{R}^*)$ is of the form $a + b\mathrm{D}$. Type IIa forgeries can be dealt with in exactly the same way as Type II forgeries in the proof of Theorem 1.

Now, consider a Type II forgery that is not a Type IIa forgery. For such a forgery, the initial preimage of $\mathcal{R}^*$ is a polynomial that involves the indeterminants $\mathrm{R}_1, \mathrm{R}_2, \ldots$. However, before the attack ends, all of these variables must be substituted via signing queries—indeed, if the attack ends with a forgery, we must have $\pi^{-1}(\mathcal{R}^*) = (s^*)^{-1}(h^* + t^*\mathrm{D})$.

Renaming variables as necessary, suppose that at the time $\mathcal{R}^*$ is initially generated, we have $\pi^{-1}(\mathcal{R}^*) = a + b\mathrm{D} + c_1\mathrm{R}_1 + \cdots + c_\ell\mathrm{R}_\ell$, where the c_i's are nonzero, and that during the attack, we substitute $\mathrm{R}_i \mapsto s_i^{-1}(h_i + t_i\mathrm{D})$ for $i = 1, \ldots, \ell$, **in that order**. Let us define a **Type IIb forgery** to be one with

$$
\frac{h_1}{t_1} = \cdots = \frac{h_\ell}{t_\ell} = \frac{h^*}{t^*}, \tag{3}
$$

and we define a **Type IIc forgery** to be a Type II forgery that is neither Type IIa or IIb.

We can use a Type IIb forger to break the ratio resistance of *Hash*. Note that the initial preimage of $\mathcal{R}^*$ cannot be of the form $\pm\mathrm{R}_k$, as otherwise this would be a Type I forgery; in particular, the group element $\mathcal{R}^*$ must be generated at random via a group oracle query made directly by the adversary. Therefore, given the ratio-resistance challenge ρ, we **guess the group oracle query that produces** $\mathcal{R}^*$, pick one of the variables R_i arbitrarily from among the variables $\mathrm{R}_1, \mathrm{R}_2, \ldots, \mathrm{R}_\ell$ appearing in $\pi^{-1}(\mathcal{R}^*)$ at that time $\mathcal{R}^*$ is generated, and run the sampler on input $t^* = t_i/\rho$ to generate $\mathcal{R}^*$. This is the adversary $\mathcal{B}_{\mathrm{IIb}}$ in Theorem 3. Note that adversary $\mathcal{B}_{\mathrm{IIb}}$ will succeed if its guess at $\mathcal{R}^*$ was correct, regardless of which of the variables R_i it chooses.

We can use a Type IIc forger to break the random-preimage resistance of *Hash*. This is the adversary $\mathcal{B}_{\mathrm{IIc}}$ in Theorem 3. To understand the design of adversary $\mathcal{B}_{\mathrm{IIc}}$, consider a Type IIc forgery. For $i = 0, \ldots, \ell$, define

$$A_i := a + \sum_{j \leq i} c_j h_j / s_j \quad \text{and} \quad B_i := b + \sum_{j \leq i} c_j t_j / s_j.$$

At the end of the attack, we must have $\pi^{-1}(\mathcal{R}^*) = A_\ell + B_\ell \mathsf{D}$, and so the forgery must satisfy:

$$A_\ell = (s^*)^{-1} h^* \quad \text{and} \quad B_\ell = (s^*)^{-1} t^*. \tag{4}$$

These two equations imply $A_\ell = B_\ell \cdot h^*/t^*$, and using the fact that $A_\ell = A_{\ell-1} + c_\ell h_\ell / s_\ell$ and $B_\ell = B_{\ell-1} + c_\ell t_\ell / s_\ell$, we can rewrite this as

$$(A_{\ell-1} - B_{\ell-1} h_\ell / t_\ell) = \underbrace{(B_{\ell-1} + s_\ell^{-1} c_\ell t_\ell)}_{=B_\ell}(h^*/t^* - h_\ell/t_\ell). \tag{5}$$

From (5), it is clear that either

(a) $A_{\ell-1} \neq B_{\ell-1} \cdot h_\ell / t_\ell$,
(b) $A_{\ell-1} = B_{\ell-1} \cdot h^*/t^*$ and $h_\ell / t_\ell = h^*/t^*$, or
(c) $B_\ell = 0$.

By repeating the above argument, and because we are assuming that (3) does not hold, we see that either

(i) $A_{i-1} \neq B_{i-1} \cdot h_i / t_i$ and $A_i = B_i \cdot h^*/t^*$ for some $i = 1, \ldots, \ell$, or
(ii) $B_i = 0$ for some $i = 1, \ldots, \ell$.

If we wish, we can categorize these as Type IIc(i) and IIc(ii) forgeries. Note that for a Type IIc(i) forgery, we may also assume that $h_j / t_j = h^*/t^*$ for $j = i+1, \ldots, \ell$, but we do not use this fact here.

The probability if a Type IIc(i) forgery can be bounded by

$$UN \cdot \mathrm{RPRadv}[\mathcal{B}_{\mathrm{IIc}}, Hash] + O(UN/q).$$

The random-preimage adversary $\mathcal{B}_{\mathrm{IIc}}$ works by **guessing $\mathcal{R}^*$ and then guessing the index i at which condition (i) above occurs.** Analogous to (5), we have

$$(A_{i-1} - B_{i-1} h_i / t_i) = (B_{i-1} + s_i^{-1} c_i t_i)(h^*/t^* - h_i/t_i). \tag{6}$$

At the time the substitution $\mathsf{R}_i \mapsto s_i^{-1}(h_i + t_i \mathsf{D})$ is made, all of the terms appearing in (6), besides s_i and h^*, are already fixed. Moreover, we are assuming the left hand side of (6) is nonzero. This implies there is a one-to-one correspondence: for every h^* such that $h^*/t^* - h_i/t_i \neq 0$ there exists a unique s_i^{-1} such that $B_{i-1} + s_i^{-1} c_i t_i \neq 0$ and *vice versa*. Adversary $\mathcal{B}_{\mathrm{IIc}}$ uses its challenge as the value of h^* and solves (6) for s_i^{-1}. Note that there are (at most) two values of h^* for which this will fail, one that satisfies $h^*/t^* - h_i/t_i = 0$ and the other that makes $s_i^{-1} = 0$.

The probability of a Type IIc(ii) forgery is easily seen to be at most $(UN)/(q-1)$. $\qquad\square$

Notes. 1. This scheme cannot be secure if we allow raw signing queries. Here is one simple attack. Suppose we get a presignature $\mathcal{R}$ with $t := \bar{C}(\mathcal{R})$ and we compute $\mathcal{R}^* = 2\mathcal{R}$. Let $h^* = Hash(m^*)$ be the hash of a message m^* for which we want to forge a signature. We solve $h/t = h^*/t^*$ for h and ask for a raw signature on h using presignature $\mathcal{R}$, obtaining the signature (s,t). We then compute s^* satisfying $(s^*)^{-1}t^* = cts^{-1}$, so (s^*, t^*) is a forgery on m^*.

2. More generally, we really do need to assume that given t and t^*, it is hard to find preimages of h and h^* such that $h/t = h^*/t^*$ holds, as otherwise, essentially the same attack can be applied. Thus, ratio resistance is essential.

3. An attacker could try the above attack with $\mathcal{R}^* = 2\mathcal{R}, 3\mathcal{R}, \ldots$, obtaining many candidates for t^* to combine with many candidates for h and h^*. This would give us a multiplicative version of the 3-sum problem, for which there is no known attack that is significantly better than birthday (see [15]).

7.1   ECDSA with Presignatures and Additive Key Derivation

Now suppose we combine presignatures with additive key derivation. Here, we assume that `presig` queries take no input as before, but the signing queries take as input an index k that specifies the presignature to use, along with a message m_k and the tweak e_k.

We define $\text{CMA}^{\text{ggm}}_{\text{akd,ps}}\text{adv}[\mathcal{A}, \mathcal{S}, \mathfrak{E}]$ to be adversary $\mathcal{A}$'s advantage in winning this modified CMA game in the EC-GGM. We can still prove security of ECDSA in this setting using stronger intractability assumptions for $Hash$.

Let us first consider the symbolic simulation of the signing oracle. Using the notation established above, $h_k := Hash(m_k)$ and $t_k := \bar{C}(\mathcal{R}_k)$. We want to choose $s_k \in \mathbb{Z}_q^*$ at random and then substitute $s_k^{-1}(h_k + t_k e_k + t_k \mathsf{D})$, rather than $s_k^{-1}(h_k + t_k \mathsf{D})$ for R_k in all polynomials in $Domain(\pi)$ that involve R_k. The proof of Lemma 2 goes through unchanged.

Definition 7 (4sum1 intractability). *Let $Hash$ be a hash function whose output space is $\mathbb{Z}_q$. Let $\mathfrak{E} \subseteq \mathbb{Z}_q$. Let $\mathcal{A}$ be an adversary. We define* 4sum1adv$[\mathcal{A}, Hash, \mathfrak{E}]$ *to be the advantage of $\mathcal{A}$ in breaking the **4sum1 property** of $Hash$ with respect to the set $\mathfrak{E}$. This is defined as the probability that $\mathcal{A}$ wins the following game.*

- *The challenger chooses $t \in \mathbb{Z}_q$ uniformly at random and gives t to $\mathcal{A}$.*
- *$\mathcal{A}$ outputs m, e, m^*, e^*, where $e, e^* \in \mathfrak{E}$.*
- *We say $\mathcal{A}$ **wins the game** if $h + te = h^* + te^*$, where $e \neq e^*$ and $h := Hash(m)$ and $h^* := Hash(m^*)$.*

Definition 8 (4sum2 intractability). *Let $Hash$ be a hash function whose output space is $\mathbb{Z}_q$. Let $\mathfrak{E} \subseteq \mathbb{Z}_q$. Let $\mathcal{A}$ be an adversary. We define* 4sum2adv$[\mathcal{A}, Hash, \mathfrak{E}]$ *to be the advantage of $\mathcal{A}$ in breaking the **4sum2 property** of $Hash$ with respect to the set $\mathfrak{E}$. This is defined as the probability that $\mathcal{A}$ wins the following game.*

- *The adversary asks the challenger for many random samples in $\mathbb{Z}_q^*$, and the adversary chooses one such sample $t \in \mathbb{Z}_q^*$.*

- *The challenger chooses $t^* \in \mathbb{Z}_q^*$ at random and gives t^* to $\mathcal{A}$.*
- *$\mathcal{A}$ outputs m, e, m^*, e^*, where $e, e^* \in \mathfrak{E}$.*
- *We say $\mathcal{A}$ **wins the game** if $h/t + e = h^*/t^* + e^*$, where $(m, e) \neq (m^*, e^*)$ and $h := Hash(m)$ and $h^* := Hash(m^*)$.*

Theorem 4. *Let $\mathcal{A}$ be an adversary attacking $\mathcal{S}_{ecdsa}$ as in Definition 2 with* **additive key derivation and presignatures** *that makes at most N presignature, signing, or group queries, of which N_{psig} are presignature requests. Let U denote the maximum number of unused presignatures at any point in time. Then there exist adversaries $\mathcal{B}_{Ia}$, $\mathcal{B}_{Ib}$, $\mathcal{B}_{IIa}$, $\mathcal{B}_{IIb}$, and $\mathcal{B}_{IIc}$, and $\mathcal{B}_{III}$, whose running times are essentially the same as $\mathcal{A}$ plus $O(UN)$, such that $\mathrm{CMA}_{akd,ps}^{ggm}adv[\mathcal{A}, \mathcal{S}_{ecdsa}, \mathfrak{E}]$ is bounded by*

$$
\begin{aligned}
&\mathrm{CRadv}[\mathcal{B}_{Ia}, Hash] + (4 + o(1))N_{psig} \cdot \mathrm{4sum1adv}[\mathcal{B}_{Ib}, Hash, \mathfrak{E}] \\
&+ (4 + o(1))N|\mathfrak{E}| \cdot \mathrm{RPRadv}[\mathcal{B}_{IIa}, Hash] + (4 + o(1))N \cdot \mathrm{4sum2adv}[\mathcal{B}_{IIb}, Hash, \mathfrak{E}] \\
&+ UN|\mathfrak{E}| \cdot \mathrm{RPRadv}[\mathcal{B}_{IIc}, Hash] + \mathrm{ZPRadv}[\mathcal{B}_{III}, Hash] + O(N^2/q).
\end{aligned}
$$

Also, adversary $\mathcal{B}_{IIb}$ obtains $O(N_{psig})$ random samples from its challenger.

Proof. We categorize forgeries as Types Ia, Ib, IIa, IIb, IIc, and III: Types Ia and Ib are as in Theorem 2, Types IIa–IIc are as in Theorem 3, and Type III is as in Theorem 1.

The analysis we did for Type Ia and III forgeries in Sect. 6 goes through here without any change. Also, the analysis we did for Type II forgeries in Sect. 6 carries over here for Type IIa forgeries.

Type Ib Forgeries. We get a Type Ib forgery if and only if the Eq. (1) holds with $e \neq e^*$. Without presignatures, the adversary had to commit to h and e before learning t, but with presignatures, the adversary is free to choose h and e, along with h^* and e^*, *after* learning t. Indeed, we see that creating a Type Ib forgery is essentially equivalent to breaking the 4sum1 property in Definition 7. We can easily use such a forger to break the 4sum1 property as follows: given the challenge t in the 4sum1 game, we **guess the relevant presignature**, set $t_k := t$ and run the sampler on t to get $\mathcal{R}_k$. This gives us $\mathcal{B}_{Ib}$ in Theorem 4.

Type IIb and IIc forgeries. Everything goes through exactly as in Theorem 3, but with h_i replaced by $\Delta_i := h_i + t_i e_i$ and h^* replaced by $\Delta^* := h^* + t^* e^*$. In particular, we categorize Type IIb forgeries as those where

$$
\frac{\Delta_1}{t_1} = \cdots = \frac{\Delta_k}{t_k} = \frac{\Delta^*}{t^*}.
$$

We can easily use a Type IIb forger to break the 4sum2 property as follows. In the first stage of the attack game in Definition 8, we use the random samples given by the 4sum2-challenger to generate all the presignatures we need using the sampling algorithm. With overwhelming probability, $O(N_{\mathrm{psig}})$ random samples will suffice. We then **guess the group operation that produces** $\mathcal{R}^*$. At the time this group operation is performed, we choose one of the variables R_i appearing in $\pi^{-1}(\mathcal{R}^*)$ arbitrarily and select t in the attack game in Definition 8 to the corresponding sample t_i. We then obtain t^* from our 4sum2-challenger and run the sampling algorithm on t^* to get $\mathcal{R}^*$. A Type IIb forgery will give us the values m, e, m^*, e^* we need to win the attack game in Definition 8. This is adversary $\mathcal{B}_{\mathrm{IIb}}$ in Theorem 4.

The adversary $\mathcal{B}_{\mathrm{IIc}}$ in Theorem 4 is exactly the same as $\mathcal{B}_{\mathrm{IIc}}$ in Theorem 3, but with h_k replaced by Δ_k and h^* replaced by Δ^*, and where we also have to guess the tweak e^*.   □

Notes. 1. Just as in the case of presignatures without additive key derivation, this scheme cannot be secure if we allow raw signing queries.
2. In the full version [12], we provide an alternative analyisis in terms of concrete security properties of the hash function used to derive tweaks.

How Strong Are the 4sum1 and 4sum2 Properties? Consider first the 4sum1 property. If we just choose e and e^* arbitrarily, then viewing *Hash* as a random oracle, then analogous to the birthday attack, we can find m and m^* satisfying the required relation in time $O(\sqrt{q})$. However, by exploiting the fact that we also have control over e and e^*, we can beat the birthday attack.

Indeed, suppose we view *Hash* as a random oracle, and the elements of $\mathfrak{E}$ are randomly chosen. Then this problem is no harder than the 4-sum problem studied in Wagner [19] and elsewhere [2, 15]. Wagner gave an algorithm to solve this problem that beats the birthday attack. In the full version [12], we sketch Wagner's algorithm, adapted to our setting. One consequence of this is that if $|\mathfrak{E}| = \Theta(q^{1/3})$, then we can solve this 4-sum problem and forge a signature in time $O(q^{1/3})$. The attack works as follows.

- Make one presignature query to get the group element $\mathcal{R}$ and let $t := \bar{C}(\mathcal{R})$.
- Use Wagner's algorithm to find m, e, m^*, e^* such that $h + te = h^* + te^*$, where $e \neq e^*$ and $h := Hash(m)$ and $h^* := Hash(m^*)$.
- Now ask for a signature using this presignature on message m with tweak e.
- This signature is also a signature on m^* with tweak e^*.

The $O(q^{1/3})$ work is time spent computing hashes of messages and tweaks (which themselves may well just be hashes), and performing hash table lookups. Mitigating against this attack is (i) the fact that the $O(q^{1/3})$ time must be done *between* the time that the presignature is generated and the time that the adversary asks for a signature using that presignature, and (ii) the fact that the attack takes space $O(q^{1/3})$ (but see [2,15] for time-space trade-offs).

We stress that this $O(q^{1/3})$ attack requires just one presignature and one corresponding signature. It is also easily seen that the 4sum2 property is also no harder than a 4-sum problem.

8   ECDSA with Re-randomized Presignatures

We saw the ECDSA with presignatures leads to potential vulnerabilities, especially when combined with additive key derivation. At the very least, we require additional intractability assumptions. In this section, we explore a variant in which the presignatures are **re-randomized** when used for signing. For threshold ECDSA implementations, this re-randomization maintains most of the benefits of presignatures; however, it also maintains most of the security properties that we had without presignatures, both in the settings with and without additive key derivation.

So now a presignature is of the form $(r', \mathcal{R}')$, where $r' \xleftarrow{\$} \mathbb{Z}_q$ and $\mathcal{R}' \leftarrow r'\mathcal{G}$. As before, when processing a request to sign a message, we can allocate one such precomputed pair and use it to finish the computation of the signature. However, instead of using the presignature directly, we *re-randomize* it, computing $\delta \xleftarrow{\$} \mathbb{Z}_q$, and using $(r, \mathcal{R}) := (r' + \delta, \mathcal{R}' + \delta\mathcal{G})$ as the presignature. Crucially, the value of δ is given to the adversary as an output of the signing request.

Notes. 1. The reason why we insist on giving δ to the adversary is that a protocol implementing a distributed signing service may ultimately reveal δ. This allows us to reduce the security of such a distributed protocol to this primitive. Depending on how the distributed signing service is implemented, generating δ may or may not introduce extra latency.
2. Instead of generating δ at random, it could also be obtained by deriving it as a hash of $\mathcal{R}'$ and the signing request. The results we present here could be adapted to this setting, especially if we model the hash as a random oracle. While the security results would be somewhat weaker than if δ is generated at random, they would still be significantly stronger than not using any re-randomization at all.

A Lazy Simulator. We start with the analog of Lazy-Sim in Fig. 4, but now with re-randomized presignatures. Figure 6 gives the details of **Lazy-Sim**.

1. Initialization:
   (a) $\pi \leftarrow \{(0, \mathcal{O})\}$.
   (b) $d \xleftarrow{\$} \mathbb{Z}_q^*$
   (c) invoke $(\mathtt{map}, 1)$ to obtain $\mathcal{G}$
   (d) invoke $(\mathtt{map}, d)$ to obtain $\mathcal{D}$
   (e) $k \leftarrow 0$; $K \leftarrow \emptyset$
   (f) return $(\mathcal{G}, \mathcal{D})$
2. To process a group oracle query $(\mathtt{map}, i)$:
   (a) if $i \notin Domain(\pi)$:
       i. $\mathcal{P} \xleftarrow{\$} E^*$;
          while $\mathcal{P} \in Range(\pi)$ do: $\mathcal{P} \xleftarrow{\$} E^*$
       ii. add $(-i, -\mathcal{P})$ and $(i, \mathcal{P})$ to π
   (b) return $\pi(i)$
3. To process a group oracle query $(\mathtt{add}, \mathcal{P}_1, \mathcal{P}_2)$:
   (a) for $j = 1, 2$: if $\mathcal{P}_j \notin Range(\pi)$:
       i. $i \xleftarrow{\$} \mathbb{Z}_q^*$;
          while $i \in Domain(\pi)$ do: $i \xleftarrow{\$} \mathbb{Z}_q^*$
       ii. add $(-i, -\mathcal{P}_j)$ and $(i, \mathcal{P}_j)$ to π
   (b) invoke $(\mathtt{map}, \pi^{-1}(\mathcal{P}_1) + \pi^{-1}(\mathcal{P}_2))$ and return the result

4. To process a presignature request:
   (a) $k \leftarrow k + 1$
   (b) $r_k' \xleftarrow{\$} \mathbb{Z}_q$
   (c) invoke $(\mathtt{map}, r_k')$ to get $\mathcal{R}_k'$
   (d) $K \leftarrow K \cup \{k\}$; return $\mathcal{R}_k'$
5. To process a request to sign m_k using presignature number $k \in K$:
   (a) $K \leftarrow K \setminus \{k\}$
   (b) $\delta_k \xleftarrow{\$} \mathbb{Z}_q$
   (c) $r_k \leftarrow r_k' + \delta_k$
   (d) if $r_k = 0$ then return $fail$
   (e) invoke $(\mathtt{map}, r_k)$ to get $\mathcal{R}_k$
   (f) $t_k \leftarrow \bar{C}(\mathcal{R}_k) \in \mathbb{Z}_q$
   (g) $h_k \leftarrow Hash(m_k) \in \mathbb{Z}_q$
   (h) if $t_k = 0$ or $h_k + t_k d = 0$ then return $fail$
   (i) $s_k \leftarrow r_k^{-1}(h_k + t_k d)$
   (j) return $(s_k, t_k, \mathcal{R}_k, \delta_k)$

Fig. 6. Lazy-Sim (with re-randomized presignatures)

A Symbolic Simulator. We define a **symbolic** simulation of the attack game, which is the analog of Symbolic-Sim in Fig. 5. As in Fig. 5, $Domain(\pi)$ will now consist of polynomials of the form $a + b\mathsf{D} + c_1 \mathsf{R}_1 + c_2 \mathsf{R}_2 + \cdots$, where $a, b, c_1, c_2, \ldots \in \mathbb{Z}_q$, and $\mathsf{D}, \mathsf{R}_1, \mathsf{R}_2, \ldots$ are indeterminants. Here, D symbolically represents the value of d, and R_k symbolically represents the value of r_k' (and *not* r_k). Figure 7 gives the details of **Symbolic-Sym**.

Lemma 3. *The difference between the adversary's forging advantage in the Lazy-Sim and Symbolic-Sim games (as described in Figs. 6 and 7) is $O(N^2/q)$.*

The proof of Lemma 3 follows the same lines as that of Lemma 2, and we leave the details to the reader.

We define $\mathrm{CMA}_{\mathrm{rrps}}^{\mathrm{ggm}}\mathrm{adv}[\mathcal{A}, \mathcal{S}, \mathfrak{E}]$ to be adversary $\mathcal{A}$'s advantage in winning this modified CMA game in the EC-GGM.

Theorem 5. *Let $\mathcal{A}$ be an adversary attacking $\mathcal{S}_{\mathrm{ecdsa}}$ as in Definition 2 with* ***re-randomized presignatures*** *that makes at most N presignature, signing, or group queries. Let U denote the maximum number of* unused *presignatures at any point in time. Then there exist adversaries $\mathcal{B}_\mathrm{I}$, $\mathcal{B}_{\mathrm{IIa}}$, $\mathcal{B}_{\mathrm{IIbc}}$, and $\mathcal{B}_{\mathrm{III}}$, whose running times are essentially the same as $\mathcal{A}$ plus $O(UN)$, such that $\mathrm{CMA}_{\mathrm{rrps}}^{\mathrm{ggm}}\mathrm{adv}[\mathcal{A}, \mathcal{S}_{\mathrm{ecdsa}}]$ is bounded by*

$$\mathrm{CRadv}[\mathcal{B}_\mathrm{I}, Hash] + (4 + o(1))N \cdot \mathrm{RPRadv}[\mathcal{B}_{\mathrm{IIa}}, Hash]$$
$$+ N \cdot \mathrm{RPRadv}[\mathcal{B}_{\mathrm{IIbc}}, Hash] + \mathrm{ZPRadv}[\mathcal{B}_{\mathrm{III}}, Hash] + O(N^2/q).$$

1. Initialization:
   (a) $\pi \leftarrow \{(0, \mathcal{O})\}$.
   (b) invoke $(\mathtt{map}, 1)$ to obtain $\mathcal{G}$
   (c) invoke $(\mathtt{map}, \mathsf{D})$ to obtain $\mathcal{D}$
   (d) $k \leftarrow 0$; $K \leftarrow \emptyset$
   (e) return $(\mathcal{G}, \mathcal{D})$
2. To process a group oracle query $(\mathtt{map}, i)$:
   (a) if $i \notin Domain(\pi)$:
       i. $\mathcal{P} \xleftarrow{\$} E^*$;
          if $\mathcal{P} \in Range(\pi)$ then abort
       ii. add $(-i, -\mathcal{P})$ and $(i, \mathcal{P})$ to π
   (b) return $\pi(i)$
3. To process a group oracle query $(\mathtt{add}, \mathcal{P}_1, \mathcal{P}_2)$:
   (a) for $j = 1, 2$: if $\mathcal{P}_j \notin Range(\pi)$:
       i. $i \xleftarrow{\$} \mathbb{Z}_q^*$;
          if $i \in Domain(\pi)$ then abort
       ii. add $(-i, -\mathcal{P}_j)$ and $(i, \mathcal{P}_j)$ to π
   (b) invoke $(\mathtt{map}, \pi^{-1}(\mathcal{P}_1) + \pi^{-1}(\mathcal{P}_2))$ and return the result

4. To process a presignature request:
   (a) $k \leftarrow k + 1$
   (b) invoke $(\mathtt{map}, \mathsf{R}_k)$ to get $\mathcal{R}'_k$
   (c) $K \leftarrow K \cup \{k\}$; return $\mathcal{R}'_k$
5. To process a request to sign m_k using presignature number $k \in K$:
   (a) $K \leftarrow K \setminus \{k\}$
   (b) $\delta_k \xleftarrow{\$} \mathbb{Z}_q$
   (c) if $\mathsf{R}_k + \delta_k \in Domain(\pi)$ then abort
   (d) invoke $(\mathtt{map}, \mathsf{R}_k + \delta_k)$ to obtain $\mathcal{R}_k$
   (e) $t_k \leftarrow \bar{C}(\mathcal{R}_k)$
   (f) if $t_k = 0$ then abort
   (g) $h_k \leftarrow Hash(m_k) \in \mathbb{Z}_q$
   (h) $s_k \xleftarrow{\$} \mathbb{Z}_q^*$
   (i) substitute $s_k^{-1}(h_k + t_k\mathsf{D}) - \delta_k$ for R_k throughout $Domain(\pi)$, and abort if any two polynomials collapse
   (j) return $(s_k, t_k, \mathcal{R}_k, \delta_k)$

Fig. 7. Symbolic-Sim (with re-randomized presignatures)

Proof. We categorize forgeries just as in Theorem 3, but we lump Types IIb and IIc into a single Type IIbc. Forgeries of types I, IIa, and III are handled just as in Theorem 3.

For forgeries of type IIbc, just as in Theorem 3, we suppose that at the time $\mathcal{R}^*$ is initially generated, we have $\pi^{-1}(\mathcal{R}^*) = a + b\mathsf{D} + c_1\mathsf{R}_1 + \cdots + c_\ell\mathsf{R}_\ell$, where the c_i's are nonzero; however, during the attack, we substitute $\mathsf{R}_i \mapsto s_i^{-1}(h_i + t_i\mathsf{D}) - \delta_i$ for $i = 1, \ldots, \ell$, again, in that order. For $i = 0, \ldots, \ell$, define

$$A_i := a + \sum_{j \leq i} c_j(h_j/s_j - \delta_j) \quad \text{and} \quad B_i := b + \sum_{j \leq i} c_j t_j/s_j.$$

Equation (5) then becomes

$$(A_{\ell-1} - B_{\ell-1}h_\ell/t_\ell - c_\ell\delta_\ell) = (B_{\ell-1} + s_\ell^{-1}c_\ell t_\ell)(h^*/t^* - h_\ell/t_\ell). \tag{7}$$

At the time the substitution $\mathsf{R}_\ell \mapsto s_\ell^{-1}(h_\ell + t_\ell\mathsf{D}) - \delta_\ell$ is made, all of the terms appearing in (7), besides δ_ℓ, s_ℓ, and h^*, are already fixed. Therefore, the left-hand side of (7) will vanish with probability $1/q$, and as long as this does not happen, we can use this Type IIbc forger to break random-preimage resistance. Indeed, just as we argued in the proof of Theorem 3, there is a one-to-one correspondence: for every h^* such that $h^*/t^* - h_\ell/t_\ell \neq 0$ there exists a unique s_ℓ^{-1} such that $B_{\ell-1} + s_\ell^{-1}c_\ell t_\ell \neq 0$ and *vice versa*. We use this the given random-preimage challenge as the value of h^* and solve (7) for s_ℓ^{-1}. □

Notes. 1. With re-randomized presignatures, we again obtain security with respect to raw signing queries (allowing arbitrary, unconstrained $h_k \in \mathbb{Z}_q$).
2. One sees from the proof of Theorem 5 that we only need that the randomizer δ_k is sufficiently unpredictable—it need not be uniformly distributed over $\mathbb{Z}_q$.

8.1 ECDSA with Re-randomized Presignatures and Additive Key Derivation

Now suppose we combine re-randomized presignatures with additive key derivation. We define $\mathrm{CMA}^{\mathrm{ggm}}_{\mathrm{akd,rrps}}\mathrm{adv}[\mathcal{A}, \mathcal{S}, \mathfrak{E}]$ to be adversary $\mathcal{A}$'s advantage in winning this modified CMA game in the EC-GGM.

Theorem 6. *Let $\mathcal{A}$ be an adversary attacking $\mathcal{S}_{\mathrm{ecdsa}}$ as in Definition 2 with* ***additive key derivation and re-randomized presignatures*** *that makes at most N presignature, signing, or group queries, of which N_{psig} are presignature queries. Let U denote the maximum number of unused presignatures at any point in time. Then there exist adversaries $\mathcal{B}_{\mathrm{Ia}}$, $\mathcal{B}_{\mathrm{Ib}}$, $\mathcal{B}_{\mathrm{IIa}}$, $\mathcal{B}_{\mathrm{IIc}}$, and $\mathcal{B}_{\mathrm{III}}$, whose running times are essentially the same as $\mathcal{A}$ plus $O(UN)$, such that $\mathrm{CMA}^{\mathrm{ggm}}_{\mathrm{akd,rrps}}\mathrm{adv}[\mathcal{A}, \mathcal{S}_{\mathrm{ecdsa}}, \mathfrak{E}]$ is bounded by*

$$\mathrm{CRadv}[\mathcal{B}_{\mathrm{Ia}}, Hash] + (4 + o(1))N_{\mathrm{sig}}|\mathfrak{E}| \cdot \mathrm{RPRadv}[\mathcal{B}_{\mathrm{Ib}}, Hash]$$
$$+ (4 + o(1))N|\mathfrak{E}| \cdot \mathrm{RPRadv}[\mathcal{B}_{\mathrm{IIa}}, Hash] + N|\mathfrak{E}| \cdot \mathrm{RPRadv}[\mathcal{B}_{\mathrm{IIbc}}, Hash]$$
$$+ \mathrm{ZPRadv}[\mathcal{B}_{\mathrm{III}}, Hash] + O(N^2/q).$$

Proof. Forgeries are categorized just as in Theorem 4, but we lump Types IIb and IIc into a single Type IIbc. Type Ia and Ib forgeries are handled just as in Theorem 2. Type IIa forgeries are handled just like Type II forgeries in Theorem 2. Type III forgeries are handled just as in Theorem 1.

For Type IIbc forgeries, everything goes through exactly as in Theorem 5, but with h_i replaced by $\Delta_i := h_i + t_i e_i$ and h^* replaced by $\Delta^* := h^* + t^* e^*$, and the adversary $\mathcal{B}_{\mathrm{IIbc}}$ has to guess e^*. □

Notes. 1. With re-randomized presignatures, we again obtain security with respect to raw signing queries (allowing arbitrary, unconstrained $h_k, e_k \in \mathbb{Z}_q$).
2. Just in Theorem 5, it is not essential that δ_k is uniformly distributed over $\mathbb{Z}_q$—it only needs to be sufficiently unpredictable.
3. In the full version [12], we provide an alternative analysis in terms of concrete security properties of the hash function used to derive tweaks.

9 Homogeneous Key Derivation

We propose a new key derivation technique (a similar construction was given in [13] for completely different purposes). This derivation technique is still essentially linear, and so enjoys many of the same advantages of additive key derivation, including (i) the ability to derive public keys from a master public key, and (ii) the ability to efficiently implement the scheme as a threshold signature scheme.

The basic idea is this. The master secret key is now a random pair $(d, d') \in \mathbb{Z}_q \times \mathbb{Z}_q$, and the corresponding master public key is the pair $(\mathcal{D}, \mathcal{D}') :=$

$(d\mathcal{G}, d'\mathcal{G}) \in E \times E$. For a given "tweak" $e \in \mathbb{Z}_q$, the corresponding derived secret key is $d + ed' \in \mathbb{Z}_q$ and the corresponding derived public key is $\mathcal{D} + e\mathcal{D}'$.

We consider homogeneous key derivation without presignatures, with presignatures, and with re-randomized presignatures.

As we will see, we can prove stronger results with homogeneous key derivation than we could with additive key derivation. In particular, we will not need to assume that the tweaks come from some predetermined set $\mathfrak{E} \subseteq \mathbb{Z}_q$. As such, we will assume that a tweak $e \in \mathbb{Z}_q$ is derived from the hash function $Hash$ as $e \leftarrow Hash(id)$, where id is an arbitrary identifier. Here, $Hash$ is the same hash function used by ECDSA; however, it could also be a different hash function (the only requirement is that this hash function maps into $\mathbb{Z}_q$ and is collision resistant). The signing algorithm will take as input both a message m and an identifier id. In the forgery attack game, a forgery consists of a valid signature (s^*, t^*) on a message m^* and an identifier id^*, subject to the constraint that the signing oracle was not invoked with the same message/identifier pair (m^*, id^*).

9.1   Homogeneous Key Derivation Without Presignatures

The lazy simulation in Fig. 2 is modified as follows: (i) In the initialization step, the challenger chooses $(d, d') \in \mathbb{Z}_q \times \mathbb{Z}_q$ at random, invokes $(\mathtt{map}, d)$ and $(\mathtt{map}, d')$ to obtain $\mathcal{D}$ and $\mathcal{D}'$. The challenger gives $(\mathcal{G}, \mathcal{D}, \mathcal{D}')$ to the adversary. (ii) In a signing request, the adversary supplies an identifier id in addition to a message m, and the tweak $e \in \mathbb{Z}_q$ is computed as $e \leftarrow Hash(id)$. To process such a signing request, the challenger carries out the same logic, but with $d + ed'$ replacing d in steps 4(f) and 4(g).

To verify a signature with respect to a tweak e^*, where $e^* := Hash(id^*)$, the signature is verified with respect to the public key $\mathcal{D} + e^*\mathcal{D}'$.

The symbolic simulation in Fig. 3 is modified as follows: (i) In the initialization step, the challenger invokes $(\mathtt{map}, \mathsf{D})$ and $(\mathtt{map}, \mathsf{D}')$ to obtain $\mathcal{D}$ and $\mathcal{D}'$. The challenger gives $(\mathcal{G}, \mathcal{D}, \mathcal{D}')$ to the adversary. Here, D and D' are distinct indeterminants. (ii) In a signing request, the adversary supplies an identifier id in addition to a message m, and the tweak $e \in \mathbb{Z}_q$ is computed as $e \leftarrow Hash(id)$. To process such a signing request, the challenger carries out the same logic, but with $\mathsf{D} + e\mathsf{D}'$ replacing D in step 4(g).

It is easy to prove that Lemma 1 carries over to this setting without change. We leave this to the reader.

We define $\mathrm{CMA}_{\mathrm{hkd}}^{\mathrm{ggm}}\mathsf{adv}[\mathcal{A}, \mathcal{S}]$ to be adversary $\mathcal{A}$'s advantage in winning this modified CMA game in the EC-GGM. We can prove the following analog of Theorem 2. As the reader will notice, the statement of this theorem is almost the same as Theorem 1.

Theorem 7. *Let $\mathcal{A}$ be an adversary attacking $\mathcal{S}_{\mathrm{ecdsa}}$ as in Definition 2 with **homogeneous key derivation** that makes at most N signing or group queries. Then there exist adversaries $\mathcal{B}_{\mathrm{I}}$, $\mathcal{B}_{\mathrm{II}}$, and $\mathcal{B}_{\mathrm{III}}$, whose running times are essentially the same as $\mathcal{A}$, such that*

$$\text{CMA}^{\text{ggm}}_{\text{hkd}} \text{adv}[\mathcal{A}, \mathcal{S}_{\text{ecdsa}}] \leq \text{CRadv}[\mathcal{B}_{\text{I}}, \text{Hash}] + (4 + o(1))N \cdot \text{RPRadv}[\mathcal{B}_{\text{II}}, \text{Hash}]$$
$$+ \text{ZPRadv}[\mathcal{B}_{\text{III}}, \text{Hash}] + O(N^2/q).$$

Proof. We categorize forgeries as Type I, II, or III just as in Theorem 1.
For a Type I forgery, for $\eta \in \{\pm 1\}$, we have

$$(s^*)^{-1}(h^* + t\text{D} + te^*\text{D}') = \eta s^{-1}(h + t\text{D} + te\text{D}').$$

This gives us three equations:

$$(s^*)^{-1}h^* = \eta s^{-1}h, \quad (s^*)^{-1}t = \eta s^{-1}t, \quad \text{and} \quad (s^*)^{-1}te^* = \eta s^{-1}te.$$

These three equations imply $h^* = h$ and $e^* = e$. This immediately gives us the
adversary $\mathcal{B}_{\text{I}}$ in Theorem 7 that breaks the collision resistance of *Hash*, either of
the form $Hash(m^*) = Hash(m)$ or $Hash(id^*) = Hash(id)$.
For a Type II forgery, if $\pi^{-1}(\mathcal{R}^*) = a + b\text{D} + b'\text{D}'$, we have

$$a + b\text{D} + b'\text{D}' = (s^*)^{-1}(h^* + t^*\text{D} + t^*e^*\text{D}').$$

This gives us three equations:

$$a = (s^*)^{-1}h^*, \quad b = (s^*)^{-1}t^*, \quad \text{and} \quad b' = (s^*)^{-1}t^*e^*.$$

Just as in Theorem 1, we obtain $b \neq 0$, $a \neq 0$, and $t^* = h^*a^{-1}b$. In addition, we
have $b' = be^*$. So just as in Theorem 1, we obtain an adversary $\mathcal{B}_{\text{II}}$ that breaks
the random-preimage resistance of *Hash*.
For a Type III forgery, just as in Theorem 1, we obtain an adversary $\mathcal{B}_{\text{III}}$ that
breaks the zero-preimage resistance of *Hash*.   □

Note. The above analysis shows that the scheme is secure even with a "raw"
signing oracle.

9.2   Homogeneous Key Derivation with Presignatures

The lazy simulation in Fig. 4 is modified as follows: (i) In the initialization step,
the challenger chooses $(d, d') \in \mathbb{Z}_q \times \mathbb{Z}_q$ at random, invokes $(\texttt{map}, d)$ and $(\texttt{map}, d')$
to obtain $\mathcal{D}$ and $\mathcal{D}'$. The challenger gives $(\mathcal{G}, \mathcal{D}, \mathcal{D}')$ to the adversary. (ii) In a
signing request, the adversary supplies an identifier id_k in addition to a message
m_k, and the tweak $e_k \in \mathbb{Z}_q$ is computed as $e_k \leftarrow Hash(id_k)$. To process such
a signing request, the challenger carries out the same logic, but with $d + e_kd'$
replacing d in steps 5(c) and 5(d).
To verify a signature with respect to a tweak e^*, where $e^* := Hash(id^*)$, the
signature is verified with respect to the public key $\mathcal{D} + e^*\mathcal{D}'$.
The symbolic simulation in Fig. 5 is modified as follows: (i) In the initial-
ization step, the challenger invokes $(\texttt{map}, \text{D})$ and $(\texttt{map}, \text{D}')$ to obtain $\mathcal{D}$ and $\mathcal{D}'$.
The challenger gives $(\mathcal{G}, \mathcal{D}, \mathcal{D}')$ to the adversary. Here, D and D' are distinct indeterminants. (ii) In a signing request, the adversary supplies an identifier id_k in

addition to a message m_k, and the tweak $e_k \in \mathbb{Z}_q$ is computed as $e_k \leftarrow Hash(id_k)$. To process such a signing request, the challenger carries out the same logic, but with $D + e_k D'$ replacing D in step 5(d).

It is easy to prove that Lemma 2 carries over to this setting without change. We leave this to the reader.

We define $\text{CMA}_{\text{hkd,ps}}^{\text{ggm}}\text{adv}[\mathcal{A}, \mathcal{S}]$ to be adversary $\mathcal{A}$'s advantage in winning this modified CMA game in the EC-GGM. We can prove the following analog of Theorem 4. As the reader will notice, the statement of this theorem is almost the same as Theorem 3.

Theorem 8. *Let $\mathcal{A}$ be an adversary attacking $\mathcal{S}_{\text{ecdsa}}$ as in Definition 2 with* **homogenous key derivation and presignatures** *that makes at most N presignature, signing, or group queries. Let U denote the maximum number of unused presignatures at any point in time. Then there exist adversaries $\mathcal{B}_{\text{I}}$, $\mathcal{B}_{\text{IIa}}$, $\mathcal{B}_{\text{IIb}}$, $\mathcal{B}_{\text{IIc}}$, and $\mathcal{B}_{\text{III}}$, whose running times are essentially the same as $\mathcal{A}$ plus $O(UN)$, such that $\text{CMA}_{\text{hkd,ps}}^{\text{ggm}}\text{adv}[\mathcal{A}, \mathcal{S}_{\text{ecdsa}}]$ is bounded by*

$$\text{CRadv}[\mathcal{B}_{\text{I}}, Hash] + N \cdot \text{RPRadv}[\mathcal{B}_{\text{IIa}}, Hash]$$
$$+ (4 + o(1))N \cdot \text{RRadv}[\mathcal{B}_{\text{IIb}}, Hash] + UN \cdot \text{RPRadv}[\mathcal{B}_{\text{IIc}}, Hash]$$
$$+ \text{ZPRadv}[\mathcal{B}_{\text{III}}, Hash] + O(N^2/q).$$

Proof. We categorize forgeries as Type I, IIa, IIb, IIc, or III essentially as in Theorem 3.

Everything goes through the same as in the proof of Theorem 7, except for the analysis of Type II forgeries.

Consider the point in time when the adversary queries the group oracle to obtain $\mathcal{R}^*$ for the first time. Let us call this a **Type IIa** forgery if at this time, $\pi^{-1}(\mathcal{R}^*)$ is of the form $a + bD + b'D'$. Type IIa forgeries can be dealt with in exactly the same way as Type II forgeries in the proof of Theorem 7.

Now, consider a Type II forgery that is not a Type IIa forgery. For such a forgery, the initial preimage of $\mathcal{R}^*$ is a polynomial that involves the indeterminants $R_1, R_2, \ldots$. However, before the attack ends, all of these variables must be substituted via signing queries, so that if the attack ends with a forgery, we must have $\pi^{-1}(\mathcal{R}^*) = (s^*)^{-1}(h^* + t^*D + t^*e^*D')$.

Just as in Theorem 3, we suppose that at the time $\mathcal{R}^*$ is initially generated, we have $\pi^{-1}(\mathcal{R}^*) = a + bD + c_1 R_1 + \cdots + c_\ell R_\ell$, where the c_i's are nonzero; however, during the attack, we substitute $R_i \mapsto s_i^{-1}(h_i + t_i D + t_i e_i D')$ for $i = 1, \ldots, \ell$, again, in that order. For $i = 0, \ldots, \ell$, define

$$A_i := a + \sum_{j \leq i} c_j h_j / s_j, \quad B_i := b + \sum_{j \leq i} c_j t_j / s_j, \quad \text{and} \quad B_i' := b' + \sum_{j \leq j} c_j t_j e_j / s_j.$$

A forgery must satisfy:

$$A_\ell = (s^*)^{-1} h^*, \quad B_\ell = (s^*)^{-1} t^*, \quad \text{and} \quad B_\ell' = (s^*)^{-1} t^* e^*. \tag{8}$$

Note that the first of these two equations are identical to the two equations in (4) in the proof of Theorem 3. Indeed, we can complete the proof just as in Theorem 3, where Type IIb and IIc forgeries are defined in the same way.   □

Note. Unlike as in Theorem 7, we see that this scheme is *insecure* if we allow a "raw" signing oracle.

9.3   Homogeneous Key Derivation with Re-randomized Presignatures

The lazy simulation in Fig. 6 is modified as follows: (i) In the initialization step, the challenger chooses $(d, d') \in \mathbb{Z}_q \times \mathbb{Z}_q$ at random, invokes $(\mathtt{map}, d)$ and $(\mathtt{map}, d')$ to obtain $\mathcal{D}$ and $\mathcal{D}'$. The challenger gives $(\mathcal{G}, \mathcal{D}, \mathcal{D}')$ to the adversary. (ii) In a signing request, the adversary supplies an identifier id_k in addition to a message m_k, and the tweak $e_k \in \mathbb{Z}_q$ is computed as $e_k \leftarrow Hash(id_k)$. To process such a signing request, the challenger carries out the same logic, but with $d + e_k d'$ replacing d in steps 5(h) and 5(i).

To verify a signature with respect to a tweak e^*, where $e^* := Hash(id^*)$, the signature is verified with respect to the public key $\mathcal{D} + e^*\mathcal{D}'$.

The symbolic simulation in Fig. 7 is modified as follows: (i) In the initialization step, the challenger invokes $(\mathtt{map}, \mathsf{D})$ and $(\mathtt{map}, \mathsf{D}')$ to obtain $\mathcal{D}$ and $\mathcal{D}'$. The challenger gives $(\mathcal{G}, \mathcal{D}, \mathcal{D}')$ to the adversary. Here, D and D' are distinct indeterminants. (ii) In a signing request, the adversary supplies an identifier id_k in addition to a message m_k, and the tweak $e_k \in \mathbb{Z}_q$ is computed as $e_k \leftarrow Hash(id_k)$. To process such a signing request, the challenger carries out the same logic, but with $\mathsf{D} + e_k \mathsf{D}'$ replacing D in step 5(i).

It is easy to prove that Lemma 3 carries over to this setting without change. We leave this to the reader.

We define $\mathrm{CMA}^{\mathrm{ggm}}_{\mathrm{hkd,rrps}}\mathrm{adv}[\mathcal{A}, \mathcal{S}]$ to be adversary $\mathcal{A}$'s advantage in winning this modified CMA game in the EC-GGM. We can prove the following analog of Theorem 6. As the reader will notice, the statement of this theorem is almost the same as Theorem 5.

Theorem 9. *Let $\mathcal{A}$ be an adversary attacking $\mathcal{S}_{\mathrm{ecdsa}}$ as in Definition 2 with* **homogeneous key derivation and re-randomized presignatures** *that makes at most N presignature, signing, or group queries. Let U denote the maximum number of* unused *presignatures at any point in time. Then there exist adversaries $\mathcal{B}_{\mathrm{I}}$, $\mathcal{B}_{\mathrm{IIa}}$, $\mathcal{B}_{\mathrm{IIc}}$, and $\mathcal{B}_{\mathrm{III}}$, whose running times are essentially the same as $\mathcal{A}$ plus $O(UN)$, such that $\mathrm{CMA}^{\mathrm{ggm}}_{\mathrm{hkd,rrps}}\mathrm{adv}[\mathcal{A}, \mathcal{S}_{\mathrm{ecdsa}}]$ is bounded by*

$$\mathrm{CRadv}[\mathcal{B}_{\mathrm{I}}, Hash] + (4 + o(1))N \cdot \mathrm{RPRadv}[\mathcal{B}_{\mathrm{IIa}}, Hash]$$
$$+ N \cdot \mathrm{RPRadv}[\mathcal{B}_{\mathrm{IIc}}, Hash] + \mathrm{ZPRadv}[\mathcal{B}_{\mathrm{III}}, Hash] + O(N^2/q).$$

Proof. We categorize forgeries as Type I, IIa, IIbc, or III essentially as in Theorem 5.

The proof follows the same outline as that of Theorem 8, except for the analysis of Type IIbc forgeries, which follows the same outline as in Theorem 5.

Note. The above analysis shows that the scheme is secure even with a "raw" signing oracle.

References

1. Bar-Ilan, J., Beaver, D.: Non-cryptographic fault-tolerant computing in constant number of rounds of interaction. In: PODC 1989, pp. 201–209 (1989)
2. Bernstein, D.J., Lange, T., Niederhagen, R., Peters, C., Schwabe, P.: Implementing Wagner's generalized birthday attack against the SHA-3 round-1 candidate FSB. Cryptology ePrint Archive, Report 2009/292 (2009). https://ia.cr/2009/292
3. Boneh, D., Lynn, B., Shacham, H.: Short signatures from the Weil pairing. In: Boyd, C. (ed.) ASIACRYPT 2001. LNCS, vol. 2248, pp. 514–532. Springer, Heidelberg (2001). https://doi.org/10.1007/3-540-45682-1_30
4. Brown, D.R.L.: Generic groups, collision resistance, and ECDSA. Des. Codes Crypt. **35**, 119–152 (2002)
5. Canetti, R., Makriyannis, N., Peled, U.: UC non-interactive, proactive, threshold ECDSA. Cryptology ePrint Archive, Report 2020/492 (2020). https://ia.cr/2020/492
6. Certicom Research: Sec 2: Recommended elliptic curve domain parameters (2010). version 2.0, http://www.secg.org/sec2-v2.pdf
7. Damgård, I., Jakobsen, T.P., Nielsen, J.B., Pagter, J.I., Østergård, M.B.: Fast threshold ECDSA with honest majority. Cryptology ePrint Archive, Report 2020/501 (2020). https://ia.cr/2020/501
8. Das, P., Erwig, A., Faust, S., Loss, J., Riahi, S.: The exact security of BIP32 wallets. Cryptology ePrint Archive, Report 2021/1287 (2021). https://ia.cr/2021/1287
9. The DFINITY Team: The internet computer for geeks. Cryptology ePrint Archive, Report 2022/087 (2022). https://ia.cr/2022/087
10. Fersch, M., Kiltz, E., Poettering, B.: On the provable security of (EC)DSA signatures. In: 2016 ACM SIGSAC, pp. 1651–1662. ACM (2016)
11. Gennaro, R., Goldfeder, S.: One round threshold ECDSA with identifiable abort. Cryptology ePrint Archive, Report 2020/540 (2020). https://ia.cr/2020/540
12. Groth, J., Shoup, V.: On the security of ECDSA with additive key derivation and presignatures. Cryptology ePrint Archive, Report 2021/1330 (2021). https://ia.cr/2021/1330
13. Gutoski, G., Stebila, D.: Hierarchical deterministic bitcoin wallets that tolerate key leakage. Cryptology ePrint Archive, Report 2014/998 (2014), https://ia.cr/2014/998
14. Nechaev, V.I.: Complexity of a determinate algorithm for the discrete logarithm. Math. Notes **55**(2), 165–172 (1994). translated from Matematicheskie Zametki, 55(2):91–101, 1994
15. Nikolić, I., Sasaki, Yu.: Refinements of the k-tree algorithm for the generalized birthday problem. In: Iwata, T., Cheon, J.H. (eds.) ASIACRYPT 2015. LNCS, vol. 9453, pp. 683–703. Springer, Heidelberg (2015). https://doi.org/10.1007/978-3-662-48800-3_28
16. Shoup, V.: Lower bounds for discrete logarithms and related problems. In: Fumy, W. (ed.) EUROCRYPT 1997. LNCS, vol. 1233, pp. 256–266. Springer, Heidelberg (1997). https://doi.org/10.1007/3-540-69053-0_18

17. National Institute of Standards and Technology: Digital signature standard (DSS). Federal Information Processing Publication 186–4 (2013). https://doi.org/10.6028/NIST.FIPS.186-4

18. Stern, J., Pointcheval, D., Malone-Lee, J., Smart, N.P.: Flaws in applying proof methodologies to signature schemes. In: Yung, M. (ed.) CRYPTO 2002. LNCS, vol. 2442, pp. 93–110. Springer, Heidelberg (2002). https://doi.org/10.1007/3-540-45708-9_7

19. Wagner, D.: A generalized birthday problem. In: Yung, M. (ed.) CRYPTO 2002. LNCS, vol. 2442, pp. 288–304. Springer, Heidelberg (2002). https://doi.org/10.1007/3-540-45708-9_19

20. Wuille, P.: Hierarchical deterministic wallets (2020). https://github.com/bitcoin/bips/blob/master/bip-0032.mediawiki

21. Yuen, T.H., Yiu, S.-M.: Strong known related-key attacks and the security of ECDSA. In: Liu, J.K., Huang, X. (eds.) NSS 2019. LNCS, vol. 11928, pp. 130–145. Springer, Cham (2019). https://doi.org/10.1007/978-3-030-36938-5_8

Secure Multiparty Computation
with Free Branching

Aarushi Goel[1], Mathias Hall-Andersen[2], Aditya Hegde[1],
and Abhishek Jain[1(✉)]

[1] Johns Hopkins University, Baltimore, USA
{aarushig,ahegde,abhishek}@cs.jhu.edu
[2] Aarhus University, Aarhus, Denmark
ma@cs.au.dk

Abstract. We study secure multi-party computation (MPC) protocols for branching circuits that contain multiple sub-circuits (i.e., branches) and the output of the circuit is that of single "active" branch. Crucially, the identity of the active branch must remain hidden from the protocol participants.

While such circuits can be securely computed by evaluating each branch and then multiplexing the output, such an approach incurs a communication cost linear in the size of the entire circuit. To alleviate this, a series of recent works have investigated the problem of reducing the communication cost of branching executions inside MPC (without relying on fully homomorphic encryption). Most notably, the stacked garbling paradigm [Heath and Kolesnikov, CRYPTO'20] yields garbled circuits for branching circuits whose size only depends on the size of the largest branch. Presently, however, it is not known how to obtain similar communication improvements for secure computation involving *more than two parties*.

In this work, we provide a generic framework for branching multi-party computation that supports *any number of parties*. The communication complexity of our scheme is proportional to the size of the largest branch and the computation is linear in the size of the entire circuit. We provide an implementation and benchmarks to demonstrate practicality of our approach.

1 Introduction

Secure multiparty computation (MPC) [5,9,20,40] is an interactive protocol that allows a group of mutually distrusting parties to jointly compute a function over their private inputs without revealing anything beyond the output of the function. Over the years, significant progress has been made towards improving the efficiency of MPC protocols [3,11,12,16,21–25,33,39] to make them practically viable.

While a wide variety of techniques for efficiency improvements have been developed in different settings based on the corruption threshold, communication model or security guarantee, a common aspect of most modern efficient protocols in all

© International Association for Cryptologic Research 2022
O. Dunkelman and S. Dziembowski (Eds.): EUROCRYPT 2022, LNCS 13275, pp. 397–426, 2022.
https://doi.org/10.1007/978-3-031-06944-4_14

of these settings is that they *circuit representation* of the function. A limitation of such protocols, however, is that their total communication complexity is at least linear in the size of the circuit. Known techniques for getting sub-linear communication in the circuit size rely on computationally heavy tools such as fully-homomorphic encryption (FHE) [19] or homomorphic secret sharing (HSS) [7]. While there have been recent advancements in improving the efficiency of these methods, they are still far from being practical in many use cases.

As a result, the efficiency of existing efficient protocols is highly dependent on how succinctly a function can be represented using circuits. This is clearly not ideal, since circuits are often not the most efficient way of representing many functions. A common example of such functions are ones that include some kind of *conditional* control flow instructions. When evaluating such functions, a circuit-based MPC will incur communication dependent on the size of the *entire* circuit, while in reality we only need to evaluate the "active" path (i.e., the path that is actually executed based on the conditional) in the circuit.

It is therefore useful to design efficient MPC protocols for useful classes of functions, where the total communication between the parties only depends on the "active" parts, rather than the entire circuit.

MPC for Conditional Branches. In this work, we focus on one such class of functions, namely, ones that contain conditional branches. As discussed in [29], a real world example of an application that consists of conditional branches is where a set of servers collectively provide k services and the clients can pay and avail any one of their services (depending on their requirements), without revealing to the servers which service they are availing. Similarly, control flow instructions are also integral to any kind of programming and as observed in [27], many kinds of control flow instructions (including repeated and/or nested loops) can be refactored into conditional branches. Such refactorings often result in a *large* number of conditional branches. For such functions, designing MPC protocols where the total communication only depends on the size of the active branch is very useful.

Recently, in a sequence of works [26,27], Heath and Kolsnekov made progress in this direction in the two-party setting. They design garbled circuit based *two-party* semi-honest protocols for evaluating functions with conditional branches, where the total communication only depends on the size of the largest branch. In the *multiparty* setting, however, no such protocols are currently known. The recent works of [28,30] design MPC for conditional branches where they reduce the number of public-key operations required to evaluate conditional branches; however, the total communication in their protocols still depends on the size of all branches. Furthermore, all these protocols only work for Boolean circuits.

Given this state of the art, we consider the following question in this work:

Does there exist an efficient multiparty protocol for securely computing conditional branches, where the total communication only depends on the size of the largest branch?

We remark that all of the above mentioned prior works only focus on the semi-honest setting. The task of designing analogous *maliciously-secure* protocols remains unexplored (both in the two-party and multi-party settings). In this work, we also consider this question.

1.1   Our Contributions

We design the first *multiparty* computation protocols for conditional branches, where the communication complexity only depends on the size of the largest branch. Our protocols can support arbitrary number of parties and corruptions. We present both constant and non-constant round variants.

I. Non-constant Round Branching MPC. Our first contribution is a *semi-honest* MPC for conditional branches, where the communication complexity only depends on the size of the largest branch. This protocol is capable of computing arithmetic circuits over any field or ring. The round complexity of this protocol depends on the depth of the circuit.

We present this protocol as a generic compiler that can transform a large class of admissible[1] MPC protocols into ones for conditional branches that achieve the aforementioned communication complexity. Several existing concretely efficient protocols including MASCOT [33], SPDZ2k [12], Overdrive [34], TinyOT [18] and [25], [13] can be used with this compiler.

In particular, by instantiating our compiler with a semi-honest admissible (dishonest-majority) MPC protocol with communication complexity $\mathsf{CC}(|C|)$ (where C is the circuit being evaluated), we obtain the following result:

Informal Theorem 1. *Let λ be the security parameter. There exists a semi-honest secure MPC for evaluating conditional branches, that can tolerate arbitrary corruptions and that achieves communication complexity of $O(\mathsf{CC}(|C_{\mathsf{max}}|) + n^2 k\lambda + n^2|C_{\mathsf{max}}|)$, where k is the number of branches in the conditional.*

We also implement this protocol to test its concrete efficiency and compare it to state-of-the-art MPC protocols. More details are provided later in this section.

Extension to Malicious Security. We also present an extension of this protocol to the case of malicious adversaries. Asymptotically, its communication complexity is similar to the semi-honest protocol, except that it incurs a multiplicative overhead dependent on a statistical security parameter.

We view this construction as initial evidence that efficient branching MPC with malicious security is possible. However, we believe that there is significant scope for future improvements towards achieving good concrete efficiency.

II. Constant Round Branching MPC. Our next contribution is a *constant round* MPC for conditional branches, where the communication complexity only

---

[1] We require the underlying MPC to be such that it evaluates the circuit in a gate-by-gate manner and maintains an invariant that for every intermediate wire in the circuit, the parties collectively hold a sharing of the value induced on that wire during evaluation.

depends on the size of the largest branch. This protocol is based on a *multiparty garbling* approach [2] and only supports boolean circuits.

We also present this protocol in the form of a general compiler. Namely, given a MPC protocol with communication complexity $CC(|C|)$ for evaluating a circuit C, we get the following result:

Informal Theorem 2. *Let λ be the security parameter. There exists a constant-round, semi-honest secure MPC for evaluating conditional branches (represented as Boolean circuits), that can tolerate arbitrary corruptions and that achieves communication complexity of $O(|CC(\lambda|C_{max}|) + n^2k\lambda + n^2\lambda|C_{max}|)$, where k is the number of branches in the conditional.*

To obtain both of the above results, we adopt a fundamentally different approach as compared to prior works [26–28, 30] in this area. Specifically, prior works require the parties to locally evaluate *all* the branches. In contrast, in our approach, the parties select the "active" branch and *only execute that branch*. A detailed overview our approach can be found in the next section.

III. Comparison and Performance Evaluation. To gauge practicality, we implement our non-constant round *semi-honest* compiler and instantiate it using two kinds of protocols:

- *Quadratic Dependence on the Number of Parties:* MP-SPDZ is a common MPC library that contains implementations of the SPDZ protocol [16] and its descendants. All of the protocols in this library have total communication with quadratic dependence on the number of parties. We instatiate our compiler with an implementation of MASCOT [33] from this library without modification. Our code is agnostic to which protocol the MPC library is configured; this helps demonstrates that our techniques are generic and blockbox. We run benchmarks over simulated LAN and WAN settings. We show that our compiled protocol outperforms naïvely evaluating all the branches in parallel using MASCOT for as few as 8 branches.
- *Linear Dependence on the Number of Parties:* We implement an optimized variant of our compiler that incurs a linear additive overhead in the number of parties, instead of a quadratic overhead. We then test the efficiency of our compiler when instantiated with the CDN protocol [13], which only has a linear dependence on the number of parties. For this, we first implement the CDN protocol. To the best of our knowledge, this is the first known implementation of CDN. Similar to the previous case, we show that our compiled protocol (instantiated using CDN) outperforms naïvely evaluating all the branches in parallel using CDN for 8 branches.

2 Technical Overview

Background. All recent works [26–28, 30] in this area are based on the same principle approach – *the parties evaluate all branches, albeit, only the "active"* *branch is evaluated on real inputs, while the remaining branches are all evaluated on fake/garbage values.*

For instance, in the two-party setting, [26,27], which are based on a garbled circuit based approach, one of the parties garbles all the k branches. It then "stacks" these garblings into a compressed form that is proportional to the length of the largest branch in the circuit. Using some additional information sent by the garbler, the evaluator is able to reconstruct k different garbled circuits, only one of which is a valid garbling of the "active" branch, and the remaining are random strings (or some garbage material). Unaware of the active branch, the evaluator evaluates the k garbled circuits w.r.t. different branches to obtain k different output labels. These output labels are then filtered with the help of a "multiplexer" to obtain the correct output. Overall, this approach reduces the communication to only depend on the size of the largest branch (the computation complexity, however, is still large).

In the multiparty setting, both [28,30], follow the same principle approach. These protocols have separate preprocessing and online phases. They require parties to evaluate all branches (including the inactive ones) in the online phase over 0 or some random values and leverage this fact to get savings in the preprocessing phase. As a result, communication in the preprocessing phase only depends on the size of one branch, but the communication in the online phase still depends on the size of all the branches.

Indeed, it is unclear how to extend the stacked garbling approach used in [26,27] to get similar savings in communication in the multiparty setting. Recall that the garbler in stacked garbling is required to garble all branches and hence its computation *depends on the size of all branches.* This means that naive approaches that involve distributing the role of the garbler amongst multiple parties are a non-starter as they will incur *communication* proportional to the size of all branches. In order to design a multiparty protocol with similar communication savings as in stacked garbling, we therefore adopt a fundamentally different approach.

Our Approach. In our approach, *the parties select which branch to execute in a "privacy-preserving" manner and only execute that branch.* To facilitate this private selection, both of our constructions (in the non-constant round and constant-round settings) employ a common tool – a variant of oblivious linear evaluation that we refer to as *oblivious inner product* (OIP). In particular, our protocols make use of OIPs with (small) *constant rate.* We show that such OIPs can be easily constructed using low-rate linearly homomorphic encryption schemes, which are known from a variety of assumptions [8,15,17,38].

In the sequel, we first describe the main ideas underlying our non-constant round constructions. We then proceed to describe our constant-round construction.

2.1 Non-constant Round Branching MPC

We start with the observation that the problem of computing conditional branches bears some similarities to the problem of private function evaluation

(PFE) [31,35,36]. Recall that in PFE, one party has the function and the remaining parties provide inputs. This, in some sense is reminiscent of the problem that we have at hand, albeit with some differences. In particular, in our case, while none of the parties actually knows which function/branch is "active", they all know the set that this branch belongs to. Moreover, the parties collectively hold information about which of these functions to evaluate. This can be viewed as a *distributed variant of PFE*. In light of this observation, we build upon some ideas previously used in the PFE literature.

Private Function Evaluation. In PFE, the function is only known to one of the parties (say party P_1). The security requirements in standard PFE are very similar to that in MPC, with the only additional requirement that the function must remain hidden from all other parties. To achieve this, Mohassel and Sadeghian [35] observe that in order to hide a function that is represented in the form of a circuit, there are two components that need to remain hidden – (1) The wire-configuration of the circuit, i.e., how the gates connect with each other, and (2) the function (i.e., addition or multiplication) implemented by each gate in the circuit. They propose a strategy to conceal the above components of a circuit in order to achieve function privacy (without relying on universal circuits). In particular, they start with MPC protocols that work over some kind of secret shares (additive/threshold/authenticated) and evaluate any given circuit in a gate-by-gate manner. These protocols maintain the invariant that for every intermediate wire in the circuit, all parties hold a sharing of the value induced on that wire during evaluation. Many concretely efficient protocols such as [12,16,22,25,33], satisfy these requirements. [35] propose the following modifications to such MPC protocols to obtain a PFE protocol:

1. *Hiding Wire Configuration:* Each intermediate wire in the circuit has two end points – (1) one is the *source gate*, for which it acts as the outgoing wire and (2) the other is the *destination gate*, for which it acts as the incoming wire. As discussed earlier, for hiding the wire configuration, we need to hide the gate connections, i.e., we want to hide the mapping between the source and destination of each wire in the circuit. For this, [35] assign two unique labels to each wire w. One is an outgoing label based on its source gate and second is an incoming label based on whether it acts as left or right input wire to its destination gate. Let π denote the mapping between these incoming and outgoing labels, i.e., let $\pi(i) = j$ denote that a wire that has incoming label i has an outgoing label j. In PFE, this mapping π is only known to the function folding party.

   In order to hide this mapping, [35] devise a mechanism to mask the outputs value of each gate and unmask them based on π when this value is used for evaluating the destination gate of this wire. This is executed by sampling an input mask and an output mask for every wire in the circuit. Let $\mathsf{in}_1, \ldots, \mathsf{in}_W$ and $\mathsf{out}_1, \ldots, \mathsf{out}_W$ be the set of these input and output masks, where W is the total number of wires in the circuit. In the preprocessing phase, with the help of the function holding party and the underlyin MPC, the parties compute $\Delta_w = \mathsf{in}_w - \mathsf{out}_{\pi(w)}$ for every $w \in [W]$. These Δ_w values are revealed to function holding party in the clear. This processing information helps the parties in using appropriately permuted input and output masks to mask and unmask wire values during evaluation in the online phase. In more detail, the online phase proceeds as follows:

- Upon evaluating each gate g, the parties use output masks to mask all the outgoing wires of the gate. Let the outgoing wires have labels c and d respectively, and let u_c and u_d denote these masked outputs. These masked outputs are revealed to all parties in the clear.
- For evaluating a particular gate g, where the two input wires have incoming wire labels a and b, the function holding party computes $A = u_{\pi(a)} + \Delta_a$ and $B = u_{\pi(b)} + \Delta_b$ and sends it to all the parties. The parties subtract their shares of inp_a and inp_b from these values to get a sharing of the actual values on which to evaluate gate g.

2. *Hiding Gate Functions:* This is relatively easier. Assume that our arithmetic circuit representation of the function only consists of addition and multiplication gates, let $\mathsf{type}_g = 0$ (and $\mathsf{type}_g = 1$ resp.) denote that gate g is an addition gate (and multiplication gate resp.). For each gate g with incoming wires a and b, we can use the underlying MPC to compute both shares of $a + b$ and $a \cdot b$. The function holding party P_1 can secret share type_g using the underlying MPC and the parties can then choose between shares of $a + b$ and $a \cdot b$ by computing the following using the underlying MPC:

$$(1 - [\mathsf{type}_g])([a + b]) + \mathsf{type}_g([a \cdot b]),$$

where we denote $[x]$ as a sharing of a value x using the secret sharing scheme used by the underlying MPC. This allows the parties to evaluate the correct function, without revealing it.

Our Semi-honest Protocol. In our setting, the parties know the description of all the branches in the conditional and have a secret sharing of the index of the active branch. In order to hide the identity of the active branch, similar to the above approach, we need to hide both the wire configuration and the gate functions of the active branch. We start by listing the barriers in directly adapting the above approach to our setting and then proceed to discuss how we resolve them.

- In the preprocessing phase, computing Δ requires the function holding party to input π to the underlying MPC. In our setting, no party knows the exact value of π.
- In the online phase, A and B values are computed locally by the function holding party in PFE since it already knows the mapping π. This is again a problem in our setting.
- Finally, in order to hide the gate functions in the online phase, the value of each type_g secret shared by the function holding party. But as above, neither party in our setting knows this value.

In order to overcome the above barriers, we crucially rely on the fact that in our setting, while no single party knows the function (or the mapping π), they all know the set that the function belongs to. In other words, given a set of k branches $C_1, \ldots, C_k$, all the parties can locally compute the mappings $\pi_1, \ldots, \pi_k$ corresponding to each branch. Moreover, the parties also have a secret sharing of the index of the active branch. Let α be the index of the active branch. Our first idea towards resolving the above barriers to is to somehow allow the parties combine their shares of α with $\pi_1, \ldots, \pi_k$ to get a sharing of π_α. However, since the size of $\pi_1, \ldots, \pi_k$ depends on the size of all branches, a naive implementation of this computation will incur communication that depends on the size of $\pi_1, \ldots, \pi_k$.

We get around this by using a new variant of oblivious linear evaluation, which we refer to as oblivious inner product. We now outline our main ideas:

- **Sharing of α:** We work with a unary representation of the index α. In other words, we assume each party have k secret shares, where the αth share is a sharing of 1, while all others are sharings of 0s. Let these shares be denoted by $[b_1], \ldots, [b_k]$

- **Input/Output Masks:** In the preprocessing phase, we use the underlying MPC to sample random input and output masks $\mathsf{in}_1, \ldots, \mathsf{in}_W$ and $\mathsf{out}_1, \ldots, \mathsf{out}_W$, where W is the number of wires in the largest branch. Each party, now locally permutes its shares of input masks based on the k mappings $\pi_1, \ldots, \pi_k$. In more detail, given sharings $[\mathsf{out}_1], \ldots, [\mathsf{out}_W]$, for each $m \in [k]$, the parties locally compute sharings $[\mathsf{out}_{\pi_m(1)}], \ldots, [\mathsf{out}_{\pi_m(W)}]$. Lets denote each $[\mathsf{out}_{\pi_m(1)}], \ldots, [\mathsf{out}_{\pi_m(W)}]$ by $[\overrightarrow{\mathsf{out}_{\pi_m}}]$. If instead of computing shares of π_α, we directly compute re-randomized shares of $[\overrightarrow{\mathsf{out}_{\pi_\alpha}}]$, then the parties can simply compute their shares of Δ_w values as follows

$$\forall w \in [W], [\Delta_w] = [\mathsf{in}_w] - [\mathsf{out}_{\pi_\alpha(w)}]$$

- **Oblivious Inner Product:** For computing re-randomized shares $[\overrightarrow{\mathsf{out}_{\pi_\alpha}}]$, we use a primitive called oblivious inner product (OIP). This is a protocol between two-parties, called the sender and receiver and bears resemblance to oblivious linear evaluation. The sender has inputs $m_0, \ldots, m_k$ and the receiver has inputs $b_1, \ldots, b_k$. At the end of the protocol, the receiver learns $m_0 + \sum_{i \in [k]} b_i m_i$ and the sender learns nothing.

We use this primitive and a GMW [20] style approach to obtain shares of $\overrightarrow{\mathsf{out}_{\pi_\alpha}}$ as follows: for each pair of parties in the protocol, we run an instance of OIP, where one party acts as the sender and the other acts as the receiver. The inputs of the sender party to this OIP are its shares of $[\overrightarrow{\mathsf{out}_{\pi_1}}], \ldots, [\overrightarrow{\mathsf{out}_{\pi_W}}]$ and a random value X, while the inputs of the receiver are its shares of the unary representation of α. At the end, each party P_i computes its share of $\overrightarrow{\mathsf{out}_{\pi_\alpha}}$ by adding the outputs of each OIP instance where it acted as the receiver and subtracting each X sampled in the OIP instance where it acted as the sender. It is easy to see that these resulting shares are indeed shares of $\overrightarrow{\mathsf{out}_{\pi_\alpha}}$.

However, note that while the length of the output of each OIP in our case only depends on the size of the largest branch, the length of sender inputs depends on the size of all branches. Therefore, in order to design an MPC protocol where the overall communication is only proportional to the size of the largest branch, we must use an OIP where the communication only depends on the length of receiver inputs and the output, but is independent of the length of sender inputs. We show that such OIPs can be constructed using linearly homomorphic encryption with constant rate.

– **Online Phase:** Now that we have sharing of Δ_w values that was computed using the mapping π corresponding to the active branch, we can compute shares of the A and B values as follows:

$$[A] = \sum_{m \in [k]} [b_1]u_{\pi_1(a)} + [\Delta_a] \quad \text{and} \quad [B] = \sum_{m \in [k]} [b_1]u_{\pi_1(b)} + [\Delta_b]$$

We note that most linearly homomorphic secret sharing schemes allow such computations to be done non-interactively and hence it does not incur any overhead in the communication complexity. Shares of type_g for every gate g can also be computed in a similar manner.

We present a formal description of this protocol in Sect. 5.

Extension to Malicious Security. While the basic outline of our protocol remains the same, even in the malicious setting, we need to do a little more work to make the above protocol secure against a malicious adversary. In particular, we need to ensure that the inputs used by the parties in the OIP instances are consistent with values/shares computed by them using the underlying MPC. For this we propose to add the following consistency checks:

Receiver's Input Consistency. We start by using an OIP that is secure against a malicious reciever. In order to ensure that receiver uses valid sharings of the active branch, we implement a kind of MAC check using the underlying MPC. In particular, in the OIP execution, the sender samples $k + 1$ random values and appends them to its inputs. Now when the receiver computes the output of the OIP, it also learns an inner product of these random values with its shares of the active branch (we refer to this as the MAC value for this OIP). We now use the underlying MPC to compute the exact same value. In particular, the sender sends the $k + 1$ random values that it sampled in the OIP as input to the underlying MPC, while the receiver sends the MAC value learnt from the output of the OIP. We allow the underlying MPC to now check if the MAC value indeed corresponds to an inner product of the receivers shares of the active branch and the random values input by the sender. We note that since the length of the receiver's input is independent of the size of all branches, computing this MAC value inside the MPC does not incur too much overhead.

Sender's Input Consistency. Recall that the inputs of the sender to the OIP depend on the size of all branches, and hence we cannot hope to use the kind of check that we used for ensuring receiver consistency. Moreover, since the length of the sender message is much shorter than the length of its inputs, we also cannot hope to use an OIP with malicious sender security that can somehow extract the sender's inputs. Therefore, instead we continue to work with an OIP that is secure against a semi-honest sender but augment it with a cut-and-choose style approach. In particular, we sample multiple copies of the masks and compute delta values using OIPs for each of those copies. We also ask the sender to commit (using compressive commitments) to the inputs and randomness used for computing each of its sender messages. At the end of all OIP instantiations, we use the underlying MPC to sample a random subset and reveal the shares of masks of all parties for that subset. The senders also send the randomness used by them in the sender messages of this opened subset. Given this information, the parties can verify if the senders behaved honestly and used consistent shares in the opened instances. We use the remaining unopened instances to run multiple copies of the online phase and take a majority to decide the final output. Due to the use of cut-and-choose, the communication complexity of our maliciously secure protocol is proportional to $\delta \times$ the cost of computing the largest branch. We defer a formal description of this protocol to the full-version of this paper.

2.2   Constant Round (Semi-honest) Protocol

Beaver, Micali, and Rogaway (BMR) [2] proposed a general template for constructing *constant round* MPC from existing generic *non-constant round* MPC. The main observations underlying their technique were – (1) round complexity of more generic non-constant round protocols depends on the depth of the function being computed and (2) garbling [40] a functionality/circuit is a constant depth procedure.

The parties can leverage these observations to first execute a *garbling phase*, where they compute a garbled circuit of the function (that they wished to evaluate) using the non-constant round protocol. This phase will require a constant number of rounds. Given this garbled circuit, they then proceed to the *evaluation phase*, where each party locally evaluates the garbled circuit to learn the output. This phase requires no interaction and hence the overall protocol runs in a constant number of rounds.

More concretely, in the garbling phase, the parties collectively sample two keys $k_{w,0}, k_{w,1}$ for every wire w in the circuit. The garbled table for each gate g in the circuit with incoming wires a, b and outgoing wire c, consists of the following four rows, corresponding to $\alpha, \beta \in \{0, 1\}$:

$$ct_{\alpha,\beta} = \mathsf{PRF}_{k_{a,\alpha}}(g) + \mathsf{PRF}_{k_{b,\beta}}(g) + k_{c,g(\alpha,\beta)}$$

Branching MPC using BMR Template. The generality of the BMR approach immediately makes it compatible with our non-constant round semi-honest protocol (from Sect. 2.1). Indeed, in the garbling phase, parties can use that protocol to compute a garbled circuit for the active branch. During the evaluation phase, however, since the parties do not know which branch the garbled circuit corresponds to, they can evaluate it for every branch and obtain the corresponding output wire labels. Note that only the labels obtained by evaluating w.r.t. to the active branch actually correspond to a *valid set of abels*. Finally, via interaction, parties can determine the output corresponding to the "valid" set of output labels. The complexity of this last step is independent of the circuit size and only depends on the number of branches times the output length.

While this yields a simple baseline constant round MPC for conditional branches, it is highly inefficient. Since no party knows the keys $k_{a,\alpha}, k_{b,\beta}$ in their entirety, they must evaluate the PRF (on these keys) inside an MPC protocol. Since, the circuit representations of PRF's are typically massive, this protocol is unlikely to be concretely efficient. As such, for concrete efficiency, we require a protocol that only makes a *black-box* use of cryptography.

Towards Black-Box use of Cryptography. Damgård and Ishai [14] proposed a variant of the above BMR template that enables parties to evaluate the PRF outside the MPC, thereby only making a black-box use of cryptography.

Specifically, in their approach, each party P_i samples two keys $k_{w,0}^i, k_{w,1}^i$ for every wire w in the circuit. In other words, the cumulative keys associated with every wire is a concatenation of all the parties' keys. The garbled table for each gate g in the circuit with incoming wires a, b and outgoing wire c, consists of the following $4 \cdot n$ rows, corresponding to $\alpha, \beta \in \{0,1\}$ and $i \in [n]$:

$$ct_{\alpha,\beta}^i = \bigoplus_{m=1}^n \mathsf{PRF}_{k_{a,\alpha}^m}(g\|i) \; + \; \bigoplus_{m=1}^n \mathsf{PRF}_{k_{b,\beta}^m}(g\|i) + k_{c,g(\alpha,\beta)}^i$$

It is easy to see that unlike the BMR approach, here the parties are only required to evaluate the PRF on their own keys, which can be done locally and the resulting PRF evaluation can be fed as input to the underlying MPC implementing the garbling functionality.

In our setting, however, this approach posits a fundamental barrier. Recall that for evaluating conditional branches, we want to garble the active branch without revealing the index of the active branch. For this, while garbling any gate (say the jth gate), it is imperative that the parties remain oblivious to both the functionality associated with it and its incoming and outgoing wires. As a result, the parties are unaware of which keys $k_{a,\alpha}^i, k_{b,\beta}^i$ to use for computing the corresponding ciphertexts, and hence cannot evaluate the PRF on those keys *locally*. A natural approach to overcome this problem is to perform this evaluation within an MPC; however, we are then back to the realm of non-black-box use of cryptography. As such it is unclear how to directly adapt this approach to our setting, while making a black-box use of cryptography.

Garbling using Key-Homomorphic PRFs. To overcome the above barrier, we explore the work of Ben-Efraim et al. [4] who presented an alternative template for multiparty garbling, using *key-homomorphic* PRFs. These are PRFs with the following property: $\mathsf{PRF}_{k_1}(m) \tilde{+} \mathsf{PRF}_{k_2}(m) = \mathsf{PRF}_{k_1 \tilde{\cdot} k_2}(m)$, where $\tilde{+}$ and $\tilde{\cdot}$ are some operations. As before, each party samples two keys for every wire in the circuit and given such a PRF, the parties the compute each ciphertext as follows:

$$ct_{\alpha,\beta} = \widetilde{\sum}_{m\in[n]} \left(\mathsf{PRF}_{k^m_{a,\alpha}}(g) \tilde{+} \mathsf{PRF}_{k^m_{b,\beta}}(g) \right) \tilde{+} \left(\widetilde{\prod}_{m\in[n]} k^m_{c,g(\alpha,\beta)} \right)$$

It is easy to see that similar to the previous approach, each party here is only required to evaluate the PRF on its own key, which can be done locally. At first, it might seem that in our setting, the same problem (as before) still persists. Indeed, for local PRF evaluation, the parties are required to know which key to use, which as discussed earlier is not possible when the parties are required to obliviously garble one of the conditional branches. However, we observe that homomorphism of the PRF can be leveraged here to resolve this problem.

Lets assume that the parties start by ordering the gates and wires in every branch in some canonical order. Now, when garbling the jth gate of the active branch, they must choose the appropriate keys from all the keys associated with the jth gate in every branch. We also assume that the parties have a sharing of the unary representation of the index associated with the active branch. The parties can now use multiple instances of OIP (as in our non-constant round protocols) to obtain shares of the keys associated with the two incoming wires of the jth gate in the active branch.

Consider a key homomorphic PRF where both $\tilde{+}$ and $\tilde{\cdot}$ are the same operation associated with the reconstruction algorithm of the secret sharing scheme used in the undelying MPC, i.e., $[\mathsf{PRF}_k(m)] = \mathsf{PRF}_{[k]}(m)$. This PRF can now be used along with the above observation to compute a garbling of the active branch as follows: for simplicity let's assume that each branch is of the same size and has W wires. The parties start by collectively sampling $2W$ keys. For garbling the jth gate, for each $\alpha,\beta \in \{0,1\}$, they use OIPs to compute shares $[k_{a,\alpha}], [k_{b,\beta}]$ and $[k_{c,g(\alpha,\beta)}]$, where a, b are the incoming and c is the outgoing wire of the jth gate in the active branch and g is the function computed by this gate. Parties can now locally evaluate the PRF on these shares and use the underlying MPC to compute shares of the ciphertexts as follows:

$$[ct_{\alpha,\beta}] = \mathsf{PRF}_{[k_{a,\alpha}]}(j) + \mathsf{PRF}_{[k_{b,\beta}]}(j) + [k_{c,g(\alpha,\beta)}]$$

Upon computing this garbled circuit for the active branch, similar to the baseline solution, parties evaluate it w.r.t. all the branches and then run a "mini-MPC" to filter out the valid labels and determine the final output.

Instantiating Key Homomorphic PRF. Most existing dishonest majority MPC protocols [12,16,22,25,33] use additive secret sharing. To use the above ideas with such protocols, we need an additively key-homomorphic PRF, i.e., where $\mathsf{PRF}_{k_1}(m) + \mathsf{PRF}_{k_2}(m) = \mathsf{PRF}_{k_1+k_2}(m)$. Unfortunately, key homomorphic PRFs are currently only known from the DDH assumption [6,37] and those PRFs do not achieve a similar additive homomorphism.

Ben-Efraim et al. [4] observed that instead of a PRF, it suffices to use a (decisional) ring LWE based random function here. This function is of the form:

$F = f_k : \mathcal{R}_p \to \mathcal{R}_p | f_k(a) = a \cdot k + e$, where $p = 2N + 1$ is a prime, N is a power of two, $\mathcal{R}_p = \mathbb{Z}_p[X]/(X^N + 1)$ and a, k, and e are polynomials in the ring and the coefficients of e come from a gaussian distribution. Since a is public, it is easy to see that given additive shares of the key k and error e, it is possible for the parties to locally compute shares of the above function. As is standard when using LWE/RLWE, encrypting using such a random function typically requires multiplying the message (before adding it to the output of this function) with the size of the range from which the message comes from. In the case of garbling, since both the message and keys come from the same distribution, as shown in [4], this requires choosing the parameters carefully and additionally requires sampling the keys from a gaussian distribution. However, since the parties only need to compute additive shares of these keys and errors, this can be done easily by requiring the parties to sample their shares from appropriate distributions. We defer more details to Sect. 6.

3 Oblivious Inner Product

In this section, we define a variant of oblivious linear evaluation (OLE), which we refer to as *oblivious inner product* (OIP). OIP is a protocol between two parties, called the *sender* and *receiver* respectively. The sender has inputs $(\overrightarrow{m_0}, \ldots, \overrightarrow{m_k})$ in some domain (say $\mathcal{D}^m$), and receiver has inputs $(b_1, \ldots, b_k)$ in the same domain $\mathcal{D}$. At the end of the protocol, the receiver should learn $\overrightarrow{m_0} + \sum_{i \in [k]} b_i \overrightarrow{m_i}$ and nothing more, while the sender should learn nothing about the reciever inputs $b_1, \ldots, b_k$.

For our constructions, we consider two variants of OIP, a *semi-honest* version and one that is secure against a *malicious receiver*. We now define the syntax and the security guarantees of a two-message OIP protocol in the plain model. The definitions can be naturally extended to the CRS model.

Definition 1 (Two-Message Oblivious Inner Product). *A two-message oblivious inner product between a receiver* R *and a sender* S *is defined by a tuple of 3 PPT algorithms* $(\mathsf{OIP_R}, \mathsf{OIP_S}, \mathsf{OIP_{out}})$. *Let* λ *be the security parameter. The receiver computes* $\mathsf{msg_R}, \rho$ *as the evaluation of* $\mathsf{OIP_R}(1^\lambda, (b_1, \ldots, b_k))$, *where* $(b_1, \ldots, b_k) \in \mathcal{D}^k$ *is the receiver's input. The receiver sends* $\mathsf{msg_R}$ *to the sender. The sender then computes* $\mathsf{msg_S}$ *as the evaluation of* $\mathsf{OIP_S}(1^\lambda, \mathsf{msg_R}, (\overrightarrow{m_0}, \ldots, \overrightarrow{m_k}))$, *where* $(\overrightarrow{m_0}, \ldots, \overrightarrow{m_k}) \in \mathcal{D}^{m \times (k+1)}$ *are sender's inputs. The sender sends* $\mathsf{msg_S}$ *to the receiver. Finally, the receiver computes the output by evaluating* $\mathsf{OIP_{out}}(\rho, \mathsf{msg_R}, \mathsf{msg_S})$.

A semi-honest OIP satisfies correctness, security against semi-honest receiver *and* semi-honest sender, *while the malicious variant satisfies* correctness, security *against semi-honest sender and malicious receiver, which are defined as follows:*

- **Correctness:** *For each* $(\overrightarrow{m_0}, \ldots, \overrightarrow{m_k}) \in \mathcal{D}^{m \times (k+1)}$ *and* $(b_1, \ldots, b_k) \in \mathcal{D}^k$, *the following holds*

$$\Pr\left[\begin{array}{c|c} (\rho, \mathsf{msg_R}) \leftarrow \mathsf{OIP_R}\left(1^\lambda, (b_1, \ldots, b_k)\right) & \\ \mathsf{msg_S} \leftarrow \mathsf{OIP_S}\left(1^\lambda, \mathsf{msg_R}, (\overrightarrow{m_0}, \ldots, \overrightarrow{m_k})\right) & \mathsf{OIP_{out}}\left(\rho, \mathsf{msg_R}, \mathsf{msg_S}\right) = \overrightarrow{m_0} + \sum_{i \in [k]} b_i \overrightarrow{m_i} \end{array}\right] = 1.$$

- **Security against Semi-Honest Sender:** *The following holds for any* $(b_1, \ldots, b_k) \in \mathcal{D}^k$ *and* $(b'_1, \ldots, b'_k) \in \mathcal{D}^k$, *where* $\exists i \in [k]$ *s.t.* $b_i \neq b'_i$

$$\left\{ (\mathsf{msg_R}, \rho) \leftarrow \mathsf{OIP_R}\left(1^\lambda, (b_1, \ldots, b_k)\right) \mid \mathsf{msg_R} \right\} \approx_c \left\{ (\mathsf{msg'_R}, \rho') \leftarrow \mathsf{OIP_R}\left(1^\lambda, (b'_1, \ldots, b'_k)\right) \mid \mathsf{msg_R} \right\}.$$

- **Security against Semi-Honest Receiver:** *For every PPT adversary* $\mathcal{A}$ *corrupting the receiver, there exists a PPT simulator* $\mathcal{S_R}$ *such that for any choice of* $(b_1, \ldots, b_k) \in \mathcal{D}^k$ *and* $(\overrightarrow{m_0}, \ldots, \overrightarrow{m_k}) \in \mathcal{D}^{m \times (k+1)}$, *the following holds:*

$$\mathsf{OIP_S}\left(1^\lambda, \mathsf{msg_R}, (\overrightarrow{m_0}, \ldots, \overrightarrow{m_k})\right) \approx_c \mathcal{S_R}(1^\lambda, \rho, \mathsf{msg_R}, \overrightarrow{m_0} + \sum_{i \in [k]} b_i \overrightarrow{m_i}),$$

where $(\mathsf{msg_R}, \rho) \leftarrow \mathsf{OIP_R}(1^\lambda, (b_1, \ldots, b_k))$.

- **Security against a Malicious Receiver:** *For every PPT adversary* $\mathcal{A}$ *corrupting the receiver, there exists a PPT simulator* $\mathcal{S_R} = (\mathcal{S}_\mathsf{R}^1, \mathcal{S}_\mathsf{R}^2)$, *such that for any choice of* $(\overrightarrow{m_0}, \ldots, \overrightarrow{m_k}) \in \mathcal{D}^{m \times (k+1)}$, *the following holds:*

$$\left| \Pr\left[\mathsf{IDEAL}_{\mathcal{S_R}, \mathcal{F}_{\mathsf{OIP}}}(1^\lambda, \overrightarrow{m_0}, \ldots, \overrightarrow{m_k}) = 1\right] - \Pr\left[\mathsf{REAL}_{\mathcal{A}, \mathsf{OIP}}(1^\lambda, \overrightarrow{m_0}, \ldots, \overrightarrow{m_k}) = 1\right] \right| \leq \frac{1}{2} + \mathsf{negl}(\lambda).$$

Where experiments $\mathsf{IDEAL}_{\mathcal{S_R}, \mathcal{F}_{\mathsf{OIP}}}$ *and* $\mathsf{REAL}_{\mathcal{A}, \mathsf{OIP}}$ *are defined as follows:*

Exp $\mathsf{IDEAL}_{\mathcal{S_R}, \mathcal{F}_{\mathsf{OIP}}}\left(1^\lambda, \overrightarrow{m_0}, \ldots, \overrightarrow{m_k}\right)$:

- $\mathsf{msg_R} \leftarrow \mathcal{A}(1^\lambda)$
- $(b_1, \ldots, b_k) \leftarrow \mathcal{S}_\mathsf{R}^1(1^\lambda, \mathsf{msg_R})$
- $\mathsf{out} \leftarrow \mathcal{F}_{\mathsf{OIP}}(\overrightarrow{m_0}, \ldots, \overrightarrow{m_k}, b_1, \ldots, b_k)$
- $\mathsf{msg_S} \leftarrow \mathcal{S}_\mathsf{R}^2(1^\lambda, \mathsf{out}, \mathsf{msg_R})$
- Output $\mathcal{A}(\mathsf{msg_S})$

Exp $\mathsf{REAL}_{\mathcal{S_R}, \mathcal{F}_{\mathsf{OIP}}}\left(1^\lambda, \overrightarrow{m_0}, \ldots, \overrightarrow{m_k}\right)$:

- $\mathsf{msg_R} \leftarrow \mathcal{A}(1^\lambda)$
- $\mathsf{msg_S} \leftarrow \mathsf{OIP_S}\left(1^\lambda, \mathsf{msg_R}, (\overrightarrow{m_0}, \ldots, \overrightarrow{m_k})\right)$
- Output $\mathcal{A}(\mathsf{msg_S})$

We present a construction of such OIPs from linearly homomorphic encryption in the full-version of this paper. We show that if the underlying linearly homomorphic encryption has rate-1, then so does the OIP protocol.

4   MPC Interface

As discussed in the introduction, all of our compilers make use of an underlying secure computation protocol with certain properties. In this section, we describe the properties that we want from these underlying protocols.

We model these requirements as a reactive functionality (denoted as $\mathcal{F}_{\mathsf{mpc}}$). At a high level, we require secret sharing based MPC that evaluate a given circuit in a gate-by-gate manner and maintain an invariant that the parties hold a secret sharing of the values induced on each intermediate wire in the circuit. A formal description of this reactive functionality appears in Fig. 1.

For ease of notation, in our protocol descriptions, we shall let $[varid]$ denote the value stores by the functionality under $(varid, a)$; and we will write $[z] = [x] + [y]$ as a shorthand for calling **Add** and $[z] = [x] \cdot [y]$ as a shorthand for calling **Multiply**. And by abuse of notation, we will let $varid$ denote the value, x, of the data item held in location $(varid, x)$. We use $[x]_i$ to denote the share of x given to party P_i in the underlying MPC.

To the best of our knowledge, most secret sharing based protocols [12,13, 16,25,33] securely implement this reactive functionality in the presence of a malicious adversary who can corrupt arbitrary number of parties. Moreover, most of these protocols are capable of evaluating circuits over any field/ring.

It is easy to see that any such secret sharing based MPC that evaluates the circuit in a gate-by-gate manner and maintains the invariant that parties hold shares of all intermediate wires in the circuit will trivially have support for the **Initialize Input, Initialize constant, Add, Add by const, Multiply, Multiply by const, Function** and **Output Private Shares** calls. Moreover, since the multiplication in these protocols typically requires parties to actually generate and compute shares of random values, the **Random** call is also implemented by these protocols. We now discuss how the remaining calls can be implemented in both the semi-honest and malicious settings.

Semi-honest Setting. The only other calls used in our semi-honest protocols are **Random Bit** and **Output**. As observed in some of these protocols, **Random Bit** is also very easy to implement (especially in the semi-honest setting). This is done by requiring each party P_i to randomly sample $b_i \in \{1, -1\}$ and secret share it amongst all the parties. The parties then add all the shares obtained from all parties (let the resulting shares be $[s]$) and then compute $\frac{[s]+1}{2}$. The resulting shares will be of a random bit. **Share Zero** can be realized with semi-honest security by having every party secret share 0 and then requiring each party to locally sum up its shares. Finally, it is easy to see that the **Output** call can also be easily implemented, since the parties actually hold shares of all intermediate values. To reconstruct the output, they can simply broadcast their respective shares to all parties and then run the reconstruction algorithm.

Malicious Setting. While protocols such as SPDZ [16] and its descendants [12, 25,33] (that use MACs w.r.t. a global key) delegate the check that ensures that these shares are indeed consistent with the "correct" values to the end of the protocol, we show that these protocols still securely implement all remaining calls in the $\mathcal{F}_{\mathsf{mpc}}$ functionality.

Intuitively, since these protocols delegate the malicious security/consistency checks to the end the protocol, the only place where we need to ensure that the shares held by the parties for any particular wire are indeed consistent and correct is when those values are reconstructed or are used outside of this MPC protocol, i.e., in the OIP and when the outcome of OIP is returned to the MPC. The subcalls inside $\mathcal{F}_{\mathsf{mpc}}$ that are really affected by this are **Initialize Input, Random, Share Zero, Check Zero** and **Output Shares** and **Output**. As discussed above, **Initialize Input** and **Random** are already implemented by these protocols.

- **Check Zero:** For this sub-call, we observe that given authenticated additive shares $([x_1], [m_1])$, $([x_2], [m_2])$, with $m_1 = k * x_1$, $m_2 = k * x_2$ where k is the global MAC key, parties can compute $[m] = [m_1] - [m_2]$ locally, followed by having each player P_i first commit and then broadcast its share $[m]_i$ to reconstruct $[m]$ and check if $m = \sum_i m_i = 0$.

- **Share Zero:** For this we can augment the semi-honest **Share Zero** protocol described above with an asymptotically efficient batch-wise check to ensure malicious security. Specifically, to verify the outputs of the ℓ semi-honest **Share Zero** calls $[x_1], \ldots, [x_\ell]$, parties can publicly sample ℓ random values $\{r_i\}_{i=1}^{\ell}$ and compute a random linear combination $[r] = \sum_{i=1}^{\ell} r_i [x_i]$ followed by running the **Check Zero** call on $[r]$ and a trivial sharing of 0 (each party P_i's share is 0).

- **Output and Output Share:** As discussed above authenticated shares in the above protocols are of the form $([x], [m])$, where $m = k * x$ and k is the global MAC key. For both of these sub-calls, the parties first broadcast their shares $[x]$ and reconstruct. Then the parties can compute $x \cdot [k]$ and run **Check Zero** to check if the resulting shares reconstruct to the same value as the shares $[m]$. This is very similar to "MAC check" subprotocol already implemented in [33].

We note that the above proposed protocols only reveal shares $[x]$ and not $[m]$. Indeed, revealing all shares of both x an m will trivially give away the global MAC key and make the protocol insecure. To make this compatible with our maliciously secure protocol, we assume that when the parties use the shares generated via $\mathcal{F}_{\mathsf{mpc}}$ outside of $\mathcal{F}_{\mathsf{mpc}}$ (i.e., to compute the OIP messages), they can do so on the "unauthenticated shares", i.e., on only the $[x]$ part and not on the $[m]$ part. Now, before, using the shares obtained as output of this OIP in $\mathcal{F}_{\mathsf{mpc}}$, we can make them "authenticated" by computing the corresponding $[m]$ shares for this output. This can be done trivially, since the parties hold a secret sharing of the global MAC key. This is a standard approach used in many of the above protocols including MASCOT [33].

Moreover, we remark that the above proposed modification does not cause our compiler or the compiled protocols to be insecure in any way. This is because, the authentication mechanism used on the shares is only specific to $\mathcal{F}_{\mathsf{mpc}}$ and not to the primitives used outside of it. As a result, outside of $\mathcal{F}_{\mathsf{mpc}}$, an adversary can easily modify the authenticated shares in whatever way they want. Hence, in principle the following strategies are equivalent – (1) where the computations done outside of $\mathcal{F}_{\mathsf{mpc}}$ are performed on authenticated shares. (2) where the computations done outside of $\mathcal{F}_{\mathsf{mpc}}$ are performed on unauthenticated shares, but we authenticate the output of those computations before they are used in $\mathcal{F}_{\mathsf{mpc}}$ again.

Functionality $\mathcal{F}_{\mathsf{mpc}}$

Initialize Input: On input $(initinp, varid, P_i)$ from P_i (for each $i \in [n]$) with a fresh identifier $varid$ the functionality stores $(varid, [x])$.

Initialize constant: On input $(initconst, constid, c)$ from each P_i ($i \in [n]$) with a fresh identifier $varid$ the functionality stores $(const, c)$.

Random: On command $(rand, varid)$ from all parties, with a fresh identifier $varid$, the functionality selects a random value r, stores $(varid, [r])$ and sends the respective share $[r]_i$ to party P_i (for each $i \in [n]$)

Random Bit: On command $(bitrand, varid)$ from all parties, with a fresh identifier $varid$, the functionality selects a random bit $b \in \{0, 1\}$, stores $(varid, [b])$ and sends the respective share $[b]_i$ to party P_i (for each $i \in [n]$)

ShareZero: On command $(sharezero, varid)$ from all parties, with a fresh identifier $varid$, the functionality computes, stores $(varid, [0])$ and sends the respective share $[0]_i$ to party P_i (for each $i \in [n]$).

Add: On command $(add, varid_1, varid_2, varid_3)$ from all parties (if $varid_1$, $varid_2$ are present in memory and $varid_3$ is not), the functionality retrieves $(varid_1, [x]), (varid_2, [y])$ and stores $(varid_3, [x + y])$.

Add by const: On command $(add, constid_1, varid_2, varid_3)$ from all parties (if $constid_1$, $varid_2$ are present in memory and $varid_3$ is not), the functionality retrieves $(constid_1, c), (varid_2, [x])$ and stores $(varid_3, [c + x])$.

Multiply: On input $(mult, varid_1, varid_2, varid_3)$ from all parties (if $varid_1$, $varid_2$ are present in memory and $varid_3$ is not), the functionality retrieves $(varid_1, [x]), (varid_2, [y])$ and stores $(varid_3, [x \cdot y])$.

Multiply by const: On command $(mult, constid_1, varid_2, varid_3)$ from all parties (if $constid_1$, $varid_2$ are present in memory and $varid_3$ is not), the functionality retrieves $(constid_1, c), (varid_2, [x])$ and stores $(varid_3, [c \cdot x])$.

Function: On input $(func, f, varid_1, \dots, varid_n, varid_{out})$ from all parties, the functionality retrieves $(varid_1, [x_1]), \dots, (varid_n, [x_n])$ and stores $(varid_{out}, [f(x_1, \dots, x_n)])$.

Output Shares: On input $(outshare, varid)$ from all parties, the functionality retrieves $(varid, [x])$ and outputs all shares $[x]$ to all parties.

Output Private Shares: On input $(outprivshare, varid)$ from all parties, the functionality retrieves $(varid, [x])$ and outputs the respective share $[x]_i$ to party P_i (for each $i \in [n]$).

Check Zero: On input $(fcheckzero, varid_1, varid_2)$ from all parties, the functionality retrieves $(varid_1, [x_1]), (varid_2, [x_2])$ and outputs 1 w.h.p if $x_1 = x_2$ and otherwise it outputs 0 and aborts.

Output: On input $(out, varid)$ from all honest parties (if $varid$ is present in memory), the functionality retrieves $(varid, [x])$ and outputs x to all players.

Fig. 1. A required ideal functionality for MPC

5 Non-constant Round Semi-honest Branching MPC

In this section, we present our semi-honest compiler for distributed computation of a circuit with conditional branches.

Let the circuit/function be such that it consists of an initial sub-function f_1, followed by the k branches and then a sub-function f_2. We assume that the parties have access to $\mathcal{F}_{\mathsf{mpc}}$ (see Fig. 1). When evaluated using $\mathcal{F}_{\mathsf{mpc}}$, the output of f_1 is a secret sharing of the inputs to the branching part and a secret sharing of the unary representation of the index associated with the branch that needs to be executed (henceforth referred to as the active branch). The output of the branching part is a secret sharing of the inputs to the function f_2.

Given a circuit C, we assume that the parties decide on some canonical ordering of the gates in the circuit, such that gate i only takes as inputs the values output by the gates $j < i$. We assume w.l.o.g. that the ith gate in C has fan-in 2 and the outgoing wire of any gate can act as the incoming wire for any number of gates.[2]

For simplicity, we assume that all branches are of the same size and have G gates. Our protocol can be easily extended to the scenario where the branches are of varying sizes by suitably padding the smaller branches with fake gates. Let ℓ be the length of inputs to the branching part of the function. For evaluating this part, we assume that there are ℓ input gates that are common to all branches. We set both the incoming and outgoing labels for the wires coming out of these gates as $1, \ldots, \ell$ respectively. For each branch $m \in [k]$, and each gate i in this branch, we assign outgoing label $i + \ell$ to the wire coming out of this gate and incoming labels $\ell + 2i - 1$ and $\ell + 2i$ respectively to its two incoming wires. Therefore, we assume that the number of unique outgoing labels assigned in a branch are $G + \ell$, while the total number of unique incoming labels assigned in a branch are $W = 2G + \ell$. We present a slightly optimized version of the protocol described in the introduction, namely that only requires parties to sample 1 mask per wire, instead of 2 masks.

Let π be the mapping corresponding to a circuit C that maps incoming labels to the outgoing labels of each wire in C. For instance, $\pi(i)$ corresponds to the outgoing label of the wire with incoming label i. Let $\mathsf{C}_1, \ldots, \mathsf{C}_k$ be the circuit representations of the k branches and let $\{\pi_1, \ldots, \pi_k\}$ be the corresponding mappings associated with these branches. Finally, we assume that the circuits and inputs are defined over some field $\mathbb{F}$.

Protocol. The parties start by invoking $(func, f_1, x_1, \ldots, x_n, \mathsf{inp}_1, \ldots, \mathsf{inp}_\ell, b_1, \ldots, b_k)$ in $\mathcal{F}_{\mathsf{mpc}}$ on their original inputs $x_1, \ldots, x_n$, to obtain shares of inputs to the branching part $[\mathsf{inp}_1], \ldots, [\mathsf{inp}_\ell]$, where $|\ell|$ is the total input length and shares $[b_1], \ldots, [b_k]$, where $b_1 \ldots b_k$ is the unary representation of the index associated with the active branch. Given these shares, parties run the protocol presented in Fig. 2. The output of this protocol is a secret sharing of the inputs to f_2 (i.e., the last part of the circuit). Let m be the length of these inputs. The parties finally invoke $(func, f_2, y_1, \ldots, y_m, \mathsf{out})$ and (out, out) in $\mathcal{F}_{\mathsf{mpc}}$ to learn the final output out.

Optimization. A naive implementation of the online phase in the above protocol will result in a round complexity that depends on the maximum number of gates in any particular branch. This can be improved to be proportional to the maximum multiplicative depth of any branch by using a simple optimization. For simplicity, lets assume that all branches have the same depth and each layer of each branch contains the same number of gates. We know that the gates on level ℓ only depend on the outgoing wires of gates on layers $< \ell$. We can therefore evaluate all the gates in a particular level in parallel. This simple idea can also be extended to the case where the branches have different depths and widths. In

---

[2] Our compiler can work with circuits that have gates with arbitrary fan-out. In our construction, it suffices to view such gates as having a single outgoing wire that acts as the incoming wire for multiple gates. Hence, we only assign a single label to the outgoing wire of each gate.

Semi-Honest Protocol

The protocol is described in the $\mathcal{F}_{\mathsf{mpc}}$-hybrid model. Parties have shares of inputs to the branches, i.e., $[\mathsf{inp}_1], \ldots, [\mathsf{inp}_\ell]$ and shares of a unary representation of the active branch, i.e., $[b_1], \ldots, [b_k]$.

- **Pre-processing Phase:**
  1. **Sample masks:** For each input and gate $g \in [\ell + G]$, parties invoke $(rand, \mathsf{mask}_g)$ in $\mathcal{F}_{\mathsf{mpc}}$ to obtain shares $[\mathsf{mask}_g]$. For each branch $m \in [k]$, let $\overrightarrow{[\mathsf{mask}_{\pi_m}]} = [\mathsf{mask}_{\pi_m(1)}] \| \ldots \| [\mathsf{mask}_{\pi_m(W)}]$.
  2. **Shares of zeros:** For each $w \in [W]$ and $i \in [n]$, parties invoke $(sharezero, X_{w,i})$ in $\mathcal{F}_{\mathsf{mpc}}$ to get shares $[X_{w,i}]$, where $X_{w,i} = 0$. For each $i \in [n]$, let $\overrightarrow{[X_i]} = [X_{1,i}] \| \ldots \| [X_{W,i}]$.
  3. **Pairwise OIP:** Each pair of parties P_R and P_S ($\forall \mathsf{R}, \mathsf{S} \in [n]$) engage in a two-message semi-honest OIP as follows, where P_R acts as the receiver and P_S acts as the sender:
     - **Receiver:** P_R computes $(\rho, \mathsf{msg}_\mathsf{R}) \leftarrow \mathsf{OIP}_\mathsf{R}(1^\lambda, [b_1]_\mathsf{R}, \ldots, [b_k]_\mathsf{R})$ and sends msg_R to P_S.
     - **Sender:** P_S computes $\mathsf{msg}_\mathsf{S} \leftarrow \mathsf{OIP}_\mathsf{S}(1^\lambda, \mathsf{msg}_\mathsf{R}, \overrightarrow{[X_\mathsf{R}]}_\mathsf{S}, \overrightarrow{[\mathsf{mask}_{\pi_1}]}_\mathsf{S}, \ldots, \overrightarrow{[\mathsf{mask}_{\pi_k}]}_\mathsf{S})$ and sends msg_S to P_R.
     - **Output:** P_R computes $\overrightarrow{\mathsf{share}_{\mathsf{R},\mathsf{S}}} \leftarrow \mathsf{OIP}_{\mathsf{out}}(\rho, \mathsf{msg}_\mathsf{R}, \mathsf{msg}_\mathsf{S})$.
  4. **Δ values:** Each party P_i (for $i \in [n]$) computes $\overrightarrow{[\Delta]}_i = \sum_{j \in [n]} \overrightarrow{\mathsf{share}_{j,i}}$, where $\overrightarrow{[\Delta]} = [\Delta_1] \| \ldots \| [\Delta_W]$.
- **Online Phase :**
  1. **Inputs:** For each input wire $i \in [\ell]$, parties compute $[u_i] = [\mathsf{inp}_i] + [\mathsf{mask}_i]$. and invoke (out, u_i) in $\mathcal{F}_{\mathsf{mpc}}$ to obtain u_i in the clear.
  2. **Circuit Evaluation:** For each gate $g \in [G]$, let $\mathsf{left} = \ell + 2g - 1$ and $\mathsf{right} = \ell + 2g$ be the incoming wire labels of its input wires. Let $\mathsf{type}_{m,g}$ be the gate type for gate g in C_m ($\forall m \in [k]$), where $\mathsf{type}_{m,g} = 0$ denotes an addition gate and $\mathsf{type}_{m,g} = 1$ denotes a multiplication gate. Parties compute the following using $\mathcal{F}_{\mathsf{mpc}}$:
     (a) For $w \in \{\mathsf{left}, \mathsf{right}\}$, compute $[y_w] = \sum_{m=1}^{k} (u_{\pi_m(w)} \cdot [b_m]) + [\Delta_w]$.
     (b) Compute $[\mathsf{type}_g] = \sum_{m=1}^{k} (\mathsf{type}_{m,g} \cdot [b_m])$
     (c) Compute $[z_g] = (1 - [\mathsf{type}_g])([y_\mathsf{left}] + [y_\mathsf{right}]) + [\mathsf{type}_g]([y_\mathsf{left}] \cdot [y_\mathsf{right}])$.
     (d) Compute $[u_{\ell+g}] = [z_g] + [\mathsf{mask}_{\ell+g}]$ and invoke (out, u_s) in $\mathcal{F}_{\mathsf{mpc}}$ to obtain u_s in the clear.
  3. **Output:** For each output gate g, compute $[z_g] = \sum_{m=1}^{k} (u_{\pi_m(w)} \cdot [b_m]) + [\Delta_w]$.

Fig. 2. Semi-honest compiler

that case, let x_ℓ (and y_ℓ resp.) be the minimum (and maximum resp.) number of gates on level ℓ in any branch. We can evaluate the first x_ℓ gates in parallel. Then in the next round we can evaluate the $y_\ell - x_\ell + x_{\ell+1}$ gates in parallel. This ensures that the overall round complexity of the online phase will only depend on the depth of the branches.

Complexity Analysis. We now analyze the communication complexity of the above semi-honest protocol. If we use a rate-1 OIP, the communication complexity in the pre-processing phase is $O(n^2|C_{max}|+n^2k\lambda)$, where $|C_{max}|$ is the size of the largest branch. In the online phase for each gate we perform both addition and multiplication and then choose between the two. As a result we perform 2 multiplications per gate. The communication complexity of the online phase is $O(2 \times \mathsf{CC}(|C_{max}|))$, where $\mathsf{CC}(|C_{max}|)$ is the communication complexity incurred upon evaluating C_{max} using the underlying MPC.

Overall, given the above protocol and optimizations, we obtain the following result. Due to space constraints, we defer the security proof of this construction to the full-version of this paper.

Theorem 1. *Let λ be the security parameter and $\mathcal{F}$ be a function class consisting of functions of the form $f(\overrightarrow{x}) = f_2(f_{\mathsf{br}}(f_1(\overrightarrow{x})))$, where $f_{\mathsf{br}} := \{g_1, \ldots, g_k\}$ is a function consisting of k conditional branches, defined as $f_{\mathsf{br}}(i, \overrightarrow{x}) = g_i(\overrightarrow{x})$. Assuming the existence of a rate-1 two-message semi-honest secure OIP (see Definition 1), there exists an MPC protocol in the $\mathcal{F}_{\mathsf{mpc}}$-hybrid model (see Sect. 4) for computing any $f \in \mathcal{F}$ that achieves semi-honest security against an arbitrary number of corruptions and incurs a communication overhead of $O(n^2(k\lambda + |C_{\mathsf{max}}|))$.*

In the full-version of this paper, we show that a rate-1 two-message semi-honest secure OIP can be constructed from rate-1 linearly homomorphic encryption. Such encryptions are known [8,15,17,38] from a variety of assumptions including LWE, Ring LWE and DDH assumption.

6   Constant Round Semi-honest Branching MPC

In this section we present our constant round semi-honest protocol for distributed computation of a branching circuit.

As discussed in the technical overview, we instantiate a random function based on the RLWE assumption for our protocol that works as an approximate key homomorphic PRF. We briefly recall the variant of the decisional RLWE hardness assumption stated by Ben-Efraim et al. [4]. Let $p = 2N + 1$ be a prime, where N, called the dimension or security parameter, is a power of 2. Let $\mathcal{R}_p = \mathbb{Z}_p[X]/(X^N + 1)$ be the polynomial ring over $\mathbb{Z}_p$ modulo $X^N + 1$. We start by recalling the decisional RLWE assumption.

Definition 2 (Decisional Ring LWE Problem). *Any non-uniform PPT adversary cannot distinguish between $\{(a_i, b_i)\}_{i \in I}$ and $\{(a_i, a_i \cdot k + \delta_i)\}_{i \in I}$ with non-negligible probability where $\{a_i\}_{i \in I}$, $\{b_i\}_{i \in I}$ and k are chosen uniformly at random from $\mathcal{R}_p$ and the coeffecients of $\{e_i\}_{i \in I}$ are sampled from χ, a spherical Gaussian distribution.*

By transforming to the Hermite normal form, the RLWE assumption also holds if k is chosen from a spherical Gaussian distribution. In general, it is also necessary to bound the number of samples $|I|$; say $|I| = O(1)$ or $|I| = O(\log N)$.

Our protocol follows the BMR approach which involves sampling a pair of keys k_w^0, k_w^1 for each wire w in the circuit. A garbled table is then constructed for each gate such that the key corresponding to the value on the output wire is encrypted using the keys corresponding to the input values. Since the position of each ciphertext in the garbled table leaks information about its plaintext, a private random mask bit $\gamma_w \in \{0,1\}$ is sampled for each wire w and the masks for the input wires are used to permute the rows of the garbled table for each gate. Let the external value β_w on a wire be the plaintext value ρ_w on the wire masked with the mask γ_w i.e., $\beta_w = \rho_w \oplus \gamma_w$. Then, the masks on the input wires are used to permute the rows of the garbled table such that the external values on the input wires can be used to index into the required row of the garbled table. Thus, to ensure that parties decrypt the correct row when evaluating the circuit, the mask for the output wire has to also be included in the ciphertext for each row. We use the approach of Ben-Efraim et al. [4], where the last coordinate of the keys k_w^0, k_w^1 for each wire are set to 0, which slightly reduces security, and the external value is embedded into this coordinate during encryption. We use $k \| e$ to denote that the bit e was embedded in the last coordinate of the key k.

As observed in [4], since the plaintext and key come from the same set when computing the ciphertexts for the garbled table, we sample coefficients for both the keys and errors from Gaussian distribution χ, similar to the RLWE errors to ensure that decryption is possible. Moreover, Ben-Efraim et al. [4] also show that overall, it suffices to use just $8 \cdot f_{\text{out}}$ distinct public random elements of the form $A_g^{u,v}$ from the ring, where f_{out} is the maximal fan-out of the circuit.

The garbling phase is presented in Fig. 3 and the evaluation phase is presented in Fig. 4. We adopt similar notation to the semi-honest protocol presented in Fig. 2 and use incoming and outgoing labels for each wire. Let ℓ be the number of input wires to the branching part of the function, we set the incoming and outgoing labels for these wires to be $1, \ldots, \ell$. For gate g in each branch, we set the outgoing wire label to be $\ell + g$, the left incoming wire label to be $\ell + 2g - 1$ and the right incoming wire label to be $\ell + 2g$. We also let π_m for each $m \in [k]$ to be the mapping that maps incoming labels to the outgoing labels of each wire for the m-th branch.

Finally, we remark that we require the underlying MPC protocol that securely realizes $\mathcal{F}_{\text{mpc}}$ to run in constant number of rounds for constant depth circuits. This is to ensure that our protocol has constant number of rounds. This is true for most secret sharing based protocols that evaluate the circuit in a gate-by-gate manner.

Complexity Analysis. We assume that the size of the ring $\mathcal{R}_p$ is in $O(\lambda)$. If we use a rate-1 semi-honest secure OIP, the communication complexity in the garbling phase is $O(n^2|C_{\text{max}}| + n^2 k \lambda \text{CC}(\lambda |C_{\text{max}}|))$, where $|C_{\text{max}}|$ is the size of the largest branch and $\text{CC}(\lambda |C_{\text{max}}|)$ is the communication complexity incurred upon evaluating C_{max} using the underlying MPC. In the evaluation phase, the communication cost incurred is for reconstructing $O(\lambda |C_{\text{max}}|)$ shares corresponding to the garbling material.

Garbling Phase of the Constant Round Semi-Honest Protocol

The protocol is described in the $\mathcal{F}_{\mathsf{mpc}}$-hybrid model which computes over $\mathcal{R}_p$. The parties have shares of a unary representation of the active branch, i.e., $[b_1], \dots, [b_k]$. For each gate $g \in [G]$, let $\mathsf{left}_g = \ell + 2g - 1$ and $\mathsf{right}_g = \ell + 2g$ be the incoming wire labels of its input wires and let $\mathsf{out}_g = \ell + g$ be the outgoing wire.

1. **Sample masks:** For each input and gate $g \in [\ell + G]$, the parties invoke $(randbit, \gamma_g)$ in $\mathcal{F}_{\mathsf{mpc}}$ to obtain shares $[\gamma_g]$. For each branch $m \in [k]$, let $[\overrightarrow{\gamma_{\pi_m}}] = [\gamma_{\pi_m(1)}] \| \cdots \| [\gamma_{\pi_m(W)}]$.
2. **Sample keys:** For each $g \in [\ell+G]$, and $j \in \{0,1\}$ each party P_i (for $i \in [n]$) locally samples its share $[k_g^j]_i \leftarrow \chi^N$ and sets the last coordinate of its share to 0.
3. **Compute LWE expansions:** For each $u, v \in \{0,1\}$, $g \in [G]$ each party P_i (for $i \in [n]$) locally samples $\delta_{m,g}^{u,v,i} \leftarrow \chi^N$ and computes $[\psi_{m,g}^{u,v}]_i = A_g^{u,v} \cdot ([k_{\pi_m(\mathsf{left}_g)}]_i + [k_{\pi_m(\mathsf{right}_g)}]_i) + \delta_{m,g}^{u,v,i}$. Let $[\overrightarrow{\psi_m}] = [\psi_{m,1}^{0,0}] \| [\psi_{m,1}^{0,1}] \| [\psi_{m,1}^{1,0}] \| [\psi_{m,1}^{1,1}] \| \cdots \| [\psi_{m,G}^{0,0}] \| [\psi_{m,G}^{0,1}] \| [\psi_{m,G}^{1,0}] \| [\psi_{m,G}^{1,1}]$.
4. **Shares of zero:** For each $i \in [n]$ and $j \in [W + 4G]$, the parties invoke $(sharezero, X_{j,i})$ in $\mathcal{F}_{\mathsf{mpc}}$ to get shares $[X_{j,i}]$, where $X_{j,i} = 0$. For each $i \in [n]$, let $[\overrightarrow{X_i}] = [X_{1,i}] \| \cdots \| [X_{W+4G,i}]$.
5. **Pairwise OIP:** Each pair of parties P_R and P_S ($\forall \mathsf{R}, \mathsf{S} \in [n]$) engage in a two-message semi-honest OIP as follows, where P_R acts as the receiver and P_S acts as the sender:
   - **Receiver:** P_R computes $(\rho, \mathsf{msg}_\mathsf{R}) \leftarrow \mathsf{OIP}_\mathsf{R}(1^\lambda, [b_1]_\mathsf{R}, \dots, [b_k]_\mathsf{R})$ and sends msg_R to P_S.
   - **Sender:** For each $m \in [1,k]$ let $[\overrightarrow{x_m}] = [\overrightarrow{\gamma_{\pi_m}}] \| [\overrightarrow{\psi_m}]$. P_S computes $\mathsf{msg}_\mathsf{S} \leftarrow \mathsf{OIP}_\mathsf{S}(1^\lambda, \mathsf{msg}_\mathsf{R}, [\overrightarrow{X_\mathsf{R}}]_\mathsf{S}, [\overrightarrow{x_1}]_\mathsf{S}, \dots, [\overrightarrow{x_k}]_\mathsf{S})$ and sends msg_S to P_R.
   - **Output:** P_R computes $\overrightarrow{\mathsf{share}_{\mathsf{R},\mathsf{S}}} \leftarrow \mathsf{OIP}_\mathsf{out}(\rho, \mathsf{msg}_\mathsf{R}, \mathsf{msg}_\mathsf{S})$.

   For each $i \in [n]$, P_i computes $[\overrightarrow{\Gamma}] \| [\overrightarrow{\Psi}] = \sum_{j \in [n]} \overrightarrow{\mathsf{share}_{j,i}}$ where $\overrightarrow{\Gamma} = \Gamma_1 \| \cdots \| \Gamma_W$ and $\overrightarrow{\Psi} = \Psi_1^{0,0} \| \cdots \| \Psi_G^{1,1}$.
6. **Garble active branch:** Let $\mathsf{type}_{m,g}$ be the gate type for gate g in C_m ($\forall m \in [k]$), where $\mathsf{type}_{m,g} = 0$ denotes an XOR gate and $\mathsf{type}_{m,g} = 1$ denotes an AND gate. Parties do the following for each $g \in [G]$
   (a) Compute $[\mathsf{type}_g] = \sum_{i=m}^k (\mathsf{type}_{m,g} \cdot [b_m])$.
   (b) For each $u, v \in \{0,1\}$ let $e_{u,v,g}^{\mathsf{xor}} = u \oplus \Gamma_{\mathsf{left}_g} \oplus v \oplus \Gamma_{\mathsf{right}_g} \oplus \gamma_{\mathsf{out}_g}$, $e_{u,v,g}^{\mathsf{and}} = ((u \oplus \Gamma_{\mathsf{left}_g}) \wedge (v \oplus \Gamma_{\mathsf{right}_g})) \oplus \gamma_{\mathsf{out}_g}$, $e_g^{u,v} = \mathsf{type}_g(e_{u,v,g}^{\mathsf{and}} - e_{u,v,g}^{\mathsf{xor}}) + e_{u,v,g}^{\mathsf{xor}}$ and $K_g^{u,v} = e_g^{u,v}(k_{\mathsf{out}_g}^1 - k_{\mathsf{out}_g}^0) + k_{\mathsf{out}_g}^0$. For each $u, v \in \{0,1\}$, compute $[K_g^{u,v} \| e_g^{u,v}]$ using $\mathcal{F}_{\mathsf{mpc}}$.
   (c) For each $u, v \in \{0,1\}$ compute $[C_g^{u,v}] = [\Psi_g^{u,v}] + \lceil \sqrt{p} \rceil [K_g^{u,v} \| e_g^{u,v}]$.

Fig. 3. Garbling phase of the constant round (semi-honest) protocol

Overall, given the above protocol and optimizations, we obtain the following result. Due to space constraints, we defer the security proof of this construction to the full-version of this paper.

Evaluation Phase of the Constant Round Semi-Honest Protocol

The protocol is described in the $\mathcal{F}_{\mathsf{mpc}}$-hybrid model. The parties have shares of the inputs to the branches, i.e., $[\mathsf{inp}_1], \ldots, [\mathsf{inp}_\ell]$ and shares of a unary representation of the active branch, i.e., $[b_1], \ldots, [b_k]$.

1. For each input wire $w \in [\ell]$ parties compute $[\beta_w] = [\mathsf{inp}_w] \oplus [\gamma_w]$ and invoke $(out, [\beta_w])$ in $\mathcal{F}_{\mathsf{mpc}}$ to obtain β_w. For each $w \in [\ell]$, let $\beta_{1,w} = \ldots = \beta_{k,w} = \beta_w$.
2. For each input wire $w \in [\ell]$ parties invoke $(out, [k_w^{\beta_w}])$ in $\mathcal{F}_{\mathsf{mpc}}$ to obtain $k_w^{\beta_w}$. For each $w \in [\ell]$, let $K_{1,w}^{\beta_w} = \ldots = K_{k,w}^{\beta_w} = k_w^{\beta_w}$.
3. For each $u, v \in \{0, 1\}$ and $g \in [G]$ parties invoke $(out, [C_g^{u,v}])$ in $\mathcal{F}_{\mathsf{mpc}}$ to obtain $C_g^{u,v}$.
4. For each $m \in [k]$ and $g \in [G]$, parties compute $C_g^{u,v} - A_g^{u,v} \cdot \left(K_{m,\pi_m(\mathsf{left}_g)}^{u} + K_{m,\pi_m(\mathsf{right}_g)}^{v} \right)$, where $u = \beta_{m,\pi_m(\mathsf{left}_g)}$ and $v = \beta_{m,\pi_m(\mathsf{right}_g)}$, and divide it by $\lceil \sqrt{p} \rceil$ to remove the error and recover $K_{m,\mathsf{out}_g}^{\beta_{m,\mathsf{out}_g}} \| \beta_{m,\mathsf{out}_g}$.
5. For each output gate g, parties compute $[z_g] = \sum_{m=1}^{k} \beta_{m,\mathsf{out}_g} [b_m] \oplus [\gamma_g]$ using $\mathcal{F}_{\mathsf{mpc}}$.

Fig. 4. Evaluation phase of the constant round (semi-honest) protocol

Theorem 2. *Let λ be the security parameter and $\mathcal{F}$ be a function class consisting of functions of the form $f(\overrightarrow{x}) = f_2(f_{\mathsf{br}}(f_1(\overrightarrow{x})))$, where $f_{\mathsf{br}} := \{g_1, \ldots, g_k\}$ is a function consisting of k conditional branches, defined as $f_{\mathsf{br}}(i, \overrightarrow{x}) = g_i(\overrightarrow{x})$. Assuming that a rate-1 two-message semi-honest secure OIP exists (see Definition 1) and that the decisional RLWE problem holds (see Definition 2), there exists a constant-round MPC protocol in the $\mathcal{F}_{\mathsf{mpc}}$-hybrid model (see Sect. 4) for computing any $f \in \mathcal{F}$ that achieves semi-honest security against an arbitrary number of corruptions and incurs a communication overhead of $O(n^2 \lambda(k + |C_{\mathsf{max}}|))$.*

Note that if we instatiate the rate-1 two-message semi-honest secure OIP using a rate-1 RLWE-based linearly homomorphic encryption, then the above theorem yields a protocol that only relies on the hardness of decisional RLWE.

7   Implementation

We implement and benchmark our semi-honest non-constant round protocol from Sect. 5. The code is publicly available at https://github.com/rot256/research-branching-mpc. In addition to the code and instructions used for benchmarking, the repository also contains the raw data used in this paper and scripts used to create the plots.

7.1   How We Benchmark

Underlaying MPC. We implement tour semi-honest compiler on top of two different multi-party computation protocols.

1. *Quadratic Dependence on the Number of Parties.* A semi-honest variant of MASCOT [33] (MASCOT without sacrificing and message authentication codes) over the prime field $\mathbb{F}_{2^{16}+1} = \mathbb{Z}/(\text{0x10001 } \mathbb{Z})$ provided by MP-SPDZ [32] (called "semi-party.x"). We simply invoke the MP-SPDZ implementation as a black-box: wrapping each instance of "semi-party.x" in a program which provides provides inputs/outputs to the party. Since MP-SPDZ povides a universal interface our implementation is agnostic with regards to the underlying MPC implementation: any reactive MPC in MP-SPDZ which allows computation over $\mathbb{F}_{2^{16}+1}$ could be swapped in with ease.
2. *Linear Dependence on the Number of Parties.* A batched semi-honest version of CDN [13] where we instantiate the linearly homomorphic encryption using the same ring LWE parameters described above. We implement this ourselves again using the Lattigo (more information below) library for the RLWE components.

CDN Implementation. We implement a semi-honest batched version of CDN, instantiating the linearly homomorphic encryption using the same parameters described above (the same as the OIP). To reduce the overhead (computational/communication) induced by the homomorphic encryption we execute multiplications in batches of 2^{12} (the dimension of the ring used for RLWE), by packing 2^{12} independent shares (over 0x10001) into a single ciphertext and execute the CDN multiplication protocol on these in parallel. The decryption threshold is the full set of parties. The CDN implement is included in the same repository. To the best of our knowledge, this is the first known implementation of CDN.

Instantiating OIP and Ring LWE Parameters. In our implementation, we use an optimized version of OIP. We observe that the $O(n^2)$ overhead incurred from the use of pairwise-OIPs can be driven down to $O(n)$, if instead of a regular linearly homomorphic encryption, we use a threshold linearly homomorphic encryption (TLHE). TLHE are linearly homomorphic encryptions that comprise of a single public-key and where each party holds a "share" of the secret key. This share of the secret key can be used by the parties to decrypt to a share of the plaintext. As shown in [10], the keys for RLWE based threshold linearly homomorphic encryption can be setup very efficiently by the parties in a couple of rounds. At a high level, this observation allows us to reuse the sender and receiver messages of each party across multiple OIP instantiations and as a result, overall, each party only needs to send one receiver message and one sender message.

Recall that in our semi-honest protocol, the receiver and sender messages in all OIP instances are computed using the same shares of the index associated with the active branch and the masks. Each party can compute its receiver message by encrypting its shares of $b_1, \ldots, b_k$. Similarly, for the sender message, each party can compute an inner-product of these encryptions received from all parties and its shares of the permuted masks. Finally, all parties can add all the sender messages (which are also ciphertexts) received from all parties. This gives them an encryption of the permuted masks for the active branch. Now each party can run threshold decryption using its share of the secret-key to obtain a sharing of the resulting inner-product.

We use BFV [17] over a cyclotomic ring of index 2^{13} and dimension 2^{12}, i.e. $R[X]/(X^{2^{12}} + 1)$ where: $Q_1 := \texttt{0x7ffffec001}, Q_2 := \texttt{0x8000016001}, P := \texttt{0x40002001}, N := Q_1 Q_2 P, R := \mathbb{Z}/(N\mathbb{Z})$. This gives us a linearly homomorphic encryption scheme for vectors $\vec{v} \in (\mathbb{F}_{2^{16}+1})^{2^{12}}$, which additionally allows (full) threshold decryption. We use the $\texttt{Lattigo}$ [1] library to implement all the RLWE components.

Benchmarking Platform. All benchmarks were run on a laptop with an Intel i7-11800H CPU (@ 2.3 GHz) and 64 GB of RAM. All networking is over the loopback interface and network latency was simulated using traffic control ($\texttt{tc}$) on Linux. We also do not restrict the bandwidth when comparing running times – note that this constitutes a relative "worst-case scenario" for our results: as our technique reduces communication, the relative performance gain for many branches would only increase by restricting bandwidth.

How The Branches Were Generated. During our benchmark each branch contained 2^{16} uniformly random gates: each gate is a multiplication/addition gate with probability $1/2$. We benchmark using "layered circuits", meaning each level contains 2^{12} gates which can be evaluated in parallel (to reduce the number of rounds). Subject to the layering constraint, the wiring is otherwise random: the inputs to each gate are sampled uniformly at random from all previous outputs (not just those in the last layer). We believe this distribution over circuits form a realistic benchmark for the expected performance across many real-world applications.

Averaging. We run all benchmarks 10 times and take the average.

7.2   Comparison of Communication Complexity

In Fig. 5, we compare the communication complexity of our technique to the naïve baseline solution of evaluating each branch in parallel using the underlying MPC. For the baseline solution we do not consider the additional overhead of multiplexing the output, i.e., selecting the output of the active branch.

Looking at Fig. 5 (a)/(b), we observe that our technique improves communication over the baseline for both CDN and MASCOT with 3 parties when the number of branches is ≥ 8. For less than 8 branches the communication overhead of the RLWE-based OIP and the need to evaluate universal gates (requiring the base-MPC to compute 3 multiplications) outweighs the communication saving of only executing the active branch. Upon reflection 8 branches is about the lowest number of branches we could hope to see savings for: recall that each branch contains $\approx 2^{15}$ multiplications[3], therefore the parallel execution of 6 branches requires the same number of multiplications as that of the 2^{16} universal gates used in our technique. As expected we also observe that the communication of our technique remains (nearly[4]) constant for any number of branches.

Lastly we fix the number of branches to 16 and plot (in Fig. 5 (c)) the communication complexity of our technique for a varying number of parties, as expected the communication of our compiler applied to MASCOT increases quadratically, while our technique preserves the linearly increasing communication of CDN; constant per-party communication (and computation).

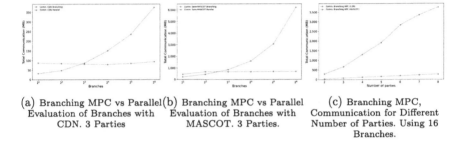

(a) Branching MPC vs Parallel Evaluation of Branches with CDN. 3 Parties   (b) Branching MPC vs Parallel Evaluation of Branches with MASCOT. 3 Parties.   (c) Branching MPC, Communication for Different Number of Parties. Using 16 Branches.

Fig. 5. Communication Complexity of Branching MPC compared to the base-line of evaluating each branch in parallel.

7.3   Comparison of Running Time

From Fig. 6 and Fig. 7, we observe that for sufficiently many branches our technique also reduces running time over the baseline for both CDN and semi-honest MASCOT. This is also expected: after the relatively high constant overhead of our technique, the marginal cost of adding another branch (of length ℓ) is that of: (1) $O(\ell)$ linear operations in the underlying MPC. (2) $O(\ell)$ $\langle ciphertext \rangle \times \langle plaintext \rangle$ operations in the RLWE based homomorphic encryption scheme. (3) $O(\ell)$ $\langle ciphertext \rangle + \langle ciphertext \rangle$ operations in the RLWE based homomorphic encryption scheme (Fig. 8).

The first one introduces a very small cost (essentially that of reading the branch), the second is dominated by the cost of doing a number theoretic transform (NTT) on the plaintext (the players local share), which again is essentially that of computing a small constant number of fixed-size FFTs. We note that the NTTs are computed on random shares and could be relegated to a precomputation phase. The final ciphertext/ciphertext addition is just a constant number of entry-wise additions of vectors in a small prime field – the cost of which is miniscule. Looking at Fig. 6 and Fig. 7 we observe that this marginal

---

[3] Since the type of each gate in each branch is sampled uniformly at random.

[4] It grows slightly, since the unary representation of the selection wire must be shared/computed. However the computation of the branch completely dominates the communication.

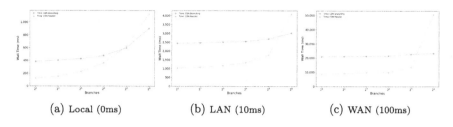

Fig. 6. Running time of Branching MPC with CDN.

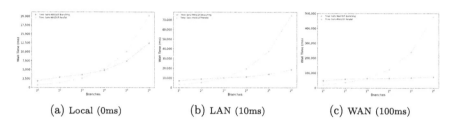

Fig. 7. Running time of Branching MPC with Semi-Honest MASCOT.

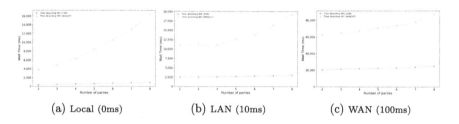

Fig. 8. Running time of Branching MPC for Different Number of Parties.

computational cost (of doing NTTs) has a higher influence when the network latency is low and quickly becomes insignificant as the latency increases.

Acknowledgements. We thank the anonymous reviewers of EUROCRYPT 2022 for their helpful comments. The first, third and forth authors are supported in part by an NSF CNS grant 1814919, NSF CAREER award 1942789 and Johns Hopkins University Catalyst award. The second author is funded by Concordium Blockhain Research Center, Aarhus University, Denmark. The third author is additionally supported by NSF CNS-1653110, NSF CNS-1801479, a Google Security & Privacy Award and DARPA under Agreements No. HR00112020021 and Agreements No. HR001120C0084. Any opinions, findings and conclusions or recommendations expressed in this material are those of the author(s) and do not necessarily reflect the views of the United States Government or DARPA.

References

1. Lattigo v2.2.0. Online: http://github.com/ldsec/lattigo, July 2021. EPFL-LDS
2. Beaver, D., Micali, S., Rogaway, P.: The round complexity of secure protocols (extended abstract). In: 22nd ACM STOC, pp. 503–513. ACM Press, May 1990
3. Beck, G., Goel, A., Jain, A., Kaptchuk, G.: Order-C secure multiparty computation for highly repetitive circuits. In: Canteaut, A., Standaert, F.-X. (eds.) EUROCRYPT 2021. LNCS, vol. 12697, pp. 663–693. Springer, Cham (2021). https://doi.org/10.1007/978-3-030-77886-6_23
4. Ben-Efraim, A., Lindell, Y., Omri, E.: Efficient scalable constant-round MPC via garbled circuits. In: Takagi, T., Peyrin, T. (eds.) ASIACRYPT 2017. LNCS, vol. 10625, pp. 471–498. Springer, Cham (2017). https://doi.org/10.1007/978-3-319-70697-9_17
5. Ben-Or, M., Goldwasser, S., Wigderson, A.: Completeness theorems for non-cryptographic fault-tolerant distributed computation (extended abstract). In: 20th ACM STOC, pp. 1–10. ACM Press, May 1988
6. Boneh, D., Lewi, K., Montgomery, H., Raghunathan, A.: Key homomorphic PRFs and their applications. In: Canetti, R., Garay, J.A. (eds.) CRYPTO 2013. LNCS, vol. 8042, pp. 410–428. Springer, Heidelberg (2013). https://doi.org/10.1007/978-3-642-40041-4_23
7. Boyle, E., Gilboa, N., Ishai, Y.: Breaking the circuit size barrier for secure computation under DDH. In: Robshaw, M., Katz, J. (eds.) CRYPTO 2016. LNCS, vol. 9814, pp. 509–539. Springer, Heidelberg (2016). https://doi.org/10.1007/978-3-662-53018-4_19
8. Castagnos, G., Laguillaumie, F.: Linearly homomorphic encryption from DDH. In: Nyberg, K. (ed.) CT-RSA 2015. LNCS, vol. 9048, pp. 487–505. Springer, Cham (2015). https://doi.org/10.1007/978-3-319-16715-2_26
9. Chaum, D., Crépeau, C., Damgård, I.: Multiparty unconditionally secure protocols (Abstract). In: Pomerance, C. (ed.) CRYPTO 1987. LNCS, vol. 293, p. 462. Springer, Heidelberg (1988). https://doi.org/10.1007/3-540-48184-2_43
10. Chen, M., et al.: Diogenes: lightweight scalable RSA modulus generation with a dishonest majority. Cryptology ePrint Archive, Report 2020/374 (2020). https://eprint.iacr.org/2020/374
11. Chida, K., et al.: Fast large-scale honest-majority MPC for malicious adversaries. In: Shacham, H., Boldyreva, A. (eds.) CRYPTO 2018. LNCS, vol. 10993, pp. 34–64. Springer, Cham (2018). https://doi.org/10.1007/978-3-319-96878-0_2
12. Cramer, R., Damgård, I., Escudero, D., Scholl, P., Xing, C.: SPDZ2k: efficient MPC mod 2^k for dishonest majority. Cryptology ePrint Archive, Report 2018/482 (2018). https://eprint.iacr.org/2018/482
13. Cramer, R., Damgård, I., Nielsen, J.B.: Multiparty computation from threshold homomorphic encryption. In: Pfitzmann, B. (ed.) EUROCRYPT 2001. LNCS, vol. 2045, pp. 280–300. Springer, Heidelberg (2001). https://doi.org/10.1007/3-540-44987-6_18
14. Damgård, I., Ishai, Y.: Constant-round multiparty computation using a black-box pseudorandom generator. In: Shoup, V. (ed.) CRYPTO 2005. LNCS, vol. 3621, pp. 378–394. Springer, Heidelberg (2005). https://doi.org/10.1007/11535218_23
15. Damgård, I., Jurik, M.: A generalisation, a simplification and some applications of Paillier's probabilistic public-key system. In: Kim, K. (ed.) PKC 2001. LNCS, vol. 1992, pp. 119–136. Springer, Heidelberg (2001). https://doi.org/10.1007/3-540-44586-2_9

16. Damgård, I., Pastro, V., Smart, N., Zakarias, S.: Multiparty computation from somewhat homomorphic encryption. In: Safavi-Naini, R., Canetti, R. (eds.) CRYPTO 2012. LNCS, vol. 7417, pp. 643–662. Springer, Heidelberg (2012). https://doi.org/10.1007/978-3-642-32009-5_38

17. Fan, J., Vercauteren, F.: Somewhat practical fully homomorphic encryption. Cryptology ePrint Archive, Report 2012/144 (2012). https://eprint.iacr.org/2012/144

18. Frederiksen, T.K., Keller, M., Orsini, E., Scholl, P.: A unified approach to MPC with preprocessing using OT. In: Iwata, T., Cheon, J.H. (eds.) ASIACRYPT 2015. LNCS, vol. 9452, pp. 711–735. Springer, Heidelberg (2015). https://doi.org/10.1007/978-3-662-48797-6_29

19. Gentry, C.: Fully homomorphic encryption using ideal lattices. In: Mitzenmacher, M. (ed.) 41st ACM STOC, pp. 169–178. ACM Press, May/June 2009

20. Goldreich, O., Micali, S., Wigderson, A.: How to play any mental game or a completeness theorem for protocols with honest majority. In: Aho, A. (ed.) 19th ACM STOC, pp. 218–229. ACM Press, May 1987

21. Gordon, S.D., Starin, D., Yerukhimovich, A.: The more the merrier: reducing the cost of large scale MPC. In: Canteaut, A., Standaert, F.-X. (eds.) EUROCRYPT 2021. LNCS, vol. 12697, pp. 694–723. Springer, Cham (2021). https://doi.org/10.1007/978-3-030-77886-6_24

22. Goyal, V., Li, H., Ostrovsky, R., Polychroniadou, A., Song, Y.: ATLAS: efficient and scalable MPC in the honest majority setting. In: Malkin, T., Peikert, C. (eds.) CRYPTO 2021. LNCS, vol. 12826, pp. 244–274. Springer, Cham (2021). https://doi.org/10.1007/978-3-030-84245-1_9

23. Goyal, V., Polychroniadou, A., Song, Y.: Unconditional communication-efficient MPC via Hall's marriage theorem. In: Malkin, T., Peikert, C. (eds.) CRYPTO 2021. LNCS, vol. 12826, pp. 275–304. Springer, Cham (2021). https://doi.org/10.1007/978-3-030-84245-1_10

24. Goyal, V., Song, Y.: Malicious security comes free in honest-majority MPC. Cryptology ePrint Archive, Report 2020/134 (2020). https://eprint.iacr.org/2020/134

25. Hazay, C., Orsini, E., Scholl, P., Soria-Vazquez, E.: Concretely efficient large-scale MPC with active security (or, TinyKeys for TinyOT). In: Peyrin, T., Galbraith, S. (eds.) ASIACRYPT 2018. LNCS, vol. 11274, pp. 86–117. Springer, Cham (2018). https://doi.org/10.1007/978-3-030-03332-3_4

26. Heath, D., Kolesnikov, V.: Stacked garbling - garbled circuit proportional to longest execution path. In: Micciancio, D., Ristenpart, T. (ed.) CRYPTO 2020, Part II, vol. 12171 of LNCS, pp. 763–792. Springer, Heidelberg, August 2020. https://doi.org/10.1007/978-3-030-56880-1_27

27. Heath, D., Kolesnikov, V.: LogStack: stacked garbling with $O(b \log b)$ computation. In: Canteaut, A., François-Xavier Standaert, editors, *EUROCRYPT 2021, Part III*, volume 12698 of *LNCS*, pages 3–32. Springer, Heidelberg, October 2021 . https://doi.org/10.1007/978-3-030-77883-5_1

28. Heath, D., Kolesnikov, V., Peceny, S.: MOTIF: (almost) free branching in GMW - via vector-scalar multiplication. In: Moriai, S., Wang, H. (eds.) ASIACRYPT 2020. Part III, vol. 12493 of LNCS, pp. 3–30. Springer, Heidelberg (2020). https://doi.org/10.1007/978-3-030-64840-4_1

29. Heath, D., Kolesnikov, V., Peceny, S.: Garbling, stacked and staggered - faster k-out-of-n garbled function evaluation. In: Tibouchi, M., Wang, H. (eds.) Advances in Cryptology - ASIACRYPT 2021 - 27th International Conference on the Theory and Application of Cryptology and Information Security, Singapore, 6–10 December 2021, Proceedings, Part II, vol. 13091 of Lecture Notes in Computer Science, pp. 245–274. Springer (2021). https://doi.org/10.1007/978-3-030-92075-3

30. Heath, D., Kolesnikov, V., Peceny, S.: Masked triples- amortizing multiplication triples across conditionals. In: Garay, J.A. (ed.) PKC 2021. LNCS, vol. 12711, pp. 319–348. Springer, Cham (2021). https://doi.org/10.1007/978-3-030-75248-4_12

31. Katz, J., Malka, L.: Constant-round private function evaluation with linear complexity. In: Lee, D.H., Wang, X. (eds.) ASIACRYPT 2011. LNCS, vol. 7073, pp. 556–571. Springer, Heidelberg (2011). https://doi.org/10.1007/978-3-642-25385-0_30

32. Keller, M.: MP-SPDZ: a versatile framework for multi-party computation. In: Proceedings of the 2020 ACM SIGSAC Conference on Computer and Communications Security (2020)

33. Keller, M., Orsini, E., Scholl, P.: MASCOT: faster malicious arithmetic secure computation with oblivious transfer. In: Weippl, E.R., Katzenbeisser, S., Kruegel, C., Myers, A.C., Halevi, S. (eds.) ACM CCS 2016, pp. 830–842. ACM Press, October 2016

34. Keller, M., Pastro, V., Rotaru, D.: Overdrive: making SPDZ great again. In: Nielsen, J.B., Rijmen, V. (eds.) EUROCRYPT 2018. LNCS, vol. 10822, pp. 158–189. Springer, Cham (2018). https://doi.org/10.1007/978-3-319-78372-7_6

35. Mohassel, P., Sadeghian, S.: How to hide circuits in MPC an efficient framework for private function evaluation. In: Johansson, T., Nguyen, P.Q. (eds.) EUROCRYPT 2013. LNCS, vol. 7881, pp. 557–574. Springer, Heidelberg (2013). https://doi.org/10.1007/978-3-642-38348-9_33

36. Mohassel, P., Sadeghian, S., Smart, N.P.: Actively secure private function evaluation. In: Sarkar, P., Iwata, T. (eds.) ASIACRYPT 2014. LNCS, vol. 8874, pp. 486–505. Springer, Heidelberg (2014). https://doi.org/10.1007/978-3-662-45608-8_26

37. Naor, M., Pinkas, B., Reingold, O.: Distributed Pseudo-random functions and KDCs. In: Stern, J. (ed.) EUROCRYPT 1999. LNCS, vol. 1592, pp. 327–346. Springer, Heidelberg (1999). https://doi.org/10.1007/3-540-48910-X_23

38. Peikert, C., Vaikuntanathan, V., Waters, B.: A framework for efficient and composable oblivious transfer. In: Wagner, D. (ed.) CRYPTO 2008. LNCS, vol. 5157, pp. 554–571. Springer, Heidelberg (2008). https://doi.org/10.1007/978-3-540-85174-5_31

39. Wails, R., Johnson, A., Starin, D., Yerukhimovich, A., Gordon, S.D.: Stormy: statistics in Tor by measuring securely. In: Cavallaro, L., Kinder, J., Wang, X.F., Katz, J. (eds.) ACM CCS 2019, pp. 615–632. ACM Press, November 2019

40. Yao, A.C.-C.: How to generate and exchange secrets (extended abstract). In: 27th FOCS, pp. 162–167. IEEE Computer Society Press, October 1986

Secure Multiparty Computation with Sublinear Preprocessing

Elette Boyle[1]([✉]), Niv Gilboa[2], Yuval Ishai[3], and Ariel Nof[3]

[1] Reichman University (IDC Herzliya), and NTT Research, Herzliya, Israel
eboyle@alum.mit.edu
[2] Ben-Gurion University, Beersheba, Israel
gilboan@bgu.ac.il
[3] Technion, Haifa, Israel
{yuvali,ariel.nof}@cs.technion.ac.il

Abstract. A common technique for enhancing the efficiency of secure multiparty computation (MPC) with dishonest majority is via *preprocessing*: In an offline phase, parties engage in an input-independent protocol to securely generate correlated randomness. Once inputs are known, the correlated randomness is consumed by a "non-cryptographic" and highly efficient online protocol.

The correlated randomness in such protocols traditionally comes in two flavors: multiplication triples (Beaver, Crypto '91), which suffice for security against semi-honest parties, and *authenticated* multiplication triples (Bendlin et al., Eurocrypt '11, Damgård et al., Crypto '12) that yield efficient protocols against malicious parties.

Recent constructions of pseudorandom correlation generators (Boyle et al., Crypto '19, '20) enable concretely efficient secure generation of multiplication triples with *sublinear communication complexity*. However, these techniques do not efficiently apply to authenticated triples, except in the case of secure two-party computation of arithmetic circuits over large fields.

In this work, we propose the first *concretely efficient* approach for (malicious) MPC with preprocessing in which the offline communication is *sublinear* in the circuit size. More specifically, the offline communication scales with the *square root* of the circuit size.

From a feasibility point of view, our protocols can make use of any secure protocol for generating (unauthenticated) multiplication triples together with any *additive* homomorphic encryption. We propose concretely efficient instantiations (based on strong but plausible "linear-only" assumptions) from existing homomorphic encryption schemes and pseudorandom correlation generators.

Our technique is based on a variant of a recent protocol of Boyle et al. (Crypto '21) for MPC with preprocessing. As a result, our protocols inherit the succinct correlated randomness feature of the latter protocol.

© International Association for Cryptologic Research 2022
O. Dunkelman and S. Dziembowski (Eds.): EUROCRYPT 2022, LNCS 13275, pp. 427–457, 2022.
https://doi.org/10.1007/978-3-031-06944-4_15

1   Introduction

Protocols for secure multiparty computation (MPC) [2,18,28,44] enable a set of parties with private inputs to compute a joint function of their inputs while revealing nothing but the output. Optimizing the asymptotic and concrete efficiency of MPC protocols has been the topic of a large body of work. The question is particularly challenging when considering security against *malicious* adversaries, who can actively corrupt parties.

A successful approach for the design of such protocols is to employ *preprocessing*. Before the inputs are known, the parties run an offline protocol to generate correlated secret randomness, which is consumed by a lightweight and typically "non-cryptographic" (or "information-theoretic") online protocol.[1] This model, known also as the offline/online model, is in particular appealing when no honest majority can be guaranteed, since it allows to push the heavy "cryptographic" part of the protocol to the offline phase, minimizing the cost of the online protocol. Originating from the work of Beaver [1], who showed how to use "multiplication triples" for secure arithmetic computation with dishonest majority, many protocols for secure computation make extensive use of correlated randomness [3,11,20–24,31,39].

Most of the above works design protocols in the preprocessing model with security against *malicious* adversaries. A powerful recurring technique uses homomorphic MACs to authenticate the values produced by the online protocol [3,23]; the resulting correlation is a form of "authenticated" multiplication triples. Indeed, the so-called "SPDZ" line of work serves as a leading approach in this area, spawning a range of optimizations, implementations, and improvements, e.g. [5,17,20,35,36]. Another recent approach includes compilers based on sublinear distributed zero-knowledge [6,14]. As per design, in all these protocols the bulk of the work lies in the preprocessing phase. In particular, the typical communication complexity of this phase in existing protocols is by orders of magnitude higher than the size of the circuit being evaluated.

Recent constructions of *pseudorandom correlation generators* (PCGs) [8–10] demonstrate promising potential for improving the communication demands of certain preprocessing procedures. PCGs provide a means for parties to locally expand short correlated seeds into long pseudorandom instances of certain correlations, without communication. Indeed, recent PCG constructions based on Learning Parity with Noise (LPN) or its Ring-LPN variant enable *concretely efficient* secure generation of many multiplication triples, with *sublinear communication* and good concrete efficiency, including the secure generation of the seeds [9,10]. This directly yields a practical, sublinear-communication preprocessing for MPC with semi-honest security.

However, these techniques do not generally apply to the more complex correlation of *authenticated* multiplication triples, necessary for extending this app-

---

[1] This can be formalized by requiring the existence of alternative correlated randomness, which is computationally indistinguishable from the one generated by the offline protocol, and given which the entire protocol is information-theoretically secure.

roach to protocols with malicious security. Concretely efficient PCGs for authenticated triples exist only in the limited setting of 2-party correlations over large fields [10].[2] Using PCG-generated pairwise authenticated triples in the style of "BDOZ" [3] may be feasible for arithmetic circuits and a small number of parties, but result in online communication that scales quadratically in the number of parties. In the case of 2-party evaluation of Boolean circuits, PCGs for OT can be used to generate multiplication triples over $\mathbb{F}_2$, enabling semi-honest online protocols with 2 bits per party per gate, whereas for malicious security one needs to communicate 2 elements of a big finite field per gate.

To conclude, current PCG machinery cannot be efficiently used to generate *authenticated* triples that support an online protocol that scales linearly with the number of parties, or alternatively even 2-party protocols for Boolean circuits. Consequently, all practical protocols for MPC with preprocessing in these settings require the communication complexity of preprocessing to be much bigger than the circuit size.

1.1   Our Results

We provide new feasibility and concrete efficiency results for secure multiparty computation (MPC) in the dishonest majority setting. Our general approach can be instantiated to give the first practical *sublinear-communication* methods for generating "SPDZ-style" correlations, in the sense of achieving malicious security with an online phase that is both non-cryptographic and has linear communication in both the circuit size and the number of parties.

Our approach does not require authenticated multiplication triples as in SPDZ [23], but rather makes use of only semi-honest (non-authenticated) triples together with additional preprocessing material that builds on a variant of a recent protocol of Boyle et al. [14]. As a consequence, our protocols inherit the succinct correlated randomness feature of the latter protocol—that is, the additional preprocessing material (beyond multiplication triples) is only sublinear in the circuit size. From a concrete efficiency point of view, our approach is also attractive for Boolean circuits in the 2-party case, as there are no concretely efficient PCG for generating binary authenticated triples, whereas PCG for OT can generate binary non-authenticated triples.

More concretely, our protocols support secure computation in the preprocessing model of arithmetic circuits over any finite field or ring $\mathbb{Z}_{2^k}$. We say that the online phase is "information theoretic" (or "non-cryptographic") in the sense that the correlated randomness distribution D is computationally indistinguishable from some distribution D' for which executing the online phase with D' induces true information theoretic security. The offline preprocessing phase has communication that scales with the *square root* of the circuit size. Our protocol

---

[2] While these limitations can in some cases be circumvented [9,25,40], this comes at a big additional cost.

can make use of any secure protocol for generating (unauthenticated) multiplication triples, together with any additively homomorphic encryption.[3]

This constitutes a new feasibility result.

Theorem 1 (Sublinear-setup MPC with preprocessing, informal). *Let C be an arithmetic circuit of size $|C|$ (counting multiplication gates, inputs and outputs) over a ring R, where R is either a finite field $\mathbb{F}$ or the ring $\mathbb{Z}_{2^k}$. Then, there exists a secure n-party MPC protocol in the preprocessing model that computes C with security against up to $n-1$ malicious parties and the following features:*

- SUBLINEAR OFFLINE COMMUNICATION, *consisting of a number of R-elements that scales as $O(\sqrt{|C|})$.*
- INFORMATION-THEORETIC ONLINE PHASE
- PER-PARTY ONLINE COMMUNICATION *that does not grow with n: namely, $O(|C|)$ R-elements.*

Security is based on the assumptions underlying two cryptographic building blocks:

- *additively homomorphic encryption;*
- *sublinear-communication protocol for semi-honest generation of pseudorandom (un-authenticated) multiplication triples over R: e.g., implied by LPN.*

Note that the information-theoretic nature of the online phase makes the task of achieving sublinear offline communication highly nontrivial, as opposed to trivial solution approaches which simply ignore the offline phase (zero offline communication) and perform a complete secure computation in the online phase.

We additionally propose concretely efficient instantiations of our main theorem (based on strong but plausible "linear-only" assumptions) from existing homomorphic encryption schemes and existing pseudorandom correlation generators.

The overhead of our online phase is quite modest and in many settings is dominated by the communication of the semi-honest baseline protocol, even over a fast 1 Gbps network, e.g. for an arithmetic circuit of 2^{20} gates over a prime field of 60 bits (and soundness error 2^{-50}).

1.2   Technical Overview

Starting Point: Distributed Zero Knowledge and BGIN'21. We follow in line with a collection of recent prior works using sublinear distributed zero knowledge machinery toward low-communication solutions for compiling semi-honest to malicious security [6,12–14].

The high-level structure of these protocols is as follows. Within the protocol, the parties begin by running the underlying semi-honest secure protocol aside

---

[3] Implied, e.g., by any of the Quadratic Residuosity, Learning with Errors, or Decisional Composite Residuosity assumptions.

from the final step. Then, before exchanging the final messages and revealing outputs, the parties first jointly execute a verification phase in which correctness of the first phase is asserted. This is done by generating and verifying *zero knowledge proofs on distributed data* (hereafter "Distributed zero knowledge"), which can be done with sublinear proof size for simple languages [6]. Distributed zero knowledge (DZK) proofs consider a setting with a single prover and multiple verifiers, who each hold pieces of the statement; the prover sends a share of the proof to each verifier, and the verifiers interact amongst themselves in order to verify the proof.

The specific structure and use of the DZK proof system within the MPC protocol application varies across works: either each party acts separately as prover to assert his own proper behavior [6,12,14], or the parties jointly emulate the prover on the collective set of generated values, which no single party knows in full [6,14].

A complication arises in any multi-party setting with more than a single corrupted party, as collusion may take place between a proving and a verifying entity. In order to provide soundness, the statement being proved must be somehow robustly held across parties, such that a corrupt verifier cannot modify his piece of the statement to enable the proof to improperly be accepted. Such robustness is natural in the case of MPC with an honest majority, where the honest parties themselves holds sufficient information to determine the (secret) statement. For the case of dishonest majority, ensuring robustness is less clear. A main idea of [14] (hereafter referred to as "BGIN'21") is that correlated randomness generated during preprocessing can be designed so as to function as an additional "dealer" party whose actions must be determined independent of the inputs, but whose behavior is *guaranteed to be honest*.

Of course, for this approach to work, it is crucial that the correlated randomness is indeed generated honestly. In the idealized preprocessing model, as considered in [14], this comes for free: the parties are assumed to be given honestly generated samples from the correlated randomness from an ideal honest dealer. Our challenge is to remove this assumption, and to generate these values as part of the protocol in a manner that still suffices for overall security, in *sublinear communication*. Moreover, we would like to do so without resorting to expensive general-purpose tools such as fully homomorphic encryption. Instead, we will rely on any *additively homomorphic* encryption. Doing so will require us to modify the BGIN'21 correlation and protocol in the process.

The BGIN'21 Dealer (Slightly Modified). Consider the DZK joint prover emulation approach. After the semi-honest execution, the parties wish to jointly prove that for every multiplication gate, the shares they hold of the output wire correspond correctly to the shares they hold of the two input wires. To compress this into a single verification instead of $|C|$, the parties sample random coefficients α^g for each multiplication gate g, and instead verify that this random linear combination of all gate-checks indeed verifies. This reduces the challenge to proving that single degree-2 multivariate polynomial evaluates to 0 on $O(|C|)$ secret-shared inputs.

To achieve this, each party takes part in 3 phases: (1) "Joint-Prover," computing its contribution of the jointly generated proof of correctness, (2) "Verifier query," jointly generating a verifier query challenge (a form of coin toss protocol), and (3) "Verifier answer," performing its role as one of the multiple verifiers.

The dealer (in addition to generating the semi-honest correlation material) must effectively perform each of these actions acting as an additional honest party, and commit to its answers to be revealed in the online phase. Concretely, for arithmetic circuit C over ring R, the dealer must perform the following generation tasks:

1. **Semi-honest multiplication triples** (for semi-honest computation): For each gate g, additive shares of random $r_1^g, r_2^g \in R$ and $r_1^g \cdot r_2^g \in R$.
2. **Random compressing coefficients:** Selecting random (or sufficiently high-entropy) linear coefficients α^g for each gate g, so that correctness of all multiplication gates can be checked in a compressed manner via a random linear α^g-combination of the individual verification polynomials. A concise description of all α^g is shared across the parties to be revealed and reconstructed in the online phase during verification. In [14], each α^g is taken to be the gth power of single random value $\alpha \leftarrow R$.
3. **Prover contribution:** The "dealer party's share" of the jointly computed DZK proof. This consists of simply proof-size many random share values $s_i \in R$, secret shared to the parties in such a way that the value of each s_i cannot be changed by malicious parties in the online phase.
4. **Verifier query generation:** Random polynomial evaluation point $\tau \in R$.
5. **Verifier answer contribution:** Computation of verifier query answer as a function of the dealer's share of the statement (a function of items 1 and 2), its shares of the proof (item 3), and the verifier query (item 4).

When using a D-ZK proof with multiple rounds of interaction (as in BGIN'21), Step 3 above is replaced by a sequence of: (a) generating random Verifier challenges, and (b) computing the Prover contribution to this round of interaction.

Some parts of items 1–5 above are not a problem toward our goal. As discussed, recent constructions of PCGs enable concretely efficient secure generation of many semi-honest multiplication triples with sublinear communication [9,10], taking care of item 1. In addition, we can easily support sampling and committing to random shares and of a random point as in items 3 & 4.

The problems are items 2 and 5. In the current state as in BGIN'21, the computation of item 5 requires performing a secure computation that is both linear in the circuit size, *and* high degree. The degree comes from multiple places: from the high powers of α^g, from the recursive DZK proof structure (typically executed interactively), and the DZK verifier answer procedure which is computed as a function on top of these (already high-degree) expressions.

Expressing Dealer with Bilinear Structure. We thus devise a new approach. Our idea is to modify the BGIN'21 protocol, so as to make the corresponding items

2–5 of dealer computation expressible as a single *bilinear* pairing computation between two types of values: (1) ones that are (already) held additively secret shared across the parties, e.g. from the semi-honest multiplication triples, and (2) a small, sublinear-size set of other secret values.

Given this structure, we can securely emulate the dealer with low communication using additively homomorphic encryption. Namely, the parties will generate *encryptions* of the small set of secret values (requiring sublinear communication, comparable to the small number of values). Then they homomorphically compute encrypted shares of the desired paired output using the public ciphertexts and their additive shares, *without* communication. Since the size of the dealer's output is short—equivalently, the bilinear maps are highly compressing—the parties can then execute a standard protocol for jointly decrypting the resulting ciphertexts, again with sublinear communication.

In turn, it hence remains to achieve the above structural goal for the dealer's computation.

First, we observe that replacing the recursive multi-round DZK with a simpler non-recursive DZK construction of [6] (albeit with $\sqrt{|C|}$ instead of $\log |C|$ communication cost) immediately alleviates one source of cost. The new prover and verifier procedures become simply degree 2. In particular, in this construction, the computation of a verifier's answer corresponds to interpreting $\sqrt{|C|}$-size collections of symbols from the proof and statement as coefficients of a polynomial, and evaluating each at the point τ chosen as the verifier query (in dealer Step 4). Said in different words, each polynomial evaluation is an inner product between the corresponding $\sqrt{|C|}$-length coefficient vector with the vector formed by the corresponding $\sqrt{|C|}$ powers $\tau^0, \tau^1, \ldots, \tau^{\sqrt{|C|}}$ of τ. Note that while there are several different blocks of symbols, they are each inner-producted with the *same* powers-of-τ vector.

If we could reach a state where the symbols of the proof and statement were held as additive secret shares, then we would in fact have reached our goal, where the powers-of-τ form the sublinear-size set of other values (to be encrypted). However, this is not yet the case. This is because the "statement" that must be proved is formed by the α^g-*linear-compressed combination* of the multiplication triple values, as opposed to the values themselves.

It is worth emphasizing an important difference between our setting and typical usage of the α^g-linear-compression technique, which is employed broadly in protocol design. Typically, coefficients α^g are chosen *after* the parties are already committed to their the semi-honest protocol execution, in which case there is no need for secrecy, and they are simply public values. In contrast, in this setting (as in BGIN'21), for the dealer to function as an honest party, the selection of these coefficients must be made already in the *preprocessing* phase, but kept secret through the semi-honest protocol execution. In turn, the traditionally simple linear compression here constitutes a nontrivial secure computation.

In fact, because of this, there is a problem even if the parties *already* somehow held secret shares of random values α^g. This is because multiplication by a coefficient α^g still amounts to an additional degree of secure multiplication. Since computation of the dealer's contribution to the verification polynomial already requires degree 2 terms, this additional multiplication pushes out of hope for turning the computation into a bilinear operation.

Instead, we identify a new method for computing the same overall verification polynomial evaluation expression between the "dealer" party and online parties, which enables pushing more work to the online parties, but which means that the linear combination coefficients do not need to be used by the dealer at all in his calculations. (In some sense, this comes from an alternative perspective and goal than from BGIN'21, which focused primarily on optimizing the online portion of the protocol while assuming an honest dealer.) This step uses the fact that the online parties hold secret shares not only of the masks r_1, r_2 of the input wires of any multiplication gate, but also shares of their product, $r_1 r_2$, leveraging the specific structure of semi-honest multiplication triples. In particular, terms in the verification polynomial of the form $\alpha^g r_1 r_2$, which were computed by the dealer in BGIN'21, can be jointly computed by the online parties if the α^g is made public, using the $(r_1 r_2)$ additive shares.

In doing so, we not only remove the extra secure multiplication of scaling by the α^g, but also the remaining question of how these coefficients α^g should be generated. What results is a successful expression of the dealer in the desired bilinear form, between additively secret shared values and powers of τ, which we will denote by π_{BL}.

Putting the Pieces Together. Obtaining the feasibility result follows in a few steps.

We prove that the above-described modifications to the dealer's ideal functionality still suffice, with corresponding adjustments in the online portion, to yield security in the overall protocol.

Combining the above ideas, we then obtain a *semi-honest* secure protocol that securely evaluates the (new) dealer functionality with sublinear communication. Namely, the parties: (1) run the sublinear-communication protocol for semi-honest generation of pseudorandom (un-authenticated) multiplication triples; (2) run a secure protocol for randomly sampling τ (as dictated by the [6] DZK; either from the ring R, or an extension ring if R is small) and generating AHE encryptions c_i of the powers $\tau^0, \tau^1, \ldots, \tau^{\sqrt{|C|}}$, (3) locally evaluate encrypted shares of the bilinear form π_{BL} by computing the compressing linear combination of the AHE ciphertexts c_i with the corresponding secret shares of the relevant values; (4) exchanging the resulting output-share ciphertexts and additively combining across parties, resulting in encryptions of the outputs of π_{BL}; and (5) executing a secure protocol for jointly decrypting the resulting ciphertexts.

In order to achieve the same dealer emulation with *malicious* security, we leverage a generic communication-preserving compiler of Naor and Nissim [38] (building on [28,37]). Using this compiler a semi-honest secure protocol can be compiled into a maliciously secured protocol for the same functionality with sublinear additive communication cost. Since the compiler only requires collision-resistant hash functions, which are implied by additively homomorphic encryption [32], this does not require introducing new assumptions. This implies the final result. In the full version of the paper, we propose a maliciously secure protocol with concrete efficiency that is based on making two stronger, but quite plausible, assumptions on the AHE: being "linear-only" and having a threshold encryption variant. See discussion at the end of Sect. 6.

2   Preliminaries

Notation. Let $P_1, \ldots, P_n$ be the parties participating in the protocol. We use $[n]$ to denote the set $\{1, \ldots, n\}$. Let R be a ring which is either a finite field $\mathbb{F}$ or the ring $\mathbb{Z}_{2^k}$ and let $|R|$ be its size. Finally, let κ be the security parameter. We use bold letters to represent vectors and $\boldsymbol{v}[j]$ to denote the jth entry of the vector $\boldsymbol{v}$. When we write $\boldsymbol{u} \cdot \boldsymbol{v}$ we refer to the *inner product* between the two vectors. We use $[\![x]\!]$ to denote an additive sharing of x. When we write $[\![\boldsymbol{x}]\!]$, we mean that *each* entry in $\boldsymbol{x}$ is additively shared across the parties.

2.1   Security Definitions

In our setting, there is a set of n parties who wish to jointly run some computation. We assume that all parties are connected via point-to-point secure channels, which enable them to send messages to each other. In this work, we will typically consider secure computation of arithmetic circuits (with addition and multiplication gates) over a finite ring R, where R can either be fixed or be given as part of the circuit description. In particular, the case of Boolean circuits is captured by $R = \mathbb{F}_2$. For security, we use the standard ideal/real world definition from [16,27].

MPC with Preprocessing. Our main result refers to an MPC protocol that employs a "cryptographic" input-independent offline protocol, followed by a "non-cryptographic" input-dependent online protocol. As a building block, we will rely on MPC protocols in a hybrid model in which the offline protocol is replaced by an ideal source of correlated randomness $\mathcal{D}$ that is generated by a trusted dealer.

In this correlated randomness model, we consider protocols for arithmetic circuits that offer security up to an "additive" attack on intermediate wires in the circuits. Most information-theoretic protocols that offer the weaker form of *semi-honest* security also satisfy this notion of security with additive attacks.

We formalize the notion of "security-up-to-additive-attacks" [26], in the setting of MPC with dishonest majority in the correlated randomness model. This security model applies to the class $\mathcal{F}$ of arithmetic circuits over a ring R, and allows the ideal-world adversary $\mathcal{S}$ to (blindly) pick a tampering function that adds a chosen value from R for each wire of the circuit. Concretely, we allow additive attacks on *input wires to multiplication gates and on the circuit's output wires*. The trusted party in the ideal world then determines the output of the honest parties by computing the circuit over the parties' inputs, applying the chosen additive error to each wire.

MPC with non-cryptographic Online Phase. An MPC protocol in the preprocessing model is similar to the above model of MPC with correlated randomness, except that the correlated randomness $\mathcal{D}$ is securely generated by an *offline protocol*, instead of being distributed by a trusted dealer. As before, the correlated randomness $\mathcal{D}$ can then be consumed by an online protocol. The main advantage of this offline-online paradigm is that it allows the online protocol to be "non-cryptographic" (or information-theoretic), which typically translates to good concrete efficiency. We formalize this notion by requiring that the correlated randomness produced by an honest execution of the offline protocol can be replaced by a *computationally indistinguishable* distribution $\mathcal{D}$, such that given $\mathcal{D}$, the online protocol is *information-theoretically* secure.

Definition 1 (PMPC with non-cryptographic online phase). *Let $\mathcal{F}$ be the class of n-party functionalities represented by arithmetic circuits C. An MPC protocol for $\mathcal{F}$ with preprocessing and non-cryptographic online phase (or PMPC protocol for short) is defined by a pair of protocols $\Pi = (\Pi_{\mathsf{offline}}, \Pi_{\mathsf{online}})$ such that:*

- *Π_{offline} is invoked with public inputs $(1^\kappa, 1^n, 1^{|C|}, R)$, where $|C|$ is the size of an arithmetic circuit $C \in \mathcal{F}$ over $\mathcal{R}$. It terminates with each party P_i outputting a local random output $\mathbf{Z}_i$.*
- *Π_{online} is invoked on public inputs $(1^\kappa, 1^n, C)$ and local inputs $(\mathbf{Z}_i, x_i)$ held by each P_i and ends with P_i outputting y_i.*

We make the following security requirements:

- *The protocol obtained by first running Π_{offline} and then Π_{online} securely realizes $\mathcal{F}$.*
- *There exists an ideal correlation generator $\mathcal{D}(1^\kappa, 1^n, 1^{|C|}, \mathcal{R})$, outputting $(\mathbf{Z}_1', ..., \mathbf{Z}_n')$, such that:*
  1. *The output of $\mathcal{D}$ is computationally indistinguishable from the output of an honest execution of Π_{offline}.*
  2. *If we feed Π_{online} with the output of $\mathcal{D}$, the resulting protocol realizes $\mathcal{F}$ with statistical (information-theoretic) security.*

In fact, to capture a minimal notion of MPC with non-cryptographic online phase, it suffices to relax the latter requirement (on Π_{online} with $\mathcal{D}$) to information-theoretic *semi-honest* security. However, the protocols we consider here satisfy the stronger property.

2.2   Fully Linear Proof Systems

A main technical building block in [14] is a *fully linear* proof system [6], enabling information-theoretic sublinear-communication zero-knowledge proofs on secret-shared or distributed input statements. In a nutshell, *zero-knowledge fully linear interactive oracle proof* (zk-FLIOP) is an information-theoretic proof system in which a prover P wishes to prove that some statement about an input x to a verifier V. In each round of the protocol, P produces a proof which, together with x, can be queried by V using *linear queries* only. Then, a public random challenge is generated and the parties proceed to the next round. At the end, the verifier V accepts or rejects based on the answers it received to its queries.

Definition 2 (Public-coin zk-FLIOP [6]**).** *A public-coin fully linear interactive proof system over R with ρ-round and ℓ-query and message length $(u_1, \ldots, u_\rho) \in \mathbb{N}^t$, consists of a randomized prover algorithm P and a deterministic verifier algorithm V. Let the input to P be $x \in R^m$ and let $r_0 = \bot$. In each round $i \in [\rho]$:*

1. *P outputs a proof $\pi_i \in R^{u_1}$, computed as a function of x, $r_1, \ldots, r_{i-1}$ and $\pi_1, \ldots, \pi_{i-1}$.*
2. *A random public challenge r_i is chosen uniformly from a finite set S_i.*
3. *ℓ linear oracle queries $q_1^i, \ldots, q_\ell^i \in R^{m+u_i}$ are determined based on $r_1, \ldots, r_i$. Then, V receives ℓ answers $(\langle q_1^i, x || \pi_i \rangle, \ldots, \langle q_\ell^i, x || \pi_i \rangle)$.*

At the end of round ρ, V outputs accept *or* reject *based on the random challenges and all the answers to the queries.*

Let $\mathcal{L} \subseteq R^m$ be an efficiently recognizable language. We say that ρ-round ℓ-query interactive fully linear protocol $(P_{\mathsf{FLIOP}}, V_{\mathsf{FLIOP}})$ over R is zero-knowledge fully linear interactive oracle proof system for $\mathcal{L}$ with soundness error ϵ if it satisfies the following properties:

- COMPLETENESS: *If $x \in \mathcal{L}$, then V_{FLIOP} always outputs* accept.
- SOUNDNESS: *If $x \notin \mathcal{L}$, then for all P^*, the probability that V_{FLIOP} outputs* accept *is at most $2^{-\epsilon}$.*
- ZERO KNOWLEDGE: *There exists a simulator $\mathcal{S}_{\mathsf{FLIOP}}$ such that for all $x \in \mathcal{L}$ it holds that $\mathcal{S}_{\mathsf{FLIOP}} \equiv \mathsf{view}_{[P_{\mathsf{FLIOP}}(x), V_{\mathsf{FLIOP}}]}(V_{\mathsf{FLIOP}})$ (where the verifier's view $\mathsf{view}_{[P_{\mathsf{FLIOP}}(x), V_{\mathsf{FLIOP}}]}(V_{\mathsf{FLIOP}})$ consists of $\{r_i\}_{i \in [\rho]}$, $\{(q_1^i, \ldots, q_\ell^i)\}_{i \in [\rho]}$ and $(\langle q_1^i, x || \pi_i \rangle, \ldots, \langle q_\ell^i, x || \pi_i \rangle)_{i \in [\rho]}$.*

In this paper, we will use this tool for degree-d languages. That is, languages for which membership can be checked using a degree-d polynomial. The following theorem, which will be used by us, states that for degree-d languages, there are zk-FLIOP protocols with sublinear communication and rounds in the size of the input and number of monomials.

Theorem 2 ([6]). *Let $q : R^m \to R$ be a polynomial of degree-d with M monomials, and let $\mathcal{L}_q = \{x \in R^m \mid q(x) = 0\}$. Let ϵ be the required soundness error. Then, there is a zk-FLIOP for $\mathcal{L}_q$ with the following properties:*

- CONSTANT ROUNDS, $d = 2$: *It has 1 round, proof length $O(\eta \sqrt{m})$, challenge length $O(\eta)$ and the number of queries is $O(\sqrt{m})$, where $\eta = \log_{|R|}\left(\frac{\sqrt{m}}{\epsilon}\right)$*

when R is a finite field, and $\eta = \log_2\left(\frac{\sqrt{m}}{\epsilon}\right)$ when $R = \mathbb{Z}_{2^k}$. The computational complexity is $\tilde{O}(M)$ and the proof generation is a degree-2 function of the input x and the prover's secret randomness, determined by the circuit C and the public randomness.

- LOGARITHMIC ROUNDS, $d \geq 2$: It has $O(\log M)$ rounds, proof length $O(d\eta \log M)$, challenge length $O(\eta \log M)$ and the number of queries is $O(d + \log M)$, where $\eta = \log_{|R|}\left(\frac{d\log m}{\epsilon}\right)$ when R is a finite field, and $\eta = \log_2\left(\frac{d\log m}{\epsilon}\right)$ when $R = \mathbb{Z}_{2^k}$. The computational complexity is $O(dM)$.

2.3   Additively-Homomorphic Encryption (AHE)

Our main protocol can be based on any *additively homomorphic encryption* (AHE) scheme. An AHE scheme consists of algorithms (Gen, Enc, Dec, Add) such that (Gen, Enc, Dec) satisfy the usual correctness and semantic security requirements of a public-key encryption scheme, and Add enables to add (more generally, linearly combine) a vector of encrypted messages.

More concretely, Gen is a key-generation algorithm which takes as input the security parameter 1^κ and outputs a pair of secret and public keys (sk, pk), where pk includes a description of a finite plaintext ring R, Enc is an encryption algorithm which takes the public key pk and a message $m \in R$ as inputs and outputs a ciphertext c, Dec is a deterministic decryption algorithm which takes the secret key sk and ciphertext c as inputs and outputs a message m (or a symbol $\perp$ in case of failure), and the randomized algorithm Add takes as input ciphertexts $\{c_j \in \mathsf{Enc}_{pk}(m_j)\}_{j\in[M]}$ and ring elements $a_0, \ldots, a_M \in R$ and outputs a *fresh* ciphertext $c \in_R \mathsf{Enc}_{pk}(a_0 + \sum_{j=1}^{M} a_j \cdot m_j)$. We use the notation Add$\left((a_k)_{k=0}^{M}, (c_k)_{k=1}^{M}\right)$ for this operation. When we simply want to add M ciphertexts (i.e., $a_0 = 0$ and $a_k = 1$ for each $k \geq 1$), we simply write Add$(c_1, \ldots, c_M)$.

The above definition captures a simple version of AHE in which one can combine an unbounded number of encrypted messages and the resulting ciphertext is distributed identically to a fresh encryption of the correct value. This notion can be satisfied by standard number-theoretic encryption schemes such as the Goldwasser-Micali scheme [29] or its generalized version due to Benaloh [19]. To accommodate other instantiations, such lattice-based schemes [33,42], or using Pailler's encryption scheme [41] over a chosen plaintext modulus, one needs to slightly relax the definition to allow a statistical error in the output of Add that depends on the number of ciphertexts that are combined. While we chose the strict definition for simplicity, our results can be extended to use the relaxed variants of AHE that support such alternative instantiations.

2.4   Ideal Functionalities and Basic Building Blocks

$\mathcal{F}_{\mathrm{coin}}$ - *Coin Tossing.* This ideal functionality who gives the parties fresh random coins. It can be implemented using any secure coin tossing protocol. In the context of our protocol, we can minimize the number of calls to $\mathcal{F}_{\text{coin}}$ by having the parties call $\mathcal{F}_{\text{coin}}$ once to obtain a seed from which they can locally derive a long vector of ring elements.

$\mathcal{F}_{\text{bc}}$ - *Broadcast with Selective Abort.* This ideal functionality allows the parties to deliver a message msg to all the other parties, while giving the adversary the ability to cause any party to abort. Therefore, whenever we say throughout the paper that P_i broadcasts a message, we mean that it sends a message to all parties via $\mathcal{F}_{\text{bc}}$. This functionality can be easily implemented by having P_i sends its message to all the parties, and then running an additional round where all parties compare the message they received. To amortize away the second-round comparison, a standard optimization technique is to batch the check for many messages by taking a random linear combination of all these message before the end of the protocol.

Authenticated Secret Sharing $\langle \cdot \rangle$. In some cases, we will need the parties to hold a secret sharing of x in an authenticated way, i.e., that allows the parties to securely reveal (with abort) the secret. We denote by $\langle x \rangle$ such a secret sharing and denote by open the opening procedure which receives $\langle x \rangle$ and guarantee that at the end either the parties will obtain x or abort the protocol (up to a negligible failure probability). To implement this over a field, one can use SPDZ-style information-theoretic MACs [3,23]. We stress that this tool is used a *sublinear* number of times in our protocol, and so its cost is amortized away.

3   The BGIN Compiler [14]

In this section, we review the verification procedure of Boyle et al.(BGIN) [14], that enables compiling a semi-honest protocol in the pre-processing model into a maliciously secured protocol, with sublinear additional amount of correlated randomness. There are two conditions that the semi-honest protocol should satisfy for the compiler to work:

1. ADDITIVE SECURITY: The adversary is restricted to only adding errors to a set of wires W in the circuit.
2. "STAR-SHARING" COMPLIANCE: For each circuit's wire $w \in W$, the parties hold a masked value $\hat{x}_w = x_w - r_w$ and additive shares of the mask r_w. The dealer knows r_w and its shares.

For formal definition, we refer the reader to [14]. The above requirements are satisfied by the semi-honest protocol based on Beaver triples [1]. Here the set W consists of all input wires for multiplication gates and output wires of the circuit. To maintain the star-sharing invariant in the circuit-independent version of the protocol, the parties first locally convert their star shares on each input wire to a multiplication gate, into *additive* shares of the output. Then, they can carry-out linear operations over the additive shares. When they arrive to the next input wire to a multiplication gate, they interact to reveal the masked input and so on.

To achieve malicious security, SPDZ-style [23] protocols use authenticated Beaver triples. This means that for each multiplication gate g, the parties receive from the dealer shares of $(r_1, r_2, r_1 \cdot r_2)$ and $(r_1 \cdot \theta, r_2 \cdot \theta, r_1 \cdot r_2 \cdot \theta)$, where θ is a global secret key. To achieve statistical security of κ bits, the MACed triple should be generated over a large ring (e.g., if the computation is carried-out over $\mathbb{F}_2$, then the MACed triple should be over $\mathbb{F}_{2^\kappa}$). This implies a correlated randomness overhead of $O(|C| \cdot \kappa)$ ring elements for small fields.

The novel verification protocol of BGIN [14] avoids this and requires the dealer to provide only sublinear amount of correlated randomness beyond the semi-honest protocol. The idea works as follows. For each wire $w \in W$, the parties need to verify the consistency of the values shared on this wire, with the values shared on the wires that precede it. In other words, the parties verify that they hold a sharing of the correct value on w, given the sharings they hold on wires that feed w. Specifically, let G_w be the set of multiplication gates that feed w (i.e., that between their output wire and w there are no other multiplication gates). For each $g \in G_w$, let x_1^g, x_2^g be the two input wires to g. The parties wish to verify that $x_w - \sum_{g \in G_w} x_1^g \cdot x_2^g = 0$. Instead, it suffices for the parties to verify that

$$
p = \sum_{w \in W} \alpha_w \cdot \left(x_w - \sum_{g \in G_w} x_1^g \cdot x_2^g \right)
$$

$$
= \sum_{w \in W} \alpha_w \cdot \left(\hat{x}_w + r_w - \sum_{g \in G_w} (\hat{x}_1^g + r_1^g) \cdot (\hat{x}_2^g + r_2^g) \right) = 0 \tag{1}
$$

where the α_ws are random elements given to the parties by the dealer (it suffices for the dealer to give a seed α from which all randomness is derived).

Next, note that each gate g_ℓ can feed several wires. For each multiplication gate g_ℓ, let W^{g_ℓ} be the set of wires w for which $g_\ell \in G_w$ (i.e., that g_ℓ's output feed these wires). Then, let $\gamma_\ell = \sum_{w \in W^{g_\ell}} \alpha_w$. Thus, Eq. (1) can be written as

$$
p = \sum_{w \in W} \alpha_w \cdot (\hat{x}_w + r_w) - \sum_{g_\ell \in \mathsf{mult}} \gamma_\ell \cdot ((\hat{x}_1^{g_\ell} + r_1^{g_\ell}) \cdot (\hat{x}_2^{g_\ell} + r_2^{g_\ell}))
$$

$$
= \sum_{w \in W} \alpha_w \cdot \hat{x}_w - \sum_{g_\ell \in \mathsf{mult}} \gamma_\ell \cdot (\hat{x}_1^{g_\ell} \cdot \hat{x}_2^{g_\ell}) + \sum_{w \in W} \alpha_w \cdot r_w
$$

$$
- \sum_{g_\ell \in \mathsf{mult}} \gamma_\ell \cdot (\hat{x}_1^{g_\ell} \cdot r_2^{g_\ell} + \hat{x}_2^{g_\ell} \cdot r_1^{g_\ell}) + \sum_{g_\ell \in \mathsf{mult}} \gamma_\ell \cdot (r_1^{g_\ell} \cdot r_2^{g_\ell})
$$

Now, setting

$$
\Lambda = \sum_{w \in W} \alpha_w \cdot \hat{x}_w - \sum_{g_\ell \in \mathsf{mult}} \gamma_\ell \cdot (\hat{x}_1^{g_\ell} \cdot \hat{x}_2^{g_\ell}) \tag{2}
$$

$$
\Gamma_i = \sum_{w \in W} \alpha_w \cdot r_{w,i} - \sum_{g_\ell \in \mathsf{mult}} \gamma_\ell \cdot (\hat{x}_1^{g_\ell} \cdot r_{2,i}^{g_\ell} + \hat{x}_2^{g_\ell} \cdot r_{1,i}^{g_\ell}) \tag{3}
$$

and $\Omega = \sum\limits_{g_\ell \in \mathsf{mult}} \gamma_\ell \cdot (r_1^{g_\ell} \cdot r_2^{g_\ell})$, it follows that checking that $p = 0$ is equivalent to checking that $\Lambda + \sum_{i=1}^{n} \Gamma_i + \Omega - 0$.

Observe that the parties can locally compute Λ, each party P_i can locally compute Γ_i and the dealer can locally compute Ω. Leveraging this, the verification protocol in [14] works thus as follows:

1. Each party P_i computes Λ and Γ_i, while the dealer computes Ω.
2. The dealer star shares Ω to the parties by sending $\hat{\Omega} = \Omega - \omega$ and also hands a mask s_i to each party P_i.
3. Each party P_i star shares Γ_i to the parties by broadcasting $\hat{\Gamma}_i = \Gamma_i - s_i$.
4. Each party P_i proves that it shared the correct Γ_i using a zk-FLIOP proof system (see explanation below).
5. If all proofs terminated successfully, then the dealer sends $\sum_{i=1}^{n} s_i + \omega$ to all parties.
6. The parties locally compute p and check equality to 0. If it holds, the parties output accept. Otherwise, they output reject.

The two main observations here are: (i) Γ_i is computed via a 2-degree polynomial. Thus, by Theorem 2, there exists a zk-FLIOP to prove that Eq. (3) holds. (ii) All inputs to the zk-FLIOP are either known to *all* parties or known to the dealer. Thus, we can run the zk-FLIOP by letting P_i emulate the prover's role, and letting all the other parties *together with the dealer* emulate the verifier's role. Specifically, the prover star-shares the proof across the parties and the dealer, and then each verifier makes the linear queries over its shares of the proof and the inputs. The fact that each piece of information is known to an honest participant (i.e., an honest party or the dealer) is what guarantee soundness. Leveraging the fact that from Theorem 2 the amount of communication in the proof can be made sublinear, we have that the amount of data sent by the verifying dealer is also sublinear in the size of the statement which, in our case, is similar to the size of the computed circuit. Finally, since all the computations made by the dealer in this protocol are over random data, it follows that the dealer can preprocess its messages and secret share it to the parties in an authenticated way, before the online computation begins. Overall, the amount of correlated randomness given to the parties for this protocol is sublinear.

Distributing the Dealer. The authors in [14] did not provide a distributed protocol to compute the dealer. Instead, they viewed the dealer's role as a circuit to be computed, and proposed to compute it using any general-purposed MPC. Then, they showed that the number of multiplication gates in the dealer's circuit is approximately $4|C| + n \cdot 2|C|$ for n parties. That is, the size of the dealer's circuit grows linearly with circuit C and the number of parties n.

4   A New Simplified Verification Protocol

In this section, we present a modified verification protocol that will allow us eventually to distribute the dealer with sublinear communication. Our primary aim is to make the computation performed by the dealer be low depth (i.e., it is possible to represent the dealer using a low-depth circuit). A secondary goal is to make the size of the dealer's circuit be independent of the number of parties.

To this end, we first observe that the parties can locally compute an additive sharing of Ω as well. This holds since γ_ℓ is public and they hold shares of $r_1^{g_\ell} \cdot r_2^{g_\ell}$ (these are part of the semi-honest correlated randomness). It follows that now

$$\Gamma_i = \sum_{w \in W} \alpha_w \cdot r_{w,i} - \sum_{g_\ell \in \text{mult}} \gamma_\ell \cdot \left(\hat{x}_1^{g_\ell} \cdot r_{2,i}^{g_\ell} + \hat{x}_2^{g_\ell} \cdot r_{1,i}^{g_\ell} + (r_1 \cdot r_2)_i^{g_\ell} \right)$$

Next, instead of letting each party prove that it star-shared the correct Γ_i, we will run a single proof where the parties emulate together the role of the zk-FLIOP prover. The dealer, however, still serves as a verifier, but now only *once* instead of n times. The goal now will be to prove that $\Gamma = \sum_{i=1}^n \Gamma_i$ is correct. That is, that

$$\Gamma = \sum_{w \in W} \alpha_w \cdot r_w - \sum_{g_\ell \in \text{mult}} \gamma_\ell \cdot (\hat{x}_1^{g_\ell} \cdot r_2^{g_\ell} + \hat{x}_2^{g_\ell} \cdot r_1^{g_\ell} + (r_1 \cdot r_2)^{g_\ell}) \qquad (4)$$

is correct given the star shares of Γ and the inputs. Our protocol to prove this is based on the constant round zk-FLIOP construction from [6] (the first item in Theorem 2) and requires $O(\sqrt{|C|})$ communication (and so $O(\sqrt{|C|})$ correlated randomness from the dealer). The idea is as follows. First, observe that letting

$$\boldsymbol{a} = ((\alpha_w)_{w \in W}, (-\gamma_\ell \cdot \hat{x}_1^{g_\ell}, -\gamma_\ell \cdot \hat{x}_2^{g_\ell}, -\gamma_\ell)_{g_\ell \in \text{mult}}) \qquad (5)$$

and

$$\boldsymbol{b} = ((r_w)_{w \in W}, (r_2^{g_\ell}, r_1^{g_\ell}, (r_1 \cdot r_2)^{g_\ell})_{g_\ell \in \text{mult}}) \qquad (6)$$

we have that $\Gamma = \boldsymbol{a} \cdot \boldsymbol{b}$ *where* $\boldsymbol{a}$ *is known to the parties and* $\boldsymbol{b}$ *is known to the dealer.* Note that both vectors are of size $|W| + 3|\text{mult}| = 5|\text{mult}| = 5|C|$. In our verification protocol, each party P_i first computes Γ_i and then star-shares it to the other parties, by broadcasting $\hat{\Gamma}_i = \Gamma_i - t_i$ to the other parties. Then, the parties locally compute $\hat{\Gamma} = \sum_{i=1}^n \hat{\Gamma}_i$. The parties then wish to verify that

$$\hat{\Gamma} + t - \boldsymbol{a} \cdot \boldsymbol{b} = 0 \qquad (7)$$

where $t = \sum_{i=1}^n t_i$. The main observation here is that Eq. (7) represents a 2-degree polynomial over the inputs $\boldsymbol{a}, \boldsymbol{b}, \hat{\Gamma}, s$. Thus, by Theorem 2, there exists a zk-FLIOP to prove that Eq. (7) holds, where the proof's size is sublinear in the size of the input. However, unlike the BGIN compiler [14], here there does not exist a single prover who knows the entire input. We thus need to let the parties *emulate* jointly the role of the prover. In particular, the parties can locally compute additive shares of the proof and then star-share them to the other parties (exactly as with Γ_i). To enable this, we use the constant round zk-FLIOP from Theorem 2, where the proof generation itself is a degree-2 function of the input and prover's randomness. Since in Eq. (7) each input is either known to all parties, or, known to the dealer and *additivley* shared across the parties, it follows that each party can locally compute an additive share of the proof. As for the verifiers, the zk-FLIOP queries can be made over their shares, since the queries are linear. As in the BGIN compiler, we crucially rely on the fact that in our protocol, each piece of information (i.e., the inputs and the proof) is known either by each party or by the dealer, and so we can use the dealer as a verifier as well. By the linearity of the queries, it thus follow that the queries' answers can be reconstructed by each party and the dealer alone, thereby guaranteeing that an honest party will receive the correct answers. This means that if cheating took place and the statement is incorrect, then by the soundness property of the zk-FLIOP, it will be detected by any honest verifier (except for a small probability). As for privacy, the zero-knowledge property together with the fact that each party sees only masked values, guarantee that no private information is leaked during the execution.

Π_{vrfy}: Let $(\mathsf{P}_{\mathsf{FLIOP}}, \mathsf{V}_{\mathsf{FLIOP}})$ be a zk-FLIOP protocol with 1 round, ℓ queries, and message length $u \in \mathbb{N}$ for the polynomial in Eq. (7).

1. The trusted dealer $\mathcal{D}$:
    (a) Chooses a random mask $t_i \in \mathbb{F}$ for each $i \in [n]$ and hands it to P_i
    (b) Chooses a random mask $s_i \in \mathbb{F}^u$ for each $i \in [n]$ and hands it to P_i.
2. The parties call $\mathcal{F}_{\mathsf{coin}}$ to receive α_w for each $w \in W$ (recall that W is the set of the circuit's output wire and multiplication gates' output wires). Alternatively, the parties call $\mathcal{F}_{\mathsf{coin}}$ to receive α and expand it to α_w by setting $\alpha_w = \alpha^w$ or via a PRG.
3. The parties locally compute Λ (see Eq. (2)).
4. Each party P_i computes Γ_i and star-shares it to the parties by broadcasting $\hat{\Gamma}_i = \Gamma_i - t_i$.
5. The parties locally compute $\hat{\Gamma} = \sum_{i=1}^{n} \hat{\Gamma}_i$ (note that $\hat{\Gamma} = \Gamma - t$ where $t = \sum_{i=1}^{n} t_i$).
6. The parties jointly prove that Γ is correct:
    Let $I = (\hat{\Gamma}, t, \boldsymbol{a}, \boldsymbol{b})$ be the vector of inputs to the zk-FLIOP protocol. Let $I^P = (\hat{\Gamma}, 0, \boldsymbol{a}, 0)$ (i.e., a vector obtained by replacing all inputs not known to all parties in I with 0) and $I^D = (0, t, 0, \boldsymbol{b})$ (i.e., a vector obtained by replacing all inputs not known to the dealer in I with 0).
    Observe that: $I = I^P + I^D$.
    (a) Let $\pi = \mathsf{P}_{\mathsf{FLIOP}}(I)$ be the proof generated by the prover in the zk-FLIOP protocol. Then, each party P_i locally computes its share of the proof π^i and broadcasts $\hat{\pi}^i = \pi^i - s_i$ to all the other parties.
    (b) The dealer $\mathcal{D}$ choose a random challenge τ and hands to the parties.
    (c) Let $\hat{\pi} = \sum_{i=1}^{n} \hat{\pi}^i$ and $s = \sum_{i=1}^{n} s_i$. Let $q_1, \ldots, q_\ell$ be the query vector determined by $\mathsf{V}_{\mathsf{FLIOP}}$ based on τ. Then, the parties locally compute

$$\hat{a}_1, \ldots, \hat{a}_\ell \leftarrow \langle q_1, \boldsymbol{I}^P || \hat{\pi} \rangle, \ldots, \langle q_\ell, \boldsymbol{I}^P || \hat{\pi} \rangle$$

whereas the dealer computes

$$\tilde{a}_1, \ldots, \tilde{a}_\ell \leftarrow \langle q_1, \boldsymbol{I}^D || s \rangle, \ldots, \langle q_\ell, \boldsymbol{I}^D || s \rangle.$$

(d) The dealer $\mathcal{D}$ hands $\tilde{a}_1, \ldots, \tilde{a}_\ell$ to the parties, who locally compute

$$a_1 = \hat{a}_1 + \tilde{a}_1, \ldots, \quad a_\ell = \hat{a}_\ell + \tilde{a}_\ell$$

(e) The parties run the decision predicate of V_{FLIOP} on $a_1, \ldots, a_\ell$. If any party received reject, then it output reject. Otherwise, the parties proceed to the next step.

7. The parties locally compute $\hat{p} = \Lambda + \hat{\Gamma}$.
8. The dealer hands the parties t.
9. The parties locally compute that $p = \hat{p} + t$. If $p = 0$, they output accept. Otherwise, they output abort.

We begin by proving correctness, soundness and privacy for Π_{vrfy}, when Π_{vrfy} is ran over a finite field $\mathbb{F}$. The proof appears in the full version.

Proposition 1. *Assume that Π_{vrfy} is executed over a finite field $\mathbb{F}$, let W be the set of all output wires and input wires to multiplication gates and let Δ_w be the additive error on wire $w \in W$. Then, Π_{vrfy} satisfies the following properties:*

1. CORRECTNESS: *If $\forall w \in W : \Delta_w = 0$ and all parties follow the protocol's instructions, then the honest parties always output* accept.
2. SOUNDNESS: *If $\exists w \in W : \Delta_w \neq 0$, then the honest parties output* accept *with probability at most $\frac{|W|}{|\mathbb{F}|} + \epsilon$, where ϵ is the soundness error of the zk-FLIOP protocol.*
3. PRIVACY: *For any adversary $\mathcal{A}$ controlling a subset of parties T of size$\leq$ $n - 1$, there exists a simulator $\mathcal{S}$ who receives $(\hat{x}_w, \Delta_w, r_{w,i})_{w \in W}$ and $\{(r_1 \cdot r_2)_i^{g_\ell}\}_{g_\ell \in \text{mult}}$ for all $i \in T$ as input, and outputs a transcript view$_\mathcal{S}$ such that* view$_\mathcal{S} \equiv$ view$_\mathcal{A}^{\Pi_{\text{vrfy}}}$.

Working Over Small Fields or the Ring $\mathbb{Z}_{2^k}$. The soundness error of our protocol depends on the size of the field $\mathbb{F}$. When we compute the circuit over small fields, it is possible to run Π_{vrfy} over an extension field to reduce the error. This is carried-out by lifting each input to the verification protocol into the extension field. Suppose that we want the error to be $2^{-\sigma}$. Then, one can choose an extension field $\tilde{\mathbb{F}}$ such that $\frac{|W|}{|\mathbb{F}|} + \epsilon \leq 2^{-\sigma}$.

Similarly, when the circuit is computed over the ring $\mathbb{Z}_{2^k}$, we will run Π_{vrfy} over the extension ring $\mathbb{Z}_{2^k}[x]/f(x)$, i.e., the ring of polynomials with coefficients from $\mathbb{Z}_{2^k}$ modulo a polynomial $f(x)$ which is of the right degree and is irreducible over $\mathbb{Z}_2$. As shown in [6,12], taking f of degree d, the number of roots of a polynomial of degree δ over $\mathbb{Z}_{2^k}[x]/f(x)$ is at most $2^{(k-1)d}\delta + 1$. Thus, the probability that $p = 0$ is at most $\frac{2^{(k-1)d} \cdot (|W|)}{2^{kd}} \approx \frac{|W|}{2^d}$. Hence, by choosing d appropriately, we can achieve a desired soundness error.

From an Online to an Offline Dealer. In Π_{vrfy} the dealer only sends messages that depend on random data. Therefore, it can preprocess all its messages and secret share it to the parties in an authenticated way. This includes the masks t_i, the masks s_i and its share of the queries' answers.

Complexity. The amount of correlated randomness that we obtain depends on the size of the proof u and the size of the queries' answers ℓ in the zk-FLIOP emulation. By Theorem 2 both ℓ and u is square-root of the input's size to the relation given in Eq. (7). Thus, the amount of correlated randomness is $O(\sqrt{|W|})$.

The communication cost of the protocol per party includes star sharing Γ_i, sending the share of the proof π^i and opening the correlated randomness which is shared in an authenticated way. Thus, it depends on the size of the proof and size of the correlated randomness. Hence, as the correlated randomness, it is of size $O(\sqrt{|W|})$.

Finally, the computational work includes computing the random coefficients α_w, computing Λ, and the work in the zk-FLIOP protocol. The number of arithmetic operations for the first two computations is linear in the size of $|W|$, whereas by Theorem 2, the number of operations for the latter is $\tilde{O}(M)$, where M is the number of monomials in Eq. (7). As the number of monomials is $O(|W|)$, we obtain that the computaional work is $\tilde{O}(|W|)$.

Summing the above and using Theorem 2 we obtain:

Proposition 2. *Let ε be a statistical error bound. Then, Protocol Π_{vrfy} has communication cost of $O(\sqrt{|W|} \cdot \kappa)$ per party, computational work $\tilde{O}(|W|)$ and the amount of correlated randomness provided by the dealer is $O(\sqrt{|W|} \cdot \kappa)$, where $\kappa = \log_{|\mathbb{F}|}\left(\frac{\sqrt{|W|}}{\varepsilon}\right)$ when the input is defined over a finite field $\mathbb{F}$, $\kappa = \log_2\left(\frac{\sqrt{|W|}}{\varepsilon}\right)$ when the input is defined over the ring $\mathbb{Z}_{2^k}$ (where W is the set of the ciruit's output wires and input wires to multiplication gates).*

4.1   A Concrete Instantiation for the Zk-FLIOP Protocol

In this section, we present a concrete instantiation for the constant round zk-FLIOP protocol used in Π_{vrfy} based on the fully linear PCP construction given in [6]. Consider a prover $\mathcal{P}$ who wants to prove that $c - \boldsymbol{a} \cdot \boldsymbol{b} = 0$ to a verifier V, where $\boldsymbol{a}$ and $\boldsymbol{b}$ are vector of elements of size m.

To prove the correctness of the statement, the vectors $\boldsymbol{a}$ and $\boldsymbol{b}$ are divided into M vectors, i.e., $\boldsymbol{a} = \boldsymbol{a}_1||\cdots||\boldsymbol{a}_M$ and $\boldsymbol{b} = \boldsymbol{b}_1||\cdots||\boldsymbol{b}_M$. This means that the statement to be proven can be written as $c - \sum_{k=1}^{M} \boldsymbol{a}_k \cdot \boldsymbol{b}_k$. Denote the number of elements in each vector by L, and so $L \cdot M = m$.

The first step of $\mathcal{P}$ is to choose random vectors $\boldsymbol{a}_0$ and $\boldsymbol{b}_0$. The, define L polynomials of degree-M such that:

$$\forall e \in [L] : f_e(0) = \boldsymbol{a}_0[e], \ldots, f_e(M) = \boldsymbol{a}_M[e].$$

That is, the evaluation of f_e on the point k is the eth entry of the vector $\boldsymbol{a}_k$. Similarly, define additional L polynomials of degree-M by setting:

$$\forall e \in [L] : g_e(0) = \boldsymbol{b}_0[e], \ldots, g_e(M) = \boldsymbol{b}_M[e].$$

Next, define an additional polynomial q by letting $q(x) = \sum_{e=1}^{L} f_e(x) \cdot g_e(x)$. By the way q is defined it follows that:

- For each $k \in \{0, \ldots, M\}$ it holds that $q(k) = \boldsymbol{a}_k \cdot \boldsymbol{b}_k$
- The degree of q is $2M$.

To fully define q the prover $\mathcal{P}$ thus computes M more additional points on q. This can be done by first interpolating the f_e and g_e polynomials to compute these polynomials on the points $M + 1, \ldots, 2M$ and then computing $q(x)$ for each $x \in \{M + 1, \ldots, 2M\}$.

The protocol then proceeds as follows:

1. **Proof**: The prover $\mathcal{P}$ defines the proof by setting

$$\pi = \left(\{f_e(0)\}_{e=1}^{L}, \{g_e(0)\}_{e=1}^{L}, q(0), \ldots, q(2M) \right)$$

2. **Challenge**: A random point τ is chosen (such that $\tau \notin \{0, \ldots, M\}$).
3. **Query**: The linear queries over the proof and inputs are defined such that the verifier V is given:
    - For each $e \in [L]$: $f_e(\tau)$ and $g_e(\tau)$.
    - $q(\tau)$
    - $c - \sum_{k=1}^{M} q(k)$
4. **Decision**: The verifier V checks that
    (a) $q(\tau) = \sum_{e=1}^{L} f_e(\tau) \cdot g_e(\tau)$
    (b) $c - \sum_{k=1}^{M} q(k) = 0$
    If both equations hold, then V outputs accept. Otherwise, it outputs reject.

Observe that in check 4a, the verifier ensures that P defined the proof correctly, i.e., computed the polynomial q honestly. Then, it can verify that the statement holds via check 4b. Note also that privacy (zero-knowledge) is maintained in this protocol by the additional random point defined for each polynomial (i.e., $f_e(0)$ and $g_e(0)$). These random points make the evaluation of each polynomial on the point τ look completely random.

Soundness. A malicious prover can succeed only if check 4a passes although $q(x)$ is not defined correctly. By the Schwartz-Zippel lemma, this event can happen when working over a finite field with probability bounded by $\frac{2M}{|\mathbb{F}|}$.

When the statement is defined over the ring $\mathbb{Z}_{2^k}$, then the verification protocol itself is executed over the extension ring $\mathbb{Z}_{2^k}[x]/f(x)$ (see above). In this case, if f is of degree d, then the cheating probability is bounded by $\frac{2^{(k-1)d} \cdot (2M)}{2^{kd}} \approx \frac{2M}{2^d}$.

Concrete Costs. Recall that L and M are parameter to choose under the constraint that $m = L \cdot M$. If we set $L = M = \sqrt{m}$, the cost becomes sublinear in m. Concretely, the size of the proof is $2L + 2M + 1 = 4\sqrt{m} + 1$. In addition, the size of the answers to the queries is $2L + 2 = 2\sqrt{m} + 2$.

Plugging in the above into our protocol, recall that $m = |W| + 3|\text{mult}|$ (see Eq. (5) and (6)). Now, in the emulation of the zk-FLIOP in Π_{vrfy}, the parties communicate to star-share their additive shares of the proof π^i and communicate to reconstruct the queries' answers (here the parties open the shared masks of the answers which was given to them by the dealer). Overall, the communication cost is therefore roughly $6\sqrt{|W|+3|\mathsf{mult}|}+2$ elements sent by each party to the other parties.

The amount of correlated randomness handed by the dealer, however, is exactly $2\sqrt{|W|+3|\mathsf{mult}|}+1$ elements. This is due to the fact that the dealer acts only as a verifier and does not hold a share of the proof (more accurately, the dealer only provides masks for the shares of the proof held by the parties; however, this is private randomness which is not required to be shared across the parties).

4.2   The Dealer's Ideal Functionality $\mathcal{F}_{\mathsf{Dealer}}$

Based on the concrete instantiation described in the previous section, we now define an ideal functionality for the trusted dealer. Later, when we show how to distribute the dealer's work, we will show how to securely compute this functionality.

Recall that the dealer's work includes the following: (i) choosing random masks for the circuit's wires as part of the semi-honest correlated randomness; (ii) choosing random private masks for the parties to mask Γ_i and to mask the additive shares of the proof π^i; (iii) choosing a random challenge τ and (iv) computing the zk-FLIOP queries' answers based on i,ii and iii.

Observe that (iv) involves computing a random point on many polynomials. Recall that in the zk-FLIOP protocol, the verifier should receive $f_e(\tau), g_e(\tau)$ for each $e \in [L]$ and $q(\tau)$. The first $2L$ polynomials are of degree M, whereas q is of degree $2M$. In our protocol, the f polynomials correspond to the vector $\boldsymbol{a}$ (see Eq. (5)), which is being determined in the online computation and is known to *all* parties. In contrast, the g polynomials correspond to the vector $\boldsymbol{b}$ (see Eq. (6)) which is known to the dealer. Finally, the polynomial q is star-shared across the parties, meaning that it is additively shared between each party and the dealer.

To define the ideal functionality in a simple way, we first define a procedure π_{BL} that performs the bilinear computation between the coefficients of a set of polynomials and the powers of a point, which is what required to evaluate these polynomials on the point.

$\pi_{\mathsf{BL}}(\vec{G}, \tau, d)$:

1. Parse $\vec{G}$ as vectors $\vec{G}_1 \| \vec{G}_2 \| \ldots$ of size $d+1$.
2. For each $\vec{G}_e$: Let g_e be a degree-d polynomial defined using the points $\vec{G}_e[0], \ldots, \vec{G}_e[d]$. Then, covert the points into polynomial coefficients $\beta_{e,0}, \ldots, \beta_{e,d}$.
3. Compute $\tau, \ldots, \tau^d$.
4. For each polynomial g_e, return $y_e = \sum_{j=0}^d \beta_{e,j} \cdot \tau^d$

Fig. 1. The procedure π_{BL}

Next, observe that in our protocol, some values are given to the parties at the beginning of the protocol, whereas some values are revealed during the execution. In the definition of the functionality, we split the outputs into three types:

1. Values that are given to the parties in the clear before the beginning of the protocol.
2. Values that are additively shared across the parties at the beginning of the protocol. These are marked using our notation $[\![\cdot]\!]$.
3. Values that should be revealed during the execution to the parties. To realize this, the dealer can secret share these values in an authenticated way. These values are marked using the notation $\langle\cdot\rangle$. As explained in Sect. 2.4, one can realize it via SPDZ-style information-theoretic MACs [3,23].

The dealer's ideal functionality to produce correlated randomness for both the semi-honest computation and the verification protocol is formally defined in Functionality 3.

FUNCTIONALITY 3 (The Ideal Functionality $\mathcal{F}_{\mathsf{Dealer}}$)

Let mult be the set of multiplication gates. Denote by W_I, W_{mult} and W_o the set of the circuit's input wires, the set of input wires to multiplication gates and the set of the circuit's output wires, respectively. Let M and L be parameters given to the functionality. Let $\mathcal{A}$ be the ideal-world adversary controlling a set of parties of size$\leq n - 1$.
The functionality $\mathcal{F}_{\mathsf{Dealer}}$ works as follows:

- For each wire $w \in W_I \cup W_{\mathsf{mult}} \cup W_o$ sample a random $r_w \in R$.
  Sample random masks $s_0, \ldots, s_{2M} \in R$.
  Sample a random $\boldsymbol{b}_0 \in R^L$
  Sample a random point $\tau \in R$.
- Let $\boldsymbol{b} = ((r_w)_{w \in W_{\mathsf{mult}} \cup W_o}, (r_2^{g_\ell}, r_1^{g_\ell}, (r_1 \cdot r_2)^{g_\ell})_{g_\ell \in \mathsf{mult}})$.
  Then, split $\boldsymbol{b}$ into M vectors of size L, i.e., $\boldsymbol{b} = \boldsymbol{b}_1 || \cdots || \boldsymbol{b}_M$.
- For each $e \in [L]$: let $\boldsymbol{G}_e$ be a vector of size $M + 1$ defined as $\boldsymbol{G}_e = \boldsymbol{b}_0[e] || \cdots || \boldsymbol{b}_M[e]$.
  Set $\boldsymbol{G} = \boldsymbol{G}_1 || \cdots || \boldsymbol{G}_L$. Then, compute: $y_1, \ldots, y_L \leftarrow \pi_{\mathsf{BL}}(\boldsymbol{G}, \tau, M)$ (see Fig. 1).
- Let $\boldsymbol{S} = (s_0, \ldots, s_{2M})$. Then, compute $z \leftarrow \pi_{\mathsf{BL}}(\boldsymbol{S}, \tau, 2M)$ (see Fig. 1) and $s = \sum_{k=1}^{M} s_k$.
- Give the parties

$$(\{\langle r_w \rangle\}_{w \in W_I \cup W_0}, [\![\boldsymbol{b}]\!], [\![\boldsymbol{b}_0]\!], [\![\boldsymbol{S}]\!], \langle y_1 \rangle, \ldots, \langle y_L \rangle, \langle \tau \rangle, \langle s \rangle, \langle z \rangle)$$

while letting $\mathcal{A}$ choose the corrupted parties' shares.

Comparison with BGIN [14]. A drawback of our verification protocol compared to [14] is that we have $O(\sqrt{C} \cdot n)$ communication per party and they have $O(\log(|C|) \cdot n)$ communication. Nevertheless, in both protocols, communication is sublinear in the size of the circuit. Our main advantage is in the work of the dealer. First, the size of the dealer's circuit (i.e., number of multiplications operations) does not depend on the number of parties n, which gives rise to efficient implementation even for large number of parties. Much more important is the fact that our dealer is represented by computation of *low-depth*. We will explore this property in Sect. 6 and see how it is crucial for achieving the goal of distributing the dealer with sublinear communication. We stress that the dealer in [14] *cannot* be represented this way. To see this, it suffices to recall that in their work the dealer needs to compute $\sum_{g_\ell \in \mathsf{mult}} \gamma_\ell \cdot (r_1^{g_\ell} \cdot r_2^{g_\ell})$. This implies that it needs to compute the coefficients γ_ℓ and so the random coefficient α_w for each wire w. To avoid linear correlated randomness, the authors in [14] suggested to use a single α from which all α_w are derived by computing: $\alpha_w = \alpha^w$. This yields a computation with depth that is linear in the size of the circuit, which makes it impossible to use the techniques presented in the next sections. In our protocol, the dealer does not need to compute anything based on the random coefficients and so this is completely avoided.

5 Online Computation with a Trusted Dealer

We are now ready to present the main protocol to compute any arithmetic circuits with malicious security in the $\mathcal{F}_{\mathsf{Dealer}}$-hybrid model (i.e., in the presence of a trusted dealer that gives the parties the correlated randomness). Informally, our protocol takes a secure-up-to-additive attack and star-sharing compliant protocol, and compiles it into malicious security, by adding a verification step, where the parties run the protocol Π_{vrfy} from Sect. 4. The formal description appears in the full version of this paper.

Concrete Costs. We estimate the concrete communication and computation overhead of our verification protocol compared to the base semi-honest protocol. The communication overhead is a small additive term that is completely dominated by the communication complexity of the semi-honest protocol. The concrete computational overhead of the verification protocol for arithmetic circuits is often dominated by the communication cost of the semi-honest protocol even when the traffic is exchanged over a fast 1 Gbps network. To make our following estimates somewhat easier we assume an imbalance between the degree of each polynomial M, which is set to $M = \sqrt{|C|}$, and the number of polynomials $L = 5\sqrt{|C|}$.

In the verification protocol, the parties communicate to star-share Γ_i and then emulate the zk-FLIOP. When using the instantiation presented in Sect. 4.1, each party sends roughly $4L = 20\sqrt{|C|}$ elements to star-share its share of the proof. Then, the parties need to open the correlated randomness, which yields $2M = 2\sqrt{|C|}$ additional elements sent per party (see the end of Sect. 4.1). Overall, each party sends approximately $22\sqrt{|C|}$ elements. This overhead is dominated by the cost of the baseline semi-honest protocol (which requires interaction for each gate) even for moderately large circuits.

The computational cost of a party is dominated by interpolation to compute M extra points on each of L polynomials of degree M. Polynomial interpolation can be efficiently performed by the Discrete Fourier Transform (DFT) and therefore the total computation is dominated by L DFT operations. To give one data point, consider an arithmetic circuit of size $|C| = 2^{20}$ over $\mathbb{F}_p$, such that p is a 60-bit prime and 2^{10} divides $p - 1$. In this setting, the soundness error is $\approx \frac{M}{|C|} = 2^{-50}$. Based on Shoup [43], a single multiplication of polynomials of degree $M = \sqrt{|C|} = 2^{10}$ over $\mathbb{F}_p$ takes 56 μs on a single standard core. The multiplication requires three DFT operations, one on each input polynomial and then one inverse DFT (which is also a DFT) to return the output polynomial to coefficient representation. Extrapolating these numbers to our case of a single DFT, it is safe to estimate that the interpolation of a single polynomial takes at most 20 μs, and interpolating $L = 5 \cdot 2^{10}$ polynomials requires at most 100 ms.

The communication cost of the semi-honest protocol is two field elements per multiplication gate for a total of $120 \cdot 2^{20}$ bits. Even if the underlying network has 1 Gbps bandwidth then the total time for communication is roughly 120 ms which exceeds the time for computation.

6 Distributing the Dealer with Sublinear Communication

We are now ready to show how to compute the dealer's functionality $\mathcal{F}_{\mathsf{Dealer}}$. The main observation behind our offline protocol is that, given a circuit C, the dealer's computation can be described using the next four steps:

1. Sample a vector $\boldsymbol{b}$ of semi-honest correlated randomness.
2. Sample a vector $\boldsymbol{v}$ of ring elements of size $O(\sqrt{|C|})$ using an arithmetic circuit of size $O(\sqrt{|C|})$.
3. Compute a bilinear function over $\boldsymbol{b}$ and $\boldsymbol{v}$ which outputs $O(\sqrt{|C|})$ ring elements. Denote the output vector by $\boldsymbol{y}$.
4. Give the parties $[\![\boldsymbol{b}]\!]$ and a subset of entries of $\boldsymbol{v}\|\boldsymbol{y}$. Some of the entries may be secret shared (and possibly authenticated).

To see this, recall that the dealer needs to evaluate $O(\sqrt{|C|})$ polynomials on a random point τ. This can be done by computing a vector of the powers of τ, i.e., $(\tau, \tau^2, \ldots, \tau^{2M})$ and then multiplying the coefficients of each polynomial with this vector. Note that the task of computing $2M$ powers of τ is represented by a circuit of size $O(\sqrt{|C|})$ since $M = O(\sqrt{|C|})$. It should be noted that $\boldsymbol{b}$ consists of points on these polynomials and not coefficients, and so the dealer is required to do the conversion first.

We now proceed to describe a protocol which emulates the dealer. The idea behind the protocol is that we will generate encryptions of the powers of τ via an additively-homomorphic encryption scheme (AHE). Then, the parties can compute locally the bilinear operation, obtaining an encrypted version of the result, which can then be decrypted.

To this end, we define several ideal functionalities that will be used in the protocol.

The Ideal Functionality $\mathcal{F}_{\mathsf{triples}}$. This ideal functionality will be used to generate the semi-honest correlated randomness of the protocol, which consists of m multiplication triples. The $\mathcal{F}_{\mathsf{triples}}$ functionality can be realized with polylogarithmic communication complexity (in m) and good concrete efficiency via pseudorandom correlation generators (PCGs) based on Ring-LPN [10].

FUNCTIONALITY 4 (The Ideal Functionality $\mathcal{F}_{\mathsf{triples}}$)

Functionality $\mathcal{F}_{\mathsf{triples}}$ works with parties $P_1, \ldots, P_n$ and an ideal-world adversary § controlling a strict subset of the parties with indexes $I \subset [n]$ as follows:
Upon receiving the command (Init, m) from all parties, it waits to receive $r_{1,i}^\ell, r_{2,i}^\ell, r_{3,i}^\ell$ for each $i \in I$ and $\ell \in [m]$ from §. Then, it chooses for each $\ell \in [m]$ and $j \in [n] \setminus I$ random $r_{1,j}^\ell, r_{2,j}^\ell, r_{3,j}^\ell$ under the constraint that

$$\sum_{i=1}^n r_{3,i}^\ell = \sum_{i=1}^n r_{1,i}^\ell \cdot \sum_{i=1}^n r_{2,i}^\ell$$

Then, it hands $(r_{1,i}^\ell, r_{2,i}^\ell, r_{3,i}^\ell)_{\ell \in [m]}$ to party P_i.

The Ideal Functionality $\mathcal{F}_{\mathsf{EncPowers}}^{\mathsf{AHE}}$. The next ideal functionality gives the parties encryptions of the powers of τ. It also gives an authenticated secret sharing of τ. In addition, it samples the masks that are used in the online verification protocol and secret shares the sum of them in an authenticated way. Recall that we can realize authenticated secret sharing with information-theoretic MACs, and so generating it can be represented by a small constant-size circuit.

FUNCTIONALITY 5 (The Ideal Functionality $\mathcal{F}_{\mathsf{EncPowers}}^{\mathsf{AHE}}$)

Functionality $\mathcal{F}_{\mathsf{EncPowers}}^{\mathsf{AHE}}$ works with parties $P_1, \ldots, P_n$ as follows:

- Upon receiving the command Init from all parties, the functionality runs $\mathsf{Gen}(1^\kappa)$ to obtain (sk, pk), Then, it chooses shares sk_i for each $i \in [n]$ such that $sk = \sum_{i=1}^n sk_i$ and sends pk, sk_i to party P_i.
- Upon receiving the command $(compute, M)$ from all parties the functionality:
  1. Chooses a random τ, computes $\tau^2, \ldots, \tau^{2M}$ and $c_1, \ldots, c_{2M} = \mathsf{Enc}_{pk}(\tau), \ldots, \mathsf{Enc}_{pk}(\tau^{2M})$.
  2. Chooses random $s_0, \ldots, s_{2M}$ and computes $s = \sum_{k=1}^M s_k$.
  Then, it hands $\{[\![s_k]\!]\}_{k=0}^{2M}, c_1, \ldots, c_{2M}, \langle \tau \rangle, \langle s \rangle$ to the parties.

The parties compute the encryption of powers of τ using a simple, iterative protocol, beginning with a shared value $\mathsf{Enc}_{pk}(1)$, which is an encryption of $\tau^0 = 1$. Next, each party chooses its random share τ_i of τ. To compute $\mathsf{Enc}_{pk}(\tau^{j+1})$ given $\mathsf{Enc}_{pk}(\tau^j)$ and τ_i, each party homomorphically computes $\mathsf{Enc}_{pk}(\tau^j \cdot \tau_i)$ and sends the result to the other parties. Upon receiving all ciphertexts, each party homomorphically evaluates $\mathsf{Enc}_{pk}(\tau^j \cdot \sum_{i=1}^n \tau_i) = \mathsf{Enc}_{pk}(\tau^{j+1})$. Overall, this functionality can be computed with communication of $O(M \cdot \mathrm{poly}(\kappa, n)) = O(\sqrt{|C|} \cdot \mathrm{poly}(\kappa, n))$ ring elements. To achieve malicious security, we can use generically communication-preserving compilers; see below.

The ideal functionality $\mathcal{F}_{\mathsf{AuthDec}}^{\mathsf{AHE}}$. This functionality receives a ciphertext c from all parties and the secret-key share sk_i from each P_i and outputs $\langle u \rangle$ where $u = \mathsf{Dec}_{sk}(c)$ and $sk = \sum_{i=1}^n sk_i$ (i.e., the parties receive authenticated secret sharing of u). Note that it can be realized by a protocol with cost that is *independent* of the size of the computed circuit.

Realizing $\mathcal{F}_{\mathsf{Dealer}}$ with Semi-honest Security. Using the above functionalities it is easy to describe a semi-honest protocol to compute $\mathcal{F}_{\mathsf{Dealer}}$.

$\varPi_{\mathsf{dealer}}^{\mathsf{SH}}$: Upon receiving a description of the circuit C as an input:

1. Sample semi-honest correlated randomness: the parties call $\mathcal{F}_{\mathsf{triples}}$ to receive $(r_{1,i}^{g_\ell}, r_{2,i}^{g_\ell}, r_{3,i}^{g_\ell})_{g_\ell \in \mathsf{mult}}$. For each input and output wire w of the circuit, each party P_i samples a random $r_{w,i}$ and then the parties generate $\langle r_w \rangle$ where $r_w = \sum_{i=1}^n r_{w,i}$.
2. The parties call $\mathcal{F}_{\mathsf{EncPowers}}^{\mathsf{AHE}}$ to receive back $sk_i, \{[\![s_k]\!]\}_{k=0}^{2M}, c_1, \ldots, c_{2M}, \langle \tau \rangle, \langle s \rangle$.
3. Each party P_i samples $\boldsymbol{b}_{0,i} \in R^L$ and then uses the shares $\boldsymbol{b}_{0,i}, \{r_{w,i}\}_{w \in W}, (r_{1,i}^{g_\ell}, r_{2,i}^{g_\ell}, r_{3,i}^{g_\ell})_{g_\ell \in \mathsf{mult}}$ to define the M-degree polynomials $g_{e,i}$ for each $e \in [L]$, and the shares $\{s_{k,i}\}_{k=0}^{2M}$ to define the $2M$-degree polynomial $\tilde{q}_i$. Then, each party locally converts its shares of the points on these polynomials to shares of the coefficients.
   Denote the coefficients of g_e (for each $e \in [L]$) by $g_{e,0}, \ldots, g_{e,M}$ and of $\tilde{q}$ by $\tilde{q}_0, \ldots, \tilde{q}_{2M}$.
4. For each $e \in [L]$, each party P_i locally computes
   $\mathsf{Enc}_{pk}(g_{e,i}(\tau)) \leftarrow \mathsf{Add}\left((g_{e,k,i})_{k \in \{0,\ldots,M\}}, (c_k)_{k \in [M]}\right)$.
   Similarly, each P_i computes
   $\mathsf{Enc}_{pk}(\tilde{q}_i(\tau)) \leftarrow \mathsf{Add}\left((\tilde{q}_{k,i})_{k \in \{0,\ldots,2M\}}, (c_k)_{k \in [2M]}\right)$.
5. Each P_i sends $\{\mathsf{Enc}_{pk}(g_{e,i}(\tau))\}_{e \in [L]}, \mathsf{Enc}_{pk}(\tilde{q}_i(\tau))$ to all the other parties.
6. The parties locally compute $\{\mathsf{Enc}_{pk}(g_e(\tau))\}_{e \in [L]}, \mathsf{Enc}_{pk}(\tilde{q}(\tau))$ by adding the received ciphertexts.
7. The parties obtain $\{\langle g_e(\tau) \rangle\}_{e \in [L]}$ and $\langle \tilde{q}(\tau) \rangle$ by calling $\mathcal{F}_{\mathsf{AuthDec}}^{\mathsf{AHE}}$. Denote $\langle \boldsymbol{y} \rangle = (\langle g_1(\tau) \rangle, \ldots, \langle g_L(\tau) \rangle)$ and $\langle z \rangle = \langle \tilde{q}(\tau) \rangle$

Output: Each party outputs his share of $\boldsymbol{b}, \boldsymbol{b}_0$ and $\{s_k\}_{k=0}^{2M}$, and his authenticated shares of τ, s, $\boldsymbol{y}$ and z.

Proposition 3. *Assuming the AHE scheme is semantically secure, protocol $\varPi_{\mathsf{dealer}}^{\mathsf{SH}}$ realizes $\mathcal{F}_{\mathsf{Dealer}}$ with semi-honest security in the ($\mathcal{F}_{\mathsf{triples}}, \mathcal{F}_{\mathsf{EncPowers}}^{\mathsf{AHE}}, \mathcal{F}_{\mathsf{AuthDec}}^{\mathsf{AHE}}$)-hybrid model.*

The proof can be found in the full version. As discussed above, $\mathcal{F}_{\mathsf{EncPowers}}^{\mathsf{AHE}}$ can be realized using a protocol with sublinear cost in the size of the computed circuit, while $\mathcal{F}_{\mathsf{AuthDec}}^{\mathsf{AHE}}$ can be realized with constant cost. Given $\mathcal{F}_{\mathsf{AuthDec}}^{\mathsf{AHE}}$ is called to decrypt sublinear amount of ciphertexts, the total cost of calling $\mathcal{F}_{\mathsf{dec}}$ is also sublinear. Thus, we get the following:

Corollary 1 (Distributing the dealer with semi-honest security). *Given (1) semi-honest protocol realizing $\mathcal{F}_{\text{triples}}$ to compute m multiplication triples with communication $\alpha(\kappa, n, m, R)$, and (2) a semantically-secure AHE scheme, there exists a protocol that securely realizes $\mathcal{F}_{\text{Dealer}}$ in the semi-honest model with communication per party of $O(\sqrt{|C|}) \cdot \text{poly}(n, \kappa)$ ring elements and $\alpha(\kappa, n, |C|, R)$ additional bits.*

Achieving Malicious Security. In the context of feasibility, one can easily obtain a malicious security variant of Corollary 1 by applying the communication-efficient GMW-style compiler of Naor and Nissim [38] (building on [28,37]). Using this compiler, a semi-honest secure protocol can be compiled into a maliciously secured protocol for the same functionality with sublinear additive communication cost of $\text{poly}(\kappa, n, \log |C|, \log |R|)$ bits per party. Since the compiler only requires collision-resistant hash functions, which are implied by additively homomorphic encryption [32], this does not require introducing new assumptions. Note that the compiler also respects an augmented correlated randomness functionality that allows the adversary to pick its own output shares as we require in this work. We thus obtain the following:

Theorem 6 (Distributing the dealer with malicious security). *Given (1) semi-honest protocol realizing $\mathcal{F}_{\text{triples}}$ to compute m multiplication triples with communication $\alpha(\kappa, m, R)$, and (2) a semantically-secure AHE scheme, there exists a protocol that securely realizes $\mathcal{F}_{\text{Dealer}}$ in the malicious model with communication per party of $O(\sqrt{|C|}) \cdot \text{poly}(n, \kappa)$ ring elements and $\alpha(\kappa, n, |C|, R) + \text{poly}(\kappa, n, \log |C|, \log |R|)$ additional bits.*

Conclusion: MPC with Sublinear Preprocessing and Non-cryptographic Online Phase. To obtain our main result, we combine the offline protocol of Theorem 6 with the online protocol described in Sect. 5, instantiated with Beaver's semi-honest MPC protocol [1] based on multiplication triples. This yields a protocol which satisfies the notion of Preprocessing MPC from Definition 1, where the offline communication complexity of Π_{offline} scales with $\sqrt{|C|}$ and the online communication and correlated randomness are the same as those of the baseline semi-honest protocol up to a sublinear additive term. The protocol relies on AHE, together with any low-communication protocol (e.g., one based on PCG) for generating random (unauthenticated) multiplication triples.

Theorem 7 (Sublinear preprocessing from AHE+triples). *Let f be an n-party functionality represented by an arithmetic circuit C over a ring R. Then, given (1) semi-honest protocol realizing m unauthenticated multiplication triples (see $\mathcal{F}_{\text{triples}}$) with communication $\alpha(\kappa, n, m, R)$, and (2) an AHE scheme over R, there exists a PMPC protocol $(\Pi_{\text{offline}}, \Pi_{\text{online}})$ for f with non-cryptographic online phase (see Definition 1) with the following efficiency measures:*

- *The communication per party in Π_{offline} is $O(\sqrt{|C|}) \cdot \text{poly}(n, \kappa)$ ring elements and $\alpha(\kappa, n, |C|, R) + \text{poly}(\kappa, n, \log |C|, \log |R|)$ additional bits;*

- *The communication per party in Π_{online} is $O(|C|) + O(\sqrt{|C|}) \cdot \text{poly}(n, \kappa)$ ring elements.*

Ingredient (1) in Theorem 7 can be instantiated with a PCG based on LPN or Ring-LPN [10] for better concrete efficiency, with $\alpha(\kappa, n, |C|, R) = n^2 \cdot \text{poly}(\kappa) \cdot (\log|C| + \log|R|)$ bits of communication. Using this instantiation, the total communication cost of Π_{offline} is $O(\sqrt{|C|}) \cdot \text{poly}(n, \kappa)$ ring elements.

Improving Concrete Efficiency. The protocol described previously for distributing the dealer uses generic tools to compile the semi-honest protocol to a malicious protocol. This approach is sufficient for good asymptotic efficiency, but not necessarily for good concrete efficiency. In the full version of the paper, we propose a maliciously secure protocol with improved performance that is based on making two stronger, but quite plausible, assumptions on the AHE: being "linear-only" and having a threshold encryption variant.

An AHE is "linear-only", or more precisely has Linear Targeted Malleability [4,7], if linear functions, and only linear functions, can be computed homomorphically on the ciphertexts. It is widely assumed that popular AHE schemes such as Goldwasser-Micali [29], Paillier [41] and even certain parameter ranges for lattice based encryption systems [15] are all "linear-only". Encryption schemes with a threshold variant enable parties to share a secret key and distributively decrypt a ciphertext without interaction. Systems with such a threshold variant include GM [34], Paillier [30] and lattice based systems via noise flooding.

The proposed protocol to distribute the dealer assuming a circuit over a field $\mathbb{F}$ executes a generically malicious secure protocol for the generation of powers of τ and then the rest of the previous semi-honest protocol. The parties proceed by threshold decryption of the ciphertexts. The adversary can add errors to the decrypted values, which might even depend on the evaluation point τ. However, due to Linear Targeted Malleability the probability that any attack on the protocol does not cause an honest party to abort after verification in the online phase is $\Theta\left(\frac{M}{|\mathbb{F}|}\right)$. The complexity of the protocol is dominated by roughly $5|C|$ homomorphic operations and threshold decryption of $5\sqrt{|C|}$ ciphertexts.

Acknowledgments. We thank the Eurocrypt reviewers for helpful comments. E. Boyle supported by a Google Research Scholar Award, AFOSR Award FA9550-21-1-0046, ERC Project HSS (852952), and ERC Project NTSC (742754). N. Gilboa supported by ISF grant 2951/20, ERC grant 876110, and a grant by the BGU Cyber Center. Y. Ishai supported by ERC Project NTSC (742754), BSF grant 2018393, and ISF grant 2774/20. A. Nof supported by ERC Project NTSC (742754).

References

1. Beaver, D.: Efficient multiparty protocols using circuit randomization. In: Feigenbaum, J. (ed.) CRYPTO 1991. LNCS, vol. 576, pp. 420–432. Springer, Heidelberg (1992). https://doi.org/10.1007/3-540-46766-1_34

2. Ben-Or, M., Goldwasser, S., Wigderson, A.: Completeness theorems for non-cryptographic fault-tolerant distributed computation (extended abstract). In: STOC (1988)
3. Bendlin, R., Damgård, I., Orlandi, C., Zakarias, S.: Semi-homomorphic encryption and multiparty computation. In: Paterson, K.G. (ed.) EUROCRYPT 2011. LNCS, vol. 6632, pp. 169–188. Springer, Heidelberg (2011). https://doi.org/10.1007/978-3-642-20465-4_11
4. Bitansky, N., Chiesa, A., Ishai, Y., Paneth, O., Ostrovsky, R.: Succinct non-interactive arguments via linear interactive proofs. In: Theory of Cryptography Conference, pp. 315–333 (2013)
5. Block, A.R., Maji, H.K., Nguyen, H.H.: Secure computation with constant communication overhead using multiplication embeddings. In: Chakraborty, D., Iwata, T. (eds.) Progress in Cryptology - INDOCRYPT, vol. 11356 of Lecture Notes in Computer Science, pp. 375–398 (2018)
6. Boneh, D., Boyle, E., Corrigan-Gibbs, H., Gilboa, N., Ishai, Y.: Zero-knowledge proofs on secret-shared data via fully linear PCPs. In: Boldyreva, A., Micciancio, D. (eds.) CRYPTO 2019. LNCS, vol. 11694, pp. 67–97. Springer, Cham (2019). https://doi.org/10.1007/978-3-030-26954-8_3
7. Boneh, D., Ishai, Y., Sahai, A., Wu, D.J.: Lattice-based SNARGs and their application to more efficient obfuscation. In: Annual International Conference on the Theory and Applications of Cryptographic Techniques, pp. 247–277 (2017)
8. Boyle, E., et al.: Efficient two-round OT extension and silent non-interactive secure computation. In: ACM CCS (2019)
9. Boyle, E., Couteau, G., Gilboa, N., Ishai, Y., Kohl, L., Scholl, P.: Efficient pseudo-random correlation generators: silent OT extension and more. In: Boldyreva, A., Micciancio, D. (eds.) CRYPTO 2019. LNCS, vol. 11694, pp. 489–518. Springer, Cham (2019). https://doi.org/10.1007/978-3-030-26954-8_16
10. Boyle, E., Couteau, G., Gilboa, N., Ishai, Y., Kohl, L., Scholl, P.: Efficient pseudorandom correlation generators from Ring-LPN. In: Micciancio, D., Ristenpart, T. (eds.) CRYPTO 2020. LNCS, vol. 12171, pp. 387–416. Springer, Cham (2020). https://doi.org/10.1007/978-3-030-56880-1_14
11. Boyle, E., Gilboa, N., Ishai, Y.: Secure computation with preprocessing via function secret sharing. In: Hofheinz, D., Rosen, A. (eds.) TCC 2019. LNCS, vol. 11891, pp. 341–371. Springer, Cham (2019). https://doi.org/10.1007/978-3-030-36030-6_14
12. Boyle, E., Gilboa, N., Ishai, Y., Nof, A.: Practical fully secure three-party computation via sublinear distributed zero-knowledge proofs. In: ACM CCS (2019)
13. Boyle, E., Gilboa, N., Ishai, Y., Nof, A.: Efficient fully secure computation via distributed zero-knowledge proofs. In: Moriai, S., Wang, H. (eds.) ASIACRYPT 2020. LNCS, vol. 12493, pp. 244–276. Springer, Cham (2020). https://doi.org/10.1007/978-3-030-64840-4_9
14. Boyle, E., Gilboa, N., Ishai, Y., Nof, A.: Sublinear GMW-Style compiler for MPC with preprocessing. In: Malkin, T., Peikert, C. (eds.) CRYPTO 2021. LNCS, vol. 12826, pp. 457–485. Springer, Cham (2021). https://doi.org/10.1007/978-3-030-84245-1_16
15. Brakerski, Z., Gentry, C., Vaikuntanathan, V.: (Leveled) fully homomorphic encryption without bootstrapping. ACM Trans. Comput. Theory (TOCT) 6(3), 1–36 (2014)
16. Canetti, R.: Security and composition of multiparty cryptographic protocols. J. Cryptol. 13(1), 143–202 (2000)
17. Catalano, D., Raimondo, M.D., Fiore, D., Giacomelli, I.: Monz2ka: fast maliciously secure two party computation on z2k. IACR Cryptology ePrint Archive (2019)

18. Chaum, D., Crépeau, C., Damgård, I.: Multiparty unconditionally secure protocols (extended abstract). In: STOC (1988)

19. Cohen, J.D., Fischer, M.J.: A robust and verifiable cryptographically secure election scheme (extended abstract). In: FOCS 1985, pp. 372–382 (1985)

20. Cramer, R., Damgård, I., Escudero, D., Scholl, P., Xing, C.: SPD$\mathbb{Z}_{2^k}$: efficient MPC mod 2^k for dishonest majority. In: Shacham, H., Boldyreva, A. (eds.) CRYPTO 2018. LNCS, vol. 10992, pp. 769–798. Springer, Cham (2018). https://doi.org/10.1007/978-3-319-96881-0_26

21. Damgård, I., Keller, M., Larraia, E., Pastro, V., Scholl, P., Smart, N.P.: Practical covertly secure MPC for dishonest majority – Or: breaking the SPDZ limits. In: Crampton, J., Jajodia, S., Mayes, K. (eds.) ESORICS 2013. LNCS, vol. 8134, pp. 1–18. Springer, Heidelberg (2013). https://doi.org/10.1007/978-3-642-40203-6_1

22. Damgård, I., Nielsen, J.B., Nielsen, M., Ranellucci, S.: The TinyTable protocol for 2-party secure computation, or: gate-scrambling revisited. In: Katz, J., Shacham, H. (eds.) CRYPTO 2017. LNCS, vol. 10401, pp. 167–187. Springer, Cham (2017). https://doi.org/10.1007/978-3-319-63688-7_6

23. Damgård, I., Pastro, V., Smart, N., Zakarias, S.: Multiparty computation from somewhat homomorphic encryption. In: Safavi-Naini, R., Canetti, R. (eds.) CRYPTO 2012. LNCS, vol. 7417, pp. 643–662. Springer, Heidelberg (2012). https://doi.org/10.1007/978-3-642-32009-5_38

24. Damgård, I., Zakarias, S.: Constant-overhead secure computation of Boolean circuits using preprocessing. In: TCC (2013)

25. Abram, D., Scholl, P.: Low-communication multiparty triple generation for SPDZ from ring-LPN. In: PKC 2022 (2022)

26. Genkin, D., Ishai, Y., Prabhakaran, M., Sahai, A., Tromer, E.: Circuits resilient to additive attacks with applications to secure computation. In: STOC (2014)

27. Goldreich, O.: The Foundations of Cryptography - volume 2, Basic Applications. Cambridge University Press (2004)

28. Goldreich, O., Micali, S., Wigderson, A.: How to play any mental game or a completeness theorem for protocols with honest majority. In: STOC (1987)

29. Goldwasser, S., Micali, S.: Probabilistic encryption. J. Comput. Syst. Sci. **28**(2), 270–299 (1984)

30. Hazay, C., Mikkelsen, G.L., Rabin, T., Toft, T., Nicolosi, A.A.: Efficient RSA key generation and threshold Paillier in the two-party setting. J. Cryptol. **32**(2), 265–323 (2019)

31. Ishai, Y., Kushilevitz, E., Meldgaard, S., Orlandi, C., Paskin-Cherniavsky, A.: On the power of correlated randomness in secure computation. In: Sahai, A. (ed.) TCC 2013. LNCS, vol. 7785, pp. 600–620. Springer, Heidelberg (2013). https://doi.org/10.1007/978-3-642-36594-2_34

32. Ishai, Y., Kushilevitz, E., Ostrovsky, R.: Sufficient conditions for collision-resistant hashing. In: Kilian, J. (ed.) TCC 2005. LNCS, vol. 3378, pp. 445–456. Springer, Heidelberg (2005). https://doi.org/10.1007/978-3-540-30576-7_24

33. Juvekar, C., Vaikuntanathan, V., Chandrakasan, A.P.: GAZELLE: A low latency framework for secure neural network inference. In: USENIX Security 2018, pp. 1651–1669 (2018)

34. Katz, J., Yung, M.: Threshold cryptosystems based on factoring. In: International Conference on the Theory and Application of Cryptology and Information Security, pp. 192–205 (2002)

35. Keller, M., Orsini, E., Scholl, P.: MASCOT: faster malicious arithmetic secure computation with oblivious transfer. In: ACM CCS (2016)

36. Keller, M., Pastro, V., Rotaru, D.: Overdrive: making SPDZ great again. In: EUROCRYPT (2018). https://doi.org/10.1007/978-3-319-78372-7_6
37. Kilian, J.: A note on efficient zero-knowledge proofs and arguments (extended abstract). In: ACM STOC, pp. 723–732 (1992)
38. Naor, M., Nissim, K.: Communication preserving protocols for secure function evaluation. In: ACM STOC, pp. 590–599 (2001)
39. Nielsen, J.B., Nordholt, P.S., Orlandi, C., Burra, S.S.: A new approach to practical active-secure two-party computation. In: Safavi-Naini, R., Canetti, R. (eds.) CRYPTO 2012. LNCS, vol. 7417, pp. 681–700. Springer, Heidelberg (2012). https://doi.org/10.1007/978-3-642-32009-5_40
40. Orlandi, C., Scholl, P., Yakoubov, S.: The rise of Paillier: homomorphic secret sharing and public-key silent OT. In: Canteaut, A., Standaert, F.-X. (eds.) EUROCRYPT 2021. LNCS, vol. 12696, pp. 678–708. Springer, Cham (2021). https://doi.org/10.1007/978-3-030-77870-5_24
41. Paillier, P.: Public-key cryptosystems based on composite degree residuosity classes. In: International Conference on the Theory and Applications of Cryptographic Techniques, pp. 223–238 (1999)
42. Regev, O.: On lattices, learning with errors, random linear codes, and cryptography. In: STOC 2005, pp. 84–93 (2005)
43. Shoup, V.: Arithmetic software libraries. https://www.shoup.net/papers/akl-chapter.pdf
44. Yao, A.C.: How to generate and exchange secrets (extended abstract). In: FOCS (1986)

Practical Non-interactive Publicly Verifiable Secret Sharing with Thousands of Parties

Craig Gentry[1], Shai Halevi[1(✉)], and Vadim Lyubashevsky[2]

[1] Algorand Foundation, New York, NY, USA
shaih@alum.mit.edu
[2] IBM Research, Ruschlikon, Switzerland

Abstract. Non-interactive publicly verifiable secret sharing (PVSS) schemes enables (re-)sharing of secrets in a decentralized setting in the presence of malicious parties. A recently proposed application of PVSS schemes is to enable permissionless proof-of-stake blockchains to "keep a secret" via a sequence of committees that share that secret. These committees can use the secret to produce signatures on the blockchain's behalf, or to disclose hidden data conditioned on consensus that some event has occurred. That application needs very large committees with thousands of parties, so the PVSS scheme in use must be efficient enough to support such large committees, in terms of both computation and communication. Yet, previous PVSS schemes have large proofs and/or require many exponentiations over large groups.

We present a non-interactive PVSS scheme in which the underlying encryption scheme is based on the learning with errors (LWE) problem. While lattice-based encryption schemes are very fast, they often have long ciphertexts and public keys. We use the following two techniques to conserve bandwidth: First, we adapt the Peikert-Vaikuntanathan-Waters (PVW) encryption scheme to the multi-receiver setting, so that the bulk of the parties' keys is a common random string. The resulting scheme yields $\Omega(1)$ amortized plaintext/ciphertext rate, where concretely the rate is $\approx 1/60$ for 100 parties, $\approx 1/8$ for 1000 parties, and approaching $1/2$ as the number of parties grows. Second, we use bulletproofs over a DL-group of order about 256 bits to get compact proofs of correct encryption/decryption of shares.

Alternating between the lattice and DL settings is relatively painless, as we equate the LWE modulus with the order of the group. We also show how to reduce the the number of exponentiations in the bulletproofs by applying Johnson-Lindenstrauss-like compression to reduce the dimension of the vectors whose properties must be verified.

An implementation of our PVSS with 1000 parties showed that it is feasible even at that size, and should remain so even with one or two order of magnitude increase in the committee size.

ⓒ International Association for Cryptologic Research 2022
O. Dunkelman and S. Dziembowski (Eds.): EUROCRYPT 2022, LNCS 13275, pp. 458–487, 2022.
https://doi.org/10.1007/978-3-031-06944-4_16

1   Introduction

A publicly-verifiable secret-sharing scheme (PVSS) lets a dealer share a secret among a committee of shareholders, in such a way that everyone (not just the shareholders) can verify that the secret was shared properly and be assured that it is recoverable. A *noninteractive* PVSS scheme lets the sender broadcast just a single message to the entire universe, from which the shareholders can get their shares and everyone else can check that sharing was properly done.[1] A *proactive* PVSS scheme further enables passing the secret from one committee of shareholders to the next, so that (a) the secret remains hidden from an adversary that only controls a minority in each committee, and (b) everyone can check that the secret is passed properly between consecutive committees.

Such protocols play crucial role in distributed cryptography, and were studied extensively in the literature [11,14,16,20,22,23,28,31–33,37,50–52,54,56]. They were also recently proposed as enablers of secure computation on large-scale distributed networks such as public blockchains [7,31]. Unfortunately, existing PVSS schemes in the literature fall short of what is needed for general-purpose secure computation in large-scale systems, where committees may scale to hundreds or even thousands of parties [7,26]. See related work in Sect. 1.1.

In this work we propose a new system for (proactive, noninteractive) PVSS, that remains feasible even with huge committees. In asymptotic terms, with security parameter λ and k-party committees, the PVSS protocol that we propose has the dealer and each committee member perform only $O(\lambda + k)$ exponentiations and broadcast $O(\lambda + k)$ scalars in $\mathbb{Z}_p$ and $O(\log(\lambda + k))$ group elements. (In addition, each party needs to perform $O(\lambda^2 + \lambda k)$ scalar multiplications in $\mathbb{Z}_p$, which comes to dominate the running time.)

In terms of actual numbers, we wrote a preliminary, single-threaded, implementation of our system and tested it on committees of up to 1000 members.[2] With a 1000-member committee, the dealer runs in about 40 s (single-threaded) and broadcasts a single message of size less than 300KB, while each committee member requires about 20 s to obtain its share and verify the proofs. As we explain in the sequel, this system can be extended to a proactive PVSS protocol for very large-scale systems, where the wall-clock time to refresh a secret is measured in just a few minutes.

We also point out that while our goal of using LWE encryption was motivated by practical consideration, a side effect is that the *secrecy* of the PVSS scheme is preserved even against quantum attackers. This protects the PVSS scheme from potential "harvest-and-decrypt" attacks using future quantum computers. This feature may be especially important for blockchain applications, where all the data is "harvested" by design.

---

[1] Clearly such schemes must rely on some form of PKI.

[2] The implementation should also support committees that are one or two orders of magnitude larger, with only a mild increase in runtime.

1.1   The PVSS Problem and Related Work

Verifiable secret sharing (VSS) was introduced by Chor et al. [16], with the objective of making secret sharing robust against malicious parties – i.e., a malicious dealer distributing incorrect shares, or malicious shareholders submitting incorrect shares in the reconstruction protocol.

Stadler [54] introduced publicly verifiable secret sharing (PVSS), in which the correctness of shares is verifiable by everyone (not just shareholders). As Stadler notes, the idea appears implicitly in earlier works. Chor et al.'s VSS protocol [16] happened to be publicly verifiable. GMW [28] also includes a PVSS protocol (Sect. 3.3), in which shareholders generate public keys independently, and the encrypter sends encryptions of shares of the secret to the shareholders, together with NIZK proofs that the ciphertexts are well-formed and indeed encrypt shares. These early schemes can be made non-interactive, by using NIZKs with the PVSS protocol in [28], or by applying the Fiat-Shamir heuristic to the Σ-protocols in [54].

Later PVSS works focused primarily on improving the efficiency of non-interactive ZK proofs for the ciphertexts, and minimizing the assumptions underlying those proofs [11,14,20,22,23,31–33,37,50–52,56]. Below, we will focus on PVSS schemes that follow the GMW approach to PVSS, where shareholders receive shares encrypted under their own independently generated public keys. In [48], this approach to PVSS is called "threshold encryption with transparent setup". We can categorize these PVSS schemes according to what underlying encryption scheme they use to encrypt shares. For the most part, these schemes all use 1) Paillier encryption, 2) ElGamal encryption of scalars "in the exponent", 3) pairing-based encryption of elements of the source group of the bilinear map, or 4) lattice-based encryption.

Paillier encryption [45] might at first appear ill-suited to PVSS in the "threshold encryption with transparent setup" setting, as shareholders have different Paillier public keys, and therefore have incompatible plaintext spaces that make it awkward to prove relationships among shares. However, this problem can be overcome by using a common interval that is inside the plaintext spaces of all of the Paillier keys, and using a proof system that proves (among other things) that the encrypted message is indeed within this interval. Camenisch and Shoup [14] build an encryption scheme with verifiable encryption and decryption, based on Paillier's decision composite residuosity assumption, that uses such an "interval" approach; the Σ-protocols for verifiable encryption and decryption each require only $O(1)$ exponentiations.[3] Recently, Lindell et al. [37] used essentially a version of Camenisch-Shoup to construct a PVSS scheme with $O(k)$ exponentiations per committee member (during re-sharing), for committees of size k (see Sect. 6.2).[4] Later schemes using variants of Paillier to encrypt PVSS shares include [23,33,51]. All of these PVSS schemes have the usual disadvantage of schemes related to Paillier, namely that exponentiations are expensive,

---

[3] In earlier work, Fouque and Stern [20] informally present a somewhat similar scheme.

[4] Lindell et al. also constructed a scheme that avoids Paillier, but with much higher bandwidth.

as the exponentiations are over a group whose size should in principle be about $\exp(O(\lambda^3))$ for security parameter λ to maintain sufficient security against the number field sieve, and which in practice is much larger than, say, an elliptic curve group with comparable security (against classical computers). Also, the size of the proofs is linear in the size of the ciphertexts.

PVSS schemes that encrypt shares "in the exponent" include [31,37,52]. In those schemes, recovering the secret itself requires solving DL, which is only possible when the secret is small. For example, Groth's PVSS scheme [30,31], affiliated with the Dfinity blockchain, shares the secret for BLS signing [9] by dividing it "into small chunks, which can be encrypted in the exponent and later extracted using the Baby-step Giant-step method". That scheme employs a weak range proof to demonstrate that the chucks in the exponent are small enough to be recovered. The scheme has numerous optimizations, such as using the same randomness for ciphertexts in the multi-receiver setting. The paper [31] mentions an implementation, but does not provide details.

Bilinear-map-based PVSS schemes can verifiably encrypt source group elements, as opposed to scalars [19,55]. An advantage of these schemes is that proofs of smallness – such as those needed in Camenisch-Shoup and Groth's PVSS scheme – are unnecessary, as the bilinear map makes verifiable encryption very natural [8,21]. A disadvantage is that these schemes are limited to settings where one is content to have the secret be a source group element – e.g., as when the secret is being used as a signing or decryption key in a pairing-based cryptosystem.

Lattice-based encryption schemes can encrypt large scalars, and have encryption and decryption procedures that are much faster than group-based schemes.[5] The main disadvantage of lattice-based schemes is high bandwidth, as lattice-based ciphertexts and public keys are in the order of kilobytes. The high bandwidth issue, however, can often be amortized away, since many plaintexts can be packed into a single ciphertext, as in the Peikert-Vaikuntanathan-Waters encryption scheme [47]. In principle, ciphertext expansion in lattice-based schemes can be arbitrarily small [12]. Also, very small ciphertext expansion (e.g., close to 2) can be compatible with very high performance that can be orders of magnitude better than Paillier-based schemes [24]. (See also [43,44], cf. [53].)

Proving that lattice-based ciphertexts are well-formed requires proofs of smallness (for vectors that should be small, such as the secret key, encryption randomness). Some lattice-based schemes [17,36] have used the approach of decomposing the coefficients of the vectors into their binary representations, and then proving that each purported bit in the representation is indeed in $\{0,1\}$. Alternatively, one can use an approach somewhat similar to Camenisch-Shoup: a Σ-protocol that proves that a vector is inside a certain ball by revealing a statistically masked version of that vector. In the lattice setting, Lyubashevsky [38] showed how to use rejection sampling to reduce the required size gap between

---

[5] Of course, this statement refers to basic, possibly additively homomorphic lattice-based encryption schemes, not fully homomorphic encryption.

the masking vector and masked vector. Some other works on proofs of smallness are: [5,18].

In this paper, we are motivated in part by the blockchain setting, where PVSS can help enable a blockchain to "keep a secret" [7] that it can use to sign or decrypt conditioned upon events, but where bandwidth is at a premium. Currently, blockchains almost exclusively use proof systems based on QAPs [29, 46] or bulletproofs [13], because these have the most concise proofs.[6]

1.2   An Overview of Our PVSS Construction

We assume we have a PKI, in which each party (and potential shareholder) has independently generated its own key pair for public-key encryption. Based on this PKI, our goal is to design a practical non-interactive PVSS scheme that allows a dealer to share a secret by verifiably (in zero-knowledge) encrypting shares of the secret to a "committee" of shareholders under their keys. The scheme should also allow each committee member to act as a dealer and verifiably "re-share" its share to the next committee of shareholders. We use Shamir secret sharing, though essentially any linear secret sharing will do.

Our PVSS scheme arises out of two design choices – namely, 1) to use lattice-based encryption, and 2) to use bulletproofs. Below, we explain these choices and their consequences.

Lattice-Based Encryption. Lattice-based encryption is a good fit for PVSS, not only because it is exceptionally fast, but also because its disadvantages turn out *not* to be big problems in the PVSS setting. One apparent disadvantage is that lattice-based encryption has long public keys and ciphertexts. However, in the multi-receiver setting of PVSS, this disadvantage can be amortized away by adapting the Peikert-Vaikuntanathan-Waters (PVW) encryption scheme [47] to the multi-receiver setting. Another apparent disadvantage is that, for lattice-based PVSS, proving that ciphertexts are well-formed requires zero-knowledge proofs of smallness – e.g., that the "noise" in the ciphertexts is small. However, as we have seen in Sect. 1.1, PVSS and verifiable encryption schemes based on Paillier and ElGamal "in the exponent" also employ weak range proofs, and therefore they have no advantage over lattices here.

We briefly review the PVW lattice-based encryption scheme, as used in our PVSS scheme. The scheme uses a public random matrix A that is common to all parties. Each party i generates a secret vector s_i, and sets $\mathbf{b}_i = \mathbf{s}_i \cdot A + \mathbf{e}_i$ to be its public key.[7] The parties' public key vectors (say that there are k of them) are collected into a matrix B. The collective public key of the PVSS system is

---

[6] Despite being compact, bulletproofs have linear verification complexity. The Dory scheme [35] is similar to bulletproofs, but with logarithmic verification complexity.

[7] In the real scheme, each user creates several such vectors, but we defer this discussion to the body of the paper.

$\begin{bmatrix} A \\ B \end{bmatrix}$. The encryption of a message vector $\mathbf{m} = (m_1, \ldots, m_k) \in \mathbb{Z}_q^k$ is

$$\begin{bmatrix} A \\ B \end{bmatrix} \mathbf{r} + \begin{bmatrix} \mathbf{e}_1 \\ \mathbf{e}_2 \end{bmatrix} + \begin{bmatrix} \mathbf{0} \\ \mathbf{m} \end{bmatrix} = \begin{bmatrix} \mathbf{c}_1 \\ \mathbf{c}_2 \end{bmatrix}, \tag{1}$$

where $\mathbf{r}, \mathbf{e}_1, \mathbf{e}_2$ are vectors with small coefficients and all operations take place in $\mathbb{Z}_q$. A committee member will use this scheme to encrypt k re-shares of its share to the next k-member committee.[8]

Note how well the PVW scheme is suited to the multi-receiver setting. In the basic setting of (single-user) Regev encryption [49], each user has its own matrix A as part of its public key, while here A is amortized across all parties. Moreover, note that an encryption to an extra user costs just an extra element in $\mathbb{Z}_q$. When the number of users becomes large, the ciphertext expansion factor becomes a small constant.

As far as we know, ours is the first use of the PVW lattice-based encryption scheme in the multi-receiver setting. Proving the security of PVW in this setting is subtle: when decrypting each user implicitly obtains the inner product of $\mathbf{s}_i$ and $\mathbf{r}$, which leaks something about $\mathbf{r}$. One therefore needs to show that, for practical parameters, the secrets are still hidden despite the leakage. We cover this issue in Sect. 2.3.

Bulletproofs. Our second design choice is to use bulletproofs. We are aiming for a PVSS scheme that can be used on a blockchain, as blockchains provide an especially compelling platform for PVSS. Linear-size proofs are not suitable for blockchains, as such proofs (which might appear in many blocks) need to be downloaded and verified by everyone that is confirming the blockchain state. For this reason, proof systems in use on actual blockchains are almost exclusively based on QAPs [29, 46] or bulletproofs [13]. Bulletproofs have some advantages over proof systems based on QAPs, such as being based on more natural assumptions, not requiring bilinear maps, and having only linear (versus quasi-linear) prover time complexity. Bulletproofs also work over small groups (a feature not shared by PVSS schemes based on Paillier encryption).

Recently, Bootle et al. [10] described a variant of bulletproofs based on lattice problems. In this variant, the proofs are not as compact, but proof generation and verification presumably would be faster. As future work, it may be interesting to investigate how using this variant affects the performance of our scheme.

Using Lattice-Based Encryption and Bulletproofs Together. Now our goal is to construct a proof system, ultimately based on bulletproofs, that allows a shareholder to prove that incoming and outgoing PVW ciphertexts correctly encrypt re-shares associated to its share.

---

[8] For convenience, we have described the system as having only k members total, but consecutive k-member committees could be non-overlapping subsets of a larger set of parties.

As a first step to make our encryption scheme and bulletproofs compatible, we set our LWE modulus q to be the order of the bulletproof group. The plaintext space of our encryption scheme – i.e., the space the shares live in – is also $\mathbb{Z}/(q\mathbb{Z})$.[9] Now we "simply" need to create a commitment of the messages and prove that the ciphertext encrypts them. After this, all the proofs can be done using bulletproofs. The main contribution of this work is a collection of techniques, optimized for efficiency, to prove that a lattice encryption is valid and that the message corresponds to some DL committed value.

In more detail, we create a Pedersen commitment to all the coefficients of $\mathbf{r}, \mathbf{e}_i$, and $\mathbf{m}$. We now would like to prove that the committed values satisfy the linear relationship in (1). Also, very importantly, we need a proof that $\mathbf{r}$ and $\mathbf{e}_i$ have small coefficients. Proving exact relationships is the bread and butter of bulletproofs. We handle proofs of smallness in a multi-stage process that carefully calibrates the transition from "lattice world" to "bulletproof world". Namely, in some cases, we first reduce the dimension of the vectors involved, and instead prove that this dimension-reduced vector has small coefficients. This dimension reduction in turn reduces the number of exponentiations we eventually need to perform in the bulletproof world. Before moving to bulletproof world, we also invoke a lattice-based (without bulletproofs) proof of smallness with a large gap. While this proof is "slacky", it is sufficient to prove certain expressions do not "wrap" modulo q, so that we can now consider these expressions over $\mathbb{Z}$. Now that we have reduced the dimension and are assured that mod-q statements can be lifted to statements over $\mathbb{Z}$, we can use bulletproofs to prove the exact l_2 norm of the vectors. We provide additional techniques to hide the exact l_2 norm if only a bound on the norm is desired. The bulletproofs for the linear relationships and for smallness are aggregated to the extent possible. Details are provided below.

Dimension Reduction and Slacky Lattice-Based Proofs of Smallness. Our dimension reduction technique is based on the Johnson-Lindenstrauss lemma [34]. The idea is that for all vectors $\mathbf{v}$, we have $\|\mathbf{v}R\| \approx \sqrt{n}\|\mathbf{v}\|$, where R is an n-column matrix whose entries are chosen from a normal distribution of variance 1. When R is chosen in this way, the distribution of $\|\mathbf{v}R\|^2$ follows the chi-squared distribution and its confidence intervals are known. When the coefficients of R are instead chosen from a discrete distribution over $\{0, \pm 1\}$ where the probability of 0 is $1/2$, one can heuristically verify that these confidence intervals are bounded by the continuous ones.[10] If we would like to be in a $1 - 2^{-128}$ interval, then R can have around 256 columns and then the ratio between the smallest value of $\|\mathbf{v}R\|$ and the largest is under 4. This means that we can project an arbitrary-dimensional vector into just 256 dimensions and

---

[9] Unlike the more standard LWE encryption in which the message also needs to be small, we use a version of the scheme implicit in [27] where the messages can be arbitrarily large in $\mathbb{Z}_q$, but the length of $\vec{m}$ has to increase to encode all of the message. We describe this in Sect. 2.2.

[10] There are concrete bounds for tails of some of these distributions (e.g. [1]), but they are asymptotic and are looser than necessary for our concrete parameters.

prove the ℓ_2 norm of the resulting vector, and be within a small factor of the correct result. And, of course, the projection operation is linear. The concrete bounds for the dimension-reduction technique are described in Sect. 3.2.

Everything in the above discussion was based on the fact that we were working over the integers, rather than over $\mathbb{Z}_q$. When working modulo q, it is possible that $\mathbf{v}$ has a large norm, but $\mathbf{v}R \bmod q$ has a small one. This event can clearly only occur if the coefficients of $\mathbf{v}$ are large enough that multiplication with R causes a wraparound modulo q. It is therefore important to show that this does not happen, and we do this in the manner as in the lattice-based proofs from [41]. We now explain how the technique applies to our context. The main idea is to show that all the elements of $\mathbf{v}$ are not too big. This seems a bit circular, as our goal is already to prove that $\|\mathbf{v}\|$ is small. But our requirement now is not to get a very tight bound on the norm, but simply to show that all the elements of $\mathbf{v}$ are small enough to not cause a wrap around. For this, one employs a simple fact that is sometimes useful in lattice cryptography [6, Lemma 2.3], which states that if a vector $\mathbf{v}$ has a large coefficient, then for any $y \in \mathbb{Z}_q$, $\langle \mathbf{v}, \mathbf{r} \rangle + y \bmod q$ has a large coefficient with probability at least $1/2$, where the coefficients of $\mathbf{r}$ are randomly chosen from $\{0, \pm 1\}$ as above. One would therefore prove that the coefficients of $\mathbf{v}$ are small by committing to some masking vector $\mathbf{y}$, receiving a 128-column matrix R as a challenge, and then outputting $\mathbf{v}R + \mathbf{y}$. The purpose of $\mathbf{y}$ is to hide $\mathbf{v}$, and so some rejection sampling [39] is necessary to keep the distribution of $\mathbf{v}R + \mathbf{y}$ independent of $\mathbf{v}$. Note that the gap between the actual ℓ_∞ norm of $\mathbf{v}$ and that of what we can prove is increased by a factor of at least the dimension of $\mathbf{v}$. This is because the ℓ_∞ norm is not well-preserved under transformations and also due to the masking which is needed because we will actually be outputting the value $\mathbf{v}R + \mathbf{y}$. This is much larger than the factor of approximately 4 in the ℓ_2-dimension reduction above, and this is why we only employ this technique for proving that no wrap-around occurs.

In the context of our encryption scheme, instead of proving that the *long* vectors $\mathbf{e}_i$ (with dimension dependent on the number of users) have small norm, we can instead prove that the *short* 256-dimensional vector

$$\left(\begin{bmatrix} \mathbf{c}_1 \\ \mathbf{c}_2 \end{bmatrix} - \begin{bmatrix} A \\ B \end{bmatrix} \mathbf{r} - \begin{bmatrix} \mathbf{0} \\ \mathbf{m} \end{bmatrix} \right) \cdot R \tag{2}$$

has small norm. Also, we prove that $\mathbf{r} \cdot R$ has small norm instead of $\mathbf{r}$. Other purportedly short vectors are handled in the same way. For example, each of the k new committee members needs to prove that the public key $\mathbf{b}_i = \mathbf{s}_i A + \mathbf{e}_i$ is properly created. The combination of these techniques is described throughout Sect. 3.

Bulletproofs and Precise Proofs of Smallness. Suppose now that we want to prove a tighter upper bound β on the squared ℓ_2 norm of a vector $\mathbf{v} = (v_1, \ldots, v_k)$. (Proving tighter bounds allows us to use tighter parameters in our lattice-based encryption scheme.) Assume β is an integer. First, we pick a vector $\mathbf{x}$ such that the squared l_2 norm of the concatenated vector $\mathbf{v}\|\mathbf{x}$ is exactly β.

For the vector $\mathbf{x}$, 4 coefficients suffice, as the non-negative integer $\beta - \sum v_i^2$ can always be expressed as the sum of at most 4 squares. We then use the "slacky" techniques above to prove that there is no wraparound modulo q in the computation of the squared l_2 norm of $\mathbf{v}\|\mathbf{x}$. Then, we commit to $\mathbf{v}\|\mathbf{x}$, and use bulletproofs to prove the exact quadratic relation.

We can aggregate the relations that we prove using bulletproofs – e.g., these exact proofs of smallness are combined together with proofs of the linear equations in (1).

1.3   Organization

In Sect. 2 we describe our lattice-based encryption scheme, and discuss the extension of PVW to the multi-receiver setting. In Sect. 3 we present the size-proof protocols that we use in our scheme and their parameters. In Sect. 4, we provide details about our implementation. In the long version [25] we describe in more detail the various sub-protocols that the parties run locally, for key-generation, encryption, decryption, and secret re-sharing, explain how to aggregate aggregate the bulletproof instances from all these components into just two bulletproof instances, and finally put all these components together in a (proactive) publicly-verifiable secret-sharing protocol.

2   The Underlying Encryption Scheme

In this section we develop the encryption scheme that is used by our protocol, starting from a (variant of) PVW encryption [47] and specializing it to our needs.

Below we denote integers and scalars by lowercase letters, vectors by bold lowercase letters, and matrices by uppercase letters. Vectors are considered row vectors by default. (Parameters are denoted by either lowercase English or lowercase Greek letters). For integers x, q, we denote by $x \bmod q$ the unique integer $x' \in [-\frac{q}{2}, +\frac{q}{2})$ such that $x' = x \pmod{q}$. We denote vectors by bold-lowercase letters, and it will usually be evident from context whether they are row or column. The l_2 and l_∞ norms of a vector $\mathbf{v}$ are denoted $\|\mathbf{v}\|_2, \|\mathbf{v}\|_\infty$, respectively. For a matrix A, we let $\|A\|_2$, (resp. $\|A\|_\infty$) denote the largest l_2, (resp. l_∞) norm of any row in A.

2.1   Learning with Errors (LWE)

The LWE problem was introduced by Regev [49]. In the decision variant, the adversary is given pairs (A, B) where A is chosen uniformly from $\mathbb{Z}_q^{k \times m}$, and it needs to distinguish the cases where:

- B is chosen uniformly at random in $\mathbb{Z}_q^{n \times m}$, or
- B is set as $B := SA + E \bmod q$, where the entries of S, E are chosen from some public distributions χ_s, χ_e over $\mathbb{Z}_q$ that output integers of magnitude much smaller than q with overwhelming probability.

This problem is believed to be hard for many different settings of the parameters $k, m, n, q, \chi_s, \chi_e$. For some of them it is even proven to be as hard as solving some "famous" lattice problems in the worst case. In this work we assume that this problem is (exponentially) hard when the χ's are uniform distributions on integers is some symmetric interval $[\pm\sigma]$ with $\sigma \ll q/2$. The specific parameters that we use were chosen according to the LWE hardness estimator of Albrecht et al. [3], see more details in The long version [25]. Also in our protocol we always use $k = m$, so we drop the distinction between these parameters in the sequel.

2.2   Variants of Regev Encryption

In [49], Regev described a public-key encryption scheme whose security is based on the hardness of decision-LWE. Later, Peikert, Vaikuntanathan and Waters (PVW) described in [47] a variant with improved plaintext-to-ciphertext expansion ratio. Our protocol is based on a variant of the PVW construction. Underlying it is the following "approximate encryption" scheme, where decryption only recovers a noisy version of the plaintext:

Key-generation. The key-owner chooses a random $A \leftarrow \mathbb{Z}_q^{k \times k}$, $S \leftarrow \chi_s^{n \times k}$ and $E \leftarrow \chi_e^{n \times k}$ and computes $B := SA + E \bmod q$. The secret key is S and the public key is (A, B), which is pseudorandom under the decision LWE assumption.

Encryption. To encrypt an n-vector $\mathbf{x} \in \mathbb{Z}_q^n$, the encryptor chooses $\mathbf{r} \leftarrow \chi_s^k$, $\mathbf{e}_1 \leftarrow \chi_e^k$, $\mathbf{e}_2 \leftarrow \chi_e^n$, and sets $\mathbf{c}_1 := A\mathbf{r} + \mathbf{e}_1 \bmod q$ and $\mathbf{c}_2 := B\mathbf{r} + \mathbf{e}_2 + \mathbf{x} \bmod q$. The ciphertext is $(\mathbf{c}_1, \mathbf{c}_2)$, which is again pseudorandom under the decision LWE assumption.

Decryption. To decrypt (approximately), the key-owner outputs $\mathbf{x}' := \mathbf{c}_2 - S\mathbf{c}_1 \bmod q$. Substituting all the terms one can check that

$$\mathbf{x}' = \big((SA + E)\mathbf{r} + \mathbf{e}_2 + \mathbf{x}\big) - S(A\mathbf{r} + \mathbf{e}_1) = \mathbf{x} + \overbrace{E\mathbf{r} + \mathbf{e}_2 - S\mathbf{e}_1}^{\mathbf{e}'},$$

where for appropriate choices of χ_s, χ_e we will have $\|\mathbf{e}'\|_\infty \ll q$.

Plaintext Encoding. To be able to fully recover the plaintext, Regev encryption uses some form of error-correction that allows the decryptor to compute $\mathbf{x}$ from the noisy $\mathbf{x}'$. Most variants of Regev encryption use encoding based on scaling, but for us it is more convenient to use a different form of encoding[11] (which was implicit in the homomorphic encryption scheme of Gentry, Sahai and Waters [27]). We encode a plaintext vector $\mathbf{x}^* \in \mathbb{Z}_q^n$ by a higher-dimension $\mathbf{x} \in \mathbb{Z}_q^{\ell n}$ that includes not just $\mathbf{x}^*$ but also a large multiple of it. Let $\Delta := \lfloor\sqrt{q}\rfloor$ and $\mathbf{g} := (\Delta, 1) \in \mathbb{Z}_q^2$. The dimension-$n$ vector $(x_1, \ldots, x_n) \in \mathbb{Z}_q^n$ is encoded in the vector $(x_1\mathbf{g}| \ldots |x_n\mathbf{g}) \in \mathbb{Z}_q^{2n}$.

---

[11] The reason that this encoding method is better for us, is that it allows us to work only with $\mathbb{Z}_q$ elements. In other variants of Regev encryption one usually must work with both $\mathbb{Z}_q$ and $\mathbb{Z}_p$ for some $p \ll q$.

More generally, we could use a parameter $\ell \geq 2$ and set $\Delta := \lfloor \sqrt[\ell]{q} \rfloor$ and the "gadget vector" $\mathbf{g} := (\Delta^{\ell-1}, \ldots, \Delta, 1) \in \mathbb{Z}_q^\ell$. We then encode a vector $(x_1, \ldots, x_n)$ in the higher-dimension $(x_1\mathbf{g}| \ldots | x_n\mathbf{g}) \in \mathbb{Z}_q^{n\ell}$. The larger we set the parameter ℓ, the more redundant the encoded vector becomes, which lets us tolerate larger noise and still recover the original vector. (On the other hand, we need to increase the number of rows in the secret key from n to ℓn.) Specifically, for each entry x_i in the original plaintext vector, the approximate-decryption above yields a noisy ℓ-vector $\mathbf{x}' = x\mathbf{g} + \mathbf{e}$ mod q, and x_i can then recovered using the decoding procedure from Fig. 1.

Decode$((x_1', \ldots, x_\ell') \in \mathbb{Z}_q^\ell)$:	# $x_i' = x\Delta^{\ell-i} + e_i$ mod q
1. For $i = 1, \ldots, \ell-1$	
$\quad$ let $y_i := x_{i+1}' - \Delta x_i'$ mod q	# $y_i = e_i - \Delta e_{i+1}$ (**w/o mod-q reduction**)
2. Set $z := \sum_{i=1}^{\ell-1} \Delta^{\ell-i-1} \cdot y_i$	# telescopic cancellation, $z = e_1 - \Delta^{\ell-1} e_\ell$
3. Set $e := z$ mod $\Delta^{\ell-1}$	# $e = e_1$
4. Output $(x_1' - e)/\Delta^{\ell-1}$	# $= x$

Fig. 1. The plaintext decoding procedure

As long as all the e_i's are bounded in magnitude below $q/2(\Delta+1) \approx \Delta^{\ell-1}/2$, then the equality $y_i = e_i - \Delta e_{i+1}$ in Row 2 holds not only modulo q but also over the integers. In that case we also have $z = e_1 - \Delta^{\ell-1} e_\ell$ over the integers, and since $|e_1| < \Delta^{\ell-1}/2$ then also $e = e_1$ in Row 3 holds over the integers, so we recover the correct output x.

For our implementation we stuck to the setting $\ell = 2$, which is somewhat simpler to implement. In general, however, setting a slightly larger value (such as $\ell = 4$) may lead to somewhat better parameters, since it can tolerate larger noise and therefore smaller lattice dimension for the same security level. We leave exploring this direction to future work.

2.3 The Multiparty Setting

A very useful property of the scheme above is that the i'th plaintext value x_i can be recovered using only rows $\{1 + (i-1)\ell, \ldots, i\ell\}$ of the secret key matrix S (indexing start at 1). To wit, denote by S_i the sub-matrix of S consisting only of these rows, and let $\mathbf{c}_{2,i}$ be the sub-vector of $\mathbf{c}_2$ consisting of entries $\{1 + (i-1)\ell, \ldots, i\ell\}$, then x_i can be recovered by setting $\mathbf{x}' := \mathbf{c}_{2,i} - S_i\mathbf{c}_1 \in \mathbb{Z}_q^\ell$, then using the decoding procedure from Fig. 1.

It is therefore possible to use the encryption scheme above in a multiparty setting, where all parties share the same random matrix A (a common-random-string which is chosen by a trusted party during setup), and each party i chooses its own secret key $S \leftarrow \chi_s^{\ell \times k}$ and noise $E_i \leftarrow \chi_e^{\ell \times k}$, and computes its own public key $B_i := S_i A + E_i$ mod q.

The global public key is then set to include the matrix A, followed by all the B_i's in order (which are viewed as sub-matrices of the public-key matrix B from above). Encryption works just as above, with the plaintext vector $\mathbf{x} \subset \mathbb{Z}_q^n$ viewed as having one plaintext element $x_i \in \mathbb{Z}_q$ destined to each party i. For decryption, each party i uses its secret key S_i to get the noise vector $\mathbf{x}_i' = x_i\mathbf{g} + \mathbf{e}_i$, then apply the decoding procedure from Fig. 1 to recover x_i from $\mathbf{x}_i'$.

LWE with Leakage. The multiparty setting above brings up a new problem: what happens when some of the parties are dishonest and deviate from the pre-scribed distribution for choosing their public keys? The issue is that encryption uses the same vector $\mathbf{r}$ for encrypting all the plaintext elements to all the parties. When party i is dishonest and B_i is chosen adversarially, seeing $B_i\mathbf{r} + \mathbf{e}_i$ may leak information about $\mathbf{r}$ to the adversary, potentially making it possible for it to distinguish some other $B_j\mathbf{r} + \mathbf{e}_j$ from random and maybe learn something about the plaintext encrypted for party j.

Luckily, some characteristics of our application make it possible to counter this threat. In particular, each party i in our protocol is required to prove that its public key is "well formed". Namely it must provide a proof of knowledge of S_i, E_i such that $B_i := S_iA + E_i \bmod q$, and moreover where the l_2 norm of the rows in S_i, E_i is bounded by some known bounds β_s, β_e, respectively. In this setting, we can reduce security to plain LWE (without any leakage), as long as the encryptor chooses $\mathbf{e}_2$ from a somewhat wider distribution than $\mathbf{e}_1$.

Fix the LWE parameters $k, n, q, \chi_s, \chi_{e1}$, and let $\rho_s, \rho_s \in \mathbb{R}$ be factors that bound the size of vector from χ_s, χ_{e1}, respectively, along any fixed direction. Specifically, we require that for any fixed $\mathbf{v} \in \mathbb{Z}_q^k$, choosing $\mathbf{s} \leftarrow \chi_s^k$ and $\mathbf{e} \leftarrow \chi_e^k$ we get

$$|\langle \mathbf{v}, \mathbf{s} \rangle| \le \rho_s \cdot \|\mathbf{v}\|_2 \text{ and } |\langle \mathbf{v}, \mathbf{e} \rangle| \le \rho_e \cdot \|\mathbf{v}\|_2,$$

except perhaps with a probability negligible in κ. Let $\beta_s, \beta_e \in \mathbb{R}$ be the bounds that the parties in our protocol must prove, and let χ_{e2} be another noise distri-bution over $\mathbb{Z}$, which is wide enough so that χ_{e2} is statistically close[12] to $\chi_{e2} + \delta$ for any fixed integer offset $\delta \le \lceil \rho_s\beta_e + \rho_e\beta_s \rceil$. Then consider the following game between an adversary and a challenger:

- The challenger chooses, sends to the adversary a random matrix $A \in \mathbb{Z}_q^{k \times k}$.
- The adversary chooses $S \in \mathbb{Z}_q^{n \times k}$ and $E \in \mathbb{Z}_q^{n \times k}$, subject to the constraint that the l_2 norm of each row in S, E is bounded by β_s, β_e, respectively. The adversary sets $B = SA + E \bmod q$ and sends S, E, B to the challenger.[13]
- The challenger chooses $\mathbf{r} \leftarrow \chi_s^k, \mathbf{e}_1 \leftarrow \chi_{e1}^k, \mathbf{e}_2 \leftarrow \chi_{e2}^k$, and a uniformly random vector $\mathbf{u} \in \mathbb{Z}_q^k$. It also tosses a coin $\sigma \in \{0, 1\}$.
  If $\sigma = 1$ then the challenger sets $\mathbf{c}_1 := A\mathbf{r} + \mathbf{e}_1 \bmod q$ and $\mathbf{c}_2 := B\mathbf{r} + \mathbf{e}_2 \bmod q$.
  If $\sigma = 0$ then the challenger sets $\mathbf{c}_1 := \mathbf{u}$ and $\mathbf{c}_2 := S\mathbf{c}_1 + \mathbf{e}_2 \bmod q$.

---

[12] Up to a distance negligible in κ.

[13] The adversary sends not only B but also S, E to the challenger, since in our protocol it will have to prove knowledge of these matrices so they can be extracted from it.

- The challenger sends $(\mathbf{c}_1, \mathbf{c}_2)$ to the adversary, and the adversary outputs a guess σ' for σ.

Lemma 2.1. *Let the parameters $k, n, q, \chi_s, \chi_{e1},$ and $\rho_s, \rho_s, \chi_{e2}$ be as above. Then under the hardness of decision-LWE with parameters k, n, χ_s, χ_{e1}, the adversary in the game above has only a negligible advantage in guessing the value of σ.*

Proof. Substituting all the variables above, we have

$$
\begin{aligned}
(A\mathbf{r} + \mathbf{e}_1, B\mathbf{r} + \mathbf{e}_2) &= \left(A\mathbf{r} + \mathbf{e}_1, (SA + E)\mathbf{r} + \mathbf{e}_2\right) \\
&= \left(A\mathbf{r} + \mathbf{e}_1, S(A\mathbf{r} + \mathbf{e}_1) - S\mathbf{e}_1 + E\mathbf{r} + \mathbf{e}_2\right) \quad (3) \\
&\stackrel{(s)}{\approx} \left(A\mathbf{r} + \mathbf{e}_1, S(A\mathbf{r} + \mathbf{e}_1) + \mathbf{e}_2\right) \stackrel{(c)}{\approx} \left(\mathbf{u}, S\mathbf{u} + \mathbf{e}_2\right). \quad (4)
\end{aligned}
$$

The last relation follows directly from the hardness of decision LWE with these parameters. To see why the penultimate relation holds, note that $\|E\mathbf{r} - S\mathbf{e}\|_\infty \leq \rho_s \beta_e + \rho_e \beta_s$ except with a negligible probability, and therefore $\mathbf{e}_2$ is statistically close to $E\mathbf{r} - S\mathbf{e}_1 + \mathbf{e}_2$.

Semantic Security in the Multiparty Setting. Lemma 2.1 implies that we can get semantic security for the honest parties in our protocol, even if the dishonest parties deviate from the prescribed distribution for choosing their public keys. (As long as they successfully prove knowledge of S, E as above.)

To that end, we modify the encryption procedure from Sect. 2.2 so that it uses the wider noise χ_{e2} rather than χ_e when choosing the noise vector $\mathbf{e}_2$. We then view the CRS matrix *together with all the honest public keys* as the matrix A from the lemma, and the dishonest public keys are viewed as the matrix B from the lemma. We note that with this view, the matrix A is pseudorandom from the adversary's perspective. Lemma 2.1 tells us that $A\vec{r} + \vec{e}_1$ is indistinguishable from random even given $B\mathbf{r} + \mathbf{e}_2$, and the encryption scheme uses the part of $A\vec{r} + \vec{e}_1$ corresponding to the honest parties' public keys to mask the plaintext values for these parties, hence we get semantic security.

How Wide Must χ_{e2} Be? Lemma 2.1 requires that χ_{e2} is very wide, enough to "flood" the term $\delta := E\mathbf{r} - S\mathbf{e}$, i.e., larger by at least the (statistical) security parameter. In our application, however, making χ_{e2} very wide is costly: For security of 128 bits, adding one bit to the width of χ_{e2} increases by about 40 the dimension of the LWE secret that we need to use. (So making it (say) 50-bit wider will increase the dimension by almost 2000.)

However, in our setting it seems likely that setting χ_{e2} only slightly larger than (the expected size of) δ is safe, since the encryption randomness and noise are only used once, and the adversary gets at most $t < 1000$ samples from the "leakage". We therefore took a pragmatic approach, making χ_{e2} only large enough so the distributions χ_{e2}^t and $\chi_{e2}^t + \delta$ are "not too far". Specifically, we set it large enough to ensure that the Rényi divergence between them is a small constant. While this is not enough to prove that decision-LWE remains hard, it is enough to show that the search problem remains hard. As we are not aware of any attack on decision-LWE that does not go via full recovery of the LWE secret, we take it as a strong indication of security even in our setting.

In more detail, in the long version [25] we establish a high-probability bound on the l_∞ norm of δ (call it μ). We use the heuristic of modeling χ_{e2} as a zero-mean Normal random variable with variance σ^2 (where σ is the parameter that we need to set). Using analysis similar to [2,4], we bound the Rényi divergence of order α between χ_{e2}^t and $\chi_{e2}^t + \delta$ by $\rho := \exp\left(\alpha\pi t \cdot (\mu/\sigma)^2\right)$, and use the probability-preservation property of Rényi divergence to conclude that for any event $E(\mathbf{v})$ that depends on a vector $\mathbf{v}$, we have

$$\Pr_{\mathbf{v} \leftarrow \chi_{e2}^t}[E(\mathbf{v})] \geq \Pr_{\mathbf{v} \leftarrow \chi_{e2}^t + \delta}[E(\mathbf{v})]^{\alpha/(\alpha-1)}/\rho.$$

In particular the above holds for the event in which the adversary finds the LWE-secret $\mathbf{r}$. Setting $\sigma = b\sqrt{2\pi t}$ and using (say) $\alpha = 2$, yields $\rho = \exp(1) = e$ and hence $\Pr_{\mathbf{v} \leftarrow \chi_{e2}^t}[E(\mathbf{v})] \geq \Pr_{\mathbf{v} \leftarrow \chi_{e2}^t + \delta}[E(\mathbf{v})]^2/e$. By the hardness of search-LWE, the probability on the left-hand side is negligible, and hence so is the probability on the right-hand side.

2.4   An Optimization: Using Module-LWE over Small Rings

As is common in lattice-based cryptosystems, we gain efficiency by using operations over higher-degree algebraic ring rather than directly over the integers. In our multiparty setting parties use ℓ-row public key (to enable or input encoding), so instead we use operations over a ring of dimension ℓ, namely $R_\ell = \mathbb{Z}[X]/(X^{\ell+1})$. (We also denote $R_{\ell,q} = R/qR = \mathbb{Z}_q[X]/(X^{\ell+1})$.) (Recall that our implementation uses $\ell = 2$, and more generally we may use slightly larger value such as $\ell = 4$.) This means that the parties' secret-key and noise vectors can now be specified using half as many scalars, so in our protocols the parties will need to commit and prove relations for half as many variables. The scheme thus needs to choose low-norm elements in R_ℓ, which is done by choosing their representation in the power basis using the same distributions $\chi_s, \chi_{e1}, \chi_{e2}$ over $\mathbb{Z}_q$. Below we use the same notations $\chi_s, \chi_{e1}, \chi_{e2}$ for both the $\mathbb{Z}$ distribution and the induced distributions over R_ℓ.

2.5   The Encryption Scheme in Our Protocol

Using all the components above, we describe here explicitly the encryption scheme as we use it in our protocol:

Parameters. Denote by n the number of parties and $t < n/2$ bound the number of dishonest parties. For LWE we have a modulus q, The dimension k of the LWE secrets and noise vectors, and the secret- and noise-distributions $\chi_s, \chi_{e1}, \chi_{e2}$.

We also have the redundancy parameter ℓ, and we denote $\mathsf{n} = n\ell$, $\mathsf{t} = t\ell$, and $\mathsf{k} = k\ell$. Let $\Delta = \lfloor \sqrt[\ell]{q} \rfloor$ and let the "gadget vector" be $\mathbf{g} = (\Delta^{\ell-1}, \ldots, \Delta, 1) \in \mathbb{Z}_q^\ell$, representing the element $g \in R_{\ell,q}$.

Common Reference String. A random matrix $A \leftarrow R_q^{k \times k}$.

Key-Generation. Each party i chooses the secret key and noise vectors in R_q^k, $\mathbf{s}_i \leftarrow \chi_s^k$ and $\mathbf{e}_i \leftarrow \chi_{e1}^k$, sets $\mathbf{b}_i := \mathbf{s}_i A + \mathbf{e}_i \in R_{\ell,q}$ as its public key, and broadcasts it to everyone.

Encryption. The global public key consists of the matrix A and all the $\mathbf{b}_i$'s. Let $B \in R_{\ell,q}^{n \times k}$ be a matrix whose rows are all the $\mathbf{b}_i$'s in order. Given n plaintext scalars $x_1, \ldots, x_n \in \mathbb{Z}_q$, we encode them in a vector $\mathbf{x} = (x_1, \ldots, x_n)g \in R_{\ell,q}^n$. Namely we encode each x_i as the element $x_i g \in R_{\ell,q}$. The encryptor chooses three vectors $\mathbf{r} \leftarrow \chi_s^k$, $\mathbf{e}_1 \leftarrow \chi_{e1}^k$, and $\mathbf{e}_2 \leftarrow \chi_{e2}^k$, and computes the ciphertext vectors

$$\mathbf{c}_1 := A\mathbf{r}^T + \mathbf{e}_1^T \bmod q, \text{ and } \mathbf{c}_2 := B\mathbf{r}^T + \mathbf{e}_2^T + \mathbf{x}^T \bmod q.$$

Decryption. On ciphertext $(\mathbf{c}_1, \mathbf{c}_2)$ and secret key $\mathbf{s}_i$, party i uses the approximate decryption procedure to compute $\mathbf{y} := \mathbf{c}_2 - \langle \mathbf{s}_i, \mathbf{c}_1 \rangle \bmod q$. This yields $\mathbf{y} = xg + e$ for some scalar $x \in \mathbb{Z}_q$ and small noise element $e \in R_{q,\ell}$, which can also be written as a vector equation $\mathbf{y} = x\mathbf{g} + \mathbf{e} \bmod q$. The decryptor then uses the decoding procedure from Fig. 1 w to recover the scalar x.

The discussion above implies that this scheme is correct as long as the decryption noise is smaller than $\Delta^{\ell-1}/2$, and and it offers semantic security for the honest parties under module-LWE (with leakage if χ_{e2} does not completely drown the other noise terms.)

3   Proofs of Smallness

Our scheme relies on parties committing to various vectors and broadcasting publicly-verifiable proofs about them. Some of the statements that are proven are simple linear constraints (e.g., when a party proves that it re-shared its secret properly). But most of the proofs that we use are proofs-of-smallness, when the prover needs to convince everyone that the norms of its vectors are bounded by some public bounds.

The main reason for proving smallness is that lattice-based cryptosystems only provide correctness guarantees when certain quantities are small enough. Another reason to use proofs-of-smallness is because the underlying proof systems that we use are only capable of proving constraints modulo some integer parameter P (e.g., discrete-logarithm-based commitments and proofs). To prove the same constraints over the integers, we augment these underlying proofs by also proving smallness of the relevant values, to establish that no wraparound modulo P occurs.

A publicly verifiable proof of smallness protocol lets a prover commit to a vector and convince everyone that the committed vector is smaller than some public bound. Such proofs are parametrized by the norm in question (l_2 or l_∞) and a gap parameter $\gamma \geq 1$. Completeness of such proofs for a bound b only holds when the vector of the honest prover has norm bounded by b/γ, while soundness ensures that even cheating provers cannot pass verification if their vector has norm larger than b. Such protocols can be modeled as special cases of the commit-and-prove functionality (e.g., [15]), except that the constraint enforced on honest parties is more strict than that for dishonest parties. This is captured in the functionality $\mathcal{SML}_l[\gamma]$ from Fig. 2.

Parameters: norm $l \in \{l_2, l_\infty\}$ and gap $\gamma \geq 1$

The functionality maintains a list $\vec{w}$ of (vector,commitment) pairs, initially empty.

Commitment. Upon receiving $(\mathsf{commit}, sid, \mathbf{w} \in \mathbb{Z}^d, c \in \{0,1\}^*)$ from the prover, if $\vec{w}$ does not contain any pairs with the commitment value c then add the pair $(\mathbf{w}, c)$ to $\vec{w}$, and send the message $(\mathsf{receipt}, sid, c, d)$ to everyone.

Proof. Given a message $(\mathsf{prove}, sid, c, b \in \mathbb{R})$ from the prover, if $\vec{w}$ contains a pair $(\mathbf{w}, c)$ such that
  - either the prover is honest and $\|\mathbf{v}\|_l \leq b/\gamma$,
  - or the prover is dishonest and $\|\mathbf{v}\|_l \leq b$,

then send the message $(\mathsf{proof}, sid, c, b)$ to everyone. (Otherwise, ignore the message.)

Fig. 2. The proof-of-smallness functionality $\mathcal{SML}_l[\gamma]$

3.1 Underlying Commit-and-Prove Systems

Our scheme makes extensive use of underlying commit-and-prove systems, that let parties commit to integer values and prove relations among these committed values. Specifically, these systems lets a prover convince everyone of the veracity of two types of constraints:

Linear Constraints. The prover commits to the secret vector $\mathbf{x}$, then given the public vector $\mathbf{a}$ it reveal the scalar b and proves that $\sum_i a_i x_i = b \pmod{P}$.

Quadratic Constraints. The prover commits to $(\mathbf{x}|\mathbf{y})$, then given the public offset vectors[14] $\mathbf{u}, \mathbf{v}$ it reveals the scalar b and proves that $\sum (x_i+u_i)(y_i+v_i) = b \pmod{P}$.

In our implementation we use Pedersen commitments to vectors, and small variations of the Bulletproof protocol [13]. (In this case the parameter P is the order of the hard-discrete-logarithm group.) The Bulletproof variants that we use are described in the long version [25], where we also show how to use some homomorphic properties in order to aggregate them.

We note that for the systems that we use, proving linear constraints is cheaper than proving quadratic constraints, roughly because the prover only needs to commit to $\mathbf{x}$ rather than to both $\mathbf{x}$ and $\mathbf{y}$. We therefore strive to only prove

---

[14] See Sect. 3.1 for the reason for the offset vectors.

quadratic constraints on *low-dimension vectors*, which leads to noticeable savings. The main novel tool that we use for that purpose, and which we believe will find other applications, is in showing how to use the Johnson-Lindenstrauss lemma to reduce the dimension of the vectors on which we need to perform quadratic proofs. That is, we replace a quadratic proof on a high-dimension vector with a linear proof on that vector, combined with a quadratic proof on a low-dimension one (i.e. 256-dimensional). See more details later in this section.

l_2 **Norm Proofs Modulo P.** In our scheme we often use commit-and-prove protocols for quadratic constraints to prove the l_2-norm of a vector modulo P, which is not entirely straightforward. Naively, we could try to let the prover commit to $(\mathbf{x}|\mathbf{x})$ and then directly use the underlying quadratic proofs to prove that $\sum_i x_i^2 = b^2 \pmod{P}$. This naive protocol doesn't quite work, however, since a cheating prover may commit to two different vectors $(\mathbf{x}|\mathbf{x}')$ rather than to the same vector twice. One solution could be to add linear proofs to establish that $x_i = x_i'$ for all i, but that could become expensive (as it may require commitments to each x_i separately).

Instead, after the prover commits to $(\mathbf{x}|\mathbf{x}') \in \mathbb{Z}_P^{2d}$ and publishes the bound b, the verifier chooses at random an offset vector $\mathbf{u} \in \mathbb{Z}_P^d$, and the prover uses the underlying quadratic proof protocol to prove that $\sum_i (x_i + u_i)(x_i - u_i) = b^2 - \|\mathbf{u}\|^2$ $\pmod{P}$. It is easy to see that if a cheating prover commits to some $(\mathbf{x}|\mathbf{x}')$ with $\mathbf{x} \neq \mathbf{x}'$, then this last constraint would only hold with probability $1/P$. In our implementation we let the verifier choose only a single random scalar $u \in \mathbb{Z}_P$, then use the offset vector $\mathbf{u} = (1, u, u^2, \ldots, u^{d-1})$. Again it is easy to see that in this case, if $\mathbf{x} \neq \mathbf{x}'$ then the constraint only holds with probability at most d/P.

3.2   Tails of Distributions and the Johnson-Lindenstrauss Lemma

As we mentioned above, an important component in our scheme is projecting high-dimension vectors down to lower dimension using the Johnson-Lindenstrauss Lemma. Namely, instead of directly proving smallness of a high-dimension vector $\mathbf{w}$, we choose a random rectangular matrix R, prove smallness of the lower-dimension $\mathbf{v} = \mathbf{w}R$, and use Johnson-Lindenstrauss to argue that this implies also tight approximation for the norm of the original $\mathbf{w}$. (Specifically, the distribution $\mathcal{D}$ that we use for the entries of R has $\mathcal{D}(0) = 1/2$ and $\mathcal{D}(\pm 1) = 1/4$.)

To obtain very tight bounds, we use a heuristic that roughly states that the tail of the distribution on $\|\mathbf{w}R\|$ can be bounded as if the entries of R were chosen from the zero-mean continuous Normal distribution of the same variance. A strong justification for this heuristic comes from the analysis of Achlioptas [1], who proved that for an arbitrary vector $\mathbf{w}$ and $R \leftarrow \mathcal{D}^{n \times k}$, *all the moments* of the induced distribution over $\|\mathbf{w}R\|^2$ are bounded by the corresponding moments of the distribution $\|\mathbf{w}R'\|^2$ where the entries of R' are chosen from the corresponding zero-mean continuous Normal distribution. This intuitively implies that the tails of the continuous distribution are fatter, and so bounding them will imply bounds on the discrete distribution. This intuition generally holds except that the discretization may cause some minor discrepancies that vanish exponentially with the dimension k. See more discussion in the long version [25]. This heuristic lets us use the following bounds when setting concrete parameters:

Fact 3.1. *Let $\mathcal{N}$ be the continuous normal distribution centered at 0 with variance 1, and $\chi^2[k]$ be the χ^2 distribution with k degrees of freedom.[15] Then for every vector $\mathbf{w} \in \mathbb{Z}^d$ it holds that:*

$$\Pr_{\mathbf{r} \leftarrow \mathcal{N}^d}\left[\left|\left\langle \mathbf{w}, \frac{1}{\sqrt{2}}\mathbf{r}\right\rangle\right| > 9.75 \cdot \|\mathbf{w}\|\right] = \Pr_{y \leftarrow \mathcal{N}}\left[|y| > 9.75 \cdot \sqrt{2}\right] < 2^{-141}.$$

$$\Pr_{R \leftarrow \mathcal{N}^{d \times 256}}\left[\left\|\frac{1}{\sqrt{2}}\mathbf{w}R\right\|^2 < 30 \cdot \|\mathbf{w}\|^2\right] = \Pr_{y \leftarrow \chi^2[256]}[y < 60] < 2^{-128}.$$

$$\Pr_{R \leftarrow \mathcal{N}^{d \times 256}}\left[\left\|\frac{1}{\sqrt{2}}\mathbf{w}R\right\|^2 > 337 \cdot \|\mathbf{w}\|^2\right] = \Pr_{y \leftarrow \chi^2[256]}[y > 674] < 2^{-128}.$$

Corollary 3.2. *[heuristic] Let $\mathcal{D}$ be a distribution on $\{0, \pm 1\}$ such that $\mathcal{D}(1) = \mathcal{D}(-1) = \frac{1}{4}$ and $\mathcal{D}(0) = \frac{1}{2}$. Under the heuristic substitution of $\mathcal{D}$ with $\frac{1}{\sqrt{2}}\mathcal{N}$, for every vector $\mathbf{w} \in \mathbb{Z}^d$:*

$$\Pr_{\mathbf{r} \leftarrow \mathcal{D}^d}\left[|\langle \mathbf{w}, \mathbf{r}\rangle| > 9.75 \cdot \|\mathbf{w}\|\right] \lessapprox 2^{-141},$$
$$\Pr_{R \leftarrow \mathcal{D}^{d \times 256}}[\|\mathbf{w}R\|^2 < 30 \cdot \|\mathbf{w}\|^2] \lessapprox 2^{-128},$$
$$\Pr_{R \leftarrow \mathcal{D}^{d \times 256}}[\|\mathbf{w}R\|^2 > 337 \cdot \|\mathbf{w}\|^2] \lessapprox 2^{-128},$$

where $\lessapprox$ denotes a heuristic bound.

3.3 A Modular Johnson-Lindenstrauss Variant

In some cases we need a high probability bounds on the size of $\mathbf{w}R \bmod P$ rather than the size of $\mathbf{w}R$ itself. When the bound that we seek is sufficiently smaller than P, we get this as an easy corollary:

Corollary 3.3. *Fix $d, P \in \mathbb{Z}$ and a bound $b \leq P/45d$, and let $\mathbf{w} \in [\pm P/2]^d$ with $\|\mathbf{w}\| \geq b$. Let $\mathcal{D}[0] = 1/2$ and $\mathcal{D}[\pm 1] = 1/4$, then $\Pr_{R \leftarrow \mathcal{D}^{d \times 256}}[\|\mathbf{w}R \bmod P\| < b\sqrt{30}] < 2^{-128}$.*

Proof. We have two cases:

- The first case is when $\|\mathbf{w}\|_\infty \geq P/4d$. Let i be an index of an entry in $\mathbf{w}$ with magnitude at least $P/4d$, and consider any column of R (denoted $\mathbf{r}$): After choosing all but the i'th entry in $\mathbf{r}$, at most one of the three values $\{0, \pm 1\}$ yields $|\langle \mathbf{w}, \mathbf{r}\rangle \bmod P| < P/8d$. Hence the probability that all the columns of

---

[15] The χ^2 distribution with k degrees of freedom is the distribution of $\sum_{i=1}^{k} x_i^2$ where $x_i \leftarrow \mathcal{N}$.

R yield entries smaller than $P/8d$ is at most $(1/2)^{256}$. Since $b \leq P/45d$ then $P/8d > b\sqrt{30}$ and therefore

$$\Pr_{R \leftarrow \mathcal{D}^{d \times 256}} [\|\mathbf{w}R \bmod P\| < b\sqrt{30}] \leq \Pr_{R} [\|\mathbf{w}R \bmod Pq\| < P/8d] \leq 2^{-256}.$$

– The second case is when $\|\mathbf{w}\|_\infty < P/4d$. Here with probability one we have $\mathbf{w}R \in [\pm P/2]^{256}$, so mod-$P$ reduction has no effect and the assertion follows directly from Corollary 3.2.

3.4   Approximate Proofs of Smallness

A tool from previous work that will be used as a subroutine in most of our new proofs is a zero-knowledge proof that proves that a committed vector has small coefficients. We use the approximate proofs of l_∞-smallness of Lyubashevsky et al. [42] (which also utilize rejection sampling, as is common in lattice-based proofs). This proof system has a fairly large gap between the l_∞ norm of the vector used by honest provers and what the prover can prove. But this gap will not show up in the rest of our scheme, because these proofs are only used to show that there is no wraparound modulo P (after which we use an exact proof for l_2 norm modulo P). The main feature of this proof is that the dimension of the transmitted vector is just 128, irrespective of how long the vector whose smallness we would like to prove.

To bound the size of a vector $\mathbf{w}$, the prover commits to $\mathbf{w}$ and to a masking vector $\mathbf{y}$ (chosen at random to be somewhat larger than $\mathbf{w}$), and sends the commitments to the verifier. The verifier chooses a small random matrix R, and the prover opens $\mathbf{z} = \mathbf{w}R + \mathbf{y}$ (and convinces the verifier that it is indeed the right $\mathbf{z}$ wrt $\mathbf{w}$ and $\mathbf{y}$), and the verifier checks that $\mathbf{z}$ is small. Soundness relies on the following lemma.

Lemma 3.4 ([42], Lemma 2.5). *Fix $q, d \in \mathbb{Z}$ and any two vectors $\mathbf{y} \in [\pm q/2]^{128}$ and $\mathbf{w} \in [\pm q/2]^d$. Let $\mathcal{D}[0] = 1/2$ and $\mathcal{D}[\pm 1] = 1/4$, then choosing $R \leftarrow \mathcal{D}^{d \times 128}$ we have*

$$\Pr_{R} \left[\|\mathbf{w}R + \mathbf{y} \bmod q\|_\infty < \frac{1}{2}\|\mathbf{w}\|_\infty \right] < 2^{-128}. \square$$

Describing the proof system in more detail, we use a hard-DL group of order P for the underlying commit-and-prove protocols, as follows. The prover holds a vector $\mathbf{w}$, and the verifier holds a discrete-log-based commitment to $\mathbf{w}$ (e.g., Pedersen). The goal of the protocol is to prove that $\mathbf{w}$ has l_∞ norm bounded by some known b, where for the honest prover we assume that $\|\mathbf{w}\|_\infty \leq b/\gamma$ (with γ our gap parameter).

0. We use security parameter $\lambda = 128$ and the size gap is $\gamma = 2 \cdot 9.75\lambda\sqrt{d} < 2500\sqrt{d}$.
1. The prover has a vector $\mathbf{w} \in \mathbb{Z}^d$ of bounded size $\|\mathbf{w}\|_\infty \leq b/\gamma$, and the verifier knows a commitment to $\mathbf{w}$.

2. The prover chooses a uniform masking vector $\mathbf{y} \leftarrow [\ \pm\lceil\frac{b}{2}(1 + \frac{1}{\lambda})\rceil\ ]^\lambda$ and sends to the verifier a commitment to $\mathbf{y}$.

3. Let $\mathcal{D}(0) = 1/2$ and $\mathcal{D}(\pm1) = 1/4$, the verifier chooses $R \leftarrow \mathcal{D}^{d\times\lambda}$ and sends it to the prover.

4. The prover computes $\mathbf{u} := \mathbf{w}R$ and $\mathbf{z} := \mathbf{u} + \mathbf{y}$. It restarts the protocol from Step 2 if either $\|\mathbf{u}\|_\infty > b/2\lambda$ or $\|\mathbf{z}\|_\infty > b/2$.

   If the two tests above passed, then the prover sends $\mathbf{z}$ to the verifier along with a ZKPOK that indeed $\mathbf{z} = \mathbf{w}R + \mathbf{y} \pmod{P}$.

5. The verifier accepts if the ZKPOK succeeds, and in addition $\|\mathbf{z}\|_\infty \leq b/2$.

Lemma 3.5. *The protocol above is an approximate proof-of-smallness for the l_∞ norm, with size gap $\gamma < 2500\sqrt{d}$.*

Proof. The honest prover has $\|\mathbf{w}\|_\infty \leq b/\gamma$, so by the first part of Claim 3.2 and the union bound, we have that $\|\mathbf{u}\|_\infty \leq 9.75\sqrt{d}\|\mathbf{w}\|_\infty \leq 9.75\sqrt{d}b/\gamma < b/2\lambda$ except with probability $2^7 \cdot 2^{-141} = 2^{-134}$. A restart due to this check therefore only happens with negligible probability.

Conditioned on $\|\mathbf{u}\|_\infty \leq b/2\lambda$, the rejection sampling check for $\|\mathbf{u} + \mathbf{y}\|_\infty \leq b/2$ leaks nothing about $\mathbf{u}$ (or $\mathbf{w}$), by [39]. Furthermore, using the analysis from [40, Section 5.2], the probability of the prover restarting due to this check is about $1 - \frac{1}{e} \approx 0.63$. Hence the expected number of repetitions is constant.

It is left to show soundness, so consider a cheating prover with $\|\mathbf{w}\|_\infty > b$. By Lemma 3.4 such prover has probability at most 2^{-128} of getting $\|\mathbf{w}R + \mathbf{y} \bmod P\|_\infty \leq b/2$, regardless of $\mathbf{y}$. This completes the proof.

3.5 Exact Proofs of Smallness

Using the protocol from Sect. 3.4, combined with a sum-of-squares proof, we can get an efficient exact proofs of smallness, provided that the bound b that we need to prove is sufficiently smaller than $\sqrt{P}$. Roughly, to prove that a value x has magnitude smaller than some public bound b, it is sufficient to show that $b^2 - x^2$ is non-negative,[16] which can be done by representing it as a sum of squares: After committing to x, the prover finds and commits to four other integers $\alpha, \beta, \gamma, \delta$ such that $b^2 - x^2 = \alpha^2 + \beta^2 + \gamma^2 + \delta^2$. The prover uses the underlying commit-and-prove systems to show that this equality holds modulo P, and also uses the approximate proof from above to show that the numbers are small enough so that they do not trigger a wraparound modulo P. Taken together, this means that this constraint holds over the integers, hence proving that indeed $|x| < b$.

In our implementation we actually use a slightly more general version, where the prover may wish to amortize over m instances of this problem. The upside of amortizing is that he will only need one l_∞ proof (as opposed to one per vector). The downside is that the size-bounds that we can prove this way are slightly more restricted, since the gap in the approximate proofs grows with (the square root of) the total dimension of all the vectors combined.

---

[16] More generally, to show that $x \in [a, b]$ it is sufficient to show that $(x - a)(b - x)$ is non-negative.

The protocol is described below. In this description we assume that commitments to different vectors can be combined to a single commitment for the concatenated vector (as needed for the underlying proofs systems). This clearly holds for the Pedersen commitments that we use in our implementation.

1. The prover has m vectors $\mathbf{w}_1, \ldots \mathbf{w}_m \in \mathbb{Z}^d$, and the verifier has commitments to all these vectors. For each vector $\mathbf{w}_i$, the prover wants to prove that $\|\mathbf{w}_i\| \leq b_i$ (where the b_i's are public).
   Denote $b = \max_i b_i$, and assume that $b < \sqrt{P}/(3536(d+4)\sqrt{m})$.
2. For each $\mathbf{w}_i$, the prover finds four non-negative integers $\alpha_i, \beta_i, \gamma_i, \delta_i$ such that $\alpha_i^2 + \beta_i^2 + \gamma_i^2 + \delta_i^2 = b_i^2 - \|\mathbf{w}_i\|^2$.
   Let $\mathbf{u}_i := (\alpha_i, \beta_i, \gamma_i, \delta_i)$ and $\mathbf{v}_i := (\mathbf{w}_i | \mathbf{u}_i) \in \mathbb{Z}^{d+4}$. The prover sends to the verifier commitments to all the $\mathbf{u}_i$'s, and they both combine them with the commitments to $\mathbf{w}_i$'s to get commitment for the $\mathbf{v}_i$'s.
3. The prover provides a ZKPOK that for all i, $\|v_i\|^2 = b_i^2 \pmod{P}$ (cf. Sect. 3.1).
4. The prover provides an l_∞ ZKPOK showing that
   $$\|(\mathbf{v}_1|\cdots|\mathbf{v}_m)\|_\infty < \sqrt{P/2(d+4)}.$$

Lemma 3.6. *If $b = \max_i b_i < \sqrt{P}/(3536(d+4)\sqrt{m})$, then the protocol above is correct, and a zero-knowledge proof of knowledge that $\|\mathbf{w}_i\| \leq b_i$ for all i.*

Proof. ZK follows from the ZK of the two underlying proofs.

For soundness, note that proving statement (3) implies that for all the $\mathbf{v}_i$'s we have $\|\mathbf{v}_i\|_\infty < \sqrt{P/2(d+4)}$, and therefore $\|\mathbf{v}_i\|^2 = \sum_{j=1}^{d+4} \mathbf{v}_{i,j}^2 < P/2$. This implies that statement (2) holds over the integers and not just modulo P, hence $b_i^2 - \|\mathbf{w}_i\|^2$ is positive.

The only thing left to show is that the bound $b = \max_i b_i$ is small enough to allow the use of the l_∞ approximate proof from Sect. 3.4 To prove that all the coefficients in the concatenated vector $(\mathbf{v}_1|\cdots|\mathbf{v}_m)$ of dimension $m(d+4)$ are of size at most $\sqrt{P/2(d+4)}$ using that proof, the honest prover must have all the coefficients smaller than $\sqrt{P/2(d+4)}/\gamma$, where $\gamma = 2500\sqrt{m(d+4)}$. Hence we need

$$b \leq \frac{\sqrt{P/2(d+4)}}{2500\sqrt{m(d+4)}} = \sqrt{P}/\left(\sqrt{2} \cdot 2500 \cdot (d+4)\sqrt{m}\right) \approx \sqrt{P}/\left(3536(d+4)\sqrt{m}\right),$$

which is exactly the bound in the statement of the lemma.

As a side remark, if we can tolerate a one-bit leakage on each $\|\mathbf{w}_i\|^2$, then the prover can instead find *three integers* $\alpha_i, \beta_i, \gamma_i$ such that $\alpha_i^2 + \beta_i^2 + \gamma_i^2 = b_i^2 - \|\mathbf{w}_i\|^2 \pm 1$ (such three integers always exist since every integer which is congruent to 1 or 2 modulo 4 is a sum of three squares). The prover then does the same proof as above, but sending $\delta_i = \pm 1$ to the verifier in the clear. (We do not use this option in our protocol.)

Exact Proofs of Smallness with Larger Bounds. In our scheme we sometimes need to prove exact bounds on vectors with entries that are larger than the bound above. To do that, we let the prover break each coefficients into (say) two digits of size $\leq \lceil \sqrt{b} \rceil$, commit to these digits and prove exact smallness for them separately, and then prove that combining these digits indeed yields the original coefficient.

Namely, the honest prover has a dimension-d vector $\mathbf{w}$ with $\|\mathbf{w}\| \leq b$, and the verifier has a commitment to $\mathbf{w}$. The prover uses radix $\phi \in \mathbb{Z}$, chosen as small as possible subject to $\phi^2 - \phi \geq b\sqrt{d}/2$. It breaks $\mathbf{w}$ into two "digit vectors", $\mathbf{w}^{lo} := \mathbf{w} \bmod \phi$ (with entries in $[\pm\phi/2]$) and $\mathbf{w}^{hi} := (\mathbf{w} - \mathbf{w}^{lo})/\phi$. It commits to these vectors, produces a linear-constraint proof showing that $\mathbf{w} = \rho \cdot \mathbf{w}^{hi} + \mathbf{w}^{lo}$ (mod P), and uses the exact proof protocol from above to prove that

$$\|\mathbf{w}^{lo}\| \leq \sqrt{d} \cdot \phi/2, \text{ and } \|\mathbf{w}^{hi}\| \leq b/\phi + \sqrt{d}/2. \tag{5}$$

To see why the last inequality must hold, observe that

$$\|\mathbf{w}^{hi}\| = \|\mathbf{w} - \mathbf{w}^{lo}\|/\phi \leq (\|\mathbf{w}\| + \|\mathbf{w}^{lo}\|)/\phi \leq (b + \phi\sqrt{d}/2)/\phi = b/\phi + \sqrt{d}/2.$$

Let $b^* := \sqrt{P}/(3536(d+4)\sqrt{m})$ be the bound that we need in order to be able to use the exact proofs from above. The condition $\phi^2 - \phi \geq b\sqrt{d}/2$ ensures that $b/\phi + \sqrt{d}/2 \leq \sqrt{d} \cdot \phi/2$, so we can use the above proofs as long as we are able to set the radix ϕ small enough such that $\sqrt{d} \cdot \phi/2 \leq b^*$. It is not hard to verify that when $\sqrt{b} < b^* \cdot (4/d)^{3/4} - (4/d)^{1/4}$, the two conditions $\phi^2 - \phi \geq b\sqrt{d}/2$ and $\sqrt{d} \cdot \phi/2 \leq b^*$ can always be satisfied.[17]

Combining the two bounds from Eq. (5) and the linear-relation proof, we can therefore conclude that the size of the original $\mathbf{w}$ is bounded by

$$\|\mathbf{w}\| \leq \phi\|\mathbf{w}^{hi}\| + \|\mathbf{w}^{lo}\| \leq \phi(b/\phi + \sqrt{d}/2) + \phi\sqrt{d}/2 = b + \phi\sqrt{d}.$$

Therefore, this technique induces a multiplicative size gap of $\gamma = 1 + \frac{\phi\sqrt{d}}{b}$ between what the honest prover holds and what we can conclude about the vector of a cheating prover. (In our setting this gap will be minuscule.)

We remark that when using this technique, the prover needs to commit to more vectors and prove quadratic constraints on them, incurring a somewhat higher computational cost. Also, in the amortized setting, we can deal with a mix of some "small" and "large" vectors by breaking into digits only the large vectors and keeping the small vectors intact.

Approximate Proofs of Smallness for l_2 Norm. The protocol in the previous section for proving that $\|\mathbf{w}\| \leq b$ require proving quadratic constraints on the $\mathbf{v}_i$'s to show that $\|\mathbf{v}_i\|^2 = b_i^2$, which may be costly. We note, however, that a simple application of Corollary 3.2 allows us to reduce the number of coefficients that are involved in the quadratic proof to $256 + 4 = 260$, regardless

---

[17] Jumping ahead, in our setting we have $b^* > 2^{104}$ and $d = 256$, so we can handle bounds up to $b \approx 2^{190}$. The bounds that we actually need to prove will all be much much smaller.

of the dimension of $\mathbf{w}$. The price that we pay is a small gap between what we can prove and what the honest prover actually uses (and the restriction on the bound that the protocol supports becomes somewhat smaller).

The idea is to first project the d-dimensional vector down to a 256-dimensional one by setting $\mathbf{u} = \mathbf{w}R$, for a random matrix R, and then apply the proof from the previous section to the projected vector $\mathbf{u}$. Using Corollary 3.2, an exact bound on $\|\mathbf{u}\|$ yields a very narrow range for the bound on $\|\mathbf{w}\|$. In our protocol, however, we use a more general form of this approximate proof, which is tailored to proving LWE relations, as we described next.

3.6 Proofs of Smallness for LWE

In the encryption scheme from Sect. 2.5, the prover sometimes has an LWE instance $\mathbf{b} = \mathbf{s}A + \mathbf{e} \pmod{q}$, and it needs to prove that $\mathbf{s}, \mathbf{e}$ are small. While the prover can commit to $\mathbf{s}, \mathbf{e}$ and use the proofs above, in this case we can save about half the cost by skipping the commitment to $\mathbf{e}$, since $\mathbf{e}$ is implicitly committed by seeing the commitment to $\mathbf{s}$ and knowing A and $\mathbf{b}$.

Below we describe this more efficient protocol, for the case $q = P$ (with P the parameter of the underlying commit-and-prove systems). In fact we need a slightly more general variant that includes a committed "offset vector", and as in previous sections we also let the prover amortize over m such proofs. We also use the technique from Sect. 3.5 to handle vectors with larger norm by splitting the projected vectors into high and low digits.

In more detail, both prover and verifier know public matrices $A_i \in \mathbb{Z}_P^{k_i \times d_i}$, $i = 1, \ldots, m$ and bounds b_i, b'_i, and let γ be the size gap (to be defined below). The prover has vectors $\mathbf{s}_i \in \mathbb{Z}_P^k$ and $\mathbf{e}_i, \mathbf{x}_i \in \mathbb{Z}_P^{d_i}$, where $\|\mathbf{s}_i\| \leq b_i/\gamma$ and $\|\mathbf{e}_i\| \leq b'_i/\gamma$. The $2m$ vectors $\mathbf{s}_i, \mathbf{e}_i$ are partitioned into a set L of m_l "large" vectors and a set S of m_s "small" ones (so $m_l + m_s = 2m$). The designation of which vector belongs to what set is also public.

To simplify notations somewhat, below we assume that the LWE secrets are all "small" and the noise vectors are all "large", which would be the case in our application. The protocol can be easily extended to handle an arbitrary mix of "large" and "small", but the notations get rather awkward.

Let $\beta := \sqrt{P}/(\sqrt{2} \cdot 2500 \cdot 260 \cdot \sqrt{m_s + 2m_l}) \approx \sqrt{P}/(2^{19.9}\sqrt{m_s + 2m_l})$. For correctness of the protocol below, we require that the the bounds on the "small" vectors in S all satisfy $b_i \leq \beta/\sqrt{30}$. For the "large" vectors in L, let $b_* = \min_i(b'_i)$ (i.e., the smallest "large" bound) and $b^* = \max_i(b'_i)$, and we require that $8b^*/\sqrt{b_*} \leq \beta$.

The radix for breaking integers into digits is set to $\phi \in \mathbb{Z}$, taken as large as possible subject to $\sqrt{30b_*}/\phi + 8 \geq 8\phi$, specifically we use $\phi := \lfloor \sqrt{b_* \cdot 30/64} \rfloor$. Denoting $\gamma_1 := \sqrt{337/30} \leq 3.36$ and $\gamma_2 := 1 + \frac{16\phi}{\sqrt{30b_*}} < 1 + \frac{2}{\sqrt{b_*}}$, the size-gap that the protocol below achieves is $\gamma_1 \cdot \gamma_2$.[18] The protocol proceeds as follows:

0. For all i, let $\hat{b}_i := \sqrt{30}\, b_i/\gamma_2$ and $\hat{b}_i^{hi} := (\sqrt{30}\, b'_i/\phi + \sqrt{256}/2)/\gamma_2 = (\sqrt{30}\, b'_i/\phi + 8)/\gamma_2$, and also let $\hat{b}^{lo} := \sqrt{256}\phi/(2\gamma_2) = 8\phi/\gamma_2$.

---

[18] In our setting we have $b_* > 2^{90}$, so the term $\frac{2}{\sqrt{b_*}}$ is insignificant.

1. The prover sets $\mathbf{b}_i := \mathbf{s}_i A_i + \mathbf{e}_i + \mathbf{x}_i \bmod P$ for all i, and sends to the verifier the $\mathbf{b}_i$'s and also commitments to the $\mathbf{s}_i$'s and $\mathbf{x}_i$'s.
2. Let $\mathcal{D}[0] = 1/2$ and $\mathcal{D}[\pm 1] = 1/4$. The verifier chooses $R_i \leftarrow \mathcal{D}^{k_i \times 256}$ and $R'_i \leftarrow \mathcal{D}^{d_i \times 256}$, and sends to the prover.
3. The prover computes $\mathbf{u}_i := \mathbf{s}_i R_i$, $\mathbf{v}_i := \mathbf{e}_i R'_i$. If $\|u_i\| > \sqrt{30} b_i / \gamma_2$ or $\|v_i\| > \sqrt{30} b'_i / \gamma_2$ then the prover aborts.

    Otherwise it splits the $\mathbf{v}_i$'s into digits, $\mathbf{v}_i^{lo} = \mathbf{v}_i \bmod \phi$ (with entries in $[\pm \phi/2]$), and $\mathbf{v}_i^{hi} = (\mathbf{v}_i - \mathbf{v}_i^{lo})/\phi$.
    The prover commits to all the $\mathbf{u}_i$'s, $\mathbf{v}_i^{lo}$'s, and $\mathbf{v}_i^{hi}$'s and sends to the verifier.
4. the parties then engage in the following ZKPOK protocols:
    A. Exact smallness proofs (cf. Sect. 3.5): For all i the prover proves that $\|\mathbf{u}_i\| \leq \hat{b}_i$, $\|\mathbf{v}_i^{lo}\| \leq \hat{b}^{lo}$, and $\|\mathbf{v}_i^{hi}\| \leq \hat{b}_i^{hi}$.
    B. Linear-constraint proofs for the projected LWE secrets, $\mathbf{s}_i R_i = \mathbf{u}_i$ (mod P) for all i.
    C. Linear-constraint proof for the LWE relation: For each all i it proves that
    $$\mathbf{b}_i R'_i = \mathbf{s}_i A_i R'_i + \phi \mathbf{v}_i^{hi} + \mathbf{v}_i^{lo} + \mathbf{x}_i R'_i \quad (\bmod P).$$
5. The verifier accepts if all the proofs passed.

Lemma 3.7. *Assume that the dimensions and bounds satisfy the following conditions:*

- *For vectors in S we have $b_i \leq \beta/\sqrt{30}$, and for vectors in L we have $8b^*/\sqrt{b_*} \leq \beta$.*
- *For all i, $b_i \leq P/45k_i$ and $b'_i \leq P/45d_i$.*

Then the protocol is correct ZKPOK, proving that $\mathbf{b}_i = \mathbf{s}_i A_i + \mathbf{e}_i + \mathbf{x}_i \bmod P$ holds for some $\|\mathbf{s}_i\| \leq b_i$ and $\|\mathbf{e}_i\| \leq b'_i$. The size gap for both the $\mathbf{s}_i$'s and $\mathbf{e}_i$'s is $\gamma := \sqrt{337/30} \cdot (1 + \frac{16\phi}{b^*}) \leq 3.36(1 + \frac{20}{\sqrt{b^*}})$.

Proof. ZK follows from the ZK of all the components. For completeness, first note that since the honest prover has $\mathbf{s}_i \leq b_i/\gamma$ and $\mathbf{s}_i \leq b'_i/\gamma$ then by Corollary 3.2 the prover only aborts in Step 3 with negligible probability.

We also need to show that the bounds used in Step 4A satisfy the constraints from Lemma 3.6. As we have $m_s + 2m_l$ projected vectors $\mathbf{u}_i, \mathbf{v}_i \in \mathbb{Z}_P^{256}$, we need to ensure that the bounds $\hat{b}_i, \hat{b}_i^{hi}, \hat{b}^{lo}$ that are used in the exact-smallness proofs do not exceed $\sqrt{P}/(\sqrt{2} \cdot 2500 \cdot 260 \sqrt{m_s + 2m_l}) = \beta$. For vectors in S we have $b_i \leq \beta/\sqrt{30}$ and therefore $\hat{b}_i \leq \sqrt{30} b_i \leq \beta$. For vectors in L, recall that we set $\phi = \lfloor \sqrt{b_* \cdot 30/64} \rfloor$ to get $\hat{b}_i^{hi} \geq \hat{b}^{lo}$, and since $b'_i \leq b^*$ we get:

$$\hat{b}^{lo} \leq \hat{b}_i^{hi} \leq (\sqrt{30}\, b'_i/\phi + 8)/\gamma_2 \leq \frac{(\sqrt{30}\, b^* + 8\phi)/\phi}{(\sqrt{30}\, b_* + 16\phi)/(\sqrt{30}\, b_*)}$$

$$= \frac{\sqrt{30}\, b^* + 8\phi}{\sqrt{30}\, b_* + 16\phi} \cdot \frac{\sqrt{30}\, b_*}{\lfloor \sqrt{b_* \cdot 30/64} \rfloor}$$

$$\leq (b^*/b_*) \cdot 8\sqrt{b_*} = 8b^*/\sqrt{b_*} \leq \sqrt{P}/(\sqrt{2} \cdot 2500 \cdot 260 \cdot \sqrt{m_s + 2m_l}).$$

It remains to prove soundness. Due to the proofs in Step 4 we can extract concrete $\mathbf{s}_i, \mathbf{x}_i, \mathbf{u}_i, \mathbf{v}_i^{hi}, \mathbf{v}_i^{lo}$ even from cheating provers. For each i, we can therefore define $\mathbf{e}_i := \mathbf{b}_i - \mathbf{s}_i A_i - \mathbf{x}_i \bmod P \in [\pm P/2]^{d_i}$ (so the constraint $\mathbf{b}_i = \mathbf{s}_i A_i + \mathbf{e}_i + \mathbf{x}_i$ (mod P) holds by definition). All we need to show, then, is that $\|\mathbf{s}_i\| \leq b_i$ and $\|\mathbf{e}_i\| \leq b_i'$.

Due to constraint 4C, it holds by definition of $\mathbf{e}_i$ that $(\phi \mathbf{v}^{hi} + \mathbf{v}^{lo}) = \mathbf{e}_i R_i'$ (mod P). Letting $\mathbf{v}_i := \phi \mathbf{v}^{hi} + \mathbf{v}^{lo}$, the bounds that we proved on the size of $\|\mathbf{v}^{hi}\|$ and $\|\mathbf{v}^{lo}\|$, together with the setting $\gamma_2 = 1 + 16\phi/(\sqrt{30} b_*) \geq 1 + 16\phi/(\sqrt{30} b_i')$, imply that

$$\|\mathbf{v}_i\| \leq \phi \hat{b}_i^{hi} + \hat{b}^{lo} = (\sqrt{30}\, b_i' + 8\phi)/\gamma_2 + 8\phi/\gamma_2 \leq \frac{\sqrt{30}\, b_i' + 16\phi}{1 + 16\phi/(\sqrt{30} b_i')} = \sqrt{30} b_i'.$$

Since $b_i \leq P/45 k_i$ and $b_i' \leq P/45 d_i$ then we can use Corollary 3.3. By this corollary, it must be the case that $\|\mathbf{s}_i\| \leq b_i$ and $\|\mathbf{e}_i\| \leq b_i'$ for all i, or else we would only have negligible probability of getting $\|\mathbf{u}_i\| \leq b_i \sqrt{30}$ or $\|\mathbf{v}_i\| \leq b_i' \sqrt{30}$. This completes the proof.

Using Different ϕ_i for Different LWE Equations. The protocol above uses the same radix ϕ for all the "large" vectors, adding an extra factor of b^*/b_* in the conditions of Lemma 3.7. In our application this factor does not make a difference, but it can be avoided by using a different radix $\phi_i = \lfloor \sqrt{b_i' \cdot 30/64} \rfloor$ for splitting the i'th "large" vector $\mathbf{v}_i$. This would have the effect of only requiring $8\sqrt{b^*} \leq \beta$ (rather than $8 b^*/\sqrt{b_*} \leq \beta$).

Sharing LWE Secrets Across Instances. When using the proof above in our protocol, we often need to prove multiple LWE instances for the same LWE secret. For example the same secret key is used in both the proof of key generation and the proof of decryption.

In this case, the prover will only send a single commitment to that LWE secret $\mathbf{s}$, the verifier will only send a single challenge matrix R, and the parties will only run a single exact-smallness proof for $\mathbf{u} = \mathbf{s}R$ in Step 4A and a single instance of the linear proof for it in Step 4B. On the other hand, they will run a separate instance of the proof in Step 4C for each LWE relation. The bounds will remain exactly as in Lemma 3.7 (although in this case we may have $m_s + 2m_l < 2m$).

Proofs for Module-LWE. As mentioned in Sect. 2.4, our implementation actually uses Module-LWE over a low dimension extension field $\mathbb{F}_{p^\ell}$ rather than over the integers (specifically we use $\ell = 2$).

The proofs-of-smallness protocols above can easily be extended to this case, treating $\mathbf{b} = \mathbf{s}A + \mathbf{e}$ (mod q) as an equation over the $\mathbb{F}_{p^\ell}$, which can be written as $B = SA' + E$ (mod P) in matrix notation over the integers.

Given A' and B, every entry in E can be expressed as an affine expression in the entries of S, and moreover, the entries in S are all known linear combinations of the (representation over $\mathbb{Z}_p$ of) $\mathbf{s}$. We can therefore arrange the entries of E in a vector $\tilde{\mathbf{e}}$, and get a new equation over the integers $\tilde{\mathbf{b}} = \mathbf{s}\tilde{A} + \tilde{\mathbf{e}}$ (mod P), which we can prove using the protocol above.

4   Implementation and Performance

In the long version [25] we describe how to put the techniques from the previous sections together into a PVSS scheme. We implemented the components above in C++, with operations in the Curve 25519 using libsodium and operations in $\mathbb{F}_{p^2}$ using NTL. The implementation is available under MIT license from https://github.com/shaih/cpp-lwevss. Our implementation is still quite naive, operating single-threaded, and making direct call to the exponentiation routines of libsodium without any optimizations for multi-exponentiations.

We run this program on an old server that we had access to, featuring Intel Xeon CPU, E5-2698 v3 running at 2.30GHz (which is a Haswell processor) with 32 cores and 250GB RAM. The software configurations included libsodium 1.0.18, NTL version 11.3.0, and GMP version 6.2.0, all compiled with gcc 7.3.1 and running on CentOS Linux 7, kernel version 3.10.0.

The performance results with number of parties from 128 to 1024 are summarized in Tables 1 and 2. In Table 1 we specify for each setting the time spent in each of the high-level subroutine: key-generation, encryption, decryption, proving, and verifying. We also specify there the number of scalar-point multiplications (denoted #exp) performed in each subroutine, and the total RAM consumption. In Table 2 we specify for each setting the running-time spent in some of

Table 1. Performance results with 128–1024 parties, by high-level subroutine.

# of parties	Keygen time(sec)	Encrypt time(sec)	Decrypt time(ms)	Prove		Verify		RAM
				# exp	time(sec)	# exp	time(sec)	usage
128	5.1	4.2	1.4	80392	22.9	23145	15.3	2.26 GB
256	5.2	4.4	1.4	82608	23.7	23451	15.9	2.73 GB
512	5.2	5.0	1.4	84030	25.3	24063	17.4	3.74 GB
1024	5.3	5.8	1.4	87524	28.2	24939	20.0	5.28 GB

the lower-level subroutines: In particular the time spent by vector-matrix multiplication by the CRS matrix over Z_q, and the time spend performing scalar-point multiplications on the curve.

Table 2. Running time (seconds) with 128–1024 parties, by low-level subroutine.

# of parties	Prover			Verifier		
	multiply by CRS	Point-scalar multiply	Total time	Multiply by CRS	Point-scalar multiply	Total time
128	15.2	9.6	32.2	6.1	2.8	15.3
256	15.3	9.9	33.3	6.1	2.8	15.9
512	15.8	10.1	35.5	6.4	2.9	17.4
1024	16.1	10.5	39.4	6.5	3.0	20.0

As can be seen in Table 2, only about 25–30% of the prover time and about 15% of the verifier time was spent performing scalar-point multiplications on the curve. The reason is that the number of these curve operations is linear in the dimensions k, while the number of scalar multiplications modulo q is quadratic (since we compute a few vector-matrix multiplications.) We also note that switching to a structured CRS matrix (by moving to operations over dimension-k extension field/ring and relying on ring-LWE) would have reduced the multiply-by-CRS time, making it insignificant. Implementing this optimization could yield an almost $2\times$ speedup for the prover and about $1.5\times$ speedup for the verifier. It is clear from these tables that this PVSS scheme is quite feasible, even for committees with many hundreds of parties and with our rather naive, single-thread implementation.

References

1. Achlioptas, D.: Database-friendly random projections: Johnson-lindenstrauss with binary coins. J. Comput. Syst. Sci. **66**(4), 671–687 (2003). https://doi.org/10.1016/S0022-0000(03)00025-4, special Issue on PODS 2001
2. Agrawal, S., Stehlé, D., Yadav, A.: Towards practical and round-optimal lattice-based threshold and blind signatures. IACR Cryptol. ePrint Arch. 2021, 381 (2021). https://eprint.iacr.org/2021/381
3. Albrecht, M.R., Player, R., Scott, S.: On the concrete hardness of learning with errors. J. Math. Cryptol. **9**, 169–203 (2015). https://doi.org/10.1515/jmc-2015-0016, https://bitbucket.org/malb/lwe-estimator/src/master/
4. Bai, S., Lepoint, T., Roux-Langlois, A., Sakzad, A., Stehlé, D., Steinfeld, R.: Improved security proofs in lattice-based cryptography: using the Rényi divergence rather than the statistical distance. J. Cryptol. **31**(2), 610–640 (2017). https://doi.org/10.1007/s00145-017-9265-9
5. Baum, C., Damgård, I., Larsen, K.G., Nielsen, M.: How to prove knowledge of small secrets. In: Robshaw, M., Katz, J. (eds.) CRYPTO 2016. LNCS, vol. 9816, pp. 478–498. Springer, Heidelberg (2016). https://doi.org/10.1007/978-3-662-53015-3_17
6. Baum, C., Lyubashevsky, V.: Simple amortized proofs of shortness for linear relations over polynomial rings. IACR Cryptol. ePrint Arch, p. 759 (2017)
7. Benhamouda, F., et al.: Can a public blockchain keep a secret? In: TCC (2020). https://eprint.iacr.org/2020/464. https://doi.org/10.1007/978-3-030-64375-1_10
8. Boneh, D., Gentry, C., Lynn, B., Shacham, H.: Aggregate and verifiably encrypted signatures from bilinear maps. In: Biham, E. (ed.) EUROCRYPT 2003. LNCS, vol. 2656, pp. 416–432. Springer, Heidelberg (2003). https://doi.org/10.1007/3-540-39200-9_26
9. Boneh, D., Lynn, B., Shacham, H.: Short signatures from the Weil pairing. In: International conference on the theory and application of cryptology and information security, pp. 514–532. Springer (2001). https://doi.org/10.1007/s00145-004-0314-9
10. Bootle, J., Chiesa, A., Sotiraki, K.: Sumcheck arguments and their applications. In: Advances in Cryptology – CRYPTO 2021: 41st Annual International Cryptology Conference, CRYPTO 2021, Virtual Event, August 16–20, 2021, Proceedings, Part I, 742–773 (2021). https://doi.org/10.1007/978-3-030-84242-0_26
11. Boudot, F., Traoré, J.: Efficient publicly verifiable secret sharing schemes with fast or delayed recovery. In: Varadharajan, V., Mu, Y. (eds.) ICICS 1999. LNCS, vol. 1726, pp. 87–102. Springer, Heidelberg (1999). https://doi.org/10.1007/978-3-540-47942-0_8

12. Brakerski, Z., Döttling, N., Garg, S., Malavolta, G.: Leveraging linear decryption: rate-1 fully-homomorphic encryption and time-lock puzzles. In: Hofheinz, D., Rosen, A. (eds.) TCC 2019. LNCS, vol. 11892, pp. 407–437. Springer, Cham (2019). https://doi.org/10.1007/978-3-030-36033-7_16

13. Bünz, B., Bootle, J., Boneh, D., Poelstra, A., Wuille, P., Maxwell, G.: Bulletproofs: short proofs for confidential transactions and more. In: 2018 IEEE Symposium on Security and Privacy, SP 2018, Proceedings, 21–23 May 2018, San Francisco, California, USA, pp. 315–334. IEEE Computer Society (2018). https://doi.org/10.1109/SP.2018.00020

14. Camenisch, J., Shoup, V.: Practical verifiable encryption and decryption of discrete logarithms. In: Boneh, D. (ed.) CRYPTO 2003. LNCS, vol. 2729, pp. 126–144. Springer, Heidelberg (2003). https://doi.org/10.1007/978-3-540-45146-4_8

15. Canetti, R., Lindell, Y., Ostrovsky, R., Sahai, A.: Universally composable two-party and multi-party secure computation. In: 34th ACM STOC, pp. 494–503. ACM Press, May 2002. https://doi.org/10.1145/509907.509980

16. Chor, B., Goldwasser, S., Micali, S., Awerbuch, B.: Verifiable secret sharing and achieving simultaneity in the presence of faults. In: 26th Annual Symposium on Foundations of Computer Science (SFCS 1985), pp. 383–395. IEEE (1985)

17. Costa, N., Martínez, R., Morillo, P.: Proof of a shuffle for lattice-based cryptography. In: Lipmaa, H., Mitrokotsa, A., Matulevičius, R. (eds.) NordSec 2017. LNCS, vol. 10674, pp. 280–296. Springer, Cham (2017). https://doi.org/10.1007/978-3-319-70290-2_17

18. del Pino, R., Lyubashevsky, V.: Amortization with fewer equations for proving knowledge of small secrets. In: Katz, J., Shacham, H. (eds.) CRYPTO 2017. LNCS, vol. 10403, pp. 365–394. Springer, Cham (2017). https://doi.org/10.1007/978-3-319-63697-9_13

19. D'Souza, R., Jao, D., Mironov, I., Pandey, O.: Publicly verifiable secret sharing for cloud-based key management. In: Bernstein, D.J., Chatterjee, S. (eds.) INDOCRYPT 2011. LNCS, vol. 7107, pp. 290–309. Springer, Heidelberg (2011). https://doi.org/10.1007/978-3-642-25578-6_21

20. Fouque, P.-A., Stern, J.: One round threshold discrete-log key generation without private channels. In: Kim, K. (ed.) PKC 2001. LNCS, vol. 1992, pp. 300–316. Springer, Heidelberg (2001). https://doi.org/10.1007/3-540-44586-2_22

21. Fuchsbauer, G.: Commuting signatures and verifiable encryption. In: Paterson, K.G. (ed.) EUROCRYPT 2011. LNCS, vol. 6632, pp. 224–245. Springer, Heidelberg (2011). https://doi.org/10.1007/978-3-642-20465-4_14

22. Fujisaki, E., Okamoto, T.: A practical and provably secure scheme for publicly verifiable secret sharing and its applications. In: International Conference on the Theory and Applications of Cryptographic Techniques, pp. 32–46. Springer (1998). https://doi.org/10.1007/BFb0054115

23. Gennaro, R., Goldfeder, S.: Fast multiparty threshold ECDSA with fast trustless setup. In: Proceedings of the 2018 ACM SIGSAC Conference on Computer and Communications Security, pp. 1179–1194 (2018)

24. Gentry, C., Halevi, S.: Compressible FHE with applications to PIR. In: Hofheinz, D., Rosen, A. (eds.) TCC 2019. LNCS, vol. 11892, pp. 438–464. Springer, Cham (2019). https://doi.org/10.1007/978-3-030-36033-7_17

25. Gentry, C., Halevi, S., Lyubashevsky, V.: Practical non-interactive publicly verifiable secret sharing with thousands of parties. https://eprint.iacr.org/2021/1397 (2021)

26. Gentry, C., Halevi, S., Magri, B., Nielsen, J.B., Yakoubov, S.: Random-index PIR and applications. In: Nissim, K., Waters, B. (eds.) Theory of Cryptography. TCC 2021. LNCS, vol. 13044. Springer, Cham (2021). https://doi.org/10.1007/978-3-030-90456-2_2

27. Gentry, C., Sahai, A., Waters, B.: Homomorphic encryption from learning with errors: Conceptually-simpler, asymptotically-faster, attribute-based. In: Canetti, R., Garay, J.A. (eds.) Advances in Cryptology - CRYPTO 2013 - 33rd Annual Cryptology Conference, 18–22 August 2013, Santa Barbara, CA, USA. Proceedings, Part I. Lecture Notes in Computer Science, vol. 8042, pp. 75–92. Springer (2013). https://doi.org/10.1007/978-3-642-40041-4_5

28. Goldreich, O., Micali, S., Wigderson, A.: Proofs that yield nothing but their validity or all languages in np have zero-knowledge proof systems. J. ACM (JACM) 38(3), 690–728 (1991)

29. Groth, J.: On the size of pairing-based non-interactive arguments. In: Annual International Conference on the Theory and Applications of Cryptographic Techniques, pp. 305–326. Springer (2016). https://doi.org/10.1007/978-3-662-49896-5_11

30. Groth, J.: Applied crypto: introducing noninteractive distributed key generation (2021). https://medium.com/dfinity/applied-crypto-one-public-key-for-the-internet-computer-ni-dkg-4af800db869d

31. Groth, J.: Non-interactive distributed key generation and key resharing. Cryptology ePrint Archive, Report 2021/339 (2021). https://eprint.iacr.org/2021/339

32. Heidarvand, S., Villar, J.L.: Public verifiability from pairings in secret sharing schemes. In: Avanzi, R.M., Keliher, L., Sica, F. (eds.) SAC 2008. LNCS, vol. 5381, pp. 294–308. Springer, Heidelberg (2009). https://doi.org/10.1007/978-3-642-04159-4_19

33. Jhanwar, M.P., Venkateswarlu, A., Safavi-Naini, R.: Paillier-based publicly verifiable (non-interactive) secret sharing. Des. Codes Cryptograph. 73(2), 529–546 (2014). https://doi.org/10.1007/s10623-014-9952-6

34. Johnson, W.B., Lindenstrauss, J.: Extensions of Lipschitz mappings into a Hilbert space 26. Contemporary mathematics 26 (1984)

35. Lee, J.: Dory: efficient, transparent arguments for generalised inner products and polynomial commitments. In: Nissim, K., Waters, B. (eds.) Theory of Cryptography. TCC 2021. LNCS, vol. 13043. Springer, Cham (2021). https://doi.org/10.1007/978-3-030-90453-1_1

36. Libert, B., Ling, S., Mouhartem, F., Nguyen, K., Wang, H.: Zero-knowledge arguments for matrix-vector relations and lattice-based group encryption. In: International Conference on the Theory and Application of Cryptology and Information Security, pp. 101–131. Springer (2016). https://doi.org/10.1007/978-3-662-53890-6_4

37. Lindell, Y., Nof, A.: Fast secure multiparty ECDSA with practical distributed key generation and applications to cryptocurrency custody. In: ACM CCS 18, pp. 1837–1854. ACM Press (2018). https://doi.org/10.1145/3243734.3243788

38. Lyubashevsky, V.: Lattice-based identification schemes secure under active attacks. In: Cramer, R. (ed.) PKC 2008. LNCS, vol. 4939, pp. 162–179. Springer, Heidelberg (2008). https://doi.org/10.1007/978-3-540-78440-1_10

39. Lyubashevsky, V.: Fiat-Shamir with aborts: applications to lattice and factoring-based signatures. In: Matsui, M. (ed.) ASIACRYPT 2009. LNCS, vol. 5912, pp. 598–616. Springer, Heidelberg, December 2009. https://doi.org/10.1007/978-3-642-10366-7_35

40. Lyubashevsky, V.: Basic lattice cryptography: encryption and Fiat-Shamir signatures. https://www.tinyurl.com/latticesurvey. Accessed Apr 2021 (2020)

41. Lyubashevsky, V., Nguyen, N.K., Seiler, G.: Practical lattice-based zero-knowledge proofs for integer relations. In: CCS, pp. 1051–1070. ACM (2020). https://doi.org/10.1145/3372297.3417894

42. Lyubashevsky, V., Nguyen, N.K., Seiler, G.: Shorter lattice-based zero-knowledge proofs via one-time commitments. In: Garay, J.A. (ed.) Public-Key Cryptography - PKC 2021, Part I. Lecture Notes in Computer Science, vol. 12710, pp. 215–241. Springer (2021). https://doi.org/10.1007/978-3-030-75245-3_9

43. Melchor, C.A., Barrier, J., Fousse, L., Killijian, M.O.: XPIR: private information retrieval for everyone. Proc. Privacy Enhancing Technol. **2016**, 155–174 (2016)

44. Olumofin, F., Goldberg, I.: Revisiting the computational practicality of private information retrieval. In: Danezis, G. (ed.) FC 2011. LNCS, vol. 7035, pp. 158–172. Springer, Heidelberg (2012). https://doi.org/10.1007/978-3-642-27576-0_13

45. Paillier, P.: Public-key cryptosystems based on composite degree residuosity classes. In: Stern, J. (ed.) EUROCRYPT 1999. LNCS, vol. 1592, pp. 223–238. Springer, Heidelberg (1999). https://doi.org/10.1007/3-540-48910-X_16

46. Parno, B., Howell, J., Gentry, C., Raykova, M.: Pinocchio: nearly practical verifiable computation. In: 2013 IEEE Symposium on Security and Privacy, pp. 238–252. IEEE (2013). https://doi.org/10.1109/SP.2013.47

47. Peikert, C., Vaikuntanathan, V., Waters, B.: A framework for efficient and composable oblivious transfer. In: Wagner, D.A. (ed.) Advances in Cryptology - CRYPTO 2008, 28th Annual International Cryptology Conference, Santa Barbara, CA, USA, 17–21 August 2008. Proceedings. Lecture Notes in Computer Science, vol. 5157, pp. 554–571. Springer (2008). https://doi.org/10.1007/978-3-540-85174-5_31

48. Rambaud, M., Urban, A.: Almost-asynchronous MPC under honest majority, revisited. IACR Cryptol. ePrint Arch. **2021**, 503 (2021)

49. Regev, O.: On lattices, learning with errors, random linear codes, and cryptography. J. ACM **56**(6), 34:1–34:40 (2009). http://doi.acm.org/10.1145/1568318.1568324

50. Reyzin, L., Smith, A., Yakoubov, S.: Turning hate into love: compact homomorphic ad hoc threshold encryption for scalable MPC. In: International Symposium on Cyber Security Cryptography and Machine Learning, pp. 361–378. Springer (2021). https://doi.org/10.1007/978-3-030-78086-9_27

51. Ruiz, A., Villar, J.L.: Publicly verifiable secret sharing from Paillier's cryptosystem. In: WEWoRC 2005-Western European Workshop on Research in Cryptology. Gesellschaft für Informatik eV (2005)

52. Schoenmakers, B.: A simple publicly verifiable secret sharing scheme and its application to electronic voting. In: Annual International Cryptology Conference, pp. 148–164. Springer (1999). https://doi.org/10.1007/3-540-48405-1_10

53. Sion, R., Carbunar, B.: On the computational practicality of private information retrieval. In: Proceedings of the Network and Distributed Systems Security Symposium, pp. 2006–06. Internet Society (2007)

54. Stadler, M.: Publicly verifiable secret sharing. In: Advances in Cryptology - EUROCRYPT '96, International Conference on the Theory and Application of Cryptographic Techniques, 12–16 May 1996, Saragossa, Spain, Proceeding. Lecture Notes in Computer Science, vol. 1070, pp. 190–199. Springer (1996). https://doi.org/10.1007/3-540-68339-9_17

55. Wu, T.Y., Tseng, Y.M.: A pairing-based publicly verifiable secret sharing scheme. J. Syst. Sci. Complex. **24**(1), 186–194 (2011)

56. Young, A., Yung, M.: A PVSS as hard as discrete log and shareholder separability. In: Kim, K. (ed.) PKC 2001. LNCS, vol. 1992, pp. 287–299. Springer, Heidelberg (2001). https://doi.org/10.1007/3-540-44586-2_21

Homomorphic Encryption

Sine Series Approximation of the Mod Function for Bootstrapping of Approximate HE

Charanjit S. Jutla$^{(\boxtimes)}$ and Nathan Manohar

IBM T. J. Watson Research Center, Yorktown Heights, NY, USA
csjutla@us.ibm.com, nmanohar@ibm.com

Abstract. While it is well known that the sawtooth function has a point-wise convergent Fourier series, the rate of convergence is not the best possible for the application of approximating the mod function in small intervals around multiples of the modulus. We show a different sine series, such that the sine series of order n has error $O(\epsilon^{2n+1})$ for approximating the mod function in ϵ-sized intervals around multiples of the modulus. Moreover, the resulting polynomial, after Taylor series approximation of the sine function, has small coefficients, and the whole polynomial can be computed at a precision that is only slightly larger than $-(2n+1)\log\epsilon$, the precision of approximation being sought. This polynomial can then be used to approximate the mod function to almost arbitrary precision, and hence allows practical CKKS-HE bootstrapping with arbitrary precision. We validate our approach by an implementation and obtain 100 bit precision bootstrapping as well as improvements over prior work even at lower precision.

1 Introduction

The work of [8,9] presented a new homomorphic encryption (HE) scheme for approximate arithmetic (called the CKKS-HE scheme) over real/complex numbers. The CKKS-HE scheme was considerably more efficient than other schemes for approximately evaluating arithmetic circuits and leveraged properties of approximate arithmetic to achieve these efficiency gains. One of the key insights was to treat the homomorphic encryption error as part of the approximate arithmetic error, and, thus, no additional mechanism was required to round away the homomorphic encryption error after decryption. The CKKS-HE scheme has found many applications, among them privacy-preserving machine learning and secure genome analysis (see [4,15–17,19,22] for some examples).

However, the initial CKKS-HE scheme was only capable of evaluating low-depth circuits since it lacked a bootstrapping procedure to "refresh" the ciphertext modulus to enable further homomorphic computation. This was remedied when [7] introduced the first bootstrapping procedure for the CKKS-HE scheme.

N. Manohar—Work done while this author was at the University of California, Los Angeles.

O. Dunkelman and S. Dziembowski (Eds.): EUROCRYPT 2022, LNCS 13275, pp. 491–520, 2022.
https://doi.org/10.1007/978-3-031-06944-4_17

This involved viewing a ciphertext ct with a small modulus q as a ciphertext with respect to the largest modulus q_L and then homomorphically computing coefficient rounding modulo q to obtain a new ciphertext ct' that encrypts approximately the same message as ct with respect to a larger modulus q_ℓ, enabling further homomorphic computation. Thus, a challenge here is to compute the mod function homomorphically, which is not easily representable via an arithmetic circuit. In fact, the mod function modulo q on the interval $[-Kq, Kq]$ for some integer K is not even a continuous function. However, [7] made the clever observation that in the CKKS-HE scheme, we have an upper bound m on the size of the message, which can be made much smaller than q. In this situation, we actually only need to be able to compute the mod function on points in $[-Kq, Kq]$ that are a distance at most m from a multiple of q. In this case, the mod function is periodic with period q and is linear on each of the small intervals around a multiple of q. Figure 1 shows the mod function along with the small intervals for approximation.

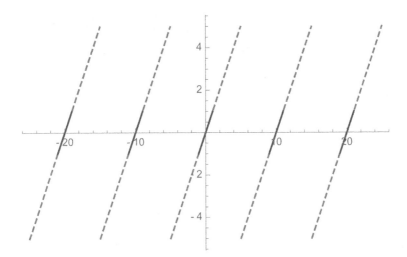

Fig. 1. The mod function with modulus $q = 10$. The solid red lines represent the small intervals on which we need to approximate. (Color figure online)

The work of [7] further observed that the mod function $[t]_q$ on these intervals can be approximated via a scaled sine function $S(t) = \frac{q}{2\pi} \sin\left(\frac{2\pi t}{q}\right)$. This approximation introduces an inherent error that depends on the message upper bound m. Let ϵ denote the ratio $\frac{m}{q}$. Then, it can be shown that

$$|[t]_q - S(t)| \leq \frac{2\pi^2}{3} q\epsilon^3.$$

If ϵ is small enough, then this error can be sufficiently small for use in bootstrapping provided that $S(t)$ can be well-approximated by a low degree polynomial. The work of [7] along with several followup works [6,12] proceeded to provide methods of approximating this scaled sine function (or scaled cosine function in the case of [12]) by a low-degree polynomial, which can then be plugged into the bootstrapping procedure of [7]. However, due to the inherent error between the mod function $[t]_q$ and the scaled sine function $S(t)$, this approach has a "fundamental error" that will occur regardless of how $S(t)$ is approximated. One of the problems with this is that in order for the error to be $O(1)$ (and, therefore, not destroy the message), m must be $O(q^{2/3})$. This means that we must begin bootstrapping while the size of the encrypted message is considerably smaller than q, which is a source of inefficiency in the bootstrapping procedure, particularly in applications that require high precision. An even greater problem is that when homomorphically computing the mod function, we must treat $qI + m$ for some integer I as the input, which we refer to as the bootstrapping plaintext. The issue with this is that if q is significantly larger than m, then since the number of modulus bits "consumed" by each homomorphic multiplication of the mod function is the size of the bootstrapping plaintext, these homomorphic multiplications will consume significantly more modulus bits than normal homomorphic operations. Thus, it is *inefficient* to obtain high-precision bootstrapping by simply increasing q to decrease ϵ. Instead, in order to obtain high-precision bootstrapping, it is beneficial to obtain good polynomial approximations to the mod function for fixed ϵ. An additional challenge to obtaining high-precision bootstrapping is that the approximation to the mod function must be representable by a *low-degree* polynomial. If the degree of the polynomial is too high, evaluating it homomorphically may consume almost all of the ciphertext modulus, leaving the ciphertext after bootstrapping incapable of performing many homomorphic operations. Compounding this challenge is the fact that the coefficients of the low-degree polynomial approximation to the mod function must additionally be small. This is because if the coefficients are large, when evaluating the polynomial, the basis polynomials must be computed to higher precision to ensure the stability of the computation, since errors introduced by approximate arithmetic are amplified by large coefficients.

The reason obtaining high-precision bootstrapping for CKKS-HE is important is that one of the main applications for CKKS-HE is privacy-preserving machine learning. However, many ML algorithms require high precision computation in order to converge. This may be especially true during the learning phase of neural networks, which involves back propagation and integer division by private integers. Additional nonlinear steps involve pooling functions, threshold functions, etc. Moreover, due to their high depth, computing these ML algorithms homomorphically without bootstrapping is infeasible. Thus, for privacy-preserving ML applications, high-precision bootstrapping is required.

Recently, the works of [18] and [13] were able to bypass the "fundamental error" in the approximation of the mod function by a scaled sine function to obtain higher-precision bootstrapping. [18] attempts to avoid the scaled sine function by finding the optimal minimax polynomial of a fixed degree that approximates the mod function via algorithmic search. They use a variant of the Remez algorithm [21] to obtain an approximation to the optimal minimax polynomial of a given degree that approximates the modular reduction function on the union of intervals containing points close to multiples of q. Unfortunately, as observed by [18], the size of the coefficients of these polynomials are too large to enable high-precision bootstrapping. They then show that by using a composition of sine/cosine and the inverse sine function and using the Remez algorithm to algorithmically search for good polynomial approximations to these functions, one can obtain higher-precision bootstrapping, but their bootstrapping method has only been shown to obtain 40 bit message precision in the latest version of their work. [13] avoids the "fundamental error" by finding direct polynomial approximations of the mod function on small intervals around the modulus via a new technique called modular Lagrange interpolation. The coefficients of these polynomials were small enough to enable high-precision bootstrapping. However, the coefficients were still large enough that in order to evaluate the polynomial approximations, one would need to operate at a higher precision than the bootstrapping plaintext. Ultimately, this fact corresponded to the bootstrapping procedure losing additional levels, since the computations during bootstrapping were operating at a higher precision. The authors are able to obtain 67 bit precision bootstrapping in the latest version of their work.

1.1   This Work

In this work, we show how to obtain arbitrary precision bootstrapping via a different method from that of [13] and more in line with the original sine function approach of [7]. Instead of approximating the mod function directly, we first approximate the mod function by a sine series and then approximate the sine function by its Taylor series (more precisely, the Taylor series of e^{ix}). This is then followed by a series of squarings to approximate the other terms in the sine series. We show that the sine series converges to the mod function in small intervals around the modulus. In particular, our sine series of order n has error $O(\epsilon^{2n+1})$ for approximating the mod function in ϵ-sized intervals around multiples of the modulus.

Thus, we avoid the fundamental error of the scaled sine approach and are able to obtain an approximation with arbitrarily small error in the desired intervals. Furthermore, the coefficients of the sine series are small (in fact, they have norm <2). This, combined with the fact that the Taylor series expansion of $\sin x$ has small coefficients, leads to a polynomial approximation of the mod function with small coefficients. Due to these small coefficients, the whole polynomial can be computed at a precision only slightly larger than $(-2n-1)\log \epsilon$, the precision of the approximation being sought.

We validate our approach by an implementation and obtain 100 bit precision bootstrapping as well as improvements over prior work even at lower precision.

1.2   Problem Overview

Here, we provide a brief overview of the challenges of approximating the mod function for use in CKKS-HE bootstrapping. We provide a thorough overview of the bootstrapping procedure in Sect. 3. The goal of CKKS-HE bootstrapping is to take a ciphertext ct at the lowest level and bring it up to the highest level so that homomorphic computation can continue. In other words, we wish to obtain a ciphertext ct′ such that

$$\langle \mathsf{ct}, \mathsf{sk} \rangle \bmod q \approx \langle \mathsf{ct}', \mathsf{sk} \rangle \bmod q_\ell,$$

where q is the lowest level modulus and q_ℓ represents a higher level modulus. Since errors accumulated during homomorphic computation are not eliminated by decryption in CKKS-HE, the goal is not to reduce the error in the cipher-text, but, rather, to increase the modulus so that more computations can be performed. If one simply views the ciphertext ct as operating at the highest level q_L, then it follows that $\langle \mathsf{ct}, \mathsf{sk} \rangle \bmod q_L = qI + m$. The magnitude of I can be upper bounded and $m \ll q$ and, thus, the challenge then becomes to compute mod q on small intervals near multiples of q (we defer additional complications such as computing on slots vs. coefficients to Sect. 3). Since CKKS-HE can compute homomorphic additions and multiplications, we need a polynomial approximation to the mod function. However, there are three crucial criteria that are relevant to the bootstrapping application.

- **Error:** The error of the approximation contributes additional error to the message m, which, if large, will cause a loss in plaintext precision.
- **Degree:** The degree of the polynomial approximation determines the multiplicative depth required to evaluate it. A larger multiplicative depth corresponds to losing more modulus levels and, thus, if too large, the polynomial will not be able to be evaluated homomorphically.
- **Coefficient Magnitude:** The size of the coefficients of the polynomial approximation determine the "evaluation precision" at which one must operate during bootstrapping. Larger coefficients correspond to a larger "evaluation precision" in order to maintain numerical stability, which, in turn, corresponds to losing more modulus bits per level.

Thus, it is critical that we obtain good low-degree polynomial approximations to the mod function in small intervals around multiples of the modulus that additionally have small coefficients. Moreover, as discussed previously, it is important the ratio $m/q = \epsilon$ is not too small, since then the size of the bootstrapping plaintext $qI + m$ will be significantly larger than m, and homomorphically evaluating the approximation to the mod function will consume a large number of modulus bits. Thus, one can think of ϵ as fixed to be, say 2^{-10}.

1.3   Sine Series

As mentioned previously, several prior approaches to CKKS-HE bootstrapping approximated the mod function via a scaled sine function. For simplicity, we will ignore the scaling for the moment and try to obtain a good approximation to the mod 2π function. Thus, prior works used $\sin x$ as an approximation of this function and noted that, for $|x| < \epsilon$, the error of approximation is $O(\epsilon^3)$. It is well-known that the Fourier series of the mod function (or sawtooth function) converges everywhere except the discontinuities. Unfortunately, the rate of convergence is too slow, and the Fourier series does not give a good approximation when the number of terms is small. Instead, we will approximate the mod function by a different sine series such that it converges to the mod function near multiples of the modulus very quickly. As a warmup, suppose we added a $\sin 2x$ term to our approximation of the mod function. If we can determine coefficients β_1 and β_2 such that the Taylor series expansion of $\beta_1 \sin x + \beta_2 \sin 2x$ is $x + x^5 p(x)$ for some polynomial $p(x)$, then for $|x| < \epsilon$, the error of approximation is $O(\epsilon^5)$, an improvement on $\sin x$. Thus, looking at the x and x^3 terms in the Taylor series expansions of $\sin x$ and $\sin 2x$, we wish to determine β_1, β_2 such that $\beta_1 + 2\beta_2 = 1$ (so that the coefficient of x is 1) and $\beta_1 + 2^3\beta_2 = 0$ (so that the coefficient of x^3 is 0). This can be solved to yield $\beta_1 = 4/3, \beta_2 = -1/6$. This intuition can then be extended to give an n-term sine series with error $O(\epsilon^{2n+1})$. We will show that the β_i's are small and, thus, the resulting low-degree polynomial approximation has small coefficients. Moreover, we will show that the constants hiding in the big-O notation are reasonable, and the dependence on n is minor.

1.4 On Approximating Arcsine

An alternative way to view our result is that having computed the periodic function $\sin x$, our sine series allows us to compute arcsin (of $\sin x$) using an angle-multiplication computation. In other words, since we showed above that $x = 4/3 \sin x - 1/6 \sin 2x + O(x^5)$ (for small x, and hence small $\sin x$), then equivalently $\arcsin y = 4/3\, y - 1/6\, d(y) + O(y^5)$, where d is a function such that $d(\sin x) = \sin 2x$. However, $d(\sin x)$ is not a simple polynomial function of $\sin x$ (as opposed to the easy double-angle formula for $\cos x$), and this way of computing $\arcsin y$ cannot use a simple polynomial of y. While good polynomial approximations of $\arcsin y$ might exist (for small y), there seems no simple methodology to obtain this. Instead, [18] use the Remez algorithm to obtain a best fit low degree polynomial approximation of arcsin. This algorithmic approach has the drawback that while the polynomial degree maybe small, the coefficients of the polynomial output by Remez algorithm can be of arbitrary size. Fortunately, [18] report that the coefficients are small enough to obtain 40-bit precision bootstrapping, although it is not clear if this holds in general.

Our approach is different, as we utilize the potential of CKKS-HE to compute on complex numbers. Thus, instead of first computing $\sin x$ and then its arcsin, we first compute the periodic function e^{ix} (using its Taylor series approximation) and then compute its logarithm. Thus, given that $x = 4/3 \sin x - 1/6 \sin 2x + O(x^5)$, we also get that $x = \text{Im}(4/3\, e^{ix} - 1/6\, e^{2ix}) + O(x^5)$ (for small x). Most importantly, it is a polynomial in its argument (i.e. e^{ix}) with small coefficients. Thus, this allows for an easy homomorphic computation.

1.5   Organization

In Sect. 2, we formalize the above intuition and prove explicit error bounds for the sine series approximation of the mod function. In Sect. 3, we overview the bootstrapping procedure for CKKS-HE. In Sect. 4, we explain how to approximate the sine series by a low-degree polynomial for bootstrapping. In Sect. 5, we implement bootstrapping using our sine series approximation and give performance metrics and comparisons with prior approaches.

2   Sine Series Approximation

In this section, we will show the following theorem and corollaries, giving a sine series approximation to the mod function in small intervals around the modulus that can be used for CKKS-HE bootstrapping.

Theorem 1. *For every $n \geq 1$, there exists a sequence of rational numbers $\beta_1, \ldots \beta_n$ such that for every ϵ, $0 < \epsilon < 2/\sqrt{n}$, for every $|x| < \epsilon$,*

$$\left| x - \sum_{k=1}^{n} \beta_k \sin(kx) \right| < e^2 * (n+1) * (\epsilon/2)^{2n+1}$$

Using the periodicity of the sine function, we immediately arrive at the following corollary.

Corollary 1. *For every $n \geq 1$, there exists a sequence of rational numbers $\beta_1, \ldots \beta_n$ such that for every ϵ, $0 < \epsilon < 2/\sqrt{n}$, for every integer m, for every x such that $|x - 2m\pi| < \epsilon$,*

$$\left| (x \bmod 2\pi) - \sum_{k=1}^{n} \beta_k \sin(kx) \right| < e^2 * (n+1) * (\epsilon/2)^{2n+1}$$

A further simple manipulation leads to the following scaled version of the corollary.

Corollary 2. *For every $n \geq 1$, there exists a sequence of rational numbers $\beta_1, \ldots \beta_n$ such that for every ϵ, $0 < \epsilon < \frac{1}{\pi\sqrt{n}}$, for every integer $q \geq 1$, for every integer m, for every x such that $|x - m * q| < \epsilon * q$,*

$$\left| (x \bmod q) - \frac{q}{2\pi} * \sum_{k=1}^{n} \beta_k \sin(2\pi k * x/q) \right| < \frac{e^2 * q}{2\pi} * (n+1) * (\epsilon\pi)^{2n+1}$$

Determining the β_i's: To prove Theorem 1, for each n, we will determine the rational numbers $\{\beta_i\}_{i \in [n]}$. In particular, these are *not* the same as the Fourier coefficients of the sawtooth function, as we are focused on x that is potentially much smaller than the period of the sawtooth function. Recall that we wish to determine $\{\beta_i\}_{i \in [n]}$ such that the resulting sine series has a Taylor series expansion of the form $x + x^{2n+1}p(x)$ for some polynomial $p(x)$. In particular, there are no terms of degree $< 2n + 1$ (except for x). These constraints give a system of equations that can be solved to determine the β_i's.

We begin by formalizing this intuition. For every $n > 0$, for every sequence of n distinct integers $\mathbf{a} = (a_1, ..., a_n)$, let $V^{(n)}(\mathbf{a})$ denote the Vandermonde matrix of $\mathbf{a}$, i.e. it is the $n \times n$ matrix with the (i,j)-th element a_i^{j-1} (for $i,j \in [1..n]$). Define $S^{(n)}(\mathbf{a})$ to be the $n \times n$ matrix with the (i,j)-th element a_i^{2j-1}, i.e. each row is the odd powers of the elements of $\mathbf{a}$. Note that the first column of this matrix is just $\mathbf{a}$. Also, define a related matrix $\hat{S}^{(n)}(\mathbf{a})$ to be the $n \times n$ matrix which is same as $S^{(n)}(\mathbf{a})$ except that the first column (i.e. $\mathbf{a}$) is replaced by $(2n+1)$-th powers of $\mathbf{a}$. In other words, the $(i,1)$-th element of this matrix is $a_i^{(2n+1)}$.

Let $\boldsymbol{\beta} = (\beta_1, \beta_2, \dots, \beta_n)$ be an n-vector of rational numbers. For the sine series approximation, we would like to determine $\boldsymbol{\beta}$ so that the transpose of the matrix $S^{(n)}(\mathbf{a})$ multiplied by $\boldsymbol{\beta}$ is a vector with all entries zero except the first, which is one. Since β_i refers to the coefficient of the $\sin(a_i x)$ term in the sine series, the above requirement ensures that when we Taylor expand each sine term in the sine series about the origin (or a multiple of 2π) and sum the terms, the resulting polynomial will be $x + x^{2n+1}p(x)$ for some polynomial $p(x)$. Thus, the $x^3, x^5, \dots, x^{2n-1}$ terms in the Taylor series expansions of the $\sin(ix)$'s cancel out. We note that since our sine series will include $\sin x, \sin 2x, \sin 3x, \dots$ terms, we will later instantiate $\mathbf{a}$ with $(1, 2, \dots, n)$. The required condition is drawn below.

$$
\begin{pmatrix} a_1 & a_2 & \cdots & a_n \\ a_1^3 & a_2^3 & \cdots & a_n^3 \\ & & \vdots & \\ a_1^{2n-1} & a_2^{2n-1} & \cdots & a_n^{2n-1} \end{pmatrix} \cdot \begin{pmatrix} \beta_1 \\ \beta_2 \\ \vdots \\ \beta_n \end{pmatrix} = \begin{pmatrix} 1 \\ 0 \\ \vdots \\ 0 \end{pmatrix} \tag{1}
$$

Let d_i denote the $(i,1)$-th minor of $S^{(n)}(\mathbf{a})$. In other words, the list $\{d_i\}_i$ is the list of minors of the first column of $S^{(n)}(\mathbf{a})$.

Lemma 1.

$$
\beta_i = (-1)^{i+1} * \frac{d_i}{\det(S^{(n)}(\mathbf{a}))}.
$$

Proof. From the above equation, $\boldsymbol{\beta}$ is just the first column of the inverse of $(S^{(n)}(\mathbf{a}))^T$. Note that the $(i,1)$-th element of the inverse of the transpose of $S^{(n)}(\mathbf{a})$ is $(-1)^{i+1} * d_i$ divided by the determinant of $S^{(n)}(\mathbf{a})$.

We now give an explicit formula for the determinant of $S^{(n)}(\mathbf{a})$. We will also give an explicit formula for the determinant of $\hat{S}^{(n)}(\mathbf{a})$, which will be of use later. We will use the well-known fact that the determinant of the Vandermonde matrix is given by the following formula.

$$
\det(V^{(n)}(\mathbf{a})) = \prod_{i=1}^{n} \prod_{1 \le j < i} (a_i - a_j).
$$

Lemma 2. *The determinant of the matrix $S^{(n)}(\mathbf{a})$ is*

$$\left(\prod_{i=1}^{n} a_i\right) * \prod_{i=1}^{n} \prod_{1 \leq j < i} (a_i^2 - a_j^2).$$

The determinant of the matrix $\hat{S}^{(n)}(\mathbf{a})$ is

$$(-1)^{n-1} * \det(S^{(n)}(\mathbf{a})) * \prod_{i=1}^{n} a_i^2.$$

Proof. We will first focus on the matrix $S^{(n)}(\mathbf{a})$. For computing the determinant, for each row i, we get a contribution of a factor a_i towards the determinant, and the remaining matrix is then just a Vandermonde matrix with all powers of a_i^2. Thus,

$$\det(S^{(n)}(\mathbf{a})) = \left(\prod_{i=1}^{n} a_i\right) * \det(V^{(n)}(\mathbf{a}')),$$

where $\mathbf{a}' = (a_1^2, \ldots, a_n^2)$. The result then follows from the well-known determinant of Vandermonde matrices.

As for the claim for the matrix $\hat{S}^{(n)}(\mathbf{a})$, first consider a modified matrix that is obtained by moving the first column to the last. Since this can be accomplished by $(n-1)$ column exchanges, the determinant of the modified matrix is $(-1)^{n-1}$ times the determinant of $\hat{S}^{(n)}(\mathbf{a})$. Furthermore, the determinant of the modified matrix is easily related to determinant of $S^{(n)}(\mathbf{a})$ by noting that i-th row in the modified matrix is a_i^2 times the i-th row in $S^{(n)}(\mathbf{a})$.

We observe from the formula for the determinant of $S^{(n)}(\mathbf{a})$ that if the sequence of integers $\mathbf{a}$ are in increasing order and lower bounded by one, then the determinant of $S^{(n)}(\mathbf{a})$ is positive. We now show the following lemma, characterizing the β_i's.

Lemma 3. *For the matrix $S^{(n)}(\mathbf{a})$ with $\mathbf{a}$ set to the sequence of integers from one to n,*

$$\beta_1 = \frac{2n}{n+1} < 2$$

and, for $i \geq 2$

$$|\beta_i| < 1.$$

Moreover, the β_i's alternate in sign and decrease in magnitude as i increases. That is,

$$|\beta_{i+1}| < |\beta_i|$$

for all $i \in [n]$, $\beta_{2j+1} > 0$, and $\beta_{2j} < 0$.

Proof. We will show this using the formula for β_i from Lemma 1. By definition,

$$
d_i = \det \begin{pmatrix}
a_1^3 & a_1^5 & \cdots & a_1^{2n-1} \\
a_2^3 & a_2^5 & \cdots & a_2^{2n-1} \\
& & \vdots & \\
a_{i-1}^3 & a_{i-1}^5 & \cdots & a_{i-1}^{2n-1} \\
a_{i+1}^3 & a_{i+1}^5 & \cdots & a_{i+1}^{2n-1} \\
& & \vdots & \\
a_n^3 & a_n^5 & \cdots & a_n^{2n-1}
\end{pmatrix}
$$

Thus,

$$
d_i = \left(\prod_{j=1, j \neq i}^{n} a_j^2 \right) * \det(S^{(n-1)}(\mathbf{a}')),
$$

where $\mathbf{a}'$ is $\mathbf{a}$ with a_i removed. Thus,

$$
\beta_i = (-1)^{i+1} * \frac{\left(\prod_{j=1, j \neq i}^{n} a_j^2 \right)}{a_i * \left(\prod_{j=1}^{i-1}(a_i^2 - a_j^2) \right) * \left(\prod_{j=i+1}^{n}(a_j^2 - a_i^2) \right)}.
$$

We observe that every term in the above expression is positive except for $(-1)^{i+1}$ and, thus, the β_i's alternate sign with $\beta_{2j+1} > 0$ and $\beta_{2j} < 0$. It follows that

$$
\beta_1 = \frac{2(n!)^2}{(n+1)!(n-1)!} = \frac{2n}{n+1} < 2.
$$

Moreover, for $i \geq 2$,

$$
|\beta_i| = \frac{1}{i} * \frac{2(n!)^2}{(2n)!} * \binom{2n}{n+i}.
$$

Observe that $|\beta_{i+1}| < |\beta_i|$. Moreover, since $\binom{2n}{n+i} < \binom{2n}{n}$ for $i \geq 2$, it follows that

$$
|\beta_i| < \frac{2}{i} \leq 1
$$

for $i \geq 2$.

Bounding the Error: A First Attempt. Having characterized the β_i's, we now turn our focus to bounding the error between $f(x) = \sum_{k=1}^{n} \beta_k \sin(kx)$ and x for $|x| < \epsilon$. We note that $f(x)$ is an analytic function since it is the sum of analytic functions and, therefore, its Taylor series converges to $f(x)$. Thus, taking the Taylor series expansion of $f(x)$ around 0,

$$
f(x) = x + \sum_{m=2n+1}^{\infty} \frac{f^{(m)}(0)}{m!} x^m.
$$

We can bound $|x - f(x)|$ for $|x| < \epsilon$ using the Lagrange remainder term of the $2n$-th Taylor polynomial of $f(x)$. Thus,

$$|x - f(x)| = \left| \frac{f^{(2n+1)}(\xi)}{(2n+1)!} x^{2n+1} \right|$$

for some real number ξ between 0 and x. We have that

$$f^{(2n+1)}(x) = \pm \sum_{k=1}^{n} \beta_k k^{2n+1} \cos(kx).$$

Upper bounding $f^{(2n+1)}(\xi)$ gives

$$|x - f(x)| < \sum_{k=1}^{n} |\beta_k| k^{2n+1} \frac{|x^{2n+1}|}{(2n+1)!}.$$

By Lemma 3, $\beta_k < 2/k$, which gives

$$|x - f(x)| < |x^{2n+1}| * \frac{2}{(2n+1)!} * \sum_{k=1}^{n} k^{2n}.$$

This then gives an upper bound of $\epsilon^{2n+1} * \frac{2*n*n^{2n}}{(2n+1)!}$, and no better than $\epsilon^{2n+1} * \frac{2*n^{2n}}{(2n+1)!} \approx (\epsilon/2)^{2n+1} * e^{2n} / (\sqrt{\pi(n+1)} * n)$ However, we will now show that a more sophisticated, yet elementary, approach that improves upon this bound by approximately a factor of e^{2n}, essentially giving us an upper bound of $(\epsilon/2)^{2n+1}$.

A Better Bound via the Alternating Series Test. To obtain a better error bound, we will show that the Taylor series expansion of our sine series satisfies Leibniz's alternating series test. This will enable us to bound the error of the sine series $f(x)$ from the mod function by the $(2n+1)$-th term in the Taylor series expansion (the first nonzero term after x). We can write the Taylor series expansion of $f(x)$ as $x - \sum_{m=n+1}^{\infty} (-1)^m * b_m$, where

$$b_m = \sum_{j=1}^{n} \beta_j * \frac{(jx)^{2m-1}}{(2m-1)!}. \tag{2}$$

To bound the error, we will show, for any x in the domain of approximation, that the series $\sum_{m=n+1}^{\infty} (-1)^m * b_m$ satisfies the alternating series test. The alternating series test requires that the b_m satisfy the following three conditions.

1. $\lim_{m \to \infty} b_m = 0$
2. All b_m are positive (or all b_m are negative)
3. $|b_m| \geq |b_{m+1}|$ for all natural numbers $m \geq n+1$.

Theorem 2. *Alternating Series Test [Leibniz]. If the series above satisfies the alternating series test then $\sum_{m=n+1}^{\infty} (-1)^m * b_m$ converges. Moreover, for all $k \geq 0$,*

$$\left| \sum_{m=n+1}^{\infty} (-1)^m * b_m - \sum_{m=n+1}^{n+1+k-1} (-1)^m * b_m \right| \leq |b_{n+1+k}|.$$

We will show the following lemma.

Lemma 4. (Main Lemma) *For every $|x| < 2/\sqrt{n}$, the above series given by b_m satisfies the Leibniz alternating series test.*

A Naive Proof Attempt. We briefly explain why the following naive approach to proving this lemma fails. For simplicity, assume that n is odd, so that β_n is positive and β_{n-1} is negative by Lemma 3. Then, the naive approach would be to prove that

$$\beta_n * \frac{(n * x)^{2m-1}}{(2m-1)!} + \beta_{n-1} * \frac{((n-1) * x)^{2m-1}}{(2m-1)!}$$

(and similarly paired other terms) decreases as m increases, starting from $m = n + 1$. Since powers of $n * x$ are larger than powers of $(n - 1) * x$, this would eventually be true for some $m > n + 1$. However, since $|\beta_n| < |\beta_{n-1}|$ and β_{n-1} is negative (see Lemma 3), this is not necessarily true at $m = n + 1$. In fact, calculations show that this indeed fails for a few terms beyond $m = n+1$. Thus, a more advanced approach is required to prove that the Leibniz test holds starting at $m = n + 1$. We will show that the test holds for $|x| < 2/\sqrt{n}$.

Preparing for the Proof. We prove Lemma 4 in the next subsection, but first we show several additional lemmas which will assist us in the proof of Lemma 4.

Define $V^{(n,k)}(\mathbf{a})$ to be an $n \times n$ matrix, which is same as the Vandermonde matrix $V^{(n)}(\mathbf{a})$ except the last column is replaced by the $(n - 1 + k)$-th powers (instead of the $(n - 1)$-th powers).

Let $h_k(\mathbf{a})$ be the *complete homogeneous symmetric polynomial* of degree k in $\mathbf{a}$ given by

$$h_k(\mathbf{a}) = \sum_{1 \leq i_1 \leq \ldots \leq i_k \leq n} a_{i_1} * \cdots * a_{i_k}.$$

The base polynomial $h_0(\mathbf{a})$ is taken to be one. Note that the polynomials $h_k(\mathbf{a})$ differ from the elementary symmetric polynomials $e_k(\mathbf{a})$, since in the latter the summation is taken over $1 \leq i_1 < \ldots < i_k \leq n$. The following lemma is a consequence of the well known *generating series* of the complete homogeneous symmetric polynomials, but we give a simple proof for completeness in Supplementary Material A.

Lemma 5. *For any $k \geq 0$, any $\mathbf{a}$ of length $n > 0$, and an independent formal variable t,*

$$\sum_{j=0}^{k} h_j(\mathbf{a})t^j = \prod_{i=1}^{n}\sum_{j=0}^{k}(ta_i)^j \mod t^{k+1}.$$

Lemma 6. *For $k \geq 1$, the determinant of the matrix $V^{(n,k)}(\mathbf{a})$ is*

$$\det(V^{(n)}(\mathbf{a})) * h_k(\mathbf{a})$$

Proof. Fix any $k \geq 1$. Consider an $n \times n$ matrix M which is same as $V^{(n,k)}(\mathbf{a})$ except that the last row is powers of an indeterminate x. In other words the last row is $(x^0, x^1, ..., x^{n-2}, x^{n-1+k})$. Let $\mathbf{a}'$ stand for the $(n-1)$ length truncation of $\mathbf{a}$. Treating the elements of $\mathbf{a}'$ as scalars, the determinant of the matrix M is a polynomial in x of degree $n - 1 + k$. Call this polynomial $f(x)$. Since the determinant of a matrix with two equal (or even scaled by a constant) rows is zero, the polynomial $f(x)$ has roots $\mathbf{a}'$. Thus,

$$f(x) = g(x) * \prod_{i=1}^{n-1} (x - a_i), \tag{3}$$

where $g(x)$ is a polynomial (to be determined) of degree k . However, $f(x)$, the degree $n - 1 + k$ polynomial, has zero coefficients for all monomials x^j with j in $[n-1..n-1+k-1]$. If we introduce a new formal variable $t = 1/x$, then the above Eq. (3) can be written as

$$\tilde{f}(t) = \tilde{g}(t) * \prod_{i=1}^{n-1} (1 - ta_i). \tag{4}$$

where $\tilde{f}$ (resp. $\tilde{g}$) is the polynomial f (resp. g) with coefficients reversed. Note, all the zero coefficients of $f(x)$ described above imply that coefficient of monomial t^j in $\tilde{f}(t)$ is zero for every j in $[1..k]$, and the constant term in $\tilde{f}(t)$ is f_{n-1+k}, where f_{n-1+k} denotes the coefficient of x^{n-1+k} in $f(x)$. Thus, $\tilde{f}(t) = f_{n-1+k}$ mod t^{k+1}. Considering Eq. (4) modulo t^{k+1}, we get

$$f_{n-1+k} * \prod_{i=1}^{n-1} (1 - ta_i)^{-1} = \tilde{g}(t) \text{ mod } t^{k+1}. \tag{5}$$

The above equation is well-formed as inverse of $(1 - ta_i)$ modulo t^{k+1} is well-defined. Indeed, it is easy to check that $(1 - ta_i) * \sum_{j=0}^{k} (ta_i)^j$ is 1 mod t^{k+1}. Hence, we also get,

$$f_{n-1+k} * \prod_{i=1}^{n-1} \sum_{j=0}^{k} (ta_i)^j = \tilde{g}(t) \text{ mod } t^{k+1}. \tag{6}$$

Since $g(x)$ is of degree k, $\tilde{g}(t)$ has degree at most k as well. Denote by $\tilde{g}_j$ the coefficient of t^j in $\tilde{g}_j$, which is same as g_{k-j}. Then, by comparing coefficients of t^j on both sides, by Lemma 5 we get that for each $j \in [0..k]$,

$$g_{k-j} = \tilde{g}_j = f_{n-1+k} * h_j(\mathbf{a}').$$

Thus, having determined $g(x)$, we also have $f(x)$ by (3). Letting $x = a_n$, then we get

$$\det (V^{(n,k)}(\mathbf{a})) = f(a_n)$$

$$= \prod_{i=1}^{n-1} (a_n - a_i) * g(a_n)$$

$$= \prod_{i=1}^{n-1} (a_n - a_i) * f_{n-1+k} * \sum_{j=0}^{k} a_n^{k-j} h_j(\mathbf{a}')$$

$$= \prod_{i=1}^{n-1} (a_n - a_i) * f_{n-1+k} * h_k(\mathbf{a})$$

$$= \det(V^{(n)}(\mathbf{a})) * h_k(\mathbf{a}),$$

where the last equality follows by noting that the top coefficient of $f(x)$, i.e. f_{n-1+k} is the (n, n)-minor of $V^{(n,k)}(\mathbf{a})$, which is same as the (n, n)-minor of Vandermonde matrix $V^{(n)}(\mathbf{a})$, which, in turn, is $(-1)^{n+n} * \det \ V^{(n-1)}(\mathbf{a}')$.

Lemma 7. For $\mathbf{a} = (1^2, 2^2, 3^2, \dots, n^2)$, for all $k \geq 0$,

$$\frac{h_{k+1}(\mathbf{a})}{h_k(\mathbf{a})} \leq n^3.$$

Proof. First note that $h_{k+1}(\mathbf{a}) = \sum_{i=1}^{n} a_i * h_k(\mathbf{a}_{(i)})$, where $\mathbf{a}_{(i)}$ is $\mathbf{a}$ restricted to first i entries. Since a_i are monotonically increasing, it follows that $h_{k+1}(\mathbf{a}) \leq n * a_n * h_k(\mathbf{a})$, from which the claim follows.

Lemma 8. For the matrix $S^{(n)}(\mathbf{a})$ with $\mathbf{a}$ set to the sequence of integers from one to n, let β_i be given by the formula in Lemma 1. Then,

$$\sum_{i=1}^{n} \beta_i * i^{2n+1} = (-1)^{n-1} * (n!)^2.$$

Proof. With $\mathbf{a}$ set to the sequence of integers from one to n, $\sum_{i=1}^{n} \beta_i * i^{2n+1}$ is the inner product of the first column of $\hat{S}^{(n)}(\mathbf{a})$ and $\boldsymbol{\beta}$. In the following, the i-th column of a matrix M will be denoted by M_i, and the (i, j)-th entry of M will be denoted by $M_{i,j}$. Thus, using Lemma 1, we have

$$\sum_{i=1}^{n} \beta_i * i^{2n+1} = \boldsymbol{\beta}^\top \cdot (\hat{S}^{(n)}(\mathbf{a}))_1$$

$$= \frac{1}{\det(S^{(n)}(\mathbf{a}))} * \sum_{i=1}^{n}(-1)^{i+1} d_i * (\hat{S}^{(n)}(\mathbf{a}))_{i,1}$$

$$= \frac{\det(\hat{S}^{(n)}(\mathbf{a}))}{\det(S^{(n)}(\mathbf{a}))}$$

$$= (-1)^{n-1} * \prod_{i=1}^{n} a_i^2$$

$$= (-1)^{n-1} * (n!)^2,$$

where we have used Lemma 2 in the second-to-last equality.

2.1   Alternating Series Test (Proof of Main Lemma)

Having shown Lemmas 6, 7, and 8, we are now ready to prove the main lemma (Lemma 4).

Proof. (of Lemma 4) In this proof, we will fix $\mathbf{a}$ to be the sequence of integers from 1 to n. Note, each b_m can be written as $b_m = c_m * \frac{x^{2m-1}}{(2m-1)!}$, where $c_m = \sum_{j=1}^{n} \beta_j * j^{2m-1}$. We now prove the three properties required of b_m so that the series $\sum_{m=n+1}^{\infty}(-1)^m * b_m$ satisfies the alternating series test.

1. We show that b_m goes to zero, as m goes to infinity. Since n is fixed and all β_i are bounded by Lemma 3, we just need to show that for every x in the domain of approximation, for every $j \in [n]$, $\frac{(jx)^{2m-1}}{(2m-1)!}$ goes to zero as m goes to infinity. Since the domain of approximation is bounded, $|x|$ itself is bounded. Since, $k! \geq e(k/e)^k$, the above is upper bounded by $e^{-1} * (jx * e/(2m-1))^{2m-1}$, which goes to zero as m goes to infinity.
2. To show that all b_m are positive (or all are negative), it suffices to show that all c_m are positive (or all c_m are negative). As a warmup, we first focus on c_{n+1} (i.e. m set to $n+1$). By Lemma 8, this quantity is simply $(-1)^{(n-1)} * (n!)^2$ and hence is positive if n is odd, and negative when n is even.
   Let $\hat{S}^{(n,k)}(\mathbf{a})$ be the matrix that is the same as $\hat{S}^{(n)}(\mathbf{a})$ except that the first column is replaced by the $(2n-1+2k)$ powers of $\mathbf{a}$. Thus, $\hat{S}^{(n,1)}(\mathbf{a})$ is same as $\hat{S}^{(n)}(\mathbf{a})$. As in the proof of Lemma 8,

$$c_{n+k} = \sum_{i=1}^{n} \beta_i * i^{2n-1+2k}$$

$$= \boldsymbol{\beta}^\top \cdot (\hat{S}^{(n,k)}(\mathbf{a}))_1$$

$$= \frac{1}{\det(S^{(n)}(\mathbf{a}))} * \sum_{i=1}^{n} (-1)^{i+1} d_i * (\hat{S}^{(n,k)}(\mathbf{a}))_{i,1}$$

$$= \frac{\det(\hat{S}^{(n,k)}(\mathbf{a}))}{\det(S^{(n)}(\mathbf{a}))}$$

To give an expression for $\det(\hat{S}^{(n,k)}(\mathbf{a}))$, we will use Lemma 6. To use this lemma, we first relate $\hat{S}^{(n,k)}(\mathbf{a})$ to $V^{n,k}(\mathbf{a})$. Recall, the first column of $\hat{S}^{(n,k)}(\mathbf{a})$ is $(2n-1+2k)$ powers of $\mathbf{a}$. Also, for other columns, the (i,j)-th entry is a_i^{2j-1} ($2 \le j \le n$). Since $k \ge 1$, each entry in the i-th row has at least one power of a_i, and hence the determinant of $\hat{S}^{(n,k)}(\mathbf{a})$ is $\prod_{i=1}^{n} a_i$ times the determinant of a new matrix M, which has as its first column $(2n+2(k-1))$ powers of $\mathbf{a}$, and all other columns as $2(j-1)$-th powers of $\mathbf{a}$ ($2 \le j \le n$). Let $\mathbf{a}^{(2)}$ be the sequence $\mathbf{a}$, but with each entry squared. Then this matrix M is same as the matrix $V^{n,k-1}(\mathbf{a}^{(2)})$ but with the first and last column exchanged. Thus, using Lemma 6, it follows that $\det(\hat{S}^{(n,k)}(\mathbf{a}))$ is

$$(-1)^{n-1} * h_{k-1}(\mathbf{a}^{(2)}) * \prod_{i=1}^{n} \prod_{1 \le j < i} (a_i^2 - a_j^2) * \prod_{i=1}^{n} a_i^3,$$

From Lemma 2, we also have that the determinant of $S^{(n)}(\mathbf{a})$ is

$$\left(\prod_{i=1}^{n} a_i \right) * \prod_{i=1}^{n} \prod_{1 \le j < i} (a_i^2 - a_j^2).$$

Recalling that a_i is just i, we thus have that for $k \ge 1$, all c_{n+k} are positive if n is odd, and all c_{n+k} are negative if n is even.

3. We now show that $|b_m| \ge |b_{m+1}|$ for all $m \ge n+1$. We have,

$$\frac{|b_{m+1}|}{|b_m|} = \frac{(-1)^{n-1} * h_{m+1-(n+1)}(\mathbf{a}^{(2)}) * \prod_{i=1}^{n} \prod_{1 \le j < i}(a_i^2 - a_j^2) * \prod_{i=1}^{n} a_i^3 * \frac{x^{2m+1}}{(2m+1)!}}{(-1)^{n-1} * h_{m-(n+1)}(\mathbf{a}^{(2)}) * \prod_{i=1}^{n} \prod_{1 \le j < i}(a_i^2 - a_j^2) * \prod_{i=1}^{n} a_i^3 * \frac{x^{2m-1}}{(2m-1)!}}$$

$$= \frac{h_{m+1-(n+1)}(\mathbf{a}^{(2)}) * \frac{x^{2m+1}}{(2m+1)!}}{h_{m-(n+1)}(\mathbf{a}^{(2)}) * \frac{x^{2m-1}}{(2m-1)!}}$$

$$= \frac{h_{m+1-(n+1)}(\mathbf{a}^{(2)})}{h_{m-(n+1)}(\mathbf{a}^{(2)})} * \frac{x^2}{2m(2m+1)}$$

$$\le n^3 * \frac{x^2}{2m(2m+1)} \quad \text{(by Lemma 7)}$$

$$\le 1 \quad \text{(for } |x| < 2/\sqrt{n}\text{)}.$$

We are now ready to prove Theorem 1.

Proof. (of Theorem 1) Let β_k, for $k \in [1..n]$, be defined as in Eq. (1) with **a** set to the sequence of numbers from 1 to n. From the Taylor series expansion of the sine series, which converges since the sine series is analytic, it follows that

$$\sum_{k=1}^{n} \beta_k \sin(kx) = x - \sum_{m=n+1}^{\infty} (-1)^m * b_m,$$

where b_m are defined in Eq. (2), i.e. $b_m = \sum_{k=1}^{n} \beta_k * \frac{(kx)^{2m-1}}{(2m-1)!}$. Thus, by Lemma 4 and Leibniz's alternating series test (Theorem 2), we have for $|x| < 2/\sqrt{n}$,

$$\left| x - \sum_{k=1}^{n} \beta_k \sin(kx) \right| \le |b_{n+1}|$$

$$= \left| \sum_{k=1}^{n} \beta_k * \frac{(kx)^{2n+1}}{(2n+1)!} \right|$$

$$= \frac{|x^{2n+1}|}{(2n+1)!} * \left| \sum_{k=1}^{n} \beta_k * k^{2n+1} \right|$$

$$= \frac{(n!)^2}{(2n+1)!} * |x^{2n+1}|,$$

where we used Lemma 8 in the last equality.

Restricting $|x| < \epsilon$, Theorem 1 follows from the fact that

$$\frac{(n!)^2}{(2n+1)!} \epsilon^{2n+1} < \frac{((n+1)/e)^{2n+2} e^2}{((2n+1)/e)^{2n+1}} \epsilon^{2n+1}$$

$$= e * (n+1) * \left(\frac{n+1}{2n+1} \right)^{2n+1} * \epsilon^{2n+1}$$

$$= e * (n+1) * \left(\frac{2n+2}{2n+1} \right)^{2n+1} * \left(\frac{\epsilon}{2} \right)^{2n+1}$$

$$< e^2 * (n+1) * \left(\frac{\epsilon}{2} \right)^{2n+1},$$

where we have used the fact that

$$\left(\frac{n}{e} \right)^n < n! < \left(\frac{n+1}{e} \right)^{n+1} e$$

for all $n \ge 1$ and that $(1 + 1/n)^n < e$ for all $n \ge 1$.

3 Application to Bootstrapping for Approximate HE

In Sect. 1, we explained that approximating the mod function on small intervals around the modulus is a necessary step in bootstrapping for approximate homomorphic encryption (CKKS). In this section, we will briefly overview the bootstrapping procedure for the CKKS-HE scheme introduced in [7].

Notation and Necessary Preliminaries: Let M be a power of 2 and $\Phi_M(X) = X^N + 1$ be the Mth cyclotomic polynomial of degree $N = M/2$. Let $\mathcal{R} = \mathbb{Z}[X]/\Phi_M(X)$. For an integer q, let $\mathcal{R}_q = \mathbb{Z}_q[X]/\Phi_M(X)$. Using the canonical embedding σ, it is possible to map an element $m(X) \in \mathcal{R}$ into $\mathbb{C}^N$ by evaluating $m(X)$ at the Mth primitive roots of unity. Using the same canonical embedding, it is also possible to define an isometric ring isomorphism between $\mathcal{S} = \mathbb{R}[X]/\Phi_M(X)$ and $\mathbb{C}^{N/2}$, where for an element $m(X) \in \mathcal{S}$, it has the canonical embedding norm $||m||_\infty^{\mathsf{can}} = ||\sigma(m)||_\infty$.

Overview of the CKKS-HE Scheme: The CKKS-HE scheme [9] is an HE scheme for approximate arithmetic over real/complex numbers. Its security is based on the ring-LWE (RLWE) assumption. The message space of the scheme is polynomials $m(X)$ in $\mathcal{R}$ with $||m||_\infty^{\mathsf{can}} < q/2$ for a prime q. Using the canonical embedding and appropriate scaling, one can map a vector in $\mathbb{C}^{N/2}$ of fixed precision into $\mathcal{R}$. The fact that canonical embedding induces an isometric ring isomorphism between $\mathcal{S}$ and $\mathbb{C}^{N/2}$ implies that operations on the message space $\mathcal{R}$ map to the same operations performed coordinate-wise on $\mathbb{C}^{N/2}$. Thus, the CKKS-HE scheme supports packing $N/2$ complex numbers into a single plaintext and operating on them in single instruction multiple data (SIMD) manner. Please refer to [9] for more details on this encoding procedure. We will refer to $m(X) \in \mathcal{R}$ as the plaintext/message and the corresponding vector in $\mathbb{C}^{N/2}$ as the plaintext "slots."

A ciphertext ct encrypting a message $m \in \mathcal{R}$ is an element of $\mathcal{R}_{q_\ell}^2$ for some $\ell \in \{0, \ldots, L\}$. ℓ refers to the "level" of the ciphertext. In [9], $q_\ell = p^\ell * q$ for primes p and q. However, q_ℓ can be set in other ways (such as via an RNS basis [8]). The decryption structure is $\langle \mathsf{ct}, \mathsf{sk} \rangle \bmod q_\ell = m + e$ for some small error $e \in \mathcal{R}$. Observe that there is no way to remove e and some of the least significant bits of m are unrecoverable. A fresh ciphertext is generated at the highest level L. Homomorphic operations increase the magnitude of the error and the message and one must apply a rescaling procedure or modular reduction to bring a ciphertext to a lower level to continue homomorphic computation. Eventually, a ciphertext is at the lowest level (an element of $\mathcal{R}_q^2$), and no further operations can be performed.

Bootstrapping Procedure for CKKS-HE: [7] introduced the first bootstrapping procedure for the CKKS-HE scheme. Subsequent works [5,6,11,12] improved various aspects of bootstrapping, but the overall procedure remains the same. The goal is to take a ciphertext at the lowest level and bring it up to a higher level so that homomorphic computation can continue. Thus, given a ciphertext ct at the lowest level, we want to obtain another ciphertext ct$'$ such that

$$\langle \mathsf{ct}, \mathsf{sk} \rangle \bmod q \approx \langle \mathsf{ct}', \mathsf{sk} \rangle \bmod q_\ell$$

for some $\ell > 1$. For simplicity in the following, we will include the starting decryption error in the message m. That is, we will assume that $\langle \mathsf{ct}, \mathsf{sk} \rangle \bmod q = m$.

Bootstrapping is done via the following sequence of steps:

1. **Modulus Raising:** By simply considering ct as a ciphertext at the highest level, it follows that $\langle \mathsf{ct}, \mathsf{sk} \rangle \bmod q_L = qI + m$ for some $I \in \mathcal{R}$.
2. **Coefficients to Slots:** We need to perform the modular reduction on the polynomial coefficients of $t = qI + m$. However, recall that homomorphic computations evaluate coordinate-wise on the plaintext "slots," not the polynomial coefficients. Thus, we need to transform our ciphertext so that the polynomial coefficients are in the "slots." This can be done by evaluating a linear transformation homomorphically.
3. **Compute the Mod Function:** We need a procedure to compute/approximate the mod function homomorphically. This is a significant challenge since we can only compute arithmetic operations homomorphically.
4. **Slots to Coefficients:** Finally, we need to undo the coefficients to slots step. This can be done by homomorphically evaluating the inverse of the previous linear transform.

Observe that if we can approximate the mod function, then the above procedure will give us a ct' at some higher level ℓ that decrypts to $m + e$ for some small error e. Since we are dealing with approximate arithmetic, this error from bootstrapping can be absorbed into the other errors that occur during approximate arithmetic and homomorphic evaluation. We can upper bound $|I| < K$ for some integer K so that we only need to approximate the mod function on the interval $[-Kq - m, Kq + m]$, where we have overloaded notation to make m an upper bound on the size of the message.

4 Evaluating the Sine Series Approximation of the Mod Function

In order to use the sine series approximation of the mod function given by Corollary 2 for bootstrapping, we must approximate the sine series by a low-degree polynomial, since the CKKS-HE scheme cannot compute sine directly. In this section, using our sine series approximation of the mod function and the well-known Taylor series expansion of the sine function, we will give explicit low-degree polynomial approximations of the mod function on small intervals around multiples of the modulus to (almost) arbitrary precision. The resulting polynomials have small coefficients, as the Taylor series of the sine function has small coefficients, and the sine series itself has small coefficients by Lemma 3. Recall that small coefficients are beneficial in contrast to large coefficients, as in the latter case one is forced to compute the different power monomials to much higher precision in order to obtain an accurate polynomial evaluation. This, in turn, causes the computational precision that we must operate at during bootstrapping to be higher, which causes each "level" to consume more bits of the modulus. We next explain how we evaluate the sine series and then determine the degree and evaluation precision required for the Taylor series approximation of sine.

Evaluating the Sine Series: To evaluate the sine series, we first compute a Taylor series approximation of e^{ix} (recall that CKKS-HE allows us to compute over complex numbers). We can obtain an approximation to $\sin x$ by extracting the imaginary part. The other higher order $\sin kx$ terms can be obtained conveniently by computing e^{ikx} from e^{ix} and extracting the imaginary part. As for computing the Taylor series approximation of the sine function, note that the domain of approximation is small intervals around ℓq, where $\ell \in [-K..K]$ and q is the modulus. The bound K comes from the bound on the Hamming-weight of the secret key and is typically 12 to 32. If our input is $X = x + \ell q$ for some small offset x and $\ell \in [-K..K]$, our goal is to compute $e^{i(2\pi(x+\ell q)/q)}$. This then requires a Taylor series that has powers of $2\pi(x + \ell q)/q$, which can be more than one. Earlier works noted that one can instead first compute $e^{i(2\pi(x+\ell q)/(q2^r))}$ using a Taylor series expansion (for some $r > 0$) and then compute $e^{i(2\pi(x+\ell q)/q)}$ using r squarings.

Determining the Degree of the Taylor Series Approximation: Next, we must determine the degree to which we compute the Taylor series expansion of $e^{2\pi i(x+\ell q)/(q2^r)}$. The Taylor series expansion is

$$\sum_{m=0}^{\infty} (2\pi i(x + \ell q)/(q2^r))^m/m!.$$

We now determine for which range of values of $(x+\ell q)$ the above restricted to the sine terms, i.e. the imaginary terms or odd powers of x, satisfies the alternating series test (so that the partial series error can be bound by the absolute value of the next missing term). Thus, we need to determine the conditions under which

$$1 > \frac{(2\pi|(x + \ell q)|/(q2^r))^{(2m+1)}/(2m + 1)!}{(2\pi|(x + \ell q)|/(q2^r))^{(2m-1)}/(2m - 1)!}$$

$$= \frac{(2\pi|(x + \ell q)|/(q2^r))^2}{(2m + 1)(2m)}$$

Assuming $x \ll q$ and $2^r \approx K + 1$, the above holds when $m > \pi$. Thus, if the Taylor series is computed partially up to any degree $2m - 1$, then the error in the approximation of sine is at most

$$(2\pi)^{2m+1}/(2m + 1)! < (2\pi e/(2m + 1))^{2m+1},$$

which is at most $2^{-(2m+1)}$ if we require that $m > 2\pi e$.

Thus, having computed $\sin(2\pi(x+\ell q)/(q2^r))$ partially up to m terms, we now investigate the error for the higher order terms in the sine series, i.e. $\sin(2\pi k(x + \ell q)/q)$ for $k \geq 1$. If the error in the approximation of the original term is small, say $\delta \ll 1$, then the error for this k-th term is approximately $k2^r * \delta$ (as it requires $r + \log k$ squarings). Thus, the total error in the sine series due to the Taylor series approximation of $\sum_{k=1}^n \beta_k \sin(2\pi k(x + \ell q)/q)$ is upper bounded in absolute value by $\sum_{k=1}^n |\beta_k| * k2^r \delta$, which is approximately $(K+1)\delta \sum_{k=1}^n |\beta_k| * k$, which is at most $n^2(K + 1)\delta$ by Lemma 3, which, in turn, is at most $n^2(K + 1)2^{-(2m+1)}$.

Finally, using Corollary 2, the total error in the mod function approximation, for an input $X = x + \ell q$ with $\ell \in [-K..K]$ and $|x| < \epsilon * q$ for any $\epsilon < 1/\pi\sqrt{n}$ is

$$(q/2\pi) * n^2(K + 1)2^{-(2m+1)} + \frac{e^2 * q}{2\pi} * (n + 1) * (\epsilon * \pi)^{2n+1}.$$

Thus, it makes sense to have m about $-n \log_2(\epsilon * \pi)$ (which is typically greater than $2\pi e$ for $n > 1$; if this value is less than $2\pi e$, then the above analysis must be redone for potentially a larger r).

Determining the Evaluation Precision: We must also determine the precision to which to evaluate the polynomials. Setting $Y = 2\pi(x + \ell q)/(q2^r)$, we observe that the degree m Taylor expansion of $e^{2\pi i(x+\ell q)/(q2^r)}$ is simply the polynomial

$$\sum_{j=0}^m (iY)^j/j!.$$

Recall that we have chosen r so that $|Y| < 1$. Moreover, setting $c_j = i^j/j!$, the polynomial becomes $\sum_{j=0}^m c_j Y^j$, where $|c_j| \leq 1$. We need to determine the precision to which we evaluate the powers Y^j (we will first evaluate the Y^{2^j}'s by repeated squaring and then use these powers to evaluate all intermediate powers). Let Y^j denote the exact values and let $\tilde{Y}^j$ denote the approximated values (to some precision to be determined). Suppose we evaluate the powers Y^j up to w bits (and simply chop off the additional bits). Then, $|\tilde{Y} - Y| < 2^{-w}$. Computing $\tilde{Y}^2$ by squaring $\tilde{Y}$ and rounding, we have that $\tilde{Y}^2$ differs from Y^2 by at most $\approx 2 * 2^{-w}$. To see this, note that $\tilde{Y} = Y \pm \delta$, where $\delta < 2^{-w}$. Then, $\tilde{Y}^2 = Y^2 \pm 2Y\delta + \delta^2 < Y^2 \pm 2\delta + \delta^2 \approx Y^2 \pm 2 * 2^{-w}$. By an analogous argument, it follows that $\tilde{Y}^j$ differs from Y^j by at most approximately $j * 2^{-w}$. Thus, the error of $\sum_{j=0}^m c_j \tilde{Y}^j$ is bounded by

$$\sum_{j=0}^m j * 2^{-w} * \frac{1}{j!} = \sum_{j=1}^m \frac{2^{-w}}{(j-1)!} < e * 2^{-w}.$$

Thus, to obtain error 2^{-d}, it suffices to compute the powers $\tilde{Y}^j$ to precision w for $w > d + \log_2 e$, only slightly higher than the minimum precision d required to obtain this approximation.

In the above, we saw that having small coefficients c_j (and coefficients that decrease in magnitude as j increases) enabled the approximation of the polynomial $\sum_{j=0}^m c_j Y^j$ by evaluating the powers of Y to precision only a couple bits larger than the minimum precision required for the desired error. This is crucial during bootstrapping as a higher evaluation precision directly corresponds to losing more bits of the modulus during the polynomial evaluation. In contrast, suppose that the c_j's were large and bounded in magnitude $|c_j| < 2^k$ for some k. Then, if the powers of Y are evaluated to precision w, the error of the polynomial evaluation is bounded by

$$\sum_{j=0}^m j * 2^{-w} * 2^k < \frac{m(m+1)}{2} * 2^{k-w}.$$

Thus, to obtain error 2^{-d}, the powers of Y would need to be evaluated to precision $w > d + k + 2 \log m - 1$. Note the additional dependence on both k and the number of terms m.

5 Implementation

To demonstrate the applicability of our polynomial approximation to high precision bootstrapping for approximate homomorphic encryption, we updated the bootstrapping procedure of the HEAAN library [1] to utilize our sine series during the "Compute the Mod Function" step (see Sect. 3). Additionally, we updated HEAAN to use the quadmath library, since we wanted to achieve bootstrapping error smaller than the precision of a double. We ran our implementation[1] using a PC with an AMD Ryzen 5 3600 3.6 GHz 6-Core CPU.

Table 1 gives our bootstrapping results for sine series of various orders. As before, ϵ represents the ratio p/q, where p is an upper bound on the size of the message (including any errors associated from the approximate arithmetic and prior homomorphic operations) and q is the size of the modulus prior to bootstrapping. In Table 1, ϵ is set to 2^{-10}. The Hamming weight of the secret key is set to $h = 256$, so that on average K is about $\sqrt{h} = 16$. However, our implementation can handle K as large as 31. q_L denotes the modulus of the largest level, which is the modulus of a fresh ciphertext prior to any homomorphic operations. N denotes the ring dimension, which we increase as q_L increases to maintain 128-bit security [2,3,10]. Results in this table were obtained using 8 slots, and the dependence on a larger number of slots is reported below. $q_{\ell'}$ denotes the modulus of the ciphertext after bootstrapping. The reported error is the decryption error after performing bootstrapping. In other words, if the decryption before bootstrapping would have resulted in message slot value M, then the decryption after bootstrapping would result in a message slot value M' such that $|M' - M| \le \beta_{bs}|M|$. As can be seen from Table 1, for $\log_2 p = 80$ and $\log_2 p = 100$, the bootstrapping error is essentially zero. This is because the

---

[1] The source code is available upon request.

Table 1. High-Precision Bootstrapping Results for $\epsilon = 2^{-10}$. The Hamming weight of the secret key is set to $h = 256$. The errors reported are for K up to 31.

Input Precision[†] $\log_2 p$	Sine Series Order	Modulus (Fresh) $\log_2 q_L$	Ring Dim. N	Boot Prec.	Modulus (After) $\log_2 q_{\ell'}$	Error (Boot.) $\beta_{\mathsf{bs}} = \mathrm{err}/p$	Runtime[††] (secs)
30	2	1200	2^{16}	55	344	2^{-25}	22
50	3	1600	2^{16}	75	531	2^{-45}	32
60	4	2400	2^{17}	85	1008	2^{-54}	119
80	5	2400	2^{17}	105	583	$< 2^{-80}$	129
100	6	3000	2^{17}	125	843	$< 2^{-100}$	167

[†]The modulus q_ℓ of the ciphertext prior to bootstrapping is p/ϵ. The number of bits of q_ℓ is $p - \log \epsilon = p + 10$, and bootstrapping (computational) precision is set to $(p - \log \epsilon + \log_2 K) + 10$.

[††]Includes runtime of "Coefficients to Slots" and "Slots to Coefficients" steps. Number of slots fixed to be 8 so that the "Compute the Mod Function" step dominates runtime. Results reported are from an AMD Ryzen 5 3600 3.6 GHz 6-Core CPU using quadmath, NTL and GMP software libraries

bootstrapping procedure is performed at a precision that is ten bits more than the number of bits required to represent $M + Kq$ (i.e. the value which needs to be reduced mod q).

Recall that the sine series approach begins by approximating e^{ix} using a Taylor series approximation, since CKKS-HE allows computation on complex numbers. In this particular implementation, we approximated $e^{ix/K}$ to degree 63 using the Paterson-Stockmeyer polynomial evaluation optimization [20] and then performed $\log K$ squarings to obtain an approximation of e^{ix}. Below, we report results for other variants for approximating e^{ix}.

We see that our methodology is capable of achieving high precision bootstrapping, with the resulting message precision as large as 100 bits. Prior to our work, the highest precision bootstrapping of CKKS was the recent work of [13] which could achieve a resulting message precision of up to 67 bits. However, that result was only for $K = 12$ and secret key Hamming weight $h = 64$, whereas our 100 bit precision bootstrapping is for $h = 256$ and can handle K up to 31. Observe that using a sparser key (in addition to weakening security) reduces the number of intervals required for approximation, making the approximation easier. Thus, we view our result as a substantial improvement for bootstrapping in settings where high precision is required, such as the inference step of a convolution neural network or even the learning stage of the neural network. As mentioned earlier, since CKKS is for approximate arithmetic, it is only possible to have unlimited computation for stable computations that do not lose precision. However, even such stable computations lose precision in early stages prior to convergence. Thus, it is important to begin such computations with high precision and, later, one can switch to smaller precision during the stable regime.

Table 2. Timing and Error Dependence on Number of Slots. In this table $\epsilon = 2^{-10}$, $\log_2 p = 80$, and the sine series order is fixed to $n = 5$.

Num Slots	Input Precision $\log_2 p$	Sine Series Order	Modulus (Fresh) $\log_2 q_L$	Ring Dim. N	Boot. prec.	Modulus (After) $\log_2 q_{\ell'}$	Error (Boot.) $\beta_{bs} = err/p$	Runtime[††] (secs)
8	80	5	2400	2^{17}	105	583	$< 2^{-80}$	129
16	80	5	2400	2^{17}	105	583	$< 2^{-80}$	151
32	80	5	2400	2^{17}	105	583	2^{-72}	178
64	80	5	2400	2^{17}	105	583	2^{-71}	208
128	80	5	2400	2^{17}	105	583	2^{-69}	269
256	80	5	2400	2^{17}	105	583	2^{-69}	308
512	80	5	2400	2^{17}	105	583	2^{-68}	484
1024	80	5	2400	2^{17}	105	583	$2^{-66.5}$	847
2048	80	5	2400	2^{17}	105	583	$2^{-65.5}$	1477

[††] Includes runtime of "Coefficients to Slots" and "Slots to Coefficients" steps. For all rows, the mod function evaluation time is almost the same at 82 secs

5.1   Time and Error Dependence on the Number of Slots

As the number of slots is increased, the time of the mod function evaluation step during bootstrapping remains the same (assuming we use at most $N/4$ slots, so that all the polynomial coefficients can be packed into a single ciphertext during the "Coefficients To Slots" step). However, the linear transforms that send the coefficients to slots and vice versa take a substantial hit since their runtime scales with the number of slots. Since the linear transforms also involve more rotations, key-switchings, multiplications by constants, and additions, for every doubling of the number of slots, the bootstrapping error also increases proportionately. However, since our error is so low, the error for a high number of slots still remains low enough to be termed high-precision. This dependence of runtime and bootstrapping error is reported in Table 2 for one particular parameter, where the sine series is of order five. Observe that for 8 and 16 slots, our bootstrapping method gives essentially no error. However, for a larger number of slots, the error slowly increases as it is dominated by the error introduced during the linear transform steps. We note that the runtime increases quite substantially as the number of slots increases. This poor performance is due to the fact that the implementation of the linear transform step used in the HEAAN library [1] scales poorly as the number of slots increases. The work [6] showed how to improve the runtime of the linear transform step at the cost of losing more ciphertext modulus bits, but their implementation is not public. The work [5] also recently improved the performance of the linear transform step further. It would be interesting to have an implementation that combined our sine series approximation of the mod function with the linear transform evaluation algorithms of [5].

5.2   Comparison with Basic Sine and Other Variants

While the implementation results reported in Table 1 used a Taylor series approximation of degree 63 of $e^{ix/K}$, the implementation in [1] instead used a degree 7 approximation of $e^{ix/K*2^4}$ followed by 4 additional squarings. We investigated if we could use a similar approach for the sine series, as the different order sine terms are obtained by squarings of e^{ix} anyways. We found that for small precision, i.e. $\log_2 p \leq 40$, this approach can lead to a faster implementation while yielding effectively the same error. However, for $\log_2 p \geq 50$, this approach led to substantially worse error. For example, at $\log_2 p = 50$, the error increased from 2^{-45} to 2^{-30}. But, as mentioned, for smaller $\log_2 p$ we get the following improvements. First of all, the basic sine approach (i.e. $n = 1$) with $r = 4$ and degree 7 Taylor series yields an error of 2^{-19} for $\log_2 p = 30$. If the fresh modulus used is 1600 bits, then the modulus after bootstrapping has 795 bits. The time taken is 10.5 s. Interestingly, with sine series of order two, i.e. $n = 2$, using the same approach we get an error of 2^{-26}, with modulus after bootstrapping having 685 bits. Moreover, the time taken is 10.7 s. Yet another implementation, with a degree 31 Taylor series approximation, and $r = 0$, also yields error 2^{-25}, but takes time 16.5 s. However, the modulus after bootstrapping has more bits at 744 bits. Regardless, it seems that the sine series of order two with a degree 7 Taylor series and $r = 4$ seems to be beneficial at low precision.

We also experimented with different values of ϵ, in particular ϵ set to 2^{-5}, 2^{-10}, 2^{-15}, 2^{-20}. The errors at each input precision were not much different, and, in fact, $\epsilon = 2^{-10}$ seems to be the best option.

Table 3. Comparison with [18]. Note, [18] cites results for $K = 25$, whereas our results are for K up to 31.

| | [18] | | | This work | |
Key Hamming Weight (h)	Ciphertext Bits Lost	Bootstrapping Precision (bits)	Key Hamming Weight (h)	Ciphertext Bits Lost	Bootstrapping Precision (bits)
192	1080	40.5	256	1069	44
N/A	N/A	N/A	256	1392	53
N/A	N/A	N/A	256	1817	80
N/A	N/A	N/A	256	2157	100

5.3   Comparison with Other Prior Works

The work [6] followed an interesting approach of obtaining Chebyshev interpolants of the scaled sine function. In particular, using the Taylor series of $\sin(2\pi K \cos x)$, they obtained approximations of $\sin(2\pi K x)$ in terms of Chebyshev polynomials. Furthermore, this approach also leads to an almost optimal minmax polynomial approximation, as well as yielding small coefficients. Since

Table 4. Comparison with Modular Lagrange Interpolation [13]. Note, [13] cites results for $K = 12$, whereas our results are for K up to 31.

	[13]			This work		
Input Precision	Key Hamming Weight (h)	Ciphertext Bits Lost	Error (Boot.)	Key Hamming Weight (h)	Ciphertext Bits Lost	Error (Boot.)
30	64	935	2^{-24}	256	856	2^{-25}
50	64	1725	2^{-46}	256	1069	2^{-45}
60	64	1800	2^{-54}	256	1392	2^{-54}
80	64	2150	2^{-63}	256	1817	$< 2^{-80}$
100	N/A	N/A	N/A	256	2157	$< 2^{-100}$

the scaling K is already incorporated in the function, it removes the $\log K$ squarings required in [7] and in this work. However, Chebyshev interpolants do not readily submit to the Paterson-Stockmeyer evaluation optimization and while [6] did show a variant of this method, it leads to coefficients increasing in size. Thus, as explained in Sect. 3, this then requires a larger computational precision that leads to loss of many more (ciphertext modulus) bits per multiplication depth in the bootstrapping circuit. For a direct comparison of our approach to [6], we take data from Tables 2, 3 and 4 from that work, as their implementation is unfortunately not public, and note that the best approximation they obtain has error 2^{-21} for data set IV*. A look at our Table 1 shows that the worst error we obtain is 2^{-25} for $\log_2 p = 30$. The number of ciphertext (modulus) bits lost for that error is $1200 - 344 = 856$, whereas [6] loses $1240 - 43 * 6 = 982$ bits. Moreover, our implementation can handle K up to 31 since we set the secret key Hamming weight $h = 256$, whereas [6] gives results for $K = 12$ and use $h = 64$. Thus, our approach is clearly better at even this low precision.

In [12], the authors obtain better approximation error than [6] by leveraging the fact the approximation is only needed in small intervals around multiples of the modulus. However, their approach also uses a baby-step giant-step, or alternately the Paterson-Stockmeyer variant applied to Chebyshev polynomials that can lead to a blowup in the size of coefficients. The authors do not give details on the number of ciphertext (modulus) bits lost in the bootstrapping procedure, nor is their implementation public. The maximum bootstrapping precision they achieve is 18.5 bits.

In [18], the authors report high-precision bootstrapping using a composition of sine/cosine and arcsine. The polynomials to approximate these functions are found via algorithmic search using the Remez algorithm (which gives no guarantee on the size of the coefficients), and the authors do not provide any details on the size of these coefficients apart from noting that they "are small enough not to distort the messages." Moreover, their implementation is not public. The authors report a practical implementation of up to 40-bits precision bootstrapping. In Table 3, we compare our results with theirs using the relevant available information in their paper. We note that [18] gives an implementation of

RNS-CKKS [8], which improves performance over the original CKKS implementation by utilizing an RNS basis. This introduces an additional challenge of having to ensure that rescaling errors are small, but this can be done without significantly increasing error, and, in fact, the recent work [14] shows a method of managing the scaling factor so that homomorphic multiplication error in RNS-CKKS is about the same as that of the original CKKS scheme.

The work [13] gives a direct approximation of the mod function, i.e. without going through the sine function, and hence bypasses the fundamental error of the sine function approach. Thus, they can get arbitrarily high precision, and they also show that the coefficients of their polynomial approximation are not too large. Nevertheless, the coefficients are large enough that our approach beats [13]. Moreover, they only give implementation numbers for $K = 12$, and for $K = 31$, the number of ciphertext modulus bits lost during bootstrapping would be higher. In Table 4, we compare their results with ours for $\epsilon = 2^{-10}$ and various plaintext precisions.

The recent work [5] optimized the performance of bootstrapping for RNS-CKKS. They introduce a scale-invariant polynomial evaluation method as well as a "double hoisting" technique for evaluating the homomorphic linear transforms. These techniques improve the performance of bootstrapping considerably and are compatible with our sine series approximation of the mod function. Moreover, to the best of our knowledge, [5] gives the first public implementation of full RNS-CKKS with bootstrapping. We note that they do not focus on obtaining better approximations to the mod function and utilize previous techniques and variants thereof to perform the "Compute the Mod Function" step in bootstrapping. Their maximum bootstrapping precision achieved is 32.6 bits, but we stress that this was not the focus of their work. An interesting direction would be to combine both their bootstrapping optimizations with our sine series approximation of the mod function.

Acknowledgements. Nathan Manohar is supported in part from a Simons Investigator Award, DARPA SIEVE award, NTT Research, NSF Frontier Award 1413955, BSF grant 2012378, a Xerox Faculty Research Award, a Google Faculty Research Award, and an Okawa Foundation Research Grant. This material is based upon work supported by the Defense Advanced Research Projects Agency through Award HR00112020024.

A   Proof of Lemma 5

Lemma 5 (restated). For any $k \geq 0$, any $\mathbf{a}$ of length $n > 0$, and an independent formal variable t,

$$\sum_{j=0}^{k} h_j(\mathbf{a}) t^j = \prod_{i=1}^{n} \sum_{j=0}^{k} (t a_i)^j \bmod t^{k+1}.$$

Proof. We prove this lemma by induction over n. The base case for $n = 1$ follows as $h_j(a) = a^j$ for every j in $[0..k]$. Suppose the lemma holds for $n - 1$. Then, let $\mathbf{a}'$ be truncation of $\mathbf{a}$ to its first $n - 1$ components. We have, modulo t^{k+1},

$$\prod_{i=1}^{n}\sum_{j=0}^{k}(ta_i)^j = \sum_{z=0}^{k}(ta_n)^z * \prod_{i=1}^{n-1}\sum_{j=0}^{k}(ta_i)^j$$

$$= \sum_{z=0}^{k}t^z a_n^z * \sum_{j=0}^{k}h_j(\mathbf{a'})t^j$$

$$= \sum_{j=0}^{k}\sum_{z=0}^{k}a_n^z * h_j(\mathbf{a'})t^{j+z}$$

$$= \sum_{z=0}^{k}\sum_{j=0}^{k}a_n^z * h_j(\mathbf{a'})t^{j+z}$$

$$= \sum_{z=0}^{k}\sum_{j=0}^{k-z}a_n^z * h_j(\mathbf{a'})t^{j+z}$$

$$= \sum_{z=0}^{k}\sum_{j'=z}^{k}a_n^z * h_{j'-z}(\mathbf{a'})t^{j'}$$

$$= \sum_{z=0}^{k}\sum_{k\geq j';\, j'\geq z}a_n^z * h_{j'-z}(\mathbf{a'})t^{j'}$$

$$= \sum_{z\leq k;\, j'\leq k;\, z\geq 0;\, z\leq j'}a_n^z * h_{j'-z}(\mathbf{a'})t^{j'}$$

$$= \sum_{j'=0}^{k}\sum_{z=0}^{j'}a_n^z * h_{j'-z}(\mathbf{a'})t^{j'}$$

$$= \sum_{j'=0}^{k}h_{j'}(\mathbf{a})t^{j'}$$

References

1. HEAAN. https://github.com/snucrypto/HEAAN
2. Albrecht, M.R.: On dual lattice attacks against small-secret LWE and parameter choices in HElib and SEAL. In: Coron, J.-S., Nielsen, J.B. (eds.) EUROCRYPT 2017. LNCS, vol. 10211, pp. 103–129. Springer, Cham (2017). https://doi.org/10.1007/978-3-319-56614-6_4
3. Albrecht, M.R., Player, R., Scott, S.: On the concrete hardness of Learning with Errors. J. Math. Cryptol. **9**(3), 169–203 (2015). http://www.degruyter.com/view/j/jmc.2015.9.issue-3/jmc-2015-0016/jmc-2015-0016.xml
4. Bergamaschi, F., Halevi, S., Halevi, T.T., Hunt, H.: Homomorphic training of 30,000 logistic regression models. In: Deng, R.H., Gauthier-Umaña, V., Ochoa, M., Yung, M. (eds.) ACNS 2019. LNCS, vol. 11464, pp. 592–611. Springer, Cham (2019). https://doi.org/10.1007/978-3-030-21568-2_29

5. Bossuat, J.-P., Mouchet, C., Troncoso-Pastoriza, J., Hubaux, J.-P.: Efficient bootstrapping for approximate homomorphic encryption with non-sparse keys. In: Canteaut, A., Standaert, F.-X. (eds.) EUROCRYPT 2021. LNCS, vol. 12696, pp. 587–617. Springer, Cham (2021). https://doi.org/10.1007/978-3-030-77870-5_21

6. Chen, H., Chillotti, I., Song, Y.: Improved Bootstrapping for Approximate Homomorphic Encryption. In: Ishai, Y., Rijmen, V. (eds.) EUROCRYPT 2019. LNCS, vol. 11477, pp. 34–54. Springer, Cham (2019). https://doi.org/10.1007/978-3-030-17656-3_2

7. Cheon, J.H., Han, K., Kim, A., Kim, M., Song, Y.: Bootstrapping for approximate homomorphic encryption. In: Nielsen, J.B., Rijmen, V. (eds.) EUROCRYPT 2018. LNCS, vol. 10820, pp. 360–384. Springer, Cham (2018). https://doi.org/10.1007/978-3-319-78381-9_14

8. Cheon, J.H., Han, K., Kim, A., Kim, M., Song, Y.: A full RNS variant of approximate homomorphic encryption. In: Selected Areas in Cryptography - SAC 2018 (2018)

9. Cheon, J.H., Kim, A., Kim, M., Song, Y.: Homomorphic encryption for arithmetic of approximate numbers. In: Takagi, T., Peyrin, T. (eds.) ASIACRYPT 2017. LNCS, vol. 10624, pp. 409–437. Springer, Cham (2017). https://doi.org/10.1007/978-3-319-70694-8_15

10. Curtis, B.R., Player, R.: On the feasibility and impact of standardising sparse-secret LWE parameter sets for homomorphic encryption. In: Brenner, M., Lepoint, T., Rohloff, K. (eds.) Proceedings of the 7th ACM Workshop on Encrypted Computing & Applied Homomorphic Cryptography, WAHC@CCS 2019, London, UK, 11–15 November 2019, pp. 1–10. ACM (2019). https://doi.org/10.1145/3338469.3358940

11. Han, K., Hhan, M., Cheon, J.H.: Improved homomorphic discrete Fourier transforms and FHE bootstrapping. IEEE Access 7, 57361–57370 (2019)

12. Han, K., Ki, D.: Better bootstrapping for approximate homomorphic encryption. In: Jarecki, S. (ed.) CT-RSA 2020. LNCS, vol. 12006, pp. 364–390. Springer, Cham (2020). https://doi.org/10.1007/978-3-030-40186-3_16

13. Jutla, C.S., Manohar, N.: Modular Lagrange Interpolation of the Mod Function for Bootstrapping of Approximate HE. Cryptology ePrint Archive, Report 2020/1355 (2020). https://eprint.iacr.org/2020/1355

14. Kim, A., Papadimitriou, A., Polyakov, Y.: Approximate Homomorphic Encryption with Reduced Approximation Error. IACR Cryptol. ePrint Arch, p. 1118 (2020). https://eprint.iacr.org/2020/1118

15. Kim, A., Song, Y., Kim, M., Lee, K., Cheon, J.H.: Logistic regression model training based on the approximate homomorphic encryption. BMC Med. Genom. 11(4), 83 (2018). https://doi.org/10.1186/s12920-018-0401-7

16. Kim, M., et al.: Ultra-Fast Homomorphic Encryption Models enable Secure Outsourcing of Genotype Imputation. bioRxiv (2020)

17. Kim, M., Song, Y., Wang, S., Xia, Y., Jiang, X.: Secure logistic regression based on homomorphic encryption: design and evaluation. JMIR Med. Inform. 6(2), e19 (2018). http://www.ncbi.nlm.nih.gov/pubmed/29666041

18. Lee, J.-W., Lee, E., Lee, Y., Kim, Y.-S., No, J.-S.: High-precision bootstrapping of RNS-CKKS homomorphic encryption using optimal minimax polynomial approximation and inverse sine function. In: Canteaut, A., Standaert, F.-X. (eds.) EUROCRYPT 2021. LNCS, vol. 12696, pp. 618–647. Springer, Cham (2021). https://doi.org/10.1007/978-3-030-77870-5_22

19. Masters, O., et al.: Towards a homomorphic machine learning big data pipeline for the financial services sector. In: RWC (2020)

20. Paterson, M.S., Stockmeyer, L.J.: On the number of nonscalar multiplications necessary to evaluate polynomials. SIAM J. Comput. **2**, 60–66 (1973)
21. Remez, E., G.: Sur la determination des polynomes d'approximation de degre' donnee'. Comm. of the Kharkov Math. Soc. **10**(196), 41–63 (1934)
22. Sav, S., et al.: POSEIDON: Privacy-Preserving Federated Neural Network Learning (2020)

Limits of Polynomial Packings for $\mathbb{Z}_{p^k}$ and $\mathbb{F}_{p^k}$

Jung Hee Cheon[1,2] and Keewoo Lee[1($\boxtimes$)]

[1] Seoul National University, Seoul, Republic of Korea
{jhcheon,activecondor}@snu.ac.kr
[2] Crypto Lab Inc., Seoul, Republic of Korea

Abstract. We formally define polynomial packing methods and initiate a unified study of related concepts in various contexts of cryptography. This includes homomorphic encryption (HE) packing and reverse multiplication-friendly embedding (RMFE) in information-theoretically secure multi-party computation (MPC). We prove several upper bounds and impossibility results on packing methods for $\mathbb{Z}_{p^k}$ or $\mathbb{F}_{p^k}$-messages into $\mathbb{Z}_{p^t}[x]/f(x)$ in terms of (i) packing density, (ii) level-consistency, and (iii) surjectivity. These results have implications on recent development of HE-based MPC over $\mathbb{Z}_{2^k}$ secure against actively corrupted majority and provide new proofs for upper bounds on RMFE.

Keywords: Packing method · Homomorphic encryption · Secure multi-party computation · Reverse multiplication-friendly embedding · $\mathbb{Z}_{p^k}$

1 Introduction

HE Packing. Homomorphic encryption (HE), which allows computations on ciphertexts without decryption, is such a versatile tool that it is often referred as the holy grail of cryptography. After Gentry's breakthrough [23], HE has undergone extensive study and development. HE is now considered to be exploitable in real-life applications (e.g. privacy-preserving machine learning [28]) and regarded as a core building block in various cryptographic primitives (e.g. secure multiparty computation [21]).

One drawback of contemporary lattice-based HE schemes [4,22] is that their plaintext space is of the form $\mathbb{Z}_q[x]/\Phi_M(x)$, as their security is based on Ring Learning with Errors (RLWE) [30]. That is, these schemes are homomorphic with regards to the addition and multiplication of polynomial ring $\mathbb{Z}_q[x]/\Phi_M(x)$. This raises a question of how to *homomorphically* encode messages into the plaintexts, as our data are usually binary bits, integers, fixed/floating point numbers, or at least $\mathbb{Z}_p$ and $\mathbb{F}_{p^k}$.

Among a number of works on how to encode data into HE plaintexts [8,10–12], Smart-Vercauteren [33,34] first introduced the idea of *packing* several $\mathbb{Z}_p$ (or $\mathbb{F}_{p^k}$) elements into the HE plaintext space $\mathbb{Z}_p[x]/\Phi_M(x)$ via CRT[1] ring isomor-

---

[1] Chinese Remainder Theorem.

© International Association for Cryptologic Research 2022
O. Dunkelman and S. Dziembowski (Eds.): EUROCRYPT 2022, LNCS 13275, pp. 521–550, 2022.
https://doi.org/10.1007/978-3-031-06944-4_18

phism with *well-chosen* prime p. Their simple yet powerful technique enables SIMD[2]-like optimizations and enhances amortized performance. That is, with a polynomial packing method, we can securely compute on *multiple* $\mathbb{Z}_p$-messages simultaneously by homomorphically computing on a *single* packed HE plaintext in $\mathbb{Z}_p[x]/\Phi_M(x)$. In particular, through the packing, the complex multiplicative structure of $\mathbb{Z}_p[x]/\Phi_M(x)$ embeds the more handy coordinate-wise multiplication (a.k.a. Hadamard product) of $\mathbb{Z}_p^n$, where n denotes the number of packed messages. Packing has now become a standard technique in HE research, and it is not too much to say that the performance of HE applications are determined by how well packings are utilized.

However, this conventional packing method has a limitation: it cannot (efficiently) pack $\mathbb{Z}_{2^k}$-messages.[3] This limitation has recently attracted attention due to development of secure multi-party computation (MPC) over $\mathbb{Z}_{2^k}$ secure against actively corrupted majority by SPD$\mathbb{Z}_{2^k}$ [15]. SPD$\mathbb{Z}_{2^k}$ follows the framework of HE-based MPC protocol SPDZ [21], while targeting $\mathbb{Z}_{2^k}$-messages rather than prime field $\mathbb{Z}_p$-messages, with a motivation from the fact that $\mathbb{Z}_{2^k}$ arithmetic matches closely what happens on standard CPUs. In this context, Overdrive2k [31] and MHz2k [13], whose goal are efficient constructions of HE-based MPC over $\mathbb{Z}_{2^k}$, came up with new and more involved polynomial packing methods for $\mathbb{Z}_{2^k}$-messages (Sect. 4).

RMFE in Perfectly Secure MPC. Another context where polynomial packings appear is *information-theoretically secure MPC* (or perfectly secure MPC). A main tool in this area is Shamir's linear secret sharing scheme(LSSS). A cumbersome fact when using LSSS is that the number of shares is restricted by the field where computation takes place.[4] Thus, it is standard to *lift* the computation to a larger field which supports enough number of shares, but this causes substantial overheads. In their seminal work [5], Cascudo-Cramer-Xing-Yuan first defined and studied *reverse multiplication-friendly embedding (RMFE)* which is, roughly speaking, an embedding of several elements of small finite field into a larger finite field while providing *somewhat* homomorphism of degree-2. Note that an RMFE can be indeed viewed as a polynomial packing $\mathbb{F}_{p^k}^n \to \mathbb{F}_{p^d} \cong \mathbb{F}_p[x]/f(x)$, where p is a prime and $f(x) \in \mathbb{F}_p[x]$ is an irreducible polynomial of degree d. Surprisingly, [5] constructed *constant-rate* RMFEs, leveraging algebraic geometry, and applied them to remove logarithmic overhead in amortized communication complexity which appears to enable Shamir's secret sharing. Since [5], RMFE has become a standard tool in information-theoretically secure MPC, to achieve *linear* amortized communication cost while preserving optimal corruption tolerance: [3,7,17,18,20,32].

---

[2] Single Instruction, Multiple Data.
[3] The original method of [33] does not consider packings for $\mathbb{Z}_{p^k}$. Gentry-Halevi-Smart [24] later generalized the method to support such packing. However, this method achieves only considerably low efficiency. See Sect. 4.1.
[4] Indeed, the number of evaluation points is bounded by the size of the field.

In [16], the notion of RMFE was extended to *over Galois rings* for construction of efficient perfectly secure MPC over $\mathbb{Z}_{p^k}$. Again, RMFE over Galois rings for $\mathbb{Z}_{p^k}$-messages can be viewed as a polynomial packing $\mathbb{Z}_{p^k}^n \rightarrow GR(p^k, d) \cong \mathbb{Z}_{p^k}[x]/f(x)$, where p is a prime and $f(x) \in \mathbb{Z}_{p^k}[x]$ is a degree-d irreducible polynomial in $\mathbb{F}_p[x]$.

Other Contexts. Other than HE and perfectly secure MPC, there are still more areas where polynomial packings are used for amortization: correlation extraction for secure computation [2], zk-SNARK [6], etc. Moreover, we believe that polynomial packing will be even more prominent and universal tool for efficiency and practicality in the future: (i) RLWE-based cryptosystems are emerging, where plaintexts are $\mathbb{Z}_q[x]/\Phi_M(x)$; (ii) Secure computation is emerging, where some parts of protocols need to be large or of certain form due to security or mathematical properties required, whereas where we actually want to compute in is (extremely) small and typical such as $\mathbb{F}_2$ or $\mathbb{Z}_{2^{32}}$.

1.1 Our Contribution

Unified Definition and Survey. In this work, we formally define polynomial packing methods, which can be understood as (somewhat) homomorphic encoding for copies of a small ring, e.g. $\mathbb{Z}_p$ or $\mathbb{F}_{p^k}$, into a larger ring, e.g. $\mathbb{Z}_q[x]/f(x)$, (Sect. 3.1). The notion of polynomial packing unifies forementioned concepts in various contexts of cryptography, including HE packing and RMFE in perfectly secure MPC. Then, we gather existing packing methods in one place. This includes RMFE (Sect. 2.3 and 3.1), classic HE packing methods (Sect. 3.1), and recent development occurred in HE-based MPC over $\mathbb{Z}_{2^k}$ (Sect. 4). We also provide *decomposition* lemmas which suggest that it is enough to study packing methods for $\mathbb{Z}_{p^k}^n$ (or $\mathbb{F}_{p^k}^n$) into $\mathbb{Z}_{p^t}[x]/f(x)$ where $t \geq k$ and p is prime, instead of general case of $\mathbb{Z}_P^n$ (or $\mathbb{F}_P^n$) into $\mathbb{Z}_Q[x]/f(x)$ where $P, Q \in \mathbb{Z}^+$ (Sect. 3.2). The results also rule out the possibility of using composite modulus for better packing.

Upper Bounds and Impossibility. We prove several upper bounds and impossibility results on packing methods for $\mathbb{Z}_{p^k}$ or $\mathbb{F}_{p^k}$-messages into $\mathbb{Z}_{p^t}[x]/f(x)$.

- Upper Bounds on Packing Density (Sect. 5): We evaluate the efficiency of packing methods by packing density which measures how densely the messages are packed in (plaintext) polynomials (Definition 5). We prove that, when a packing method provides somewhat homomorphism upto degree-D polynomials, the packing density is roughly upper bounded by $1/D$ (Theorem 1 and 2). These results have several implications:

  - The packing method of MHz2k [13] achieves nearly optimal density in some sense when using their parameters (Example 6). Our results justify the *lifting* of MHz2k packing (See Sect. 4.3).

- We provide the first upper bound on RMFE over Galois ring for $\mathbb{Z}_{p^k}$-messages (Example 7).
- We provide a new proof for upper bound on RMFE, which can be extended to higher-degree settings unlike the previous proof (Example 10).
- Impossibility of Level-consistency (Sect. 6): The notion of level-consistency captures the property whether packings are decodable in an identical way at different multiplicative levels (Definition 6). The level-consistency is a desirable feature as it allows homomorphic computation between different packing levels. We prove sufficient and necessary conditions on parameters to allow a level-consistent packing method. These results have the following implications:
  - HELib packing [26] (a.k.a. GHS packing [24], See Sect. 4.1) is essentially the optimal method to use in *fully* homomorphic encryption(FHE) (Example 14).
  - It is impossible to construct efficient level-consistent packing methods in most cases. This justifies the use of *level-dependent* packings in SPDZ-like MPC protocols over $\mathbb{Z}_{2^k}$ [13,31] and highlights the usefulness of the trick proposed by MHz2k [13], which closed the gap between the level-consistent and level-dependent packing methods in so-called *reshare* protocol. (See Sect. 6.1.)
- Impossibility of Surjectivity (Sect. 7): For a packing method into $\mathcal{R}$, the notion of surjectivity captures the condition whether every element of $\mathcal{R}$ is decodable (Definition 8). This distinction is essential when designing a cryptographic protocol with the packing method in a malicious setting, where an adversary might freely deviate from the protocol. If there is an element in $\mathcal{R}$ which fails to decode, a malicious adversary might make use of the element to illegitimately learn information of other parties, if such invalid packings are not properly handled. We prove sufficient and necessary conditions on parameters to allow a surjective packing method. Our results suggest that it is impossible to construct a meaningful surjective packing method in most cases. This justifies the use of *non*-surjective packings and the need of ZKPoMK[5], which ensures an HE ciphertext encrypts a validly packed plaintext, in SPDZ-like MPC protocols over $\mathbb{Z}_{2^k}$ [13,31].

2   Preliminaries

2.1   Notations and Terminologies

In this paper, we only consider finite commutative rings with unity. Thus, we omit the long description and simply refer them as rings. Readers must understand the term *ring* as finite commutative rings with unity, even if not explicitly stated. In addition, we only consider monic polynomials when defining quotient rings. Thus, we omit description on *monic* property throughout the paper for

---

[5] Zero-knowledge proof of message knowledge.

readability. Readers must understand any polynomials defining quotient rings as monic polynomials, even if not explicitly stated.

This paper carefully distinguishes between the use of the terms *message* and *plaintext*. Messages are those we really want to compute with. On the other hand, plaintexts are defined by encryption scheme (particularly, HE schemes) we are using. In this paper, messages are in $\mathbb{Z}_{p^k}$ or $\mathbb{F}_{p^k}$ and plaintexts are in $\mathbb{Z}_q[x]/f(x)$.

For prime fields, we use both notations $\mathbb{F}_p$ and $\mathbb{Z}_p$, depending on whether we want to emphasize that it is a field or that it is the ring of integer modulo p. The multiplicative order of b modulo a is denoted as $\mathrm{ord}_a(b)$. We use $\mathrm{Inv}_a(b)$ to denote the smallest positive integer which is a multiplicative inverse of b modulo a. We use $\odot$ to denote the coordinate-wise multiplication (a.k.a. Hadamard product) in products of rings. In a product of rings R^n, the element e_i denotes a standard unit vector whose i-th coordinate is 1 and the other coordinates are 0. We denote the M-th cyclotomic polynomial as $\Phi_M(x)$ and the Euler's totient function as $\phi(\cdot)$. We use $GR(p^k, d)$ to denote the Galois ring, a degree-d extension of $\mathbb{Z}_{p^k}$. We use notations $[n] := \{1, 2, \cdots, n\}$ and $[0, n] := \{0, 1, \cdots, n\}$.

2.2 Polynomial Factorizations

Here, we briefly review some basic facts on polynomial factorizations in $\mathbb{Z}_{p^k}[x]$. First, recall Hensel lifting (or Hensel's lemma).

Lemma 1 (Hensel Lifting). *Let $f(x) \in \mathbb{Z}_{p^k}[x]$ be a monic polynomial which factors into $\prod_{i=1}^{r} g_i(x)^{\ell_i}$ in $\mathbb{F}_p[x]$, where $g_i(x)$ are distinct irreducible polynomials. Then there exist pairwise coprime monic polynomials $f_1(x), \cdots, f_r(x) \in \mathbb{Z}_{p^k}[x]$ such that $f(x) = \prod_{i=1}^{r} f_i(x)$ in $\mathbb{Z}_{p^k}[x]$ and $f_i(x) = g_i(x)^{\ell_i} \pmod{p}$, for all $i \in [r]$.*

When $\gcd(M, p) = 1$, $\Phi_M(x)$ factors into $\prod_{i=1}^{r} g_i(x)$ in $\mathbb{F}_p[x]$, where $g_i(x)$ are distinct irreducible polynomials of degree $d := \mathrm{ord}_M(p)$. Thus, $\phi(M) = r \cdot d$ holds. To see this, consider a primitive M-th root of unity in a sufficiently large extension field of $\mathbb{F}_p$. Then, it is easy to see that the number of its conjugates is d which coincides with the degree of its minimal polynomial. Applying Hensel's lemma, we have a factorization $\Phi_M(x) = \prod_{i=1}^{r} f_i(x)$ in $\mathbb{Z}_{p^k}[x]$, where $\deg(f_i) = d$ and $f_i(x) = g_i(x) \pmod{p}$. Accordingly, we have a CRT ring isomorphism $\mathbb{Z}_{p^k}[x]/\Phi_M(x) \cong \prod_{i=1}^{r} \mathbb{Z}_{p^k}[x]/f_i(x)$. Each $\mathbb{Z}_{p^k}[x]/f_i(x)$ is often referred to as a CRT *slot* of $\mathbb{Z}_{p^k}[x]/\Phi_M(x)$.

2.3 RMFE

Reverse multiplication-friendly embeddings (RMFE) were first defined and studied in-depth by [5].[6] At a high level, RMFEs are embeddings of several elements

---

[6] Nonetheless, this object was also previously studied in [2] to amortize oblivious linear evaluations (OLE) into a larger extension field for correlation extraction problem in MPC. However, their construction achieved only sublinear density.

of small finite field into a larger finite field, while providing *somewhat* homomorphism of degree-2.

Definition 1 (RMFE). *A pair of maps* (φ, ψ) *is called an* $(n, d)_{p^k}$*-reverse multiplication-friendly embedding (RMFE) if it satisfies the following.*

- *The map* $\varphi : \mathbb{F}_{p^k}^n \to \mathbb{F}_{p^{kd}}$ *is* $\mathbb{F}_{p^k}$*-linear.*
- *The map* $\psi : \mathbb{F}_{p^{kd}} \to \mathbb{F}_{p^k}^n$ *is* $\mathbb{F}_{p^k}$*-linear.*
- *For all* $\boldsymbol{a}, \boldsymbol{b} \in \mathbb{F}_{p^k}^n$, *it holds* $\psi(\varphi(\boldsymbol{a}) \cdot \varphi(\boldsymbol{b})) = \boldsymbol{a} \odot \boldsymbol{b}$.

Surprisingly, [5] constructed families of $(n, d)_{p^k}$-RMFE where the density n/d converges to some *constant*, for arbitrary prime power p^k, leveraging algebraic geometry. That is, [5] constructed *constant-rate* RMFEs. For instance, we have a family of $(n, d)_2$-RMFE with $n/d \to 0.203$ from [5]. Since this seminal work, RMFE has become a standard tool in information-theoretically secure MPC, to achieve *linear* amortized communication cost while preserving optimal corruption tolerance: [3,5,7,17,18,20,32]. RMFE was also leveraged in zk-SNARK context recently [6].

Recently in [16], RMFE *over Galois rings* was first defined and studied. It is a natural generalization of RMFE over fields to Galois rings.

Definition 2 (RMFE over Galois Ring). *A pair of maps* (φ, ψ) *is called an* $(n, d)_{p^r}$*-RMFE over modulus* p^k *if it satisfies the following.*

- *The map* $\varphi : GR(p^k, r)^n \to GR(p^k, d)$ *is* $GR(p^k, r)$*-linear.*
- *The map* $\psi : GR(p^k, d) \to GR(p^k, r)^n$ *is* $GR(p^k, r)$*-linear.*
- *For all* $\boldsymbol{a}, \boldsymbol{b} \in GR(p^k, r)^n$, *it holds* $\psi(\varphi(\boldsymbol{a}) \cdot \varphi(\boldsymbol{b})) = \boldsymbol{a} \odot \boldsymbol{b}$

The authors also showed that any $(n, d)_{p^r}$-RMFE over fields can be naturally lifted upto an $(n, d)_{p^r}$-RMFE over modulus p^k. That is, there are *asymptotically good* RMFE also in the Galois ring setting.

Their goal was to construct efficient $(n, d)_p$-RMFEs over modulus p^k for $\mathbb{Z}_{p^k}$-messages as a building block for more efficient information-theoretically secure MPC over $\mathbb{Z}_{p^k}$. More generally, it seems there are very limited applications where messages in Galois ring (except $\mathbb{Z}_{p^k}$ or $\mathbb{F}_{p^k}$) play important roles. Thus, in our work, we focus on $(n, d)_p$-RMFE over modulus p^k for $\mathbb{Z}_{p^k}$-messages. Note that this case can be interpreted as packing $\mathbb{Z}_{p^k}$-messages into $GR(p^k, d) \cong \mathbb{Z}_{p^k}[x]/f(x)$ for some degree-d $f(x) \in \mathbb{Z}_{p^k}[x]$ which is irreducible modulo p.

3   Packing: Definitions and Basic Facts

In this section, we formally define *packings* and related concepts which are our main interests in this work. Some basic examples of packing methods are introduced for illustrative purpose. We also present some propositions which allow us to modularize our study of packing methods. We begin with a formal definition of packing.

3.1 Definitions and Basic Examples

Definition 3 (Packing). *Let R and $\mathcal{R}$ be rings. We call a pair of algorithms* (Pack, Unpack) *a packing method for n R-messages into $\mathcal{R}$, if it satisfies the following.*

- Pack *is an algorithm (possibly probabilistic) which, given $\boldsymbol{a} \in R^n$ as an input, outputs an element of $\mathcal{R}$.*
- Unpack *is a deterministic algorithm which, given $a(x) \in \mathcal{R}$ as an input, outputs an element of R^n or $\perp$ denoting a failure.*
- Unpack(Pack($\boldsymbol{a}$)) $= \boldsymbol{a}$ *holds for all $\boldsymbol{a} \in R^n$ with probability 1.*

For simplicity, the definition is presented a bit generally. In this paper, we are mostly interested in the cases where R is $\mathbb{Z}_p$ with $p \in \mathbb{Z}^+$ (or a finite field $\mathbb{F}_{p^k}$) and $\mathcal{R}$ is a polynomial ring $\mathbb{Z}_q[x]/f(x)$ with $q \in \mathbb{Z}^+$ and monic $f(x)$.

Notice that in Definition 3 the ring structure is not considered. Packing methods are interesting only when algebraic structures of the rings come in, since otherwise a packing is nothing more than a vanilla data encoding. The following definition of *degree* captures quality of (somewhat) homomorphic correspondence between packed messages and a packing. In this work, we are interested in packings of at least degree-2.

Definition 4 (Degree-D Packing). *Let $\mathcal{P} = (\mathsf{Pack}_i, \mathsf{Unpack}_i)_{i=1}^D$ be a collection of packing methods for R^n into $\mathcal{R}$. We call $\mathcal{P}$ a degree-D packing method, if it satisfies the following for all $1 \le i \le D$:*

- *If $a(x), b(x)$ satisfy $\mathsf{Unpack}_i(a(x)) = \boldsymbol{a}$, $\mathsf{Unpack}_i(b(x)) = \boldsymbol{b}$ for $\boldsymbol{a}, \boldsymbol{b} \in R^n$, then $\mathsf{Unpack}_i(a(x) \pm b(x)) = \boldsymbol{a} \pm \boldsymbol{b}$ holds;*
- *If $a(x), b(x)$ satisfy $\mathsf{Unpack}_s(a(x)) = \boldsymbol{a}$, $\mathsf{Unpack}_t(b(x)) = \boldsymbol{b}$ for $\boldsymbol{a}, \boldsymbol{b} \in R^n$ and $s, t \in \mathbb{Z}^+$ such that $s + t = i$, then $\mathsf{Unpack}_i(a(x) \cdot b(x)) = \boldsymbol{a} \odot \boldsymbol{b}$ holds.*

Notice that the definition is heavy on the use of Unpack rather than Pack. Some readers might find it unnatural to define a property of *packing* methods with their *unpacking* structures. However, this is how things are. For instance, given that a collection of unpacking algorithms $(\mathsf{Unpack}_i)_{i=1}^D$ allows a degree-D packing method, it is trivial to find an appropriate collection of packing algorithms $(\mathsf{Pack}_i)_{i=1}^D$: we can just define Pack_i as an algorithm which randomly outputs a preimage of the input regarding Unpack_i. On the other hand, if a collection of packing algorithms $(\mathsf{Pack}_i)_{i=1}^D$ is given, it requires non-trivial computations to find an appropriate collection of packing algorithms $(\mathsf{Unpack}_i)_{i=1}^D$ in this case. In this regard, definitions and proofs coming up are also aligned to Unpack rather than Pack.

Here are some direct but noteworthy consequences of the definition.

Remark 1. Note that the definition implies that $\mathsf{Unpack}_i(c \cdot a(x)) = c \cdot \boldsymbol{a}$ holds for all $c \in \mathbb{Z}$ with probability 1. In particular, $\mathsf{Unpack}_i(0) = \boldsymbol{0}$.

Remark 2. A packing method $\mathcal{P} = (\mathsf{Pack}_i, \mathsf{Unpack}_i)_{i=1}^D$ is of degree-D, only if $\mathcal{P}' = (\mathsf{Pack}_i, \mathsf{Unpack}_i)_{i=1}^{D'}$ is a degree-D' packing method for all $D' < D$.

The following are some basic examples of packing methods. More sophisticated examples are introduced in Sect. 4.

Example 1 (Coefficient Packing). Let $f(x)$ be a degree-d monic polynomial in $\mathbb{Z}_p[x]$. Define Pack as a bijection which maps $(a_0, \cdots, a_{d-1}) \in \mathbb{Z}_p^d$ to $\sum_{i=0}^{d-1} a_i \cdot x^i \in \mathbb{Z}_p[x]/f(x)$. Define Unpack as the inverse of Pack. Then, (Pack, Unpack) is a degree-1 packing method for $\mathbb{Z}_p^d$ into $\mathbb{Z}_p[x]/f(x)$. We often refer this method as *coefficient packing*. As coefficient packing is already too good, we do not further examine degree-1 packing methods in this paper. Note that this method also applies to $\mathbb{F}_{p^k}$-messages if degree-1 is sufficient, since $\mathbb{F}_{p^k}^n$ is isomorphic to $\mathbb{Z}_p^{kn}$ as $\mathbb{Z}_p$-modules.

Example 2 (Conventional HE Packing). When making use of lattice-based HE schemes, where the plaintext space is of the form $\mathbb{Z}_p[x]/\Phi_M(x)$, it is standard to choose prime p such that $p = 1 \pmod M$ (and M as a power-of-two to enable efficient implementations). Then, $\Phi_M(x)$ fully splits in $\mathbb{Z}_p[x]$, and $\mathbb{Z}_p[x]/\Phi_M(x) \cong \mathbb{Z}_p^{\phi(M)}$ holds. The isomorphism induces a natural packing method, which is of degree-∞, i.e. degree-D for any $D \in \mathbb{Z}^+$. This packing is more than good in several aspects, but has quite heavy restrictions on parameters. In particular, the method does not allow packing $\mathbb{Z}_{2^k}$-messages.

Example 3 (HE Packing for $\mathbb{F}_{p^d}$). If one want to pack $\mathbb{F}_{p^d}$-messages when making use of lattice-based HE schemes, we often choose M so that $\Phi_M(x)$ factorizes into r distinct degree-d irreducible polynomials in $\mathbb{Z}_p[x]$. Then, we have $\mathbb{Z}_p[x]/\Phi_M(x) \cong \mathbb{F}_{p^d}^r$. As Example 2, this isomorphism induces a natural packing method which is of degree-∞, but has even heavier restriction on parameters.

Example 4 (RMFE). Essentially, an RMFE is nothing more than a degree-2 packing method for copies of a finite field $\mathbb{F}_{p^k}$ into a larger finite field $\mathbb{F}_{p^d} \cong \mathbb{Z}_p[x]/f(x)$, where p is a prime and $f(x)$ is a monic degree-d irreducible polynomial in $\mathbb{Z}_p[x]$. The only additional requirement is that the packing algorithm at level-1 and unpacking algorithm at level-2 must be $\mathbb{Z}_p$-linear functions. However, any degree-2 packing method can be easily transformed to satisfy the requirement.

Example 5 (RMFE over Galois Ring). Essentially, an RMFE over Galois ring for $\mathbb{Z}_{p^k}$-messages is nothing more than a degree-2 packing method for copies of $\mathbb{Z}_{p^k}$ into a larger Galois ring $GR(p^k, d) \cong \mathbb{Z}_{p^k}[x]/f(x)$, where p is a prime and $f(x)$ is a degree-d irreducible polynomial in $\mathbb{Z}_p[x]$.

Lastly, we define *packing density* which measures efficiency of packing methods. It measures how dense messages are packed in a single packing.

Definition 5 (Packing Density). *For a packing method for R^n into $\mathcal{R}$, we define its* packing density *as $\log(|R|^n)/\log(|\mathcal{R}|)$.*

Example 1, 2, and 3 have perfect packing density of 1. However, we will see that these are very special cases. In most cases such perfect packing density is not achievable, and even moderate packing density is hard to achieve.

3.2 Decomposition Lemmas

In this subsection, we state and prove several necessary conditions on existence of certain packing methods. The following propositions allow us to modularize our study and focus on the case of packings into $\mathbb{Z}_{p^t}[x]/f(x)$.

Proposition 1. *Let R be a ring with characteristic p and $\mathcal{R}$ be a ring with characteristic q. There exists a degree-0 packing method* (Pack, Unpack) *for R^n into $\mathcal{R}$ only if p divides q.*

Proof. Let $a(x)$ be an output of Pack($\mathbf{1}$). Then, Unpack($q \cdot a(x)$) $= q \cdot \mathbf{1}$ by Remark 1. Meanwhile, $q \cdot a(x) = 0$ in $\mathcal{R}$. Thus, $q \cdot \mathbf{1} = \mathbf{0}$ in R^n, by Remark 1.$\square$

Proposition 2. *Let R be a ring with characteristic p. Let $q = q_1 \cdot q_2$, where $p|q_1$ and $\gcd(q_1, q_2) = 1$. There exists a degree-D packing method $\mathcal{P}$ for R^n into $\mathbb{Z}_q[x]/f(x)$, if and only if there exists a degree-D packing method $\mathcal{P}'$ for R^n into $\mathbb{Z}_{q_1}[x]/f(x)$.*

Proof (Sketch). Suppose $(\mathsf{Pack}_i, \mathsf{Unpack}_i)_{i=1}^{D}$ is a degree-D packing method $\mathcal{P}$ for R^n into $\mathbb{Z}_q[x]/f(x)$. Let $a(x)$ satisfy $\mathsf{Unpack}_i(a(x)) = \boldsymbol{a}$ for some $\boldsymbol{a} \in R^n$ and $1 \leq i \leq D$. We can identify $a(x)$ with $(a_1(x), a_2(x)) \in \mathbb{Z}_{q_1}[x]/f(x) \times \mathbb{Z}_{q_2}[x]/f(x)$ via CRT isomorphism. Now, consider multiplying a constant $\mathrm{Inv}_{q_1}(q_2) \cdot q_2$. Observe the following.

- $(\mathrm{Inv}_{q_1}(q_2) \cdot q_2) \cdot \boldsymbol{a} = (\mathrm{Inv}_p(q_2) \cdot q_2) \cdot \boldsymbol{a} = \boldsymbol{a} \in R^n$
- $(\mathrm{Inv}_{q_1}(q_2) \cdot q_2) \cdot a_1(x) = 1 \cdot a_1(x) = a_1(x) \in \mathbb{Z}_{q_1}[x]/f(x)$
- $(\mathrm{Inv}_{q_1}(q_2) \cdot q_2) \cdot a_2(x) = \mathrm{Inv}_{q_1}(q_2) \cdot 0 = 0 \in \mathbb{Z}_{q_2}[x]/f(x)$

Thus, if $\mathsf{Unpack}_i(a(x)) = \mathsf{Unpack}_i(a_1(x), a_2(x)) = \boldsymbol{a}$ then $\mathsf{Unpack}_i(a_1(x), 0) = \boldsymbol{a}$. Then, we can construct $\mathcal{P}'$ with appropriate projections and injections. The other direction is more direct. For the full proof, see the full version [14].$\square$

Proposition 3. *Let $p = p_1 \cdot p_2$ and $q = q_1 \cdot q_2$, satisfying $p_1|q_1$, $p_2|q_2$, and $\gcd(q_1, q_2) = 1$. There exists a degree-D packing method $\mathcal{P}$ for $\mathbb{Z}_p^n$ into $\mathcal{R} := \mathbb{Z}_q[x]/f(x)$, if and only if there exist degree-D packing methods $\mathcal{P}^{(j)}$ for $\mathbb{Z}_{p_j}^n$ into $\mathcal{R}_j := \mathbb{Z}_{q_j}[x]/f(x)$ for $j = 1, 2$.*

Proof (Sketch). Suppose $(\mathsf{Pack}_i, \mathsf{Unpack}_i)_{i=1}^{D}$ is a degree-D packing method $\mathcal{P}$ for $\mathbb{Z}_p^n$ into $\mathcal{R}$. Let $a(x) \in \mathcal{R}$ satisfy $\mathsf{Unpack}_i(a(x)) = \boldsymbol{a}$ for some $\boldsymbol{a} \in \mathbb{Z}_p^n$ and $1 \leq i \leq D$. We can identify $a(x)$ with $(a_1(x), a_2(x)) \in \mathcal{R}_1 \times \mathcal{R}_2$ and $\boldsymbol{a}$ with $(\boldsymbol{a}_1, \boldsymbol{a}_2) \in \mathbb{Z}_{p_1}^n \times \mathbb{Z}_{p_2}^n$ via CRT isomorphisms. Now, consider multiplying a constant $\mathrm{Inv}_{q_1}(q_2) \cdot q_2$. Observe the following.

- $(\mathrm{Inv}_{q_1}(q_2) \cdot q_2) \cdot \boldsymbol{a}_1 = (\mathrm{Inv}_{p_1}(q_2) \cdot q_2) \cdot \boldsymbol{a}_1 = \boldsymbol{a}_1 \in \mathbb{Z}_{p_1}^n$
- $(\mathrm{Inv}_{q_1}(q_2) \cdot q_2) \cdot \boldsymbol{a}_2 = \mathrm{Inv}_{q_1}(q_2) \cdot \boldsymbol{0} = \boldsymbol{0} \in \mathbb{Z}_{p_2}^n$
- $(\mathrm{Inv}_{q_1}(q_2) \cdot q_2) \cdot a_1(x) = 1 \cdot a_1(x) = a_1(x) \in \mathcal{R}_1$
- $(\mathrm{Inv}_{q_1}(q_2) \cdot q_2) \cdot a_2(x) = \mathrm{Inv}_{q_1}(q_2) \cdot 0 = 0 \in \mathcal{R}_2$

That is, if $\mathsf{Unpack}_i(a_1(x), a_2(x)) = (\boldsymbol{a}_1, \boldsymbol{a}_2)$ then $\mathsf{Unpack}_i(a_1(x), 0) = (\boldsymbol{a}_1, \boldsymbol{0})$. The similar holds for $j = 2$. Then, we can construct $\mathcal{P}^{(1)}$ and $\mathcal{P}^{(2)}$ with appropriate projections and injections. The other direction is more direct. For the full proof, see the full version of this paper [14]. □

According to Proposition 1 and 2, to study degree-D packing methods for copies of a finite field $\mathbb{F}_{p^k}$ into $\mathbb{Z}_q[x]/f(x)$, it is enough to study degree-D packing methods into $\mathbb{Z}_{p^t}[x]/f(x)$ for some $t \geq 1$. The similar holds for packing methods for copies of $\mathbb{Z}_p$ according to Proposition 1, 2, and 3. That is, to study degree-D packing methods for copies of $\mathbb{Z}_p$ into $\mathbb{Z}_q[x]/f(x)$ where p is an arbitrary integer, it is enough to study degree-D packing methods for $\mathbb{Z}_{p^k}^n$ into $\mathbb{Z}_{p^t}[x]/f(x)$ for some $t \geq k$ where p is a prime.

Therefore, from now on, we focus on packing methods for $\mathbb{Z}_{p^k}^n$ or $\mathbb{F}_{p^k}^n$ into $\mathbb{Z}_{p^t}[x]/f(x)$ where p is a prime. (Afterwards, p is a fixed prime, even if it is not explicitly stated.) This is not only because they are the most interesting case containing $\mathbb{Z}_{2^k}$ and $\mathbb{F}_{2^k}$, but also because they play roles as building blocks when constructing general packing methods (Proposition 2, 3). We note that the properties of packing methods, which we examine in the following sections (level-consistency in Sect. 6 and surjectivity in Sect. 7), are preserved by the constructions in Proposition 2 and 3.

4   More Examples

In continuation of Sect. 3.1, we give more examples on packing methods. The following examples are degree-2 packing methods for $\mathbb{Z}_{2^k}$-messages, which are (or can be) used to construct HE-based MPC protocol over $\mathbb{Z}_{2^k}$ following the approach of SPDZ [21]. Most of definitions and statements in this paper are motivated from these examples.

4.1   HELib Packing

In Example 2, we introduced the conventional HE packing method for $\mathbb{Z}_q$-messages into $\mathbb{Z}_q[x]/\Phi_M(x)$, where M is a power-of-two and $q = 1 \pmod{M}$. However, it is not always applicable, e.g. if we consider $\mathbb{Z}_{2^k}$-messages. The problem here is that $\Phi_M(X)$ never fully splits in $\mathbb{Z}_{2^k}$. One way to detour this problem is the following. It was first proposed by Gentry-Halevi-Smart [24] and generalized by Halevi-Shoup [26] to optimize *bootstrapping* procedure for fully homomorphic encryption (particularly, for HELib [25]). In this paper, we will refer this method as HELib packing.

To construct a packing method for $\mathbb{Z}_{p^k}$-messages into $\mathbb{Z}_{p^k}[x]/\Phi_M(x)$, choose M to satisfy $\gcd(M, p) = 1$. Let $\Phi_M(x)$ factor into r distinct degree-d irreducible polynomials in $\mathbb{Z}_p[x]$, where $d := \mathrm{ord}_M(p)$. Then, we have the factorization $\Phi_M(x) = \prod_{i=1}^r f_i(x)$ in $\mathbb{Z}_{p^k}[x]$ via Hensel lifting and the CRT ring isomorphism $\mathbb{Z}_{p^k}[x]/\Phi_M(x) \cong \prod_{i=1}^r \mathbb{Z}_{p^k}[x]/f_i(x)$. The packing algorithm Pack puts i-th $\mathbb{Z}_{p^k}$-message at the constant term of $\mathbb{Z}_{2^k}[x]/f_i(x)$ and puts zeroes at the other coefficients. Define Unpack as the inverse of Pack. It is easy to see that (Pack, Unpack) defines a degree-∞ packing method. However, the HELib packing achieves very low packing density $1/d$.

4.2   Overdrive2k Packing

To design an efficient HE-based MPC protocol over $\mathbb{Z}_{2^k}$, Overdrive2k [31] constructed a degree-2 packing method for $\mathbb{Z}_{2^k}^n$ into $\mathbb{Z}_{2^k}[x]/\Phi_M(x)$, where M is odd (so yielding a CRT ring isomorphism $\mathbb{Z}_{2^k}[x]/\Phi_M(x) \cong \prod_{i=1}^{r} \mathbb{Z}_{2^k}[x]/f_i(x)$ with $\deg(f_i) = d$). For construction, they considered the following problem. Consider a subset A of $[0, d-1]$ with $A = \{a_1, \cdots, a_m\}$ so that $2a_i \neq a_j + a_k$ for all $(i, i) \neq (j, k)$ and $a_i + a_j < d$ for all i, j. The problem is to find the maximum value of $m = |A|$ with A for given d.[7] Given a solution m and A for given d, the packing algorithm of Overdrive2k at level-1 put i-th m messages in $\mathbb{Z}_{2^k}$ at the coefficients of x^{a_i} of an element in $\mathbb{Z}_{2^k}[x]/f_i(x)$ for $a_i \in A$ and put zeroes at the other coefficients. Then, via the ring homomorphism, we can pack $r \cdot m$ messages into a plaintext achieving the packing density of m/d. The authors Overdrive2k noted that the packing density of their method seems to follow the trend of approximately $d^{0.6}/d$.

Since the set A is carefully designed, if we multiply two packed plaintexts, the $(2 \cdot a_i)$-th coefficient of the result equals the multiplied value of a_i-th coefficients of the original plaintexts. That is, Overdrive2k packing is of degree-2. Note that Overdrive2k packing naturally extends to arbitrary degree-2 packing methods for $\mathbb{Z}_{p^k}^n$ into $\mathbb{Z}_{p^k}[x]/f(x)$.

4.3   MHz2k Packing

To further improve the packing density of Overdrive2k, MHz2k [13] construct a degree-2 packing method for $\mathbb{Z}_{2^k}$-messages into $\mathbb{Z}_{2^t}[x]/\Phi_M(x)$, where t is slightly larger than k. Their core idea is to pack messages at *evaluation points* via interpolation unlike Overdrive2k which rather pack at coefficients. The caveat here is, however, that the polynomial interpolation on $\mathbb{Z}_{2^k}$ is not always possible, e.g. there is no $f(x) \in \mathbb{Z}_{2^k}$ satisfying $f(0) = 1$ and $f(2) = 0$ simultaneously. In this context, they propose the *tweaked interpolation*, where they lift the target points of $\mathbb{Z}_{2^k}$ upto a larger ring $\mathbb{Z}_{2^{k+\delta}}$, multiplying an appropriate power-of-two to eliminate the effect of non-invertible elements.

Let $t = k + 2\delta$ and $\mathbb{Z}_{2^t}[x]/\Phi_M(x)$ factors into $\prod_{i=1}^{r} \mathbb{Z}_{2^t}[x]/f_i(x)$ via CRT, where $f_i(x)$ are all of degree-d. The packing algorithm at level-1 perform tweaked interpolation on i-th $\lfloor \frac{d+1}{2} \rfloor$ $\mathbb{Z}_{2^k}$-messages $\{\mu_{ij}\}$, so that we have $L_i(x) \in \mathbb{Z}_{2^t}[x]$ which satisfies (i) $\deg(L_i) \leq \lfloor \frac{d-1}{2} \rfloor$ and (ii) $L_i(j) = \mu_{ij} \cdot 2^\delta$. Then, put $L_i(x)$ in the i-th CRT slot of $\mathbb{Z}_{2^t}[x]/\Phi_M(x)$, i.e. $\mathbb{Z}_{2^t}[x]/f_i(x)$. This gives us a packing density of roughly $k/(2k + 2d)$. Since the degree condition on $L_i(x)$ and extra δ in the modulus are designed to avoid degree overflow and modulus overflow, when the product of two packings is given, we can decode the homomorphically

---

[7] Similar problems were also considered in other cryptography literature [2, 18, 29]. For more detailed discussions, see the full version [14].

multiplied messages without any loss of information. That is, we can unpack at level-2 by evaluating points on each CRT slot and observing the upper k bits of outputs.

Note that MHz2k packing can be naturally extended to a degree-D packing method for $\mathbb{Z}_{p^k}$-messages into $\mathbb{Z}_{p^t}[x]/\Phi_M(x)$ with $\gcd(M, p) = 1$ of density roughly

$$\frac{k}{D \cdot (k + \frac{d}{p-1})}.$$

4.4   Comparison

In this subsection, we compare some properties of the examples previously given in this section. These features are motivations of the definitions and results in later sections. This subsection is summarized in Table 1.

Table 1. Comparisons on degree-2 packing methods for $\mathbb{Z}_{2^k}$-messages

Method	HELib	Overdrive2k	MHz2k
Level-consistency	Consistent	Dependent	Dependent
$t \stackrel{?}{=} k$	$t = k$	$t = k$	$t > k$
Density	$1/d$	$\approx d^{0.6}/d$	$\approx k/(2k + 2d)$

Notice that, in HELib packing which is of degree-∞, packing algorithms and unpacking algorithms are identical for all level. We will later refer these kind of packings as *level-consistent* packings (Sect. 6). However, in Overdrive2k and MHz2k packing, the packing algorithm differs for each level. For example, in Overdrive2k packing, messages are coefficients of x^{a_i}'s at level-1, and coefficients of $x^{2 \cdot a_i}$'s at level-2. We will later refer these kind of packings as *level-dependent* packings (Sect. 6).

One big difference of MHz2k packing from the previous packings is that it uses larger modulus for polynomial ring than that of messages. The other packing methods are sort of coefficient packing, making it no use of increasing the modulus for polynomial ring. This difference will serve as one of the topics in Sect. 5 (e.g. Example 6).

Note that degree-2 MHz2k packing reaches density of nearly $1/2$ when k is sufficiently larger than d. This is true for typical parameters used in HE-based MPC over $\mathbb{Z}_{2^k}$: $k = 64, 128, 196$ and $d \leq 20$. In Sect. 5, we will show that MHz2k packing achieves a certain form of near-optimality (Example 6).

We now examine common features of these methods. Note that there are *invalid* packings regarding to these packing methods. For example, in HELib packing, $a(x) \in \mathbb{Z}_{2^k}[x]/\Phi_M(x)$ is not a valid packing, i.e. $\mathsf{Unpack}(a(x)) = \perp$, if $a(x)$ modulo $f_i(x)$ is not a constant. We will later refer these kind of packings as non-*surjective* packings (Sect. 7).

Also notice that all these packings leverage CRT ring isomorphism, which is a natural and convenient way to achieve parallelism. They pack messages into each CRT slot in an identical and independent manner. We refer packing methods following this approach as *CRT packings*.

5 Bounds on Packing Density

In this section, we examine upper bounds on packing density of degree-D packing methods for $\mathbb{Z}_{p^k}$ and $\mathbb{F}_{p^k}$, where p is a prime (See Sect. 3.2).

5.1 Algebraic Background

We first remark some algebraic facts, which enable proofs in the following subsections.

Proposition 4. *When R is a principal ideal ring (PIR), every submodule of a free R-module of rank n can be finitely generated with n generators.*

Proof. See the full version of this paper [14]. □

Remark 3. Note that $\mathbb{Z}_{p^t}$ is a local PIR. Consider $\mathcal{R} := \mathbb{Z}_{p^t}[x]/f(x)$ as a free $\mathbb{Z}_{p^t}$-module with the rank $\deg(f)$. Then by Nakayama's lemma, the cardinality of minimal generating sets is a well-defined invariant for submodules of $\mathcal{R}$.

Let $\mathcal{A}$ be a linearly independent subset of $\mathcal{R}$. Then, since the span $\langle \mathcal{A} \rangle$ is a submodule of $\mathcal{R}$ with a minimal generating set $\mathcal{A}$, inequality $\deg(f) \geq |\mathcal{A}|$ holds by Proposition 4.

5.2 Packing Density of $\mathbb{Z}_{p^k}$-Message Packings

In this subsection, we examine upper bounds on packing density of degree-D $\mathbb{Z}_{p^k}$-message packings. We begin with an upper bound for degree-1 packing methods: we cannot pack copies of $\mathbb{Z}_{p^k}$ more than the degree of the quotient polynomial. Unlike the simple and plausible statement, the proof is quite involved. In particular, it depends on Remark 3. The following proposition says that we cannot reduce the degree of quotient polynomial significantly and tower the packings along a large modulus. Notice that there are no restriction on t and $f(x)$.

Proposition 5. *There exists a degree-1 packing method for $\mathbb{Z}_{p^k}^n$ into $\mathcal{R} := \mathbb{Z}_{p^t}[x]/f(x)$ with $k \leq t$, only if $n \leq \deg(f)$.*

Proof. Let $(\mathsf{Pack}_1, \mathsf{Unpack}_1)$ be a degree-1 packing method for $\mathbb{Z}_{p^k}^n$ into $\mathcal{R}$. For each $i \in [n]$, choose $a_i(x) \in \mathcal{R}$ such that $\mathsf{Unpack}_1(a_i(x)) = e_i$. View $\mathcal{R}$ as a free $\mathbb{Z}_{p^t}$-module of rank $\deg(f)$, and consider the submodule $\langle a_1(x), \cdots, a_n(x) \rangle$. By linear homomorphic property (Remark 1), when $\sum_{i=1}^{n} c_i \cdot a_i(x) = 0$ for some $c_i \in \mathbb{Z}_{p^t}$, then $c_i = 0 \pmod{p^k}$ must hold. Thus, $\{a_1(x), \cdots, a_n(x)\}$ is a minimal generating set of $\langle a_1(x), \cdots, a_n(x) \rangle$, and therefore $n \leq \deg(f)$ holds (Remark 3). □

In the rest of this subsection, we narrow our scope to packing methods for $\mathbb{Z}_{p^k}^n$ into $\mathbb{Z}_{p^k}[x]/f(x)$ with the same modulus. Indeed, this setting is less general. Nonetheless, our results still have interesting consequences (See Example 6–9). The following is a small remark on packings of non-zero elements modulo p in this setting.

Remark 4. Let $(\mathsf{Pack}_i, \mathsf{Unpack}_i)_{i=1}^D$ be a degree-D packing method for $\mathbb{Z}_{p^k}^n$ into $\mathcal{R} := \mathbb{Z}_{p^k}[x]/f(x)$. For any $i \in [D]$, if $\mathsf{Unpack}_i(a(x)) = \boldsymbol{a}$ for some $\boldsymbol{a} \in \mathbb{Z}_{p^k}^n$ which is non-zero modulo p, then $a(x)$ is also non-zero modulo p. Otherwise, $\mathsf{Unpack}_i(p^{k-1} \cdot a(x)) = \mathsf{Unpack}_i(0) = \boldsymbol{0} \neq p^{k-1} \cdot \boldsymbol{a}$, contradicting the linear homomorphic property (Remark 1). In particular, when $f(x)$ is an irreducible polynomial in $\mathbb{Z}_p[x]$, such $a(x)$ is a unit in $\mathcal{R}$.

Roughly speaking, our main result is that we cannot pack more than d/D $\mathbb{Z}_{p^k}$-messages into $\mathbb{Z}_{p^k}[x]/f(x)$ while satisfying degree-D homomorphic property, where $d = \deg(f)$. Intuitively, the statement can be understood as that we must pack the inputs into lower d/D coefficients since reduction by the quotient polynomial act as randomization and will ruin the structure of packing. However, the proof is much more involved since we have to handle all possible packing methods. Notice that the following theorem subsumes Proposition 5 as the $D = 1$ case in the $t = k$ setting. The essence of the proof is a generic construction of a large set which is required to be linearly independent regardless of specific structures of packing methods.

Theorem 1. *There exists a degree-D packing method for $\mathbb{Z}_{p^k}^n$ into $\mathcal{R} := \mathbb{Z}_{p^k}[x]/f(x)$ where $f(x) \in \mathbb{Z}_{p^k}[x]$ is a degree-d irreducible polynomial modulo p, only if $d \geq D \cdot (n-1) + 1$.*

Proof. Let $(\mathsf{Pack}_i, \mathsf{Unpack}_i)_{i=1}^D$ be a degree-D packing method for $\mathbb{Z}_{p^k}^n$ into $\mathcal{R}$. For each $i \in [n]$, choose $a_i(x) \in \mathcal{R}$ such that $\mathsf{Unpack}_1(a_i(x)) = \boldsymbol{e}_i$. Let us denote $\mathcal{A}^{(r,s)} := \{a_1(x)^r \cdot a_j(x)^s\}_{1 < j \leq n}$. For example, $\mathcal{A}^{(0,D)} = \{a_2(x)^D, \cdots, a_n(x)^D\}$, $\mathcal{A}^{(D,0)} = \{a_1(x)^D\}$, and $\mathcal{A}^{(1,D-1)} = \{a_1(x)a_2(x)^{D-1}, \cdots, a_1(x)a_n(x)^{D-1}\}$.

Step 1: Consider the following set of level-t packings.

$$\mathcal{A}_t := \bigcup_{\substack{r+s=t \\ 0<s}} \mathcal{A}^{(r,s)}$$

We will show that $\mathcal{A}_t$ is linearly independent in $\mathcal{R}$ for all $t \leq D$ by induction on t. The case where $t = 1$ is true by the linear homomorphic property at level-1 (Remark 1): $\mathcal{A}_1 = \{a_2(x), \cdots, a_n(x)\}$ (See also Proposition 5).

Suppose $\mathcal{A}_t$ is linearly independent for some $t < D$. View $\mathcal{A}_{t+1}$ as $\mathcal{A}^{(0,t+1)} \cup a_1(x) \cdot \mathcal{A}_t$. Suppose $\sum_{a_\alpha(x) \in \mathcal{A}_{t+1}} (c_\alpha \cdot a_\alpha(x)) = 0$, for some $c_\alpha \in \mathbb{Z}_{p^k}$. Then, by linear homomorphic property at level-$(t+1)$, $c_\alpha = 0$ must hold for all $a_\alpha(x) \in \mathcal{A}^{(0,t+1)}$, since elements of $a_1(x) \cdot \mathcal{A}_t$ unpack to $\boldsymbol{0}$ and $\mathcal{A}^{(0,t+1)}$ unpacks to a linearly independent set by construction. Subsequently, we have again the following equality:

$$\sum_{a_\alpha(x) \in a_1(x) \cdot \mathcal{A}_t} (c_\alpha \cdot a_\alpha(x)) = 0.$$

Meanwhile, since $a_1(x)$ is a unit in $\mathcal{R}$ (Remark 4) and $\mathcal{A}_t$ is linearly independent by induction hypothesis, $c_\alpha = 0$ must also hold for all $a_\alpha(x) \in a_1(x) \cdot \mathcal{A}_t$. Thus, $\mathcal{A}_t$ is linearly independent in $\mathcal{R}$ for all $t \leq D$.

Step 2: Now consider the set $\mathcal{A} := \mathcal{A}_D \cup \{a_1(x)^D\}$, which coincides with $\{a_1(x)^D, \cdots, a_n(x)^D\} \cup a_1(x) \cdot \mathcal{A}_{D-1}$. Suppose $\sum_{a_\alpha(x) \in \mathcal{A}} (c_\alpha \cdot a_\alpha(x)) = 0$, for some $c_\alpha \in \mathbb{Z}_{p^k}$. Then, by linear homomorphic property at level-D, $c_\alpha = 0$ must hold for all $a_\alpha(x) \in \{a_1(x)^D, \cdots, a_n(x)^D\}$, since elements of $a_1(x) \cdot \mathcal{A}_{D-1}$ unpack to $\mathbf{0}$ and $\{a_1(x)^D, \cdots, a_n(x)^D\}$ unpacks to a linearly independent set by construction. Subsequently, we have again the following equality:

$$\sum_{a_\alpha(x) \in a_1(x) \cdot \mathcal{A}_{D-1}} (c_\alpha \cdot a_\alpha(x)) = 0.$$

Meanwhile, since $a_1(x)$ is a unit in $\mathcal{R}$ and $\mathcal{A}_{D-1}$ is linearly independent by Step 1, $c_\alpha = 0$ must also hold for all $a_\alpha(x) \in a_1(x) \cdot \mathcal{A}_{D-1}$. Thus, $\mathcal{A}$ is linearly independent, and therefore $d \geq |\mathcal{A}| = D(n-1) + 1$ must hold (Remark 3). □

The following are direct consequences of our theorem.

Example 6. Degree-D packing methods for $\mathbb{Z}_{p^k}$-messages into $\mathbb{Z}_{p^k}[x]/f(x)$, where $f(x)$ is a degree-d irreducible polynomial modulo p, have packing density of no larger than $\frac{1}{D} + \frac{1}{d} \cdot (1 - \frac{1}{D})$. Consequently, degree-$D$ *CRT* packing methods for $\mathbb{Z}_{p^k}$-messages into $\mathbb{Z}_{p^k}[x]/f(x)$, where $f(x)$ factors into r distinct irreducible factors modulo p, have packing density of no larger than $\frac{1}{D} + \frac{r}{\deg(f)} \cdot (1 - \frac{1}{D})$ (Sect. 4.4). In particular, degree-D CRT packing methods for $\mathbb{Z}_{2^k}$-messages into $\mathbb{Z}_{2^t}[x]/\Phi_M(x)$, where M is odd and $\Phi_M(x)$ factors into distinct degree-d irreducible factors modulo p, have packing density of no larger than $\frac{1}{D} + \frac{1}{d} \cdot (1 - \frac{1}{D})$.

That is, when parameters are carefully chosen, the MHz2k packing already nearly reach the optimal packing density for packing methods for $\mathbb{Z}_{p^k}$-messages into $\mathbb{Z}_{p^k}[x]/f(x)$ (Sect. 4.3). Thus, if one wants to construct a degree-D packing method for $\mathbb{Z}_{2^k}$-messages into $\mathbb{Z}_{2^t}[x]/\Phi_M(x)$ with substantially better density than the MHz2k packing, the only possibility is choosing $t > k$ or not employing the CRT approach.

Example 7 (RMFE over Galois Ring). Consider RMFE *over Galois rings* for copies of $\mathbb{Z}_{p^k}$ into a larger Galois ring isomorphic to $\mathbb{Z}_{p^k}[x]/f(x)$, which is exactly the setting of Theorem 1. The theorem states that such RMFE cannot have packing density larger than $\frac{1}{2} + \frac{1}{2\deg(f)}$. To the best of our knowledge, this is the first upper bound result on packing density of RMFE over Galois rings. Our theorem also yields upper bounds on packing density of degree-D generalization of RMFE over Galois rings.

Example 8. For $D > 1$, consider degree-D packing methods for $\mathbb{Z}_{p^k}$-messages into $\mathbb{Z}_{p^t}[x]/f(x)$, where $f(x)$ is irreducible modulo p. By Proposition 5, when $t > k$, we cannot achieve a perfect packing density 1. When $t = k$, we cannot achieve a perfect packing density 1 unless $\deg(f) = 1$, by Theorem 1. That is, there is no perfect degree-D packing method for $\mathbb{Z}_{p^k}$-messages into $\mathbb{Z}_{p^t}[x]/f(x)$, when $f(x)$ is irreducible modulo p and $\deg(f) > 1$.

Example 9. For $D > 1$, consider degree-D packing methods for $\mathbb{Z}_{p^k}$-messages into $\mathbb{Z}_{p^t}[x]/f(x)$, where $f(x)$ is square-free modulo p. By Example 8, there is no perfect degree-D CRT packing method for $\mathbb{Z}_{p^k}$-messages into $\mathbb{Z}_{p^t}[x]/f(x)$, unless $f(x)$ splits into distinct linear factors. In particular, there is no perfect degree-D CRT packing method for $\mathbb{Z}_{2^k}$-messages into $\mathbb{Z}_{2^t}[x]/\Phi_M(x)$ when M is odd.

5.3 Packing Density of $\mathbb{F}_{p^k}$-Message Packings

In this subsection, we examine upper bounds on packing density of degree-D $\mathbb{F}_{p^k}$-message packings. We begin with an upper bound for degree-1 packing methods, which is an analogue of Proposition 5. Unlike the simple and plausible statement, the proof is quite involved. In particular, it depends on Remark 3. The following proposition says that we cannot reduce the degree of quotient polynomial significantly and tower the packings along a large modulus. Notice that there are no restriction on t and $f(x)$.

Proposition 6. *There exists a degree-1 packing method for $\mathbb{F}_{p^k}^n$ into $\mathcal{R} := \mathbb{Z}_{p^t}[x]/f(x)$, only if $n \cdot k \leq \deg(f)$.*

Proof. Let $(\mathsf{Pack}_1, \mathsf{Unpack}_1)$ be a degree-1 packing method for $\mathbb{F}_{p^k}^n$ into $\mathcal{R}$. Fix a basis of $\mathbb{F}_{p^k}$ as $\{\beta_1, \cdots, \beta_k\}$. For each $i \in [n]$ and $j \in [k]$, choose $a_{ij}(x) \in \mathcal{R}$ such that $\mathsf{Unpack}_1(a_{ij}(x)) = \beta_j \cdot e_i$. View $\mathcal{R}$ as a free $\mathbb{Z}_{p^t}$-module of rank $\deg(f)$, and consider the submodule $\langle a_{ij}(x)\rangle_{i\in[n],j\in[k]}$. By linear homomorphic property (Remark 1), when $\sum_{i=1}^n c_{ij} \cdot a_{ij}(x) = 0$ for $c_i \in \mathbb{Z}_{p^t}$, then $c_i = 0 \pmod{p}$ must hold. Thus, $\{a_{ij}(x)\}_{i\in[n],j\in[k]}$ is a minimal generating set of $\langle a_{ij}(x)\rangle_{i\in[n],j\in[k]}$, and therefore $n \cdot k \leq \deg(f)$ holds (Remark 3). □

In the rest of this subsection, we narrow our scope to packing methods for $\mathbb{F}_{p^k}^n$ into $\mathbb{Z}_p[x]/f(x)$ with the prime modulus. Indeed, this setting is less general. Nonetheless, our results still have interesting consequences (See Example 10–13).

Our main result in this subsection is the following theorem, which is a finite field analogue of Theorem 1. However, it is much more involved since we must also handle the multiplicative structure inside $\mathbb{F}_{p^k}$. Notice that our theorem subsumes Proposition 6 as the $D = 1$ case in the $t = 1$ setting. The essence of the proof is again a generic construction of a large set which is required to be linearly independent regardless of specific structures of packing methods.

Theorem 2. *Let $\mathcal{B} := \{\beta_1, \cdots, \beta_k\}$ be a basis of $\mathbb{F}_{p^k}$ as a $\mathbb{F}_p$-vector space. There exists a degree-D packing method for $\mathbb{F}_{p^k}^n$ into $\mathcal{R} := \mathbb{Z}_p[x]/f(x)$ where*

$f(x) \in \mathbb{Z}_p[x]$ is a degree-d irreducible polynomial modulo p, only if the following inequality holds.

$$d \geq \dim\langle\beta_1^D, \cdots, \beta_k^D\rangle + (n-1)\sum_{t=1}^{D}\dim\langle\beta_1^t, \cdots, \beta_k^t\rangle$$

Proof (Sketch). Similar to the proof of Theorem 1. See the full version [14]. □

To have a more concrete bound, we prove the following proposition. Let $\sigma_{p^k}^{(t)}$ denote the multiplicative order of p modulo $\frac{p^k-1}{\gcd(p^k-1,t)}$.

Proposition 7. *Let β be a primitive element of $\mathbb{F}_{p^k}$. Regarding the primitive element basis $\{1, \beta, \beta^2, \cdots, \beta^{k-1}\}$, the following equality holds.*

$$\dim\langle 1^t, \beta^t, \beta^{2t}, \cdots, \beta^{(k-1)t}\rangle = \sigma_{p^k}^{(t)}$$

Proof. Observe that $\dim\langle 1^t, \beta^t, \beta^{2t}, \cdots, \beta^{(k-1)t}\rangle$ is equal to the degree of the minimal polynomial of β^t in $\mathbb{F}_p[x]$. The degree of the minimal polynomial of β^t is again equal to the length of the orbit of β^t regarding Frobenius map $x \mapsto x^p$. Since β is a primitive element, we are finding the smallest $s \in \mathbb{Z}^+$ satisfying $t = t \cdot p^s \pmod{p^k - 1}$, which is $\sigma_{p^k}^{(t)}$ by definition. □

Corollary 1. *There exists a degree-D packing method for $\mathbb{F}_{p^k}^n$ into $\mathcal{R} := \mathbb{Z}_p[x]/f(x)$ where $f(x) \in \mathbb{Z}_p[x]$ is a degree-d irreducible polynomial modulo p, only if the following inequality holds.*

$$d \geq \sigma_{p^k}^{(D)} + (n-1)\sum_{t=1}^{D}\sigma_{p^k}^{(t)}$$

Proof. Choose a primitive element β of $\mathbb{F}_{p^k}$ and apply Theorem 2 on the basis $\{1, \beta, \beta^2, \cdots, \beta^{k-1}\}$ with the help of Proposition 7. □

The following are some consequences of our main result.

Example 10 (RMFE). Note that $\sigma_{p^k}^{(1)}$ and $\sigma_{p^k}^{(2)}$ are always k. Then, by Corollary 1, degree-2 packing methods for $\mathbb{F}_{p^k}$-messages into $\mathbb{Z}_p[x]/f(x)$, where $f(x)$ is a degree-d irreducible polynomial, have packing density of no larger than $\frac{1}{2} + \frac{k}{2d}$. That is, packing density of RMFE is upper bounded by $\frac{1}{2} + \frac{k}{2d}$. This is a known result (See [17]). However, previous proofs do not extend to higher-degree cases (See Example 12) or to the Galois ring case (See Example 7).

Example 11 (Degree-2 Packing). By Example 10, degree-2 CRT packing methods for $\mathbb{F}_{p^k}$-messages into $\mathbb{Z}_p[x]/f(x)$, where $f(x)$ factors into r distinct irreducible factors, have packing of no larger than $\frac{1}{2} + \frac{r \cdot k}{2\deg(f)}$ (Sect. 4.4). In particular, degree-2 CRT packing methods for $\mathbb{F}_{2^k}$-messages into $\mathbb{Z}_2[x]/\Phi_M(x)$, where M is odd and $\Phi_M(x)$ factors into distinct degree-d irreducible factors modulo 2, have packing density of no larger than $\frac{1}{2} + \frac{k}{2d}$.

Suppose one wants to design a degree-2 packing method for $\mathbb{F}_{p^k}$-messages into $\mathbb{Z}_{p^t}[x]/f(x)$ which has a packing density substantially larger than $1/2$. Note that choosing $t \geq 2$ already yields packing density no larger than $1/2$ by Proposition 6. Thus, only possibility is not employing the CRT approach.

Example 12 (Degree-3 Packing). Note that $\sigma_{p^k}^{(3)}$ is always k, except the case of $p^k = 4$. Then, by Corollary 1, degree-3 packing methods for $\mathbb{F}_{p^k}$-messages into $\mathbb{Z}_p[x]/f(x)$, where $f(x)$ is a degree-d irreducible polynomial, have packing density of no larger than $\frac{1}{3} + \frac{2k}{3d}$, unless $p^k = 4$. Consequently, degree-3 *CRT* packing methods for $\mathbb{F}_{p^k}$-messages into $\mathbb{Z}_p[x]/f(x)$, where $f(x)$ factors into r distinct irreducible factors, have packing density of no larger than $\frac{1}{3} + \frac{2r \cdot k}{3 \deg(f)}$. In particular, degree-3 CRT packing methods for $\mathbb{F}_{2^k}$-messages into $\mathbb{Z}_2[x]/\Phi_M(x)$, where M is odd and $\Phi_M(x)$ factors into distinct degree-d irreducible factors modulo 2, have packing density of no larger than $\frac{1}{3} + \frac{2k}{3d}$, given $k \neq 2$.

Suppose one wants to design a degree-3 packing method for $\mathbb{F}_{p^k}$-messages into $\mathbb{Z}_{p^t}[x]/f(x)$ which has a packing density substantially larger than $1/3$. Note that choosing $t \geq 3$ already yields packing density no larger than $1/3$ by Proposition 6. Thus, only possibility is choosing $t = 2$ or not employing the CRT approach.

Example 13. By the same arguments as in Example 8 and 9, we have the following: For $D > 1$, there is no perfect degree-D packing method for $\mathbb{F}_{p^k}$-messages into $\mathbb{Z}_{p^t}[x]/f(x)$, when $f(x)$ is irreducible modulo p and $\deg(f) > 1$. Thus, there is no perfect degree-D CRT packing method for $\mathbb{F}_{p^k}$-messages into $\mathbb{Z}_{p^t}[x]/f(x)$, unless $f(x)$ splits into distinct linear factors. In particular, there is no perfect degree-D CRT packing method for $\mathbb{F}_{2^k}$-messages into $\mathbb{Z}_{2^t}[x]/\Phi_M(x)$ when M is odd.

6   Level-Consistency

In this section, we define and examine the concept of *level-consistency*, which is a favorable property for a packing method to have. Our main results are necessary and sufficient conditions for a polynomial ring to allow a level-consistent packing method for $\mathbb{Z}_{p^k}$ and $\mathbb{F}_{p^k}$, where p is a prime (See Sect. 3.2). They limit the achievable efficiency of level-consistent packing methods, yielding the impossiblity of designing an efficient packing methods while satisfying level-consistency.

6.1   Definition and Basic Facts

Definition 6. *For $D > 1$, a degree-D packing method* $(\mathsf{Pack}_i, \mathsf{Unpack}_i)_{i=1}^{D}$ *is called* level-consistent *if* Unpack_i *is all identical for $1 \leq i \leq D$. Otherwise, we say a packing method is* level-dependent.

The notion of level-consistency captures the property whether packings are decodable in an identical way at different levels (Proposition 8). In an algebraic viewpoint, a level-consistent packing has a single Unpack for all levels, which is a *ring homomorphism* defined on where it does not abort. The level-consistency is a desirable feature, as it allows homomorphic computation between different packing levels. On the other hand, when working with level-dependent packing methods, we must be careful about whether the operands are packed in the same packing level as we perform homomorphic computation on packed messages.

For instance, Overdrive2k [31] and MHz2k [13] design and utilize $\mathbb{Z}_{2^k}$-message packing methods, which are *level-dependent*, to construct HE-based MPC protocols over $\mathbb{Z}_{2^k}$ following the approach of SPDZ [21]. Their level-dependency complicates the so-called *reshare* protocol which re-encrypts a *level-zero* HE ciphertext to a *fresh* ciphertext allowing two-level HE to be sufficient for their purpose. The problem here is that a masking HE ciphertext is used twice in the reshare protocol: once to mask the input ciphertext of level-zero and once to reconstruct the fresh ciphertext of level-one by subtracting it. While the difference of HE levels can be managed easily with modulus-switching, that of the packing levels seems to be problematic.

In order to remedy this issue caused by level-dependency, Overdrive2k and MHz2k had to come up with their own solutions. Overdrive2k provides two masking ciphertexts having the *same messages* but in *different packing*: one with level-zero packing and the other with level-one packing. However, this solution substantially degrades the efficiency of the protocol. MHz2k resolves this issue by a technical trick which does not cause any extra cost, closing the gap between the level-consistent and level-dependent packing methods in this case.

This issue does not arise in SPDZ-family [1, 19, 21, 27] over a finite field $\mathbb{Z}_p$, where the conventional packing method is already level-consistent (See Example 2). For detailed discussion, refer to [13]. In a later subsection, we prove the impossibility of designing an efficient $\mathbb{Z}_{2^k}$-message packings while satisfying level-consistency. This justifies the use of *level-dependent* packings in SPDZ-like MPC protocols over $\mathbb{Z}_{2^k}$ and highlights the usefulness of the trick proposed by MHz2k [13].

The following proposition says that a level-consistent packing method can be trivially extended to an arbitrary degree.

Proposition 8. *A level-consistent degree-D packing method $\mathcal{P}$ can be extended to a level-consistent degree-D' packing method $\mathcal{P}'$ for arbitrary $D' > D$.*

Proof. When $\mathcal{P}$ is $(\mathsf{Pack}_i, \mathsf{Unpack})_{i=1}^D$, just define $\mathcal{P}'$ as $(\mathsf{Pack}_1, \mathsf{Unpack})_{i=1}^{D'}$. □

A crucial tool when dealing with a level-consistent packing method is idempotents. We extensively leverage the concept of idempotents and their properties when proving our main results on level-consistency. Here, we list properties of idempotents which are used afterwards.

Proposition 9. *Let R be a finite ring. For all $a \in R$, there exists a positive integer s such that a^s is idempotent, i.e. $a^{2s} = a^s$.*

Proof. See the full version of this paper [14].   □

Proposition 10. *Let R and $\mathcal{R}$ be rings. Let $\mathcal{P}$ be a level-consistent packing method for R^n into $\mathcal{R}$ with identical unpacking algorithms* Unpack. *For any idempotent $\boldsymbol{a} \in R^n$, there exists an idempotent $a(x) \in \mathcal{R}$ such that* Unpack$(a(x)) = \boldsymbol{a}$.

Proof. First, extend $\mathcal{P}$ to a degree-D packing method for a sufficiently large D (Proposition 8). Let $\boldsymbol{a} \in R^n$ be idempotent. Choose an element $\tilde{a}(x) \in \mathcal{R}$ such that Unpack$(\tilde{a}(x)) = \boldsymbol{a}$. By Proposition 9, there exists $s \in \mathbb{Z}^+$ such that $a(x) := \tilde{a}(x)^s$ is idempotent in $\mathcal{R}$. Then, Unpack$(a(x)) = $ Unpack$(\tilde{a}(x)^s) = \boldsymbol{a}^s = \boldsymbol{a}$ holds.
                                                                                   □

Proposition 11. *For a prime p, let $\mathcal{R} := \mathbb{Z}_{p^t}[x]/f(x)$ and $f(x) = g(x)^\ell$ (mod p), where $g(x)$ is an irreducible polynomial in $\mathbb{F}_p[x]$. Then, an idempotent element of $\mathcal{R}$ is either 0 or 1.*

Proof. See the full version of this paper [14].   □

Another tool which is useful when dealing with level-consistent packing methods is nilpotents. The following proposition says any nilpotent must unpack to a nilpotent, given it is a valid packing regarding to a level-consistent method.

Proposition 12. *Let R and $\mathcal{R}$ be rings, and let $\mathcal{P}$ be a level-consistent packing method for R^n into $\mathcal{R}$ with identical unpacking algorithms* Unpack. *For any nilpotent $a(x) \in \mathcal{R}$,* Unpack$(a(x))$ *outputs a nilpotent $\boldsymbol{a} \in R^n$ or a failure $\perp$.*

Proof. Suppose Unpack$(a(x))$ outputs $\boldsymbol{a} \in R^n$. Let s be a positive integer such that $a(x)^s = 0$ in $\mathcal{R}$. Extend $\mathcal{P}$ to a degree-s packing method (Proposition 8). Then, $\boldsymbol{a}^s = $ Unpack$(a(x)^s) = $ Unpack$(0) = \boldsymbol{0}$ holds.   □

Lastly, we introduce the notion of *one-to-one* packing which plays an important role in the proof of our main result.

Definition 7 (One-to-one Packing). *Let R and $\mathcal{R}$ be rings. We say a packing method* (Pack$_i$, Unpack$_i$)$_{i=1}^D$ *for R^n into $\mathcal{R}$ is one-to-one, if there is unique $a(x) \in \mathcal{R}$ such that* Unpack$_i(a(x)) = \boldsymbol{a}$ *for all $\boldsymbol{a} \in R^n$ and $i \in [D]$.*

6.2 Level-Consistency in $\mathbb{Z}_{p^k}$-Message Packings

Our main result on level-consistency in $\mathbb{Z}_{p^k}$-message packings is the following theorem. Our theorem illustrates a necessary condition for a surjective packing method for $\mathbb{Z}_{p^k}$-messages to exist. As mentioned, the proof regards the notion of idempotents (Proposition 10, 11).

Theorem 3. *For a prime p, let $f(x) \in \mathbb{Z}_{p^t}[x]$ have exactly r distinct irreducible factors in $\mathbb{Z}_p[x]$. There exists a level-consistent packing method for $\mathbb{Z}_{p^k}^n$ into $\mathbb{Z}_{p^t}[x]/f(x)$ only if $n \leq r$.*

Proof. Let $f(x)$ be factorized into $\prod_{i=1}^{r} \bar{f}_i(x)$ in $\mathbb{Z}_p[x]$, where each $\bar{f}_i(x)$ is a power of a distinct irreducible polynomial in $\mathbb{Z}_p[x]$. The factorization can be lifted upto $\mathbb{Z}_{p^t}[x]$ via Hensel lifting. Let $f(x) = \prod_{i=1}^{r} f_i(x)$, where $f_i(x) \in \mathbb{Z}_{p^t}[x]$ is the Hensel lift of $\bar{f}_i(x)$ satisfying $\bar{f}_i(x) = f_i(x) \pmod{p}$. By Proposition 11, there are 2^r idempotents in $\mathbb{Z}_{p^t}[x]/f(x) \approx \prod_{i=1}^{r} \mathbb{Z}_{p^t}[x]/f_i(x)$, namely $\{0,1\}^r$. Also note that there are 2^n idempotents in $\mathbb{Z}_{p^k}^n$, namely $\{0,1\}^n$.

By Proposition 10, for each idempotent $\boldsymbol{a}$ of $\mathbb{Z}_{p^k}^n$, there is a distinct idempotent $a(x)$ of $\mathbb{Z}_{p^t}[x]/f(x)$ such that $\mathsf{Unpack}(a(x)) = \boldsymbol{a}$. Thus, the number of idempotents in $\mathbb{Z}_{p^k}^n$ cannot be larger than that of $\mathbb{Z}_{p^t}[x]/f(x)$, and $n \leq r$ holds. $\qquad\square$

The following are some consequences of Theorem 3. We begin with an optimality result for HELib packing (Sect. 4.1).

Example 14. Essentially, Theorem 3 asserts that HELib packing offers the optimal packing density if level-consistency is required. As level-consistency is more than a favorable feature for *fully* homomorphic encryption(FHE), our result reassures that HELib packing is an excellent packing method to use for FHE, and it strongly justifies long line of researches based on such packing method [9,24,26].

The following examples illustrate the hardness of designing an efficient HE packing method for $\mathbb{Z}_{2^k}$-messages while satisfying level-consistency. We have similar results for $\mathbb{Z}_{p^k}$-messages with $p \neq 2$.

Example 15. When $M = 2^m$, since $\Phi_M(x) = (x+1)^{2^{m-1}}$ in $\mathbb{F}_2[x]$, we can pack at most one copy of $\mathbb{Z}_{2^k}$ into $\mathbb{Z}_{2^t}[x]/\Phi_M(x)$ while satisfying level-consistency.

Example 16. When M is an odd, $\Phi_M(x)$ factors into a product of distinct irreducible polynomials of degree $d = \mathrm{ord}_M(2)$ in $\mathbb{F}_2[x]$. Let $\phi(M) = r \cdot d$. Then, we can pack at most r copies of $\mathbb{Z}_{2^k}$ into $\mathbb{Z}_{2^t}[x]/\Phi_M(x)$ while satisfying level-consistency. Note that, since $d > \log M$ by definition, $r < \phi(M)/\log M$.

Example 17. When $M = 2^s \cdot M'$, where M' is an odd, $\Phi_M(x) = \Phi_{M'}(-x^{2^{s-1}}) = \Phi_{M'}(x)^{2^{s-1}}$ in $\mathbb{F}_2[x]$. Thus, we cannot pack more copies of $\mathbb{Z}_{2^k}$ into $\mathbb{Z}_{2^t}[x]/\Phi_M(x)$ than $\mathbb{Z}_{2^t}[x]/\Phi_{M'}(x)$ while satisfying level-consistency.

Theorem 3 also yields the impossibility of level-consistent RMFEs over Galois ring for $\mathbb{Z}_{p^k}$-messages.

Example 18. In $GR(p^t, d) \cong \mathbb{Z}_{p^t}[x]/f(x)$ with a degree-d $f(x)$ which is irreducible modulo p, we can pack at most one copy of $\mathbb{Z}_{p^k}$ while satisfying level-consistency. That is, there is no meaningful level-consistent RMFE over Galois ring for $\mathbb{Z}_{p^k}$-messages.

On the other side, we have the following theorem with a constructive proof, which asserts that the necessary condition in Theorem 3 is also a sufficient one.

Theorem 4. *If there are r distinct irreducible factors of $f(x) \in \mathbb{Z}_{p^t}[x]$ in $\mathbb{F}_p[x]$, then there is a level-consistent packing method for $\mathbb{Z}_{p^k}^r$ into $\mathbb{Z}_{p^t}[x]/f(x)$.*

Proof. Let $f(x)$ be factorized into $\prod_{i=1}^{s} g_i(x)^{\ell_i}$ in $\mathbb{F}_p[x]$, where $s \geq r$ and each $g_i(x)$ is distinct irreducible polynomial in $\mathbb{F}_p[x]$. The factorization can be lifted upto $\mathbb{Z}_{p^k}[x]$ via Hensel lifting. Let $f(x) = \prod_{i=1}^{s} f_i(x)$, where $f_i(x) \in \mathbb{Z}_{p^k}[x]$ is the Hensel lift of $g_i(x)^{\ell_i}$ satisfying $f_i(x) = g_i(x)^{\ell_i} \pmod{p}$. Then, we can identify $\mathbb{Z}_{p^k}[x]/f(x)$ with $\prod_{i=1}^{s} \mathbb{Z}_{p^k}[x]/f_i(x)$ via the CRT ring isomorphism.

There is a trivial ring monomorphism $\psi : \mathbb{Z}_{p^k}^r \to \mathbb{Z}_{p^k}[x]/f(x)$ defined as the following.

$$\psi(a_1, \cdots, a_r) = (a_1, \cdots, a_r, 0, \cdots, 0) \in \prod_{i=1}^{s} \mathbb{Z}_{p^k}[x]/f_i(x)$$

Define the function $\psi^{-1} : \mathbb{Z}_{p^k}[x]/f(x) \to \mathbb{Z}_{p^k}^r \cup \{\bot\}$ as the following.

$$\psi^{-1}(a(x)) = \begin{cases} \boldsymbol{a}, & \text{if there is } \boldsymbol{a} \in \mathbb{Z}_{p^k}^r \text{ such that } \psi(\boldsymbol{a}) = a(x) \\ \bot, & \text{otherwise} \end{cases}$$

Let π_k and ι_k denote the projection and injection between $\mathbb{Z}_{p^t}[x]/f(x)$ and $\mathbb{Z}_{p^k}[x]/f(x)$ respectively. Define $\mathsf{Pack} := \iota_k \circ \psi$ and $\mathsf{Unpack} := \psi^{-1} \circ \pi_k$ (Fig. 1). Then, it is straightforward that $(\mathsf{Pack}, \mathsf{Unpack})$ is a level-consistent packing method.   □

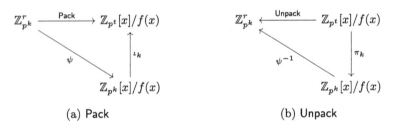

(a) Pack   (b) Unpack

Fig. 1. Definitions of Pack and Unpack in Theorem 4

6.3   Level-Consistency in $\mathbb{F}_{p^k}$-Message Packings

Our main result on level-consistency in $\mathbb{F}_{p^k}$-message packings is the following theorem. It is a finite field analogue of Theorem 3 which is on $\mathbb{Z}_{p^k}$-message packings. Our theorem illustrates a necessary condition for a level-consistent packing method for $\mathbb{F}_{p^k}$-messages to exist.

Theorem 5. *Let r be the number of distinct irreducible factors of $f(x) \in \mathbb{Z}_{p^t}[x]$ in $\mathbb{F}_p[x]$ whose degrees are multiples of k. There exists a level-consistent packing method $\mathbb{F}_{p^k}^n$ into $\mathbb{Z}_{p^t}[x]/f(x)$ only if $n \leq r$.*

Proof (Sketch). Then, using Proposition 12 with the fact that **0** is the only nilpotent element in $\mathbb{F}_{p^k}^n$, we can modify given (Pack, Unpack) to a level-consistent packing method (Pack$'$, Unpack$'$) for $\mathbb{F}_{p^k}^n$ into $\mathbb{F}_p[x]/\hat{g}(x)$, where $\hat{g}(x)$ is the largest square-free factor of $f(x)$.

Moreover, we can find $g(x)$, a divisor of $\hat{g}(x)$, such that for any $a(x) \in \mathbb{F}_p[x]/\hat{g}(x)$ satisfying Unpack$'(a(x)) = \mathbf{0}$, it holds that $a(x) = 0 \pmod{g(x)}$. That is, we can again modify (Pack$'$, Unpack$'$) into a level-consistent *one-to-one* packing method (Pack$''$, Unpack$''$) for $\mathbb{F}_{p^k}^n$ into $\mathbb{F}_p[x]/g(x)$. Then, by arguments on multiplicative orders with help of Proposition 10 and 11, we can eventually prove that $g(x)$ must have n distinct irreducible factors in $\mathbb{F}_p[x]$ whose degrees are multiples of k, in order to such (Pack$''$, Unpack$''$) to exist. For the full proof, see the full version of this paper [14].   □

The following are some consequences of Theorem 5. They illustrate the hardness of designing an efficient HE packing method for $\mathbb{F}_{2^k}$-messages while satisfying level-consistency. We have similar results for $\mathbb{F}_{p^k}$-messages with $p \neq 2$.

Example 19. When $M = 2^m$, since $\Phi_M(x) = (x+1)^{2^{m-1}}$ in $\mathbb{F}_2[x]$, we can only pack copies of $\mathbb{F}_2$ into $\mathbb{Z}_{2^t}[x]/\Phi_M(x)$ while satisfying level-consistency. Even in that case, we can pack at most one copy of $\mathbb{F}_2$.

Example 20. When M is an odd, $\Phi_M(x)$ factors into a product of distinct irreducible polynomials of degree $d = \text{ord}_M(2)$ in $\mathbb{F}_2[x]$. Let $\phi(M) = r \cdot d$. Then, we can only pack copies of $\mathbb{F}_{2^k}$ such that $k | d$ into $\mathbb{Z}_{2^t}[x]/\Phi_M(x)$ while satisfying level-consistency. In that case, we can pack at most r copies of $\mathbb{F}_{2^k}$. Note that, since $d > \log M$ by definition, $r < \phi(M)/\log M$. For instance, if one wants to pack $\mathbb{F}_{2^8}$ into $\mathbb{Z}_{2^t}[x]/\Phi_M(x)$ with an odd M while satisfying level-consistency, then one must choose M such that $\text{ord}_M(2)$ is a multiple of 8.

Example 21. When $M = 2^s \cdot M'$, where M' is an odd, $\Phi_M(x) = \Phi_{M'}(-x^{2^{s-1}}) = \Phi_{M'}(x)^{2^{s-1}}$ in $\mathbb{F}_2[x]$. Thus, we cannot pack more copies of $\mathbb{F}_{2^k}$ into $\mathbb{Z}_{2^t}[x]/\Phi_M(x)$ than $\mathbb{Z}_{2^t}[x]/\Phi_{M'}(x)$ while satisfying level-consistency.

Theorem 5 also yields the impossibility of level-consistent RMFEs.

Example 22. In $\mathbb{F}_{p^d} \cong \mathbb{Z}_p[x]/f(x)$ with a degree-d irreducible $f(x)$, we can pack at most one copy of $\mathbb{F}_{p^k}$ while satisfying level-consistency. Furthermore, if $k \nmid d$, we cannot pack even a single copy of $\mathbb{F}_{p^k}$ into $\mathbb{F}_{p^d}$ while satisfying level-consistency. That is, there is no meaningful level-consistent RMFE.

On the other side, we have the following theorem with a constructive proof, which asserts that the necessary condition in Theorem 5 is also a sufficient one.

Theorem 6. *Suppose there are r distinct irreducible factors of $f(x) \in \mathbb{Z}_{p^t}[x]$ in $\mathbb{F}_p[x]$ whose degrees are multiples of k. Then, there exists a level-consistent packing method $\mathbb{F}_{p^k}^r$ into $\mathbb{Z}_{p^t}[x]/f(x)$.*

Proof (Sketch). Similar to the proof of Theorem 4. See the full version [14].   □

7 Surjectivity

In this section, we define and examine the concept of *surjectivity*, which is a favorable property for a packing method to have. Our main results are necessary and sufficient conditions for a polynomial ring to allow a surjective packing method for $\mathbb{Z}_{p^k}$ and $\mathbb{F}_{p^k}$, where p is a prime (See Sect. 3.2). They limit the achievable efficiency of surjective packing methods, yielding the impossiblity of designing an efficient packing methods while satisfying surjectivity.

7.1 Definition and Basic Facts

Definition 8 (Surjective Packing). *Let $\mathcal{R}$ be a ring. We say a degree-D packing method $(\mathsf{Pack}_i, \mathsf{Unpack}_i)_{i=1}^{D}$ into $\mathcal{R}$ is surjective[8] if there is no $a(x) \in \mathcal{R}$ such that $\mathsf{Unpack}_1(a(x)) = \bot$.*

For a packing method for R^n into $\mathcal{R}$, the notion of surjectivity captures the condition whether every element of $\mathcal{R}$ is decodable. This distiction is essential when designing a cryptographic protocol with the packing method in a malicious setting, where an adversary might freely deviate from the protocol. If there is $a(x) \in \mathcal{R}$ such that $\mathsf{Unpack}_1(a(x)) = \bot$, a malicious adversary might make use of $a(x)$, when one is supposed to use a valid packing according to the protocol. The deviation may not only harm the correctness of the protocol, but also may leak information of honest parties, if such invalid packings are not properly handled.

For instance, Overdrive2k [31] and MHz2k [13] design and utilize $\mathbb{Z}_{2^k}$-message packings which are *not* surjective to construct HE-based MPC protocols over $\mathbb{Z}_{2^k}$ following the approach of SPDZ [21]. In order to mitigate the *invalid* packings, they perform ZKPoMK (Zero-Knowledge Proof of Message Knowledge) to ensure an HE ciphertext encrypts a validly packed plaintext.[9] ZKPoMK do not appear in SPDZ-family [1,19,21,27] over a finite field $\mathbb{Z}_p$, where the conventional packing method is already surjective with perfect packing density (See Example 2). In a later subsection, we prove the impossibility of designing an efficient $\mathbb{Z}_{2^k}$-message packings while satisfying surjectivity. This justifies the use of *non*-surjective packings and the need of ZKPoMK in SPDZ-like MPC protocols over $\mathbb{Z}_{2^k}$.

The following proposition says that the definition of surjectivity trivially extends to all levels. The fact is used throughout this section.

Proposition 13. *Suppose $(\mathsf{Pack}_i, \mathsf{Unpack}_i)_{i=1}^{D}$ is a degree-D surjective packing method for R^n into $\mathcal{R}$. Then, there is no $a(x) \in \mathcal{R}$ such that $\mathsf{Unpack}_i(a(x)) = \bot$, for all $i \in [D]$.*

Proof. By surjectivity and multiplicative homomorphic property, it holds that $\mathsf{Unpack}_2(a(x)) = \mathsf{Unpack}_1(1) \odot \mathsf{Unpack}_1(a(x)) \in R^n$, for all $a(x) \in \mathcal{R}$. Likewise, we can proceed inductively upto $\mathsf{Unpack}_D(\cdot)$. □

---

[8] In a sense that any element of $\mathcal{R}$ *could* be an image of $\mathsf{Pack}_1(\cdot)$.

[9] ZKPoMK was first conceptualized in MHZ2k [13], but it is also performed in Overdrive2k [31] implicitly. For detailed discussion, refer to [13].

A crucial fact when dealing with a surjective packing method is the following proposition on zero-sets. We extensively use the proposition when proving our main results on surjectivity.

Proposition 14 (Zero-set Ideal). *Let R and $\mathcal{R}$ be rings. For $D > 1$, let $(\mathsf{Pack}_i, \mathsf{Unpack}_i)_{i=1}^D$ be a degree-D surjective packing method for R^n into $\mathcal{R}$. Let Z_i be the set consisting of elements $a(x) \in \mathcal{R}$ such that $\mathsf{Unpack}_i(a(x)) = \mathbf{0}$. Then, $Z = Z_1 = \cdots = Z_D$ for some ideal Z of $\mathcal{R}$. Moreover, $|Z| = |\mathcal{R}|/|R|^n$.*

Proof. By Proposition 13 and multiplicative homomorphic property, $\mathcal{R} \cdot Z_i \subset Z_{i+1}$ holds for $i < D$. Since $1 \in \mathcal{R}$, $Z_i \subset \mathcal{R} \cdot Z_i$ holds, and therefore $Z_i \subset \mathcal{R} \cdot Z_i \subset Z_{i+1}$. By Proposition 13 and additive homomorphic property, Z_i's have the same size, namely $|Z_i| = |\mathcal{R}|/|R|^n$. Thus, $Z_i = \mathcal{R} \cdot Z_i = Z_{i+1}$ holds. We can now put $Z := Z_1 = \cdots = Z_D$. Moreover, since $\mathcal{R} \cdot Z = Z$ holds, Z is an ideal of $\mathcal{R}$. □

7.2 Surjectivity in $\mathbb{Z}_{p^k}$-Message Packings

Our main result on surjectivity in $\mathbb{Z}_{p^k}$-message packings is the following theorem. Our theorem illustrates a necessary condition for a surjective packing method for $\mathbb{Z}_{p^k}$-messages to exist.

Theorem 7. *Let $\tilde{r}$ be the number of linear factors of $f(x) \in \mathbb{Z}_{p^t}[x]$ in $\mathbb{Z}_{p^k}[x]$ which are mutually distinct modulo p. For $D > 1$, there exists a degree-D surjective packing method $\mathbb{Z}_{p^k}^n$ into $\mathbb{Z}_{p^t}[x]/f(x)$ only if $n \leq \tilde{r}$.*

Proof (Sketch). Let $(\mathsf{Pack}_i, \mathsf{Unpack}_i)_{i=1}^D$ be a degree-D surjective packing method for $\mathbb{Z}_{p^k}^n$ into $\mathbb{Z}_{p^t}[x]/f(x)$. For all $b(x) \in \mathbb{Z}_{p^t}[x]/f(x)$, since $\mathsf{Unpack}_i(b(x)) = \mathbf{b}$ for some $\mathbf{b} \in \mathbb{Z}_{p^k}^n$ by surjectivity (Proposition 13), $\mathsf{Unpack}_i(p^k \cdot b(x)) = \mathbf{0}$ holds. Thus, we can construct a degree-D surjective packing method $(\mathsf{Pack}_i', \mathsf{Unpack}_i')_{i=1}^D$ for $\mathbb{Z}_{p^k}^n$ into $\mathbb{Z}_{p^k}[x]/f(x)$ with appropriate projections and injections. Then, we repeatedly apply Proposition 14 to show that, for each unit vector $\mathbf{e}_i \in \mathbb{Z}_{p^k}^n$, there exists $a_i(x) \in \mathbb{Z}_{p^k}[x]/f(x)$ such that (i) $\mathsf{Unpack}_1'(a_i(x)) = \mathbf{e}_i$ (ii) $a_i(x)$ is non-zero at exactly one CRT slot. Eventually, again with Proposition 14, we can couple each $a_i(x)$ with distinct linear factors of $f(x) \in \mathbb{Z}_{p^k}[x]$. For a full proof, see the full version of this paper [14]. □

Before we proceed, we state a simple fact on irreducibility of $\Phi_{2^m}(x)$ over a power-of-two modulus.

Proposition 15 (Irreducibility of $\Phi_{2^m}(x)$). *For $M = 2^m$, cyclotomic polynomial $\Phi_M(x)$ is irreducible modulo 4, i.e. there are no $f(x), g(x) \in \mathbb{Z}_4[x]$ such that $f(x) \cdot g(x) = \Phi_M(x)$ (mod 4) and $\deg(f), \deg(g) \geq 1$.*

Proof. See the full version of this paper [14]. □

The following are some consequences of Theorem 7. They illustrate the impossibility of designing a surjective HE packing method for $\mathbb{Z}_{2^k}$-messages with cyclotomic polynomials. We have similar results for $\mathbb{Z}_{p^k}$-messages with $p \neq 2$.

Example 23. When $M = 2^m$, by Proposition 15, we cannot pack any copies of $\mathbb{Z}_{2^k}$ into $\mathbb{Z}_{2^t}[x]/\Phi_M(x)$ while satisfying surjectivity and degree-2 homomorphism.

Example 24. When M is an odd, $\Phi_M(x)$ factors into a product of distinct irreducible polynomials of degree $d = \mathrm{ord}_M(2)$ in $\mathbb{F}_2[x]$. Thus, we cannot pack any copies of $\mathbb{Z}_{2^k}$ into $\mathbb{Z}_{2^t}[x]/\Phi_M(x)$ while satisfying surjectivity and degree-2 homomorphism.

Example 25. When $M = 2^s \cdot M'$, where M' is an odd, $\Phi_M(x) = \Phi_{M'}(-x^{2^{s-1}})$ in $\mathbb{Z}[x]$. Thus, by Example 24, we cannot pack any copies of $\mathbb{Z}_{2^k}$ into $\mathbb{Z}_{2^t}[x]/\Phi_M(x)$ while satisfying surjectivity and degree-2 homomorphism.

Theorem 7 also yields the impossibility of surjective RMFEs over Galois ring for $\mathbb{Z}_{p^k}$-messages.

Example 26. In $GR(p^t, d) \cong \mathbb{Z}_{p^t}[x]/f(x)$ with a degree-d $f(x)$ which is irreducible modulo p, we cannot pack any copy of $\mathbb{Z}_{p^k}$ while satisfying surjectivity, unless $d = 1$. That is, there is no meaningful surjective RMFE over Galois ring for $\mathbb{Z}_{p^k}$-messages.

On the other side, we have the following theorem with a constructive proof, which asserts that the necessary condition in Theorem 7 is also a sufficient one.

Theorem 8. *Suppose there are r linear factors of $f(x) \in \mathbb{Z}_{p^t}[x]$ in $\mathbb{Z}_{p^k}[x]$ which are mutually distinct modulo p. Then, there exists a surjective packing method $\mathbb{Z}_{p^k}^r$ into $\mathbb{Z}_{p^t}[x]/f(x)$.*

Proof. Let $g(x) \in \mathbb{Z}_{p^k}[x]$ be the product of such r linear factors of $f(x)$ in $\mathbb{Z}_{p^k}[x]$. Then, there is a CRT ring isomophism $\psi : \mathbb{Z}_{p^k}^r \xrightarrow{\cong} \mathbb{Z}_{p^k}[x]/g(x)$. Let π_k and ι_k denote the projection and injection between $\mathbb{Z}_{p^t}[x]/f(x)$ and $\mathbb{Z}_{p^k}[x]/f(x)$, and let π_g and ι_g denote those of $\mathbb{Z}_{p^k}[x]/f(x)$ and $\mathbb{Z}_{p^k}[x]/g(x)$ respectively.

Define $\mathsf{Pack} := \iota_k \circ \iota_g \circ \psi$ and $\mathsf{Unpack} := \psi^{-1} \circ \pi_h \circ \pi_k$ (Fig. 2). Then, it is straightforward that $(\mathsf{Pack}, \mathsf{Unpack})$ is a surjective packing method.   □

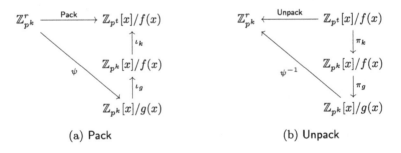

(a) Pack   (b) Unpack

Fig. 2. Definitions of Pack and Unpack in Theorem 8

7.3   Surjectivity in $\mathbb{F}_{p^k}$-Message Packings

Our main result on surjectivity in $\mathbb{F}_{p^k}$-message packings is the following theorem. It is a finite field analogue of Theorem 7 which is on $\mathbb{Z}_{p^k}$-message packings. Our theorem illustrates a necessary condition for a surjective packing method for $\mathbb{F}_{p^k}$-messages to exist.

Theorem 9. *Let r be the number of distinct degree-k irreducible factors of $f(x) \in \mathbb{Z}_{p^t}[x]$ in $\mathbb{F}_p[x]$. For $D > 1$, there exists a degree-D surjective packing method $\mathbb{F}_{p^k}^n$ into $\mathbb{Z}_{p^t}[x]/f(x)$ only if $n \le r$.*

Proof (Sketch). Let $(\mathsf{Pack}_i, \mathsf{Unpack}_i)_{i=1}^D$ be a degree-D surjective packing method for $\mathbb{F}_{p^k}^n$ into $\mathbb{Z}_{p^t}[x]/f(x)$. For all $b(x) \in \mathbb{Z}_{p^t}[x]/f(x)$, since $\mathsf{Unpack}_i(b(x)) = \boldsymbol{b}$ for some $\boldsymbol{b} \in \mathbb{F}_{p^k}^n$ by surjectivity (Proposition 13), $\mathsf{Unpack}_i(p \cdot b(x)) = \boldsymbol{0}$ holds. Thus, we can construct a degree-D surjective packing method $(\mathsf{Pack}_i', \mathsf{Unpack}_i')_{i=1}^D$ for $\mathbb{F}_{p^k}^n$ into $\mathbb{F}_p[x]/f(x)$ with appropriate projections and injections.

By Proposition 14 and the fact that $\mathcal{R} := \mathbb{F}_p[x]/f(x)$ is a principal ideal ring, the zero-set ideal can be set as $Z = \breve{g}(x) \cdot \mathcal{R}$ for some $\breve{g}(x) \in \mathbb{F}_p[x]$ which divides $f(x)$. Let $g(x) := f(x)/\breve{g}(x)$. Then, using $\mathcal{R}/Z \cong \mathbb{F}_p[x]/g(x)$, we can construct a degree-D surjective packing method $(\mathsf{Pack}_i'', \mathsf{Unpack}_i'')_{i=1}^D$ for $\mathbb{F}_{p^k}^n$ into $\mathbb{F}_p[x]/g(x)$ with appropriate projections and injections. Note that $\deg(g) = k \cdot n$ since $|\mathcal{R}/Z| = p^{kn}$ by Proposition 14. Then by a counting argument on zero-divisors, we can show that $g(x)$ must factor into n distinct degree-k irreducible polynomials to allow such packing. For the full proof, see the full version [14]. $\square$

The following are some consequences of Theorem 9. They illustrate the hardness of designing an efficient HE packing method for $\mathbb{F}_{2^k}$-messages while satisfying surjectivity. We have similar results for $\mathbb{F}_{p^k}$-messages with $p \neq 2$.

Example 27. When $M = 2^m$, since $\Phi_M(x) = (x+1)^{2^{m-1}}$ in $\mathbb{F}_2[x]$, we can only pack copies of $\mathbb{F}_2$ into $\mathbb{Z}_{2^t}[x]/\Phi_M(x)$ while satisfying surjectivity and degree-2 homomorphism. Even in that case, we can pack at most one copy of $\mathbb{F}_2$.

Example 28. When M is an odd, $\Phi_M(x)$ factors into a product of distinct irreducible polynomials of degree $d = \mathrm{ord}_M(2)$ in $\mathbb{F}_2[x]$. Let $\phi(M) = r \cdot d$. Then, we can only pack copies of $\mathbb{F}_{2^d}$ into $\mathbb{Z}_{2^t}[x]/\Phi_M(x)$ while satisfying surjectivity and degree-2 homomorphism. In that case, we can pack at most r copies of $\mathbb{F}_{2^d}$. Note that, since $d > \log M$ by definition, $r < \phi(M)/\log M$.

For instance, if one wants to pack $\mathbb{F}_{2^8}$ into $\mathbb{Z}_{2^t}[x]/\Phi_M(x)$ with an odd M while satisfying the conditions, then one must choose M such that $\mathrm{ord}_M(2) = 8$. However, such M cannot be larger than $(2^8 - 1)$ and might be too small for a secure parameter of HE.

Example 29. When $M = 2^s \cdot M'$, where M' is an odd, $\Phi_M(x) = \Phi_{M'}(-x^{2^{s-1}}) = \Phi_{M'}(x)^{2^{s-1}}$ in $\mathbb{F}_2[x]$. Thus, we cannot pack more copies of $\mathbb{F}_{2^k}$ into $\mathbb{Z}_{2^t}[x]/\Phi_M(x)$ than $\mathbb{Z}_{2^t}[x]/\Phi_{M'}(x)$ while satisfying surjectivity and degree-2 homomorphism.

Meanwhile, using such M can be useful when packing copies of a small field: it enables to meet certain level of HE security by enlarging the degree of the ring. See Example 28.

Theorem 9 also yields the impossibility of surjective RMFEs.

Example 30. In $\mathbb{F}_{p^d} \cong \mathbb{Z}_p[x]/f(x)$ with a degree-d irreducible $f(x)$, we cannot pack even a single copy of $\mathbb{F}_{p^k}$ while satisfying surjectivity and degree-2 homomorphism, if $k \neq d$. That is, there is no meaningful surjective RMFE.

On the other side, we have the following theorem with a constructive proof, which asserts that the necessary condition in Theorem 9 is also a sufficient one.

Theorem 10. *If there are r distinct degree-k irreducible factors of $f(x) \in \mathbb{Z}_{p^t}[x]$ in $\mathbb{F}_p[x]$, then there exists a surjective packing method $\mathbb{F}_{p^k}^r$ into $\mathbb{Z}_{p^t}[x]/f(x)$.*

Proof (Sketch). Similar to the proof of Theorem 8. See the full version [14]. □

Acknowledgement. The authors thank Dongwoo Kim for insightful discussions on packing methods, Donggeon Yhee for discussions on Proposition 7, and Minki Hhan for constructive comments on an earlier version of this work. The authors also thank the reviewers of Eurocrypt 2022 who provided thoughtful suggestions to improve the earlier version of this paper. This work was supported by Institute of Information & Communications Technology Planning & Evaluation (IITP) grant funded by the Korea government (MSIT) (No. 2020-0-00840, Development and Library Implementation of Fully Homomorphic Machine Learning Algorithms supporting Neural Network Learning over Encrypted Data).

References

1. Baum, C., Cozzo, D., Smart, N.P.: Using TopGear in overdrive: a more efficient ZKPoK for SPDZ. In: Paterson, K.G., Stebila, D. (eds.) SAC 2019. LNCS, vol. 11959, pp. 274–302. Springer, Cham (2020). https://doi.org/10.1007/978-3-030-38471-5_12

2. Block, A.R., Maji, H.K., Nguyen, H.H.: Secure computation based on leaky correlations: high resilience setting. In: Katz, J., Shacham, H. (eds.) CRYPTO 2017. LNCS, vol. 10402, pp. 3–32. Springer, Cham (2017). https://doi.org/10.1007/978-3-319-63715-0_1

3. Block, A.R., Maji, H.K., Nguyen, H.H.: Secure computation with constant communication overhead using multiplication embeddings. In: Chakraborty, D., Iwata, T. (eds.) INDOCRYPT 2018. LNCS, vol. 11356, pp. 375–398. Springer, Cham (2018). https://doi.org/10.1007/978-3-030-05378-9_20

4. Brakerski, Z., Gentry, C., Vaikuntanathan, V.: (Leveled) fully homomorphic encryption without bootstrapping. In: Proceedings of the 3rd Innovations in Theoretical Computer Science Conference, pp. 309–325 (2012)

5. Cascudo, I., Cramer, R., Xing, C., Yuan, C.: Amortized complexity of information-theoretically secure MPC revisited. In: Shacham, H., Boldyreva, A. (eds.) CRYPTO 2018. LNCS, vol. 10993, pp. 395–426. Springer, Cham (2018). https://doi.org/10.1007/978-3-319-96878-0_14

6. Cascudo, I., Giunta, E.: On interactive oracle proofs for Boolean R1CS statements. Cryptology ePrint Archive, Report 2021/694 (2021)

7. Cascudo, I., Gundersen, J.S.: A secret-sharing based MPC protocol for Boolean circuits with good amortized complexity. In: Pass, R., Pietrzak, K. (eds.) TCC 2020. LNCS, vol. 12551, pp. 652–682. Springer, Cham (2020). https://doi.org/10.1007/978-3-030-64378-2_23

8. Castryck, W., Iliashenko, I., Vercauteren, F.: Homomorphic SIM^{2}D operations: single instruction much more data. In: Nielsen, J.B., Rijmen, V. (eds.) EUROCRYPT 2018. LNCS, vol. 10820, pp. 338–359. Springer, Cham (2018). https://doi.org/10.1007/978-3-319-78381-9_13

9. Chen, H., Han, K.: Homomorphic lower digits removal and improved FHE bootstrapping. In: Nielsen, J.B., Rijmen, V. (eds.) EUROCRYPT 2018. LNCS, vol. 10820, pp. 315–337. Springer, Cham (2018). https://doi.org/10.1007/978-3-319-78381-9_12

10. Chen, H., Laine, K., Player, R., Xia, Y.: High-precision arithmetic in homomorphic encryption. In: Smart, N.P. (ed.) CT-RSA 2018. LNCS, vol. 10808, pp. 116–136. Springer, Cham (2018). https://doi.org/10.1007/978-3-319-76953-0_7

11. Cheon, J.H., Jeong, J., Lee, J., Lee, K.: Privacy-preserving computations of predictive medical models with minimax approximation and non-adjacent form. In: Brenner, M., et al. (eds.) FC 2017. LNCS, vol. 10323, pp. 53–74. Springer, Cham (2017). https://doi.org/10.1007/978-3-319-70278-0_4

12. Cheon, J.H., Kim, A., Kim, M., Song, Y.: Homomorphic encryption for arithmetic of approximate numbers. In: Takagi, T., Peyrin, T. (eds.) ASIACRYPT 2017. LNCS, vol. 10624, pp. 409–437. Springer, Cham (2017). https://doi.org/10.1007/978-3-319-70694-8_15

13. Cheon, J.H., Kim, D., Lee, K.: MHz2k: MPC from HE over $\mathbb{Z}_{2^k}$ with new packing, simpler Reshare, and better ZKP. In: Malkin, T., Peikert, C. (eds.) CRYPTO 2021. LNCS, vol. 12826, pp. 426–456. Springer, Cham (2021). https://doi.org/10.1007/978-3-030-84245-1_15

14. Cheon, J.H., Lee, K.: Limits of polynomial packings for $\mathbb{Z}_{p^k}$ and $\mathbb{F}_{p^k}$. Cryptology ePrint Archive, Report 2021/1033 (2021)

15. Cramer, R., Damgård, I., Escudero, D., Scholl, P., Xing, C.: SPD$\mathbb{Z}_{2^k}$: efficient MPC mod 2^k for dishonest majority. In: Shacham, H., Boldyreva, A. (eds.) CRYPTO 2018. LNCS, vol. 10992, pp. 769–798. Springer, Cham (2018). https://doi.org/10.1007/978-3-319-96881-0_26

16. Cramer, R., Rambaud, M., Xing, C.: Asymptotically-good arithmetic secret sharing over $\mathbb{Z}/p^\ell\mathbb{Z}$ with strong multiplication and its applications to efficient MPC. In: Malkin, T., Peikert, C. (eds.) CRYPTO 2021. LNCS, vol. 12827, pp. 656–686. Springer, Cham (2021). https://doi.org/10.1007/978-3-030-84252-9_22

17. Cramer, R., Xing, C., Yuan, C.: On the complexity of arithmetic secret sharing. In: Pass, R., Pietrzak, K. (eds.) TCC 2020. LNCS, vol. 12552, pp. 444–469. Springer, Cham (2020). https://doi.org/10.1007/978-3-030-64381-2_16

18. Dalskov, A., Lee, E., Soria-Vazquez, E.: Circuit amortization friendly encodings and their application to statistically secure multiparty computation. In: Moriai, S., Wang, H. (eds.) ASIACRYPT 2020. LNCS, vol. 12493, pp. 213–243. Springer, Cham (2020). https://doi.org/10.1007/978-3-030-64840-4_8

19. Damgård, I., Keller, M., Larraia, E., Pastro, V., Scholl, P., Smart, N.P.: Practical covertly secure MPC for dishonest majority – or: breaking the SPDZ limits. In: Crampton, J., Jajodia, S., Mayes, K. (eds.) ESORICS 2013. LNCS, vol. 8134, pp. 1–18. Springer, Heidelberg (2013). https://doi.org/10.1007/978-3-642-40203-6_1

20. Damgård, I., Larsen, K.G., Nielsen, J.B.: Communication lower bounds for statistically secure MPC, with or without preprocessing. In: Boldyreva, A., Micciancio, D. (eds.) CRYPTO 2019. LNCS, vol. 11693, pp. 61–84. Springer, Cham (2019). https://doi.org/10.1007/978-3-030-26951-7_3

21. Damgård, I., Pastro, V., Smart, N., Zakarias, S.: Multiparty computation from somewhat homomorphic encryption. In: Safavi-Naini, R., Canetti, R. (eds.) CRYPTO 2012. LNCS, vol. 7417, pp. 643–662. Springer, Heidelberg (2012). https://doi.org/10.1007/978-3-642-32009-5_38

22. Fan, J., Vercauteren, F.: Somewhat practical fully homomorphic encryption. Cryptology ePrint Archive, Report 2012/144 (2012)

23. Gentry, C.: Fully homomorphic encryption using ideal lattices. In: Proceedings of the Forty-First Annual ACM Symposium on Theory of Computing, pp. 169–178 (2009)

24. Gentry, C., Halevi, S., Smart, N.P.: Better bootstrapping in fully homomorphic encryption. In: Fischlin, M., Buchmann, J., Manulis, M. (eds.) PKC 2012. LNCS, vol. 7293, pp. 1–16. Springer, Heidelberg (2012). https://doi.org/10.1007/978-3-642-30057-8_1

25. Halevi, S., Shoup, V.: Helib. Retrieved from HELib (2014). https://github.com.homenc/HElib

26. Halevi, S., Shoup, V.: Bootstrapping for HElib. In: Oswald, E., Fischlin, M. (eds.) EUROCRYPT 2015. LNCS, vol. 9056, pp. 641–670. Springer, Heidelberg (2015). https://doi.org/10.1007/978-3-662-46800-5_25

27. Keller, M., Pastro, V., Rotaru, D.: Overdrive: making SPDZ great again. In: Nielsen, J.B., Rijmen, V. (eds.) EUROCRYPT 2018. LNCS, vol. 10822, pp. 158–189. Springer, Cham (2018). https://doi.org/10.1007/978-3-319-78372-7_6

28. Kim, A., Song, Y., Kim, M., Lee, K., Cheon, J.H.: Logistic regression model training based on the approximate homomorphic encryption. BMC Med. Genomics 11(4), 23–31 (2018)

29. Lipmaa, H.: Progression-free sets and sublinear pairing-based non-interactive zero-knowledge arguments. In: Cramer, R. (ed.) TCC 2012. LNCS, vol. 7194, pp. 169–189. Springer, Heidelberg (2012). https://doi.org/10.1007/978-3-642-28914-9_10

30. Lyubashevsky, V., Peikert, C., Regev, O.: On ideal lattices and learning with errors over rings. In: Gilbert, H. (ed.) EUROCRYPT 2010. LNCS, vol. 6110, pp. 1–23. Springer, Heidelberg (2010). https://doi.org/10.1007/978-3-642-13190-5_1

31. Orsini, E., Smart, N.P., Vercauteren, F.: Overdrive2k: efficient secure MPC over $\mathbb{Z}_{2^k}$ from somewhat homomorphic encryption. In: Jarecki, S. (ed.) CT-RSA 2020. LNCS, vol. 12006, pp. 254–283. Springer, Cham (2020). https://doi.org/10.1007/978-3-030-40186-3_12

32. Polychroniadou, A., Song, Y.: Constant-overhead unconditionally secure multiparty computation over binary fields. In: Canteaut, A., Standaert, F.-X. (eds.) EUROCRYPT 2021. LNCS, vol. 12697, pp. 812–841. Springer, Cham (2021). https://doi.org/10.1007/978-3-030-77886-6_28

33. Smart, N.P., Vercauteren, F.: Fully homomorphic encryption with relatively small key and ciphertext sizes. In: Nguyen, P.Q., Pointcheval, D. (eds.) PKC 2010. LNCS, vol. 6056, pp. 420–443. Springer, Heidelberg (2010). https://doi.org/10.1007/978-3-642-13013-7_25

34. Smart, N.P., Vercauteren, F.: Fully homomorphic SIMD operations. Des. Codes Cryptogr. 71(1), 57–81 (2014). https://doi.org/10.1007/s10623-012-9720-4

High-Precision Bootstrapping for Approximate Homomorphic Encryption by Error Variance Minimization

Yongwoo Lee[1,2], Joon-Woo Lee[2], Young-Sik Kim[3(✉)], Yongjune Kim[4], Jong-Seon No[2], and HyungChul Kang[1]

[1] Samsung Advanced Institute of Technology, Suwon-si, Gyeonggi-do, Korea
{yw0803.lee,hc1803.kang}@samsung.com
[2] Department of Electrical and Computer Engineering, INMC, Seoul National University, Seoul, Korea
joonwoo3511@ccl.snu.ac.kr, jsno@snu.ac.kr
[3] Department of Information and Communication Engineering, Chosun University, Gwangju, Korea
iamyskim@chosun.ac.kr
[4] Department of Electrical Engineering and Computer Science, DGIST, Daegu, Korea
yjk@dgist.ac.kr

Abstract. The Cheon-Kim-Kim-Song (CKKS) scheme (Asiacrypt'17) is one of the most promising homomorphic encryption (HE) schemes as it enables privacy-preserving computing over real (or complex) numbers. It is known that bootstrapping is the most challenging part of the CKKS scheme. Further, homomorphic evaluation of modular reduction is the core of the CKKS bootstrapping. As modular reduction is not represented by the addition and multiplication of complex numbers, approximate polynomials for modular reduction should be used. The best-known techniques (Eurocrypt'21) use a polynomial approximation for trigonometric functions and their composition. However, all the previous methods are based on an indirect approximation, and thus it requires lots of multiplicative depth to achieve high accuracy. This paper proposes a direct polynomial approximation of modular reduction for CKKS bootstrapping, which is optimal in error variance and depth. Further, we propose an efficient algorithm, namely the lazy baby-step giant-step (BSGS) algorithm, to homomorphically evaluate the approximate polynomial, utilizing the lazy relinearization/rescaling technique. The lazy-BSGS reduces the computational complexity by half compared to the ordinary BSGS algorithm. The performance improvement for the CKKS scheme by the proposed algorithm is verified by implementation using HE libraries. The implementation results show that the proposed method has a multiplicative depth of 10 for modular reduction to achieve the state-of-the-art accuracy, while the previous methods have depths of 11 to 12. Moreover, we achieve higher accuracy within a small multiplicative depth, for example, 93-bit within multiplicative depth 11.

© International Association for Cryptologic Research 2022
O. Dunkelman and S. Dziembowski (Eds.): EUROCRYPT 2022, LNCS 13275, pp. 551–580, 2022.
https://doi.org/10.1007/978-3-031-06944-4_19

Keywords: Bootstrapping · Cheon-Kim-Kim-Song (CKKS) scheme · Fully homomorphic encryption (FHE) · Privacy-preserving machine learning (PPML) · Signal-to-noise ratio (SNR)

1   Introduction

Homomorphic encryption (HE) is a specific class of encryption schemes that enables computation over encrypted data. The Cheon-Kim-Kim-Song (CKKS) scheme [12] is one of the highlighted fully homomorphic encryption (FHE) schemes as it supports efficient computation on real (or complex) numbers, which are the usual data type for many applications such as deep learning. As the other HE schemes are designed for different domains, the CKKS scheme is known to be the most efficient for real numbers. For example, Brakerski-Fan-Vercauteren (BFV) [5,6,17] and Brakerski-Gentry-Vaikuntanathan (BGV) [4] schemes are designed for integer messages in $\mathbb{Z}_q$, and FHEW/TFHE [13–15] are designed for binary circuits.

Gentry's blueprint of bootstrapping provides the idea of homomorphic re-encryption of ciphertext. In CKKS bootstrapping, the modular reduction by an integer is performed homomorphically. However, the modular reduction function is not represented by the addition and multiplication of complex numbers. Hence, an approximate polynomial of trigonometric functions is used in prior arts [3,7,9,18,24], which have two limitations in practice: i) these are indirect approximations, which require larger multiplicative depths, and ii) the measure of approximation error is minimax-base (minimizing the upper bound of the approximation error). This paper shows that the minimax polynomial does not guarantee the minimax bootstrapping error. We propose that the error variance would be a better measure than the minimax error, especially for bootstrapping.

The CKKS scheme provides the trade-off between the efficiency and precision of messages as encrypted data of the CKKS scheme inherently has noise. Errors in encrypted data are propagated and added along with homomorphic operations. Hence, the error should be carefully measured when we design a circuit for efficiency and security in CKKS. Moreover, as attacks against CKKS have recently been proposed [11,26,27], reducing errors of the CKKS scheme becomes more crucial to mitigate the risk of the attacks.

1.1   Our Contributions

This paper contains contributions to the high-precision bootstrapping of the CKKS scheme. We propose i) a method to find the optimal approximate polynomial for the modular reduction in bootstrapping and ii) an efficient algorithm for homomorphic evaluation of polynomials.

First, we propose the optimal approximate polynomial for CKKS bootstrapping in the aspect of signal-to-noise ratio (SNR), which improves the precision of CKKS bootstrapping. As a result, we can reserve more levels after bootstrapping while achieving the best-known precision, where the level of a ciphertext is defined as the number of successive multiplications that can be performed to the ciphertext without bootstrapping. The proposed approximate polynomial has the following three features: i) an optimal measure of error for CKKS bootstrapping: we show that an approximate polynomial that achieves the least error variance is also optimal for CKKS bootstrapping in the aspect of SNR. ii) a direct approximation: the approximate polynomial of modular reduction is directly obtained from the whole polynomial space of degree n, i.e., P_n, using the error variance-minimizing method, and thus it has less multiplicative depths compared to the previous methods (In other words, less bootstrapping is required for the same circuit.) iii) reduction of error from noisy calculation: in the polynomial evaluation over CKKS, each polynomial basis has an error. Unlike previous bootstrapping methods, the proposed method minimizes the errors introduced by noisy basis as well as the approximation error.

Second, we propose a novel variant of the baby-step giant-step (BSGS) algorithm, called the lazy-BSGS algorithm, which reduces the number of relinearizations by half compared to ordinary BSGS algorithms. The proposed lazy-BSGS algorithm is more efficient for higher degree polynomial. The proposed approximate polynomial has a high degree, while the previous methods use a composition of small-degree polynomials. Thus, the lazy-BSGS algorithm makes the evaluation time of the proposed polynomial comparable to the previous methods.

Note for the First Contribution. Previous methods utilized the minimax approximate polynomial of modular reduction function for bootstrapping to reduce the bootstrapping error [18,24]. However, in CKKS bootstrapping, a linear transformation on slot values, called SLOTTOCOEFF, is performed, and its resulting ciphertext is the sum of thousands of noisy values. Since many noisy values are added, the upper bound on the final error value is loose. Hence, we propose to minimize the error variance instead of the upper bound on the error.

Besides the approximation error, each polynomial basis also has an error in CKKS, and it is amplified when we multiply large coefficients of the approximate polynomial. The previous approximation method could not control these errors with the approximate polynomial coefficients. Thus, they used the trigonometric function and double angle formula instead, to make the approximation degree small [3,18,24]. This indirect approximation results in larger multiplicative depths. It is preferred to reserve more levels after bootstrapping as it can reduce the number of bootstrapping in the whole system; moreover, the number of remaining levels after bootstrapping is also important for an efficient circuit design of algorithms using CKKS, for example, in [23], the depth of activation layer is optimized for the levels after bootstrapping. The proposed method minimizes the basis error variance as well as the approximation error variance, so it has less multiplicative depths compared to the previous composition of trigonometric functions. To the best of our knowledge, this is the first method to find the optimal approximate polynomial that minimizes both the approximation error and the error in the basis at the same time.

We show that from the learning with error (LWE) assumption, the input of approximate polynomial follows a distribution similar to Irwin-Hall distribution, regardless of the security. The proposed method exploits this property to improve the approximation accuracy. Also, we derive an analytical solution for our error variance-minimizing approximate polynomial, while the previous minimax approximate polynomial was obtained by iterative algorithms [18,24].

Note for the Second Contribution. As rescaling and relinearization introduce additional errors, it is desirable to perform them as late as possible. In addition, the number of rescalings/relinearizations is also reduced by reordering the operations to delay the relinearization/rescaling. This technique, the so-called lazy rescaling/relinearization technique, has been applied to reduce the computational complexity in [1,8,22]. We propose a rigorous analysis on lazy rescaling and relinearization in the BSGS algorithm. Moreover, we propose the algorithm to find the optimal approximate polynomial, which fits the lazy-BSGS algorithm for odd functions.

1.2 Related Works

Bootstrapping of the CKKS Scheme. Since the CKKS bootstrapping was firstly proposed in [9], the Chebyshev interpolation has been applied to the homomorphic evaluation of modular reduction [7,18]. Then, a technique for direct approximation was proposed using the least squares method [25] and Lagrange interpolation [19]. However, the magnitudes of coefficients of those approximate polynomials are too large. The algorithm to find minimax approximate polynomial using improved multi-interval Remez algorithm and the use of arcsin to reduce approximation error of the modular reduction were presented in [24]. The bootstrapping for the non-sparse-key CKKS scheme was proposed, and the computation time for homomorphic linear transformations was significantly improved by using double hoisting in [3]. Julta and Manohar proposed to use sine series approximation [20], but as there exists a linear transformation from sine series $\{\sin(kx)\}$ to power of sine functions $\{\sin(x)^k\}$, this method is also based on trigonometric functions.

Attacks on the CKKS Scheme and High-Precision Bootstrapping. An attack to recover the secret key using the error pattern after decryption was recently proposed by Li and Micciancio [26], and thus it becomes more crucial to reduce the error in CKKS. One possible solution to this attack is to add a huge error, so-called the noise flooding technique [16] or perform rounding after decryption to make the plaintext error-free [26]. In order to use the noise flooding technique, the CKKS scheme requires much higher precision, and the bootstrapping error is the bottleneck of precision. Although a lot of research is required on how to exploit the bootstrapping error for cryptanalysis of CKKS, the high-precision bootstrapping is still an interesting topic [3,20,24,25].

1.3 Organization of This Paper

The remainder of the paper is organized as follows. In Sect. 2, we provide the necessary notations and SNR perspective on error. The CKKS scheme and its bootstrapping algorithm are summarized in Sect. 3. We provide a new method to find the optimal direct approximate polynomials for the CKKS scheme and also show its optimality in Sect. 4. Section 5 provides the novel lazy-BSGS algorithm for the efficient evaluation of approximate polynomial for CKKS bootstrapping. The implementation results and comparison for precision and timing performance for the CKKS bootstrapping are given in Sect. 6. Finally, we conclude the paper in Sect. 7.

2   Preliminaries

2.1   Basic Notation

Vectors are denoted in boldface, such as $\boldsymbol{v}$, and all vectors are column vectors. Matrices are denoted by boldfaced capital letters, i.e., $\mathbf{M}$. We denote the inner product of two vectors by $\langle \cdot, \cdot \rangle$ or simply $\cdot$. $\lceil \cdot \rfloor$, $\lfloor \cdot \rfloor$, and $\lceil \cdot \rceil$ denote the rounding, floor, and ceiling functions, respectively. $[m]_q$ is the modular reduction, i.e., the remainder of m dividing by q. $x \leftarrow \mathcal{D}$ denotes the sampling x according to a distribution $\mathcal{D}$. When a set is used instead of distribution, x is sampled uniformly at random among the set elements. Random variables are denoted by capital letters such as X. $E[X]$ and $Var[X]$ denote the mean and variance of random variable X, respectively. For a function f, $Var[f(X)]$ can be simply denoted by $Var[f]$. $\|\boldsymbol{a}\|_2$ and $\|\boldsymbol{a}\|_\infty$ denote the L-2 norm and the infinity norm, and when the input is a polynomial, those denote the norm of coefficient vector. We denote the supreme norm of a function $\|f\|_{\mathsf{sup}} := \sup_{t \in \mathcal{D}} |f(t)|$ for a given domain $\mathcal{D}$.

Let $\Phi_M(X)$ be the M-th cyclotomic polynomial of degree N, and when M is a power of two, $M = 2N$, and $\Phi_M(X) = X^N + 1$. Let $\mathcal{R} = \mathbb{Z}/\langle \Phi_M(X) \rangle$ be the ring of integers of a number field $\mathcal{S} = \mathbb{Q}/\langle \Phi_M(X) \rangle$, where $\mathbb{Q}$ is the set of rational numbers and we write $\mathcal{R}_q = \mathcal{R}/q\mathcal{R}$. A polynomial $a(X) \in \mathcal{R}$ can be denoted by a by omitting X when it is obvious. Since the multiplicative depth of a circuit is crucial in CKKS, from here on, the multiplicative depth is referred to as depth.

2.2   The CKKS Scheme

The CKKS scheme and its residual number system (RNS) variants [10,18] provide operations on encrypted complex numbers, which are done by the canonical embedding and its inverse. Recall that the canonical embedding Emb of $a(X) \in \mathbb{Q}/\langle \Phi_M(X) \rangle$ into $\mathbb{C}^N$ is the vector of the evaluation values of a at the roots of $\Phi_M(X)$ and Emb^{-1} denotes its inverse. Let π denote a natural projection from $\mathbb{H} = \{(z_j)_{j \in \mathbb{Z}_M^*} : z_j = \overline{z_{-j}}\}$ to $\mathbb{C}^{N/2}$, where $\mathbb{Z}_M^*$ is the multiplicative group of integer modulo M. The encoding and decoding are defined as follows.

– $\mathsf{Ecd}(\boldsymbol{z}; \Delta)$: For an $(N/2)$-dimensional vector $\boldsymbol{z}$, the encoding returns

$$m(X) = \mathsf{Emb}^{-1}\left(\lfloor \Delta \cdot \pi^{-1}(\boldsymbol{z}) \rceil_{\mathsf{Emb}(\mathcal{R})}\right) \in \mathcal{R},$$

where Δ is the scaling factor and $\lfloor \cdot \rceil_{\mathsf{Emb}(\mathcal{R})}$ denotes the discretization into an element of $\mathsf{Emb}(\mathcal{R})$.

– $\mathsf{Dcd}(m; \Delta)$: For an input polynomial $m(X) \in \mathcal{R}$, output a vector

$$z = \pi(\Delta^{-1} \cdot \mathsf{Emb}(m)) \in \mathbb{C}^{N/2},$$

where its entry of index j is given as $z_j = \Delta^{-1} \cdot m(\zeta_M^j)$ for $j \in T$, ζ_M is the M-th root of unity, and T is a multiplicative subgroup of $\mathbb{Z}_M^*$ satisfying $\mathbb{Z}_M^*/T = \{\pm 1\}$. Alternatively, this can be basically represented by multiplication by an $N/2 \times N$ matrix $\mathbf{U}$ whose entries are $\mathbf{U}_{ji} = \zeta_j^i$, where $\zeta_j := \zeta_M^{5^j}$.

For a real number σ, $\mathcal{DG}(\sigma^2)$ denotes the distribution in $\mathbb{Z}^N$, whose entries are sampled independently from the discrete Gaussian distribution of variance σ^2. $\mathcal{HWT}(h)$ is the set of signed binary vectors in $\{0, \pm 1\}^N$ with Hamming weight h. Suppose that we have ciphertexts of level l for $0 \leq l \leq L$.

The RNS-CKKS scheme performs all operations in RNS. The ciphertext modulus $Q_l = q \cdot \prod_{i=1}^{l} p_i$ is used, where p_i's are chosen as primes that satisfy $p_i = 1 \pmod{2N}$ to support efficient number theoretic transform (NTT). We note that $Q_0 = q$ is greater than p as the final message's coefficients should not be greater than the ciphertext modulus q. For a faster computation, we use the hybrid key switching technique in [18]. First, for predefined dnum, a small integer, we define partial products $\left\{ \tilde{Q}_j \right\}_{0 \leq j < \mathsf{dnum}} = \left\{ \prod_{i=j\alpha}^{(j+1)\alpha-1} p_i \right\}_{0 \leq j < \mathsf{dnum}}$, for a small integer $\alpha = \lceil (L+1)/\mathsf{dnum} \rceil$. For a ciphertext with level l and $\mathsf{dnum}' = \lceil (l+1)/\alpha \rceil$, we define [18]

$$\mathcal{WD}_l(a) = \left(\left[a \frac{\tilde{Q}_0}{Q_l} \right]_{\tilde{Q}_0}, \cdots, \left[a \frac{\tilde{Q}_{\mathsf{dnum}'-1}}{Q_l} \right]_{\tilde{Q}_{\mathsf{dnum}'-1}} \right) \in \mathcal{R}^{\mathsf{dnum}'},$$

$$\mathcal{PW}_l(a) = \left(\left[a \frac{Q_l}{\tilde{Q}_0} \right]_{Q_l}, \cdots, \left[a \frac{Q_l}{\tilde{Q}_{\mathsf{dnum}'-1}} \right]_{Q_l} \right) \in \mathcal{R}_{Q_l}^{\mathsf{dnum}'}.$$

Then, for any $(a, b) \in \mathcal{R}_{Q_l}^2$, we have

$$\langle \mathcal{WD}_l(a), \mathcal{PW}_l(b) \rangle = a \cdot b \pmod{Q_l}.$$

Then, the operations in the RNS-CKKS scheme are defined as follows:

– $\mathsf{KeyGen}(1^\lambda)$:
  • Given the security parameter λ, we choose a power-of-two M, an integer h, an integer P, a real number σ, and a maximum ciphertext modulus Q, such that $Q \geq Q_L$.
  • Sample the following values: $s \leftarrow \mathcal{HWT}(h)$.
  • The secret key is $\mathsf{sk} := (1, s)$.

– $\mathsf{KSGen}_{\mathsf{sk}}(s')$: For auxiliary modulus $P = \prod_{i=0}^{k} p_i' \approx \max_j \tilde{Q}_j$, sample $a_k' \leftarrow \mathcal{R}_{PQ_L}$ and $e_k' \leftarrow \mathcal{DG}(\sigma^2)$. Output the switching key

$$\mathsf{swk} := (\mathsf{swk}_0, \mathsf{swk}_1) = (\{b_k'\}_{k=0}^{\mathsf{dnum}'-1}, \{a_k'\}_{k=0}^{\mathsf{dnum}'-1}) \in \mathcal{R}_{PQ_L}^{2 \times \mathsf{dnum}'},$$

where $b_k' = -a_k' s + e_k' + P \cdot \mathcal{PW}(s')_k \pmod{PQ_L}$.

- • Set the evaluation key as $\mathsf{evk} := \mathsf{KSGen}_{\mathsf{sk}}(s^2)$.
- $\mathsf{Enc}_{\mathsf{sk}}(m)$: Sample $a \leftarrow \mathcal{R}_{Q_L}$ and $e \leftarrow \mathcal{DG}(\sigma^2)$. The output ciphertext is

$$\mathsf{ct} = (-a \cdot s + e + m, a) \, (\mathrm{mod} \ Q_L),$$

where $\mathsf{sk} = (1, s)$. There is also a public-key encryption method [12], but omitted here.

- $\mathsf{Dec}_{\mathsf{sk}}(\mathsf{ct})$: Output $\bar{m} = \langle \mathsf{ct}, \mathsf{sk} \rangle$.
- $\mathsf{Add}(\mathsf{ct}_1, \mathsf{ct}_2)$: For $\mathsf{ct}_1, \mathsf{ct}_2 \in \mathcal{R}_{Q_l}^2$, output $\mathsf{ct}_{\mathsf{add}} = \mathsf{ct}_1 + \mathsf{ct}_2 \, (\mathrm{mod} \ Q_l)$.
- $\mathsf{Mult}(\mathsf{ct}_1, \mathsf{ct}_2)$: For $\mathsf{ct}_1 = (b_1, a_1)$ and $\mathsf{ct}_2 = (b_2, a_2) \in \mathcal{R}_{Q_l}^2$, return

$$\mathsf{ct}_{\mathsf{mult}} = (d_0, d_1, d_2) := (b_1 b_2, a_1 b_2 + a_2 b_1, a_1 a_2) \, (\mathrm{mod} \ Q_l).$$

- $\mathsf{RL}_{\mathsf{evk}}(d_0, d_1, d_2)$: For a three-tuple ciphertext (d_0, d_1, d_2) corresponding to secret key $(1, s, s^2)$, return $(d_0, d_1) + \mathsf{KS}_{\mathsf{evk}}((0, d_2))$.
- $\mathsf{cAdd}(\mathsf{ct}_1, \boldsymbol{a}; \Delta)$: For $\boldsymbol{a} \in \mathbb{C}^{N/2}$ and a scaling factor Δ, output $\mathsf{ct}_{\mathsf{cadd}} = \mathsf{ct} + (\mathsf{Ecd}(\boldsymbol{a}; \Delta), 0)$.
- $\mathsf{cMult}(\mathsf{ct}_1, \boldsymbol{a}; \Delta)$: For $\boldsymbol{a} \in \mathbb{C}^{N/2}$ and a scaling factor Δ, output $\mathsf{ct}_{\mathsf{cmult}} = \mathsf{Ecd}(\boldsymbol{a}; \Delta) \cdot \mathsf{ct}$.
- $\mathsf{RS}(\mathsf{ct})$: For $\mathsf{ct} \in \mathcal{R}_{Q_l}^2$, output $\mathsf{ct}_{\mathsf{RS}} = \lfloor p_l^{-1} \cdot \mathsf{ct} \rceil \, (\mathrm{mod} \ q_{l-1})$.
- $\mathsf{KS}_{\mathsf{swk}}(\mathsf{ct})$: For $\mathsf{ct} = (b, a) \in \mathcal{R}_{Q_l}^2$ and $\mathsf{swk} := (\mathsf{swk}_0, \mathsf{swk}_1)$, output

$$\mathsf{ct}_{\mathsf{KS}} = \left(b + \left\lfloor \frac{\langle \mathcal{WD}_l(a), \mathsf{swk}_0 \rangle}{P} \right\rceil, \left\lfloor \frac{\langle \mathcal{WD}_l(a), \mathsf{swk}_1 \rangle}{P} \right\rceil \right) \, (\mathrm{mod} \ Q_l).$$

The key-switching techniques are used to provide various operations such as complex conjugate and rotation. To remove the error introduced by approximate scaling factors, one can use different scaling factors for each level as given in [21], or we can use the scale-invariant method proposed in [3] for polynomial evaluation. We note that (FullRNS-)HEAAN and SEAL are (dnum = 1) and (dnum = $L + 1$) cases, respectively, and Lattigo supports for arbitrary dnum.

2.3   Signal-to-Noise Ratio Perspective of the CKKS Scheme

There has been extensive research on noisy media in many areas such as wireless communications and data storage. In this perspective, the CKKS scheme can be considered as a noisy media; encryption and decryption correspond to transmission and reception, respectively. The message in a ciphertext is the signal, and the final output has additive errors due to ring-LWE (RLWE) security, rounding, and approximation.

The SNR is the most widely-used measure of signal quality, which is defined as the ratio of the signal power to the noise power as follows:

$$\mathrm{SNR} = \frac{E[S^2]}{E[N^2]},$$

where S and N denote the signal (message) and noise (error), respectively. As shown in the definition, the higher SNR corresponds to the better quality.

A simple way to increase SNR is to increase the signal power, but it would be limited due to regulatory or physical constraints. The CKKS scheme has the same problem; a larger scaling factor should be multiplied to the message to increase the message power, but if one uses a larger scaling factor, the ciphertext level decreases, or larger parameters should be used for security. Hence, to increase SNR, it is beneficial to reduce the noise power in the CKKS scheme rather than increasing the signal power.

Error estimation of the CKKS scheme so far has been focused on the high-probability upper bound of the error after several operations [9, 12] and also minimax for approximation [24]. However, the bound becomes quite loose as the homomorphic operation continues, and its statistical significance may diminish. Thus, we maximize SNR in this paper, which is equivalent to minimizing error variance when the scaling factor is fixed.

3   Bootstrapping of the CKKS Scheme

3.1   Outline of the CKKS Bootstrapping

There are extensive studies for bootstrapping of the CKKS scheme [3,7,9,18–20,24,25]. The CKKS bootstrapping consists of the following four steps: MODRAISE, COEFFTOSLOT, EVALMOD, and SLOTTOCOEFF.

Modulus Raising (MODRAISE). MODRAISE increases the ciphertext modulus to a larger modulus. Let ct be the ciphertext satisfying $m(X) = [\langle \mathsf{ct}, \mathsf{sk} \rangle]_q$. Then we have $t(X) = \langle \mathsf{ct}, \mathsf{sk} \rangle = qI(X) + m(X) \equiv m(X) \pmod{q}$ for $I(X) \in \mathcal{R}$ with a high-probability bound $\|I(X)\|_\infty < K = \mathcal{O}(\sqrt{h})$. The following procedure aims to calculate the remaining coefficients of $t(X)$ when dividing by q.

Homomorphic Evaluation of Encoding (COEFFTOSLOT). Homomorphic operations are performed in plaintext slots, but we need component-wise operations on coefficients. Thus, to deal with $t(X)$, we should put polynomial coefficients in plaintext slots. In COEFFTOSLOT step, $\mathsf{Emb}^{-1} \circ \pi^{-1}$ is performed homomorphically using matrix multiplication [9], or FFT-like hybrid method [7]. Then, we have two ciphertexts encrypting $\mathbf{z}'_0 = (t_0, \ldots, t_{\frac{N}{2}-1})$ and $\mathbf{z}'_1 = (t_{\frac{N}{2}}, \ldots, t_{N-1})$ (when the number of slots is small, we can put $\mathbf{z}'_0$ and $\mathbf{z}'_1$ in a ciphertext, see [9]), where t_j denotes the j-th coefficient of $t(X)$. The matrix multiplication is composed of three steps [9]: i) rotate ciphertexts, ii) multiply diagonal components of matrix to the rotated ciphertexts, and iii) sum up the ciphertexts.

Evaluation of the Approximate Modular Reduction (EVALMOD). An approximate evaluation of the modular reduction function is performed in this step. As additions and multiplications cannot represent the modular reduction function, an approximate polynomial for $[\cdot]_q$ is used. For approximation, it is desirable to control the message size to ensure $m_i \leq \epsilon \cdot q$ for a small ϵ [9].

Homomorphic Evaluation of Decoding (SLOTTOCOEFF). SLOTTOCOEFF is the inverse operation of COEFFTOSLOT. Since the matrix elements do not have to be precise as much in CoeffToSlot, we can use a smaller scaling factor here [3]. In SlotToCoeff, the ciphertext is multiplied by the CRT matrix $\mathbf{U}$, whose elements have magnitudes of one. Thus, the N errors in slots are multiplied by a constant of size one and then added.

3.2 Polynomial Approximation of Modular Reduction

Previous works approximated the modular reduction function as $\frac{q}{2\pi} \sin\left(\frac{2\pi t}{q}\right)$ [7, 9, 18]. Approximate polynomial of sine function is found by using Taylor expansion of exponent function and $e^{it} = \cos(t) + i \cdot \sin(t)$ in [9]. The Chebyshev approximation of sine function improved the approximation in [7]. The modified Chebyshev approximation in cosine function and the double-angle formula reduced the error and evaluation time in [18]. However, in these approaches, the sine function is used, and thus there is still the fundamental approximation error, that is,

$$\left| m - \frac{q}{2\pi} \sin(2\pi \frac{m}{q}) \right| \leq \frac{q}{2\pi} \cdot \frac{1}{3!} \left(\frac{2\pi |m|}{q} \right)^3.$$

Direct-approximation methods were proposed in [19, 25], but their coefficients are large and amplify errors of polynomial basis. A composition with inverse sine function that offers a trade-off between the precision and the remaining level was proposed to remove the fundamental approximation error between the sine function and the modular reduction [24]. However, the evaluation of inverse sine function has a considerable multiplicative depth.

Those prior researches tried to find the minimax approximate polynomial p_n, which minimizes $\|f - p_n\|_{\mathsf{sup}}$, where f is the function to approximate, such as sine function [7, 9, 18, 24]. Lee et al. proposed the multi-interval Remez algorithm [24], which is an iterative method to find minimax approximate polynomial of an arbitrary piece-wise continuous function.

3.3 Baby-Step Giant-Step Algorithms

There are several baby-step giant-step algorithms for a different purpose in the context of HE. In this paper, BSGS only refers to the polynomial evaluation algorithm proposed in [18] and its variants. The BSGS algorithm is presented in Algorithm 1 composed of SetUp, BabyStep, and GiantStep. SetUp calculates all the polynomial bases required to evaluate the given polynomial. The GiantStep divides the input polynomial by a polynomial of degree $2^i k$ and calls GiantStep recursively for its quotient and remainder, where $i \leq \lfloor \log(\deg/k) \rfloor$ for an integer k, and deg is the degree of the polynomial. When the given polynomial has a degree less than k, it calls BabyStep, and it evaluates the given polynomial of a small degree, namely a baby polynomial.

Originally, Han and Ki proposed to use a power-of-two k [18], and Lee et al. generalized k to an arbitrary even number and proposed to omit even-degree terms for odd polynomial,[1] which reduces the number of ciphertext-ciphertext

---

[1] This technique appears in their first version in Cryptology ePrint Archive.

Algorithm 1. BSGS Algorithm [18,24]

Instance: A ciphertext ct of t, a polynomial $p(X) = \sum_i c_i \cdot T_i(X)$.
Output: A ciphertext encrypting $p(t)$.

1: Let l be the smallest integer satisfying $2^l k > n$ for an even number k.
2: **procedure** SETUP(ct, l, k)
3:    ct$_i \leftarrow$ encryption of $T_i(t)$
4:    ct$_{2^i k} \leftarrow$ encryption of $T_{2^i k}(t)$ ▷ for $0 \leq i < l$.
5: **end procedure**
6: **procedure** BABYSTEP($p(X), \{ct_i\}, k$)
7:    **return** $\sum_j c_j \cdot ct_j$ ▷ baby polynomials.
8: **end procedure**
9: **procedure** GIANTSTEP($p(X), \{ct_i\}, l, k$)
10:     **if** $deg(p) < k$ **then**
11:         **return** BABYSTEP($p(X), \{ct_i\}, k$)
12:     **end if**
13:     Find $q(X), r(X)$ s.t. $p(X) = q(X) \cdot T_{2^i k}(X) + r(X)$
14:     ct$_q \leftarrow$ GIANTSTEP($q(X), \{ct_i\}, l, k$)
15:     ct$_r \leftarrow$ GIANTSTEP($r(X), \{ct_i\}, l, k$)
16:     **return** ct$_q \cdot$ ct$_{2^i k}$ + ct$_r$
17: **end procedure**

---

multiplications [24]. The number of ciphertext-ciphertext multiplications is given as

$$k - 2 + l + 2^l$$

in general, and

$$\lfloor \log(k-1) \rfloor + k/2 - 2 + l + 2^l$$

for odd polynomials, where $\deg < k \cdot 2^l$ is satisfied. Also, Bossuat *et al.* improved to do more recursion for high-degree terms [3] to optimize the multiplicative depth. In the BSGS algorithm of Bossuat *et al.*, we can evaluate a polynomial of degree up to $2^d - 1$ within multiplicative depth d by applying $O(\log k)$ additional multiplications.

4 Optimal Approximate Polynomial of Modular Reduction for Bootstrapping of the CKKS Scheme

This section proposes a new method to find the optimal approximate polynomial of the modular reduction function for the CKKS bootstrapping, considering the noisy computation nature of the CKKS Scheme. The optimality of the proposed approximate polynomial is proved, and statistics of input for an approximate polynomial are also analyzed to improve the approximation.

4.1 Error Variance-Minimizing Polynomial Approximation

We use the variance of error as the objective function for the proposed polynomial approximation and show that it is also optimal for CKKS bootstrapping.

As described later in the following subsections, the error in the noisy polynomial basis, namely the basis error, might be amplified by coefficients of the approximate polynomial. Thus, the magnitude of its coefficients should be small, and using the generalized least square method, the optimal coefficient vector c^* of the approximate polynomial is obtained as

$$c^* = \arg\min_c \left(Var[e_{\mathsf{aprx}}] + \sum w_i c_i^2 \right), \tag{1}$$

where e_{aprx} is the approximation error, and the constant values w_i are determined by the basis error given by CKKS parameters such as key Hamming weight, number of slots, and scaling factor.

We call the proposed approximate polynomial obtained by (1) as the *error variance-minimizing approximate polynomial*, and we derived an analytic solution. We note that the optimized solution attempts to minimize the variance of the approximation error as well as the variance of amplified basis error. The error variance-minimizing approximate polynomial is described in detail by taking bootstrapping as a specific example in the following subsection. It is worth noting that the approximation can be applied arbitrary function.

4.2 Optimality of the Proposed Direct Approximate Polynomial

In this subsection, we show that the proposed error variance-minimizing approximate polynomial is optimal for CKKS bootstrapping in the following aspects. First, we show that an approximate polynomial that minimizes the error variance after EVALMOD also minimizes the bootstrapping error variance, and thus it is optimal in terms of SNR. Next, we show that the direct approximation to the modular reduction allows a more accurate approximation than previous indirect approximations using trigonometric functions [3,7,9,18,24] for fixed multiplicative depth.

Error-Optimality of the Proposed Approximate Polynomial in CKKS Bootstrapping. Here, we show that error variance-minimizing approximate polynomial guarantees the minimal error after bootstrapping in the aspect of SNR, while the minimax approach in [3,7,9,18,24] does not guarantee the minimax error after bootstrapping. In EVALMOD, the operations between different slots do not happen, and thus we can assume that the error in each slot is independent. The SLOTTOCOEFF is the homomorphic operation of decoding, and the decoding of $m(X)$ is given as $(m(\zeta_0), m(\zeta_1), \ldots, m(\zeta_{N/2-1}))$. Hence, the error in the j-th slot after SLOTTOCOEFF is given as $e_{\mathsf{boot},j}(\zeta_j) = \sum_{i=0}^{N-1} e_{\mathsf{mod},i} \cdot \zeta_j^i$ which is the sum of thousands of independent random variables, where $e_{\mathsf{mod},i}$ denotes the error in the i-th slot after EVALMOD and $|\zeta_j| = 1$.

The minimax approximate polynomial minimizes $\|e_{\mathsf{aprx}}(t)\|_{\mathsf{sup}}$ [7,24]. In this case, we have $e_{\mathsf{mod},i} = e_{\mathsf{aprx}}(t_i) + e_{\mathsf{noise},i}$, where t_i is the i-th slot value after COEFFTOSLOT and $e_{\mathsf{noise},i}$ is the random error by the noisy polynomial basis of CKKS. Hence, the minimax approximation minimizes $\max \left(\left| e_{\mathsf{aprx}}(t_i) \cdot \zeta_j^i \right| \right) =$

$\|e_{\mathsf{aprx}}(t_i)\|_{\mathsf{sup}}$, not $\max\left(\left|e_{\mathsf{boot},j}\right|\right)$. In other words, we observe that the final bootstrapping error is $e_{\mathsf{boot},j}$, and we have

$$\max\left(\left|e_{\mathsf{boot},j}\right|\right) = \max\left(\left|\sum_{i=0}^{N-1} e_{\mathsf{mod},i} \cdot \zeta_j^i\right|\right) = \max\left(\left|\sum_{i=0}^{N-1} \left(e_{\mathsf{aprx}}(t_i) + e_{\mathsf{noise},i}\right) \cdot \zeta_j^i\right|\right)$$

$$\leq \max\left(\left|\sum_{i=0}^{N-1} e_{\mathsf{aprx}}(t_i) \cdot \zeta_j^i\right|\right) + \max\left(\left|\sum_{i=0}^{N-1} e_{\mathsf{noise},i} \cdot \zeta_j^i\right|\right), \qquad (2)$$

where

$$\max\left(\left|\sum_{i=0}^{N-1} e_{\mathsf{aprx}}(t_i) \cdot \zeta_j^i\right|\right) \leq \left\|\zeta_j^0 \cdot e_{\mathsf{aprx}}\right\|_{\mathsf{sup}} + \cdots + \left\|\zeta_j^{N-1} \cdot e_{\mathsf{aprx}}\right\|_{\mathsf{sup}}.$$

Hence, the minimax approximate polynomial does not guarantee the minimum infinity norm of bootstrapping error but provides an upper bound only for the approximation error term. Besides, it is challenging to optimize polynomial coefficients for noisy basis in the existing minimax approximation.

In contrast, the proposed error variance-minimizing approximate polynomial minimizes $Var[e_{\mathsf{mod},j}]$. Thus, it also minimizes the final bootstrapping error $Var[e_{\mathsf{boot},j}]$, as

$$Var[e_{\mathsf{boot},j}] = Var[e_{\mathsf{mod},0} \cdot \zeta_j^0] + \cdots + Var[e_{\mathsf{mod},N-1} \cdot \zeta_j^{(N-1)}].$$

The above equation implies that minimizing the variance of the approximate error is optimal to reduce the bootstrapping error of the CKKS scheme in the aspect of SNR. Due to the characteristics of SLOTTOCOEFF, we have the tight value of the variance of bootstrapping error, while the minimax provides an upper bound of infinity norm. In other words, we can optimize our objective function by the proposed error variance-minimizing approximate polynomial, whereas the minimax approach optimizes an upper bound (the right-hand side of (2)) instead of the bootstrapping error (the left-hand side of (2)).

Depth Optimality of Direct Approximation. As shown in (1), the proposed method approximates the objective function directly, while the prior works approximate trigonometric functions [3,7,9,18,24]. Let $P_{\mathsf{deg}} \subset \mathbb{C}[X]$ be the set of all polynomials whose degree is less than or equal to deg. When we perform a direct approximation, the algorithm finds an approximate polynomial among all elements of P_{deg}, and its multiplicative depth is $\lceil\log(\mathsf{deg})\rceil$.

When we use the approximation of trigonometric function, the search space of the approximation algorithm is much more limited. For example, as in [3,24], suppose that we use the double angle formula twice and approximate polynomial for cosine and arcsine of degree deg_1 and deg_2, respectively. Then the search space is

$$\left\{f_2 \circ g \circ f_1 | f_1 \in P_{\mathsf{deg}_1}, f_2 \in P_{\mathsf{deg}_2}, \text{ and } g(x) = (x^2 - 1)^2 - 1\right\}.$$

We can see that the search space is much smaller than $P_{4\mathsf{deg}_1\mathsf{deg}_2}$, and its multiplicative depth is $\lceil\log(\mathsf{deg}_1 + 1)\rceil + 2 + \lceil\log(\mathsf{deg}_2 + 1)\rceil \geq \lceil\log(4\mathsf{deg}_1\mathsf{deg}_2 + 1)\rceil$.

Hence, the direct approximation in $P_{4\deg_1\deg_2}$ has more chance to find a better approximation as well as it has less multiplicative depth.

4.3 Noisy Polynomial Basis and Polynomial Evaluation in the CKKS Scheme

Let $\{\phi_0(x), \phi_1(x), \ldots, \phi_n(x)\}$ denote a polynomial basis of degree n such that every $\phi_k(t)$ is odd for an odd k. When a polynomial $p(x) = \sum c_i \phi_i(x)$ is evaluated homomorphically, it is expected that the result is $p(x) + e$ for a small error e. In the CKKS scheme, there exists an error in encrypted data, and thus, each $\phi_i(x)$ contains independent $e_{\mathsf{basis},i}$, namely the basis error. Thus, the output is

$$\sum c_i(\phi_i(x) + e_{\mathsf{basis},i}) = p(x) + \sum c_i e_{\mathsf{basis},i}.$$

In general, $\sum c_i e_{\mathsf{basis},i}$ is small as $e_{\mathsf{basis},i}$ are small. However, when $|c_i|$ are much greater than $p(x)$, $\sum c_i e_{\mathsf{basis},i}$ dominates $p(x)$.

The basis errors, $e_{\mathsf{basis},i}$ are introduced by rescaling, key switching, and encryption errors, which are independent of the message. Each $\phi_i(x)$ is usually obtained from smaller-degree polynomials, and thus there may be some correlation between $e_{\mathsf{basis},i}$'s. If we assume that each $e_{\mathsf{basis},i}$ is independent, then the variance of $\sum c_i \cdot e_{\mathsf{basis},i}$ becomes $\sum c_i^2 \cdot Var(e_{\mathsf{basis},i})$ and w_i in (1) corresponds to $Var(e_{\mathsf{basis},i})$. The experiments in Sect. 6 support that our approximation with this independence assumption obtains accurate approximations for bootstrapping in practice. In other words, we do not need exact distributions of $e_{\mathsf{basis},i}$ in practice.

In conclusion, the magnitude of c_i's should be controlled when we find an approximate polynomial. A high-degree approximate polynomial for modular reduction and piece-wise cosine function has large coefficients magnitude in previous works [19,24]. There have been series of studies in approximate polynomials in the CKKS scheme [3,7,12,18,19,24,25], but the errors amplified by coefficients were not considered in the previous studies.

4.4 Optimal Approximate Polynomial for Bootstrapping and the Magnitude of Its Coefficients

The most depth-consuming and noisy part of bootstrapping is EVALMOD. In this subsection, we show how to find the optimal approximate polynomial for EVALMOD in the aspect of SNR. By scaling the modular reduction function $[\cdot]_q$ by $\frac{1}{q}$, we define

$$f_{\mathsf{mod}} : \bigcup_{i=-K+1}^{K-1} I_i \to [-\epsilon, \epsilon], \text{ that is, } f_{\mathsf{mod}}(t) = t - i \text{ if } t \in I_i,$$

where $I_i = [i - \epsilon, i + \epsilon]$ for an integer $-K < i < K$. Here, ϵ denotes the ratio of the maximum coefficient of the message polynomial and the ciphertext modulus, that is, $|m_i/q| \le \epsilon$, where m_i denotes a coefficient of $m(X)$. Let T be the random variable of input t of $f_{mod}(t)$. Then, $T = R + I$, where R is the random variable of the rational part r, and I is the random variable of the integer part i. We note that $\Pr_T(t) = \Pr_I(i) \cdot \Pr_R(r)$ is satisfied for $t = r + i$ as i and r are independent and $\bigcup_i I_i = [-\epsilon, \epsilon] \times \{0, \pm 1, \ldots, \pm(K-1)\}$, where $\Pr_T, \Pr_I$, and $\Pr_R$ are the probability mass functions or probability density functions of T, I, and R, respectively.

The approximation error for t is given as

$$e_{aprx}(t) = p(t) - f_{mod}(t) = p(t) - (t - i),$$

where a polynomial $p(t) = \sum c_i \phi_i(t)$ approximates $f_{mod}(t)$. We can set $p(t)$ as an odd function because $f_{mod}(t)$ is odd. Then the variance of e_{aprx} is given as

$$Var[e_{aprx}] = E[e_{aprx}^2] = \int_t e_{aprx}(t)^2 \cdot \Pr_T(t)\, dt$$

$$= \sum_{-K < i < K} \Pr_I(i) \int_{t=i-\epsilon}^{i+\epsilon} e_{aprx}(t)^2 \cdot \Pr_R(t - i)\, dt,$$

where the mean of e_{aprx} is zero by assuming that $\Pr_T(t)$ is even. It is noted that the integral can be directly calculated or approximated by the sum of discretized values as in [25].

The basis error $\sum c_i^2 \cdot Var(e_{basis,i})$ is also added as discussed in Subsect. 4.3. We generalize $Var(e_{basis,i})$ by w_i. Then, we find $\boldsymbol{c}^*$ such that

$$\boldsymbol{c}^* = \arg\min_{\boldsymbol{c}} \left(Var[e_{aprx}] + \sum w_i c_i^2 \right), \tag{3}$$

and its solution satisfies

$$\nabla_{\boldsymbol{c}} \left(Var[e_{aprx}] + \sum w_i c_i^2 \right) = 0,$$

where $\boldsymbol{c} = (c_1, c_3, \ldots, c_n)$ and $\boldsymbol{w} = (w_1, w_3, \ldots, w_n)$ are coefficient and weight constant vectors, respectively. We note that the objective function is convex.

It is noted that $Var(e_{basis,i})$ may differ by i, and thus, a precise adjustment of the magnitude of polynomial coefficients can be made by multiple weight constants, w_i's. The following theorem states that we can find the approximate polynomial for $p(t)$ efficiently; the computation time of solving this system of linear equations is the same as that of finding an interpolation polynomial for given points. It will be faster than the improved multi-interval Remez algorithm [24], as the Remez algorithm requires an interpolation per each iteration.

Theorem 1. *There exists a polynomial-time algorithm that finds the odd polynomial $p(t) = \sum c_i \phi_i(t)$ satisfying*

$$\arg\min_{\boldsymbol{c}} \left(Var[e_{aprx}] + \sum w_i c_i^2 \right),$$

when $\Pr_T(t)$ is an even function.

Proof. By substituting $p(t) = \sum c_i \phi_i(t)$ from $Var[e_{\mathsf{aprx}}] = E[e_{\mathsf{aprx}}^2] = E[f_{\mathsf{mod}}(t)^2] - 2E[f_{\mathsf{mod}}(t) \cdot p(t)] + E[p(t)^2]$, we have

$$\frac{\partial}{\partial c_j} Var[e_{\mathsf{aprx}}] = -2E[f_{\mathsf{mod}}(t)\phi_j(t)] + 2\sum_i c_i \cdot E[\phi_i(t)\phi_j(t)].$$

Therefore, one can find $\boldsymbol{c}^* = \arg\min_{\boldsymbol{c}} \left(Var[e_{\mathsf{aprx}}] + \sum w_i c_i^2 \right)$ by solving the following system of linear equations:

$$(\mathbf{T} + \boldsymbol{w}\mathbf{I}) \cdot \boldsymbol{c} = \boldsymbol{y}, \tag{4}$$

where $\boldsymbol{w}$ is a diagonal matrix where $\boldsymbol{w}_{ii} = w_i$,

$$\mathbf{T} = \begin{bmatrix} E[\phi_1 \cdot \phi_1] & E[\phi_1 \cdot \phi_3] & \dots & E[\phi_1 \cdot \phi_n] \\ E[\phi_3 \cdot \phi_1] & E[\phi_3 \cdot \phi_3] & \dots & \vdots \\ \vdots & & \ddots & \vdots \\ E[\phi_n \cdot \phi_1] & E[\phi_n \cdot \phi_3] & \dots & E[\phi_n \cdot \phi_n] \end{bmatrix}, \text{ and } \boldsymbol{y} = \begin{bmatrix} E[f_{\mathsf{mod}} \cdot \phi_1] \\ E[f_{\mathsf{mod}} \cdot \phi_3] \\ \vdots \\ E[f_{\mathsf{mod}} \cdot \phi_n] \end{bmatrix}.$$

$E[\phi_i \cdot \phi_j]$ and $E[f_{\mathsf{mod}} \cdot \phi_i]$ are integral of polynomials, which are easily calculated. Also, the equation can be simplified by the linear transformation from monomial basis to ϕ, and thus, the approximation of other functions is readily obtained.

$\square$

4.5   Statistical Characteristics of Modular Reduction

The input distribution of the proposed approximate polynomial, represented by Pr_I and Pr_R, is required to find $\mathbf{T}$ and $\boldsymbol{y}$. Unfortunately, in HE, it is not always possible to utilize the message distribution as it might be related to security. However, we observe and analyze that the major part of the input distribution of approximate polynomial is unrelated to the security.

After MODRAISE, the plaintext in the ciphertext $\mathsf{ct} = (b, a)$ is given as

$$t(X) = q \cdot I(X) + m(X) = \langle \mathsf{ct}, \mathsf{sk} \rangle \left(\bmod\ X^N + 1 \right),$$

where sk has Hamming weight h and each coefficient of a ciphertext (b, a) is an element of $\mathbb{Z}_q$. The RLWE assumption states that a ciphertext is uniformly distributed over $\mathcal{R}_q^2$, and thus each coefficient of b and a is distributed uniformly at random. In other words, coefficients of $b + a \cdot s$ follow the well-known Irwin-Hall distribution. Especially, it is a sum of $h + 1$ independent and identically distributed uniform random variables.

We note that one can exploit the distribution of I without security concerns. This is because the probability distribution Pr_I is given by the RLWE assumption (that b and a are uniformly distributed), regardless of the message distribution. Also, the implementation results in Sect. 6 show that we can achieve high approximation accuracy of the proposed approximate polynomial using Pr_I even if we set to the worst-case of Pr_R.

Table 1. Experimental result and theoretical probability mass function of I when $h = 192$

i	$\mathrm{Pr}_I(i)$ Experiment	Theory	i	$\mathrm{Pr}_I(i)$ Experiment	Theory	i	$\mathrm{Pr}_I(i)$ Experiment	Theory
0	$9.94 \cdot 10^{-2}$	$9.91 \cdot 10^{-2}$	± 8	$1.36 \cdot 10^{-2}$	$1.37 \cdot 10^{-2}$	± 16	$3.34 \cdot 10^{-5}$	$3.48 \cdot 10^{-5}$
± 1	$9.64 \cdot 10^{-2}$	$9.61 \cdot 10^{-2}$	± 9	$8.02 \cdot 10^{-3}$	$8.10 \cdot 10^{-3}$	± 17	$1.16 \cdot 10^{-5}$	$1.23 \cdot 10^{-5}$
± 2	$8.78 \cdot 10^{-2}$	$8.76 \cdot 10^{-2}$	± 10	$4.44 \cdot 10^{-3}$	$4.50 \cdot 10^{-3}$	± 18	$3.84 \cdot 10^{-6}$	$4.09 \cdot 10^{-6}$
± 3	$7.52 \cdot 10^{-2}$	$7.51 \cdot 10^{-2}$	± 11	$2.30 \cdot 10^{-3}$	$2.34 \cdot 10^{-3}$	± 19	$1.20 \cdot 10^{-6}$	$1.27 \cdot 10^{-6}$
± 4	$6.05 \cdot 10^{-2}$	$6.05 \cdot 10^{-2}$	± 12	$1.12 \cdot 10^{-3}$	$1.15 \cdot 10^{-3}$	± 20	$3.40 \cdot 10^{-7}$	$3.71 \cdot 10^{-7}$
± 5	$4.58 \cdot 10^{-2}$	$4.58 \cdot 10^{-2}$	± 13	$5.15 \cdot 10^{-4}$	$5.26 \cdot 10^{-4}$	± 21	$9.41 \cdot 10^{-8}$	$1.01 \cdot 10^{-7}$
± 6	$3.25 \cdot 10^{-2}$	$3.26 \cdot 10^{-2}$	± 14	$2.20 \cdot 10^{-4}$	$2.27 \cdot 10^{-4}$	± 22	–	$2.58 \cdot 10^{-8}$
± 7	$2.17 \cdot 10^{-2}$	$2.18 \cdot 10^{-2}$	± 15	$8.84 \cdot 10^{-5}$	$9.15 \cdot 10^{-5}$	± 23	–	$6.15 \cdot 10^{-8}$

We can numerically obtain the distribution of I or analytically derive its distribution. Table 1 is the probability mass function of I, obtained numerically using SEAL and analytically derived by using Irwin-Hall distribution. It is shown that the experimental results and our probability analysis using the Irwin-Hall distribution agree. In previous researches, a heuristic assumption is used, and a high-probability upper bound $K = O(\sqrt{h})$ for $\|I\|_\infty$ is used for polynomial approximation [3,9,18,24], but they could not utilize the distribution of I.

For Pr_R, we can set the worst-case scenario; message $m(X)$ is uniformly distributed over $\|m\|_\infty < \epsilon \cdot q$, as it results in the most significant entropy of the message. The experimental results in Sect. 6 show that even though the worst-case scenario is used and the distribution of $m(X)$ is different from the actual one, the error value in the proposed method is comparable to the prior arts [3,24] while consuming less depth. Also, in the experiment of [3], a uniformly distributed message is used to simulate the bootstrapping error and utilized the fact that $m(X)$ is highly probable to be in the center to use a small-degree arcsine Taylor expansion. We note that we can also heuristically assume a specific distribution in our bootstrapping when we specify Pr_R for (1) and improve the precision.

5   Lazy Baby-Step Giant-Step Algorithm

This section proposes error and complexity optimization when evaluating the error variance-minimizing approximate polynomial in bootstrapping. There are two optimizations: First, we show that the error variance-minimizing approximate polynomial is odd, and thus, we can ignore the even-degree terms. Second, we propose a novel evaluation algorithm, namely the lazy-BSGS algorithm, to reduce the computational complexity of EvalMod.

5.1   Reducing Error and Complexity Using Odd Function Property

When the approximate polynomial is an odd function, we can save time for both homomorphically evaluating and finding the polynomial. Moreover, by omitting the even-degree terms, we can reduce the approximate error and basis errors.

Error Variance-Minimizing Polynomial for an Odd Function. This subsection shows that the variance-minimizing polynomial is an odd function, where $\Pr_T(t)$ is even. Using an odd polynomial, we can reduce the approximation error and the computation time to find the proposed approximate polynomial. First of all, we only need to integrate over the positive domain when obtaining each element of (4). Second, the number of operations to evaluate the approximate polynomial can also be reduced by omitting even-degree terms when using the lazy-BSGS algorithm Algorithm 2 in the following subsection. Finally, the basis error is also reduced as only half of the terms are added.

The following theorem shows that when the objective of polynomial approximation such as $f_{\mathsf{mod}}(t)$ is odd and the probability density function is even, the error variance-minimizing approximate polynomial is also an odd function.

Theorem 2. *If $\Pr_T(t)$ is an even function and $f(t)$ is an odd function, the error variance-minimizing approximate polynomial for $f(t)$ is an odd function.*

Proof. Existence and uniqueness: Equation (3) is a quadratic polynomial for the coefficients c, and thus there exists one and only solution.

Oddness: Let P_m be the subspace of the polynomials of degree at most m and $f_m(t)$ denote the unique element in P_m that is closest to $f(t)$ in terms of the variance of difference. Then, $Var[-f(-t) - p(t)] + \sum w_i c_i^2$ is minimized when $p(t) = -f_m(-t)$, because

$$
\begin{aligned}
Var\left[-f(-t) - p(t)\right] &= \int_t (-f(-t) - p(t))^2 \cdot Pr(t)dt \\
&= \int_{-u} -(f(u) + p(-u))^2 \cdot Pr(-u)du \\
&= \int_u (f(u) - (-p(-u)))^2 \cdot Pr(u)du \\
&= Var\left[f(t) - (-p(-t))\right],
\end{aligned}
$$

and the squares of coefficients of $f_m(t)$ and $-f_m(-t)$ are the same. As the error variance-minimizing approximate polynomial is unique, we conclude $f_m(t) = -f_m(-t)$.

$\square$

5.2 Lazy Baby-Step Giant-Step Algorithm

In this subsection, we propose a new algorithm that efficiently evaluates arbitrary polynomials over the CKKS scheme, namely the lazy-BSGS algorithm in Algorithm 2, and we extend it to the odd polynomials. We apply the lazy relinearization and rescaling technique [1,2,8,22] to the BSGS algorithm to improve its time complexity and error performance. For example, when we evaluate a polynomial of degree 711 by using the ordinary BSGS algorithm in [18], 58 non-scalar multiplications are required; however, when we use the odd-BSGS

Algorithm 2. Lazy-BSGS Algorithm

Instance: A ciphertext ct of t, a polynomial $p(X)$ of degree deg.
Output: A ciphertext encrypting $p(t)$.

1: Let l be the smallest integer satisfying $2^l k > n$ for an even number k.
2: **procedure** SETUPLAZY(ct, l, k)
3:     **for** $i = 2; i < k; i \leftarrow 2i$ **do**
4:         $\text{ct}_i \leftarrow 2 \cdot \text{ct}_{i/2}\text{ct}_{i/2} - 1$
5:         $\text{ct}_i \leftarrow \text{RL}(\text{ct}_i)$
6:     **end for**
7:     **for** $i = 3; i < k; i \leftarrow i + 1$ **do**
8:         $i_0, i_1 \leftarrow 2^{\lfloor \log i \rfloor}, i - 2^{\lfloor \log i \rfloor}$
9:         $\text{ct}_{i_0} \leftarrow \text{RL}(\text{ct}_{i_0})$
10:         $\text{ct}_i \leftarrow 2 \cdot \text{ct}_{i_0}\text{ct}_{i_1} - \text{ct}_{i_0 - i_1}$
11:     **end for**
12:     **if** $k/2$ is even **then**   ▷ To reduce the error, see Fig. 2
13:         $\text{ct}_k \leftarrow 2 \cdot \text{ct}_{k/2+1}\text{ct}_{k/2-1} - \text{ct}_2$
14:     **else**
15:         $\text{ct}_k \leftarrow 2 \cdot \text{ct}_{k/2}\text{ct}_{k/2} - 1$
16:     **end if**
17:     $\text{ct}_k \leftarrow \text{RL}(\text{ct}_k)$
18:     **for** $i = 2k; i < \text{deg}; i \leftarrow 2i$ **do**
19:         $i_0, i_1 \leftarrow 2^{\lfloor \log i \rfloor}, i - 2^{\lfloor \log i \rfloor}$
20:         $\text{ct}_i \leftarrow 2 \cdot \text{ct}_{i/2}\text{ct}_{i/2} - 1$
21:         $\text{ct}_i \leftarrow \text{RL}(\text{ct}_i)$
22:     **end for**
23:     $\{\text{ct}_i\} \leftarrow$ encryptions of $T_i(t)$
24:     $\{\text{ct}_{2^i k}\} \leftarrow$ encryptions of $T_{2^i k}(t)$
25: **end procedure**
26: **procedure** GIANTSTEPLAZY($p(X), \{\text{ct}_i\}, l, k$)
27:     **if** $deg(p) < k$ **then**
28:         **return** BABYSTEP($p(X), \{\text{ct}_i\}, k$)
29:     **end if**
30:     Find $q(X), r(X)$ s.t. $p(X) = q(X) \cdot T_{2^i k}(X) + r(X)$
31:     $\text{ct}_q \leftarrow$ GIANTSTEP($q(X), \{\text{ct}_i\}, l, k$)
32:     $\text{ct}_r \leftarrow$ GIANTSTEP($r(X), \{\text{ct}_i\}, l, k$)
33:     $\text{ct}_q \leftarrow \text{RL}(\text{ct}_q)$
34:     **return** $\text{ct}_q \cdot \text{ct}_{2^i k} + \text{ct}_r$
35: **end procedure**

---

algorithm [24], 46 non-scalar multiplications are required. Moreover, the lazy relinearization method reduces the number of relinearizations to 33, which is the same number of relinearizations for a polynomial of degree 220 using the ordinary BSGS algorithm.

The relinearization and rescaling introduce additional errors in the CKKS scheme, and the error propagates along with homomorphic operations. Hence, we should delay the relinearization and rescaling to reduce the error of the resulting ciphertext. Moreover, those operations, especially relinearization, require many

NTTs, and thus it requires lots of computation. For some circuits, we can reduce the numbers of relinearizations and rescalings by delaying them. We observe that we can perform plaintext addition, ciphertext addition, and scalar multiplication to a ciphertext before relinearization.

A ciphertext is a three-tuple $(d_0, d_1, d_2) \in \mathcal{R}^3_{q_L}$ such that $\langle (d_0, d_1, d_2), (1, s, s^2) \rangle$ $= m + e$. A plaintext $u \in \mathcal{R}$ can be multiplied homomorphically by calculating $(u \cdot d_0, u \cdot d_1, u \cdot d_2)$, but we note that the error is amplified by the magnitude of u. When we add a ciphertext (b, a) to (d_0, d_1, d_2), we get $(d_0 + b, d_1 + a, d_2)$. However, as the scaling factor of ciphertext is changed along with homomorphic operations, we should make sure that the scaling factors of the two ciphertexts are identical when we add two ciphertexts. If not, we can multiply a constant, Δ_1/Δ_2, to a ciphertext which has a smaller scaling factor and then add, where Δ_1 is the larger scaling factor, and Δ_2 is the smaller scaling factor. Alternatively, we can use the scaling factor management technique proposed in [21].

We propose the lazy-BSGS algorithm, which reduces the numbers of rescalings and relinearizations, and we analyze its computational complexity. Here, we rigorously analyze the number of relinearizations as its complexity is much higher than other operations, and we note that the number of rescalings is also similar. As we use the Chebyshev polynomial of the first kind as the polynomial basis, we explain the lazy-BSGS algorithm with Chebyshev polynomial. For the sake of brevity, we denote ciphertext-ciphertext multiplication by $\cdot$, and the ciphertext of $T_j(t_0)$ is denoted by ct_j, where T_j is Chebyshev polynomial of the first kind with degree j.

SETUP finds all the Chebyshev polynomials of degree less than or equal to k, and $T_{2^i k}$ for $i < l$, for given parameter k and l. We use $T_a = 2 \cdot T_{2^i} \cdot T_{a-2^i} - T_{2^{i+1}-a}$ to find ct_a, where $i = \lfloor \log(a) \rfloor$. We note that one can alternatively use multiplication of odd degree polynomials to reduce the basis error, which is presented in Subsect. 5.4.

First, we find ct_{2^i} for $i < k$, and these are used to find other Chebyshev bases with degrees less than k. Thus, we rescale and relinearize them, which requires $\lfloor \log(k-1) \rfloor$ rescalings and relinearizations. When calculating $\mathsf{ct}_a = 2 \cdot \mathsf{ct}_{2^i} \cdot \mathsf{ct}_{a-2^i} - \mathsf{ct}_{2^{i+1}-a}$, if ct_{a-2^i} is a three-tuple ciphertext, we relinearize it (and rescale it if needed.) We note that the lazy rescaling makes it possible to accurately subtract $\mathsf{ct}_{2^{i+1}-a}$ from $2 \cdot \mathsf{ct}_{2^i} \cdot \mathsf{ct}_{a-2^i}$ without level consumption as follows. We do not rescale $\mathsf{ct}_{2^i} \cdot \mathsf{ct}_{a-2^i}$ here, and thus the scaling factor of $2 \cdot \mathsf{ct}_{2^i} \cdot \mathsf{ct}_{a-2^i}$ is maintained as $\approx q^2$. Obviously, the level of $\mathsf{ct}_{2^{i+1}-a}$ is larger than that of $\mathsf{ct}_{2^i} \cdot \mathsf{ct}_{a-2^i}$. When their scaling factors are different, we multiply $(\Delta_{2^i} \cdot \Delta_{a-2^i}) \cdot p_l/\Delta_{2^{i+1}-a}$ to $\mathsf{ct}_{2^{i+1}-a}$ and rescale if $\Delta_{2^{i+1}-a} \approx q^2$, or multiply $(\Delta_{2^i} \cdot \Delta_{a-2^i})/\Delta_{2^{i+1}-a}$ if $\Delta_{2^{i+1}-a} \approx q$, where Δ_j denotes the scaling factor of ct_j, and p_l is the last prime of modulus chain for ct_{a-2^i}. Now, the scaling factors of $\mathsf{ct}_{2^{i+1}-a}$ and $2\mathsf{ct}_{2^i} \cdot \mathsf{ct}_{a-2^i}$ are the same, and thus we can subtract them without additional error from the difference of scale.

To evaluate $\mathsf{ct}_{2^i} \cdot \mathsf{ct}_{a-2^i}$, we need to relinearize ct_{a-2^i} if it is not relinearized yet. Hence, we need relinearized ct_j's for $j < 2^{\lfloor \log k-1 \rfloor - 1}$ to find ct_i for all

$i < 2^{\lfloor \log k-1 \rfloor}$. Moreover, if $k \geq 2^{\lfloor \log k-1 \rfloor} + 2^{\lfloor \log k-1 \rfloor-1}$, we need $k - 2^{\lfloor \log k-1 \rfloor} + 2^{\lfloor \log k-1 \rfloor-1}$ more relinearizations. Each $\mathsf{ct}_{2^i k}$ should be relinearized as it is used for multiplication in GIANTSTEP, which requires l relinearizations. In conclusion, we do

$$\lfloor \log(k-1) \rfloor + (2^{\lfloor \log k-1 \rfloor-1} - 1) + l$$

relinearizations in SETUP. If $k \geq 2^{\lfloor \log k-1 \rfloor} + 2^{\lfloor \log k-1 \rfloor-1}$, $\left(k - 3 \cdot 2^{\lfloor \log k-1 \rfloor-1}\right)$ additional relinearizations are required.

BABYSTEP performs only plaintext multiplication and addition. Hence, it does not require relinearization in our lazy-BSGS algorithm, but the scale for baby-step polynomial coefficients should be adequately scaled to make the added ciphertexts have identical scaling factors, but this process does not involve additional computation at all. Note that the resulting ciphertext of BABYSTEP is not relinearized, i.e., it has size 3.

In GIANTSTEP, the ct_q is relinearized before multiplied to $\mathsf{ct}_{2^i k}$. Hence, the number of relinearizations is $2^{l-1} + 2^{l-2} + \cdots + 1 = 2^l - 1$, and the final result is not relinearized. Thus, we perform relinearization once more right before SLOTTOCOEFF.

Finally, the number of relinearizations in lazy-BSGS is

$$\lfloor \log(k-1) \rfloor + (2^{\lfloor \log k-1 \rfloor-1} - 1) + l + 2^l$$

if $k < 2^{\lfloor \log k-1 \rfloor} + 2^{\lfloor \log k-1 \rfloor-1}$ and otherwise

$$\lfloor \log(k-1) \rfloor + \left(2^{\lfloor \log k-1 \rfloor-1} - 1\right) + l + 2^l + \left(k - 3 \cdot 2^{\lfloor \log k-1 \rfloor-1}\right).$$

Lazy-BSGS for Odd Polynomial. We can naturally extend the lazy-BSGS for the odd polynomials. Here, SETUP finds all the odd-degree Chebyshev polynomials of degrees less than k. To find an odd-degree Chebyshev polynomial, we need an even-degree Chebyshev polynomial because the multiplication of odd-degree Chebyshev polynomials is not an odd-degree polynomial. Hence, we use T_{2^i} to find ct_a, where $i = \lfloor \log(a) \rfloor$, and thus we rescale and relinearize them, which requires $\lfloor \log(k-1) \rfloor$ rescaling and relinearization. Thus, the number of relinearizations in lazy-BSGS for odd polynomial is

$$\lfloor \log(k-1) \rfloor + (2^{\lfloor \log k-1 \rfloor-1}/2 - 1) + l + 2^l$$

if $k < 2^{\lfloor \log k-1 \rfloor} + 2^{\lfloor \log k-1 \rfloor-1}$ and otherwise

$$\lfloor \log(k-1) \rfloor + \left(2^{\lfloor \log k-1 \rfloor-1}/2 - 1\right) + l + 2^l + \left(k - 3 \cdot 2^{\lfloor \log k-1 \rfloor-1}\right)/2.$$

Using the error variance-minimizing approximate polynomial in bootstrapping requires evaluating a polynomial with a higher degree than the previous composition methods. However, the lazy-BSGS algorithm reduces the time complexity by half, compared to ordinary BSGS mentioned in Sect. 2. As a result, the lazy-BSGS algorithm makes the time complexity of evaluating our polynomial comparable to the previous algorithm. Figure 1 compares our lazy-BSGS algorithm, odd-BSGS algorithm [24], and the original BSGS algorithm [18].

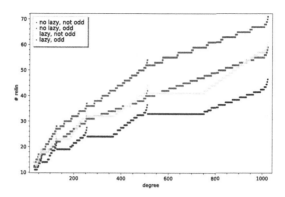

Fig. 1. Number of relinearizations for the variants of BSGS algorithms.

The lazy-BSGS algorithm is given in Algorithm 2 in detail. We note that the methods in [3] should be applied for optimal depth and scale-invariant evaluation, but we omit it for the sake of brevity. However, we note that Fig. 1 considers the depth optimization in [3], and thus, the number of relinearizations is high when the degree is close to a power of two. The BSGS coefficients are pre-computed for optimal parameters k and l to minimize the complexity.

5.3 Error Variance-Minimizing Approximate Polynomial for BSGS Algorithm

In this subsection, we propose a method to find the variance-minimizing approximate polynomial for the odd-BSGS algorithm. We generalize the amplified basis error and find the variance-minimizing coefficients for the odd-BSGS algorithm. The numerical method to select the weight constantly is also proposed.

BSGS Algorithm Coefficients and Minimizing the Approximation Error Variance. In the lazy-BSGS algorithm, we divide the given polynomial by $T_{2^i k}$ and evaluate its quotient and remainder. Hence, each polynomial basis is multiplied by a divided coefficient, not c_i. We define $\boldsymbol{d}$ by the vector of coefficients multiplied to the basis in BABYSTEP, in other words, we have 2^l polynomials in BABYSTEP such that $p_i^{\mathsf{baby}}(t) = \sum_{j \in \{1,3,\ldots,k-1\}} d_{i,j} T_j(t)$ for $i = 0, 1, \ldots, 2^l - 1$, and $\boldsymbol{d} = (d_{0,1}, d_{0,3}, \ldots, d_{2^l-1,\deg-k\cdot2^{l-1}})$.

We should reduce the magnitude of $\boldsymbol{d}$, to reduce the basis error. Let $p(t) = \sum c_i T_i(t)$, and then, $\boldsymbol{c}$ and $\boldsymbol{d}$ have the following linearity:

$$\boldsymbol{c} = \mathbf{L} \cdot \boldsymbol{d} = \begin{bmatrix} \mathbf{A}_{2^{l-1}k} \end{bmatrix} \cdot \begin{bmatrix} \mathbf{A}_{2^{l-2}k} & \mathbf{0} \\ \mathbf{0} & \mathbf{A}_{2^{l-2}k} \end{bmatrix} \cdots \begin{bmatrix} \mathbf{A}_k & & \\ & \ddots & \\ & & \mathbf{A}_k \end{bmatrix} \cdot \boldsymbol{d}, \qquad (5)$$

where

$$\mathbf{A}_k = \begin{bmatrix} \mathbf{I}_{k/2} & \frac{1}{2}\mathbf{J}_{k/2} \\ \mathbf{0} & \frac{1}{2}\mathbf{I}_{k/2} \end{bmatrix},$$

$\mathbf{I}_{k/2}$ is the $k/2 \times k/2$ identity matrix, and $\mathbf{J}_{k/2}$ is the $k/2 \times k/2$ exchange matrix. Hence, the linear equation to find the error variance-minimizing approximate polynomial (4) is modified for the BSGS algorithm as

$$(\mathbf{L}^\mathsf{T}\mathbf{TL} + w\mathbf{I}) \cdot \boldsymbol{d} = \boldsymbol{y}. \tag{6}$$

Generalization of Weight Constant. Let E_p be a function of $\boldsymbol{d}$, which is the variance of basis error amplified by the BSGS algorithm. We simplify E_p by a heuristic assumption that T_i's are independent and the encryptions of $T_k(t), \ldots, T_{2^{l-1}k}(t)$ have small error. Let $\hat{T}_i$ be the product of all $T_{2^j k}$'s multiplied to p_i in the giant step, for example, $\hat{T}_0 = 1$ and $\hat{T}_3 = T_k T_{2k}$. Considering the error multiplied by $d_{i,j}$, $e_j \cdot \hat{T}_i$ is the dominant term as T_i has zero mean for odd integer i as it is an odd polynomial. Thus, we can say that

$$E_p \approx \sum_i \sum_j d_{i,j}^2 E[\hat{T}_i^2] Var[e_{\mathsf{basis},j}],$$

a quadratic function of $\boldsymbol{d}$. In other words, we have $E_p = \boldsymbol{d}^\mathsf{T}\mathbf{H}\boldsymbol{d}$, where $\mathbf{H}$ is a diagonal matrix that $\mathbf{H}_{ki+j,ki+j} = E[\hat{T}_i^2]Var[e_{\mathsf{basis},j}]$. Thus, (3) is generalized as

$$\boldsymbol{c}^* = \arg\min_{\boldsymbol{c}} \left(Var[e_{\mathsf{aprx}}] + E_p\right).$$

Equation (5) gives us that the optimal coefficient $\boldsymbol{d}^*$ satisfies

$$(\mathbf{L}^\mathsf{T}\mathbf{TL} + \mathbf{H})\,\boldsymbol{d}^* = \mathbf{L}^\mathsf{T}\boldsymbol{y}. \tag{7}$$

Numerical Method of Finding Optimal Approximate Polynomial. Instead of finding E_p, a simple numerical method can also be used. In practice, the numerical method shows good error performance in the implementation in Subsect. 6.1. We can let $w_i = w$ for all i and find w numerically. When w increases, the magnitude of coefficients decreases, and $Var[e_{\mathsf{aprx}}]$ increases, and thus its sum is a convex function of w. The magnitude of the basis errors that are amplified by coefficients $\boldsymbol{d}$ has the order of the rescaling error whose variance is $\frac{2n(h+1)}{12 \cdot q^2}$, where n is the number of slots. In other words, we adjust w to minimize

$$Var[e_{\mathsf{aprx}}] + w \cdot \|\boldsymbol{d}\|_2^2, \tag{8}$$

where $w \approx \frac{2n(h+1)}{12 \cdot q^2}$. The odd-BSGS coefficients $\boldsymbol{d}$, which minimize (8), satisfy

$$(\mathbf{L}^\mathsf{T}\mathbf{TL} + w\mathbf{I})\boldsymbol{d} = \mathbf{L}^\mathsf{T}\boldsymbol{y}.$$

Lemma 1 (Rescaling error [9]). *The error variance of rescaling error is $\frac{2n(h+1)}{12}$, where h is key Hamming weight and n is the number of slots.*

We can fine-tune w by a numerical method of performing bootstrapping and measure the bootstrapping error variance, and then adjust w. Once we decide on $\boldsymbol{d}$, it becomes just part of the implementation; one can even hard-wire it.

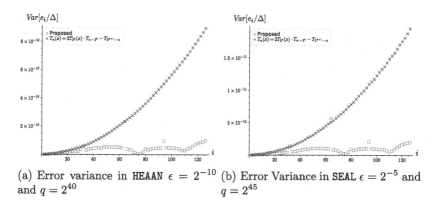

(a) Error variance in HEAAN $\epsilon = 2^{-10}$ and $q = 2^{40}$

(b) Error Variance in SEAL $\epsilon = 2^{-5}$ and $q = 2^{45}$

Fig. 2. Variance of basis error in $T_i(t)$ for even i using HEAAN (a) and SEAL (b) libraries with various parameters, where $h = 64$.

5.4   Basis Error Variance Minimization for Even-Degree Terms

In this subsection, we show that the even-degree Chebyshev polynomials in CKKS have huge errors and propose a method to find a small-error Chebyshev polynomial. In the BSGS algorithm, we use even-degree Chebyshev polynomials, namely, $T_{2^i k}(t)$. For depth and simplicity, we usually obtain $T_a(t)$ by using

$$T_a(t) = 2 \cdot T_{2^i}(t) \cdot T_{a-2^i}(t) - T_{2^{i+1}-a}(t),$$

where $i = \lfloor \log(a) \rfloor$. Let ct_i be the ciphertext of message $T_i(t)$ with scaling factor Δ, and it contains error $e_{\mathsf{basis},i}$. Then, the error in ct_{i+j} obtained by $\mathsf{ct}_{i+j} = 2\mathsf{ct}_i \cdot \mathsf{ct}_j - \mathsf{ct}_{|i-j|}$ is given as

$$(2T_i(t)e_{\mathsf{basis},j} + 2T_j(t)e_{\mathsf{basis},i})\Delta + 2e_{\mathsf{basis},i}e_{\mathsf{basis},j} - e_{\mathsf{basis},|i-j|}. \tag{9}$$

As $\Delta \gg e_{\mathsf{basis},i}, e_{\mathsf{basis},j}$, the dominant term of error variance in (9) is

$$Var[2T_i(t)e_{\mathsf{basis},j} + 2T_j(t)e_{\mathsf{basis},i}]$$
$$\approx 4E[T_i(t)^2]Var[e_{\mathsf{basis},j}] + 4E[T_j(t)^2]Var[e_{\mathsf{basis},i}]. \tag{10}$$

As a simple example, it is shown that $E[T_i(t)^2]$ is close to one when i is an even number for low-degree polynomials, where t is a value after COEFFTOSLOT. Meanwhile, $E[T_i(t)]$ is zero and $Var[T_i(t)]$ is a small value when i is odd. Thus, following to (10), the error remains large when it is multiplied by an even-degree Chebyshev polynomial in the calculation of the next Chebyshev polynomial. Therefore, when a is even, ct_a should be calculated by $\mathsf{ct}_a = 2\mathsf{ct}_{2^i-1} \cdot \mathsf{ct}_{a+1-2^i} - \mathsf{ct}_{2^{i+1}-2-a}$ rather than $\mathsf{ct}_a = 2\mathsf{ct}_{2^i} \cdot \mathsf{ct}_{a-2^i} - \mathsf{ct}_{2^{i+1}-a}$. Also, it is noted that, for the above reasons, the power-of-two polynomials should have a large basis error.

Figure 2 shows the experimental results of the variance of error in encryption of $T_i(t)$ for even i's, where t is the output value of COEFFTOSLOT.

Table 2. The second moment of $T_i(t)$ when t is value after SLOTTOCOEFF and $N = 2^{15}$

i		0	1	2	3	4	5	6	7	8	9
$E[T_i(t)^2]$	$h = 192$	1.00	0.035	0.905	0.187	0.718	0.361	0.579	0.457	0.520	0.491
	$h = \sqrt{N}$	1.00	0.013	0.950	0.105	0.828	0.239	0.696	0.358	0.596	0.426

Square mark and × mark legends are the results with and without operation reordering, respectively. In other words, square marks are results from $ct_a = 2ct_{2^i-1} \cdot ct_{a-2^i+1} - ct_{2^{i+1}-2-a}$ for even a. The experimental result in Fig. 2 supports our argument that multiplying even-degree Chebyshev polynomials amplifies the error. We can see that the basis error is significantly improved by reordering operations. For example, the variance of error in ct_{74} is reduced to $1/1973$ compared to that of without reordering (Fig. 2).

6   Performance Analysis and Comparison

In this section, several implementation results and comparisons for the previous bootstrapping algorithms are presented. The bootstrapping using the proposed approximate polynomial is implemented on the well-known HE library Lattigo, as Lattigo is the only open-source library that supports bootstrapping of RNS-CKKS at the time of writing. We also provide a proof-of-concept implementation of bootstrapping with high precision such as 93 bits, based on the HEAAN library.

6.1   Error Analysis

Weight Parameter and Approximation Error. In Subsect. 5.3, we discussed analytic and numerical solutions for error variance-minimizing approximate polynomial. In this subsection, these methods are implemented and verified. We confirm that the numerical method in Subsect. 5.3 finds a polynomial that is very close but has a slightly larger error than that of the optimal one, and $w \approx \frac{(h+1)2n}{q^2 12}$, where n is the number of slots.

The experimental results are shown in Fig. 3 with parameters $N = 2^{16}, h = 64$, and the slot size $n = 2^3$. The blue lines with triangular legend show the error by polynomial approximation as $2n \cdot q^2 \cdot Var[e_{\mathsf{aprx}}]$. The green lines with × mark legend show the amplified basis errors as $2n \cdot q^2 \cdot E_p$, and the red lines with square legend are for the mean square of bootstrapping errors without scale obtained by experiments using the proposed approximate polynomial in (8). The gray dot line is the variance of bootstrapping error without scale, achieved by the analytic solution of the error variance-minimizing approximate polynomial (7) of the same degree, which is the lower bound of bootstrapping error variance. The reason for multiplying the above result by $2n$ is because of SLOTTOCOEFF as discussed in Subsect. 4.2. For the worst-case assumption, we assume that m is distributed uniformly at random.

In Fig. 3, the sum of blue lines with triangular legend and green lines with × mark legend meets the red lines with the square legend. In other words, it shows

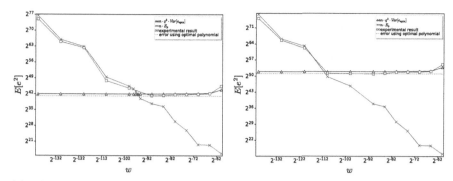

(a) Theoretical and experimental variances of errors when $p = 2^{40}$

(b) Theoretical and experimental variance of errors when $p = 2^{45}$

Fig. 3. The theoretical variance of the approximation error, amplified basis error, and experimental results implemented in HEAAN. Polynomials of degree 81 are used. (Color figure online)

that the theoretical derivation and experimental results are agreed upon. It can also be seen that it is possible to obtain an approximate polynomial with a small error with the proposed numerical method, but the error is slightly larger than that of the analytical solution. It is noted that the optimal w is close to the variance of the rescaling error $\frac{(h+1)2n}{q^2 12}$.

Polynomial Degree and Minimum Error. This subsection presents the experimental result of the approximate error variance of the proposed error variance-minimizing approximate polynomial for the given degree and constant w. In the above paragraphs, we show that when $w \approx \frac{(h+1)2n}{q^2 12}$, the variance of approximation error achieves the optimality. Unlike the previous methods that find the approximate polynomial without considering the CKKS parameters, the proposed approximation algorithm finds an approximate polynomial that is optimal for the given parameter of the CKKS scheme, such as the number of slots, key Hamming weight, and scaling factor.

In Fig. 4, we represent the variance of approximation error with $w = \frac{(h+1)2n}{q^2 12}$, where $\|m/q\|_\infty < 2^{-5}$. $w = 2^{-104}$ corresponds to $q \approx 2^{60}$ and slot size $n = 2^{14}$. $w = 2^{-200}$ corresponds to $q \approx 2^{109}$ for the same slot size. In this figure, we can see that the proposed method approaches the maximal accuracy of polynomial approximation for $q \approx 2^{60}$ within depth 10. Moreover, we can see that the proposed error variance-minimizing approximate polynomial achieves approximate error variance 2^{-209} within depth only 11.

6.2 Comparison of Bootstrapping and High-Precision Bootstrapping

Experimental Result of Bootstrapping Error. The proposed method is implemented using Lattigo, and it is compared with the most accurate bootstrapping techniques in the literature [3,24] in Table 3. In this table, the proposed

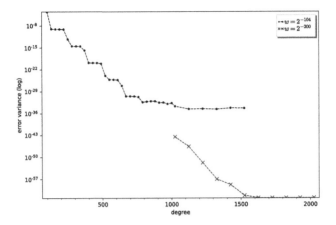

Fig. 4. Error variance of the proposed polynomial, for $w = 2^{-104}$ and 2^{-200}.

Table 3. Comparison of the variance of bootstrapping error of the proposed error variance-minimizing polynomial and prior arts. Columns "cos" and "sin^{-1}" are for the degree of the approximate polynomial of each, and "double" is for the number of double angle formulas of cosine applied. The proposed method uses direct approximation, so the degree of the approximate polynomial is indicated by f_{mod}.

Algorithm	h	N	n	$\log QP_L$	λ	$\log q$	$\log p$	$\log \|r\|_\infty$	EvalMod cos	Double	sin^{-1}	Depth	#relin	$Var[e_{\mathsf{boot}}]$	Bit prec.	Runtime(s)
[24]	192	2^{16}	2^{14}	1553	≈ 128	60	50	-10	68	2	5	12	24	$2^{-64.5}$	32.6	451.5
[3]	192	2^{16}	2^{14}	1547	≈ 128	60	45	-5	62	2	7	11	24	$2^{-62.6}$	31.6	22.8
				1547	≈ 128	60	45	-5	62	2	3	10	22	$2^{-44.4}$	22.4	25.3
Proposed	192	2^{16}	2^{14}	1487	> 128	60	45	-5	f_{mod}: 711			10	33	$2^{-62.1}$	31.4	28.3
Proposed (high prec^2.)	192	2^{17}	2^{12}	–	–	115	102	-5	f_{mod}: 1625			11	46	$2^{-185.4}$	93.03	–
	192	2^{17}	2^{3}	–	–	115	106	-5						$2^{-199.0}$	100.11	–

error variance-minimizing polynomial directly approximates f_{mod}, and the previous methods approximate the cosine function and use the double-angle formula. For a high precision achieved in [3, 24], approximate polynomials of $\frac{1}{2\pi} \arcsin(t)$ by multi-interval Remez algorithm and Taylor expansion are evaluated, respectively, and the evaluation of those algorithms consumes three more levels. For a fair comparison, we fix the message precision as ≈ 31-bits and compare the depth of modular reduction. The timing result is measured using Intel Xeon Silver 4210 CPU @ 2.20 GHz, single core. The scale-invariant evaluation [3] is also applied for a precise evaluation. The same parameter set as [3] is used for the proposed method, and thus the same levels are consumed for CoeffToSlot and SlotToCoeff.

In the experiment, we sample each slot value $a + bi \in \mathbb{C}$, where a and b are uniformly distributed over $[-1, 1]$, and thus, from the central limit theorem, the coefficient of the encoded plaintext follows a Gaussian distribution. On the other hand, the proposed error variance-minimizing approximate polynomial is obtained under assumption that the coefficients of plaintext are distributed uniformly at random, that is, $\Pr_R(r) = \frac{1}{2\epsilon}$ for all $r \in [-\epsilon, \epsilon]$ as a worst-case assumption discussed in Sect. 4. We note that the difference of message distribution for approximation and actual experiment is a harsh environment for the proposed error variance minimizing approximate polynomial.

The first three rows of Table 3 show that the proposed method requires less depth compared to the prior arts. This is due to the indirect approximation using trigonometric functions of previous methods. Compared to the previous method with the same depth of 10, our method has 9-bit higher precision. In another aspect, the proposed approximate polynomial achieves the same precision as the previous methods by only the depth of 10. The proposed bootstrapping consumes one to two fewer levels in EVALMOD, thus we used smaller parameters in the experiment which improves security. We can utilize the additional level depending on the application, for example, one can exploit it for efficient circuit design to reduce the total number of bootstrapping of the whole system (e.g., inference of privacy-preserving deep learning [23],) or we might speed up COEFFTOSLOT or SLOTTOCOEFF using this remaining level. However, in terms of bootstrapping runtime for ≈ 31-bit precision, our method is slower than previous methods due to the evaluation of high-degree polynomial. Our algorithm is more advantageous for higher precision as it is efficiently scalable, which is discussed in the next subsection.

Comparison of Numerical and Analytical Error. Experiments in Fig. 3 show that the error variance-minimizing approximate polynomial has $Var[e_{\mathsf{aprx}}] + \sum w_i d_i^2 = 2^{-103.33}$ when $w = 2^{-104}$. We can easily find the expected bootstrapping error variance with this value. The error variance is multiplied by $2n$ in SLOTTOCOEFF; thus, the error variance after SLOTTOCOEFF should be $2^{-88.33}$. The scaling factor in bootstrapping is $\approx q$, and thus, the error without scaling is $2^{-88.33} \cdot q^2 \approx 2^{31.67}$. The scaling factor of a message is $\approx 2^{45}$, and thus the expected bootstrapping error variance is $2^{31.67}/p^2 \approx 2^{-58.33}$. Compared with the experimental result in Table 3, $2^{-61.12}$, we can see that the numerical result roughly meets the analysis. The difference seems to be due to various methods to reduce the error introduced in Sect. 5.

Scalability and High-Precision Bootstrapping. The last two rows in Table 3 represent the proof-of-concept implementation of high-precision CKKS bootstrapping[2]. In the table, we can see that the proposed method achieves high precision such as 93-bit with 2^{12} slots. It is worth noting that our method uses the same depth as previous methods [3,24], but achieves much higher accuracy. We use the variance-minimizing approximate polynomial of degree 1625 with parameter $w = 2^{-200}$ which minimizes (8) (the minimum value is $\approx 2^{-209}$), as

---

[2] It is implemented using a multi-precision CKKS library HEAAN which supports rescaling by an arbitrary-length integer. As this proof-of-concept implementation is only interested in high precision, we omitted runtime and parameter QP_L (as a side note, $(h, N, \log QP_L) = (192, 2^{17}, 3069)$ achieves 128-bit security [3].) We note that the implementation is slow due to the non-RNS nature of HEAAN and has less level due to the use of dnum = 1.

shown in Fig. 4. We can also say that bottleneck of bootstrapping error is the scaling factor, not the approximation.

The previous bootstrapping methods so far cannot achieve such high accuracy, and even if so, it will have a huge multiplicative depth to perform a high-degree polynomial approximation. Julta and Manohar proposed sine series approximation and 100-bit accuracy CKKS bootstrapping using their approximation which consumes modulus of 2^{2157} (see Table 1 in [20]). In contrast, due to the direct approximation of the proposed method, it has much less depth compared to indirect approximations, and thus we can achieve the same accuracy (shown in the last row or Table 3) with modulus about 2^{1495}, which corresponds to 6 more levels after bootstrapping. Also, the proposed lazy-BSGS algorithm reduces the number of relinearizations; the previous BSGS algorithm for odd polynomial [24] requires 66 relinearizations to evaluate polynomial of degree 1625.

This high accuracy is essential in the presence of the Li-Micciancio attack [26]. The "noise flooding" method is currently the only known way to make CKKS provably secure against Li-Micciancio attack, but it was impractical with bootstrapping as it makes CKKS noisy by losing about 30–40 bits of accuracy [26]. Although a lot of research is required on how to exploit the bootstrapping error for cryptanalysis, at least, we can directly apply the noise flooding technique [16] with the high-precision bootstrapping.

7   Conclusion

In this paper, we have two contributions for accurate and fast bootstrapping of CKKS scheme, that is, we proposed i) a method to find the optimal approximate polynomial of modular reduction for bootstrapping and its analytical solution, and ii) a more efficient algorithm to homomorphically evaluate a high-degree polynomial. The proposed error variance-minimizing approximate polynomial guarantees the minimum error after bootstrapping in the aspect of SNR; in contrast, the previous minimax approximation does not guarantee the minimum infinity norm of the bootstrapping error. Moreover, we proposed an efficient algorithm, the lazy-BSGS algorithm, to evaluate the approximate polynomial. The lazy-BSGS algorithm reduces the number of relinearizations by half compared to the ordinary BSGS algorithm, and the error is also reduced. We also proposed the algorithm to find the error variance-minimizing approximate polynomial designed for the lazy-BSGS algorithm.

The proposed algorithm reduces the level consumption of the most depth-consuming part of bootstrapping, approximate modular reduction. Thus we can reserve more levels after bootstrapping or we can use the level to speed up bootstrapping. The number of the levels after bootstrapping is significant for efficient circuit design of algorithms using CKKS [23], as well as it reduces the number of bootstrappings.

The bootstrapping performance improvement by the proposed algorithm was verified by an implementation. The implementation showed that we could reduce the multiplicative depth of modular reduction in CKKS bootstrapping while achieving the best-known accuracy. Also, we discussed that the proposed method achieves the CKKS bootstrapping with very high accuracy, so we can directly apply the noise flooding technique to the CKKS scheme for IND-CPA^D security.

Acknowledgements. We would like to thank anonymous reviewers of Crypto 2021 and Eurocrypt 2022 for their suggestions and comments which improves the paper.

References

1. Blatt, M., Gusev, A., Polyakov, Y., Rohloff, K., Vaikuntanathan, V.: Optimized homomorphic encryption solution for secure genome-wide association studies. BMC Med. Genomics **13**(7), 1–13 (2020)
2. Boemer, F., Costache, A., Cammarota, R., Wierzynski, C.: nGraph-HE2: a high-throughput framework for neural network inference on encrypted data. In: The ACM Workshop on Encrypted Computing & Applied Homomorphic Cryptography, pp. 45–56 (2019)
3. Bossuat, J.-P., Mouchet, C., Troncoso-Pastoriza, J., Hubaux, J.-P.: Efficient bootstrapping for approximate homomorphic encryption with non-sparse keys. In: Canteaut, A., Standaert, F.-X. (eds.) EUROCRYPT 2021. LNCS, vol. 12696, pp. 587–617. Springer, Cham (2021). https://doi.org/10.1007/978-3-030-77870-5_21
4. Brakerski, Z., Gentry, C., Vaikuntanathan, V.: (Leveled) fully homomorphic encryption without bootstrapping. ACM Trans. Comput. Theory (TOCT) **6**(3), 1–36 (2014)
5. Brakerski, Z., Vaikuntanathan, V.: Fully homomorphic encryption from ring-LWE and security for key dependent messages. In: Rogaway, P. (ed.) CRYPTO 2011. LNCS, vol. 6841, pp. 505–524. Springer, Heidelberg (2011). https://doi.org/10.1007/978-3-642-22792-9_29
6. Brakerski, Z., Vaikuntanathan, V.: Efficient fully homomorphic encryption from (standard) LWE. SIAM J. Comput. **43**(2), 831–871 (2014)
7. Chen, H., Chillotti, I., Song, Y.: Improved bootstrapping for approximate homomorphic encryption. In: Ishai, Y., Rijmen, V. (eds.) EUROCRYPT 2019. LNCS, vol. 11477, pp. 34–54. Springer, Cham (2019). https://doi.org/10.1007/978-3-030-17656-3_2
8. Chen, H., Kim, M., Razenshteyn, I., Rotaru, D., Song, Y., Wagh, S.: Maliciously secure matrix multiplication with applications to private deep learning. In: Moriai, S., Wang, H. (eds.) ASIACRYPT 2020. LNCS, vol. 12493, pp. 31–59. Springer, Cham (2020). https://doi.org/10.1007/978-3-030-64840-4_2
9. Cheon, J.H., Han, K., Kim, A., Kim, M., Song, Y.: Bootstrapping for approximate homomorphic encryption. In: Nielsen, J.B., Rijmen, V. (eds.) EUROCRYPT 2018. LNCS, vol. 10820, pp. 360–384. Springer, Cham (2018). https://doi.org/10.1007/978-3-319-78381-9_14
10. Cheon, J.H., Han, K., Kim, A., Kim, M., Song, Y.: A full RNS variant of approximate homomorphic encryption. In: Cid, C., Jacobson Jr., M. (eds.) SAC 2018. LNSC, vol. 11349, pp. 347–368 Springer, Cham (2018). https://doi.org/10.1007/978-3-030-10970-7_16
11. Cheon, J.H., Hhan, M., Hong, S., Son, Y.: A hybrid of dual and meet-in-the-middle attack on sparse and ternary secret LWE. IEEE Access **7**(89), 497–506 (2019)

12. Cheon, J.H., Kim, A., Kim, M., Song, Y.: Homomorphic encryption for arithmetic of approximate numbers. In: Takagi, T., Peyrin, T. (eds.) ASIACRYPT 2017. LNCS, vol. 10624, pp. 409–437. Springer, Cham (2017). https://doi.org/10.1007/978-3-319-70694-8_15

13. Chillotti, I., Gama, N., Georgieva, M., Izabachène, M.: Faster packed homomorphic operations and efficient circuit bootstrapping for TFHE. In: Takagi, T., Peyrin, T. (eds.) ASIACRYPT 2017. LNCS, vol. 10624, pp. 377–408. Springer, Cham (2017). https://doi.org/10.1007/978-3-319-70694-8_14

14. Chillotti, I., Gama, N., Georgieva, M., Izabachène, M.: TFHE: fast fully homomorphic encryption over the torus. J. Cryptol. **33**(1), 34–91 (2020)

15. Ducas, L., Micciancio, D.: FHEW: bootstrapping homomorphic encryption in less than a second. In: Oswald, E., Fischlin, M. (eds.) EUROCRYPT 2015. LNCS, vol. 9056, pp. 617–640. Springer, Heidelberg (2015). https://doi.org/10.1007/978-3-662-46800-5_24

16. Ducas, L., Stehlé, D.: Sanitization of FHE ciphertexts. In: Fischlin, M., Coron, J.-S. (eds.) EUROCRYPT 2016. LNCS, vol. 9665, pp. 294–310. Springer, Heidelberg (2016). https://doi.org/10.1007/978-3-662-49890-3_12

17. Fan, J., Vercauteren, F.: Somewhat practical fully homomorphic encryption. Cryptology ePrint Archive 2012/144 (2012)

18. Han, K., Ki, D.: Better bootstrapping for approximate homomorphic encryption. In: Cryptographers' Track at the RSA Conference, pp. 364–390 (2020)

19. Jutla, C.S., Manohar, N.: Modular Lagrange interpolation of the mod function for bootstrapping for approximate HE. Cryptology ePrint Archive 2020/1355 (2020)

20. Jutla, C.S., Manohar, N.: Sine series approximation of the mod function for bootstrapping of approximate HE. Cryptology ePrint Archive 2021/572 (2021)

21. Kim, A., Papadimitriou, A., Polyakov, Y.: Approximate homomorphic encryption with reduced approximation error. In: Galbraith, S.D. (ed.) CT-RSA 2022. LNCS, vol. 13161, pp. 120–144. Springer, Cham (2022). https://doi.org/10.1007/978-3-030-95312-6_6

22. Kim, M., Song, Y., Li, B., Micciancio, D.: Semi-parallel logistic regression for GWAS on encrypted data. BMC Med. Genomics **13**(7), 1–13 (2020)

23. Lee, J.W., et al.: Privacy-preserving machine learning with fully homomorphic encryption for deep neural network. IEEE Access (2021). https://ieeexplore.ieee.org/abstract/document/9734024

24. Lee, J.-W., Lee, E., Lee, Y., Kim, Y.-S., No, J.-S.: High-precision bootstrapping of RNS-CKKS homomorphic encryption using optimal minimax polynomial approximation and inverse sine function. In: Canteaut, A., Standaert, F.-X. (eds.) EUROCRYPT 2021. LNCS, vol. 12696, pp. 618–647. Springer, Cham (2021). https://doi.org/10.1007/978-3-030-77870-5_22

25. Lee, Y., Lee, J.W., Kim, Y.S., No, J.S.: Near-optimal polynomial for modular reduction using L2-norm for approximate homomorphic encryption. IEEE Access **8**(144), 321–330 (2020)

26. Li, B., Micciancio, D.: On the security of homomorphic encryption on approximate numbers. In: Canteaut, A., Standaert, F.-X. (eds.) EUROCRYPT 2021. LNCS, vol. 12696, pp. 648–677. Springer, Cham (2021). https://doi.org/10.1007/978-3-030-77870-5_23

27. Son, Y., Cheon, J.H.: Revisiting the hybrid attack on sparse and ternary secret LWE. Cryptology ePrint Archive 2019/1019 (2019)

Rubato: Noisy Ciphers for Approximate Homomorphic Encryption

Jincheol Ha[1], Seongkwang Kim[2(✉)], Byeonghak Lee[1], Jooyoung Lee[1(✉)], and Mincheol Son[1]

[1] KAIST, Daejeon, Korea
{smilecjf,lbh0307,hicalf,encrypted.def}@kaist.ac.kr
[2] Samsung SDS, Seoul, Korea
seongkwang.kim23@gmail.com

Abstract. A transciphering framework converts a symmetric ciphertext into a homomorphic ciphertext on the server-side, reducing computational and communication overload on the client-side. In Asiacrypt 2021, Cho et al. proposed the RtF framework that supports approximate computation.

In this paper, we propose a family of *noisy* ciphers, dubbed Rubato, with a novel design strategy of introducing noise to a symmetric cipher of a low algebraic degree. With this strategy, the multiplicative complexity of the cipher is significantly reduced, compared to existing HE-friendly ciphers, without degrading the overall security. More precisely, given a moderate block size (16 to 64), Rubato enjoys a low multiplicative depth (2 to 5) and a small number of multiplications per encrypted word (2.1 to 6.25) at the cost of slightly larger ciphertext expansion (1.26 to 1.31). The security of Rubato is supported by comprehensive analysis including symmetric and LWE cryptanalysis. Compared to HERA within the RtF framework, client-side and server-side throughput is improved by 22.9% and 32.2%, respectively, at the cost of only 1.6% larger ciphertext expansion.

Keywords: Homomorphic encryption · Transciphering framework · Stream cipher · HE-friendly cipher

1 Introduction

Real-world data typically contain some errors from their true values since they are represented by real numbers rather than bits or integers. Even in the case that input data are represented by exact numbers without approximation, one might have to approximate intermediate values during data processing for efficiency. Therefore, it would be practically relevant to support approximate computation over encrypted data. The CKKS encryption scheme [24] provides the desirable

---

S. Kim—This work was done while S. Kim was a PhD student at KAIST.

J. Lee—This work was supported by the National Research Foundation of Korea (NRF) grant funded by the Korea government (MSIT) (No. 2021R1F1A1047146).

© International Association for Cryptologic Research 2022
O. Dunkelman and S. Dziembowski (Eds.): EUROCRYPT 2022, LNCS 13275, pp. 581–610, 2022.
https://doi.org/10.1007/978-3-031-06944-4_20

feature using an efficient encoder for real numbers. Due to this feature, CKKS achieves good performance in various applications, for example, to securely evaluate machine learning algorithms on a real dataset [17,55].

Unfortunately, current HE schemes including CKKS commonly suffer from heavy computational and memory overload. The encryption/decryption speed is relatively slow compared to conventional encryption schemes, and it implies that HE is inadequate for bulk encryption. Also, ciphertext expansion seems to be an intrinsic problem of homomorphic encryption due to the noise used in the encryption algorithm. Although the ciphertext expansion has been significantly reduced down to the order of hundreds in terms of the ratio of a ciphertext size to its plaintext size since the invention of the batching technique [38], it does not seem to be acceptable from a practical viewpoint. Furthermore, this ratio becomes even worse when it comes to encryption of a short message; encryption of a single bit might result in a ciphertext of a few megabytes.

1.1 Transciphering and HE-friendly Ciphers

TRANSCIPHERING FRAMEWORK. To address the issue of computational overload and the ciphertext expansion, a hybrid framework, also called a *transciphering framework*, has been proposed for exact computation [54]. It basically converts a symmetric ciphertext $c = E_k(m)$ to a homomorphic ciphertext $Enc^{HE}(m)$ by homomorphically evaluating the cipher. For approximate computation, Cho et al. [25] proposed a new transciphering framework, dubbed the RtF framework (see Fig. 1). We give a brief description of the RtF framework in the following.

For a given message vector $m \in \mathbb{R}^n$, a client encrypts an encoded message $\lfloor \Delta \cdot m \rceil \in \mathbb{Z}_q^n$ using a symmetric cipher E over $\mathbb{Z}_q$ with a secret key $k \in \mathbb{Z}_q^n$ and a nonce nc; this secret key is encrypted using the FV encryption algorithm Enc^{FV}. The resulting ciphertexts $c = E_k(m)$, the FV-encrypted symmetric key $Enc^{FV}(k)$, and the nonce nc are stored in the server. When the server wants to compute $Enc^{CKKS}(m)$ (for computation over encrypted data), the server homomorphically evaluates the server-side conversion of the RtF framework, securely obtaining $Enc^{CKKS}(m)$.

Given a symmetric cipher with low multiplicative depth and complexity, a transciphering framework provides the following advantages on the client-side.

- A client does not need to encrypt all its data using an HE algorithm (except the symmetric key). All the data can be encrypted using only a symmetric cipher, significantly saving computational resources in terms of time and memory.
- Symmetric encryption does not result in ciphertext expansion, so the communication overhead between the client and the server will be significantly low compared to using any homomorphic encryption scheme alone.

All these merits come at the cost of computational overload on the server-side. That said, this trade-off would be worth considering in practice since servers are typically more powerful than clients.

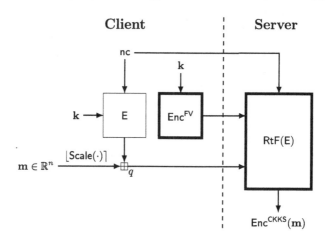

Fig. 1. A simplified diagram of the RtF transciphering framework. Homomorphic operations are performed in the boxes with thick lines.

Although a transciphering framework can be considered at any place where HE is used, it is not a panacea for every privacy problem since it takes more time than HE-only until $\mathsf{Enc}^{\mathsf{HE}}(\mathbf{m})$ is finally obtained. We suggest two appropriate scenarios for transciphering frameworks in the full version of this paper [43].

HE-FRIENDLY CIPHERS. Symmetric ciphers are built on top of linear and nonlinear layers, and in a conventional environment, there has been no need to take different design principles for the two types of layers with respect to their implementation cost. However, when a symmetric cipher is combined with BGV/FV-style HE schemes [18,34] in a transciphering framework, homomorphic addition becomes way cheaper than homomorphic multiplication in terms of computation time and noise growth. With this observation, the efficiency of an HE-friendly cipher is evaluated by its multiplicative complexity and depth. In an arithmetic circuit, its multiplicative complexity is represented by the number of multiplications (ANDs in the binary case). Multiplicative depth is the depth of the tree that represents the arithmetic circuit, closely related to the noise growth in the HE-ciphertexts. These two metrics have brought a new direction in the design of symmetric ciphers: to use simple nonlinear layers at the cost of highly randomized linear layers as adopted in the design of FLIP [53] and Rasta [27].

1.2   Our Contribution

Designing a symmetric cipher can be seen as a trade-off between security and efficiency. A designer should identify important cost metrics of the targeted platform (e.g., x86, ARM, and HE), and focus on optimizing them within a given security level. When it comes to HE-friendly ciphers, one of the most important cost metrics is the time for evaluating the cipher while homomorphically encrypted, typically translated to multiplicative depth and complexity in the literature. To optimize such metrics, quadratic S-boxes [6], random linear layers [53], and nonlinear layers with high-degree inverses [27] have been used.

In this regard, the LWE encryption has promising properties as an HE-friendly cipher since it is based on a linear combination of key material, while noise prevents algebraic attacks. However, straightforward application of the LWE encryption has a disadvantage on the client-side; in the LWE encryption, $(\mathbf{a}, b = \langle \mathbf{a}, \mathbf{s} \rangle + e)$ is sampled from an LWE distribution, where $\mathbf{a}$ should be freshly generated by a pseudorandom function for every encryption. It makes the LWE encryption too costly on the client-side compared to conventional symmetric encryption.

In this work, we propose a new HE-friendly cipher, dubbed Rubato, as a cost-effective trade-off between the LWE encryption and conventional symmetric encryption in a transciphering framework for approximate homomorphic encryption. In particular, when the RtF transciphering framework [25] is used, we can add noise only with a partial loss of precision. For a *low-degree* keyed function $\mathsf{E}_{\mathbf{k}} : \mathbb{Z}_q^k \to \mathbb{Z}_q^\ell$, each sample is of the form

$$(\mathbf{a}, \mathsf{E}_{\mathbf{k}}(\mathbf{a}) + \mathbf{e})$$

where $\mathbf{e} \in \mathbb{Z}_q^\ell$ is sampled from a discrete Gaussian distribution, and $\mathbf{a}$ is generated by an extendable output function (XOF) with a nonce. We remark that such a noisy cipher is not suitable for transciphering of exact data since the server might lose some information on the original message after transciphering. In Table 1, we compare Rubato to existing HE-friendly ciphers operating on modular domains assuming 128-bit security and the same modulus q.

Table 1. Comparison of HE-friendly ciphers operating on modular domains, where the modulus q is set to 25 bits. "#(Key words)" is the number of key words in $\mathbb{Z}_q$ and "#(Multiplications)" (resp. "Random bits") is the number of multiplications (resp. random bits) required to generate a single component of a ciphertext.

Cipher	Masta	HERA	Pasta	LWE	Rubato
#(Key words)	16	16	64	1024	64
Multiplicative depth	7	10	5	0	2
#(Multiplications)	7	10	9.81	0	2.1
Random bits	400	150	250	25600	80
Source	[42]	[25]	[30]	[58]	**This work**

Since Rubato is a combination of a conventional symmetric cipher and the LWE encryption, we analyze its security in two ways: symmetric cryptanalysis and LWE cryptanalysis. We apply the symmetric cryptanalysis by guessing all the noise, while LWE cryptanalysis is considered by linearizing monomials to new variables. From extensive analysis, we recommend a set of parameters for various applications.

Our implementation of Rubato combined with the RtF transciphering framework can be found in a public repository both for the client side[1] and the server side[2]. When Rubato and HERA are compared in the RtF framework, client-side and server-side throughput is improved by 22.9% and 32.2%, respectively, at the cost of only 1.6% larger ciphertext expansion.

1.3 Related Work

Since the transciphering framework has been introduced [54], early works have been focused on the homomorphic evaluation of popular symmetric ciphers (e.g., AES [38], SIMON [48], and PRINCE [31]). Such ciphers have been designed without any consideration of their arithmetic complexity, so the performance of their homomorphic evaluation was not satisfactory.

LowMC [6], being the first HE-friendly cipher, aims to minimize the depth and the number of AND gates, but its low multiplicative depth makes it vulnerable to algebraic attacks [26,28,57]. Due to these attacks, its parameters have been updated, and the resulting cipher is now called LowMCv3. Canteaut et al. [19] claimed that stream ciphers would be advantageous in terms of online complexity compared to block ciphers, and proposed a new stream cipher Kreyvium. However, its practical relevance is limited since the multiplicative depth (with respect to the secret key) keeps growing as keystreams are generated.

The FLIP stream cipher [53] is based on a novel design strategy that its permutation layer is randomly generated for every encryption without increasing the algebraic degree in its secret key. Furthermore, it has been reported that FiLIP [52], a generalized instantiation of FLIP, can be efficiently evaluated with the TFHE scheme [45]. Rasta [27] is a stream cipher aiming at higher throughput at the cost of high latency using random linear layers, which are generated by an extendable output function. Dasta [44], a variant of Rasta using affine layers with lower entropy, boosts up the client-side computation. Masta [42], another variant of Rasta operating on a modular domain, improves upon Rasta in terms of the throughput on both the client and server side. Dobraunig et al. [30] formally defined hybrid homomorphic encryption and proposed another variant Pasta of Rasta operating on a modular domain, improving performance upon Masta.

Cho et al. [25] proposed a transciphering framework for approximate homomorphic encryption, called RtF, which is composed of a stream cipher over modular domain and conversion from FV to CKKS. The stream cipher HERA was proposed in the same paper as a building block of the RtF framework. The HERA cipher is based on a new design strategy – the key schedule is randomized while linear layers are fixed – which is claimed to be efficient on both sides.

In order to reduce the ciphertext expansion when encrypting short messages, Chen et al. [21] proposed an efficient LWEs-to-RLWE conversion method which enables transciphering to the HE-ciphertexts (including CKKS): small messages can be encrypted by LWE-based symmetric encryption with a smaller ciphertext

---

[1] https://github.com/KAIST-CryptLab/Rubato.
[2] https://github.com/KAIST-CryptLab/RtF-Transciphering.

size (compared to RLWE-based encryption), and a collection of LWE ciphertexts can be repacked to an RLWE ciphertext to perform a homomorphic evaluation. Lu et al. [50] proposed a faster LWEs-to-RLWE conversion algorithm in a hybrid construction of FHEW [32] and CKKS, dubbed PEGASUS, where the conversion is possible for a larger number of slots.

2   Preliminaries

2.1   Notations

Throughout the paper, bold lowercase letters (resp. bold uppercase letters) denote vectors (resp. matrices). For a real number r, $\lfloor r \rceil$ denotes the nearest integer to r, rounding upwards in case of a tie. For an integer q, we identify $\mathbb{Z}_q$ with $\mathbb{Z} \cap (-q/2, q/2]$, and for any real number z, $[z]_q$ denotes the mod q reduction of z into $(-q/2, q/2]$. The notation $\lfloor \cdot \rceil$ and $[\cdot]_q$ are extended to vectors (resp. polynomials) to denote their component-wise (resp. coefficient-wise) reduction. For a complex vector $\mathbf{x}$, its ℓ_p-norm is denoted by $\|\mathbf{x}\|_p$. When we say ℓ_p-norm of a polynomial, it means that the ℓ_p-norm of the coefficient vector of the polynomial. For a measurable subset $S \subset \mathbb{R}^d$, vol(S) is the volume of S.

Usual dot products of vectors are denoted by $\langle \cdot, \cdot \rangle$. We denote the multiplicative group of $\mathbb{Z}_q$ by $\mathbb{Z}_q^\times$. The set of strings of arbitrary length over a set S is denoted by S^*. For two vectors (strings) $\mathbf{a}$ and $\mathbf{b}$, their concatenation is denoted by $\mathbf{a}\|\mathbf{b}$. For a set S, we will write $a \leftarrow S$ to denote that a is chosen from S uniformly at random. For a probability distribution $\mathcal{D}$, $a \leftarrow \mathcal{D}$ denotes that a is sampled according to the distribution $\mathcal{D}$. Unless stated otherwise, all logarithms are to the base 2.

2.2   Lattice Background

Let $\mathbf{B} \in \mathbb{R}^{m \times n}$ be a full rank matrix. The lattice $L(\mathbf{B})$ generated by $\mathbf{B}$ is defined by $L(\mathbf{B}) = \{\mathbf{B} \cdot \mathbf{x} : \mathbf{x} \in \mathbb{Z}^n\}$. The matrix $\mathbf{B}$ is called a basis of $L(\mathbf{B})$. The i-th successive minimum $\lambda_i(L)$ of a lattice L is the smallest value t such that at least i linearly independent lattice vectors of length $\leq t$ exist in L. The shortest vector problem (SVP) is finding a shortest non-zero vector of L from a given basis. The γ-unique shortest vector problem (γ-uSVP) is finding the shortest non-zero vector of L provided that $\lambda_2(L) > \gamma\lambda_1(L)$. The γ-bounded distance decoding (BDD$_\gamma$) problem is finding a lattice point in L closest to a target vector $\mathbf{t}$ provided that dist$(\mathbf{t}, L) := \min_{\mathbf{x} \in L}$ dist$(\mathbf{t}, \mathbf{x}) \leq \gamma \cdot \lambda_1(L)$.

HERMITE FACTOR.   Given an n-dimensional lattice L with a basis $\mathbf{B}$, a *root-Hermite factor* δ of the basis $\mathbf{B}$ is defined by $\delta^{n-1} = \|\mathbf{b}_1\|/(\det(L(\mathbf{B}))^{1/n}$ where $\mathbf{b}_1$ is the shortest vector of the basis and $\det(L(\mathbf{B})) = \sqrt{\mathbf{B}^\mathsf{T}\mathbf{B}}$. If δ is smaller, then the basis includes a shorter vector in the lattice.

GAUSSIAN HEURISTIC.   Gaussian heuristic (GH) is a heuristic on how many lattice points are contained in a *nice* object. Given a measurable set $S \subset \mathbb{R}^n$ and a full-rank lattice $L \subset \mathbb{R}^n$, the number of lattice points of L in S is approximated by $\#(S \cap L) = \mathrm{vol}(S)/\det(L)$. If S is an n-dimension ball of radius R, then the equation becomes $\#(S \cap L) = v_n R^n / \det(L)$ where v_n is the volume of the unit n-ball. With this heuristic, the norm of the shortest vector of L can be approximated by

$$GH(L) = \left(v_n^{-1} \det(L)\right)^{\frac{1}{n}}.$$

For random lattices, GH is precise within the error at most 5% [37].

GEOMETRIC SERIES ASSUMPTION. Schnorr claimed that the Gram-Schmidt orthogonalized norm of a BKZ-reduced basis behaves as a geometric series, which is called geometric series assumption (GSA) [60]. For a BKZ-reduced basis $\mathbf{B} = [\mathbf{b}_1, \cdots, \mathbf{b}_n]$ and its orthogonalization $\mathbf{B}^* = [\mathbf{b}_1^*, \cdots, \mathbf{b}_n^*]$, it satisfies that $\|\mathbf{b}_1^*\|/\|\mathbf{b}_i^*\| = r^{i-1}$ for all $1 \le i \le n$ where r is a constant.

2.3   Learning with Errors

Let n and q be positive integers. Let χ be a probability distribution over $\mathbb{Z}$. For an unknown vector $\mathbf{s} \in \mathbb{Z}_q^n$, the LWE (learning with errors) distribution $L_{\mathbf{s},\chi}$ over $\mathbb{Z}_q^n \times \mathbb{Z}_q$ is obtained by sampling a vector $\mathbf{a} \leftarrow \mathbb{Z}_q^n$ and an error $e \leftarrow \chi$, and outputting

$$(\mathbf{a}, b = [\langle \mathbf{a}, \mathbf{s} \rangle + e]_q) \in \mathbb{Z}_q^n \times \mathbb{Z}_q.$$

The search-LWE problem is to find $\mathbf{s} \in \mathbb{Z}_q^n$ when independent samples $(\mathbf{a}_i, b_i)$ are obtained according to $L_{\mathbf{s},\chi}$. The decision-LWE problem is to distinguish the distribution $L_{\mathbf{s},\chi}$ from the uniform distribution over $\mathbb{Z}_q^n \times \mathbb{Z}_q$.

For a positive real $\alpha > 0$, the discrete Gaussian distribution $D_{\alpha q}$ is a probability distribution on $\mathbb{Z}$ defined by

$$\Pr\left[y \leftarrow D_{\alpha q} : y = x\right] \propto \exp\left(-\pi x^2/(\alpha q)^2\right)$$

for each $x \in \mathbb{Z}$. The discrete Gaussian distribution is a popular candidate of the distribution χ.

2.4   RtF Transciphering Framework

We briefly introduce the RtF framework [25], which enables the transciphering of approximate data. The RtF framework works as follows. On the client-side, a real message vector $\mathbf{m} \in \mathbb{R}^n$ is scaled up and rounded off into $\mathbb{Z}_q$. Then, the client encrypts the scaled message $\widetilde{\mathbf{m}} \in \mathbb{Z}_q^n$ using a stream cipher E over $\mathbb{Z}_q$. This "E-ciphertext" will be sent to the server with a nonce nc and an FV-encrypted secret key $\mathcal{K}$ of E.

On the server-side, it first evaluates the stream cipher E homomorphically from nonces $\{nc_i\}_i$ and the FV-encrypted key $\mathcal{K}$. Then the server performs the linear transformation $\mathsf{SlotToCoeff}^{\mathsf{FV}}$, obtaining the resulting FV-ciphertext $\mathcal{Z}$ that contains the keystreams of E in its coefficients. This process is called the offline phase since evaluating $\mathcal{Z}$ is possible only with nonces and $\mathcal{K}$.

After receiving E-ciphertexts $\{\mathbf{c}_i = \mathsf{E}_{\mathbf{k}}(\widetilde{\mathbf{m}}_i)\}_i$, the server starts its online phase. Computing an FV-ciphertext $\mathcal{C}$ having the E-ciphertexts on its coefficients and subtracting $\mathcal{Z}$ from $\mathcal{C}$, the server obtains the FV-ciphertext $\mathcal{X}$ of $\{\widetilde{\mathbf{m}}_i\}_i$ in its coefficients. Finally, the server CKKS-bootstraps $\mathcal{X}$ to translate it into the corresponding CKKS-ciphertext of $\{\mathbf{m}_i\}_i$ in its slots. Since the messages $\{\mathbf{m}_i\}_i$ should be moved from the coefficients to the slots, the last step of the bootstrapping, SlotToCoeff^{CKKS}, can be omitted. As a result, the server will be able to approximately evaluate any circuit on the CKKS-ciphertexts. The detailed description of the RtF framework can be found in the full version [43].

3 Rubato: A Family of Noisy Ciphers

3.1 Specification

The Rubato cipher is designed to be flexible in block size so that it offers a more suitable choice of parameters for various applications. The block size n is the square of a positive integer v, which defines the size of matrices in linear layers. The stream cipher Rubato for λ-bit security takes as input a symmetric key $\mathbf{k} \in \mathbb{Z}_q^n$, a nonce $\mathsf{nc} \in \{0,1\}^\lambda$, and returns a keystream $\mathbf{k}_{\mathsf{nc}} \in \mathbb{Z}_q^\ell$ for some $\ell < n$, where the nonce is fed to the underlying extendable output function (XOF) that outputs an element in $(\mathbb{Z}_q^n)^*$. In a nutshell, Rubato is defined as follows.

$$\mathsf{Rubato}[\mathbf{k},\mathsf{nc}] = \mathsf{AGN} \circ \mathsf{Fin}[\mathbf{k},\mathsf{nc},r] \circ \mathsf{RF}[\mathbf{k},\mathsf{nc},r-1] \circ \cdots \circ \mathsf{RF}[\mathbf{k},\mathsf{nc},1] \circ \mathsf{ARK}[\mathbf{k},\mathsf{nc},0]$$

where the i-th round function $\mathsf{RF}[\mathbf{k},\mathsf{nc},i]$ is defined as

$$\mathsf{RF}[\mathbf{k},\mathsf{nc},i] = \mathsf{ARK}[\mathbf{k},\mathsf{nc},i] \circ \mathsf{Feistel} \circ \mathsf{MixRows} \circ \mathsf{MixColumns}$$

and the final round function Fin is defined as

$$\mathsf{Fin}[\mathbf{k},\mathsf{nc},r] =$$
$$\mathsf{Tr}_{n,\ell} \circ \mathsf{ARK}[\mathbf{k},\mathsf{nc},r] \circ \mathsf{MixRows} \circ \mathsf{MixColumns} \circ \mathsf{Feistel} \circ \mathsf{MixRows} \circ \mathsf{MixColumns}$$

for $i = 1, 2, \ldots, r-1$ (see Fig. 2).

KEY SCHEDULE. The round key schedule can be simply seen as a component-wise product between random values and the master key $\mathbf{k}$, where the uniformly random values in $\mathbb{Z}_q^\times$ are obtained from a certain extendable output function XOF with an input nc. Given a sequence of the outputs from XOF, say $\mathbf{rc} = (\mathbf{rc}_0, \ldots, \mathbf{rc}_r) \in (\mathbb{Z}_q^n)^{r+1}$, ARK is defined as follows.

$$\mathsf{ARK}[\mathbf{k},\mathsf{nc},i](\mathbf{x}) = \mathbf{x} + \mathbf{k} \bullet \mathbf{rc}_i$$

for $i = 0, \ldots, r$, and $\mathbf{x} \in \mathbb{Z}_q^n$, where $\bullet$ (resp. $+$) denotes component-wise multiplication (resp. addition) modulo q. The extendable output function XOF might be instantiated with a sponge-type hash function SHAKE [33].

LINEAR LAYERS. Each linear layer is the composition of MixColumns and MixRows. Similarly to HERA, MixColumns (resp. MixRows) multiplies a certain $v \times v$ MDS matrix $\mathbf{M}_v$ to each column (resp. row) of the state as in Fig. 4a and

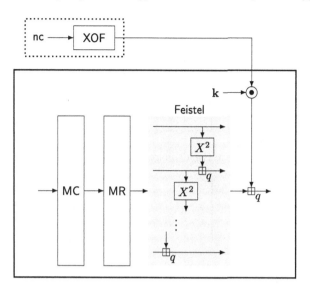

Fig. 2. The round function of Rubato. Operations in the box with dotted (resp. thick) lines are public (resp. secret). "MC" and "MR" represent MixColumns and MixRows, respectively.

Fig. 4b, where the state of Rubato is also viewed as a $v \times v$-matrix over $\mathbb{Z}_q$ (see Fig. 3). The MDS matrix $\mathbf{M}_v$ for $v = 4, 6, 8$ is defined as follows.

$$\mathbf{y}_4 = [2, 3, 1, 1]$$
$$\mathbf{y}_6 = [4, 2, 4, 3, 1, 1]$$
$$\mathbf{y}_8 = [5, 3, 4, 3, 6, 2, 1, 1]$$

$$\mathbf{M}_v = \begin{bmatrix} \mathbf{y}_v \\ \mathrm{ROT}^1(\mathbf{y}_v) \\ \vdots \\ \mathrm{ROT}^{v-1}(\mathbf{y}_v) \end{bmatrix}$$

where $\mathrm{ROT}^i(\mathbf{y})$ is the rotation to the right of $\mathbf{y}$ by i components. Therefore, $\mathbf{M}_v$ is a circulant matrix derived from $\mathbf{y}_v$.

NONLINEAR LAYERS. The nonlinear map Feistel is a Feistel network in a row, which was proposed in [30]. For $\mathbf{x} = (x_1, \ldots, x_n) \in \mathbb{Z}_q^n$, we have

$$\mathsf{Feistel}(\mathbf{x}) = (x_1, x_2 + x_1^2, x_3 + x_2^2, \ldots, x_n + x_{n-1}^2).$$

It is naturally bijective and of degree 2.

TRUNCATION. The truncation function $\mathsf{Tr}_{n,\ell} : \mathbb{Z}_q^n \to \mathbb{Z}_q^\ell$ is just a truncation of the last $n - \ell$ words. For $\mathbf{x} = (x_1, \ldots, x_n) \in \mathbb{Z}_q^n$, we have

$$\mathsf{Tr}_{n,\ell}(\mathbf{x}) = (x_1, \ldots, x_\ell).$$

$$\begin{array}{|c|c|c|c|}
\hline
x_{1,1} & x_{1,2} & \cdots & x_{1,v} \\
\hline
x_{2,1} & x_{2,2} & \cdots & x_{2,v} \\
\hline
\vdots & \vdots & \ddots & \vdots \\
\hline
x_{v,1} & x_{v,2} & \cdots & x_{v,v} \\
\hline
\end{array}$$

Fig. 3. State of Rubato. Each square stands for the component in $\mathbb{Z}_q$.

$$\begin{bmatrix} y_{1,c} \\ y_{2,c} \\ \vdots \\ y_{v,c} \end{bmatrix} = \mathbf{M}_v \cdot \begin{bmatrix} x_{1,c} \\ x_{2,c} \\ \vdots \\ x_{v,c} \end{bmatrix} \qquad\qquad \begin{bmatrix} y_{c,1} \\ y_{c,2} \\ \vdots \\ y_{c,v} \end{bmatrix} = \mathbf{M}_v \cdot \begin{bmatrix} x_{c,1} \\ x_{c,2} \\ \vdots \\ x_{c,v} \end{bmatrix}$$

(a) MixColumns   (b) MixRows

Fig. 4. Definition of MixColumns and MixRows. For $c \in \{1, 2, \ldots, v\}$, x_{ij} and y_{ij} are defined as in Fig. 3.

Although we know that the truncation function makes some part of the last ARK and MixRows meaningless, we write it in this way for brevity. We recommend to instantiate $\mathsf{Tr}_{n,\ell} \circ \mathsf{ARK}[\mathbf{k}, \mathsf{nc}, r] \circ \mathsf{MixRows}$ as a whole in real implementation.

ADDING GAUSSIAN NOISE. At the very last of the cipher, we add Gaussian noise to every component. From an one-dimensional discrete Gaussian distribution $D_{\alpha q}$ with zero mean and variance $(\alpha q)^2 / 2\pi$, we sample ℓ elements $e_1, \ldots, e_\ell \leftarrow D_{\alpha q}$ independently. For $\mathbf{x} = (x_1, \ldots, x_\ell) \in \mathbb{Z}_q^\ell$, we have

$$\mathsf{AGN}(\mathbf{x}) = (x_1 + e_1, \ldots, x_\ell + e_\ell).$$

ENCRYPTION MODE. When a keystream of k blocks (in $(\mathbb{Z}_q^\ell)^k$) is needed for some $k > 0$, the "inner-counter mode" can be used; for $\mathsf{ctr} = 0, 1, \ldots, k-1$, one computes

$$\mathbf{z}[\mathsf{ctr}] = \mathsf{Rubato}\,[\mathbf{k}, \mathsf{nc}\|\mathsf{ctr}]\,(\mathbf{ic}),$$

where $\mathbf{ic}$ denotes a constant $(1, 2, \ldots, n) \in \mathbb{Z}_q^n$. For a given message vector $\mathbf{m} \in (\mathbb{R}^\ell)^k$, encryption by Rubato is defined by

$$\mathbf{c} = \lfloor \Delta \cdot \mathbf{m} \rceil + \mathbf{z} \pmod{q}$$

where $\Delta \in \mathbb{R}$ is a scaling factor.

3.2 Parameter Selection

In this section, we recommend some sets of parameters and concrete instantiation of Rubato. Some sets of parameters are selected in Table 2. The notations in the table follow those in Sect. 3.1. We give three types of parameters: S, M, and L. These imply the size of blocks.

Table 2. Selected parameters of Rubato.

Parameter	λ	n	ℓ	$\lceil \log q \rceil$	αq	r
Par-80S	80	16	12	26	11.1	2
Par-80M	80	36	32	25	2.7	2
Par-80L	80	64	60	25	1.6	2
Par-128S	128	16	12	26	10.5	5
Par-128M	128	36	32	25	4.1	3
Par-128L	128	64	60	25	4.1	2

When choosing the modulus q, we consider the effect of noise on precision. For a discrete Gaussian distribution $D_{\alpha q}$, the size of noise is expectedly $\mathbb{E}_{e \leftarrow D_{\alpha q}} [\,|e|\,]$. Suppose we obtain p-bit average precision while using the RtF framework with some deterministic cipher (e.g., HERA [25]). It means that, a given message x and the message after transciphering x', $|x - x'| < 1/2^p$. Then, the expected loss of precision bits is upper bounded by

$$p + \log_2 \left[\mathbb{E}_{e \leftarrow D_{\alpha q}} [1/2^p + e/\Delta] \right].$$

In our instantiation, we enlarge the modulus q to compensate this loss of precision.

The choice of the scaling factor Δ should vary along with the $\|\mathbf{m}\|_1$, where $\mathbf{m} \in \mathbb{R}^*$ is a message vector. In our experiment (see Sect. 5), we constrain $\|\mathbf{m}\|_1 \leq 1$ and choose $\Delta = q/16$ for the RtF framework [25]. If someone manipulates a message $\|\mathbf{m}\|_1 \leq s$, it is appropriate to choose $\Delta = q/(16 \cdot s)$.

3.3 Design Rationale

The main observation behind our design is that adding noise increases the algebraic degree of a cipher. Suppose that we are given LWE samples $\{(\mathbf{a}_i, b_i = \langle \mathbf{a}_i, \mathbf{s} \rangle + e_i)\}_i$. In Arora-Ge attack [9], an attacker establishes an equation

$$\prod_{e=-t\alpha q}^{t\alpha q} (b_i - \langle \mathbf{a}_i, \mathbf{s} \rangle - e) = 0$$

in order to solve the LWE instance, where $t \in \mathbb{R}$ determines the adversarial success probability. In this way, the noisy linear equation becomes a polynomial equation of degree $(2t\alpha q + 1)$. If the linear equation $\langle \mathbf{a}, \mathbf{s} \rangle$ is replaced by a polynomial $F(\mathbf{a}, \mathbf{s})$ of degree d, the Arora-Ge equation becomes of degree $d(2t\alpha q + 1)$.

We choose the discrete Gaussian distribution for sampling noise since the cryptanalysis of LWE has been extensively studied under the discrete Gaussian assumption. In the main body of the stream cipher, we use building blocks from HERA [25] and Pasta [30]. For linear layers and the key schedule, we follow the style of HERA. Although we are aware of generic ways of constructing an MDS matrix [40,41], those approaches result in a matrix with large components. We keep the component of matrices $\mathbf{M}_v$ as small as possible for efficiency. When enlarging the block size n, we computationally find $v \times v$ MDS matrices since we cannot keep the original linear layer of HERA.

For nonlinear layers, Cho et al. [25] claimed that a nonlinear layer whose inverse is of a high degree mitigates algebraic MitM attacks. As there has not been any known quadratic function with the inverse of a high degree over $\mathbb{Z}_q$, a cubic S-box has been used in HERA, which leads to a larger multiplicative depth. After truncation was proposed for an alternative countermeasure for an algebraic MitM attack [29], Dobraunig et al. [30] proposed a Feistel structure for HE-friendly ciphers. Since the Feistel structure is vulnerable to algebraic MitM attacks, a cubic function for the last nonlinear layer and truncation are adopted to Pasta. As we thought that deploying both the cubic function and truncation is superfluous, we conclude that truncation without the cubic function is sufficient for Rubato.

4   Security Analysis

In this section, we provide the security analysis of Rubato. We summarize the analysis result in Table 3. We omit too costly attacks (i.e., time complexity larger than 2^{1000} for all the parameters) such as trivial linearization and interpolation attacks. We computed the complexity of each attack by using Wolfram Mathematica and made the source codes publicly available in our repository[3]. In the full version [43], we give some additional plots on the security analysis.

ASSUMPTIONS AND THE SCOPE OF ANALYSIS. In this work, we will consider the standard "secret-key model", where an adversary arbitrarily chooses a nonce and obtains the corresponding keystream without any information on the secret key. The related-key and the known-key models are beyond the scope of this paper.

Since Rubato takes as input counters, an adversary is not able to control the differences of the inputs. Nonces can be adversarially chosen, while they are also fed to the extendable output function, which is modeled as a random oracle. So one cannot control the difference of the internal variables. For this reason, we believe that our construction is secure against any type of chosen-plaintext attacks including (higher-order) differential, truncated differential, invariant subspace trail, and cube attacks. A recent generalization of an integral attack [15] requires only a small number of chosen plaintexts, while it is not applicable to Rubato within the security bound.

---

[3] https://github.com/KAIST-CryptLab/Rubato.

Table 3. The log of the complexity of the attacks on Rubato. The upward sign ($\uparrow$) implies that the complexity is larger than 2^{1000}. The linear algebra constant ω is assumed to be 2.

Parameter	GCD	Gröbner	LC	Lattice	Arora-Ge
Par-80S	393.6	80.04	155.9	760.5	80.04
Par-80M	878.6	84.55	249.9	$\uparrow$	80.37
Par-80L	$\uparrow$	82.73	349.8	$\uparrow$	82.73
Par-128S	411.9	128.1	311.7	$\uparrow$	128.1
Par-128M	880.7	128.1	249.9	$\uparrow$	128.1
Par-128L	$\uparrow$	169.6	349.8	$\uparrow$	129.6

4.1   Cryptanalysis Based on Symmetric Primitive Analysis

Most of the symmetric cryptanalysis assumes that a targeted cipher is a deterministic algorithm. Symmetric cryptanalysis is to find some statistical or algebraic characteristics of the function which is distinguished from its ideal counterpart. However, as the Gaussian noise is added at the end of the cipher, Rubato should be seen as a random sampling. For this reason, most of the conventional symmetric cryptanalysis are not directly applicable to Rubato. Nevertheless, by guessing all the noise, an attacker can try to analyze Rubato using symmetric key cryptanalysis. Since the noise is sampled from discrete Gaussian distribution $D_{\alpha q}$, it is always advantageous for an attacker to guess that the noise is zero when the data are sufficiently given. We denote the probability such that a sample from $D_{\alpha q}$ is zero by $\varepsilon_0 = \Pr\left[e \leftarrow D_{\alpha q} : e = 0\right]$.

4.1.1   Trivial Linearization
Trivial linearization is to solve a system of linear equations by replacing all monomials with new variables. When applied to the r-round Rubato cipher, the number of monomials appearing in this system is upper bounded by

$$S = \sum_{i=0}^{2^r} \binom{n+i-1}{i}.$$

Therefore, at most S equations will be enough to solve this system of equations. All the monomials of degree at most 2^r are expected to appear after r rounds of Rubato (as explained in detail in the full version [43]). Therefore, by guessing $e = 0$, we can conclude that this attack requires $O(S^\omega / \varepsilon_0^S)$ time, where $2 \leq \omega \leq 3$. Since the success probability is too small for $r \geq 1$, it will never be a dominant attack.

4.1.2 GCD Attack

The GCD attack seeks to compute the greatest common divisor (GCD) of univariate polynomials, and it can be useful for a cipher operating on a large field with its representation being a polynomial in a single variable. This attack can be extended to a system of multivariate polynomial equations by guessing all the key variables except one. For r-round Rubato, the complexity of the GCD attack is estimated as $O(q^{n-1}r^2 2^r)$ even if there is no noise. For a security parameter $\lambda \leq 256$, Rubato will be secure against the GCD attack even with a single round as long as $n \geq 16$.

4.1.3 Gröbner Basis Attack

The Gröbner basis attack is an attack by solving a system of equations by computing a Gröbner basis of the system. If such a Gröbner basis is found, then the variables can be eliminated one by one after carefully converting the order of monomials. We refer to [8] for details. In the literature, security against Gröbner basis attack is bounded by the time complexity for Gröbner basis computing.

Suppose that an attacker wants to solve a system of m polynomial equations in n variables over a field $\mathbb{F}_q$,

$$f_1(x_1, \ldots, x_n) = f_2(x_1, \ldots, x_n) = \cdots = f_m(x_1, \ldots, x_n) = 0.$$

The complexity of computing a Gröbner basis of such system is known to be

$$O\left(\binom{n + d_{reg}}{d_{reg}}^\omega \right)$$

in terms of the number of operations over the base field, where $2 \leq \omega \leq 3$ and d_{reg} is the *degree of regularity* [14]. With the degree of regularity, one can see how many degrees of polynomial multiples will be needed to find the Gröbner basis. Unfortunately, it is hard to compute the exact degree of regularity for a generic system of equations. When the number of equations is larger than the number of variables, the degree of regularity of a *semi-regular sequence* can be computed as the degree of the first non-positive coefficient in the Hilbert series

$$\mathrm{HS}(z) = \frac{1}{(1-z)^n} \times \prod_{i=1}^{m} (1 - z^{d_i}).$$

As it is conjectured that most sequences are semi-regular [35], we analyze the security of Rubato against the Gröbner basis attack under the (semi-)regular assumption.

HYBRID APPROACH. One can take a hybrid approach between the guess-and-determine attack and the algebraic attack [13]. Guessing some variables makes the system of equations overdetermined. An overdetermined system becomes easier to solve; the complexity of the hybrid approach after g guesses is given as

$$O\left(q^g \binom{n - g + d_g}{d_g}^\omega \right)$$

where d_g is the degree of regularity after g guesses.

APPLICATION TO Rubato. For the Gröbner basis attack, re-arranging equations may lead to a significant impact on the attack complexity. For example, one may set a system of equations using only plaintext-ciphertext pairs or set a system of equations with new variables standing for internal states. The former will be a higher-degree system in fewer variables, while the latter will be a lower-degree system in more variables.

From a set of nonce-plaintext-ciphertext triples $\{(\mathsf{nc}_i, \mathbf{m}_i, \mathbf{c}_i)\}_i$, an attacker will be able to establish an overdetermined system of equation

$$f_1(k_1, \ldots, k_n) = f_2(k_1, \ldots, k_n) = \cdots = f_m(k_1, \ldots, k_n) = 0$$

where $k_i \in \mathbb{Z}_q$ is the i-th component of the key variable. The degree of regularity of the system is computed as the degree of the first non-positive coefficient in

$$\left(1 - z^{2^r}\right)^{m-n} \left(\sum_{i=0}^{2^r - 1} z^i\right)^n$$

where r is the number of rounds. The larger number of equations implies a smaller degree of regularity. Since the summation does not have any negative term, one easily sees that the degree d_{reg} of regularity cannot be smaller than 2^r. We conservatively lower bound the time complexity when there is no noise by

$$O\left(\binom{n + 2^r}{2^r}^\omega\right)$$

regardless of the number of equations. Since at least n equations are required for the unique root, we can conclude that this attack requires n data and

$$O\left(\binom{n + 2^r}{2^r}^\omega \varepsilon_0^{-n}\right)$$

time. We note that the hybrid approach always has worse complexity.

Instead of a system of equations of degree 2^r, one can establish a system of $((r-1)n + \ell)k$ quadratic equations in $n(r-1)k + n$ variables, where k is the block length of each query. To get the unique root, it requires that $k \geq n/\ell$. Then, the complexity is

$$O\left(\binom{n(r-1)k + n + d_{reg}(r, k)}{d_{reg}(r, k)}^\omega \varepsilon_0^{-\ell k}\right)$$

where the degree $d_{reg}(r, k)$ of regularity is computed under the semi-regular assumption.

Although we explain that the truncation can prevent MitM attack, MitM attack is not a "never-applicable" attack for Rubato. Suppose $\mathbf{y} = (y_1, \ldots, y_\ell)$ be a keystream. By creating new variables $x_{\ell+1}, \ldots, x_n$, an attacker can make n MitM equations in $2n - \ell$ variables $k_1, \ldots, k_n, x_{\ell+1}, \ldots, x_n$. Denoting the first

$\lfloor r/2 \rfloor$-round function by F and the last $\lceil r/2 \rceil$-round function except for $\mathsf{Tr}_{n,\ell}$ and AGN by G,

$$\mathsf{Rubato}[\mathbf{k}, \mathsf{nc}_1] = (y_1, \ldots, y_\ell)$$
$$G \circ F[\mathbf{k}, \mathsf{nc}_1] = (y_1 - e_1, \ldots, y_\ell - e_\ell, x_{\ell+1}, \ldots, x_n)$$
$$F[\mathbf{k}, \mathsf{nc}_1] = G^{-1}(y_1 - e_1, \ldots, y_\ell - e_\ell, x_{\ell+1}, \ldots, x_n) \tag{1}$$

where e_i's are guessed noise. Equation 1 is of degree $2^{\lceil r/2 \rceil}$ so that the lower bound of the degree of regularity is also $2^{\lceil r/2 \rceil}$. Similarly as above, to get the unique root, the queried block length k should satisfy $n + k(n - \ell) \le nk$. Then, the time complexity is lower bounded by

$$O\left(\binom{n + (n - \ell)k + 2^{\lceil r/2 \rceil}}{2^{\lceil r/2 \rceil}}^\omega \varepsilon_0^{-\ell k} \right).$$

4.1.4   Interpolation Attack

The interpolation attack is to establish an encryption polynomial in plaintext variables without any information on the secret key and to distinguish it from a random permutation [46]. It is known that the data complexity of this attack depends on the number of monomials in the polynomial representation of the cipher.

For the r-round Rubato cipher, let $\mathbf{rc} = (\mathbf{rc}_0, \ldots, \mathbf{rc}_r) \in (\mathbb{Z}_q^n)^{r+1}$ be a sequence of the outputs from XOF. For $i = 0, \ldots, r$, $\mathbf{rc}_i$ is evaluated by a polynomial of degree 2^{r-i}. As we expect that the r-round Rubato cipher has almost all monomials of degree $\le 2^r$ in its polynomial representation, the number of monomials is lower bounded by

$$\sum_{j=0}^{r} \sum_{i=0}^{2^j} \binom{n + i - 1}{i}.$$

Similarly as the trivial linearization, the success probability is too small for $r \ge 1$, it will never be a dominant attack.

4.1.5   Linear Cryptanalysis

Linear cryptanalysis was originally introduced for binary spaces [51], but it can also be applied to non-binary spaces [11]. Similarly to binary ciphers, for an odd prime number q, the linear probability of a cipher $\mathsf{E} : \mathbb{Z}_q^n \to \mathbb{Z}_q^n$ with respect to input and output masks $\mathbf{a}, \mathbf{b} \in \mathbb{Z}_q^n$ can be defined by

$$\mathsf{LP}^{\mathsf{E}}(\mathbf{a}, \mathbf{b}) = \left| \mathbb{E}_{\mathbf{m}} \left[\exp \left\{ \frac{2\pi i}{q} \left(-\langle \mathbf{a}, \mathbf{m} \rangle + \langle \mathbf{b}, \mathsf{E}(\mathbf{m}) \rangle \right) \right\} \right] \right|^2$$

where $\mathbf{m}$ follows the uniform distribution on $\mathbb{Z}_q^n$. When E is a random permutation, the expected linear probability is defined by $\mathsf{ELP}^{\mathsf{E}}(\mathbf{a}, \mathbf{b}) = \mathbb{E}_{\mathsf{E}}[\mathsf{LP}^{\mathsf{E}}(\mathbf{a}, \mathbf{b})]$.

Then, the number of samples required for linear cryptanalysis is known to be $1/\mathrm{ELP}^{\mathsf{E}}(\mathbf{a}, \mathbf{b})$. In order to ensure the security against linear cryptanalysis, it is sufficient to bound the maximum linear probability $\max_{\mathbf{a} \neq 0, \mathbf{b}} \mathrm{ELP}^{\mathsf{E}}(\mathbf{a}, \mathbf{b})$.

APPLICATION TO Rubato. Although it seems that the linear cryptanalysis cannot be applied to Rubato directly because of the noise, we give a security bound for linear cryptanalysis assuming no noise. There are two applications of linear cryptanalysis on Rubato according to how to take the input variables: the XOF output variables or the key variables. In the first case, unlike traditional linear cryptanalysis, the probability of any linear trail of Rubato depends on the key since it is multiplied by the input. It seems infeasible to make a plausible linear trail without any information on the key material.

In the second case, the attack is reduced to solving an LWE-like problem as follows; given pairs $(\mathsf{nc}_i, \mathbf{y}_i)$ such that $\mathsf{Rubato}(\mathbf{k}, \mathsf{nc}_i) = \mathbf{y}_i$, one can establish

$$\langle \mathbf{b}, \mathbf{y}_i \rangle = \langle \mathbf{a}, \mathbf{k} \rangle + e_i$$

for some vectors $\mathbf{a} \neq \mathbf{0}, \mathbf{b} \in \mathbb{Z}_q^n$ and error e_i sampled according to a certain distribution χ. An attacker requires $1/\mathrm{ELP}^{\mathsf{E}}(\mathbf{a}, \mathbf{b})$ samples to distinguish χ from the uniform distribution [11].

Lemma 1. *For any* $\mathbf{a} = (a_1, \ldots, a_n) \neq \mathbf{0}, \mathbf{b} = (b_1, \ldots, b_n) \in \mathbb{Z}_q^n$ *such that* $\mathsf{hw}(b_2, b_3, \ldots, b_n) = h$, *the linear probability of* Feistel *is*

$$\mathrm{LP}^{\mathsf{Feistel}}(\mathbf{a}, \mathbf{b}) \leq \frac{1}{q^h}.$$

Proof. By the definition, we have

$\mathrm{LP}^{\mathsf{Feistel}}(\mathbf{a}, \mathbf{b})$

$$= \left| \mathbb{E}_{\mathbf{m}} \left[\exp \left\{ \frac{2\pi i}{q} \left(-\langle \mathbf{a}, \mathbf{m} \rangle + \langle \mathbf{b}, \mathsf{Feistel}(\mathbf{m}) \rangle \right) \right\} \right] \right|^2$$

$$= \left| \mathbb{E}_{\mathbf{m}} \left[\exp \left\{ \frac{2\pi i}{q} \left(\sum_{k=1}^{n-1} (-a_k m_k + b_k m_k + b_{k+1} m_k^2) + (-a_n + b_n) m_n \right) \right\} \right] \right|^2$$

$$= \left| \mathbb{E}_{m_n} \left[\exp \left\{ \frac{2\pi i}{q} \left((-a_n + b_n) m_n \right) \right\} \right] \right|^2$$

$$\times \prod_{i=1}^{n-1} \left| \mathbb{E}_{m_i} \left[\exp \left\{ \frac{2\pi i}{q} \left((-a_i + b_i) m_i + b_{i+1} m_i^2 \right) \right\} \right] \right|^2.$$

Carlitz and Uchiyama [20] proved that

$$\left| \sum_{x=0}^{q-1} \exp \left(\frac{2\pi i}{q} \cdot p(x) \right) \right| \leq (r-1)\sqrt{q}$$

for any polynomial $p(x)$ of degree r over $\mathbb{Z}_q$. Therefore, we have

$$\left| \mathbb{E}_{m_i} \left[\exp \left\{ \frac{2\pi i}{q} \left((-a_i + b_i) m_i + b_{i+1} m_i^2 \right) \right\} \right] \right|^2 \leq \left| \frac{1}{q} \cdot \sqrt{q} \right|^2 \leq \frac{1}{q}$$

and it implies that

$$\text{LP}^{\text{Feistel}}(\mathbf{a}, \mathbf{b}) \leq \frac{1}{q^h}.$$

$\square$

Since the branch number of the linear layer of Rubato is $2v$ (as shown in the full version [43]), we can conclude that an r-round Rubato cipher provides λ-bit security against linear cryptanalysis when $q^{(2v-2)\cdot\lfloor\frac{r}{2}\rfloor} > 2^\lambda$.

4.1.6   Differential Cryptanalysis and Its Variants

Since Rubato takes counters as input, an adversary is not able to control the differences of its inputs. Nonces can be adversarially chosen, while they are also fed to the extendable output function, which is modeled as a random oracle. So one cannot control the difference of the internal variables. For this reason, we believe that our construction will be secure against any type of chosen-plaintext attack including (higher-order) differential, truncated differential, invariant subspace trail, and cube attacks.

Nonetheless, to prevent an unsuspected differential-related attack, we present a computation of a differential characteristic in the following. Given a pair $\mathbf{a}, \mathbf{b} \in \mathbb{Z}_q^n$, the differential probability of Feistel is defined by

$$\text{DP}^{\text{Feistel}}(\mathbf{a}, \mathbf{b}) = \frac{1}{q^n} \cdot \left|\{\mathbf{x} \in \mathbb{Z}_q^n : \text{Feistel}(\mathbf{x} + \mathbf{a}) - \text{Feistel}(\mathbf{x}) = \mathbf{b}\}\right|.$$

So $\text{DP}^{\text{Feistel}}(\mathbf{a}, \mathbf{b})$ is determined by the number of solutions to $\text{Feistel}(\mathbf{x} + \mathbf{a}) - \text{Feistel}(\mathbf{x}) = \mathbf{b}$.

Lemma 2. *For any* $\mathbf{a} = (a_1, \ldots, a_n) \neq \mathbf{0}, \mathbf{b} = (b_1, \ldots, b_n) \in \mathbb{Z}_q^n$ *such that* $\text{hw}(a_1, a_2, \ldots, a_{n-1}) = h$, *the differential probability of* Feistel *is*

$$\text{DP}^{\text{Feistel}}(\mathbf{a}, \mathbf{b}) \leq \frac{1}{q^h}.$$

Proof. Our goal is to find the maximum number of solutions to the equation

$$\text{Feistel}(\mathbf{x} + \mathbf{a}) - \text{Feistel}(\mathbf{x}) = (a_1, 2a_1x_1 + a_1^2 + a_2, \ldots, 2a_nx_{n-1} + a_{n-1}^2 + a_n) = \mathbf{b}.$$

For $i \leq n-1$, the equation $2a_ix_i + a_i^2 + a_{i+1} = b_i$ has a unique solution $x_i = (b_i - a_i^2 - a_{i+1}) \cdot (2a_i)^{-1}$ if $a_i \neq 0$ and the equation has maximally q solutions if $a_i = 0$. For $i = n$, the variable x_n is free so that the maximal number of solution is q. It implies that

$$\text{DP}^{\text{Feistel}}(\mathbf{a}, \mathbf{b}) \leq \frac{1}{q^h}.$$

$\square$

Since the branch number of the linear layer of Rubato is $2v$ (as shown in the full version [43]), we can conclude that an r-round Rubato cipher provides λ-bit security against differential cryptanalysis when $q^{(2v-2)\cdot\lfloor\frac{r}{2}\rfloor} > 2^\lambda$.

4.2   Cryptanalysis Based on LWE Analysis

As Rubato is not an LWE instance, algorithms solving LWE are not directly applied to Rubato. However, if someone considers a single component of a keystream block of Rubato as

$$\left((a_{\mathbf{u}})_{\mathbf{u}}, \sum_{\mathbf{u}} a_{\mathbf{u}} \mathbf{k}^{\mathbf{u}} + e \right) \tag{2}$$

where $\mathbf{u} = (u_1, \ldots, u_n) \in \mathbb{Z}_{\geq 0}^n$, and $\mathbf{k}^{\mathbf{u}} = \prod_i k_i^{u_i}$ implies a monomial with degree $\mathbf{u}$, it becomes an LWE instance with the linearized variables whose dimension is

$$S_{n,r} = \sum_{i=1}^{2^r} \binom{n+i-1}{i}$$

where $2^r < q$.

In this section, we will denote notations in a linearized way. For example, we denote Rubato samples by $(\mathbf{A}, \mathbf{c} = \mathbf{A}\mathbf{s} + \mathbf{e})$ where $\mathbf{s}$ stands for the vector $(\mathbf{k}^{\mathbf{u}})_{\mathbf{u}}$ and $\mathbf{A}$ stands for a set of $(a_{\mathbf{u}})_{\mathbf{u}}$ in a certain monomial order.

We remark that we do not explore potential vulnerabilities which can arise from combining symmetric key cryptanalysis and LWE cryptanalysis. We analyze each attack in its original way, not in a mixed way. For example, in our analysis, all the LWE cryptanalysis except Arora-Ge attack [9] assume that $(a_{\mathbf{u}})_{\mathbf{u}}$ is independently sampled from the uniform distribution over $\mathbb{Z}_q$, which is not the case for Rubato.

4.2.1   Exhaustive Search

The most naive approach for solving LWE is the exhaustive search. Given m samples $(\mathbf{A}, \mathbf{c})$, an attacker guesses noise $\mathbf{e} = (e_1, \ldots, e_m)$ and finds $\mathbf{s}$ satisfying $\mathbf{A}\mathbf{s} = \mathbf{c} - \mathbf{e}$ where $\mathbf{A}$ is required to have a left inverse. To attack Rubato, the attacker needs to guess at least $(2t\alpha q + 1)^{S_{n,r}}$ times for success probability $\Pr\left[e \leftarrow D_{\alpha q} : |e_i| \leq t\alpha q \text{ for all } i \right]$ where the expected time complexity is upper bounded by $\varepsilon_0^{S_{n,r}}$. Since the success probability is too small for $r \geq 1$, it will never be a dominant attack.

There is a meet-in-the-middle (MitM) approach mentioned in [10], which is a time-memory trade-off of the exhaustive search. For the same reason, the MitM approach cannot be a dominant attack.

4.2.2   Lattice Attacks

Reduction to a lattice problem is one way to solve LWE. To solve a lattice problem, an attacker needs a short enough basis of the given lattice. This short basis is obtained by using a lattice reduction algorithm such as the BKZ algorithm [23,59].

CORE-SVP HARDNESS OF BKZ ALGORITHMS. The BKZ algorithm is a lattice reduction algorithm that uses an (approximate-)SVP oracle of small dimension

β. This algorithm repeatedly calls the SVP oracle as a subroutine to find the shortest vectors in the projected lattice of dimension β. An output from the BKZ-β algorithm is called a "BKZ$_\beta$-reduced basis". The SVP oracle can be instantiated using sieving algorithms or enumeration algorithms.

Unfortunately, it is difficult to predict how many calls will be made to the SVP oracle in the BKZ algorithm. So, we analyze the security of Rubato against the BKZ algorithm using a single call, in which case the underlying hardness assumption is called *core-SVP hardness* [7]. Table 4 compares the expected time complexity of the BKZ algorithm for various instantiations of the SVP oracle in terms of BKZ block size β and root-Hermite factor δ. For Lindner and Peikert [49] and Albrecht et al. [3], the time complexity is estimated by extrapolating their experimental running time of the BKZ algorithm using enumeration methods. For the remaining instantiations, the complexity analysis is theoretically based on the cost of a single call to the SVP-oracle.

When it comes to the quality of a BKZ$_\beta$-reduced basis, Chen [22] gave a limit

$$\lim_{N \to \infty} \delta = \left(v_\beta^{-\frac{1}{\beta}} \right)^{\frac{1}{\beta-1}} \approx \left(\frac{\beta}{2\pi e} (\pi \beta)^{\frac{1}{\beta}} \right)^{\frac{1}{2(\beta-1)}} \tag{3}$$

for the root-Hermite factor δ assuming the Gaussian heuristic and the geometric series assumption. Chen also gave an experimental proof that this limit is a reasonable choice when N is finite. As another estimate of δ for a BKZ$_\beta$-reduced basis, the *lattice rule of thumb* [56], which says $\delta = \beta^{\frac{1}{2\beta}}$, is often used in the literature. We will opt for Chen's limit when we compute β from a fixed value of δ.

Table 4. Expected time complexity of the BKZ algorithm for various instantiations of the SVP oracle in terms of BKZ block size β and root-Hermite factor δ.

Instantiation of the SVP oracle	Complexity (in log)
Lindner and Peikert [49]	$\frac{1.8}{\log \delta} - 110$
Albrecht et al. [3]	$\frac{0.009}{\log^2 \delta} - 27$
Enumeration [2]	$\frac{\beta \log \beta}{8} - 0.654\beta + 25.84$
Classical Sieve [12]	$0.292\beta + o(\beta)$
Quantum Sieve [47]	$0.265\beta + o(\beta)$

PRIMAL ATTACK. Primal attack is the strategy of solving the search-LWE problem via solving the bounded distance decoding (BDD) problem. Given m samples $(\mathbf{A}, \mathbf{c} = \mathbf{As} + \mathbf{e})$ following $L_{\mathbf{s},\chi}$, one can see that $\mathbf{c}$ is near the lattice $L(\mathbf{A})$. Finding the nearest lattice point from $\mathbf{c}$ is equivalent to finding the secret vector $\mathbf{s}$ when $\mathbf{A}$ is (left) invertible. If $\mathbf{A}$ is not invertible, it is sufficient to gather a few more samples.

In order to solve the derived BDD problem, there are two approaches: enumeration [37,49] and reduction to unique-SVP (uSVP) [4,5]. Since the enumeration method is treated as a subroutine in the BKZ algorithm, we do not take it into account as a direct solver of the BDD problem.

The second approach, the reduction to uSVP, was firstly proposed by Albrecht et al. [4]. The main idea of the approach is to solve SVP of the larger lattice $L = L(\mathbf{B})$ of basis

$$\mathbf{B} = \begin{pmatrix} \mathbf{A} & \mathbf{c} \\ \mathbf{0} & u \end{pmatrix}$$

where $u = \text{dist}(\mathbf{c}, L(\mathbf{A}))$. This lattice contains an unusually small vector $(\mathbf{e}, -u)$, which implies the gap $\lambda_2(L)/\lambda_1(L)$ is large. Assuming Gaussian heuristic and linear independence of $\mathbf{A}$, Göpfert [39] showed that an attacker can create the $\lambda_2(L)/\lambda_1(L)$-gap greater than

$$\frac{\min\left\{q, q^{1-N/m}\sqrt{\frac{m}{2\pi e}}\right\}}{\sqrt{m} \cdot \frac{\alpha q}{\sqrt{2\pi}}}.$$

As a lattice reduction satisfying $\lambda_2(L)/\lambda_1(L) > \tau\delta^m$ for some constant $\tau \le 1$ is sufficient to solve a uSVP instance [36], this approach requires log root-Hermite factor

$$\log \delta = \frac{\log^2(\tau\alpha\sqrt{e})}{4N \log q}$$

if $\min\left\{q, q^{1-N/m}\sqrt{\frac{m}{2\pi e}}\right\} = q^{1-N/m}\sqrt{\frac{m}{2\pi e}}$. Although experimental evidence suggests $\tau \le 0.4$ [36], we set $\tau = 1$ for the conservative choice of parameters.

Alkim et al. gave an alternative success condition of the attack [7]. Denoting $d = m + N + 1$ and $\sigma = \alpha q/\sqrt{2\pi}$, the requirement is that

$$\sigma\sqrt{\beta} \le \delta^{2\beta-d}q^{m/d}$$

where δ is computed by Eq. 3. We take both into account along with the parameter $N = S_{n,r}$.

DUAL ATTACK. The dual attack, also called the short integer solution (SIS) strategy, is an attack finding small vector $\mathbf{w} \in \mathbb{Z}_q^m$ such that $\mathbf{w}^\mathsf{T}\mathbf{A} \equiv 0 \pmod{q}$. Given m samples $(\mathbf{A}, \mathbf{c})$ from $L_{\mathbf{s},\chi}$, finding a short vector satisfying $\mathbf{w}^\mathsf{T}\mathbf{A} \equiv \mathbf{0} \pmod{q}$ leads to

$$\mathbf{w}^\mathsf{T}\mathbf{c} = \mathbf{w}^\mathsf{T}(\mathbf{A}\mathbf{s} + \mathbf{e}) = \mathbf{w}^\mathsf{T}\mathbf{e}$$

where the last term is small. The short vector $\mathbf{w}$ should satisfy

$$\|\mathbf{w}\|_2 = \frac{1}{\alpha}\sqrt{\frac{\ln(1/\epsilon)}{\pi}}$$

in order to distinguish $L_{\mathbf{s},\chi}$ from random with advantage ϵ [49]. By the definition of the root-Hermite factor δ, the attack requires that

$$\log \delta = \frac{\log^2\left(\frac{1}{\alpha}\sqrt{\frac{\ln(1/\epsilon)}{\pi}}\right)}{4N \log q}$$

for the LWE instance parametrized by N, α, and q. When evaluating the security of Rubato, we set $N = S_{n,r}$ and $\epsilon \approx 1/23$.

4.2.3 BKW Attack

The original BKW algorithm was proposed for solving the learning parity with noise (LPN) problem [16] by Blum, Kalai, and Wasserman. Regev pointed out that the BKW algorithm can be used for solving LWE, and Albrecht et al. [3] gave the formal analysis of the BKW algorithm for LWE. We briefly explain the BKW attack on LWE, and we refer to [3] for more details.

The BKW attack is a lattice-version of Gaussian elimination parametrized by a and b. Suppose there is an LWE distribution $L_{\mathbf{s},\chi}$ where $\chi = D_{\alpha q}$ is parametrized by the dimension N and the modulus q. Given enough samples $(\mathbf{A}, \mathbf{c})$ from $L_{\mathbf{s},\chi}$, the BKW attack first reduces $\mathbf{A}$ to a kind of block diagonal matrix. The width of the block is b and there will be an $a = \lceil N/b \rceil$ blocks.

As samples from $L_{\mathbf{s},\chi}$ intrinsically include noise, too many additions or subtractions between samples result in a useless equation. Instead, the attacker gathers $(q^b - 1)/2$ samples having all nonzero values up to sign in the first block. Denote this table of samples by T^1. If $L_{\mathbf{s},\chi}$ outputs a sample $(\mathbf{a}_i, c_i)$ which has the same first block in T^1, the attacker makes $(\mathbf{a}_i, c_i)$ to have all-zero first block by adding/subtracting the sample in T^1. Similarly, the attacker can gather $(q^b - 1)/2$ samples having all-zero first block and all nonzero values up to sign in the second block. Denote this table of samples by T^2. By repeating the same process, the attacker can construct a matrix of the form

$$\begin{pmatrix} T^1 & & & & & & & & \\ 0 & \cdots & 0 & T^2 & & & & & \\ 0 & \cdots & 0 & 0 & \cdots & 0 & T^3 & & \\ \vdots & \ddots & \vdots & \vdots & \ddots & \vdots & & & \\ 0 & \cdots & 0 & 0 & \cdots & 0 & 0 & \cdots & 0 & T^{a-1} \\ 0 & \cdots & 0 & 0 & \cdots & 0 & 0 & \cdots & 0 & 0 & T^a \\ 0 & \cdots & 0 & 0 & \cdots & 0 & 0 & \cdots & 0 & \cdots & 0 & M \end{pmatrix}.$$

After solving a lattice problem with respect to M, the attacker can perform back substitution for the remaining parts.

The time complexity of this attack to solve search-LWE is

$$\left(\frac{q^b - 1}{2} \right) \cdot \left(\frac{a(a-1)}{s} \cdot (N+1) \right) + \left\lceil \frac{q^b}{2} \right\rceil \cdot \left(\left\lceil \frac{N}{d} \right\rceil + 1 \right) \cdot d \cdot a + \mathrm{poly}(N)$$

where $d = N - \lfloor N/b \rfloor$. The parameter a should satisfy $a \leq \log(\alpha^{-2})$ in order to distinguish $L_{\mathbf{s},\chi}$ from random [56]. We compute the concrete complexity by using $a = \log(\alpha^{-2})$ without the polynomial terms. As $N = S_{n,r}$ for Rubato, the complexity of the attack is at least $2^{S_{n,r} \log q / (-2 \log \alpha)}$.

4.2.4   Arora-Ge Attack

Arora and Ge proposed an algebraic algorithm to solve the search-LWE problem [9]. The main idea of this attack is that, given LWE samples $\{(\mathbf{a}_i, b_i)\}_i$, the errors fall into some interval $[-t\alpha q, t\alpha q]$ for some large enough t so that the equations

$$\prod_{e=-t\alpha q}^{t\alpha q} (b_i - \langle \mathbf{a}_i, \mathbf{s} \rangle - e) = 0$$

holds. Although the complexity of this attack for LWE is well-organized in [1], we independently describe the lower bound of complexity as the equations are different from LWE.

When guessing noise, an attacker may control the range of guesses to minimize the cost of attacks since the noise is not uniformly distributed. We denote the probability such that a sample from discrete Gaussian $D_{\alpha q}$ lies in the interval $[-t\alpha q, t\alpha q]$ by

$$\varepsilon_t = \Pr\left[e \leftarrow D_{\alpha q} : |e| \leq t\alpha q\right].$$

Since this probability determines the complexity of many attacks, we find the minimum of the complexity among $\{t : -3\sqrt{2\pi} \leq t \leq 3\sqrt{2\pi}\}$ which is equivalent to the range of 6 times the standard deviation.

Let $\mathsf{E}_i(\cdot)$ denote the i-th component of the Rubato cipher without noise. Then, by using Arora-Ge attack, an attacker can make a set of equations as follows. Given m nonce-plaintext-ciphertext triples $\{(\mathsf{nc}_j, \mathbf{m}_j, \mathbf{c}_j)\}_j$,

$$\left\{ \prod_{e_{i,j}=-t\alpha q}^{t\alpha q} (\mathbf{c}_{j,i} - \mathsf{E}_i(\mathsf{nc}_j, \mathbf{m}_j) - e_{i,j}) = 0 \right\}_{\substack{1 \leq i \leq \ell \\ 1 \leq j \leq m}} \tag{4}$$

where $\mathbf{c}_{j,i}$ is the i-th component of $\mathbf{c}_j$. These equations are for the key variable $\mathbf{k}$ of total degree $2^r(2t\alpha q + 1)$.

Now, we give a lower bound of the complexity of solving Eq. 4 by using Gröbner basis attack. As discussed in Sect. 4.1.3, we can conservatively assume the degree of regularity of Eq. 4 is $2^r(2t\alpha q + 1)$ regardless of the number of nonce-plaintext-ciphertext triples. We have the time complexity at least

$$O\left(\binom{n + 2^r(2t\alpha q + 1)}{2^r(2t\alpha q + 1)}^{\omega} \varepsilon_t^{-c} \right)$$

where c should be larger than or equal to n to get the unique root. This complexity formula also lower bounds the trivial linearization approach to solving Eq. 4.

MEET-IN-THE-MIDDLE APPROACH.   Similar to most of the algebraic attacks, one can try to use the MitM approach for Arora-Ge attack. From Eq. 1, the attacker can build the Arora-Ge equations as follows.

$$\left\{ \prod_{(e_{i,j})_i \in C_j} (F_i[\mathbf{k}, \mathsf{nc}_j] - (G^{-1})_i(y_1 - e_{1,j}, \ldots, y_\ell - e_{\ell,j}, x_{\ell+1}, \ldots, x_n)) = 0 \right\}_{1 \leq j \leq m}$$

where
$$C_j := \left\{ (e_1, \ldots, e_\ell) \in \mathbb{Z}^\ell : -t\alpha q \leq e_i \leq t\alpha q \text{ for all } i \right\},$$

F_i and $(G^{-1})_i$ are the i-th components of F and G^{-1} respectively. These equations are of degree $2^{\lceil r/2 \rceil}(2t\alpha q + 1)^\ell$ so that the lower bound of the degree of regularity also is $2^{\lceil r/2 \rceil}(2t\alpha q + 1)^\ell$. Similarly as above, to get the unique root, the queried block length k should satisfy $n + k(n - \ell) \leq nk$. Then, the time complexity is lower bounded by

$$O\left(\binom{n + (n - \ell)k + 2^{\lceil r/2 \rceil}(2t\alpha q + 1)^\ell}{2^{\lceil r/2 \rceil}(2t\alpha q + 1)^\ell}^\omega \varepsilon_t^{-\ell k} \right).$$

We give some plots of the complexity of the Arora-Ge attack according to the choice of t in the full version [43].

5   Performance Evaluation

In this section, we evaluate the performance of the RtF framework combined with the Rubato cipher in terms of encryption speed and ciphertext expansion. The source codes of server-side computation are developed in Golang version 1.16.4 with Lattigo library[4] which implements RNS (residue number system) variants of the FV and the CKKS schemes. For the HE parameters, we use the RtF parameter Par-128a in [25], which uses the arcsin function. For completeness, we summarize the HE parameters in the full version [43]. The source codes of client-side computation are developed in C++17, using GNU C++ 7.5.0 compiler with AVX2 instruction set. For the instantiation of the XOF, we use AES128 in counter-mode as well as SHAKE256 in openssl library[5] and XKCP library[6], respectively. Our experiments are done in AMD Ryzen 7 2700X @ 3.70 GHz single-threaded with 64 GB memory.

5.1   Benchmark and Comparison

We measure the performance of the RtF framework along with Rubato, distinguishing two different parts: the client-side and the server-side. The client-side latency includes time for generating pseudorandom numbers (needed to generate a single keystream in $\mathbb{Z}_q^n$), keystream generation from Rubato, message scaling, rounding, and vector addition over $\mathbb{Z}_q$. Since generating pseudorandom numbers from XOF takes significant time on the client-side, we measure the client-side performance according to the instantiations of the XOF.

On the server-side, the latency is divided into offline and online phases as described in Sect. 2.4. The offline latency includes time for randomized key schedule, homomorphic evaluation of the keystreams from Rubato, and the linear

---

[4] https://github.com/ldsec/lattigo.
[5] https://github.com/openssl/openssl.
[6] https://github.com/XKCP/XKCP.

transformation SlotToCoeff^{FV}. The online latency includes computing the FV-ciphertext containing the symmetric ciphertexts in its coefficients, homomorphic subtraction, and the modified CKKS-bootstrapping process in the RtF framework (called HalfBoot). We measure the latency until the first HE-ciphertext comes out, while the throughput is measured until all the n HE-ciphertexts come out. Because the XOF running time does not affect the server-side performance as significantly as it does on the client-side, we only use SHAKE256 instantiation for a fair comparison with previous results. We note that our evaluation does not take into account key encryption since the encrypted key will be used over multiple sessions once it is computed. For the same reason, the initialization process of the HE schemes is not considered.

Table 5. Client-side performance of the RtF transciphering framework with Rubato.

Set	AES128		SHAKE256	
	Latency (cycle)	Throughput (C/B)	Latency (cycle)	Throughput (C/B)
Par-80S	2154	72.63	5906	199.1
Par-80M	3644	49.36	11465	143.5
Par-80L	4957	32.97	16679	110.9
Par-128S	3076	103.6	10446	351.8
Par-128M	4381	55.10	14292	179.7
Par-128L	5323	35.70	16920	113.5

We summarize our implementation results in Table 5 and Table 6. In Table 5, the client-side latency and throughput for each instantiation of the XOF are given. Table 6 includes ciphertext expansion ratio (CER), time-relevant measurements, and precision. One can see that a larger parameter implies higher throughput at the cost of higher latency on both sides. As Rubato needs a substantial amount of random bits, the client-side performance is significantly influenced by the choice of XOF. On the server-side, we note that Rubato only affects the offline latency while the online latency is affected by the efficiency of CKKS bootstrapping.

Table 6. Server-side performance of the RtF transciphering framework with Rubato.

Set	CER	Latency		Throughput (KB/s)	Precision (bits)
		Offline (s)	Online (s)		
Par-80S	1.31	21.48	19.75	6.676	18.8
Par-80M	1.25	37.44	19.71	7.032	19.0
Par-80L	1.25	85.65	19.79	6.520	19.1
Par-128S	1.31	50.78	20.28	6.083	18.8
Par-128M	1.26	68.47	19.88	6.666	18.9
Par-128L	1.26	86.34	20.09	6.712	18.9

COMPARISON. We compare the result of `Par-128L` to the recent implementation of HERA [25], LWEs-to-RLWE conversions [50], and CKKS itself. The comparison is summarized in Table 7. The result of HERA is obtained from the paper. The source codes of LWEs-to-RLWE conversion are taken from the `OpenPegasus` library[7]. As `OpenPegasus` library does not include symmetric LWE encryption, we implement (seeded) symmetric LWE encryption with AVX2-optimized SHAKE256. We use `Lattigo` library for CKKS encryption.

Table 7. Comparison of the RtF transciphering framework with Rubato to previous environments supporting homomorphic encryption of approximate numbers. All the experiments are done with 128-bit security. Parameter N in parentheses implies the dimension of LWE. The parameter p stands for the bits of precision.

Scheme	N	ℓ	Ctxt. Exp.		Client		Server		p
			Ctxt. (KB)	Ratio	Lat. (μs)	Thrp. (MB/s)	Lat. (s)	Thrp. (KB/s)	
RtF-Rubato	2^{16}	2^{16}	0.183	1.26	4.585	31.04	106.4	6.712	18.9
RtF-HERA [25]	2^{16}	2^{16}	0.055	1.24	1.520	25.26	141.58	5.077	19.1
LWE [50]	$2^{16}(2^{10})$	2^{10}	0.007	4.84	21.91	0.051	65.88	0.010	9.3
CKKS	2^{14}	2^{14}	468	23.25	9656	2.035	None		19.1

In this table, the security parameter λ is set to 128. For the fairness of comparison, the remaining levels after transciphering are all set to be 7. For all experiments, we sample the domain of each component of the message vector from the uniform distribution over $(-1, 1)$. When computing the ciphertext expansion ratio, we use the formula $\log q/(p + 1)$, which excludes the effect of sending a public nonce. Multiple use of different nonces can be dealt with a counter so that the effect of a nonce to the ratio is asymptotically zero.

Since the `OpenPegasus` library supports only selected sets of parameters in terms of the number of slots and the ciphertext modulus (at the point of submission), we implemented LWEs-to-RLWE for $N = 2^{16}$ and $\ell = 2^{10}$ which does not provide exactly the same functionality as ours with full available slots.

One can see that Rubato with the RtF framework outperforms HERA with respect to the both-side throughput, while it has a worse CER and ciphertext size compared to HERA. Also, Rubato outperforms the LWEs-to-RLWE conversion with respect to CER, ciphertext size and client-side performance, achieving the main purpose of the transciphering framework. Compared to the CKKS-only environment, Rubato with the RtF framework has better CER and client-side performance, while the CKKS-only environment requires no additional computation.

---

[7] https://github.com/Alibaba-Gemini-Lab/OpenPEGASUS

References

1. Albrecht, M., Cid, C., Faugère, J.C., Fitzpatrick, R., Perret, L.: On the complexity of the Arora-Ge algorithm against LWE. In: SCC 2012 - Third International Conference on Symbolic Computation and Cryptography, pp. 93–99, July 2012
2. Albrecht, M.R., Bai, S., Li, J., Rowell, J.: Lattice reduction with approximate enumeration oracles. In: Malkin, T., Peikert, C. (eds.) CRYPTO 2021. LNCS, vol. 12826, pp. 732–759. Springer, Cham (2021). https://doi.org/10.1007/978-3-030-84245-1_25
3. Albrecht, M.R., Cid, C., Faugère, J.C., Fitzpatrick, R., Perret, L.: On the complexity of the BKW algorithm on LWE. Des. Codes Crypt. **74**(2), 325–354 (2015)
4. Albrecht, M.R., Fitzpatrick, R., Göpfert, F.: On the efficacy of solving LWE by reduction to unique-SVP. In: Lee, H.-S., Han, D.-G. (eds.) ICISC 2013. LNCS, vol. 8565, pp. 293–310. Springer, Cham (2014). https://doi.org/10.1007/978-3-319-12160-4_18
5. Albrecht, M.R., Göpfert, F., Virdia, F., Wunderer, T.: Revisiting the expected cost of solving uSVP and applications to LWE. In: Takagi, T., Peyrin, T. (eds.) ASIACRYPT 2017. LNCS, vol. 10624, pp. 297–322. Springer, Cham (2017). https://doi.org/10.1007/978-3-319-70694-8_11
6. Albrecht, M.R., Rechberger, C., Schneider, T., Tiessen, T., Zohner, M.: Ciphers for MPC and FHE. In: Oswald, E., Fischlin, M. (eds.) EUROCRYPT 2015. LNCS, vol. 9056, pp. 430–454. Springer, Heidelberg (2015). https://doi.org/10.1007/978-3-662-46800-5_17
7. Alkim, E., Ducas, L., Pöppelmann, T., Schwabe, P.: Post-quantum key exchange: a new hope. In: SEC 2016, pp. 327–343. USENIX Association, USA (2016)
8. Aly, A., Ashur, T., Ben-Sasson, E., Dhooghe, S., Szepieniec, A.: Design of symmetric-key primitives for advanced cryptographic protocols. IACR Trans. Symmetric Cryptol. **2020**(3) (2020)
9. Arora, S., Ge, R.: New algorithms for learning in presence of errors. In: Aceto, L., Henzinger, M., Sgall, J. (eds.) ICALP 2011. LNCS, vol. 6755, pp. 403–415. Springer, Heidelberg (2011). https://doi.org/10.1007/978-3-642-22006-7_34
10. Bai, S., Galbraith, S.D.: Lattice decoding attacks on binary LWE. In: Susilo, W., Mu, Y. (eds.) ACISP 2014. LNCS, vol. 8544, pp. 322–337. Springer, Cham (2014). https://doi.org/10.1007/978-3-319-08344-5_21
11. Baignères, T., Stern, J., Vaudenay, S.: Linear cryptanalysis of non binary ciphers. In: Adams, C., Miri, A., Wiener, M. (eds.) SAC 2007. LNCS, vol. 4876, pp. 184–211. Springer, Heidelberg (2007). https://doi.org/10.1007/978-3-540-77360-3_13
12. Becker, A., Ducas, L., Gama, N., Laarhoven, T.: New directions in nearest neighbor searching with applications to lattice sieving. In: Proceedings of the Twenty-Seventh Annual ACM-SIAM Symposium on Discrete Algorithms, pp. 10–24. SIAM (2016)
13. Bettale, L., Faugere, J.C., Perret, L.: Hybrid approach for solving multivariate systems over finite fields. J. Math. Cryptol. **3**(3), 177–197 (2009)
14. Bettale, L., Faugère, J.C., Perret, L.: Solving polynomial systems over finite fields: improved analysis of the hybrid approach. In: Proceedings of the 37th International Symposium on Symbolic and Algebraic Computation, ISSAC 2012. Association for Computing Machinery (2012)
15. Beyne, T., et al.: Out of oddity – new cryptanalytic techniques against symmetric primitives optimized for integrity proof systems. In: Micciancio, D., Ristenpart, T. (eds.) CRYPTO 2020. LNCS, vol. 12172, pp. 299–328. Springer, Cham (2020). https://doi.org/10.1007/978-3-030-56877-1_11

16. Blum, A., Kalai, A., Wasserman, H.: Noise-tolerant learning, the parity problem, and the statistical query model. J. ACM **50**(4), 506–519 (2003)
17. Boura, C., Gama, N., Georgieva, M., Jetchev, D.: Simulating homomorphic evaluation of deep learning predictions. In: Dolev, S., Hendler, D., Lodha, S., Yung, M. (eds.) CSCML 2019. LNCS, vol. 11527, pp. 212–230. Springer, Cham (2019). https://doi.org/10.1007/978-3-030-20951-3_20
18. Brakerski, Z., Gentry, C., Vaikuntanathan, V.: (Leveled) Fully homomorphic encryption without bootstrapping. In: Proceedings of the 3rd Innovations in Theoretical Computer Science Conference, pp. 309–325. ACM (2012)
19. Canteaut, A., et al.: Stream ciphers: a practical solution for efficient homomorphic-ciphertext compression. J. Cryptol. **31**(3), 885–916 (2018)
20. Carlitz, L., Uchiyama, S.: Bounds for exponential sums. Duke Math. J. **24**(1), 37–41 (1957)
21. Chen, H., Dai, W., Kim, M., Song, Y.: Efficient homomorphic conversion between (Ring) LWE ciphertexts. In: Sako, K., Tippenhauer, N.O. (eds.) ACNS 2021. LNCS, vol. 12726, pp. 460–479. Springer, Cham (2021). https://doi.org/10.1007/978-3-030-78372-3_18
22. Chen, Y.: Réduction de Réseau et Sécurité Concrète du Chiffrement Complètement Homomorphe. Ph.D. thesis (2013). thèse de doctorat dirigée par Nguyen, Phong-Quang Informatique Paris 7 2013
23. Chen, Y., Nguyen, P.Q.: BKZ 2.0: better lattice security estimates. In: Lee, D.H., Wang, X. (eds.) ASIACRYPT 2011. LNCS, vol. 7073, pp. 1–20. Springer, Heidelberg (2011). https://doi.org/10.1007/978-3-642-25385-0_1
24. Cheon, J.H., Kim, A., Kim, M., Song, Y.: Homomorphic encryption for arithmetic of approximate numbers. In: Takagi, T., Peyrin, T. (eds.) ASIACRYPT 2017. LNCS, vol. 10624, pp. 409–437. Springer, Cham (2017). https://doi.org/10.1007/978-3-319-70694-8_15
25. Cho, J., et al.: Transciphering framework for approximate homomorphic encryption. In: Tibouchi, M., Wang, H. (eds.) ASIACRYPT 2021. LNCS, vol. 13092, pp. 640–669. Springer, Cham (2021). https://doi.org/10.1007/978-3-030-92078-4_22
26. Dinur, I., Liu, Y., Meier, W., Wang, Q.: Optimized interpolation attacks on LowMC. In: Iwata, T., Cheon, J.H. (eds.) ASIACRYPT 2015. LNCS, vol. 9453, pp. 535–560. Springer, Heidelberg (2015). https://doi.org/10.1007/978-3-662-48800-3_22
27. Dobraunig, C., et al.: Rasta: a cipher with low ANDdepth and few ANDs per bit. In: Shacham, H., Boldyreva, A. (eds.) CRYPTO 2018. LNCS, vol. 10991, pp. 662–692. Springer, Cham (2018). https://doi.org/10.1007/978-3-319-96884-1_22
28. Dobraunig, C., Eichlseder, M., Mendel, F.: Higher-order cryptanalysis of LowMC. In: Kwon, S., Yun, A. (eds.) ICISC 2015. LNCS, vol. 9558, pp. 87–101. Springer, Cham (2016). https://doi.org/10.1007/978-3-319-30840-1_6
29. Dobraunig, C., Grassi, L., Guinet, A., Kuijsters, D.: CIMINION: symmetric encryption based on Toffoli-gates over large finite fields. In: Canteaut, A., Standaert, F.-X. (eds.) EUROCRYPT 2021. LNCS, vol. 12697, pp. 3–34. Springer, Cham (2021). https://doi.org/10.1007/978-3-030-77886-6_1
30. Dobraunig, C., Grassi, L., Helminger, L., Rechberger, C., Schofnegger, M., Walch, R.: Pasta: a case for hybrid homomorphic encryption. Cryptology ePrint Archive, Report 2021/731 (2021). https://ia.cr/2021/731
31. Doröz, Y., Shahverdi, A., Eisenbarth, T., Sunar, B.: Toward practical homomorphic evaluation of block ciphers using prince. In: Böhme, R., Brenner, M., Moore, T., Smith, M. (eds.) FC 2014. LNCS, vol. 8438, pp. 208–220. Springer, Heidelberg (2014). https://doi.org/10.1007/978-3-662-44774-1_17

32. Ducas, L., Micciancio, D.: FHEW: bootstrapping homomorphic encryption in less than a second. In: Oswald, E., Fischlin, M. (eds.) EUROCRYPT 2015. LNCS, vol. 9056, pp. 617–640. Springer, Heidelberg (2015). https://doi.org/10.1007/978-3-662-46800-5_24

33. Dworkin, M.J.: SHA-3 standard: permutation-based hash and extendable-output functions. Technical report. National Institute of Standards and Technology (2015)

34. Fan, J., Vercauteren, F.: Somewhat practical fully homomorphic encryption. IACR Cryptology ePrint Archive, Report 2012/144 (2012). https://eprint.iacr.org/2012/144

35. Fröberg, R.: An inequality for Hilbert series of graded algebras. Mathematica Scandinavica **56**, 117–144 (1985)

36. Gama, N., Nguyen, P.Q.: Predicting lattice reduction. In: Smart, N. (ed.) EUROCRYPT 2008. LNCS, vol. 4965, pp. 31–51. Springer, Heidelberg (2008). https://doi.org/10.1007/978-3-540-78967-3_3

37. Gama, N., Nguyen, P.Q., Regev, O.: Lattice enumeration using extreme pruning. In: Gilbert, H. (ed.) EUROCRYPT 2010. LNCS, vol. 6110, pp. 257–278. Springer, Heidelberg (2010). https://doi.org/10.1007/978-3-642-13190-5_13

38. Gentry, C., Halevi, S., Smart, N.P.: Homomorphic evaluation of the AES circuit. In: Safavi-Naini, R., Canetti, R. (eds.) CRYPTO 2012. LNCS, vol. 7417, pp. 850–867. Springer, Heidelberg (2012). https://doi.org/10.1007/978-3-642-32009-5_49

39. Göpfert, F.: Securely instantiating cryptographic schemes based on the learning with errors assumption. Ph.D. thesis, Technische Universität, Darmstadt (2016)

40. Grassi, L., Khovratovich, D., Rechberger, C., Roy, A., Schofnegger, M.: POSEIDON: a new hash function for zero-knowledge proof systems. In: 30th USENIX Security Symposium (USENIX Security 2021), pp. 519–535. USENIX Association, August 2021

41. Guo, J., Peyrin, T., Poschmann, A.: The PHOTON family of lightweight hash functions. In: Rogaway, P. (ed.) CRYPTO 2011. LNCS, vol. 6841, pp. 222–239. Springer, Heidelberg (2011). https://doi.org/10.1007/978-3-642-22792-9_13

42. Ha, J., et al.: Masta: an HE-friendly cipher using modular arithmetic. IEEE Access **8**, 194741–194751 (2020)

43. Ha, J., Kim, S., Lee, B., Lee, J., Son, M.: Rubato: noisy ciphers for approximate homomorphic encryption (Full Version). To appear in the IACR Cryptology ePrint Archive (2022)

44. Hebborn, P., Leander, G.: Dasta - alternative linear layer for Rasta. IACR Trans. Symmetric Cryptol. **2020**(3), 46–86 (2020)

45. Hoffmann, C., Méaux, P., Ricosset, T.: Transciphering, using FiLIP and TFHE for an efficient delegation of computation. In: Bhargavan, K., Oswald, E., Prabhakaran, M. (eds.) INDOCRYPT 2020. LNCS, vol. 12578, pp. 39–61. Springer, Cham (2020). https://doi.org/10.1007/978-3-030-65277-7_3

46. Jakobsen, T., Knudsen, L.R.: The interpolation attack on block ciphers. In: Biham, E. (ed.) FSE 1997. LNCS, vol. 1267, pp. 28–40. Springer, Heidelberg (1997). https://doi.org/10.1007/BFb0052332

47. Laarhoven, T.: Search problems in cryptography: from fingerprinting to lattice sieving. Ph.D. thesis, Mathematics and Computer Science, February 2016, proefschrift

48. Lepoint, T., Naehrig, M.: A comparison of the homomorphic encryption schemes FV and YASHE. In: Pointcheval, D., Vergnaud, D. (eds.) AFRICACRYPT 2014. LNCS, vol. 8469, pp. 318–335. Springer, Cham (2014). https://doi.org/10.1007/978-3-319-06734-6_20

49. Lindner, R., Peikert, C.: Better key sizes (and attacks) for LWE-based encryption. In: Kiayias, A. (ed.) CT-RSA 2011. LNCS, vol. 6558, pp. 319–339. Springer, Heidelberg (2011). https://doi.org/10.1007/978-3-642-19074-2_21

50. Lu, W., Huang, Z., Hong, C., Ma, Y., Qu, H.: PEGASUS: bridging polynomial and non-polynomial evaluations in homomorphic encryption. In: 2021 IEEE Symposium on Security and Privacy (SP), pp. 1057–1073. IEEE Computer Society, May 2021

51. Matsui, M.: Linear cryptanalysis method for DES cipher. In: Helleseth, T. (ed.) EUROCRYPT 1993. LNCS, vol. 765, pp. 386–397. Springer, Heidelberg (1994). https://doi.org/10.1007/3-540-48285-7_33

52. Méaux, P., Carlet, C., Journault, A., Standaert, F.-X.: Improved filter permutators for efficient FHE: better instances and implementations. In: Hao, F., Ruj, S., Sen Gupta, S. (eds.) INDOCRYPT 2019. LNCS, vol. 11898, pp. 68–91. Springer, Cham (2019). https://doi.org/10.1007/978-3-030-35423-7_4

53. Méaux, P., Journault, A., Standaert, F.-X., Carlet, C.: Towards stream ciphers for efficient FHE with low-noise ciphertexts. In: Fischlin, M., Coron, J.-S. (eds.) EUROCRYPT 2016. LNCS, vol. 9665, pp. 311–343. Springer, Heidelberg (2016). https://doi.org/10.1007/978-3-662-49890-3_13

54. Naehrig, M., Lauter, K., Vaikuntanathan, V.: Can homomorphic encryption be practical? In: Proceedings of the 3rd ACM Workshop on Cloud Computing Security Workshop, pp. 113–124. ACM (2011)

55. Park, S., Byun, J., Lee, J., Cheon, J.H., Lee, J.: HE-friendly algorithm for privacy-preserving SVM training. IEEE Access 8, 57414–57425 (2020)

56. Player, R.: Parameter selection in lattice-based cryptography. Ph.D. thesis, Royal Holloway, University of London (2018)

57. Rechberger, C., Soleimany, H., Tiessen, T.: Cryptanalysis of low-data instances of full LowMCv2. IACR Trans. Symmetric Cryptol. 2018(3), 163–181 (2018)

58. Regev, O.: On lattices, learning with errors, random linear codes, and cryptography. J. ACM 56(6), 1–40 (2009)

59. Schnorr, C.P., Euchner, M.: Lattice basis reduction: improved practical algorithms and solving subset sum problems. Math. Program. 66(1), 181–199 (1994)

60. Schnorr, C.P.: Lattice reduction by random sampling and birthday methods. In: Alt, H., Habib, M. (eds.) STACS 2003. LNCS, vol. 2607, pp. 145–156. Springer, Heidelberg (2003). https://doi.org/10.1007/3-540-36494-3_14

Field Instruction Multiple Data

Khin Mi Mi Aung[1](ID), Enhui Lim[1(✉)](ID), Jun Jie Sim[2(✉)](ID),
Benjamin Hong Meng Tan[1(✉)](ID), Huaxiong Wang[2](ID), and Sze Ling Yeo[1]

[1] Institute for Infocomm Research, Agency for Science, Technology and Research
(A*STAR), Singapore, Singapore
{mi_mi_aung,lim_enhui,benjamin_tan}@i2r.a-star.edu.sg
[2] School of Physical and Mathematical Sciences, Nanyang Technological University,
Singapore, Singapore
junjie005@e.ntu.edu.sg, hxwang@ntu.edu.sg

Abstract. Fully homomorphic encryption (FHE) has flourished since it
was first constructed by Gentry (STOC 2009). Single instruction multiple data (SIMD) gave rise to efficient homomorphic operations on vec-
tors in $(\mathbb{F}_{t^d})^\ell$, for prime t. RLWE instantiated with cyclotomic polynomials of the form $X^{2^N} + 1$ dominate implementations of FHE due to
highly efficient fast Fourier transformations. However, this choice yields
very short SIMD plaintext vectors and high degree extension fields, e.g.
$\ell < 100, d > 100$ for small primes ($t = 3, 5, \ldots$).

In this work, we describe a method to encode more data on top of
SIMD, *Field Instruction Multiple Data*, applying reverse multiplication
friendly embedding (RMFE) to FHE. With RMFE, length-k $\mathbb{F}_t$ vectors
can be encoded into $\mathbb{F}_{t^d}$ and multiplied once. The results have to be
recoded (decoded and then re-encoded) before further multiplications
can be done. We introduce an FHE-specific technique to additionally
evaluate arbitrary linear transformations on encoded vectors for free
during the FHE recode operation. On top of that, we present two optimizations to unlock high degree extension fields with small t for homomorphic computation: r-fold RMFE, which allows products of up to 2^r
encoded vectors before recoding, and a three-stage recode process for
RMFEs obtained by composing two smaller RMFEs. Experiments were
performed to evaluate the effectiveness of FIMD from various RMFEs
compared to standard SIMD operations. Overall, we found that FIMD
generally had $> 2\times$ better (amortized) multiplication times compared
to FHE for the same amount of data, while using almost $k/2\times$ fewer
ciphertexts required.

Keywords: Homomorphic encryption · Finite extension fields ·
Reverse multiplication friendly embeddings · Single instruction
multiple data

Work was done while Sze Ling Yeo was at the Institute for Infocomm Research.

O. Dunkelman and S. Dziembowski (Eds.): EUROCRYPT 2022, LNCS 13275, pp. 611–641, 2022.
https://doi.org/10.1007/978-3-031-06944-4_21

1   Introduction

Fully homomorphic encryption (FHE) has seen a lot of improvements since it was first realized by Gentry [24]. Currently, there are four main schemes in wide use, Brakerski-Gentry-Vaikunathan (BGV) [5], Brakerski-Fan-Vercauteren (BFV) [4,22], Cheon-Kim-Kim-Song (CKKS) [11] and FHEW/TFHE [14,15,21]. The first two schemes support finite field operations, the CKKS scheme supports approximate arithmetic of numbers and the FHEW/TFHE family operates over bits or low-precision numbers.

Most implementations of FHE, such as SEAL [36], PALISADE [35] and Lattigo [33] focus on the case where BGV and BFV are instantiated with power-of-two cyclotomic polynomial moduli. These parameters enjoy highly efficient arithmetic due to negacyclic fast fourier transforms (FFT). However, small primes such as $t = 3, 5, 7, 11$ are not useful in these cases due to the unfriendly decomposition of the plaintext space into very few slots with a slot algebra corresponding to finite fields of high extension degree. Therefore, use of BGV and BFV focused on word-sized homomorphic encryption which uses large primes of 32 or more bits, integer and fractional encodings proposed in [8,16,19,20] and an alternate "polynomial modulus" for high-precision integer arithmetic in [3,10].

Various papers have been published on the use of finite extension fields of low to medium extension degree (≤ 64) for homomorphic computation, which we elaborate on in a later section on related work. However, there remains a lack of techniques that unlock the use of high degree extension fields for homomorphic computation, which would lead to improvements for small-prime arithmetic circuits due to the faster arithmetic enabled by negacyclic FFT.

OUR CONTRIBUTIONS. In this work, we introduce field instruction multiple data (FIMD), a method to encode more data into FHE ciphertexts by leveraging the inherent *vector of extension fields* plaintext structure from SIMD. We add another level of packing to FHE, embedding a vector of base/intermediate field elements into each slot of a SIMD plaintext such that homomorphic operations can be performed on the encoded vectors. Field addition, multiplication and linearized polynomial evaluations correspond to component-wise addition, multiplication, and linear maps on the encrypted vectors.

To that end, we apply reverse multiplication friendly embedding (RMFE) defined by Cascudo et al. [7] to FHE. RMFE allows us to encode a length-k vector of small field elements $(\mathbb{F})^k$ into a single element of a larger extension field $\mathbb{E}/\mathbb{F}$. Products of these extension field elements then "correspond" to component-wise multiplication on the underlying vectors. However, this process is not a homomorphism and thus cannot support an arbitrary number of multiplications. To address this limitation in MPC, Cascudo et al. [7] defined a recoding protocol ReEncode which decodes and re-encodes field elements in one go after each MPC multiplication so that it can be used in subsequent multiplications.

The key to applying RMFEs to FHE is that the encode, decode, and recoding (i.e. decode then re-encode) operations are $\mathbb{F}$-linear maps between $(\mathbb{F})^k$ and $\mathbb{E}$. Such maps can be represented by linearized polynomials and therefore evaluated in FHE using low-noise Frobenius automorphisms. Furthermore, we show that rotations, shifts and even arbitrary linear transformations M on the encrypted vector can be done for free by modifying the recode operation into a composition of decode, M, and encode. This gives FIMD more flexibility than SIMD in terms of the overhead of linear transformations over the plaintext space but FIMD requires the recode operation after multiplications. Crucially, we exploit the fact that the recode operation in FHE is non-interactive and does not require any pre-processing. Performing arbitrary linear transformations during the ReEncode protocol of Cascudo et al. [7] would be almost impossible because randomness specific to any desired linear transformation has to be prepared beforehand.

Besides that, we propose r-fold RMFE to amortize the overhead of the homomorphic RMFE recode operation over several multiplications, at the cost of lower packing efficiency. Instead of decoding after a single multiplication, r-fold RMFE allows up to encodings of 2^r vectors to be multiplied together before decoding. With an additional requirement that field elements encoding multiplications of fewer than 2^r vectors can be added together, r-fold RMFE can allow multivariate polynomials of degree up to 2^r to be evaluated before decoding. This generalization of RMFE could be of independent interest.

On top of that, we introduce a three-stage process for recoding operations for RMFEs composed of two component RMFEs. Exploiting the fact that such RMFEs is built on a tower of field extensions $\mathbb{F} \subset \mathbb{E}_1 \subset \mathbb{E}_2$, we apply three linear maps $\psi_{\mathsf{out}} : \mathbb{E}_2 \to (\mathbb{E}_1)^{k_{\mathsf{out}}}$, $\phi_{\mathsf{out}} : (\mathbb{E}_1)^{k_{\mathsf{out}}} \to \mathbb{E}_2$, and $\pi'_{\mathsf{in}} : (\mathbb{E}_1)^{k_{\mathsf{out}}} \to (\mathbb{E}_1)^{k_{\mathsf{out}}}$, each of which have lower degree than the recoding map $\pi : \mathbb{E}_2 \to \mathbb{E}_2$. All together, this approach reduces the number of Frobenius automorphisms needed compared to the standard recode process.

Finally, we perform several experiments to compare the efficiency of the various flavors of RMFE introduced in this work against each other and standard FHE multiplications. FIMD improves the performance of FHE for small plaintext moduli, not only achieving more than $2\times$ faster multiplications amortized but also using up to $k/2\times$ fewer ciphertexts in the whole process.

RELATED WORK. Exploiting finite fields for homomorphic computation was first considered by Kim et al. [32]. They showed that equality of two encrypted integers could be efficiently computed using Fermat's Little Theorem. For more complex operations, Jäschke and Armknecht [31] explored using addition and multiplication in extension fields to compute integer addition but found them lacking. Leveraging the vector space nature of extension fields, Tan et al. [39] proposed the extract then compute method for comparison of encrypted integers. Illiashenko and Zucca [30] took advantage of the nature of comparison polynomials, reaching comparable efficiency to THFE-based methods for homomorphic comparisons.

Studies were also done for encoding integers and fixed-point numbers such that arithmetic was efficient. Dowlin et al. [19] considered decomposing integers and fractional numbers into base-2 representations and then encoding them as polynomials for fast arithmetic. Costache et al. [16] then showed that the two methods of Dowlin et al. were isomorphic and derived lower bounds for the representation to support homomorphic computation. This was further extended by Castryck et al. [8] to a more flexible encoding based on Laurent polynomials and more fine-grained decomposition of the FHE plaintext space with composite plaintext modulus. In another direction, Chen et al. [10] proposed to replace the plaintext modulus t with $X - b$ for some base b. This yields the plaintext space $\mathbb{Z}/(b^n + 1)\mathbb{Z}$ which enables high-precision arithmetic. Bootland et al. [3] generalized this to support complex-valued data by considering polynomials of the form $X^m + b$.

Lastly, RMFE was studied to improve MPC over finite fields. Cascudo et al. [7] used it to improve the amortized communication complexity of MPC protocols at the expense of the size of the field; previous work had to reduce the adversary threshold instead. Concurrently, Block et al. [2] applied it to achieve more efficient batched multiplications in MPC over binary fields. Since then, RMFE has been generalized to support MPC over Galois rings by Cramer et al. [17] and alternatively into circuit-amortization friendly embeddings to evaluate more complex circuits in a single multiplication by Dalskov et al. [18]. For HE-based MPC over $\mathbb{Z}_{2^k}$, methods were devised for protocols Overdrive2k [34] and MHz2k [12] for packing $\mathbb{Z}_{2^k}$-messages into polynomials, supporting depth-1 homomorphic correspondence.

2   Preliminaries

2.1   Fully Homomorphic Encryption

A leveled fully homomorphic encryption (FHE) scheme is a homomorphic encryption scheme that supports evaluation of circuits of at most depth L, for some pre-defined non-negative integer L. Encryptions of messages m will be denoted with $\overline{m}$ to emphasize their underlying encrypted messages. We will use $\mathcal{P}$ to denote the space of possible messages for the FHE scheme.

- $(pk, evk, sk) \leftarrow \mathsf{KeyGen}(1^\lambda, 1^L)$: Given security and level parameters λ and L as inputs, output a public key pk, secret key sk and evaluation key evk.
- $c = \overline{m} \leftarrow \mathsf{Enc}(pk, m)$: Given a public key pk and message $m \in \mathcal{P}$ as inputs, output a ciphertext $c = \overline{m}$ that encrypts m.
- $m' \leftarrow \mathsf{Dec}(sk, c)$: Given a secret key sk and ciphertext c as inputs, and outputs a message $m' \in \mathcal{P}$.
- $c' \leftarrow \mathsf{Eval}(evk, f, \overline{m_1}, ..., \overline{m_n})$: Given evaluation key evk, function $f : \mathcal{P}^n \rightarrow \mathcal{P}$ and encryption $\overline{m_1}, ..., \overline{m_n}$ of ciphertexts $m_1, ..., m_n \in \mathcal{P}$, output a ciphertext c' such that $\mathsf{Dec}(sk, c') = f(m_1, ..., m_n)$.

Usually, the Eval algorithm uses sub-routines of which the most common ones are homomorphic addition and multiplication.

- $c^+ \leftarrow \mathsf{EvalAdd}(evk, \overline{m_1}, \overline{m_2})$: Given an evaluation key evk and two ciphertexts $\overline{m_1}, \overline{m_2}$ as inputs, output a ciphertext $c^+ = \overline{m_1 + m_2}$, encrypting the sum of the encrypted input messages.

– $c^\times \leftarrow$ EvalMul($evk, \overline{m_1}, \overline{m_2}$): Given an evaluation key evk and two ciphertexts $\overline{m_1}, \overline{m_2}$ as inputs, output a ciphertext $c^\times = \overline{m_1 \times m_2}$, encrypting the product of the encrypted input messages.

For all known (leveled) FHE schemes, which are based on (Ring) Learning with Error ((R)LWE) problems, ciphertexts are noisy encryptions of their underlying plaintext. This means that only a limited number of computations can be performed before the noise in the ciphertexts overwhelms the data and the result is unusable.

Single Instruction Multiple Data (SIMD). Let $R = \mathbb{Z}[X]/\Phi_m(X)$, where $\Phi_m(X)$ is the m-th cyclotomic polynomial and $R_q = R/qR$. Generation two FHE schemes such as BGV and BFV typically use plaintext spaces of the form $\mathcal{P} = R_t$ for some prime t. Smart and Vercauteren [37] noted that, if t and m are co-prime, $\Phi_m(X) \equiv \prod_{i=1}^{\ell} f_i(X) \bmod t$, with $\deg f_i(X) := d = \phi(m)/\ell$ for all $i \in \{1, \ldots, \ell\}$. They proposed single instruction multiple data (SIMD), simultaneously operating on vectors of messages, for FHE by exploiting the following ring isomorphisms

$$\mathcal{P} = R_t \cong \mathbb{Z}_t[X]/\langle f_1(X)\rangle \times \mathbb{Z}_t[X]/\langle f_2(X)\rangle \times \cdots \times \mathbb{Z}_t[X]/\langle f_\ell(X)\rangle \cong \prod_{i=1}^{\ell} \mathbb{F}_{t^d}.$$

These isomorphisms are a result of applying the Chinese Remainder Theorem on the polynomial ring $\mathbb{Z}[X]/\Phi_m(X)$ with the decomposition of $\Phi_m(X)$ into its irreducible factors modulo t. From this, vectors in $(\mathbb{F}_{t^d})^\ell$ can be encoded in a single ciphertext and enjoy homomorphic component-wise $\mathbb{F}_{t^d}$ addition and multiplications. Furthermore, the elements within the vectors can be moved around via ring automorphisms $\kappa : X \mapsto X^\kappa$, for $\kappa \in \mathbb{Z}_m^*$. In particular, for prime t, the automorphism $X \mapsto X^t$ corresponds to a component-wise Frobenius map on plaintext vectors. Halevi and Shoup [29] present a thorough introduction on the SIMD plaintext structure. Thus, with SIMD, we have a third sub-routine for intra-vector data manipulation through homomorphic automorphisms.

– $c^* \leftarrow$ EvalAut($evk, \kappa, \overline{m}$): Given an evaluation key evk, ciphertext $\overline{m}$ and automorphism $\kappa \in \mathbb{Z}_m^*$, output a ciphertext $c^* = \overline{\kappa(m)}$.

This third sub-routine, more specifically the Frobenius automorphism, is key to the effective application of finite extension fields for homomorphic computation. In practice, multiple powers of the Frobenius automorphism, typically the set of $\{t^i\}_{i=1}^{d-1}$ will be needed and techniques have been developed to optimize the computational complexity and evaluation key sizes for evaluating more than one automorphism on a single ciphertext [28]. Besides that, through EvalAut and multiplicative masks, basic data movement of shifts and rotations on encoded vectors $\mathbf{x} = (x_1, \ldots, x_\ell) \in (\mathbb{F}_{t^d})^\ell$.

– $c' \leftarrow$ FHE.EvalShift($evk, \rho, \overline{\mathbf{x}}$): Let $\rho < 0$ denote a left shift and $\rho \geq 0$ denote a right shift. Using FHE.EvalAut defined above, output the ciphertext

$$c' = \begin{cases} \overline{(x_{|\rho|}, \ldots, x_\ell, 0, \ldots, 0)}, & \text{if } \rho < 0; \\ \overline{(0, \ldots, 0, x_1, \ldots, x_{\ell-\rho})}, & \text{otherwise.} \end{cases}$$

– $c' \leftarrow$ FHE.EvalRot$(evk, \rho, \overline{\mathbf{x}})$: Let $\rho < 0$ denote a left rotation and $\rho \geq 0$ denote a right rotation. Using FHE.EvalAut defined above, output the ciphertext

$$c' = \begin{cases} \overline{(x_{|\rho|}, ..., x_\ell, x_1, ..., x_{|\rho|-1})}, & \text{if } \rho < 0; \\ \overline{(x_{\ell-\rho+1}, ..., x_\ell, x_1, ..., x_{\ell-\rho})}, & \text{otherwise.} \end{cases}$$

2.2 Finite Extension Fields

Let q be a prime power. Extension fields $\mathbb{F}_{q^w}$ are $\mathbb{F}_q$-vector spaces of dimension w. A q-*linearized polynomial* $f(Y)$ is a polynomial of the form

$$f(Y) = f_0 + f_1 Y^{q^1} + f_2 Y^{q^2} + \cdots + f_{z-1} Y^{q^{z-1}} \in \mathbb{F}_q[Y],$$

where any non-zero coefficient of f is attached to a monomial Y^{q^a} for some positive integer a. In the following lemma, we review how $\mathbb{F}_q$-linear maps between subspaces of $\mathbb{F}_{q^w}$ can be expressed as q-linearized polynomials.

Lemma 1. *Let V and W be $\mathbb{F}_q$-linear subspaces of $\mathbb{F}_{q^w}$, and let $T : V \to W$ be an $\mathbb{F}_q$-linear map. Then, there exists a unique q-linearized polynomial $f_T(Y)$ with $\deg f_T \leq q^{\dim(V)}$, such that for any $\alpha \in V$, $f_T(\alpha) = T(\alpha)$.*

Proof. Let $\{\alpha_1, \alpha_2, \ldots, \alpha_k\}$ be a basis for V, and let A denote the Moore matrix given by

$$\begin{bmatrix} \alpha_1 & \alpha_2 & \cdots & \alpha_k \\ \alpha_1^q & \alpha_2^q & \cdots & \alpha_k^q \\ \vdots & \vdots & \cdots & \vdots \\ \alpha_1^{q^{k-1}} & \alpha_2^{q^{k-1}} & \cdots & \alpha_k^{q^{k-1}} \end{bmatrix}.$$

Evaluation of a q-linearized polynomial is clearly $\mathbb{F}_q$-linear, so for $f_T(\alpha) = T(\alpha)$ to hold for any α, $f_T(Y)$ must have coefficients $f_0, f_1, \ldots, f_{k-1}$ such that the following matrix equation holds:

$$\begin{bmatrix} f_0 & f_1 & \cdots & f_{k-1} \end{bmatrix} A = \begin{bmatrix} T(\alpha_1) & T(\alpha_2) & \cdots & T(\alpha_k) \end{bmatrix}.$$

Since $\alpha_1, \alpha_2, \ldots, \alpha_k$ are linearly independent, A has a nonzero determinant by [26, Lemma 1.3.3]. A is also a square matrix, so its inverse A^{-1} always exists. Thus $f_0, f_1, \cdots, f_{k-1}$ is found by computing $\begin{bmatrix} T(\alpha_1) & T(\alpha_2) & \cdots & T(\alpha_k) \end{bmatrix} A^{-1}$. From this computation it is also clear that $f_T(Y)$ is unique. The proof is complete.

For FHE schemes with plaintext space $\mathcal{P} \cong (\mathbb{F}_{t^d})^\ell$, homomorphic evaluation of component-wise t-linearized polynomials can be easily done using EvalAut. Each monomial Y^{t^i} can be homomorphically computed with EvalAut$(evk, t^i, \overline{Y})$, without multiplications and therefore almost no depth.

– $c' \leftarrow$ EvalLinearMap$(evk, f_T, \overline{m})$: For simplicity, we use $\overline{m_1} + \overline{m_2}$ to denote EvalAdd$(evk, \overline{m_1}, \overline{m_2})$ for FHE ciphertexts $\overline{m_1}, \overline{m_2}$ and $a \cdot \overline{m}$ to mean the product of a plaintext a and ciphertext $\overline{m}$. Then, let $f_T(X) = \sum_{i=0}^{d-1} a_i X^{t^i}$ and output $c' := \sum_{i=0}^{d-1} a_i \cdot$ EvalAut$(evk, p^i, \overline{m}) = \overline{\sum_{i=0}^{d-1} a_i m^{t^i}}$.

2.3 Reverse Multiplication Friendly Embeddings

Introduced by Cascudo et al. [7] and concurrently studied by Block et al. [2], reverse multiplication friendly embeddings (RMFE) are methods of embedding $(\mathbb{F}_t)^k$ into $\mathbb{F}_{t^d}$ such that component-wise multiplication in the vector space (denoted with $*$) corresponds to multiplication over the field.

Definition 1. *Let q be a prime power and $\mathbb{F}_q$ denote the finite field of q elements. For integers $k, w \geq 1$, a $(k, w)_q$-RMFE is a pair of $\mathbb{F}_q$-linear maps, (ϕ, ψ), where $\phi : (\mathbb{F}_q)^k \to \mathbb{F}_{q^w}$ and $\psi : \mathbb{F}_{q^w} \to (\mathbb{F}_q)^k$ such that for all $\mathbf{x}, \mathbf{y} \in (\mathbb{F}_q)^k$,*

$$\mathbf{x} * \mathbf{y} = \psi(\phi(\mathbf{x}) \cdot \phi(\mathbf{y})).$$

There are two approaches to constructing RMFEs, polynomial interpolation, and algebraic function fields. From these, others can be obtained by composing these base constructions appropriately.

RMFEs from Polynomial Interpolation. The core idea is that a vector $\mathbf{x} = (x_1, ..., x_k) \in (\mathbb{F}_q)^k$ can be encoded as a polynomial $f \in \mathbb{F}_q[X]$ via interpolation, that is, we require that $f(P_i) = x_i$ for some fixed set of points $\{P_i \in \mathbb{F}_q\}$. Hence products of polynomials, when evaluated at the points $\{P_i\}$, yield component-wise products of the vectors corresponding to each polynomial. The following theorem constructs an RMFE that can then be constructed based on this principle. The caveat is the value of k is limited by the number of points available in $\mathbb{F}_q$.

Theorem 1 ([7, **Lemma 4**]). *For a base finite field $\mathbb{F}_q$ and $1 \leq k \leq q + 1$, there exists a $(k, 2k - 1)_q$-RMFE.*

Proof. Let $\mathbb{F}_q[X]_{\leq m}$ denote the set of polynomials in $\mathbb{F}_q[X]$ whose degree is at most m and define ∞_{m+1} as a formal symbol such that $f(\infty_{m+1})$ is the coefficient of X^m for $f \in \mathbb{F}_q[X]_{\leq m}$. Let $P_1, ..., P_k$ be pair-wise distinct elements in $\mathbb{F}_q \cup \{\infty_k\}$ and let α be a root of a monic irreducible polynomial $F(X)$ of degree $2k - 1$. Then $\mathbb{F}_{q^{2k-1}} \cong \mathbb{F}_q(\alpha) \cong \mathbb{F}_q[X]/(F(X))$.

Polynomial interpolation yields the following $\mathbb{F}_q$-vector space isomorphism between $\mathbb{F}_q[X]_{\leq k-1}$ and $(\mathbb{F}_q)^k$:

$$\mathcal{E}_1 : \mathbb{F}_q[X]_{\leq k-1} \to (\mathbb{F}_q)^k; \quad f \mapsto (f(P_1), ..., f(P_k)).$$

The evaluation embedding into $(\mathbb{F}_q)^k$ can be extended naturally to any set of polynomials of a limited degree. In particular, for polynomials in $\mathbb{F}_q[X]_{\leq 2k-2}$,

$$\mathcal{E}_1' : \mathbb{F}_q[X]_{\leq 2k-2} \to (\mathbb{F}_q)^k; \quad f \mapsto (f(P_1'), ..., f(P_k')),$$

where $P_i' := P_i$ if $P_i \in \mathbb{F}_q$ and $P_i' := \infty_{2k-1}$ if $P_i = \infty_k$. Finally, we use the following isomorphism to map polynomials to the extension field $\mathbb{F}_{q^{2k-1}}$,

$$\mathcal{E}_2 : \mathbb{F}_q[X]_{\leq 2k-2} \to \mathbb{F}_{q^{2k-1}}; \quad f = \sum_{i=0}^{2k-2} f_i X^i \mapsto f(\alpha) = \sum_{i=0}^{2k-2} f_i \alpha^i.$$

The $(k, 2k - 1)_q$-RMFE is obtained by defining $\phi = \mathcal{E}_2 \circ \mathcal{E}_1^{-1}$, where $\mathcal{E}_2$ is restricted to the subset $\mathbb{F}_q[X]_{\leq k-1}$, and $\psi = \mathcal{E}_1' \circ \mathcal{E}_2^{-1}$. To see the correctness of the procedure, let $f_x = \mathcal{E}_1^{-1}(\mathbf{x}), f_y = \mathcal{E}_1^{-1}(\mathbf{y})$ be the polynomial encoding of the vectors $\mathbf{x}, \mathbf{y} \in (\mathbb{F}_q)^k$. $\mathcal{E}_2^{-1}(\phi(\mathbf{x}) \cdot \phi(\mathbf{y})) = f_{\mathbf{x}} f_{\mathbf{y}}$, since there is no overflow on the monomials X^i. Therefore,

$$\begin{aligned}
\psi(\phi(\mathbf{x}) \cdot \phi(\mathbf{y})) &= \mathcal{E}_1'(f_{\mathbf{x}} f_{\mathbf{y}}) \\
&= (f_{\mathbf{x}} f_{\mathbf{y}}(P_1), ..., f_{\mathbf{x}} f_{\mathbf{y}}(P_k)) \\
&= (f_{\mathbf{x}}(P_1) f_{\mathbf{y}}(P_1), ..., f_{\mathbf{x}}(P_k) f_{\mathbf{y}}(P_k)) \\
&= \mathbf{x} * \mathbf{y}.
\end{aligned}$$

Algebraic Function Fields. A function field $K/\mathbb{F}_q$ is an algebraic extension of the rational function field $\mathbb{F}_q(X)$, which contains all fractions of polynomials in $\mathbb{F}_q[X]$. Every function field K has an infinite set of "points" called *places*, denoted by P and has a degree $\deg P$. The number of places with a given degree is finite and in particular, places P of $\deg P = 1$ are called *rational*.

For functions $f \in K$ and a place P, either f has a pole at P (i.e. $(1/f)(P) = 0$), or f can be evaluated at P and $f(P)$ can be thought of as an element of $\mathbb{F}_{q^{\deg P}}$. The elements of the function field K always have the same number of zeroes and poles, up to multiplicity, called the order. For any two functions f, g that do not have poles at P,

1. $\lambda(f(P)) = (\lambda f)(P)$, for every $\lambda \in \mathbb{F}_q$;
2. $f(P) + g(P) = (f + g)(P)$ and
3. $f(P) \cdot g(P) = (f \cdot g)(P)$.

A *divisor* is a formal sum of places, $G = \sum c_P P$, with $c_P \in \mathbb{Z}$ and only finitely many $c_P \neq 0$. This set of places also is called the support of G and denoted with $supp(G)$. Just like places, a divisor G has a degree, $\deg G := \sum c_P \deg P \in \mathbb{Z}$. For any function $f \in K \backslash \{0\}$, there is a *principal divisor* associated to f, denoted with (f). Roughly speaking, this principal divisor has the form $(f) = \sum a_P P$, where $a_P = o$ if f has a zero of order o at P, $a_P = -o$ if f has a pole of order o at P and $a_P = 0$ if P is neither a zero or pole of f.

The Riemann-Roch space associated with a divisor, $G = \sum c_P P$, is denoted by $\mathcal{L}(G) = \{0\} \cup \{f \in K \backslash \{0\} \mid (f) + G = \sum a_P P$ and $a_P \geq 0, \forall P\}$. It is the set of all functions in K that have poles and zeroes at the set of places prescribed by G along with the zero function. To be more precise, every function $f \in \mathcal{L}(G)$ has a zero of order at least $|c_P|$ at the places P if $c_P \leq 0$ and can have a pole of order of at most c_P at the places P with $c_P \geq 0$. For any other place $Q \notin supp(G)$, $f(Q) \in \mathbb{F}_{q^{\deg Q}}$. This space is a vector space over $\mathbb{F}_q$ and its dimension $\ell(G)$ is not more than $\deg G + 1$ [6, Lemma 2.51].

Another important fact is that given $f, g \in \mathcal{L}(G)$, the product $f \cdot g$ resides in $\mathcal{L}(2G)$. For every function field K, there is a non-negative integer associated with it called the genus, denoted with $g(K) := \max_G \deg G - \ell(G) + 1$ where G runs over all divisors of K.

From Polynomial Interpolation to Function Fields. To give more intuition for the more abstract RMFEs from algebraic function fields, we sketch how RMFEs from the rational function field $\mathbb{F}_q(Y)$ parallel the RMFEs obtained from polynomial interpolation. The points $P_i \in \mathbb{F}_q$ of polynomial interpolation can be understood as univariate polynomials $(Y - P_i)$, which are *rational* places in $\mathbb{F}_q(Y)$, and ∞ roughly corresponding to the place $(1/Y)$. More general places in $\mathbb{F}_q(Y)$ include the ideals $Q = (f(Y))$, where f are irreducible polynomials. The degree of such a place Q is equal to the degree of the polynomial $f(Y)$.

Recall that in interpolation RMFEs, vectors were mapped to polynomials in $\mathbb{F}_q[X]_{\leq 2k-2}$. In rational function field RMFEs, this corresponds to mapping vectors to functions living in a particular subset of the Riemann-Roch space $\mathcal{L}(G)$ of some divisor G, such that G does not have the places $\{(Y - P_i)\}$ in its support. To embed functions from $\mathcal{L}(G)$ into $\mathbb{F}_{q^w}$, we "evaluate" them at a fixed place $R = (f(Y))$ whose degree is w. This evaluation corresponds to considering the residues of our functions, modulo $f(Y)$.

RMFEs from Algebraic Function Fields. Here, we state the properties of RMFEs that can be obtained from algebraic function fields. Proofs for the following theorems and corollaries can be found in [7].

Theorem 2 ([7, **Lemma 6**]). *Let $K/\mathbb{F}_q$ be an algebraic function field with genus g and k distinct rational places $P_1, ..., P_k$. Let G be a divisor of K such that $\mathrm{supp}(G) \cap \{P_1, ..., P_k\} = \emptyset$ and $\ell(G) - \ell(G - \sum_{i=1}^{k} P_i) = k$. If there exists a place R with $w = \deg R > 2 \deg G$, then there exists a $(k, w)_q$-RMFE.*

In particular, the conditions of Theorem 2 are satisfied as long as there is a place of sufficiently high degree.

Corollary 1 ([7, **Corollary 1**]). *Let $K/\mathbb{F}_q$ be an algebraic function field of genus g and suppose that there are k distinct rational places $(P_1, ..., P_k)$ and a place of degree $w \geq 2k + 4g - 1$. Then, there exists a $(k, w)_q$-RMFE.*

Finally, we state how RMFEs can be composed to yield more RMFEs.

Theorem 3 ([7, **Lemma 5**]). *Suppose $(\phi_{\mathsf{in}}, \psi_{\mathsf{in}})$ is a $(k_{\mathsf{in}}, w_{\mathsf{in}})_q$-RMFE and $(\phi_{\mathsf{out}}, \psi_{\mathsf{out}})$ is a $(k_{\mathsf{out}}, w_{\mathsf{out}})_{q^{w_{\mathsf{in}}}}$-RMFE. (ϕ, ψ) is a $(k_{\mathsf{in}} k_{\mathsf{out}}, w_{\mathsf{in}} w_{\mathsf{out}})_q$-RMFE, where*

$$\phi : (\mathbb{F}_q)^{k_{\mathsf{in}} k_{\mathsf{out}}} \longrightarrow \mathbb{F}_{q^{w_{\mathsf{in}} w_{\mathsf{out}}}}$$

$$\begin{pmatrix} x_1, & ..., & x_{k_{\mathsf{in}}}, \\ x_{k_{\mathsf{in}}+1}, & ..., & x_{2k_{\mathsf{in}}}, \\ \vdots & \ddots & \vdots \\ x_{k_{\mathsf{in}}(k_{\mathsf{out}}-1)+1}, & ..., & x_{k_{\mathsf{in}} k_{\mathsf{out}}} \end{pmatrix} \mapsto \phi_{\mathsf{out}} \begin{pmatrix} \phi_{\mathsf{in}}(x_1, ..., x_{k_{\mathsf{in}}}), \\ \phi_{\mathsf{in}}(x_{k_{\mathsf{in}}+1}, ..., x_{2k_{\mathsf{in}}}), \\ ..., \\ \phi_{\mathsf{in}}(x_{k_{\mathsf{in}}(k_{\mathsf{out}}-1)+1}, ..., x_{k_{\mathsf{in}} k_{\mathsf{out}}}) \end{pmatrix}$$

and

$$\psi : \mathbb{F}_{q^{w_{\mathsf{in}} w_{\mathsf{out}}}} \to (\mathbb{F}_q)^{k_{\mathsf{in}} k_{\mathsf{out}}}$$

$$\alpha \mapsto \psi_{\mathsf{out}}(\alpha) = (u_1, ..., u_{k_{\mathsf{out}}}) \in (\mathbb{F}_{q^{w_{\mathsf{in}}}})^{k_{\mathsf{out}}} \mapsto (\psi_{\mathsf{in}}(u_1), ..., \psi_{\mathsf{in}}(u_{k_{\mathsf{out}}})) \in (\mathbb{F}_q)^{k_{\mathsf{in}} k_{\mathsf{out}}}.$$

3   Field Instruction Multiple Data (FIMD)

In this section, we present how RMFE and SIMD can be combined to encode and work on more data in a single FHE ciphertext. Then, we describe an extension to RMFE that removes the need to recode after each multiplication, at the expense of more expensive recoding operations. Finally, we introduce some optimizations tailored to composite RMFEs.

3.1   RMFE with FHE

The BGV and BFV FHE schemes offer the plaintext space $\mathcal{P} \cong \prod_{i=1}^{\ell} \mathbb{F}_{t^d}$. Typical FHE-based secure computation systems only use base field operations and pack an $\mathbb{F}_t$ element in each slot. RMFE unlocks the full capacity of $\mathcal{P}$ by introducing a "new" dimension in $\mathcal{P}$ hidden within the $\mathbb{F}_{t^d}$ algebra of each SIMD slot. Homomorphic extension field operations such as addition, multiplication, and linearized polynomials are exploited to work with encrypted vectors from $(\mathbb{F}_q)^k$ within each plaintext slot, where $q^w \leq t^d$. With RMFE, we use "extension field instructions" to process data, yielding a *field instruction multiple data* (FIMD) system.

Throughout this section, let (ϕ, ψ) be a $(k, w)_q$-RMFE. We first describe the core encoding and decoding functionality of FIMD.

- $\mu \in \mathbb{F}_{t^d} \leftarrow \mathsf{FIMD.Encode}(\mathbf{x} = (x_1, ..., x_{\ell \cdot k}) \in (\mathbb{F}_q)^{\ell \cdot k})$: For $i = 1, ..., \ell$, let
  $\mathbf{x}_i = (x_{(i-1)k+1}, ..., x_{i \cdot k}) \in (\mathbb{F}_q)^k$.
  1. Embed each $\mathbf{x}_i$ into $\mathbb{F}_{q^w}$ with ϕ to obtain $\hat{\mathbf{x}} = (\phi(\mathbf{x}_1), ..., \phi(\mathbf{x}_\ell)) \in (\mathbb{F}_{q^w})^\ell$;
  2. Encode $\hat{\mathbf{x}}$ into $\mu \in \mathcal{P}$ with the SIMD isomorphism.
- $\mathbf{m} \in (\mathbb{F}_q)^{\ell \cdot k} \leftarrow \mathsf{FIMD.Decode}(\mu \in \mathcal{P})$:
  1. Decode μ to the SIMD plaintext vector $\hat{\mathbf{m}} = (\mu_1, ..., \mu_\ell) \in (\mathbb{F}_{q^w})^\ell$;
  2. Apply ψ to the components of $\hat{\mathbf{m}}$ separately to compute the final output
     $\mathbf{m} = (\psi(\mu_1), ..., \psi(\mu_\ell)) \in (\mathbb{F}_q)^{\ell \cdot k}$.

The μ from FIMD.Encode is then encrypted with the FHE scheme into $\overline{\mu}$ for use in encrypted processing. Similarly, the input to FIMD.Decode comes from decrypted FHE ciphertexts that contain RMFE-encoded vectors.

Arithmetic Operations. The main operations in FHE are homomorphic addition and multiplication. Addition is straightforward in FIMD but multiplication requires a little more work to achieve. Because RMFE only supports one multiplication after embedding, the resulting data cannot be used without first decoding and re-encoding it. A re-encoding protocol was proposed by Cascudo et al. [7] to refresh secret-shared RMFE-encoded field elements and we require a similar operation with FHE. Crucially, the $\mathbb{F}_q$-linear nature of ϕ and ψ means that they can be composed to obtain a recode map, $\pi := \phi \circ \psi$.

Evaluating π on encrypted RMFE-encoded data is done by homomorphically evaluating the q-linearized polynomial f_π from applying Lemma 1 to π. Let evk denote the evaluation keys for the BGV/BFV FHE scheme and μ_1, μ_2 obtained from FIMD.Encode, then the basic homomorphic FIMD operations are as follows.

- $c' \leftarrow$ FIMD.Recode(evk, c): Output $c' =$ FHE.EvalLinearMap(evk, f_π, c).
- $c^+ \leftarrow$ FIMD.EvalAdd($evk, \overline{\mu_1}, \overline{\mu_2}$): Output $c^+ =$ FHE.EvalAdd($evk, \overline{\mu_1}, \overline{\mu_2}$).
- $c^\times \leftarrow$ FIMD.EvalMul($evk, \overline{\mu_1}, \overline{\mu_2}$):
  1. Compute $c =$ FHE.EvalMul($evk, \overline{\mu_1}, \overline{\mu_2}$);
  2. Output $c^\times =$ FIMD.Recode(evk, c).

Moving Data within Encrypted RMFE-Encoded Vectors. With SIMD, data in the various slots can be moved around using the automorphisms $\kappa \in \mathbb{Z}_m^*$. Rotations of the components are achieved with EvalAut using the appropriate automorphisms, κ, and shifts computed by first masking the irrelevant slots and rotating the result. Similar operations can be done with RMFE-encoded vectors and in fact, RMFE supports even more complex intra-vector manipulations.

This is possible due to the $\mathbb{F}_q$-linearity of ϕ and ψ. Any $\mathbb{F}_q$-linear map τ : $(\mathbb{F}_q)^k \to (\mathbb{F}_q)^k$ can be applied on $\mathbf{x}$ of $\phi(\mathbf{x})$ by sandwiching it between ϕ and ψ, as $\phi \circ \tau \circ \psi$. This generalizes the recode operation, which has the identity map id between ϕ and ψ. In this way, arbitrary linear transformations on individual RMFE components in FIMD can be folded into homomorphic multiplication and thus done for free in many situations. Let f'_τ be the polynomial from Lemma 1 for $\phi \circ \tau \circ \psi$.

- $c^{\times'} \leftarrow$ FIMD.EvalMul'($evk, \tau, \overline{m_1}, \overline{m_2}$):
  1. Compute $c =$ FHE.EvalMul($evk, \overline{\mu_1}, \overline{\mu_2}$);
  2. Output $c^\times =$ FHE.EvalLinearMap(evk, f'_τ, c).

Rotations and Shifts for FIMD-Encoded Vectors. With the complete FIMD technique, where RMFE and SIMD are combined, we focus on how to compute rotations and shifts on $\mathcal{P}$, interpreted as the space of vectors $(\mathbb{F}_q)^{k \cdot \ell}$. For any plaintext $\mathbf{x} = (x_1, ..., x_{k \cdot \ell}) \in (\mathbb{F}_q)^{k \cdot \ell}$, FIMD encodes it into $\hat{\mathbf{x}} = (\phi(\mathbf{x}_1), ..., \phi(\mathbf{x}_\ell))$, where $\mathbf{x}_i = (x_{(i-1)k+1}, ..., x_{i \cdot k})$ for $1 \le i \le \ell$. To achieve rotations or shifts on the entire vector, we split the process into two steps.

First, we execute a set of RMFE-only data movement operations followed by a set of SIMD-only data movement operations. If we only move by small steps ($<k$), usually there would be one portion of the data that will move to an adjacent SIMD-slot and another that stays in the same SIMD-slot. More generally, each $\mathbf{x}_i$ can be partitioned into two parts, one that moves by z SIMD-slots and the other that moves by $z + 1$ SIMD-slots to the left or right, for some $z = 0, ..., \ell - 1$. If any of $z, z + 1$ goes beyond $\ell + 1$, those components should be wrapped around the other side of the vector for rotations and discarded for shifts. This is accomplished by using the appropriate SIMD data movement operation, FHE.EvalRot for the former and FHE.EvalShift for the latter.

For example, when rotating data one slot to the left, the first component of $\mathbf{x}_i$, $x_{(i-1)k+1}$ will be moved into last component of $\mathbf{x}_{i-1}$, whereas all other components remain in $\mathbf{x}_i$ but are moved 1 slot to the left, i.e. $(x_{(i-1)k+2}, ..., x_{i \cdot k}, y)$, where y would come from $\mathbf{x}_{i+1}$. On the other hand, moving by $k + 1$ slots to the left means that $x_{(i-1)k+1}$ will be moved to slot $i - 2$ and $(x_{(i-1)k+2}, ..., x_{i \cdot k}, y)$ moved to slot $i - 1$.

- $c' \leftarrow$ FIMD.EvalRot(evk, ρ, c): Let $|\rho| = \rho_{\mathsf{SIMD}}k + \rho_{\mathsf{RMFE}}$.
  - If $\rho_{\mathsf{RMFE}} = 0$, output $c' =$ FHE.EvalRot(evk, ρ, c).
  - Otherwise, $\rho_{\mathsf{RMFE}} > 0$. Let τ_0 and τ_1 be $\mathbb{F}_q$-linear maps on $(\mathbb{F}_q)^k$ with $\tau_0(\mathbf{z}) = (z_{\rho_{\mathsf{RMFE}}+1}, ..., z_k, 0, ..., 0)$ and $\tau_1(\mathbf{z}) = (0, ..., 0, z_1, ..., z_{\rho_{\mathsf{RMFE}}})$ for $\mathbf{z} = (z_1, ..., z_k)$.
    1. Compute ciphertexts $c_{\tau_0} =$ FHE.EvalLinearMap(evk, f_{τ_0}, c) and $c_{\tau_1} =$ FHE.EvalLinearMap(evk, f_{τ_1}, c);
    2. Positive (negative) ρ mean rotation to the right (left). To move data correctly, for $i = 0, 1$,
       $\rho > 0$: compute $c'_{\tau_i} =$ FHE.EvalRot$(evk, \rho_{\mathsf{SIMD}} - i, c_{\tau_i})$;
       $\rho < 0$: compute $c'_{\tau_i} =$ FHE.EvalRot$(evk, -\rho_{\mathsf{SIMD}} - (1 - i), c_{\tau_i})$.
    3. Output $c' =$ FIMD.EvalAdd$(evk, c'_{\tau_0}, c'_{\tau_1})$.
- $c' \leftarrow$ FIMD.EvalShift(evk, ρ, c): Follow the steps of FIMD.EvalRot(evk, ρ, c), replacing FHE.EvalRot with FHE.EvalShift.

3.2 r-fold RMFE

Among the possible plaintext spaces $(\mathbb{F}_{t^d})^\ell$ available in the BGV/BFV FHE schemes, the possible set of (d, ℓ) can be very diverse. Many times, t is chosen so that $d = 1$ and ℓ is maximized. However, this requires large t because $d = 1 \Leftrightarrow t \mid (m - 1)$, where m refers to the m-th cyclotomic polynomial $\Phi_m(X)$ in $\mathcal{P} = \mathbb{Z}_t[X]/\Phi_m(X)$.

In the case for small $t = 2, 3, 5, 7, ...$, we can choose m to minimize d but it is not always possible. More specifically, most HE implementations support cyclotomic polynomials of the form $\Phi_m(X) = X^{m/2} + 1$, where $m = 2^N$ for some positive integer N. For such m, small primes tend to have very high d in the range of $m/4, ..., m/32$, which using $m = 32768$ as an example, would translate to $d \in \{512, 1024, 2048, 4096\}$. With such high d, using FHE.EvalLinearMap after each multiplication would be prohibitively expensive and alternatives are needed.

Instead of just 1 multiplication before decoding, we generalize RMFE to an embedding that allows r-fold multiplications before decoding is strictly necessary. This means that products of up to 2^r encoded vectors can be done before ψ is applied by multiplying the vectors pair-wise recursively.

Definition 2. *Let q be a prime power and $\mathbb{F}_q$ denote the finite field of q elements. For integers $k, w, r \geq 1$, a $(k, w, r)_q$-RMFE is a pair of $\mathbb{F}_q$-linear maps, (ϕ, ψ), where $\phi : (\mathbb{F}_q)^k \to \mathbb{F}_{q^w}$ and $\psi : \mathbb{F}_{q^w} \to (\mathbb{F}_q)^k$ such that for any 2^r vectors $\mathbf{x_1}, ..., \mathbf{x_{2^r}} \in (\mathbb{F}_q)^k$,*

$$\mathop{\text{\Large$*$}}_{i=1}^{2^r} \mathbf{x_i} = \psi \left(\prod_{i=1}^{2^r} \phi(\mathbf{x_i}) \right).$$

This allows us to effectively amortize the expensive recoding step over several multiplications instead, although this reduces the packing capacity as we will show. Besides that, in practice, linear map evaluations incur some noise increase and reducing the number of recoding steps also reduces the noise overhead of FIMD multiplications.

With this new property, it is desirable to be able to add intermediate products of r-fold RMFE-encoded vectors, regardless of the number of multiplications these products have undergone. This way, we can easily perform degree-r multivariate polynomial evaluations simultaneously on all components of r-fold RMFE-encoded vectors. While it is not a strict requirement in Definition 2, we will focus on constructions that support this. To that end, we need an additional condition on algebraic function field RMFEs to ensure inter-operability between encoded vectors that go through a different number of multiplications.

Definition 3. *Let $K/\mathbb{F}_q$ be an algebraic function field. A divisor, $G = \sum a_P P$ in K, is called positive if $a_P \geq 0$ for all P.*

For a positive divisor G, $\mathcal{L}(G)$ is the set of functions that may have poles of order at most a_P at the places P with $a_P \neq 0$ in G. This means that $\mathcal{L}(xG) \subseteq \mathcal{L}(yG)$ for any $x \leq y$, since functions in $\mathcal{L}(xG)$ can only have poles of order less than $x \cdot a_P \leq y \cdot a_P$.

Theorem 4 (Extending Theorem 2). *Let $K/\mathbb{F}_q$ be an algebraic function field with genus g and k distinct rational places $P_1, ..., P_k$. Let G be a positive divisor of K such that $\mathrm{supp}(G) \cap \{P_1, ..., P_k\} = \emptyset$ and $\ell(G) - \ell(G - \sum_{i=1}^{k} P_i) = k$. If there exists a place R with $w = \deg R > 2^r \deg G$, then there exists a $(k, w, r)_q$-RMFE.*

Proof. As before, we have the evaluation map from $\mathcal{L}(G)$ to the rational places,

$$\mathcal{E}_1 : \mathcal{L}(G) \to (\mathbb{F}_q)^k; f \mapsto (f(P_1), ..., f(P_k)).$$

We choose a k-dimensional subspace $W \subset \mathcal{L}(G)$ such that $\mathcal{E}_1$ restricted to W is an isomorphism between W and $(\mathbb{F}_q)^k$ for encoding. Then, with $f(R)$ denoting the evaluation of any $f \in K$ at R, the RMFE encode map is given by

$$\phi : \mathcal{E}_1(W) \cong (\mathbb{F}_q)^k \to \mathbb{F}_{q^w}; \quad (f(P_1), ..., f(P_k)) \mapsto f(R).$$

With a positive divisor, all $\mathcal{L}(xG) \subseteq \mathcal{L}(2^r G)$ and so we focus on the largest space, $\mathcal{L}(2^r G)$. We define the following injective $\mathbb{F}_q$-linear map (since $\deg R > \deg 2^r G$ as well),

$$\mathcal{E}_2 : \mathcal{L}(2^r G) \to \mathbb{F}_{q^w}; \quad f \mapsto f(R).$$

To obtain the RMFE decode map ψ, we first consider the map from the image of $\mathcal{E}_2$ to the input space,

$$\psi' : \mathrm{Im}(\mathcal{E}_2) \subseteq \mathbb{F}_{q^w} \to (\mathbb{F}_q)^k; \quad f(R) \mapsto (f(P_1), ..., f(P_k)).$$

Because $\mathcal{E}_2$ is injective, $f \in \mathcal{L}(2^r G)$ is uniquely determined by $f(R)$ and we linearly extend ψ' to all of $\mathbb{F}_{q^w}$ to get ψ.

The correctness of the construction follows for the same reasons in the proof of Theorem 2. With a positive divisor G, any RMFE-encoded vectors that undergone some number of multiplications would lie in $\mathcal{L}(xG) \subseteq \mathcal{L}(2^r G)$ for some $x \leq 2^r$ and thus can be added together in the "ambient" space $\mathcal{L}(2^r G)$.

Corollary 2 (Extending Corollary 1). *Let $K/\mathbb{F}_q$ be an algebraic function field of genus g and suppose that there are k distinct rational places $(P_1, ..., P_k)$ and a place of degree $w \geq 2^r k + 2^{r+1} g - 2^r + 1$. Then, there exists a $(k, w, r)_q$-RMFE.*

Proof. Like the proof of Corollary 1, we choose a divisor G of degree $k + 2g - 1$, whose support is disjoint from $(P_1, ..., P_k)$. Now, to apply Theorem 4 we require $w = \deg R > 2^r \deg G$, and therefore can get a $(k, w, r)_q$-RMFE as long as $w > 2^r(k + 2g - 1)$. ∎

FIMD with r-Fold RMFE. We tag ciphertexts with a *RMFE level*, augmenting a standard BGV/BFV ciphertext c into (c, η), where η denotes the number of multiplications that have been done on c since the data was first RMFE-encoded. This is to keep track of how many multiplications a ciphertext can tolerate without recoding before being rendered useless by excessive multiplications.

Let (ϕ, ψ) be a $(k, w, r)_q$-RMFE and we use rFIMD to denote the combination of r-fold RMFE with SIMD packing methods. First, we highlight the modifications needed when encrypting and decrypting r-fold RMFE vectors.

- $(c, 0) \leftarrow$ rFIMD.Encrypt$(pk, \mathbf{x} = (x_1, ..., x_{\ell \cdot k}) \in (\mathbb{F}_t)^{\ell \cdot k})$:
  1. Compute $\hat{\mathbf{x}} = $ FIMD.Encode$(\mathbf{x} = (x_1, ..., x_{\ell \cdot k}))$.
  2. Encrypt $\hat{\mathbf{x}}$ and output $(c = $ FHE.Encrypt$(pk, \hat{\mathbf{x}}), 0)$.
- $\mathbf{m} \leftarrow$ rFIMD.Decrypt$(sk, (c, \eta))$:
  1. If $\eta > r$, abort and output $\perp$. Otherwise, continue to Step 2.
  2. Decrypt the ciphertext to obtain $\mu = $ FHE.Decrypt(sk, c).
  3. Decode μ and output $\mathbf{m} = $ FIMD.Decode$(\mu) \in (\mathbb{F}_t)^{\ell \cdot k}$.

Homomorphic operations remain mostly unchanged, especially for addition. The only difference is that the RMFE level of output ciphertexts has to be accounted for. As a side effect of shifts and rotations of RMFE-encoded data being modified recodings, any data movement operation in rFIMD with $\rho = \rho_{\mathsf{SIMD}} k + \rho_{\mathsf{RMFE}}$ with $\rho_{\mathsf{RMFE}} \neq 0$ would reset the RMFE level to zero.

- $(c^+, \eta) \leftarrow$ rFIMD.EvalAdd$(evk, (c_1, \eta_1), (c_2, \eta_2))$: Set $\eta = \max(\eta_1, \eta_2)$ and output $(c^+ = $ FIMD.EvalAdd$(evk, c_1, c_2), \eta)$.
- $(c^\times, \eta) \leftarrow$ rFIMD.EvalMul$(evk, (c_1, \eta_1), (c_2, \eta_2))$: Let $\eta' = \max(\eta_1, \eta_2) + 1$. We distinguish between two cases, $\eta' = r$ and $\eta' < r$.
  1. If $\eta' = r$, compute the recoded result $c^\times = $ FIMD.EvalMul(evk, c_1, c_2) and output $(c^\times, 0)$.
  2. Otherwise, $\eta' < r$ and output $(c^\times = $ FHE.EvalMul$(evk, c_1, c_2), \eta')$.
- $(c', \eta') \leftarrow$ rFIMD.EvalShift$(evk, \rho, (c, \eta))$: Let $\rho = \rho_{\mathsf{SIMD}} k + \rho_{\mathsf{RMFE}}$.
  Return $(c' = $ FIMD.EvalShift$(evk, \rho, c), \eta')$, where $\eta' = 0$ if $\rho_{\mathsf{RMFE}} \neq 0$ and $\eta' = \eta$ otherwise.
- $(c', \eta) \leftarrow$ rFIMD.EvalRot$(evk, \rho, (c, \eta))$: Let $\rho = \rho_{\mathsf{SIMD}} k + \rho_{\mathsf{RMFE}}$.
  Return $(c' = $ FIMD.EvalRot$(evk, \rho, c), \eta')$, where $\eta' = 0$ if $\rho_{\mathsf{RMFE}} \neq 0$ and $\eta' = \eta$ otherwise.

3.3   Composite RMFE with FHE

Recall from Theorem 3 that composite RMFEs $(k_{in}k_{out}, w_{in}w_{out})_q$ are built from two component RMFEs, an "inner" $(k_{in}, w_{in})_q$-RMFE and "outer" $(k_{out}, w_{out})_{q^{w_{in}}}$-RMFE with the maps (ϕ_{in}, ψ_{in}) and (ϕ_{out}, ψ_{out}) respectively. This allows us to design a three-stage method for recoding that leverages the simpler linear maps (ϕ_{in}, ψ_{in}) and (ϕ_{out}, ψ_{out}). However, it also presents complications for extending the r-fold property to composite RMFEs, which we describe and address at the end of the section by relaxing the recoding requirements for composite RMFEs.

Exploiting the Intermediate Extension. The key difference between standard and composite RMFEs is the tower of field extensions of $\mathbb{F}_q$ underlying composite RMFEs, $\mathbb{F}_q \subseteq \mathbb{E}_1 = \mathbb{F}_{q^{w_{in}}} \subseteq \mathbb{E}_2 = \mathbb{F}_{q^{w_{in}w_{out}}}$. Furthermore, their respective extension degrees $[\mathbb{E}_1 : \mathbb{F}_q] = w_{in}$ and $[\mathbb{E}_2 : \mathbb{E}_1] = w_{out}$ are smaller than the direct extension $[\mathbb{E}_2 : \mathbb{F}_q] = w_{in}w_{out}$. This means that $\mathbb{E}_1$-linear maps on $\mathbb{E}_2$ and $\mathbb{F}_q$-linear maps on $\mathbb{E}_1$ correspond to $|\mathbb{E}_1|$- and $|\mathbb{F}_q|$-linearized polynomials of lower degrees and thus easier to evaluate.

We propose a three-stage recode process for composite RMFEs, exploiting the intermediate field $\mathbb{E}_1$. Let $\mathbf{x} = (\mathbf{x}_1, ..., \mathbf{x}_{k_{out}})$, $\mathbf{y} = (\mathbf{y}_1, ..., \mathbf{y}_{k_{out}}) \in (\mathbb{F}_q)^{k_{in}k_{out}}$ be vectors to be encoded, where $\mathbf{z}_i = (z_{(i-1)k_{in}+1}, ..., z_{ik_{in}}) \in (\mathbb{F}_q)^{k_{in}}$ for $\mathbf{z} \in \{\mathbf{x}, \mathbf{y}\}$. Denoting with $\alpha \in \mathbb{E}_2$ the result of $\phi(\mathbf{x}) \cdot \phi(\mathbf{y})$, we perform recoding in the following manner,

1. Compute $\psi_{out}(\alpha) = (\phi_{in}(\mathbf{x}_1) \cdot \phi_{in}(\mathbf{y}_1), ..., \phi_{in}(\mathbf{x}_{k_{out}}) \cdot \phi_{in}(\mathbf{y}_{k_{out}})) \in (\mathbb{E}_1)^{k_{out}}$.
2. Apply the recode map $\pi_{in} = \phi_{in} \circ \psi_{in}$ to each component of $\psi_{out}(\alpha)$, recoding the intermediate field elements from the "inner" RMFE.

$$\left(\pi_{in}\left(\phi_{in}(\mathbf{x}_i) \cdot \phi_{in}(\mathbf{y}_i) \right) \right)_{i=1}^{k_{out}} = (\phi_{in}(\mathbf{x}_1 * \mathbf{y}_1), ..., \phi_{in}(\mathbf{x}_{k_{out}} * \mathbf{y}_{k_{out}})) \in (\mathbb{E}_1)^{k_{out}}$$

3. Encode the resulting vector $(\phi_{in}(\mathbf{x}_1 * \mathbf{y}_1), ..., \phi_{in}(\mathbf{x}_{k_{out}} * \mathbf{y}_{k_{out}}))$ with ϕ_{out}, getting $\alpha' = \phi_{out}((\phi_{in}(\mathbf{x}_1 * \mathbf{y}_1), ..., \phi_{in}(\mathbf{x}_{k_{out}} * \mathbf{y}_{k_{out}}))) \in \mathbb{E}_2$.

Three-Stage Recode for FIMD. As with standard recode, we evaluate linear maps in each stage. However, Stages 1 and 3 work over an $\mathbb{E}_1$-vector space while Stage 2 work over an $\mathbb{F}_q$-vector space. Stages 1 and 3 correspond to applying the "outer" RMFE decoding and encoding maps, ψ_{out}, ϕ_{out} respectively. These would correspond to evaluating two $q^{w_{in}}$-linearized polynomials, one per map, following Lemma 1.

Let ϕ'_{in} and ψ'_{in} denote extensions of ϕ_{in} and ψ_{in} to $\mathbb{F}_q$-linear maps over $(\mathbb{E}_1)^{k_{out}}$ that perform component-wise encoding and decoding of the $\mathbb{E}_1$ elements. In the second stage, notice that the map

$$\pi'_{in} : (\mathbb{E}_1)^{k_{out}} \rightarrow (\mathbb{E}_1)^{k_{out}}$$
$$(\alpha_1, ..., \alpha_{k_{out}}) \mapsto \phi'_{in}(\psi'_{in}((\alpha_1, ..., \alpha_{k_{out}})))$$
$$= (\phi_{in}(\psi_{in}(\alpha_1)), ..., \phi_{in}(\psi_{in}(\alpha_{k_{out}})))$$

is $\mathbb{F}_q$-linear since $(\mathbb{E}_1)^{k_{\text{out}}}$ is the product of k_{out} copies of the $\mathbb{F}_q$-vector space $\mathbb{E}_1$ and π is the product of k_{out} copies of π_{in}. Thus, we can evaluate one q-linearized polynomial to achieve Stage 2.

In fact, as with the recode operation with standard RMFEs, we can view π'_{in} as a recode operation over the entire input vector space $\mathbb{F}_q^{k_{\text{in}} k_{\text{out}}}$. Then, we can similarly enhance the three-stage recode process to also evaluate arbitrary linear transformations τ over elements in $\mathbb{F}_q^{k_{\text{in}} k_{\text{out}}}$.

$$\pi'_{\text{in},\tau} : (\mathbb{E}_1)^{k_{\text{out}}} \to (\mathbb{E}_1)^{k_{\text{out}}}$$

$$(\alpha_1, \ldots, \alpha_{k_{\text{out}}}) \mapsto \phi'_{\text{in}} \left(\tau \left(\psi'_{\text{in}} \left((\alpha_1, \ldots, \alpha_{k_{\text{out}}}) \right) \right) \right)$$

With this, we get an alternate FIMD multiplication algorithm for composite RMFEs. Similar to FIMD.EvalMul' in Sect. 3.1, we can evaluate arbitrary linear transformations τ during FIMD multiplication. This is achieved by replacing $f_{\pi'_{\text{in}}}$ with the appropriate linearized polynomial for $\pi'_{\text{in},\tau}$ in Stage 2 of FIMD.Recode3S.

- $c' \leftarrow$ FIMD.Recode3S(evk, c): Let $f_{\psi_{\text{out}}}$, $f_{\pi'_{\text{in}}}$, and $f_{\phi_{\text{out}}}$ denote the linearized polynomials required in the three stage recoding process.
  1. Compute $c^{(1)} = $ FHE.EvalLinearMap($evk, f_{\psi_{\text{out}}}, c$).
  2. Compute $c^{(2)} = $ FHE.EvalLinearMap($evk, f_{\pi'_{\text{in}}}, c^{(1)}$).
  3. Output $c' = $ FHE.EvalLinearMap($evk, f_{\phi_{\text{out}}}, c^{(2)}$).
- $c^{\times} \leftarrow$ FIMD.EvalMul^c(evk, c_1, c_2):
  1. Compute $c = $ FHE.EvalMul(evk, c_1, c_2).
  2. Output $c^{\times} = $ FIMD.Recode3S(evk, c).

As with standard RMFEs, r-fold RMFEs can be composed just like the original RMFE.

Theorem 5 (Composite r-fold RMFE). *Let $(\phi_{\text{in}}, \psi_{\text{in}})$ be a $(k_{\text{in}}, w_{\text{in}}, r)_q$-RMFE and $(\phi_{\text{out}}, \psi_{\text{out}})$ be a $(k_{\text{out}}, w_{\text{out}}, r)_{q^{w_{\text{in}}}}$-RMFE. Then, their composition in the manner of Theorem 3, denoted with (ϕ, ψ), is a $(k_{\text{in}} k_{\text{out}}, w_{\text{in}} w_{\text{out}}, r)_q$-RMFE.*

The proof of this is exactly the same as $(k, w)_q$-RMFE composition, since the composition of $\mathbb{F}_q$-linear maps are $\mathbb{F}_q$-linear and field elements decode to component-wise products of their respective encoded input vectors after each decode step. If both $(\phi_{\text{in}}, \psi_{\text{in}})$ and $(\phi_{\text{out}}, \psi_{\text{out}})$ allow mixing "intermediate" products, then the composed r-fold RMFE (ϕ, ψ) will also have this property.

Relaxing the r-fold Property for Composite RMFEs. Recode can be delayed up until 2^r encoded vectors are multiplied for any r-fold RMFEs. However, r-fold RMFEs from Theorem 5 is less space-efficient than r-fold RMFEs derived from Theorem 4. This is due to the fact that r-fold RMFEs have $w > 2^r \cdot k$ and so a composite r-fold RMFE from Theorem 5 would typically have $w_{\text{in}} w_{\text{out}} > (2^{2r}) \cdot k_{\text{in}} k_{\text{out}}$ per Corollary 2. With FHE, $w_{\text{in}} w_{\text{out}}$ is generally a dependent variable – t and m are the main parameters – rendering r-fold composite RMFEs almost unusable.

To remedy this situation, we relax the r-fold property such that for composite r-fold RMFEs, one can perform a less expensive "outer" recode after r'-fold multiplications for some $r' \mid r$ and only do a complete recode process after r-fold multiplications.

Theorem 6 (Composite r-fold RMFE, Relaxed Recode). *Let $(\phi_{\mathsf{in}}, \psi_{\mathsf{in}})$ be a $(k_{\mathsf{in}}, w_{\mathsf{in}}, r)_q$-RMFE and $(\phi_{\mathsf{out}}, \psi_{\mathsf{out}})$ be a $(k_{\mathsf{out}}, w_{\mathsf{out}}, r')_{q^{w_{\mathsf{in}}}}$-RMFE, for some $r' \mid r$. Then, their composition following Theorem 3, denoted with (ϕ, ψ), is a $(k_{\mathsf{in}}k_{\mathsf{out}}, w_{\mathsf{in}}w_{\mathsf{out}}, r)_q$-RMFE, provided $\pi_{\mathsf{out}} = \phi_{\mathsf{out}} \circ \psi_{\mathsf{out}}$ is evaluated on encoded elements after every r'-fold multiplications.*

Proof. Let ϕ'_{in} and ψ'_{in} denote extensions of the "inner" RMFE encode and decode maps to act component-wise on vectors in $(\mathbb{E}_1)^{k_{\mathsf{out}}}$. Suppose we have 2^r inputs, $\mathbf{x}_i = (x_{1,i}, ..., x_{k_{\mathsf{in}}k_{\mathsf{out}},i})$ for $1 \leq i \leq 2^r$ and let their respective encodings be $\alpha_i = \phi_{\mathsf{out}}(\phi'_{\mathsf{in}}(\mathbf{x}_i))$. Any intermediate result after r'-fold multiplications β would need to be refreshed with $\beta' = \pi_{\mathsf{out}}(\beta)$. Otherwise, further multiplications would fail to correctly decode with ψ_{out} and thus similarly fail to decode with ψ. Finally, observe that the map ψ_{in} tolerates up to $2^r \geq 2^{r'}$ multiplications. Therefore, any intermediate product γ would decode correctly with $\psi'_{\mathsf{in}}(\psi_{\mathsf{out}}(\gamma))$ as long as they have been "outer recoded" after every r'-fold multiplications.

Thus, the "outer" RMFE is no longer restricted to be r-fold and can even be a standard $(k_{\mathsf{out}}, w_{\mathsf{out}})_q$-RMFE if we are willing to perform an "outer" recode after each multiplication. In that case, the overhead between composite and standard r-fold RMFEs would be almost identical. Assuming we are using a composite r-fold RMFE with components $(\phi_{\mathsf{in}}, \psi_{\mathsf{in}})$ and $(\phi_{\mathsf{out}}, \psi_{\mathsf{out}})$ of $(k_{\mathsf{in}}, w_{\mathsf{in}}, r)_q$ and $(k_{\mathsf{out}}, w_{\mathsf{out}}, r')_q$-RMFEs respectively, we have

- $(c^\times, \rho) \leftarrow \mathsf{rFIMD.EvalMul}^c(evk, (c_1, \rho_1), (c_2, \rho_2))$: Let $\rho' = \max(\rho_1, \rho_2) + 1$ and $\pi_{\mathsf{out}} = \phi_{\mathsf{out}} \circ \psi_{\mathsf{out}}$.
  1. Compute $c = \mathsf{FHE.EvalMul}(evk, c_1, c_2)$.
  2. Then, we consider three cases based on ρ'.
     (a) If $\rho' = r$, output $(c^\times = \mathsf{FIMD.Recode3S}(evk, c), 0)$.
     (b) Else, if $\rho' \mid r'$, output $(c^\times = \mathsf{FHE.EvalLinearMap}(evk, \pi_{\mathsf{out}}, c), \rho')$.
     (c) Otherwise, output (c, ρ').

4   RMFE Parameter Selection with FHE

In this section, we describe how parameters should be chosen for RMFE with FHE. As introduced in Sect. 2.1, for chosen t and m, the FHE plaintext space is $(\mathbb{F}_{t^d})^\ell$, where $d \cdot \ell = \phi(m)$. Therefore, we are limited to $(k, w, r)_q$-RMFEs where $q^w \leq t^d$ and q is some power of t.

For the various forms of RMFE discussed in previous sections, the main parameter is the function field K used in Theorems 2 and 4. First, we introduce the Hasse-Weil bound, which gives an upper bound on the number of rational places of a function field. For every function field K, there is a unique non-singular projective curve C associated with it. It was shown that there is a one-to-one correspondence between the points on the curve C and the rational places of K.

Table 1. Possible $(k, \deg R, r)_q$-RMFE parameters

Function field	Base field, $\mathbb{F}_q$	Genus, g	Max. k, η	$\deg G$	Min. $\deg R$, r-fold
Rational (P)	$\mathbb{F}_t$	0	$= t + 1$	$k - 1$	$2^r(k-1) + 1$
Elliptic (E)	$\mathbb{F}_t$	1	$\leq t + 1 + 2\sqrt{t}$	$k + 1$	$2^r(k+1) + 1$
Hermitian (H)	$\mathbb{F}_{t^2}$	$\frac{t(t-1)}{2}$	$= t^3 + 1$	$k + t^2 - t - 1$	$2^r(\deg G) + 1$

Lemma 2 (Hasse-Weil Bound, [38, Theorem 5.2.3]). *Let $K/\mathbb{F}_q$ be an algebraic function field with genus g. The number of rational places of K, η, satisfies*

$$|\eta - (q+1)| \leq 2g\sqrt{q}.$$

A collection of curves that satisfy the Hasse-Weil bound can be found at [23].

Packing Density. The packing density of an RMFE instantiation can be defined as w/k. Cascudo et al. showed that there existed families of RMFEs with good asymptotic packing density.

Theorem 7 ([7, Theorem 5]). *There exists a family of $(k, w)_t$-RMFE with $k \to \infty$ and $w = O(k)$. More concretely,*

$$\frac{w}{k} \to 2 + \frac{4}{A(t)},$$

where $A(t)$ is Ihara's constant of $\mathbb{F}_t$.

We extend the definition of packing density to FIMD by computing d/k and not w/k because the FHE plaintext space is fixed to extension degree d with the choice of t and m. A smaller number means that the FIMD instantiation can effectively use a larger portion of the underlying field.

Function Fields for Efficient RMFE for FHE. To make good use of the finite extension fields available from SIMD, we consider the following function fields that yield RMFEs with w/k close to 2. Details of the possible RMFEs enabled by these function fields are given in Table 1. The minimum degree of the place R is derived from Corollaries 1 and 2.

- Rational Function Field, $F_t(X)$: Corresponding to choosing the projective line as the underlying curve.
- "Elliptic" Function Fields, $F_t[X,Y]/C$: C is an appropriate elliptic curve that approaches the Hasse-Weil bound.
- Hermitian Function Field, $F_{t^2}[X,Y]/C$: $C = Y^t + Y - X^{t+1}$ is the Hermitian curve, and the function field satisfies the Hasse-Weil bound exactly.

When using Hermitian curves, note that the FHE slot degree d is effectively halved as the base field of the Hermitian function field is $\mathbb{F}_q = \mathbb{F}_{t^2}$.

Existence of Higher Degree Place R. Given a function field $K/\mathbb{F}_q$, the choice of w is dependent on whether K even admits a place R with $\deg R = w$. The following lemma gives conditions for the existence of places of a given degree.

Lemma 3 ([38, **Corollary 5.2.10 (b), (c)**]). *Let $K/\mathbb{F}_q$ be an algebraic function field with genus g.*

1. If $g = 0$, then there exists a place of degree w, for all $w \geq 1$.
2. If $g \geq 1$, it is sufficient that w satisfies

$$2g + 1 \leq q^{\frac{w-1}{2}}(q^{\frac{1}{2}} - 1),$$

for there to exist a place R of degree w.

The function fields from Table 1 have relatively small values of g, ensuring us a wide selection of w. More explicitly, let w_0 be the value derived from Lemma 3 such that for all $w \geq w_0$, Lemma 3 guarantees the existence of a place of degree w for a given function field. Table 2 records the values of w_0 for each of the function fields from Table 1.

Table 2. Lower bound on degree of places guaranteed to exist by Lemma 3

Function field	w_0
Rational (P)	1
Elliptic (E)	$2(\log_t 3 - \log_t(t^{1/2} - 1)) + 1$
Hermitian (H)	$\log_t \left(t + \frac{1}{t-1}\right) + 1$

Composite RMFEs for FHE. For composite RMFEs, r-fold or otherwise, there are more considerations for the choices of component RMFEs. If we do not need the r-fold property, we could choose component RMFEs, $(k_{\mathsf{in}}, w_{\mathsf{in}})$ and $(k_{\mathsf{out}}, w_{\mathsf{out}})$ such that the complexity of each stage of FIMD.Recode3S is about the same. This entails balancing $w_{\mathsf{in}} \cdot k_{\mathsf{out}}$ with w_{out} as these determine the degree of the linear maps computed in Stage 2 and Stages 1 and 3 respectively.

For composite r-fold RMFEs, the main choices are in the sizes of r' and k_{out}. Larger r' means fewer recoding operations but reduces the potential packing efficiency, while k_{out} determines how expensive the "outer" recoding operation would be. An option is to have cheap "outer" recodes and a more expensive three-stage recode since the latter would be amortized over r-fold multiplications.

5   Experiment Results

In this section, we discuss the results of our experiments on the performance of standard and r-fold RMFEs, as well as the three-stage recode optimization for composite (r-fold) RMFEs. The experiment platform is an Intel® Xeon® Platinum 8170 with maximum turbo frequency of 3.7 GHz and 192 GB RAM. We do not use multi-threading for the experiments in this section.

Table 3. FHE plaintext spaces for various primes with $\Phi_{8192}(X)$

Plaintext modulus, t	# SIMD slots, ℓ	Extension degree, d
3	2	2048
7	4	1024
17	8	512
31	16	256

Throughout this section, we use $\Phi_{8192}(X) = X^{4096} + 1$ and various plaintext modulus t. Magma was used to implement the RMFEs and compute the necessary data to use with HElib. The capacity parameter in HElib is set to 99 and yields a maximum ciphertext bit-width of <159. Estimations with the lwe-estimator of Albrecht et al. [1] shows the FHE instance achieving at least 80-bit security. Table 3 shows the decomposition of the plaintext space for $m = 8192$ with respect to various primes. We split our experiments into two main categories: FIMD with basic and composite (r-fold) RMFE.

rFIMD Implementation Details. The main component of rFIMD is the recode operation, which consists of evaluating one or more linear maps on FHE ciphertexts to refresh the RMFE encoding encrypted within them. To that end, we generated the key-switching matrices for all necessary automorphisms in the recode operation, which is at most, w matrices for a $(k, w, r)_q$-RMFE. This allows us to fully exploit the hoisting technique of Halevi and Shoup [28]. We evaluate each linear map in the recode operation by first hoisting the input ciphertext and then computing the required automorphisms one by one to minimize the number of ciphertexts in memory. Besides that, due to the large noise increases from the recode computation, we apply modulus switching to rescale the resulting ciphertext. This reduces the ciphertext modulus based on the current estimated noise levels and improves the performance of multiplications down the line.

5.1   Experimental Results for Basic (r)FIMD

A list of the parameters used for basic RMFEs is shown in Table 4. These parameters are chosen by maximizing k for each function field and they also support r-fold variants for small $r \in \{1, 2, 4\}$. Note that Hermitian function fields were not considered for $t = 17, 31$, as $\deg G$ would exceed d. We also had to reduce k for $t = 31$ with higher r values for the same reason that $\deg G$ would exceed d. We denote an RMFE parameter set by t-$curve\_type$, where $curve\_type \in \{P, E, H\}$ indicates the rational (P for projective line), elliptic and Hermitian function fields respectively. For example, 17-P represents the case where $t = 17$ and the RMFE is instantiated with the rational function field.

The first set of experiments compared the performance and noise impact of (r)FIMD multiplication to FHE multiplication. We prepared one (r)FIMD ciphertext and one FHE ciphertext, which was repeatedly squared until their

Table 4. Basic RMFE parameters

t	d	K	Parameter (P) set	Curve	k	d/k	w
3	2048	Projective	3-P	–	4	512	7
		Elliptic	3-E	$y^2 - x^3 - 2x - 1$	7	293	17
		Hermitian	3-H	$y^3 + y - x^4$	28	73.1	67
7	1024	Projective	7-P	–	8	128	15
		Elliptic	7-E	$y^2 - x^3 - 3$	13	78.8	29
		Hermitian	7-H	$y^7 + y - x^8$	214	4.79	511
17	512	Projective	17-P	–	18	28.4	35
		Elliptic	17-E	$y^2 - x^3 - 3x$	26	19.7	55
31	256	Projective	31-P	–	16.0	8.0	63
					32.0	16.0	31
		Elliptic	31-E	$y^2 - x^3 - 3$	14	18.3	89
					43	5.95	31

capacities were exhausted. The time taken to complete this process as well as the overall number of multiplications that were done were recorded. For better comparison against (r)FIMD multiplications, we took as many timings from the last few FHE multiplications onwards, so that the same number of multiplications are compared. This is because HElib implements the BGV scheme whose multiplications become cheaper due to the use of modulus switching after each multiplication for noise control. The complete set of basic (r)FIMD experiments are described in Table 11, furnished in Appendix A. As we observe a similar trend across the different parameter sets, a subcollection will be used to facilitate the discussion about the experiment results in Table 5.

In general, (r)FIMD multiplications take much longer to complete than FHE multiplications. We observe a trend of better amortized (r)FIMD multiplication speedup as r increases. The speedup is primarily attributed to the decrease in (r)FIMD multiplication time as the number of recodes performed is reduced. Sometimes, recoding is not necessary as no more operations can be executed after the maximum FIMD multiplications are achieved. Table 5 show that by suppressing the recodes for P Sets 3-H and 7-H, we are able to obtain an amortized speedup of more than 20× and 11× respectively. This shows that recode is indeed an expensive operation that should be used sparingly.

We also see that higher k values are needed to see benefits with (r)FIMD. These k values are dependent on the type of the function field, with RMFEs from Hermitian function fields yielding the highest k, for any fixed r. Hence, it is beneficial to perform fewer recodes while maximizing the value of k for a basic (r)FIMD instantiation. Note that the number of multiplications supported for any ciphertext varies slightly, due to variance in the noise generated in fresh ciphertexts.

Table 5. Selected experiments comparing (r)FIMD and FHE multiplication performance for basic RMFEs

P Set	k	r	Max # rFIMD Mult	Max # FHE Mult	rFIMD Mult (sec)	FHE Mult (sec)	Speedup v.s. k FHE Mult
3-H	28	1	3	5	3.59	0.0245	0.191×
		2	4	5	2.31	0.0355	0.431×
		4	4	5	0.900	0.0400	1.24×
		4*	4	5	0.0541	0.0389	20.1×
7-P	8	1	3	5	3.74	0.0242	0.0516×
		2	4	5	2.40	0.0359	0.120×
		4	4	5	1.16	0.0378	0.261×
		4*	4	5	0.0431	0.0404	11.0×
7-H	214	1	3	5	1.83	0.0238	2.79×
17-P	18	1	2	5	1.16	0.0245	0.380×
		2	4	5	1.12	0.0348	0.558×
		4	4	5	0.428	0.0381	1.61×
31-E	43	1	2	4	0.578	0.0236	1.76×
	43	2	3	4	0.382	0.0251	2.82×
	14	4*	3	4	0.0258	0.0263	14.3×

*No recodes were performed

Furthermore, our implementation of homomorphic linear map evaluation computes one monomial at a time and consumes it immediately; leaving $0.5k\times$ fewer ciphertexts (during peak operation) in memory compared to FHE. This can be adjusted to trade off improved FIMD multiplication speeds by computing several monomials at once using multiple cores. We observed that the recode operation roughly consumes the noise budget of one multiplication, implying that the standard RMFEs defined in Sect. 2.3 would yield about 1/2 the number of FHE multiplications. Overall, r-fold RMFEs have an important role in balancing FIMD multiplication performance and retaining a sizable proportion of multiplications for any given capacity.

5.2   Experimental Results for Composite RMFE

As Table 3 shows, it is very difficult to work with small primes as the extension degrees of their plaintext slot algebra are exceedingly high (>1000). Therefore, we investigated the effectiveness of composite RMFEs for FIMD in such cases. For our choice of $m = 8192$, it would not be meaningful to use composite RMFEs for $t = 17, 31$ and we focus on $t = 3, 7$ in this section. Due to the high degree, it is very expensive to generate the recode map π and so we focus on the three-stage recode process described in Sect. 3.3.

Just like the previous section, we consider the packing density of a composite RMFE instantiation with d/k, where $k = k_{in} \cdot k_{out}$. The degree $d' = [\mathbb{E}_1 : \mathbb{F}_q]$ is chosen as the next largest power-of-two from w_{in}. For larger r-fold values, we can adjust the intermediate degree accordingly. We identify a composite RMFE parameter set by a prefix C, e.g. C7-E, and present the parameters used in the experiments to follow in Table 6.

Table 6. Composite RMFE parameters

t	d	K	P set	Curve	$(k_{total}, d/k_{total})$
3	2048	Projective	C3-P	–	$(8, 256)$, $(16, 128)$, $(32, 64)$, $(64, 32)$, $(128, 16)$, $(256, 8)$, $(512, 4)$
		Elliptic	C3-E	$y^2 - x^3 - 2x - 1$	$(24, 85.3)$, $(48, 42.7)$, $(64, 32)$, $(96, 21.3)$, $(128, 16)$, $(192, 10.7)$, $(384, 5.33)$
		Hermitian	C3-H	$y^3 + y - x^4$	$(24, 85.3)$, $(44, 46.5)$, $(48, 42.7)$, $(88, 23.2)$, $(96, 21.3)$, $(108, 19.0)$, $(276, 11.6)$, $(216, 216)$
7	1024	Projective	C7-P	–	$(32, 32)$, $(64, 16)$, $(128, 8)$, $(256, 4)$
		Elliptic	C7-E	$y^2 - x^3 - 3$	$(26, 39.4)$, $(48, 21.3)$, $(52, 19.7)$, $(96, 10.7)$, $(104, 9.85)$, $(208, 4.92)$
		Hermitian	C7-H	$y^7 + y - x^8$	$(64, 16)$

In this second set of experiments, we compared the performance and noise impact of FIMD multiplication with composite RMFEs to FHE multiplication. Similar to the previous experiment, we repeatedly squared FIMD and FHE ciphertext until their capacities were exhausted and recorded the time taken as well as how many squarings could be done.

As illustrated in Table 12 in Appendix A, composite RMFEs are more expensive than basic RMFE and standard FHE. Composite RMFEs, however, offer a greater amortized speedup than basic RMFEs over standard FHE multiplications due to the increase in packing capacity (i.e. lower d/k_{total}). We make a few observations on some of the trends in the results, presenting them with tables featuring appropriate subcollections of Table 12 below.

Our first observation is that there is a slight advantage in choosing an intermediate field such that its extension degree $d' = [\mathbb{E}_1 : \mathbb{F}_q] > [\mathbb{E}_2 : \mathbb{E}_1]$. Considering the results presented in Table 7, we see that a larger d' value, over the same k_{total}, resulted in more than 10% savings in (r)FIMD multiplication time. This is supported by the fact that the 3-stage recode process requires evaluating two $\mathbb{E}_1$-linear maps in Steps 1 and 3 of FIMD.Recode3S and only one $\mathbb{F}_q$-linear map in Step 2. Using larger $\mathbb{E}_1$ reduces the computation time in Steps 1 and 3 while increasing the computation time in Step 2 and we expect that a ratio close to $2 : 1$ for $[\mathbb{E}_1 : \mathbb{F}_q] : [\mathbb{E}_2 : \mathbb{E}_1]$ would be best for three-stage recode performance in our implementation.

Table 7. Effect of intermediate field size on composite RMFEs

P set	k_{total}	$(k_{\text{in}}, r_{\text{in}})_q$	$(k_{\text{out}}, r_{\text{out}})_{q^{d'}}$	rFIMD Mult (sec)	Speedup v.s. FHE Mult
C7-P	64	$(4,2)_7$	$(16,2)_{7^{16}}$	0.4663130	3.396230
		$(8,2)_7$	$(8,2)_{7^{32}}$	0.4076150	3.734270

We consider the effect of fixing either r_{in} and r_{out}, while fixing d', on composite RMFEs. A subcollection of the experiments where we fixed r_{out} and d', while varying r_{in}, that supports our observation can be found in Table 8. We observe that similar to basic RMFEs, (r)FIMD multiplication timings generally decrease with larger r_{in}. In our implementation, after each (r)FIMD multiplication, the ciphertext capacity drops by similar amounts regardless of recoding type (outer or full). With larger r_{in}, some full recodes are replaced by outer recodes, thereby reducing the time taken. However, due to the smaller k_{total} that accompanies this increase, overall amortized speedup against FHE multiplication actually decreased.

Table 8. Effect of r_{in} for Composite RMFEs, Keeping r_{out} and d' fixed

P set	$(k_{\text{in}}, r_{\text{in}})_q$	$(k_{\text{out}}, r_{\text{out}})_{q^{d'}}$	k_{total}	Max rFIMD Mult	rFIMD Mult (sec)	Speedup v.s. k_{total} FHE Mult
C3-E	$(2,2)_3$	$(64,1)_{3^{16}}$	128	2	1.4284200	1.138740
	$(6,1)_3$	$(64,1)_{3^{16}}$	384	2	2.4344100	1.954400
C3-H	$(3,2)_3$	$(16,1)_{3^{64}}$	48	2	0.4838210	1.189630
	$(11,1)_3$	$(16,1)_{3^{64}}$	176	2	1.1126300	1.891190
	$(11,2)_3$	$(8,1)_{3^{128}}$	88	2	0.4557780	2.271160
	$(27,1)_3$	$(8,1)_{3^{128}}$	216	2	1.0570600	2.641760

On the other hand, Table 9 features a subcollection of experiments fixing r_{in} and d' while varying r_{out}. We generally get a decrease in (r)FIMD multiplication times as r_{out} increases. This is consistent with earlier trends seen in basic RMFEs and composite RMFEs with fixed r_{out}.

Looking at the parameter sets 7-H and C7-P, we also conclude that three-stage recode is more efficient than direct recode for composite RMFEs. Although we could not compute the direct recode map for C7-P, we approximate its performance by extending from 7-H in Table 10. The theoretical w_{total} for C7-P is $16 \cdot 63 = 1008$, which roughly corresponds to the number of monomials in

Table 9. Effect of r_{out} for Composite RMFEs, Keeping r_{in} and d' fixed

P set	$(k_{\mathsf{in}}, r_{\mathsf{in}})_q$	$(k_{\mathsf{out}}, r_{\mathsf{out}})_{q^{d'}}$	Max rFIMD Mult	rFIMD Mult (sec)	Speedup v.s. FHE Mult
C3-P	$(4,3)_3$	$(16,2)_{3^{32}}$	3	0.5992640	2.602520
	$(4,3)_3$	$(32,1)_{3^{32}}$	2	0.2796210	11.709300
C3-E	$(2,2)_3$	$(32,2)_{3^{16}}$	3	0.8984420	1.212720
	$(2,2)_3$	$(64,1)_{3^{16}}$	2	1.4284200	1.138740
	$(6,1)_3$	$(32,2)_{3^{16}}$	2	1.3726500	2.065650
	$(6,1)_3$	$(64,1)_{3^{16}}$	2	2.4344100	1.954400
C3-H	$(3,1)_3$	$(16,2)_{3^{32}}$	2	0.7272080	0.935283
	$(3,1)_3$	$(32,1)_{3^{32}}$	2	1.2001000	1.107840
	$(11,1)_3$	$(8,2)_{3^{64}}$	2	0.6007660	1.847700
	$(11,1)_3$	$(16,1)_{3^{64}}$	2	1.1126300	1.891190
	$(27,1)_3$	$(4,2)_{3^{128}}$	2	0.5804140	2.261520
	$(27,1)_3$	$(8,1)_{3^{128}}$	2	1.0570600	2.641760
C7-P	$(8,1)_7$	$(16,2)_{7^{16}}$	1	0.5346350	3.126460
	$(8,1)_7$	$(32,1)_{7^{16}}$	1	0.7542980	4.484790

Table 10. Comparing Three-Stage Recode and Direct Recode

P set	k	w	r	Max rFIMD Mult	rFIMD Mult (sec)	1 rFIMD Mult (sec)
7-H	214	511	1	3	1.83	0.610
C7-P	$8 \cdot 32 = 256$	$16 \cdot 63 = 1008$	$(1,1)$	1	0.754	0.754

its direct recode map. We extrapolate the FIMD multiplication timing for C7-P with direct recode by adjusting the multiplication time for 7-H by a factor of $1008/511 \approx 1.97$ as $w = 511$ for 7-H. 7-H took 1.83 s for 3 multiplications which give an average of 0.610 s per multiplication. One multiplication in C7-P took an average of 0.754 s which is almost twice as fast as the adjusted time of $0.610 \cdot 1.97 \approx 1.20$ s.

6   Conclusion and Future Work

In this work, we present a method that allows small primes to be used with the BGV and BFV FHE schemes without compromising on the amount of data that can be packed into a ciphertext. Specifically, we adapted reverse multiplication friendly embedding (RMFE) to FHE. To that end, we introduced an

FHE-specific technique to compute a linear transformation on encoded vectors for free during the recode process. Additionally, we proposed two extensions to RMFE targeting FHE plaintext spaces with high extension degree fields, namely r-fold RMFE and a three-stage recode process for composite RMFE. r-fold RMFE supports correct decoding of products of up to 2^r encoded vectors at the expense of requiring a higher field degree w for the embedding, capitalizing on the fact that the fixed d of FHE is often too high for small primes to fully utilize for standard RMFEs. Composite RMFEs, on the other hand, let us "split" a large extension field into a tower of smaller fields. This tower of fields is exploited in a three-stage recode, where each stage goes between pairs of fields that are smaller extensions and thereby use operations of lower complexity.

Our experiments show that FIMD multiplication is noisier than FHE multiplications, typically using the capacity of two FHE multiplications. On the other hand, FIMD multiplications have a lower amortized time and need only two ciphertexts to multiply more data. We also find that composite RMFEs, while applicable to high-degree (>1000) extension fields, are difficult to use in practice. Generating the direct recode map is very time-consuming but the three-stage recode process requires as much capacity as almost 3 FHE multiplications. That said, we approximated the performance of direct recode and found that three-stage recode does improve multiplication times, but significantly increased noise consumption. A middle ground needs to be found for using composite RMFEs, which would entail using "inner" and "outer" RMFEs with some amount of r and r'-fold respectively.

This paper represents the beginning of applying RMFE to FHE, and much work remains to be done. A first direction would be adapting the methods of [13] to FIMD and potentially improve downstream applications of FHE. Another important task is to adapt RMFE for Galois rings, which was explored by Cramer et al. [17] for MPC, to FHE. Crucially, the bootstrapping techniques of Gentry et al. [25], Halevi and Shoup [27] and Chen and Han [9] for BGV and BFV demand plaintext algebras that are Galois rings. Finally, developing RMFEs from other classes of algebraic function fields is necessary to better understand how best to perform homomorphic computation with high-degree extension fields.

A   Complete Experiment Results

A.1   Basic RMFE

Table 11. Comparison of FIMD and FHE multiplication performance for basic RMFEs

P Set	k	r	Max # rFIMD Mult	Max # FHE Mult	rFIMD Mult (sec)	FHE Mult (sec)	Speedup v.s. k FHE Mult
3-P	4	1	3	6	7.84	0.0170	0.00868×
		2	4	5	4.54	0.0337	0.0297×
		4	4	5	1.75	0.0369	0.0845×
		4*	4	5	0.0475	0.0370	3.12×
3-E	7	1	3	6	7.16	0.0180	0.0176×
		2	4	6	4.58	0.0276	0.0421×
		4	4	5	1.70	0.0478	0.197×
		4*	4	5	0.0469	0.0373	5.57×
3-H	28	1	3	5	3.59	0.0245	0.191×
		2	4	5	2.31	0.0355	0.431×
		4	4	5	0.900	0.0400	1.24×
		4*	4	5	0.0541	0.0389	20.1×
7-P	8	1	3	5	3.74	0.0242	0.0516×
		2	4	5	2.40	0.0359	0.120×
		4	4	5	1.16	0.0378	0.261×
		4*	4	5	0.0431	0.0404	11.0×
7-E	13	1	3	5	3.71	0.0244	0.0853×
		2	4	5	2.31	0.0359	0.202×
		4	4	5	0.931	0.0384	0.536×
		4*	4	5	0.0478	0.0404	20.1×
7-H	214	1	3	5	1.83	0.0238	2.79×
17-P	18	1	2	5	1.16	0.0245	0.380×
		2	4	5	1.12	0.0348	0.558×
		4	4	5	0.428	0.0381	1.61×
17-E	26	1	2	5	1.16	0.0252	0.565×
		2	4	5	0.961	0.0434	1.17×
		4	4	5	0.421	0.0389	2.40×
31-P	32	1	2	4	0.579	0.0231	1.28×
	32	2	3	4	0.384	0.0259	2.16×
	16	4	3	4	0.0262	0.0254	15.5×
31-E	43	1	2	4	0.578	0.0236	1.76×
	43	2	3	4	0.382	0.0251	2.82×
	14	4	3	4	0.0258	0.0263	14.3×

*No recodes were performed

A.2 Composite RMFE

Table 12. Comparison of FIMD and FHE multiplication performance for composite RMFEs, with the three-stage recode process of Sect. 3.3

P Set	$(k_{in}, r_{in})_q$	$(k_{out}, r_{out})_{q^{d'}}$	Max rFIMD Mult	Max FHE Mult	rFIMD Mult (sec)	FHE Mult (sec)	Speedup v.s. FHE Mult
C3-P	$(2,2,3)_3$	$(28,3,55)_{3^8}$	3	6	0.7074590	0.0174873	1.384240
	$(4,1,7)_3$	$(64,2,127)_{3^8}$	2	5	1.6718600	0.0129312	1.980060
	$(4,1,7)_3$	$(128,1,255)_{3^8}$	1	5	1.7500500	0.0124286	3.636160
	$(4,2,7)_3$	$(64,1,127)_{3^{16}}$	2	5	1.1955500	0.0126123	2.700630
	$(4,3,7)_3$	$(16,2,31)_{3^{32}}$	3	5	0.1890470	0.0350566	11.86810
	$(4,3,7)_3$	$(32,1,63)_{3^{32}}$	2	5	0.2501270	0.0248627	12.72320
	$(4,4,7)_3$	$(8,2,15)_{3^{64}}$	3	5	0.0966742	0.0340547	11.272400
	$(4,4,7)_3$	$(16,1,31)_{3^{64}}$	2	5	0.1409130	0.0233469	10.603700
	$(4,6,7)_3$	$(2,2,3)_{3^{256}}$	4	5	0.0882771	0.0365346	3.310900
	$(4,6,7)_3$	$(4,1,7)_{3^{256}}$	3	6	0.1059930	0.0175280	2.645920
C3-E	$(2,2,7)_3$	$(32,2,63)_{3^{16}}$	3	6	0.8984420	0.0170243	1.212720
	$(2,2,7)_3$	$(64,1,127)_{3^{16}}$	2	5	1.4284200	0.0127079	1.138740
	$(6,1,15)_3$	$(32,2,63)_{3^{16}}$	2	5	1.3726500	0.0147678	2.065650
	$(6,1,15)_3$	$(64,1,127)_{3^{16}}$	2	6	2.4344100	0.0123901	1.954400
	$(6,2,15)_3$	$(16,2,31)_{3^{32}}$	3	5	0.8059610	0.0338111	4.027320
	$(6,2,15)_3$	$(32,1,63)_{3^{32}}$	2	5	1.0435400	0.0129588	2.384290
	$(6,3,15)_3$	$(8,2,15)_{3^{64}}$	3	6	0.5079130	0.0164912	1.558490
	$(6,3,15)_3$	$(16,1,31)_{3^{64}}$	2	6	0.1632760	0.0168873	9.929100
	$(6,4,15)_3$	$(4,2,7)_{3^{128}}$	3	5	0.0692145	0.0332331	11.523500
	$(6,4,15)_3$	$(8,1,15)_{3^{128}}$	2	5	0.0893559	0.0248044	13.324400
C3-H	$(3,1,17)_3$	$(16,2,31)_{3^{32}}$	2	6	0.7272080	0.0141697	0.935283
	$(3,1,17)_3$	$(32,1,63)_{3^{32}}$	2	6	1.2001000	0.0138491	1.107840
	$(3,2,17)_3$	$(8,2,15)_{3^{64}}$	3	6	0.4109670	0.0276301	1.613570
	$(3,2,17)_3$	$(16,1,31)_{3^{64}}$	2	5	0.4838210	0.0119909	1.189630
	$(11,1,33)_3$	$(8,2,15)_{3^{64}}$	2	6	0.6007660	0.0126140	1.847700
	$(11,1,33)_3$	$(16,1,31)_{3^{64}}$	2	6	1.1126300	0.119557	1.891190
	$(11,2,33)_3$	$(4,2,7)_{3^{128}}$	3	6	0.3776890	0.0258704	3.013850
	$(11,2,33)_3$	$(8,1,15)_{3^{128}}$	2	5	0.4557780	0.117630	2.271160
	$(27,1,65)_3$	$(4,2,7)_{3^{128}}$	2	5	0.5804140	0.0121539	2.261520
	$(27,1,65)_3$	$(8,1,15)_{3^{128}}$	2	5	1.0570600	0.0129282	2.641760
C7-P	$(4,2,7)_7$	$(16,2,31)_{7^{16}}$	3	5	0.4663130	0.0247454	3.396230
	$(4,2,7)_7$	$(32,1,63)_{7^{16}}$	2	5	0.5249380	0.0129875	3.166860
	$(8,1,15)_7$	$(16,2,31)_{7^{16}}$	1	5	0.5346350	0.0130587	3.126460
	$(8,1,15)_7$	$(32,1,63)_{7^{16}}$	1	5	0.7542980	0.0132143	4.484790
	$(8,2,15)_7$	$(8,2,15)_{7^{32}}$	3	5	0.4076150	0.0237835	3.734270
	$(8,2,15)_7$	$(16,1,31)_{7^{32}}$	2	5	0.5056360	0.0129546	3.279410
	$(8,3,15)_7$	$(4,2,7)_{7^{64}}$	3	5	0.2652440	0.0235409	2.840060
	$(8,3,15)_7$	$(8,1,15)_{7^{64}}$	2	5	0.0908312	0.0126516	8.914370
C7-E	$(6,2,15)_7$	$(8,2,15)_{7^{32}}$	3	5	0.4115960	0.0246697	2.876960
	$(6,2,15)_7$	$(16,1,31)_{7^{32}}$	2	6	0.5140520	0.0129425	2.417030
	$(13,1,29)_7$	$(8,2,15)_{7^{32}}$	2	5	0.5879160	0.0124884	2.209150
	$(13,1,29)_7$	$(16,1,31)_{7^{32}}$	1	5	0.7183080	0.0126397	3.660070
	$(13,3,29)_7$	$(2,2,3)_{7^{128}}$	3	5	0.2556120	0.0242098	2.462540
	$(13,3,29)_7$	$(4,1,7)_{7^{128}}$	2	5	0.0623321	0.0255382	21.305100
C7-H	$(32,1,147)_7$	$(2,1,3)_{7^{256}}$	2	6	0.5453260	0.0135578	1.591150

References

1. Albrecht, M.R., Player, R., Scott, S.: On the concrete hardness of learning with errors. J. Math. Cryptol. **9**(3), 169–203 (2015)
2. Block, A.R., Maji, H.K., Nguyen, H.H.: Secure computation with constant communication overhead using multiplication embeddings. In: Chakraborty, D., Iwata, T. (eds.) INDOCRYPT 2018. LNCS, vol. 11356, pp. 375–398. Springer, Cham (2018). https://doi.org/10.1007/978-3-030-05378-9_20
3. Bootland, C., Castryck, W., Iliashenko, I., Vercauteren, F.: Efficiently processing complex-valued data in homomorphic encryption. J. Math. Cryptol. **14**(1), 55–65 (2020)
4. Brakerski, Z.: Fully homomorphic encryption without modulus switching from classical GapSVP. In: Safavi-Naini, R., Canetti, R. (eds.) CRYPTO 2012. LNCS, vol. 7417, pp. 868–886. Springer, Heidelberg (2012). https://doi.org/10.1007/978-3-642-32009-5_50
5. Brakerski, Z., Gentry, C., Vaikuntanathan, V.: (Leveled) fully homomorphic encryption without bootstrapping. In: ITCS 2012, pp. 309–325. ACM (2012)
6. Cascudo, I.: On asymptotically good strongly multiplicative linear secret sharing. Ph.D. thesis, Universidad de Oviedo, July 2010
7. Cascudo, I., Cramer, R., Xing, C., Yuan, C.: Amortized complexity of information-theoretically secure MPC revisited. In: Shacham, H., Boldyreva, A. (eds.) CRYPTO 2018, Part III. LNCS, vol. 10993, pp. 395–426. Springer, Cham (2018). https://doi.org/10.1007/978-3-319-96878-0_14
8. Castryck, W., Iliashenko, I., Vercauteren, F.: Homomorphic SIM^2D operations: single instruction much more data. In: Nielsen, J.B., Rijmen, V. (eds.) EUROCRYPT 2018, Part I. LNCS, vol. 10820, pp. 338–359. Springer, Cham (2018). https://doi.org/10.1007/978-3-319-78381-9_13
9. Chen, H., Han, K.: Homomorphic lower digits removal and improved FHE bootstrapping. In: Nielsen, J.B., Rijmen, V. (eds.) EUROCRYPT 2018, Part I. LNCS, vol. 10820, pp. 315–337. Springer, Cham (2018). https://doi.org/10.1007/978-3-319-78381-9_12
10. Chen, H., Laine, K., Player, R., Xia, Y.: High-precision arithmetic in homomorphic encryption. In: Smart, N.P. (ed.) CT-RSA 2018. LNCS, vol. 10808, pp. 116–136. Springer, Cham (2018). https://doi.org/10.1007/978-3-319-76953-0_7
11. Cheon, J.H., Kim, A., Kim, M., Song, Y.: Homomorphic encryption for arithmetic of approximate numbers. In: Takagi, T., Peyrin, T. (eds.) ASIACRYPT 2017, Part I. LNCS, vol. 10624, pp. 409–437. Springer, Cham (2017). https://doi.org/10.1007/978-3-319-70694-8_15
12. Cheon, J.H., Kim, D., Lee, K.: MHz2k: MPC from HE over $\mathbb{Z}_{2^k}$ with new packing, simpler reshare, and better ZKP. In: Malkin, T., Peikert, C. (eds.) CRYPTO 2021, Part II. LNCS, vol. 12826, pp. 426–456. Springer, Cham (2021). https://doi.org/10.1007/978-3-030-84245-1_15
13. Cheon, J.H., Kim, M., Kim, M.: Search-and-compute on encrypted data. In: Brenner, M., Christin, N., Johnson, B., Rohloff, K. (eds.) FC 2015. LNCS, vol. 8976, pp. 142–159. Springer, Heidelberg (2015). https://doi.org/10.1007/978-3-662-48051-9_11
14. Chillotti, I., Gama, N., Georgieva, M., Izabachène, M.: Faster fully homomorphic encryption: bootstrapping in less than 0.1 seconds. In: Cheon, J.H., Takagi, T. (eds.) ASIACRYPT 2016, Part I. LNCS, vol. 10031, pp. 3–33. Springer, Heidelberg (2016). https://doi.org/10.1007/978-3-662-53887-6_1

15. Chillotti, I., Gama, N., Georgieva, M., Izabachène, M.: Faster packed homomorphic operations and efficient circuit bootstrapping for TFHE. In: Takagi, T., Peyrin, T. (eds.) ASIACRYPT 2017, Part I. LNCS, vol. 10624, pp. 377–408. Springer, Cham (2017). https://doi.org/10.1007/978-3-319-70694-8_14

16. Costache, A., Smart, N.P., Vivek, S., Waller, A.: Fixed-point arithmetic in SHE schemes. In: Avanzi, R., Heys, H. (eds.) SAC 2016. LNCS, vol. 10532, pp. 401–422. Springer, Heidelberg (2016). https://doi.org/10.1007/978-3-319-69453-5

17. Cramer, R., Rambaud, M., Xing, C.: Asymptotically-good arithmetic secret sharing over $\mathbb{Z}/p^\ell\mathbb{Z}$ with strong multiplication and its applications to efficient MPC. In: Malkin, T., Peikert, C. (eds.) CRYPTO 2021, Part III. LNCS, vol. 12827, pp. 656–686. Springer, Cham (2021). https://doi.org/10.1007/978-3-030-84252-9_22

18. Dalskov, A., Lee, E., Soria-Vazquez, E.: Circuit amortization friendly encodingsand their application to statistically secure multiparty computation. In: Moriai, S., Wang, H. (eds.) ASIACRYPT 2020, Part III. LNCS, vol. 12493, pp. 213–243. Springer, Cham (2020). https://doi.org/10.1007/978-3-030-64840-4_8

19. Dowlin, N., Gilad-Bachrach, R., Laine, K., Lauter, K., Naehrig, M., Wernsing, J.: Manual for using homomorphic encryption for bioinformatics. Technical report. MSR-TR-2015-87, Microsoft Research, November 2015. https://www.microsoft.com/en-us/research/publication/manual-for-using-homomorphic-encryption-for-bioinformatics/, accessed 27 September 2021

20. Dowlin, N., Gilad-Bachrach, R., Laine, K., Lauter, K., Naehrig, M., Wernsing, J.: CryptoNets: applying neural networks to encrypted data with high throughput and accuracy. Technical report, Microsoft, February 2016

21. Ducas, L., Micciancio, D.: FHEW: bootstrapping homomorphic encryption in less than a second. In: Oswald, E., Fischlin, M. (eds.) EUROCRYPT 2015, Part I. LNCS, vol. 9056, pp. 617–640. Springer, Heidelberg (2015). https://doi.org/10.1007/978-3-662-46800-5_24

22. Fan, J., Vercauteren, F.: Somewhat practical fully homomorphic encryption. Cryptology ePrint Archive, Report 2012/144 (2012)

23. van der Geer, G., Howe, E.W., Lauter, K.E., Ritzenthaler, C.: Tables of curves with many points (2009). http://www.manypoints.org. Accessed 20 Sept 2021

24. Gentry, C.: Fully homomorphic encryption using ideal lattices. In: Proceedings of the Forty-First Annual ACM Symposium on Theory of Computing, STOC 2009, pp. 169–178. Association for Computing Machinery (2009)

25. Gentry, C., Halevi, S., Smart, N.P.: Fully homomorphic encryption with polylog overhead. In: Pointcheval, D., Johansson, T. (eds.) EUROCRYPT 2012. LNCS, vol. 7237, pp. 465–482. Springer, Heidelberg (2012). https://doi.org/10.1007/978-3-642-29011-4_28

26. Goss, D.: Basic Structures of Function Field Arithmetic. Springer, Berlin (1998)

27. Halevi, S., Shoup, V.: Bootstrapping for HElib. In: Oswald, E., Fischlin, M. (eds.) EUROCRYPT 2015, Part I. LNCS, vol. 9056, pp. 641–670. Springer, Heidelberg (2015). https://doi.org/10.1007/978-3-662-46800-5_25

28. Halevi, S., Shoup, V.: Faster homomorphic linear transformations in HElib. In: Shacham, H., Boldyreva, A. (eds.) CRYPTO 2018, Part I. LNCS, vol. 10991, pp. 93–120. Springer, Cham (2018). https://doi.org/10.1007/978-3-319-96884-1_4

29. Halevi, S., Shoup, V.: Design and implementation of HElib: a homomorphic encryption library. Cryptology ePrint Archive, Report 2020/1481 (2020). https://eprint.iacr.org/2020/1481

30. Iliashenko, I., Zucca, V.: Faster homomorphic comparison operations for BGV and BFV. PoPETs **2021**(3), 246–264 (2021). https://doi.org/10.2478/popets-2021-0046

31. Jäschke, A., Armknecht, F.: (Finite) field work: choosing the best encoding of numbers for FHE computation. In: Capkun, S., Chow, S.S.M. (eds.) CANS 2017. LNCS, vol. 11261, pp. 482–492. Springer, Cham (2018). https://doi.org/10.1007/978-3-030-02641-7_23

32. Kim, M., Lee, H.T., Ling, S., Wang, H.: On the efficiency of FHE-based private queries. IEEE Trans. Dependable Secure Comput. **15**(2), 357–363 (2018)

33. Lattigo v2.2.0. Online, July 2021. http://github.com/ldsec/lattigo. ePFL-LDS

34. Orsini, E., Smart, N.P., Vercauteren, F.: Overdrive2k: efficient secure MPC over $\mathbb{Z}_{2^k}$ from somewhat homomorphic encryption. In: Jarecki, S. (ed.) CT-RSA 2020. LNCS, vol. 12006, pp. 254–283. Springer, Cham (2020). https://doi.org/10.1007/978-3-030-40186-3_12

35. PALISADE lattice cryptography library (release 1.11.5), September 2021. https://gitlab.com/palisade/palisade-release. pALISADE Project

36. Microsoft SEAL (release 3.6), November 2020. https://github.com/Microsoft/SEAL. Microsoft Research, Redmond, WA

37. Smart, N.P., Vercauteren, F.: Fully homomorphic SIMD operations. Des. Codes Crypt. **71**(1), 57–81 (2014)

38. Stichtenoth, H.: Algebraic Function Fields and Codes, 2nd edn. Springer, New York (2008)

39. Tan, B.H.M., Lee, H.T., Wang, H., Ren, S.Q., Aung, K.M.M.: Efficient private comparison queries over encrypted databases using fully homomorphic encryption with finite fields. IEEE Trans. Depend. Secure Comput. **18**, 2861–2874 (2020)

Obfuscation

Cryptanalysis of Candidate Obfuscators for Affine Determinant Programs

Li Yao[1]([✉]), Yilei Chen[2,3], and Yu Yu[1,3]

[1] Shanghai Jiao Tong University, Shanghai 200240, China
pegasustianma@gmail.com
[2] Tsinghua University, Beijing 100084, China
[3] Shanghai Qi Zhi Institute, Shanghai 200232, China

Abstract. At ITCS 2020, Bartusek et al. proposed a candidate indistinguishability obfuscator ($i\mathcal{O}$) for affine determinant programs (ADPs). The candidate is special since it directly applies specific randomization techniques to the underlying ADP, without relying on the hardness of traditional cryptographic assumptions like discrete-log or learning with errors. It is relatively efficient compared to the rest of the $i\mathcal{O}$ candidates. However, the obfuscation scheme requires further cryptanalysis since it was not known to be based on any well-formed mathematical assumptions.

In this paper, we show cryptanalytic attacks on the $i\mathcal{O}$ candidate provided by Bartusek et al. Our attack exploits the weakness of one of the randomization steps in the candidate. The attack applies to a fairly general class of programs. At the end of the paper we discuss plausible countermeasures to defend against our attacks.

Keywords: Indistinguishability obfuscation · Cryptanalysis · Affine determinant program

1 Introduction

Indistinguishability Obfuscation ($i\mathcal{O}$) [7] is a probabilistic polynomial-time algorithm that transforms a circuit C into an obfuscated circuit $C' = i\mathcal{O}(C)$ while preserving the functionality. In addition, for any functionally equivalent circuits C_1 and C_2 of the same size, $i\mathcal{O}(C_1)$ and $i\mathcal{O}(C_2)$ are computationally indistinguishable. $i\mathcal{O}$ is a powerful cryptographic primitive with a wide variety of applications in cryptography and complexity theory. Indeed indistinguishability obfuscation, when combined with a minimal cryptographic primitive (one-way functions), is generally regarded as "crypto complete", implying almost all cryptographic applications currently known (e.g., [10,17,32,38]).

Despite the remarkable success in basing cryptographic applications on $i\mathcal{O}$, constructing efficient and provably secure $i\mathcal{O}$ remains a long-standing open problem in cryptography. While still far from the ultimate goal, many $i\mathcal{O}$ candidates have been provided in the past eight years. They can be generally classified as follows:

© International Association for Cryptologic Research 2022
O. Dunkelman and S. Dziembowski (Eds.): EUROCRYPT 2022, LNCS 13275, pp. 645–669, 2022.
https://doi.org/10.1007/978-3-031-06944-4_22

CANDIDATES FROM MULTILINEAR MAPS. The initial $i\mathcal{O}$ candidates are built based on multilinear maps (a.k.a. graded encodings) [18,20,24]. Starting from the first $i\mathcal{O}$ candidate of Garg et al. [21], these candidates have gone through several rounds of break-and-repair. (see, e.g. [6,14–16,26,37]). To date, some variants of the original candidate of Garg et al. [21] remain secure, but no security proofs were known for any of those variants without using strong idealized models.

CANDIDATES FROM SUCCINCT FUNCTIONAL ENCRYPTION. A remarkable line of works has been dedicated to building $i\mathcal{O}$ from succinct functional encryption schemes, which can then be based on well-founded assumptions, including LPN, DLIN in pairing and PRG in NC^0 [3,4,11,22,29–31,33–36]. They build $i\mathcal{O}$ via a series of reductions and take advantage of many cryptographic primitives, including attribute-based encryption, fully homomorphic encryption, FE for quadratic functions, homomorphic secret-sharing, universal circuits, etc. The downside of those candidates is that the overall constructions are complicated and far from efficient.

CANDIDATES BASED ON NON-STANDARD LATTICE ASSUMPTIONS. We also have lattice-based candidates without using pairing or multilinear maps. [12,13,23] construct candidates based on a strong circular-security assumption. [39] shows that oblivious LWE sampling implies $i\mathcal{O}$ and gives a candidate based on a circularity-like conjecture. Unfortunately, [25] provides counterexamples to both assumptions. Apart from the circularity-based candidates, some works try to base $i\mathcal{O}$ on Noisy Linear FE [1,2]. Recent work [19] improves on [39] by basing iO on succinct LWE sampling, a weaker notion. It presents a candidate whose security is related to the hardness of solving systems of polynomial equations. The security of all these candidates relies on non-standard assumptions.

CANDIDATE FOR AFFINE DETERMINANT PROGRAM. Finally, a special candidate obfuscator, which is the focus of this work, is provided by Bartusek et al. [8] for obfuscating affine determinant programs. An affine determinant program (ADP): $\{0,1\}^n \to \{0,1\}$ is specified by a tuple of square matrices $(\mathbf{A}, \mathbf{B}_1, \mathbf{B}_2, \ldots, \mathbf{B}_n)$ over $\mathbb{F}_q$ and a function $\mathsf{Eval} : \mathbb{F}_q \to \{0,1\}$. It evaluates on input $\mathbf{x} \in \{0,1\}^n$ and produces an output $\mathsf{Eval}(\det(\mathbf{A} + \sum_{i\in[n]} x_i\mathbf{B}_i))$. Non-uniform log-space computations (denoted by L/poly) can be transformed into polynomial-size ADPs. Since $\mathsf{NC}^1 \subseteq \mathsf{L/poly}$, an obfuscator for such ADPs can serve as an obfuscator for NC^1 circuits, which implies general purpose $i\mathcal{O}$ additionally assuming the existence of fully homomorphic encryption [21].

The obfuscation candidate based on ADP is unique since it is the only unbroken candidate to date that does not rely on any traditional cryptographic assumptions like discrete-log or LWE. The candidate is also relatively simple to describe. In addition, the current quantum techniques do not seem to show special advantage in breaking the ADP-based candidate. So if LWE is broken by a quantum algorithm in future, the obfuscation candidate for ADP might be the only living $i\mathcal{O}$ candidate against quantum computers.

The idea of using the ADP program model for obfuscation was also used in the earlier paper of Bartusek et al. [9] for obfuscating conjunctions, where they can achieve provable security based on standard cryptographic assumptions. However, obfuscating a general program requires significantly different ideas. Indeed, the lack of security reduction from any well-formed assumption also means that the security of the candidate in [8] requires more investigation.

1.1   Main Result

In this work, we show cryptanalytic attacks against the $i\mathcal{O}$ candidate of Bartusek et al. [8]. Our attack can be seen as a variant of the "mod 4 attack" mentioned in [8, Section 9.3]. The "mod 4 attack" was originally discussed in [8, Section 9.3] as an attack for breaking a simpler version of the obfuscation scheme. It was also the motivation of adding a layer of randomization called Random Local Substitutions (RLS). However, we show that even with the RLS they provide, we can still manipulate the "mod 4 attack" in some other way to break the $i\mathcal{O}$ candidate.

To explain what kind of programs our attack applies to, let us describe the necessary and sufficient conditions separately. The *necessary* condition of the programs where our attack applies is that we can efficiently find four inputs of the form $\mathbf{x}_1 = \mathtt{a0b0c}, \mathbf{x}_2 = \mathtt{a1b0c}, \mathbf{x}_3 = \mathtt{a0b1c}, \mathbf{x}_4 = \mathtt{a1b1c}$ s.t. the program outputs the same value on these inputs, where $\mathbf{a}, \mathbf{b}, \mathbf{c}$ are some fixed strings of arbitrary length. Our attack will exactly run on those four inputs. The *sufficient* conditions are more complex to describe in their general forms. They deal with the minors of the matrices used in the ADPs to be obfuscated. Here let us mention a simple sufficient condition, that is, if two of the matrices among the n are all zero. Namely, for $1 \leq i < j \leq n$, $\mathbf{B}_i = \mathbf{B}_j = \mathbf{0}$. If so then we can distinguish the obfuscated version of such programs with those of functionally equivalent ADPs with $\mathbf{B}_i \neq \mathbf{0}$ or $\mathbf{B}_j \neq \mathbf{0}$. The general sufficient conditions relax the constraint such that we do not require the underlying branching program to contain all-zero matrices. This makes our attack work for a fairly general class of programs. However, as mentioned, the precise conditions on which our attack applies is a bit complicated. We refer readers to Sect. 5.3 for details.

At the end of the paper we provide some revisions of the RLS randomization which plausibly defends the obfuscation scheme against our attack. Let us also remark that the witness encryption candidate in [8] is constructed via a somewhat different methodology, to which our attack does not apply.

1.2   Our Ideas in a Nutshell

To obfuscate an ADP, Bartusek et al. [8] sample independent even noises and add them to each entry of $\{\mathbf{A}, \mathbf{B}_{i \in [n]}\}$. However, they also notice that the adversary can extract the parities of the noises by computing the determinant first and then computing the result mod 4 after adding noises. The coefficients of the parities are minors of $\mathbf{A} + \sum_{i \in [n]} x_i \mathbf{B}$, which are known to the adversary.

To defend against the attack, they introduce Random Local Substitutions, aiming to substitute the ADP P chosen by the adversary with another ADP $P' = \mathsf{RLS}(P)$, while preserving the functionality.

The intuition that how the RLS comes to rescue is that by applying RLS to P the adversary cannot learn minors of $\mathbf{A}' + \sum_{i \in [n]} x_i \mathbf{B}'_i$, where $\{\mathbf{A}', \mathbf{B}'_{i \in [n]}\}$ are matrices of $\mathsf{RLS}(P)$. However, as we will show in this paper, it is not necessary to learn the coefficients of the parities to carry out the attack. We sketch the idea of our attack below.

Our attack starts from a well-crafted kind of ADP. Consider the simplest case where $n = 2$. We observe that if for $i \in \{1, 2\}$, $\mathbf{B}_i$ of P is a zero matrix, then $\mathbf{B}'_i$ of $P' = \mathsf{RLS}(P)$ will also be a zero matrix. Therefore, if for all $i, \mathbf{B}_i$ is a zero matrix, then for all $\mathbf{x}$, the minors of $\mathbf{A}' + \sum_{i \in [n]} x_i \mathbf{B}'_i$ remain the same. Therefore, we can add four parity equations together to cancel out the unknown coefficients (the equal minors), i.e., $\forall x : 4x \equiv 0 \mod 4$. We refer to Sect. 5.1 for how we cancel out the coefficients and other details about the attack.

We further generalize the above attack by relaxing the limitation that $\mathbf{B}_i$ of P are all zero matrices. By comparing the minors before and after the RLS, we notice that the RLS may not bring much uncertainty to the minors of $\mathbf{A}' + \sum_{i \in [n]} x_i \mathbf{B}'_i$, especially when $\mathbf{B}_{i \in [n]}$ are sparse matrices. In Sect. 5.2, we figure out the exact condition on which the minors of $\mathbf{A}' + \sum_{i \in [n]} x_i \mathbf{B}'_i$ remain the same for different $\mathbf{x}$, regardless of the randomness injected by the RLS. Thus, our attack is similarly applicable to all ADPs satisfying the condition.

2   Preliminaries

Let $\mathbb{Z}, \mathbb{N}^+$ be the set of integers and positive integers respectively. For $n \in \mathbb{N}^+$, we let $[n]$ denote the set $\{1, \ldots, n\}$. For $p \in \mathbb{N}^+$, We denote $\mathbb{Z}/p\mathbb{Z}$ by $\mathbb{Z}_p$ and denote the finite field of prime order p by $\mathbb{F}_p$. A vector $\mathbf{v} \in \mathbb{F}_p^n$ (represented in column form by default) is written as a bold lower-case letter and we denote its i-th element by $v_i \in \mathbb{F}_p$. A matrix $\mathbf{A} \in \mathbb{F}_p^{n \times m}$ is written as a bold capital letter and we denote the entry at position (i, j) by $(\mathbf{A})_{i,j}$. For any set of matrices $\mathbf{A}_1, \ldots, \mathbf{A}_n$ of potentially varying dimensions, let $\mathsf{diag}(\mathbf{A}_1, \ldots, \mathbf{A}_n)$ be the block diagonal matrix with the $\mathbf{A}_i$ on the diagonal, and zeros elsewhere.

We use the usual Landau notations. A function $f(\cdot)$ is said to be negligible if $f(n) = n^{-\omega(1)}$ and we denote it by $f(n) = \mathsf{negl}(n)$. We write $D_1 \approx_C D_2$ if no computationally-bounded adversary can distinguish between D_1 and D_2 except with advantage negligible in the security parameter.

2.1   Indistinguishability Obfuscation

Definition 1 (Indistinguishability Obfuscator [7]). *A uniform PPT machine $i\mathcal{O}$ is an indistinguishability obfuscator for a circuit class $\{\mathcal{C}_\lambda\}$ if the following conditions are satisfied:*

- *(Strong Functionality Preservation) For all security parameters $\lambda \in \mathbb{N}^+$, for all $C \in \mathcal{C}_\lambda$,*

$$\Pr_{C' \leftarrow i\mathcal{O}(\lambda, C)} [\forall x, C'(x) = C(x)] \geq 1 - \text{negl}(\lambda).$$

- *For any non-uniform PPT distinguisher D, there exists a negligible function α such that the following holds: for all $\lambda \in \mathbb{N}^+$, for all pairs of circuits $C_0, C_1 \in \mathcal{C}_\lambda$, we have that if $C_0(x) = C_1(x)$ for all input x and $|C_0| = |C_1|$ (where $|C|$ denotes the size of a circuit), then*

$$|\Pr\left[D\left(i\mathcal{O}\left(\lambda, C_0\right)\right) = 1\right] - \Pr\left[D\left(i\mathcal{O}\left(\lambda, C_1\right)\right) = 1\right]| \leq \alpha(\lambda).$$

3 Affine Determinant Programs

In this section we describe a way of representing L/poly computations as polynomial-size ADPs [5,28]. We start with the definitions of L/poly computations, Branching Programs (BPs) and ADPs, followed by the connections among them.

Definition 2 (Non-uniform Logarithmic-space Turing Machines). *A logarithmic-space Turing machine with polynomial-sized advice is a logarithmic-space Turing machine M^* (i.e. a machine using a logarithmic amount of writable memory space) as well as an infinite collection of advice strings $\{a_n\}_{n \in \mathbb{N}}$ of polynomial size (i.e. $|a_n| = O(n^c)$ for some c). (M^*, a_n) decides a language $L^* \subset \{0, 1\}^*$ if*

$$\forall x \in \{0, 1\}^*, M^*(x, a_{|x|}) = \chi_{L^*}(x)$$

(where $\chi_{L^*}(x)$ is the indicator function for L^*, i.e. $\chi_{L^*}(x) = 1$ if and only if $x \in L^*$). The set of languages decided by of logarithmic-space Turing machines with polynomial-sized advice is denoted by L/poly; we refer to (M^*, a_n) as an L/poly machine.

Definition 3 (Branching Programs). *A branching program is defined by a directed acyclic graph $G(V, E)$, two special vertices $s, t \in V$, and a labeling function ϕ assigning to each edge in E a literal (i.e., x_i or $\overline{x}_i$) or the constant 1. Its size is defined as $|V| - 1$. Each input assignment $\mathbf{x} = (x_1, \ldots, x_n)$ naturally induces an unlabeled subgraph $G_\mathbf{x}$, whose edges include every $e \in E$ such that $\phi(e)$ is satisfied by $\mathbf{x}$. An accepting path on input x is a directed $s - t$ path in the graph $G_\mathbf{x}$. BP is said to be deterministic if for every $\mathbf{x}$, the out-degree of every vertex in $G_\mathbf{x}$ is at most 1. Thus, an deterministic branching program computes the function $f : \{0, 1\}^n \rightarrow \{0, 1\}$, such that $f(\mathbf{x}) = 1$ if and only if the number of accepting paths on $\mathbf{x}$ is 1.*

Definition 4 (Affine Determinant Programs). *An affine determinant program is parameterized by an input length n, a width ℓ, and a finite field $\mathbb{F}_p$. It is comprised of an affine function $L : \{0, 1\}^n \rightarrow \mathbb{F}_p^{\ell \times \ell}$ along with an evaluation function Eval : $\mathbb{F}_p \rightarrow \{0, 1\}$. The affine function L is specified by an $(n+1)-$tuple of $\ell \times \ell$ matrices $L = (\mathbf{A}, \mathbf{B}_1, \ldots, \mathbf{B}_n)$ over $\mathbb{F}_p$ so that $L(\mathbf{x}) := \mathbf{A} + \sum_{i \in [n]} x_i \mathbf{B}_i.$*

On input $\mathbf{x} \in \{0,1\}^n$, $\mathsf{ADP}_{L,\mathsf{Eval}}(\mathbf{x})$ *is computed as* $\mathsf{Eval}(\det(L(\mathbf{x})))$. *Typically, we use one of the following* Eval *functions.*

- $\mathsf{Eval}_{=0}(y) \stackrel{\text{def}}{=} \begin{cases} 1, & y = 0 \\ 0, & y \neq 0 \end{cases}$.

- $\mathsf{Eval}_{\neq 0}(y) \stackrel{\text{def}}{=} \begin{cases} 1, & y \neq 0 \\ 0, & y = 0 \end{cases}$.

- $\mathsf{Eval}_{\mathsf{parity}}(y) \stackrel{\text{def}}{=} y \bmod 2$.

Transformation Between L/poly *Computations and Deterministic* $\mathsf{BP}s$. Suppose we have an $s(n)$-space bounded non-uniform deterministic Turing machine, its configuration graph on an input of length n is bounded by $2^{O(s^*(n))}$, where $s^*(n) = \max\{s(n), \lceil \log(n) \rceil, \lceil \log(a(n)) \rceil\}$ and $a(n)$ is the length of the advice. Then we can construct a deterministic branching program G^n to simulate the Turing machine. G^n has a vertex for each of the configurations that is reachable from the start configuration. The edge $e_{j,k}$ is labeled by x_i if configuration j can reach configuration k in one step when $x_i = 1$. The label $\bar{x}_i$ is defined analogously. The label 1 means that configuration j can always reach configuration k in one step. G^n is acyclic as we can require the Turing machine to count the steps taken and record it on the work tape. It is easy to see that $G^n_{\mathbf{x}}$ has a $s-t$ path if and only if the Turing machine accepts on input $\mathbf{x}$. On the other hand, after putting description of a deterministic branching program on the advice tape, finding a $s-t$ path in the BP can be computed in log-space since the out degree of every vertex is at most 1 for any $\mathbf{x}$. Due to these facts, we can conclude that polynomial-size deterministic BPs equal to L/poly computations.

Encoding $\mathsf{BP}s$ *as* $\mathsf{ADP}s$. Suppose there is a branching program of size ℓ computing a Boolean function f, where each input induces at most one accepting path[1]. We can represent the branching program as an adjacency matrix of size $(\ell + 1) \times (\ell + 1)$. Each element in the matrix is 0, 1 or some variable (x_i or $\bar{x}_i$). We denote the adjacency matrix by $M(\mathbf{x})$. $M(\mathbf{x})$ is 0 below the main diagonal (including main diagonal) since a branching program can be view as a DAG. Then we modify the main diagonal elements of $M(\mathbf{x})$ to -1 and delete the leftmost column and lowermost row. We denote the resulting $\ell \times \ell$ matrix by $L(\mathbf{x})$. For all $\mathbf{x} \in \{0,1\}^n$, We have $\det(L(\mathbf{x})) = f(\mathbf{x})$. Then we set $\mathbf{A} = L(\mathbf{0})$, $\mathbf{B}_i = L(\mathbf{1}_i) - \mathbf{A}$, where $\mathbf{0}$ is the input whose bits are all 0 and $\mathbf{1}_i$ is the input whose i's bit is 1 and 0 everywhere else. For all $\mathbf{x} \in \{0,1\}^n$, We have $L(\mathbf{x}) = \mathbf{A} + \sum_{i \in [n]} x_i \mathbf{B}_i$. This immediately gives us an ADP for the branching program. The evaluation function is $\mathsf{Eval}_{\neq 0}$. We use the following theorem to show the correctness of the encoding. For more details we refer readers to [27].

---

[1] Here, we actually define a new class of branching programs that can be seen as a generalization of the deterministic BPs whose out degree of every vertex is not limited by 1 for all $\mathbf{x}$. This new notion can be helpful when obfuscating ADPs.

Theorem 1 (Imported Theorem [27]). *Let $\mathbf{A}_G$ be the $a \times a$ adjacency matrix of a DAG G (over $GF(p)$). For any two vertices s, t in G, let $n_{s,t}^p$ denote the number of distinct s-t paths in G modulo p, and for any $a \times a$ matrix $\mathbf{A}$, let $\mathbf{A}_{(i,j)}$ denote the $(a-1) \times (a-1)$ matrix obtained by removing the ith row and the jth column from $\mathbf{A}$. Then for any two vertices s, t the following assertion hold:*

$$n_{s,t}^p = \det{}_p(\mathbf{I} - \mathbf{A}_G)^{-1} \det{}_p((\mathbf{I} - \mathbf{A}_G)_{(t,s)}).$$

The entries in the main diagonal of $(\mathbf{I} - \mathbf{A}_G)$ are all 1s. Therefore, $\det_p(\mathbf{I} - \mathbf{A}_G)^{-1} = 1$.

Example. We give a small example for a BP/ADP for a 3-bit function that computes $x_1 \vee x_3 = 1$ (see Fig. 1(a)). First, we delete the rejection configuration and related edges. Then we apply topological sorting on the remaining 4 configurations. If there are two edges between any two configurations, we replace them by an edge labeled by "1". Now we can obtain a branching program corresponding to the Turing machine (see Fig. 1(b)). The $M(\mathbf{x}), L(\mathbf{x})$ of the branching program is

$$M(\mathbf{x}) = \begin{bmatrix} 0 & x_1 & 1-x_1 & 0 \\ 0 & 0 & 0 & 1 \\ 0 & 0 & 0 & x_3 \\ 0 & 0 & 0 & 0 \end{bmatrix}, L(\mathbf{x}) = \begin{bmatrix} x_1 & 1-x_1 & 0 \\ -1 & 0 & 1 \\ 0 & -1 & x_3 \end{bmatrix}.$$

and the resulting ADP is

$$\mathbf{A} = \begin{bmatrix} 0 & 1 & 0 \\ -1 & 0 & 1 \\ 0 & -1 & 0 \end{bmatrix}, \mathbf{B}_1 = \begin{bmatrix} 1 & -1 & 0 \\ 0 & 0 & 0 \\ 0 & 0 & 0 \end{bmatrix}, \mathbf{B}_2 = \begin{bmatrix} 0 & 0 & 0 \\ 0 & 0 & 0 \\ 0 & 0 & 0 \end{bmatrix}, \mathbf{B}_3 = \begin{bmatrix} 0 & 0 & 0 \\ 0 & 0 & 0 \\ 0 & 0 & 1 \end{bmatrix}.$$

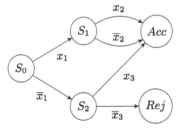
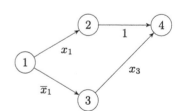

(a) configuration transition diagram of an L/poly Turing machine (input length is 3)

(b) a branching program

Fig. 1. A transformation between L/poly computations and BPs

Other examples can be found in, e.g., [8, Section 4].

4   The BIJMSZ $i\mathcal{O}$ Scheme

In this section we recall the $i\mathcal{O}$ scheme proposed by Bartusek, Ishai, Jain, Ma, Sahai, and Zhandry [8]. The scheme works by additionally applying the following four transformations in sequence to an ADP. These transformations are functionality-preserving. Readers who are familiar with the scheme can safely skip this section. Looking ahead, our attack will exploit the weakness of Transformation 1 and 2.

4.1   Transformation 1: Random Local Substitutions

The goal of Random Local Substitutions (RLS) is to inject entropy into the branching program by adding some vertices and modifying edges in a somewhat random way[2]. We denote the resulting BP by $M'(\mathbf{x})$. Specifically, we can add a vertex $v_{j,k}$ for each pair (v_j, v_k). For convenience, we only consider the 2×2 submatrices of $M'(\mathbf{x})$ with row indexed by v_j, $v_{j,k}$ and column indexed by $v_{j,k}$, v_k. Denote this matrix by $M'^{(j,k)}(\mathbf{x})$. If the edge between v_j, v_k is labeled by 1, then $M'^{(j,k)}(\mathbf{x})$ has following 4 choices (the last one is special as it is the only one which can change the label between v_j and v_k, we will analyze it separately in our attack):

$$\begin{bmatrix} 0 & 1 \\ 0 & 0 \end{bmatrix}, \begin{bmatrix} 1 & 1 \\ 0 & 0 \end{bmatrix}, \begin{bmatrix} 0 & 1 \\ 0 & 1 \end{bmatrix}, \begin{bmatrix} 1 & 0 \\ 0 & 1 \end{bmatrix}.$$

If there is no edge between v_j, v_k, then $M'^{(j,k)}(\mathbf{x})$ has following 3 choices:

$$\begin{bmatrix} 0 & 0 \\ 0 & 0 \end{bmatrix}, \begin{bmatrix} 1 & 0 \\ 0 & 0 \end{bmatrix}, \begin{bmatrix} 0 & 0 \\ 0 & 1 \end{bmatrix}.$$

If the edge between v_j, v_k is labeled by x_i, then $M'^{(j,k)}(\mathbf{x})$ has following 12 choices:

$$\begin{bmatrix} 0 & x_i \\ 0 & 0 \end{bmatrix}, \begin{bmatrix} 0 & x_i \\ 0 & 1 \end{bmatrix}, \begin{bmatrix} 0 & x_i \\ 0 & x_i \end{bmatrix}, \begin{bmatrix} 0 & x_i \\ 0 & \overline{x}_i \end{bmatrix}, \begin{bmatrix} 1 & x_i \\ 0 & 0 \end{bmatrix}, \begin{bmatrix} 1 & 0 \\ 0 & x_i \end{bmatrix},$$

$$\begin{bmatrix} x_i & x_i \\ 0 & 0 \end{bmatrix}, \begin{bmatrix} x_i & x_i \\ 0 & \overline{x}_i \end{bmatrix}, \begin{bmatrix} x_i & 0 \\ 0 & x_i \end{bmatrix}, \begin{bmatrix} x_i & 0 \\ 0 & 1 \end{bmatrix}, \begin{bmatrix} \overline{x}_i & x_i \\ 0 & 0 \end{bmatrix}, \begin{bmatrix} \overline{x}_i & x_i \\ 0 & x_i \end{bmatrix}.$$

If the edge between v_j, v_k is labeled by $\overline{x}_i$, then $M'^{(j,k)}(\mathbf{x})$ also has 12 choices, which is analogous to labeled by x_i. We can swap x_i and $\overline{x}_i$ in above matrices to obtain the 12 choices.

One can easily check that the above transformation does not change the amount of path from v_j to v_k. Namely, it is functionality-preserving[3].

---

[2] The transformation is actually applied to an ADP. We describe it by BP because BP is a DAG and thus can be better understood. You can understand the RLS here in this way: it decodes the input ADP back to a BP first, then it does the transformation and encodes the resulting BP as the final ADP.

[3] There are many potential ways of applying RLS. The RLS transformation here is the candidate given in [8].

Example. We start from the example branching program in Sect. 3 and add a intermediate vertex for every two vertices (see Fig. 2(a)). Then we reassign the labels of the edges as described above. We show a possible result of RLS in Fig. 2(b). The ADP corresponding to the figure is

$$
\mathbf{A}' = \begin{bmatrix}
0 & 1 & 1 & 0 & 0 & 0 & 0 & 0 & 0 \\
-1 & 0 & 0 & 1 & 0 & 0 & 0 & 0 & 0 \\
0 & -1 & 0 & 0 & 0 & 0 & 1 & 0 & 0 \\
0 & 0 & -1 & 0 & 0 & 0 & 0 & 0 & 0 \\
0 & 0 & 0 & -1 & 0 & 1 & 0 & 0 & 0 \\
0 & 0 & 0 & 0 & -1 & 0 & 1 & 0 & 0 \\
0 & 0 & 0 & 0 & 0 & -1 & 0 & 0 & 1 \\
0 & 0 & 0 & 0 & 0 & 0 & -1 & 0 & 0 \\
0 & 0 & 0 & 0 & 0 & 0 & 0 & -1 & 1
\end{bmatrix}, \mathbf{B}'_1 = \begin{bmatrix}
0 & 0 & 0 & 1 & 0 & 0 & 0 & 0 & 0 \\
0 & 0 & 0 & -1 & 0 & 0 & 0 & 0 & 0 \\
0 & 0 & 0 & 0 & 0 & 0 & -1 & 0 & 0 \\
0 & 0 & 0 & 0 & 0 & 0 & 0 & 0 & 0 \\
0 & 0 & 0 & 0 & 0 & 0 & 0 & 0 & 0 \\
0 & 0 & 0 & 0 & 0 & 0 & 0 & 0 & 0 \\
0 & 0 & 0 & 0 & 0 & 0 & 0 & 0 & 0 \\
0 & 0 & 0 & 0 & 0 & 0 & 0 & 0 & 0 \\
0 & 0 & 0 & 0 & 0 & 0 & 0 & 0 & 0
\end{bmatrix},
$$

$$
\mathbf{B}'_2 = \begin{bmatrix}
0 & 0 & 0 & 0 & 0 & 0 & 0 & 0 & 0 \\
0 & 0 & 0 & 0 & 0 & 0 & 0 & 0 & 0 \\
0 & 0 & 0 & 0 & 0 & 0 & 0 & 0 & 0 \\
0 & 0 & 0 & 0 & 0 & 0 & 0 & 0 & 0 \\
0 & 0 & 0 & 0 & 0 & 0 & 0 & 0 & 0 \\
0 & 0 & 0 & 0 & 0 & 0 & 0 & 0 & 0 \\
0 & 0 & 0 & 0 & 0 & 0 & 0 & 0 & 0 \\
0 & 0 & 0 & 0 & 0 & 0 & 0 & 0 & 0 \\
0 & 0 & 0 & 0 & 0 & 0 & 0 & 0 & 0
\end{bmatrix}, \mathbf{B}'_3 = \begin{bmatrix}
0 & 0 & 0 & 0 & 0 & 0 & 0 & 0 & 0 \\
0 & 0 & 0 & 0 & 0 & 0 & 0 & 0 & 0 \\
0 & 0 & 0 & 0 & 0 & 0 & 0 & 0 & 0 \\
0 & 0 & 0 & 0 & 0 & 0 & 0 & 0 & 0 \\
0 & 0 & 0 & 0 & 0 & 0 & 0 & 0 & 0 \\
0 & 0 & 0 & 0 & 0 & 0 & 0 & 0 & 0 \\
0 & 0 & 0 & 0 & 0 & 0 & 0 & 0 & 0 \\
0 & 0 & 0 & 0 & 0 & 0 & 0 & 1 & 1 \\
0 & 0 & 0 & 0 & 0 & 0 & 0 & 0 & -1
\end{bmatrix}.
$$

(vertices are sorted in lexicographical order, i.e. $v_1, v_{1,2}, v_{1,3}, v_{1,4}, v_2, v_{2,3}, \cdots$).

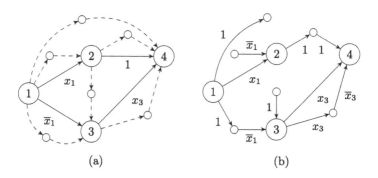

(a)   (b)

Fig. 2. Random local substitutions

4.2   Transformation 2: Small Even-Valued Noise

This transformation takes advantage of the fact that for any polynomial $g : \mathbb{Z}^n \to \mathbb{Z}$, and for any $\{e_i \in \mathbb{Z}\}_{i \in [n]}$, it holds that

$$
g(x_1, x_2, \ldots, x_n) \equiv g(x_1 + 2e_1, x_2 + 2e_2, \ldots, x_n + 2e_n) \mod 2
$$

Therefore, when taking an ADP as input, we can add independent random even numbers as the noise term to each entry of $\{\mathbf{A}, \{\mathbf{B}_i\}_{i\in[n]}\}$. We denote the resulting matrices by $\{\mathbf{A}+2\mathbf{E}_0, \{\mathbf{B}_i+2\mathbf{E}_i\}_{i\in[n]}\}$. The evaluation function also needs to change from $\mathsf{Eval}_{\neq 0}$ to $\mathsf{Eval}_{\mathsf{parity}}$.

The bound for the error terms and the modulus p must be set carefully to guarantee correctness and security. In particular, the noise term are relatively small compared to the modulus p (although both are super-polynomial) so that for any $y_1, ..., y_n \in \{0, 1\}$:

$$\left(\det \left((\mathbf{A}+2\mathbf{E}_0) + \sum_{i\in[n]} y_i(\mathbf{B}_i + 2\mathbf{E}_i)\right) \bmod p \right) \bmod 2 = \det(\mathbf{A} + \sum_{i\in[n]} y_i \mathbf{B}_i) \bmod 2$$

In other words, the noise term in an honest evaluation does not wrap around mod p.

4.3   Transformation 3: Block-Diagonal Matrices

Ideally, when obfuscating an ADP, we need to force the adversary to evaluate the program in the way we want. This goal is achieved by adding some randomness in the matrices. Only an honest evaluation can cancel out the randomness and reveal the output. Other combination of the matrices will leave the randomness intact, hiding all useful information of the origin ADP. This can be accomplished by sampling $2n$ random matrices $\{\mathbf{G}_i, \mathbf{H}_i\}_{i\in[n]}$ of determinant 1. We will append each $\mathbf{G}_i$ to $\mathbf{A}$ along the diagonal, and then append $\mathbf{H}_i - \mathbf{G}_i$ to $\mathbf{B}_i$ in the ith slot along the diagonal. We denote the resulting matrices by $\{\mathsf{diag}(\mathbf{A}, \mathbf{G}_1, \mathbf{G}_2, \ldots, \mathbf{G}_n), \{\mathsf{diag}(\mathbf{B}_i, \mathbf{0}, \mathbf{0}, \ldots, \mathbf{0}, \mathbf{H}_i - \mathbf{G}_i, \mathbf{0}, \ldots, \mathbf{0}, \mathbf{0})\}_{i\in[n]}\}$.

4.4   Transformation 4: AIK Re-randomization

The re-randomization step a la. [5] is applied twice in the obfuscation, once after taking the second transformation and again after taking the third transformation. In both steps, we left- and right-multiply each matrices with uniformly random matrices $\mathbf{R}, \mathbf{S}$ respectively such that $\det(\mathbf{R}) \cdot \det(\mathbf{S}) = 1$.

To summarize, the final obfuscation is

$$\mathbf{R}' \left(\mathsf{AddDiag}\left(\mathbf{R}\left(\mathsf{AddNoise}(\mathsf{RLS}(\mathsf{ADP})) \right) \mathbf{S} \right) \right) \mathbf{S}'.$$

5   Our Attack

The BIJMSZ obfuscation scheme consists of three transformations along with the re-randomization step. Among the three transformations, the purpose of adding block-diagonal matrices is preventing adversary from evaluating program dishonestly (e.g. Computing $\mathbf{A} + 3\mathbf{B}_1$); adding even-valued noise is meant to convert possibly low-rank matrices into full-rank ones. The re-randomization step is meant to hide information other than the determinant and rank of the matrices.

Therefore, after applying these two transformations and the re-randomization step, we expect that the leakage only comes from the determinant of $\mathbf{A} + \sum_{i \in [n]} x_i \mathbf{B}_i$. Indeed, our attack is based on the following observations about the determinant.

Key Observations. The adversary can get extra information by computing $\det(\mathbf{A} + \sum_{i \in [n]} x_i \mathbf{B}_i) \bmod 4$, namely, first computing the determinant over $\mathbb{Z}_p$, then computing the result mod 4. Note that we can ignore modulo p when analyzing our attack since we always add matrices of the ADPs together honestly, i.e. compute $\mathbf{A} + \sum_{i \in [n]} x_i \mathbf{B}_i$ where $x_i \in \{0, 1\}$. In this case, the determinant will never wrap around mod p. See Sect. 4.2.

The idea of computing $\det(\mathbf{A} + \sum_{i \in [n]} x_i \mathbf{B}_i) \bmod 4$ was also observed by Bartusek et al. [8, Section 9.3], where they suggest that computing such a value is useful for extracting the parities of the noise terms. The reason that Bartusek et al. introduce the RLS transformation is precisely to prevent this attack.

However, if the RLS transformation does not inject randomness into some matrices, then we can still extract information by computing the determinant modulo 4. Indeed, we observe that the RLS candidate given in [8, Section 8.1.1] is not guaranteed to inject randomness into every matrix. Specifically, if we have a program $\{\mathbf{A}, \mathbf{B}_1 = \mathbf{0}\}$, the program after RLS will be $\{\mathbf{A}', \mathbf{B}_1' = \mathbf{0}\}$. Namely, when applying RLS on a zero matrix $\mathbf{B}$, it only increases the dimension of the $\mathbf{B}$ matrix, and the resulting matrix remains a zero matrix.

5.1 Base Case

Running Example. Consider an ADP $(\mathbf{A}, \mathbf{B}_1, \mathbf{B}_2)$ computing $f : \{0, 1\}^2 \to 1$ that is in one of the following forms:

1. $\mathbf{B}_1 = \mathbf{B}_2 = \mathbf{0}$;
2. $\mathbf{B}_1 \neq \mathbf{0}$ or $\mathbf{B}_2 \neq \mathbf{0}$.

First, apply RLS to the ADP and denote the resulting ADP by $(\mathbf{A}', \mathbf{B}_1', \mathbf{B}_2')$. Let $L'(\mathbf{x}) = \mathbf{A}' + \sum_i x_i \mathbf{B}_i'$. In case 1, we have $\mathbf{B}_1' = \mathbf{B}_2' = \mathbf{0}$, whereas $\mathbf{B}_1' \neq \mathbf{0}$ or $\mathbf{B}_2' \neq \mathbf{0}$ in case 2. Then applying the AddNoise operation to $(\mathbf{A}', \mathbf{B}_1', \mathbf{B}_2')$, hoping that the choice of ADP is masked by the operation. We let $(\mathbf{A}'' = \mathbf{A}' + 2\mathbf{E}_0, \mathbf{B}_1'' = \mathbf{B}_1' + 2\mathbf{E}_1, \mathbf{B}_2'' = \mathbf{B}_2' + 2\mathbf{E}_2)$ denote the resulting ADP and evaluate the ADP by computing $\det(L''(\mathbf{x}))$, where $L''(\mathbf{x}) = \mathbf{A}'' + \sum_i x_i \mathbf{B}_i''$. We omit the AddDiag operation as well as the re-randomization step since they will not change $\det(\mathbf{A}'' + \sum_i x_i \mathbf{B}_i'')$. We have

Theorem 2.

$$
\begin{aligned}
\det(\mathbf{A}'' + \sum_{i \in [n]} x_i \mathbf{B}_i'') & \\
\equiv \det(L'(\mathbf{x})) + \sum_{j \in [\ell'], k \in [\ell']} (2e_{j,k}^{(0)} + \sum_i x_i 2e_{j,k}^{(i)}) \det(L'(\mathbf{x})_{(j,k)}) & \mod 4
\end{aligned}
\tag{1}
$$

where $L'(\mathbf{x})_{(j,k)}$ is a matrix obtained by deleting the jth row and k^{th} column of $L'(\mathbf{x})$, $e_{j,k}^{(i)}$ is the (j,k) element of $\mathbf{E}_i$ and ℓ' is the dimension of $L'(\mathbf{x})$.

To see the correctness of the equation, first we only need to consider constant terms and linear terms of the noises. Quadratic terms or terms with higher degree will be cancelled out by modulo 4 since noises are all even numbers. Then we notice that when computing $\det(\mathbf{M} + 2\mathbf{E})$ for a matrix $\mathbf{M}$ and a noise matrix $\mathbf{E}$, the constant terms of noises are equal to $\det(\mathbf{M})$; the linear terms of noises can be divided into non-intersecting parts, each part only relevant to one entity of $\mathbf{E}$. For the (j,k) element of $\mathbf{E}$ which is denoted by $e_{j,k}$, the linear term of $e_{j,k}$ is $e_{j,k} \cdot \det(\mathbf{M}_{(j,k)})$. We can obtain Eq. (1) by replacing $\mathbf{M}$ with $L'(\mathbf{x})$ and $\mathbf{E}$ with $2\mathbf{E}_0 + 2\sum_i x_i \mathbf{E}_i$.

To formally prove Theorem 2, we prove the following lemma.

Lemma 1. *For any $\ell \geq 2$, $\mathbf{A} \in \mathbb{Z}^{\ell \times \ell}$, and any $\mathbf{E} \in \mathbb{Z}^{\ell \times \ell}$, we have*

$$\det(\mathbf{A} + 2\mathbf{E}) = \det(\mathbf{A}) + \sum_{j \in [\ell], k \in [\ell]} 2e_{j,k} \det(\mathbf{A}_{(j,k)}) \pmod 4 \qquad (2)$$

where $e_{j,k}$ is the $(j,k)^{th}$ entry of $\mathbf{E}$, $\mathbf{A}_{(j,k)} \in \mathbb{Z}^{(\ell-1) \times (\ell-1)}$ is a matrix obtained by deleting the jth row and the kth column of $\mathbf{A}$.

Proof. Recall the Laplace expansion for determinant: for any matrix $\mathbf{V} \in \mathbb{R}^{\ell \times \ell}$, for any $k \in [\ell]$,

$$\det(\mathbf{V}) = \sum_{j \in [\ell]} (-1)^{j+k} v_{j,k} \det(\mathbf{V}_{(j,k)}) \qquad (3)$$

We prove Lemma 1 by induction. For the base case of $\ell = 2$,

$$\det(\mathbf{A} + 2\mathbf{E})$$
$$= (a_{1,1} + 2e_{1,1}) \cdot (a_{2,2} + 2e_{2,2}) - (a_{1,2} + 2e_{1,2}) \cdot (a_{2,1} + 2e_{2,1})$$
$$\equiv_{(1)} (a_{1,1}a_{2,2} - a_{1,2}a_{2,1}) + 2(e_{1,1}a_{2,2} + e_{2,2}a_{1,1} - e_{1,2}a_{2,1} - e_{2,1}a_{1,2}) \pmod 4$$
$$\equiv \det(\mathbf{A}) + \sum_{j \in [\ell], k \in [\ell]} (-1)^{j+k} 2e_{j,k} \det(\mathbf{A}_{(j,k)}) \pmod 4$$
$$\equiv_{(2)} \det(\mathbf{A}) + \sum_{j \in [\ell], k \in [\ell]} 2e_{j,k} \det(\mathbf{A}_{(j,k)}) \pmod 4,$$
$$(4)$$

where (1) is obtained by dropping the multiples of 4, (2) is obtained by dropping the -1 sign since $-2e = 2e \pmod 4$ for every $e \in \mathbb{Z}^4$.

---

[4] For the same reason, we will ignore the sign of the minors in the rest of this paper.

For $\ell \geq 3$,

$$\det(\mathbf{A} + 2\mathbf{E})$$
$$= \sum_{j \in [\ell]} (-1)^{j+1}(a_{j,1} + 2e_{j,1}) \cdot \det((\mathbf{A} + 2\mathbf{E})_{(j,1)})$$
$$\equiv_{(1)} \det(\mathbf{A}) + \sum_{j \in [\ell]} (2e_{j,1}) \cdot \det((\mathbf{A})_{(j,1)}) +$$
$$\sum_{j \in [\ell]} a_{j,1} \cdot \left(\sum_{i \in [\ell], i \neq j, k \in [\ell], k \neq 1} 2e_{i,k} \det((\mathbf{A}_{(i,k)})_{(j,1)}) \right) \pmod 4 \tag{5}$$
$$\equiv_{(2)} \det(\mathbf{A}) + \sum_{j \in [\ell], k \in [\ell]} 2e_{j,k} \det(\mathbf{A}_{(j,k)}) \pmod 4$$

where (1) uses the induction hypothesis, (2) is obtained by fixing each $e_{j,k}$ and regrouping the terms of $\mathbf{A}_{(j,k)}$.

Therefore Theorem 2 holds:

$$\det(\mathbf{A}'' + \sum_{i \in [n]} x_i \mathbf{B}_i'')$$
$$\equiv \det(L'(\mathbf{x})) + \sum_{j \in [\ell'], k \in [\ell']} (2e_{j,k}^{(0)} + \sum_i x_i 2e_{j,k}^{(i)}) \det(L'(\mathbf{x})_{(j,k)}) \mod 4 \tag{6}$$

Let us now show how to use Theorem 2 to distinguish two programs.

Case 1. We have $L'(00) = L'(10) = L'(01) = L'(11)$ since $\mathbf{B}_1' = \mathbf{B}_2' = \mathbf{0}$. Thus, we can write $\det(L''(\mathbf{x})) \mod 4$ as:

$\det(L''(00)) \equiv \det(L'(00)) + \sum_{j,k}(2e_{j,k}^{(0)}) \det(L'(00)_{(j,k)}) \mod 4$
$\det(L''(10)) \equiv \det(L'(00)) + \sum_{j,k}(2e_{j,k}^{(0)} + 2e_{j,k}^{(1)}) \det(L'(00)_{(j,k)}) \mod 4$
$\det(L''(01)) \equiv \det(L'(00)) + \sum_{j,k}(2e_{j,k}^{(0)} + 2e_{j,k}^{(2)}) \det(L'(00)_{(j,k)}) \mod 4$
$\det(L''(11)) \equiv \det(L'(00)) + \sum_{j,k}(2e_{j,k}^{(0)} + 2e_{j,k}^{(1)} + 2e_{j,k}^{(2)}) \det(L'(00)_{(j,k)}) \mod 4$

Then we sum them all:

$\det(L''(00)) + \det(L''(01)) + \det(L''(10)) + \det(L''(11))$
$\equiv 4 \det(L'(00)) + \sum_{j,k}(8e_{j,k}^{(0)} + 4e_{j,k}^{(1)} + 4e_{j,k}^{(2)}) \det(L'(00)_{(j,k)}) \mod 4$
$\equiv 0 \mod 4$

Case 2. We do computations analogous to case 1. However, in this case, we do not have $L'(00) = L'(10) = L'(01) = L'(11)$ any more. As the result, we cannot combine the $2e_{j,k}^{(i)} \det(L'(\mathbf{x})_{(j,k)})$ terms. Therefore, when computing $\sum_{\mathbf{x} \in \{0,1\}^2} \det(L''(\mathbf{x})) \mod 4$, the result may be either 0 or 2, both with probability $1/2$. As we will show in Sect. 5.2, we can achieve $\sum_{\mathbf{x} \in \{0,1\}^2} \det(L''(\mathbf{x})) \equiv 0 \mod 4$ by setting $\mathbf{A}, \mathbf{B}_1, \mathbf{B}_2$ carefully even when $\mathbf{B}_1 \neq \mathbf{0} \wedge \mathbf{B}_2 \neq \mathbf{0}$. However, for most of ADPs, the result of the equation will be either 0 or 2, both with probability $1/2$. So it is easy to find such ADPs which can be distinguished from case 1.

In conclusion, we can guess the random choice of ADP with probability at least $3/4$ by computing $\sum_{\mathbf{x}\in\{0,1\}^2} \det(L''(\mathbf{x})) \mod 4$. We guess case 1 when the result is 0. Otherwise, we guess case 2.

5.2   Advanced Case

In the base case we have shown that an ADP with two matrices being 0s can be distinguished from a functionally equivalent ADP with non-zero matrices at the same input bits. Such a condition is quite restricted, as it can be easily prevented by, for example, adding a dummy non-zero entry at the diagonal of each matrix. So it is natural to raise the following question:

Can we apply the attack without forcing $\mathbf{B}_1 = \mathbf{B}_2 = \mathbf{0}$?

The answer is yes. To see why, we observe that the attack in the base case crucially uses the fact that we can combine the $2e_{j,k}^{(i)} \det(L'(\mathbf{x})_{(j,k)})$ terms when they are equal across different inputs. Namely, for any $\mathbf{x_1}, \mathbf{x_2} \in \{0,1\}^2$, $\hat{L}'(\mathbf{x_1}) = \hat{L}'(\mathbf{x_2})$, where $\hat{\mathbf{M}}$ is the minor matrix of $\mathbf{M}^{\ell\times\ell}$, i.e.

$$\hat{\mathbf{M}} = \begin{bmatrix} \det(\mathbf{M}_{(1,1)}) \ \det(\mathbf{M}_{(1,2)}) \ \cdots \ \det(\mathbf{M}_{(1,\ell)}) \\ \det(\mathbf{M}_{(2,1)}) \ \det(\mathbf{M}_{(2,2)}) \ \cdots \ \det(\mathbf{M}_{(2,\ell)}) \\ \vdots \qquad\qquad \vdots \qquad \ddots \qquad \vdots \\ \det(\mathbf{M}_{(\ell,1)}) \ \det(\mathbf{M}_{(\ell,2)}) \ \cdots \ \det(\mathbf{M}_{(\ell,\ell)}) \end{bmatrix}.$$

Let us remark that instead of defining $\hat{\mathbf{M}}$ as a matrix, we can define it as any ordered set $\{\det(\mathbf{M}_{(i,j)})\}$. However, writing it as a matrix is a convenient notation.

In the base case, we assume the entire matrices of $L'(\mathbf{x_i})$, for $i = 1,2,3,4$, are equal to each other. However, for the attack to work **we only require** $\hat{L}'(\mathbf{x_i})$, **for** $i = 1,2,3,4$, **to be equal to each other**. The rest of the section is devoted to analyzing the relationship between $\hat{L}'(\mathbf{x})$ and $\hat{L}(\mathbf{x})$ and figure out that to what extent the entries of $\hat{L}'(\mathbf{x})$ are unpredictable after applying RLS on $L(\mathbf{x})$.

Let us first classify the vertices of the graphs we are dealing with.

Theorem 3. *Vertices in* $L'(\mathbf{x})$ *can be classified into two categories: original vertices and intermediate vertices. The entries of* $\hat{L}'(\mathbf{x})$ *have the following cases:*

1. $\forall s,j \in [\ell+1]$ *satisfying* $s \le \ell$ *and* $j > 1$, $\hat{L}'(\mathbf{x})[v_s, v_j] = \hat{L}(\mathbf{x})[v_s, v_j]^5$.
2. $\forall s,i,j \in [\ell+1]$ *satisfying* $s \le \ell$ *and* $i < j$, $\hat{L}'(\mathbf{x})[v_s, v_{i,j}] = \hat{L}(\mathbf{x})[v_s, v_j] \cdot L'(\mathbf{x})[v_{i,j}, v_j]$.
3. $\forall s,t,j \in [\ell+1]$ *satisfying* $s < t$ *and* $j > 1$, $\hat{L}'(\mathbf{x})[v_{s,t}, v_j] = \hat{L}(\mathbf{x})[v_s, v_j] \cdot L'(\mathbf{x})[v_s, v_{s,t}]$.

---

[5] Recall that when encoding a BP into an ADP, the lowermost row and the leftmost column are deleted. Thus, if the dimension of $L(\mathbf{x})$ is ℓ, the number of nodes should be $\ell + 1$.

4. $\forall s,t,i,j \in [\ell+1]$ satisfying $s < t$ and $i < j$,

$\hat{L}'(\mathbf{x})[v_{s,t}, v_{i,j}]_{(v_{s,t}\neq v_{i,j})} = \hat{L}(\mathbf{x})[v_s, v_j] \cdot L'(\mathbf{x})[v_{i,j}, v_j] \cdot L'(\mathbf{x})[v_s, v_{s,t}]$.

5. $\forall i,j \in [\ell+1]$ satisfying $i < j$,

$$\hat{L}'(\mathbf{x})[v_{i,j}, v_{i,j}] = \begin{cases} \det(L(\mathbf{x})), & L(\mathbf{x})[v_i, v_j] = 0 \text{ or } L'(\mathbf{x})[v_i, v_j] = 1 \\ \det(L(\mathbf{x})_{(v_i,v_j)=0}), & L(\mathbf{x})[v_i, v_j] = 1 \text{ and } L'(\mathbf{x})[v_i, v_j] = 0 \end{cases}$$

where $\mathbf{M}[v_i, v_j]$ is the entry in the row corresponding to v_i (row v_i for short) and the column corresponding to v_j (column v_j for short) of $\mathbf{M}$, $\mathbf{M}_{(v_i,v_j)=0}$ is a matrix obtained by modifying the (v_i, v_j) entry of $\mathbf{M}$ to 0 and $v_{i,j}$ is the intermediate vertex between v_i and v_j, as we defined in Sect. 4.1.

Proof. We prove the theorem by showing following 4 lemmas.

Lemma 2. $\forall s,j \in [\ell+1]$ satisfying $s \leq \ell$ and $j > 1$, $\hat{L}'(\mathbf{x})[v_s, v_j] = \hat{L}(\mathbf{x})[v_s, v_j]$.

Proof. Comparing $L'(\mathbf{x})_{(v_s,v_j)}$ with $L(\mathbf{x})_{(v_s,v_j)}$, there are mainly two kinds of differences: 1) $L'(\mathbf{x})_{(v_s,v_j)}$ have rows and columns corresponding to intermediate vertices. 2) $L'(\mathbf{x})_{(v_s,v_j)}[v_i, v_t]$ may not equal to $L(\mathbf{x})_{(v_s,v_j)}[v_i, v_t]$. To be specific, recall that if $L(\mathbf{x})[v_i, v_t] = 1$, the RLS will set $L'(\mathbf{x})[v_i, v_t] = 0$ with probability $1/4$. Thus, if we delete the intermediate vertices as well as related edges one by one and recover the values between original vertices at the same time, we can convert $L'(\mathbf{x})_{(v_s,v_j)}$ to $L(\mathbf{x})_{(v_s,v_j)}$. To prove the lemma, we only need to prove that the determinant remains unchanged during the conversion. We use $v_{i,t}$ to denote the intermediate vertex to be deleted. There are broadly 2 cases in the conversion:

LABEL BETWEEN ORIGINAL VERTICES DELETED OR UNCHANGED. In this case, we do not need to recover the label between original vertices (namely, the label between v_i and v_t). Also, we can find row $v_{i,t}$ or column $v_{i,t}$ with only nonzero entry -1 at $(v_{i,t}, v_{i,t})$. Therefore, Computing the expansion of $\det(L'(\mathbf{x})_{(v_s,v_j)})$ by row $v_{i,t}$ or column $v_{i,t}$ is equal to computing the determinant after deleting row $v_{i,t}$ and column $v_{i,t}$. See Fig. 3(a) and (b).

LABEL BETWEEN ORIGINAL VERTICES CHANGED. This case can be transformed to the first one by adding row $v_{i,k}$ to row v_i or adding column $v_{i,k}$ to column v_k, which keeps the determinant unchanged as well as recovers the label between v_i and v_t. See Fig. 3(c).

Lemma 3. $\forall i,j \in [\ell+1]$ satisfying $i < j$, $\hat{L}'(\mathbf{x})[v_*, v_{i,j}] = \hat{L}(\mathbf{x})[v_*, v_j] \cdot L'(\mathbf{x})[v_{i,j}, v_j]$,
where v_* is either an original vertex or an intermediate vertex, $v_* \neq v_{i,j}$ and $v_* \neq v_1$.

Proof. We notice that row $v_{i,j}$ of $L'(\mathbf{x})_{(v_*,v_{i,j})}$ has the only possible nonzero entry at $(v_{i,j}, v_j)$. We can expand $\det(L'(\mathbf{x})_{(v_*,v_{i,j})})$ by row $v_{i,j}$. The result is $L'(\mathbf{x})[v_{i,j}, v_j] * \det((L'(\mathbf{x})_{(v_*,v_{i,j})})_{(v_{i,j},v_j)})$. We can rewrite $(L'(\mathbf{x})_{(v_*,v_{i,j})})_{(v_{i,j},v_j)}$ as $(L'(\mathbf{x})_{(v_*,v_j)})_{(v_{i,j},v_{i,j})}$, namely, the matrix obtained by deleting row $v_{i,j}$ and column $v_{i,j}$ of $L'(\mathbf{x})_{(v_*,v_j)}$. As we showed in the proof of Lemma 2, $\det(L'(\mathbf{x})_{(v_*,v_j)})$ equals to $\det((L'(\mathbf{x})_{(v_*,v_j)})_{(v_{i,j},v_{i,j})})$. See Fig. 4.

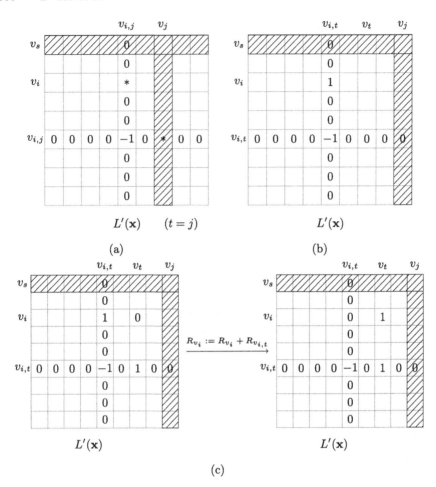

Fig. 3. Minors unrelated to any intermediate vertex

Lemma 4. $\forall s, t \in [\ell + 1]$ satisfying $s < t, \hat{L}'(\mathbf{x})[v_{s,t}, v_*] = \hat{L}(\mathbf{x})[v_s, v_*] \cdot L'(\mathbf{x})[v_s, v_{s,t}]$.
where v_* is either an original vertex or an intermediate vertex, $v_* \neq v_{s,t}$ and $v_* \neq v_{\ell+1}$.

We omit the proof as it is analogous to Lemma 3.

Lemma 5. $\forall i, j \in [\ell + 1]$ satisfying $i < j$, $\hat{L}'(\mathbf{x})[v_{i,j}, v_{i,j}] = \det(L(\mathbf{x})_{(v_i,v_j)=L'(\mathbf{x})[v_i,v_j]})$.

Proof. As we showed in the proof of Lemma 2, we have a conversion that deletes all intermediate vertices and recovers labels between original vertices. However, the label between v_i and v_j is an exception. To recover the label, we need to add row $v_{i,j}$ to row v_i or add column $v_{i,j}$ to column v_j. Unfortunately, both row

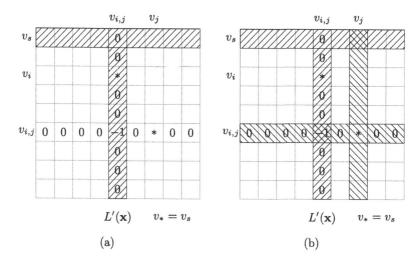

Fig. 4. Minor related to some intermediate vertex

$v_{i,j}$ and column $v_{i,j}$ are deleted in $L'(\mathbf{x})_{(v_{i,j},v_{i,j})}$. As the result, there's no way that we can recover the label. Therefore, after the conversion, we will obtain a matrix whose (v_i, v_j) entry may be the only different entry compared with $L(\mathbf{x})$. To be specific, if $L(\mathbf{x})[v_i, v_j] = 1$ and $L'(\mathbf{x})[v_i, v_j] = 0$, the (v_i, v_j) entry of the resulting matrix is 0.

This completes the proof of Theorem 3.

With Theorem 3 we can find the necessary and sufficient condition for $\hat{L}'(\mathbf{x_1}) = \hat{L}'(\mathbf{x_2})$, where $\mathbf{x_1}, \mathbf{x_2}$ are two different inputs. In fact, we have

Theorem 4. *For $L(\mathbf{x_1})$ and $L(\mathbf{x_2})$ satisfying following conditions, we can conclude that $\hat{L}'(\mathbf{x_1}) = \hat{L}'(\mathbf{x_2})$ regardless of the randomness injected by the RLS:*

1. $\hat{L}(\mathbf{x_1}) = \hat{L}(\mathbf{x_2})$.
2. $\forall i, j \in [\ell + 1]$ *satisfying* $i \leq \ell$ *and* $j > 1$ *and* $L(\mathbf{x_1})[v_i, v_j] \neq L(\mathbf{x_2})[v_i, v_j]$, *the entries in the ith row and j^{th} column of $\hat{L}(\mathbf{x_1})$ are all 0s.*
3. $\forall i, j \in [\ell + 1]$ *satisfying* $i < j$,

$$\det(L(\mathbf{x_1})_{(v_i, v_j)=0}) = \det(L(\mathbf{x_1})) = \det(L(\mathbf{x_2})) = \det(L(\mathbf{x_2})_{(v_i, v_j)=0}).$$

Proof. We will analyse these three conditions one by one.

First, we require that $\hat{L}(\mathbf{x_1}) = \hat{L}(\mathbf{x_2})$. The reason is that for any pair of original vertices v_i, v_j, $\hat{L}'(\mathbf{x})[v_i, v_j] = \hat{L}(\mathbf{x})[v_i, v_j]$. (See Theorem 3, the first case.)

Then, we compute $\Delta L(\mathbf{x_1}, \mathbf{x_2}) = L(\mathbf{x_1}) - L(\mathbf{x_2})$. The nonzero entries in $\Delta L(\mathbf{x_1}, \mathbf{x_2})$ represent the differences between $L(\mathbf{x_1})$ and $L(\mathbf{x_2})$. If $\Delta L(\mathbf{x_1}, \mathbf{x_2})[v_i, v_j] \neq 0$, the difference may be propagated into $(v_i, v_{i,j})$, $(v_{i,j}, v_j)$ and (v_i, v_j) of $\Delta L'(\mathbf{x_1}, \mathbf{x_2})$ after applying RLS (see Fig. 5). We notice that row $v_{i,j}$ entries of $\hat{L}'(x)$ depend on $L'(\mathbf{x})[v_i, v_{i,j}]$ (marked in north east lines) and column $v_{i,j}$ entries of $\hat{L}'(x)$ depend on $L'(\mathbf{x})[v_{i,j}, v_j]$ (marked in north west lines).

So the difference may cause entries in row $v_{i,j}$ or column $v_{i,j}$ (except $(v_{i,j}, v_{i,j})$, which we will discuss later) of $\Delta\hat{L}'(\mathbf{x_1}, \mathbf{x_2})$ to be nonzero. Fortunately, these entries of $\hat{L}'(\mathbf{x})$ also depend on row v_i entries and column v_j entries of $\hat{L}(\mathbf{x})$. To be specific, if row v_i entries and column v_j entries of $\hat{L}(\mathbf{x})$ are all zero, row $v_{i,j}$ entries and column $v_{i,j}$ entries of $\hat{L}'(x)$ are all zero (except $(v_{i,j}, v_{i,j})$), whatever the entries of $L'(\mathbf{x})$ are. (See Theorem 3, the second to the forth case.) Therefore, we further require that for any nonzero entry of $\Delta L(\mathbf{x_1}, \mathbf{x_2})[v_i, v_j]$, row v_i entries and column v_j entries of $\hat{L}(\mathbf{x_1})$ are all zero.

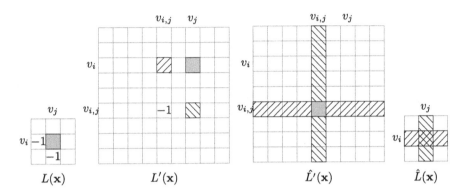

Fig. 5. The relationship among (minor) matrices before and after the RLS

Finally, we analyze the condition for $\Delta\hat{L}'(\mathbf{x_1}, \mathbf{x_2})[v_{i,j}, v_{i,j}] = 0$. If $L(\mathbf{x_1})[v_i, v_j] = L(\mathbf{x_2})[v_i, v_j] = 0$, we have $\hat{L}'(\mathbf{x_1})[v_{i,j}, v_{i,j}] = \det(L(\mathbf{x_1}))$, $\hat{L}'(\mathbf{x_2})[v_{i,j}, v_{i,j}] = \det(L(\mathbf{x_2}))$. Therefore, we require $\det(L(\mathbf{x_1})) = \det(L(\mathbf{x_2}))$. If $L(\mathbf{x_1})[v_i, v_j] = L(\mathbf{x_2})[v_i, v_j] = 1$, with probability $1/4$, we have $\hat{L}'(\mathbf{x_1})[v_{i,j}, v_{i,j}] = \det(L(\mathbf{x_1})_{(v_i, v_j)=0})$, $\hat{L}'(\mathbf{x_2})[v_{i,j}, v_{i,j}] = \det(L(\mathbf{x_2})_{(v_i, v_j)=0})$. We further require $\det(L(\mathbf{x_1})_{(v_i, v_j)=0}) = \det(L(\mathbf{x_2})_{(v_i, v_j)=0})$. (See Theorem 3, the fifth case.) If $L(\mathbf{x_1})[v_i, v_j] = 0, L(\mathbf{x_2})[v_i, v_j] = 1$, we require $\det(L(\mathbf{x_1})) = \det(L(\mathbf{x_2})_{(v_i, v_j)=0})$. If $L(\mathbf{x_1})[v_i, v_j] = 1, L(\mathbf{x_2})[v_i, v_j] = 0$, we require $\det(L(\mathbf{x_1})_{(v_i, v_j)=0}) = \det(L(\mathbf{x_2}))$.

This completes the proof of Theorem 4.

Running Example. Let us start with defining a family of ADPs to which our attack could apply[6]. Since we only need 4 inputs to carry out our attack, we can fix the other $n - 2$ input bits. w.l.o.g. we assume that x_1 and x_2 are unfixed. $\forall$ ADP P in the family, there exists an assignment $\mathbf{a} \in \{0,1\}^{n-2}$ to the values of $x_3 x_4 \dots x_n$ respect to P, s.t. the program matches the following pattern:

---

[6] The family of ADPs here is only a subset of all ADPs our attack could apply.

$$L(x_1 x_2 \mathbf{a}) = \begin{bmatrix} 0 & 0 & \cdots & 0 & 1 & 0 \\ -1 & * & \cdots & * & * & 0 \\ 0 & -1 & \cdots & * & * & 0 \\ \vdots & \vdots & \ddots & \vdots & \vdots & \vdots \\ 0 & 0 & \cdots & -1 & * & 0 \\ 0 & 0 & \cdots & 0 & -1 & 0 \end{bmatrix}.$$

where $*$ is a wildcard and represents one element in $\{0, 1, x_1, \overline{x_1}, x_2, \overline{x_2}\}$.

Next, we will show that

$$\sum_{\mathbf{x} \in \{00\mathbf{a}, 10\mathbf{a}, 01\mathbf{a}, 11\mathbf{a}\}} \det(L''(\mathbf{x})) \equiv 0 \mod 4.$$

First, we have

$$\hat{L}(x_1 x_2 \mathbf{a}) = \begin{bmatrix} 0 & 0 & \cdots & 0 & 1 \\ 0 & 0 & \cdots & 0 & 0 \\ \vdots & \vdots & \ddots & \vdots & \vdots \\ 0 & 0 & \cdots & 0 & 0 \\ 0 & 0 & \cdots & 0 & 1 \end{bmatrix}.$$

Namely, $\det(L(x_1 x_2 \mathbf{a})_{(i,j)}) = \begin{cases} 1, & (i = 1 \vee i = \ell) \wedge j = \ell \\ 0, & otherwise \end{cases}$. To see why,

notice that the rightmost column of $\hat{L}(x_1 x_2 \mathbf{a})$ is an all-zero column, thus $\det(L(x_1 x_2 \mathbf{a})_{(i,j)}) = 0$ for $j < \ell$. Moreover, we can add the topmost and lowermost rows of $\hat{L}(x_1 x_2 \mathbf{a})$ together to obtain an all-zero row, thus $\det(L(x_1 x_2 \mathbf{a})_{(i,j)}) = 0$ for $1 < i < \ell$. It is easy to check that $\det(L(x_1 x_2 \mathbf{a})_{(1,\ell)}) = \det(L(x_1 x_2 \mathbf{a})_{(\ell,\ell)}) = 1$.

Then, nonzero entries in $\Delta L(\mathbf{x_1 a}, \mathbf{x_2 a})$ depend on $x_1, \overline{x_1}, x_2$ and $\overline{x_2}$ entries in $L(x_1 x_2 \mathbf{a})$, where $\mathbf{x_1}, \mathbf{x_2} \in \{0, 1\}^2 \wedge \mathbf{x_1} \neq \mathbf{x_2}$. These entries are marked by $*$ in the matrix above. Therefore, we hope that entries in 2nd-$(\ell - 1)^{th}$ rows, 2nd-$(\ell - 1)^{th}$ columns of $\hat{L}(\mathbf{x} \in \{00\mathbf{a}, 10\mathbf{a}, 01\mathbf{a}, 11\mathbf{a}\})$ are all zero, which is exactly the case.

Finally, only entries marked by $*$ may be modified from 1 to 0 after RLS. Since entries in the rightmost column of $L(x_1 x_2 \mathbf{a})$ are always all zero, we can conclude that $\det(L(x_1 x_2 \mathbf{a})) = \det(L(x_1 x_2 \mathbf{a})_{(i,j)=0}) = 0$, where $i, j \in [\ell]$ and $L(x_1 x_2 \mathbf{a})[i, j] = *$ according to the above matrix.

We also give a concrete example:

$$L(\mathbf{x}) = \begin{bmatrix} 0 & \overline{x_3} & 0 & x_3 & 0 \\ -1 & 0 & x_4 & 0 & \overline{x_4} \\ 0 & -1 & \overline{x_1} & 0 & 0 \\ 0 & 0 & -1 & x_2 & 0 \\ 0 & 0 & 0 & -1 & \overline{x_3} \end{bmatrix}, L(x_1 x_2 \mathbf{a}) \atop {\mathbf{a}=11} = \begin{bmatrix} 0 & 0 & 0 & 1 & 0 \\ -1 & 0 & 1 & 0 & 0 \\ 0 & -1 & \overline{x_1} & 0 & 0 \\ 0 & 0 & -1 & x_2 & 0 \\ 0 & 0 & 0 & -1 & 0 \end{bmatrix}.$$

$L(\mathbf{x})$ computes $\overline{x_1} \wedge x_2 \wedge \overline{x_3}$, i.e. the output depends on x_1 and x_2. Therefore, in advanced case attack, we don't require the output bit to ignore some input bits, unlike in the base case attack.

Let us remark that the successful condition of our attack can be further relaxed. For example, if $\det(L(01)_{(v_2,v_3)=0})$ $((v_2,v_3)$ corresponding to the $(2,2)$ entry of $L(\mathbf{x}))$ did not equal to $\det(L(00))$ while $\det(L(01)) = \det(L(00))$, then $\hat{L}'(01)[v_{2,3},v_{2,3}] = \hat{L}'(00)[v_{2,3},v_{2,3}]$ still holds with probability $3/4$. As a result, the advantage that we can distinguish the ADP in the example from another functionally equivalent ADP after obfuscation will decrease by a factor of $3/4$, which is still noticeable.

5.3   The Scope of the Attack

In the end let us discuss

What kind of programs does the attack apply to?

We are afraid that we cannot give an exact and succinct answer to this question. The reason is when analysing ADPs, we focus on constraints on determinants and minors. However, the connection between these constraints and functionality is unclear. Moreover, with constraints on 4 inputs (we only need 4 inputs to apply the attack), it is difficult to figure out what the whole function looks like.

Therefore, we choose to describe the necessary condition and the sufficient condition separately. The necessary condition of the attack is to find 4 inputs $\mathbf{x}_1 = \mathbf{a}0\mathbf{b}0\mathbf{c}, \mathbf{x}_2 = \mathbf{a}1\mathbf{b}0\mathbf{c}, \mathbf{x}_3 = \mathbf{a}0\mathbf{b}1\mathbf{c}, \mathbf{x}_4 = \mathbf{a}1\mathbf{b}1\mathbf{c}$ s.t. the program outputs the same value on these inputs where $\mathbf{a}, \mathbf{b}, \mathbf{c}$ are some fixed strings of arbitrary length. The sufficient condition of the attack is that for the 4 inputs mentioned above, we always have $\hat{L}'(\mathbf{x}_1) = \hat{L}'(\mathbf{x}_2) = \hat{L}'(\mathbf{x}_3) = \hat{L}'(\mathbf{x}_4)$ regardless of the randomness injected by the RLS. This condition is satisfiable when the plaintext ADP satisfies the conditions in Theorem 4.

We also notice that the attack can be further generalized. Recall that in the above attack, we require $\hat{L}'(00) = \hat{L}'(10) = \hat{L}'(01) = \hat{L}'(11)$. But why we need the equality of these four minor matrices? When looking back to Sect. 5.1, on the high level, we can write the idea of our attack as

$$\begin{bmatrix} e_{j,k}^{(0)} & e_{j,k}^{(1)} & e_{j,k}^{(2)} \end{bmatrix} \begin{bmatrix} 1\;1\;1\;1 \\ 0\;1\;0\;1 \\ 0\;0\;1\;1 \end{bmatrix} \begin{bmatrix} \det(L'(00)_{(j,k)}) \\ \det(L'(10)_{(j,k)}) \\ \det(L'(01)_{(j,k)}) \\ \det(L'(11)_{(j,k)}) \end{bmatrix} = 0 \quad \mathrm{mod}\ 2.$$

To make the equation hold regardless of the choice of $e_{j,k}^{(0)}, e_{j,k}^{(1)}$ and $e_{j,k}^{(2)}$, the equality of these four minor matrices is necessary. However, if we have $2^b (b > 2)$ inputs, we will not require the equality of minor matrices. Take $b = 3$ as an example, the idea of our attack can be written as:

$$
\begin{bmatrix} e_{j,k}^{(0)} & e_{j,k}^{(1)} & e_{j,k}^{(2)} & e_{j,k}^{(3)} \end{bmatrix}
\begin{bmatrix} 1 & 1 & 1 & 1 & 1 & 1 & 1 & 1 \\ 0 & 1 & 0 & 0 & 1 & 1 & 0 & 1 \\ 0 & 0 & 1 & 0 & 1 & 0 & 1 & 1 \\ 0 & 0 & 0 & 1 & 0 & 1 & 1 & 1 \end{bmatrix}
\begin{bmatrix} \det(L'(000)_{(j,k)}) \\ \det(L'(100)_{(j,k)}) \\ \det(L'(010)_{(j,k)}) \\ \det(L'(001)_{(j,k)}) \\ \det(L'(110)_{(j,k)}) \\ \det(L'(101)_{(j,k)}) \\ \det(L'(011)_{(j,k)}) \\ \det(L'(111)_{(j,k)}) \end{bmatrix} = 0 \quad \mathrm{mod}\ 2.
$$

Therefore, for $\hat{L}'(\mathbf{x} \in \{0,1\}^3)$ satisfying following four conditions:

1. $\hat{L}'(000)+\hat{L}'(100)+\hat{L}'(010)+\hat{L}'(001)+\hat{L}'(110)+\hat{L}'(101)+\hat{L}'(011)+\hat{L}'(111) = \mathbf{0}$ mod 2
2. $\hat{L}'(100) + \hat{L}'(110) + \hat{L}'(101) + \hat{L}'(111) = \mathbf{0}$ mod 2
3. $\hat{L}'(010) + \hat{L}'(110) + \hat{L}'(011) + \hat{L}'(111) = \mathbf{0}$ mod 2
4. $\hat{L}'(001) + \hat{L}'(101) + \hat{L}'(011) + \hat{L}'(111) = \mathbf{0}$ mod 2

we have

$$
\sum_{\mathbf{x}\in\{0,1\}^3} \det(L''(\mathbf{x})) \equiv 0 \quad \mathrm{mod}\ 4.
$$

To conclude, if we cannot find four inputs satisfying the conditions in Theorem 4, it is still possible to find eight or more inputs that are capable of applying the "mod 4" attack.

6   A Plausible Fix and Further Discussions

In this section, we describe a possible approach of preventing our attack. Intuitively, the reason for the attack to work is that the RLS transformation does not inject enough randomness into the original ADP. To be specific, if the edge between v_j and v_k is labeled 0 or 1 before RLS, the edges among v_j, v_k and $v_{j,k}$ are never labelled x_i or $\overline{x}_i$ after RLS.

Therefore, a natural way of fixing the attack is to get around this limitation. If the edge between v_j, v_k is labeled by 1, then $M'^{(j,k)}(\mathbf{x})$ has the following extra choices:

$$
\begin{bmatrix} x_i & 1 \\ 0 & \overline{x}_i \end{bmatrix}, \begin{bmatrix} \overline{x}_i & 1 \\ 0 & x_i \end{bmatrix}, \begin{bmatrix} x_i & 1 \\ 0 & 0 \end{bmatrix}, \begin{bmatrix} 0 & 1 \\ 0 & x_i \end{bmatrix}, \begin{bmatrix} \overline{x}_i & 1 \\ 0 & 0 \end{bmatrix}, \begin{bmatrix} 0 & 1 \\ 0 & \overline{x}_i \end{bmatrix}.
$$

If there is no edge between v_j, v_k, then $M'^{(j,k)}(\mathbf{x})$ has following extra choices:

$$
\begin{bmatrix} x_i & 0 \\ 0 & \overline{x}_i \end{bmatrix}, \begin{bmatrix} \overline{x}_i & 0 \\ 0 & x_i \end{bmatrix}, \begin{bmatrix} x_i & 0 \\ 0 & 0 \end{bmatrix}, \begin{bmatrix} 0 & 0 \\ 0 & x_i \end{bmatrix}, \begin{bmatrix} \overline{x}_i & 0 \\ 0 & 0 \end{bmatrix}, \begin{bmatrix} 0 & 0 \\ 0 & \overline{x}_i \end{bmatrix}.
$$

We use the example in Sect. 4.1 to show the revision of the RLS (see Fig. 6, changes compared with Fig. 2(b) are marked in red color).

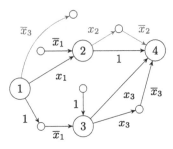

Fig. 6. The revision of the RLS (Color figure online)

With the revision we can defend against the base case attack since it effectively makes the B matrices non-zero. But how about the advanced case? Suppose that the label between $v_{j,\ell}$ and v_ℓ is x_i or $\overline{x}_i$ after the RLS (this is always possible in the revision of the RLS). As the result, $\forall \mathbf{x}, \mathbf{y}$ satisfying $x_i \neq y_i$, $L'(\mathbf{x})[v_{j,\ell}, v_\ell] \neq L'(\mathbf{y})[v_{j,\ell}, v_\ell]$. Recall that $\hat{L}'(\mathbf{x})[v_1, v_{j,\ell}] = \hat{L}(\mathbf{x})[v_1, v_\ell] \cdot L'(\mathbf{x})[v_{j,\ell}, v_\ell]$. In addition, we always have $\hat{L}(\mathbf{x})[v_1, v_\ell] = 1$. We can conclude that $\hat{L}'(\mathbf{x})[v_1, v_{j,\ell}] \neq \hat{L}'(\mathbf{y})[v_1, v_{j,\ell}]$. Namely, the revision can prevent the equality of the minors and thus defend against the advanced case attack.

We also notice the necessity of setting up connection between security parameter λ and the RLS transformation. The amount of randomness of the RLS introduced in [8] only depends on the matrix size of ADP. Even for the revision of the RLS we mentioned above (as it is), the amount of randomness only depends on the input length and the matrix dimension.

Therefore, for programs with very small input lengths and matrix dimensions, the adversary can guess the output of RLS correctly with some probability that is independent of λ, in which situation the adversary could break the $i\mathcal{O}$ scheme with non-negligible probability. A simple way of preventing this attack is applying RLS iteratively for λ times. Adding more intermediate vertices is another possible solution.

Let us remark that the revision of RLS we provide merely prevents the attack we describe in this paper, it should not be viewed as a candidate with enough confidence.

We cannot even ensure that with the above revision the $i\mathcal{O}$ scheme can be secure against all "modulo 4 attacks". We leave it as future work to give an RLS candidate with concrete parameters in some restricted adversarial model that is provably secure against known attacks. For example, it will be interesting to provide a candidate with provable security against all "modulo 4 attacks".

Acknowledgments. We thank anonymous reviewers for their helpful comments. Y.C. is supported by Tsinghua University start-up funding and Shanghai Qi Zhi Institute. Yu Yu was supported by the National Key Research and Development Program of China (Grant Nos. 2020YFA0309705 and 2018YFA0704701) and the National Natural Science Foundation of China (Grant Nos. 62125204 and 61872236). Yu Yu also acknowledges the support from the XPLORER PRIZE.

References

1. Agrawal, S.: Indistinguishability obfuscation without multilinear maps: new methods for bootstrapping and instantiation. In: Ishai, Y., Rijmen, V. (eds.) EUROCRYPT 2019. LNCS, vol. 11476, pp. 191–225. Springer, Cham (2019). https://doi.org/10.1007/978-3-030-17653-2_7

2. Agrawal, S., Pellet-Mary, A.: Indistinguishability obfuscation without maps: attacks and fixes for noisy linear FE. In: Canteaut, A., Ishai, Y. (eds.) EUROCRYPT 2020. LNCS, vol. 12105, pp. 110–140. Springer, Cham (2020). https://doi.org/10.1007/978-3-030-45721-1_5

3. Ananth, P., Jain, A., Lin, H., Matt, C., Sahai, A.: Indistinguishability obfuscation without multilinear maps: new paradigms via low degree weak pseudorandomness and security amplification. In: Boldyreva, A., Micciancio, D. (eds.) CRYPTO 2019. LNCS, vol. 11694, pp. 284–332. Springer, Cham (2019). https://doi.org/10.1007/978-3-030-26954-8_10

4. Ananth, P., Jain, A.: Indistinguishability obfuscation from compact functional encryption. In: Gennaro, R., Robshaw, M. (eds.) CRYPTO 2015. LNCS, vol. 9215, pp. 308–326. Springer, Heidelberg (2015). https://doi.org/10.1007/978-3-662-47989-6_15

5. Applebaum, B., Ishai, Y, Kushilevitz, E.: Cryptography in NC^0. In: 45th FOCS, pp. 166–175. IEEE (2004)

6. Barak, B., Garg, S., Kalai, Y.T., Paneth, O., Sahai, A.: Protecting obfuscation against algebraic attacks. In: Nguyen, P.Q., Oswald, E. (eds.) EUROCRYPT 2014. LNCS, vol. 8441, pp. 221–238. Springer, Heidelberg (2014). https://doi.org/10.1007/978-3-642-55220-5_13

7. Barak, B., et al.: On the (Im)possibility of obfuscating programs. In: Kilian, J. (ed.) CRYPTO 2001. LNCS, vol. 2139, pp. 1–18. Springer, Heidelberg (2001). https://doi.org/10.1007/3-540-44647-8_1

8. Bartusek, J., Ishai, Y., Jain, A., Ma, F., Sahai, A., Zhandry, M.: Affine determinant programs: a framework for obfuscation and witness encryption. In: 11th ITCS, pp. 82:1–82:39. LIPIcs (2020)

9. Bartusek, J., Lepoint, T., Ma, F., Zhandry, M.: New techniques for obfuscating conjunctions. In: Ishai, Y., Rijmen, V. (eds.) EUROCRYPT 2019. LNCS, vol. 11478, pp. 636–666. Springer, Cham (2019). https://doi.org/10.1007/978-3-030-17659-4_22

10. Bitansky, N., Paneth, O., Rosen, A.: On the cryptographic hardness of finding a Nash equilibrium. In: 56th FOCS, pp. 1480–1498. IEEE (2015)

11. Bitansky N., Vaikuntanathan V.: Indistinguishability obfuscation from functional encryption. In: 56th FOCS, pp. 171–190. IEEE (2015)

12. Brakerski, Z., Döttling, N., Garg, S., Malavolta, G.: Candidate iO from homomorphic encryption schemes. In: Canteaut, A., Ishai, Y. (eds.) EUROCRYPT 2020. LNCS, vol. 12105, pp. 79–109. Springer, Cham (2020). https://doi.org/10.1007/978-3-030-45721-1_4

13. Brakerski, Z., Döttling, N., Garg, S., Malavolta, G.: Factoring and pairings are not necessary for io: Circular-secure LWE suffices. Cryptology ePrint Archive, Report 2020/1024 (2020). https://eprint.iacr.org/2020/1024

14. Brakerski, Z., Rothblum, G.N.: Virtual black-box obfuscation for all circuits via generic graded encoding. In: Lindell, Y. (ed.) TCC 2014. LNCS, vol. 8349, pp. 1–25. Springer, Heidelberg (2014). https://doi.org/10.1007/978-3-642-54242-8_1

15. Chen, Y., Gentry, C., Halevi, S.: Cryptanalyses of candidate branching program obfuscators. In: Coron, J.-S., Nielsen, J.B. (eds.) EUROCRYPT 2017. LNCS, vol. 10212, pp. 278–307. Springer, Cham (2017). https://doi.org/10.1007/978-3-319-56617-7_10

16. Cheon, J.H., Han, K., Lee, C., Ryu, H., Stehlé, D.: Cryptanalysis of the multilinear map over the integers. In: Oswald, E., Fischlin, M. (eds.) EUROCRYPT 2015. LNCS, vol. 9056, pp. 3–12. Springer, Heidelberg (2015). https://doi.org/10.1007/978-3-662-46800-5_1

17. Cohen, A., Holmgren, J., Nishimaki, R., Vaikuntanathan, V., Wichs, D.: Watermarking cryptographic capabilities. In: 48th STOC, pp. 1115–1127. ACM (2016)

18. Coron, J.-S., Lepoint, T., Tibouchi, M.: Practical multilinear maps over the integers. In: Canetti, R., Garay, J.A. (eds.) CRYPTO 2013. LNCS, vol. 8042, pp. 476–493. Springer, Heidelberg (2013). https://doi.org/10.1007/978-3-642-40041-4_26

19. Devadas, L., Quach, W., Vaikuntanathan, V., Wee, H., Wichs, D.: Succinct LWE sampling, random polynomials, and obfuscation. In: Nissim, K., Waters, B. (eds.) TCC 2021. LNCS, vol. 13043, pp. 256–287. Springer, Cham (2021). https://doi.org/10.1007/978-3-030-90453-1_9

20. Garg, S., Gentry, C., Halevi, S.: Candidate multilinear maps from ideal lattices. In: Johansson, T., Nguyen, P.Q. (eds.) EUROCRYPT 2013. LNCS, vol. 7881, pp. 1–17. Springer, Heidelberg (2013). https://doi.org/10.1007/978-3-642-38348-9_1

21. Garg, S., Gentry, C., Halevi, S., Raykova, M., Sahai, A., Waters, B.: Candidate indistinguishability obfuscation and functional encryption for all circuits. In: 54th FOCS, pp. 40–49. IEEE (2013)

22. Gay, R., Jain, A., Lin, H., Sahai, A.: Indistinguishability obfuscation from simple-to-state hard problems: new assumptions, new techniques, and simplification. In: Canteaut, A., Standaert, F.-X. (eds.) EUROCRYPT 2021. LNCS, vol. 12698, pp. 97–126. Springer, Cham (2021). https://doi.org/10.1007/978-3-030-77883-5_4

23. Gay, R., Pass, R.: Indistinguishability obfuscation from circular security. In: 53rd STOC, pp. 736–749. ACM (2021)

24. Gentry, C., Gorbunov, S., Halevi, S.: Graph-induced multilinear maps from lattices. In: Dodis, Y., Nielsen, J.B. (eds.) TCC 2015. LNCS, vol. 9015, pp. 498–527. Springer, Heidelberg (2015). https://doi.org/10.1007/978-3-662-46497-7_20

25. Hopkins, S., Jain, A., Lin, H.: Counterexamples to new circular security assumptions underlying iO. In: Malkin, T., Peikert, C. (eds.) CRYPTO 2021. LNCS, vol. 12826, pp. 673–700. Springer, Cham (2021). https://doi.org/10.1007/978-3-030-84245-1_23

26. Hu, Y., Jia, H.: Cryptanalysis of GGH map. In: Fischlin, M., Coron, J.-S. (eds.) EUROCRYPT 2016. LNCS, vol. 9665, pp. 537–565. Springer, Heidelberg (2016). https://doi.org/10.1007/978-3-662-49890-3_21

27. Ishai, Y., Kushilevitz, E.: Private simultaneous messages protocols with applications. In: 5th ISTCS, pp. 174–183. IEEE (1997)

28. Ishai, Y., Kushilevitz, E.: Perfect constant-round secure computation via perfect randomizing polynomials. In: Widmayer, P., Eidenbenz, S., Triguero, F., Morales, R., Conejo, R., Hennessy, M. (eds.) ICALP 2002. LNCS, vol. 2380, pp. 244–256. Springer, Heidelberg (2002). https://doi.org/10.1007/3-540-45465-9_22

29. Jain, A., Lin, H., Matt, C., Sahai, A.: How to leverage hardness of constant-degree expanding polynomials over $\mathbb{R}$ to build $i\mathcal{O}$. In: Ishai, Y., Rijmen, V. (eds.) EUROCRYPT 2019. LNCS, vol. 11476, pp. 251–281. Springer, Cham (2019). https://doi.org/10.1007/978-3-030-17653-2_9

30. Jain, A., Lin, H., Sahai, A.: Indistinguishability obfuscation from well-founded assumptions. In: 53rd STOC, pp. 60–73. ACM (2021)
31. Jain, A., Lin, H., Sahai, A.: Indistinguishability Obfuscation from LPN over $F_{-}p$, DLIN, and PRGs in $NC^{\wedge}0$. Cryptology ePrint Archive, Report 2021/1334 (2021). https://eprint.iacr.org/2021/1334
32. Koppula, V., Lewko, A.B., Waters, B.: Indistinguishability obfuscation for turing machines with unbounded memory. In: 47th STOC, pp. 419–428. ACM (2015)
33. Lin, H.: Indistinguishability obfuscation from constant-degree graded encoding schemes. In: Fischlin, M., Coron, J.-S. (eds.) EUROCRYPT 2016. LNCS, vol. 9665, pp. 28–57. Springer, Heidelberg (2016). https://doi.org/10.1007/978-3-662-49890-3_2
34. Lin, H.: Indistinguishability obfuscation from SXDH on 5-linear maps and locality-5 PRGs. In: Katz, J., Shacham, H. (eds.) CRYPTO 2017. LNCS, vol. 10401, pp. 599–629. Springer, Cham (2017). https://doi.org/10.1007/978-3-319-63688-7_20
35. Lin, H., Tessaro, S.: Indistinguishability obfuscation from trilinear maps and block-wise local PRGs. In: Katz, J., Shacham, H. (eds.) CRYPTO 2017. LNCS, vol. 10401, pp. 630–660. Springer, Cham (2017). https://doi.org/10.1007/978-3-319-63688-7_21
36. Lin, H., Vaikuntanathan, V.: Indistinguishability obfuscation from DDH-like assumptions on constant-degree graded encodings. In: 57th FOCS, pp. 11–20. IEEE (2016)
37. Miles, E., Sahai, A., Zhandry, M.: Annihilation attacks for multilinear maps: cryptanalysis of indistinguishability obfuscation over GGH13. In: Robshaw, M., Katz, J. (eds.) CRYPTO 2016. LNCS, vol. 9815, pp. 629–658. Springer, Heidelberg (2016). https://doi.org/10.1007/978-3-662-53008-5_22
38. Sahai, A., Waters, B.: How to use indistinguishability obfuscation: deniable encryption, and more. In: 46th STOC, pp. 475–484. ACM (2014)
39. Wee, H., Wichs, D.: Candidate obfuscation via oblivious LWE sampling. In: Canteaut, A., Standaert, F.-X. (eds.) EUROCRYPT 2021. LNCS, vol. 12698, pp. 127–156. Springer, Cham (2021). https://doi.org/10.1007/978-3-030-77883-5_5

Indistinguishability Obfuscation from LPN over $\mathbb{F}_p$, DLIN, and PRGs in NC⁰

Aayush Jain[1(✉)], Huijia Lin[2], and Amit Sahai[3]

[1] NTT Research and Carnegie Mellon University, Pittsburgh, USA
aayushja@andrew.cmu.edu
[2] University of Washington, Seattle, USA
rachel@cs.washington.edu
[3] UCLA, Los Angeles, USA
sahai@cs.ucla.edu

Abstract. In this work, we study what minimal sets of assumptions suffice for constructing indistinguishability obfuscation ($i\mathcal{O}$). We prove:

Theorem(Informal): *Assume sub-exponential security of the following assumptions:*

– the Learning Parity with Noise (LPN) assumption over general prime fields $\mathbb{F}_p$ with polynomially many LPN samples and error rate $1/k^\delta$, where k is the dimension of the LPN secret, and $\delta > 0$ is any constant;

– the existence of a Boolean Pseudo-Random Generator (PRG) in NC⁰ with stretch $n^{1+\tau}$, where n is the length of the PRG seed, and $\tau > 0$ is any constant;

– the Decision Linear (DLIN) assumption on symmetric bilinear groups of prime order.

Then, (subexponentially secure) indistinguishability obfuscation for all polynomial-size circuits exists. Further, assuming only polynomial security of the aforementioned assumptions, there exists collusion resistant public-key functional encryption for all polynomial-size circuits.

This removes the reliance on the Learning With Errors (LWE) assumption from the recent work of [Jain, Lin, Sahai STOC'21]. As a consequence, we obtain the first fully homomorphic encryption scheme that does not rely on any lattice-based hardness assumption.

Our techniques feature a new notion of randomized encoding called Preprocessing Randomized Encoding (PRE), that essentially can be computed in the exponent of pairing groups. When combined with other new techniques, PRE gives a much more streamlined construction of $i\mathcal{O}$ while still maintaining reliance only on well-studied assumptions.

1 Introduction

Indistinguishability obfuscation ($i\mathcal{O}$) for general programs computable in polynomial time [12] enables us to hide all implementation-specific details about any program while preserving its functionality. $i\mathcal{O}$ is a fundamental and powerful primitive, with a plenthra of applications in cryptography and beyond. It is

© International Association for Cryptologic Research 2022
O. Dunkelman and S. Dziembowski (Eds.): EUROCRYPT 2022, LNCS 13275, pp. 670–699, 2022.
https://doi.org/10.1007/978-3-031-06944-4_23

hence extremely important to investigate how to build $i\mathcal{O}$, based on as *minimal assumptions* as possible, and via as *simple constructions* as possible. Advances on understanding what assumptions imply $i\mathcal{O}$ and simplification of $i\mathcal{O}$ constructions have immediate implications on the rest of cryptography through the many applications of $i\mathcal{O}$. So far, through the accumulation of extensive research by a large community since the first mathematical candidate $i\mathcal{O}$ proposal by [19] (see the survey in [20] and references therein), we recently saw the first construction of $i\mathcal{O}$ [30] based on four well-studied assumptions: Learning With Errors (LWE) [38], Decisional Linear assumption (DLIN) [11] over bilinear groups, Learning Parity with Noise (LPN) over $\mathbb{F}_p$ [25], and the existence of a Pseudo-Random Generator (PRG) in NC^0 [21].

While the work of Jain, Lin and Sahai [30] settles the feasibility of $i\mathcal{O}$ on solid assumptions, much still awaits be answered, even on the front of feasibility. A fundamental question to study next is:

"What minimal sets of well-studied assumptions suffice to construct $i\mathcal{O}$?"

From a complexity theoretic perspective, studying the minimal sets of sufficient assumptions helps deepen our understanding of the nature and structure of $i\mathcal{O}$, as well as understanding the power of these sufficient assumptions (via the many applications of $i\mathcal{O}$). It also serves as a test-bed for new ideas and techniques, and may lead to new ways of constructing $i\mathcal{O}$ and other primitives.

As we embark upon this question, it is important to keep an open mind. The answers may not be unique – there may be different minimal combinations of assumptions that are sufficient for $i\mathcal{O}$, and we do not know what the future may bring. Perhaps LWE alone is enough, or perhaps not. The answers may not be what we expect. Unexpected answers may teach us just as much as (if not more than) the answers that confirm our expectations. Our work here presents one such answer that challenges expectations, and at the same time, simplifies the overall architecture needed to construct $i\mathcal{O}$ from well-studied assumptions.

Our Result. We improve upon the $i\mathcal{O}$ construction of [30] by removing their reliance on LWE. We thus obtain $i\mathcal{O}$ based on the following three assumptions, which generates interesting consequences that we discuss below.

Theorem 1 (Informal). Assume sub-exponential security of the following assumptions:

- the Learning Parity with Noise (LPN) assumption over general prime fields $\mathbb{F}_p$ with polynomially many LPN samples and error rate $1/k^\delta$, where k is the dimension of the LPN secret, and $\delta > 0$ is any constant;
- the existence of a Boolean Pseudo-Random Generator (PRG) in NC^0 with stretch $n^{1+\tau}$, where n is the length of the PRG seed, and $\tau > 0$ is any constant;
- the Decision Linear (DLIN) assumption on symmetric bilinear groups of prime order.

Then, (subexponentially secure) indistinguishability obfuscation for all polynomial-size circuits exists. Assuming only polynomial security of the assumptions above yields polynomially secure functional encryption for all polynomial-size circuits.

It is interesting to note that of the three assumptions above, only one of them is known to imply public-key encryption or key agreement on its own – the DLIN assumption. Even assuming the other two assumptions simultaneously, it is not known how to build key agreement or any other "public key" primitive. (Recall that known constructions of public-key encryption from LPN require relatively sparse errors, that is, $\delta \geq \frac{1}{2}$ in our language above [2,10].) Thus, this work removes one, namely LWE, of the two public-key assumptions in [30], making a first step towards understanding the minimal set of assumptions underlying $i\mathcal{O}$.

Lattices vs. (Pairing + LPN over $\mathbb{F}_p$ + PRG in NC^0). An immediate consequence of our theorem is that the combination of bilinear pairing, LPN over $\mathbb{F}_p$, and constant-locality PRG is sufficient for building all the primitives that are implied by $i\mathcal{O}$ or Functional Encryption (FE) (and other assumptions that are implied by one of the three assumptions). This, somewhat surprisingly, includes *Fully Homomorphic Encryption (FHE)* that support homomorphic evaluation of (unbounded) polynomial-size circuits, through the construction by [17] that shows FHE can be built from subexponentially secure $i\mathcal{O}$ and rerandomizable encryption, which is implied by the DLIN assumption. It also includes Attribute Based Encryption (ABE) that support policies represented by (unbounded) polynomial-size circuits, which is a special case of functional encryption. To this day, the only known constructions of FHE and ABE for circuits are based on the hardness of lattice-type problems – either directly from problems like LWE or Ring LWE, or slightly indirectly via problems such as the approximate GCD problem [18]. Our work hence yields the first alternative pathways towards these remarkable primitives.

Corollary 2 (Informal). Assume the same assumptions as in the Theorem 1. Then, fully homomorphic encryption and attribute-based encryption for all polynomial-sized circuits exist.

Beyond FHE and ABE, lattice problems and techniques have been at the heart of nearly every work over the past decade attempting to achieve advanced cryptographic feasibility goals. Our theorem shows that, through $i\mathcal{O}$, the combination of pairing groups, LPN over $\mathbb{F}_p$, and constant-locality PRG is just as powerful as (and potentially more powerful than) lattice techniques for achieving feasibility goals.

We emphasize that our result complements instead of replaces lattice-based constructions. It also gives rise to several exciting open directions for future work, such as, can we obtain *direct* constructions of FHE or ABE (not via $i\mathcal{O}$ or FE) from the trio of assumptions? And, is there any formal relationship between these assumptions and lattice assumptions (e.g., BDD, SVP etc.)?

Streamlining $i\mathcal{O}$ Construction. In our minds, an equally important contribution of our work is streamlining of the construction of $i\mathcal{O}$ from well-studied assumptions. Current surviving $i\mathcal{O}$ proposals are all highly complex. They usually start with building a minimal tool and then transform it to $i\mathcal{O}$ through a number of sophisticated transformations in the literature. Take the recent construction of $i\mathcal{O}$ in [30] as an example. It starts with 1) building a 1-key secret-key FE scheme for NC^0 with sublinearly compact ciphertext, that is only weakly $(1 - 1/\mathsf{poly}(\lambda))$-secure, then 2) lift the function class to handle circuits via transformations in [7,32,37], 3) amplify security via [20], 4) turn secret-ley FE to public-key FE via [13], 5) transform FE with sublinear-size ciphertext to FE with sublinear-time encryption [22,35], and finally 6) construct $i\mathcal{O}$ from public-key FE for circuits with sublinear-time encryption [6,14]. While there exist alternative transformations for each of the steps, and other constructions of $i\mathcal{O}$ may omit some of the steps, it is a widely recognized problem that existing $i\mathcal{O}$ constructions are complex.

Our new construction of $i\mathcal{O}$, while removing the reliance of LWE, also removes the reliance on most transformations used in previous constructions. Starting from a known and simple partially hiding functional encryption scheme based on DLIN by [40], we construct a public-key FE for NC^1 with sublinear-time encryption, and then lift the function class from NC^1 to P using Yao's garbled circuits as done in [7,32,37], which can be transformed into a public key which implies $i\mathcal{O}$ via [6,14].

To enable our results, we propose and achieve the new notion of *Preprocessed Randomized Encodings (*PRE*)*. Roughly speaking, PRE allows for preprocessing the input $\mathbf{x}$ and random coins $\mathbf{r}$ into *preprocessed input* $(\mathsf{PI}, \mathsf{SI})$ where PI is public and SI is private, so that, later a randomized encoding of $(f, \mathbf{x})$ can be computed by polynomials with only degree 2 in SI, and constant degree in PI, over general prime field $\mathbb{F}_p$. PRE guarantees that the preprocessed input $(\mathsf{PI}, \mathsf{SI})$ can be computed in time sublinear in the size of the circuit f and the randomized encoding together with PI hides the actual input $\mathbf{x}$.

We now proceed to an overview of our techniques.

2 Technical Overview

FE Bootstrapping. A common thread in many recent $i\mathcal{O}$ constructions [4,5, 7,8,20,27,28,30,32–34,36] is FE bootstrapping – transformations that lift FE for computing simple functions in NC^0 to full fledged functional encryption for polynomial-sized circuits. Such an FE scheme in turn implies $i\mathcal{O}$ by the works of [6,14].

More specifically, functional encryption is an advanced form of public key encryption, which allows generating functional secret keys associated with a specific function $f : \{0,1\}^n \to \{0,1\}^m$, denoted as SK_f, such that, decrypting a ciphertext $\mathsf{CT}(\mathbf{x})$ using this secret key reveals only the output $f(\mathbf{x})$, and nothing else about the encrypted input $\mathbf{x}$. To imply $i\mathcal{O}$, it suffices to have FE for NC^1 with the following properties:

- It supports publishing a single functional decryption key SK_C, for a circuit $C : \{0,1\}^n \rightarrow \{0,1\}^m$ where every output bit is computable by a formula of fixed size $\mathsf{poly}(\lambda)$ in the security parameter. The overall size of C is $\mathsf{poly}(\lambda) \cdot m$.
- It is crucial that FE has encryption that runs in time sublinear in the size of the circuit C: $T_{\mathsf{Enc}} = \mathsf{poly}(\lambda) \cdot m^{1-\epsilon}$ – we refer to this property as **sublinear time-succinctness**.

In contrast, FE with encryption that takes time polynomial in the circuit size is just equivalent to vanilla public key encryption [23,39]. An intermediate level of efficiency known as **sublinear size-succinctness** only requires the ciphertext size to be sublinear $|\mathsf{CT}(\mathbf{x})| = \mathsf{poly}(\lambda) \cdot m^{1-\epsilon}$, without restricting the encryption time. It has been shown that FE with sublinear size-succinctness in fact implies FE with sublinear time-succinctness, but additionally assuming LWE [22,35]. In this work, one of our technical contributions is presenting a direct way of constructing FE with sublinear *time*-succinctness without LWE.

To reach the above powerful FE via bootstrapping, we start with FE schemes supporting the most expressive class of functions that we know how to build from standard assumptions. Partially-hiding functional encryption generalizes the syntax of functional encryption to allow a public input PI that does not need to be hidden in addition to the secret input SI. Furthermore, decryption reveals only $h(\mathsf{PI}, \mathsf{SI})$, where h is the function for which the functional decryption key is generated. So far, from standard assumptions over bilinear maps of order p (e.g. DLIN), prior works [20,28,40] constructed PHFE for polynomials h over $\mathbb{Z}_p$ that have constant degree in the public input PI and only degree-2 in the private input SI. We say such a polynomial h has degree-$(O(1), 2)$.

$$h(\mathsf{PI}, \mathsf{SI}) = \sum_{j,k} g_{j,k}(\mathsf{PI}) \cdot x_j \cdot x_k \quad \mathrm{mod}\ p, \quad \text{where } g_{j,k} \text{ has constant degree}$$

Furthermore, known PHFE schemes enjoy strong simulation security and their encryption runs in time linear in the length of the input: $T_{\mathsf{Enc}} = (|\mathsf{PI}| + |\mathsf{SI}|)\mathsf{poly}(\lambda)$. Both these properties will be instrumental later.

Perhaps the most straightforward way of bootstrapping FE for simple functions to FE for complex functions is using the former to compute a Randomized Encoding (RE) π of the complex function $C(\mathbf{x})$, from which the output can be derived. It seems, then, that all we need is an RE that can be securely evaluated using degree-$(O(1), 2)$ PHFE. Unfortunately, this idea immediately hits a key barrier: Known RE encoding algorithms $\mathsf{Encode}_C(\mathbf{x}; \mathbf{r})$ have at least locality 4 and hence degree 4 (over $\mathbb{Z}_p$) in $\mathbf{x}$ and $\mathbf{r}$, both of which must be kept private. Making the degree smaller has been a long-standing open question. To circumvent this issue, we formalize a new notion of degree-$(O(1), 2)$ randomized encoding that crucially relies on *input preprocessing*.

Preprocessed Randomized Encoding. The key properties of a preprocessed Randomized Encoding (PRE) scheme are: *(i)* encodings can be generated using degree-$(O(1), 2)$ polynomials h on pre-processed inputs $(\mathsf{PI}, \mathsf{SI})$; and *(ii)* the input preprocessing has *sublinear time succinctness*. More precisely, the syntax of PRE is described below.

Preprocessed Randomized Encoding

- PRE.PreProc$(p, \mathbf{x}) \rightarrow (\mathsf{PI}, \mathsf{SI})$. The preprocessing algorithm converts an input $\mathbf{x} \in \{0, 1\}^n$ and random tape $\mathbf{r}$ into a preprocessed input $(\mathsf{PI}, \mathsf{SI})$ over $\mathbb{Z}_p$. It is important that preprocessing does not depend on the circuit to be encoded later (but only an upper bound on its size). It must satisfy **sublinear time-succinctness** in the sense that preprocessing time is sublinear in the size of the computation, $T_{\mathsf{PreProc}} = m^{1-\epsilon}\mathsf{poly}(\lambda)$.
- PRE.Encode$(C, \mathsf{PI}, \mathsf{SI}) = \pi$. The encoding algorithm takes a circuit C of size $m\mathsf{poly}(\lambda)$ and a preprocessed input $(\mathsf{PI}, \mathsf{SI})$, and produces a binary randomized encoding π. PRE.Encode$_C$ can be computed by a polynomial mapping over $\mathbb{Z}_p$ with constant degree in PI and degree 2 in SI.
- PRE.Decode$(\pi) = \mathbf{y}$. The decoding algorithm decodes the output $\mathbf{y} = C(\mathbf{x})$ from π.

Indistinguishability security: PRE guarantees that (PI, π) generated from $(C, \mathbf{x}_0)$ or $(C, \mathbf{x}_1)$ are indistinguishable as long as $C(\mathbf{x}_0) = C(\mathbf{x}_1)$.

If we had such PRE, we can easily construct the desired powerful FE as follows:

$$\text{FE.SK} : \quad \text{PHFE.SK}_h \text{ , where } h(\mathsf{PI}, \mathsf{SI}) = \text{PRE.Encode}_C(\mathsf{PI}, \mathsf{SI}) = \pi$$

$$\text{FE.CT} : \quad \text{PHFE.CT}(\mathsf{PI}, \mathsf{SI}) \text{ , where } (\mathsf{PI}, \mathsf{SI}) \leftarrow \text{PRE.PreProc}(p, \mathbf{x})$$

The simulation security of the underlying PHFE guarantees that the only information revealed is PI, π. Hence by the indistinguishability security of pRE, FE ciphertexts of inputs $\mathbf{x}_0, \mathbf{x}_1$ that produce the same outputs are indistinguishable. For *time succinctness*, since the preprocessing takes sublinear time $m^{1-\epsilon}\mathsf{poly}(\lambda)$ and PHFE encryption takes time proportional to the length of the preprocessed inputs, which is also sublinear, we have that FE encryption has sublinear time succinctness.

2.1 Challenges to Constructing Preprocessed Randomized Encoding

We now explain how to construct PRE for NC^1. The main challenges are making sure that: *(i)* encoding is only degree 2 in the private preprocessed input SI; and *(ii)* preprocessing has sublinear time-succinctness. Towards this, our starting point is to consider a known randomized encoding scheme for NC^1 that has constant *locality* and *sublinear randomness* (explained next), and somehow modify it so that it can enjoy degree-$(O(1), 2)$ encoding. Such a constant-degree RE scheme can be obtained by combining a constant-locality RE, such as [41], with a PRG in NC^0. The encoding algorithm works as $\pi = \mathsf{Encode}'_C(\mathbf{x}; \mathbf{r}' = \mathsf{PRG}(\mathbf{r}))$, where the random tape has sublinear length $|\mathbf{r}| = m^{1-\tau}\mathsf{poly}(\lambda)$ if the Encode' algorithm uses a linear number of random coins $|\mathbf{r}'| = O(m)\mathsf{poly}(\lambda)$ and PRG has appropriate polynomial stretch. We call this property *sublinear randomness*; it is needed because the PRE encoding algorithm is *deterministic* and hence the sublinearly short preprocessed input $(\mathsf{PI}, \mathsf{SI})$ must encode all the randomness needed for producing the encoding. Observe that Encode' has constant locality (and hence degree) in $(\mathbf{x}, \mathbf{r})$, but the locality is much higher than 2.

High-Level Approach for PRE: So how can we use preprocessing to reduce the encoding degree to just 2 in private proprocessed inputs? We start by adapting several ideas from [30] that were used to construct objects called structured-seed PRGs, to constructing our desired PRE. Here is the high-level approach:

- Since the public input PI is supposed to hide $\mathbf{x}' = \mathbf{x}, \mathbf{r}$, we will set PI as an encryption HEEnc($\mathbf{x}'$) of $\mathbf{x}'$ using a special-purpose homomorphic encryption scheme.
- We set SI to contain the secret key of this homomorphic encryption and some other "preprocessed information" about the encryption. Crucially, we need to ensure that PI, SI can be computed by a circuit of size sublinear in size of C.
- Given PI, SI, the encode algorithm Encode first takes PI and homomorphically evaluate Encode′ to obtain an output encryption HEEnc(π). Then, it takes SI and decrypts HEEnc(π) to obtain π. We will ensure that homomorphic evaluation of a locality-d function Encode′ is a degree d operation on PI, and crucially decryption is a degree 2 operation in SI (and has at most constant degree in HEEnc(π)). Because of this, Encode will have degree-$(O(1), 2)$.

Instantiation via LPN *Over* $\mathbb{F}_p$. An example of such a homomorphic encryption scheme is based on LPN over $\mathbb{F}_p$.

$$\mathsf{PI} = \mathsf{HEEnc}(\mathbf{x}') = (\mathbf{A}, \mathbf{b} = \mathbf{sA} + \mathbf{e} + \mathbf{x}' \mod p)$$

where the dimension dim is polynomially related with λ, but relatively small as we describe below. We sample $\mathbf{A} \leftarrow \mathbb{Z}_p^{\dim \times |\mathbf{x}'|}$, $\mathbf{s} \leftarrow \mathbb{Z}_p^{1 \times \dim}$, and the errors $\mathbf{e}$ is chosen so that each coordinate is non-zero with probability $\dim^{-\delta}$ for any constant $\delta > 0$ associated with the LPN over $\mathbb{F}_p$ assumption.

To come up with SI for decryption. We observe that for every locality-d polynomial h the following equation holds:

$$h(\mathbf{b} - \mathbf{As}) = h(\mathbf{x}' + \mathbf{e})$$

The LHS of the equation tells us that if we include in SI all degree-d monomials of $\mathbf{s}$, namely, $\mathsf{SI} = (1||\mathbf{s})^{\otimes d}$, then the above quantity can be computed by a polynomial that is degree d in PI $= (\mathbf{A}, \mathbf{b})$ and in fact linear in SI. By choosing dim to be polynomially smaller than $|\mathbf{x}|$, the above SI will still be sufficiently succinct for our purposes. The RHS of the equation tells us that the error $\mathbf{e}$ is sparse, and h depends only on a constant number d variables, and thus with probability $1 - O(\dim^{-\delta})$, we have $h(\mathbf{x}' + \mathbf{e}) = h(\mathbf{x}')$. This almost matches what we want, except that decryption has a noticable error probability $O(\dim^{-\delta})$.

To correct the decryption errors, the key observation is that for a polynomial mapping Encode′$_C$ with long outputs, the error vector $\mathsf{Corr} = \mathsf{Encode}'_C(\mathbf{x}' + \mathbf{e}) - \mathsf{Encode}'_C(\mathbf{x}')$ is sparse: only a $O(\dim^{-\delta})$ fraction of elements in Corr are non-zero. Prior work [30] developed a technique for "compressing" such sparse vector Corr into (U, V) of sublinear length $|U, V| = m^{1-\epsilon}\mathsf{poly}(\lambda)$. From U, V, Corr can be expanded out using only degree 2. Therefore, by adding (U, V) to SI, we can decrypt and then correct errors in the output with just degree-2 computation in U, V.

$$\mathsf{SI} = (1||\mathbf{s})^{\otimes d}, U, V$$

However, the compression mechanism of [30] only guarantees that U, V are *size-succinct*, but are not time-succinct, and in fact, constructing them takes time linear in the circuit size m.

Barriers to Time-Succinctness: Unfortunately, the above approach cannot achieve time-succinctness for the following reasons: The preprocessing algorithm needs to compute the errors $\mathsf{Corr} = \mathsf{Encode}'_C(\mathbf{x}' + \mathbf{e}) - \mathsf{Encode}'_C(\mathbf{x}')$ in the decryption output. Though the error vector is sparse, every element could be wrong with $\Omega(\dim^{-\delta})$ probability, depending on the LPN noises $\mathbf{e}$ used to encrypt $\mathbf{x}'$ and the input-output dependency graph of the function Encode'_C computed. Therefore, the circuit implementing the preprocessing must have Encode'_C stored. This creates two problems: *(i)* the proprocessing time (in the circuit model) is at least $|C|$, and more subtly, *(ii)* the proprocessing depends on C.

In the previous work of [30], they deal with the first issue by invoking the transformation from size-succinct FE to time-succinct FE [22,35] assuming LWE. The second issue is not a problem, since they construct structured-seed PRG and only apply the aforementioned technique to a fixed PRG in NC^0. However, structured-seed PRG alone is not enough for FE bootstrapping, and they need to additionally rely on FHE based on LWE, and the security amplification technique of [20] which again relies on LWE[1].

In this work, to streamline the construction of $i\mathcal{O}$, and to weaken the underlying assumptions, we want to construct PRE that directly achieves time-succinctness. Next, we discuss how to address the first issue above using the idea of *amortization*.

Key Idea: Amortization. To get around the hurdle that preprocessing a single input $\mathbf{x}$ seems to inherently take time proportional to $|C|$, we ask a simpler question: can we "batch-preprocess" in sublinear time? To make it precise, say we have k input vectors $\mathbf{x}_1, \ldots, \mathbf{x}_k$ each of dimension n, and we are interested in learning $h(\mathbf{x}_1), \ldots, h(\mathbf{x}_k)$ w.r.t. a polynomial mapping $h : \{0,1\}^n \to \{0,1\}^{m'}$ with constant locality. Can we batch-process $\{\mathbf{x}_1, \ldots, \mathbf{x}_k\}$ into a public and a secret input $(\mathsf{PI}, \mathsf{SI})$ in time sublinear in $m' \cdot k$, such that each $h(\mathbf{x}_i)$ can be computed with constant degree in PI and degree 2 in SI. Our answer is *Yes!*

Furthermore, in order to get around the subtler problem that preprocessing depends on Encode'_C, we will consider a version of amortized preprocessing for

---

[1] Besides [20], there are other works that contain FE security amplification techniques [4,5,26]. However, it has been recently acknowledged that there is a common issue in these techniques due to an incorrect application of the leakage simulation lemma. The work of [20] circumvents the use leakage simulation lemma, but achieves only weaker security amplification, which nevertheless is still sufficient for constructing $i\mathcal{O}$.

computing polynomials h that have a fixed set of monomials $\mathcal{Q} = \{Q_1, \ldots, Q_{m'}\}$. We say that $h(\mathbf{x}_1, \cdots, \mathbf{x}_k)$ has monomial pattern $\mathcal{Q}$ if it has form:

$$h(\mathbf{x}_1, \cdots, \mathbf{x}_k) = \sum_{i,j} \eta_{i,j} Q_j(\mathbf{x}_i) \bmod p \text{ , where } \eta_{i,j} \text{ are integer coefficients} \quad (1)$$

The preprocessing is then allowed to depend on the monomials $\mathcal{Q}$, but not the polynomials h to be computed later. We formalize this tool called Preprocessed Polynomial Encoding (PPE) below.

Preprocessed Polynomial Encoding

- PPE.PreProc$(p, \mathcal{Q}, \mathbf{x}_1, \cdots, \mathbf{x}_k) \rightarrow$ (PI, SI). Given a collection of constant degree-d monomials, $\mathcal{Q} = \{Q_1, \ldots, Q_{m'}\}$, the preprocessing algorithm converts a batch of k inputs $\{\mathbf{x}_i \in \{0,1\}^n\}_{i \in [k]}$ into a preprocessed input (PI, SI) over $\mathbb{Z}_p$. It satisfies **sublinear time-succinctness** in the sense that preprocessing time is sublinear in $m' \cdot k$.
- PPE.Decode$(p, \mathcal{Q}, h, \text{PI}, \text{SI}) = y$. The decoding algorithm decodes the output

$$y = h(\mathbf{x}_1, \cdots, \mathbf{x}_k) = \sum_{i,j} \eta_{i,j} Q_j(\mathbf{x}_i) \bmod p \ .$$

Indistinguishability security: PPE guarantees that PI for any two different inputs $\mathbf{x}_1, \cdots, \mathbf{x}_k$ and $\mathbf{x}'_1, \cdots, \mathbf{x}'_k$ are indistinguishable.

Next we need to answer two questions: *(i)* Can we construct PPE?; and *(2)* Is this amortization useful to construct PRE? Below, we answer the second question first.

Constructing PRE *Using (Amortized)* PPE. In order to construct PRE scheme, we need a randomized encoding scheme (with sublinear randomness) with an encoding algorithm Encode$'_C$ that is exactly the kind of polynomials that PPE can handle (Eq. 1). Then, we can simply use the PPE preprocessing as the PRE preprocessing. More precisely, there should exist a universal set of monomials $\mathcal{Q}$, such that, for every complex circuit C,

$$\mathsf{Encode}'_C(\mathbf{x}, \mathbf{r})7 = \left\{ h_l(\mathbf{x}_1, \cdots, \mathbf{x}_k) = \sum_{i,j} \eta_{l,i,j} Q_j(\mathbf{x}_i) \bmod p \right\}_l$$

where $\eta_{l,i,j}$'s depend on C, but Q_j's do not.

We construct such an RE for NC^1, denoted as ARE, using Yao's garbling scheme [41] and a PRG in NC^0. Recall that we consider circuits $C : \{0,1\}^n \rightarrow \{0,1\}^{m=m'k}$ where every output bit is computable by a formula of fixed size, say λ. We can divide C into k chunks $C_1, \ldots, C_k$ where circuit C_i computes the ith chunk of outputs of C and has size $m'\lambda$, and then we can garble each of the chunks separately.

$$\mathsf{ARE.Encode}(C, \mathbf{x}, \mathbf{r}_1, \ldots, \mathbf{r}_k) = \mathsf{Yao.Gb}(C_1, \mathbf{x}; \mathsf{PRG}(\mathbf{r}_1)), \ldots, \mathsf{Yao.Gb}(C_{k'}, \mathbf{x}; \mathsf{PRG}(\mathbf{r}_k)),$$

The idea is viewing $\{\mathbf{x}_i = (\mathbf{x}, \mathbf{r}_i)\}$ as the k inputs to be batch processed. But, do the functions $\{\mathsf{Yao.Gb}(C_i, \star, \star)\}$ share a universal set of monomials? Unfortunately, this is not the case since the computation of each garbled table depends on the gates in C_i. To solve this problem, we modify our approach to garble the universal circuit and treat C_i's as part of input to be garbled. More precisely,

$$\mathsf{ARE.Encode}(C, \mathbf{x}, \mathbf{r}_1, \ldots, \mathbf{r}_k) = \mathsf{Yao.Gb}(U, (C_1, \mathbf{x}), \mathsf{PRG}(\mathbf{r}_1)), \ldots, \mathsf{Yao.Gb}(U, (C_k, \mathbf{x}), \mathsf{PRG}(\mathbf{r}_k)),$$

where U is a universal circuit that takes as input $C_i, \mathbf{x}$ and outputs $C_i(\mathbf{x})$. Now the computation of the garbled tables no longer depend on C_i, neither does the input garbling of $\mathbf{x}$. The only part that depends on C_i is the input garbling of C_i, which looks like $(1 - C_{ij})l_0 + C_{ij}l_1$, for every bit of description of C_i. Examining more closely, we see that the monomials for computing the labels are in fact universal, and C_i only affects the coefficients that combine these monomials. This is exactly the type of polynomials that PPE can handle.

Note that our ARE only handles NC^1 circuits because they can be written as formulas. In a formula, every wire w feeds into a single gate g as an input wire. Hence, it suffices to use a PRG with linear stretch to expand the label for wire w into pseudorandom masks used for creating the garbled table for g. If the fan-out were unbounded, we would need a PRF in order to generate the pseudorandom masks for all the gates that wire w feeds into. However, we do not have PRF with constant locality. More details are provided in Sect. 5, where we also show that the size of the garbling is linear in $|C| = m\lambda$ and the total input length $|\mathbf{x}' = (\mathbf{x}, \mathbf{r})|$ is sublinear in m.

2.2 Constructing Proprocessed Polynomial Encoding

We now construct our key technical tool PPE. For simplicity, in this overview, we will focus on computing just the a collection of degree d monomials $\mathcal{Q} = \{Q_i(\mathbf{x}_j)\}_{i \in [m'], j \in [k]}$, as it illustrates the idea behind our preprocessing procedure, and polynomials with monomial pattern $\mathcal{Q}$ can be computed in the same degree as the monomials. Similar to before, the public preprocessed input PI contains a LPN encryption of each $\mathbf{x}_j$, that is,

$$\mathsf{PI} = \{\mathsf{HEEnc}(\mathbf{x}_j) = (\mathbf{A}_j, \mathbf{b}_j = \mathbf{s}\mathbf{A}_j + \mathbf{e}_j + \mathbf{x}_j)\}_{j \in [k]},$$

where $\mathbf{A}_j \leftarrow \mathbb{Z}_p^{n \times k}$, $\mathbf{s} \leftarrow \mathbb{Z}_p^{1 \times k}$, and $\mathbf{e}_j \in \mathbb{Z}_p^k$ where each coordinate is zero with probability $k^{-\delta}$. Here we set the LPN dimension to k, which is set to be polynomially related to but polynomially smaller than n. Given PI, we can homomorphically evaluate all monomials in $\mathcal{Q}$ to obtain encryption of the outputs $\{\mathsf{HEEnc}(Q_i(\mathbf{x}_j))\}_{i,j}$.

Next, we construct SI so that these ciphertexts can be decypted and errors can be corrected. For decryption, SI includes all degree d monomials in the secret key $\mathbf{s}$, $\mathsf{SI}_0 = (1\|\mathbf{s})^{\otimes d}$, so that one can obtain the erroneous outputs $\{Q_i(\mathbf{x}_j + \mathbf{e}_j)\}_{i,j}$. Next, think of the errors Corr as arranged in a $m' \times k$ matrix, where $\mathsf{Corr}[i, j] = Q_i(\mathbf{x}_j + \mathbf{e}_j) - Q_i(\mathbf{x}_j)$. We do not compress the entire matrix Corr in one shot, nor compressing it column by column, the new idea is compressing it row by row. Each row, denoted by Corr_i, has dimension k and contains the errors related to computing a single monomial Q_i on all inputs $\{\mathbf{x}_j\}_j$,

$$\mathsf{Corr}_i = \{Q_i(\mathbf{x}_j + \mathbf{e}_j) - Q_i(\mathbf{x}_j)\}_{j\in[k]} \; .$$

If we can compress each Corr_i into SI_i in (amortized) sublinear time $(k^{1-\Omega(1)})\mathsf{poly}(\lambda)$, then the overall time for computing $\mathsf{SI} = (\mathsf{SI}_0, \mathsf{SI}_1, \cdots, \mathsf{SI}'_m)$ is $(k^{1-\Omega(1)} \cdot \frac{m}{k})\mathsf{poly}(\lambda)$, sublinear in $m' \cdot k$. Given such SI, we can indeed correct all errors in degree 2 and obtain the desired outputs $\{Q_i(\mathbf{x}_j)\}_{i,j}$.

The Compressed Version SI_i. So what is special about compressing each row Corr_i? The key is that elements in one row $\{\mathsf{Corr}[i,j]\}_j$ are all *independent*, because the value $\mathsf{Corr}[i,j]$ depends on $\mathbf{e}_j, \mathbf{x}_j$, which is independent for different j's. In comparison, note that this is not the case for elements in one column $\{\mathsf{Corr}[i,j]_i\}$. This is because two different monomials Q_i and $Q_{i'}$ may depend on the same input variable, say the k'th, and hence $\mathsf{Corr}[i,j]$ and $\mathsf{Corr}[i',j]$ both depend on the same noise $e_{j,k}$ used for hiding $x_{j,k}$. The independence and the fact that each element $\mathsf{Corr}[i,j]$ is non-zero with probability $O(k^{-\delta})$ imply that each row Corr_i has $O(k^{1-\delta})$ non-zero elements with overwhelming probability.

We rely on both the sparsity of and independence of elements in Corr_i to compress it. Let's first see how the compressed version SI_i looks like. We assign elements in Corr_i into $T = k^{1-\delta}$ square matrices $\{\mathbf{M}_{i,\gamma}\}_{\gamma\in[T]}$, each of size $(t = k^{\delta/2}) \times (t = k^{\delta/2})$. The assignment can be arbitrary as long as every element $\mathsf{Corr}[i,j]$ is assigned to a unique location in one of the matrices $\mathbf{M}_{i,j_1}[j_2, j_3]$. We denote by ϕ this assignement, $\phi(j) = (j_1, j_2, j_3)$. Observe that on average, each matrix $\mathbf{M}_{i,\gamma}$ contains less than 1 non-zero entries. By the independence of elements in Corr_i again, every matrix $\mathbf{M}_{i,\gamma}$ has at most λ non-zero entries, with overwhelming probability in λ. Thus, every matrix $\mathbf{M}_{i,\gamma}$ has rank less than λ and can be decomposed into $\mathbf{U}_{i,\gamma}, \mathbf{V}_{i,\gamma} \in \mathbb{Z}_p^{t\times\lambda}$ such that $\mathbf{M}_{i,\gamma} = \mathbf{U}_{i,\gamma} \cdot \mathbf{V}_{i,\gamma}^\top$. The compressed version $\mathsf{SI}_i = \{\mathbf{U}_{i,\gamma}, \mathbf{V}_{i,\gamma}\}_{\gamma\in[t_1]}$ contains exactly these $\mathbf{U}, \mathbf{V}$ matrices, and the value of $Q_i(\mathbf{x}_j)$ can be computed in degree $(O(1), 2)$ from PI, SI_0 and SI_i as follows:

$$Q_i(\mathbf{x}_j) = Q_i(\mathbf{b}_j - \mathbf{s}\mathbf{A}_j) - \big(\mathsf{Corr}[i,j] = \mathbf{M}_{i,j_1}[j_2, j_3]\big)$$
$$= Q_i(\mathbf{b}_j - \mathbf{s}\mathbf{A}_j) - \big(\mathbf{U}_{i,j_1} \cdot \mathbf{V}_{i,j_1}^\top\big)[j_2, j_3]$$

The size of $\mathsf{SI}_i = O(T \times t \times \lambda) = O(k^{1-\delta} \times k^{\delta/2} \times \lambda) = O(k^{1-\delta/2}\lambda)$ is sublinear in k as desired.

Computing of SI_i *in Sublinear Time.* We now show that beyond being size-succinct, each SI_i can also be computed in time sublinear in k in an amortized fashion. More precisely, we show that the collection of $\mathsf{SI}_1, \ldots, \mathsf{SI}_{m'}$ can be computed by a circuit of size $(nk^2 + m'k^{1-\delta/2})\mathsf{poly}(\lambda)$, which is sublinear in $m' \cdot k$ when k is set appropriately. We break down the task of computing $\mathsf{SI}_1, \ldots, \mathsf{SI}_{m'}$ in two steps.

1. Clearly, to compute each SI_i in amortized sublinear time in k, we cannot afford to compute the entire row Corr_i which has dimension k. Instead, we compute the list NZCorr_i of non-zero entries in Corr_i only, which has size $O(k^{1-\delta})$. More precisely, NZCorr_i consists of tuples of the form

$$\mathsf{NZCorr}_i = \{(j, \ \phi(j) = (j_1, j_2, j_3), \ \mathsf{Corr}[i, j]) \mid j \in [k], \ \mathsf{Corr}_i[j] \neq 0\} \ .$$

That is, it contains the index j of the non-zero entries in Corr_i, the matrix location they are assigned to $\mathbf{M}_{i,j_1}[j_2, j_2]$, and the value of the error $\mathsf{Corr}[i, j]$. Moreover, the list is sorted in ascending order with respect to coordinate j_1, so that tuples with the same value j_1 appear contiguously.
2. In the second step, we use these special lists $\{\mathsf{NZCorr}_i\}$ to compute SI_i.

Let's see how to do each step in amortized sublinear time, starting with the easier second step.

The Second Step: Given NZCorr_i, we can compute SI_i in time $\mathsf{poly}(\lambda)(k^{1-\delta/2})$. This is done by making a single pass on NZCorr_i and generating rows and columns of $\{\mathbf{U}_{i,\gamma}, \mathbf{V}_{i,\gamma}\}_{\gamma \in [T]}$ "on the fly". We can start by initializing these matrices with zero entries. Then for the ℓ'th tuple $(j, \phi(j) = (j_1, j_2, j_3), \mathsf{Corr}[i, j])$ in NZCorr_i, we set $\mathbf{U}_{i,j_1}[j_2, \ell] = \mathsf{Corr}[i, j]$ and $\mathbf{V}_{i,j_1}[j_3, \ell] = 1$. Since each matrix $\mathbf{M}_{i,\gamma}$ gets assigned at most λ non-zero entries, the index ℓ ranges from 1 up to λ, fitting the dimension of $\mathbf{U}$'s, and $\mathbf{V}$'s. Hence, this way of generating $\mathbf{U}_{i,\gamma}$ and $\mathbf{V}_{i,\gamma}$ guarantees that $\mathbf{M}_{i,\gamma} = \mathbf{U}_{i,\gamma} \mathbf{V}_{i,\gamma}^\top$.

The First Step: Next, we first illustrate how to generate all lists $\{\mathsf{NZCorr}_i\}_{i \in [m']}$ in sublinear time in $m'k$, in the Random Access Memory (RAM) model. The first sub-step is collecting information related to all the non-zero elements in the LPN errors $\{\mathbf{e}_j\}_{j \in [k]}$ used to encrypt the inputs $\{\mathbf{x}_j\}_{j \in [k]}$. More precisely, for every coordinate $l \in [n]$ in an input, form the list

$$\mathsf{NZInp}_l = \{(j, x_{j,l}, e_{j,l}) \mid e_{j,l} \neq 0\}_{j \in [k]} \ .$$

That is, NZInp_l contains the index j of each input $\mathbf{x}_j$, such that, the l'th element $x_{j,l}$ is blinded by a non-zero error $e_{j,l} \neq 0$, as well as the values $x_{j,l}, e_{j,l}$ of the input and error elements. Tuples in this list are sorted in ascending order with respect to coordinate j. Note that these lists can be computed in time $O(nk)$.

Now, think of a database that contains all $\{\mathsf{NZInp}_l\}_l$ and inputs $\{\mathbf{x}_j\}_j$, which can be randomly accessed. The second sub-step makes a pass over all monomials $Q_1, \ldots Q_{m'}$. Each monomial Q_i depends on at most d variables (out of n variables), say Q_i depends on variables at coordinates $\{l_1, \ldots, l_d\}$. For every monomial Q_i, with random access to the database, make a single pass on lists $\mathsf{NZInp}_{l_1}, \ldots, \mathsf{NZInp}_{l_d}$ and generate NZCorr_i on the fly. The fact that every list NZInp_l is sorted according to j ensures that the time spent for each Q_i is $O(k^{1-\delta})$. Thus, in the RAM model $\{\mathsf{NZCorr}_i\}_i$ can be constructed in sublinear time $O(m'k^{1-\delta})$. All we need to do now is coming up with a circuit to do the same.

Circuit Conversion. To obtain such a circuit, we examine each and every step inside the above RAM program and then replace them by suitable (sub)circuits, while preserving the overall running-time. Since the conversion is very technical, we refer the reader to the full version for details, and only highlight some of the tools used in the conversion. We make extensive use of sorting circuits of almost linear size [1] and Turing machine to circuit conversions. For example, at some point we have to replace RAM memory lookups by circuits. To do so, we prove the following simple lemma about RAM look up programs. A RAM lookup program $P_{q,N}^{\mathsf{lookup}}$ indexed with a number $N \in \mathbb{N}$ and a number $q \in \mathbb{N}$ is a program with the following structure: It takes as input q indices $\{i_1, \ldots, i_q\}$ and a database $\mathsf{DB} \in \{0,1\}^N$ and it outputs $\{\mathsf{DB}[i_1], \ldots, \mathsf{DB}[i_q]\}$. We show that this can be implemented efficiently by a circuit:

Lemma 3. *Let $q, N \in \mathbb{N}$. A RAM lookup program $P_{q,N}^{\mathsf{RAM}}$ (that looks up q indices from a database of size N) can be implemented by an efficiently uniformly generatable boolean circuit of size $O((q + N)\mathsf{poly}(\log_2(q \cdot N)))$ for some polynomial* poly.

Please see the full version [29] for how we use the above lemma and other technical details.

Outline. This completes are technical overview. In the main body, we present three abstractions PPE, ARE and PRE. In the full version, we show how to combine these abstractions along with a partially hiding FE scheme to build a sublinear functional encryption. The outline is summarized in Fig. 1.

3   Preliminaries

We now set up some notations that will be used throughout the paper. Throughout, we will denote the security parameter by λ. For any distribution $\mathcal{X}$, we denote by $x \leftarrow \mathcal{X}$ the process of sampling a value x from the distribution $\mathcal{X}$. Similarly, for a set X we denote by $x \leftarrow X$ the process of sampling x from the uniform distribution over X. For an integer $n \in \mathbb{N}$ we denote by $[n]$ the set $\{1, .., n\}$. Throughout, when we refer to polynomials in security parameter, we mean constant degree polynomials that take positive value on non-negative inputs. We denote by $\mathsf{poly}(\lambda)$ an arbitrary polynomial in λ satisfying the above requirements of non-negativity.

We use standard Landau notations. We will also use $\widetilde{O}$, where for any function $a(n, \lambda)$, $b(n, \lambda)$, we say that $a = \widetilde{O}(b)$ if $a(n, \lambda) = O(b(n, \lambda)\mathsf{poly}(\lambda, \log_2 n))$ for some polynomial poly. A function $\mathsf{negl} : \mathbb{N} \to \mathbb{R}$ is negligible if $\mathsf{negl}(\lambda) = \lambda^{-\omega(1)}$. Further, the negl is subexponentially small if $\mathsf{negl}(\lambda) = 2^{-\lambda^{\Omega(1)}}$.

We denote vectors by bold-faced letters such as $\mathbf{b}$ and $\mathbf{u}$. Matrices will be denoted by capitalized bold-faced letters for such as $\mathbf{A}$ and $\mathbf{M}$. For any $k \in \mathbb{N}$, we denote by the notation $\mathbf{v}^{\otimes k} = \underbrace{\mathbf{v} \otimes \cdots \otimes \mathbf{v}}_{k}$ the standard tensor product. This contains all the monomials in the variables inside $\mathbf{v}$ of degree exactly k.

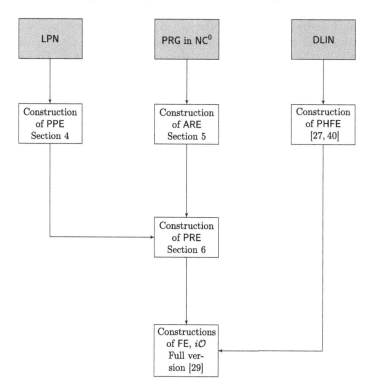

Fig. 1. Flowchart depicting the technical outline.

Multilinear Representation of Polynomials and Representation over $\mathbb{Z}_p$. A straightforward fact from analysis of boolean functions is that every NC^0 function $F : \{0,1\}^n \to \{0,1\}$ can be represented by a unique constant degree multilinear polynomial $f \in \mathbb{Z}[\mathbf{x} = (x_1, \ldots, x_n)]$, mapping $\{0,1\}^n$ to $\{0,1\}$. At times, we consider a mapping of such polynomial $f \in \mathbb{Z}[\mathbf{x}]$ into a polynomial g over $\mathbb{Z}_p[\mathbf{x}]$ for some prime p. This is simply obtained by reducing the coefficients of f modulo p and then evaluating the polynomial over $\mathbb{Z}_p$. Observe that $g(\mathbf{x}) = f(\mathbf{x}) \mod p$ for every $\mathbf{x} \in \{0,1\}^n$ as $f(\mathbf{x}) \in \{0,1\}$ for every such $\mathbf{x}$. Furthermore, given any NC^0 function F, finding these representations take polynomial time.

Computational Indistinguishability. We now describe how computational indistinguishability is formalized.

Definition 4 (ϵ-indistinguishability). *We say that two ensembles $\mathcal{X} = \{\mathcal{X}_\lambda\}_{\lambda \in \mathbb{N}}$ and $\mathcal{Y} = \{\mathcal{Y}_\lambda\}_{\lambda \in \mathbb{N}}$ are ϵ-indistinguishable where $\epsilon : \mathbb{N} \to [0, 1]$ if for every probabilistic polynomial time adversary $\mathcal{A}$ it holds that: For every sufficiently large $\lambda \in \mathbb{N}$,*

$$\left| \Pr_{x \leftarrow \mathcal{X}_\lambda} [\mathcal{A}(1^\lambda, x) = 1] - \Pr_{y \leftarrow \mathcal{Y}_\lambda} [\mathcal{A}(1^\lambda, y) = 1] \right| \leq \epsilon(\lambda).$$

We say that two ensembles are computationally indistinguishable if they are ϵ-indistinguishable for $\epsilon(\lambda) = \mathsf{negl}(\lambda)$ for some negligible negl, and that two ensembles are sub-exponentially indistinguishable if they are ϵ-indistinguishable for $\epsilon(\lambda) = 2^{-\lambda^c}$ for some positive real number c.

Assumptions. We make use of three assumptions. We state the two assumptions LPN and PRG below, which are used to build the components which are new to this paper. Please see [30] for a formal definition of DLIN.

Definition 5 (δ-LPN (Assumption, [9,15,16,24])). *Let $\delta \in (0, 1)$. We say that the δ-LPN Assumption is true if the following holds: For any constant $\eta_p > 0$, any function $p : \mathbb{N} \to \mathbb{N}$ s.t., for every $\ell \in \mathbb{N}$, $p(\ell)$ is a prime of ℓ^{η_p} bits, any constant $\eta_n > 0$, we set $p = p(\ell)$, $n = n(\ell) = \ell^{\eta_n}$, and $r = r(\ell) = \ell^{-\delta}$, and we require that the following two distributions are computationally indistinguishable:*

$$\left\{ (\mathbf{A}, \mathbf{b} = \mathbf{s} \cdot \mathbf{A} + \mathbf{e}) \mid \mathbf{A} \leftarrow \mathbb{Z}_p^{\ell \times n}, \ \mathbf{s} \leftarrow \mathbb{Z}_p^{1 \times \ell}, \ \mathbf{e} \leftarrow \mathcal{D}_r^{1 \times n}(p) \right\}_{\ell \in \mathbb{N}}$$

$$\left\{ (\mathbf{A}, \mathbf{u}) \mid \mathbf{A} \leftarrow \mathbb{Z}_p^{\ell \times n}, \ \mathbf{u} \leftarrow \mathbb{Z}_p^{1 \times n} \right\}_{\ell \in \mathbb{N}}$$

In addition, we say that subexponential δ-LPN holds if the two distributions above are subexponentially indistinguishable.

The second assumption we use is of that of an existence of Boolean PRG in NC^0 with polynomial stretch.

Definition 6 *(Pseudorandom Generator).* *A stretch-$m(\cdot)$ pseudorandom generator is a Boolean function $\mathsf{PRG} : \{0,1\}^* \to \{0,1\}^*$ mapping n-bit inputs to $m(n)$-bit outputs (also known as the stretch) that is computable by a uniform p.p.t. machine, and for any non-uniform p.p.t adversary $\mathcal{A}$ there exist a negligible function negl such that, for all $n \in \mathbb{N}$*

$$\left| \Pr_{r \leftarrow \{0,1\}^n} [\mathcal{A}(\mathsf{PRG}(r)) = 1] - \Pr_{z \leftarrow \{0,1\}^m} [\mathcal{A}(z) = 1] \right| < \mathsf{negl}(n).$$

Further, a PRG is said to be in NC^0 if PRG is implementable by a uniformly efficiently generatable NC^0 circuit. PRG is said to have polynomial stretch if $m(n) = n^{1+\Omega(1)}$. Finally, PRG is said to be subexponentially secure if $\mathsf{negl}(n) = O(\exp(-n^{\Omega(1)}))$.

Remark 7. In the candidate constructions, typically there is a sampling algorithm that samples the description of PRG, and this property of computational indistinguishability is expected to hold with probability $1 - o(1)$ over the choice of PRG. Such a PRG will give us an existential result. Constructively, this issue can be addressed by constructing our FE scheme with multiple instantiations of PRG so that with overwhelming probability, at least one of the FE schemes we build is secure, and then using an FE combiner [3,31].

4   Preprocessed Polynomial Encoding

In this section, we formally define a PPE scheme. Before we formally define the notion we introduce the function class $\mathcal{F}_{\mathsf{PPE}}$. We first define the notion of a degree d monomial pattern $\mathcal{Q}$ over n variables which is just a collection of monomials of degree at most d.

Definition 8 (*d-monomial pattern and monomials*). *For an integer $d > 0$, and an integer $n > d \in \mathbb{N}$, we say $\mathcal{Q}$ is a d-monomial pattern over n variables, if $\mathcal{Q} = \{Q_1, \ldots, Q_m\}$, where for every $i \in [m]$, we have that $0 < |Q_i| \leq d$, and each Q_i is a distinct subset of $[n]$. For any input $\mathbf{x} \in \{0,1\}^n$ and a set $Q \subseteq [n]$, define $\mathsf{Mon}_Q(\mathbf{x}) = \prod_{i \in Q} x_i$ to be the monomial in $\mathbf{x}$ corresponding to the set Q. Thus, for any input $\mathbf{x}$, a d-monomial pattern $\mathcal{Q} = \{Q_1, \ldots, Q_m\}$ over n variables defines m monomials of degree at most d.*

We denote by $\Gamma_{d,n}$ the set of all d-monomial patterns over n variables.

Definition 9 (**Polynomial Class $\mathcal{F}_{\mathsf{PPE}}$**). *For a constant $d \in \mathbb{N}$, the family of classes of polynomials $\mathcal{F}_{\mathsf{PPE},d} = \{\mathcal{F}_{\mathsf{PPE},d,n_{\mathsf{PPE}},\mathcal{Q},k_{\mathsf{PPE}}}\}_{d \leq n_{\mathsf{PPE}} \in \mathbb{N}, \mathcal{Q} \in \Gamma_{d,n_{\mathsf{PPE}}}, k_{\mathsf{PPE}} \in [N]}$ consists of polynomials $f \in \mathcal{F}_{\mathsf{PPE},d,n_{\mathsf{PPE}},\mathcal{Q},k_{\mathsf{PPE}}}$ of the following kind: f is defined by a sequence of integers $(\zeta_i^{(j)})_{j \in [k_{\mathsf{PPE}}], i \in [m_{\mathsf{PPE}}]}$. It takes as input $\mathbf{x}$ consisting of k_{PPE} blocks $\mathbf{x} = (\mathbf{x}^{(1)}, \ldots, \mathbf{x}^{(k_{\mathsf{PPE}})})$ each of n_{PPE} variables, and has form:*

$$f(\mathbf{x}) := \sum_{j \in [k_{\mathsf{PPE}}],\ Q_i \in \mathcal{Q}} \zeta_i^{(j)} \mathsf{Mon}_{Q_i}(\mathbf{x}^{(j)}),$$

where $\mathcal{Q}$ is a d-monomial pattern with $|\mathcal{Q}| = m_{\mathsf{PPE}}$.

In a nutshell, $\mathcal{F}_{\mathsf{PPE}}$ consists of polynomials that take as input a k_{PPE} blocks of inputs of size n_{PPE}, and computes all polynomials that are linear combination of some fixed constant degree d monomials on those inputs governed by a set $\mathcal{Q}$. Looking ahead, for the PPE scheme we will require that the size of the circuit computing $(\mathsf{PI}, \mathsf{SI})$ will be sublinear in $|\mathcal{Q}| \cdot k_{\mathsf{PPE}}$.

Definition 10 (Syntax of PPE). *For any constant $d > 0$, a PPE scheme for function class $\mathcal{F}_{\mathsf{PPE},d}$ consists of the following p.p.t. algorithms:*

- *$(\mathsf{PI}, \mathsf{SI}) \leftarrow \mathsf{PreProc}(1^{n_{\mathsf{PPE}}}, 1^{k_{\mathsf{PPE}}}, p, \mathcal{Q}, \mathbf{x} \in \mathbb{Z}_p^{n_{\mathsf{PPE}} \cdot k_{\mathsf{PPE}}})$: The randomized Pre-processing algorithm takes as input the block length parameter n_{PPE}, the number of blocks parameter k_{PPE}, a prime p, a d-monomial pattern on n_{PPE} variables $\mathcal{Q}$ of size m_{PPE}, and an input $\mathbf{x} \in \mathbb{Z}_p^{n_{\mathsf{PPE}} \cdot k_{\mathsf{PPE}}}$. It processes it to output two strings, a public string PI and a private string SI. Both these strings are vectors over $\mathbb{Z}_p$. We denote by $\ell_{\mathsf{PPE}} = \ell_{\mathsf{PPE}}(n_{\mathsf{PPE}}, m_{\mathsf{PPE}}, k_{\mathsf{PPE}})$ the combined dimension of $(\mathsf{PI}, \mathsf{SI})$ over $\mathbb{Z}_p$.*
- *$y \leftarrow \mathsf{Eval}(f \in \mathcal{F}_{\mathsf{PPE},d,n_{\mathsf{PPE}},\mathcal{Q},k_{\mathsf{PPE}}}, (\mathsf{PI}, \mathsf{SI}))$: The deterministic evaluation algorithm takes as input the description of a function $f \in \mathcal{F}_{d,n_{\mathsf{PPE}},\mathcal{Q},k_{\mathsf{PPE}}}$ and a pre-processed input $(\mathsf{PI}, \mathsf{SI})$. It outputs $y \in \mathbb{Z}_p$.*

The correctness requirement is completely straightforward namely y should be equal to $f(\mathbf{x})$ with high probability.

Definition 11 ((Statistical) Correctness of PPE). *Let $d > 0$ be a constant integer, a PPE scheme for the function class $\mathcal{F}_{d,\mathsf{PPE}}$ satisfies correctness if: For every $k_{\mathsf{PPE}} \in \mathbb{N}$, $n_{\mathsf{PPE}} = k^{\Theta(1)}$, and $\mathcal{Q} \in \Gamma_{d,n_{\mathsf{PPE}}}$ with $m_{\mathsf{PPE}} \geq 1$ sets, any function $f \in \mathcal{F}_{d,\mathsf{PPE},n_{\mathsf{PPE}},\mathcal{Q},k_{\mathsf{PPE}}}$, any prime p and any input $\mathbf{x} \in \mathbb{Z}_p^{n_{\mathsf{PPE}} \cdot k_{\mathsf{PPE}}}$:*

$$\Pr\left[\mathsf{Eval}(f, (\mathsf{PI}, \mathsf{SI})) = f(\mathbf{x}) \bmod p \big| (\mathsf{PI}, \mathsf{SI}) \leftarrow \mathsf{PreProc}(1^{n_{\mathsf{PPE}}}, 1^{k_{\mathsf{PPE}}}, p, \mathcal{Q}, \mathbf{x})\right]$$
$$\geq 1 - O(\exp(-k_{\mathsf{PPE}}^{\Omega(1)}))$$

Note that we require correctness to hold when k_{PPE} is large enough, we will also require the security to hold for large values of k_{PPE}. The next definition we discuss is that of security. The security definition roughly requires that for any input $\mathbf{x} \in \mathbb{Z}_p^{n_{\mathsf{PPE}} \cdot k_{\mathsf{PPE}}}$, the public part of the computed pre-processed input while pre-processing $\mathbf{x}$ is computationally indistinguishable to the public part of the pre-processed input when the pre-processing is done for the input $0^{n_{\mathsf{PPE}} \cdot k_{\mathsf{PPE}}}$.

Definition 12 (Security of PPE). *Let $d > 0$ be an integer constant. A PPE scheme is secure, if the following holds: Let $\beta > 0$ be any constant and p : $\mathbb{N} \to \mathbb{N}$ be any function that on input an integer r, outputs an r^β bit prime. Let $n_{\mathsf{PPE}} = k_{\mathsf{PPE}}^{\Theta(1)}$ be any polynomial in k_{PPE}. Let $p = p(k_{\mathsf{PPE}})$ and $\{\mathbf{x}_{k_{\mathsf{PPE}}}\}_{k_{\mathsf{PPE}} \in \mathbb{N}}$ be any ensemble of inputs where each $\mathbf{x}_{k_{\mathsf{PPE}}} \in \mathbb{Z}_p^{n_{\mathsf{PPE}} \cdot k_{\mathsf{PPE}}}$ and $\{\mathcal{Q}_{k_{\mathsf{PPE}}}\}_{k_{\mathsf{PPE}} \in \mathbb{N}}$ be ensemble of monomial patterns with $\mathcal{Q}_{k_{\mathsf{PPE}}} \in \Gamma_{d,n_{\mathsf{PPE}}}$ with size $m_{\mathsf{PPE}} \geq 1$. Then for $k_{\mathsf{PPE}} \in \mathbb{N}$, it holds that for any probabilistic polynomial time adversary, following distributions are computationally indistinguishable with the advantage bounded by $\mathsf{negl}(k_{\mathsf{PPE}})$.*

$$\left\{ \mathsf{PI} \mid (\mathsf{PI}, \mathsf{SI}) \leftarrow \mathsf{PreProc}(1^{n_{\mathsf{PPE}}}, 1^{k_{\mathsf{PPE}}}, p, \mathcal{Q}_{k_{\mathsf{PPE}}}, \mathbf{x}_{k_{\mathsf{PPE}}}) \right\}_{k_{\mathsf{PPE}}}$$

$$\left\{ \mathsf{PI} \mid (\mathsf{PI}, \mathsf{SI}) \leftarrow \mathsf{PreProc}(1^{n_{\mathsf{PPE}}}, 1^{k_{\mathsf{PPE}}}, p, \mathcal{Q}_{k_{\mathsf{PPE}}}, 0^{n_{\mathsf{PPE}} \cdot k_{\mathsf{PPE}}}) \right\}_{k_{\mathsf{PPE}}}$$

Further, the scheme is said to be subexponentially secure if $\mathsf{negl}(k_{\mathsf{PPE}}) = \exp(-k_{\mathsf{PPE}}^{\Omega(1)})$.

Definition 13 (Sublinear Pre-processing Efficiency). *Let $d > 0$ be a constant integer. We say that* PPE *scheme for* $\mathcal{F}_{\mathsf{PPE},d}$ *satisfies sublinear efficiency if there exists a polynomial* poly *and constants* $c_1, c_2, c_3 > 0$ *such that for* $n_{\mathsf{PPE}}, k_{\mathsf{PPE}} \in \mathbb{N}$, $\mathcal{Q} \in \Gamma_{d, n_{\mathsf{PPE}}}$ *with size* $m_{\mathsf{PPE}} \geq 1$ *and a prime p the size of the circuit computing* $\mathsf{PreProc}(1^{n_{\mathsf{PPE}}}, 1^{k_{\mathsf{PPE}}}, p, \mathcal{Q}, \cdot)$ *is* $t_{\mathsf{PPE}} = O((n_{\mathsf{PPE}} \cdot k_{\mathsf{PPE}}^{c_1} + m_{\mathsf{PPE}} \cdot k_{\mathsf{PPE}}^{1-c_2} + k_{\mathsf{PPE}}^{c_3})\mathsf{poly}(\log_2 p))$.

The reason we call this requirement as sublinear pre-processing efficiency is that if $m_{\mathsf{PPE}} = n_{\mathsf{PPE}}^{1+\Omega(1)}$, then, one can find a small enough $k_{\mathsf{PPE}} = n_{\mathsf{PPE}}^{\Omega(1)}$ such that $t_{\mathsf{PPE}} = \tilde{O}((m_{\mathsf{PPE}}k_{\mathsf{PPE}})^{1-\Omega(1)})$ where $\tilde{O}$ hides polynomial factors in $\log_2 p$. Finally we present the requirement that the evaluation for any function f, can be done by a constant degree polynomial g_f that is just degree two in SI.

Definition 14 (Complexity of Evaluation). *Let $d \in \mathbb{N}$ be any constant. We require that* PPE *scheme for* $\mathcal{F}_{\mathsf{PPE},d}$ *satisfies the following. We require that for every $k_{\mathsf{PPE}} \in \mathbb{N}$, $n_{\mathsf{PPE}} = k_{\mathsf{PPE}}^{\Theta(1)}$, and $\Gamma \in \Gamma_{d, n_{\mathsf{PPE}}}$ of size $m_{\mathsf{PPE}} \geq 1$, any prime p, any input $\mathbf{x} \in \mathbb{Z}_p^{n_{\mathsf{PPE}} \cdot k_{\mathsf{PPE}}}$, any pre-processed input $(\mathsf{PI}, \mathsf{SI}) \leftarrow \mathsf{PreProc}(1^{n_{\mathsf{PPE}}}, 1^{k_{\mathsf{PPE}}}, p, \Gamma, \mathbf{x})$, and any $f \in \mathcal{F}_{d, n_{\mathsf{PPE}}, \mathcal{Q}, k_{\mathsf{PPE}}}$, the following relation is satisfied:*

$$\mathsf{Eval}(f, (\mathsf{PI}, \mathsf{SI})) = g_{f, \mathcal{Q}}(\mathsf{PI}, \mathsf{SI}) \mod p$$

where $g_{f, \mathcal{Q}}(\cdot, \cdot)$ is an efficiently computable (multivariate) polynomial over $\mathbb{Z}_p$ of degree $O(d)$ in PI and degree 2 in SI.

4.1 PPE Construction Details

In this section, we present our construction of PPE scheme. Before delving into the construction, we describe the list of notations that will be useful:

- Parameters $t_1 = \lceil k^{1-\delta} \rceil$ and $T = \lceil k^{\delta/2} \rceil$. Observe that $2 \cdot k_{\mathsf{PPE}} \geq t_1 \cdot T^2 \geq k_{\mathsf{PPE}}$.
- t is the slack parameter. It is set as $k_{\mathsf{PPE}}^{\frac{\delta}{10}}$,
- **Map ϕ:** We define an injective map ϕ which canonically maps k_{PPE} elements into t_1 buckets (equivalently called as a matrices in the text below), each having a size of $T \times T$. For every $j \in [k_{\mathsf{PPE}}]$, $\phi(j) = (j_1, (j_2, j_3))$ where $j_1 \in [t_1]$, $(j_2, j_3) \in [T] \times [T]$. Such a map can be computed in time polynomial in $\log_2 k_{\mathsf{PPE}}$ and can be computed by first dividing $j \in [k_{\mathsf{PPE}}]$ by t_1 and setting its remainder as j_1. Then the quotient of this division is further divided by T. The quotient and the remainder of this division are set as (j_2, j_3).

Construction of PPE

$(\mathsf{PI}, \mathsf{SI}) \;\leftarrow\; \mathsf{PreProc}(1^{n_{\mathsf{PPE}}}, 1^{k_{\mathsf{PPE}}}, p, \mathcal{Q} = (Q_1, \ldots, Q_{m_{\mathsf{PPE}}}), \mathbf{x})$: Below we describe the pseudo-code. We show how to construct a circuit for the same when we talk about preprocessing efficiency property of the scheme. Perform the following steps:

- Parse $\mathbf{x} = (\mathbf{x}_1, \ldots, \mathbf{x}_{k_{\mathsf{PPE}}})$ where each $\mathbf{x}_j \in \mathbb{Z}_p^{n_{\mathsf{PPE}}}$. Parse $\mathbf{x}_j = (x_{j,1}, \ldots, x_{j,n_{\mathsf{PPE}}})$.
- The overall outline is the following: We first show how to sample components $\mathsf{PI}' = (\mathsf{PI}_1, \ldots, \mathsf{PI}_{k_{\mathsf{PPE}}})$, and then how to sample SI along with a boolean variable flag. PI will be set as $(\mathsf{flag}, \mathsf{PI}')$.
- **Sampling** $\mathsf{PI}' = (\mathsf{PI}_1, \ldots, \mathsf{PI}_{k_{\mathsf{PPE}}})$: Sample $\mathbf{s} \leftarrow \mathbb{Z}_p^{k_{\mathsf{PPE}}}$. For every $i \in [n_{\mathsf{PPE}}]$, and $j \in [k_{\mathsf{PPE}}]$:
  1. Sample $\mathbf{a}_{j,i} \leftarrow \mathbb{Z}_p^{k_{\mathsf{PPE}}}$.
  2. Sample $e_{j,i} \leftarrow \mathsf{Ber}(k_{\mathsf{PPE}}^{-\delta}) \cdot \mathbb{Z}_p$. Denote $\mathbf{e}_j = (e_{j,1}, \ldots, e_{j,n_{\mathsf{PPE}}})$.
  3. Compute $b_{j,i} = \langle \mathbf{a}_{j,i}, \mathbf{s} \rangle + e_{j,i} + x_{j,i} \mod p$.
  For $j \in [k_{\mathsf{PPE}}]$, set $\mathsf{PI}_j = \{\mathbf{a}_{j,i}, b_{j,i}\}_{i \in [n_{\mathsf{PPE}}]}$.
- **Sampling** SI: SI has $m_{\mathsf{PPE}} + 1$ components. That is, $\mathsf{SI} = (\mathsf{SI}_0, \ldots, \mathsf{SI}_{m_{\mathsf{PPE}}})$. Set $\mathsf{SI}_0 = (1, \mathbf{s})^{\otimes \lceil \frac{d}{2} \rceil}$. We now show how to compute SI_r for $r \in [m_{\mathsf{PPE}}]$.
  1. For $j \in [k_{\mathsf{PPE}}]$, compute $\mathsf{Corr}_{r,j} = \mathsf{Mon}_{Q_r}(\mathbf{x}_j) - \mathsf{Mon}_{Q_r}(\mathbf{x}_j + \mathbf{e}_j)$.
  2. Initialize for every $\gamma \in [t_1]$, matrices $\mathbf{M}_{r,\gamma}$ in $\mathbb{Z}_p^{T \times T}$ with zero entries.
  3. For $j \in [k_{\mathsf{PPE}}]$, compute $\phi(j) = (j_1, (j_2, j_3))$ and set $\mathbf{M}_{r,j_1}[j_2, j_3] = \mathsf{Corr}_{r,j}$. If any matrix $\mathbf{M}_{r,\gamma}$ for $\gamma \in [t_1]$, has more than t non-zero entries, then set $\mathsf{flag}_r = 0$. Otherwise, set $\mathsf{flag}_r = 1$.
  4. If $\mathsf{flag}_r = 1$, then, for $\gamma \in [t_1]$, compute matrices $\mathbf{U}_{r,\gamma}, \mathbf{V}_{r,\gamma}^\top \in \mathbb{Z}_p^{T \times t}$ such that $\mathbf{M}_{r,\gamma} = \mathbf{U}_{r,\gamma} \cdot \mathbf{V}_{r,\gamma}$. Otherwise for every $\gamma \in [t_1]$, set $\mathbf{U}_{r,\gamma}, \mathbf{V}_{r,\gamma}$ to be matrices with zero-entries.
  5. Set $\mathsf{SI}_r = \{\mathbf{U}_{r,\gamma}, \mathbf{V}_{r,\gamma}\}_{\gamma \in [t_1]}$.
- **Sampling flag:** For every $i \in [n_{\mathsf{PPE}}]$, let $\mathsf{Set}_i = \{j \in [k_{\mathsf{PPE}}] | e_{j,i} \neq 0\}$. If any of these sets have size outside the range $[k_{\mathsf{PPE}}^{1-\delta} - t k_{\mathsf{PPE}}^{\frac{1-\delta}{2}}, k_{\mathsf{PPE}}^{1-\delta} + t k_{\mathsf{PPE}}^{\frac{1-\delta}{2}}]$, set $\mathsf{flag} = 0$. Otherwise, set $\mathsf{flag} = \min\{\mathsf{flag}_r\}_{r \in [m]}$.

$y \leftarrow \mathsf{Eval}(f, (\mathsf{PI}, \mathsf{SI}))$: Parse $\mathsf{PI} = (\mathsf{flag}, \mathsf{PI}_1, \ldots, \mathsf{PI}_{k_{\mathsf{PPE}}})$ where $\mathsf{PI}_j = \{\mathbf{a}_{j,i}, b_{j,i}\}_{i \in [n_{\mathsf{PPE}}]}$. Similarly, parse $\mathsf{SI} = (\mathsf{SI}_0, \ldots, \mathsf{SI}_{m_{\mathsf{PPE}}})$. Here $\mathsf{SI}_0 = (1, \mathbf{s})^{\otimes \lceil \frac{d}{2} \rceil}$ and $\mathsf{SI}_r = \{\mathbf{U}_{r,\gamma}, \mathbf{V}_{r,\gamma}\}_{\gamma \in [t_1]}$ for $r \in [m_{\mathsf{PPE}}]$. Parse $\mathbf{x} = (\mathbf{x}_1, \ldots, \mathbf{x}_{k_{\mathsf{PPE}}})$ and $f(\mathbf{x}) = \sum_{r \in [m_{\mathsf{PPE}}], j \in [k_{\mathsf{PPE}}]} \mu_{r,j} \mathsf{Mon}_{Q_r}(\mathbf{x}_j)$ for $\mu_{r,j} \in \mathbb{Z}$. Output:

$$g_{f,\mathcal{Q}}(\mathsf{PI}, \mathsf{SI}) = \sum_{r \in [m_{\mathsf{PPE}}], j \in [k_{\mathsf{PPE}}]} \mu_{r,j} w_{r,j}(\mathsf{PI}, \mathsf{SI}),$$

where the polynomial $w_{r,j}(\mathsf{PI},\mathsf{SI})$ is the following:

$$w_{r,j}(\mathsf{PI},\mathsf{SI}) = \mathsf{flag} \cdot (\mathsf{Mon}_{Q_r}(b_{j,1} - \langle \mathbf{a}_{j,1},\mathbf{s} \rangle, \dots, b_{j,n_{\mathsf{PPE}}} - \langle \mathbf{a}_{j,n_{\mathsf{PPE}}},\mathbf{s} \rangle))$$
$$+ \mathsf{flag} \cdot \mathbf{U}_{r,j_1} \cdot \mathbf{V}_{r,j_1}[j_2,j_3],$$

where $\phi(j) = (j_1,(j_2,j_3))$. We remark that the polynomial above is written as a function of $\mathbf{s}$ and not SI_0, however, since we always mean $\mathsf{SI}_0 = (1,\mathbf{s})^{\otimes \lceil \frac{d}{2} \rceil}$, we treat this polynomial as some degree-2 polynomial in SI_0.

Remark 15. The only difference to the scheme described in the overview is that the scheme also uses a boolean variable flag. flag will be 1 with overwhelming probability, and is set to 0 when "certain" low probability events happen. As described earlier, the size of the input $(\mathsf{PI},\mathsf{SI})$ is already sublinear. Later, we describe how even the time to compute it is sublinear.

In the full version [29], we argue correctness, efficiency, complexity and security properties.

Summing Up: From the above theorems, we have the following result:

Theorem 16. *Assuming δ-LPN assumption (Definition 5) holds for any constant $\delta > 0$, then there exists a PPE scheme satisfying Definition 10. Further, if the assumption is subexponentially secure, then so is the resulting PPE scheme.*

5 Amortized Randomized Encoding

We now formally define the notion of an amortized RE scheme (which we will denote by ARE). The notion is designed to be exactly compatible with a PPE scheme. The function class $\mathcal{F}_{\mathsf{ARE}}$ is identical to the class for the PRE scheme $\mathcal{F}_{\mathsf{PRE}}$. Namely, $\mathcal{F}_{\mathsf{ARE}} = \{\mathcal{F}_{\mathsf{ARE},n_{\mathsf{ARE}},m_{\mathsf{ARE}},k_{\mathsf{ARE}},\lambda}\}_{n_{\mathsf{ARE}},k_{\mathsf{ARE}},m_{\mathsf{ARE}},\lambda \in \mathbb{N}}$ consists of all circuits $C : \{0,1\}^{n_{\mathsf{ARE}}} \to \{0,1\}^{m_{\mathsf{ARE}} \cdot k_{\mathsf{ARE}}}$ where every bit of the output is computed by a Boolean formula of size λ (circuits where each gate has a single fan-out). Such an ARE scheme has the following syntax:

Definition 17 (Syntax of ARE). *An ARE scheme consists of the following p.p.t. algorithms:*

- Encode$(C \in \mathcal{F}_{\mathsf{ARE},n_{\mathsf{ARE}},m_{\mathsf{ARE}},k_{\mathsf{ARE}},\lambda}, \mathbf{x} \in \{0,1\}^{n_{\mathsf{ARE}}}) \to \mathbf{y}$. *The encoding algorithm is a randomized algorithm that takes as input a circuit $C \in \mathcal{F}_{\mathsf{ARE},n_{\mathsf{ARE}},m_{\mathsf{ARE}},k_{\mathsf{ARE}},\lambda}$ along with an input $\mathbf{x} \in \{0,1\}^{n_{\mathsf{ARE}}}$. It outputs a string $\mathbf{y} \in \{0,1\}^*$.*
- Decode$(1^\lambda, 1^{n_{\mathsf{ARE}}}, 1^{m_{\mathsf{ARE}}}, 1^{k_{\mathsf{ARE}}}, \mathbf{y}) \to \mathbf{z}$: *The deterministic decode algorithm takes as input a string $\mathbf{y}$. It outputs $\mathbf{z} \in \perp \cup \{0,1\}^{m_{\mathsf{ARE}} \cdot k_{\mathsf{ARE}}}$.*

An ARE scheme satisfies the following properties.

Definition 18 ((Perfect) Correctness of ARE). *A* ARE *scheme for the function class* $\mathcal{F}_{\mathsf{ARE}}$ *satisfies correctness if: For every polynomials* $n_{\mathsf{ARE}}(\cdot)$, $m_{\mathsf{ARE}}(\cdot), k_{\mathsf{ARE}}(\cdot)$, *every* $\lambda \in \mathbb{N}$, *let* $n_{\mathsf{ARE}} = n_{\mathsf{ARE}}(\lambda), m_{\mathsf{ARE}} = m_{\mathsf{ARE}}(\lambda), k_{\mathsf{ARE}} = k_{\mathsf{ARE}}(\lambda)$. *Then, for every* $\mathbf{x} \in \{0,1\}^{n_{\mathsf{ARE}}}$, $C \in \mathcal{F}_{\mathsf{ARE}, n_{\mathsf{ARE}}, m_{\mathsf{ARE}}, k_{\mathsf{ARE}}, \lambda}$:

$$\Pr\left[\mathsf{Decode}(1^\lambda, 1^{n_{\mathsf{ARE}}}, 1^{m_{\mathsf{ARE}}}, 1^{k_{\mathsf{ARE}}}, \mathbf{y}) = C(\mathbf{x}) \big| \mathbf{y} \leftarrow \mathsf{Encode}(C, \mathbf{x})\right] = 1$$

Definition 19 (Indistinguishability Security). *We say that* ARE *scheme is secure if the following holds: Let* $\lambda \in \mathbb{N}$ *be the security parameter, and* $n_{\mathsf{ARE}}, m_{\mathsf{ARE}}, k_{\mathsf{ARE}} = \Theta(\lambda^{\Theta(1)})$ *be polynomials in* λ. *For every sequence* $\{C, \mathbf{x}_0, \mathbf{x}_1\}_\lambda$ *where* $\mathbf{x}_0, \mathbf{x}_1 \in \{0,1\}^{n_{\mathsf{ARE}}}$ *and* $C \in \mathcal{F}_{\mathsf{ARE}, n_{\mathsf{ARE}}, m_{\mathsf{ARE}}, k_{\mathsf{ARE}}, \lambda}$ *with* $C(\mathbf{x}_0) = C(\mathbf{x}_1)$, *it holds that for* $\lambda \in \mathbb{N}$ *the following distributions are computationally indistinguishable*

$$\{\mathbf{y} \mid \mathbf{y} \leftarrow \mathsf{ARE.Encode}(C, \mathbf{x}_0)\}$$
$$\{\mathbf{y} \mid \mathbf{y} \leftarrow \mathsf{ARE.Encode}(C, \mathbf{x}_1)\}$$

Further, we say that ARE *is subexponentially secure the above distributions are subexponentially indistinguishable.*

Efficiency Properties. We require that such an ARE scheme is compatible with a PPE scheme. Namely, the encoding operation $\mathsf{Encode}(C, \cdot)$ uses a constant degree d-monomial pattern $\mathcal{Q}$ of small size $m'_{\mathsf{ARE}} = O((n_{\mathsf{ARE}} + m_{\mathsf{ARE}})\mathsf{poly}(\lambda))$ over $n'_{\mathsf{ARE}} = O((n_{\mathsf{ARE}} + m_{\mathsf{ARE}}^{1-\Omega(1)})\mathsf{poly}(\lambda))$ variables such that every bit is computable using those monomials. Namely:

Definition 20 (Efficiency). *We require that there exists constants* $d \in \mathbb{N}, c_1, c_2 > 0$, *such that the following holds. For any* $\lambda \in \mathbb{N}$ *and any* $n_{\mathsf{ARE}}, k_{\mathsf{ARE}}, m_{\mathsf{ARE}} = \lambda^{\Omega(1)}$, *there exists an efficiently samplable degree* d-monomial pattern $\mathcal{Q}$ *of size* $m'_{\mathsf{ARE}} = O((n_{\mathsf{ARE}} + m_{\mathsf{ARE}})\lambda^{c_1})$ *such that for any circuit* $C \in \mathcal{F}_{\mathsf{ARE}, n_{\mathsf{ARE}}, m_{\mathsf{ARE}}, k_{\mathsf{ARE}}, \lambda}$ *and input* $\mathbf{x} \in \{0,1\}^{n_{\mathsf{ARE}}}$, $\mathsf{Encode}(C, \mathbf{x}; \mathbf{r}) \to \mathbf{y} \in \{0,1\}^T$ *satisfies the following requirements:*

- *Parse* $\mathbf{r} = (\mathbf{r}_1, \ldots, \mathbf{r}_{k_{\mathsf{ARE}}})$ *where each component is of equal size. Let* $\mathbf{a}_i = (\mathbf{x}, \mathbf{r}_i)$. *Then the length of* $\mathbf{a}_i \in \{0,1\}^{n'_{\mathsf{ARE}}}$ *is* $n'_{\mathsf{ARE}} = O((n_{\mathsf{ARE}} + m_{\mathsf{ARE}}^{1-c_2})\lambda^{c_1})$.
- *For* $i \in [T]$, *each* $y_i = \sum_{Q \in \mathcal{Q}, j \in [k_{\mathsf{ARE}}]} \mu_{i,Q,j} \cdot \mathsf{Mon}_Q(\mathbf{a}_j)$ *for efficiently samplable* $\mu_{i,Q,j} \in \mathbb{Z}$.

The first property is to ensure that $\mathbf{a}_i$ for $i \in [k_{\mathsf{ARE}}]$ will be the k_{ARE} blocks that will be preprocessed by the PPE scheme in our construction of PRE. The monomial pattern used by the PRE will be $\mathcal{Q}$, and it will be used to compute $\mathbf{y}$.

5.1 Construction Details

In Fig. 2, we now give the formal construction of the ARE scheme. We establish some useful notations and recall the tools we need.

Notation and Ingredients: $\lambda \in \mathbb{N}$ is the security parameter, $n_{\mathsf{ARE}}, m_{\mathsf{ARE}}, k_{\mathsf{ARE}}$ are parameters associated with the function class $\mathcal{F}_{\mathsf{ARE}, n_{\mathsf{ARE}}, m_{\mathsf{ARE}}, k_{\mathsf{ARE}}}$.

Tool: We use a PRG in NC^0 (denoted by G) that stretches $t^{1-\epsilon}$ bits to t bits (t is set below). We also use a PRG in NC^0 (denoted by H) that stretches λ bits to $2 \cdot \lambda + 2$ bits. Denote by H_0 the function that computes first half of the output of H and by H_1 the function that computes the other half.
We set $n'_{\mathsf{ARE}} = (n_{\mathsf{ARE}} + m_{\mathsf{ARE}}^{1-\epsilon})\mathsf{poly}(\lambda)$ for a large enough polynomial poly. We will set $t = n'_{\mathsf{ARE}} - n_{\mathsf{ARE}}$.

Universal Formula Implementing a Formula: Let $U = U_{m_{\mathsf{ARE}}\lambda, n_{\mathsf{ARE}}, m_{\mathsf{ARE}}}$: $\{0,1\}^{m_{\mathsf{ARE}} \cdot \lambda} \times \{0,1\}^{n_{\mathsf{ARE}}} \rightarrow \{0,1\}^{m_{\mathsf{ARE}}}$ be the universal circuit formula for evaluating Boolean formulas with n_{ARE}-bit inputs, m_{ARE}-bit outputs, and size $m_{\mathsf{ARE}} \cdot \lambda$. In particular, $U(C_i, \mathbf{x}) = C_i(\mathbf{x})$ for circuits C_i and input $\mathbf{x}_i$ satisfying the requirements. The size of each U is $\tilde{O}(n_{\mathsf{ARE}} + m_{\mathsf{ARE}})$, where $\tilde{O}$ hides polynomial factors in $\log n_{\mathsf{ARE}}, \log n_{\mathsf{ARE}}, \lambda$. Since $n_{\mathsf{ARE}}, m_{\mathsf{ARE}}$ are all polynomials in λ, we ignore its dependence on logarithmic factors.

In full version [29], we discuss why all the properties are satisfied. Thus, we have the following theorem:

Theorem 21. *Assuming the existence of a boolean PRG in NC^0 with a stretch $n^{1+\epsilon}$ for some constant $\epsilon > 0$ where n is the input length to the PRG (see Definition 6), then there exists an ARE scheme satisfying Definition 17. Further, if the PRG is subexponentially secure, then so is ARE.*

6   Preprocessed Randomized Encoding

In this section, we define a Preprocessed Randomized Encoding scheme. We define and build it for the following function class:

Function Class: The function class $\mathcal{F}_{\mathsf{PRE}} = \{\mathcal{F}_{\mathsf{PRE}, n_{\mathsf{PRE}}, m_{\mathsf{PRE}}, k_{\mathsf{PRE}}, \lambda}\}_{n_{\mathsf{PRE}}, m_{\mathsf{PRE}}, k_{\mathsf{PRE}} \in \mathsf{Poly}, \lambda \in \mathbb{N}}$ is indexed with three polynomials $n_{\mathsf{PRE}}, m_{\mathsf{PRE}}, k_{\mathsf{PRE}} : \mathbb{N} \rightarrow \mathbb{N}$ and a parameter $\lambda \in \mathbb{N}$. We define this function class to be exactly $\mathcal{F}_{\mathsf{FE}, n_{\mathsf{PRE}}, m_{\mathsf{PRE}} \cdot k_{\mathsf{PRE}}, \lambda}$, consisting of all Boolean formulas with $n_{\mathsf{PRE}}(\lambda)$ input bits and $m_{\mathsf{PRE}}(\lambda) \cdot k_{\mathsf{PRE}}(\lambda)$ output bits where every output bit is computed by a Boolean formula of size λ.

Definition 22 (Syntax of Preprocessed Randomized Encoding). *A preprocessed randomized encoding scheme PRE for the function class $\mathcal{F}_{\mathsf{PRE}}$ contains the following polynomial time algorithms:*

- *PRE.PreProc$(1^\lambda, 1^{n_{\mathsf{PRE}}}, 1^{m_{\mathsf{PRE}}}, 1^{k_{\mathsf{PRE}}}, p, \mathbf{x} \in \{0,1\}^{n_{\mathsf{PRE}}}) \rightarrow (\mathsf{PI}, \mathsf{SI})$. The preprocessing algorithm takes as inputs the security parameter λ, input length $1^{n_{\mathsf{PRE}}}$, output block length $1^{m_{\mathsf{PRE}}}$, number of output blocks parameter $1^{k_{\mathsf{PRE}}}$ a prime p and an input $\mathbf{x} \in \{0,1\}^n$. It outputs preprocessed input $(\mathsf{PI}, \mathsf{SI}) \in \mathbb{Z}_p^{\ell_{\mathsf{PRE}}}$, where PI is the public part and SI is the private part of the input.*

The ARE scheme

Encode $\mathsf{Encode}(C, \mathbf{x}, \mathbf{r})$: Parse $C = (C_1, \ldots, C_{k_{\mathsf{ARE}}})$ such that $C_i : \{0,1\}^{n_{\mathsf{ARE}}} \to \{0,1\}^{m_{\mathsf{ARE}}}$ is the Boolean formula computing the ith chunk of output of C of size m_{ARE}. The size of circuit C_i is $m_{\mathsf{ARE}}\lambda$. Parse $\mathbf{r} = (\mathbf{r}_1, \ldots, \mathbf{r}_{k_{\mathsf{ARE}}})$ where $\mathbf{r}_i \in \{0,1\}^{n'_{\mathsf{ARE}} - n_{\mathsf{ARE}}}$. Set $\mathbf{a}_i = (\mathbf{x}, \mathbf{r}_i) \in \{0,1\}^{n'_{\mathsf{ARE}}}$ for $i \in [k_{\mathsf{ARE}}]$. For every $\kappa \in [k_{\mathsf{ARE}}]$, compute Π_κ as follows:

- Using G expand $\mathbf{r}_\kappa$ into $(\sigma, \mathbf{b})$ of length $(n_{\mathsf{ARE}} + m_{\mathsf{ARE}})\mathsf{poly}(\lambda)$. Here σ will be used as labels to produce garbling of $U(C_\kappa, \mathbf{x})$ and $\mathbf{b}$ will be used as permutation bits for every wire in the circuit U. Precisely, for every wire w in U, we let $\sigma_{w,0}, \sigma_{w,1} \in \{0,1\}^\lambda$ be the two labels for the wire, and $b_w \in \{0,1\}$ the permutation bit for the wire.
- (Input wire labels for C_κ and $\mathbf{x}$) Generate input labels of $(C_\kappa, \mathbf{x})$. That is for every input wire $w_{ckt,i}$ for $i \in [m_{\mathsf{ARE}} \cdot \lambda]$ and $w_{inp,j}$ for $j \in [n_{\mathsf{ARE}}]$.

$$\mathsf{Lab}_{C_\kappa,i} = \sigma_{w_{ckt,i},0}(1 - C_{\kappa,i}) + \sigma_{w_{ckt,i},1}(C_{\kappa,i})\|C_{\kappa,i} \oplus b_{w_{ckt,i}},$$

$$\mathsf{Lab}_j = \sigma_{w_{inp,j},0}(1 - x_j) + \sigma_{w_{inp,j},1}(x_j)\|x_j \oplus b_{w_{inp,j}}$$

Above $C_{\kappa,i}$ is i^{th} bit of the circuit description.
- Compute garbled tables for U. That is, for every gate **gate** in U with input wires w_1, w_2 and output wire w_3, output the following garbled table.

$$T_{\mathsf{gate}} = \begin{pmatrix} \mathsf{H}_0(\sigma_{w_1,b_{w_1}}) \oplus \mathsf{H}_0(\sigma_{w_2,b_{w_2}}) \oplus \left(\sigma_{w_3,g(b_{w_1},b_{w_2})}\|g(b_{w_1},b_{w_2}) \oplus b_{w_3}\right) \\ \mathsf{H}_1(\sigma_{w_1,b_{w_1}}) \oplus \mathsf{H}_0(\sigma_{w_2,\bar{b}_{w_2}}) \oplus \left(\sigma_{w_3,g(b_{w_1},\bar{b}_{w_2})}\|g(b_{w_1},\bar{b}_{w_2}) \oplus b_{w_3}\right) \\ \mathsf{H}_0(\sigma_{w_1,\bar{b}_{w_1}}) \oplus \mathsf{H}_1(\sigma_{w_2,b_{w_2}}) \oplus \left(\sigma_{w_3,g(\bar{b}_{w_1},b_{w_2})}\|g(\bar{b}_{w_1},b_{w_2}) \oplus b_{w_3}\right) \\ \mathsf{H}_1(\sigma_{w_1,\bar{b}_{w_1}}) \oplus \mathsf{H}_1(\sigma_{w_2,\bar{b}_{w_2}}) \oplus \left(\sigma_{w_3,g(\bar{b}_{w_1},\bar{b}_{w_2})}\|g(\bar{b}_{w_1},\bar{b}_{w_2}) \oplus b_{w_3}\right) \end{pmatrix} \tag{2}$$

- Let $w_{out,\gamma}$ for $\gamma \in [m_{\mathsf{ARE}}]$ denote the wires for output. Generate output translation table $\mathsf{OutTab} = \{(0, \sigma_{w_{out,\gamma},0}), (1, \sigma_{w_{out,\gamma},1})\}_{\gamma \in [m_{\mathsf{ARE}}]}$. Set $\Pi_\kappa = \{\mathsf{Lab}_{C_\kappa,i}, \mathsf{Lab}_j, T_{\mathsf{gate}}, \mathsf{OutTab}\}_{i \in [m_{\mathsf{ARE}} \cdot \lambda], \, j \in [n_{\mathsf{ARE}}], \, \mathsf{gate} \in \mathsf{gate}(U)}$. The output of the encode operation is $\Pi = \{\Pi_\kappa\}_{\kappa \in [k_{\mathsf{ARE}}]}$.

Decode $\mathsf{Decode}(\Pi = (\Pi_1, \ldots, \Pi_{k_{\mathsf{ARE}}}))$: Compute and output $\mathbf{y}_\kappa = \mathsf{YaoDecode}(\Pi_\kappa)$ for $\kappa \in [k_{\mathsf{ARE}}]$.

Fig. 2. ARE scheme description

- $\mathsf{PRE.Encode}(C, (\mathsf{PI}, \mathsf{SI})) = \mathbf{y}$. *The encoding algorithm takes inputs a circuit $C \in \mathcal{F}_{\mathsf{PRE},n_{\mathsf{PRE}},m_{\mathsf{PRE}},k_{\mathsf{PRE}},\lambda}$, and preprocessed input $(\mathsf{PI}, \mathsf{SI})$. It outputs a binary encoding $\mathbf{y}$.*
- $\mathsf{PRE.Decode}(\mathbf{y}) = \mathsf{out}$. *The decoding algorithm takes as input an encoding $\mathbf{y}$ and outputs a binary output out.*

Remark 23. Note that we could have defined the primitive without a parameter k_{PRE} by considering formulas with output length m_{PRE} as described in the high-level overview earlier. This is only done because this notation will align well with rest of the primitives that we use and build in this paper. Instead of requiring the size of the circuit computing the preprocessing to be proportional to $m_{\mathsf{PRE}}^{1-\epsilon}$ for some constant $\epsilon > 0$, we will require it to be proportional to $m_{\mathsf{PRE}} \cdot k_{\mathsf{PRE}}^{1-\epsilon}$. By setting k_{PRE} to be sufficiently large function of m_{PRE}, this will ensure the size of the circuit computing the preprocessing is sublinear in $m_{\mathsf{PRE}} \cdot k_{\mathsf{PRE}}$

In this paper, we care about constructions where for the function class above, $n_{\mathsf{PRE}}, m_{\mathsf{PRE}}$ and k_{PRE} are all polynomially related with λ, that is, of magnitude $\lambda^{\Theta(1)}$. Further, the output block length is super-linear in the input length, that is, $m_{\mathsf{PRE}} = n_{\mathsf{PRE}}^{1+\epsilon}$ for some constant $\epsilon > 0$.

Correctness and Security Requirements

Definition 24 (Correctness). *We say that* PRE *is correct if the following holds: For every* $\lambda \in \mathbb{N}$, $n_{\mathsf{PRE}}, m_{\mathsf{PRE}}, k_{\mathsf{PRE}} = \Theta(\lambda^{\Theta(1)})$, p *a prime,* $\mathbf{x} \in \{0,1\}^{n_{\mathsf{PRE}}}$, *and* $C \in \mathcal{F}_{\mathsf{PRE}, n_{\mathsf{PRE}}, m_{\mathsf{PRE}}, k_{\mathsf{PRE}}, \lambda}$.

$$\Pr[\mathsf{Decode}(\mathsf{Encode}(C, \mathsf{PreProc}(1^\lambda, 1^{n_{\mathsf{PRE}}}, 1^{m_{\mathsf{PRE}}}, 1^{k_{\mathsf{PRE}}}, p, \mathbf{x}))) = C(\mathbf{x})] \geq 1 - \exp(-\lambda^{\Omega(1)}).$$

Definition 25 (Indistinguishability Security). *We say that* PRE *scheme is secure if the following holds: Let* $\beta, c_1, c_2, c_3 > 0$ *be arbitrary constants, and* $p : \mathbb{N} \to \mathbb{N}$ *be any function that takes as input any integer* r *and outputs a* r^β *bit prime and* $n_{\mathsf{PRE}}(r) = r^{c_1}$, $m_{\mathsf{PRE}}(r) = r^{c_2}$ *and* $k_{\mathsf{PRE}} = r^{c_3}$ *be three polynomials. Let* $\{C, \mathbf{x}_0, \mathbf{x}_1\}_{\lambda \in \mathbb{N}}$ *be any ensemble where* $\mathbf{x}_0, \mathbf{x}_1 \in \{0,1\}^{n_{\mathsf{PRE}}(\lambda)}$ *and* $C \in \mathcal{F}_{\mathsf{PRE}, n_{\mathsf{PRE}}(\lambda), m_{\mathsf{PRE}}(\lambda), k_{\mathsf{PRE}}(\lambda), \lambda}$ *with* $\mathbf{y} = C(\mathbf{x}_0) = C(\mathbf{x}_1)$. *Then it holds that for any* $\lambda \in \mathbb{N}$, *and letting* $p = p(\lambda)$, $n_{\mathsf{PRE}} = n_{\mathsf{PRE}}(\lambda)$, $m_{\mathsf{PRE}} = m_{\mathsf{PRE}}(\lambda)$ *and* $k_{\mathsf{PRE}} = k_{\mathsf{PRE}}(\lambda)$ *it holds that the following distributions are computationally indistinguishable*

$$\left\{ (\mathsf{PI}, \mathbf{y}) \mid (\mathsf{PI}, \mathsf{SI}) \leftarrow \mathsf{PRE.PreProc}(1^\lambda, 1^{n_{\mathsf{PRE}}}, 1^{m_{\mathsf{PRE}}}, 1^{k_{\mathsf{PRE}}}, p, \mathbf{x}_0), \ \mathbf{y} \leftarrow \mathsf{PRE.Encode}(C, \mathsf{PI}, \mathsf{SI}) \right\}$$

$$\left\{ (\mathsf{PI}, \mathbf{y}) \mid (\mathsf{PI}, \mathsf{SI}) \leftarrow \mathsf{PRE.PreProc}(1^\lambda, 1^{n_{\mathsf{PRE}}}, 1^{m_{\mathsf{PRE}}}, 1^{k_{\mathsf{PRE}}}, p, \mathbf{x}_1), \ \mathbf{y} \leftarrow \mathsf{PRE.Encode}(C, \mathsf{PI}, \mathsf{SI}) \right\}$$

Further, we say that PRE *is subexponentially secure the above distributions are subexponentially indistinguishable.*

The Efficiency and Complexity Requirements

Definition 26 (Sublinear Efficiency of PRE). *We require that there exists a polynomial* poly *and constants* $c_1, c_2, c_3 > 0$ *such that for every polynomials* $n_{\mathsf{PRE}}, m_{\mathsf{PRE}}$ *and* k_{PRE} *and every security parameter* $\lambda \in \mathbb{N}$, *every prime* p, *the (randomized) circuit* $D(\cdot)$ *that on input* $\mathbf{x} \in \{0,1\}^{n_{\mathsf{PRE}}}$ *computes* $\mathsf{PRE.PreProc}(1^\lambda, 1^{n_{\mathsf{PRE}}}, 1^{m_{\mathsf{PRE}}}, 1^{k_{\mathsf{PRE}}}, p, \mathbf{x})$ *has size bounded by* $((n_{\mathsf{PRE}} + m_{\mathsf{PRE}}^{1-c_1})k_{\mathsf{PRE}}^{c_2} + m_{\mathsf{PRE}}k_{\mathsf{PRE}}^{1-c_3})\mathsf{poly}(\lambda, \log p)$.

In particular, this implies that when $m_{\mathsf{PRE}} = m_{\mathsf{PRE}}(\lambda) = \Theta(\lambda^{\Theta(1)})$, $n_{\mathsf{PRE}} = O(m_{\mathsf{PRE}}^{1-\epsilon})$ *for some constant* $\epsilon \in (0,1)$, *then, there exists some constant* $c > 0, \gamma(c_1, c_2, c_3, c) > 0$ *such that when* $k_{\mathsf{PRE}} = n_{\mathsf{PRE}}^c$, *then the size of* D *is bounded by* $(m_{\mathsf{PRE}} \cdot k_{\mathsf{PRE}})^{1-\gamma} \cdot \mathsf{poly}(\lambda, \log p)$).

Definition 27 (Complexity of Encoding). *We require that for every polynomials* $n_{\mathsf{PRE}}, m_{\mathsf{PRE}}, k_{\mathsf{PRE}}$, *every security parameter* $\lambda \in \mathbb{N}$, *every* $C \in \mathcal{F}_{\mathsf{PRE}, n_{\mathsf{PRE}}, m_{\mathsf{PRE}}, k_{\mathsf{PRE}}, \lambda}$, *and every prime* p, *there exists a polynomial mapping* f *satisfying the following:*

- *For every input* $\mathbf{x} \in \{0,1\}^{n_{\mathsf{PRE}}}$, *and every* $(\mathsf{PI}, \mathsf{SI}) \leftarrow \mathsf{PreProc}(1^\lambda, 1^{n_{\mathsf{PRE}}}, 1^{m_{\mathsf{PRE}}}, 1^{k_{\mathsf{PRE}}}, p, \mathbf{x})$,

$$f(\mathsf{PI}, \mathsf{SI}) \bmod p = \mathsf{PRE}.\mathsf{Encode}(C, (\mathsf{PI}, \mathsf{SI})) .$$

- *There is a universal constant* $d \in \mathbb{N}$ *independent of all parameters, s.t.,* f *has degree* d *in* PI *and degree 2 in* SI.
- f *can be uniformly and efficiently generated from* $\lambda, n_{\mathsf{PRE}}, m_{\mathsf{PRE}}, k_{\mathsf{PRE}}, p, C$.

6.1 Construction of Preprocessed Randomized Encoding

The construction of a PRE scheme is really straightforward. We simply compose PPE with ARE. Let's take a look at it formally. Let the function class we are interested in is $\mathcal{F}_{\mathsf{PRE}, n_{\mathsf{PRE}}, m_{\mathsf{PRE}}, k_{\mathsf{PRE}}, \lambda}$ where λ is the security parameter and $n_{\mathsf{PRE}}, m_{\mathsf{PRE}}, k_{\mathsf{PRE}}$ are polynomials in the security parameter. Let p denote the prime to be used for the PRE scheme.

Ingredients: We make use of two ingredients:

1. A ARE scheme. Let $d > 0$ be the constant degree which is the degree of evaluation of the PRE scheme. We set:
   - $n_{\mathsf{ARE}} = n_{\mathsf{PRE}}$,
   - $m_{\mathsf{ARE}} = m_{\mathsf{PRE}}$,
   - $k_{\mathsf{ARE}} = k_{\mathsf{PRE}}$,
   - $m'_{\mathsf{ARE}} = (n_{\mathsf{PRE}} + m_{\mathsf{PRE}}) \cdot \lambda^{c_1}$,
   - $n'_{\mathsf{ARE}} = (n_{\mathsf{PRE}} + m_{\mathsf{PRE}}^{1-c_2})\lambda^{c_1}$, where $c_1, c_2 > 0$ are constants associated with the efficiency requirements of ARE. Let $\mathcal{Q}_{\mathsf{ARE}}$ be the d-monomial pattern of size m'_{ARE} over n'_{ARE} variables associated with the encoding operation.
2. A PPE scheme, where we set:
   - The prime to be used as p,
   - $n_{\mathsf{PPE}} = n'_{\mathsf{ARE}}$,
   - $m_{\mathsf{PPE}} = m'_{\mathsf{ARE}}$,
   - Set the monomial pattern $\mathcal{Q}_{\mathsf{PPE}} = \mathcal{Q}_{\mathsf{ARE}} = \mathcal{Q}$. The degree of the monomial pattern is d,
   - Let $d' = O(d)$ be the constant degree of the polynomial $g_f(\cdot) = \mathsf{PPE}.\mathsf{Eval}(f, \cdot) \bmod p$ used to evaluate any polynomial $f \in \mathcal{F}_{d, \mathsf{PPE}, n_{\mathsf{PPE}}, \mathcal{Q}, k_{\mathsf{PPE}}}$.

We now describe our construction in Fig. 3:

The PRE scheme

Preprocessing $\mathsf{PRE}.\mathsf{PreProc}(1^\lambda, 1^{n_{\mathsf{PRE}}}, 1^{m_{\mathsf{PRE}}}, 1^{k_{\mathsf{PRE}}}, p, \mathbf{x} \in \{0,1\}^{n_{\mathsf{PRE}}})$: Run the following steps:

- Sample uniformly randomness $\mathbf{r}_1, \ldots, \mathbf{r}_{k_{\mathsf{ARE}}} \in \{0,1\}^{n'_{\mathsf{ARE}} - n_{\mathsf{ARE}}}$ used for running $\mathsf{ARE}.\mathsf{Encode}(\cdot, \mathbf{x}, \mathbf{r})$. Set $\mathbf{a}_i = (\mathbf{x}, \mathbf{r}_i)$ for $i \in [k_{\mathsf{ARE}}]$. Here $\mathbf{a}_i \in \{0,1\}^{n'_{\mathsf{ARE}} = n_{\mathsf{PPE}}}$.
- Compute $(\mathsf{PI}, \mathsf{SI}) \leftarrow \mathsf{PPE}.\mathsf{PreProc}(1^{n_{\mathsf{PPE}}}, 1^{k_{\mathsf{PPE}}}, p, \mathcal{Q}, \mathbf{a})$. Output $\mathsf{PI} = \mathsf{PI}$ and $\mathsf{SI} = \mathsf{SI}$.

Encoding $\mathsf{PRE}.\mathsf{Encode}(C, (\mathsf{PI}, \mathsf{SI}))$: Run the following steps:

- By the efficiency property of ARE, for any circuit $C \in \mathcal{F}_{\mathsf{ARE}, n_{\mathsf{ARE}}, m_{\mathsf{ARE}}, k_{\mathsf{ARE}}, \lambda}$, for $i \in [T]$ where T is the output length of $\mathsf{ARE}.\mathsf{Encode}(C, \cdot)$, the ith output bit of $\mathsf{ARE}.\mathsf{Encode}(C, \cdot)$ is computable by an efficiently generatable polynomial $f_i \in \mathcal{F}_{\mathsf{PPE}, d, n_{\mathsf{PPE}}, \mathcal{Q}, k_{\mathsf{PPE}}}$. Let g_{f_i} be the degree $(d', 2)$-polynomial evaluating $\mathsf{PPE}.\mathsf{Eval}(f_i, \cdot)$. Compute $y_i = \mathsf{PPE}.\mathsf{Eval}(f_i, \mathsf{PI}, \mathsf{SI}) = g_{f_i}(\mathsf{PI}, \mathsf{SI})$. Output $\mathbf{y} = (y_1, \ldots, y_T)$.

Decode $\mathsf{PRE}.\mathsf{Decode}(\mathbf{y})$: Run and output $\mathsf{ARE}.\mathsf{Decode}(\mathbf{y}) = \mathbf{z}$.

Fig. 3. The description of the PRE scheme.

In the full version, we argue various properties associated with a PRE scheme. Thus, we have the following theorem:

Theorem 28. *Assume that there exists two constant $\delta, \epsilon > 0$ such that:*

- *δ-LPN assumption (Definition 5) holds,*
- *There exists a PRG in NC^0 with a stretch $n^{1+\epsilon}$ where n is the length of the input (Definition 6),*

Then, there exists a PRE scheme (Definition 22). Further, assuming the underlying assumptions are subexponentially secure, then so is the resulting PRE scheme.

7 Summing Up

In the full version [29], we use a PRE scheme and combine it with a partially hiding functional encryption, to build a sublinear functional encryption for Boolean formulas and then bootstrap it to $i\mathcal{O}$ using prior results. Thus, we prove:

Theorem 29. *If there exists constants $\delta, \tau > 0$ such that:*

- *δ-LPN assumption holds (Definition 5),*
- *There exists a PRG in NC^0 with a stretch of $n^{1+\tau}$ where n is length of the input (Definition 6),*
- *The DLIN assumption over prime order symmetric bilinear groups holds.*

Then, there exists a sublinear functional encryption scheme for circuits. Further if the underlying assumptions are subexponentially secure, then there exists a secure indistinguishability obfuscation for all circuits.

Acknowledgements. Aayush Jain is supported by NTT Research, a grant from CyLab security and privacy institute and a start-up package by the computer science department at CMU.

Huijia Lin is supported by NSF grants CNS- 2026774, CNS-1936825 (CAREER), Simons JP Morgan Faculty Award, and a Simons collaboration grant on algorithmic fairness.

Amit Sahai is supported in part from a Simons Investigator Award, DARPA SIEVE award, NTT Research, NSF Frontier Award 1413955, BSF grant 2012378, a Xerox Faculty Research Award, a Google Faculty Research Award, and an Okawa Foundation Research Grant. This material is based upon work supported by the Defense Advanced Research Projects Agency through Award HR00112020024.

The views expressed are those of the authors and do not reflect the official policy or position of the Department of Defense, DARPA, ARO, Simons, Intel, Okawa Foundation, ODNI, IARPA, DIMACS, BSF, Xerox, the National Science Foundation, NTT Research, Google, J.P. Morgan or the U.S. Government.

References

1. Ajtai, M., Komlós, J., Szemerédi, E.: An $O(n \log n)$ sorting network. In: 15th ACM STOC, pp. 1–9. ACM Press (April 1983)
2. Alekhnovich, M.: More on average case vs approximation complexity. In: 44th FOCS, pp. 298–307. IEEE Computer Society Press (October 2003)
3. Ananth, P., Badrinarayanan, S., Jain, A., Manohar, N., Sahai, A.: From FE combiners to secure MPC and back. In: Hofheinz, D., Rosen, A. (eds.) TCC 2019, Part I. LNCS, vol. 11891, pp. 199–228. Springer, Cham (2019). https://doi.org/10.1007/978-3-030-36030-6_9
4. Ananth, P., Jain, A., Lin, H., Matt, C., Sahai, A.: Indistinguishability obfuscation without multilinear maps: new paradigms via low degree weak pseudorandomness and security amplification. In: Boldyreva, A., Micciancio, D. (eds.) CRYPTO 2019, Part III. LNCS, vol. 11694, pp. 284–332. Springer, Cham (2019). https://doi.org/10.1007/978-3-030-26954-8_10
5. Ananth, P., Jain, A., Sahai, A.: Indistinguishability obfuscation without multilinear maps: IO from LWE, bilinear maps, and weak pseudorandomness. IACR Cryptology ePrint Archive 2018/615 (2018)
6. Ananth, P., Jain, A.: Indistinguishability obfuscation from compact functional encryption. In: Gennaro, R., Robshaw, M. (eds.) CRYPTO 2015, Part I. LNCS, vol. 9215, pp. 308–326. Springer, Heidelberg (2015). https://doi.org/10.1007/978-3-662-47989-6_15
7. Ananth, P., Jain, A., Sahai, A.: Indistinguishability obfuscation from functional encryption for simple functions. Eprint 2015/730 (2015)
8. Ananth, P., Sahai, A.: Projective arithmetic functional encryption and indistinguishability obfuscation from degree-5 multilinear maps. In: Coron, J.-S., Nielsen, J.B. (eds.) EUROCRYPT 2017, Part I. LNCS, vol. 10210, pp. 152–181. Springer, Cham (2017). https://doi.org/10.1007/978-3-319-56620-7_6
9. Applebaum, B., Avron, J., Brzuska, C.: Arithmetic cryptography: extended abstract. In: Roughgarden, T. (ed.) ITCS 2015, pp. 143–151. ACM (January 2015)
10. Applebaum, B., Brakerski, Z.: Obfuscating circuits via composite-order graded encoding. In: Dodis, Y., Nielsen, J.B. (eds.) TCC 2015, Part II. LNCS, vol. 9015, pp. 528–556. Springer, Heidelberg (2015). https://doi.org/10.1007/978-3-662-46497-7_21

11. Ballard, L., Green, M., de Medeiros, B., Monrose, F.: Correlation-resistant storage via keyword-searchable encryption. Cryptology ePrint Archive, Report 2005/417 (2005). http://eprint.iacr.org/2005/417
12. Barak, B., et al.: On the (im)possibility of obfuscating programs. In: Kilian, J. (ed.) CRYPTO 2001. LNCS, vol. 2139, pp. 1–18. Springer, Heidelberg (2001). https://doi.org/10.1007/3-540-44647-8_1
13. Bitansky, N., Nishimaki, R., Passelègue, A., Wichs, D.: From Cryptomania to Obfustopia through secret-key functional encryption. In: Hirt, M., Smith, A. (eds.) TCC 2016, Part II. LNCS, vol. 9986, pp. 391–418. Springer, Heidelberg (2016). https://doi.org/10.1007/978-3-662-53644-5_15
14. Bitansky, N., Vaikuntanathan, V.: Indistinguishability obfuscation from functional encryption. In: Guruswami, V. (ed.) 56th FOCS, pp. 171–190. IEEE Computer Society Press (October 2015)
15. Blum, A., Furst, M., Kearns, M., Lipton, R.J.: Cryptographic primitives based on hard learning problems. In: Stinson, D.R. (ed.) CRYPTO 1993. LNCS, vol. 773, pp. 278–291. Springer, Heidelberg (1994). https://doi.org/10.1007/3-540-48329-2_24
16. Boyle, E., Couteau, G., Gilboa, N., Ishai, Y.: Compressing vector OLE. In: Lie, D., Mannan, M., Backes, M., Wang, X. (eds.) ACM CCS 2018, pp. 896–912. ACM Press (October 2018)
17. Canetti, R., Lin, H., Tessaro, S., Vaikuntanathan, V.: Obfuscation of probabilistic circuits and applications. In: Dodis, Y., Nielsen, J.B. (eds.) TCC 2015, Part II. LNCS, vol. 9015, pp. 468–497. Springer, Heidelberg (2015). https://doi.org/10.1007/978-3-662-46497-7_19
18. van Dijk, M., Gentry, C., Halevi, S., Vaikuntanathan, V.: Fully homomorphic encryption over the integers. In: Gilbert, H. (ed.) EUROCRYPT 2010. LNCS, vol. 6110, pp. 24–43. Springer, Heidelberg (2010). https://doi.org/10.1007/978-3-642-13190-5_2
19. Garg, S., Gentry, C., Halevi, S., Raykova, M., Sahai, A., Waters, B.: Candidate indistinguishability obfuscation and functional encryption for all circuits. In: 54th FOCS, pp. 40–49. IEEE Computer Society Press (October 2013)
20. Gay, R., Jain, A., Lin, H., Sahai, A.: Indistinguishability obfuscation from simple-to-state hard problems: new assumptions, new techniques, and simplification. In: Canteaut, A., Standaert, F.-X. (eds.) EUROCRYPT 2021, Part III. LNCS, vol. 12698, pp. 97–126. Springer, Cham (2021). https://doi.org/10.1007/978-3-030-77883-5_4
21. Goldreich, O.: Candidate one-way functions based on expander graphs. In: Goldreich, O. (ed.) Studies in Complexity and Cryptography. Miscellanea on the Interplay between Randomness and Computation. LNCS, vol. 6650, pp. 76–87. Springer, Heidelberg (2011). https://doi.org/10.1007/978-3-642-22670-0_10
22. Goldwasser, S., Kalai, Y.T., Popa, R.A., Vaikuntanathan, V., Zeldovich, N.: Reusable garbled circuits and succinct functional encryption. In: Boneh, D., Roughgarden, T., Feigenbaum, J. (eds.) Symposium on Theory of Computing Conference, STOC 2013, Palo Alto, CA, USA, June 1–4, 2013, pp. 555–564. ACM (2013). http://doi.acm.org/10.1145/2488608.2488678
23. Gorbunov, S., Vaikuntanathan, V., Wee, H.: Functional encryption with bounded collusions via multi-party computation. In: Safavi-Naini, R., Canetti, R. (eds.) CRYPTO 2012. LNCS, vol. 7417, pp. 162–179. Springer, Heidelberg (2012). https://doi.org/10.1007/978-3-642-32009-5_11
24. Ishai, Y., Prabhakaran, M., Sahai, A.: Founding cryptography on oblivious transfer – efficiently. In: Wagner, D. (ed.) CRYPTO 2008. LNCS, vol. 5157, pp. 572–591. Springer, Heidelberg (2008). https://doi.org/10.1007/978-3-540-85174-5_32

25. Ishai, Y., Prabhakaran, M., Sahai, A.: Secure arithmetic computation with no honest majority. In: Reingold, O. (ed.) TCC 2009. LNCS, vol. 5444, pp. 294–314. Springer, Heidelberg (2009). https://doi.org/10.1007/978-3-642-00457-5_18

26. Jain, A., Korb, A., Manohar, N., Sahai, A.: Amplifying the security of functional encryption, unconditionally. In: Micciancio, D., Ristenpart, T. (eds.) CRYPTO 2020, Part I. LNCS, vol. 12170, pp. 717–746. Springer, Cham (2020). https://doi.org/10.1007/978-3-030-56784-2_24

27. Jain, A., Lin, H., Matt, C., Sahai, A.: How to leverage hardness of constant-degree expanding polynomials over $\mathbb{R}$ to build $i\mathcal{O}$. In: Ishai, Y., Rijmen, V. (eds.) EUROCRYPT 2019, Part I. LNCS, vol. 11476, pp. 251–281. Springer, Cham (2019). https://doi.org/10.1007/978-3-030-17653-2_9

28. Jain, A., Lin, H., Sahai, A.: Simplifying constructions and assumptions for $i\mathcal{O}$. IACR Cryptology ePrint Archive 2019/1252 (2019). https://eprint.iacr.org/2019/1252

29. Jain, A., Lin, H., Sahai, A.: Indistinguishability obfuscation from LPN over f_p, dlin, and prgs in nc$^\wedge$0. IACR Cryptology ePrint Archive 2021/1334 (2021). https://eprint.iacr.org/2021/1334

30. Jain, A., Lin, H., Sahai, A.: Indistinguishability obfuscation from well-founded assumptions. In: Khuller, S., Williams, V.V. (eds.) 53rd Annual ACM SIGACT Symposium on Theory of Computing, Virtual Event, STOC 2021, Italy, June 21–25, 2021, pp. 60–73. ACM (2021)

31. Jain, A., Manohar, N., Sahai, A.: Combiners for functional encryption, unconditionally. In: Canteaut, A., Ishai, Y. (eds.) EUROCRYPT 2020, Part I. LNCS, vol. 12105, pp. 141–168. Springer, Cham (2020). https://doi.org/10.1007/978-3-030-45721-1_6

32. Lin, H.: Indistinguishability obfuscation from constant-degree graded encoding schemes. In: Fischlin, M., Coron, J.-S. (eds.) EUROCRYPT 2016, Part I. LNCS, vol. 9665, pp. 28–57. Springer, Heidelberg (2016). https://doi.org/10.1007/978-3-662-49890-3_2

33. Lin, H.: Indistinguishability obfuscation from SXDH on 5-linear maps and locality-5 PRGs. In: Katz, J., Shacham, H. (eds.) CRYPTO 2017, Part I. LNCS, vol. 10401, pp. 599–629. Springer, Cham (2017). https://doi.org/10.1007/978-3-319-63688-7_20

34. Lin, H., Matt, C.: Pseudo flawed-smudging generators and their application to indistinguishability obfuscation. IACR Cryptology ePrint Archive 2018/646 (2018)

35. Lin, H., Pass, R., Seth, K., Telang, S.: Output-compressing randomized encodings and applications. In: Kushilevitz, E., Malkin, T. (eds.) TCC 2016, Part I. LNCS, vol. 9562, pp. 96–124. Springer, Heidelberg (2016). https://doi.org/10.1007/978-3-662-49096-9_5

36. Lin, H., Tessaro, S.: Indistinguishability obfuscation from bilinear maps and blockwise local PRGs. Cryptology ePrint Archive, Report 2017/250 (2017). http://eprint.iacr.org/2017/250

37. Lin, H., Vaikuntanathan, V.: Indistinguishability obfuscation from DDH-like assumptions on constant-degree graded encodings. In: Dinur, I. (ed.) 57th FOCS, pp. 11–20. IEEE Computer Society Press (October 2016)

38. Regev, O.: On lattices, learning with errors, random linear codes, and cryptography. In: Gabow, H.N., Fagin, R. (eds.) 37th ACM STOC, pp. 84–93. ACM Press (May 2005)

39. Sahai, A., Seyalioglu, H.: Worry-free encryption: functional encryption with public keys. In: Proceedings of the 17th ACM Conference on Computer and Communications Security, pp. 463–472. ACM (2010)

40. Wee, H.: Functional encryption for quadratic functions from k-Lin, revisited. In: Pass, R., Pietrzak, K. (eds.) TCC 2020, Part I. LNCS, vol. 12550, pp. 210–228. Springer, Cham (2020). https://doi.org/10.1007/978-3-030-64375-1_8

41. Yao, A.C.C.: How to generate and exchange secrets (extended abstract). In: FOCS, pp. 162–167 (1986)

Incompressible Cryptography

Jiaxin Guan[1]([✉])([iD]), Daniel Wichs[2,3], and Mark Zhandry[1,3]([iD])

[1] Princeton University, Princeton, NJ 08544, USA
jiaxin@guan.io
[2] Northeastern University, Boston, MA 02115, USA
[3] NTT Research, Inc., Sunnyvale, CA 94085, USA

Abstract. *Incompressible encryption* allows us to make the ciphertext size flexibly large and ensures that an adversary learns nothing about the encrypted data, even if the decryption key later leaks, unless she stores essentially the entire ciphertext. *Incompressible signatures* can be made arbitrarily large and ensure that an adversary cannot produce a signature on *any* message, even one she has seen signed before, unless she stores one of the signatures essentially in its entirety.

In this work, we give simple constructions of both incompressible public-key encryption and signatures under minimal assumptions. Furthermore, large incompressible ciphertexts (resp. signatures) can be decrypted (resp. verified) in a streaming manner with low storage. In particular, these notions strengthen the related concepts of *disappearing encryption and signatures*, recently introduced by Guan and Zhandry (TCC 2021), whose previous constructions relied on sophisticated techniques and strong, non-standard assumptions. We extend our constructions to achieve an optimal "rate", meaning the large ciphertexts (resp. signatures) can contain almost equally large messages, at the cost of stronger assumptions.

1 Introduction

Security breaches are ubiquitous. Therefore, it is natural to wonder: will encrypted messages remain secure, even if the secret decryption key is later leaked? Forward secrecy deals exactly with this problem, but requires either multi-round protocols or key updates, both of which may be undesirable in many scenarios. And in the usual time-bounded adversary model, unfortunately, such limitations are inherent: an adversary can simply store the ciphertext and wait for the secret key to leak, at which point it can easily decrypt.

Incompressible encryption. In this work we ask: can we force a would-be "save-it-for-later adversary" to actually store the ciphertext in its entirety, for the entire length of time it is waiting for the secret key to leak? At a minimum such storage may be inconvenient, and for very large files or long time frames, it may

J. Guan—Part of this research was conducted while this author was a research intern at NTT Research, Inc.

O. Dunkelman and S. Dziembowski (Eds.): EUROCRYPT 2022, LNCS 13275, pp. 700–730, 2022.
https://doi.org/10.1007/978-3-031-06944-4_24

be prohibitively costly. Even for short messages, one may artificially increase the ciphertext size, hopefully forcing the adversary to use much more storage than message length. We may therefore hope that such an *incompressible encryption scheme* maintains the privacy of messages even if the secret key is later revealed.

Remark 1. For an illustrative example, an individual with a gigabit internet connection can transmit $\sim10\,\text{TB}$ per day, potentially much more than their own storage. Of course many entities will have $10\,\text{TB}$ or even vastly more, but an incompressible scheme would force them to devote $10\,\text{TB}$ to storing a particular ciphertext for potentially years until the key is revealed. Across millions or billions of people, even powerful adversaries like state actors would only be able to devote such storage to a small fraction of victims.

Unfortunately, traditional public key encryption schemes are not incompressible; an adversary may be able to store only a short digest of the ciphertext and still obtain non-trivial information about the plaintext once the secret key is leaked. For example, for efficiency reasons, hybrid encryption is typically used in the public key setting, where the encryption of a message m may look like:

$$(\mathsf{Enc}(\mathsf{pk}, s), G(s) \oplus m) \ .$$

Here, s is a short seed, and G is a pseudorandom generator used to stretch the random seed into a pseudorandom pad for the message m. A save-it-for-later adversary need not store the entire ciphertext; instead, they can store just $\mathsf{Enc}(\mathsf{pk}, s)$ as well as, say, the first few bits of $G(s) \oplus m$. Once the secret key is revealed, they can learn s and then recover the first few bits of m. This may already be enough to compromise the secrecy of m. Such an attack is especially problematic if we wanted to artificially increase the ciphertext size by simply padding the message and appending dummy bits, since then the first few bits of m would contain the entire secret plaintext.

The compressibility issue is not limited to the scheme above: we could replace $G(s) \oplus m$ with a different efficient symmetric key encryption scheme such as CBC-mode encryption, and essentially the same attack would work. The same goes for bit encryption as well.

Incompressible public key encryption instead requires that if the adversary stores anything much smaller than the ciphertext, the adversary learns absolutely nothing about the message, even if the secret key later leaks.

Remark 2. We note that plain public key encryption does have *some* incompressibility properties. In particular, it is impossible, in a plain public key encryption scheme, for the adversary to significantly compress the ciphertext and later be able to reconstruct the original ciphertext. However, this guarantee implies nothing about the privacy of the underlying message should the key leak.

Incompressible Signatures. A canonical application of signatures is to prevent man-in-the-middle attacks: by authenticating each message with a signature, one is assured that the messages were not tampered with. However, a man-in-the-middle can always *delay* sending an authenticated message, by storing it for later. The only way to block such attacks in the usual time-bounded adversary model is to use multi-round protocols, rely on synchronized clocks and timeouts, or have the recipients keep state, all of which may be undesirable. We therefore also consider the case of incompressible *signatures*, which force such a delaying adversary to actually store the entire signature for the duration of the delay.

In slightly more detail, in the case of plain signatures, a forgery is a signature on any *new* message, one the adversary did not previously see signed. The reason only new signed messages are considered forgeries is because an adversary can simply store a valid signature it sees, and later reproduce it. An *incompressible* signature, essentially, requires that an adversary who produces a valid signature on an existing message must have actually stored a string almost as large as the signature. By making the signatures long, we may hope to make it prohibitively costly to maintain such storage. As in the case of encryption, existing signature schemes do not appear to offer incompressible security; indeed, it is usually desired that signatures are very short.

Feature: Low-storage for streaming honest users. Given that communication will be inconveniently large for the adversary to store, a desirable feature of incompressible ciphertexts and signatures is that they can be sent and received with low storage requirements for the honest users. In such a setting, the honest users would never store the entire ciphertext or signature, but instead generate, send, and process the communication bit-by-bit in a streaming fashion.

Feature: High rate. With incompressible ciphertexts and signatures, communication is set to be deliberately large. If the messages themselves are also large, it may be costly to further blow up the communication in order to achieve incompressibility. Therefore, a desirable feature is to have the rate—the ratio of the maximum message length to the communication size—be as close to 1 as possible. In this way, for very large messages, there is little communication overhead to make the communication incompressible.

1.1   Prior Work

Dziembowski [Dzi06b] constructed information-theoretically secure symmetric-key incompressible encryption (referred to as forward-secure encryption) via randomness extractors. The focus of our work is on public-key encryption and signature schemes, which inherently cannot be information-theoretically secure.[1]

---

[1] The symmetric-key scheme of [Dzi06b] also only offers one-time security. However, a simple hybrid argument shows that this implies many-time security, where the adversary can compress each of many ciphertexts *separately* and later sees the secret key. However, it inherently does not offer any security if the adversary can *jointly* compress many ciphertexts, even if the compressed value is much smaller than a single ciphertext! In contrast, public-key incompressible encryption automatically ensures security in such setting via a simple hybrid argument.

Very recently, Guan and Zhandry [GZ21] define and construct what they call *disappearing* public key encryption and digital signatures. Their notions are very similar to ours, except with an important distinction: they assume both honest and malicious parties operate as space-bounded streaming algorithms throughout their operation. Honest users are assumed to have a somewhat lower storage bound than the adversary's.

In terms of the functionality requirement for honest users, their model corresponds to the low-storage streaming variant of incompressible cryptography. However, in terms of the security requirement, disappearing cryptography is somewhat weaker, since it restricts the adversary to also be space-bounded throughout its entire operation, and observe the ciphertexts/signatures produced by the cryptosystem in a streaming manner. On the other hand, incompressible cryptography allows the adversary to observe each ciphertext/signature in its entirety and compute on it using an unrestricted amount of local memory, but then store some small compressed version of it afterwards. Some disappearing schemes may be insecure in the incompressible threat model: for example, one of the disappearing ciphertext schemes from [GZ21] could potentially even be based on *symmetric key* cryptography, despite being a public key primitive.[2] Yet public key incompressible ciphertexts easily imply public key encryption, which is believed to be stronger than symmetric key cryptography [IR90].

In summary, incompressible cryptography with low-storage streaming is also disappearing, but the reverse direction does not hold.

Guan and Zhandry explain several interesting applications of disappearing ciphertexts and signatures, including deniable encryption [CDNO97]. Here, one imagines that the secret key holder is coerced into revealing their key. In order to protect the contents of an encrypted message, traditional deniable encryption allows the key holder to generate a fake key that causes the ciphertext to decrypt to any desired value. Unfortunately, such receiver-deniable encryption is impossible in the standard model [BNNO11]. Disappearing ciphertexts offer a solution, since the contents are protected without even faking the key, as the space-bounded attacker is unable to store the ciphertext.

However, in addition to achieving a weaker security model than incompressible cryptography, the schemes of [GZ21] are based on non-standard heuristic assumptions. In particular:

- Their schemes are built from a novel object called *online obfuscation*, a very strong proposed form of program obfuscation in the bounded storage setting. While [GZ21] gives plausible candidate constructions, the constructions are complex and it is unclear how to prove security. It is even plausible that the notion of online obfuscation is *impossible*.
- One of their candidates requires, at a minimum, standard-model virtual grey box (VGB) obfuscation [BCKP14], which is stronger even than indistinguishability obfuscation [BGI+01], already one of the strongest known assumptions

---

[2] It's not hard to see that one-way functions, and therefore symmetric key cryptography, are implied by disappearing ciphertexts, since the secret key can be information-theoretically recovered from the public key.

in cryptography. And even assuming VGB, the security remains unproven. Their other candidate could plausibly be information-theoretic (but again, currently not proven), but is limited to a quadratic separation between the ciphertext/signature size and the honest users' storage.
- Their encryption and signature schemes involve ciphertexts/signatures that are significantly larger than the messages, and so their schemes are low "rate" when the messages are large.

To summarize, prior to this work it was not known how to achieve disappearing/incompressible public-key encryption/signatures with provable security even under very strong assumptions such as indistinguishability obfuscation!

1.2   Our Results

We give new positive results for incompressible cryptography:

- Under the minimal assumption of standard-model public key encryption, we construct a simple incompressible public key encryption scheme. The scheme supports streaming with constant storage, independent of the ciphertext size. As a special case, we achieve provably secure disappearing ciphertexts with optimal honest-user storage and under mild assumptions, significantly improving on [GZ21]. The ciphertext size is $|c| = |S| + |m| \times \mathsf{poly}(\lambda)$, where $|S|$ is the adversary's storage, $|m|$ the message size, and λ the security parameter.
- Under the minimal assumption of one-way functions, we construct incompressible signatures. Our scheme supports streaming with constant storage, independent of the signature size. Thus we also achieve provably secure disappearing signatures under minimal assumptions, again significantly improving on [GZ21]. The total communication (message length plus signature size) is $|S| + |m| + \mathsf{poly}(\lambda)$.
- Under standard-model indistinguishability obfuscation (iO), we construct "rate 1" incompressible public-key encryption, where $|c| = |S| + \mathsf{poly}(\lambda)$ and the message length can be as large as roughly $|S|$. In particular, for very large messages, the ciphertext size is roughly the same as the message size.

  The public keys of our scheme are small, but the secret keys in this scheme are at least as large as the message, which we explain is potentially inherent amongst provably-secure high-rate schemes.

  Along the way, we give the first rate-1 construction of functional encryption for circuits, where $|c| = |m| + \mathsf{poly}(\lambda)$.
- We consider a notion of "rate-1" incompressible signatures, where the total communication is only $|S| + \mathsf{poly}(\lambda)$, and the message can be as large as roughly $|S|$. Note that the signature by itself must have size at least $|S|$ for incompressibility (since m may be compressible), and so if we separately send the message and signature, the total communication would be at least $|S| + |m|$, which is not rate 1. Instead, we just send a signature and require the message to be efficiently extractible from the signature.

We show that rate-1 incompressible signatures are *equivalent* to incompressible encodings, defined by Moran and Wichs [MW20]. By relying on the positive results of [MW20], we obtain such signatures under either the Decisional Composite Residuosity (DCR) or Learning With Errors (LWE) assumption, in either the CRS or random oracle model. The random oracle version supports low-space streaming, as does the CRS model if we assume the (large) CRS is streamed. On the other hand, by relying on the negative results of [MW20], we conclude that a provably secure rate-1 construction in the standard model is unlikely.

1.3   Other Related Work

Bounded Storage Model. Guan and Zhandry [GZ21] is set in Maurer's [Mau92] Bounded Storage Model (BSM), which leverages bounds on the adversary's storage to enable applications. Most prior work in the BSM is about achieving unconditionally secure schemes for the types of scenarios for which we already have computationally secure schemes in the standard model (CPA encryption [CM97, AR99, Lu02, Raz17, GZ19], Key Agreement [CM97, GZ19, DQW21], Oblivious Transfer [CCM98, Din01, DHRS04, GZ19, DQW21], etc.). Time-stamping [MST04] is perhaps the first application of the BSM beyond achieving information-theoretic security by assuming additional computational assumptions. Similarly, our work, as well Guan and Zhandry [GZ21], considers scenarios for which computationally secure schemes in the standard model are impossible and which only make sense in the BSM (public-key encryption where the adversary gets the secret key after seeing the ciphertext, signature schemes where the adversary cannot sign messages whose signatures she has previously observed). Our results necessarily rely on computational assumptions.

Big-Key Cryptography in the Bounded Retrieval Model. The study of big-key cryptography in the Bounded Retrieval Model (BRM) has evolved through a series of works [Dzi06a, DLW06, CDD+07, ADW09, ADN+10, BKR16]. The high-level difference is that in the BRM, the secret keys are made large to prevent exfiltration, while the communication (e.g., ciphertexts, signatures) are kept small. Incompressible cryptography is the reverse: we make the communication large to prevent an adversary from being able to remember it in its entirety, while the secret key is ideally small. On a technical level, while there are some high-level similarities such as relying on a combination of computational and information-theoretic techniques, the concrete schemes are quite different.

Symmetric Cryptography with Memory-Bounded Adversaries. There has been various studies into the symmetric-key setting where the adversaries are memory-bounded. For instance, the work by Rivest [Riv97] introduces *all-or-nothing encryption*, a symmetric-key encryption scheme such that only knowing some individual bits of the ciphertext reveals no information about the message. This is similar to the forward-secure encryption due to [Dzi06b], except that in forward-secure encryption, the adversary is allowed to compute an arbitrary function (with a small-sized output) of the ciphertext, instead of only knowing a few individual bits of it. So all-or-nothing encryption can be thought of as disappearing encryption in the symmetric-key setting, whereas forward-secure encryption is cloaser the a symmetric-key incompressible encryption. The work by Zaverucha [Zav15] further extends the idea of all-or-nothing encryption, constructing a password-based encryption scheme. Building on this, the work by Biryukov and Khovratovich [BK16] constructs memory-hard encryption by combing the idea from [Zav15] together with an external memory-hard function, which allows for high memory bounds even with a small block size. All of these prior works are in the symmetric-key setting, and it is not obvious how to extend them to the public-key setting as we study in this paper.

1.4   Technical Overview

Incompressible Encryption. We first consider incompressible public key encryption. The syntax is identical to that of standard-model encryption, but the security game is different:

1. The challenger first gives the adversary the public key.
2. The adversary then produces two messages m_0, m_1.
3. The challenger encrypts one of the two messages, as the ciphertext c.
4. Now the adversary produces a state s of size somewhat smaller than c.
5. The challenger then reveals the secret key.
6. The adversary, given only the small state s but also the secret key, now makes a guess for which message was encrypted.

Note that, except for the size of the state s being bounded between Steps 4 and 6, the size of the adversary's storage is unbounded. It is also easy to see that this definition implies standard semantic security of public-key encryption.

Remark 3. Note that this security definition is quite similar to that of disappearing public key encryption by Guan and Zhandry [GZ21] with two distinctions. Firstly, in the disappearing encryption security experiment, there is no Step 4 as above. Instead, the adversary is bounded by some space *throughout the entire experiment*. Additionally, functionality wise, disappearing encryption requires the protocol to be executable by honest parties with some space bound lower than the adversary's storage. In our setting, we do not consider this to be an inherent requirement, but rather a desirable feature that some of our schemes satisfy. As we will see in Remark 4, this feature is incompatible with rate-1 schemes, and hence we will drop it in that setting.

Our Solution. We give a construction of incompressible encryption in Sect. 3, under the minimal assumption of generic public key encryption.

We describe our solution using *functional* encryption (FE), which is a form of public key encryption where the secret key holder can give out function secret keys for functions f; a function secret key allows for learning $f(m)$ but nothing else about the message. For our application, we only need a very special case of single-key functional encryption, which we instantiate with a simple and potentially practical construction from generic public key encryption scheme. Our incompressible encryption scheme works as follows:

- The public key is just the public key for the underlying FE scheme. The secret key is a function secret key for the function f_v defined as

$$f_v(s,b) = \begin{cases} s & \text{if } b = 0 \\ s \oplus v & \text{if } b = 1 \end{cases}$$

  where the value v is chosen uniformly at random and hard-coded into f_v. Here, s, v are reasonably short strings, whose length will be discussed shortly.
- To encrypt m, choose a random s, and compute $c \leftarrow \mathsf{FE.Enc}(\mathsf{FE.mpk}, (s, 0))$ as an encryption of $(s, 0)$ under the FE scheme. Then choose a large random string R. Interpret s as the pair (s', t), where t is a string of length equal to the message length, and s' is the seed for a strong extractor. Then compute $z = \mathsf{Extract}(R; s') \oplus t \oplus m$. The final ciphertext is (c, R, z).
- To decrypt, use the FE secret key to recover $s = (s', t)$ from c. Then recover $m = z \oplus \mathsf{Extract}(R; s') \oplus t$.

We can generate and transmit the string R in a streaming fashion. We can then use an online extractor [Vad03] so that $\mathsf{Extract}(R; s')$ can be computed without having to store R in its entirety. Note that R is the only "big" component of the ciphertext, so encryption and decryption therefore require small space.

We prove security through a hybrid argument. First, we use FE security to switch to c being generated as $c \leftarrow \mathsf{FE.Enc}(\mathsf{FE.mpk}, (s \oplus v, 1))$. Since this c decrypts equivalently under the secret key, this change is indistinguishable.

We then observe that the string $u = s \oplus v$ being encrypted under the FE scheme, as well as the string z included in the final ciphertext, are both just uniformly random strings. We can therefore delay the generation of the secret key and v until the very end of the experiment. Now we think of the adversary's state (as well as some other small values needed to complete the simulation) as a leakage on the large random string R. Since the adversary's storage is required to be small compared to R, R has min-entropy conditioned on this leakage. This means we can invoke the randomness guarantee of the randomness extractor to replace $\mathsf{Extract}(R; s')$ with a uniform random string. At this point, m is one-time-padded with a uniform string, and therefore information-theoretically hidden.

We explain how to instantiate the functional encryption scheme. Since the adversary only ever sees a single secret key, we can build such a functional encryption scheme generically from public key encryption, using garbled circuit techniques [GVW12]. On the other hand, our functional encryption scheme only needs to support an extremely simple linear function. We show a very simple and potentially practical solution from any public key encryption scheme.

Remark 4. We note that our scheme has a less-than-ideal rate, since the ciphertext size is at least as large as the adversary's storage *plus* the length of the message. Low rates, however, are inherent to schemes supporting low-storage streaming. Indeed, the storage requirements of the honest users must be at least as large as the message, and in the high-rate case this means the honest users must be capable of storing the entire ciphertext. This remains true *even if the message itself is streamed bit-by-bit*, which can be seen as follows: by incompressibility, the decrypter cannot start outputting message bits until essentially the entire stream has been sent. Otherwise, an attacker can store a short prefix of the ciphertext, and then when it gets the secret key mimic the decrypter until it outputs the first message bit. Now, at the point right before the decrypter outputs the first message bit, the entire contents of the message must be information-theoretically contained within the remaining communication (which is short) and the decrypter's state, since the decrypter ultimately outputs the whole message. Thus the decrypter's state must be almost as large as the message.

A rate-1 solution. We now discuss how we achieve a rate-1 scheme, using indistinguishability obfuscation. This is our most complicated construction, and we only give a brief overview here with the full construction in Sect. 4.

The central difficulty in achieving a rate-1 scheme is that we cannot guarantee a ciphertext with large information-theoretic entropy. Indeed, the ciphertext must be almost as small as the message, so there is little room for added entropy on top of the message. But the message itself, while large, many not have much entropy. Therefore, our approach of using randomness extraction to extract a random string from the ciphertext will not work naively.

Our solution, very roughly, is to have the large random value in the *secret key*. Using a delicate argument, we switch to a hybrid where the ciphertext is just an encryption of large randomness R, and the secret key contains the message, masked by a string extracted from R. Now we can mimic the low-rate case, arguing that given the small state produced by the adversary, R still has min-entropy. Thus, the message m is information-theoretically hidden.

The result is that we achieve an incompressible encryption scheme whose rate matches the rate of the underlying functional encryption scheme. Unlike the low-rate case, our FE scheme appears to need the full power of FE for circuits, since it will be evaluating cryptographic primitives such as PRGs and extractors. Unfortunately, all existing FE schemes for general circuits, even using iO, have poor rate. For example, if we look at the original iO scheme of [GGH+13], the ciphertext contains *two* plain public key encryption encryptions of the message, *plus* a NIZK proof of consistency. The result is that the rate is certainly at most 1/3. Another construction due to [BCP14] sets the ciphertext to be an obfuscated program containing the message; since known obfuscation schemes incur a large blowup, the scheme is not rate-1.

We give a novel rate-1 FE scheme (with many key security), by building on ideas from [BZ14]. They build an object called private linear broadcast encryption (PLBE), which can be seen as a special case of FE for simple comparison functionalities. However, their approach readily generalizes to more complex functionalities. The problem with their construction is that their proof incurs a security loss proportional to the domain size. In their case, the domain is polynomial and this is not a problem. But in our case, the domain is the message space, which is exponential. One may hope to use complexity leveraging, but this would require setting the security parameter to be at least as large as the message. However, this will not give a rate-1 scheme since the ciphertext is larger than the message by an additive factor linear in the security parameter.

We therefore devise new techniques for proving security with just a polynomial loss, even for large messages, thus giving the first rate-1 FE scheme for general circuits, from iO and one-way functions. Details in Sect. 7.

Remark 5. We note that the final construction of rate-1 incompressible encryption has very short public keys, but large secret keys. We therefore leave as an interesting open question devising a scheme that also has short secret keys. However, achieving such a scheme with provable security under standard assumptions appears hard. Indeed, cryptographic assumptions typically make no restrictions on the adversary's storage. The issue is that the message itself may have little entropy, and so to prove that a ciphertext is incompressible it seems the computational assumptions will be used to transition to a hybrid where the ciphertext has nearly full entropy (indeed, this is how our proof works). But this transition happens without space bounds, meaning the reduction actually is capable of decrypting the ciphertext and recovering the message once the key is revealed. Yet in this hybrid the ciphertext was "used up" in order to make it high-entropy, and it seems the only place left to embed the message is the secret key (again, this is how our proof works). If the message is large, it therefore seems the secret key must be large as well. We believe this intuition can be formalized as a black-box separation result, similarly to analogous results of [Wic13], but we leave this for future work.

Incompressible Signatures. An incompressible signature scheme is defined by the following experiment:

1. The challenger first gives the adversary the public key.
2. The adversary makes repeated signing queries on arbitrary messages. In response, the challenger produces a signature on the message.
3. After observing many signatures, the adversary must produce a small state s of size somewhat smaller than a single signature.
4. Next, the adversary, is given the small state s, and wins if it produces a valid signature on *any* message, potentially even one used in a prior signing query.

Note that, except for the size of the state s being bounded between Steps 3 and 4, the size of the adversary's storage is unbounded.

Remark 6. This definition is also quite similar to that of disappearing signature due to Guan and Zhandry [GZ21] except for two differences. For disappearing signatures, the security experiment does not have Step 3 as above, and instead requires the adversary to be bounded by some space *throughout the entire experiment*. Functionality wise, disappearing signature requires the scheme can be run by honest parties with a space bound somewhat lower that the adversary's storage, whereas we don't require that for incompressible signatures.

Our Solution. We give a very simple construction of incompressible signatures in Sect. 5. To sign m, first choose a large uniformly random string R, and then compute $\sigma \leftarrow \mathsf{Sign}(\mathsf{sk}, (R, m))$, where Sign is a standard-model signature scheme. The overall signature is then (R, σ). Verification is straightforward.

Both signing and verification can be evaluated in a low-space streaming fashion, provided Sign can be evaluated as such. One can always assume this property of Sign: first hash the message using a streaming-friendly hash function such as Merkle-Damgård, and then sign the hash. Since the hash is small and computing the hash requires low-space, the overall signing algorithm is low space.

For security, consider an adversary which produces a small state s somewhat smaller than the length of R. Since R is random, it will be infeasible for the adversary to re-produce R in Step 4. Therefore, any valid signature must have an R different than any of the messages previously signed. But this then violates the standard unforgeability of Sign.

A rate-1 solution. In Sect. 6, we modify the above construction to get a rate-1 solution. We note that "rate" here has to be defined carefully. In the above solution, the signature size is independent of the message size, and so it seems that the signature has good rate. However, communication will involve both the signature *and* the message, and so the total length of the communication will be significantly larger than the message. We therefore want that the *total communication* length is only slightly longer than the message being signed.

On the other hand, if the message is very long, one may naturally wonder whether we can just sign the message using any standard-model signature scheme, and have the resulting communication be rate-1. However, a long message may in fact be compressible. What we want is to achieve rate-1 total communication, and incompressibility, even if the message may be compressed.

We therefore define a rate-1 incompressible signature as an incompressible signature where the signature is only slightly longer than the message, and where there is a procedure to extract the message from the signature. In this way, all that needs to be sent is the signature itself, and therefore the total communication remains roughly the same as the message.

Equivalence to incompressible encodings. We next demonstrate that incompressible signatures are equivalent to incompressible encodings [MW20]. These are public encoding schemes where the encoding encodes a message into a codeword c that is only slightly longer than the message. From c, the original message can be recovered using a decoding procedure. For security, the adversary then receives the codeword as well as the message, tries to compress the codeword into a small storage s. Then the adversary, given s *and the message*, tries to recover the exact codeword c.

A rate-1 incompressible signature (with small public keys) gives an incompressible encoding: to encode a message, simply generate a new public/secret key pair, and sign the message. The codeword c is then the public key together with the signature. Decoding and security follow readily from the message extraction procedure and security of the incompressible signature.

In the other direction, to sign a message, first incompressibly encode the message and then sign the result using a standard-model signature scheme. The final signature is the codeword together with the standard-model signature. Extraction follows from the decoding procedure. If the incompressible encoding supports low-space streaming, so does the signature scheme. For security, since the adversary cannot produce the original codeword that was signed due to the security of the incompressible encoding, they must produce some other codeword. But a valid signature would also contain a standard-model signature on this new codeword, violating the security of the signature scheme.

Moran and Wichs [MW20] instantiate incompressible encodings under either the Decisional Composite Residuosity (DCR) or Learning With Errors (LWE) assumptions, in either the CRS or random oracle models. We observe that their incompressible encodings simply break the message into blocks of length $\mathsf{poly}(\lambda)$ and encode each block separately; as such they can be easily streamed in low space, though the CRS-based scheme would need the CRS to be streamed as well. We obtain the incompressible signatures under the same assumptions in the same models, with low-space streaming.

We also note that we can have the signer generate the CRS and include it in the public key, giving a standard-model incompressible encoding scheme with large public keys. Note that such a scheme is not immediately equivalent to incompressible encodings, since the codeword contains the public key, and would therefore be too large.

On the other hand, [MW20] show that a CRS or random oracle is somewhat necessary, by giving a black box separation relative to falsifiable assumptions in the standard model. Due to our equivalence, this implies such a black box impossibility for incompressible signatures in the standard model as well.

2   Preliminaries

Min-Entropy Extractor. Recall the definition for average min-entropy:

Definition 1 (Average Min-Entropy). *For two jointly distributed random variables (X, Y), the average min-entropy of X conditioned on Y is defined as*

$$H_\infty(X|Y) = -\log \mathbf{E}_{y \xleftarrow{\$} Y}[\max_x \Pr[X = x|Y = y]].$$

Lemma 1 ([DRS04]). *For random variables X, Y where Y is supported over a set of size T, we have $H_\infty(X|Y) \geq H_\infty(X, Y) - \log T \geq H_\infty(X) - \log T$.*

Definition 2 (Extractor [Nis90]). *A function $\mathsf{Extract} : \{0,1\}^n \times \{0,1\}^d \to \{0,1\}^m$ is a (k, ϵ) strong average min-entropy extractor if, for all jointly distributed random variables (X, Y) where X takes values in $\{0,1\}^n$ and $H_\infty(X|Y) \geq k$, we have that $(U_d, \mathsf{Extract}(X; U_d), Y)$ is ϵ-close to (s, U_m, Y), where U_d and U_m are uniformly random strings of length d and m respectively.*

Remark 7. Any strong randomness extractor is also a strong *average* min-entropy extractor, with a constant loss in ϵ.

Digital Signatures. We also generalize the syntax of a signature scheme, which will ultimately be necessary to achieve a meaningful high "rate". Instead of producing a signature that is sent along side the message, we would implicitly embed or *encode* the message into the signature. The signature is then all that is sent to the receiver, from which the message can be decoded and verified. Any standard signature scheme can readily be viewed in our generalized syntax by just calling (m, σ) the "signature."

A public key signature scheme for message space $\{0,1\}^{L_m}$ and signature space $\{0,1\}^{L_\sigma}$ is a tuple of PPT algorithms $\Pi = (\text{Gen}, \text{Sign}, \text{Ver})$ such that:

- $\text{Gen}(1^\lambda) \to (\text{vk}, \text{sk})$ samples a verification key vk, and a signing key sk.
- $\text{Sign}(\text{sk}, m) \to \sigma$ takes as input the signing key sk and a message m, and computes a signature σ *that implicitly contains the message* m.
- $\text{Ver}(\text{vk}, \sigma) \to m/\bot$ takes as input the verification key vk and a signature σ, and outputs either the message m or $\bot$. Outputting m means that the signature verifies, and outputting $\bot$ means that the signature is invalid.

Definition 3 (Correctness). *For all* $\lambda \in \mathbb{N}$ *and message* $m \in \{0,1\}^{L_m}$, *let* $(\text{vk}, \text{sk}) \leftarrow \text{Gen}(1^\lambda)$, *then we have* $\Pr[\text{Ver}(\text{vk}, \text{Sign}(\text{sk}, m)) = m] \geq 1 - \text{negl}(\lambda)$.

We modify the security experiment slightly by asking the adversary to output a signature σ instead of a message-signature pair, and the adversary wins the game if and only if $\text{Ver}(\text{vk}, \sigma) \notin \{\bot, m_1, \ldots, m_q\}$ where m_i's are the previously queried messages. The "rate" of the signature scheme is defined to be L_m/L_σ.

Functional Encryption. For our constructions we also need single-key game-based functional encryption. Let λ be the security parameter. Let $\{\mathcal{C}_\lambda\}$ be a class of circuits with input space $\mathcal{X}_\lambda$ and output space $\mathcal{Y}_\lambda$. A functional encryption scheme for the circuit class $\{\mathcal{C}_\lambda\}$ is a tuple of PPT algorithms $\text{FE} = (\text{Setup}, \text{KeyGen}, \text{Enc}, \text{Dec})$ defined as follows:

- $\text{Setup}(1^\lambda) \to (\text{mpk}, \text{msk})$ takes as input the security parameter λ, and outputs the master public key mpk and the master secret key msk.
- $\text{KeyGen}(\text{msk}, C) \to \text{sk}_C$ takes as input the master secret key msk and a circuit $C \in \{\mathcal{C}_\lambda\}$, and outputs a function key sk_C.
- $\text{Enc}(\text{mpk}, m) \to \text{ct}$ takes as input the public key mpk and a message $m \in \mathcal{X}_\lambda$, and outputs the ciphertext ct.
- $\text{Dec}(\text{sk}_C, \text{ct}) \to y$ takes as input a function key sk_C and a ciphertext ct, and outputs a value $y \in \mathcal{Y}_\lambda$.

We can analogously define the "rate" of an FE scheme to be the ratio between the message length to the ciphertext length. We require correctness and security of a functional encryption scheme.

Definition 4 (Correctness). *A functional encryption scheme* FE = (Setup, KeyGen, Enc, Dec) *is said to be correct if for all* $C \in \{\mathcal{C}_\lambda\}$ *and* $m \in \mathcal{X}_\lambda$:

$$\Pr\left[y = C(m) : \begin{matrix}(\mathsf{mpk}, \mathsf{msk}) \leftarrow \mathsf{Setup}(1^\lambda) \\ \mathsf{sk}_C \leftarrow \mathsf{KeyGen}(\mathsf{msk}, C) \\ \mathsf{ct} \leftarrow \mathsf{Enc}(\mathsf{mpk}, m) \\ y \leftarrow \mathsf{Dec}(\mathsf{sk}_C, \mathsf{ct})\end{matrix}\right] \geq 1 - \mathsf{negl}(\lambda).$$

Consider the following *Semi-Adaptive Security Experiment*, $\mathsf{Dist}_{\mathsf{FE},\mathcal{A}}^{\mathsf{SemiAdpt}}(\lambda)$:

– Run FE.Setup(1^λ) to obtain (mpk, msk) and sample a random bit $b \leftarrow \{0,1\}$.
– On input 1^λ and mpk, The adversary $\mathcal{A}$ submits the challenge query consisting of two messages m_0 and m_1. It then receives $\mathsf{ct} \leftarrow \mathsf{FE.Enc}(\mathsf{mpk}, m_b)$.
– The adversary now submits a circuit $C \in \{\mathcal{C}_\lambda\}$ s.t. $C(m_0) = C(m_1)$, and receives $\mathsf{sk}_C \leftarrow \mathsf{FE.KeyGen}(\mathsf{msk}, C)$.
– The adversary $\mathcal{A}$ outputs a guess b' for b. If $b' = b$, we say that the adversary succeeds and experiment outputs 1. Otherwise, the experiment outputs 0.

Definition 5 (Single-Key Semi-Adaptive Security). *For security parameter* λ, *a functional encryption scheme* FE = (Setup, KeyGen, Enc, Dec) *is said to have single-key semi-adaptive security if for all PPT adversaries* $\mathcal{A}$:

$$\Pr\left[\mathsf{Dist}_{\mathsf{FE},\mathcal{A}}^{\mathsf{SemiAdpt}}(\lambda) = 1\right] \leq \frac{1}{2} + \mathsf{negl}(\lambda).$$

We can also consider *selective* security, where the adversary only receives mpk *after* sending the challenge messages. We can also consider *many-time* semi-adaptive/selective security, where the adversary is able to adaptively query for as many sk_C as it would like, provided they all occur after the challenge query.

3   Incompressible Encryption: Our Basic Construction

Here we show how to construct an incompressible public key encryption scheme with low "rate", i.e. the ratio of the message size to the ciphertext size. First, we define what it means for a public key encryption scheme to be *incompressible*.

3.1   Definition

We give the definition of incompressible encryption, which is based on the similar definition of disappearing encryption [GZ21]. For security parameters λ and S, an incompressible public key encryption scheme with message space $\{0,1\}^{L_m}$ and ciphertext space $\{0,1\}^{L_{ct}}$ is a tuple of PPT algorithms $\Pi = (\mathsf{Gen}, \mathsf{Enc}, \mathsf{Dec})$.

Remark 8. For the original disappearing PKE defined in [GZ21], it is additionally required that Gen, Enc, and Dec can be run in space $N \ll L_{ct}$. Here, we will consider schemes that have both large and small space.

The rest of the syntax of an incompressible PKE scheme is identical to that of a classical PKE scheme. The "rate" of the PKE scheme is simply L_m/L_{ct}.

For the security definition, consider the following indistinguishability experiment for an adversary $\mathcal{A} = (\mathcal{A}_1, \mathcal{A}_2)$:

Incompressible Encryption Security Experiment $\mathsf{Dist}_{\mathcal{A},\Pi}^{\mathsf{IncomEnc}}(\lambda)$:

1. The adversary $\mathcal{A}_1$, on input 1^λ, outputs a space bound 1^S.
2. Run $\mathsf{Gen}(1^\lambda, 1^S)$ to obtain keys $(\mathsf{pk}, \mathsf{sk})$.
3. Sample a uniform bit $b \in \{0,1\}$.
4. The adversary is then provided the public key pk.
5. The adversary replies with the challenge query consisting of two messages m_0 and m_1, receives $\mathsf{ct} \leftarrow \mathsf{Enc}(\mathsf{pk}, m_b)$.
6. $\mathcal{A}_1$ produces a state st of size at most S.
7. The adversary $\mathcal{A}_2$ is given the tuple $(\mathsf{pk}, \mathsf{sk}, m_0, m_1, \mathsf{st})$ and outputs a guess b' for b. If $b' = b$, we say that the adversary succeeds and the output of the experiment is 1. Otherwise, the experiment outputs 0.

Definition 6 (Incompressible Encryption Security). *For security parameters λ and S, a public key encryption scheme $\Pi = (\mathsf{Gen}, \mathsf{Enc}, \mathsf{Dec})$ has incompressible encryption security if for all PPT adversaries $\mathcal{A} = (\mathcal{A}_1, \mathcal{A}_2)$:*

$$\Pr\left[\mathsf{Dist}_{\mathcal{A},\Pi}^{\mathsf{IncomEnc}}(\lambda) = 1\right] \leq \frac{1}{2} + \mathsf{negl}(\lambda).$$

Remark 9. The original Disappearing Ciphertext Security [GZ21] has a very similar security notion, except that the adversary has a space bound of S *throughout the entire experiment*, and that the ciphertext is a long stream sent bit by bit. Notice that our definition of Incompressible Encryption Security is a strictly stronger security definition than Disappearing Ciphertext Security.

3.2 Construction

Construction 1. *Given* $\mathsf{FE} = (\mathsf{Setup}, \mathsf{KeyGen}, \mathsf{Enc}, \mathsf{Dec})$ *a single-key selectively secure functional encryption scheme with a rate of* ρ_{FE} *and a strong average min-entropy extractor* $\mathsf{Extract} : \{0,1\}^n \times \{0,1\}^d \rightarrow \{0,1\}^{L_m}$, *with* $d = \mathsf{poly}(\lambda)$ *and* $n = S + \mathsf{poly}(\lambda)$ *the construction* $\Pi = (\mathsf{Gen}, \mathsf{Enc}, \mathsf{Dec})$ *works as follows:*

- $\mathsf{Gen}(1^\lambda, 1^S)$: *First, obtain* $(\mathsf{FE.mpk}, \mathsf{FE.msk}) \leftarrow \mathsf{FE.Setup}(1^\lambda)$. *Then, generate the secret key for the following function* f_v *with a hardcoded* $v \in \{0,1\}^{d+L_m}$:

$$f_v(s' = (s,t), \mathsf{flag}) = \begin{cases} s' & \text{if } \mathsf{flag} = 0 \\ s' \oplus v & \text{if } \mathsf{flag} = 1 \end{cases}.$$

  Output $\mathsf{pk} = \mathsf{FE.mpk}$ *and* $\mathsf{sk} = \mathsf{FE.sk}_{f_v} \leftarrow \mathsf{FE.KeyGen}(\mathsf{FE.msk}, f_v)$.
- $\mathsf{Enc}(\mathsf{pk}, m)$: *Sample a random tuple* $s' = (s,t)$ *where* $s \in \{0,1\}^d$ *is used as a seed for the extractor and* $t \in \{0,1\}^{L_m}$ *is used as a one-time pad. The ciphertext consists of three parts:* $\mathsf{FE.ct} \leftarrow \mathsf{FE.Enc}(\mathsf{FE.mpk}, (s', 0))$, *a long randomness* $R \in \{0,1\}^n$, *and* $z = \mathsf{Extract}(R; s) \oplus t \oplus m$.

- Dec(sk, ct $= (\text{FE.ct}, R, z)$): *First, obtain* $s' \leftarrow \text{FE.Dec}(\text{FE.sk}_{f_v}, \text{FE.ct})$, *and then use the seed* s *to compute* $\text{Extract}(R; s) \oplus z \oplus t$ *to recover* m.

Note that if Extract is an *online* extractor [Vad03], then encryption and decryption can be run in a low-space streaming fashion, by first sending FE.ct, then streaming R, and then sending z. The rate of this construction is

$$\frac{L_m}{L_{\text{ct}}} = L_m \left(\frac{d + L_m + 1}{\rho_{\text{FE}}} + n + L_m \right)^{-1} = \frac{1}{(1/\rho_{\text{FE}} + 1) + S/L_m} - o(1).$$

Theorem 1. *Assuming the existence of a functional encryption scheme with single-key selective security and a rate of* $1/\text{poly}(\lambda)$, *and a* $(\text{poly}(\lambda), \text{negl}(\lambda))$ *average min-entropy extractor, there exists an incompressible PKE with ciphertext size* $S + L_m + \text{poly}(\lambda) + \text{poly}(\lambda)L_m$, *public key size* $\text{poly}(\lambda)$ *and secret key size* $\text{poly}(\lambda)$. *It supports streaming decryption using* $L_m + \text{poly}(\lambda)$ *bits of memory.*

3.3   Proof of Security

We organize our proof of security into a sequence of hybrids.

Sequence of Hybrids

- H_0: The original incompressible encryption security experiment $\text{Dist}_{A,\Pi}^{\text{IncomEnc}}$, where the bit b in the experiment is fixed to be 0.
- H_1: In step 5, instead of computing $\text{FE.ct} \leftarrow \text{FE.Enc}(\text{FE.mpk}, (s', 0))$, compute $\text{FE.ct} \leftarrow \text{FE.Enc}(\text{FE.mpk}, (s' \oplus v, 1))$.
- H_2: In step 2, only sample $(\text{FE.mpk}, \text{FE.msk}) \leftarrow \text{FE.Setup}(1^\lambda)$. In step 5, after receiving the challenge query, sample uniformly random $z \in \{0,1\}^{L_m}$, $u \in \{0,1\}^{d+L_m}$, $R \in \{0,1\}^n$ and send back $\text{FE.ct} \leftarrow \text{FE.Enc}(\text{FE.mpk}, (u, 1))$, R, and z as the ciphertext. In step 7, sample a uniformly random $s \in \{0,1\}^d$, and compute $t = \text{Extract}(R; s) \oplus z \oplus m_0$, and $v = s' \oplus u$ where s' is the tuple (s, t). Use this v to compute $\text{sk} = \text{FE.sk}_{f_v} \leftarrow \text{FE.KeyGen}(\text{FE.msk}, f_v)$.
- H_3: In step 7, sample a uniformly random $r \in \{0,1\}^{L_m}$ and compute $t = r \oplus z \oplus m_0$ instead.
- H_4: Swap the bit b in the security experiment to be 1 instead of 0.
- H_5: Switch back to the case where $t = \text{Extract}(R; s) \oplus z \oplus m_1$.
- H_6: Switch back to the case where we produce sk in step 2 instead of step 5.
- H_7: Switch the FE ciphertext back to the real one $\text{FE.Enc}(\text{FE.mpk}, (s', 0))$. Notice here we're at the original incompressible encryption security experiment, where the bit b is fixed to be 1.

Proof of Hybrid Arguments

Lemma 2. *If the functional encryption scheme* FE *has single-key selective security, then no PPT adversary can distinguish between* H_0 *and* H_1 *(respectively* H_6 *and* H_7*) with non-negligible probability.*

Proof. Here we will prove the case for H_0 and H_1. The case for H_6 and H_7 follows analogously. This is by a simple reduction to the single-key selective security of the functional encryption scheme. If an adversary $\mathcal{A}$ is able to distinguish between H_0 and H_1, we show how to construct an adversary $\mathcal{A}'$ that breaks security of the functional encryption scheme FE. The only difference between H_0 and H_1 is that in H_0 the adversary receives an encryption of $(s', 0)$, while in H_1 the adversary receives an encryption of $(s' \oplus v, 1)$. But notice that $f_v(s', 0) = s' = f_v(s' \oplus v, 1)$, so the adversary $\mathcal{A}$ is able to distinguish between two FE ciphertexts that have the same functional output on function f_v, for which it has a secret key. This directly breaks the underlying functional encryption security. Concretely, $\mathcal{A}'$ works as follows by using $\mathcal{A} = (\mathcal{A}_1, \mathcal{A}_2)$ as a subroutine:

- On input 1^λ, sample uniform values s' and v, and submit the challenge query $\mathsf{FE}.m_0 = (s', 0)$ and $\mathsf{FE}.m_1 = (s' \oplus v, 1)$ to the challenger. Receive $\mathsf{FE.mpk}$ and $\mathsf{FE.ct}$ in response.
- Send 1^λ to $\mathcal{A}_1$ and receive 1^S.
- Send $\mathsf{FE.mpk}$ to $\mathcal{A}_1$, receive challenge query m_0 and m_1, and respond with $\mathsf{FE.ct}$, R and z, where R is a random string of length $S + \mathsf{poly}(\lambda)$, and $z = \mathsf{Extract}(R; s) \oplus t \oplus m_0$. The adversary $\mathcal{A}_1$ produces a state st. Notice that the only component that's different for H_0 and H_1 is $\mathsf{FE.ct}$, and it does not depend on the challenge query from $\mathcal{A}_1$. R and z remain unchanged.
- Send f_v to the challenger and receive $\mathsf{FE.sk}_{f_v}$. Forward $\mathsf{sk} = \mathsf{FE.sk}_{f_v}$ to $\mathcal{A}_2$ together with $(\mathsf{FE.mpk}, m_0, m_1, \mathsf{st})$.
- If $\mathcal{A}_2$ outputs that it is in H_0, output 0. Otherwise, output 1.

It is straightforward to verify that if $\mathcal{A}$ wins the game, $\mathcal{A}'$ wins as well.   □

Lemma 3. *No adversary can distinguish between H_1 and H_2 (respectively H_5 and H_6) with non-negligible probability.*

Proof. We prove the case for H_1 and H_2, the case for H_5 and H_6 follows analogously. Since pk does not depend on sk, and sk is not used until in step 7, now instead of fixing f_v (and thus $\mathsf{sk} = \mathsf{FE.sk}_{f_v}$) in step 2, we sample it lazily in step 7. Our new sampling procedure in H_2 makes the following two changes to H_1: First, in H_1, we sample a uniform t and compute $z = \mathsf{Extract}(R; s) \oplus t \oplus m_0$, while in H_2, we sample a uniform z and compute $t = \mathsf{Extract}(R; s) \oplus z \oplus m_0$. This is just a change of variables, and gives two identical distributions. Second, in H_1 we sample a uniform v and encrypt $u = v \oplus s'$, while in H_2 we encrypt a uniform u and compute $v = u \oplus s'$. Again, these are identical distributions. Thus, no adversary can distinguish between H_1 and H_2 with non-negligible probability. □

Lemma 4. *If the extractor $\mathsf{Extract}$ is a $(\mathsf{poly}(\lambda), \mathsf{negl}(\lambda))$ average min-entropy extractor, then no adversary that produces a state st of size at most S can distinguish between H_2 and H_3 (resp. H_4 and H_5) with non-negligible probability.*

Proof. We prove the case for H_2 and H_3. The other case follows naturally.

Here let the random variables $X = R$, and $Y = (\mathsf{FE.mpk}, \mathsf{FE.msk}, m_0, m_1, u, z)$ and $Z = \mathsf{st}$. By Lemma 1, we have

$$H_\infty(X|Y, Z) \geq \min_y H_\infty(X|Y = y, Z) \geq \min_y H_\infty(X|Y = y) - S = \mathsf{poly}(\lambda).$$

The last equality above follows since $X = R$ is a uniformly random string, independent of Y, of length $S + \mathsf{poly}(\lambda)$. By extractor security, no adversary can distinguish $(s, \mathsf{Extract}(R; s), Y, Z)$ from (s, U_{L_m}, Y, Z) except with $\mathsf{negl}(\lambda)$ probability. Since we now sample $u \leftarrow U_{L_m}$, no adversary can now distinguish between $t = \mathsf{Extract}(R; s) \oplus z \oplus m_0$ and $t = u \oplus z \oplus m_0$, i.e. H_2 and H_3. □

Lemma 5. *No adversary can distinguish H_3 from H_4 with non-zero probability.*

Proof. Notice that the only difference between H_3 and H_4 is that in H_3 we have $t = r \oplus z \oplus m_0$ while in H_4 we have $t = r \oplus z \oplus m_1$, where r is uniformly random. Thus t is uniformly random in both cases, and H_3 and H_4 are identical. □

Theorem 2. *If FE is a functional encryption scheme with single-key selective security, and $\mathsf{Extract}$ is a $(\mathsf{poly}(\lambda), \mathsf{negl}(\lambda))$ average min-entropy extractor, then Construction 1 has incompressible encryption security.*

Proof. The lemmas above show a sequence of hybrids where no PPT adversary that produces a state with size at most S can distinguish one from the next with non-negligible probability. The first hybrid H_0 corresponds to the incompressible encryption security game where $b = 0$, and the last one H_7 corresponds to the case where $b = 1$. The security of the indistinguishability game follows. □

3.4   Instantiating Our FE

We now give a simple construction of functional encryption for our needed functionality. Recall that our functions f_v have the form $f_v(s, \mathsf{flag}) = s \oplus (\mathsf{flag} \cdot v)$.

Construction 2. *Let $(\mathsf{Gen}', \mathsf{Enc}', \mathsf{Dec}')$ be a public key encryption scheme. Our scheme $\mathsf{FE} = (\mathsf{Setup}, \mathsf{KeyGen}, \mathsf{Enc}, \mathsf{Dec})$ for message length $n + 1$ is defined as:*

- $\mathsf{Setup}(1^\lambda)$: *For $i \in \{1, \ldots, n\}, b \in \{0, 1\}$, run $(\mathsf{pk}_{i,b}, \mathsf{sk}_{i,b}) \leftarrow \mathsf{Gen}'(1^\lambda)$. Output $(\mathsf{mpk} = (\mathsf{pk}_{i,b})_{i,b}, \mathsf{msk} = (\mathsf{sk}_{i,b})_{i,b})$.*
- $\mathsf{KeyGen}(\mathsf{msk}, f_v) = (\mathsf{sk}_{i,v_i})_i$.
- $\mathsf{Enc}(\mathsf{mpk}, (s, \mathsf{flag}))$: *For $i \in \{1, \ldots, n\}, b \in \{0, 1\}$, compute $c_{i,b} = \mathsf{Enc}'(\mathsf{pk}_{i,b}, s_i \oplus (\mathsf{flag} \cdot b))$. Output $c = (c_{i,b})_{i,b}$.*
- $\mathsf{Dec}(\mathsf{sk}_{f_v}, c)$: *Output $x = x_1 x_2 \cdots x_n$ where $x_i = \mathsf{Dec}'(\mathsf{sk}_{i,v_i}, c_{i,v_i})$*

For correctness, note that $x_i = s_i \oplus (\mathsf{flag} \cdot v_i)$, and therefore $x = s \oplus (\mathsf{flag} \cdot v) = f_v(s, \mathsf{flag})$. Note that the rate of this scheme is $1/\mathsf{poly}(\lambda)$. Thus the overall rate of our incompressible encryption scheme is $1/\mathsf{poly}(\lambda)$.

Theorem 3. *If $(\mathsf{Gen}', \mathsf{Enc}', \mathsf{Dec}')$ is a CPA secure public key encryption scheme, then Construction 2 is single key semi-adaptively secure for the functions f_v.*

Proof. Consider a single key semi-adaptive adversary for Construction 2. Let $m_0 = (s_0, \mathsf{flag}_0), m_1 = (s_1, \mathsf{flag}_1)$ be the challenge messages. For a fixed flag bit, f_v is injective. Therefore, if $m_0 \neq m_1$, it must be that $\mathsf{flag}_0 \neq \mathsf{flag}_1$. Then if the adversary's secret key query is on f_v, we must have $v = s_0 \oplus s_1$. Thus the two possibilities for the challenge ciphertext are the same for c_{i,v_i}, but encrypt opposite bits in $c_{i,1-v_i}$. Since the adversary never gets to see the secret keys $\mathsf{sk}_{i,1-v_i}$, a simple hybrid argument shows that flipping these bits is indistinguishable. □

Corollary 1. *Assuming the existence of a CPA secure public key encryption scheme and a $(\mathsf{poly}(\lambda), \mathsf{negl}(\lambda))$ average min-entropy extractor, there exists an incompressible PKE with ciphertext size $S + L_m + \mathsf{poly}(\lambda) + \mathsf{poly}(\lambda)L_m$, public key size $\mathsf{poly}(\lambda)$ and secret key size $\mathsf{poly}(\lambda)$. Furthermore, it supports streaming decryption using $L_m + \mathsf{poly}(\lambda)$ bits of memory.*

4   Rate-1 Incompressible Encryption

Here, we construct incompressible encryption with an optimal rate of $1 - o(1)$, i.e. the message length is (almost) the same as the ciphertext length.

4.1   Construction

For our construction, we require a functional encryption scheme with single-key semi-adaptive security and a rate of 1, a strong average min-entropy extractor, and a secure pseudorandom generator (PRG). Our construction works as follows.

Construction 3. *Given* $\mathsf{FE} = (\mathsf{Setup}, \mathsf{KeyGen}, \mathsf{Enc}, \mathsf{Dec})$ *a rate-1 functional encryption scheme satisfying single-key semi-adaptive security,* $\mathsf{Extract} : \{0,1\}^{L_m} \times \{0,1\}^d \to \{0,1\}^n$ *a strong average min-entropy extractor where* $d, n = \mathsf{poly}(\lambda)$, *and* $\mathsf{PRG} : \{0,1\}^n \to \{0,1\}^{L_m}$ *a secure PRG, the construction* $\Pi = (\mathsf{Gen}, \mathsf{Enc}, \mathsf{Dec})$ *works as follows:*

- $\mathsf{Gen}(1^\lambda, 1^S)$: *First, obtain* $(\mathsf{FE.mpk}, \mathsf{FE.msk}) \leftarrow \mathsf{FE.Setup}(1^\lambda)$. *Then, generate the secret key for the following function* $f_{v,s}$ *with a hardcoded large random pad* $v \in \{0,1\}^{L_m}$ *and a small extractor seed* $s \in \{0,1\}^d$:

$$f_{v,s}(x, \mathsf{flag}) = \begin{cases} x & \textit{if } \mathsf{flag} = 0 \\ \mathsf{PRG}(\mathsf{Extract}(x; s)) \oplus v & \textit{if } \mathsf{flag} = 1 \end{cases}.$$

   Output $\mathsf{pk} = \mathsf{FE.mpk}$ *and* $\mathsf{sk} = \mathsf{FE.sk}_{f_{v,s}} \leftarrow \mathsf{FE.KeyGen}(\mathsf{FE.msk}, f_{v,s})$. *Set* $L_m = S + \mathsf{poly}(\lambda)$.
- $\mathsf{Enc}(\mathsf{pk}, m)$: *The ciphertext is simply an encryption of* $(m, 0)$ *using the underlying* FE *scheme, i.e.* $\mathsf{FE.ct} \leftarrow \mathsf{FE.Enc}(\mathsf{FE.mpk}, (m, 0))$.
- $\mathsf{Dec}(\mathsf{sk}, \mathsf{ct})$: *Decryption also corresponds to* FE *decryption. The output is simply* $\mathsf{FE.Dec}(\mathsf{FE.sk}_{f_{v,s}}, \mathsf{ct}) = f_{v,s}(m, 0) = m$ *as desired.*

Let ρ_{FE} be the rate of FE. Then the ciphertext size is $(L_m + 1)/\rho_{\mathsf{FE}}$ and the rate of our incompressible encryption scheme is $\rho_\Pi = \rho_{\mathsf{FE}}/(1 + L_m^{-1})$. If $\rho_{\mathsf{FE}} = 1 - o(1)$, then $\rho_\Pi = 1 - o(1)$ as well.

Theorem 4. *Assuming the existence of a functional encryption scheme with single-key semi-adaptive security and a rate of $1 - o(1)$, and a $(\mathsf{poly}(\lambda), \mathsf{negl}(\lambda))$ average min-entropy extractor, there exists an incompressible PKE with message size of up to $S - \mathsf{poly}(\lambda)$, ciphertext size $S + \mathsf{poly}(\lambda)$, public key size $\mathsf{poly}(\lambda)$ and secret key size $\mathsf{poly}(S, \lambda)$.*

4.2 Proof of Security

We organize our proof of security into a sequence of hybrids.

Sequence of Hybrids

- H_0: The original incompressible encryption security experiment $\mathsf{Dist}_{\mathcal{A},\Pi}^{\mathsf{IncomEnc}}$, where the bit b in the experiment is fixed to be 0.
- H_1: Instead of fixing v and s in step 2 of the security experiment, lazily sample v and s in step 7 where we need to provide sk. Also, instead of sampling v directly, first sample a uniformly random $u \in \{0,1\}^{L_m}$, and then compute $v = u \oplus m_0$.
- H_2: We further modify how we sample v. Now instead of sampling a random u, we sample a random PRG key $k \in \{0,1\}^n$, and set $v = \mathsf{PRG}(k) \oplus m_0$.
- H_3: We once more modify how we sample v. We now sample a long randomness $R \in \{0,1\}^{L_m}$ and use that to compute $v = \mathsf{PRG}(\mathsf{Extract}(R; s)) \oplus m_0$.
- H_4: In step 5, set the ciphertext to be $\mathsf{FE.ct} \leftarrow \mathsf{FE.Enc}(\mathsf{FE.mpk}, (R, 1))$.
- H_5: In step 7, revert to computing $v = \mathsf{PRG}(k) \oplus m_0$ for a uniform k.
- H_6: In step 7, revert to computing $v = u \oplus m_0$ for a uniform u.
- H_7: Switch the bit b of the experiment from 0 to 1.
- H_8: In step 7, sample v as $\mathsf{PRG}(k) \oplus m_1$.
- H_9: In step 7, sample v as $\mathsf{PRG}(\mathsf{Extract}(R; s)) \oplus m_1$.
- H_{10}: In step 5, change the ciphertext back to $\mathsf{FE.ct} \leftarrow \mathsf{FE.Enc}(\mathsf{FE.mpk}, (m_1, 0))$.
- H_{11}: In step 7, sample v as $\mathsf{PRG}(k) \oplus m_1$.
- H_{12}: In step 7, sample v as $u \oplus m_1$.
- H_{13}: Sample a uniform v back at the beginning of the experiment in step 2. Notice that now we're back at the original incompressible encryption security experiment, where the bit b is fixed to be 1.

For the proofs of the hybrids and Theorem 4, please refer to the full version.

5 Incompressible Signatures: Our Basic Construction

5.1 Definition

Here we give the definition of *incompressible* signatures. An incompressible signature scheme $\Pi = (\mathsf{Gen}, \mathsf{Sign}, \mathsf{Ver})$ takes an additional space parameter S, and in addition to the standard model signature security (where the adversary has unbounded space throughout the game), we also require *incompressible signature security* that utilizes the following experiment for adversary $\mathcal{A} = (\mathcal{A}_1, \mathcal{A}_2)$:

Signature Forgery Experiment $\mathsf{SigForge}_{\mathcal{A}, \Pi}^{\mathsf{IncomSig}}(\lambda)$:

- The adversary $\mathcal{A}_1$, on input 1^λ, outputs a space bound 1^S.
- Run $\mathsf{Gen}(1^\lambda, 1^S)$ to obtain keys $(\mathsf{vk}, \mathsf{sk})$.
- The adversary $\mathcal{A}_1$ is given the public key vk.
- For $q = \mathsf{poly}(\lambda)$ rounds, $\mathcal{A}_1$ submits a message m, and receives $\sigma \leftarrow \mathsf{Sign}(\mathsf{sk}, m)$. At the end of the last round, $\mathcal{A}_1$ produces a state st of size at most S.
- The adversary $\mathcal{A}_2$ is given the public key vk, the state st, and all the queried messages m, and outputs a signature σ'. If $\mathsf{Ver}(\mathsf{vk}, \sigma')$ outputs $\bot$, output 0. Otherwise, output 1.

Notice that traditionally, we would require $\mathsf{Ver}(\mathsf{vk}, \sigma')$ to be distinct from the messages m's queried before, but here we have no such requirement. With this experiment in mind, we now define the additional security requirement for an incompressible signature scheme.

Definition 7 (Incompressible Signature Security). *For security parameters λ and S, an incompressible signature scheme $\Pi = (\mathsf{Gen}, \mathsf{Sig}, \mathsf{Ver})$ has incompressible signature security, if for all PPT adversaries $\mathcal{A} = (\mathcal{A}_1, \mathcal{A}_2)$:*

$$\Pr\left[\mathsf{SigForge}_{\mathcal{A}, \Pi}^{\mathsf{IncomSig}}(\lambda) = 1\right] \leq \mathsf{negl}(\lambda).$$

5.2 Construction

We present a very simple construction from classical public key signature schemes.

Construction 4. *Let λ, S be security parameters. Given $\mathsf{Sig} = (\mathsf{Gen}, \mathsf{Sign}, \mathsf{Ver})$ a classical public key signature scheme with message space $\{0,1\}^{n+L_m}$ where $n = S + \mathsf{poly}(\lambda)$ and rate ρ', we construct an incompressible signature scheme $\Pi = (\mathsf{Gen}, \mathsf{Sign}, \mathsf{Ver})$ as follows:*

- $\mathsf{Gen}(1^\lambda, 1^S)$: *Run $\mathsf{Sig.Gen}(1^\lambda)$ to obtain $(\mathsf{Sig.vk}, \mathsf{Sig.sk})$. Output $\mathsf{vk} = \mathsf{Sig.vk}$ and $\mathsf{sk} = \mathsf{Sig.sk}$.*
- $\mathsf{Sign}(\mathsf{sk}, m)$: *Sample randomness $R \in \{0,1\}^n$, and output $\sigma \leftarrow \mathsf{Sig.Sign}(\mathsf{Sig.sk}, (R, m))$.*
- $\mathsf{Ver}(\mathsf{vk}, \sigma)$: *Run $M \leftarrow \mathsf{Sig.Ver}(\mathsf{Sig.vk}, \sigma)$. If $M = \bot$, output $\bot$. Otherwise, if $M = (R, m)$, output m.*

Sig can be computed in an low-space streaming fashion, since we can hash the message in low space first using Merkle-Damgård. Then Construction 5 can readily be computed with low space streaming. The rate of this construction is

$$\frac{L_m}{L_\sigma} = \frac{L_m}{(S + L_m)/\rho'} = \rho'(1 + S/L_m)^{-1}.$$

5.3   Proof of Security

Theorem 5. *Assuming the existence of a secure public key signature scheme with rate ρ', there exists an incompressible signature scheme with signature size $\rho'(S + L_m + \mathsf{poly}(\lambda))$, public key size $\mathsf{poly}(\lambda)$ and secret key size $\mathsf{poly}(\lambda)$. Furthermore, it supports streaming computation using $\mathsf{poly}(\lambda)$ bits of memory.*

Proof. We show this through a reduction proof. Concretely, we show how one can use an adversary $\mathcal{A} = (\mathcal{A}_1, \mathcal{A}_2)$ that breaks the incompressible signature security as a subroutine to build an adversary $\mathcal{A}'$ the breaks the underlying classical Sig scheme. The adversary $\mathcal{A}'$ works as follows:

- Send 1^λ to $\mathcal{A}_1$, receive 1^S, and set $n = S + \mathsf{poly}(\lambda)$.
- Receive vk from the challenger, and forward it to $\mathcal{A}_1$.
- For each signing query m_i made by $\mathcal{A}_1$, sample a random $R_i \in \{0,1\}^n$ and make a query (R_i, m_i) to the challenger. Receive back σ_i and forward it directly to $\mathcal{A}_1$.
- When $\mathcal{A}_1$ produces a state st, send vk, st and all the signing queries $\{m_i\}_i$ to $\mathcal{A}_2$. Output what $\mathcal{A}_2$ outputs as σ'.

Notice that if $\mathcal{A}$ wins, that means $\mathsf{Ver}(\mathsf{vk}, \sigma') = (R', m') \neq \perp$. If $m' \notin \{m_i\}_i$, then (R', m') is a pair not queried before by $\mathcal{A}'$, and thus $\mathcal{A}'$ wins the game. If $m' = m_j$ for some j, then we argue that with overwhelming probability $R' \neq R_j$, and hence $\mathcal{A}'$ wins as well. Indeed this is true since

$$H_\infty(R_j | \mathsf{st}, \mathsf{vk}, \{m_i\}_i) \geq S + \mathsf{poly}(\lambda) - S = \mathsf{poly}(\lambda).$$

Therefore R_j is unpredictable conditioned on $\mathcal{A}_2$'s view, so the probability of $\mathcal{A}_2$ producing some $R' = R_j$ is negligible. ☐

6   Rate-1 Incompressible Signatures

6.1   Incompressible Encoding

Moran and Wichs [MW20] give the definition for incompressible encodings and show construction based on either the Decisional Composite Residuosity (DCR) or Learning With Errors (LWE) assumptions. We modify the definition slightly to better accommodate the syntax in this paper.

Definition 8 (Incompressible Encodings [MW20]). *Let λ be security parameters. An incompressible encoding scheme for message space $\{0,1\}^{L_m}$ and codeword space $\{0,1\}^{L_c}$ is a pair of PPT algorithms $\mathsf{Code} = (\mathsf{Enc}, \mathsf{Dec})$ that utilizes the following syntax:*

- $\mathsf{Enc}(1^\lambda, m) \to c$ *on input the security parameter and a message, outputs a codeword c.*
- $\mathsf{Dec}(c) \to m$ *on input a codeword, outputs the decoded message m.*

The "rate" of the incompressible encoding is L_m/L_c.[3]

We additionally require correctness and S-incompressibility[4]:

Definition 9 (Correctness). *For all* $\lambda \in \mathbb{N}$ *and* $m \in \mathcal{M}$, $\Pr[\mathsf{Dec}(\mathsf{Enc}(1^\lambda, m)) = m] \geq 1 - \mathsf{negl}(\lambda)$.

Next, consider the following experiment for adversary $\mathcal{A} = (\mathcal{A}_1, \mathcal{A}_2)$:

Codeword Compression Experiment $\mathsf{Comp}_{\mathcal{A},\mathsf{Code}}^{\mathsf{IncomCode}}(\lambda, S)$:

- On input 1^λ, the adversary $\mathcal{A}_1$ submits a message m and auxiliary input aux. It receives $c \leftarrow \mathsf{Enc}(1^\lambda, m)$, and produces a state st of size at most S.
- The adversary $\mathcal{A}_2$ is given the state st, the message m, and the auxiliary information aux; it produces a codeword c'. Output 1 if and only if $c' = c$.

Definition 10 (S-Incompressibility). *For security parameter* λ, *we require that for all PPT adversary* $\mathcal{A} = (\mathcal{A}_1, \mathcal{A}_2)$:

$$\Pr\left[\mathsf{Comp}_{\mathcal{A},\mathsf{Code}}^{\mathsf{IncomCode}}(\lambda, S) = 1\right] \leq \mathsf{negl}(\lambda).$$

6.2 Construction

Now we show how we modify Construction 4 to get an incompressible signature scheme with a rate of 1. Essentially we can think of the procedure of attaching a long random string in Construction 4 as a form of an incompressible encoding with a poor rate. Here we just need to replace it with an incompressible encoding with a rate of 1.

Construction 5. *Let* λ, S *be security parameters. Given* $\mathsf{Sig} = (\mathsf{Gen}, \mathsf{Sign}, \mathsf{Ver})$ *a classical signature scheme with rate 1, and* $\mathsf{Code} = (\mathsf{Enc}, \mathsf{Dec})$ *an incompressible encoding scheme with rate 1 and S-incompressibility, we construct an incompressible signature scheme* $\Pi = (\mathsf{Gen}, \mathsf{Sign}, \mathsf{Ver})$ *as follows:*

- $\mathsf{Gen}(1^\lambda, 1^S)$: *Run* $\mathsf{Sig}.\mathsf{Gen}(1^\lambda)$ *to obtain* $(\mathsf{Sig.vk}, \mathsf{Sig.sk})$. *Output* $\mathsf{vk} = \mathsf{Sig.vk}$ *and* $\mathsf{sk} = \mathsf{Sig.sk}$.
- $\mathsf{Sign}(\mathsf{sk}, m)$: *First compute the codeword* $c \leftarrow \mathsf{Code}.\mathsf{Enc}(1^\lambda, m)$, *and then compute* $\sigma \leftarrow \mathsf{Sig}.\mathsf{Sign}(\mathsf{Sig.sk}, c)$.
- $\mathsf{Ver}(\mathsf{vk}, \sigma)$: *Run* $c \leftarrow \mathsf{Sig}.\mathsf{Ver}(\mathsf{Sig.vk}, \sigma)$. *If* $c = \bot$, *output* $\bot$. *Otherwise, output* $m \leftarrow \mathsf{Code}.\mathsf{Dec}(c)$.

The rate of our scheme is the product of the rates of the incompressible encoding and standard-model signature scheme. We can construct a classical signature scheme with rate $1 - o(1)$ from any one-way function by hashing the message using a universal one-way hash function, and then signing the hash value. Our incompressible signatures therefore have rate $1 - o(1)$, in the CRS or random oracle model. The following is proved in the full version:

---

[3] This is equivalent to the α-expansion property as defined in [MW20] for $\alpha = L_c/L_m$.

[4] This is equivalent to β-incompressibility as defined in [MW20] for $\beta = S$.

Theorem 6. *Assuming the existence of a secure public key signature scheme with rate 1 and an incompressible encoding scheme with rate 1, there exists an incompressible signature scheme with signature size L_m, public key size $\mathsf{poly}(\lambda)$ and secret key size $\mathsf{poly}(\lambda)$. Furthermore, it supports streaming computation using $\mathsf{poly}(\lambda)$ bits of memory, assuming either the random oracle model, or the streaming of the CRS in the CRS model.*

6.3 Equivalence to Incompressible Encoding

Lastly, we quickly show that incompressible signatures are equivalent to incompressible encodings (plus one-way functions) by showing how to construct an incompressible encoding scheme from an incompressible signature scheme.

Construction 6. *Let λ be a security parameter. Given* $\mathsf{Sig} = (\mathsf{Gen}, \mathsf{Sign}, \mathsf{Ver})$ *an incompressible signature scheme with rate 1 and small verification keys, we construct an incompressible encoding scheme $\Pi = (\mathsf{Enc}, \mathsf{Dec}, \mathsf{Ver})$ as follows:*

- $\mathsf{Enc}(1^\lambda, m)$: *Sample* $(\mathsf{Sig.vk}, \mathsf{Sig.sk}) \leftarrow \mathsf{Sig.Gen}(1^\lambda, 1^S)$, *and then compute* $\sigma \leftarrow \mathsf{Sig.Sign}(\mathsf{Sig.sk}, m)$. *Output* $c = (\mathsf{Sig.vk}, \sigma)$.
- $\mathsf{Dec}(c = (\mathsf{Sig.vk}, \sigma))$: *Simply output* $m \leftarrow \mathsf{Sig.Ver}(\mathsf{Sig.vk}, \sigma)$.

The codeword length is the signature length (equal to message length if Sig has rate 1) plus the length of the verification length. Hence the rate is 1 if the verification keys are short. Correctness follows directly from the correctness of the signature scheme. Security also follows directly: if an adversary using a state st of size at most S is able to produce $c' = c$, then it has also produced a valid signature σ and hence wins the incompressible signature security game. Therefore, by Construction 5 and 6, incompressible signatures and incompressible encodings (plus one-way functions) are equivalent.

7 Constructing Rate-1 Functional Encryption

Here, we build rate-1 functional encryption (FE). For our application, we only need one key security. However, our construction satisfies many-key security, though we need indistingishability obfuscation (iO). We leave it as an open question whether such high-rate *single key* FE can be built from standard tools.

Our construction is based on the techniques of Boneh and Zhandry [BZ14], who build from iO something called private linear broadcast encryption, which is a special case of general FE. A number of issues arise in generalizing their construction to general functions, which we demonstrate how to handle.

7.1 Building Blocks

Definition 11 (Indistinguishability Obfuscation [BGI+01]). *An indistinguiability obfuscator iO for a circuit class $\{\mathcal{C}_\lambda\}$ is a PPT uniform algorithm satisfying the following conditions:*

- **Functionality**: *For any $C \in \mathcal{C}_\lambda$, then with probability 1 over the choice of $C' \leftarrow i\mathcal{O}(1^\lambda, C)$, $C'(x) = C(x)$ for all inputs x.*
- **Security**: *For all pairs of PPT adversaries (S, D), if there exists a negligible function α such that*

$$\Pr[\forall x, C_0(x) = C_1(x) : (C_0, C_1, \sigma) \leftarrow S(\lambda)] > 1 - \alpha(\lambda)$$

then there exists a negligible function β such that

$$\left| \Pr[D(\sigma, i\mathcal{O}(\lambda, C_0)) = 1] - \Pr[D(\sigma, i\mathcal{O}(\lambda, C_1)) = 1] \right| < \beta(\lambda)$$

When $\mathcal{C}_\lambda$ is the class of all polynomial-size circuits, we simply call $i\mathcal{O}$ an indistinguishability obfuscator. There are several known ways to construct indistinguishability obfuscation:

- Garg et al. [GGH+13] build the first candidate obfuscation from cryptographic multilinear maps.
- Provably from novel strong circularity assumptions [BDGM20, GP21, WW20]
- Provably from "standard" assumptions [JLS21]: (sub-exponentially secure) LWE, LPN over fields, bilinear maps, and constant-locality PRGs

Definition 12 (Puncturable PRF [BW13, KPTZ13, BGI14]**).** *A puncturable PRF with domain $\mathcal{X}_\lambda$ and range $\mathcal{Y}_\lambda$ is a pair (Gen, Punc) where:*

- Gen(1^λ) *outputs an efficiently computable function* PRF $: \mathcal{X}_\lambda \to \mathcal{Y}_\lambda$
- Punc$($PRF$, x)$ *takes as input a function* PRF *and an input $x \in \mathcal{X}_\lambda$, and outputs a "punctured" function* PRF$^{\overline{x}}$.
- **Correctness**: *With probability 1 over the choice of* PRF $\leftarrow$ Gen(1^λ),

$$\mathsf{PRF}^{\overline{x}}(x') = \begin{cases} \mathsf{PRF}(x') & \text{if } x' \neq x \\ \bot & \text{if } x' = x \end{cases}$$

- **Security**: *For all $x \in \mathcal{X}_\lambda$, $($PRF$^{\overline{x}}$, PRF$(x))$ is computationally indistinguishable from $($PRF$^{\overline{x}}, y)$, where* PRF $\leftarrow$ Gen(1^λ) *and $y \leftarrow \mathcal{Y}_\lambda$.*

Such puncturable PRFs can be built from any one-way function [GGM86].

We now give a new definition of a type of signature scheme with a *single-point binding* (SPB) property. This allows, given a message m, for generating a fake verification key together with a signature on m. The fake verification key and signature should be indistinguishable from the honest case. Yet there are no signatures on messages other than m relative to the fake verification key. [BZ14] implicitly constructs such signatures from iO and one-way functions, but with a logarithmic message space, which was good enough for their special-purpose FE scheme. In our case, we need to handle very large exponential message spaces. The problem with [BZ14]'s approach is that the security loss is proportional to the message space; to compensate requires assuming (sub)exponential hardness, and also setting the security parameter to be larger than the message length. This results in the signature size being polynomial in the message size, resulting in a low-rate FE scheme. SPB signatures avoid the exponential loss, so we can keep the security parameter small, resulting in a rate-1 FE scheme.

Definition 13. *A single-point binding (SPB) signature is a quadruple of algorithms* (Gen, Sign, Ver, GenBind) *where* Gen, Sign, Ver *satisfy the usual properties of a signature scheme. Additionally, we have the following:*

- $(\mathsf{vk}, \sigma) \leftarrow \mathsf{GenBind}(1^\lambda, m)$ *takes as input a message m, and produces a verification key* vk *and signature σ.*
- *For any messages m and with overwhelming probability over the choice of* $(\mathsf{vk}, \sigma) \leftarrow \mathsf{GenBind}(1^\lambda, m)$, $\mathsf{Ver}(\mathsf{vk}, \sigma') \in \{m, \bot\}$ *for any σ'. That is, there is no message $m' \neq m$ such that there is a valid signature of m' relative to* vk.
- *For any m,* $\mathsf{GenBind}(1^\lambda, m)$ *and* $(\mathsf{vk}, \mathsf{Sign}(\mathsf{sk}, m))$ *are indistinguishable, where* $(\mathsf{vk}, \mathsf{sk}) \leftarrow \mathsf{Gen}(1^\lambda)$. *Note that this property implies that* $\mathsf{Ver}(\mathsf{vk}, \sigma)$ *accepts and output m, when* $(\mathsf{vk}, \sigma) \leftarrow \mathsf{GenBind}(1^\lambda, m)$.

We explain how to construct SPB signatures in the full version of the paper, either from leveled FHE (and hence LWE), or from iO and one-way functions.

Our Rate-1 FE Scheme. We now give our rate-1 FE scheme:

Construction 7. *Let $i\mathcal{O}$ be an indistinguishability obfuscator,* Gen *be a PRF,* (Gen′, Sig, Ver) *a signature scheme, and* $\mathsf{PRG} : \{0,1\}^\lambda \to \{0,1\}^{2\lambda}, \mathsf{PRG}' : \{0,1\}^\lambda \to \{0,1\}^{L_m}$ *be a PRG.*

- $\mathsf{Setup}(1^\lambda)$*: Sample* $\mathsf{PRF} \leftarrow \mathsf{Gen}(1^\lambda)$. *Set* $\mathsf{msk} = \mathsf{PRF}$ *and* $\mathsf{mpk} = i\mathcal{O}(1^\lambda, P_{\mathsf{Enc}})$, *where P_{Enc} is the program given in Fig. 1.*
- $\mathsf{KeyGen}(\mathsf{msk}, f)$*: output* $\mathsf{sk}_f \leftarrow i\mathcal{O}(1^\lambda, P_{\mathsf{Dec},f})$, *where $P_{\mathsf{Dec},f}$ is the program given in Fig. 2.*
- $\mathsf{Enc}(\mathsf{mpk}, m)$*: Choose a random r, and evaluate* $(t, v) \leftarrow \mathsf{mpk}(r)$. *Then parse* $v = (w, u)$. *Set* $c = \mathsf{PRG}'(w) \oplus m$. *Next run* $(\mathsf{vk}, \mathsf{sk}) \leftarrow \mathsf{Gen}'(1^\lambda; u)$, *using u as the random coins for* Gen′. *Compute* $\sigma \leftarrow \mathsf{Sign}(\mathsf{sk}, c)$. *Output* (t, σ).
- $\mathsf{Dec}(sk_f, (t, \sigma)) = \mathsf{sk}_f(t, \sigma)$

Inputs: r **Constants:** PRF 1. $t \leftarrow \mathsf{PRG}(r)$. 2. $v \leftarrow \mathsf{PRF}(t)$. 3. Output (t, v).	**Inputs:** t, σ **Constants:** PRF 1. $(w, u) \leftarrow \mathsf{PRF}(t)$. 2. $(\mathsf{vk}, \mathsf{sk}) \leftarrow \mathsf{Gen}'(1^\lambda; u)$. 3. $c \leftarrow \mathsf{Ver}(\mathsf{vk}, c, \sigma)$. If $c = \bot$, abort and output $\bot$. 4. Output $f(\mathsf{PRG}'(w) \oplus c)$.

Fig. 1. The program P_{Enc}.   **Fig. 2.** The program $P_{\mathsf{Dec},f}$.

Correctness follows immediately from the correctness of the various components. Notice that the ciphertext size is $L_m + \mathsf{poly}(\lambda)$, provided the signature scheme outputs short signatures. Therefore, construction 7 has rate $1 - o(1)$.

Provided the random coins for (Gen′, Sign, Ver) are independent of the message length, P_{Enc} has size $\mathsf{poly}(\lambda)$, independent of the message length. If Gen′, Sign can be evaluated in a low-space streaming fashion, then so can Enc.

7.2   Proof of Security

Sequence of Hybrids

- H_0: This is the FE security experiment, where the bit b in the experiment is fixed to be 0. Note that in this hybrid, the challenge ciphertext is generated as (t^*, σ^*), where $r^* \leftarrow \{0,1\}^\lambda$, $t^* \leftarrow \mathsf{PRG}(r^*)$, $(w^*, u^*) \leftarrow \mathsf{PRF}(t^*)$, $x^* \leftarrow \mathsf{PRG}'(w^*)$, $c^* \leftarrow x^* \oplus m_0$, $(\mathsf{vk}^*, \mathsf{sk}^*) \leftarrow \mathsf{Gen}'(1^\lambda; u^*)$, and $\sigma^* \leftarrow \mathsf{Sign}(\mathsf{sk}^*, c^*)$.
- H_1: This is identical to H_0, except that we now generate t^* uniformly at random: $t^* \leftarrow \{0,1\}^{2\lambda}$.
- H_2: This is the same as H_1, except that we change the way we generate $\mathsf{mpk}, \mathsf{sk}_f$. First compute $\mathsf{PRF}^{\overline{t^*}} \leftarrow \mathsf{Punc}(\mathsf{PRF}, t^*)$, $(w^*, u^*) \leftarrow \mathsf{PRF}(t^*)$. Then let $(\mathsf{vk}^*, \mathsf{sk}^*) \leftarrow \mathsf{Gen}'(1^\lambda; u^*)$ and $x^* = \mathsf{PRG}(w^*)$. We now compute $\mathsf{mpk} \leftarrow i\mathcal{O}(1^\lambda, P_{\mathsf{Enc}}^{\mathrm{punc}})$ and answer secret key queries with $\mathsf{sk}_f \leftarrow i\mathcal{O}(1^\lambda, P_{\mathsf{Dec}}^{\mathrm{punc}})$. Here, $P_{\mathsf{Enc}}^{\mathrm{punc}}$ and $P_{\mathsf{Dec},f}^{\mathrm{punc}}$ are the programs in Figs. 3 and 4
- H_3: This is identical to H_2, except that now we generate w^*, u^* uniformly at random, instead of $(w^*, u^*) \leftarrow \mathsf{PRF}(t^*)$.
- H_4: This is identical to H_3 except that we now generate x^* uniformly at random instead of $x^* \leftarrow \mathsf{PRG}(w^*)$.
- H_5: This is identical to H_4, except for the following changes:
  - We generate c^* uniformly at random at the beginning of the experiment.
  - After the challenge query, we generate $x^* = c^* \oplus m_0$. Note that x^* is the only place m_0 enters the experiment.
- H_6: This is identical to H_5, except now we generate $(\mathsf{vk}^*, \sigma^*) \leftarrow \mathsf{GenBind}(1^\lambda, c^*)$.
- H_7 through H_{13}: Hybrid H_{7+i} is identical to H_{6-i}, except that m_0 is replaced with m_1. Thus H_{13} is the FE security experiment where b is fixed to be 1.

Inputs: $m; r$

Constants: $\mathsf{PRF}^{\overline{t^*}}$, t^*

1. $t \leftarrow \mathsf{PRG}(r)$. If $t = t^*$, immediately abort and output $\bot$.

2. $v \leftarrow \mathsf{PRF}^{\overline{t^*}}(t)$.
3. Output (t, v).

Fig. 3. The program $P_{\mathsf{Enc}}^{\mathrm{punc}}$. Differences from P_{Enc} highlighted in yellow. (Color figure onine)

Inputs: t, σ

Constants: $\mathsf{PRF}_1^{\overline{t^*}}, \mathsf{PRF}_2^{\overline{t^*}}, t^*, x^*, \mathsf{vk}^*$

1. If $t \neq t^*$, skip to Step 2. If $t = t^*$, run $c \leftarrow \mathsf{Ver}(\mathsf{vk}^*, \sigma)$;

   if $c = \bot$, abort and output $\bot$, otherwise abort and output $f(x^* \oplus c)$.
2. $(w, u) \leftarrow \mathsf{PRF}^{\overline{t^*}}(t)$
3. $(\mathsf{vk}, \mathsf{sk}) \leftarrow \mathsf{Gen}'(1^\lambda; u)$.
4. $c \leftarrow \mathsf{Ver}(\mathsf{vk}, c, \sigma)$. If $c = \bot$, abort and output $\bot$.
5. Output $f(\mathsf{PRG}(w) \oplus c)$.

Fig. 4. The program $P_{\mathsf{Dec}, f}^{\mathsf{punc}}$. Differences from $P_{\mathsf{Enc}, f}$ highlighted in yellow. (Color figure onine)

For the proofs of the hybrid arguments, please refer to the full version.

References

[ADN+10] Alwen, J., Dodis, Y., Naor, M., Segev, G., Walfish, S., Wichs, D.: Public-Key encryption in the bounded-retrieval model. In: Gilbert, H. (ed.) EUROCRYPT 2010. LNCS, vol. 6110, pp. 113–134. Springer, Heidelberg (2010). https://doi.org/10.1007/978-3-642-13190-5_6

[ADW09] Alwen, J., Dodis, Y., Wichs, D.: Leakage-resilient public-key cryptography in the bounded-retrieval model. In: Halevi, S. (ed.) CRYPTO 2009. LNCS, vol. 5677, pp. 36–54. Springer, Heidelberg (2009). https://doi.org/10.1007/978-3-642-03356-8_3

[AR99] Aumann, Y., Rabin, M.O.: Information theoretically secure communication in the limited storage space model. In: Wiener, M. (ed.) CRYPTO 1999. LNCS, vol. 1666, pp. 65–79. Springer, Heidelberg (1999). https://doi.org/10.1007/3-540-48405-1_5

[BCKP14] Bitansky, N., Canetti, R., Kalai, Y.T., Paneth, O.: On virtual grey box obfuscation for general circuits. In: Garay, J.A., Gennaro, R. (eds.) CRYPTO 2014. LNCS, vol. 8617, pp. 108–125. Springer, Heidelberg (2014). https://doi.org/10.1007/978-3-662-44381-1_7

[BCP14] Boyle, E., Chung, K.-M., Pass, R.: On extractability obfuscation. In: Lindell, Y. (ed.) TCC 2014. LNCS, vol. 8349, pp. 52–73. Springer, Heidelberg (2014). https://doi.org/10.1007/978-3-642-54242-8_3

[BDGM20] Brakerski, Z., Döttling, N., Garg, S., Malavolta, G.: Candidate iO from homomorphic encryption schemes. In: Canteaut, A., Ishai, Y. (eds.) EUROCRYPT 2020. LNCS, vol. 12105, pp. 79–109. Springer, Cham (2020). https://doi.org/10.1007/978-3-030-45721-1_4

[BGI+01] Barak, B., Goldreich, O., Impagliazzo, R., Rudich, S., Sahai, A., Vadhan, S., Yang, K.: On the (Im)possibility of obfuscating programs. In: Kilian, J. (ed.) CRYPTO 2001. LNCS, vol. 2139, pp. 1–18. Springer, Heidelberg (2001). https://doi.org/10.1007/3-540-44647-8_1

[BGI14]   Boyle, E., Goldwasser, S., Ivan, I.: Functional signatures and pseudorandom functions. In: Krawczyk, H. (ed.) PKC 2014. LNCS, vol. 8383, pp. 501–519. Springer, Heidelberg (2014). https://doi.org/10.1007/978-3-642-54631-0_29

[BK16]   Biryukov, A., Khovratovich, D.: Egalitarian computing. In: Holz, T., Savage, S. (eds.) USENIX Security 2016, pp. 315–326. USENIX Association (2016)

[BKR16]   Bellare, M., Kane, D., Rogaway, P.: Big-key symmetric encryption: resisting key exfiltration. In: Robshaw, M., Katz, J. (eds.) CRYPTO 2016. LNCS, vol. 9814, pp. 373–402. Springer, Heidelberg (2016). https://doi.org/10.1007/978-3-662-53018-4_14

[BNNO11] Bendlin, R., Nielsen, J.B., Nordholt, P.S., Orlandi, C.: Lower and upper bounds for deniable public-key encryption. In: Lee, D.H., Wang, X. (eds.) ASIACRYPT 2011. LNCS, vol. 7073, pp. 125–142. Springer, Heidelberg (2011). https://doi.org/10.1007/978-3-642-25385-0_7

[BW13]   Boneh, D., Waters, B.: Constrained pseudorandom functions and their applications. In: Sako, K., Sarkar, P. (eds.) ASIACRYPT 2013. LNCS, vol. 8270, pp. 280–300. Springer, Heidelberg (2013). https://doi.org/10.1007/978-3-642-42045-0_15

[BZ14]   Boneh, D., Zhandry, M.: Multiparty key exchange, efficient traitor tracing, and more from indistinguishability obfuscation. In: Garay, J.A., Gennaro, R. (eds.) CRYPTO 2014. LNCS, vol. 8616, pp. 480–499. Springer, Heidelberg (2014). https://doi.org/10.1007/978-3-662-44371-2_27

[CCM98]   Cachin, C., Crépeau, C., Marcil, J.: Oblivious transfer with a memory-bounded receiver. In: 39th FOCS, pp. 493–502. IEEE Computer Society Press (1998)

[CDD+07] Cash, D., Ding, Y.Z., Dodis, Y., Lee, W., Lipton, R., Walfish, S.: Intrusion-resilient key exchange in the bounded retrieval model. In: Vadhan, S.P. (ed.) TCC 2007. LNCS, vol. 4392, pp. 479–498. Springer, Heidelberg (2007). https://doi.org/10.1007/978-3-540-70936-7_26

[CDNO97] Canetti, R., Dwork, C., Naor, M., Ostrovsky, R.: Deniable encryption. In: Kaliski, B.S. (ed.) CRYPTO 1997. LNCS, vol. 1294, pp. 90–104. Springer, Heidelberg (1997). https://doi.org/10.1007/BFb0052229

[CM97]   Cachin, C., Maurer, U.: Unconditional security against memory-bounded adversaries. In: Kaliski, B.S. (ed.) CRYPTO 1997. LNCS, vol. 1294, pp. 292–306. Springer, Heidelberg (1997). https://doi.org/10.1007/BFb0052243

[DHRS04] Ding, Y.Z., Harnik, D., Rosen, A., Shaltiel, R.: Constant-round oblivious transfer in the bounded storage model. In: Naor, M. (ed.) TCC 2004. LNCS, vol. 2951, pp. 446–472. Springer, Heidelberg (2004). https://doi.org/10.1007/978-3-540-24638-1_25

[Din01]   Ding, Y.Z.: Oblivious transfer in the bounded storage model. In: Kilian, J. (ed.) CRYPTO 2001. LNCS, vol. 2139, pp. 155–170. Springer, Heidelberg (2001). https://doi.org/10.1007/3-540-44647-8_9

[DLW06]   Di Crescenzo, G., Lipton, R., Walfish, S.: Perfectly secure password protocols in the bounded retrieval model. In: Halevi, S., Rabin, T. (eds.) TCC 2006. LNCS, vol. 3876, pp. 225–244. Springer, Heidelberg (2006). https://doi.org/10.1007/11681878_12

[DQW21]   Dodis, Y., Quach, W., Wichs, D.: Speak much, remember little: cryptography in the bounded storage model, revisited. Cryptology ePrint Archive, Report 2021/1270 (2021). https://ia.cr/2021/1270

[DRS04] Dodis, Y., Reyzin, L., Smith, A.: Fuzzy extractors: how to generate strong keys from biometrics and other noisy data. In: Cachin, C., Camenisch, J.L. (eds.) EUROCRYPT 2004. LNCS, vol. 3027, pp. 523–540. Springer, Heidelberg (2004). https://doi.org/10.1007/978-3-540-24676-3_31

[Dzi06a] Dziembowski, S.: Intrusion-resilience via the bounded-storage model. In: Halevi, S., Rabin, T. (eds.) TCC 2006. LNCS, vol. 3876, pp. 207–224. Springer, Heidelberg (2006). https://doi.org/10.1007/11681878_11

[Dzi06b] Dziembowski, S.: On forward-secure storage. In: Dwork, C. (ed.) CRYPTO 2006. LNCS, vol. 4117, pp. 251–270. Springer, Heidelberg (2006). https://doi.org/10.1007/11818175_15

[GGH+13] Garg, S., Gentry, C., Halevi, S., Raykova, M., Sahai, A., Waters, B.: Candidate indistinguishability obfuscation and functional encryption for all circuits. In: 54th FOCS, pp. 40–49. IEEE Computer Society Press (2013)

[GGM86] Goldreich, O., Goldwasser, S., Micali, S.: How to construct random functions. J. ACM **33**(4), 792–807 (1986)

[GP21] Gay, R., Pass, R.: Indistinguishability obfuscation from circular security. In: Proceedings of the 53rd Annual ACM SIGACT Symposium on Theory of Computing, STOC 2021, pp. 736–749 (2021)

[GVW12] Gorbunov, S., Vaikuntanathan, V., Wee, H.: Functional encryption with bounded collusions via multi-party computation. In: Safavi-Naini, R., Canetti, R. (eds.) CRYPTO 2012. LNCS, vol. 7417, pp. 162–179. Springer, Heidelberg (2012). https://doi.org/10.1007/978-3-642-32009-5_11

[GZ19] Guan, J., Zhandary, M.: Simple schemes in the bounded storage model. In: Ishai, Y., Rijmen, V. (eds.) EUROCRYPT 2019. LNCS, vol. 11478, pp. 500–524. Springer, Cham (2019). https://doi.org/10.1007/978-3-030-17659-4_17

[GZ21] Guan, J., Zhandry, M.: Disappearing cryptography in the bounded storage model. In: Theoretical Cryptography Conference (2021). https://ia.cr/2021/406

[IR90] Impagliazzo, R., Rudich, S.: Limits on the provable consequences of one-way permutations. In: Goldwasser, S. (ed.) CRYPTO 1988. LNCS, vol. 403, pp. 8–26. Springer, New York (1990). https://doi.org/10.1007/0-387-34799-2_2

[JLS21] Jain, A., Lin, H., Sahai, A.: Indistinguishability obfuscation from well-founded assumptions. In: Proceedings of the 53rd Annual ACM SIGACT Symposium on Theory of Computing, STOC 2021, pp. 60–73 (2021)

[KPTZ13] Kiayias, A., Papadopoulos, S., Triandopoulos, N., Zacharias, T.: Delegatable pseudorandom functions and applications. In: Sadeghi, A.R., Gligor, V.D., Yung, M. (eds.) ACM CCS 2013, pp. 669–684. ACM Press (2013)

[Lu02] Lu, C.-J.: Hyper-encryption against space-bounded adversaries from online strong extractors. In: Yung, M. (ed.) CRYPTO 2002. LNCS, vol. 2442, pp. 257–271. Springer, Heidelberg (2002). https://doi.org/10.1007/3-540-45708-9_17

[Mau92] Maurer, U.M.: Conditionally-perfect secrecy and a provably-secure randomized cipher. J. Cryptol. **5**(1), 53–66 (1992). https://doi.org/10.1007/BF00191321

[MST04] Moran, T., Shaltiel, R., Ta-Shma, A.: Non-interactive timestamping in the bounded storage model. In: Franklin, M. (ed.) CRYPTO 2004. LNCS, vol. 3152, pp. 460–476. Springer, Heidelberg (2004). https://doi.org/10.1007/978-3-540-28628-8_28

[MW20] Moran, T., Wichs, D.: Incompressible encodings. In: Micciancio, D., Ristenpart, T. (eds.) CRYPTO 2020. LNCS, vol. 12170, pp. 494–523. Springer, Cham (2020). https://doi.org/10.1007/978-3-030-56784-2_17

[Nis90] Nisan, N.: Psuedorandom generators for space-bounded computation. In: 22nd ACM STOC, pp. 204–212. ACM Press (1990)

[Raz17] Raz, R.: A time-space lower bound for a large class of learning problems. In: Umans, C. (ed.) 58th FOCS, pp. 732–742. IEEE Computer Society Press (2017)

[Riv97] Rivest, R.L.: All-or-nothing encryption and the package transform. In: Biham, E. (ed.) FSE 1997. LNCS, vol. 1267, pp. 210–218. Springer, Heidelberg (1997). https://doi.org/10.1007/BFb0052348

[Vad03] Vadhan, S.P.: On constructing locally computable extractors and cryptosystems in the bounded storage model. In: Boneh, D. (ed.) CRYPTO 2003. LNCS, vol. 2729, pp. 61–77. Springer, Heidelberg (2003). https://doi.org/10.1007/978-3-540-45146-4_4

[Wic13] Wichs, D.: Barriers in cryptography with weak, correlated and leaky sources. In: Kleinberg, R.D. (ed.) ITCS 2013, pp. 111–126. ACM (2013)

[WW20] Wee, H., Wichs, D.: Candidate obfuscation via oblivious LWE sampling. Cryptology ePrint Archive, Report 2020/1042 (2020). https://eprint.iacr.org/2020/1042

[Zav15] Zaverucha, G.: Stronger password-based encryption using all-or-nothing transforms (2015)

COA-Secure Obfuscation
and Applications

Ran Canetti[1], Suvradip Chakraborty[2], Dakshita Khurana[3],
Nishant Kumar[3(✉)], Oxana Poburinnaya[4], and Manoj Prabhakaran[5]

[1] Boston University, Boston, USA
[2] ETH Zürich, Zürich, Switzerland
[3] UIUC, Champaign, USA
nkumar13@illinois.edu
[4] Boston, USA
[5] IIT Bombay, Mumbai, India

Abstract. We put forth a new paradigm for program obfuscation, where obfuscated programs are endowed with proofs of "well formedness." In addition to asserting existence of an underlying plaintext program with an attested structure, these proofs also prevent mauling attacks, whereby an adversary surreptitiously creates an obfuscated program based on secrets which are embedded in other obfuscated programs. We call this new guarantee *Chosen Obfuscation Attacks (COA) security*.

We show how to enhance a large class of obfuscation mechanisms to be COA-secure, assuming subexponentially secure IO for circuits and subexponentially secure one-way functions. To demonstrate the power of the new notion, we also use it to realize:
- A new form of software watermarking, which provides significantly broader protection than current schemes against counterfeits that pass a keyless, public verification process.
- *Completely CCA* encryption, which is a strengthening of completely non-malleable encryption.

1 Introduction

General-purpose program obfuscation (developed in [3, 7, 13, 16, 17, 20] and many other works) holds great promise for enhancing the security of software: Software can be distributed and executed without fear of exposing sensitive design secrets or keys hidden in the code. Furthermore, when executing obfuscated

R. Canetti—Supported by the DARPA SIEVE project, contract No. #HR00112020023.

S. Chakraborty—Work done while at IST Austria; supported in part by ERC grant 724307.

D. Khurana and N. Kumar—Supported in part by DARPA SIEVE project contract No. #HR00112020024, a gift from Visa Research, and a C3AI DTI award.

O. Poburinnaya—Work done in part while at Boston University.

M. Prabhakaran—Supported by a Ramanujan Fellowship and Joint Indo-Israel Project DST/INT/ISR/P-16/2017 of Dept. of Science and Technology, India.

O. Dunkelman and S. Dziembowski (Eds.): EUROCRYPT 2022, LNCS 13275, pp. 731–758, 2022.
https://doi.org/10.1007/978-3-031-06944-4_25

software, all intermediate states are guaranteed to remain hidden, even when both the hardware and the software components of the underlying platform are adversarial.

However, ubiquitous use of program obfuscation might actually make the security of software worse in other respects: Verifying properties of an obfuscated program becomes harder - it is essentially reduced to black-box testing the program. This is highly unsatisfactory, especially in situations where the source of the program is untrusted. Indeed, the very property that makes obfuscation a boon for software creators - namely the ability to hide secrets both in the code and in the functionality - is a bane for users of the software, unless those users put complete trust in the creators.

Another concern is that the use of program obfuscation makes it harder to verify whether a given program depends on other programs in "illegitimate ways", where legitimacy (and lack thereof) relates to both structural and functional dependence between programs. For instance, obfuscation might facilitate *software plagiarism* by hiding the fact that program A runs some (potentially proprietary) program B as a subroutine, without publicly disclosing this fact. Furthermore, obfuscation might facilitate hiding the fact that program A is a *mauled* version of B - i.e. that A's functionality surrepetitiously depends on the functionality of B. The latter can be a concern even regardless of how B is implemented.[1]

We define and realize a new notion of program obfuscation that addresses the above concerns. However, before we present the new notion and some applications, we point out prior approaches. To the best of our knowledge, the only existing general notion of obfuscation that provides the ability to verify properties of obfuscated programs is Verifiable Indistinguishability Obfuscation [2]. However, that notion provides only limited hiding guarantees: indistinguishability of the obfuscated versions of two functionally equivalent programs is guaranteed only if there is a short witness of their equivalence. Furthermore, it provides no guarantees against adversaries that maul honestly generated programs.

Mauling attacks have been considered in the context of non-malleability of obfuscation. Thid has so far been studied only in the context of virtual black box obfuscation of point functions and related functionalities [11,24] and is thus susceptible to strong impossiblity results [4]. In particular, no generally viable notion of non-malleable obfuscation has been proposed.

Defending against program plagiarism has been studied in the context of software watermarking [4]. However, that line of work has concentrated on detecting illicit programs that very closely preserve the functionality of the watermarked program [12] (or else preserve some cryptographic use of it [18]), and does not

---

[1] One might expect that existing notions of obfuscation, such as indistinguishability obfuscation (IO), already defend against such mauling attacks. However, this expectation fails for programs whose code includes random keys that affect the functionality. For instance, IO does not appear to rule out the possibility that an adversary, given an obfuscated version of a puncturable pseudorandom function with a random key k, manages to generate another obfuscated program that computes the same function but with key $(k + 1)$.

address more general forms of plagiarism – e.g., generating a seemingly legitimate obfuscated program that illicitly uses a given program as a subroutine, or even changes some internal parameters while preserving the overall design.

1.1 Our Contributions

We first summarize our main contributions and then elaborate on each one.

- *Definitions:* We show how to enhance a number of existing notions of program obfuscation so as to provide a strong flavor of verifiability, combined with mitigating malleability attacks. We call such enhancement "security against chosen obfuscation attacks" (or, COA security). For sake of specifity, we also formulate a self-contained notion of COA obfuscation which will be used throughout this work.[2]
- *Constructions:* We construct COA obfuscation, assuming subexponentially secure iO and one-way functions. More generally, we show how to enhance (or, fortify) any one out of a class of measures of secure obfuscation to provide COA security.
- *Applications:* COA-secure obfuscation is directly applicable in situations where a user wishes to verify some properties regarding the structure and functionality of a given obfuscated program. In addition, we use COA-secure obfuscation to construct *software watermarking* mechanisms that provide a new and powerful notion of security. Finally, we use COA-secure obfuscation to construct a *completely CCA*-secure public-key encryption scheme, which is a new notion of security that naturally strengthens *completely non-malleable* public-key encryption [14], which in turn augments non-malleability to consider mauling attacks against both the ciphertext *and the public key.*

1.2 Defining COA Obfuscation

The first main contribution of this work is in developing a security notion that incorporates meaningful secrecy, verifiability, and non-malleability guarantees, while still being realizable by general-purpose obfuscation algorithms. Several challenges face such an endeavor.

First, to let the user verify various properties of the program, we would like to emulate the effect of having a one message proof attached to the obfuscated program. Since we do not have any cryptographic setup, such a proof cannot be zero-knowledge. Still, we would like to ensure that this proof does not reveal anything about the program that is to be hidden by the obfuscation. We thus formulate a notion of hiding that's intertwined with the functionality of the obfuscated program.

Developing an appropriate notion of non-malleability proves equally challenging. In particular, it appears hard to effectively capture mauling attacks on the

---

[2] We also define a somewhat weaker variant, which only guarantees verifiability without any non-malleability guarantees. We then realize this variant with a simpler construction than the one used to obtain COA security. See more details in [8].

functionality of programs without resorting to "simulation-based" formalisms (as done in [11,24]), which would in turn be subject to general impossibility akin to VBB-obfuscation [4]. Indeed, an indistinguishability-based notion that avoids the need for a simulator appears to be warranted in order to preserve broad applicability.

We get around this difficulty by extending the notion of CCA-secure commitments (namely, commitments that are secure against chosen commitment attacks [9]) to our setting. Indeed, our notion (which is, in turn, a natural extension of security against chosen ciphertext attacks for public-key encryption [27,28] to the setting of obfuscation) provides the strongest-known viable form of non-malleability for obfuscation schemes.

That is, we consider obfuscators O that take as input a program C along with a predicate ϕ that represents some attestation on the structure and functionality of C. Next, we augment the process of executing an obfuscated program with an initial step aimed at verifying that this program "corresponds to a plaintext program that satisfies ϕ." Here, however, we somewhat relax the traditional deterministic verification process, and instead allow for *randomized* verification that, given a purported obfuscaed program $\hat{C}$, outputs either a reject symbol, or else a fully functional program $\tilde{C}$. We then require that: (a) whenever $\phi(C)$ holds, $V(O(C,\phi),\phi) = \tilde{C}$, where $\tilde{C}$ is functionally equivalent to C, and (b) For all strings $\hat{C}$ and predicates ϕ, the event where $V(\hat{C},\phi) = \tilde{C}$ where $\tilde{C} \neq \perp$, and there is no program C that is functionally equivalent to $\tilde{C}$ and such that $\phi(C)$ holds, occurs only with negligible probability.

We stress that the above definition postulates a two-step randomized process for generating a functional obfuscated program: the first step is carried out by O, while the second is carried out by V. Furthermore, while obfuscating a legitimate program C (i.e. $\phi(C) = 1$) always results with a program $\tilde{C} = V(O(C,\phi),\phi)$ that is functionally equivalent to C, an adversarially generated string $\hat{C}$ might result in a random variable $\tilde{C} = V(\hat{C},\phi)$ where different draws from $\tilde{C}$ are different programs with completely different functionalities. (Still $\phi(\tilde{C})$ holds almost always.)[3]

Finally, we would like to require that, for "sufficiently similar" programs C_0, C_1, polytime adversaries be unable to distinguish $O(C_0,\phi)$ from $O(C_1,\phi)$, *even when given access to a de-obfuscation oracle* $O^{-1}(\cdot,\phi)$. That is, we consider adversaries that are given a challenge program $C^* = O(C_b,\phi)$ for $b \leftarrow \{0,1\}$, along with access to an oracle $O^{-1}(\cdot)$ that operates as follows: If $\hat{C} = C^*$ or $V(\hat{C},\phi) = \perp$, then $O^{-1}(\hat{C}) = \perp$. Else, $O^{-1}(\hat{C}) = C$, where C is the lexicographically first program that's functionally equivalent to $\hat{C}$ and where $\phi(C)$ holds. The verification guarantee implies that (w.h.p.) such a program exists when $V(\hat{C},\phi) \neq \perp$.

It remains to determine what makes programs C_0, C_1 "sufficiently similar". Here we consider a number of variants, that correspond to existing notions of security for plain obfuscation. One natural option, corresponding to plain iO, considers any pair C_0, C_1 of equal-size, functionally equivalent programs.

---

[3] Our randomized verification step is borrowed from that of Non-Interactive Distributionally Indistinguishable (NIDI) arguments, as developed in [22]. Indeed, as there, it appears to be an essential relaxation that is crucial for realizability.

Another option, which turns out to be relatively simple to work in the context of our applications, corresponds to a slight simplification of the notion of obfucation of probabilistic circuits, specifically X-Ind-pIO [10]. That is, we consider samplers that sample triples (C_0, C_1, z), where C_0 and C_1 are programs and z is some auxiliary information. A sampler Samp is admissible for ϕ if both C_0 and C_1 satisfy ϕ, and in addition any poly size adversary A, given z and oracle access to a program, can tell whether this program is C_0 or C_1 only with sub-exponentially small advantage over $1/2$, when $(C_0, C_1, z) \leftarrow$ Samp. An obfusator (O, V) is COA Secure with respect to predicate ϕ if any polytime adversary A', that's given $C^* = O(C_b, \phi)$, z, where $((C_0, C_1, z) \leftarrow$ Samp, as well as oracle access to $O^{-1}(\cdot)$, can guess b only with advantage that's polynomially related to that of A.

The intuition for why COA security guarantees non-malleability is the same as in the case of CCA commitment and CCA encryption: An adversary that manages to "maul" its challenge progrom $\hat{C}$ into a program $\hat{C}'$ that passes verification and such that the preimages of the resulting $\tilde{C}$ and $\tilde{C}'$ are related in some non-trivial way, can readily use this ability to break COA security via applying $O^{-1}(\tilde{C}')$ to obtain the plaintext program that is related to the preimage of its challenge C^*. It is stressed that here the "non trivial relation" may include both structural and functional properties of the plaintext programs.

1.3 Applications of COA Obfuscation

COA-secure obfuscation is clearly directly applicable in situations where a user wishes to verify some properties regarding the structure and functionality of a program that is otherwise obfuscated (hence "opaque"). We further demonstrate the power of this notion via two applications: First, we define and construct a new notion of program watermarking which, while being formally incomparable with existing notions, significantly pushes the envelope of what's obtainable in this context. Second, we define and construct a new notion of completely-CCA secure encryption, nametly encryption that remain secure even in the presence of an oracle that decrypts adversarially chosen ciphertexts *with respect to adversarially chosen public keys*. In both cases, our constructions rely on COA-secure obfuscation in a crucial way.

A New Approach to Software Watermarking. Existing formulations of watermarking (e.g. [12,15]) concentrate on *preventing* the creation of "counterfeit" programs that are close in functionality to the watermarked program and yet remain unmarked. Instead, we propose a way to *publicly detect* any program that stands in some pre-determined relation with the watermarked program, and is unmarked (or carries a different mark than the watermarked program). The new notion is incomparable with the existing ones: On the one hand, the proposed notion does not rule out the possibility of creating "jail-broken programs", it only guarantees that these programs will be detectable. Still, the detection algorithm is fixed and keyless, hence detection is inherently public and universal. Furthermore, the new notion identifies a significantly larger class of "software piracy" attacks, namely those attacks where the "forbidden similarity" between the jail-broken program and the original program may be defined via some pre-determined relation that considers both the *structure* and the *functionality* of the jail-broken program and the watermarked program.

More specifically, our proposed notion of watermarking, with respect to a family $\mathcal{C}$ of programs and a relation $R(\cdot, \cdot)$, postulates a marking algorithm M and a (randomized) verification algorithm V with the following properties. The watermarking party chooses a program C from the family $\mathcal{C}$, along with a mark m, and applies M to obtain a watermarked program $\hat{C}$ such that:

(a) $V(\hat{C}) = (\tilde{C}, m)$, where $\tilde{C}$ is functionally equivalent to C. (That is, $\hat{C}$ passes verification, bears the mark m, and results in a program that's functionally equivalent to the original.)

(b) Any adversarially generated program $\hat{C}'$ where $V(\hat{C}') = (\tilde{C}', m')$ and such that there exists a program C' that's functionally equivalent to $\tilde{C}'$ and such that $R(C, C')$ holds, must have $m' = m$ except for negligible probability. (That is, if $\hat{C}'$ passes verification and the resulting program $\tilde{C}$ has a functionally equivalent "plaintext" program C' that stands in the specified relation with C, then $\hat{C}'$ has to bear the mark m.)

We note that this notion is very general, and in particular prevents potential plagiarism where the plagiarized program has very different functionality than the watermarked one, and yet uses the watermarked program as a subroutine or otherwise incorporates it in its code.

We then use subexponential COA obfuscation to construct watermarking schemes for any function family $\mathcal{C}$ and relation R where:

(a) the description of a program $C \leftarrow \mathcal{C}$ is "one way" with respect to the functionality of the program (i.e. the description is uniquely determined, yet hard to efficiently extract, given sufficiently many input-output pairs), and:

(b) R is such that whenever $R(C, C')$ holds, knowledge of C' enables breaking the one wayness of C. That is, there is an algorithm that computes the description of C, given only C' and oracle access to C. As a concrete example, we consider watermarking a PRF, where the relation R holds only if two PRF circuits use the same key; relying on a "key-injective" PRF, this can be extended to a relation R that holds whenever two PRFs agree on their outputs for some input.

Application to Completely CCA Encryption. We formulate a new notion of security for public key encryption, which we call completely CCA (CCCA) secure encryption. Our new notion of security provides a strong form of non-malleability for encryption schemes, and is a stronger variant of the notion of completely non-malleable encryption of Fischlin [14]. The latter notion of secure encryption scheme rules out non-malleability even when a man-in-the-middle adversary "mauls" an honest (public-key, ciphertext) pair to produce a new public key and a new ciphertext where the corresponding plaintext is related to the original plaintext (according to some relation **R**).

Informally, our notion of completely CCA security strengthens *CCA security* (rather than plain non-malleability) by allowing the adversary to have access to a *strong decryption oracle*. The adversary can query this decryption oracle adaptively with different (possibly related) combinations of public keys and ciphertexts. The decryption oracle brute-force finds a message and randomness string corresponding to the queried public-key/ciphertext pair (and if no such pair exists, it it returns a $\perp$). The security requirement is that the adversary must not be able to break CPA-security for a challenge public-key ciphertext pair even given unbounded queries to this oracle (as long as it does not query the oracle on the challenge pair).

As shown by Fischlin [14], even his (weaker) notion of completely non-malleable encryption is *impossible* to realize with respect to black-box simulation in the plain model (i.e., without any trusted setup assumptions). In this work we show, surprisingly, that it is possible to construct completely CCA-2 secure encryption (and hence completely non-malleable encryption) in the plain model from COA obfuscation. While the reduction is BB, the bound is avoided by the fact that we need *sub-exponential* assumptions to construct COA obfuscation to begin with.

Let us provide more detail about the new notion of CCCA encryption. We first formulate a strong variant of completely non-malleable encryption in the spirit of CCA-secure commitments. In this variant, the adversary has access to a standard decryption oracle (with respect to adversarially generated ciphertext and the original secret key), and also has access to an oracle that, essentially, takes an adversarially generated public key pk and ciphertext c, and returns a plaintext m such that c could potentially the result of encrypting m with public key pk (and some random string). We note that this is a very strong primitive, that in particular implies both completely non-malleable encryption and CCA-secure commitment.

We then show that the Sahai-Waters CCA secure encryption [29], when the obfuscation algorithm is COA-secure (with respect to a predicate ϕ that attests for the correct structure of the obfuscated program), rather than plain iO, is completely CCA secure.

We provide two alternative proofs of security of this scheme. One proof follows a blueprint similar to that of [29], with one major difference: when the adversary $\mathcal{A}$ queries the decryption oracle with a public-key ciphertext pair $(\tilde{pk}, c)$ then:

- If $\tilde{pk}$ matches the challenge public key, then there is a direct reduction to the Sahai-Waters game.
- If $\tilde{pk}$ is different from the challenge public key, then the reduction uses the COA deobfuscation oracle to decrypt the ciphertext c. In more details, the reduction first invokes $c\mathcal{O}.\mathsf{Ver}$ on $\tilde{pk}$ to obtain some program $\tilde{P}$. The verifiability property of $c\mathcal{O}$ guarantees that if $\tilde{P} \neq \perp$, then there must be a program P' such that $\tilde{P} = \mathsf{iO}(P'; r)$. Since we assume iO is injective, the reduction can then use the deobfuscation oracle $\mathcal{O}^{-1}$ on $\tilde{P}$ to recover P'. Now, from this plaintext program P' it is possible to extract "secret" PRF keys $(\mathsf{K}_1, \mathsf{K}_2)$ by reading the description of P' (this is possible since our COA fortification is defined for circuits that have some PRF keys embedded). These secret keys can then be used to decrypt c.

The second proof directly uses the notion of COA-secure obfuscation: We formulate an admissible sampler where each sample consists of two instances of the encryption program in the public key, along with an auxiliary input that enables the adversary to obtain a challenge ciphertext c^* where embedded in c^* depends on whether one has access to the first or the second instance of the encryption program. We then argue that:

(a) when the encryption programs are given as oracles, it is infeasible to distinguish the two cases, thus the sampler is admissible. (Here we essentially use the fact that the underlying symmetric encryption scheme is CCA.) We conclude that a even a COA adversary, that has access to the COA-obfuscated version of one of the two copies of the encryption algorithm, along with the same auxiliary input a de-obfuscation oracle, is still unable to distinguish the two cases.

(b) On the other hand, A CCCA attack against the scheme can be simulated by a COA adversary that has access to a COA-secure obfuscation of one of the two instances of the encryption algorithm, to the same auxiliary input as before, and to a de-obfuscation oracle that's used to respond to the de-encryption queries of the CCCA attacker. This means that such CCCA attack must fail.

1.4 Constructing COA Obfuscation

Before sketching our construction for COA obfuscation, it will be helpful to set aside the non-malleability requirement, and consider only the simpler question of fortifying an obfuscation scheme to obtain verifiability. Let $\mathcal{O}$ be an obfuscator, and let ϕ be an efficiently computable predicate on programs. Recall that the verifiable version of $\mathcal{O}$ with respect to ϕ is a pair of algorithms $(v\mathcal{O}.\mathsf{Obf}, v\mathcal{O}.\mathsf{Verify})$ such that the following holds:

- Correctness: For any program C such that $\phi(C)$ holds, if $\hat{C} \leftarrow v\mathcal{O}.\mathsf{Obf}(C)$ and $\widetilde{C} \leftarrow v\mathcal{O}.\mathsf{Verify}(\hat{C})$, then we have that $\widetilde{C}$ and C are functionally equivalent. That is, $v\mathcal{O}.\mathsf{Verify}$ "accepts" $\hat{C}$ as $\widetilde{C}$.
- Verifiability: Conversely, if $\widetilde{C}$ is the result of $v\mathcal{O}.\mathsf{Verify}(\hat{C})$ for some string $\hat{C}$, then, except with negligible probability, there exists a program C such that $\phi(C)$ holds and $\widetilde{C}$ is functionally equivalent to C, or more precisely, that $\widetilde{C}$ is in the image of $\mathcal{O}(C)$.
- Obfuscation: $v\mathcal{O}$ guarantees the same level of indistinguishability as $\mathcal{O}$. That is, there exists an efficient transformation from distinguishers between $v\mathcal{O}.\mathsf{Obf}(C_1)$ and $v\mathcal{O}.\mathsf{Obf}(C_2)$, to distinguishers between $\mathcal{O}(C_1)$ and $\mathcal{O}(C_2)$, for any distribution over pairs of programs $C_1, C_2 \in F$ that satisfy ϕ.
  (The formal definition considers distribution over (C_1, C_2, z) where z is auxiliary information that will be given to the distinguishers. Also, we shall permit the transformation to suffer a (possibly sub-exponential) quantitative loss in the level of indistinguishability.)

A useful interpretation of the pair of algorithms $(v\mathcal{O}.\mathsf{Obf}, v\mathcal{O}.\mathsf{Verify})$ is that they *together implement* $\mathcal{O}$. An intriguing side-effect of this is that the honest $v\mathcal{O}$ obfuscator (who runs $v\mathcal{O}.\mathsf{Obf}$) does not necessarily know the final obfuscated program $\widetilde{C}$ generated by $v\mathcal{O}.\mathsf{Verify}$, though it knows that it is of the form $\mathcal{O}(C)$. On the other hand, if the obfuscator is malicious, it could control the outcome of $v\mathcal{O}.\mathsf{Verify}$ to be fixed, or alternately, ensure that different runs of $v\mathcal{O}.\mathsf{Verify}$

results in obfuscations of *different programs* (without violating the verifiability condition). These "relaxations" of $v\mathcal{O}$ may appear inconsequential, since an honest obfuscator is only interested in fixing the functionality, and on the other hand, a malicious obfuscator could have randomly chosen the program it wants to obfuscate. But as we see below, these relaxations are crucial to realizing verifiability fortification.

Exploiting NIDI for Verifiability. A natural approach to obtaining verifiability would be to attach some form of a non-interactive proof to the obfuscated program, proving that it was constructed as $\mathcal{O}(C)$ for some C such that $\phi(C)$ holds. Unfortunately, NIZK is impossible without a trusted setup. The next best option would be to use a non-interactive witness indistinguishable (NIWI) proof system, which can indeed be realized without a setup [5,6,19], under a variety of assumptions. Indeed, this was the approach taken in [2]. However, since a NIWI proof can hide a witness only if alternate witnesses are available, attaching a NIWI to $\mathcal{O}(C)$ directly does not suffice; instead, [2] cleverly combines three obfuscations with a NIWI which only proves that two of them correspond to functionally equivalent programs, both satisfying the predicate (this necessitates the verifiable-equivalence restriction). By evaluating the three programs and taking the majority, the user is assured that they are using a valid $\mathcal{O}(C)$. Also, the variable witnesses introduced suffices to prevent the NIWI from breaking the indistinguishability guarantee that iO provides for pairs of functionally equivalent circuits. Unfortunately, this approach is closely tied to the specific hiding guarantee of iO, limited to functionally equivalent circuits, and further adds a technical requirement that there should be a short witness to the equivalence.

The relaxations we build into $v\mathcal{O}$ enable an alternative. Specifically, instead of attaching a proof to (one or more) programs, $v\mathcal{O}$.Verify is allowed to sample a program and a proof. This enables us to use a proof system which lets the verifier sample a statement and a proof together, where the statement comes from a distribution determined by the prover. Such a proof system was recently introduced in [22], under the name of *Non-Interactive Distributionally Indistinguishable* (NIDI) arguments. The hiding property that NIDI offers is that as long as two statement distributions are indistinguishable from each other, then adding the proofs does not break the indistinguishability (by more than a sub-exponential factor). With a statement distribution corresponding to $\mathcal{O}(C)$, we can directly use the prover and verifier in a NIDI argument as $v\mathcal{O}$.Obf and $v\mathcal{O}$.Verify.

COA Security Fortification. For defining COA-security fortification, we consider an *injective* obfuscator $\mathcal{O}$, where injectivity means that the obfuscator does not map two distinct programs to the same obfuscated program. While this property may naturally be present in obfuscators with perfect functionality preservation, it is easy to add this to an obfuscator (without affecting hiding properties) by simply attaching a perfectly binding commitment of a program to the obfuscation. The reason we shall consider the given obfuscator $\mathcal{O}$ to be injective is so that we will be able to unambiguously refer to a *de-obfuscation oracle*.

Given an injective obfuscator $\mathcal{O}$, a COA fortification of $\mathcal{O}$, denoted $c\mathcal{O} = (c\mathcal{O}.\mathsf{Obf}, c\mathcal{O}.\mathsf{Ver})$ is a pair of efficient algorithms satisfying the following properties:

- Correctness: This is similar to that in the case of verifiability fortification, except that there is no requirement for the obfuscated to satisfy any predicate. That is, for any program C, if $\hat{C} \leftarrow c\mathcal{O}.\mathsf{Obf}(C)$, then we have that $\widetilde{C} \leftarrow c\mathcal{O}.\mathsf{Ver}(\hat{C})$ such that $\widetilde{C}$ is functionally equivalent to C.

- Verifiability: Again, this property is similar to that in the case of verifiability fortification, except for the predicate. That is, if $\widetilde{C} \leftarrow c\mathcal{O}.\mathsf{Ver}(\hat{C})$ then, except with negligible probability, $\widetilde{C}$ is in the codomain of $\mathcal{O}(C)$.

- COA-secure obfuscation: COA-security is defined analogous to how CCA security is defined for encryption or (more appropriately) commitment. Consider an adversary who tries to guess $b \leftarrow \{1, 2\}$ from $\hat{C}$, where $\hat{C} \leftarrow c\mathcal{O}.\mathsf{Obf}(C_b)$, and (C_1, C_2) are a pair of programs. In a chosen obfuscation attack (COA), the adversary can create purported obfuscations $\hat{C}' \neq \hat{C}$ and have them de-obfuscated as $\mathcal{O}^{-1}(c\mathcal{O}.\mathsf{Ver}(\hat{C}'))$. Note that we require $\mathcal{O}$ to be injective so that $\mathcal{O}^{-1}$ is well-defined (it outputs $\perp$ if the input is not in the codomain of $\mathcal{O}$). Any advantage that the adversary has in guessing b with access to this deobfuscation oracle should translate to a distinguishing advantage between $\mathcal{O}(C_1)$ and $\mathcal{O}(C_2)$ (without a deobfuscation oracle).

COA-Security Fortification from Robust NIDI. Our COA-security fortification uses non-interactive CCA-secure commitments, as well as NIDI arguments. CCA-secure commitments were introduced by [9], and a non-interactive construction based on NIDI arguments was given in [22], which suffices for our purposes. However, for the NIDI arguments used in our construction, we need a stronger security guarantee than in [22], namely *robustness* – a term that we borrow from [9] where it was used in a similar sense. A robust NIDI w.r.t. an oracle $\mathbb{O}$ retains its indistinguishability preservation guarantee for distinguishers that have access to $\mathbb{O}$. We discuss the construction of robust NIDI soon after describing COA fortification.

Our COA-security fortification $c\mathcal{O}$ uses a non-interactive CCA-secure commitment scheme , and NIDI arguments for NP that are robust against the decommitment oracle for , . The obfuscation $c\mathcal{O}.\mathsf{Obf}(C)$ generates a robust NIDI proof $\hat{C}$ for the language consisting of pairs $(\widetilde{C}, c)$ where $\widetilde{C} \leftarrow \mathcal{O}(C)$ and $c \leftarrow, (C)$. Note that C is fixed, but only the distribution over $(\widetilde{C}, c)$ is determined by the NIDI prover (obfuscator). The verifier $c\mathcal{O}.\mathsf{Ver}(\hat{C})$ runs the NIDI verifier to transform $\hat{C}$ into a pair $(\widetilde{C}, c)$ (or rejects it), and then outputs $\widetilde{C}$. Note that the CCA-secure commitment c is simply discarded by the verifier. The role of this commitment is, in the proof of security, to allow running a COA adversary – which expects access to the oracle $\mathcal{O}^{-1} \circ c\mathcal{O}.\mathsf{Ver}$ – using the decommitment oracle for com.

Constructing Robust NIDI. Our construction of a robust NIDI follows the outline in [22], except that we instantiate all primitives with those that retain their security guarantees in the presence of the oracle $\mathbb{O}$. In what follows, we outline this construction.

In a nutshell, a NIDI consists of an iO-obfuscated program that obtains as input the first message of an appropriate two-message proof system (satisfying ZK with superpolynomial simulation), and outputs a statement sampled from the input distribution, together with a proof. In [22], it was shown that the resulting system hides the distribution from which statements are sampled. Our construction of robust NIDIs modifies this template by requiring the underlying iO and ZK proof to be secure in the presence of the oracle $\mathbb{O}$. For any oracle with a finite truth table, we achieve this by assuming subexponential security of the underlying primitives, e.g., by setting the iO security parameter large enough such that iO becomes secure against adversaries that store the underlying truth table.

2   Preliminaries

We use $x \leftarrow S$ to denote uniform sampling of x from the set S. $[n]$ is used to denote the set $\{1, 2, \ldots n\}$. For $x, y \in \{0, 1\}^n$, $x \circ y$ denotes the inner product of x, y, i.e. if $x = x[1 \ldots n], y = y[1 \ldots n]$, $x \circ y = \bigoplus_{i \in [n]} x_i \cdot y_i$. Functional equivalance of two circuits C_1, C_2 is denoted by $C_1 \equiv C_2$. We refer to a circuit class as $\mathcal{C} = \{\mathcal{C}_\kappa\}_{\kappa \in \mathbb{N}}$, where $\mathcal{C}_\kappa$ consists of a set of circuits. In addition, whenever we consider a circuit class, we assume that it has a corresponding efficient predicate to check membership in the class, i.e. for circuit class $\mathcal{C} = \{\mathcal{C}_\kappa\}_{\kappa \in \mathbb{N}}$, there is a corresponding efficient predicate $\phi_\mathcal{C}$ s.t. $\phi_\mathcal{C}(\kappa, C) = 1$ if $C \in \mathcal{C}_\kappa$ and 0 otherwise. For a distribution $\mathcal{D}$ on domain $\mathcal{X}$, $\mathsf{Supp}(\mathcal{D})$ denotes the support of $\mathcal{D}$ on $\mathcal{X}$. We define puncturable PRFs and key-injectivity for puncturable PRFs below:

Definition 1 (Puncturable PRF).   *For sets $\{0, 1\}^n$ and $\{0, 1\}^m$, a puncturable PRF with key space $\mathcal{K}$ consists of a tuple of algorithms* $(\mathsf{PRF.Eval}, \mathsf{PRF.Puncture}, \mathsf{PRF.pEval})$ *that satisfy the following two conditions.*

- **Functionality preserving under puncturing.** *For every $x^* \in \{0, 1\}^n$, every $x \in \{0, 1\}^n \setminus \{x^*\}$, and all $K \in \mathcal{K}$, we have:* $\mathsf{PRF.Eval}(K, x) = \mathsf{PRF.pEval}(K\{x^*\}, x)$, *where $K\{x^*\} \leftarrow \mathsf{PRF.Puncture}(K, x^*)$.*
- **Pseudorandomness at punctured points.** *For every $x^* \in \{0, 1\}^n$, every $x \in \{0, 1\}^n \setminus \{x^*\}$, and any PPT adversary $\mathcal{A}$, it holds that*

$$\Big| \Pr\left[\mathcal{A}(K\{x^*\}, \mathsf{PRF.Eval}(K, x^*)) = 1 \right] - \Pr[\mathcal{A}(K\{x^*\}, U_k) = 1] \Big| = \mathsf{negl}(\kappa),$$

where $K \leftarrow \mathcal{K}$, $K\{x^*\} \leftarrow \mathsf{PRF.Puncture}(K, x^*)$, and U_k is the uniform distribution over $\{0, 1\}^k$.

2.1   Non-Interactive Distributionally Indistinguishable (NIDI) Arguments

In a NIDI argument [22] for an NP language $\mathcal{L}$, the prover algorithm $\mathcal{P}$ is given a distribution $\mathcal{D}$ for sampling member-witness pairs, and it generates a program π

which can be used (by the verifier algorithm $\mathcal{V}$) to verifiably generate a member of the language $\mathcal{L}$. The hiding property of a NIDI is that if two distributions $\mathcal{D}_1$ and $\mathcal{D}_2$ are such that the members they generate are indistinguishable from each other (when the witnesses are held back), then the program π generated by the NIDI prover remains similarly indistinguishable, upto a "gap" ϵ. We formally recall the definition of this primitive from [22] below.

Definition 2 (Non-Interactive Distributionally-Indistinguishable (NIDI) Arguments). *A pair of PPT algorithms $(\mathcal{P}, \mathcal{V})$ is a non-interactive distributionally-indistinguishable (NIDI) argument for* NP *language $\mathcal{L}$ with associated relation $R_{\mathcal{L}}$ if there exist non-interactive algorithms $\mathcal{P}$ and $\mathcal{V}$ that satisfy:*

- **Completeness:** *For every* poly(κ)*-sampleable distribution[4] $\mathcal{D} = (\mathcal{X}, \mathcal{W})$ over instance-witness pairs in $R_{\mathcal{L}}$ such that* Supp$(\mathcal{X}) \subseteq \mathcal{L}$,

$$\pi \in \mathsf{Supp}\left(\mathcal{P}(1^\kappa, \mathcal{D})\right) \implies \mathcal{V}(1^\kappa, \pi) \in \mathsf{Supp}(\mathcal{X}).$$

- **Soundness:** *For every ensemble of polynomial-length strings $\{\pi_\kappa\}_\kappa$ there exists a negligible function μ such that*

$$\Pr_{x \leftarrow \mathcal{V}(1^\kappa, \pi_\kappa)} \left[(x \neq \perp) \wedge (x \notin \mathcal{L})\right] \leq \mu(\kappa).$$

- ϵ-**Gap Distributional Indistinguishability:** *There exists an efficient transformation T on distinguishers such that for every* poly(κ)*-sampleable pair of distributions $\mathcal{D}_0 = (\mathcal{X}_0, \mathcal{W}_0)$ and $\mathcal{D}_1 = (\mathcal{X}_1, \mathcal{W}_1)$ over instance-witness pairs in $R_{\mathcal{L}}$ where* Supp$(\mathcal{X}_0) \cup$ Supp$(\mathcal{X}_1) \subseteq \mathcal{L}$, *and every distinguisher D with*

$$\left| \Pr[D(\mathcal{P}(1^\kappa, \mathcal{D}_0)) = 1] - \Pr[D(\mathcal{P}(1^\kappa, \mathcal{D}_1)) = 1] \right| = \nu(\kappa)$$

the distinguisher $D' = T(D)$ satisfies:

$$\left| \Pr[D'(\mathcal{X}_0) = 1] - \Pr[D'(\mathcal{X}_1) = 1] \right| \geq \epsilon(\kappa) \cdot \nu(\kappa).$$

We have the following theorem from [22].

Theorem 1. *Assuming the existence of sub-exponentially secure one-way functions and sub-exponentially secure indistinguishability obfuscation, there exist* NIDI *arguments satisfying ϵ-gap distributional indistinguishability, for every $\epsilon(\kappa) = 2^{-o(\log^c \kappa)}$, for a constant $c > 1$.*

---

[4] Here, we slightly abuse notation and use $\mathcal{D}$ to also denote a circuit that on input uniform randomness, outputs a sample from the distribution $\mathcal{D}$.

2.2   CCA Commitments

A chosen-commitment attack (CCA) secure commitment scheme [9] is a commitment scheme, which remains hiding for commitments even in the presence of a (computationally inefficient) "decommitment oracle" CCA.DeCom that opens all commitments that do not match the challenge commitment. For the decommitment oracle to be well-defined, we shall require that the commitment is perfectly binding: for all r_0, r_1 and $m_0 \neq m_1$ we have that CCA.Com$(m_0; r_0) \neq$ CCA.Com$(m_1; r_1)$.

A CCA secure commitment scheme is parameterized by a message length $M = M(\kappa)$; we shall consider the message space to be $\{0, 1\}^M$, where M is polynomial. As defined below, a *non-interactive* CCA commitment scheme consists of an efficient randomized algorithm CCA.Com (with an implicit "canonical opening"). We let CCA.DeCom denote the function that maps an output of CCA.Com to the message underlying it (or $\perp$ if no such message exists).

Definition 3. *An $\epsilon(\kappa)$-secure non-interactive CCA commitment scheme over a message space $\{0, 1\}^{M(\kappa)}$ consists of a randomized algorithm CCA.Com and a deterministic algorithm CCA.DeCom, satisfying the following.*

- **Correctness.** *For all $m \in \{0, 1\}^M$ and $r \in \{0, 1\}^*$ we have that*

$$\text{CCA.DeCom}(\text{CCA.Com}(1^\kappa, m; r)) = m.$$

  (This implies perfect binding.)
- **Efficiency.** *CCA.Com runs in time* poly(κ), *while CCA.DeCom runs in time* $2^{O(\kappa)}$.
- *$\epsilon(\kappa)$-**Security.** For a message $m \in \{0, 1\}^M$ and a distinguisher $\mathcal{D}$, let*

$$p_{\mathcal{D}, m}^{\text{CCA}} = \Pr_{c \leftarrow \text{CCA.Com}(1^\kappa, m)} [\mathcal{D}^{\text{CCA.DeCom} \circ \text{Filt}_c}(1^\kappa, c) = 1],$$

  where Filt$_c$ is the identity function on all inputs except c, on which it outputs $\perp$. Then, for all polynomials s there is a negligible function ν such that, for all $m_1, m_2 \in \{0, 1\}^M$ and all distinguishers $\mathcal{D}$ of size at most $s(\kappa)$,

$$\left| p_{\mathcal{D}, m_1}^{\text{CCA}} - p_{\mathcal{D}, m_2}^{\text{CCA}} \right| \leq \epsilon(\kappa)\nu(\kappa).$$

We rely on a recent construction of non-interactive CCA commitments from [22].

Theorem 2 ([22]). *Assuming sub-exponentially secure indistinguishability obfuscation and either*

- *Sub-exponential (classical) hardness of DDH and sub-exponential quantum hardness of LWE (as used in [21]), or*
- *Sub-exponential time-lock puzzles based on the RSW assumption (as used in [26])*

there exist non-interactive CCA commitments satisfying Definition 3.

The assumptions in the aforementioned theorem can also be reduced by using time-lock puzzles based on iO and the existence of hard-to-parallelize languages.

2.3   Obfuscation

An *obfuscator* $\mathcal{O}$ is a randomized program that probabilistically maps a circuit from some family $\{\mathcal{C}_\kappa\}_{\kappa\in\mathbb{N}}$ to another functionally equivalent circuit. We shall require an obfuscator to satisfy the following correctness and efficiency properties (with probability 1):

Functionality Preservation. For all $\kappa \in \mathbb{N}$ and all $C \in \mathcal{C}_\kappa$, $\mathcal{O}(1^\kappa, C) \equiv C$ (where $\equiv$ indicates that the two circuits are functionally equivalent).

Polynomial Slowdown. There exists a polynomial p such that for all $\kappa \in \mathbb{N}$ and all $C \in \mathcal{C}_\kappa$, $|\mathcal{O}(1^\kappa, C)| \leq p(|C|)$ (where $|\cdot|$ denotes the size of a circuit).

Efficient Obfuscation. $\mathcal{O}$ is a polynomial time algorithm. Generally, we shall also assume that the circuits in $\mathcal{C}_\kappa$ are of size at most polynomial in κ.

Security. For a sampler Samp and a distinguisher D, we define, for $b \in \{1,2\}$,

$$p_{\mathcal{O},D}^{\mathsf{Samp},b} := \Pr_{\substack{(C_1,C_2,z)\leftarrow\mathsf{Samp}(1^\kappa) \\ \widetilde{C}\leftarrow\mathcal{O}(1^\kappa,C_b)}} \left[D(\widetilde{C}, z) = 1\right]$$

$$\text{and}\quad \mathsf{Adv}_{\mathcal{O},D}^{\mathsf{Samp}} := \left|p_{\mathcal{O},D}^{\mathsf{Samp},1} - p_{\mathcal{O},D}^{\mathsf{Samp},2}\right| \tag{1}$$

Then, an obfuscator $\mathcal{O}$ is said to be $(\mathcal{S}, \mathcal{D})$ secure, if for all $\mathsf{Samp} \in \mathcal{S}$ and $D \in \mathcal{D}$, $\mathsf{Adv}_{\mathcal{O},D}^{\mathsf{Samp}}$ is negligible. In particular, for *indistinguishability obfuscation* (iO), $\mathcal{S}$ is the class of samplers which output (C_1, C_2, z) where $C_1 \equiv C_2$ and $z = (C_1, C_2)$, and $\mathcal{D}$ consists of all PPT distinguishers.

Following [10],[5] below we define a class of samplers, called admissible samplers, that only requires that it is (very) hard for a PPT adversary to distinguish between oracle access to C_1 and to C_2. Here the distinguishing probability is required to be negligible even after amplifying by a factor of 2^κ, with κ being the number of bits of inputs for the circuits.

Definition 4 (Admissible Samplers). *For any adversary $\mathcal{A}$, and $b \in \{1,2\}$, let*

$$p_{\mathcal{A}}^{\mathsf{Samp},b,\kappa} := \Pr_{(C_1,C_2,z)\leftarrow\mathsf{Samp}(1^\kappa)} \left[\mathcal{A}^{C_b}(z) = 1\right]$$

$$\text{and}\quad \mathsf{Adv}_{\mathcal{A}}^{\mathsf{Samp},\kappa} := \left|p_{\mathcal{A}}^{\mathsf{Samp},1,\kappa} - p_{\mathcal{A}}^{\mathsf{Samp},2,\kappa}\right|.$$

A sampler Samp over $\mathcal{C} = \{\mathcal{C}_\kappa\}_{\kappa\in\mathbb{N}}$ where all $C \in \mathcal{C}_\kappa$ take κ-bit inputs, is called admissible if there exists a negligible function μ s.t. for any non-uniform PPT adversary $\mathcal{A}$, $\mathsf{Adv}_{\mathcal{A}}^{\mathsf{Samp},\kappa} \leq \mu(\kappa) \cdot 2^{-\kappa}$, for all sufficiently large κ.

---

[5] Admissible samplers are a special case of X-Ind sampler defined in [10], where it is parametrized by a function $X(\kappa) \leq 2^\kappa$. The definition of admissible samplers corresponds to setting $X(\kappa) = 2^\kappa$ and restricting to (deterministic) circuits taking κ-bit inputs.

We shall refer to an obfuscation scheme with respect to such admissible samplers as a pIO scheme. As shown in [10], assuming the existence of sub-exponentially secure iO and sub-exponentially secure puncturable PRFs, pIO schemes exist for any polynomial sized circuit family, that is secure against a class $\mathcal{D}$ of sub-exponential time distinguishers.

Next we define injective obfuscators.

Definition 5 (Injective Obfuscator). *An obfuscator $\mathcal{O}$ for a circuit family $\{\mathcal{C}_\kappa\}_{\kappa \in \mathbb{N}}$ is said to be* injective *if $\forall \kappa_1, \kappa_2, C_1, C_2$*

$$\mathcal{O}(1^{\kappa_1}, C_1; r_1) = \mathcal{O}(1^{\kappa_2}, C_2; r_2) \neq \perp \Rightarrow C_1 = C_2.$$

We remark that it is easy to convert any obfuscator into an injective obfuscator (without affecting its hiding properties) simply by attaching a perfectly binding commitment of the circuit to its original obfuscation.

3   New Definitions

We define COA-secure obfuscation in Sect. 3.1, and Verifiability/COA fortification for obfuscations in Sects. 3.2 and 3.3 respectively. Towards this, first, we will need the following definition of circuit samplers.

Definition 6 (ϕ-Satisfying Samplers). *Let $\mathcal{C} = \{\mathcal{C}_\kappa\}_{\kappa \in \mathbb{N}}$ be a circuit class and ϕ be a predicate. We say that a randomized algorithm* Samp *is a ϕ-satisfying sampler over $\mathcal{C}$ if, for all large enough κ,* Samp(1^κ) *outputs (C_1, C_2, z) such that, with probability 1, $C_1, C_2 \in \mathcal{C}_\kappa$ and, $\phi(C_1) = \phi(C_2) = 1$.*

3.1   COA-Secure Obfuscation

Definition 7 (Admissible ϕ-satisfying Samplers). *A sampler algorithm* Samp(1^κ) *is an* admissible ϕ-satisfying sampler over $\mathcal{C}$ *if it is both admissible (according to Definition 4) and ϕ-satisfying (according to Definition 6) over $\mathcal{C}$.*

Definition 8 (COA-Secure Obfuscation). *A COA-secure obfuscation for a circuit class $\mathcal{C} = \{\mathcal{C}_\kappa\}_{\kappa \in \mathbb{N}}$ w.r.t. a predicate ϕ is a pair of PPT algorithms $(c\mathcal{O}.\mathsf{Obf}, c\mathcal{O}.\mathsf{Ver})$ defined as follows[6]:*

- *$c\mathcal{O}.\mathsf{Obf}(1^\kappa, C, \phi) \to \widehat{C}$. This takes as input the security parameter κ, a circuit $C \in \mathcal{C}_\kappa$, a predicate ϕ, and outputs an encoding $\widehat{C}$.*
- *$c\mathcal{O}.\mathsf{Ver}(1^\kappa, \widehat{C}, \phi) \to \{\widetilde{C} \cup \perp\}$. This takes as input a string $\widehat{C}$, a predicate ϕ, and outputs either a circuit $\widetilde{C}$ or a reject symbol $\perp$.*

These algorithms satisfy the following correctness, verifiability and security properties.

---

[6] Both the algorithms $c\mathcal{O}.\mathsf{Obf}$ and $c\mathcal{O}.\mathsf{Ver}$ take as input a predicate. This is to capture the uniformity of the algorithms w.r.t. ϕ.

– **Perfect Correctness.** *For every $\kappa \in \mathbb{N}$ and circuit $C \in \mathcal{C}_\kappa$ s.t. $\phi(C) = 1$,*
if $\widetilde{C} \leftarrow c\mathcal{O}.\mathsf{Ver}(1^\kappa, c\mathcal{O}.\mathsf{Obf}(1^\kappa, C, \phi), \phi)$, then $\widetilde{C} \equiv C$.
– **Verifiability.** *For every ensemble of polynomial-length strings $\{\Pi_\kappa\}_{\kappa \in \mathbb{N}}$,*
there exists a negligible function $\nu(\cdot)$ such that:

$$\Pr_{\widetilde{C} \leftarrow c\mathcal{O}.\mathsf{Ver}(1^\kappa, \Pi_\kappa, \phi)} \left[\widetilde{C} \neq \bot \wedge \left(\nexists C \in \mathcal{C}_\kappa : \phi(C) = 1 \wedge \widetilde{C} \equiv C \right) \right] = \nu(\kappa).$$

– **COA Security.** *Let $\mathbb{O}$ be an oracle defined as follows: $\mathbb{O}(\kappa, \widetilde{C})$ outputs the*
lexicographically first circuit $C \in \mathcal{C}_\kappa$ such that $\phi(C) = 1$ and C is functionally
equivalent to $\widetilde{C}$.
For any sampler algorithm Samp, and an oracle distinguisher $\mathcal{D}$, for $b \in$
$\{1, 2\}$, let

$$q_{c\mathcal{O}, \mathcal{D}}^{\mathsf{Samp}, b, \kappa} := \Pr_{\substack{(C_1, C_2, z) \leftarrow \mathsf{Samp}(1^\kappa) \\ \widehat{C} \leftarrow c\mathcal{O}.\mathsf{Obf}(1^\kappa, C_b, \phi)}} \left[\mathcal{D}^{\mathbb{O}(\kappa, \cdot) \circ c\mathcal{O}.\mathsf{Ver}(1^\kappa, \cdot, \phi) \circ \mathsf{Filt}_{\widehat{C}}} (1^\kappa, \widehat{C}, z) = 1 \right],$$

$$\mathsf{COAAdv}_{c\mathcal{O}, \mathcal{D}}^{\mathsf{Samp}, \kappa} := \left| q_{c\mathcal{O}, \mathcal{D}}^{\mathsf{Samp}, 1, \kappa} - q_{c\mathcal{O}, \mathcal{D}}^{\mathsf{Samp}, 2, \kappa} \right|$$

where $\mathsf{Filt}_{\widehat{C}}$ denotes a function that behaves as the identity function on all
inputs except $\widehat{C}$, on which it outputs $\bot$.
Then for every admissible ϕ-satisfying sampler Samp (according to Defini-
tion 7) and any non-uniform PPT distinguisher $\mathcal{D}$, there exists a negligible
function $\mu(\cdot)$, s.t. $\mathsf{COAAdv}_{c\mathcal{O}, \mathcal{D}}^{\mathsf{Samp}, \kappa} = \mu(\kappa)$.

While the above definition of COA security is w.r.t. admissible samplers, we can also define COA security more generally as an add-on for obfuscation schemes $\mathcal{O}$ whose security could be w.r.t. other samplers. Before presenting this notion of fortifying any obfuscation scheme with COA security, we introduce a simpler (but already useful) notion of fortifying an obfuscation scheme by adding verifiability.

3.2 Verifiability Fortification for Obfuscation

Given an obfuscation scheme $\mathcal{O}$, we shall define its verifiability fortification w.r.t. a predicate ϕ as a pair of algorithms $(v\mathcal{O}.\mathsf{Obf}, v\mathcal{O}.\mathsf{Verify})$. The verification algorithm guarantees that, given a string Π (purportedly generated by $v\mathcal{O}.\mathsf{Obf}$), if $\widetilde{C} \leftarrow v\mathcal{O}.\mathsf{Verify}(\Pi)$ and $\widetilde{C} \neq \bot$, then there exists a circuit C which satisfies the predicate ϕ s.t. $\widetilde{C} = \mathcal{O}(C; r)$ for some randomness r.

Definition 9 (Verifiability Fortification for Obfuscation). *Let $\mathcal{O}$ be an obfuscator for a circuit class $\mathcal{C} = \{\mathcal{C}_\kappa\}_{\kappa \in \mathbb{N}}$ and ϕ be an efficiently computable predicate on circuits. An ϵ-gap verifiability fortification of $\mathcal{O}$ w.r.t. ϕ, is a tuple of PPT algorithms $v\mathcal{O} = (v\mathcal{O}.\mathsf{Obf}, v\mathcal{O}.\mathsf{Verify})$ that satisfy the following:*

– **Correctness.** *For every $\kappa \in \mathbb{N}$ and every circuit $C \in \mathcal{C}_\kappa$, such that $\phi(C) = 1$,*

$$\Pr_{\widetilde{C} \leftarrow v\mathcal{O}.\mathsf{Verify}(1^\kappa, v\mathcal{O}.\mathsf{Obf}(1^\kappa, C, \phi), \phi)} [\widetilde{C} \equiv C] = 1.$$

- **Verifiability.** *For every ensemble of polynomial-length strings $\{\Pi_\kappa\}_{\kappa \in \mathbb{N}}$, there exists a negligible function $\nu(\cdot)$ such that:*

$$\Pr_{\widetilde{C} \leftarrow v\mathcal{O}.\mathsf{Verify}(1^\kappa, \Pi_\kappa, \phi)} \left[\widetilde{C} \neq \perp \wedge \left(\nexists(C \in \mathcal{C}_\kappa, r) : \phi(C) = 1 \wedge \widetilde{C} = \mathcal{O}(C; r) \right) \right] = \nu(\kappa).$$

- **ϵ-Gap Indistinguishability of Obfuscated Circuits.** *There exists an efficient transformation $\mathcal{T}$ (on distinguisher circuits) such that for any ϕ-satisfying sampler* Samp *(Definition 6) over $\{\mathcal{C}_\kappa\}_\kappa$ and distinguisher $\mathcal{D}$,*

$$\mathsf{Adv}^{\mathsf{Samp}}_{\mathcal{O}, \mathcal{T}(\mathcal{D})} \geq \epsilon(\kappa) \cdot \mathsf{Adv}^{\mathsf{Samp}}_{v\mathcal{O}.\mathsf{Obf}, \mathcal{D}}$$

where $\mathsf{Adv}^{\mathsf{Samp}}_{\mathcal{O}', \mathcal{D}'}$ (for $(\mathcal{O}', \mathcal{D}') = (\mathcal{O}, \mathcal{T}(\mathcal{D}))$ or $(v\mathcal{O}.\mathsf{Obf}, \mathcal{D})$) is as defined in (1).

3.3   COA Fortification for Obfuscation

We now define COA fortification $c\mathcal{O}$ for an obfuscation scheme $\mathcal{O}$ w.r.t. a predicate ϕ. Apart from the natural correctness property, we require that $c\mathcal{O}$ satisfies verifiability w.r.t. predicate ϕ just like verifiability fortification. In addition, we want $c\mathcal{O}$ to satisfy "gap COA security", which intuitively means that any distinguisher $\mathcal{D}$ that distiguishes between $c\mathcal{O}.\mathsf{Obf}(C_1)$ and $c\mathcal{O}.\mathsf{Obf}(C_2)$ *given access to a circuit deobfuscation oracle* can be converted to a distinguisher that distinguishes $\mathcal{O}(C_1)$ from $\mathcal{O}(C_2)$ without access to any oracle. In our construction, our transformation between distinguishers is not necessarily of polynomial size in the security parameter κ – therefore, in addition to ϵ as before, we parameterize the gap security in our definition by $T = T(\kappa)$ to capture the (in)efficiency of this transformation.

Definition 10 (COA Fortification for Injective Obfuscators). *Let $\mathcal{O}$ be an injective obfuscator for a circuit class $\mathcal{C} = \{\mathcal{C}_\kappa\}_{\kappa \in \mathbb{N}}$ and ϕ be an efficiently computable predicate on circuits. A (T, ϵ)-gap COA fortification of $\mathcal{O}$ w.r.t. ϕ is a pair of PPT algorithms $c\mathcal{O} = (c\mathcal{O}.\mathsf{Obf}, c\mathcal{O}.\mathsf{Ver})$ as follows:*

- $c\mathcal{O}.\mathsf{Obf}(1^\kappa, C, \phi) \to \widehat{C}$. *This is a randomized algorithm that on input security parameter κ, a circuit $C \in \mathcal{C}_\kappa$, and a predicate ϕ, outputs an encoding $\widehat{C}$.*
- $c\mathcal{O}.\mathsf{Ver}(1^\kappa, \widehat{C}, \phi) \to \{\widetilde{C} \cup \perp\}$. *This is a randomized algorithm that on input security parameter κ, a string $\widehat{C}$, and a predicate ϕ, outputs either a circuit $\widetilde{C}$ or a reject symbol $\perp$.*

These algorithms satisfy the following correctness and security properties.

- **Perfect Correctness.** *For every $\kappa \in \mathbb{N}$ and every circuit $C \in \mathcal{C}_\kappa$ such that $\phi(C) = 1$,*

$$\Pr_{\widetilde{C} \leftarrow c\mathcal{O}.\mathsf{Ver}(1^\kappa, c\mathcal{O}.\mathsf{Obf}(1^\kappa, C, \phi), \phi)} [\exists r \ s.t. \ \widetilde{C} = \mathcal{O}(1^\kappa, C; r)] = 1$$

- **Verifiability.** *For every ensemble of polynomial-length strings* $\{\Pi_\kappa\}_{\kappa \in \mathbb{N}}$, *there exists a negligible function* $\nu(\cdot)$ *such that:*

$$\Pr_{\widetilde{C} \leftarrow c\mathcal{O}.\mathsf{Ver}(1^\kappa, \Pi_\kappa, \phi)} \left[\widetilde{C} \neq \bot \wedge \left(\nexists(C \in \mathcal{C}_\kappa, r) : \phi(C) = 1 \wedge \widetilde{C} = \mathcal{O}(1^\kappa, C; r) \right) \right] = \nu(\kappa).$$

- (T, ϵ)-**Gap Security.** *Let* $\mathcal{O}^{-1}(\widetilde{C}) = \begin{cases} C & \text{if } \exists(C \in \mathcal{C}_\kappa, r) \text{ s.t. } \widetilde{C} = \mathcal{O}(1^\kappa, C; r) \\ \bot & \text{otherwise.} \end{cases}$

(well-defined since $\mathcal{O}$ *is injective). For any* ϕ-*satisfying sampler* Samp *(see Definition 6), and an oracle circuit* $\mathcal{D}$, *for* $b \in \{1, 2\}$, *let*

$$q_{c\mathcal{O},\mathcal{D}}^{\mathsf{Samp},b} := \Pr_{\substack{(C_1, C_2, z) \leftarrow \mathsf{Samp}(1^\kappa) \\ \widehat{C} \leftarrow c\mathcal{O}.\mathsf{Obf}(1^\kappa, C_b, \phi)}} \left[\mathcal{D}^{\mathcal{O}^{-1} \circ c\mathcal{O}.\mathsf{Ver}(1^\kappa, \cdot, \phi) \circ \mathsf{Filt}_{\widehat{C}}}(1^\kappa, \widehat{C}, z) = 1 \right]$$

$$\mathsf{COAAdv}_{c\mathcal{O},\mathcal{D}}^{\mathsf{Samp}} := \left| q_{c\mathcal{O},\mathcal{D}}^{\mathsf{Samp},1} - q_{c\mathcal{O},\mathcal{D}}^{\mathsf{Samp},2} \right|$$

where $\mathsf{Filt}_{\widehat{C}}$ *denotes a function that behaves as the identity function on all inputs except* $\widehat{C}$, *on which it outputs* $\bot$.

Then, there exists a T-*sized transformation* $\mathcal{T}$ *(on distinguisher circuits) such that for any admissible sampler* Samp *over* $\{\mathcal{C}_\kappa\}_\kappa$ *and distinguisher* $\mathcal{D}$,

$$\mathsf{Adv}_{\mathcal{O},\mathcal{T}(\mathcal{D})}^{\mathsf{Samp}} \geq \epsilon(\kappa) \cdot \mathsf{COAAdv}_{c\mathcal{O},\mathcal{D}}^{\mathsf{Samp}}$$

where $\mathsf{Adv}_{\mathcal{O},\mathcal{T}(\mathcal{D})}^{\mathsf{Samp}}$ *is as defined in* (1).

Remark 1. One could consider a (possibly) stronger definition that allows the sampler Samp used in defining $\mathsf{COAAdv}_{c\mathcal{O},\mathcal{D}}^{\mathsf{Samp}}$ to also make de-obfuscation queries. We note that for worst-case indistinguishability notions for $\mathcal{O}$ (like iO), this does not make any difference, as the (non-uniform) sampler can output the optimal pair of circuits.

Remark 2. We remark that for any $T = T(\kappa) \geq \mathsf{poly}(\kappa)$, any $\epsilon = \epsilon(\kappa) \leq \mathsf{negl}(\kappa)$, (T, ϵ)-gap COA fortification for any injective (T, ϵ)-secure pIO implies COA-secure obfuscation according to Definition 8. Here (T, ϵ)-security indicates that the advantage of any $\mathsf{poly}(T)$-sized adversary in the pIO security game is at most $\mathsf{negl}(\epsilon)$.

4   Robust NIDI

Robust NIDI arguments w.r.t. an oracle $\mathbb{O}$ are an extension of NIDI arguments (Definition 2), whereby the gap distributional indistinguishability requirement of NIDI is further strengthened to hold even if the distinguisher has access to the oracle $\mathbb{O}$. (The completeness and soundness guarantees remain unchanged.) In other words, any distinguisher $\mathcal{D}^\mathbb{O}$, distinguishing the proofs generated by prover $\mathcal{P}$ on input the distributions on instance-witness pairs - $\mathcal{D}_0 = (\mathcal{X}_0, \mathcal{W}_0)$ or $\mathcal{D}_1 = (\mathcal{X}_1, \mathcal{W}_1)$, can be converted to an efficient distinguisher $T(D)^\mathbb{O}$ which distinguishes the underlying instances $\mathcal{X}_0$ or $\mathcal{X}_1$ upto a "gap" ϵ. We formally define the same below.

Definition 11 (Robust NIDI Arguments). *Let $\mathcal{L}$ be an* NP *language with an associated relation $R_{\mathcal{L}}$, and $\mathbb{O}$ be an arbitrary oracle. A NIDI argument for $\mathcal{L}$, $(\mathcal{P}, \mathcal{V})$ is said to be* robust *w.r.t. $\mathbb{O}$ if it satisfies the following:*

- *ϵ-Gap Robust Distributional Indistinguishability: There exists an efficient transformation T on distinguishers such that for every $\mathrm{poly}(\kappa)$-sampleable pair of distributions $\mathcal{D}_0 = (\mathcal{X}_0, \mathcal{W}_0)$ and $\mathcal{D}_1 = (\mathcal{X}_1, \mathcal{W}_1)$ over instance-witness pairs in $R_{\mathcal{L}}$ where $\mathsf{Supp}(\mathcal{X}_0) \cup \mathsf{Supp}(\mathcal{X}_1) \subseteq \mathcal{L}$, and every distinguisher D with*

$$\left| \Pr[D^{\mathbb{O}}(\mathcal{P}(1^\kappa, \mathcal{D}_0)) = 1] - \Pr[D^{\mathbb{O}}(\mathcal{P}(1^\kappa, \mathcal{D}_1)) = 1] \right| = \nu(\kappa)$$

the distinguisher $\widehat{D} = T(D)$ satisfies:

$$\left| \Pr[\widehat{D}^{\mathbb{O}}(\mathcal{X}_0) = 1] - \Pr[\widehat{D}^{\mathbb{O}}(\mathcal{X}_1) = 1] \right| \geq \epsilon(\kappa) \cdot \nu(\kappa).$$

We construct robust NIDI arguments for any finite[7] oracle $\mathbb{O} = \{\mathbb{O}_\kappa\}_{\kappa \in \mathbb{N}}$ by modifying the construction in [22] to ensure that all the underlying primitives remain secure in the presence of oracle $\mathbb{O}$. Our approach to achieve this is to rely on complexity leveraging, although it may be possible to leverage other axes of hardness in order to instantiate the underlying primitives with those that remain secure in the presence of $\mathbb{O}$. In the full version [8], we prove the following theorem.

Theorem 3. *Fix any finite oracle $\mathbb{O} = \{\mathbb{O}_\kappa\}_{\kappa \in \mathbb{N}}$. Assuming the existence of sub-exponentially secure one-way functions and sub-exponentially secure indistinguishability obfuscation, there exist robust NIDI arguments w.r.t. $\mathbb{O}$, satisfying ϵ-gap distributional indistinguishability, for every $\epsilon(\kappa) = 2^{-o(\log^c(\kappa))}$, for some constant $c > 1$, satisfying Definition 11.*

5   Constructing COA Secure Obfuscation

In this section, we prove the following theorem.

Theorem 4. *For any $(T(\kappa), \epsilon(\kappa))$, if there exist $\epsilon(\kappa)$-secure CCA commitments satisfying Definition 3 for which the decommitment oracle can be implemented in time $T(\kappa)$, and robust NIDIs satisfying $\epsilon(\kappa)$-gap distributional indistinguishability w.r.t. the decommitment oracle for the CCA commitments (see Definition 11), then there exists a $(T(\kappa), \epsilon(\kappa)/4)$-gap COA fortification for any injective obfuscation, satisfying Definition 10.*

Here we describe our construction, and defer its proof of security to our full version [8].

---

[7] By 'finite', we mean that there exists a constant $c > 1$ s.t. for large enough κ the oracle $\mathbb{O}_\kappa$ can be represented as a truth-table of size at most 2^{κ^c}.

Construction 1. We require the following primitives:

– Let ccacom denote an $\epsilon(\kappa)$-secure CCA commitment scheme according to Definition 3 and let $\mathbb{O}$ denote the (deterministic, inefficient) oracle that implements the CCA.DeCom algorithm for ccacom. That is, on input a commitment string ,, the oracle $\mathbb{O}$ outputs either a message $m \in \{0,1\}^*$ or $\perp$. Also, let $T = \mathsf{poly}(|m|, 2^\kappa)$ (where $|m|$ denotes the size of message space for ccacom).
– Let r-NIDI denote a robust NIDI w.r.t. oracle $\mathbb{O}$ for language $\mathcal{L}_\phi$, defined below.
– Let $\mathcal{O}$ denote the underlying obfuscator for our COA fortification. We will assume that this obfuscator is secure against $\mathsf{poly}(T)$-sized adversaries. This can be achieved by appropriately scaling the security parameter for $\mathcal{O}$, since $\mathcal{O}$ is assumed to be subexponentially secure.
– Define language $\mathcal{L}_\phi = \{\{O, c\} : \exists (C, r_1, r_2) : O = \mathcal{O}(C; r_1) \wedge c = \mathsf{ccacom}(C; r_2) \wedge \phi(C) = 1\}$

The algorithm $c\mathcal{O}.\mathsf{Obf}(1^\kappa, C, \phi)$ does the following:

– Define distribution $\mathcal{D}_C(r_1 \| r_2) = \{\mathcal{O}(C; r_1), c = \mathsf{ccacom}(C; r_2)\}$ for uniformly sampled r_1, r_2.
– Output $\pi \leftarrow \mathsf{r\text{-}NIDI}.\mathcal{P}(1^\kappa, \mathcal{D}_C, \mathcal{L}_\phi)$ computed using uniform randomness r_c.

The algorithm $c\mathcal{O}.\mathsf{Ver}(1^\kappa, \widehat{C}, \phi)$ does the following:

– Sample randomness $r_\mathcal{R}$.
– Output $y \leftarrow \mathsf{r\text{-}NIDI}.\mathcal{V}(1^\kappa, \pi; r_R)$.

In particular, for $\epsilon(\kappa) = 2^{-o(\log^c(\kappa))}$ and some constant $c > 1$, there exist $\epsilon(\kappa)$-secure CCA commitments satisfying Definition 3 for which the decommitment oracle can be implemented in time $T(\kappa)$ where $T(\kappa) = 2^{\kappa^\delta}$ for some constant $\delta > 0$, and by Theorem 3 there exist robust NIDI arguments satisfying $\epsilon(\kappa)$ gap distributional indistinguishability w.r.t. the decommitment oracle for the CCA commitments. Then, the theorem above implies that there exist $(2^{\kappa^\delta}, 2^{-o(\log^c(\kappa))})$-gap COA fortification for any injective obfuscation.

Corollary 1. *Assuming the existence of sub-exponentially secure one-way functions and sub-exponentially secure indistinguishability obfuscation, there exists COA-secure obfuscation for all polynomial-sized circuits, satisfying Definition 8.*

Proof. (Sketch) By [10], assuming the existence of sub-exponentially secure iO and sub-exponentially secure puncturable PRFs, there exist subexponentially secure pIO schemes for any polynomial sized circuit family. That is, there exists a constant $\delta > 0$ such that for $T = 2^{\kappa^\delta}$, and every $\mathsf{poly}(T)$-sized distinguisher $\mathcal{D}$, $\mathsf{Adv}^{\mathsf{Samp}}_{\mathsf{pIO}, \mathcal{D}} = \mathsf{negl}(T)$ where Samp is an admissible sampler according to Definition 4. This scheme can be made injective (while retaining T-security) by attaching a perfectly binding commitment of the circuit to its original obfuscation.

Furthermore, for $\epsilon(\kappa) = 2^{-o(\log^c(\kappa))}$ and some constant $c > 1$, there exist $\epsilon(\kappa)$-secure CCA commitments satisfying Definition 3 for which the decommitment oracle can be implemented in time $T(\kappa)$, and by Theorem 3 there exist robust NIDI arguments satisfying $\epsilon(\kappa)$ gap distributional indistinguishability w.r.t. the decommitment oracle for the CCA commitments. Then, the theorem above implies that there exist $(2^{\kappa^{\delta}}, 2^{-o(\log^c(\kappa))})$-gap COA fortification for any injective obfuscation and in particular, for the injective pIO scheme described above. This results in a COA-secure obfuscation scheme, whose correctness and verifiability are immediate from those of the COA fortification. Furthermore, by definition of fortification, this means there is a T-sized transformation T on distinguishers such that for any admissible sampler Samp and distinguisher $\mathcal{D}$,

$$\mathsf{Adv}^{\mathsf{Samp}}_{\mathcal{O}, T(\mathcal{D})} \geq \epsilon(\kappa) \cdot \mathsf{COAAdv}^{\mathsf{Samp}}_{c\mathcal{O}, \mathcal{D}}$$

This implies that for any T-sized distinguisher $\mathcal{D}$, $\mathsf{COAAdv}^{\mathsf{Samp}}_{c\mathcal{O}, \mathcal{D}} = \mathsf{negl}(\kappa)$.   □

6   Keyless Verifiable Watermarking

In this section, we describe an application of COA obfuscation to building watermarking schemes. We present a generalized abstraction called *keyless verifiable watermarking*. As a consequence we obtain watermarking for useful functionalities like PRFs as a special case of this abstraction.

In the following, we define our notion of watermarking, which generalizes the one in the recent work of Kitagawa et al. [23] to capture publicly markable and extractable watermarking schemes without setup.

Definition 12 (Keyless Verifiable Watermarking). *Let* $\mathcal{C} = \{\mathcal{C}_{\kappa}\}_{\kappa \in \mathbb{N}}$ *be a circuit class s.t.* $\mathcal{C}_{\kappa}$ *consists of circuits with input length* $n(\kappa)$ *and output length* $m(\kappa)$. *For a distribution family* $\mathcal{D}_{\mathcal{C}}$ *and a relation* R *over* $\mathcal{C}$, *a* $(\mathcal{D}_{\mathcal{C}}, R)$-*unremovable keyless verifiable watermarking scheme with a message space* $\mathcal{M} = \{\mathcal{M}_{\kappa}\}_{\kappa \in \mathbb{N}}$ *consists of two PPT algorithms* (Mark, Verify) *as follows:*

- Mark$(1^{\kappa}, C, m)$: Mark *is a randomized algorithm that takes as input a circuit* $C \in \mathcal{C}_{\kappa}$, *a message (or mark)* $m \in \mathcal{M}_{\kappa}$ *and outputs a (marked) circuit* $\widehat{C}$.
- Verify$(1^{\kappa}, \widehat{C})$: Verify *is a randomized algorithm that takes as input a (purportedly marked) circuit* $\widehat{C}$ *and outputs a pair* (C', m'), *where* C' *is a circuit or* $\bot$, *and* $m' \in \mathcal{M}_{\kappa} \cup \{\bot\}$.

They should satisfy the following properties:

- **Correctness.** *There exists a negligible function* μ *s.t. for any circuit* $C \in \mathcal{C}_{\kappa}$ *and message* $m \in \mathcal{M}_{\kappa}$ *it holds that*

$$\Pr_{(C',m') \leftarrow \mathsf{Verify}(1^{\kappa}, \mathsf{Mark}(1^{\kappa}, C, m))} [C' \not\equiv C \ \lor \ m' \neq m] \leq \mu(\kappa).$$

– $(\mathcal{D}_\mathcal{C}, R)$-**Unremovability.** *There exists a negligible function ν s.t. for every non-uniform PPT adversary $\mathcal{A}$, for all sufficiently large κ,*

$$\Pr[\mathsf{Exp}_{\mathcal{A},\mathcal{D}_\mathcal{C},R}(\kappa) = 1] \le \nu(\kappa)$$

where the experiment $\mathsf{Exp}_{\mathcal{A},\mathcal{D}_\mathcal{C},R}(\kappa)$ is defined as follows:

1. *$\mathcal{A}(1^\kappa)$ sends a message $m \in \mathcal{M}_\kappa$ to the challenger. The challenger samples a circuit $C \leftarrow \mathcal{D}_{\mathcal{C}_\kappa}$ and responds with $\widehat{C} \leftarrow \mathsf{Mark}(1^\kappa, C, m)$.*
2. *$\mathcal{A}$ outputs a circuit $\widehat{C}^*$. Let $(C^*, m^*) \leftarrow \mathsf{Verify}(1^\kappa, \widehat{C}^*)$. Then, the experiment outputs 1 iff $C^* \ne \bot$, $m^* \ne m$, and*
   - *either $\exists C' \in \mathcal{C}_\kappa$ s.t. $C' \equiv C^*$ and $R_\kappa(C', C) = 1$,*
   - *or there is no circuit in $\mathcal{C}_\kappa$ that is functionally equivalent to C^*.*

Our definition is incomparable with recent related definitions, specifically those of Cohen et al. [12] Aaronson et al. [1], where the latter proposes a unified definition to capture most prior works. Specifically, we require that a watermarking scheme has a verification algorithm that is executed before running the watermarked programs. In our definition, the adversary is considered to have removed the watermark only if it produces a circuit that verifies, and for which the corresponding circuit in the circuit family is related to the original circuit.

Our definition also strengthens the definitions from prior works (including [23] and [1]) in some crucial ways:

– Our definition eliminates the need for any key generation algorithm/public parameters.
– Our definition incorporates a guarantee that a circuit passing the verification indeed belongs to the circuit class.

In addition, our definition has a flavor of traitor-tracing security that is similar to the recent works of [18]. In particular, we say that an adversary wins the watermarking game if it removes/modifies the watermark and outputs a circuit that is *related* to the original circuit – where *related* refers to satisfying one of a large class of relations.

We shall construct a $(\mathcal{D}_\mathcal{C}, R)$-unremovable keyless verifiable watermarking scheme, when circuits drawn from $\mathcal{D}_\mathcal{C}$ are unlearnable from oracle access, but the relation R is such that a circuit becomes learnable given a related circuit (as made precise in Theorem 5). We first describe our construction before stating its security guarantee.

Construction 2. Let $\mathcal{C} = \{\mathcal{C}_\kappa\}_{\kappa \in \mathbb{N}}$ be a circuit class s.t. $\mathcal{C}_\kappa$ consists of circuits that take inputs of length $n(\kappa)$ and produce outputs of length $m(\kappa)$, and $\mathcal{M} = \{\mathcal{M}_\kappa\}_{\kappa \in \mathbb{N}}$ be a space of polynomially long messages. For any $\kappa \in \mathbb{N}$ and any $m \in \mathcal{M}_\kappa$, let $\mathcal{C}'_\kappa = \{C_m \mid C \in \mathcal{C}_\kappa, m \in \mathcal{M}_\kappa\}$, where

$$C_m(x) = \begin{cases} m || C(0) & \text{if } x = 0 \\ C(x) & \text{otherwise.} \end{cases}$$

Let circuit class $\mathcal{C}' = \{\mathcal{C}'_\kappa\}_{\kappa \in \mathbb{N}}$ be the marked circuit class and ϕ' be its membership predicate, i.e. $\phi'(C) = 1$ iff $C \in \mathcal{C}'_\kappa$ (ϕ' will internally use $\phi_\mathcal{C}$, the membership predicate of $\mathcal{C}$).

Let $c\mathcal{O} = (c\mathcal{O}.\mathsf{Obf}, c\mathcal{O}.\mathsf{Ver})$ be COA obfuscation for $\mathcal{C}'$, w.r.t. predicate ϕ' (according to Definition 8). Instantiate the watermarking scheme for $\mathcal{C}$ w.r.t. message space $\mathcal{M} = \{\mathcal{M}_\kappa\}_{\kappa \in \mathbb{N}}$ and relation R as follows:

- $\underline{\mathsf{Mark}(1^\kappa, C, m)}$: Return $c\mathcal{O}.\mathsf{Obf}(1^\kappa, C_m, \phi')$, where C_m is defined using C as above.
- $\underline{\mathsf{Verify}(1^\kappa, \widehat{C})}$: Let $C' \leftarrow c\mathcal{O}.\mathsf{Ver}(1^\kappa, \widehat{C}, \phi')$. Parse $C'(0)$ as $m\|y$, where $m \in \mathcal{M}_\kappa$ and $y \in \{0,1\}^{m(\kappa)}$. (If $C' = \perp$, or the parsing above fails, return $(\perp, \perp)$.) Construct a circuit C'' such that

$$C''(x) = \begin{cases} y & \text{if } x = 0 \\ C'(x) & \text{otherwise.} \end{cases}$$

Return (C'', m).

We provide the following theorem which captures the security of the above construction. We provide a proof of this in our full version [8].

Theorem 5. *Let $\mathcal{C} = \{\mathcal{C}_\kappa\}_{\kappa \in \mathbb{N}}$, $\mathcal{D}_\mathcal{C} = \{\mathcal{D}_{\mathcal{C}_\kappa}\}_{\kappa \in \mathbb{N}}$ and $R = \{R_\kappa\}_{\kappa \in \mathbb{N}}$ be ensembles of polynomial (in κ) sized circuits, distributions over those circuits and relations over those circuits, as follows:*

- *$\mathcal{C}_\kappa = \{E_\kappa(f, \cdot) \mid f \in \{0,1\}^{h(\kappa)}\}$, where E_κ is a polynomial sized circuit implementing a function $E_\kappa : \{0,1\}^{h(\kappa)} \times \{0,1\}^{n(\kappa)} \to \{0,1\}^{m(\kappa)}$, with $n(\kappa) \leq \kappa^c$ for a constant $c < 1$.*
- *For any circuit family $\mathcal{A} = \{\mathcal{A}_\kappa\}_{\kappa \in \mathbb{N}}$ where $\mathcal{A}_\kappa$ is of size $\mathsf{poly}(2^{n(\kappa)})$,*

$$\Pr_{C \leftarrow \mathcal{D}_{\mathcal{C}_\kappa}, C' \leftarrow \mathcal{A}_\kappa^{C(\cdot)}} [C' \equiv C] \leq \mathsf{negl}(2^{n(\kappa)}).$$

- *There is a family of polynomial (in κ) sized circuits $\mathrm{Rec} = \{\mathrm{Rec}_\kappa\}_{\kappa \in \mathbb{N}}$ such that,*

$$\Pr_{C \leftarrow \mathcal{D}_{\mathcal{C}_\kappa}} \left[\exists C' \in \mathcal{C}_\kappa, R_\kappa(C, C') = 1 \wedge \mathrm{Rec}_\kappa^{C(\cdot)}(C') \neq C \right] \leq \mathsf{negl}(\kappa).$$

Then the watermarking scheme in Construction 2 is a $(\mathcal{D}_\mathcal{C}, R)$-unremovable keyless verifiable watermarking scheme, (according to Definition 12) for circuit class $\mathcal{C}$ and message space $\mathcal{M}$.

Next, we provide the following corollary which captures PRF watermarking as special case of the above theorem.

Corollary 2. *Let $F = \{F_k(\cdot)\}_{k \in \mathcal{K}_\kappa, \kappa \in \mathbb{N}}$ be a PRF family with key-space $\mathcal{K} = \{\mathcal{K}_\kappa\}_{\kappa \in \mathbb{N}}$, and seed, input, and output lengths as polynomials $h(\kappa), n(\kappa)$ and $m(\kappa)$ respectively, such that $n(\kappa) \leq \kappa^c$ for some $c < 1$. In addition, suppose the key distribution ensemble $\mathcal{D}_\mathcal{K}$ and relation ensemble R are as follows:*

– *F is a sub-exponentially secure PRF under key distribution* $\mathcal{D}_{\mathcal{K}}$. *That is, for any adversary of size* $\mathsf{poly}(2^{n(\kappa)})$, *the following holds: (where* $\mathcal{F}(n, m) = set$ *of all functions with input length* n *and output length* m)

$$\left| \Pr_{k \leftarrow \mathcal{D}_{\mathcal{K}}, b \leftarrow \mathcal{A}^{F_k(\cdot)}(1^\kappa)} [b = 1] - \Pr_{H \leftarrow \mathcal{F}(n,m), b \leftarrow \mathcal{A}^H(1^\kappa)} [b = 1] \right| \leq \mathsf{negl}(2^{n(\kappa)})$$

– *There exists an algorithm* Rec *s.t.*

$$\Pr_{k \leftarrow \mathcal{D}_{\mathcal{K}}} \left[\exists k' \in \mathcal{K}, R_\kappa(k', k) = 1 \wedge \mathsf{Rec}_\kappa^{F_k(\cdot)}(k') \neq k \right] = \mathsf{negl}(\kappa).$$

Then the watermarking scheme for F *in construction 2 is a* $(\mathcal{D}_{\mathcal{K}}, R)$-*unremovable keyless verifiable watermarking scheme.*

As a concrete instantiation of the above corollary, we consider the following relation over PRF keys: $R_\kappa(k, k') = 1$ iff $F_k(\cdot)$ agrees with $F_{k'}(\cdot)$ on at least one input. We will use a sub-exponentially secure PRF family F, which satisfies the following *key injectivity* property:

$$\Pr_{k \leftarrow \mathcal{D}_{\mathcal{K}_\kappa}} [\exists k' \in \mathcal{K}, R_\kappa(k, k') = 1 \wedge k' \neq k] = \mathsf{negl}(\kappa).$$

where $\mathcal{D}_{\mathcal{K}_\kappa}$ denotes the key distribution for which the PRF security holds. Such PRFs can be constructed as in [12] under sub-exponential DDH and LWE assumptions. For such a PRF, $R(k, k') = 1$ iff $k = k'$ (for most k). Then, letting Rec be the identity function satisfies the condition on the relation R in the above corollary. Thus, instantiating Corollary 2 with $F_k(\cdot), \mathcal{D}_{\mathcal{K}}, R$ as defined above, we get a $(\mathcal{D}_{\mathcal{K}}, R)$-keyless verifiable watermarking scheme for F.

7   Completely CCA-secure Encryption

In this section, we introduce the notion of a completely CCA-secure public key encryption scheme. Our notion of completely CCA secure PKE is a generalization of the notion of completely non-malleable encryption put forward by [14]. The original definition of Fischlin [14] follows a simulation-based formulation. Later [30] gave a game-based formulation of completely non-malleable encryption and showed it to be equivalent to the original simulation-based definition of complete non-malleability. Our formulation of completely CCA-secure encryption also uses a game-based formulation.

Definition 13 (C-CCA-security). *An encryption scheme* $\mathcal{PKE} = ($KeyGen, Enc, Dec$)$ *is completely CCA secure if there exists a (potentially randomized) verification algorithm* KeyVerify *such that the following hold.*

– *Soundness of verification: For any string* $\hat{pk}$ *and message* x, *the probability that* KeyVerify$(\hat{pk})$ *rejects and* Enc$(\hat{pk}, x) \neq \perp$ *is negligible, i.e., there is a negligible function* $\mu(\cdot)$ *in the security parameter* κ *such that*

$$\Pr[(r_v, r_e) \leftarrow \{0, 1\}^\kappa, \mathsf{KeyVerify}(\hat{pk}; r_v) = 0 \wedge \mathsf{Enc}(\hat{pk}, x, r_e) \neq \perp)] < \mu(\kappa)$$

– *For every PPT adversary $\mathcal{A}$, $\mathsf{Adv}^{c\text{-}cca}_{\mathcal{PKE},\mathcal{A},b}(\cdot)$ is upper bounded by $\mu(\kappa)$, where*

$$\mathsf{Adv}^{c\text{-}cca}_{\mathcal{PKE},\mathcal{A},b}(\cdot) = \Pr[\mathsf{Exp}^{c\text{-}cca}_{\mathcal{PKE},\mathcal{A}}(\kappa) = 1] - \frac{1}{2}$$

and $\mathsf{Exp}^{c\text{-}cca}_{\mathcal{PKE},\mathcal{A}}(\kappa)$ is defined via the following experiment involving $\mathcal{A}$ and a (potentially inefficient) challenger $\mathcal{C}$:

1. *The challenger $\mathcal{C}$ samples $r^* \xleftarrow{\$} \{0,1\}^\kappa$ and runs $(\mathsf{pk}^*, \mathsf{sk}^*) \leftarrow \mathsf{KeyGen}(1^\kappa, r^*)$. It then returns pk^* to $\mathcal{A}$. It also samples a random bit $b \xleftarrow{\$} \{0,1\}$, computes the challenge ciphertext $c^* \leftarrow \mathsf{Enc}(\mathsf{pk}^*, b, r)$ for a random r, and returns c^* to $\mathcal{A}$.*

2. *At any point in the game, the adversary can make (multiple) decryption queries to the challenger with respect to either the given public key or different (potentially mauled) public keys. In particular, $\mathcal{A}$ gets access to an oracle $\mathcal{D}(\cdot, \cdot)$. The oracle $\mathcal{D}$ takes as input either a ciphertext c_i, or else a pair $(\tilde{\mathsf{pk}}_i, c_i)$. In the first case, if $c_i = c^*$ then $\mathcal{D}$ returns $\bot$. Else $\mathcal{D}$ returns $\mathsf{Dec}(\mathsf{sk}^*, c_i)$. In the second case, $\mathcal{D}$ first chooses a random string r. Next, if $c_i = c^*$ and $\mathsf{pk}_i = pk^*$, or else $c_i = \bot$, or $\mathsf{KeyVerify}(\mathsf{pk}_i, r) = \bot$, then $\mathcal{D}$ returns $\bot$. Otherwise, $\mathcal{D}$ brute-force finds the set of message-randomness pairs (m, r) such that $\mathsf{Enc}(\mathsf{pk}_i, m; r) = c_i$. Finally, it returns a random message from this set, or $\bot$ if this set is empty.*

3. *When $\mathcal{A}$ outputs a guess b', return 1 if $b' = b$.*

7.1   C-CCASecure PKE Scheme in the Plain Model

In this section we show how to construct a completely CCA2 secure PKE scheme in the plain model (i.e., without any set up assumption). It is known from the work of Fischlin [14] that, it is *impossible* to construct even completely non-malleable encryption schemes for general relations w.r.t. black-box simulation in the standard model. Later works [25,30] overcome this impossibility result by relying on the common random or reference string model. In this work, we show how to construct a completely CCA2 secure encryption scheme (which is stronger than complete non-malleability) in the *plain* model from COA fortification of *indistinguishability obfuscators* (iO) and one-way functions. The use of sub-exponential assumptions allow us to bypass the impossibility result of Fischlin [14]. We now present the details of our construction. The main ingredients required for our construction as follows:

Construction 3. Let $\epsilon > 0$ be an arbitrary small constant s.t. $\epsilon < \delta$ and:

– Let $F_1 : \{0,1\}^{2\kappa} \to \{0,1\}$ and $F_2 : \{0,1\}^{2\kappa+1} \to \{0,1\}^\kappa$ be two puncturable pseudo-random functions that for security parameter 1^k satisfy 2^{k^ϵ}- security against (non-uniform) adversaries.

– Let $\mathsf{G} : \{0,1\}^\kappa \to \{0,1\}^{2\kappa}$ be a PRG that's 2^{k^ϵ}- secure against (non-uniform) adversaries.

- Let $\phi(C)$ be the predicate asserting that C is a circuit of the form of Fig. 1 with F_1, F_2 and G as specified above.
- Let $\mathsf{iO} = (\mathsf{iO.Obf}, \mathsf{iO.Eval})$ be *sub-exponentially* secure injective indistinguishability obfuscation scheme that for security parameter 1^k satisfies 2^{k^ϵ}-security against (non-uniform) adversaries.
- Let $c\mathcal{O} = (c\mathcal{O}.\mathsf{Obf}, c\mathcal{O}.\mathsf{Ver})$ be a COA fortification of an underlying *injective* indistinguishability obfuscator (iO) for circuits with respect to predicate ϕ.

We construct our completely CCA-2 secure encryption scheme $\mathcal{PKE} = (\mathsf{KeyGen}, \mathsf{Enc}, \mathsf{Dec})$ as follows:

1. $\mathsf{KeyGen}(1^\kappa)$: The key generation algorithm does the following:
   - Sample puncturable PRF keys K_1 for F_1 and K_2 for F_2.
   - Generate program $P_{\mathsf{K}_1,\mathsf{K}_2}$ defined in Fig. 1.
   - Compute $\widehat{P} \leftarrow c\mathcal{O}.\mathsf{Obf}(1^\kappa, P_{\mathsf{K}_1,\mathsf{K}_2}, \phi)$.
   - Output $pk = \widehat{P}$, $sk = (\mathsf{K}_1, \mathsf{K}_2)$.

Hardwired: Puncturable PRF Keys $\mathsf{K}_1, \mathsf{K}_2$.

Input: Message $m \in \{0, 1\}$, randomness $r \in \{0, 1\}^\kappa$.
(a) Let $t = \mathsf{G}(r)$
(b) Set $c_1 = t$, $c_2 = F_1(\mathsf{K}_1, t) \oplus m$, and $c_3 = F_2(\mathsf{K}_2, c_1 | c_2)$.
(c) Output $c = (c_1, c_2, c_3)$.

Fig. 1. Program $P_{\mathsf{K}_1,\mathsf{K}_2}$.

2. $\mathsf{Enc}(pk, m \in \{0, 1\})$: The encryption algorithm does the following:
   - Sample randomness $r \in \{0, 1\}^\kappa$
   - Run the randomized verification algorithm $\widetilde{P} \leftarrow c\mathcal{O}.\mathsf{Ver}(1^\kappa, \widehat{P}, \phi)$.
   - If $\widetilde{P} \neq \bot$, run $\widetilde{P}(m; r)$ to obtain $c = (c_1, c_2, c_3)$.
3. $\mathsf{Dec}(pk, sk, c = (c_1, c_2, c_3))$: The decryption algorithm does the following:
   - Check if $c_3 \overset{?}{=} F_2(\mathsf{K}_2, c_1 | c_2)$. If the check fails, output $\bot$. Otherwise, it continues.
   - Output $m' = F_1(\mathsf{K}_1, c_1) \oplus c_2$

In [8] we also show that Complete CCA security of the above scheme holds whehever the obfuscation scheme used is COA secure as in Definition 8. That is:

Theorem 6. *Assume that the obfuscation scheme $\mathcal{O}$ in the above scheme is COA secure with respect to predicate ϕ. Then the scheme is complete CCA secure as in Definition 13.*

References

1. Aaronson, S., Liu, J., Liu, Q., Zhandry, M., Zhang, R.: New approaches for quantum copy-protection. In: Malkin, T., Peikert, C. (eds.) CRYPTO 2021. LNCS, vol. 12825, pp. 526–555. Springer, Cham (2021). https://doi.org/10.1007/978-3-030-84242-0_19

2. Badrinarayanan, S., Goyal, V., Jain, A., Sahai, A.: Verifiable functional encryption. In: Cheon, J.H., Takagi, T. (eds.) ASIACRYPT 2016. LNCS, vol. 10032, pp. 557–587. Springer, Heidelberg (2016). https://doi.org/10.1007/978-3-662-53890-6_19

3. Barak, B.: How to go beyond the black-box simulation barrier. In: 42nd Annual Symposium on Foundations of Computer Science, FOCS 2001, Las Vegas, Nevada, USA, 14–17 October 2001, pp. 106–115 (2001)

4. Barak, B., et al.: On the (im)possibility of obfuscating programs. J. ACM **59**(2):6:1–6:48 (2012)

5. Barak, B., Ong, S.J., Vadhan, S.P.: Derandomization in cryptography. SIAM J. Comput. **37**(2), 380–400 (2007)

6. Bitansky, N., Paneth, O.: ZAPs and non-interactive witness indistinguishability from indistinguishability obfuscation. In: Dodis, Y., Nielsen, J.B. (eds.) TCC 2015. LNCS, vol. 9015, pp. 401–427. Springer, Heidelberg (2015). https://doi.org/10.1007/978-3-662-46497-7_16

7. Brakerski, Z., Döttling, N., Garg, S., Malavolta, G.: Candidate iO from homomorphic encryption schemes. In: Canteaut, A., Ishai, Y. (eds.) EUROCRYPT 2020. LNCS, vol. 12105, pp. 79–109. Springer, Cham (2020). https://doi.org/10.1007/978-3-030-45721-1_4

8. Canetti, R., Chakraborty, S., Khurana, D., Kumar, N., Poburinnaya, O., Prabhakaran, M.: COA-Secure obfuscation and applications. IACR Cryptol. ePrint Arch. (2022)

9. Canetti, R., Lin, H., Pass, R.: Adaptive hardness and composable security in the plain model from standard assumptions. In: FOCS 2010, pp. 541–550 (2010)

10. Canetti, R., Lin, H., Tessaro, S., Vaikuntanathan, V.: Obfuscation of probabilistic circuits and applications. In: Dodis, Y., Nielsen, J.B. (eds.) TCC 2015. LNCS, vol. 9015, pp. 468–497. Springer, Heidelberg (2015). https://doi.org/10.1007/978-3-662-46497-7_19

11. Canetti, R., Varia, M.: Non-malleable obfuscation. In: Reingold, O. (ed.) TCC 2009. LNCS, vol. 5444, pp. 73–90. Springer, Heidelberg (2009). https://doi.org/10.1007/978-3-642-00457-5_6

12. Cohen, A., Holmgren, J., Nishimaki, R., Vaikuntanathan, V., Wichs, D.: Watermarking cryptographic capabilities. SIAM J. Comput. **47**(6), 2157–2202 (2018)

13. Devadas, L., Quach, W., Vaikuntanathan, V., Wee, H., Wichs, D.: Succinct LWE sampling, random polynomials, and obfuscation. In: Nissim, K., Waters, B. (eds.) TCC 2021. LNCS, vol. 13043, pp. 256–287. Springer, Cham (2021). https://doi.org/10.1007/978-3-030-90453-1_9

14. Fischlin, M.: Completely non-malleable schemes. In: Caires, L., Italiano, G.F., Monteiro, L., Palamidessi, C., Yung, M. (eds.) ICALP 2005. LNCS, vol. 3580, pp. 779–790. Springer, Heidelberg (2005). https://doi.org/10.1007/11523468_63

15. Garg, R., Khurana, D., Lu, G., Waters, B.: Black-box non-interactive non-malleable commitments. Cryptology ePrint Archive, Report 2020/1197 (2020). https://eprint.iacr.org/2020/1197

16. Garg, S., Gentry, C., Sahai, A., Waters, B.: Witness encryption and its applications. In: Symposium on Theory of Computing Conference, STOC 2013, Palo Alto, CA, USA, 1–4 June 2013, pp. 467–476 (2013)

17. Gay, R., Pass, R.: Indistinguishability obfuscation from circular security. In: Khuller, S., Williams, V.V. (eds.) STOC 2021: 53rd Annual ACM SIGACT Symposium on Theory of Computing, Virtual Event, Italy, 21–25 June 2021, pp. 736–749. ACM (2021)

18. Goyal, R., Kim, S., Waters, B., Wu, D.J.: Beyond software watermarking: traitor-tracing for pseudorandom functions. IACR Cryptol. ePrint Arch. 2020:316 (2020)

19. Groth, J., Ostrovsky, R., Sahai, A.: New techniques for noninteractive zero-knowledge. J. ACM **59**(3):11:1–11:35 (2012)

20. Jain, A., Lin, H., Sahai, A.: Indistinguishability obfuscation from well-founded assumptions. Cryptology ePrint Archive, Report 2020/1003 (2020). https://eprint.iacr.org/2020/1003

21. Kalai, Y.T., Khurana, D.: Non-interactive non-malleability from quantum supremacy. In: Boldyreva, A., Micciancio, D. (eds.) CRYPTO 2019. LNCS, vol. 11694, pp. 552–582. Springer, Cham (2019). https://doi.org/10.1007/978-3-030-26954-8_18

22. Khurana, D.: Non-interactive distributional indistinguishability (NIDI) and non-malleable commitments. In: Canteaut, A., Standaert, F.-X. (eds.) EUROCRYPT 2021. LNCS, vol. 12698, pp. 186–215. Springer, Cham (2021). https://doi.org/10.1007/978-3-030-77883-5_7

23. Kitagawa, F., Nishimaki, R., Yamakawa, T.: Secure software leasing from standard assumptions. arXiv preprint arXiv:2010.11186 (2020)

24. Komargodski, I., Yogev, E.: Another step towards realizing random oracles: non-malleable point obfuscation. In: Nielsen, J.B., Rijmen, V. (eds.) EUROCRYPT 2018. LNCS, vol. 10820, pp. 259–279. Springer, Cham (2018). https://doi.org/10.1007/978-3-319-78381-9_10

25. Libert, B., Yung, M.: Efficient completely non-malleable public key encryption. In: Abramsky, S., Gavoille, C., Kirchner, C., Meyer auf der Heide, F., Spirakis, P.G. (eds.) ICALP 2010. LNCS, vol. 6198, pp. 127–139. Springer, Heidelberg (2010). https://doi.org/10.1007/978-3-642-14165-2_12

26. Lin, H., Pass, R., Soni, P.: Two-round and non-interactive concurrent non-malleable commitments from time-lock puzzles. In: Umans, C. (ed.) FOCS 2017, Berkeley, CA, USA, 15–17 October 2017, pp. 576–587. IEEE Computer Society (2017)

27. Naor, M., Yung, M.: Public-key cryptosystems provably secure against chosen ciphertext attacks. In: STOC 1990, New York, NY, USA, pp. 427–437. Association for Computing Machinery (1990)

28. Rackoff, C., Simon, D.R.: Non-interactive zero-knowledge proof of knowledge and chosen ciphertext attack. In: Feigenbaum, J. (ed.) CRYPTO 1991. LNCS, vol. 576, pp. 433–444. Springer, Heidelberg (1992). https://doi.org/10.1007/3-540-46766-1_35

29. Sahai, A., Waters, B.: How to use indistinguishability obfuscation: deniable encryption, and more. In: Shmoys, D.B. (ed.) STOC 2014, New York, NY, USA, 31 May–03 June 2014, pp. 475–484. ACM (2014)

30. Ventre, C., Visconti, I.: Completely non-malleable encryption revisited. In: Cramer, R. (ed.) PKC 2008. LNCS, vol. 4939, pp. 65–84. Springer, Heidelberg (2008). https://doi.org/10.1007/978-3-540-78440-1_5

Unclonable Polymers and Their Cryptographic Applications

Ghada Almashaqbeh[1]([✉]), Ran Canetti[2], Yaniv Erlich[3], Jonathan Gershoni[4],
Tal Malkin[5], Itsik Pe'er[5], Anna Roitburd-Berman[4], and Eran Tromer[4,5]

[1] University of Connecticut, Storrs, USA
ghada@uconn.edu
[2] Boston University, Boston, USA
canetti@bu.edu
[3] Eleven Therapeutics and IDC Herzliya, Herzliya, Israel
yaniv@eleventx.com
[4] Tel Aviv University, Tel Aviv, Israel
{gershoni,roitburd}@tauex.tau.ac.il
[5] Columbia University, New York, USA
{tal,itsik,tromer}@cs.columbia.edu

Abstract. We propose a mechanism for generating and manipulating protein polymers to obtain a new type of *consumable storage* that exhibits intriguing cryptographic "self-destruct" properties, assuming the hardness of certain polymer-sequencing problems.

To demonstrate the cryptographic potential of this technology, we first develop a formalism that captures (in a minimalistic way) the functionality and security properties provided by the technology. Next, using this technology, we construct and prove security of two cryptographic applications that are currently obtainable only via trusted hardware that implements logical circuitry (either classical or quantum). The first application is a password-controlled *secure vault* where the stored data is irrecoverably erased once a threshold of unsuccessful access attempts is reached. The second is (a somewhat relaxed version of) *one time programs*, namely a device that allows evaluating a secret function only a limited number of times before self-destructing, where each evaluation is made on a fresh user-chosen input.

Finally, while our constructions, modeling, and analysis are designed to capture the proposed polymer-based technology, they are sufficiently general to be of potential independent interest.

1 Introduction

Imagine we could cryptographically create *k-time programs*, i.e., programs that can be run only some bounded number of times, and inherently self-destruct after the k-th invocation. This would open the door to a plethora of groundbreaking applications: For instance, we would be able to use even low-entropy passwords for offline data storage, because k-time programs could lock out a brute-force-search adversary after a few attempts; today this is possible only via interaction or trusted electronics.

© International Association for Cryptologic Research 2022
O. Dunkelman and S. Dziembowski (Eds.): EUROCRYPT 2022, LNCS 13275, pp. 759–789, 2022.
https://doi.org/10.1007/978-3-031-06944-4_26

Alternatively, we could release a sensitive and proprietary program (such as a well-trained ML model) and be guaranteed that the program can be used only a limited number of times, thus potentially preventing over-use, mission-creep, or reverse engineering.

Such programs can also be viewed as a commitment to a potentially exponential number of values, along with a guarantee that only few of these values are ever opened.

Indeed, k-time programs, first proposed by Goldwasser, Kalai, and Rothblum [35] are extremely powerful. What does it take to make this concept a reality? Obviously, we cannot hope to do that with pure software or classical information alone, since these are inherently cloneable. In fact, software-only k-time programs do not exist even if the program can use quantum gates [13].

In [35] it is shown that "one-out-of-two" memory gadgets, which guarantee that exactly one out of two pieces of data encoded in the gadget will be retrievable, along with circuit garbling techniques [55], suffice for building k-time programs for *any* functionality.

However, how do we obtain such memory gadgets? While Goldwasser et al. suggest a number of general directions, we are not aware of actual implementations of one-out-of-two memory gadgets other than generically tamper-proofing an entire computational component.

Can alternative technologies be explored? Also, what can be done if we only can obtain some weaker forms of such memory gadgets, that provide only limited retrievability to naive users, along with limited resilience to adversarial attacks?

More generally, where can we look for such technologies, and how can we co-develop the new technology together with the cryptographic modeling and algorithmics that will complement the technology to obtain full-fledged k-time programs, based only on minimal and better-understood assumptions on the physical gadgets, rather than by dint of complex defensive engineering?

1.1   Contributions

This work describes a cross-disciplinary effort to provide some answers to these questions, using ideas based on the current technological capabilities and limitations in synthesizing and identifying *random proteins*. We begin with a brief overview of the relevant biochemical technology and our ideas for using this technology for bounded-retrieval information storage. We then describe our algorithmic and analytical work towards constructing k-time programs and related applications, along with rigorous security analysis based on well-defined assumptions on the adversarial capabilities - both biochemical and computational.

Biochemical Background. Advances in biotechnology have allowed the custom-tailored synthesis of biological polymers for the purpose of data storage. Most effort has focused on DNA molecules, which can be synthesized as to encode digital information in their sequence of bases. DNA can be readily cloned and read with excellent fidelity, both by nature and by existing technology [12,19,27,38]. Even minute amounts of DNA can be reliably cloned - and then read - an effectively unbounded number of times, making it an excellent storage medium—too good, alas, for our goal, since it is unclear how to bound the number of times a DNA-based storage can be read.

Consider, though, a different biological polymer: proteins. These chains of amino acids can likewise represent digital information, and can be synthesized via standard (albeit more involved) lab procedures. However, reading ("sequencing") the amino acid sequence in a protein appears much more difficult: The best known lab procedure for sequencing general proteins is mass spectrometry, which requires a macroscopic pure sample, free of substantial pollution. The sequencing process then destroys the sample - the protein is chopped into small fragments which are accelerated in a detector.

Furthermore, we have no way to clone a protein that is given in a small amount. Indeed, Francis Crick's central dogma of molecular biology states: *"once 'information' has passed into protein it cannot get out again. [Information] transfer from protein to protein, or from protein to nucleic acid is impossible"* [20]. Over billions of years of evolution, no known biological system has ever violated this rule, despite the reproductive or immunological benefits this could have bestowed. Moreover, in the 63 years since that bold hypothesis (or, alternatively, challenge) was put forth, it has also stymied human ingenuity, in spite of the enormous usefulness to science and medicine that such ability would provide.

This makes proteins terrible as a general-purpose data storage medium: they cannot be read unless presented in just the right form, and they self-destruct after few reads. However, cryptography is the art of making computational lemonade out of hard lemons. Can we leverage the time-tested hardness of sequencing small amounts of proteins for useful functionality? We see a couple of approaches, leading to different functionality and applications.

Biochemical "Conditionally Retrievable Memory". As a first attempt, we consider a protein-based "conditionally retrievable memory", that stores information in a way so that retrieving the information requires knowledge of some key, and furthermore, once someone attempts to retrieve the information "too many times" with wrong keys, the information becomes irrevocably corrupted. A first attempt at implementing such a system may proceed as follows: The sender encodes the payload information into a *payload* protein, and the key into a *header* protein, which are connected into a single protein (the concrete encoding and procedures are discussed in Sect. 2). The process actually creates a macroscopic amount of such payload-header pairs, and mixes these pairs with a large quantity of *decoys* which are similarly structured but encode random keys and payloads. The resulting sample is then put in a vial, serving the role of (biological) memory.

Recovering the information from the vial can be done via a *pull-down* procedure, i.e., a chemical reaction of the sample with an antibody that attaches to a specific portion of the protein. Given the key, one can choose the correct antibody and use it to isolate the information-bearing proteins from the added ones. Then, the information can be read via mass spectrometry.

In addition, *any* meaningful attempt to obtain information from the vial would necessarily employ some sort of pull-down on some portion of the sample in the vial, and then employ mass spectrometry on the purified portion of the sample. (Indeed, performing mass spectrometry on the vial without *pull-down* will return results that are polluted by the decoys.) Furthermore, since each application of the spectrometry process needs, and then irrevocably consumes, some fixed sample mass, an adversary is effectively limited to trying some bounded number n of guesses for the key, where n depends on the initial mass of the sample in the vial and the grade of the specific spectrometer used.

Partially Retrievable Memory. The above scheme appears to be easily adaptable to the case of storing multiple key-payload pairs in the same vial, along with the random noise proteins. This variant has the intriguing feature that even a user that knows all keys can only obtain n payloads from the vial, where n is the number of pull-down-plus-mass-spectrometry operations that can be applied to the given sample.

Challenges. While the above ideas seem promising, they still leave a lot to be desired as far as a cryptographic scheme is concerned: First, we would need a more precise model that adequately captures the capabilities required from honest users of the system, as well as bounds on the feasible capabilities of potential adversaries—taking into account that adversaries might have access to significantly more high-end bio-engineering and computational tools than honest users. Next, we would need to develop algorithmic techniques that combine bio-engineering steps and computational steps to provide adequate functionality and security properties. Finally, we would need to provide security analysis that rigorously asserts the security properties within the devised model. We describe these steps next.

Formal Modeling: Consumable Tokens. The full biochemical schemes we propose involve multiple steps and are thus difficult to reason about formally. We thus distill the requisite functionality and security properties into relatively simple idealized definition of a *consumable token* in Sect. 3. In a nutshell, an $(1, n, v)$-time token is created with $2v$ values: keys $k_1, ..., k_v$ and messages $m_1, ..., m_v$, taken from domains K and M, respectively. Honest users can query a token only once, with key k'. If $k' = k_i$ for some i, then the user obtains m_i, else the user obtains $\bot$. Adversaries can query a token n times, each with a new key k'. Whenever any of keys equals k_j, the adversary obtains m_j. We assume that the size of M, K and v are fixed, independent of any security parameter.

Constructing Consumable Tokens. Our biochemical procedures provide a candidate construction for consumable tokens, but with weak parameters. They can only store a few messages, of short length, under short keys, with non-negligible completeness and soundness errors. This is in addition to the power gap between an honest recipient and an adversarial one; the former can perform *one* data retrieval attempt, while the latter might be able to perform up to n queries, for some small integer n.

Thus, employing our protein-based consumable tokens in any of the applications discussed above is not straightforward. It requires several (conventional and new) techniques to mitigate these challenges. Amplifying completeness is handled by sending several vials, instead of one, all encoding the same message. Storing long messages is handled by fragmenting a long message into several shorter ones, each of which is stored under a different header in a separate vial. The rest are more involved and were impacted by the application itself.

Bounded Query, Point Function Obfuscation for Low-entropy Passwords. Password-protected secure vaults, or digital lockers, allow encrypting a message under a low entropy password. This can be envisioned as a point function with multi-bit output where the password is the point and the message is the output. With our consumable tokens, one can store the message inside a vial with the password being mapped to a token key (or header) that is used to retrieve the message. The guarantee is that an honest recipient, who knows the password, will be able to retrieve the message using one query. While an adversary can try up to n guesses after which the token will be consumed.

However, having a non-negligible soundness error complicates the matter. We cannot use the conventional technique of sharing the message among several vials, and thus reducing the error exponentially. This is due to the fact that we have one password mapped to the keys of these tokens, so revealing the key of any of these tokens would give away the password. We thus devise a chaining technique, which effectively forces the adversary to operate on the tokens sequentially. In Sect. 4, we start with formalizing an ideal functionality for bounded-query point function obfuscation, and then detail our consumable token and chaining based construction, along with formal security proofs.

$(1, n)$-time Programs. Next we use $(1, n, v)$-consumable tokens to construct $(1, n)$-time programs, namely a system that, given a description of a program π, generates some digital rendering $\hat{\pi}$ of π, and a number of consumable tokens, that (a) allows a user to obtain $\pi(x)$ on any value x of the user's choice, and (b) even an adversary cannot obtain more information from the combination of $\hat{\pi}$ and the physical tokens, on top of $\pi(x_1), ..., \pi(x_n)$ for n adversarially chosen values $x_1, ..., x_n$.

In the case of $n = 1$ (i.e., when even an adversary can obtain only a single message out of each token), $(1, 1)$-time programs can be constructed by garbling the program π and then implementing one-out-of-two oblivious transfer for each input wire using a $(1, 1, 2)$-consumable token with $K = M = \{0, 1\}^\kappa$ [35]. However, constructing $(1, n')$-time programs from $(1, n, v)$-consumable tokens with $n > 1$ turns out to be a significantly more challenging problem, even when v is large and even when n' is allowed to be significantly larger than n (i.e., even when the bound that the construction is asked to impose on the number of x_i's for which the adversary obtains $\pi(x_i)$ is significantly larger than the number of messages that the adversary can obtain from each token): A first challenge is that plain circuit garbling provides no security as soon as it is evaluated on more than a single input (in fact, as soon as the adversary learns both labels of some wire). Moreover, even if one were to use a "perfect multi-input garbling scheme" (or, in other words VBB obfuscation [9]), naive use of consumable tokens would allow an adversary to evaluate the function on an exponential number of inputs.

Our construction combines the use of general program obfuscation (specifically, Indistinguishability Obfuscation [9,42]) together with special-purpose encoding techniques that guarantee zero degradation in the number of values that an adversary may obtain—namely $(1, n)$-time programs using our consumable tokens.

Specifically, our construction obfuscates the circuit, and uses consumable tokens to store random secret strings each of which represents an input in the circuit input domain. Without the correct strings, the obfuscated circuit will output $\bot$. Beside amplifying soundness error (luckily it is based on secret sharing for this case), our construction employs an innovative technique to address a limitation imposed by the concrete construction of consumable tokens. That is, a token can store a limited number of messages (or random strings), thus allowing to encode only a subset of the circuit inputs rather than the full input space. We use linear error correcting codes to map inputs to codewords, which are in turn used to retrieve random strings from several tokens.

We show a number of flavors of this construction, starting with a simple one that uses idealized (specifically VBB) obfuscation, followed by a more involved variant that uses only indistinguishability obfuscation $i\mathcal{O}$. We also discuss how reusable garbled circuits [34] can be used to limit the use of $i\mathcal{O}$ to a smaller and simpler circuits.

Protection from Malicious Encapsulators. Our constructions provide varying degrees of protection for an honest evaluator in face of potentially ill-structured programs. The $(1, n)$-point function obfuscation application carries the guarantee that an adversary can only obfuscate (or encapsulate) valid point functions with the range and domain specified. This is due to the fact that we use consumable tokens each of which is storing one secret message m (from a fixed domain) under a single token key (from a fixed space). The use of a wrong key (i.e., one that is not derived correctly from the password that an honest evaluator knows) will return $\bot$. The general $(1, n)$-program application only guarantees that the evaluator is given *some* fixed program, but without guarantees regarding the nature of the program. Such guarantees need to be provided in other means. A potential direction is to provide a generic non-interactive zero knowledge proof that the encapsulated program along with the input labels belong to a given functionality or circuit class.

The Analytical Model. We base our formalism and analysis within the UC security framework [15]. This appears to be a natural choice in a work that models and argues about schemes that straddle two quite different models of computation, and in particular attempt at arguing security against attacks that combine bioengineering capabilities as well as computational components. Specifically, when quantifying security we use separate security parameters: one for the bioengineering components and one for the computational ones. Furthermore, while most of the present analysis pertains to the computational components, we envision using the UC theorem to argue about composite adversaries and in particular construct composite simulators that have both bioengineering and computational components.

1.2   Related Work

Katz et al. [44] initiated the study of tamper-proof hardware tokens to achieve UC security for MPC protocols in the plain model. Several follow up works explored this direction, e.g., [18,40,41], with a foundational study in [37]. In general, two types of tokens are used: stateful [23] and stateless (or resettable) [7,22]; the latter is considered a weaker and more practical assumption than the former. In another line of work, Goldwasser et al. [35] employed one-time memory devices to build one-time programs as mentioned before. They assume that such memory devices exist without showing any concrete instantiation. Our work instead provides an instantiation for a weaker version of memory devices—$(1,n)$-time memory devices—and uses them to build $(1,n)$-time programs. Other works relied on tamper-proof smart cards to construct functionalities such as anonymous authentication and practical MPC protocols [39,45]. They assume that such cards withstand reverse-engineering or side-channel attacks. Our work, on the other hand, proposes an alternative that relies on deeper, more inherent physical phenomena that have withstood the test of nature and ingenuity. We show that even a weak level of security and functionality, far below the natural smart-card trust assumption, suffices for useful cryptographic functionalities.

Quantum computing offer an unclonability feature that poses the question of whether it can offer a solution for bounded program execution. This possibility was ruled out by Broadbent et al. [13] who proved that one-time programs, even in the quantum model, cannot be constructed without one-time memory devices. To circumvent this impossibility, Roehsner et al. [52] introduced a relaxed notion—probabilistic one-time programs—allowing for some error in the output, and showed a construction in the quantum model without requiring hardware tokens. Secure software leasing (SSL) [5] emerged as a weaker alternative for quantum copy-protection [1]. SSL deals with software piracy for quantum unlearnable circuits; during the lease period the user can run the program over any input, but not after the lease expires. Our work bounds the number of executions a user obtains regardless of the time period and can be used for learnable functions.

Another line of research explored basing cryptography on physical assumptions. For example, noisy channels [21] and tamper-evident seals [48] were used to implement oblivious transfer and bit commitments. Others built cryptographic protocols for physical problems: [32] introduced zero knowledge proof system for nuclear warhead verification and [28] presented a unified framework for such proof systems with applications to DNA profiling and neutron radiography. This has been extended in [29] to build secure physical computation in which parties have private physical inputs and they want to compute a function over these inputs. Notably, [29] uses *disposable circuits*; these are hardware tokens that can be destroyed (by the opposing party) after performing a computation. In comparison to all these works, our consumable tokens are weaker as they are used for storing short messages rather than performing a computation.

Physical unclonable functions (PUFs) [51] are hardware devices used as sources of randomness, that cannot be cloned. PUFs found several applications, such as secure storage [25], key management [43], oblivious transfer [53], and memory leakage-resilient encryption schemes [6]. The works [14] and [50] proposed models for using trusted and malicious PUFs, respectively, in the UC setting. Our tokens share the unclonability feature with PUFs, but they add the bounded query property and the ability to control the output of a data retrieval query.

Lastly, a few works investigated the use of DNA in building cryptographic primitives and storage devices. For example, a DNA-based encryption scheme was proposed in [56], while [26] focused on bio-data storage that deteriorates with time by utilizing engineered sequences of DNA and RNA, without any further cryptographic applications. Both works do not provide any formal modeling or security analysis. To the best of our knowledge, we are the first to use unclonable biological polymers—proteins—to build advanced cryptographic applications with formal treatment. Apart from storage, a more ambitious view was posed by Adleman [3] back in the 1990s, who investigated the concept of *molecular computers*. They showed how biochemical interactions can solve a combinitorial problem over a small graph encoded in molecules of DNA [2]. This leaves an open question of whether one can extend that to proteins and build stronger tokens that can securely execute a full computation.

2   Unclonable Polymer-Based Data Storage

In this section, we present an overview of the protein-based data storage construction that we use to build consumable tokens. We focus on the specifications and guarantees this construction provides rather than detailed explanation of the biology behind them. The detailed explanation, and a more complete version of this section, can be found in the full version.[1]

Protein-based Data Storage and Retrieval. Advances in biotechnology have allowed the custom-tailored synthesis of biological polymers for the purpose of data storage. Much of the effort in this new field has focused on the use of DNA, generating an arsenal of molecular protocols to store and retrieve information [12,19,27,38]. With this growing application, we became interested in the cryptographic attributes this new hardware offers. Specifically, we propose the use of proteins, in particular short amino-acid polymers or peptides, as a data storage material. Curiously, the most fundamental characteristics of proteins; they cannot be directly cloned nor can they replicate or be amplified, and that "data retrieval" is typically self-destructive, might be considered as limitations from a regular data storage point of view. However, these exact traits can confer powerful features to instantiate cryptographic primitives and protocols.

Accordingly, for storage, the digital message is encoded into the primary configuration of the peptide/protein, i.e., the sequence of the 20 natural amino

---

[1] It should be noted that we are working on a sister paper showing the details of this biological construction; will delve into the technical details of the biochemical realization and empirically analyze it under the framework established in this paper.

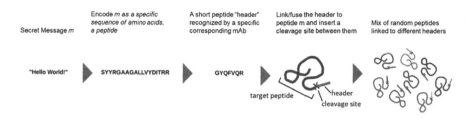

Fig. 1. General scheme for peptide-based data storage.

acids of the protein material, the "peptide-payload". To retrieve the message, the order of the amino-acids of a protein is determined, after which this sequence is decoded to reconstruct the original message. Given that our primary goal is to design a biological machinery to securely realize cryptographic primitives, we extend this basic paradigm to support data secrecy. Our proposal is based on a number of features of proteins and peptides: (i) unique peptides can be designed to comprise any string of amino acids and be physically produced with precision and at high fidelity, (ii) a peptide sample whose amino acid sequence is not known is unclonable and cannot be replicated or amplified, (iii) sequencing the peptide results in its consumption.[2]

As illustrated in Fig. 1, the peptide message, peptide-m, is conjugated to a short (<10 amino acids) peptide tag, a tag that is recognized specifically by a predetermined monoclonal antibody (mAb). Thus, the peptide tag, designated "header", corresponds to its specific mAb. Next, peptide-m is mixed with a vast variety of decoy peptide messages, all of which are peptide permutations of composition and length, each conjugated to a collection of alternative header sequences. The sender shares the secret header with the recipient, i.e., the peptide sequence of the header (this is digital data), which reveals to the recipient the identity of the correct unique mAb to be used to recover peptide-m. Then he sends a vial of the protein mix (a physical component).

For data retrieval, as shown in Fig. 2, the only possible way to decode the message is to first single out and purify peptide-m. This can be achieved by employing the unique mAb that specifically recognizes the unique header attached to peptide-m. Note that all decoy peptides and the target peptide-m are of the same general length, mass, and composition, but differing in sequence. Thus, effective purification of the desired protein from the decoys, without the matching mAb, is impossible through standard biochemical/biophysical methodologies. This achieves message secrecy in the sense that without the matching mAb, m cannot be retrieved.

Biochemical properties. Protein-based data storage enjoys several properties that we exploit in our cryptographic applications. These include the following

---

[2] Although we talk about one message in these protocols, several messages can be stored in one sample by having several peptide-ms instead of one, each of which is conjugated with a unique header and mixed with the decoys.

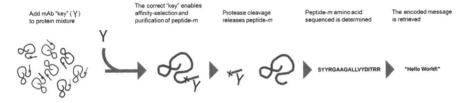

Fig. 2. Message retrieval.

(this is a high level description, more details on the biochemical features that supports these properties can be found in the full version):

– *Unclonability.* Proteins are unclonable biological polymers, meaning that given an amount of proteins one cannot replicate it to obtain a larger amount.
– *Destructive data retrieval.* Modern biology is only capable of reading protein sequences indirectly, destructively, and at lower throughput compared to DNA. The main practical strategy for reading proteins is mass spectrometry (MS) or versions thereof [8,33]. This machinery imposes several conditions on the protein sample to allow retrieving the digital data. First, the sample must contain a sufficient amount of the target protein, and second, the sample must be pure enough. Once a vial is purified and read using MS, the structure of the protein is destructed due to fragmentation.
– *Adversarial interactions.* The only known way to retrieve any information about the data stored in a vial is by pulling-down the target protein using the key (or mAb), and then sequencing this protein using MS. Thus, an adversary, who does not know the correct mAb, can only guess a candidate mAb and check if sequencing will output m. Also, when obtaining several (independent) tokens, the adversary will operate on these tokens separately, since purification and sequencing are still needed to obtain the stored data.
– *Bounded query.* The previous properties imply that a protein-based data storage allows for a finite number of data retrieval attempts after which the vial is consumed, i.e., each data retrieval attempt destroys a portion of the biological material. In our model, we account for that fact that an adversary could be more powerful that an honest recipient, e.g., she owns more advanced MS that operates at lower thresholds. This implies that the vial will allow the adversary to perform multiple data retrieval attempts, denoted as n, but an honest recipient will perform only one.
– *Message and key (header) sizes.* Proteins can store relatively short messages using short headers. In the full version, we show how to use fragmentation to store a long message using several vials instead of one, such that the header will be the concatenation of all headers used in these vials. Nonetheless, in our applications, we use consumable tokens to store cryptographic keys rather than very long messages.
– *Completeness and soundness errors.* Due to laboratory experimental (human and machine) errors, the protein-based data storage may have non-negligible

completeness and soundness errors. The former means that despite the use of the correct mAb, the target message may not be successfully retrieved. While the latter means that despite the use of an incorrect mAb, an adversary may manage to recover m. In other words, these incorrect mAb may have similar features to the correct one (what we call close keys). We amplify the completeness error on the biology side (by sending several vials all encoding the same message),[3] while we amplify the soundness error as part of the cryptographic constructions that we build in later sections.

3   The Consumable Token Functionality

We utilize the protein-based data storage to build what we call consumable tokens. A consumable token is a physical token that stores some secret messages, requires a secret key to retrieve any of these messages, and (partially) destructs after each data retrieval attempt. An honest recipient will have one data retrieval attempt, while an adversary (who could be more powerful than honest parties) may have multiple attempts. In this section, we define an ideal functionality for consumable tokens that we use in our applications. Some preliminary notions that we use in our work can be found in the full version.

Notation. We use $[n]$ as a shorthand for $\{1, 2, \ldots, n\}$. For time unit representation, we use the term "computational time step" to refer to the time needed to perform an operation in Turing machine-based modeling of computations. While we use "technologically-realizable time step" to refer to the time needed to perform an operation in physical procedures, which may involve computational algorithms as well. We use κ to denote the security parameter which encapsulates two security parameters: κ_p for physical procedures and κ_c for computational algorithms. Thus, when we say polynomial in κ, this means polynomial in the $\max\{\kappa_p, \kappa_c\}$. Lastly, boldface letters represent vectors and PPT is a shorthand for probabilistic polynomial time.

3.1   Ideal Functionality Definition

In formalizing our ideal functionality, we target an adversary class that interacts with a token only using the feasible procedure of applying token keys. Also, we adopt a deterministic approach for quantifying the closeness relation between the keys, and hence, computing the soundness error of any data retrieval attempt. In particular, each key k in the token key space has a set of close keys. Hitting any of these keys may allow retrieving the message from the token with a probability bounded by γ (the upper bound for the soundness error).

Adversary Class $\mathcal{A}$. We require the consumable token (or any cryptographic application built using this token) to be secure against an adversary that performs data retrieval (or decode) queries using token keys. This adversary, if

---

[3] At the cryptography level this is still viewed as one token that allows the honest recipient to retrieve the message with all but negligible probability.

given multiple tokens, operate on these tokens separately. To capture the fact that class $\mathcal{A}$ may have more power than the honest parties, an adversary $A \in \mathcal{A}$ can perform up to n decode queries instead of only one. This adversary is adaptive in the sense that it may choose her input based on the outputs obtained from previous interactions. Furthermore, this adversary is capable of performing digital and physical procedures.

Key Affinity Database. In order to capture the relation between the keys in the token key space $\mathcal{K}$, we use an affinity database D. Such a database is composed of rows each of which is indexed by a key $k \in \mathcal{K}$. Each row, in turn, contains a set of tuples (k', γ') where k' is a close key to k and γ' is the corresponding soundness error, such that $\gamma' \leq \gamma$. So for a token storing message m under key k, a decode query with k' allows an adversary A to obtain m with probability γ'. Recall that a token can store multiple messages each of which is tied to a different key. When these keys are selected at random, any key applied by the adversary will be close to at most one of these keys. Accordingly, in our model the ideal functionality is parameterized by the affinity database D. It consults this database for each adversarial query to decide key closeness and γ' value (if any). Furthermore, recall that for any token the soundness error is upper bounded by γ. Thus, for all queries $i \in [n]$, we require $\sum_i \gamma_i' \leq \gamma$.

Ideal Functionality. An ideal functionality for consumable tokens, denoted as $\mathcal{F}_{CT}$, is defined in Fig. 3. As shown, $\mathcal{F}_{CT}$ is parameterized by a security parameter κ, a key affinity database D, and an integer n. As noted earlier, for simplicity $\mathcal{F}_{CT}$ allows an honest party to perform one decode query, while it allows the adversary to perform up to n queries. It is straightforward to generalize to arbitrary configurations given that the power gap between honest parties and the adversary is preserved.

As shown in the figure, $\mathcal{F}_{CT}$ supports four interfaces. The first one, Encode, allows the sender P_1 to create a consumable token with ID tid encoding multiple secret messages under secret keys, all chosen by P_1, and transfer the token to P_2. To capture the fact that in real life an adversary may interrupt the communication between P_1 and P_2, $\mathcal{F}_{CT}$ asks the adversary whether to proceed. If the adversary agrees to continue, $\mathcal{F}_{CT}$ notifies P_2 about the new token, and creates a state for this token.[4] This state includes a counter j to track the number of decode queries performed so far, which is initialized to 0. It also includes two flags, hflag_1 and hflag_2, tracking whether P_1 and P_2, respectively, are honest or corrupted. These flags are set by default to 1 indicating that both parties are honest.

The second interface, Decode, allows P_2 to query the token on a key k'. If the input key matches the ith token key in $\mathbf{k}$, the corresponding message $\mathbf{m}_i$ will be returned to P_2, otherwise, $\perp$ will be returned. After the first query, where the counter j is set to 1, $\mathcal{F}_{CT}$ stops answering all future Decode queries, capturing that an honest recipient gets only one retrieval query.

---

[4] It is the responsibility of P_1 to securely share $\mathbf{k}$ with P_2.

Functionality $\mathcal{F}_{CT}$

$\mathcal{F}_{CT}$ is parameterized by a security parameter κ, a key affinity database D and a positive integer n.

Encode: Upon receiving the command $(\mathsf{Encode}, \mathsf{tid}, P_1, P_2, \mathbf{k}, \mathbf{m}, v)$ from token creator P_1, where tid is the token ID, P_2 is the token recipient, $\mathbf{k}$ is a vector of v token keys, and $\mathbf{m}$ is a vector of v messages, do: if a token with ID tid was created, end activation. Otherwise, do the following:

- Send $(\mathsf{Encode}, \mathsf{tid}, P_1, P_2)$ to the adversary.
- Upon receiving (OK) from the adversary, send $(\mathsf{Encode}, \mathsf{tid}, P_1)$ to P_2, and store $(\mathsf{tid}, P_1, P_2, \mathbf{k}, \mathbf{m}, v, j = 0, \mathsf{hflag}_1 = 1, \mathsf{hflag}_2 = 1)$.

Decode: Upon receiving the command $(\mathsf{Decode}, \mathsf{tid}, k')$ from P_2, if no token with ID tid exists, then end activation. Otherwise, retrieve $(\mathsf{tid}, P_1, P_2, \mathbf{k}, \mathbf{m}, v, j, \mathsf{hflag}_1, \mathsf{hflag}_2)$ and do the following:

- If $j > 0$, end activation. Else, increment j, and if $\exists i \in [v]$ s.t. $k' = \mathbf{k}_i$, then set $\mathsf{out} = \mathbf{m}_i$, else set $\mathsf{out} = \bot$.
- Send $(\mathsf{tid}, \mathsf{out})$ to P_2.

Corrupt-encode: Upon receiving the command $(\mathsf{Corrupt\text{-}encode}, \mathsf{tid}, k', \mathbf{m}', v)$ from the adversary, do: if a token with ID tid was created, end activation. Else, send $(\mathsf{Encode}, \mathsf{tid}, P_1)$ to P_2 and store $(\mathsf{tid}, P_1, P_2, k', \mathbf{m}', v, j = 0, \mathsf{hflag}_1 = 0, \mathsf{hflag}_2 = 1)$.

Corrupt-decode: Upon receiving the command $(\mathsf{Corrupt\text{-}decode}, \mathsf{tid}, k')$ from the adversary, if no token with ID tid was created, end activation. Else, retrieve $(\mathsf{tid}, P_1, P_2, \mathbf{k}, \mathbf{m}, v, j, \mathsf{hflag}_1, \mathsf{hflag}_2)$. If $\mathsf{hflag}_2 = 1$ and $j > 0$, or $j > n$, then end activation, else do the following:

- If $\exists i \in [v]$ s.t. $k' = \mathbf{k}_i$, then set $\mathsf{out} = \mathbf{m}_i$, else set $\mathsf{out} = \bot$ and $(\mathsf{close}, \gamma', i) = \mathsf{affinity}(D, \mathbf{k}, k')$. If $\mathsf{close} = 1$, choose $r \xleftarrow{\$} [0, 1]$ and change $\mathsf{out} = \mathbf{m}_i$ if $r \leq \gamma'$.
- Store $(\mathsf{tid}, P_1, P_2, \mathbf{k}, \mathbf{m}, v, j + 1, \mathsf{hflag}_1, \mathsf{hflag}_2 = 0)$.
- Send $(\mathsf{tid}, \mathsf{out})$ to the adversary.

Fig. 3. An ideal functionality for consumable tokens.

The third and fourth interfaces, Corrupt-encode and Corrupt-decode, are used to notify $\mathcal{F}_{CT}$ that the environment wants to corrupt any of the involved parties. Corrupting P_1 allows the adversary to encode a vector of messages $\mathbf{m}'$ under a key vector $\mathbf{k}'$, both of his choice. The state of this token will indicate that P_1 is corrupted by setting $\mathsf{hflag}_1 = 0$. On the other hand, and to capture the additional power an adversary $A \in \mathcal{A}$ has, corrupting P_2 allows the adversary to perform up to n decode queries. Moreover, trying a key $k' \neq \mathbf{k}_i$ for $i \in [v]$, gives the adversary γ' chance to obtain $\mathbf{m}_i$ if k' is close enough to key $\mathbf{k}_i$.

To depict these capabilities, $\mathcal{F}_{CT}$ tracks the number of decode queries performed so far and stops answering when this counter j reaches its maximum value n. Key closeness and soundness error are measured by invoking an algorithm called affinity that simply searches the database and checks if k' (the

---

Protocol 1 (A Physical Construction of Consumable Tokens)

Protocol 1 is parameterized by a security parameter κ, the message space $\mathcal{M}$, the header space $\mathcal{H}$, and the peptide space $\mathcal{P}$.

Encode$_{\mathsf{phys}}(\mathbf{h}, \mathbf{m})$: Given a vector of v messages $\mathbf{m} \in \mathcal{M}^v$ and a vector of v headers $\mathbf{h} \in \mathcal{H}^v$, do the following:
1. For $i \in [v]$, encode each $\mathbf{m}_i$ as a target protein peptide-$\mathbf{m}_i$.
2. For each peptide-$\mathbf{m}_i$ and $\mathbf{h}_i$, synthesize a protein sequence that concatenates them with an amount that allows retrieving $\mathbf{m}_i$ only once.
3. Mix the target proteins with a natural mixture of decoy proteins d_p selected at random from $\mathcal{P}$, and produce a protein vial S_P. Output S_P.

Decode$_{\mathsf{phys}}(h, S_P)$: Given a header $h \in \mathcal{H}$, and a protein vial S_P, do the following:
1. Immunoperciptate S_P with the mAb that recognizes h then wash out excess mixture.
2. Cleave the target protein and sequence it using MS. If MS identifies the peptides in this protein, then decode the message m (which will be one of the messages in $\mathbf{m}$) back into its digital form, and set out $= m$. Otherwise, set out $= \bot$. Output out.

Fig. 4. A physical construction of consumable tokens.

adversary's input) is listed in the close key set of any of token keys in $\mathbf{k}$. It outputs a flag close, and index i, and a soundness error value γ'. If close $= 1$, this means that k' is close to $\mathbf{k}_i$, and hence, $\mathcal{F}_{CT}$ outputs $\mathbf{m}_i$ with probability γ'.

As shown, we restrict the token to be in the hand of either an honest party or the adversary but not both at the same time. Therefore, P_2 cannot be corrupted after the honest recipient submits a decode query. Before submitting any honest decode query, corrupting P_2 is allowed, and when the environment asks for that, the value of hflag$_2$ is set to 0.

3.2   A Construction for Consumable Tokens

In this section, we present a construction for consumable tokens, shown in Fig. 4. It is based on the biological procedures used in storing and retrieving data using proteins discussed in Sect. 2. We conjecture that it securely realizes $\mathcal{F}_{CT}$.[5] In the full version, we present a mathematical (vector-based) model to abstract the biological procedures. We also show a consumable token construction (using this vector model) and formally prove its security.

---

[5] This construction is described at a high level; the biological experiments (the subject of our followup paper) will determine parameters such as required protein quantities, MS thresholds, amount of decoy proteins, etc., and falsify our conjecture.

4   Bounded-query Point Function Obfuscation

In this section, we introduce one of the cryptographic applications of consumable tokens: obfuscating bounded-query point functions with multibit output. We begin with motivating this application, after which we define a notion for bounded-query point function obfuscation, and a construction showing how consumable tokens can be used to realize this functionality.

Motivation. Program obfuscation is a powerful cryptographic concept that witnessed a large interest in the past two decades. It hides everything about a program other than what can be learned solely by running this program. A program obfuscator is a compiler that takes as input the original program, or circuit, and produces an unintelligible version that preserves functionality but hides any additional information. Program obfuscation found numerous applications, e.g., [30,31,46,49]. Barak et al. [9] initiated the first rigorous study of program obfuscation laying down several security notions. Among them, we have virtual black box (VBB), which states that all what an adversary can learn from an obfuscated program can be simulated using an oracle access to the original program. The same work showed that this notion cannot be realized for general functionalities, but can be realized for restricted function classes.

Point functions are one of these classes that has been studied thoroughly [11, 16,17,46,54]. A point function outputs 1 at a single target point x, and 0 at all points $x' \neq x$. It is useful for access control applications where providing the correct passcode grants the user an access to the system. An extended version of this function class supports a multibit output, i.e., message m, instead of a single bit. The obfuscation of this extended class is motivated by the notion of digital lockers [16]: for a message m encrypted using a low-entropy key, such as a human-generated password, the only way for an adversary to learn anything about m from its ciphertext is through an exhaustive search over the key space.

A question that arises here is whether one can strengthen this security guarantee to also prevent exhaustive search attacks. In real life access-control applications, this usually takes the form of tracking the number of login attempts and lock the user out when a maximum number is exceeded. However, this cannot be applied to digital lockers; an adversary has a copy of the ciphertext and can decrypt it for as many times as she wishes. Thus, the question becomes more about the possibility of augmenting multibit-output point function obfuscation with a bounded-query (or limited number of decryptions) capability.

We answer this question in the affirmative by instantiating a bounded-query obfuscator for point functions with multibit output using consumable tokens. We achieve that by translating the low entropy point or password p into the high entropy token key space, and setting the multibit output to be the message m encoded inside the token. The message m is obtained when the correct password p is queried, and only up to n_q queries can be performed ($n_q \in \mathbb{N}$).

4.1   Definition

We aim to build an obfuscator for multibit-output point functions with points drawn from a low entropy distribution. For password space $\mathcal{P}$ and message space

---

Functionality $\mathcal{F}_{BPO}$

$\mathcal{F}_{BPO}$ is parameterized by a security parameter κ, a class of point functions $\mathcal{I}_\kappa$, and a positive integer n_q.

Obfuscate: Upon receiving the command (Obfuscate, P_2, p, m) from party P_1 (the obfuscator), where P_2 is the evaluator, p is a password, and m is the function output (so $I_{p,m} \in \mathcal{I}_\kappa$), do: if this is not the first activation, then do nothing. Otherwise:
- Send (Obfuscate, P_1, P_2) to the adversary.
- Upon receiving (OK) from the adversary, store $(p, m, j = 0, \mathsf{hflag}_2 = 1)$ and output (Obfuscate, P_1) to P_2.

Evaluate: Upon receiving input (Evaluate, p') from P_2: if Obfuscate was not invoked yet or $j > 0$, then end activation. Otherwise, increment j, and if $p = p'$, then set $out = m$, else set $out = \perp$. Output out to P_2.

Corrupt-obfuscate: Upon receiving the command (Corrupt-obfuscate, p', m') from the adversary, do: If an Obfuscate output was generated, then end activation. Else, store $(p', m', j = 0, \mathsf{hflag}_1 = 0, \mathsf{hflag}_2 = 1)$ and output (Obfuscate, P_1) to P_2.

Corrupt-evaluate: Upon receiving the command (Corrupt-evaluate, p') from the adversary, if no stored state exists, end activation. Else, retrieve $(p, m, j, \mathsf{hflag}_2)$ and do:
- If $j = n_q$, or $\mathsf{hflag}_2 = 1$ and $j > 0$, then end activation.
- Else, increment j, set $\mathsf{hflag}_2 = 0$, and if $p' = p$, set $out = m$, else set $out = \perp$.
- Output out to the adversary.

Fig. 5. An ideal functionality for bounded-query point function obfuscation.

$\mathcal{M}$, let $I_{p,m} : \mathcal{P} \to \mathcal{M} \cup \{\perp\}$ be a point function that outputs m when queried on p and $\perp$ otherwise. Let $\mathcal{I} = \{I_{p,m} | p \in \mathcal{P}, m \in \mathcal{M}\}$ be the family of these functions. In this section, we define an ideal functionality for bounded-query point function obfuscation that allows one honest query and up to n_q function evaluations. This functionality, denoted as $\mathcal{F}_{BPO}$, is captured in Fig. 5.

As shown in the figure, $\mathcal{F}_{BPO}$ supports four interfaces. The first is Obfuscate that allows P_1 to ask for obfuscating any point function $I_{p,m}$ in the class $\mathcal{I}$ defined earlier. If the adversary agrees to continue, $\mathcal{F}_{BPO}$ notifies P_2 about the new obfuscation request and creates a state for it. As shown, this state stores a counter to track the number of evaluate queries performed so far, which is initialized to 0. It also stores two flags, hflag_1 and hflag_2 introduced before, tracking whether P_1 and P_2, respectively, are honest or corrupted. These flags are set by default to 1 indicating that both parties are honest. As noted, $\mathcal{F}_{BPO}$ allows for one obfuscation request, and hence, several instantiations are needed to create multiple obfuscated functions.

The second interface, Evaluate, allows P_2 to request evaluating the obfuscated point function over an input password p' of her choice. If this input matches the stored password p, then P_2 obtains m, and $\perp$ otherwise. $\mathcal{F}_{BPO}$ updates the counter j to be 1, and thus, all future queries will not output anything since an honest P_2 gets only one query.

The third and fourth interfaces, Corrupt-obfuscate and Corrupt-evaluate, are used to notify $\mathcal{F}_{BPO}$ that the environment wants to corrupt any of the involved parties. Corrupting P_1 allows the adversary to obfuscate any point function $I_{p,m} \in \mathcal{I}$ of her choice. The state of this obfuscation will indicate that P_1 is corrupted by setting hflag$_1$ to 0. On the other hand, corrupting P_2 allows the adversary to perform up to n_q evaluate queries over inputs of her choice. The adversary needs to invoke Corrupt-evaluate for each input evaluation, where after performing n_q queries, $\mathcal{F}_{BPO}$ will stop responding. As shown, an obfuscated function can be in the hand of either an honest party or the adversary, but not both at the same time. In particular, if an honest party performs her single evaluate query, Corrupt-evaluate will not do anything.

Beside realizing the above ideal functionality, which captures correctness and security, we require any bounded-query point function obfuscation scheme realizing $\mathcal{F}_{BPO}$ to satisfy the efficiency property defined below.

Definition 1 (Efficiency of Bounded-query point function Obfuscation). *There exists a polynomial q such that for all $\kappa \in \mathbb{N}$, all $I_{p,m} \in \mathcal{I}_\kappa$, and all inputs $p' \in \mathcal{P}$, if computing $I_{p,m}(p')$ takes t computational time steps, then the command* (Evaluate, p') *takes $q(t, \kappa)$ technologically-realizable time steps.*

4.2 Construction

A direct application of $\mathcal{F}_{CT}$ produces a construction that suffers from two limitations. First, it obfuscates a class of point functions with multibit output that is restricted in its domain; must be in the high-entropy token key space $\mathcal{K}$. Second, $\mathcal{F}_{CT}$ has a non-negligible soundness error bounded by γ, which will violate the security guarantees of $\mathcal{F}_{BPO}$. Recall that the goal is to have a construction that permits A to only perform a bounded query exhaustive search. In other words, the success probability of A in retrieving m must be only negligibly larger than the probability of guessing the correct password when performing n_q queries (e.g., $\frac{n_q}{|\mathcal{P}|} + \mathsf{negl}(\kappa)$ when using a uniform password distribution). We now show our construction in stages, where to simplify the discussion, we assume a uniform password distribution in the following paragraphs.[6]

First Attempt. An initial idea is to use a known soundness amplification technique in which m is shared among u tokens, accompanied with a mechanism to map a password $p \in \mathcal{P}$ to a set of keys $k_i \in \mathcal{K}$ for $i \in [u]$. This mapping can be built as, for example, a set of random oracles $\pi_1, \ldots, \pi_u$ each of which maps any password $p \in \mathcal{P}$ to a random string of size ρ for some $\rho \in \mathbb{N}$. So we have $\pi_i : \mathcal{P} \to \{0,1\}^\rho$ and we denote the output space of each π_i as $\mathcal{S}^\mathcal{P} \subset \{0,1\}^\rho$ such that $|\mathcal{S}^\mathcal{P}| = |\mathcal{P}|$. Each random string is then used to choose a key at random from $\mathcal{K}$. This is modeled by having the token creator P_1 use a public algorithm KeyGen that takes a random string as input and returns a token key as an output.

---

[6] Later, when proving Theorem 1, we generalize that by replacing $\frac{n_q}{|\mathcal{P}|}$ with a variable representing the probability of guessing the password using n_q queries. The value of this variable can be computed based on the underlying password distribution.

At a high level, with this construction an adversary A will need to retrieve all shares from all token instances in order to recover m. Taking the worst case scenario, meaning fixing the soundness error to be the maximum value γ, this multi-instance approach reduces the overall soundness error to γ^u. By setting u to be large enough, the soundness error becomes negligible. Furthermore, and given that each token instance allows n attempts to retrieve a share, and that all shares are needed to recover m, A will have $n_q = n$ attempts to obtain m.

However, the above analysis is flawed. The adversary A can perform what we call a *leftover attack* and utilize the relation between the keys of the u tokens (i.e., mappings of the same password) to gain a better advantage in recovering m. That is, success with any of the tokens not only reveals the message share stored in that token, but also reveals the keys of the rest of the tokens. In detail, A operates on the first token and performs up to $n - 1$ queries (by guessing passwords and mapping them to token keys using π_1). If any of these queries succeeds in retrieving m_1, then with probability at least $1 - \gamma$, A knows that the key (and hence the password guess) used in this query is the correct key k_1 (respectively, the password p). Knowing p, and the public mapping function set $\{\pi_1, \dots, \pi_u\}$ as well as KeyGen, allows A to derive the rest of the tokens keys and retrieve all shares $m_2, \dots, m_u$. On the other hand, if A does not succeed in retrieving m_1 using the first $n - 1$ queries, it operates on the second token by repeating the same strategy. In fact, A here has a better chance to guess the correct password/key since it will exclude all the passwords that did not succeed with the first token. If A succeeds in retrieving m_2, and thus p and $k_1, k_3, \dots, k_u$ as mentioned previously, then it can go back to the first token and use the last query to retrieve m_1. If it didn't succeed, A applies the same strategy to the rest of the tokens with the hope of guessing the correct password.

As noted, although the probability of retrieving all shares without correctly guessing any of the token keys is γ^u, A now has $n_q = un$ queries (instead of n) to guess the right password. Based on that, the probability of retrieving m can be computed as:[7] $\Pr[m] = \frac{un}{|\mathcal{P}|} + \left(1 - \frac{un}{|\mathcal{P}|}\right)\gamma^u$. In other words, A can retrieve m by either guessing the password correctly in any of the un queries, or by being lucky and retrieving all shares from all tokens despite using incorrect keys due to the soundness error. Although, the second term has been reduced and can be set to negligible by configuring u properly, the first term increased the advantage of A way beyond $\frac{n}{|\mathcal{P}|}$.

Our Construction. To address the leftover attack, we introduce a construction that chains the u tokens together so that in order to operate on the jth token, A would need to retrieve all m_i for $i < j$. Otherwise, A will have to guess the token key from a large space (larger than $|\mathcal{P}|$). This enables us to amplify the soundness error without increasing the total number of queries A obtains.

Towards building our construction, we introduce a modified way to map passwords to token keys. In particular, a function set $f_1, \dots, f_u$ is used to gen-

---

[7] For the jth token, the size of the password space, after excluding the passwords that were already tried, is $|\mathcal{P}| - (j - 1)n$. For simplicity, we let $|\mathcal{P}| - (j-1)n \approx |\mathcal{P}|$.

erate token keys $k_1, \ldots, k_u$ such that for $i \in [u]$ we define $f_1 : \mathcal{P} \to \mathcal{K}$ and $f_i : \mathcal{P} \times \{0,1\}^\kappa \to \mathcal{K}$ when $i > 1$. We write $k_i \leftarrow f_i(p, r_i')$, where $r_i' = r_0 \oplus \cdots \oplus r_{i-1}$ such that $r_0 = \perp$ and $r_i \leftarrow \{0,1\}^\kappa$ is a random string stored in the ith token. Each f_i first applies the mapping π_i described earlier to p and then uses the output along with the random string r_i' (for $i > 1$) to generate a token key. A concrete instantiation of f_i could be composed of a random oracle that takes $\pi_i(p) \| r_i'$ as input and outputs a random string of size ρ, then KeyGen is invoked for this random string to generate a key k_i as before.

Note that each f_i, for $i > 1$, may have an input space that is larger than the output space, i.e., $|\mathcal{P}|2^\kappa >> |\mathcal{K}|$. If this is the case (in particular, if $2^\kappa \geq |\mathcal{K}|$), this function can be instantiated to cover the full space of $\mathcal{K}$ and be a many-to-one mapping. That is, a password $p \in \mathcal{P}$ can be mapped to different keys (or to all keys in $\mathcal{K}$) by changing the random string r used when invoking f_i. Furthermore, correctly guessing the key k of any of the tokens (other than the first one) without the random string r, does not help the adversary in guessing the password p (the adversary still needs to guess r in order to recover the password).

Protocol 2, described in Fig. 6, outlines a construction that uses the above function set, along with the consumable token ideal functionality $\mathcal{F}_{CT}$, to build a bounded-query obfuscator for low-entropy point functions with multibit output.

We informally argue that this construction addresses the leftover attack described previously (again, for simplicity we assume a uniform password distribution for the moment). To see this, let an adversary A follow the same strategy as before and assume that A did not obtain $r_1 \| m_1$ while performing $(n - 1)$ queries over the first token. A now moves to the second token, performs $(n - 1)$ queries where it will succeed in guessing the key k_2 correctly with probability $\frac{n-1}{|\mathcal{K}|}$. This is different from the naive construction in which this probability is $\frac{n-1}{|\mathcal{P}|-(n-1)}$ since the previously tried passwords are excluded. In our construction, A, when it does not have r_1, has the only choice of trying keys from the full key space $\mathcal{K}$ (regardless of the password space distribution). This is due to the fact that without r_2' (where $r_2' = r_1$), A cannot compute the induced key space by $\mathcal{P}$, thus the only choice is to guess keys from $\mathcal{K}$. This probability will be negligible for a large enough $\mathcal{K}$.

Furthermore, even if A guesses the correct k_2, without the random string r_2' it will be infeasible to deduce the password p from k_2 through f_2. A needs to feed f_2 with passwords and random strings, where the latter has a space of size 2^κ. Also, under the many-to-one construction of $f_2, \ldots, f_u$, several (or even all) passwords could be mapped to k_2 due to the random string combination, which makes the task harder for A to find out the correct password. The same argument applies to the rest of the tokens because without r_1, none of the subsequent r_i' can be computed, and the only effective strategy for A is to guess keys from the key space $\mathcal{K}$. So for each of these tokens, the success probability is $\frac{n-1}{|\mathcal{K}|}$ instead of $\frac{n-1}{|\mathcal{P}|-(i-1)(n-1)}$ as in the naive scheme (again, the latter will depend on the password distribution, but the former will always be uniform). The success probability for A to retrieve m is then approximated as: $\Pr[m] \approx \frac{n}{|\mathcal{P}|} + \left(1 - \frac{n}{|\mathcal{P}|}\right)\gamma^u$.

Protocol 2 (A bounded-query obfuscation scheme for $\mathcal{I}$)

For a security parameter κ, a number of token instances u, $i \in [u]$, message $m \in \mathcal{M}$, password $p \in \mathcal{P}$, and token key space $\mathcal{K}$, let $f_1, \ldots, f_u$ be as defined before such that $f_1 : \mathcal{P} \rightarrow \mathcal{K}$, and $f_i : \mathcal{P} \times \{0,1\}^\kappa \rightarrow \mathcal{K}$ for $i > 1$, P_1 be the obfuscator, P_2 be the evaluator, and $\mathcal{F}_{CT}$ be the consumable token functionality defined in Section 3. Construct a tuple of algorithms (Obf, Eval) to obfuscate a function in $\mathcal{I}$ as follows.

Obf: on input a function $I_{p,m} \in \mathcal{I}$, P_1 does the following:
1. Use an additive secret sharing scheme to generate random shares $m_1, \ldots, m_u$ such that $m = \oplus_{i=1}^{u} m_i$.
2. Set $r_0 = \bot$.
3. For $i \in [u]$:
   (a) Generate a random string $r_i \leftarrow \{0,1\}^\kappa$.
   (b) Compute $r'_i = \oplus_{j=0}^{i-1} r_j$.
   (c) Generate a token key k_i: $k_i \leftarrow f_i(p, r'_i)$.
   (d) Generate a token ct_i, with a unique token ID tid_i, encoding $r_i \| m_i$ using k_i by sending the command (Encode, tid_i, P_1, P_2, k_i, $r_i \| m_i$, 1) to $\mathcal{F}_{CT}$.

Eval: on input an obfuscated function $o = \{ct_1, \ldots, ct_u\}$ and point $p \in \mathcal{P}$, P_2 does the following:
1. Set $r_0 = \bot$.
2. For $i \in [u]$:
   (a) Compute $r'_i = \oplus_{j=0}^{i-1} r_j$.
   (b) Generate a token key k_i: $k_i \leftarrow f_i(p, r'_i)$.
   (c) Query token ct_i using k_i to retrieve $r_i \| m_i$ by sending the command (Decode, tid_i, k_i) to $\mathcal{F}_{CT}$.
3. Compute $m = \oplus_{i=1}^{u} m_i$ and output m.

Fig. 6. A construction for a bounded-query obfuscation scheme for $\mathcal{I}$.

That is, to retrieve m, A either has to guess the password correctly using the first token, or get lucky with every token and retrieve the share it stores. As shown, this amplifies the soundness error (and can be set to negligible with sufficiently large u) without increasing the number of queries A can do.[8]

4.3 Security

Theorem 1 shows that Protocol 2 in Fig. 6 securely realizes $\mathcal{F}_{BPO}$ for the function family $\mathcal{I}$, with an arbitrary password distribution. For simplicity, we assume that the token keys k_i, the randomness r_i, and the message m are all of an equal size, which is polynomial in the security parameter κ. The proof can be found in the full version.

---

[8] Similarly, to make the presentation easier, the probability is simplified here where some terms are omitted. See the full proof in the full version.

Theorem 1. *For* $0 \leq \gamma \leq 1$, *if each of* $f_1, \ldots, f_u$ *is as defined above, then Protocol 2 securely realizes* $\mathcal{F}_{BPO}$ *for the point function family* $\mathcal{I} = \{I_{p,m} | p \in \mathcal{P}, m \in \mathcal{M}\}$ *in the* $\mathcal{F}_{CT}$-*hybrid model in the presence of any adversary* $\Lambda \subset \mathcal{A}$, *with* $n_q = n$ *and large enough* u.

Remark 1. As mentioned before, κ encapsulates a digital and a biological security parameters. Also, $\mathcal{A}$ is capable of doing computational algorithms and physical procedures, so is the simulator. In the above theorem, the simulator is computational, but it relies on $\mathcal{F}_{CT}$ whose simulator involves physical procedures. The use of UC security allows us to obtain an overall security guarantee against all physical/digital combined attacks, both in concrete and asymptotic terms.

5 $(1, n)$-time Programs

In this section, we introduce another cryptographic application of consumable tokens; $(1, n)$-programs. For such programs, completeness states that an honest party can run a program at most once, while soundness states that an adversary can run this program at most n times. Again, this can be generalized to allow for multiple honest queries given that the power gap between honest parties and the adversary is preserved. We begin with motivating this application, after which we present a construction showing how consumable tokens can be used to build $(1, n)$-programs for arbitrary functions.

Remark 2. One may argue that this application is a generalization of the bounded-query point function obfuscation. Thus, the previous section is not needed as one may construct a $(1, n)$-program for any point function. However, $(1, n)$-program guarantees that only some program was encapsulated, while the previous section guarantees that a valid point function has been encapsulated. Also, the construction shown in this section relies on a rather strong assumption, namely, indistinguishability obfuscation, that was not required in the previous section. Therefore, we present these applications separately.

Motivation. One-time (and k-time) programs allow hiding a program and limiting the number of executions to only one (or k). They can be used to protect proprietary software and to support temporary transfer of cryptographic abilities. Furthermore, k-time programs allow obfuscating learnable functions—functions that can be learned using a polynomial number of queries. By having k as a small constant, an adversary might not be able to learn the function, which makes obfuscating such a function meaningful.

Goldwasser et al. [35] showed a construction for one-time programs that combines garbled circuits with one-time memory devices. Goyal et al. [37] strengthened this result by employing stateful hardware tokens to support unconditional security against malicious recipients and senders. Bellare et al. [10] presented a compiler to compile any program into an adaptively secure one-time version. All these schemes assumed the existence of tamper-proof hardware tokens without any concrete instantiation. Dziembowski et al. [24] replaced one-time memory devices with one-time PRFs. Although they mentioned that no hardware tokens are needed, they impose physical restrictions such as inability to leak all bits of the PRF key, and limiting the number of read/write operations; it is unclear if these assumptions can be realized in practice. Goyal et al. [36] avoided the usage of hardware tokens by relying on a blockchain and witness encryption. In particular, the garbled circuit is posted on the blockchain and the input labels are encrypted using witness encryption, which can be decrypted later after mining several blocks given that the input is unique to guarantee at most one execution. Yet, requiring to store a garbled circuit on a blockchain is impractical.

We investigate the applicability of consumable tokens in constructing bounded execution programs. This is a natural direction given the bounded query capability of these tokens, and the fact that we build these tokens rather than assuming their existence. Nonetheless, the gap between an honest party and the adversary forces us to consider a slightly different notion; the $(1, n)$-program mentioned above. Thus, any application that requires the adversary to execute only on one input, like digital currencies, cannot be implemented using $(1, n)$-programs. However, applications that allow n adversarial queries, such as obfuscating learnable functions, can employ our scheme.

5.1   Definition

In this section, we define an ideal functionality for bounded-query encapsulation. This functionality, denoted as $\mathcal{F}_{BE}$, is captured in Fig. 7. The description of the interfaces, and the goal of using the flags and the counter, are very similar to what was described in the previous section for $\mathcal{F}_{BPO}$. The only difference is that instead of hiding a point function, $\mathcal{F}_{BE}$ hides an arbitrary circuit. The honest recipient can evaluate this circuit over one input, while an adversary can evaluate over up to n_q inputs. Thus, we do not repeat that here.

Beside realizing the above ideal functionality, we require any bounded-query obfuscation scheme realizing $\mathcal{F}_{BE}$ to satisfy the efficiency property defined below.

Definition 2 (Efficiency of Bounded-query Encapsulation). *There exists a polynomial p such that for all $\kappa \in \mathbb{N}$, all $C \in \mathcal{C}_\kappa$, and all inputs $x \in \{0,1\}^*$, if computing $C(x)$ takes t computational time steps, then the command (Evaluate, $\cdot$, x) takes $p(t, \kappa)$ technologically-realizable time steps.*

5.2   Construction and Security

To ease exposition, we describe our construction in an incremental way. We start with a simplified construction that handles only programs with small input space, and assumes idealized obfuscation (specifically, Virtual Black Box obfuscation [9]). Next we extend to handle programs with exponential-size domains (namely, poly-size inputs). We then replace VBB with indistinguishability obfuscation $i\mathcal{O}$. Finally, we briefly discuss how reusable garbling can reduce the use of $i\mathcal{O}$.

Functionality $\mathcal{F}_{BE}$

$\mathcal{F}_{BE}$ is parameterized by a security parameter κ, a circuit class $\mathcal{C}_\kappa$, and a positive integer n_q.

Encapsulate: Upon receiving the command (Encapsulate, P_2, C) from party P_1 (the encapsulator), where P_2 is the evaluator, and $C \in \mathcal{C}_\kappa$, do: if this is not the first activation, then do nothing. Otherwise:

- Send (Encapsulate, P_1, P_2) to the adversary.
- Upon receiving (OK) from the adversary, store the state ($C, j = 0, \mathsf{hflag}_1 = 1, \mathsf{hflag}_2 = 1$), and output (Encapsulate, P_1) to P_2.

Evaluate: Upon receiving input (Evaluate, x) from P_2, where $x \in \{0,1\}^*$: if Encapsulate was not invoked yet or $j > 0$, then end activation. Otherwise, increment j and output ($C(x)$) to P_2.

Corrupt-encapsulate: Upon receiving the command (Corrupt-encapsulate, C') from the adversary, do: If an Encapsulate output was generated, then end activation. Else, store ($C', j = 0, \mathsf{hflag}_1 = 0, \mathsf{hflag}_2 = 1$) and output (Encapsulate, P_1) to P_2.

Corrupt-evaluate: Upon receiving the command (Corrupt-evaluate, x') from the adversary, if no stored state exists, end activation. Else:

- Retrieve ($C, j, \mathsf{hflag}_1, \mathsf{hflag}_2$).
- If $\mathsf{hflag}_2 = 1$ and $j > 0$, or $j = n_q$, then end activation, else increment j, set $\mathsf{hflag}_2 = 0$, and send ($C(x')$) to the adversary.

Fig. 7. An ideal functionality for bounded-query encapsulation.

First Attempt—Using VBB. In this initial attempt, our goal is to lay down the basic idea behind our construction (rather than optimizing for efficiency). We use two tables Tab_1 and Tab_2. Tab_1 maps a program's input space $\mathcal{X}$ to the token message space $\mathcal{M}$. This table is secret and will be part of the hidden program. While Tab_2 maps $\mathcal{X}$ to the token key space $\mathcal{K}$, and it is public.

We use Prog to denote the program that encapsulates the intended circuit or simply function f, which we want to transform into a $(1, n)$-program. As shown in Fig. 8, Prog is parameterized by a table $\mathsf{Tab} : \mathcal{X} \to \mathcal{M}$, a secret key sk, and f. It has two paths: a trapdoor path and a regular one. The trapdoor path is activated when a hidden trigger in the input m is detected. In particular, this input may contain a ciphertext of the program output. On the other hand, if this ciphertext encrypts the special string $\phi^{\ell_{out}}$, where ϕ is some unique value outside the range of f and ℓ_{out} is the length of f's output, the regular path is activated. It evaluates f over $x \in \mathcal{X}$ that corresponds to the first part of m.

Protocol 3 defined in Fig. 9 shows a construction for $(1, n)$-time program for Prog using $\mathcal{F}_{CT}$. For simplicity, we assume $|\mathcal{X}| = |\mathcal{M}| = |\mathcal{K}|$, the keys in $\mathcal{K}$ are distinct (i.e., do not have any affinity relation), and that $\mathcal{F}_{CT}$ has a negligible soundness error (we discuss later how to achieve that). Bounded query is achieved via the consumable token; to evaluate over input x, the obfuscated

---

Program $\mathsf{Prog}_{\mathsf{Tab},sk,f}$

Input: m
Description:
1. Parse m as $m_0 \parallel m_1$, and set $y = \mathsf{Decrypt}(sk, m_1)$
2. Check that there exists $x \in \mathcal{X}$ such that $\mathsf{Tab}[x] = m_0$. If this is not the case then output $\perp$
3. If $y \neq \phi^{\ell_{out}}$, then output y, else, output $f(x)$

Fig. 8. The program $\mathsf{Prog}_{\mathsf{Tab},sk,f}$

program bP requires a corresponding message m that is stored inside a token. Since the table Tab_2 is secret hidden inside bP, the only way for P_2 to obtain a valid m is through the consumable token. Once the token is consumed, no more evaluations can be performed. An adversary, on the other hand, and using $\mathcal{F}_{CT}$, will be able to obtain up to n messages corresponding to n program inputs. Thus, this adversary can run bP at most n times. See the full version for an (informal) security argument of this construction.

Our Construction—Extending Program Domain and Replacing VBB with $i\mathcal{O}$. The concrete construction of a consumable token may impose limitations on the number of keys and messages that can be stored in a single token. Thus, a token may not be able to cover the full domain $\mathcal{X}$ of the program Prog. So if a single token can store a set of message $M \subset \mathcal{M}$ messages, we have $|M| < |\mathcal{X}|$. To address this issue, we modify the previous construction to use multiple tokens along with an error correcting code C. We map each $x \in \mathcal{X}$ to a codeword of length ω, and we use ω tokens to represent the program input. Each symbol in a codeword indicates which key to use with each token. By configuring C properly, this technique allows us to cover the program domain without impacting the number of program executions that (an honest or a malicious) P_2 can perform.

Concretely, we use a linear error correcting code C with minimum distance δ, meaning that the Hamming distance between any two legal codewords is at least δ. We represent each key in the set $K \subseteq \mathcal{K}$ used in creating a token, where $|K| = |M|$, as a tuple of index and value. So the set K is ordered lexicographically such that the first key in this ordered set is given index 0, and so on. Hence, a symbol in a codeword is the index of the token key to be used with the corresponding token. Based on this terminology, we work in a field of size $q = |K|$ with a code alphabet $\Sigma = \{0, \ldots, q-1\}$.

Definition 3. (Linear Codes [4]). *Let $\mathcal{F}_q$ be a finite field. A $[\omega, d, \delta]_q$ linear code is a linear subspace C with dimension d of $\mathcal{F}_q^\omega$, such that the minimum distance between any two distinct codewords $\mathbf{c}, \mathbf{c}' \in C$ is at least δ. A generating matrix G of C is a $\omega \times d$-matrix whose rows generates the subspace C.*

Protocol 3 (A $(1, n)$-time program scheme for Prog—First attempt)

For a security parameter κ, message space $\mathcal{M}$, program input space $\mathcal{X}$, and token key space $\mathcal{K}$, such that $|\mathcal{X}| = |\mathcal{M}| = |\mathcal{K}|$, let P_1 be the encapsulator, P_2 be the evaluator, $\mathcal{F}_{CT}$ as defined in Section 3 but with negligible soundness error, and Tab_1 and Tab_2 are mapping tables as defined above. Construct a tuple of algorithms $(\mathsf{Encap}, \mathsf{Eval})$ for a $(1, n)$-time program scheme as follows.

Encap: on input an arbitrary function f with input space $\mathcal{X}$ and mapping tables $\mathsf{Tab}_1 : \mathcal{X} \to \mathcal{M}$ and $\mathsf{Tab}_2 : \mathcal{X} \to \mathcal{K}$, P_1 does the following:

1. Generate a token ct, with a unique token ID tid, encoding all messages $m \in \mathcal{M}$ each using a unique key from $\mathcal{K}$. This is done by sending the command $(\mathsf{Encode}, \mathsf{tid}_i, \mathcal{K}, \mathcal{M}, |\mathcal{M}|)$ to $\mathcal{F}_{CT}$.
2. Generate a random secret key $sk \in \{0, 1\}^\kappa$.
3. Send ct, Tab_2, and $bP = \mathsf{VBB}(\mathsf{Prog}_{\mathsf{Tab}_1, sk, f})$ to P_2, where bP is an obfuscated version of the program $\mathsf{Prog}_{\mathsf{Tab}_1, sk, f}$ described in Figure 8.

Eval: on input $(1, n)\text{-Prog} = (\mathsf{ct}, \mathsf{Tab}_2, bP)$ and $x \in \mathcal{X}$, P_2 does the following:
1. Set $k' = \mathsf{Tab}_2[x]$.
2. Query token ct using k' by sending the command $(\mathsf{Decode}, \mathsf{tid}, k')$ to $\mathcal{F}_{CT}$ and obtain m.
3. Output $out = bP(m)$.

Fig. 9. A construction for a $(1, n)$-time program scheme for $\mathsf{Prog}_{\mathsf{Tab}, sk, f}$.

For any $d \leq \omega \leq q$, there exist a $[\omega, d, (\omega - d + 1)]_q$ linear code: the Reed-Solomon code [47], which we use in our construction. Let S denote the set of strings to be encoded, such that each input $x \in \mathcal{X}$ is mapped to a unique $\mathbf{s} \in S$. Using classic Reed-Solomon, to encode an input x, we first define its corresponding $\mathbf{s}$, and then we multiply $\mathbf{s}$ by the generating matrix G to generate a codeword of size ω. Using this approach, we can cover a domain size $|S| = q^{d+1}$.

Accordingly, P_1 now has to generate ω tokens, denoted as $\mathsf{ct}_0, \ldots, \mathsf{ct}_{\omega-1}$, instead of one. Each of these tokens will include all keys in K. Each key $k \in K$ will be tied to a unique message m such that m will be retrieved when a decode query using k is performed over the token. Let the messages stored in the first token be $m_{0,0}, \ldots, m_{0,q-1}$, and in the second token be $m_{1,0}, \ldots, m_{1,q-1}$, and so on. We generate these messages using a pseudorandom generator with some random seed r. In particular, we have $m_{i,j} = PRG(r)[i, j]$ for all $i \in \{0, \ldots, \omega - 1\}$ and $j \in \{0, \ldots, q - 1\}$; we picture the output of the PRG as an $\omega \times q$ matrix of substrings. Hence, $m_{0,0}$ is the substring stored at row 0 and column 0 in this matrix, which is the first substring of the PRG output, and so on.[9] Thus, to create token ct_0, P_1 will pass K and $m_{0,0}, \ldots, m_{0,q-1}$ to $\mathcal{F}_{CT}$, while for ct_1 the messages $m_{1,0}, \ldots, m_{1,q-1}$ along with K will be passed, etc.

---

[9] As we will see shortly, $m_{i,j} = PRG(r)[i, j] \parallel \phi^{n(|x| + \ell_{out})}$ assuming all $x \in \mathcal{X}$ are of the same length, but we omit that for now to ease exposure.

Program $\mathsf{Prog}_{G,n,sk,r,f}$

Input: m, x

Description:

1. Parse m as $m_0 \,\|\, \cdots \,\|\, m_{\omega-1}$, and parse each m_i as $m_i^0 \,\|\, m_i^1$
2. Use G to compute the codeword $\mathbf{c}$ that corresponds to x.
3. Check that m corresponds to a valid codeword: Let $B = PRG(r)$, if $\exists B[i, \mathbf{c}[i]] \neq m_i^0$, then output $\perp$.
4. Set $y_i = \mathsf{Decrypt}(sk, m_i^1)$ for all $i \in \{0, \ldots, \omega - 1\}$.
5. If $\exists y_i \neq \phi^{n(|x|+\ell_{out})}$, then take the first such y_i and do the following:
   - Parse y_i as $y_i^0 \,\|\, \cdots \,\|\, y_i^{n-1}$.
   - Parse each y_i^j as $y_i^{j,0} \,\|\, y_i^{j,1}$ (for $j \in \{0, \ldots, n-1\}$).
   - Output $y_i^{j,1}$ for which $y_i^{j,0} = x$.

   Else, output $f(x)$.

Fig. 10. The program $\mathsf{Prog}_{G,n,sk,r,f}$ with linear error correcting codes.

So to execute Prog over input x, P_2 first maps x to $\mathbf{s}$, and then generates the codeword $\mathbf{c}$ for $\mathbf{s}$. After that, she uses the keys with the indices included in $\mathbf{c}$ to query the corresponding tokens. For example, if $\mathbf{c} = \{5, 9, 15, \ldots\}$, then k_5 is used to query the first token to retrieve $m_0 = m_{0,5}$, k_9 is used to query the second token and retrieve $m_1 = m_{1,9}$, etc. These messages $m = m_0 \,\|\, \cdots \,\|\, m_{\omega-1}$ will be used as input to Prog to obtain the output $f(x)$. This in turn means that Prog must check that m corresponds to a valid codeword in C. We also modify the trapdoor path to allow including multiple outputs instead of one. This is needed to allow the simulator to simulate for an adversary who queries the tokens out of order. It may happen that the last query is common for two (or more) codewords (in other words, just when this query takes place, the simulator will tell that the adversary got valid codewords). Having multiple outputs (each concatenated with the x value that leads to this output) permits the simulator to embed the valid outputs for the inputs corresponding to these valid codewords.

The modified version of Prog can be found in Fig. 10 (with both the linear code and $i\mathcal{O}$ instead of VBB). We also modify the description of Prog (see Fig. 11). The parameters of the underlying error correcting code are configured in a way that produces a code C such that $|C| = |\mathcal{X}|$. As shown, the output of Encap now contains ω tokens beside the obfuscation of Prog. Eval follows the description above.

On Preserving the Number of Program Executions $(1, n)$. An honest party can query any token once. Thus, overall, she will be able to retrieve only one codeword. An adversary, on the other hand, can query each token up to n times. We want to guarantee that the $n\omega$ messages she obtains does not allow constructing more than n valid codewords. In other words, we want to ensure that to retrieve $n + 1$ codewords, at least $n\omega + 1$ distinct queries are needed.

Protocol 4 (A $(1, n)$-time program scheme for Prog)

For a security parameter κ, message space $\mathcal{M}$, input space $\mathcal{X}$, and token key space $\mathcal{K}$, let P_1 be the encapsulator, P_2 be the evaluator, $\mathcal{F}_{CT}$ be as defined in Section 3 but with negligible soundness error, $[\omega, d, \delta]_q$ be a linear code C with a generating matrix G such that $|C| = |\mathcal{X}|$, and $PRG : \{0,1\}^\kappa \to \{0,1\}^{\omega q|m|}$ be a psuedorandom generator, where $m \in \mathcal{M}$ and $|K| = q$ for $K \subseteq \mathcal{K}$. Construct a tuple of algorithms (Encap, Eval) for a $(1, n)$-time program scheme as follows.

Encap: On input an arbitrary function f with input space $\mathcal{X}$, and a linear code $[\omega, d, \delta]_q$ with generating matrix G, P_1 does the following:

1. Generate secret key $sk \in \{0,1\}^\kappa$ and a string $r \in \{0,1\}^\kappa$ both at random.
2. Generate messages $m_{i,j} = PRG(r)[i,j] \parallel \phi^{n(|x|+\ell_{out})}$ for all $i \in \{0, \ldots, \omega - 1\}$ and $j \in \{0, \ldots, q - 1\}$.
3. Generate at random token key subspace $K \subseteq \mathcal{K}$ such that $|K| = q$.
4. For $i \in \{0, \ldots, \omega-1\}$, generate a token ct_i, with a unique token ID tid_i, encoding messages $m_{i,0}, \ldots, m_{i,q-1}$ using $k_0 \ldots k_{q-1} \in K$. This is done by sending the command $(\mathsf{Encode}, tid_i, \{k_0 \ldots k_{q-1}\}, \{m_{i,0}, \ldots, m_{i,q-1}\}, q)$ to $\mathcal{F}_{CT}$.
5. Send $ct = \{ct_0, \ldots, ct_{\omega-1}\}$ and $bP = i\mathcal{O}(\mathsf{Prog}_{G,n,sk,r,f})$ to P_2, where $\mathsf{Prog}_{G,n,sk,r,f}$ is defined in Figure 10.

Eval: On input a $(1, n)\text{-}\mathsf{Prog} = (ct, bP)$ and $x \in \mathcal{X}$, P_2 does the following:

1. Map x to a codeword $\mathbf{c}$.
2. For each $i \in \{0, \ldots, \omega-1\}$, query token ct_i using $k'_{\mathbf{c}[i]}$ by sending the command $(\mathsf{Decode}, tid_i, k'_{\mathbf{c}[i]})$ to $\mathcal{F}_{CT}$ and get m_i in return.
3. Output $\mathsf{out} = bP(m_0 \parallel \cdots \parallel m_{\omega-1}, x)$.

Fig. 11. A construction for a $(1, n)$-time program scheme for $\mathsf{Prog}_{G,n,sk,r,f}$.

To formalize this notion, we define what we call a *cover*; a cover of two, or more, codewords is the set of all distinct queries needed to retrieve these codewords. For example, codewords $\mathbf{c}_1 = \{5, 4, 13, 17\}$ and $\mathbf{c}_2 = \{5, 9, 12, 18\}$ have a cover of $\{5, 4, 9, 12, 13, 17, 18\}$,[10] and so P_2 needs 7 queries to obtain the messages that correspond to these codewords from the tokens.

Definition 4. *A code $[\omega, d, \delta]_q$ is n-robust if for any $n + 1$ distinct codewords the size of the cover is at least $n\omega + 1$.*

So the robustness factor is the number of codewords an adversary can obtain. To preserve this number to be the original n that an adversary can obtain with one token, we need to configure the parameters of C to satisfy the lower bound of the cover size defined above. We show that for Reed-Solomon codes as follows (the proof can be found in the full version).

---

[10] Note that if 5 was not on the same position for both codewords then it would have been considered distinct. Different positions means that k_5 will be used with different tokens, which leads to different messages $m_{i,j}$.

Lemma 1. *For a Reed-Solomon code $[\omega, d, \delta]_q$ to be n-robust (cf. Definition 4), we must have $\omega - n(d-1) - 1 \geq 0$.*

Accordingly, we have the following theorem (the proof can be found in the full version.)

Theorem 2. *Assuming sup-exponentially secure $i\mathcal{O}$ and one-way functions, the $i\mathcal{O}$-based construction described in Fig. 11 is a $(1, n)$-time program in the $\mathcal{F}_{CT}$-hybrid model.*

Remark 3. It is an intriguing question whether we can obtain $(1, n)$-time programs without $i\mathcal{O}$. Since an adversary can evaluate over multiple inputs, we cannot use garbled circuits—evaluating a circuit over more than one input compromises security. A potential direction is to employ reusable garbling [34], and use our construction to build a $(1, n)$-time program for the circuit that encodes the inputs (which requires a secret key from the grabler). Thus, $i\mathcal{O}$ is only needed for the encoding circuit, and our consumable token limits the number of times this circuit can be evaluated, rather than obfuscating the full program as above.

Acknowledgements. This material is based upon work supported by DARPA under contracts #HR001120C00, #HR00112020023, and #D17AP00027. Any opinions, findings and conclusions or recommendations expressed in this material are those of the author(s) and do not necessarily reflect the views of the United States Government or DARPA. This research was supported in part by a grant from the Columbia-IBM center for Blockchain and Data Transparency, by JPMorgan Chase & Co., and by LexisNexis Risk Solutions. Any views or opinions expressed herein are solely those of the authors listed.

References

1. Aaronson, S.: Quantum copy-protection and quantum money. In: 2009 24th Annual IEEE Conference on Computational Complexity, pp. 229–242. IEEE (2009)
2. Adleman, L.M.: Molecular computation of solutions to combinatorial problems. Science **266**(5187), 1021–1024 (1994)
3. Adleman, L.M.: Computing with DNA. Sci. Am. **279**(2), 54–61 (1998)
4. Almashaqbeh, G., et al.: Gage mpc: bypassing residual function leakage for non-interactive mpc. PETS **2021**(4), 528–548 (2021)
5. Ananth, P., La Placa, R.L.: Secure software leasing. In: Canteaut, A., Standaert, F.-X. (eds.) EUROCRYPT 2021. LNCS, vol. 12697, pp. 501–530. Springer, Cham (2021). https://doi.org/10.1007/978-3-030-77886-6_17
6. Armknecht, F., Maes, R., Sadeghi, AR., Sunar, B., Tuyls, P.: Memory leakage-resilient encryption based on physically unclonable functions. In: Sadeghi, AR., Naccache, D. (eds.) Towards Hardware-Intrinsic Security. Information Security and Cryptography, pp. 135–164. Springer, Berlin, Heidelberg (2010). https://doi.org/10.1007/978-3-642-14452-3_6
7. Badrinarayanan, S., Jain, A., Ostrovsky, R., Visconti, I.: UC-secure multiparty computation from one-way functions using stateless tokens. In: Galbraith, S.D., Moriai, S. (eds.) ASIACRYPT 2019. LNCS, vol. 11922, pp. 577–605. Springer, Cham (2019). https://doi.org/10.1007/978-3-030-34621-8_21

8. Baldwin, M.A.: Protein identification by mass spectrometry issues to be considered. Mol. Cell. Proteom. **3**(1), 1–9 (2004)
9. Barak, B., et al.: On the (Im)possibility of obfuscating programs. In: Kilian, J. (ed.) CRYPTO 2001. LNCS, vol. 2139, pp. 1–18. Springer, Heidelberg (2001). https://doi.org/10.1007/3-540-44647-8_1
10. Bellare, M., Hoang, V.T., Rogaway, P.: Adaptively secure garbling with applications to one-time programs and secure outsourcing. In: Wang, X., Sako, K. (eds.) ASIACRYPT 2012. LNCS, vol. 7658, pp. 134–153. Springer, Heidelberg (2012). https://doi.org/10.1007/978-3-642-34961-4_10
11. Bitansky, N., Canetti, R.: On strong simulation and composable point obfuscation. In: Rabin, T. (ed.) CRYPTO 2010. LNCS, vol. 6223, pp. 520–537. Springer, Heidelberg (2010). https://doi.org/10.1007/978-3-642-14623-7_28
12. Blawat, M., et al.: Forward error correction for DNA data storage. Procedia Comput. Sci. **80**, 1011–1022 (2016)
13. Broadbent, A., Gutoski, G., Stebila, D.: Quantum one-time programs. In: Canetti, R., Garay, J.A. (eds.) CRYPTO 2013. LNCS, vol. 8043, pp. 344–360. Springer, Heidelberg (2013). https://doi.org/10.1007/978-3-642-40084-1_20
14. Brzuska, C., Fischlin, M., Schröder, H., Katzenbeisser, S.: Physically uncloneable functions in the universal composition framework. In: Rogaway, P. (ed.) CRYPTO 2011. LNCS, vol. 6841, pp. 51–70. Springer, Heidelberg (2011). https://doi.org/10.1007/978-3-642-22792-9_4
15. Canetti, R.: Universally composable security. J. ACM **67**(5), 28:1–28:94 (2020)
16. Canetti, R., Dakdouk, R.R.: Obfuscating point functions with multibit output. In: Smart, N. (ed.) EUROCRYPT 2008. LNCS, vol. 4965, pp. 489–508. Springer, Heidelberg (2008). https://doi.org/10.1007/978-3-540-78967-3_28
17. Canetti, R., Tauman Kalai, Y., Varia, M., Wichs, D.: On symmetric encryption and point obfuscation. In: Micciancio, D. (ed.) TCC 2010. LNCS, vol. 5978, pp. 52–71. Springer, Heidelberg (2010). https://doi.org/10.1007/978-3-642-11799-2_4
18. Chandran, N., Goyal, V., Sahai, A.: New constructions for UC secure computation using tamper-proof hardware. In: Smart, N. (ed.) EUROCRYPT 2008. LNCS, vol. 4965, pp. 545–562. Springer, Heidelberg (2008). https://doi.org/10.1007/978-3-540-78967-3_31
19. Church, G.M., Gao, Y., Kosuri, S.: Next-generation digital information storage in DNA. Science, p. 1226355 (2012)
20. Crick, F.H.: On protein synthesis. In: Symposia of the Society for Experimental Biology, vol. 12, p. 8 (1958)
21. Damgård, I., Kilian, J., Salvail, L.: On the (im)possibility of basing oblivious transfer and bit commitment on weakened security assumptions. In: Stern, J. (ed.) EUROCRYPT 1999. LNCS, vol. 1592, pp. 56–73. Springer, Heidelberg (1999). https://doi.org/10.1007/3-540-48910-X_5
22. Damgård, I., Scafuro, A.: Unconditionally secure and universally composable commitments from physical assumptions. In: Sako, K., Sarkar, P. (eds.) ASIACRYPT 2013. LNCS, vol. 8270, pp. 100–119. Springer, Heidelberg (2013). https://doi.org/10.1007/978-3-642-42045-0_6
23. Döttling, N., Kraschewski, D., Müller-Quade, J.: Unconditional and composable security using a single stateful tamper-proof hardware token. In: Ishai, Y. (ed.) TCC 2011. LNCS, vol. 6597, pp. 164–181. Springer, Heidelberg (2011). https://doi.org/10.1007/978-3-642-19571-6_11
24. Dziembowski, S., Kazana, T., Wichs, D.: One-time computable self-erasing functions. In: Ishai, Y. (ed.) TCC 2011. LNCS, vol. 6597, pp. 125–143. Springer, Heidelberg (2011). https://doi.org/10.1007/978-3-642-19571-6_9

25. Eichhorn, I., Koeberl, P., van der Leest, V.: Logically reconfigurable PUFs: memory-based secure key storage. In: Proceedings of the Sixth ACM Workshop on Scalable Trusted Computing, pp. 59–64 (2011)

26. El Orche, F.E., et al.: Taphonomical security:(dna) information with foreseeable lifespan. Cryptology ePrint Archive (2021)

27. Erlich, Y., Zielinski, D.: DNA fountain enables a robust and efficient storage architecture. Science **355**(6328), 950–954 (2017)

28. Fisch, B., Freund, D., Naor, M.: Physical zero-knowledge proofs of physical properties. In: Garay, J.A., Gennaro, R. (eds.) CRYPTO 2014. LNCS, vol. 8617, pp. 313–336. Springer, Heidelberg (2014). https://doi.org/10.1007/978-3-662-44381-1_18

29. Fisch, B.A., Freund, D., Naor, M.: Secure physical computation using disposable circuits. In: Dodis, Y., Nielsen, J.B. (eds.) TCC 2015. LNCS, vol. 9014, pp. 182–198. Springer, Heidelberg (2015). https://doi.org/10.1007/978-3-662-46494-6_9

30. Garg, S., Gentry, C., Halevi, S., Raykova, M.: Two-round secure MPC from indistinguishability obfuscation. In: Lindell, Y. (ed.) TCC 2014. LNCS, vol. 8349, pp. 74–94. Springer, Heidelberg (2014). https://doi.org/10.1007/978-3-642-54242-8_4

31. Garg, S., Gentry, C., Halevi, S., Raykova, M., Sahai, A., Waters, B.: Candidate indistinguishability obfuscation and functional encryption for all circuits. In: FOCS, pp. 40–49. IEEE (2013)

32. Glaser, A., Barak, B., Goldston, R.J.: A zero-knowledge protocol for nuclear warhead verification. Nature **510**(7506), 497–502 (2014)

33. Glish, G.L., Vachet, R.W.: The basics of mass spectrometry in the twenty-first century. Nat. Rev. Drug Discov. **2**(2), 140–150 (2003)

34. Goldwasser, S., Kalai, Y., Popa, R.A., Vaikuntanathan, V., Zeldovich, N.: Reusable garbled circuits and succinct functional encryption. In: ACM STOC (2013)

35. Goldwasser, S., Kalai, Y.T., Rothblum, G.N.: One-time programs. In: Wagner, D. (ed.) CRYPTO 2008. LNCS, vol. 5157, pp. 39–56. Springer, Heidelberg (2008). https://doi.org/10.1007/978-3-540-85174-5_3

36. Goyal, R., Goyal, V.: Overcoming cryptographic impossibility results using blockchains. In: Kalai, Y., Reyzin, L. (eds.) TCC 2017. LNCS, vol. 10677, pp. 529–561. Springer, Cham (2017). https://doi.org/10.1007/978-3-319-70500-2_18

37. Goyal, V., Ishai, Y., Sahai, A., Venkatesan, R., Wadia, A.: Founding cryptography on tamper-proof hardware tokens. In: Micciancio, D. (ed.) TCC 2010. LNCS, vol. 5978, pp. 308–326. Springer, Heidelberg (2010). https://doi.org/10.1007/978-3-642-11799-2_19

38. Grass, R.N., Heckel, R., Puddu, M., Paunescu, D., Stark, W.J.: Robust chemical preservation of digital information on DNA in silica with error-correcting codes. Angew. Chem. Int. Ed. **54**(8), 2552–2555 (2015)

39. Hazay, C., Lindell, Y.: Constructions of truly practical secure protocols using standardsmartcards. In: ACM CCS, pp. 491–500 (2008)

40. Hazay, C., Polychroniadou, A., Venkitasubramaniam, M.: Composable security in the tamper-proof hardware model under minimal complexity. In: Hirt, M., Smith, A. (eds.) TCC 2016. LNCS, vol. 9985, pp. 367–399. Springer, Heidelberg (2016). https://doi.org/10.1007/978-3-662-53641-4_15

41. Hazay, C., Polychroniadou, A., Venkitasubramaniam, M.: Constant round adaptively secure protocols in the tamper-proof hardware model. In: Fehr, S. (ed.) PKC 2017. LNCS, vol. 10175, pp. 428–460. Springer, Heidelberg (2017). https://doi.org/10.1007/978-3-662-54388-7_15

42. Jain, A., Lin, H., Sahai, A.: Indistinguishability obfuscation from well-founded assumptions. In: ACM STOC, pp. 60–73. ACM (2021)

43. Jin, C., Xu, X., Burleson, W.P., Rührmair, U., van Dijk, M.: Playpuf: programmable logically erasable PUFs for forward and backward secure key management. IACR Cryptol. ePrint Arch. **2015**, 1052 (2015)
44. Katz, J.: Universally composable multi-party computation using tamper-proof hardware. In: Naor, M. (ed.) EUROCRYPT 2007. LNCS, vol. 4515, pp. 115–128. Springer, Heidelberg (2007). https://doi.org/10.1007/978-3-540-72540-4_7
45. Lindell, Y.: Anonymous authentication. J. Priv. Confid. **2**(2) (2011)
46. Lynn, B., Prabhakaran, M., Sahai, A.: Positive results and techniques for obfuscation. In: Cachin, C., Camenisch, J.L. (eds.) EUROCRYPT 2004. LNCS, vol. 3027, pp. 20–39. Springer, Heidelberg (2004). https://doi.org/10.1007/978-3-540-24676-3_2
47. MacWilliams, F.J., Sloane, N.J.A.: The theory of error correcting codes, vol. 16. Elsevier (1977)
48. Moran, T., Naor, M.: Basing cryptographic protocols on tamper-evident seals. TCC **411**(10), 1283–1310 (2010)
49. Naccache, D., Shamir, A., Stern, J.P.: How to copyright a function? In: Imai, H., Zheng, Y. (eds.) PKC 1999. LNCS, vol. 1560, pp. 188–196. Springer, Heidelberg (1999). https://doi.org/10.1007/3-540-49162-7_14
50. Ostrovsky, R., Scafuro, A., Visconti, I., Wadia, A.: Universally composable secure computation with (malicious) physically uncloneable functions. In: Johansson, T., Nguyen, P.Q. (eds.) EUROCRYPT 2013. LNCS, vol. 7881, pp. 702–718. Springer, Heidelberg (2013). https://doi.org/10.1007/978-3-642-38348-9_41
51. Pappu, R., Recht, B., Taylor, J., Gershenfeld, N.: Physical one-way functions. Science **297**(5589), 2026–2030 (2002)
52. Roehsner, M.C., Kettlewell, J.A., Batalhão, T.B., Fitzsimons, J.F., Walther, P.: Quantum advantage for probabilistic one-time programs. Nat. Commun. **9**(1), 1–8 (2018)
53. Rührmair, U.: Oblivious transfer based on physical unclonable functions. In: International Conference on Trust and Trustworthy Computing, pp. 430–440 (2010)
54. Wee, H.: On obfuscating point functions. In: ACM STOC, pp. 523–532 (2005)
55. Yao, A.C.C.: How to generate and exchange secrets. In: FOCS, pp. 162–167 (1986)
56. Zhang, Y., Fu, L.H.B.: Research on DNA cryptography. In: Applied Cryptography and Network Security, vol. 357, pp. 10–5772. InTech, Rijeka, Croatia (2012)

Distributed (Correlation) Samplers: How to Remove a Trusted Dealer in One Round

Damiano Abram$^{(\boxtimes)}$, Peter Scholl, and Sophia Yakoubov

Aarhus University, Aarhus, Denmark
damiano.abram@cs.au.dk

Abstract. Structured random strings (SRSs) and correlated randomness are important for many cryptographic protocols. In settings where interaction is expensive, it is desirable to obtain such randomness in as few rounds of communication as possible; ideally, simply by exchanging one reusable round of messages which can be considered public keys.

In this paper, we describe how to generate any SRS or correlated randomness in such a single round of communication, using, among other things, indistinguishability obfuscation. We introduce what we call a *distributed sampler*, which enables n parties to sample a single public value (SRS) from any distribution. We construct a semi-malicious distributed sampler in the plain model, and use it to build a semi-malicious *public-key PCF* (Boyle *et al.*, FOCS 2020) in the plain model. A public-key PCF can be thought of as a distributed *correlation* sampler; instead of producing a public SRS, it gives each party a private random value (where the values satisfy some correlation).

We introduce a general technique called an *anti-rusher* which compiles any one-round protocol with semi-malicious security without inputs to a similar one-round protocol with active security by making use of a programmable random oracle. This gets us actively secure distributed samplers and public-key PCFs in the random oracle model.

Finally, we explore some tradeoffs. Our first PCF construction is limited to *reverse-sampleable* correlations (where the random outputs of honest parties must be simulatable given the random outputs of corrupt parties); we additionally show a different construction without this limitation, but which does not allow parties to hold secret parameters of the correlation. We also describe how to avoid the use of a random oracle at the cost of relying on sub-exponentially secure indistinguishability obfuscation.

1   Introduction

Randomness is crucial for many cryptographic protocols. Participants can generate some randomness locally (e.g. by flipping coins), but the generation of other

Supported by the Independent Research Fund Denmark (DFF) under project number 0165-00107B (C3PO), the European Research Council (ERC) under the European Unions's Horizon 2020 research and innovation programme under grant agreement No 803096 (SPEC), and a starting grant from Aarhus University Research Foundation.

O. Dunkelman and S. Dziembowski (Eds.): EUROCRYPT 2022, LNCS 13275, pp. 790–820, 2022.
https://doi.org/10.1007/978-3-031-06944-4_27

forms of randomness is more involved. For instance, a *uniform reference string* (URS) must be produced in such a way that a coalition of corrupt protocol participants—controlled by the adversary—cannot bias it too much. Even more complex is the generation of a *structured* reference string (SRS, such as an RSA modulus), which can depend on secrets (such as the modulus factorization) that should not be known to anyone.

In contrast to common reference strings, which are public, some protocols demand *correlated randomness*, where each participant holds a secret random value, but because the values must satisfy some relationship, they cannot be generated locally by the participants. An example of correlated randomness is random oblivious transfer, where one participant has a list of random strings, and another has one of those strings as well as its index in the list. Such correlated randomness often allows cryptographic protocols to run with a more efficient online phase.

Typically, in order to set up an SRS or correlated randomness without making additional trust assumptions, the parties must run a secure multi-party computation protocol, which takes several rounds of interaction. In this paper, we explore techniques that let parties sample *any* common reference string or correlation in just *one round* of interaction.

1.1 Related Work

There are a number of lines of work that can be used to generate randomness in different ways.

Universal Samplers. A universal sampler [HJK+16] is a kind of SRS which can be used to obliviously sample from any distribution that has an efficient sampling algorithm. That is, after a one-time trusted setup to generate the universal sampler, it can be used to generate arbitrary other SRSs. Hofheinz *et al.* [HJK+16] show how to build universal samplers from indistinguishability obfuscation and a random oracle, while allowing an unbounded number of adaptive queries. They also show how to build weaker forms of universal sampler in the standard model, from single-key functional encryption [LZ17]. A universal sampler is a very powerful tool, but in many cases impractical, due to the need for a trusted setup.

Non-interactive Multiparty Computation (NIMPC). Non-interactive multiparty computation (NIMPC, [BGI+14a]) is a kind of one-round protocol that allows n parties to compute any function of their secret inputs in just one round of communication. However, NIMPC requires that the parties know one another's public keys before that one round, so there is another implicit round of communication.[1] NIMPC for general functions can be constructed based on subexponentially-secure indistinguishability obfuscation [HIJ+17].

---

[1] This requirement is inherent; otherwise, an adversary would be able to take the message an honest party sent, and recompute the function with that party's input while varying the other inputs. NIMPC does allow similar recomputation attacks, but only with *all* honest party inputs fixed, which a PKI can be used to enforce.

Spooky Encryption. Spooky encryption [DHRW16] is a kind of encryption which enables parties to learn joint functions of ciphertexts encrypted under independent public keys (given one of the corresponding secret keys). In order for semantic security to hold, what party i learns using her secret key should reveal nothing about the value encrypted to party j's public key; so, spooky encryption only supports the evaluation of *non-signaling* functions. An example of a non-signaling function is any function where the parties' outputs are an additive secret sharing. Dodis *et al.* [DHRW16] show how to build spooky encryption for any such additive function from the LWE assumption with a URS (this also implies multi-party homomorphic secret sharing for general functions). In the two-party setting, they also show how to build spooky encryption for a larger class of non-signaling functions from (among other things) sub-exponentially hard indistinguishability obfuscation.

Pseudorandom Correlation Generators and Functions (PCGs and PCFs). Pseudorandom correlation generators [BCG+19a, BCG+19b, BCG+20b] and functions [BCG+20a, OSY21] let parties take a small amount of specially correlated randomness (called the *seed* randomness) and expand it non-interactively, obtaining a large sample from a target correlation. Pseudorandom correlation generators (PCGs) support only a fixed, polynomial expansion; pseudorandom correlation functions (PCFs) allow the parties to produce exponentially many instances of the correlation (via evaluation of the function on any of exponentially many inputs).

PCGs and PCFs can be built for any *additively secret shared* correlation (where the parties obtain additive shares of a sample from some distribution) using LWE-based spooky encryption mentioned above. Similarly, with two parties, we can build PCGs and PCFs for more general *reverse-samplable* correlations by relying on spooky encryption from subexponentially secure iO. PCGs and PCFs with better concrete efficiency can be obtained under different flavours of the LPN assumption, for simpler correlations such as vector oblivious linear evaluation [BCGI18], oblivious transfer [BCG+19b] and others [BCG+20b, BCG+20a].

Of course, in order to use PCGs or PCFs, the parties must somehow get the correlated seed randomness. *Public-key* PCGs and PCFs allow the parties to instead derive outputs using their independently generated public keys, which can be published in a single round of communication. The above, spooky encryption-based PCGs and PCFs are public-key, while the LPN-based ones are not. Public-key PCFs for OT and vector-OLE were recently built based on DCR and QR [OSY21]; however, these require a structured reference string consisting of a public RSA modulus with hidden factorization.

1.2   Our Contributions

In this paper, we leverage indistinguishability obfuscation to build public-key PCFs for *any* correlation. On the way to realizing this, we define several other primitives, described in Fig. 1. One of these primitives is a *distributed sampler,* which is a weaker form of public-key PCF which only allows the sampling of public randomness. (A public-key PCF can be thought of as a distributed *correlation* sampler.) Our constructions, and the assumptions they use, are mapped out in Fig. 2. We pay particular attention to avoiding the use of sub-exponentially secure primitives where possible (which rules out strong tools such as probabilistic iO [CLTV15]).

Primitive	Distribution	Output
Distributed Sampler (DS, Def. 3.1)	fixed	public
Reusable Distributed Universal Sampler ([ASY22])	any	public
Public-key PCF (pk-PCF, [OSY21])	fixed, reverse-sampleable	private
Ideal pk-PCF ([ASY22])	any	private

Fig. 1. In this table we describe one-round n-party primitives that can be used for sampling randomness. They differ in terms of whether a given execution enables sampling from *any* distribution (or just a fixed one), and in terms of whether they only output public randomness (in the form of a URS or SRS) or also return private correlated randomness to the parties.

We begin by exploring constructions secure against semi-malicious adversaries, where corrupt parties are assumed to follow the protocol other than in their choice of random coins. We build a semi-malicious distributed sampler, and use it to build a semi-malicious public-key PCF. We then compile those protocols to be secure against active adversaries. This leads to a public-key PCF that requires a random oracle, and supports the broad class of *reverse-sampleable* correlations (where, given only corrupt parties' values in a given sample, honest parties' values can be simulated in such a way that they are indistinguishable from the ones in the original sample).

We also show two other routes to public-key PCFs with active security. One of these avoids the use of a random oracle, but requires sub-exponentially secure building blocks. The other requires a random oracle, but can support general correlations, not just reverse-sampleable ones. (The downside is that it does not support correlations *with master secrets*, which allow parties to have secret input parameters to the correlation.) We defer the discussion of this last construction to the full version of this paper [ASY22, Section 7] due to space constraints.

It may seem strange to want to avoid sub-exponentially secure primitives,[2] when many candidates for indistinguishability obfuscation itself are based on subexponential assumptions [JLS21]. However, despite informal arguments [LZ17], this is not known to be inherent: earlier iO candidates are based on polynomial hardness [GGH+13] (albeit for an exponential family of assumptions), and in future we may obtain iO from a single, polynomial hardness assumption. In general, it is always preferable to require a weaker form of security from a primitive, and this also leads to better parameters in practice. The

---

[2] By sub-exponential security, we mean that no PPT adversary cannot break the security of that primitive with probability better than $2^{-\lambda^c}$ for a constant c.

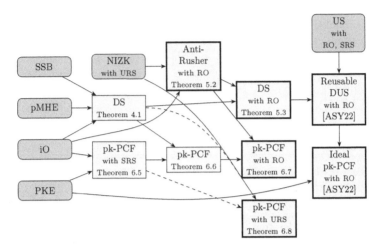

Fig. 2. In this table we describe the constructions in this paper. In pink are assumptions: they include somewhere statistically binding hash functions (SSB), multiparty homomorphic encryption with private evaluation (pMHE [AJJM20], a weaker form of multi-key FHE), indistinguishability obfuscation (iO), non-interactive zero knowledge proofs (NIZK), and universal samplers (US). In blue are constructions of distributed samplers (DS, Definition 3.1), reusable distributed universal samplers (reusable DUS, Definition 7.6) and public-key pseudorandom correlation functions (pk-PCFs, [OSY21]). Constructions with bold outlines are secure against active adversaries; the rest are secure against semi-malicious adversaries. In magenta are necessary setup assumptions. (Note that the availability of a random oracle (RO) immediately implies the additional availability of a URS.) Dashed lines denote the use of sub-exponentially secure tools. (Color figure online)

problem of removing sub-exponential assumptions from iO, or applications of iO, has been studied previously in various settings [GPSZ17, LZ17].

1.3   Technical Overview

Distributed Samplers. We start by introducing a new tool called a *distributed sampler* (DS, Sect. 3). A distributed sampler allows n parties to sample a single, public output from an efficiently sampleable distribution $\mathcal{D}$ with just one round of communication (which is modelled by the exchange of public keys).

Semi-malicious Distributed Samplers. We use multiparty homomorphic encryption with private evaluation (pMHE [AJJM20], a weaker, setup-free version of multi-key FHE) and indistinguishability obfuscation to build semi-malicious distributed samplers in the plain model (Sect. 4). In our distributed sampler construction, all parties can compute an encryption of the sample from everyones' public keys (using, among other things, the homomorphic properties of the encryption scheme), and then use an obfuscated program in party i's public key to get party i's partial decryption of the sample. The partial decryptions can then be combined to recover the sample itself. The tricky thing is that, in the proof, we must ensure that we can replace the real sample with an ideal sample. To do this, we must remove all information about the real sample from the public keys. However, pMHE secret keys are not *puncturable*; that is, there is no way to ensure that they do not reveal any information about the contents of one ciphertext, while correctly decrypting all others. We could, in different hybrids, hardcode the correct partial decryption for each of the exponentially many possible ciphertexts, but this would blow up the size of the obfuscated program. Therefore, instead of directly including a pMHE ciphertext in each party's DS public key, we have each party obfuscate an additional program which produces a new pMHE ciphertext each time it is used. This way, when we need to remove all information about a given sample, we can remove the entire corresponding secret key (via the appropriate use of puncturable PRFs and hardcoded values). This technique may be useful for other primitives, such as NIMPC [BGI+14a] and probabilistic iO [CLTV15], to avoid the use of an exponential number of hybrids.

Achieving Active Security with a Random Oracle. Upgrading to active security is challenging because we need to protect against two types of attacks: malformed messages, and rushing adversaries, who wait for honest parties' messages before sending their own. We protect against the former using non-interactive zero knowledge proofs. (This requires a URS which, though it is a form of setup, is much weaker than an SRS.) We protect against the latter via a generic transformation that we call an *anti-rusher* (Sect. 5.1). To use our anti-rusher, each party includes in her public key an obfuscated program which takes as input a hash (i.e. a random oracle output) of all parties' public keys. It then samples *new* (DS) public keys, using this hash as a PRF nonce. This ensures that even an adversary who selects her public keys after seeing the honest party public keys cannot influence the selected sample other than by re-sampling polynomially many times.

Public-key PCFs. We start by building a public-key PCF that requires an SRS (Sect. 6.3). The SRS consists of an obfuscated program that, given a nonce and n parties' public encryption keys, uses a PRF to generate correlated randomness, and encrypts each party's random output to its public key. We can then eliminate the need for a pre-distributed SRS by instead using a distributed sampler to sample it (Sect. 6.4).

Public-key PCFs without Random Oracles. The proofs of security for the constructions sketched above only require polynomially many hybrids, roughly speaking because the random oracle allows the simulator to predict and control the inputs to the obfuscated programs. We can avoid the use of the random oracle, at the cost of going through exponentially many hybrids in the proof of security, and thus requiring sub-exponentially secure primitives.

Public-key PCFs for any Correlation with a Random Oracle. Boyle *et al.* [BCG+19b] prove that a public-key PCF in the plain model that can handle *any* correlation (not just reverse-sampleable ones) must have keys at least as large as all the correlated randomness it yields. We observe that we can use a random oracle to sidestep this lower bound by deriving additional randomness from the oracle.

As a stepping stone, we introduce a different flavour of the distributed sampler, which we call the *reusable distributed universal sampler* (reusable DUS). It is *reusable* because it can be queried multiple times (without the need for additional communication), and it is *universal* because each query can produce a sample from a different distribution (specified by the querier). We build a reusable distributed universal sampler from a universal sampler, a random oracle and a distributed sampler (by using the distributed sampler to produce the universal sampler). Our last public-key PCF ([ASY22, Section 7]) then uses the reusable distributed universal sampler to sample from a distribution that first picks the correlated randomness and then encrypts each party's share under her public key.

2   Preliminaries

Notation. We denote the security parameter by λ and the set $\{1, 2, \ldots, m\}$ by $[m]$. Our constructions are designed for an ordered group of n parties $P_1, P_2, \ldots, P_n$. We will denote the set of (indexes of) corrupted parties by C, whereas its complementary, the set of honest players, is H.

We indicate the probability of an event E by $\mathbb{P}[E]$. We use the term *noticeable* to refer to a non-negligible quantity. A probability p is instead *overwhelming* if $1 - p$ is negligible. We say that a cryptographic primitive is sub-exponentially secure, if the advantage of the adversary is bounded by $2^{-\lambda^c}$ for some constant $c > 0$. When the advantage is negligible, we say that it is polynomially secure.

We use the simple arrow $\leftarrow$ to assign the output of a deterministic algorithm $\mathsf{Alg}(x)$ or a specific value a to a variable y, i.e. $y \leftarrow \mathsf{Alg}(x)$ or $y \leftarrow a$. If Alg is instead probabilistic, we write $y \xleftarrow{\$} \mathsf{Alg}(x)$ and we assume that the random tape is sampled uniformly. If the latter is set to a particular value r, we write however $y \leftarrow \mathsf{Alg}(x; r)$. We use $\xleftarrow{\$}$ also if we sample the value of y uniformly over a set X, i.e. $y \xleftarrow{\$} X$. Finally, we refer to algorithms having no input as distributions. The latter are in most cases parametrised by λ. The terms *circuit* and *program* are used interchangeably.

Used Primitives. Our work relies on the following primitives.

- *Indistinguishability Obfuscation (iO).* [BGI+01] An obfuscator is an algorithm that rearranges a circuit Cr into another program Cr' with the same input-output behaviour, but being so different that it is impossible to tell what operations Cr initially performed. Specifically, security states that it is impossible to distinguish between the obfuscation of equivalent circuits. The first indistinguishability obfuscator was designed by Garg *et al.* in [GGH+13]. Formal definitions of iO are given in [ASY22, Section 2.1].

- *Puncturable PRFs.*[KPTZ13,BW13,BGI14b] A puncturable PRF is a PRF F in which it is possible to puncture the keys in any position x. In other words, it means that from a key K, it is possible to derive another key $\hat{K}$ containing no information about $F_K(x)$ but still permitting to compute $F_K(y)$ for every $y \neq x$. It is easy to build puncturable PRF from the GGM construction [GGM86]. Formal definitions are given in [ASY22, Section 2.2].

- *Simulation-Extractable NIZKs.* [GO07] A NIZK for an NP relation $\mathcal{R}$ is a construction that allows proving the knowledge of a witness w for a statement x with only one round of interaction and without revealing any additional information about w. The zero-knowledge property is formalised by the existence of PPT simulators generating proofs without needing witnesses. The operation is performed exploiting a trapdoored CRS.
  We say that the NIZK is simulation-extractable if there exists an efficient algorithm that, in conjunction with the simulators, permits to extract the witness from any valid proof generated by the adversary.
  When the CRS is a random string of bits, we talk about NIZKs with URS. Formal definitions are given in [ASY22, Section 2.3].

- *Multiparty Homomorphic Encryption with Private Evaluation (pMHE).* MHE with private evaluation [AJJM20] is a construction that permits to evaluate circuits over encrypted values. It is possible to obtain partial decryptions with no interactions. Retrieving the actual plaintext requires however an additional round of communication as we need to pool the partial decryptions. MHE with private evaluation is a weaker version of multi-key FHE. The main differences is that there is actually no public key but only a private one that changes for every ciphertext. Furthermore, the encryption algorithm needs to know the parameters (input size, output size and depth) of the circuits we are going to evaluate. We can build pMHE from LWE [AJJM20]. Formal definitions are given in [ASY22, Section 2.4].

- *Somewhere Statistically Binding (SSB) Hashing.* [HW15] An SSB hash function is a keyed hash function with particular properties: every key hk hides an index i that specifies in which block the hash is statistically binding. Specifically, every pair of messages having the same digest under hk must coincide at the i-th block. It is possible to build SSB hash functions from fully homomorphic encryption [HW15]. Formal definitions are given in [ASY22, Section 2.5].

3 Defining Distributed Samplers

Informally speaking, a distributed sampler (DS) for the distribution $\mathcal{D}$ is a construction that allows n parties to obtain a random sample R from $\mathcal{D}$ with just one round of communication and without revealing any additional information about the randomness used for the generation of R. The output of the procedure can be derived given only the public transcript, so we do not aim to protect the privacy of the result against passive adversaries eavesdropping the communications between the parties.

If we assume an arbitrary trusted setup, building a DS becomes straightforward; we can consider the trivial setup that directly provides the parties with a random sample from $\mathcal{D}$. Obtaining solutions with a weaker (or no) trusted setup is much more challenging.

The structure and syntax of distributed samplers is formalised as follows. We then analyse different flavours of security definitions.

Definition 3.1 (n-party Distributed Sampler for the Distribution $\mathcal{D}$).
An n-party distributed sampler for the distribution $\mathcal{D}$ is a pair of PPT algorithms (Gen, Sample) *with the following syntax:*

1. Gen *is a probabilistic algorithm taking as input the security parameter $\mathbb{1}^\lambda$ and a party index $i \in [n]$ and outputting a sampler share U_i for party i. Let $\{0, 1\}^{L(\lambda)}$ be the space from which the randomness of the algorithm is sampled.*
2. Sample *is a deterministic algorithm taking as input n shares of the sampler $U_1, U_2, \ldots, U_n$ and outputting a sample R.*

In some of our security definitions, we will refer to the *one-round protocol* Π_{DS} that is induced by the distributed sampler $\mathsf{DS} = (\mathsf{Gen}, \mathsf{Sample})$. This is the natural protocol obtained from DS, where each party first broadcasts a message output by Gen, and then runs Sample on input all the parties' messages.

3.1 Security

In this section we formalise the definition of distributed samplers with relation to different security flavours, namely, semi-malicious and active. We always assume that we deal with a static adversary who can corrupt up to $n - 1$ out of the n parties. We recall that a protocol has semi-malicious security if it remains secure even if the corrupt parties behave semi-honestly, but the adversary can select their random tapes.

Definition 3.2 (Distributed Sampler with Semi-malicious Security). *A distributed sampler* (Gen, Sample) *has semi-malicious security if there exists a PPT simulator* Sim *such that, for every set of corrupt parties $C \subsetneq [n]$ and corresponding randomness $(\rho_i)_{i \in C}$, the following two distributions are computationally indistinguishable:*

$$
\left\{
\begin{array}{l}
(U_i)_{i \in [n]} \\
(\rho_i)_{i \in C}, R
\end{array}
\;\middle|\;
\begin{array}{ll}
\rho_i \xleftarrow{\$} \{0, 1\}^{L(\lambda)} & \forall i \in H \\
U_i \leftarrow \mathsf{Gen}(\mathbb{1}^\lambda, i; \rho_i) & \forall i \in [n] \\
R \leftarrow \mathsf{Sample}(U_1, U_2, \ldots, U_n) &
\end{array}
\right\}
\quad and
$$

$$
\left\{
\begin{array}{l}
(U_i)_{i \in [n]} \\
(\rho_i)_{i \in C}, R
\end{array}
\;\middle|\;
\begin{array}{l}
R \xleftarrow{\$} \mathcal{D}(\mathbb{1}^\lambda) \\
(U_i)_{i \in H} \xleftarrow{\$} \mathsf{Sim}\left(\mathbb{1}^\lambda, C, R, (\rho_i)_{i \in C}\right)
\end{array}
\right\}
$$

Observe that this definition implies that, even in the simulation, the relation

$$R = \mathsf{Sample}(U_1, U_2, \ldots, U_n)$$

holds with overwhelming probability. In other words, security requires that $(\mathsf{Gen}, \mathsf{Sample})$ securely implements the functionality that samples from $\mathcal{D}$ and outputs the result to all of the parties.

Observe that the previous definition can be adapted to passive security by simply sampling the randomness of the corrupted parties inside the game in the real world and generating it using the simulator in the ideal world.

We now define actively secure distributed samplers. Here, to handle the challenges introduced by a rushing adversary, we model security by defining an ideal functionality in the universal composability (UC) framework [Can01], and require that the protocol Π_{DS} securely implements this functionality.

Definition 3.3 (Distributed Sampler with Active Security). *Let* $\mathsf{DS} = (\mathsf{Gen}, \mathsf{Sample})$ *be a distributed sampler for the distribution* $\mathcal{D}$. *We say that* DS *has* active security *if the one-round protocol* Π_{DS} *securely implements the functionality* $\mathcal{F}_{\mathcal{D}}$ *(see Fig. 3) against a static and active adversary corrupting up to* $n - 1$ *parties.*

$$\mathcal{F}_{\mathcal{D}}$$

Initialisation. On input Init from every honest party and the adversary, the functionality activates and sets $Q := \emptyset$. (Q will be used to keep track of queries.) If all the parties are honest, the functionality outputs $R \xleftarrow{\$} \mathcal{D}(\mathbb{1}^\lambda)$ to every honest party and sends R to the adversary, then it halts.

Query. On input Query from the adversary, the functionality samples $R \xleftarrow{\$} \mathcal{D}(\mathbb{1}^\lambda)$ and creates a fresh label id. It sends (id, R) to the adversary and adds the pair to Q.

Output. On input $(\mathsf{Output}, \widehat{\mathsf{id}})$ from the adversary, the functionality retrieves the only pair $(\mathsf{id}, R) \in Q$ with $\mathsf{id} = \widehat{\mathsf{id}}$. If such pair does not exist, the functionality does nothing. Otherwise, it outputs R to every honest party and terminates.

Abort. On input Abort from the adversary, the functionality outputs $\perp$ to every honest party and terminates.

Fig. 3. Distributed sampler functionality

Remark 3.4 (Distributed Samplers with a CRS or Random Oracle). Our constructions with active security rely on a setup assumption in the form of a common reference string (CRS) and random oracle. For a CRS, we assume the algorithms $\mathsf{Gen}, \mathsf{Sample}$ are implicitly given the CRS as input, which is modelled as being sampled by an ideal setup functionality. As usual, the random oracle is modelled as an external oracle that may be queried by any algorithm or party, and programmed by the simulator in the security proof.

Observe that this definition allows the adversary to request several samples R from the functionality, and then select the one it likes the most. Our definition must allow this in order to deal with a rushing adversary who might wait for the messages $(U_i)_{i \in H}$ of all the honest parties and then locally re-generate the corrupt parties' messages $(U_i)_{i \in C}$, obtaining a wide range of possible outputs. Finally, it can broadcast the corrupt parties' messages that lead to the output it likes the most. This makes distributed samplers with active security rather useless when the distribution $\mathcal{D}$ has low entropy, i.e. when there exists a polynomial-size set S such that $\mathcal{D}(\mathbb{1}^\lambda) \in S$ with overwhelming probability. Indeed, in such cases, the adversary is able to select its favourite element in the image of $\mathcal{D}$.

On the Usefulness of Distributed Samplers with a CRS. Our distributed samplers with active security require a CRS for NIZK proofs. Since one of the main goals of the construction is avoid trusted setup in multiparty protocols, assuming the existence of a CRS, which itself is some form of setup, may seem wrong.

We highlight, however, that some types of CRS are much easier to generate than others. A CRS that depends on values which must remain secret (e.g. an RSA modulus with unknown factorization, or an obfuscated program which contains a secret key) is difficult to generate. However, assuming the security of trapdoor permutations [FLS90], bilinear maps [GOS06], learning with errors [PS19] or indistinguishability obfuscation [BP15], we can construct NIZK proofs where the CRS is just a random string of bits, i.e. a URS. In the random oracle model, such a CRS can even be generated without any interaction. So, the CRS required by our constructions is the simplest, weakest kind of CRS setup.

4   A Construction with Semi-malicious Security

We now present the main construction of this paper: a distributed sampler with semi-malicious security based on polynomially secure MHE with private evaluation and indistinguishability obfuscation. In Sect. 5, we explain how to upgrade this construction to achieve active security.

The Basic Idea. Our goal is to generate a random sample R from the distribution $\mathcal{D}$. The natural way to do it is to produce a random bit string s and feed it into $\mathcal{D}$. We want to perform the operation in an encrypted way as we need to preserve the privacy of s. A DS implements the functionality that provides samples from the underlying distribution, but not the randomness used to obtain them, so no information about s can be leaked.

We guarantee that any adversary corrupting up to $n - 1$ parties is not able to influence the choice of s by XORing n bit strings of the same length, the i-th one of which is independently sampled by the i-th party P_i. Observe that we are dealing with a semi-malicious adversary, so we do not need to worry about corrupted parties adaptively choosing their shares after seeing those of the honest players.

Preserving the Privacy of the Random String. To preserve the privacy of s, we rely on an MHE scheme with private evaluation pMHE = (Enc, PrivEval, FinDec). Each party P_i encrypts s_i, publishing the corresponding ciphertext c_i and keeping the private key sk_i secret. As long as the honest players do not reveal their partial decryption keys, the privacy of the random string s is preserved. Using the homomorphic properties of the MHE scheme, the parties are also able to obtain partial plaintexts of R without any interactions. However, we run into an issue: in order to finalise the decryption, the construction would require an additional round of communication where the partial plaintexts are broadcast.

Reverting to a One-round Construction. We need to find a way to perform the final decryption without additional interaction, while at the same time preserving the privacy of the random string s. That means revealing a very limited amount of information about the private keys $sk_1, sk_2, \ldots, sk_n$, so that it is only possible to retrieve R, revealing nothing more.

Inspired by [HIJ+17], we build such a precise tool by relying on indistinguishability obfuscation: in the only round of interaction, each party P_i additionally publishes an obfuscated *evaluation program* $EvProg_i$ containing the private key sk_i. When given the ciphertexts of the other parties, $EvProg_i$ evaluates the circuit producing the final result R and outputs the partial decryption with relation to sk_i. Using the evaluation programs, the players are thus able to retrieve R by feeding the partial plaintexts into pMHE.FinDec.

Dealing with the Leakage about the Secret Keys. At first glance, the solution outlined in the previous paragraph seems to be secure. However, there are some sneaky issues we need to deal with.

In this warm-up construction, we aim to protect the privacy of the random string s by means of the reusable semi-malicious security of the MHE scheme with private evaluation. To rely on this assumption, no information on the secret keys must be leaked. However, this is not the case here, as the private keys are part of the evaluation programs.

In the security proof, we are therefore forced to proceed in two steps: first, we must remove the secret keys from the programs using obfuscation, and then we can apply reusable semi-malicious security. The first task is actually trickier than it may seem. iO states we cannot distinguish between the obfuscation of two equivalent programs. Finding a program with the same input-output behaviour as $EvProg_i$ without it containing any information about sk_i is actually impossible, as any output of the program depends on the private key. We cannot even hard-code the partial decryptions under sk_i for all possible inputs into the obfuscated program as that would require storing an exponential amount of information, blowing up the size of $EvProg_i$.

In [HIJ+17], while constructing an NI-MPC protocol based on multi-key FHE and iO, the authors deal with an analogous issue by progressively changing the behaviour of the program input by input, first hard-coding the output corresponding to a specific input and then using the simulatability of partial decryptions to remove any dependency on the multi-key FHE secret key. Unfortunately, in our context, this approach raises additional problems. First of all, in contrast with some multi-key FHE definitions, MHE does not support simulatability of partial decryptions. Additionally, since the procedure of [HIJ+17] is applied input by input, the security proof would require exponentially many hybrids. In that case, security can be argued only if transitions between subsequent hybrids cause a subexponentially small increase in the adversary's advantage. In other words, we would need to rely on subexponentially secure primitives even if future research shows that iO does not. Finally, we would still allow the adversary to compute several outputs without changing the random strings $(s_h)_{h \in H}$ selected by the honest parties. Each of the obtained values leaks some additional information about the final output of the distributed sampler. In [HIJ+17], this fact did not constitute an issue as this type of leakage is intrinsically connected to the notion of NI-MPC.

Bounding the Leakage: Key Generation Programs. To avoid the problems described above, we introduce the idea of *key generation programs*. Each party P_i publishes an obfuscated program KGProg_i which encrypts a freshly chosen string s_i, keeping the corresponding partial decryption key secret.

The randomness used by KGProg_i is produced via a puncturable PRF F taking as a nonce the key generation programs of the other parties. In this way, any slight change in the programs of the other parties leads to a completely unrelated string s_i, ciphertext c_i and key sk_i. It is therefore possible to protect the privacy of s_i using a polynomial number of hybrids, as we need only worry about a single combination of inputs. Specifically, we can remove any information about sk_i from EvProg_i and hard-code the partial plaintext d_i corresponding to $(c_j)_{j \in [n]}$. At that point, we can rely on the reusable semi-malicious security of the MHE scheme with private evaluation, removing any information about s_i from c_i and d_i and programming the final output to be a random sample R from $\mathcal{D}$.

The introduction of the key generation programs requires minimal modifications to the evaluation programs. In order to retrieve the MHE private key, EvProg_i needs to know the same PRF key K_i used by KGProg_i. Moreover, it now takes as input the key generation programs of the other parties, from which it will derive the MHE ciphertexts needed for the computation of R. Observe that EvProg_i will also contain KGProg_i, which will be fed into the other key generation programs in a nested execution of obfuscated circuits.

Compressing the Inputs. The only problem with the construction above, is that we now have a circularity issue: we cannot actually feed one key generation program as input to another key generation program, since the programs are of the same size. This holds even if we relied on obfuscation for Turing machines, since to prove security, we would need to puncture the PRF keys in the nonces, i.e. the key generation programs of the other parties. The point at which the i-th key is punctured, which is at least as big as the program itself, must be hard-coded into KGProg_i, which is clearly too small.

Instead of feeding entire key generation programs into KGProg_i, we can input their hash, which is much smaller. This of course means that there now exist different combinations of key generation programs leading to the same MHE ciphertext-key pair (c_i, sk_i), and the adversary could try to extract information about sk_i by looking for collisions. The security of the hash function should, however, prevent this attack. The only issue is that iO does not really get along with this kind of argument based on collision-resistant hashing. We instead rely on the more iO-friendly notion of a *somewhere statistically binding* hash function $\mathsf{SSB} = (\mathsf{Gen}, \mathsf{Hash})$ [HW15].

Final Construction. We now present the formal description of our semi-maliciously secure DS. The algorithms Gen and Sample, as well as the unobfuscated key generation program $\mathcal{P}_{\mathsf{KG}}$ and evaluation program $\mathcal{P}_{\mathsf{Eval}}$, can be found in Fig. 4. In the description, we assume that the puncturable PRF F outputs pseudorandom strings (r_1, r_2, r_3) where each of r_1, r_2 and r_3 is as long as the randomness needed by $\mathcal{D}$, $\mathsf{pMHE.Enc}$, and $\mathsf{HE.PrivEval}$ respectively. Moreover, we denote by B the maximum number of blocks in the messages fed into $\mathsf{SSB.Hash}$.

Theorem 4.1. *If* $\mathsf{SSB} = (\mathsf{Gen}, \mathsf{Hash})$ *is a somewhere statistically binding hash function,* $\mathsf{pMHE} = (\mathsf{Enc}, \mathsf{PrivEval}, \mathsf{FinDec})$ *is a MHE scheme with private evaluation,* iO *is an indistinguishability obfuscator and* (F, Punct) *is a puncturable PRF, the construction in Fig. 4 is an n-party distributed sampler with semi-malicious security for the distribution* $\mathcal{D}$.

We prove Theorem 4.1 in [ASY22, Appendix A]. Observe that a distributed sampler with semi-malicious security also has passive security.

5 Upgrading to Active Security

When moving from semi-malicious to active security, there are two main issues we need to tackle: corrupt parties publishing malformed shares of the sampler, and rushing adversaries. The former can be easily dealt with by adding NIZK proofs of well-formedness to the sampler shares (for this reason, our solution relies on a URS). Rushing adversaries are a more challenging problem, and to deal with this, we rely on a random oracle.

The Problem of Rushing. In the semi-maliciously secure construction described in Sect. 4, the randomness used to generate an honest party's MHE ciphertexts and private keys is output by a PRF, which takes as input a nonce that depends on the key generation programs of all parties (including the corrupt ones). To prove security, we need to puncture the PRF key at that nonce, erasing any correlation between the MHE ciphertext and the PRF key. This can be done in the semi-malicious case, as the simulator knows the programs of the corrupted parties before it must produce those of the honest parties. In the actively secure case, we run into an issue. The adversary is able to adaptively choose the programs of the corrupted parties after seeing those of the other players, in what is called *rushing behaviour*. In the security proof, we would therefore need to puncture a PRF key without knowing the actual position where puncturing is needed.

Distributed Sampler with Semi-Malicious Security

$\mathsf{Gen}(\mathbb{1}^\lambda, i)$:

1. $K \xleftarrow{\$} \{0,1\}^\lambda$
2. $\mathsf{hk} \xleftarrow{\$} \mathsf{SSB.Gen}(\mathbb{1}^\lambda, B, 0)$
3. $\mathsf{KGProg} \xleftarrow{\$} \mathsf{iO}\big(\mathbb{1}^\lambda, \mathcal{P}_{\mathsf{KG}}[K, i]\big)$
4. $\mathsf{EvProg} \xleftarrow{\$} \mathsf{iO}\big(\mathbb{1}^\lambda, \mathcal{P}_{\mathsf{Eval}}[K, i, \mathsf{hk}, \mathsf{KGProg}]\big)$
5. Output $U := (\mathsf{hk}, \mathsf{KGProg}, \mathsf{EvProg})$.

$\mathsf{Sample}\big((U_i = (\mathsf{hk}_i, \mathsf{KGProg}_i, \mathsf{EvProg}_i))_{i \in [n]}\big)$:

1. $\forall i \in [n] : \quad d_i \leftarrow \mathsf{EvProg}_i\big((\mathsf{hk}_j, \mathsf{KGProg}_j)_{j \neq i}\big)$
2. Output $R \leftarrow \mathsf{pMHE.FinDec}\big(\tilde{\mathcal{D}}, (d_i)_{i \in [n]}\big)$

The algorithm $\tilde{\mathcal{D}}$.
Given a set of n random strings $s_1, s_2, \ldots, s_n$, perform the following operations.

1. $s \leftarrow s_1 \oplus s_2 \oplus \cdots \oplus s_n$
2. Output $R \leftarrow \mathcal{D}(\mathbb{1}^\lambda; s)$

$\mathcal{P}_{\mathsf{KG}}[K, i]$: the key generation program

Hard-coded. The private key K and the index i of the party.
Input. A hash y.

1. $(r_1, r_2, r_3) \leftarrow F_K(y)$
2. $s \leftarrow r_1$
3. $(c, \mathsf{sk}) \leftarrow \mathsf{pMHE.Enc}(\mathbb{1}^\lambda, \tilde{\mathcal{D}}.\mathsf{params}, i, s; r_2)$
4. Output c.

$\mathcal{P}_{\mathsf{Eval}}[K, i, \mathsf{hk}_i, \mathsf{KGProg}_i]$: the evaluation program

Hard-coded. The private key K, the index i of the party, the hash key hk_i, and the obfuscated key generation program KGProg_i.
Input. A set of $n-1$ pairs $(\mathsf{hk}_j, \mathsf{KGProg}_j)_{j \neq i}$ where the first element is a hash key and the second is an obfuscated key generation program.

1. $\forall j \in [n] : \quad y_j \leftarrow \mathsf{SSB.Hash}\big(\mathsf{hk}_j, (\mathsf{hk}_l, \mathsf{KGProg}_l)_{l \neq j}\big)$
2. $\forall j \neq i : \quad c_j \leftarrow \mathsf{KGProg}_j(y_j)$
3. $(r_1, r_2, r_3) \leftarrow F_K(y_i)$
4. $s_i \leftarrow r_1$
5. $(c_i, \mathsf{sk}_i) \leftarrow \mathsf{pMHE.Enc}(\mathbb{1}^\lambda, \tilde{\mathcal{D}}.\mathsf{params}, i, s_i; r_2)$
6. $d_i \leftarrow \mathsf{pMHE.PrivEval}(\mathsf{sk}_i, \tilde{\mathcal{D}}, c_1, c_2, \ldots, c_n; r_3)$
7. Output d_i.

Fig. 4. A distributed sampler with semi-malicious security

Although the issue we described above is very specific, dealing with rushing behaviour is a general problem. In a secure distributed sampler, we can program the shares of the honest parties to output an ideal sample when used in conjunction with the shares of the corrupted players. Since the latter are unknown upon generation of the honest players' shares, the immediate approach would be to program the outputs for every possible choice of the adversary. We run however into an incompressibility problem as we would need to store exponentially many ideal outputs in the polynomial-sized sampler shares.

5.1 Defeating Rushing

In this section, we present a compiler that allows us to deal with rushing behaviour without adding any additional rounds of interaction. This tool handles rushing behaviour not only for distributed samplers, but for a wide range of applications (including our public-key PCF in Sect. 6). Consider any single-round protocol with no private inputs, where SendMsg is the algorithm which party i runs to choose a message to send, and Output is an algorithm that determines each party's output (from party i's state and all the messages sent). More concretely, we can describe any such one-round protocol using the following syntax:

SendMsg($\mathbb{1}^{\lambda}, i; r_i$) $\rightarrow \mathbf{g}_i$ generates party i's message $\mathbf{g}_i$, and
Output($i, r_i, (\mathbf{g}_j)_{j \in [n]}$) $\rightarrow \mathsf{res}_i$ produces party i's output res_i.

(In the case of distributed samplers, SendMsg corresponds to Gen, and Output corresponds to Sample.)

We define modified algorithms (ARMsg, AROutput) such that the associated one-round protocol realizes an ideal functionality that first waits for the corrupted parties' randomness, and then generates the randomness and messages of the honest parties.

This functionality clearly denies the adversary the full power of rushing: the ability to choose corrupt parties' messages based on honest parties' messages. For this reason, we call it the *no-rush* functionality $\mathcal{F}_{\mathsf{NoRush}}$. However, we do allow the adversary a weaker form of rushing behaviour: *selective sampling*. The functionality allows the adversary to re-submit corrupt parties' messages as many times as it wants, and gives the adversary the honest parties' messages in response (while hiding the honest parties' randomness). At the end, the adversary can select which execution she likes the most.

Definition 5.1 (Anti-Rusher). *Let* (SendMsg, Output) *be a one-round n-party protocol where* SendMsg *needs* $L(\lambda)$ *bits of randomness to generate a message. An anti-rusher for* SendMsg *is a one-round protocol* (ARMsg, AROutput) *implementing the functionality* $\mathcal{F}_{\mathsf{NoRush}}$ *(see Fig. 5) for* SendMsg *against an active adversary.*

If (SendMsg, Output) = (Gen, Sample) is a distributed sampler with semi-malicious security, applying this transformation gives a distributed sampler with active security.

$\mathcal{F}_{\mathsf{NoRush}}$

Initialisation. Upon receiving Init from every party and the adversary, the functionality activates and enters the querying phase.

Querying phase. Upon receiving the id-th Query from the adversary, the functionality waits for r_i from every corrupted party P_i. Then, for every $h \in H$, it samples $r_h \overset{\$}{\leftarrow} \{0,1\}^{L(\lambda)}$ and computes $g_h \leftarrow \mathsf{SendMsg}(\mathbb{1}^\lambda, h; r_h)$. Finally, it stores $(r_i)_{i \in [n]}$ as the id-th set of randomness and sends $(g_h)_{h \in H}$ back to the adversary.

Output. Upon receiving Output from the adversary, the functionality waits for a value $\widehat{\mathsf{id}}$ from the adversary, and retrieves the corresponding tuple $(r_i)_{i \in [n]}$ (or outputs $\bot$ if there is no such tuple). It then outputs r_h to P_h for every $h \in H$.

Fig. 5. The anti-rushing functionality $\mathcal{F}_{\mathsf{NoRush}}$

Intuition Behind Our Anti-rushing Compiler. We define (ARMsg, AROutput) as follows. When called by party i, ARMsg outputs an obfuscated program S_i; this program takes as input a response of the random oracle, and uses it as a nonce for a PRF F_{K_i}. The program then feeds the resulting pseudorandom string r into SendMsg, and outputs whatever message SendMsg generates. Our techniques are inspired by the *delayed backdoor programming* technique of Hofheinz et al. [HJK+16], used for adaptively secure universal samplers.

The Trapdoor. In order to prove that our compiler realizes $\mathcal{F}_{\mathsf{NoRush}}$ for SendMsg, a simulator must be able to force the compiled protocol to return given outputs of SendMsg, even *after* sending messages (outputs of ARMsg) on behalf of the honest parties.

Behind its usual innocent behaviour, the program S_i hides a trapdoor that allows it to secretly communicate with the random oracle. S_i owns a key k_i for a special authenticated encryption scheme based on puncturable PRFs. Every time it receives a random oracle response as input, S_i parses it as a ciphertext-nonce pair and tries to decrypt it. If decryption succeeds, S_i outputs the corresponding plaintext; otherwise, it resumes the usual innocent behaviour, and runs SendMsg. (The encryption scheme guarantees that the decryption of random strings fails with overwhelming probability; this trapdoor is never used accidentally, but it will play a crucial role in the proof.) Obfuscation conceals how the result has been computed as long as it is indistinguishable from a random SendMsg output.

The inputs fed into $(\mathsf{S}_i)_{i \in [n]}$ are generated by querying the random oracle with the programs themselves and NIZKs proving their well-formedness. The random oracle response consists of a random nonce v and additional n blocks $(u_i)_{i \in [n]}$, the i-th one of which is addressed to S_i. The input to S_i will be the pair (u_i, v). When the oracle tries to secretly communicate a message to S_i, u_i will be a ciphertext, whereas v will be the corresponding nonce.

Given a random oracle query, using the simulation-extractability of the NIZKs, the simulator can retrieve the secrets (in particular, the PRF keys) of the corrupted parties. It can then use this information to learn the randomness used to generate the corrupted parties' messages (i.e. their outputs of SendMsg).

The simulator then needs only to encrypt these messages received from $\mathcal{F}_{\mathsf{NoRush}}$ using $(k_i)_{i \in H}$, and include these ciphertexts in the oracle response.

Formal Description of Our Anti-rushing Compiler. We now formalise the ideas we presented in the previous paragraphs. Our anti-rushing compiler is described in Fig. 7. The unobfuscated program $\mathcal{P}_{\mathsf{AR}}$ is available in Fig. 6. We assume that its obfuscation needs $M(\lambda)$ bits of randomness. Observe that $\mathcal{P}_{\mathsf{AR}}$ is based on two puncturable PRFs F and F', the first one of which is used to generate the randomness fed into SendMsg.

The second puncturable PRF is part of the authenticated encryption scheme used in the trapdoor. We assume that its outputs are naturally split into $2m$ λ-bit blocks, where $m(\lambda)$ is the size of an output of SendMsg (after padding). To encrypt a plaintext $(x^1, \ldots, x^m) \in \{0, 1\}^m$ using the key k and nonce $v \in \{0, 1\}^\lambda$, we first expand v using F'_k. The ciphertext consists of m λ-bit blocks, the j-th one of which coincides with the $(2j + x^j)$-th block output by F'. Decryption is done by reversing these operations. For this reason, we assume that the values $(u_i)_{i \in [n]}$ in the oracle responses are naturally split into m λ-bit chunks. Observe that if the j-th block of the ciphertext is different from both the $2j$-th and the $(2j + 1)$-th block output by the PRF, decryption fails.

Finally, let $\mathsf{NIZK} = (\mathsf{Gen}, \mathsf{Prove}, \mathsf{Verify}, \mathsf{Sim}_1, \mathsf{Sim}_2, \mathsf{Extract})$ be a simulation-extractable NIZK for the relation $\mathcal{R}$ describing the well-formedness of the obfuscated programs $(\mathsf{S}_i)_{i \in [n]}$. Formally, a statement consists of the pair (S_i, i), whereas the corresponding witness is the triple containing the PRF keys k_i and K_i hard-coded in S_i and the randomness used for the obfuscation of the latter.

$\mathcal{P}_{\mathsf{AR}}[\mathsf{SendMsg}, k, K, i]$

Hard-coded. The algorithm SendMsg, PRF keys k and K and the index i of the party.
Input. Oracle responses $(u, v) \in \{0, 1\}^{\lambda \cdot m(\lambda)} \times \{0, 1\}^\lambda$.

1. $(y_1^0, y_1^1, y_2^0, y_2^1, \ldots, y_m^0, y_m^1) \leftarrow F'_k(v)$
2. For every $j \in [m]$ set
$$x^j \leftarrow \begin{cases} 0 & \text{if } y_j^0 = u^j, \\ 1 & \text{if } y_j^1 = u^j, \\ \bot & \text{otherwise.} \end{cases}$$
3. If $x^j \neq \bot$ for every $j \in [m]$, output $(x^1, x^2, \ldots, x^m)$.
4. Set $r \leftarrow F_K(u, v)$.
5. Output $\mathsf{g}_i \leftarrow \mathsf{SendMsg}(\mathbb{1}^\lambda, i; r)$.

Fig. 6. The anti-rushing program

Anti-Rushing Compiler Π_{NoRush}

URS. The protocol needs a URS urs $\overset{\$}{\leftarrow}$ NIZK.Gen($\mathbb{1}^\lambda$) for the NIZK proofs.

ARMsg($\mathbb{1}^\lambda, i, \text{urs}$):

1. $k_i \overset{\$}{\leftarrow} \{0,1\}^\lambda$
2. $K_i \overset{\$}{\leftarrow} \{0,1\}^\lambda$
3. $w_i \overset{\$}{\leftarrow} \{0,1\}^{M(\lambda)}$
4. $\mathsf{S}_i \leftarrow \mathsf{iO}\big(\mathbb{1}^\lambda, \mathcal{P}_{\mathsf{AR}}[\mathsf{SendMsg}, k_i, K_i, i]; w_i\big)$ (see Fig. 6)
5. $\pi_i \overset{\$}{\leftarrow} \mathsf{Prove}\big(\mathbb{1}^\lambda, \mathsf{urs}, (\mathsf{S}_i, i), (k_i, K_i, w_i)\big)$
6. Output $\mathsf{armsg}_i := (\mathsf{S}_i, \pi_i)$.

AROutput$\big((\mathsf{armsg}_j = (\mathsf{S}_j, \pi_j))_{j \in [n]}, \mathsf{urs}\big)$:

1. If there exists $j \in [n]$ such that $\mathsf{Verify}\big(\mathsf{urs}, \pi_j, (\mathsf{S}_j, j)\big) = 0$, output $\perp$.
2. Query $(\mathsf{S}_j, \pi_j)_{j \in [n]}$ to the random oracle $\mathcal{H}$ to get $\big(v, (u_i)_{i \in [n]}\big)$.
3. $\forall i \in [n] :$ $\mathsf{g}_i \leftarrow \mathsf{S}_i(u_i, v)$.
4. Output $(\mathsf{g}_j)_{j \in [n]}$.

Fig. 7. Anti-rushing compiler

Theorem 5.2. *If* (SendMsg, Output) *is a one-round n-party protocol,* NIZK $=$ (Gen, Prove, Verify, Sim$_1$, Sim$_2$, Extract) *is a simulation-extractable NIZK with URS for the relation* $\mathcal{R}$, iO *is an indistinguishability obfuscator and* (F, Punct) *and* (F', Punct') *are two puncturable PRFs satisfying the properties described above, the protocol* $\Pi_{\text{NoRush}} = $ (ARMsg, AROutput) *described in Fig. 7 realizes* $\mathcal{F}_{\text{NoRush}}$ *for* SendMsg *in the random oracle model with a URS.*

We prove Theorem 5.2 in [ASY22, Appendix B].

Theorem 5.3. *Suppose that* DS $=$ (Gen, Sample) *is a semi-maliciously secure distributed sampler for the distribution* $\mathcal{D}$. *Assume that there exists an anti-rusher for* DS.Gen. *Then, there exists an actively secure distributed sampler for* $\mathcal{D}$.

On the Novelty of this Compiler. Observe that the idea of a compiler converting passive protocols into actively secure ones is not new. The most famous example is GMW [GMW87], which achieves this by adding ZK proofs proving the well-formedness of all the messages in the protocol. The novelty of our construction consists of doing this without increasing the number of rounds. GMW deals with rushing by requiring all the parties to commit to their randomness at the beginning of the protocol and then prove that all the messages in the interaction are consistent with the initial commitments. A passively secure one-round protocol would therefore be compiled, in the best case, into a 2-round one.

Although the techniques were inspired by [HJK+16], this work employs the ideas in a new context, generalising them to multiple players and applying them in multiparty protocols. Observe indeed that [HJK+16] devised the techniques to construct adaptively secure universal samplers. To some extent, we still use them to prevent the adversary from making adaptive choices.

6 Public-Key PCFs for Reverse-Samplable Correlations

We now consider the concept of a *distributed correlation sampler*, where the distribution $\mathcal{D}$ produces *private, correlated* outputs $R_1, R_2, \ldots, R_n$, where R_i is given only to the i-th party. This can also model the case where the distribution $\mathcal{D}$ has only one output $R = R_1 = \cdots = R_n$, which must be accessible only to the parties that took part in the computation (but not to outsiders; unlike with a distributed sampler).

PCGs and PCFs. The concept of distributed correlation samplers has been previously studied in the form of pseudorandom correlation generators (PCGs) [BCGI18, BCG+19a, BCG+19b, BCG+20b] and pseudorandom correlation functions (PCFs)[BCG+20a, OSY21]. These are tailored to distributions with n outputs, each one addressed to a different player. Specifically, they consist of two algorithms (Gen, Eval): Gen is used to generate n short correlated seeds or keys, one for each party. Eval is then used to locally expand the keys and non-interactively produce a large amount of correlated randomness, analogously to the non-correlated setting of a PRG (for PCG) or PRF (for PCF).

Both PCGs and PCFs implicitly rely on a trusted dealer for the generation and distribution of the output of Gen, which in practice can be realized using a secure multiparty protocol. The communication overhead of this computation should be small, compared with the amount of correlated randomness obtained from Eval.

If we consider a one-round protocol to distribute the output of Gen, the message of the i-th party and the corresponding randomness r_i act now as a kind of public/private key pair (r_i is necessary to retrieve the i-th output.) Such a primitive is called a *public-key PCF* [OSY21]. Orlandi *et al.* [OSY21] built public-key PCFs for the random OT and vector-OLE correlations based on Paillier encryption with a common reference string (a trusted RSA modulus). In this section, we will build public-key PCFs for general correlations, while avoiding trusted setups.

6.1 Correlation Functions and Their Properties

Instead of considering singe-output distributions $\mathcal{D}$, we now consider n-output correlations $\mathcal{C}$. We also allow different samples from $\mathcal{C}$ to themselves be correlated by some secret parameters, which allows handling correlations such as vector-OLE and authenticated multiplication triples (where each sample depends on some fixed MAC keys). This is modelled by allowing each party i to input a *master secret* mk_i into $\mathcal{C}$. These additional inputs are independently sampled by each party using an algorithm Secret.

Some Example Correlations. Previous works have focussed on a simple class of *additive correlations*, where the outputs $R_1, \ldots, R_n$ form an additive secret sharing of values sampled from a distribution. This captures, for instance, oblivious transfer, (vector) oblivious linear evaluation and (authenticated) multiplication triples, which are all useful correlations for secure computation tasks. Vector OLE and authenticated triples are also examples requiring a master secret, which is used to fix a secret scalar or secret MAC keys used to produce samples. Assuming LWE, we can construct public-key PCFs for any additive correlation [BCG+20a], using homomorphic secret-sharing based on multi-key FHE [DHRW16]. However, we do not know how to build PCFs for broader classes of correlations, except for in the two-party setting and relying on subexponentially secure iO [DHRW16].

As motivation, consider the following important types of non-additive correlations:

- *Pseudorandom secret sharing.* This can be seen as a correlation that samples sharings of uniformly random values under some linear secret sharing scheme. Even for simple t-out-of-n threshold schemes such as Shamir, the best previous construction requires $\binom{n}{t}$ complexity [CDI05].
- *Garbled circuits.* In the two-party setting, one can consider a natural garbled circuit correlation, which for some circuit C, gives a garbling of C to one party, and all pairs of input wire labels to the other party. Having such a correlation allows preprocessing for secure 2-PC, where in the online phase, the parties just use oblivious transfer to transmit the appropriate input wire labels.[3] Similarly, this can be extended to the multi-party setting, by for instance, giving n parties the garbled circuit together with a secret-sharing of the input wire labels.

For garbled circuits, it may also be useful to consider a variant that uses a master secret, if e.g. we want each garbled circuit to be sampled with a fixed offset used in the free-XOR technique [KS08].

Reverse-Samplable Correlations. The natural way to define a public-key PCF would be a one-round protocol implementing the functionality that samples from the correlation function $\mathcal{C}$ and distributes the outputs. However, Boyle *et al.* [BCG+19b] prove that for PCGs, any construction satisfying this definition in the plain model would require that the messages be at least as long as the randomness generated, which negates one of the main advantages of using a PCF. Following the approach of Boyle *et al.*, in this section we adopt a weaker definition. We require that no adversary can distinguish the real samples of

---

[3] Note that formally, in the presence of malicious adversaries, preprocessing garbled circuits in this way requires the garbling scheme to be adaptively secure [BHR12].

the honest parties from simulated ones which are *reverse sampled* based on the outputs of the corrupted players. This choice restricts the set of correlation functions to those whose outputs are efficiently reverse-samplable[4]. We formalise this property below.

Definition 6.1 (Reverse Samplable Correlation Function with Master Secrets). *An n-party correlation function with master secrets is a pair of PPT algorithms* (Secret, $\mathcal{C}$) *with the following syntax:*

- Secret *takes as input the security parameter $\mathbb{1}^\lambda$ and the index of a party $i \in [n]$. It outputs the i-th party's master correlation secret mk_i.*
- $\mathcal{C}$ *takes as input the security parameter $\mathbb{1}^\lambda$ and the master secrets $\mathsf{mk}_1, \ldots, \mathsf{mk}_n$. It outputs n correlated values $R_1, R_2, \ldots, R_n$, one for each party.*

We say that (Secret, $\mathcal{C}$) *is reverse samplable if there exists a PPT algorithm* RSample *such that, for every set of corrupted parties $C \subsetneq [n]$ and master secrets $(\mathsf{mk}_i)_{i \in [n]}$ and $(\mathsf{mk}'_h)_{h \in H}$ in the image of* Secret, *no PPT adversary is able to distinguish between $\mathcal{C}(\mathbb{1}^\lambda, \mathsf{mk}_1, \mathsf{mk}_2, \ldots, \mathsf{mk}_n)$ and*

$$
\left\{ (R_1, R_2, \ldots, R_n) \middle|
\begin{array}{l}
\forall i \in C: \quad \mathsf{mk}'_i \leftarrow \mathsf{mk}_i \\
(R'_1, R'_2, \ldots, R'_n) \xleftarrow{\$} \mathcal{C}(\mathbb{1}^\lambda, \mathsf{mk}'_1, \mathsf{mk}'_2, \ldots, \mathsf{mk}'_n) \\
\forall i \in C: \quad R_i \leftarrow R'_i \\
(R_h)_{h \in H} \xleftarrow{\$} \mathsf{RSample}\big(\mathbb{1}^\lambda, C, (R_i)_{i \in C}, (\mathsf{mk}_i)_{i \in C}, (\mathsf{mk}'_h)_{h \in H}\big)
\end{array}
\right\}
$$

Notice that indistinguishability cannot rely on the secrecy of the master secrets $(\mathsf{mk}_i)_{i \in [n]}$ and $(\mathsf{mk}'_h)_{h \in H}$, since the adversary could know their values. Furthermore, RSample does not take as input the same master secrets that were used for the generation of the outputs of the corrupted parties. The fact that indistinguishability holds in spite of this implies that the elements $(R_i)_{i \in C}$ leak no information about the master secrets of the honest players.

6.2 Defining Public Key PCFs

We now formalise the definition of public key PCF as it was sketched at the beginning of the section. We start by specifying the syntax, we will then focus our attention on security, in particular against semi-malicious and active adversaries.

Definition 6.2 (Public-Key PCF with Master Secrets). *A public-key PCF for the n-party correlation function with master secrets* (Secret, $\mathcal{C}$) *is a pair of PPT algorithms* (Gen, Eval) *with the following syntax:*

- Gen *takes as input the security parameter $\mathbb{1}^\lambda$ and the index of a party $i \in [n]$, and outputs the PCF key pair* $(\mathsf{sk}_i, \mathsf{pk}_i)$ *of the i-th party.* Gen *needs $L(\lambda)$ bits of randomness.*

---

[4] In the examples above, reverse-samplability is possible for pseudorandom secret-sharing, but not for garbled circuits, since we should not be able to find valid input wire labels when given only a garbled circuit.

$$\mathcal{G}_{\text{PCF-Corr}}(\lambda)$$

Initialisation.
1. $b \xleftarrow{\$} \{0,1\}$
2. $\forall i \in [n]: \quad (\mathsf{sk}_i, \mathsf{pk}_i) \xleftarrow{\$} \mathsf{Gen}(\mathbb{1}^\lambda, i)$
3. $\forall i \in [n]: \quad \mathsf{mk}'_i \xleftarrow{\$} \mathsf{Secret}(\mathbb{1}^\lambda, i)$
4. Activate the adversary with input $(\mathbb{1}^\lambda, (\mathsf{pk}_i)_{i \in [n]})$.

Repeated querying. On input $(\mathsf{Correlation}, x)$ from the adversary where $x \in \{0,1\}^{l(\lambda)}$, compute
1. $\forall i \in [n]: \quad R_i^0 \leftarrow \mathsf{Eval}(i, \mathsf{pk}_1, \ldots, \mathsf{pk}_n, \mathsf{sk}_i, x)$
2. $(R_i^1)_{i \in [n]} \xleftarrow{\$} \mathcal{C}(\mathbb{1}^\lambda, \mathsf{mk}'_1, \ldots, \mathsf{mk}'_n)$
3. Give $(R_1^b, R_2^b, \ldots, R_n^b)$ to the adversary.

Output. The adversary wins if its final output is b.

Fig. 8. Correctness game for the public-key PCF

– Eval *takes as input an index* $i \in [n]$, n *PCF public keys, the i-th PCF private key* sk_i *and a nonce* $x \in \{0,1\}^{l(\lambda)}$. *It outputs a value* R_i *corresponding to the i-th output of* $\mathcal{C}$.

Every public-key PCF $(\mathsf{Gen}, \mathsf{Eval})$ for $\mathcal{C}$ induces a one-round protocol $\Pi_\mathcal{C}$. This is the natural construction in which every party broadcasts pk_i output by Gen, and then runs Eval on all the parties' messages, its own private key and various nonces.

Definition 6.3 (Semi-maliciously Secure Public-Key PCF for Reverse Samplable Correlation). *Let* $(\mathsf{Secret}, \mathcal{C})$ *be an n-party, reverse samplable correlation function with master secrets. A public-key PCF* $(\mathsf{Gen}, \mathsf{Eval})$ *for* $(\mathsf{Secret}, \mathcal{C})$ *is semi-maliciously secure if the following properties are satisfied.*

– **Correctness.** *No PPT adversary can win the game* $\mathcal{G}_{\text{PCF-Corr}}(\lambda)$ *(see Fig. 8) with noticeable advantage.*
– **Security.** *There exists a PPT extractor* Extract *such that for every set of corrupted parties* $C \subsetneq [n]$ *and corresponding randomness* $(\rho_i)_{i \in C}$, *no PPT adversary can win the game* $\mathcal{G}_{\text{PCF-Sec}}^{C,(\rho_i)_{i \in C}}(\lambda)$ *(see Fig. 9) with noticeable advantage.*

Correctness requires that the samples output by the PCF are indistinguishable from those produced by $\mathcal{C}$ even if the adversary receives all the public keys. Security instead states that a semi-malicious adversary learns no information about the samples and the master secrets of the honest players except what can be deduced from the outputs of the corrupted parties themselves.

Like for distributed samplers, the above definition can be adapted to passive security by modifying the security game. Specifically, it would be sufficient to sample the randomness of the corrupted parties inside the game, perhaps relying on a simulator when $b = 1$.

$$\mathcal{G}_{\mathrm{PCF\text{-}Sec}}^{C,(\rho_i)_{i\in C}}(\lambda)$$

Initialisation.

1. $b \xleftarrow{\$} \{0,1\}$
2. $\forall h \in H: \quad \rho_h \xleftarrow{\$} \{0,1\}^{L(\lambda)}$
3. $\forall i \in [n]: \quad (\mathsf{sk}_i, \mathsf{pk}_i) \leftarrow \mathsf{Gen}(\mathbb{1}^\lambda, i; \rho_i)$
4. $(\mathsf{mk}_i)_{i\in C} \leftarrow \mathsf{Extract}(C, \rho_1, \rho_2, \ldots, \rho_n)$.
5. $\forall h \in H: \quad \mathsf{mk}'_h \xleftarrow{\$} \mathsf{Secret}(\mathbb{1}^\lambda, h)$
6. Activate the adversary with $\mathbb{1}^\lambda$ and provide it with $(\mathsf{pk}_i)_{i\in[n]}$ and $(\rho_i)_{i\in C}$.

Repeated querying. On input $(\mathsf{Correlation}, x)$ from the adversary where $x \in \{0,1\}^{l(\lambda)}$, compute

1. $\forall i \in [n]: \quad R_i^0 \leftarrow \mathsf{Eval}(i, \mathsf{pk}_1, \ldots, \mathsf{pk}_n, \mathsf{sk}_i, x)$
2. $\forall i \in C: \quad R_i^1 \leftarrow R_i^0$
3. $(R_h^1)_{h\in H} \xleftarrow{\$} \mathsf{RSample}(\mathbb{1}^\lambda, C, (R_i^1)_{i\in C}, (\mathsf{mk}_i)_{i\in C}, (\mathsf{mk}'_h)_{h\in H})$
4. Give $(R_1^b, R_2^b, \ldots, R_n^b)$ to the adversary.

Output. The adversary wins if its final output is b.

Fig. 9. Security game for the public-key PCF

In our definition, nonces are adaptively chosen by the adversary; however, in a *weak* PCF [BCG+20a], the nonces are sampled randomly or selected by the adversary ahead of time. We can define a weak public-key PCF similarly, and use the same techniques as Boyle *et al.* [BCG+20a] to convert a weak public-key PCF into a public-key PCF by means of a random oracle.

Active Security. We define actively secure public-key PCFs using an ideal functionality, similarly to how we defined actively secure distributed samplers.

Definition 6.4 (Actively Secure Public-Key PCF for Reverse Samplable Correlation). *Let* (Secret, C) *be an n-party reverse samplable correlation function with master secrets. A public-key PCF* $(\mathsf{Gen}, \mathsf{Eval})$ *for* (Secret, C) *is actively secure if the corresponding one-round protocol* Π_C *implements the functionality* $\mathcal{F}_C^{\mathsf{RSample}}$ *(see Fig. 10) against a static and active adversary corrupting up to $n-1$ parties.*

Any protocol that implements $\mathcal{F}_C^{\mathsf{RSample}}$ will require either a CRS or a random oracle; this is inherent for meaningful correlation functions, since the simulator needs to retrieve the values $(R_i)_{i\in C}$ in order to forward them to $\mathcal{F}_C^{\mathsf{RSample}}$. Therefore, some kind of trapdoor is needed.

Notice also that the algorithm RSample takes as input the master secrets of the corrupted parties. We can therefore assume that whenever the values $(R_i)_{i\in C}$ chosen by the adversary are inconsistent with $(\mathsf{mk}_i)_{i\in C}$ or with C itself, the output of the reverse sampler is $\bot$. As a consequence, an actively secure public-key PCF must not allow the corrupted parties to select these irregular outputs; otherwise distinguishing between real world and ideal world would be trivial.

$$\mathcal{F}_{\mathcal{C}}^{\mathsf{RSample}}$$

Initialisation. On input Init from every honest party and the adversary, the functionality samples $\mathsf{mk}_h \xleftarrow{\$} \mathsf{Secret}(\mathbb{1}^\lambda, h)$ for every $h \in H$ and waits for $(\mathsf{mk}_i)_{i \in C}$ from the adversary.

Correlation. On input a fresh nonce $x \in \{0,1\}^{l(\lambda)}$ from a party P_j, the functionality waits for $(R_i)_{i \in C}$ from the adversary. Then, it computes

$$(R_h)_{h \in H} \xleftarrow{\$} \mathsf{RSample}\big(\mathbb{1}^\lambda, C, (R_i)_{i \in C}, (\mathsf{mk}_i)_{i \in C}, (\mathsf{mk}_h)_{h \in H}\big),$$

sends R_j to P_j and stores $\big(x, (R_i)_{i \in [n]}\big)$. If x has already been queried, the functionality retrieves the stored tuple $\big(x, (R_i)_{i \in [n]}\big)$ and outputs R_j to P_j.

Fig. 10. The actively secure public-key PCF functionality for reverse samplable correlation

6.3   Public-Key PCF with Trusted Setup

We will build our semi-maliciously secure public-key PCF by first relying on a trusted setup and then removing it by means of a distributed sampler. A public-key PCF with trusted setup is defined by Definition 6.2 to include an algorithm Setup that takes as input the security parameter $\mathbb{1}^\lambda$ and outputs a CRS. The CRS is then provided as an additional input to the evaluation algorithm Eval, but not to the generation algorithm Gen. (If Gen required the CRS, then substituting Setup with a distributed sampler would give us a two-round protocol, not a one-round protocol.)

We say that a public-key PCF with trusted setup is semi-maliciously secure if it satisfies Definition 6.3, after minor tweaks to the games $\mathcal{G}_{\mathrm{PCF\text{-}Corr}}(\lambda)$ and $\mathcal{G}_{\mathrm{PCF\text{-}Sec}}^{C, (\rho_i)_{i \in C}}(\lambda)$ to account for the modified syntax. Notice that in the latter, the extractor needs to be provided with the CRS but not with the randomness used to produce it. If that was not the case, we would not be able to use a distributed sampler to remove the CRS. Formal definitions of public-key PCF with trusted setup are available in [ASY22, Section 6.3].

Our Public-key PCF with Trusted Setup. Our construction is based once again on iO. The key of every party i is a simple PKE pair $(\mathsf{sk}_i, \mathsf{pk}_i)$. The generation of the correlated samples and their distribution is handled by the CRS, which is an obfuscated program. Specifically, the latter takes as input the public keys of the parties and a nonce $x \in \{0,1\}^{l(\lambda)}$. After generating the master secrets $\mathsf{mk}_1, \mathsf{mk}_2, \ldots, \mathsf{mk}_n$ using Secret and the correlated samples $R_1, R_2, \ldots, R_n$ using $\mathcal{C}$, the program protects their privacy by encrypting them under the provided public keys. Specifically, R_i and mk_i are encrypted using pk_i, making the i-th party the only one able to retrieve the underlying plaintext.

The randomness used for the generation of the samples, the master secrets and the encryption is produced by means of two puncturable PRF keys k and K, known to the CRS program. The CRS program is equipped with two keys:

k and K. The first one is used to generate the master secrets; the input to the PRF is the sequence of all public keys $(\mathsf{pk}_1, \mathsf{pk}_2, \ldots, \mathsf{pk}_n))$. The master secrets remain the same if the nonce x varies. The second PRF key is used to generate the randomness fed into $\mathcal{C}$ and the encryption algorithm; here, the PRF input consists of all the program inputs. As a result, any slight change in the inputs leads to completely unrelated ciphertexts and samples.

On the Size of the Nonce Space. Unfortunately, in order to obtain semi-maliciously security, we need to assume that the nonce space is of polynomial size. In the security proof, we need to change the behaviour of the CRS program for all nonces. This is due to the fact that we cannot rely on the reverse samplability of the correlation function as long as the program contains information about the real samples of the honest players. If the number of nonces is exponential, our security proof would rely on a non-polynomial number of hybrids and therefore we would need to assume the existence of sub-exponentially secure primitives.

The Formal Description of Our Solution. Our public-key PCF with trusted setup for $(\mathsf{Secret}, \mathcal{C})$ is described in Fig. 11 together with the program $\mathcal{P}_{\mathsf{CG}}$ used as a CRS.

Our solution relies on an IND-CPA PKE scheme $\mathsf{PKE} = (\mathsf{Gen}, \mathsf{Enc}, \mathsf{Dec})$ and two puncturable PRFs F and F'. We assume that the output of the first one is naturally split into $n+1$ blocks, the initial one as big as the randomness needed by $\mathcal{C}$, the remaining ones the same size as the random tape of $\mathsf{PKE}.\mathsf{Enc}$. We also assume that the output of F' is split into n blocks as big as the randomness used by Secret.

Theorem 6.5 (Public Key PCFs with Trusted Setup). *Let* $(\mathsf{Secret}, \mathcal{C})$ *be an n-party, reverse samplable correlation function with master secrets. If* $\mathsf{PKE} = (\mathsf{Gen}, \mathsf{Enc}, \mathsf{Dec})$ *is an IND-CPA PKE scheme, iO is an indistinguishability obfuscator, (F, Punct) and (F', Punct') are puncturable PRFs with the properties described above and $l(\lambda)$ is $\mathsf{polylog}(\lambda)$, the construction presented in Fig. 11 is a semi-maliciously secure public-key PCF with trusted setup for* $(\mathsf{Secret}, \mathcal{C})$.

Furthermore, if PKE, iO, (F, Punct) *and* (F', Punct') *are sub-exponentially secure, the public-key PCF with trusted setup is semi-maliciously secure even if* $l(\lambda)$ *is* $\mathsf{poly}(\lambda)$.

In both cases, the size of the CRS and the PCF keys is $\mathsf{poly}(l)$.

We prove Theorem 6.5 in [ASY22, Appendix C].

6.4 Our Public-Key PCFs

As mentioned in the previous section, once we obtain a semi-maliciously secure public-key PCF with trusted setup, we can easily remove the CRS using a distributed sampler. We therefore obtain a public-key PCF with security against semi-malicious adversaries. If the size of the CRS and the keys of the initial construction is logarithmic in the size of the nonce space, the key length after removing the setup is still polynomial in $l(\lambda)$.

Public-Key PCF with Trusted Setup

Setup($\mathbb{1}^\lambda$)

  1. $k \xleftarrow{\$} \{0,1\}^\lambda$
  2. $K \xleftarrow{\$} \{0,1\}^\lambda$
  3. Output $\mathsf{CGP} \xleftarrow{\$} \mathsf{iO}\big(\mathbb{1}^\lambda, \mathcal{P}_{\mathsf{CG}}[k, K]\big)$

Gen($\mathbb{1}^\lambda, i$)

  1. Output $(\mathsf{sk}_i, \mathsf{pk}_i) \xleftarrow{\$} \mathsf{PKE.Gen}(\mathbb{1}^\lambda)$

Eval($i, \mathsf{CGP}, \mathsf{pk}_1, \ldots, \mathsf{pk}_n, \mathsf{sk}_i, x$)

  1. $(c_1, c_2, \ldots, c_n) \leftarrow \mathsf{CGP}(\mathsf{pk}_1, \ldots, \mathsf{pk}_n, x)$
  2. $(R_i, \mathsf{mk}_i) \leftarrow \mathsf{PKE.Dec}(\mathsf{sk}_i, c_i)$
  3. Output R_i.

$\mathcal{P}_{\mathsf{CG}}[k, K]$

Hard-coded. Two puncturable PRF keys k and K.
Input. n public keys $\mathsf{pk}_1, \ldots, \mathsf{pk}_n$ and a nonce $x \in \{0,1\}^{l(\lambda)}$.

  1. $(r, r_1, r_2, \ldots, r_n) \leftarrow F_K(\mathsf{pk}_1, \ldots, \mathsf{pk}_n, x)$.
  2. $(s_1, s_2, \ldots, s_n) \leftarrow F'_k(\mathsf{pk}_1, \ldots, \mathsf{pk}_n)$.
  3. $\forall i \in [n]: \quad \mathsf{mk}_i \leftarrow \mathsf{Secret}(\mathbb{1}^\lambda, i; s_i)$
  4. $(R_1, R_2, \ldots, R_n) \leftarrow \mathcal{C}(\mathbb{1}^\lambda, \mathsf{mk}_1, \ldots, \mathsf{mk}_n; r)$
  5. $\forall i \in [n]: \quad c_i \leftarrow \mathsf{PKE.Enc}(\mathsf{pk}_i, (R_i, \mathsf{mk}_i); r_i)$
  6. Output $c_1, c_2, \ldots, c_n$.

Fig. 11. A public-key PCF with trusted setup

Theorem 6.6 (Semi-maliciously Secure Public Key PCFs). *Let* $(\mathsf{Secret}, \mathcal{C})$ *be an n-party, reverse samplable correlation function with master secrets. Suppose that* $\mathsf{pkPCFS} = (\mathsf{Setup}, \mathsf{Gen}, \mathsf{Eval})$ *is a semi-maliciously secure public-key PCF with trusted setup for* $(\mathsf{Secret}, \mathcal{C})$*. Moreover, assume that there exists a semi-maliciously secure n-party distributed sampler for* $\mathsf{pkPCFS.Setup}$*. Then, public-key PCFs for* $(\mathsf{Secret}, \mathcal{C})$ *with semi-malicious security exist.*

We will not prove Theorem 6.6 formally. Security follows from the fact that distributed samplers implement the functionality that samples directly from the underlying distribution. From this point of view, it is fundamental that the randomness input into Setup is not given as input to the extractor of the public-key PCF pkPCFS.

Active Security in the Random Oracle Model. If we rely on a random oracle, it is easy to upgrade a semi-maliciously secure public-key PCF to active security. We can use an anti-rusher (see Sect. 5.1) to deal with rushing and malformed messages. If the key size of the semi-malicious construction is polynomial in $l(\lambda)$, after compiling with the anti-rusher, the key length is still $\mathsf{poly}(l)$. The technique described above allows us to deduce the security of our solution from the semi-malicious security of the initial public-key PCF. The result is formalised by the following theorem. Again, we will not provide a formal proof.

Theorem 6.7 (Actively Secure Public Key PCFs in the Random Oracle Model). *Let* $(\mathsf{Secret}, \mathcal{C})$ *be an n-party, reverse samplable correlation function with master secret. Assume that* $\mathsf{pkPCF} = (\mathsf{Gen}, \mathsf{Eval})$ *is a semi-maliciously secure public-key PCFs for* $(\mathsf{Secret}, \mathcal{C})$ *and suppose there exists an anti-rusher for the associated protocol. Then, actively secure public-key PCFs for* $(\mathsf{Secret}, \mathcal{C})$ *exist.*

Active Security from Sub-exponentially Secure Primitives. So far, all our constructions rely on polynomially secure primitives. However, we often work in the random oracle model. We now show that it is possible to build actively secure public-key PCFs in the URS model assuming the existence of sub-exponentially secure primitives. Furthermore, these constructions come with no restrictions on the size of the nonce space.

Our solution is obtained by assembling a sub-exponentially and semimaliciously secure public-key PCF with trusted setup with a sub-exponentially and semi-maliciously secure distributed sampler. We add witness-extractable NIZKs proving the well-formedness of the messages. Like for our semi-malicious construction, if the size of the CRS and the keys of the public-key PCF with trusted setup is polynomial in the nonce length $l(\lambda)$, after composing with the DS, the key size remains $\mathsf{poly}(l)$.

Theorem 6.8 (Actively Secure Public Key PCFs from Subexponentially Secure Primitives). *Let* $(\mathsf{Secret}, \mathcal{C})$ *be an n-party, reverse samplable correlation function with master secret. Suppose that* $\mathsf{pkPCFS} = (\mathsf{Setup}, \mathsf{Gen}, \mathsf{Eval})$ *is a sub-exponentially and semi-maliciously secure public-key PCF with trusted setup for* $(\mathsf{Secret}, \mathcal{C})$. *Assume that there exists a sub-exponentially and semi-maliciously secure n-party distributed sampler for* $\mathsf{pkPCFS.Setup}$. *If there exist simulation-extractable NIZKs with URS proving the well-formedness of the sampler shares and the PCF public keys, there exists an actively secure public-key PCF for* $(\mathsf{Secret}, \mathcal{C})$ *in the URS model.*

We prove Theorem 6.8 in [ASY22, Appendix D].

References

[AJJM20] Ananth, P., Jain, A., Jin, Z., Malavolta, G.: Multi-key fully-homomorphic encryption in the plain model. In: Pass, R., Pietrzak, K. (eds.) TCC 2020. LNCS, vol. 12550, pp. 28–57. Springer, Cham (2020). https://doi.org/10.1007/978-3-030-64375-1_2

[ASY22]   Abram, D., Scholl, P., Yakoubov, S.: Distributed (correlation) samplers: how to remove a trusted dealer in one round. Cryptology ePrint Archive, Report 2022/? (2022)

[BCG+19a] Boyle, E., et al.: Efficient two-round OT extension and silent non-interactive secure computation. In: ACM CCS 2019. ACM Press (November 2019)

[BCG+19b] Boyle, E., Couteau, G., Gilboa, N., Ishai, Y., Kohl, L., Scholl, P.: Efficient pseudorandom correlation generators: silent OT extension and more. In: Boldyreva, A., Micciancio, D. (eds.) CRYPTO 2019. LNCS, vol. 11694, pp. 489–518. Springer, Cham (2019). https://doi.org/10.1007/978-3-030-26954-8_16

[BCG+20a] Boyle, E., Couteau, G., Gilboa, N., Ishai, Y., Kohl, L., Scholl, P.: Correlated pseudorandom functions from variable-density LPN. In: 61st FOCS. IEEE Computer Society Press (November 2020)

[BCG+20b] Boyle, E., Couteau, G., Gilboa, N., Ishai, Y., Kohl, L., Scholl, P.: Efficient pseudorandom correlation generators from ring-LPN. In: Micciancio, D., Ristenpart, T. (eds.) CRYPTO 2020. LNCS, vol. 12171, pp. 387–416. Springer, Cham (2020). https://doi.org/10.1007/978-3-030-56880-1_14

[BCGI18] Boyle, E., Couteau, G., Gilboa, N., Ishai, Y.: Compressing vector OLE. In: ACM CCS 2018. ACM Press (October 2018)

[BGI+01] Barak, B., et al.: On the (im)possibility of obfuscating programs. In: Kilian, J. (ed.) CRYPTO 2001. LNCS, vol. 2139, pp. 1–18. Springer, Heidelberg (2001). https://doi.org/10.1007/3-540-44647-8_1

[BGI+14a] Beimel, A., Gabizon, A., Ishai, Y., Kushilevitz, E., Meldgaard, S., Paskin-Cherniavsky, A.: Non-interactive secure multiparty computation. In: Garay, J.A., Gennaro, R. (eds.) CRYPTO 2014. LNCS, vol. 8617, pp. 387–404. Springer, Heidelberg (2014). https://doi.org/10.1007/978-3-662-44381-1_22

[BGI14b] Boyle, E., Goldwasser, S., Ivan, I.: Functional signatures and pseudorandom functions. In: Krawczyk, H. (ed.) PKC 2014. LNCS, vol. 8383, pp. 501–519. Springer, Heidelberg (2014). https://doi.org/10.1007/978-3-642-54631-0_29

[BHR12]   Bellare, M., Hoang, V.T., Rogaway, P.: Adaptively secure garbling with applications to one-time programs and secure outsourcing. In: Wang, X., Sako, K. (eds.) ASIACRYPT 2012. LNCS, vol. 7658, pp. 134–153. Springer, Heidelberg (2012). https://doi.org/10.1007/978-3-642-34961-4_10

[BP15]   Bitansky, N., Paneth, O.: ZAPs and non-interactive witness indistinguishability from indistinguishability obfuscation. In: Dodis, Y., Nielsen, J.B. (eds.) TCC 2015. LNCS, vol. 9015, pp. 401–427. Springer, Heidelberg (2015). https://doi.org/10.1007/978-3-662-46497-7_16

[BW13]   Boneh, D., Waters, B.: Constrained pseudorandom functions and their applications. In: Sako, K., Sarkar, P. (eds.) ASIACRYPT 2013. LNCS, vol. 8270, pp. 280–300. Springer, Heidelberg (2013). https://doi.org/10.1007/978-3-642-42045-0_15

[Can01]   Canetti, R.: Universally composable security: a new paradigm for cryptographic protocols. In: Proceedings of the 42nd FOCS. IEEE Computer Society Press (October 2001)

[CDI05] Cramer, R., Damgård, I., Ishai, Y.: Share conversion, pseudorandom secret-sharing and applications to secure computation. In: Kilian, J. (ed.) TCC 2005. LNCS, vol. 3378, pp. 342–362. Springer, Heidelberg (2005). https://doi.org/10.1007/978-3-540-30576-7_19

[CLTV15] Canetti, R., Lin, H., Tessaro, S., Vaikuntanathan, V.: Obfuscation of probabilistic circuits and applications. In: Dodis, Y., Nielsen, J.B. (eds.) TCC 2015. LNCS, vol. 9015, pp. 468–497. Springer, Heidelberg (2015). https://doi.org/10.1007/978-3-662-46497-7_19

[DHRW16] Dodis, Y., Halevi, S., Rothblum, R.D., Wichs, D.: Spooky encryption and its applications. In: Robshaw, M., Katz, J. (eds.) CRYPTO 2016. LNCS, vol. 9816, pp. 93–122. Springer, Heidelberg (2016). https://doi.org/10.1007/978-3-662-53015-3_4

[FLS90] Feige, U., Lapidot, D., Shamir, A.: Multiple non-interactive zero knowledge proofs based on a single random string (extended abstract). In: Proceedings of the 31st FOCS. IEEE Computer Society Press (October 1990)

[GGH+13] Garg, S., Gentry, C., Halevi, S., Raykova, M., Sahai, A., Waters, B.: Candidate indistinguishability obfuscation and functional encryption for all circuits. In: Proceedings of the 54th FOCS. IEEE Computer Society Press (October 2013)

[GGM86] Goldreich, O., Goldwasser, S., Micali, S.: How to construct random functions. J. ACM (4) (1986)

[GMW87] Goldreich, O., Micali, S., Wigderson, A.: How to play any mental game or a completeness theorem for protocols with honest majority. In: Proceedings of the 19th ACM STOC. ACM Press (May 1987)

[GO07] Groth, J., Ostrovsky, R.: Cryptography in the multi-string model. In: Menezes, A. (ed.) CRYPTO 2007. LNCS, vol. 4622, pp. 323–341. Springer, Heidelberg (2007). https://doi.org/10.1007/978-3-540-74143-5_18

[GOS06] Groth, J., Ostrovsky, R., Sahai, A.: Non-interactive Zaps and new techniques for NIZK. In: Dwork, C. (ed.) CRYPTO 2006. LNCS, vol. 4117, pp. 97–111. Springer, Heidelberg (2006). https://doi.org/10.1007/11818175_6

[GPSZ17] Garg, S., Pandey, O., Srinivasan, A., Zhandry, M.: Breaking the subexponential barrier in obfustopia. In: Coron, J.-S., Nielsen, J.B. (eds.) EUROCRYPT 2017. LNCS, vol. 10212, pp. 156–181. Springer, Cham (2017). https://doi.org/10.1007/978-3-319-56617-7_6

[HIJ+17] Halevi, S., Ishai, Y., Jain, A., Komargodski, I., Sahai, A., Yogev, E.: Non-interactive multiparty computation without correlated randomness. In: Takagi, T., Peyrin, T. (eds.) ASIACRYPT 2017. LNCS, vol. 10626, pp. 181–211. Springer, Cham (2017). https://doi.org/10.1007/978-3-319-70700-6_7

[HJK+16] Hofheinz, D., Jager, T., Khurana, D., Sahai, A., Waters, B., Zhandry, M.: How to generate and use universal samplers. In: Cheon, J.H., Takagi, T. (eds.) ASIACRYPT 2016. LNCS, vol. 10032, pp. 715–744. Springer, Heidelberg (2016). https://doi.org/10.1007/978-3-662-53890-6_24

[HW15] Hubacek, P., Wichs, D.: On the communication complexity of secure function evaluation with long output. In: Proceedings of the ITCS 2015. ACM (January 2015)

[JLS21] Jain, A., Lin, H., Sahai, A.: Indistinguishability obfuscation from well-founded assumptions. In: Proceedings of the 53rd Annual ACM SIGACT Symposium on Theory of Computing, STOC 2021, pp. 60–73, New York, NY, USA. Association for Computing Machinery (2021)

[KPTZ13] Kiayias, A., Papadopoulos, S., Triandopoulos, N., Zacharias, T.: Delegatable pseudorandom functions and applications. In: Proceedings of the ACM CCS 2013. ACM Press (November 2013)

[KS08] Kolesnikov, V., Schneider, T.: Improved garbled circuit: free XOR gates and applications. In: Aceto, L., Damgård, I., Goldberg, L.A., Halldórsson, M.M., Ingólfsdóttir, A., Walukiewicz, I. (eds.) ICALP 2008. LNCS, vol. 5126, pp. 486–498. Springer, Heidelberg (2008). https://doi.org/10.1007/978-3-540-70583-3_40

[LZ17] Liu, Q., Zhandry, M.: Decomposable obfuscation: a framework for building applications of obfuscation from polynomial hardness. In: Kalai, Y., Reyzin, L. (eds.) TCC 2017. LNCS, vol. 10677, pp. 138–169. Springer, Cham (2017). https://doi.org/10.1007/978-3-319-70500-2_6

[OSY21] Orlandi, C., Scholl, P., Yakoubov, S.: The rise of paillier: homomorphic secret sharing and public-key silent OT. In: Canteaut, A., Standaert, F.-X. (eds.) EUROCRYPT 2021. LNCS, vol. 12696, pp. 678–708. Springer, Cham (2021). https://doi.org/10.1007/978-3-030-77870-5_24

[PS19] Peikert, C., Shiehian, S.: Noninteractive zero knowledge for NP from (plain) learning with errors. In: Boldyreva, A., Micciancio, D. (eds.) CRYPTO 2019. LNCS, vol. 11692, pp. 89–114. Springer, Cham (2019). https://doi.org/10.1007/978-3-030-26948-7_4

Author Index

Printed in the United States
by Baker & Taylor Publisher Services